T0293192

The Adaptive Markets Hypothesis

The Adaptive Markets Hypothesis

An Evolutionary Approach to Understanding Financial System Dynamics

Andrew W. Lo

Andrew W. Lo is the Charles E. and Susan T. Harris Professor at the MIT Sloan School of Management, director of the MIT Laboratory for Financial Engineering, and a principal investigator at the MIT Computer Science and Artificial Intelligence Laboratory. He is also an external faculty member of the Santa Fe Institute and a research associate of the National Bureau of Economic Research.

Ruixun Zhang

Ruixun Zhang is an Assistant Professor and Boya Young Fellow in the Department of Financial Mathematics, School of Mathematical Sciences at Peking University (PKU), with affiliations at the PKU Center for Statistical Science, the PKU National Engineering Laboratory for Big Data Analysis and Applications, the PKU Laboratory for Mathematical Economics and Quantitative Finance, and the MIT Laboratory for Financial Engineering.

OXFORD
UNIVERSITY PRESS

UNIVERSITY PRESS

Great Clarendon Street, Oxford, OX2 6DP,
United Kingdom

Oxford University Press is a department of the University of Oxford.
It furthers the University's objective of excellence in research, scholarship,
and education by publishing worldwide. Oxford is a registered trade mark of
Oxford University Press in the UK and in certain other countries

Published in the United States of America by Oxford University Press
198 Madison Avenue, New York, NY 10016, United States of America

British Library Cataloguing in Publication Data
Data available

Library of Congress Control Number: 2022947789

ISBN 9780199681143

DOI: 10.1093/oso/9780199681143.001.0001

Printed in the UK by
Bell & Bain Ltd., Glasgow

Dedicated to my mother Julia Yao Lo.
– Andrew W. Lo

Dedicated to mom, dad, and Wendy.
– Ruixun Zhang

Acknowledgements

We would like to thank Jayna Cummings for reading through an early draft of the book and helping us improve the exposition significantly. Proofreading assistance from four students, Yufan Chen, Lintong Wu, Yumin Xu, and Peishan Yu, is also greatly appreciated. We also thank Raja Dharmaraj and Jade Dixon for their assistance throughout the production process, Jayne MacArthur for copyediting the book, and Alexandra Nickerson for preparing the index.

Personal Acknowledgements (Andrew W. Lo)

The adaptive markets hypothesis (AMH) was formulated in Lo (2002a, 2004, 2005), twenty years ago, and since then has become increasingly relevant and necessary to understand both the wisdom of crowds during normal market conditions, and the madness of mobs during periods of market turmoil such as the technology bubble in 2000, the financial crisis of 2008, and, most recently, the COVID-19 pandemic.

Since then, the theory and applications of the AMH have progressed considerably, thanks to collaborations with Doyne Farmer, Mila Getmansky, Jasmina Hasanhodzic, David Hirshleifer, Amir Khandani, Peter Lee, H. Allen Orr, Dmitry Repin, Brett Steenbarger, Emanuele Viola, and especially Tom Brennan, with whom I co-authored the very first mathematical formulation of adaptive markets, as well as several follow-on studies, and Ruixun Zhang, a co-author on several of my papers with Tom and separately with me, and with whom I have the pleasure and honour of co-authoring this book.

Many other research collaborators worked with me at various stages of the long journey to the AMH, helping me to shape this idea even before it had a name. These co-authors include Emmanuel Abbe, Pablo Azar, Monica Billio, Nicholas Chan, Ely Dahan, Eric Fielding, Mark Flood, Gartheeban Ganeshapillai, Dale Gray, John Guttag, Shane Haas, Joe Haubrich, Alex Healy, Phil Hill, Jim Hutchinson, Katy Kaminski, Adlar Kim, Andrei Kirilenko, Nihal Koduri, David Larochelle, Simon Levin, William Li, Craig MacKinlay, Igor Makarov, Harry Mamaysky, Shauna Mei, Bob Merton, Mark Mueller, Loriana Pelizzon, Pankaj Patel, Tommy Poggio, Jiang Wang, and Helen Yang.

Finally, I want to thank Oxford University Press and the Saïd Business School for inviting me to deliver the Clarendon Lectures for 2013, the starting point for this book. It is an extraordinary honour to be included among the impressive list of Clarendon Lecturers, not only in finance, but also in other fields, including economics, English, law, and management studies. I was especially pleased to have delivered these lectures at the Saïd Business School; as a now twenty-six-year-old institution at a centuries-old university, it is a fascinating complex of old and new that I think is very much along the lines of the topic of this volume.

In fact, if Edward Hyde, the first Earl of Clarendon, were with us today, I believe he would have approved of the Clarendon Lectures in Finance, even though it is the newest among the Clarendon lecture series. Lord Clarendon was, at one point, very briefly, the Chancellor of the Exchequer, so finance was certainly a subject that was near and dear to his heart. I believe he would also have approved of the topic of my talks—the role of human behaviour in financial markets—because, as a politician who earned the love (as well as the ire) of his king when he was Lord Chancellor and chief minister to Charles II, he was a keen student of human psychology. I can only hope that my efforts in this domain will be as successful as his.

Andrew W. Lo

Personal Acknowledgements (Ruixun Zhang)

First and foremost, I would like to thank Andrew W. Lo for giving me the opportunity to get involved in research related to the AMH, and for the honour of co-authoring this book. Andrew has been a tremendous advisor, mentor, and role model for me throughout the years. I would not have had the joy of working on some of the exciting projects in these pages without his consistent support and encouragement. I chose to pursue an academic career because of the inspiration from the high standard and impact of Andrew's research, as well as the example by which he leads as a world-renowned scholar.

I am also grateful to the many teachers, mentors, and colleagues who have supported me, and from whom I am fortunate to have learned so much over the years. This includes Tom Brennan, Peter Carr, Dayue Chen, Richard Dudley, Weinan E, Michel Goemans, Xin Guo, David Hirshleifer, Diane Lambert, Ngaiming Mok, H. Allen Orr, Pradeep Ravikumar, Weijie Su, Xin

Sun, Changping Wang, Lie Wang, Lan Wu, Jake Xia, Jingping Yang, and Kathy Zhong.

I would also like to thank the institutions with which I have been affiliated during various stages of my career, including MIT and Peking University, for the flexible and supportive academic environment, which empowers me to work on this fascinating interdisciplinary topic.

Ruixun Zhang

Contents

II. BEHAVIOUR

III. NEURONS

IV. FINANCIAL MARKET DYNAMICS

V. FINANCIAL INSTITUTIONS AND ADAPTATION

List of Figures

List of Tables

1

Introduction and Roadmap

If an individual in January 1926 invested $1 in thirty-day US Treasury bills, one of the safest securities in the world, and continued reinvesting the proceeds month by month until June 2023, the original investment would have grown to a mere $23. Alternatively, if an individual invested $1 in the S&P 500, a much riskier investment, over the same 98-year period, this investment would have grown to $13,484, a considerably larger amount.

However, suppose that each month, an individual were able to divine in advance which of these two investments would yield a higher return that month, and took advantage of this information by switching the running total of their initial $1 investment into the higher-yielding asset. What would a $1 investment in such a 'perfect foresight' strategy become by June 2023?[1]

The startling answer is $2,721,489,288,781, over 2.7 trillion dollars (Fig. 1.1)! Despite the fact that perfect foresight in financial markets is impossible, this example suggests that even a modest ability to forecast financial asset returns will be handsomely rewarded. Of course, considerable risks are involved. Financial markets are very difficult to predict; otherwise, we would all be rich. Therefore, one of the central questions in finance—indeed, perhaps the most central question—is, 'Under what circumstances is prediction possible at all?'

The quest to understand financial markets and the behaviour of their participants has attracted an enormous amount of effort from generations of financial economists. Although a comprehensive survey of that quest is beyond the scope of this book, the most significant achievements over the past several decades include expected utility theory (von Neumann and Morgenstern, 1944), the concept of 'rational expectations' (Lucas, 1972), the efficient markets hypothesis (EMH) (Samuelson, 1965; Fama, 1970), and behavioural economics and finance (Simon, 1955; Kahneman, Slovic, and Tversky, 1982; Thaler, 1993; Shiller, 2003). While these theories mark important milestones in our understanding of financial markets, as

---

[1] We are grateful to Bob Merton for this example, which was originally included in Farmer and Lo (1999).

The Adaptive Markets Hypothesis. Andrew W. Lo and Ruixun Zhang, Oxford University Press. © Andrew W. Lo and Ruixun Zhang (2024). DOI: 10.1093/oso/9780199681143.003.0001

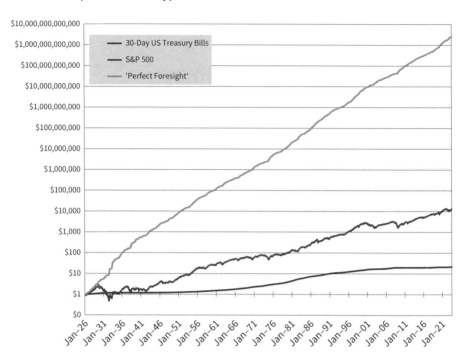

Fig. 1.1 Growth of $1 invested from January 1926 to June 2023.

demonstrated by the panoply of Nobel Prizes awarded to their authors, they do not always agree with each other. To this day, the debate of whether it is possible to 'beat the market' still attracts some of the best minds around the world, among both academics and practitioners. Stories of legendary investors like Warren Buffett and Jim Simons continue to inspire the next generation of financial talent.

However, the financial crisis of 2008 left investors, financial advisors, portfolio managers, and regulators trying to make sense of its repercussions and searching for guidance in its wake. The traditional paradigms of modern portfolio theory and the EMH now seem woefully inadequate. But simply acknowledging that investor behaviour may be irrational is of small comfort to the individuals who need to decide how to allocate their assets among increasingly erratic and uncertain investment alternatives. The reason for the strange dynamics of this state of confusion is straightforward: many market participants now question the framework in which their financial decisions are being made. Without a clear and credible narrative of what happened, how it happened, why it happened, whether it can happen again, or what to do about it, their only response is to react instinctively to the most recent crisis of the moment, which is a sure recipe for financial ruin.

In this book, we present a new narrative, one capable of reconciling rational behaviour with periods of temporary financial insanity. We call this narrative the adaptive markets hypothesis (AMH), in which intelligent but fallible investors learn from and adapt to changing environments. These ideas were described in non-technical terms for a general audience in *Adaptive Markets: Financial Evolution at the Speed of Thought* (Lo, 2017). In this companion volume, we present a more formal and systematic exposition of the theory of adaptive markets and its many applications. These include mathematical, statistical, and computational details of greater interest to academics and quantitatively oriented practitioners. In this introductory chapter, we lay out a road map for the rest of the book, so readers can focus on the parts most relevant to them based on their background and interests.

The main theme of the AMH, and of this book, is that financial markets may not always be efficient, but they are usually competitive and adaptive, varying in their *degree* of efficiency as investor populations and the financial environment change over time. We describe how the AMH can make sense of market turmoil during crises, regardless of whether they have been induced by technological (2000), financial (2008), or public health (2020) factors, as well as the emergence and popularity of the EMH in the decades prior to these crises. For practitioners, the AMH is able to reconcile the apparent contradiction between the existence of systematic behavioural biases and the difficulty of outperforming passive investment vehicles.

Contrary to the popular sentiment that emerged after the financial crisis of 2008, the EMH is not wrong—it is merely incomplete. Markets are well-behaved most of the time, but like any other human endeavour, they are not infallible. They can break down on occasion, and for understandable and predictable reasons. By viewing financial markets and their related institutions from the perspective of evolutionary biology rather than physics,[2] we can construct a much deeper and more accurate narrative of how markets work, and what we can do to prepare for their periodic failures.

The AMH is not an alternative to the EMH, but rather a broader framework that includes the EMH as a subset. There is a well-known parable about five monks who, blind from birth, encounter an elephant for the very first time and are later asked to describe it. The monk who felt the elephant's trunk insists that an elephant is just like a snake, the monk who felt the elephant's leg claims that an elephant is just like a tree, and so on. None of their individual

---

[2] For the hazards of 'physics envy' in finance, see Lo and Mueller (2010).

perspectives is wrong, but they each possess an incomplete understanding of the animal.

So, too, with financial markets. Under stable, stationary, and predictable economic conditions, markets generally work well, and the EMH serves as a reasonably good approximation to reality. Under more dynamic and stochastic environments, the EMH becomes less plausible, and behavioural regularities seem to emerge. The AMH provides an integrated and logically consistent framework for reconciling these disparate perspectives. In addition, it offers several practical insights with respect to investing in an economic climate of uncertainty and market turmoil. For example, we show in this book that the AMH is not only able to explain departures from the EMH and behavioural regularities in the marketplace, but also how markets are able to shift from the wisdom of crowds to the madness of mobs and back again. By studying the forces behind such changes, we can begin to develop more effective models for managing our investments and come closer to the ultimate goal of allocating scarce resources efficiently in order to support steady economic growth while maintaining financial stability.

1.1 Behaviour and Rationality

We start with human behaviour, which lies at the heart of any discussion of market dynamics. Human behaviour is a universally familiar notion, studied by disciplines ranging from economics and sociology to psychology and biology. However, economists have a particular view on human behaviour, informed by two schools of thought that ultimately merged into one theory of economic behaviour: the theory of expected utility.

Let us briefly examine the origins of this theory. In his 1947 PhD thesis, the legendary Paul Samuelson outlined the basic principles of utility theory. His thesis had the very modest title of *Foundations of Economic Analysis*. It was, indeed, modestly titled because it did, in fact, become the foundations of economic analysis. Meanwhile, von Neumann and Morgenstern (1944), in their *Theory of Games and Economic Behavior*, extended an axiomatic approach to the case of random payoffs in the theory of expected utility. Samuelson, at first sceptical of this theory, quickly became one of its greatest champions, combining it with his own approach. Today, every first-year PhD student in economics and finance learns the basic principles of revealed preference and the maximization of the expected value of a concave utility function, subject to a budget constraint.

Despite this dual origin, it is an interesting fact of pedagogy that, in the field of economics, the theory of expected utility is the *only* theory of behaviour that we teach our students. Psychologists, for example, are vexed with economists because they have many theories of human behaviour, whereas we have just one. Of course, there are some possible limitations to our theory, as we shall soon see.

It is clear that Samuelson had a very specific programme in his research agenda, which was to reshape economics in the mould of physics. Let us turn to Samuelson (1998), when Paul Samuelson described how he came to write the *Foundations of Economic Analysis*:

> Perhaps the most relevant of all for the genesis of *Foundations*, Edwin Bidwell Wilson (1879–1964) was at Harvard. Wilson was the great Willard Gibbs's last (and, essentially, only) protégé at Yale. He was a mathematician, a mathematical physicist, a mathematical statistician, a mathematical economist, a polymath who had done first-class work in many fields of the natural and social sciences. I was perhaps his only disciple…. I was vaccinated early to understand that economics and physics could share the same formal mathematical theorems (Euler's theorem on homogeneous functions, Weierstrass's theorems on constrained maxima, Jacobi determinant identities underlying LeChatelier reactions, etc.), while still not resting on the same empirical foundations and certainties.

Samuelson's agenda is a significant reason why all economists, the authors of this book included, suffer from what has been called 'physics envy' (Lo and Mueller, 2010). Economists would love to have three laws that explain 99% of all economic behaviour, but, in reality, we probably have 99 laws that explain 3% of all behaviour, a particular sore point among economists.

Nevertheless, this physics-based approach to economics was tremendously successful. If you consider the economic milestones that have been achieved over the last five decades—utility theory, revealed preference, general equilibrium theory, game theory, macroeconometrics, portfolio theory, rational expectations, option pricing, and, of course, the EMH—all of them grew out of this particular research programme. This body of work eventually gave rise to the term '*Homo economicus*', a mythical species of humankind embodying the highly rational decision-making processes implied by these theories.

The EMH (Samuelson, 1965; Fama, 1970), the notion that market prices 'fully reflect all available information', is an excellent illustration of *Homo economicus* at work. As one of the most influential ideas in finance, the importance of the EMH lies in the fact that the hypothesis provides very sharp conjectures about how prices should behave, not unlike Adam Smith's famous invisible hand of the market, or, more recently, the notion of 'the wisdom of crowds'. Even though none of us has all the relevant information about a given financial asset, each of us has disparate pieces of information which, when combined via the human organizational adaptation we call a 'market', yields an incredibly well-informed number that is the asset's price. It is as though *Homo economicus* has determined the price despite (or because of) the inadequacies of *Homo sapiens*.

The EMH is disarmingly simple, yet unexpectedly profound. It has inspired intense study and debate, launching literally thousands of empirical investigations of its many specific implications for human behaviour since its articulation by Eugene Fama. These implications have been confirmed so many times across so many contexts that Jensen (1978) concluded that 'there is no other proposition in economics which has more solid empirical evidence supporting it than the Efficient Market Hypothesis'. It appeared to the field that *Homo economicus* had arrived.

1.2 'Anomalies'

However, over the past several decades an accumulation of evidence from psychology, behavioural economics and finance, the cognitive neurosciences, and biology has highlighted a growing number of significant and persistent inconsistencies between *Homo economicus* and *Homo sapiens*.[3] These inconsistencies have called into question the assumptions of expected utility theory, rational expectations, equilibrium analysis, and even the law of one price, which are the foundations of efficient markets and much of the rest of neoclassical economics and finance. The financial crisis of 2008 only added more fuel to the many fires threatening the EMH edifice.

The growing body of literature that has emerged from the work of psychologists and behavioural economists has demonstrated a variety of cognitive biases in market behaviour, including loss aversion, anchoring, framing, probability matching, overconfidence, and over-reaction. Time and time again, over the course of the last three decades, researchers have documented departures from all the axiomatic assumptions that give rise to efficient markets and rational expectations. Given the centrality of the EMH in what we teach in finance, beginning in the introductions but included in all subsequent finance courses, this should give us cause for concern. If what students are currently learning is deficient in certain respects, the next generation of finance professionals are in for an unpleasant awakening when they attempt to put theory into practice. We shall return to this concern when we consider the implications of the AMH for investing and trading in Part IV of this book.

---

[3] See, for example, Kahneman, Slovic, and Tversky (1982) and Thaler (1993).

For a specific example of irrationality, consider the following behavioural anomaly: probability matching.[4] This anomaly is a rather old discovery that has rarely been discussed in recent behavioural finance contexts.

Suppose we play a simple game with a coin. I toss it a series of times, and you try to guess whether heads or tails is going to come up. If you guess correctly, I pay you a dollar, and if you guess incorrectly, you pay me a dollar. We do this many times, over and over again. Now, for the sake of argument, suppose the coin is biased: it will come up heads 75% of the time, and tails 25%. However, you do not know this in advance. All you know is that it *might* be biased.

After we play for ten or twenty trials, you begin to notice that the relative frequency of heads is actually much greater than the relative frequency of tails. What should you do, as *Homo economicus*? The optimal strategy—the profit-maximizing strategy—would be to guess heads before every toss.

It turns out that when this game is played with experimental subjects in a laboratory setting, they do not follow this optimal strategy; they do not guess heads every time. Oddly enough, they seem to randomize their choice of heads versus tails with approximately the same relative frequency as the actual coin tosses. Even more striking is when, in the midst of this experiment, the coin is secretly switched from a 75%/25% coin to a 60%/40% coin. After another twenty or thirty trials, the subject will gradually change their behaviour, ultimately matching the 60%/40% frequency as well.[5]

This might seem like a minor anomaly, but it has had significant consequences in at least one context.[6] During World War II, the US engaged in bombing missions over Germany. Before the pilots boarded their planes for their missions, they were given a choice: either wear a flak jacket that would protect them from shrapnel and air to air gunfire that would strafe the sides of these bombers, or wear a parachute that would save them in case they were shot down. In those days, pilots could not wear both, because these protective devices were too heavy. They had to choose one or the other.

It turns out that the probability of a pilot being killed by shrapnel was about 75%, and the probability of being shot down was about 25%. What should the pilots have chosen to maximize their safety? To maximize their chances of survival, they should have chosen the flak jacket every time. In fact, the

---

[4] One of the earliest papers to document this phenomenon is Grant, Hake, and Hornseth (1951).

[5] For example, we personally found strong evidence for probability matching in an experiment conducted at MIT (Lo, Marlowe, and Zhang, 2021), in which each participant played a computer game to guess the outcome of a binary lottery with a real monetary payoff. See Chapter 5 for further details.

[6] We thank the late Stephen A. Ross for providing us with this example, for which he credited Amos Tversky as the source.

pilots randomized, picking the flak jacket 75% of the time, and the parachute 25% of the time.

Even more puzzling is the fact that we find this behaviour in other animal species, including ants (Deneubourg et al., 1987; Pasteels, Deneubourg, and Goss, 1987; Hölldobler and Wilson, 1990; Kirman, 1993), bees (Harder and Real, 1987; Thuijsman et al., 1995; Keasar et al., 2002), fish (Bitterman, Wodinsky, and Candland, 1958; Behrend and Bitterman, 1961), pigeons (Graf, Bullock, and Bitterman, 1964; Young, 1981), and primates (Woolverton and Rowlett, 1998). In virtually any species able to make a choice between A and B where a randomized experiment can be constructed, we observe probability matching. For example, psychologists experimented with a species of tilapia, dividing an aquarium into two sides, left and right, and choosing which side to feed the fish from. They randomized 70% to the left and 30% to the right. You would guess that all of the tilapia would always go to the left side, but they too randomized.

Probability matching is just one example of the so-called behavioural biases or 'anomalies' among the many others mentioned above. There is more than sufficient documentation that they exist. The question is why? The behavioural finance literature often stops here, and simply concludes that, like Sasquatch, the abominable snowman, and the Loch Ness monster, *Homo economicus* is a myth. But in order for us to understand how to incorporate these anomalies and biases into our theories, we need to know why they occur and what causes them.

As the saying goes, it takes a theory to beat a theory, and anomalies by themselves are not theories. Are they merely irrational errors, or is something deeper going on?

1.3 Environment and Evolution

The compelling empirical evidence in support of market efficiency, juxtaposed with the equally compelling empirical and experimental evidence of the apparent irrationality of behavioural anomalies, suggests that human behaviour is not solely determined by economic considerations. Instead, human behaviour is the amalgam of multiple decision-making faculties—including instinct, emotion, and logic—that yield the actions we observe. But because the relative importance of these faculties varies across time and circumstances, even for a given individual, it is no wonder that, despite centuries of intense analysis and debate, there is still remarkably little consensus among economists, psychologists, and biologists as to how to model human behaviour.

What we hope to achieve in this book is to answer not only the 'why' of these seeming irrationalities, but what they mean for financial markets. We are going to reconcile the EMH with behavioural finance, and argue that neither of them is always correct, but both of them do apply. They simply do not apply at the same time with the same force. In other words, they are opposite sides of the same coin. Behavioural biases are adaptive behaviours that have been taken out of their natural context.

In Chapter 2, we present the logic behind probability matching and describe the context in which it makes perfect sense—not economic sense, but perfect behavioural sense. Our framework for the evolutionary origin of behaviour is simple enough to solve analytically but general enough to explain commonly observed behaviours in animal species ranging from ants to human beings. While these behaviours might be suboptimal from the individual's selfish perspective, from the population's perspective they are optimal in a very different sense: in the sense of maximizing survival.

From the perspective of evolution, the only thing we care about is survival. As Woody Allen put it, 'eighty percent of life is just showing up'. In fact, this is an underestimate. Biology is all about survival, and, as Charles Darwin demonstrated, variation and natural selection shape survival in the same way that they shape ecologies. Ultimately, it is the interaction between a given behaviour and its environment that determines the reproductive success of a particular behaviour.

Throughout this book we use terms that an ecologist or an evolution-ary biologist would use. We do this intentionally. They are not meant as metaphors. Instead, they are used as accurate scientific descriptions of actual processes, and we will make that case over the course of this book. The AMH is evolution applied to financial interactions, pure and simple.

1.4 The Traditional Investment Paradigm

To understand the implications of this new paradigm for financial mar-kets and investment decisions, let us consider first the most common tenets of the traditional investment paradigm. Firstly, there is a positive trade-off between risk and reward across all financial investments—that is, assets with higher risk offer a higher expected return. Secondly, this trade-off is linear, where the risk is best measured by equity beta, while excess returns are mea-sured by alpha, the average deviation of a portfolio's return from the capital asset pricing model (CAPM), or other, more recent multifactor benchmarks. Thirdly, reasonably attractive investment returns may be achieved by pas-sive, long-only, highly diversified portfolios of equities weighted by market capitalization (i.e. those containing only equity betas and no alpha). Fourthly, strategic asset allocation among asset classes is the most important decision that an investor makes when selecting a portfolio best suited to their risk tolerance and long-run investment objectives. Fifthly, and finally, all investors should be holding stocks for the long run. Collectively, these five basic principles have become the foundation of the investment management industry, influencing virtually every product and service offered by professional portfolio managers, investment consultants, and financial advisors.

Like all theories, these tenets are meant to be approximations to a much more complex reality. Their usefulness and accuracy depend on a number of implicit assumptions regarding the relationship between risk and reward, including:

A1. The relationship is linear.
A2. The relationship is static across time and circumstances.
A3. The relationship's parameters can be accurately estimated.
A4. Investors have rational expectations.
A5. Asset returns are stationary (i.e. their joint distribution is constant over time).
A6. Markets are efficient.

Each of these assumptions can be challenged on theoretical, empirical, and experimental grounds. However, all theories are, by definition, abstractions that involve simplifying assumptions. The relevant question is not whether these assumptions are literally true—they are not—but rather whether the errors they contain are sufficiently small that they can be ignored for practical purposes.

We propose that the answer to this question has changed over the past decade. From the mid-1930s to the mid-2000s—a period of relatively stable financial markets and regulations—these assumptions were reasonable approximations to US financial markets. However, the errors have greatly increased in recent years, for identifiable reasons, to the point where now they can no longer be ignored.

Figure 1.2 provides a clear illustration of this proposal, plotting the cumulative total return of the value-weighted stock market return index compiled by the University of Chicago's Center for Research in Security Prices (CRSP) from January 1926 to December 2010 on a logarithmic scale, so that the same vertical distance corresponds to the same percentage return, regardless of the time period considered. This graph shows that the US equity market was a remarkably reliable source of investment return from the mid-1930s to the mid-2000s, yielding an uninterrupted and nearly linear log-cumulative

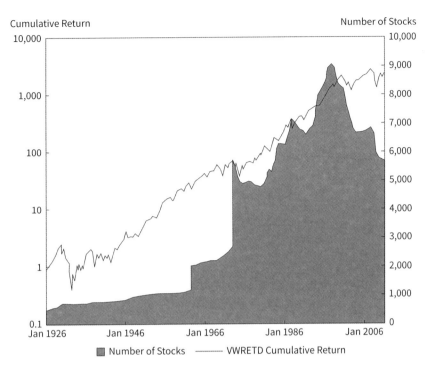

Fig. 1.2 Semi-logarithmic plot of the cumulative total return of the CRSP value-weighted return index from January 1926 to December 2010, and standard plot of the total number of stocks used in the index.

Source: Lo, A. W. (2012). Adaptive markets and the new world order (corrected May 2012). *Financial Analysts Journal* 68(2): 18–29. Reprinted with permission from the publisher, Taylor & Francis Ltd., http://www.tandfonline.com.

growth curve over these seven decades. This period, which followed the Great Depression, has sometimes been called the 'Great Modulation', because of the stability that characterized financial markets during this time.[7] This period should not be confused with the 'Great Moderation', a term coined by Stock and Watson (2002) that refers to the 1987–2007 period of lower volatility in the US business cycle, but the two concepts are clearly related. While there were certainly sizeable ups and downs over this time span, from the perspective of an investor with a 10–20-year horizon, investing in a well-diversified portfolio of US equities would have generated comparably good average returns and volatility over almost any point throughout this seventy-year period.

[7] This term also refers to the economic and regulatory reforms that were put in place in the wake of the Great Depression to modulate financial activity, including much of the US legal code that now governs the entire financial system: the Glass–Steagall Act of 1932, the Banking Act of 1933, the Securities Act of 1933, the Securities Exchange Act of 1934, the Investment Company Act of 1940, and the Investment Advisers Act of 1940.

In such a stable financial environment, assumptions A1–A6 do yield reasonable approximations to market behaviour; hence, it is not surprising that the traditional investment paradigm of a linear risk–reward trade-off, passive buy-and-hold index funds, and 60/40 asset-allocation heuristics emerged and became popular during this period. The pressing issue at hand, however, is whether the period following the Great Modulation can be ignored as a temporary anomaly—the exception that proves the rule—or if it is a harbinger of a new world order. There is mounting evidence that supports the latter conclusion.

1.5 A New World Order

Although every generation of investors is likely to consider its own environment unique and special, with its own unprecedented challenges and innovations, there are objective reasons to believe that the environment of the years since the 2008 financial crisis is significantly different from the environment of the prior seven decades. One obvious indication is volatility, something all investors became painfully aware of during the crisis.

Figure 1.3 depicts the annualized volatility of daily CRSP value-weighted index returns over trailing 125-day windows, a measure of short-term volatility. This graph shows that the aftermath of the 1929 stock market crash was an extremely volatile period, which was followed by the decades of the Great Modulation, when the volatility was considerably more muted. However, the period with the highest volatility occurred not during the Great Depression, but much more recently, during the fourth quarter of 2008, in the wake of the Lehman bankruptcy.

Additionally, other market statistics such as trading volume, market capitalization, trade execution times, and the number of listed securities and investors indicate that today's equity markets are larger, faster, and more diverse than at any other time in modern history. These lines of evidence all point to a similar conclusion: we are living in genuinely unusual times.

This pattern may well be a reflection of a much broader trend: population growth. Figure 1.4 depicts the estimated world population from 10,000 BC to the present day in logarithmic scale. As with the graph of US equities, this series also exhibits exponential growth.[8] Figure 1.4 shows three distinct

[8] World population data are obtained from the US Census Bureau's International Database. The US Census Bureau reports several sources for world population estimates from 10,000 BC to 1950, some of which include lower and upper estimates. We average these estimates to yield a single estimate for each year in which figures are available. From 1951 to 2019, the US Census Bureau provides a unique estimate per year. For further details, see www.census.gov/programs-surveys/international-programs/about/idb.html.

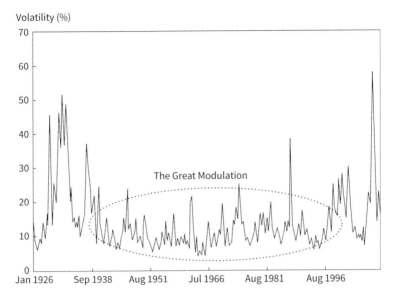

Fig. 1.3 One hundred and twenty five-day rolling-window annualized volatility of the CRSP daily value-weighted return index, from 2 January 1926 to 31 December 2010.

Source: Lo, A. W. (2012). Adaptive markets and the new world order (corrected May 2012). *Financial Analysts Journal* 68(2): 18–29. Reprinted with permission from the publisher, Taylor & Francis Ltd., http://www.tandfonline.com.

periods of human population growth over the last twelve millennia: low growth during the Stone Age from 10,000 BC to 4,000 BC, moderate growth from the start of the Bronze Age around 4,000 BC to the industrial revolution in the 1800s, and much faster growth since then. In 1900, the world population was estimated to be approximately 1.5 billion individuals (the blue dot); the 2019 estimate puts current world population at 7.7 billion (the purple dot).

Within the space of a century, we have more than quadrupled the number of inhabitants on this planet. This has had profound financial consequences. The vast majority of these individuals must work to survive, and will therefore engage in some form of life-cycle savings and investment activity during their lifetimes. This naturally increases the required scale of financial markets, as well as the complexity of the interactions among the various counterparties.

This dramatic increase in the human population is no accident. It is a direct consequence of technological innovations that have allowed our species to manipulate the natural resources in our environment to meet, and, ultimately, exceed our subsistence needs. Advances in agricultural, medical, manufacturing, transportation, information, and financial technologies have all contributed to this extraordinary run of reproductive success by *Homo sapiens*. These advances are largely the result of competitive economic forces

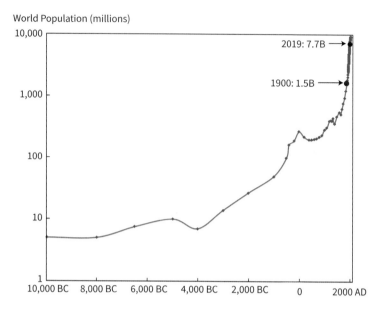

Fig. 1.4 Semi-logarithmic plot of estimated world population from 10,000 BC to 2019 AD.

Source: Lo, A. W. (2021). The financial system red in tooth and claw: 75 years of co-evolving markets and technology. *Financial Analysts Journal* 77(3): 5–33. Reprinted with permission from the publisher, Taylor & Francis Ltd., http://www.tandfonline.com.

which reward innovation, and through which less recent innovations often quickly become obsolete. This has led to a far different world today than the world of only a few decades ago.

One of the most compelling illustrations of this difference is the pair of graphs in Fig. 1.5, which display the population size, per capita gross domestic product (GDP), and average life expectancy of the world's countries at two points in time: 1900 and 2018. In 1900, the US—the largest yellow disc at the upper-right range of Fig. 1.5a—was in an enviable position, with one of the highest levels of GDP per capita and life expectancy among the major industrialized countries of the world, with only a handful of close competitors.

However, Fig. 1.5b tells a very different story: a mere twelve decades later, the US is no longer the only dominant economic force in the global economy, now surrounded by many sizeable competitors, including Japan (the large red disc close to the US) and Europe (the many orange discs to the left of the US). Meanwhile, the economic growth of the two most populous countries in the world—China (the largest red disc) and India (the largest light-blue disc)— has had enormous impacts on global trade patterns, labour supply, relative

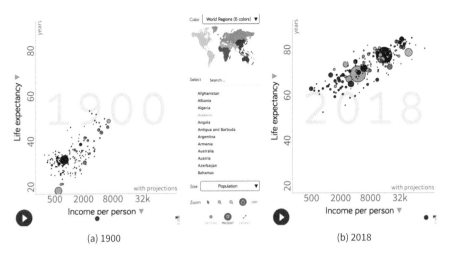

Fig. 1.5 Population, per capita GDP, and life expectancy for different countries in (a) 1900 and (b) 2018.

Source: Free material from http://www.gapminder.org.

wages and production costs, foreign exchange rates, and innovation and productivity in just the last twenty years. At the same time, decades have been added to human life expectancy, even in the poorest nations. Given these seismic economic shifts, it is no wonder that the dynamics of global financial asset prices, which ultimately must reflect the supply and demand of real assets, have become less stable in recent years. The Great Modulation is giving way to a new world order.

1.6 The Adaptive Markets Hypothesis

The large-scale economic changes of this new world order, and their political and cultural consequences, are the ultimate reasons that assumptions A1–A6 have become less plausible in the current environment, and thus why financial market dynamics are so different today than they were during the Great Modulation. Technological advances are often accompanied by unintended consequences, including pollution, global warming, and pandemic disease. It should come as no surprise that financial crises are another such unintended consequence.

Financial technology, in particular, has been a double-edged sword. It has facilitated tremendous global economic growth over past decades by gathering and channelling vast amounts of capital from asset owners in one part of the world to entrepreneurs in other parts, who are able to make better use of it.

But globally connected capital markets imply that local financial shocks will propagate more quickly to other regions, as we saw with the 2008 financial crisis, which was truly global in scope.

The AMH emerged in the context of this new world order as a more complete explanation of the behaviour of financial markets and their participants than earlier hypotheses. This theory begins with the recognition that human behaviour is a complex combination of multiple decision-making systems, of which logical reasoning is only one among several. The ability to engage in abstract thought, communicate these thoughts to others, and act in a coordinated fashion to achieve complex goals seem to be uniquely human traits that have allowed us to dominate our environment like no other species, ushering in the age of *Homo economicus* (at least according to economists). Neuroscientists have traced these abilities to a region of the brain known as the neocortex, an anatomical structure unique to mammals that is particularly large and densely connected in *Homo sapiens*.[9] On an evolutionary timescale, the neocortex is the newest component of the brain, hence its name.

However, before humans developed these impressive faculties of abstraction, we still managed to survive in a hostile and competitive world, thanks to more primitive decision-making mechanisms. One example is the fight-or-flight response, a series of near-instantaneous physiological reactions to physical threats that include increased blood pressure and blood flow to the large muscle groups, the constriction of blood vessels in other parts of the body, rapid release of nutrients such as glucose into the bloodstream, decreased appetite, digestive activity, sexual desire, tunnel vision and loss of hearing, and much faster reflexes.[10] In short, the fight-or-flight response prepares us to defend ourselves from attack by either evading our attacker or fighting to the death. This complex collection of decisions is not made voluntarily or after careful deliberation. Rather, it is a 'hardwired' automatic response found in many animal species. The evolutionary basis for its development is clear enough; if we had to weigh carefully the costs and benefits of reacting in this manner each time we were threatened, we would end up as dinner for less pensive predators.

The key insight regarding these various decision-making mechanisms is that they are not completely independent. In some cases, such as the fight-or-flight response, they work together to achieve a single purpose: a physiological reaction involving several systems that are usually independent

---

[9] See Schoenemann (2006) for a review of the literature on human brain evolution and a comparison of subcomponents of the brain across hominid species.

[10] See de Becker (1997), Zajonc (1980, 1984), and Lo (2013).

but which become highly correlated under specific circumstances. It is no coincidence that the all-too-familiar pattern of abruptly increasing correlations of previously uncorrelated activities exists in physiological phenomena as well as in financial time series—fight-or-flight responses can trigger flights to safety.

However, such coordination sometimes implies that certain decision-making components take priority over others. For example, Baumeister, Heatherton, and Tice (1994) document many instances in which an extreme emotional reaction can 'short circuit' logical deliberation, inhibiting activity in the neocortex. From an evolutionary standpoint, this makes perfect sense—emotional reactions are a call to arms that should be heeded immediately because one's personal survival may depend on it, while higher brain functions such as language and logical reasoning are suppressed until the threat is over (i.e. until the emotional reaction subsides). When being chased by a tiger, it is more advantageous to be frightened into scrambling up a tree than to be able to solve differential equations!

However, from a financial decision-making perspective, this reaction can be highly counterproductive. Adaptations like the fight-or-flight response emerged in response to physical threats, not financial losses, yet our instinctive response to both is much the same. The behavioural biases that psychologists and behavioural economists have documented are simply adaptations that have been taken out of their evolutionary context: the fight-or-flight reaction is an extremely effective decision-making system in a street fight, but it is potentially disastrous in a financial crisis.[11]

The focus of the AMH is not on any single behaviour. Rather, it focuses on how behaviour *responds* to changing market conditions. In the framework of the AMH, individuals are neither perfectly rational nor completely irrational. Instead, they are intelligent, forward-looking, competitive investors who adapt to new economic realities. When John Maynard Keynes was criticized for flip-flopping on the gold standard, he is said to have replied, 'When the facts change, sir, I change my mind; what do you do?' By modelling the *change* in behaviour as a function of the environment in which investors find themselves, it becomes clear that efficient and irrational markets are two extremes, neither of which fully captures the state of the market at any point in time.

---

[11] See Chapter 11 for a more detailed discussion of the neuroscientific perspective on financial crises, and Chapter 2 for an evolutionary framework in which various behavioural regularities such as risk aversion, loss aversion, and probability matching emerge quite naturally through the forces of natural selection.

Human responses to risk are more subtle than the fight-or-flight mechanism might imply. One striking illustration of this subtlety is the 'Peltzman effect', named after the University of Chicago economist Sam Peltzman. In a controversial empirical study on the impact of government regulations requiring the use of automobile safety devices such as seat belts, Peltzman (1975) concluded that these regulations did little to reduce the number of highway deaths because people adjusted their behaviour accordingly, presumably by driving faster and more recklessly. Although, in certain cases, the number of fatalities among the occupants of cars involved in accidents did decline over time, his analysis showed that this decline was almost entirely offset by an *increase* in the number of pedestrian deaths and nonfatal accidents. He concluded that the benefits of safety regulations were mostly negated by changes in driving behaviour. Since then, many studies have extended Peltzman's original study by considering additional safety devices such as airbags, anti-lock brakes, crumple zones, and so on. In some cases, these new studies have confirmed Peltzman's original findings after controlling for other factors such as enforcement practices, driver age, rural versus urban roads, and vehicle weight, but, in other cases, they have refuted it.[12]

These mixed results are not surprising, given the many different contexts in which we drive automobiles. For example, a harried commuter might take advantage of improved safety devices by driving faster and getting to work a few minutes earlier, but the same does not apply to visiting tourists. However, in a more recent study of the Peltzman effect, Sobel and Nesbit (2007) investigate the one driving context in which there are very few confounding factors to create mixed results, and where there is no doubt that all drivers are singularly focused on arriving at their final destination as quickly as possible: NASCAR races. Their conclusion: 'Our results clearly support the existence of offsetting behaviour in NASCAR—drivers do drive more recklessly in response to the increased safety of their automobiles.' When the only goal is to reduce driving time, it seems perfectly rational that increased safety would induce drivers to drive faster.

From a financial perspective, this confirmation of the Peltzman effect is completely consistent with basic portfolio theory: if an asset's volatility declines, but its expected return remains unchanged, investors will put more money into such an asset, other things (like correlations to other assets) being equal.

But what if safety improvements are *perceived* to be more effective than they actually are? Individuals may then end up taking more risk than they

---

[12] See, for example, Crandall and Graham (1984), Farmer et al. (1997), and Cohen and Einav (2003).

intended, simply because they feel safer than the reality of the situation. In other words, risk perception may differ from risk reality, obviously a critical factor in the 2008 financial crisis. Given the AAA ratings of collateralized debt obligations (CDOs) and the relatively short and default-free history of these new securities, investors may have thought they were safer than, in fact, they were.[13]

It is easy to see how the adaptive nature of human risk preferences can generate asset bubbles and market crashes. This is one of the most important motivations for producing and publicizing accurate, objective, and timely risk analytics in financial contexts; the negative feedback loops that risk analytics can provide are one of nature's most reliable mechanisms for maintaining system stability—'homeostasis', to use the biological term. The aggregation of these individual behavioural dynamics explains why markets are never completely efficient or irrational: they are simply adaptive.

1.7 Practical Implications

The AMH leads to a wide range of behavioural, cultural, and financial implications, which we present in more detail throughout this volume. From an investment management perspective, perhaps the most important implication is that the trade-off between risk and reward is not stable over time or circumstances, but varies as a function of the population of market participants and the business environment in which they are immersed. During periods of market dislocation—for example, when fear rules the day—investors will reduce their holdings of risky assets and move into safer investments. This will have the effect of reducing the average return on risky assets, and increasing the average return on safer ones, exactly the opposite of what rational finance predicts: the madness of mobs replaces the wisdom of crowds. However, during more 'normal' periods in which market conditions are benign (i.e. when price fluctuations are within historically observed ranges) and current events have no over-riding consequences for market valuations or the conduct of business, assumptions A1–A6 are good approximations to reality, and the wisdom of crowds returns.

---

[13] However, even in this case, the wisdom of crowds suggested an important difference between CDOs and other securities with identical credit ratings. For example, in an April 2006 publication by the *Financial Times* (Senior, 2006), Cian O'Carroll, the European head of structured products at Fortis Investments, explained why CDOs were in such high demand: 'You buy a AA-rated corporate bond you get paid LIBOR plus 20 basis points; you buy a AA-rated CDO and you get LIBOR plus 110 basis points.' Did investors wonder why CDOs were offering 90 basis points of additional yield, or where that extra yield might have been coming from? It may not have been the disciples of the EMH that were misled during these frothy times, but more likely those who were convinced they had discovered a free lunch.

If the wisdom of crowds is more common than the madness of mobs over an extended period of time, as theory and empirical evidence seem to suggest, then statistical averages over long horizons (e.g. market risk premia) will largely reflect the wisdom of crowds. However, this does not imply that the wisdom of crowds must hold at *every* point in time. There may be periods of collective fear or greed when the madness of mobs takes over, not unlike the notion of punctuated equilibria in evolutionary biology when, after long periods of evolutionary stasis, relatively sudden changes lead to extinctions and new species emerge in their aftermath.[14] It is precisely during such periods in financial history that bubbles and crashes emerge, and assumptions A1–A6 become less accurate approximations to reality.

This dynamic can be observed in the historical data, as Table 1.1 and Fig. 1.6 illustrate. Table 1.1 reports the historical means and standard deviations for the returns of stocks and bonds from January 1926 to December 2010, which confirms the traditional view that there is a positive trade-off between risk and reward. However, Fig. 1.6 shows something rather different. It depicts a 1,250-day rolling window (that is, a running average approximately five years long) of standard deviations of daily CRSP value-weighted index returns and of geometrically compounded returns, respectively representing the risk and reward in that window. As can be seen, there is a time-varying and often negative relationship between the two; in fact, the correlation between these two daily series is –59.9%!

This empirical anomaly was first documented by Black (1976), who explained it as a 'leverage effect': when equity prices decline, generating

Table 1.1 Summary statistics of long-term stock and bond returns, from January 1926 to December 2010.

Asset Class	Geometric Mean (%)	Arithmetic Mean (%)	Standard Deviation (%)
Small-company stocks	12.1	16.7	32.6
Large-company stocks	9.9	11.9	20.4
Long-term corporate bonds	5.9	6.2	8.3
Long-term government bonds	5.5	5.9	9.5
Intermediate-term government bonds	5.4	5.5	5.7
US Treasury bills	3.6	3.7	3.1

Data source: Ibbotson (2011, Table 2–1).

[14] See, for example, Eldredge and Gould (1972). This reference to punctuated equilibria is not merely an analogy—it is meant to apply quite literally to financial institutions and economic relationships, which are subject to evolutionary forces in their own right.

Percentage

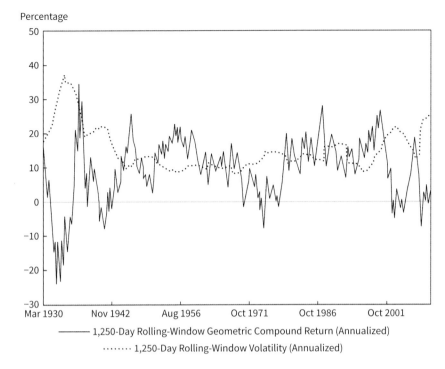

—— 1,250-Day Rolling-Window Geometric Compound Return (Annualized)

········ 1,250-Day Rolling-Window Volatility (Annualized)

Fig. 1.6 1,250-day rolling-window annualized volatility and geometric compound returns of the daily CRSP value-weighted return index from 19 March 1930 to 31 December 2010.

Source: Lo, A. W. (2012). Adaptive markets and the new world order (corrected May 2012). *Financial Analysts Journal* 68(2): 18–29. Reprinted with permission from the publisher, Taylor & Francis Ltd., http://www.tandfonline.com.

negative returns, this implies there is higher volatility in equity, because corporations with debt in their capital structure are now more highly leveraged. This explanation seems eminently plausible, except for the fact that this so-called leverage effect is still present and even *stronger* among companies entirely financed by equity (Hasanhodzic and Lo, 2019). The AMH provides an alternate explanation: sudden increases in equity volatility cause a significant portion of investors to reduce their equity holdings rapidly through a fight-or-flight response, better known in financial contexts as a 'flight to safety'. This process of divestment puts downward pressure on equity prices and upward pressure on the prices of safer assets, causing the normally positive association between risk and reward to be temporarily violated. Once these emotional responses subside, the madness of mobs is replaced by the wisdom of crowds, and the usual risk–reward relationship is restored.

The second implication of the AMH from an investment management perspective is that market efficiency is not an all-or-nothing condition, but a continuum—one that depends on the relative proportion of market participants who are making investment decisions with their prefrontal cortex versus their more instinctive faculties, such as their fight-or-flight reactions. In other words, the *degree* of market efficiency should be measured, like the energy efficiency of an air conditioner or a hot-water heater. Market efficiency is directly related to the degree to which a given set of market participants is adapted to the environment in which a market has developed. A relatively new market is likely to be less efficient than a market that has been in existence for decades, but, even in the latter case, inefficiencies can arise if either the environment shifts or the population of investors changes materially. In fact, market efficiency can be measured and managed, as many securities exchanges do routinely as part of their ongoing efforts to improve market quality. The adaptive investment perspective implies that assumptions A1–A6 should not be viewed as either true or false, but rather as approximations that may become more or less accurate as market conditions and investor populations change.

This observation leads to a third implication of the AMH, that investment policies must be formulated with these potential changes in mind, and should adapt accordingly. When assumptions A1–A6 are reasonable approximations to current conditions, traditional investment approaches are adequate, but when they break down, perhaps because of periods of extreme fear or greed, the traditional approaches may no longer be as effective. One obvious example is the notion of diversification. Diversifying one's investments across 500 individual securities—for example, the stocks in the S&P 500—was sufficient during the Great Modulation to produce relatively stable and attractive returns over extended periods of time. However, in today's environment, these 500 securities are so tightly coupled in their behaviour that they offer much lower diversification benefits than in the past. The principle of diversification is not wrong; it is simply harder to achieve in today's macro-factor driven markets. Therefore, its implementation must be adapted to the current environment (e.g. diversifying across a broader array of investments in multiple countries), and according to factor exposures instead of, or in addition to, asset classes.

A fourth investment implication of the AMH involves an important consequence of competition, innovation, and natural selection in financial markets: the transformation of alpha. Under assumptions A1–A6, alpha should always equal 0. Under the AMH, alpha can be positive from time to time, but any unique and profitable investment opportunity will eventually be adopted by many investors, in which case the alpha will either be reduced to 0 through competition, or it will reach an equilibrium level in which the risks associated with its exploitation are sufficient to limit the number of willing participants in this opportunity to some finite and sustainable number. This is one possible explanation for the relatively stable risk–reward trade-off of US equities during the Great Modulation, and why that trade-off seems to have changed in recent years: global competition across all financial markets and strategies has intensified, due to economies of scale and scope leading to greater consolidation among asset owners, and there has been mounting pressure in low-yield environments to find new sources of expected return. Even more striking examples can be found in the hedge fund industry (see Chapter 16), where alphas decay rapidly, only to reappear a few years later, after enough investors and managers have moved on to greener pastures.

Finally, the AMH offers a strikingly different implication for asset allocation than the traditional investment paradigm. In the stable environment of assumptions A1–A6, simple asset allocation rules such as a static 60/40 stock/bond portfolio will often suffice. But if there is significant volatility of volatility, and if risk premia also vary over time, then making financial decisions about one's portfolio in terms of the usual asset-based portfolio weights may not be very useful. For example, a 60% asset weight in equities may yield a volatility of $0.6 \times 0.20 = 12\%$ during normal times, but during the fourth quarter of 2008, when the VIX reached 80%, such an allocation would have yielded a volatility of approximately 48%. Given that investors are usually more concerned with risk and reward than the numerical values of their portfolio weights, the AMH suggests that denominating asset allocations in units of risk may be more useful and more stable for one's investments, particularly when assumptions A1–A6 break down. For example, if an investor is comfortable with an annualized return volatility of 10% for their entire portfolio, this can be the starting point for an asset allocation strategy in which a risk budget of 10% is allocated across several asset classes (e.g. 5% risk to equities, 3% risk to bonds, and 1% risk to commodities).[15] As the volatilities and correlations of the underlying assets change over time, the portfolio weights must change in tandem to maintain constant risk weights and portfolio volatility,

[15] The fact that the volatilities of these individual components do not add up to 10% is not a typographical error; it is a deliberate reminder that the return volatility of a portfolio is not the sum of the volatilities of the individual components, due both to correlations among the assets and to the nonlinearity of the square root function. Moreover, cash is also an investable asset, but because its nominal returns have zero volatility, cash investments will not appear in any risk budget, despite their importance for managing portfolio volatility. Therefore, the notion of a risk budget must be used with caution so as not to mislead or confuse investors.

so that the investor experiences fewer surprises with respect to their portfolio's realized risk levels, thereby reducing the potential for fight-or-flight responses.

This asset allocation strategy—which we call a risk-denominated asset allocation (RDAA) strategy—may seem like portfolio insurance and its related dynamic asset allocation strategies of the 1980s (Black and Perold, 1992; Perold and Sharpe, 1995), but there are several important differences between the two. Firstly, the motivation for an RDAA strategy is the nonstationarity of risk levels due to behavioural responses, while portfolio insurance typically assumes stationary returns, with a stable statistical profile. Changes in portfolio weights in RDAA strategies are driven by changes in the short-term volatility, but the changes in portfolio weights in portfolio insurance strategies are driven by short-term losses. Finally, the amount of time variation in the portfolio weights of an RDAA strategy is determined by the volatility of volatility. If the volatility is relatively stable, then the weights in an RDAA strategy will be relatively smooth, but the time variation in the weights of a portfolio insurance strategy is determined by the magnitude of volatility—a higher volatility will require more frequent portfolio rebalancing. Both types of strategies will yield return streams superficially correlated with each other because the losses to which portfolio insurance responds are usually accompanied by increased volatility, to which an RDAA strategy responds (Black, 1976; Hasanhodzic and Lo, 2019). As a result, RDAA and portfolio insurance strategies may change their risk levels at approximately the same time. However, the magnitude and frequency of those changes will not be the same, since they are driven by different variables, so the correlation will not be perfect, and the ultimate risk–reward profiles of the two types of strategies can be quite different.

Specifying the risk allocation in a portfolio has an additional benefit. During periods of heightened market volatility, exposure to risky assets will be reduced in order to maintain earlier levels of volatility. These periods, however, are precisely when the madness of mobs is most likely to emerge, causing the expected returns of risky assets to decline due to flights to safety. Conversely, in the traditional investment paradigm, it never pays to engage in such tactical shifts, because a market timing strategy has been shown to be virtually impossible, and therefore ineffective. By reducing exposure to risky assets from time to time, the traditional paradigm concludes that a portfolio will forgo the risk premia associated with those risky assets. This misleading conclusion highlights one of the starkest contrasts between the implications of the EMH versus the AMH: if risk premia and volatilities are constant through time, then static portfolio weights may indeed be adequate for a portfolio, but if they vary over time in response to observable market conditions, then an adaptive strategy may well be superior.

Risk-denominated portfolio weights are only part of the solution to the asset allocation problem under the AMH. Asset allocation must also consider the impact of time-varying expected returns and correlations of individual asset classes, which may be quite different under various market regimes. An integrated approach is to use adaptive statistical estimators for all the relevant parameters of an investor's environment to construct allocations that incorporate estimation error, regime shifts, institutional changes, and more realistic models of investor preferences and behaviour. This approach has the added advantage that, in stable environments, truly adaptive portfolio policies will reduce to traditional, static ones, implying little cost in implementing adaptive strategies during normal periods, yet significant benefits during market dislocations.

The practical implementation of the AMH is clearly more challenging than the simpler heuristics of the traditional investment paradigm. However, these challenges are considerably less daunting today than in decades past, given automated execution algorithms, lower trading costs, better statistical measures of time-varying parameters, improvements in trading technology, the greater liquidity of exchange-traded index futures and other derivative securities, and better educated investors and portfolio managers. Nevertheless, the increased complexity of today's investment environment is undeniable. It is a reflection not merely of recent financial crises, but of a much larger and more complex global economy to which we must learn to adapt by applying more effective financial technologies.

1.8 Organizational Structure of the Book

Having now laid out the basic ideas we hope to cover and the motivation for our approach, we are ready to dive into the details. The book is divided into five parts. We begin with the mathematical foundations of the AMH in Part I, *Foundations*, which covers the simple yet surprisingly powerful binary-choice model that we use throughout the volume to show how rational and irrational economic behaviours and financial market dynamics emerge quite naturally through evolution. The key idea is that behaviour interacts with the specific type of risk that affects reproductive success. The notion of systematic versus idiosyncratic risk—pioneered independently in the 1960s by William Sharpe, John Lintner, Jan Mossin, and Jack Treynor in the CAPM—plays a critical role in our framework, but for a completely different reason than in the CAPM. Ultimately, the difference between systematic and idiosyncratic risk is able to explain a startling number of 'anomalies' we have observed. These may be anomalous from an economic perspective—the selfish, optimizing perspective—but they make perfect sense from the biological perspective. Part I also addresses more technical aspects of our framework, including the impact of random mutations, the possibility of natural selection operating on groups rather than individuals or genes, and other aspects of evolution applied to behaviour.

We apply this framework in Part II, *Behaviour*, and show how many of the most fundamental economic behaviours that we take as given and for granted—risk aversion, cooperation, randomization, Bayesian inference, and intelligence—can be *derived* from evolutionary first principles. These same principles also show that under slightly different environmental conditions, irrational behaviours such as probability matching, loss aversion, bounded rationality, bias, and discrimination can emerge through natural selection as well. This confirms a fact well known by ecologists and evolutionary biologists: evolution is a directionless process dictated by the interactions of multiple species in a randomly shifting environment. Therefore, certain behaviours may seem highly rational, while others may seem wildly irrational, and both may very well be the product of natural selection. However, the binary choice model provides the means to identify highly specific conditions under which one type of behaviour emerges versus another, giving us hope that we will one day develop a complete quantitative understanding of behaviour among both *Homo economicus* and *Homo sapiens*.

In Part III, *Neurons*, we focus on the fundamental driver of all behaviour: the brain. We draw heavily on recent advances in the cognitive neurosciences, through which our understanding of rationality has been permanently altered when viewed from a neurophysiological perspective. This part of the book speaks directly to the issue of how economists versus psychologists and other behaviouralists think about human behaviour. Ultimately, both efficient markets and their behavioural departures can be understood through the cognitive neurosciences, laying the foundations of the AMH. In particular, we provide evidence for how human psychophysiology and emotion affect our economic and financial decision-making.

We then apply the principles of the AMH to understand how financial markets change over time, and in response to shifting environments, in several specific contexts in Part IV, *Financial Market Dynamics*. We give a novel computational view of market efficiency, then discuss some implications for the growth of relative wealth. We also provide an in-depth example of the AMH at work in the world of hedge funds, the 'Galápagos Islands' of the financial industry, where evolution happens before our very eyes. We study a very specific set of events that occurred in the hedge fund industry—the 'Quant Meltdown' of August 2007—in which we see how market participants adapt quickly and effectively to changing economic environments. These examples provide both proofs of concept for the practical relevance of the AMH to the financial system, as well as cautionary tales about the consequences of adapting too slowly.

Finally, in Part V, *Financial Institutions and Adaptation*, we take a broader perspective and consider the implications of the AMH for the financial system. Starting with a brief review of the past seventy-five years of financial history, we see that financial institutions adapt to changing business environments, and although predicting asset prices may be a challenge, predicting changes in institutions is not nearly as difficult. By focusing on the financial system as an ecosystem populated by a set of species, each with its own objectives, resources, and constraints, all of which can be measured to some degree, it is possible to develop an understanding of how that ecosystem is likely to evolve over time and across fitness landscapes. With that perspective in mind, we consider the role that financial culture has played in economic booms and busts, and how we can improve regulatory processes and economic policies to yield a more robust and resilient financial system.

Thank for your joining us on this journey to develop a deeper understanding of the AMH, and we look forward to serving as your tour guides.

PART I
FOUNDATIONS

2
The Origin of Behaviour

In this chapter, we propose a single evolutionary explanation for the origin of a number of diverse and widespread behaviours that have been observed in organisms ranging from ants to human beings, including risk aversion, risk-sensitive foraging, loss aversion, probability matching, randomization, and diversification.[1] We show here that a relatively simple framework is able to generate a surprisingly rich set of behaviours. The simplicity and generality of our model suggest that these derived behaviours are primitive and nearly universal within and across species. The framework we present in this chapter serves as the launching platform for later extensions throughout the book. It is our mathematical foundation for modelling economic behaviour from the evolutionary perspective.

Some of the behaviours we derive in this chapter have been the subject of significant controversy within both economics and psychology. These so-called 'behavioural biases' are especially pronounced when elements of risk and probability are involved. Two of the most ubiquitous of these biases are loss aversion (Tversky and Kahneman, 1974; Kahneman and Tversky, 1979)—the tendency to take a greater risk when choosing between two potential losses, and less risk when choosing between two potential gains—and probability matching, also known as the 'matching law' or 'Herrnstein's Law' (Grant, Hake, and Hornseth, 1951; Hake and Hyman, 1953; Herrnstein, 1997; Vulkan, 2000)—the tendency to choose randomly between choices matching an underlying probability distribution, for example, when asked to guess the outcomes of a series of biased coin tosses, randomly choosing heads and tails where the randomization matches the probability of the biased coin. The idea of randomizing behaviour is especially difficult to reconcile with the standard economic paradigm of expected utility theory, in which an individual's behaviour is non-stochastic, completely determined by utility functions, budget constraints, and the probability laws governing the

[1] This chapter, including the figures, is adapted with permission of World Scientific Publishing Co., Inc., from Brennan, T. J., and Lo, A. W. (2011). The origin of behavior. *Quarterly Journal of Finance* 1(01): 55–108; permission conveyed through Copyright Clearance Center, Inc.

The Adaptive Markets Hypothesis. Andrew W. Lo and Ruixun Zhang, Oxford University Press. © Andrew W. Lo and Ruixun Zhang (2024). DOI: 10.1093/oso/9780199681143.003.0002

environment. Both of these types of biases clearly imply irrationality, that is, individually suboptimal choices, yet these behaviours have been observed in thousands of geographically diverse human subjects over several decades, as well as in other animal species.

Our model consists of an initial population of individuals (not necessarily human) that live for one period of unspecified length and engage in a single binary decision that has consequences for the random number of offspring they will generate. Only the most reproductively successful behaviours will flourish due to the forces of natural selection, while less reproductively successful behaviours will disappear at exponential rates. When the uncertainty in reproductive success is systematic across these individuals, natural selection will yield behaviours that may be individually suboptimal but are optimal from the point of view of the population. However, when the reproductive uncertainty is idiosyncratic, the perspectives of the individual and the population coincide. Although this may be obvious to an evolutionary biologist, this observation yields surprisingly specific implications for the types of behaviour that are sustainable over time, behaviours that are likely to be innate to most living organisms.

A simple numerical example of one of our results will illustrate our approach. Consider a population of individuals, each facing a binary choice between one of two possible actions, *a* and *b*. Sixty per cent of the time, the environmental conditions are positive, and action *a* will lead to reproductive success, generating three offspring for the individual. Forty per cent of the time, the environmental conditions are negative, and action *a* will lead to zero offspring. Suppose action *b* has exactly the opposite outcomes—whenever *a* yields three offspring, *b* yields zero, and whenever *a* yields zero, *b* yields three. From the individual's perspective, always choosing *a*, which has the higher probability of reproductive success, will lead to more offspring, on average. However, if all individuals in the population behaved in this 'rational' manner, the first time that a negative environmental condition occurs, the entire population will become extinct. Assuming that offspring behave identically to their parents, the behaviour 'always choose *a*' cannot survive over time. For the same reason, 'always choose *b*' is also unsustainable. In fact, we show below that, in this special case, the behaviour with the highest reproductive success over time is for each individual to choose *a* 60% of the time and *b* 40% of the time, matching the probabilities of reproductive success and failure. Eventually, this behaviour will dominate the entire population.

Probability matching has long puzzled economists and psychologists because of its apparent inconsistency with basic self-interest.[2] However, probability matching is perfectly consistent with evolution, arising purely from the forces of natural selection and population growth. Moreover, for more generalized environmental conditions (i.e. more general assumptions about reproductive success), we are able to derive more general types of behaviour that involve randomization but not necessarily probability matching. These results may explain the inconsistency in the circumstances where such behaviour is observed: whether or not randomizing behaviour matches environmental probabilities depends on the relative reproductive success of the outcomes.

Our framework yields a simple and specific condition for such behaviour. Our results do not depend on how individuals arrive at their choices, whether they learn over time, or whether individuals possess a theory of mind or self-awareness about the consequences of their actions. In fact, our results do not even require individuals to possess a central nervous system.

We also show that the concepts of risk aversion and risk-sensitive foraging behaviour emerge from the same framework. Because populations grow geometrically, a sequence of 50/50 gambles yielding two or four offspring each generation will yield a slower average growth rate than sure bets of three offspring. This emerges mathematically from the simple fact that the product of two and four is smaller than the product of three and three. Although the expected number of offspring is the same for both behaviours, the riskier behaviour has slower growth in the long run. While this principle of geometric mean fitness is well known among population biologists, its implications for risk-bearing activity in economic settings have not been fully explored. For example, the fact that the preferences most likely to survive over time are those that require a higher expected fecundity in return for taking risk implies the existence of a positive evolutionary 'risk premium', which we are able to derive explicitly and quantify as a function of environmental conditions.

Our model also generates asymmetric risk preferences for gains and losses (i.e. loss aversion), resolving a longstanding debate between the disciples of von Neumann and Morgenstern's expected utility theory (von Neumann and Morgenstern, 1944; Schoemaker, 1982) and the proponents of behavioural

[2] One of the earliest papers to document this phenomenon is Grant, Hake, and Hornseth (1951). Kogler and Kühberger (2007) report 'Experimental research in simple repeated risky choices shows a striking violation of rational choice theory: the tendency to match probabilities by allocating the frequency of response in proportion to their relative probabilities.'

alternatives, such as prospect theory (Kahneman and Tversky, 1979; Tversky and Kahneman, 1981). Each of these theoretical perspectives captures different aspects of the same behaviour shaped by natural selection and population growth. Moreover, our framework provides an explanation for the apparent variability in the experimental evidence regarding loss aversion, and the nature of the reference point that demarcates risk-seeking behaviour from risk-averse behaviour: evolution shapes an individual's decision-making preferences (or mechanisms) to enhance their reproductive success, which, in turn, is determined by total wealth and not incremental wealth. Accordingly, two individuals with the same decision-making process, but different levels of net worth, may behave differently when offered the same incremental prospects.

Finally, and perhaps most significantly, our framework illustrates the role of the environment in shaping behaviour, and why certain populations appear to exhibit irrational behaviour while others do not. The difference can be traced to a single feature of the environment's impact on individual biology: systematic versus idiosyncratic sources of randomness in reproduction. In populations where environmental factors are largely systematic (i.e. where they affect the reproduction rates of all individuals in the same manner), any form of synchronization in behaviour may lead to extinction. As a result, such synchrony is unlikely to be perpetuated. In other words, if environmental risks are systematic, survival depends on the population diversifying its behaviour, so that some fraction will survive to reproduce no matter what the environment is like. In these cases, it may seem as if certain individuals are acting irrationally, since they may not be behaving optimally for a given environment. But such heterogeneous behaviour is, in fact, optimal from the perspective of the population.

If, however, environmental risks are largely idiosyncratic, then individuals engaging in identical behaviour (e.g. individually optimal behaviour), will not expose the population to extinction. Moreover, in this case, natural selection will favour the individually optimal behaviour; hence, a population of individually rational individuals will emerge. Thus, rationality is not necessarily in the eye of the (individual) beholder, but it is sometimes in the hands of systematic environmental factors.

In this chapter, we first provide a necessarily brief review of the literature on evolution and behaviour. In Section 2.1, we present our theoretical binary choice framework. Using this framework, in Section 2.2 we derive necessary and sufficient conditions under which probability matching emerges, and also show how probability matching breaks down under different environments. By making one of the two binary choices riskless, in Section 2.3, we show how risk preferences evolve. We also derive an evolutionary equity risk premium, and show how loss aversion arises naturally from these preferences. In Section 2.4, we develop further consequences from the difference between systematic and idiosyncratic risks in behaviour, showing that the former yields populations in which individuals do not always act rationally and the latter does not. Finally, we preview several extensions of our binary choice framework in Section 2.5, which we carry out in greater detail throughout this book.

Related Literature

The literature on evolution and behaviour is overwhelming, spanning the disciplines of evolutionary biology, ecology, evolutionary and social psychology, and economics, with myriad branches of relevant citations within each of these broad fields. While a comprehensive survey is well beyond the scope of this book, we will attempt to provide a representative sampling of the many related strands of this vast body of research.

Evolutionary principles are now routinely used to derive possible implications for animal behaviour. While each species has developed unique responses for addressing its particular environmental challenges, the most critical of these have been shaped by the evolutionary forces of mutation, competition, and natural selection. Although such forces operate at the individual genetic level, as described compellingly by Dawkins (1976), the path-breaking work of Hamilton (1964), Trivers (1971, 1985, 2002), Wilson (1975b), and Maynard Smith (1982, 1984) shows that evolutionary mechanisms may also explain a variety of counterintuitive social behaviours, including altruism, cooperation, kin selection, and reciprocity, among others. The field of evolutionary psychology (Pinker, 1979, 1991, 1994; Barkow, Cosmides, and Tooby, 1992; Cosmides and Tooby, 1994; Tooby and Cosmides, 1995; Gigerenzer, 2000; Buss, 2004; Ehrlich and Levin, 2005) has expanded the reach of evolution to even broader domains, such as language, culture, and religion.

Evolutionary ideas have also played an important role in economics. Thomas Malthus (1826) used a simple biological argument—the fact that populations increase at geometric rates, while natural resources increase at only arithmetic rates (at least before the nineteenth century)—to arrive at the dire economic consequences that earned the field the moniker of 'the dismal science'. Both Darwin and Wallace were aware of and apparently influenced by Malthusian arguments (see Hirshleifer (1977) for further details). In the twentieth century, Schumpeter's (1939) view of business cycles, entrepreneurs, and capitalism has an unmistakable evolutionary flavour to it;

in fact, his ideas of creative destruction and bursts of entrepreneurial activity bear a striking resemblance to natural selection and Eldredge and Gould's (1972) notion of punctuated equilibrium.

Economists and biologists have begun to explore these connections in several directions: economic extensions of sociobiology (Becker, 1976; Hirshleifer, 1977); evolutionary game theory (Maynard Smith, 1982, 1984; Weibull, 1995); an evolutionary interpretation of economic change (Nelson and Winter, 1982); economies as complex adaptive systems (Anderson, Arrow, and Pines, 1988); and the impact of uncertainty regarding the number of offspring on current consumption patterns (Arrow and Levin, 2009).

Evolutionary concepts have also appeared in the finance literature. For example, Luo (1995) explores the implications of natural selection on the futures markets, Hirshleifer and Luo (2001) consider the long-run prospects of overconfident traders in a competitive securities market, and Kogan et al. (2006) show that irrational traders can influence market prices even when their wealth becomes negligible. The literature on agent-based modelling pioneered by Arthur et al. (1997), simulating interactions among software agents programmed with simple heuristics, relies heavily on evolutionary dynamics. Finally, at least two prominent investment professionals have proposed Darwinian alternatives to explain market behaviour. In a chapter entitled 'The Ecology of Markets' (Ch. 15), Niederhoffer (1997) likens financial markets to an ecosystem, with dealers as 'herbivores', speculators as 'carnivores', and floor traders and distressed investors as 'decomposers'. Meanwhile, Bernstein (1998) makes a compelling case for active management by pointing out that the notion of equilibrium is rarely realized in practice, and that market dynamics are better explained by evolutionary processes.

In our specific context, however, the two most relevant lines of research—one from biology and the other from economics—involve the direct application of evolutionary principles to individual behaviour and preferences. In the evolutionary biology literature, Maynard Smith (1982) developed the concept of an evolutionarily stable strategy, specific behaviours that survive over time by conferring reproductive advantages or 'fitness', typically measured by the rate of population growth. Using this notion of fitness, Fretwell (1972), Cooper and Kaplan (1982), and Frank and Slatkin (1990) observe that randomizing behaviour can be advantageous in terms of maximizing geometric growth rates in the face of stochastic environmental conditions. The impact of variability in reproductive success among individuals in a population has been shown to yield a form of risk aversion, which increases average reproductive success, and the biological phenomenon known as bet-hedging, which reduces the variance of reproductive success (Slatkin, 1974; Caraco, 1980; Real, 1980; Rubenstein, 1982; Seger and Brockmann, 1987). Frank and

Slatkin (1990) propose a framework that highlights the importance of correlation between individual reproductive success in determining the path of
evolution. Meanwhile, similar results have been derived in the behavioural
ecology literature, in which the maximization of fitness via dynamic programming has been shown to yield several observed behaviours, including
risk-sensitive foraging in mammals (Real and Caraco, 1986; Stephens and
Krebs, 1986; Mangel and Clark, 1988) and seed dispersal strategies in plants
(Levin, Cohen, and Hastings, 1984; Levin et al., 2003).

In the economics literature, evolutionary principles have been used to
justify the existence of utility functions and develop implications regarding
their functional form, as in Hansson and Stuart (1990) and Robson (1996a,
2001a). (See Robson (2001b) for a comprehensive review of this literature.)
For example, in an equilibrium model of economic growth, Hansson and
Stuart (1990) derived restrictions on individual preferences about consumption, savings, and the labour supply from the forces of natural selection.
Robson (1996a) investigates expected and nonexpected utility behaviours,
finding that idiosyncratic risk-seeking may be optimal from the perspective
of the population, even though it is suboptimal from an individual perspective see also Grafen (1999); Curry (2001). Robson (2001b) argues that the
kind of predictable behaviour capable of being captured by a utility function emerged naturally as an adaptive mechanism for individuals faced with
repeated choices in a nonstationary environment. Specifically, it is argued
that early exploration in choice-making (the primary focus of our analysis),
coupled with a utility-based rule of thumb for deciding when to terminate
exploration and stay with a particular choice, leads to an evolutionarily optimal adaptation to unknown underlying distributions of outcomes. Robson
and Samuelson (2007) find that exponential discounting in utility functions
is consistent with an evolutionarily optimal growth of a population, while the
emergence of time preference is derived by Rogers (1994), Samuelson (2001),
Robson and Samuelson (2007, 2009), and Robson and Szentes (2008).

However, as Waldman (1994) observed, the individually optimal behaviour
predicted by expected utility may not always coincide with behaviour that
maximizes fitness, even when utility functions are derived from evolutionary
principles (p. 483):

Another possible outcome is that preferences do not equate utility maximization
with fitness maximization, and correspondingly evolution then does not favour
humans who are efficient utility-maximizers. Instead what happens in this case
is that evolution favours a systematic bias in the decision-making process which
moves behaviour away from the maximization of utility and toward the maximization of fitness.

Waldman (1994) provides a compelling illustration of this insight through the comparison between asexual and sexual reproduction, in which the latter yields evolutionarily stable second-best adaptations. Within our binary choice framework, we show that even under asexual reproduction, systematic 'errors' such as probability matching can persist and become dominant, despite the fact that such behaviour is suboptimal from the individual's perspective.

Our approach builds on the insights of Fretwell (1972), Maynard Smith (1982), Waldman (1994), and Robson (1996a, 2001a) in applying the well-known principle of geometric mean fitness (Dempster, 1955) to the actions of a heterogeneous population of individuals and deriving the subset of behaviours that survive. Geometric mean fitness has also appeared in the financial context as the Kelly criterion for maximizing the geometric growth rate of a portfolio with returns $\{R_1, R_2, \ldots, R_T\}$ (Kelly, 1956; Samuelson, 1971; Thorp, 1971; Cover and Thomas, 1991; Thorp, 2006):

$$\text{Max } \mathbb{E}\left[\frac{1}{T}\sum_{t=1}^{T}\log(1 + R_t)\right]. \tag{2.1}$$

However, the motivation for geometric mean fitness in financial investment is considerably less compelling than in population biology. Samuelson (1971) argued that maximizing the geometric mean return of a portfolio is optimal only for individuals with a very specific risk preference (i.e. those with logarithmic utility functions).[3]

Our framework is considerably simpler than earlier treatments, involving only a single binary choice for each individual during its lifetime, although a choice that has significant implications for the individual's reproductive success. One virtue of our framework's parsimony is the universality of its derived behaviours among living organisms.[4] Our model is simple enough to solve analytically but remarkably rich in its implications for behaviour, yielding risk aversion, probability matching, loss aversion, and more general forms of randomization in behaviour. As with most other models in the population biology literature, the individual behaviours that survive in our framework need not be optimal from the individual's perspective, and may appear to be irrational. In fact, these behaviours are merely adaptive, products of natural selection that are likely to be more primitive on

---

[3] See Chapter 15 for a more in-depth treatment of the Kelly criterion in our evolutionary framework.

[4] For example, the fact that probability matching behaviour has been observed in nonhuman subjects (see the discussions and literature cited in Chapter 1) suggests that these behaviours may have a common ancient evolutionary origin and an adaptive role that belies their apparent shortcomings.

an evolutionary timescale than the more sophisticated learned behaviours captured by Rogers (1994), Robson (1996a, 2001a), and Robson and Samuelson (2007, 2009). In this respect, our analysis complements those of the existing literature on evolutionary foundations of utility theory, providing additional evidence for the link between behaviour and natural selection at the most basic level of choice.

2.1 The Binary Choice Model

We begin with a population of individuals that live for one period, produce a random number of offspring asexually, and then die. (In the jargon of evolutionary biology, they are asexual semelparous organisms.) During their lives, individuals make only one decision: they choose one of two possible courses of action, denoted a and b. This results in one of two corresponding random numbers of offspring, x_a and x_b, described by some well-behaved probability distribution function, $\Phi(x_a, x_b)$. We assume that x_a and x_b are not perfectly correlated, otherwise, for all intents and purposes, individuals would have only one action available to them. We also assume that:

Assumption 2.1 (x_a, x_b) *and* $\log(fx_a + (1-f)x_b)$ *have finite moments up to order 2 for all* $f \in [0, 1]$.

Assumption 2.2 (x_a, x_b) *is independent and identically distributed over time, and identical for all individuals in a given generation.*

Assumptions 2.1 and 2.2 allow us to derive analytically tractable results, and are not nearly as implausible in a biological context as they would be when applied to financial data.[5] For the moment, we assume in Assumption 2.2 that x_a and x_b are the same two outcomes for all individuals in the population; in other words, if two individuals choose the same action a, both will produce the same number of random offspring, x_a. This implies that the variation in offspring due to behaviour is wholly systematic (i.e. the link between action and reproductive success is the same throughout the entire population). This assumption is highly significant, and its ramifications can

---

[5] Both assumptions can be relaxed to some degree, but at the expense of analytical simplicity. For example, Assumption 2.1 can be relaxed by considering random variables with no finite moments of any order, in which case we must turn our attention to the location and scale parameters. The assumption of an independent and identical distribution in Assumption 2.2 can also be relaxed by imposing stationarity and ergodicity, or by allowing heterogeneity in the marginal distributions while imposing mixing conditions as in White (2001). We discuss such extensions in Chapter 9.

be better understood when we consider the alternate case of idiosyncratic random offspring in Section 2.4.

2.1.1 The Role of $\Phi(x_a, x_b)$

The role of Φ is critical to our framework, as it represents the entirety of the consequences of an individual's actions on reproductive success. Embedded in Φ is the entire array of biological machinery that is fundamental to evolution (i.e. genetics and gene expression), which is of intense interest to biologists but of less direct interest to economists than the link between behaviour and reproductive success. If action a leads to higher fecundity than action b for individuals within a given population, the particular set of genes that predispose individuals to select a over b will be favoured by natural selection. In this case, those genes will survive and flourish, implying that the behaviour 'choose a over b' will also flourish. However, if a and b have identical consequences for success (i.e. $x_a \equiv x_b$), then Φ is a degenerate distribution. By asserting that Φ is a non-degenerate bivariate distribution, we have essentially defined two equivalence classes of actions that have different consequences for reproduction (i.e. all actions yielding the same reproductive fitness are considered equivalent in our framework).

The specification of Φ also captures the fundamental distinction between traditional models of population genetics (Levins, 1968; Wright, 1968; Wilson and Bossert, 1971; Dawkins, 1976) and the broader applications of evolution to behaviour (Hamilton, 1964; Trivers, 1971; Wilson, 1975b; Maynard Smith, 1982); the former focuses on the natural selection of traits (determined by genetics), while the latter focuses on the natural selection of behaviour. Although behaviour is obviously linked to genetics, the specific genes involved, their loci, and the mechanisms by which they are transmitted from one generation to the next are of less relevance to economic analysis than the ultimate consequences of behaviour for reproduction, which is captured by Φ. In the jargon of econometrics, Φ may be viewed as a 'reduced form' representation of an individual's biology, whereas the molecular biology of genetics corresponds to the 'structural form'.[6] This terminology is more than a simple analogy: it accurately summarizes the difference between our framework and the emerging field of behavioural genomics (Plomin, 1990; Plomin, Owen, and McGuffin, 1994; McGuffin, Riley, and Plomin, 2001), which attempts to map traits and behaviours to specific genes.

---

[6] Waldman (1994) uses the same terminology in his framework, in which individual traits are directly linked to reproductive success rather than specific genes.

2.1.2 Individual Behaviour

Suppose that each individual i chooses a with some probability $f \in [0, 1]$ and b with probability $1 - f$, denoted by the Bernoulli variable I_i^f. Hence, i's offspring, x_i^f, is given by:

$$x_i^f = I_i^f x_a + (1 - I_i^f) x_b, \quad I_i^f \equiv \begin{cases} 1 \;\; \text{with probability} \;\; f \\ 0 \;\; \text{with probability} \;\; 1 - f \end{cases}. \qquad (2.2)$$

We shall henceforth refer to f as the individual's 'behaviour', since it completely determines how the individual chooses between a and b. Note that, since f can be 0 or 1, we are not requiring individuals to randomize; this will be derived as a population-wide consequence of natural selection under certain conditions. Also, we ascribe no intelligence or volition to this behaviour. We are simply providing a formal representation for it, and then investigating its evolutionary prospects. To that end, we assume that offspring will behave in a manner identical to their parents (i.e. they will choose between a and b according to the same f). As a result, the population may be viewed as being composed of 'types' of individuals indexed by f that range continuously from 0 to 1, including the endpoints. In this manner, we are able to study the evolutionary dynamics of each type of individual over many generations.

2.1.3 Population Dynamics

Since our analysis involves individuals making binary decisions over time and across multiple generations, the number and type of subscripts used may sometimes seem excessive and confusing. Therefore, before considering the population dynamics we have proposed, a few clarifying comments regarding our notation may be useful.

Individuals in a given generation t are indexed by i, and generations are indexed by $t = 1, \ldots, T$. In all cases, we assume independent and identically distributed (IID) randomness over time or, equivalently, generations. Thus, on occasion, we will omit the t subscript, unless we wish to emphasize the temporal ordering of the variables, such as a recursive relation between two successive generations. A superscript f will denote the particular type of individual as defined by the decision rule, I_i^f, in Equation (2.2).

With these notational conventions in mind, we denote by n_t^f the total number of offspring of type f in generation t, which is simply the sum of all the offspring from the type-f individuals of the previous generation:

$$n_t^f \;=\; \sum_{i=1}^{n_{t-1}^f} x_{i,t}^f \;=\; \left(\sum_{i=1}^{n_{t-1}^f} I_{i,t}^f\right)x_{a,t} \;+\; \left(\sum_{i=1}^{n_{t-1}^f} (1 - I_{i,t}^f)\right)x_{b,t}, \tag{2.3}$$

$$\frac{n_t^f}{n_{t-1}^f} \;\overset{p}{=}\; f x_{a,t} \;+\; (1 - f)x_{b,t}, \tag{2.4}$$

where we have added time subscripts to the relevant variables to clarify their temporal ordering, and '$\overset{p}{=}$' in Equation (2.4) denotes equality in probability as n_{t-1}^f increases without bound,[7] which follows from the law of large numbers applied to the sum $\sum_i I_{i,t}^f/n_{t-1}^f$. (Recall that $I_{i,t}^f$ is IID across i.)[8]

Through backward recursion, the population size in Equation (2.4) of type-f individuals in generation T is given by

$$n_T^f \;\overset{p}{=}\; \prod_{t=1}^{T}(f x_{a,t} + (1 - f)x_{b,t}) \;=\; \exp\!\left(\sum_{t=1}^{T}\log(f x_{a,t} + (1 - f)x_{b,t})\right), \tag{2.5}$$

$$\frac{1}{T}\log n_T^f \;\overset{p}{=}\; \frac{1}{T}\sum_{t=1}^{T}\log(f x_{a,t} + (1 - f)x_{b,t}) \;\overset{p}{\to}\; \mathbb{E}[\log(f x_a + (1 - f)x_b)], \tag{2.6}$$

where the '$\overset{p}{\to}$' in Equation (2.6) denotes convergence in probability,[9] and follows from Kolmogorov's law of large numbers applied to the sum $\sum_t \log(f x_{a,t} + (1 - f)x_{b,t})/T$ as T increases without bound (Lewontin and Cohen, 1969). (Recall that since $(x_{a,t}, x_{b,t})$ is assumed to be IID over time, we have dropped the t subscripts in the expectation in Equation (2.6).) We have assumed that $n_0^f = 1$ without loss of generality.

Since the value of f that maximizes the population size, n_T^f, is also the value of f that maximizes $T^{-1}\log n_T^f$,[10] Equation (2.6) implies that this value converges in probability to the maximum of the following the expectation:[11]

$$\alpha(f) \;\equiv\; \mathbb{E}[\log(f x_a + (1 - f)x_b)]. \tag{2.7}$$

---

[7] See the definition in Appendix B.1.

[8] In particular, Kolmogorov's law of large numbers asserts that $\sum_i I_{i,t}^f/n_{t-1}^f$ converges almost surely to $\mathbb{E}[I_{i,t}^f] = f$. (See, for example, Serfling (1980, Ch. 1.8).)

[9] See the definition in Appendix B.1.

[10] This follows from the fact that $T^{-1}\log(n_T^f)$ is a monotone transformation n_T^f.

[11] More precisely, the value f^* that maximizes $\alpha(f)$ corresponds to a population size, $n_t^{f^*}$, that is asymptotically larger than any other population n_t^f, $f \neq f^*$, in the sense that $\text{plim}_{t\to\infty} n_t^f/n_t^{f^*} = 0$. See Section 2.1.4 for a more detailed exposition of these asymptotic properties.

This expression is simply the expectation of the log-geometric average growth rate of the population, and the value f^* that maximizes it, which we shall call the 'growth-optimal' behaviour in order to distinguish it from behaviour that may be optimal for the individual, is given by:[12]

Proposition 2.1 *Under Assumptions 2.1 and 2.2, the growth-optimal behaviour, f^*, is:*

$$f^* = \begin{cases} 1 & \text{if} \quad \mathbb{E}[x_a/x_b] > 1 \;\text{ and }\; \mathbb{E}[x_b/x_a] < 1 \\ \text{solution to Equation (2.9)} & \text{if} \quad \mathbb{E}[x_a/x_b] \geq 1 \;\text{ and }\; \mathbb{E}[x_b/x_a] \geq 1, \qquad (2.8) \\ 0 & \text{if} \quad \mathbb{E}[x_a/x_b] < 1 \;\text{ and }\; \mathbb{E}[x_b/x_a] > 1 \end{cases}$$

where f^* is defined implicitly in the second case of Equation (2.8) by

$$0 = \mathbb{E}\left[\frac{x_a - x_b}{f^* x_a + (1 - f^*)x_b}\right], \qquad (2.9)$$

and the expectations in Equations (2.6)–(2.9) are with respect to the joint distribution $\Phi(x_a, x_b)$.

The three possible behaviours in Equation (2.8) reflect the relative reproductive success of the two choices. This is a generalization of the 'adaptive coin-flipping' strategies of Cooper and Kaplan (1982). Choosing a deterministically will be optimal if choice a exhibits an unambiguously higher expected relative fecundity, just as choosing b deterministically will be optimal if the opposite is true, while randomizing between a and b will be optimal if neither choice has a clear-cut reproductive advantage. This last outcome is perhaps the most counterintuitive, because it is suboptimal from an individual's perspective, but from the perspective of the population as a whole, the individuals that have the most reproductive success over time will be those that choose randomly according to the probability f^*.[13] If, however, one choice is significantly better than the other in terms of the expected ratio of offspring, then, over time, the behaviour that will survive will be the deterministic choice, not the randomizing choice. In these extreme cases,

---

[12] Proofs of all propositions can be found in Appendix B.
[13] Cooper and Kaplan (1982) interpret this behaviour as a form of altruism because individuals seem to be acting in the interest of the population at the expense of their own fitness. However, Grafen (1999) provides a different interpretation by proposing an alternate measure of fitness, one that reflects the growth rate of the survivors.

because of the unambiguous consequences for fecundity, the deterministic choice that leads to higher reproductive success will quickly dominate the population.

The behaviour f^* that emerges through the forces of natural selection is thus quite distinct from that which emerges from the neoclassical economic framework of expected utility: expected utility theory implies deterministic behaviour.[14] Given the same environmental conditions and parameters regarding preference, the action that maximizes expected utility will be the same. In our framework, however, there are many circumstances in which f^* is strictly greater than 0 and less than 1; thus, even if the circumstances between individuals are identical, the behaviour shaped by natural selection will not be.[15]

The deterministic choices, $f^* = 0, 1$, in Proposition 2.1 may be viewed as a primitive form of herding behaviour, in which all individuals in the population choose to act in an identical manner, especially if the relative fecundities, $\mathbb{E}[x_a/x_b]$ and $\mathbb{E}[x_b/x_a]$, shift suddenly from the intermediate state in Equation (2.8) to one of the deterministic states due to rapid environmental changes, and if there is sufficient diversity of behaviour left in the population after the change occurs. This last qualification is critical, due to our assumption that offspring behave exactly as their parents. Hence, if individuals with behaviour $f = 1$ no longer exist in the population, a behaviour cannot emerge even if it is optimal from the perspective of the population. This underscores the importance of random mutations and the evolutionary advantages of sexual reproduction under stochastic environmental conditions. We examine the consequences of mutation in more detail in Chapter 3.

To an outside observer, behaviours among individuals in this population may seem heterogeneous before the shift, because these individuals are randomizing, but they will become increasingly similar after the shift, as selective pressures begin to favour deterministic behaviour over randomization, creating the appearance (but not the reality) of intentional coordination, communication, and synchronization. If the reproductive cycle is sufficiently short, this change in population-wide behaviour may seem highly responsive to environmental changes, giving the impression

---

[14] Although random utility models have been proposed by Thurstone (1927), McFadden (1973), Manski (1975), and others in the discrete choice literature (see Manski and McFadden (1981)), the source of randomness in these models is assumed to be measurement error, not the behaviour itself.

[15] In this respect, our framework differs in a fundamental way from the evolutionary models of Robson (1996a, 2001b). Robson and Samuelson (2007), and Robson and Szentes (2008), in which evolutionary arguments are used to derive specific utility functions that individuals optimize to yield particular behaviours. Although Robson (2001b) proposes the emergence of utility functions as an adaptation to repeated choices in a nonstationary environment, our framework shows that the concept of utility is not necessarily primitive to behaviour or natural selection, and there is at least one type of behaviour—randomization—that cannot be captured by standard expected utility theory.

that individuals are learning about their environment. This is, indeed, a form of learning, but it occurs at the population level, not at the individual level, and not within an individual's lifespan. Considerably more sophisticated adaptations are necessary to generate true herding and synchronization behaviour as in Hamilton (1971), Mirollo and Strogatz (1990), and Strogatz and Stewart (1993), including sensory inputs, conditional behaviour (e.g. conditioned on additional state variables), and neuroplasticity.

Proposition 2.1 may also be interpreted as a primitive form of group selection, in which natural selection appears to operate at the group level instead of, or in addition to, the level of individuals, traits, or genes (Wynne-Edwards, 1962; Sober and Wilson, 1998). However, in this case, the notion of a 'group' is determined by the interaction between behaviour and the environment: those individuals with behaviour f^* will appear to be favoured, and those with other behaviours, $f \neq f^*$, will be disadvantaged. Chapter 4 discusses extensions for group selection in greater detail.

2.1.4 Asymptotic Properties

The growth-optimal behaviour described in Equation (2.8) is simple. However, it has a direct corollary in that f^* leads to a 'winner-take-all' outcome, in which individuals of all other suboptimal types of f' will be rapidly overrun by individuals of type f^*, since the ratio of the population sizes of f' and f^* converges exponentially fast to 0, due to the optimality of f^*:

Corollary 2.1 *Under Assumptions 2.1 and 2.2, as T increases without bound, the geometric average growth rate, $(n_T^f)^{1/T}$, of the population of individuals with behaviour f converges in probability to $\exp(\alpha(f))$, and the growth optimal behaviour, f^*, will dominate the population exponentially fast since*

$$\left(\frac{n_T^{f'}}{n_T^{f^*}}\right)^{1/T} \overset{p}{=} \exp\left(\left[\alpha(f') - \alpha(f^*)\right]\right) \overset{p}{\to} 0, \tag{2.10}$$

which implies that $n_T^{f'}/n_T^{f^*} \overset{p}{\to} 0$ at an exponential rate.

This corollary confirms that the behaviour produced by the forces of natural selection is, indeed, given by Equation (2.8), and the exponential rate of convergence underlies the winner-take-all phenomenon that seems to characterize so many competitive situations (see, e.g., Frank and Cook (1995)). Whether such behaviour is deterministic or random depends entirely on the consequences of such behaviour for reproductive success.

Note that our asymptotic approach to studying the evolutionary properties of behaviour is different from the typical biologist's perspective, in that the main object of interest for us is f^*, not the population itself. In particular, the actual size of the population of type-f individuals is of less concern to us than the fact that selection will favour one particular f^*. In fact, in contrast to standard models in population dynamics that are formulated to have stable equilibria, the population size in our framework approaches either 0 or infinity in the limit, depending on the parameters of $\Phi(x_a, x_b)$.[16] Nevertheless, we can fully characterize the statistical properties of the population via the central limit theorem. Specifically, as T grows without bound, it can be shown that the suitably normalized population size, n_T^f, approaches a lognormal distribution:

Proposition 2.2 *Under Assumptions 2.1 and 2.2, as T increases without bound, the geometric average, $(n_T^f)^{1/T}$, of the population size of individuals with behaviour f converges in distribution to a lognormal random variable:*

$$\sqrt{T}\left(T^{-1}\log n_T^f - \alpha(f)\right) \overset{a}{\sim} \mathcal{N}\left(0, \sigma^2(f)\right), \tag{2.11}$$

where $\sigma^2(f) \equiv \text{Var}\left[\log(fx_a + (1-f)x_b)\right]$ and '$\overset{a}{\sim}$' denotes asymptotic equivalence in distribution.

This evolutionary basis of behaviour is the same as Seger and Brockmann's (1987) geometric mean fitness criterion, but applied directly to reproductive success, x, not to specific genes. The basic logic of Equation (2.8) is similar to the work of Maynard Smith (1982), in which mixed strategies are shown to be evolutionarily stable, but our approach is more parsimonious, and, by design, it yields broader implications for behaviour, as represented by Φ. Our derived behaviours are also distinct from those of Hansson and Stuart (1990), Robson (1996a,b, 2001a,b), Grafen (1999), Curry (2001), Samuelson (2001), and Robson and Samuelson (2007), in which evolutionary arguments are used to justify specific types of utility functions and risk preferences; in the latter cases, two individuals with identical utility functions will behave identically, whereas in our case, two individuals with identical $f^* \in (0,1)$ may make different choices at any point in time (see also Waldman (1994)).

In the sections that follow, we show that this simple binary choice framework leading to growth-optimal behaviour is able to explain a surprisingly rich set of behavioural anomalies that have been a source of controversy in

---

[16] To see why, observe that Kolmogorov's law of large numbers implies that $T^{-1}\log n_T^f$ converges almost surely to $\alpha(f) \equiv \mathbb{E}[\log(fx_a + (1-f)x_b)]$. If $\alpha(f)$ is positive, the population grows without bound, and if $\alpha(f)$ is negative, the population becomes extinct.

economics, psychology, and evolutionary biology, including more general forms of probability matching, loss aversion, and risk aversion.

2.2 Probability Matching

Using the binary choice framework, we can easily derive probability-matching behaviour as emerging solely through the forces of natural selection. We first derive the conditions that yield exact probability matching. We then generalize this result considerably, deriving conditions for approximate probability matching, as well as conditions under which probability matching does not arise.

2.2.1 Exact Probability Matching

To develop a further intuition for the binary choice model, consider the special case in which the number of offspring, (x_a, x_b), are simply Bernoulli random variables that are perfectly out of phase in each of two possible environmental states:

$$
\begin{array}{c|cc}
 & \text{State 1} & \text{State 2} \\
\text{Action} & (\text{prob. } p) & (\text{prob. } 1-p) \\
\hline
a & x_a = m & x_a = 0 \\
b & x_b = 0 & x_b = m \\
\end{array}
\qquad (2.12)
$$

With probability p, one environmental state is realized in which choice a yields $m > 0$ offspring, and choice b yields none, while with probability $1 - p$, the other environmental state is realized, in which the opposite is the case.[17] Without loss of generality, we assume that $p \in (\frac{1}{2}, 1]$ so that the environmental state in which choice a produces offspring is more likely.

In this simple case of 0 or m offspring, the expectation in Equation (2.7) can be evaluated explicitly as

$$
\alpha(f) = \log m + p \log f + (1 - p) \log(1 - f), \qquad (2.13)
$$

and the value of f that maximizes this expression is p. Despite the fact that setting $f = 1$ maximizes the likelihood that an individual is able to reproduce, such 'selfish' behaviour is not sustainable from the perspective of

---

[17] Note that the environment in this example does not satisfy Assumption 2.1 because there is a positive probability of zero offspring, implying that $\log(f x_a + (1-f)x_b)$ can have infinite moments. However, this does not affect any of the results in this chapter as long as we adopt the convention that $\log(0) = -\infty$ and, as a result, the population growth rate (Equation (2.7)) of the behaviour $f = 0$ and $f = 1$ becomes $-\infty$.

the population, because if all individuals were to behave in this way, the entire population would be wiped out the first time $x_a = 0$. Since such an extinction will almost certainly occur eventually,[18] the behaviour $f = 1$ will ultimately be eliminated from the population. In contrast, the randomizing behaviour, $f^* = p$, yields the highest possible growth rate, $I(p) = \log(mp^p(1 - p)^{(1-p)})$. Table 2.1 contains a numerical simulation of this example.

This is classic probability matching, first documented over half a century ago (Grant, Hake, and Hornseth, 1951). Since then, this behaviour has

Table 2.1 Simulated population sizes for a binary-choice model with five subpopulations in which individuals choose a with probability f and b with probability $1 - f$, where $f = 0.20, 0.50, 0.75, 0.90, 1.00$, and the initial population is 10 for each f. Reproductive uncertainty is systematic and binary, with $\text{Prob}(x_a = 3, x_b = 0) = 0.75$ and $\text{Prob}(x_a = 0, x_b = 3) = 0.25$. In this setting, probability matching, $f^* = 0.75$, is the growth-optimal behaviour.

Generation	$f = .20$	$f = .50$	$f^* = .75$	$f = .90$	$f = 1$
1	21	6	12	24	30
2	12	6	6	57	90
3	6	12	12	144	270
4	18	9	24	387	810
5	45	18	48	1,020	2,430
6	96	21	108	2,766	7,290
7	60	42	240	834	21,870
8	45	54	528	2,292	65,610
9	18	87	1,233	690	196,830
10	9	138	2,712	204	590,490
11	12	204	6,123	555	1,771,470
12	36	294	13,824	159	5,314,410
13	87	462	31,149	435	15,943,230
14	42	768	69,954	1,155	0
15	27	1,161	157,122	3,114	0
16	15	1,668	353,712	8,448	0
17	3	2,451	795,171	22,860	0
18	3	3,648	1,787,613	61,734	0
19	9	5,469	4,020,045	166,878	0
20	21	8,022	9,047,583	450,672	0
21	6	12,213	6,786,657	1,215,723	0
22	0	18,306	15,272,328	366,051	0
23	0	27,429	34,366,023	987,813	0
24	0	41,019	77,323,623	2,667,984	0
25	0	61,131	173,996,290	7,203,495	0

Source: Brennan, T. J., and Lo, A. W. (2012). An evolutionary model of bounded rationality and intelligence. *PLoS ONE* 7(11): e50310. https://doi.org/10.1371/journal.pone.0050310.

[18] If all individuals always choose a, and if (x_a, x_b) is IID over time, the probability of extinction by time t is $1 - p^t$, which approaches 1 as t increases without bound.

become so well-established among both human and nonhuman subjects that it is now referred to as the 'matching law' or 'Herrnstein's law'.[19] However, there are several notable departures from this behavioural pattern (Baum, 1974; Horne and Lowe, 1993; Kogler and Kühberger, 2007); hence, this 'law' may not be as consistent as its name might suggest. In the next section, we provide a general explanation for both probability matching behaviour and departures from it.

2.2.2 The General Case

The Bernoulli example above can be easily generalized to any arbitrary number of offspring for both choices:

$$\text{Prob}(x_a = c_{a1}, x_b = c_{b1}) \;=\; p \in [0,1],$$
$$\text{Prob}(x_a = c_{a2}, x_b = c_{b2}) \;=\; 1 - p \equiv q, \tag{2.14}$$

where we assume that $c_{ij} \geq 0$ and $c_{aj} + c_{bj} \neq 0$, $i = a, b$, and $j = 1, 2$. The condition $c_{aj} + c_{bj} \neq 0$ rules out the case where both c_{aj} and c_{bj} are 0, in which case the binary choice problem becomes degenerate, since both actions lead to extinction. Thus, the only choice that has any impact on fecundity is the non-extinction state, and the only behaviour that is sustainable is to select the action with the higher number of offspring.

The growth-optimal behaviour in this case will depend on the relationship between the probability, p, and the relative fecundity variables, $r_j \equiv c_{aj}/c_{bj}$, for each of the two possible states of the world, $j = 1, 2$.[20] Specifically, we have:

Proposition 2.3 *Under Assumptions 2.1 and 2.2, if (x_a, x_b) satisfies Equation (2.14), then the growth-optimal behaviour, f^*, is given by:*

$$f^* = \begin{cases} 1 & \text{if } r_2 \in [\, q + \frac{pq}{r_1 - p}, \infty) \text{ and } r_1 > p \\[2ex] \frac{p}{1 - r_2} + \frac{q}{1 - r_1} & \text{if } \begin{cases} r_2 \in (\frac{1}{q} - \frac{p}{q} r_1, q + \frac{pq}{r_1 - p}) \text{ and } r_1 > p, \text{ or} \\[1ex] r_2 \in (\frac{1}{q} - \frac{p}{q} r_1, \infty) \text{ and } r_1 \leq p \end{cases} \\[3ex] 0 & \text{if } r_2 \in [\, 0, \frac{1}{q} - \frac{p}{q} r_1\,]. \end{cases} \tag{2.15}$$

[19] See Hake and Hyman (1953), Herrnstein (1961), Herrnstein (1970), Bradshaw, Szabadi, and Bevan (1976), Davison and McCarthy (1988), Herrnstein and Prelec (1991), Herrnstein (1997), and Vulkan (2000).
    [20] Since c_{ij} may be 0, the ratios, r_j, may be infinite if a finite numerator is divided by 0. This poses no issues for any of the results in this chapter as long as the usual conventions involving infinity are followed. The ambiguous case of $r_j = 0/0$ is ruled out by the condition $c_{aj} + c_{bj} \neq 0$.

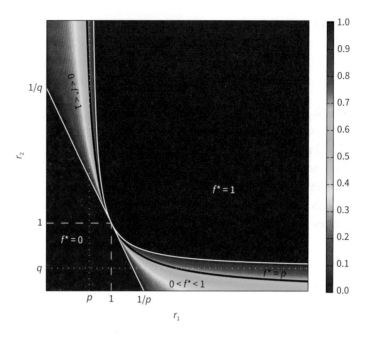

Fig. 2.1 Regions of the (r_1, r_2)-plane that imply deterministic $(f^* = 0$ or $1)$ or randomizing $(0 < f^* < 1)$ behaviour, where $r_j = c_{aj}/c_{bj}$ measures the relative fecundities of action a to action b in the two states, $j = 1, 2$. The asymptotes of the curved boundary line occur at $r_1 = p$ and $r_2 = q$. Values of r_1 and r_2 for which exact probability matching is optimal are given by the solid black curve.

Figure 2.1 illustrates the values of r_1 and r_2 that yield each of the three types of behaviours in Equation (2.15). If r_1 and r_2 are not too different, implying that the ratio of fecundities between choices a and b is not that different between the two states of the world, then random behaviour yields no evolutionary advantage over deterministic choice. In this case, the individually optimal behaviour $(f^* = 0$ or $1)$ will prevail in the population. If, however, one of the r variables is large while the other is small, then random behaviour will be more advantageous than a deterministic one from the perspective of the population. In such cases, there are times in which each choice performs substantially better than the other; hence, it is evolutionarily optimal for a population to diversify between the two choices, rather than to always choose the outcome with the highest probability of progeny in a single generation. This case is summarized in:

Corollary 2.2 *Suppose there exists a large difference between r_1 and r_2. Without loss of generality, let $r_1 \gg 0$, $r_2 \ll 1$, and $p > \frac{1}{2}$. Then under Assumptions 2.1* *and 2.2, and if (x_a, x_b) satisfies Equation (2.14), the growth-optimal behaviour is given by*

$$f^* = p(1 + O(1/r_1) + O(r_2)) \approx p. \qquad (2.16)$$

Equation (2.16) shows that if one choice is much worse than the other choice p per cent of the time, and if the other choice is much worse than the first $(1 - p)$ per cent of the time, then the first choice should be made with probability p, and the second choice should be made with probability $1-p$. The definition of 'much worse' is made precise by specifying that the values of $1/r_1$ and r_2 are both close to zero. Over time, the individuals that flourish in such a world are precisely those that engage in approximate probability matching behaviour.

This result can be further refined. When r_1 and r_2 satisfy the condition:

$$0 = p\frac{r_2}{1 - r_2} + q\frac{1}{1 - r_1}, \qquad (2.17)$$

exact probability matching behaviour arises. The solid black curve in Fig. 2.1 illustrates the locus of values for which this condition holds. The horizontal asymptote of the curve occurs at $r_2 = 0$, so as r_2 tends towards zero and r_1 becomes relatively large, exact probability matching will be optimal. (Note that the asymmetry between r_1 and r_2 is due entirely to our requirement that $f^* = p$ and $p \neq \frac{1}{2}$.) However, values of (r_1, r_2) off this curve but still within the shaded region imply random behaviour that is approximately—but not exactly—probability matching, providing a potential explanation for more complex but non-deterministic foraging patterns observed in various species (Deneubourg et al., 1987; Pasteels, Deneubourg, and Goss, 1987; Kirman, 1993; Thuijsman et al., 1995; Keasar et al., 2002).

In Chapter 5, we test this framework experimentally using human subjects facing binary choices with monetary payoffs calibrated at different values of r_1 and r_2. Although there are obviously many forces at work in determining human behaviour, even for narrowly defined tasks such as this, we find surprisingly consistent behaviour with the predictions of Equation (2.15).

2.2.3 Individually Optimal vs Growth-Optimal Behaviour

It is instructive to compare the growth-optimal behaviour of Equation (2.15) with behaviour that maximizes an individual's reproductive success, denoted by $\tilde{f}$:

Proposition 2.4 *Under Assumptions 2.1 and 2.2, and if (x_a, x_b) satisfies Equation (2.14), the individually optimal behaviour, $\tilde{f}$, is deterministic and given by*

$$\tilde{f} = \begin{cases} 1 & \text{if } r_2 > 1 + \frac{p}{q}(1 - r_1)r_3 \\ 0 & \text{if } r_2 < 1 + \frac{p}{q}(1 - r_1)r_3 \end{cases}, \quad r_3 \equiv \frac{c_{b1}}{c_{b2}}. \tag{2.18}$$

For a fixed value of r_3, the threshold in Equation (2.18) that determines the optimal individual behaviour is a line that divides the (r_1, r_2)-plane into two regions. For values of (r_1, r_2) above this line, $\tilde{f} = 1$, and for values below this line, $\tilde{f} = 0$. When $r_3 = 1$, this implies that any time the growth-optimal behaviour involves randomization, it will always be at odds with the individually optimal behaviour, $\tilde{f} = 1$. We shall return to this important special case in Section 2.3. Of course, from the perspective of the population, the growth-optimal behaviour, f^*, is independent of r_3, depending only on the relative performance of the two possible choices as measured by the relative fecundities r_1 and r_2.

We shall revisit this distinction between growth-optimal and individually optimal behaviour in Section 2.4, where we consider the case in which the randomness in offspring is idiosyncratic (i.e. (x_a, x_b) is IID across individuals, as well as across time). In this alternate environment, we will show that the growth-optimal and individually optimal behaviours are identical.

2.3 Risk Preferences

Our binary choice model can also be used to study the evolution of risk preferences, by making one of the two choices riskless. In particular, using the Bernoulli case, Equation (2.14), as our basis, suppose that choice b yields a non-random outcome, $c_{b1} = c_{b2} = c_b$ (or $r_3 = 1$). In this case, each individual is choosing between a random outcome and a certain one, where we maintain the assumption that:

$$\begin{aligned} \text{Prob}(x_a = c_{a1}, x_b = c_b) &= p \in [0, 1], \\ \text{Prob}(x_a = c_{a2}, x_b = c_b) &= 1 - p \equiv q. \end{aligned} \tag{2.19}$$

Without loss of generality, we assume that $c_{a1} < c_{a2}$. To ensure that the choice between a and b is not trivial, we require that $c_{a1} < c_b < c_{a2}$, otherwise one choice will always dominate the other trivially. For convenience, we shall parameterize c_b as a convex combination of the risky outcomes, c_{a1} and c_{a2}:

$$c_b \equiv \theta c_{a1} + (1 - \theta)c_{a2}, \ \theta \in (0, 1). \tag{2.20}$$

When $\theta = 0$, the riskless outcome is c_{a2}, which dominates the risky choice, and when $\theta = 1$, the riskless outcome is c_{a1}, which is dominated by the risky choice. As a result, $\theta \in (0, 1)$ covers the entire spectrum of possible risk–reward trade-offs in which neither choice dominates the other.

In the remainder of this section, we first derive the growth-optimal risk preferences by applying the results of Section 2.1 to Equation (2.19). Using these preferences, we then show how risk aversion emerges purely through the forces of natural selection, and derive an implied evolutionary 'risk premium' that is completely independent of any notion of economic equilibrium. Lastly, we also show how growth-optimal behaviour f^* can explain loss aversion.

2.3.1 Growth-Optimal Risk Preferences

Applying Proposition 2.3 to Equation (2.19) yields:

Corollary 2.3 *Under Assumptions 2.1 and 2.2, if (x_a, x_b) satisfies Equation (2.19), then the growth-optimal behaviour, f^*, is given by:*

$$f^* = \begin{cases} 1 & \text{if } \theta \in [\theta_o, 1) \\ \left(1 - \frac{p}{\theta}\right)\left(1 + \frac{1}{(1-\theta)(\sigma-1)}\right) & \text{if } \theta \in (p, \theta_o) , \\ 0 & \text{if } \theta \in (0, p] \end{cases} \qquad (2.21)$$

where $\theta_o \equiv p\sigma/(p\sigma + q)$, and $\sigma \equiv c_{a2}/c_{a1} > 1$.

Note that σ can be viewed as a crude measure of a's risk, thus our choice to use the symbol typically reserved for standard deviation. As θ increases from 0 to 1, the number of offspring produced by the riskless choice, b, decreases from c_{a2} to c_{a1}, making the risky choice, a, relatively more attractive. However, for values of θ from 0 to p, the risky choice is not sufficiently attractive, and the optimal behaviour is to select the sure thing ($f^* = 0$). As θ increases from p to θ_o, the optimal behaviour from the perspective of the population, f^*, is to select choice a with an increasingly higher probability. When θ exceeds the threshold θ_o, the risky choice becomes so attractive relative to the sure thing that individuals will always choose the risky alternative ($f^* = 1$). Figure 2.2 graphs this relationship between f^* and θ for three values of σ, showing that it is close to piecewise linear for $\sigma = 2$, but nonlinear for $\sigma = 100$.

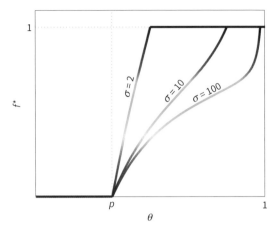

Fig. 2.2 The growth-optimal behaviour, f^*, as a function of θ for $p = 1/3$ and various levels of the ratio $\sigma = c_{a2}/c_{a1}$ of the two outcomes of the risky alternative, a. The parameter θ determines the magnitude of the payoff, $c_b = \theta c_{a1} + (1 - \theta) c_{a2}$, of the riskless alternative, b.

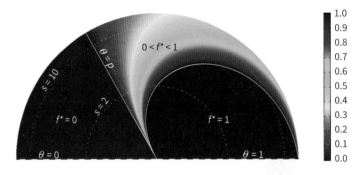

Fig. 2.3 Radial plot of the growth-optimal behaviour, f^*, for $p = 1/3$ as a function of θ, which varies from 0 to 1 clockwise around the semi-circle, and $\sigma = c_{a2}/c_{a1}$, which varies from 1 to infinity from the centre of the semi-circle to its perimeter. The parameter θ determines the magnitude of the payoff $c_b = \theta c_{a1} + (1 - \theta) c_{a2}$, of the riskless alternative, b.

Figure 2.3 provides a more complete depiction of the trade-off between σ and θ in determining the growth-optimal behaviour, f^*.

A more transparent version of the growth-optimal behaviour in Corollary 2.3 can be derived by restating Equation (2.21) in terms of the outcomes of each of the two choices, a and b. As before, let c_p and c_o denote the arithmetic and harmonic means of the a outcomes, respectively, so that

$$c_p \equiv p c_{a1} + q c_{a2} \quad \text{and} \quad c_v \equiv \frac{1}{\frac{p}{c_{a1}} + \frac{q}{c_{a2}}}. \tag{2.22}$$

The values c_o and c_p correspond to the values $\theta = \theta_o$ and $\theta = p$ in Corollary 2.3. Hence, the growth-optimal behaviour of an individual depends entirely on where the sure thing, c_b, lies in the range (c_{a1}, c_{a2}): if $c_b \in [c_{a1}, c_o]$, then the risky choice is always growth-optimal; if $c_b \in (c_o, c_p)$, randomizing between the risky choice and the safe choice is growth-optimal; and if $c_b \in [c_p, c_{a2})$, the safe choice is always growth-optimal.[21] These outcomes are illustrated in Fig. 2.4, where the green range for c_b yields the safe choice as the growth-optimal behaviour, the red range yields the risky choice, and the grey range yields randomization.

Of course, the growth-optimal behaviour also depends on p, the probability of the higher-yielding outcome in a. This dependence is implicit in the relative widths of the three ranges in Fig. 2.4. In particular, the relative width of the interval in which the riskless choice is always growth-optimal is given by p: the more likely the lower outcome of the risky asset, c_{a1}, the greater the range of values for which the certain outcome, c_b, dominates the risky outcome, c_a. The relative width of the interval in which the risky choice is always growth-optimal is given by $1/(1+\sigma p/(1-p))$, which decreases with both σ and p. As the riskiness of a or the likelihood of the lower outcome increases, the region in which the risky choice is always growth-optimal becomes smaller.

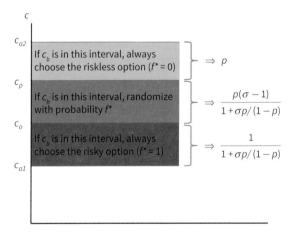

Fig. 2.4 Growth-optimal behaviour of the risky/riskless choice as a function of the magnitude of the riskless outcome, c_b. The green range for c_b indicates that the riskless choice is growth-optimal, the red range indicates that the risky choice is growth-optimal, and the grey region indicates that randomizing between the risky and riskless choices is growth-optimal. The widths of the three regions, relative to the total range, $c_{a2} - c_{a1}$, are displayed to the right of each region.

[21] Note that the ordering $c_{a1} < c_o < c_p < c_{a2}$ always holds, since the harmonic mean is less than the arithmetic mean.

For a fixed probability p, the risk parameter, σ, determines the relative magnitude of the randomization interval compared to the risky choice interval. Not surprisingly, for larger σ, the randomization interval is wider, implying there is a greater range of values of c_b for which randomizing between the risky and riskless choices is growth-optimal. We shall see another manifestation of this behaviour towards risk in the next section.

2.3.2 Risk Aversion

Our binary choice model also shows that the key property of risk aversion—the need to compensate individuals with a positive payment to induce them to accept a fair gamble (i.e. a risk premium)—arises quite naturally from natural selection. Chapter 6 discusses the evolutionary origin of risk aversion in more detail, but here we provide a short preview of the basic concepts.

Consider the risky/riskless case of Equation (2.19) in Section 2.3.1, but now let the payoffs for the risky option, a, be defined relative to the riskless payoff, c_b, of b:

$$c_{a1} \equiv c_b - d, \quad c_{a2} \equiv c_b + u, \quad u, d > 0 \tag{2.23}$$

in the special case in which the optimal behaviour, f^*, is exactly $\frac{1}{2}$, so that neither choice is selected more frequently than the other. This value implies that the growth-optimal behaviour is indifferent between the riskless payoff of b and the risky payoff of a, which, in turn, implies that the two choices must have the same consequences for population growth. In this respect, b's sure payoff may be viewed as the 'certainty equivalent' of a, an economic concept used to measure the dollar value of random payoffs.

Assuming that $p = q = \frac{1}{2}$ so that u and d are equally likely outcomes, we are then able to derive the implications of these parameter settings for u and d:

$$u = d + \frac{d^2}{c_b - d}. \tag{2.24}$$

When $u = d$, behaviour is said to be 'risk neutral', because the expected value of a is identical to the sure payoff of b. However, Equation (2.24) shows that u must exceed d by a positive amount $d^2/(c_b - d)$ in order to be consistent with the behaviour $f^* = \frac{1}{2}$. The difference between the expected values of a and b is

$$\pi \equiv \frac{d^2}{2(c_b - d)}, \tag{2.25}$$

which can be considered an evolutionary risk premium. However, unlike the risk premia of economic models of rational markets (Merton, 1980; Mehra and Prescott, 1985), which depend on the equalization of supply and demand, π arises from the fact that populations grow geometrically (see Equation (2.7)), and the factor by which the population grows, $\exp(\mathbb{E}[\log(x)])$, is always less than or equal to the expected number of offspring in a single generation, $\mathbb{E}[x]$, due to Jensen's inequality, which states that the expected value of a convex function $g(\cdot)$ of a random variable x is greater than or equal to the function of the expected value of x, or $\mathbb{E}[g(x)] \geq g(\mathbb{E}[x])$.[22] In a study on risk-sensitive foraging behaviour, Smallwood (1996) applies Jensen's inequality to derive risk-averse behaviour by first assuming that an animal's fitness is an increasing but concave function of its energy level, and then applying Jensen's inequality to foraging behaviour that yields random energy levels. Jensen's inequality implies that risky choices will always yield lower population growth than the corresponding riskless choices with identical expected values. From an evolutionary perspective, the only sustainable behaviour in which a and b are equally likely to be chosen is if the risky choice, a, yields a larger expected number of offspring than the riskless choice, b (i.e. u must always be larger than d).

This result may also explain risk aversion in nonhuman animal species such as risk-sensitive foraging behaviour. Regardless of the species, Equation (2.24) shows that when c_b is very large relative to d, the evolutionary risk premium, π, becomes negligible, since a bad outcome for a has very little impact on growth rates given the magnitude of c_b. However, when d is close to c_b, a bad outcome for a implies near sterility for that individual; hence, a substantial risk premium is required to maintain the individual's indifference between a and b.

2.3.3 Loss Aversion

Growth-optimal behaviour can also generate loss aversion, the tendency of human subjects to take less risk when choosing between two potential gains but more risk when choosing between two potential losses (Tversky and Kahneman, 1974; Kahneman and Tversky, 1979). For example, when offered the choice between investment opportunities A and B, where A is a lottery ticket paying \$1 million with a 25% probability and \$0 with 75% probability and B

---

[22] The opposite inequality holds for concave functions.

generates a sure profit of $240,000, the vast majority of MIT Sloan School of Management MBA students have chosen B in many trials over the past two decades.[23] However, when the same subjects were offered the choice between investment opportunities A′ and B′, where A′ is a lottery ticket yielding a loss of $1,000,000 with 75% probability and $0 with 25% probability and B′ generates a sure loss of $750,000, virtually all of them chose A′, the more risky alternative. Such inconsistent risk attitudes have materially adverse consequences: the most popular choices of B and A′ yield a combined outcome that is $10,000 less than A and B′, no matter how the lotteries turn out. To see why, note that the combined outcome of choices B and A′ is –$760,000 with a probability of 75%, and $240,000 with a probability of 25%, while, in contrast, the combined outcome of choices A and B′ is –$750,000 with a probability of 75%, and $250,000 with a probability of 25%. Thus, a subject choosing B and A′ expects to have an outcome that is $10,000 worse than the outcome corresponding to the choices of A and B′. Moreover, if the results of the two lotteries are perfectly correlated, then a subject choosing B and A′ obtains a combined payoff that is $10,000 lower in each possible state of the outcomes.

To see how loss aversion arises in our framework, we must first consider the relationship between monetary payoffs and reproductive success. That is, we must link an individual's financial wealth to the number of offspring that wealth affords. Only when this relationship is specified can we deduce the impact of natural selection on decisions involving financial gain or loss. We denote by $r(w)$ a 'reproduction function' that yields the number of offspring produced by an individual with total wealth w. Some elementary biological and economic considerations suggest the following three properties for $r(w)$:

Assumption 2.3 $r(w)$ *is a continuous non-decreasing function of wealth w.*

Assumption 2.4 $r(w) = 0$ *for all levels of wealth, w, below a subsistence level w_o.*

Assumption 2.5 $r(w) = \bar{c} > 0$ *for all levels of wealth, w, above an abundance level w_r.*

Assumption 2.3 states that more wealth leads to more offspring. Assumption 2.4 acknowledges the existence of a subsistence level of wealth below which an

---

[23] This example is a modification of experiments originally conducted by Tversky and Kahneman (1974) with Stanford undergraduate students using actual cash payoffs. The MIT Sloan MBA versions were based exclusively on hypothetical classroom surveys, the primary modification an increase in the dollar values of the outcomes—a very telling change that was necessitated by the fact that MBA students did not exhibit loss aversion with smaller payoffs. See the discussion in the remainder of this section for an explanation of this difference.

individual cannot produce any offspring. Lastly, Assumption 2.5 reflects the existence of environmental resource constraints that place an upper limit on the number of offspring any individual can generate, irrespective of wealth.

These assumptions seem obvious and almost trivially true,[24] yet they have surprisingly sharp implications for the properties of $r(w)$: they imply that $r(w)$ necessarily resembles the S-shaped utility functions documented experimentally by Kahneman, Slovic, and Tversky (1982) and other behavioural economists in a sense made precise by the following proposition.

Proposition 2.5 *If $r(w)$ satisfies Assumptions 2.3–2.5 and is twice continuously differentiable, then $r(w)$ is concave for sufficiently large values of w and convex for sufficiently small values of w. If $r(w)$ satisfies Assumptions 2.3–2.5 but is not continuously differentiable, then a slightly weaker result holds: there exist values $w_1 < w_2$ such that*

$$r(\lambda w + (1 - \lambda)w_1) \le \lambda r(w) + (1 - \lambda)r(w_1), \quad \text{for } w \ll w_1, \text{ and} \qquad (2.26)$$

$$r(\lambda w + (1 - \lambda)w_2) \ge \lambda r(w) + (1 - \lambda)r(w_2), \quad \text{for } w \gg w_2, \qquad (2.27)$$

where $\lambda \in [0, 1]$.

It should be remarked that an even more fundamental implication of our evolutionary model of behaviour is that an individual's relative wealth—that is, wealth relative to other members of the population—should be more important than absolute wealth, as suggested by Duesenberry (1949) and Frank (2000). This follows trivially from Corollary 2.1 and the existence of a mapping $r(w)$ between wealth and fecundity. Because evolutionary success is determined solely by relative growth rates, and assuming reasonably similar functions $r(w)$ across individuals (i.e. they have similar biological specifications and constraints), a monotonic relationship between wealth and fecundity implies that, *ceteris paribus*, natural selection will favour those individuals with higher relative wealth. Note that Duesenberry's (1949) 'relative income hypothesis' refers to income, not wealth. However, because wealth is highly correlated with cumulative income flows, the empirical phenomena associated with relative wealth should also manifest themselves in relative income, again *ceteris paribus*. Chapter 15 discusses the implications for financial growth in settings of relative wealth.

---

[24] Perhaps the least obvious of the three is the continuity assumption (Assumption 2.3), which depends on the numeraire with which wealth is measured, and how wealth interacts with the biology of reproduction. With the advent of fiat money, and given current *in vitro* fertilization technologies, we believe that continuity is a reasonable approximation to human reproduction.

With our assumptions and Proposition 2.5 in place, we may now translate monetary payoffs into number of offspring through the reproduction function, $r(w)$, and examine the impact of evolution on the behaviour of individuals choosing between dollar-denominated choices in the experimental setting described above.

Consider an experiment along the lines of Kahneman and Tversky (1979), in which an individual is asked to choose between a risky investment, A, yielding one of two final wealth levels, w_{a1} and w_{a2}, which imply reproductive outcomes $c_{a1} \equiv r(w_{a1})$ and $c_{a2} \equiv r(w_{a2})$, and a riskless investment, B, yielding a guaranteed final wealth level, w_b, which translates into the reproductive outcome $c_b \equiv r(w_b)$. Suppose that the initial wealth of the individual is modest relative to the incremental payoffs of A, so that the total wealth obtained in either outcome of A is large. Then we have:

Corollary 2.4 *Under Assumptions 2.1–2.5, if w_{a1} is sufficiently large so that $r(\cdot)$ is concave throughout the interval $[w_{a1}, w_{a2}]$, we have $r^{-1}(c_p) < w_p = pw_{a1} + qw_{a2}$, and the growth-optimal behaviour is to take the safe bet whenever w_b is in the region $\left[r^{-1}(c_p), w_{a2}\right]$, which is strictly larger than $[w_p, w_{a2}]$ by the incremental interval $\left[r^{-1}(c_p), w_p\right]$ that depends on the concavity of $r(w)$. For values of w_b below $r^{-1}(c_p)$, the growth-optimal behaviour is either to randomize or to take the risky bet, according to whether w_b is larger or smaller than $r^{-1}(c_0)$, respectively, where c_0 is defined in Equation (2.22).*

Corollary (2.4) shows that if an individual is confronted with a risky investment A that involves sufficiently large gains—so large that the relevant portion of $r(w)$ is concave—and the riskless investment B is not too small relative to the payoffs from A, but possibly smaller than the expected payoff, w_p, from A, then the growth-optimal behaviour will be to select the sure thing. These results show that an individual is risk averse when it comes to gains, preferring sure bets that pay less than the expected value of risky bets, when the individual begins with a modest level of wealth, if A and B both are able to move the individual's total wealth into the concave region of $r(w)$, and if w_b is in the nonempty range $\left[r^{-1}(c_p), w_p\right]$.

Now consider two investment alternatives, A' and B', where A' is a risky investment yielding one of two final wealth levels, w'_{a1} and w'_{a2}, which translate into reproductive outcomes $c'_{a1} \equiv r(w'_{a1})$ and $c'_{a2} \equiv r(w'_{a2})$, and B' is a riskless investment with a guaranteed final wealth level w'_b, which translates into the reproductive outcome $c'_b \equiv r(w'_b)$, and suppose that w'_{a2} is small, implying incremental losses relative to initial wealth. Then we have:

Corollary 2.5 *Under Assumptions 2.1–2.5, if w'_{a2} is sufficiently small so that $r(\cdot)$ is convex throughout the interval $\left[w'_{a1}, w'_{a2}\right]$, we have $r^{-1}(c'_p) > w'_p = pw'_{a1} + qw'_{a2}$, and the growth-optimal behaviour is either to randomize or to always take the risky bet whenever w'_b is in the region $\left[w'_{a1}, r^{-1}(c'_p)\right]$, which is strictly larger than $\left[w'_{a1}, w'_p\right]$. Moreover, the region in which the growth-optimal behaviour is to always take the risky bet, namely $\left[w'_{a1}, r^{-1}(c'_0)\right]$, may also be strictly larger than $\left[w'_{a1}, w'_p\right]$. This will occur if the function $r(w)$ is both invertible in $\left[w'_{a1}, w'_{a2}\right]$ and also sufficiently convex so its reciprocal, $1/r(w)$, is concave in this region.*

Corollary 2.5 shows that for a sufficiently extreme sure loss, w'_b, individuals will always choose the risky option, A', despite the fact that this choice may lead to an even greater loss, w'_{a1}, with probability p. In addition, individuals will always choose the risky option with some positive probability, even though the expected payoff of the risky option is less than that of the safe bet, provided that the safe payoff, w'_b, is in the nonempty region $\left[w'_p, r^{-1}(c'_p)\right]$. Moreover, they will choose the risky option with 100% probability even if the expected payoff of the risky option is less than that of the safe bet, provided that $r(w)$ is sufficiently convex so that $1/r(w)$ is concave and w'_b is in the nonempty region $\left[w'_p, r^{-1}(c'_0)\right]$. This type of behaviour for $r(w)$ will occur, for example, whenever $r(w)$ follows a power law of the form $\alpha(\beta - w)^{-\gamma}$, for $0 < \gamma < 1$.

Loss aversion arises when more risk is taken when choosing between a sure loss and a risky loss, and less risk is taken when choosing between a sure gain and a risky gain. Corollaries 2.4 and 2.5 show that such behaviour is clearly growth-optimal under Assumptions 2.3–2.5. However, our results go beyond this basic pattern, and imply that individuals will not simply choose to always take the safe bet or to always take the risky choice. Rather, there is also a region of w_b values, namely $\left[r^{-1}(c_o), r^{-1}(c_p)\right]$ or $\left[r^{-1}(c'_o), r^{-1}(c'_p)\right]$, where randomization is optimal. In addition, for suitably constructed extreme losses (i.e. tail risk), taking the risky bet deterministically is rarely optimal, and instead some degree of randomization is generally best. These results are illustrated graphically in Fig. 2.5.

Our framework may also explain some of the inconsistencies and instabilities in the experimental evidence for loss aversion. One potential source of instability is the fact that the typical experimental design offers the same fixed set of choices to all subjects in a given experiment, a standard protocol to maintain identical 'treatments' across subjects in order to render the outcomes comparable across individuals. However, if subjects make decisions based on reproductive success, then the proper method for controlled experimentation is to offer all subjects the same choices denominated in

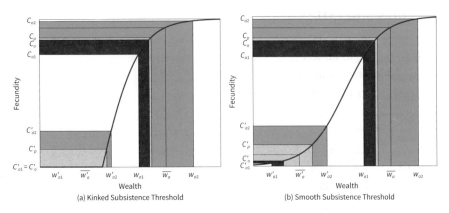

Fig. 2.5 (a) Kinked and (b) smooth subsistence thresholds in reproduction functions, $r(w)$, (in blue) relating the number of offspring, c, to monetary wealth, w. In both graphs, if w_b is in the green region, then always choosing the riskless choice, b, is growth-optimal ($f^* = 0$); if w_b is in the red region, then always choosing the risky choice, a, is growth-optimal ($f^* = 1$); and if w_b is in the grey region between red and green, randomization is growth-optimal. Wealth values denoted with primes are equal to those denoted without primes less a common fixed amount, and the colour coding is identical.

terms of reproductive success, not in the same incremental dollar wagers. Of course, without knowledge of each subject's net worth and reproduction function, it is impossible to construct such a controlled experiment even if it were economically viable. But, by offering the same fixed-dollar wagers, two sources of variation across subjects are injected into the experimental outcome: variation in the level of wealth, and variation in the reproduction function, $r(w)$. These factors may explain some of the variability in the findings of loss aversion studies across venues and subject pools.

Of course, the fact that loss aversion emerges from an evolutionary process does not imply that it is optimal from an individual investor's perspective. In fact, loss-averse behaviour is routinely singled out by professional traders as counterproductive to their objectives. For example, the phenomenon of 'doubling down' in the face of mounting losses is a common behavioural pattern among inexperienced traders, and the adage to 'cut your losses and ride your gains' is time-honoured Wall Street wisdom that is meant to correct this known tendency towards loss aversion. In this respect, loss aversion is yet another example of the evolutionary principle that individually optimal behaviour need not coincide with the growth-optimal behaviour, a distinction we address explicitly in Section 2.4.

2.4 Idiosyncratic versus Systematic Risk

So far we have assumed that the number of offspring from actions a and b are given by the same two random variables, x_a and x_b, respectively, for all individuals. In other words, we have assumed that fecundity is systematic, which implies significant differences between growth-optimal and individually optimal behaviour under certain conditions. In this section, we show that if the uncertainty in reproduction is instead idiosyncratic to each individual, the growth-optimal behaviour always coincides with individually optimal behaviour. This difference points to the central role that aggregate uncertainty plays in shaping the evolution of behaviour and preferences.[25] In this section, we first consider the case where fecundity is purely idiosyncratic, so that $(x_{a,i}, x_{b,i})$ are IID across individuals in a given generation. We then discuss the general case of both idiosyncratic and systematic fecundity.

2.4.1 Idiosyncratic Risk

As before, we denote by x_i^f the random number of offspring produced by individual i. However, suppose that:

$$x_i^f = I_i^f x_{a,i} + (1 - I_i^f) x_{b,i}, \qquad I_i^f \equiv \begin{cases} 1 & \text{with probability } f \\ 0 & \text{with probability } 1 - f \end{cases}, \quad (2.28)$$

where

Assumption 2.6 $(x_{a,i}, x_{b,i})$ *is IID over time and across individuals i in a given generation.*

In contrast to the systematic case in Equation (2.2) and Assumption 2.2, $(x_{a,i}, x_{b,i})$ are now assumed to be IID across individuals, as well as across time, and I_i^f are the same Bernoulli 0 or 1 random variables that summarize the behaviour of individual i, as defined in Section 2.1.2.

Assumption 2.6 is a seemingly small change, but it has dramatic consequences for the evolutionary dynamics of the population and growth-optimal behaviour. In this case, the randomness in the number of offspring is strictly idiosyncratic, in the sense that the correlation between the number of offspring for two individuals, i and j, is 0, even if both individuals choose the same course of action. Recall from Equation (2.2) that in the systematic case, if two individuals choose action a, both will generate the same number of random offspring, x_a (i.e. their reproductive success is perfectly correlated). Idiosyncratic fecundity implies that even if all individuals in a given population choose the same action, there will still be considerable cross-sectional variability in the number of offspring produced. This diversified outcome has a very different set of consequences for growth-optimal behaviour.

In particular, in the idiosyncratic case, the total number of offspring, n_t^f, across all type-f individuals in generation t is:

$$ n_t^f \;=\; \sum_{i=1}^{n_{t-1}^f} x_{i,t}^f \;=\; \sum_{i=1}^{n_{t-1}^f} I_{i,t}^f x_{a,i,t} \;+\; \sum_{i=1}^{n_{t-1}^f} (1 - I_{i,t}^f) x_{b,i,t}, \qquad (2.29) $$

$$ \frac{n_t^f}{n_{t-1}^f} \;\overset{p}{=}\; f\mu_a \;+\; (1-f)\mu_b, \quad \mu_a \equiv \mathbb{E}[x_{a,i}], \;\; \mu_b \equiv \mathbb{E}[x_{b,i}], \qquad (2.30) $$

where Equation (2.30) follows from the law of large numbers applied to the sums $\sum_i I_i^f x_{a,i}/m$ and $\sum_i I_i^f x_{b,i}/m$.[26] The key difference between Equation (2.4) and Equation (2.30) is that in the latter case, both the individual's choice and the number of offspring are idiosyncratic; hence, both are subject to the law of large numbers. This implies that in a large population of m individuals, even if all individuals choose action a, the outcomes will vary across individuals ($x_{a,i}$), while in the systematic case, all individuals will receive the identical number of offspring, x_a. Alternatively, in the systematic case, the number of offspring of individuals i and j is perfectly correlated, but, in the idiosyncratic case, it is perfectly uncorrelated.

This difference has significant consequences when we consider the behaviour of a group of type-f individuals over time. Adding a time subscript t as before to denote the population size of this group at time t, n_t^f, we have:

$$ \frac{n_t^f}{n_{t-1}^f} \;\overset{p}{=}\; f\mu_a \;+\; (1-f)\mu_b. \qquad (2.31) $$

[26] By construction, I_i^f and $x_{k,i}$ are independent, $k = a, b$; hence, their expected product is the product of their expectations, and Kolmogorov's law of large numbers guarantees almost sure convergence as long as they are IID and their first moments are finite

Without loss of generality, we normalize $m = 1$ at $t = 1$. Hence, the total population size in generation T is:

$$n_T^f \overset{p}{=} \left(f\mu_a + (1-f)\mu_b \right)^T, \tag{2.32}$$

$$\left(n_T^f \right)^{1/T} \overset{p}{=} \exp\left(\log(f\mu_a + (1-f)\mu_b) \right), \tag{2.33}$$

where Equation (2.33) differs from Equation (2.6) in that there is no expectation over x_a and x_b, because the idiosyncratic nature of the cross-section of individuals has eliminated the randomness in the population. This simple expression attains its optimum at the extremes of f. Thus, we have:

Proposition 2.6 *Under Assumptions 2.1 and 2.6, the growth-optimal behaviour, f^*, is given by:*

$$f^* = \begin{cases} 1 & \text{if } \mu_a > \mu_b \\ 0 & \text{if } \mu_a \leq \mu_b \end{cases}, \tag{2.34}$$

which coincides with the individually optimal behaviour, $\tilde{f}$.

Proposition 2.6 states that when the randomness in fecundity is purely idiosyncratic, the growth-optimal behaviour coincides with the individually optimal behaviour. In contrast to the case of systematic fecundity, since the outcome of each individual's decision is independent of the outcomes of the decisions of other individuals, it is exceedingly improbable for the entire population to become extinct, even if all individuals engage in identical behaviour.[27] However, when the randomness is purely systematic, the identical behaviour among individuals does lead to extinction with positive probability. Hence, the growth-optimal behaviour differs from individually optimal behaviour. If environmental challenges to reproductive success are systematic, the only type of behaviour that can survive in the long run within our framework is some form of randomization.

The difference between idiosyncratic and systematic risk affects more than behaviour; populations subjected to idiosyncratic environmental risk grow

---

[27] If we assume two states of nature, as in the case of exact probability matching (Equation (2.12)), the probability of extinction is the probability that all individuals acting individually optimally will simultaneously experience an outcome of zero offspring. Without loss of generality, if we assume $p > \frac{1}{2}$, then $\tilde{f} = f^* = 0$ (see Proposition 2.6). Hence, the probability of extinction is p^n, which approaches 0 quickly even for modest population sizes (e.g. $0.45^{50} = 4.6 \times 10^{-18}$).

much more quickly. To see why, recall from Corollary 2.1 that in the case of systematic risk, the geometric average growth rate of the growth-optimal population, f^*, is given by

$$\left(n_T^{f^*}\right)^{1/T} \stackrel{p}{=} \exp(\alpha(f^*)) \; = \; \exp\big(\mathbb{E}[\log(f^*x_a + (1 - f^*)x_b)]\big), \quad (2.35)$$

where f^* is given by Equation (2.8). In the case of idiosyncratic risk, Proposition 2.6 implies that the geometric average growth rate of the growth-optimal population, f^*, is given by the larger of μ_a and μ_b. Without loss of generality, we assume that $\mu_a > \mu_b$. We then have the following inequality:

$$\exp\big(\mathbb{E}[\log(f^*x_a + (1 - f^*)x_b)]\big) \leq \exp\big(\log \mathbb{E}[f^*x_a + (1 - f^*)x_b]\big) \quad (2.36)$$

$$= f^*\mu_a + (1 - f^*)\mu_b \; \leq \; \mu_a, \quad (2.37)$$

where Equation (2.36) follows from Jensen's inequality and Equation (2.37) is a strict inequality, unless $f^* = 1$ in the case of systematic risk.

Consider two otherwise identical populations, both of which have the same marginal distribution for (x_a, x_b), but where (x_a, x_b) is systematic in one and idiosyncratic in the other. The population with idiosyncratic risk will grow at least as fast, and typically faster, than the population with systematic risk. This holds despite the fact that the expected number of offspring, (μ_a, μ_b), is the same in both populations, and is driven by two distinct factors: Jensen's inequality and the possibility of randomizing behaviour in the case of systematic risk. Jensen's inequality is the same mechanism at work in generating risk aversion (see Section 2.3.2). An IID cross-section of individuals is able to approximate a 'riskless' rate of growth for large populations because the law of large numbers applies within a single generation, which is not the case for a population with systematic risk. The latter case is simply a consequence of the fact that in populations where randomizing behaviour is growth-optimal, a fraction of the population selects the choice with the lower expected value. Hence, this population will, by definition, grow at a slower rate than the population with systematic risk where every individual selects the choice with the higher expected value.

To develop an appreciation for the magnitude of these effects, consider the case of exact probability matching in Section 2.2.1, in which $f^* = p$, where p is the probability of state 1 in Equation (2.12). Without loss of generality, we let $p > \frac{1}{2}$. The ratio of the geometric average growth rates of the idiosyncratic and systematic cases is given by:

$$\left(\frac{n_T^{f^*=1}}{n_T^{f^*=p}}\right)^{1/T} \;\;\stackrel{a}{=}\;\; \frac{mp}{mp^p(1-p)^{1-p}} \;=\; \left(\frac{p}{1-p}\right)^{1-p}. \tag{2.38}$$

For $p = 0.6$, this ratio is 1.176, implying that the geometric average growth rate of the population with idiosyncratic risk is 17.6% greater than the population with systematic risk. While this may seem small, it implies that after fifty generations, the population size in the case of idiosyncratic risk will be approximately 3,325 times that in the case of systematic risk.

2.4.2 The General Case

We now consider the general case in which the random mechanism determining fecundity contains both systematic and idiosyncratic components. We denote by x_i^f the random number of offspring produced by individual i, and suppose that:

$$x_i^f = I_i^f x_{a,i} + (1 - I_i^f)x_{b,i}, \;\; I_i^f \;\equiv\; \begin{cases} 1 & \text{with probability } f \\ 0 & \text{with probability } 1-f \end{cases}, \tag{2.39}$$

$$x_{k,i} = y_{k,i} + z_k, \;\; k = a, b, \tag{2.40}$$

where

Assumption 2.7 $(y_{a,i}, y_{b,i})$ *is IID across individuals and over time, and* z_k *is IID over time and identical across individuals in the same generation.*

In Assumption 2.7, the idiosyncratic component, $(y_{a,i}, y_{b,i})$, is IID across individuals, as well as across time, whereas the systematic component, z_k, is the same across individuals but IID across time, and I_i^f are the same Bernoulli 0 or 1 random variables summarizing the behaviour of individual i, as defined in Section 2.1.2.

Given that I_i^f are IID across the population of individuals of type f, we have the following expression for the total number of offspring, n_t^f, across all type-f individuals in generation t:

$$n_t^f = \sum_{i=1}^{n_{t-1}^f} x_{i,t}^f = \sum_{i=1}^{n_{t-1}^f} I_i^f (y_{a,i} + z_a) + \sum_{i=1}^{n_{t-1}^f} (1 - I_i^f)(y_{b,i} + z_b), \qquad (2.41)$$

$$\frac{n_t^f}{n_{t-1}^f} \overset{p}{=} f(\mu_a + z_a) + (1 - f)(\mu_b + z_b), \ \mu_k \equiv \mathbb{E}[y_{k,i}], \ k = a, b. \qquad (2.42)$$

Note that Equation (2.42) is a combination of Equations (2.4) and (2.30), containing both stochastic and non-stochastic components, reflecting the impact of the systematic and idiosyncratic components in reproduction. This implies that as T increases without bound, the geometric average growth rate of the population of type-f individuals is well approximated by

$$\left(n_T^f\right)^{1/T} \overset{p}{=} \exp\!\left(\mathbb{E}\log(f(\mu_a + z_a) + (1 - f)(\mu_b + z_b))\right), \qquad (2.43)$$

which follows from the law of large numbers, as before. From this expression, we see that the value of f that maximizes the population size, n_T^f, is the value that maximizes the expectation:

$$\alpha(f) \equiv \mathbb{E}[\log(f(\mu_a + z_a) + (1 - f)(\mu_b + z_b))], \qquad (2.44)$$

which is virtually identical to the systematic case (Equation (2.7)), the only difference arising from the shift in mean μ_k from the idiosyncratic component, $y_{k,i}$. We then have:

Proposition 2.7 *Under Assumptions 2.1 and 2.7, the growth-optimal behaviour, f^*, is given by*

$$f^* = \begin{cases} 1 & \text{if } \mathbb{E}[w_a/w_b] > 1 \text{ and } \mathbb{E}[w_b/w_a] < 1 \\ \text{solution to Equation (2.46)} & \text{if } \mathbb{E}[w_a/w_b] \geq 1 \text{ and } \mathbb{E}[w_b/w_a] \geq 1, \\ 0 & \text{if } \mathbb{E}[w_a/w_b] < 1 \text{ and } \mathbb{E}[w_b/w_a] > 1 \end{cases} \qquad (2.45)$$

where f^* is defined implicitly in the second case of Equation (2.45) by

$$0 = \mathbb{E}\left[\frac{w_a - w_b}{f^* w_a + (1 - f^*)w_b}\right], \qquad (2.46)$$

and the expectations in Equations (2.6)–(2.9) are with respect to the joint distribution, $\Phi(w_a, w_b)$, where

$$w_k \equiv \mu_k + z_k, \ k = a, b. \qquad (2.47)$$

Proposition 2.7 shows that the general case in which an individual's action leads to random offspring with idiosyncratic and systematic components is mathematically equivalent to the systematic case with an additional shift in mean from the idiosyncratic component.

Our comparison of systematic and idiosyncratic environmental risks yields an interesting implication for populations in which the environment is heterogeneous. Consider an environment that consists of several distinct regions, some with idiosyncratic risk and others with systematic risk, and suppose that these regions are initially populated uniformly (i.e. all possible behaviours, $f \in [0, 1]$, are represented within each region). Over time, the regions that will reproduce most rapidly are those with the greatest proportion of idiosyncratic risk. This effect may give the appearance of individuals seeking out environmental conditions and niches in which the risks are more idiosyncratic, but it is merely a consequence of Jensen's inequality that requires no self-awareness, volition, or intelligence.

The differences across regions may also be interpreted as yet another form of group selection (Wynne-Edwards, 1962; Sober and Wilson, 1998), in which groups defined by regions of idiosyncratic risk are favoured. As in the case of Proposition 2.1, it is the environment—specifically, the type of reproductive risk—that determines the definition of the group on which natural selection operates.

This result also provides an intriguing normative implication: to the extent that survival is the objective and the future environment is uncertain, policies that lead to greater idiosyncratic fecundity such as biodiversity may be desirable to the population as a whole, leading to improvements in population growth rates by $f^* \mu_a + (1 - f^*)\mu_b$. We will revisit this topic in Chapter 6.

2.5 Discussion

The link between behaviour and reproductive success in a binary choice model is the key to an evolutionary explanation for several commonly observed behaviours in many animal species. While risk aversion, loss aversion, probability matching, and more general forms of randomizing behaviour may seem suboptimal for the individual, these behaviours persist over time and across many species precisely because they are optimal from the perspective of the population. Moreover, as environmental conditions change, the growth-optimal behaviour may also change in response to new selective pressures. Hence, the inexplicably erratic actions of certain species may well be adaptive rather than simply irrational.

These considerations may seem more relevant for the foraging behaviour of ants and bees than for human challenges such as investing in the stock market. After all, most decisions we face each day have little to do with our reproductive success. As a result, the relevance of f^* to economic and social behaviour may be questioned. The answer to this difficulty lies in the degree to which evolutionary pressures have a bearing on behaviour, summarized by the specification of $\Phi(x_a, x_b)$. For example, if a choice between a and b has no impact on fecundity (e.g. monetary prizes that are small in comparison to an individual's net worth), then x_a and x_b will be statistically identical, because either choice leaves the individual with the same reproductive prospects. In this case, the bivariate distribution, $\Phi(x_a, x_b)$, reduces to a univariate distribution, $\Phi(x)$, natural selection is indifferent to the choice between a and b, and f^* is indeterminate. Therefore, whether f^* is applicable to a given context is fully captured by the relationship between the behaviours of individuals and their impact on reproductive success (i.e. Φ).

One concrete illustration of how Φ plays this role is the case of loss aversion. When the dollar amounts offered to subjects in the standard loss aversion experiments are too low, loss aversion is not observed (see footnote 23). This result can be easily understood in the context of Φ: when the stakes are high, the outcomes have a measurable impact on reproductive fitness (broadly defined). Hence, one aspect of loss aversion may be observed ($f^* = 1$). But when the stakes are too low, the consequences of both choices for fitness are identical; hence, the growth-optimal behaviour has nothing to say about the outcome of the experiment.

It should be emphasized that the behaviours derived in our simple framework are primitive, both conceptually and from an evolutionary perspective. We have purposefully abstracted away the more realistic aspects of biology and behaviour such as sexual reproduction, random mutations, neuroplasticity, learning, communication, and strategic behaviour to focus on those behaviours that are primordial and common to most living organisms. By definition, those common behaviours must confer significant advantages in the face of stochastic environmental conditions. Otherwise, they would not have survived over time and become so widespread within and across species.

Of course, more complex behaviours will arise as new species emerge and evolve. Although the specific biological manifestations of behaviour are beyond the scope of our analysis, imaging and neurophysiological studies of decision-making under uncertainty in humans and primates (Breiter et al., 2001; Smith et al., 2002; Fehr and Camerer, 2007; Gold and Shadlen, 2007; Spitzer et al., 2007; Yang and Shadlen, 2007; Rangel, Camerer, and

Montague, 2008; Bossaerts, 2009; Resulaj et al., 2009; Wunderlich, Rangel, and O'Doherty, 2009; Hare et al., 2010), including studies of loss aversion (Kuhnen and Knutson, 2005; De Martino et al., 2006; Tom et al., 2007), are beginning to identify the neural mechanisms involved in these adaptations. From these studies, it is not difficult to see how sensory inputs, memory, and other neural substrates can yield a much greater variety of behaviours from which nature selects the most advantageous, including the ability to avoid probability matching altogether (Shanks, Tunney, and McCarthy, 2002). In Part III of this book, we provide more colour on how these behaviours are related to our brain from a neuroscientific perspective.

To see how such mechanisms might have arisen through the forces of natural selection, our simple binary choice model can easily be extended to allow for sexual reproduction, random mutations (see Chapter 3), and an arbitrary number of possible actions, each with its own consequences on the number of offspring. These actions can, in turn, depend on a vector of auxiliary 'state variables' $\mathbf{Z}$ (see Chapter 4). This more complex framework can generate considerably more sophisticated types of behaviour, including learning, memory (see Chapter 9), and, ultimately, the emergence of intelligence (see Chapter 8). Part II of this book explores such extensions. However, economists have implicitly incorporated these more sophisticated decision-making mechanisms through utility theory (Robson, 1996a, 2001a,b; Grafen, 1999; Bernheim and Rangel, 2009), arguing convincingly that utility functions are also shaped by the pressures of natural selection (Hansson and Stuart, 1990; Rogers, 1994; Robson, 1996b; Curry, 2001; Samuelson, 2001; Robson and Samuelson, 2007, 2009). Our current framework may be viewed as a bridge between the higher level utility-based models of human behaviour and the more primitive decision-making components that we share with other animal species.

Our framework may be useful in differentiating primitive behaviours from more refined decision-making faculties, providing us with a clearer map of the boundaries of rational economic theory versus instinctive behaviour. For example, our results show that loss aversion is not a stable phenomenon, but one that depends on the relationship between incremental risks and total net worth. As aggregate wealth in the economy declines, loss-averse behaviour is likely to be more prevalent in the population, but during periods of prosperity, other behaviours will emerge. A better understanding of this pattern may allow consumers, investors, and policymakers to manage their risks more effectively.

While species with more highly developed nervous systems may exhibit greater behavioural variation, even in those cases, primitive behaviours are still likely to be available, if not always chosen. We conjecture that such behaviours are most readily actuated under conditions similar to those of our binary choice model, namely when outcomes are significant enough to impact reproductive fitness (broadly defined), and when the effects of other variables on fitness are relatively small. These primitive behaviours may also be the basis of more modern adaptations such as boredom, thrill-seeking behaviour, rebellion, innovation, and, most recently, financial market bubbles and crashes.

Lastly, the evolutionary origin of behaviour has important implications for economics, not only in resolving the debate between the supporters of efficient markets versus those of behavioural finance, but also in providing a broader framework in which conflicts between rationality and human behaviour can be resolved in an intellectually consistent manner. Specifically, much of neoclassical economic theory is devoted to deriving the aggregate implications of individually optimal behaviour (i.e. the maximization of expected utility or profits subject to budget or production constraints). By documenting departures from individual rationality, behavioural critics have argued that rational expectations models are invalid and irrelevant. Both perspectives make valid points, but they are incomplete. The behaviours derived from the first principles in our evolutionary framework may very well be the 'animal spirits' that Keynes (1936) singled out over eight decades ago, and which are apparently still a force to be reckoned with today. Financial markets are neither efficient nor irrational. They are merely adaptive.

3
Mutation

Rationality is the key assumption behind the standard economic models of human behaviour.[1] Nevertheless, psychologists and economists alike have documented many violations of rational models in human behaviour, often referred to as 'cognitive biases' in the literature. The debate between rational models of behaviour and their systematic deviations, so-called 'irrational' behaviour, has attracted an enormous amount of research in economics, psychology, and evolutionary biology (Becker, 1962; Stanovich and West, 2000; Rabin and Thaler, 2001; McKenzie, 2003; Burnham, 2013; Gneezy and List, 2013). For instance, bounded rationality (Simon, 1955) and prospect theory (Kahneman and Tversky, 1979; Tversky and Kahneman, 1992) provide alternative perspectives for understanding human behaviour beyond the maximization of expected utility. At the same time, numerous empirical studies are devoted to understanding the relationship between individual rationality and decision-making in the real world (Hsu et al., 2005; Camerer and Fehr, 2006; Gneezy and List, 2006; Apicella et al., 2008; Dreber et al., 2009; Chen and Chen, 2011; Bednar et al., 2012; Fershtman, Gneezy, and List, 2012; Gneezy and Imas, 2014). In addition, irrational behaviour, as opposed to utility-maximizing behaviour, has been found to be useful and persistent in a variety of environments in evolution (Belavkin, 2006; Houston, McNamara, and Steer, 2007; Waksberg, Smith, and Burd, 2009; Ross and Wilke, 2011; Okasha and Binmore, 2012). However, it is unclear how these behaviours relate to standard economic theories of individual rationality, and why they emerge in some instances and not others.

In this chapter, we reconcile the two sides in the rationality debate by proposing an evolutionary explanation for irrational behaviour. A rational behaviour is a function of its particular environment, but different environments may lead to different rational behaviours in evolution. As a result,

---

[1] This chapter, including the table and figure, is adapted with permission of World Scientific Publishing Co., Inc., from Brennan, T. J., Lo, A. W., and Zhang, R. (2018). Variety is the spice of life: irrational behavior as adaptation to stochastic environments. *Quarterly Journal of Finance* 8(03): 1850009; permission conveyed through Copyright Clearance Center, Inc.

The Adaptive Markets Hypothesis. Andrew W. Lo and Ruixun Zhang, Oxford University Press. © Andrew W. Lo and Ruixun Zhang (2024). DOI: 10.1093/oso/9780199681143.003.0003

allegedly irrational behaviours not only persist in evolution, but are also necessary for the robust growth of a population in stochastic environments. Furthermore, we show that there is an optimal degree of irrationality in the population as a whole, depending on the degree of environmental randomness. In this process, mutation provides diversity to the set of behaviours in the population as a whole, and therefore acts as an important link between rational and irrational behaviour. Over time, only a certain degree of mutation and irrationality in the population will persist.

Much of the rationality debate focuses on whether the rational models can help people make better inferences and decisions in the real world (McKenzie, 2003). Rather than taking this approach, our framework provides an evolutionary explanation of seemingly irrational behaviours and different degrees of irrationality in the population. These results have widespread implications for asset pricing, corporate behaviour, and disciplines beyond finance, such as management and public policy.

For example, it is well known that apparently irrational traders persist in financial markets (De Long et al., 1990, 1991; Biais and Shadur, 2000; Hirshleifer, Subrahmanyam, and Titman, 2006; Kogan et al., 2006), and apparently irrational behaviours such as herding prevail, especially during crises (Bowe and Domuta, 2004; Drehmann, Oechssler, and Roider, 2005; Hirshleifer and Teoh, 2009). These behaviours are able to affect asset prices, creating bubbles and crashes. From the perspective of corporate finance, managers do not always form beliefs logically, and their beliefs do not convert to decisions in a consistent and rational manner (Kahneman and Tversky, 2000; Gilovich, Griffin, and Kahneman, 2002). Our model suggests that the resulting behaviours are not necessarily 'irrational', but simply the result of market evolution. In fact, behaviours normally regarded as irrational such as overconfidence (Kyle and Wang, 1997; Daniel and Titman, 1999; Hirshleifer and Luo, 2001) might even be beneficial in certain market environments.

Our framework also provides a different explanation for the entry of new firms and technologies into an industry, a well-studied phenomenon in industrial economics (Klepper and Graddy, 1990; Audretsch and Mahmood, 1994; Geroski, 1995; Mata, Portugal, and Guimaraes, 1995; Campbell, 1998). Even if new entrants appear to be suboptimal with respect to their current context, they facilitate more robust growth of the entire industry in the face of a stochastically shifting environment. Furthermore, our results yield the optimal amount of entrants as a function of environmental stability.

3.1 Environments with Mutation

We build on top of the binary choice framework described in Chapter 2, and add mutation to the standard model. In general, mutation implies that the offspring of type-f individuals are not necessarily of type f, but assume a probability distribution over all possible types. We consider a simple form of mutation: an offspring of a type-f individual mutates equally likely to all possible types.

To be more specific, we consider a space of discrete types. Let f take its value from a finite set $\{f_1, f_2, \cdots, f_{K+1}\}$, for example, $\{0, \frac{1}{K}, \frac{2}{K}, \ldots, \frac{K-1}{K}, 1\}$, where K is a positive integer. The world has $K+1$ types in total. In addition to Assumptions 2.1 and 2.2 in Chapter 2, we further assume that:

Assumption 3.1 *Each type-f individual mutates with a small probability $\varepsilon > 0$ to type $g \neq f$. Once it mutates, it mutates with equal probability $\frac{\varepsilon}{K}$ to any type $g \in \{f_1, f_2, \cdots, f_{K+1}\} \setminus \{f\}$.*

Note that Assumption 3.1 is a simple and special form of mutation. From the behavioural point of view, it is general enough to capture the most important characteristic of mutation, which is to provide the link between different types of behaviour. In this particular structure, we are able to parameterize the degree of mutation with a single parameter ε.

We would like to emphasize that each individual lives for only one period in our model, and therefore its mutant offspring may be viewed as 'new entrants' in the next generation's population, since they represent different behaviours than their predecessors. Similarly, there is no intelligence or volition ascribed to the behaviour, f; we are simply providing a formal representation for it, then investigating its evolutionary implications. To that end, the individuals choosing between a and b according to the same f may be viewed as consisting of the same type, where types are indexed by f and range continuously from 0 to 1, including the endpoints. In this manner, we are able to study the evolutionary dynamics of each type of individual over many generations.

Once mutation is introduced into the population, it is no longer possible to analyse the population dynamics of each type f separately. The entire system becomes a multi-type branching process in random environments (Smith and Wilkinson, 1969; Tanny, 1981). Let $\mathbf{n}_t = \left(n_t^{f_1}, \cdots, n_t^{f_{K+1}} \right)'$ be the column vector of number of individuals of all $K+1$ types in generation t. The following proposition describes the population dynamics between two generations.

Proposition 3.1 *Under Assumptions 2.1, 2.2, and 3.1, as n_{t-1}^g increases without bound for all types $g \in \{f_1, f_2, \cdots, f_{K+1}\}$, the element-wise ratio of the number of individuals between two generations, $\mathbf{n}_t / \mathbf{n}_{t-1}$, can be written as:*

$$\frac{\mathbf{n}_t}{\mathbf{n}_{t-1}} = \mathbf{A}_t \quad a.s. \tag{3.1}$$

where $\mathbf{A}_t \equiv \mathbf{M} \cdot \mathbf{F}_t$. Here, $\mathbf{M}$ is a constant mutation matrix:

$$\mathbf{M} = \begin{pmatrix} 1-\epsilon & \frac{\epsilon}{K} & \cdots & \frac{\epsilon}{K} \\ \frac{\epsilon}{K} & 1-\epsilon & \cdots & \frac{\epsilon}{K} \\ \vdots & \vdots & \ddots & \vdots \\ \frac{\epsilon}{K} & \frac{\epsilon}{K} & \cdots & 1-\epsilon \end{pmatrix},$$

and $\mathbf{F}_t$ is a stochastic fecundity matrix:

$$\mathbf{F}_t = \begin{pmatrix} f_1 x_{a,t} + (1-f_1)x_{b,t} & \cdots & 0 \\ \vdots & \ddots & \vdots \\ 0 & \cdots & f_{K+1}x_{a,t} + (1-f_{K+1})x_{b,t} \end{pmatrix},$$

with $0 = f_1 < f_2 < \cdots < f_{K+1} = 1$.

Equation (3.1) gives the fundamental relationship between individuals in two consecutive generations. With probability 1, $\mathbf{n}_t$ can be written as the product of two matrices and $\mathbf{n}_{t-1}$. $\mathbf{F}_t$ represents the reproducibility of different types of individuals, and $\mathbf{M}$ represents the redistribution of types because of mutation. It is a natural question to ask how $\mathbf{n}_t$ behaves in the limit. We summarize the asymptotic behaviour of the population with mutation in the following proposition.

Proposition 3.2 (growth rate) *Under Assumptions 2.1, 2.2, and 3.1, there exists a number α_ε such that*

$$\alpha_\epsilon = \lim_{T \to \infty} \frac{1}{T} \log \mathbf{c}' \mathbf{n}_T = \lim_{T \to \infty} \frac{1}{T} \log \|\mathbf{A}_t \mathbf{A}_{t-1} \cdots \mathbf{A}_1\|$$

almost surely, where $\| \cdot \|$ is any matrix norm and $\mathbf{c}$ is any vector of bounded non-negative numbers ($\mathbf{c} \neq \mathbf{0}$).

In the particular case when $\mathbf{c}$ is a vector of 1's, we obtain the growth rate of the entire population; when $\mathbf{c} = \mathbf{e}_i$ (i.e. the vector with the i-th coordinate is equal to 1, and 0 otherwise), we obtain the growth rate of the i-th type of individuals. A direct corollary of Proposition 3.2 is that all types of behaviours will grow at the same exponential rate, α_ε. This is an important difference between populations with mutation and those without it. We can understand this through the following thought experiment. Suppose a long time has elapsed. Because the positive mutation rate is fixed, any behaviour that is not favoured by the current environment will still have a fixed proportion of offspring from the behaviour of the type that grows the fastest. Therefore, the ratio of the individuals of any two behaviours can be bounded at its lower end by some positive constant, while no single behaviour can grow exponentially faster than any other behaviour. Note that α_ε is called the *maximum Liapunov characteristic exponent* of matrix $\mathbf{A}_t$ in the probability literature. Corollary 3.1 in the next section gives an estimate of α_ε.

Another difference between the populations with and without mutation is the asymptotic ratio between different types within the population. Without mutation, $\alpha(f)$ is different for different f, and therefore the ratio $n_T^f/n_T^{f^*}$ will converge to 0 for any $f \neq f^*$ (see Corollary 2.1 in Chapter 2). However, α_ε is the same for all types f in a population with mutation, and the ratio $n_T^{f_1}/n_T^{f_2}$ is typically stochastic even in the long run, as T increases without bound. We present ergodic theorems to characterize the asymptotic behaviour of this ratio in the next section.

3.1.1 Asymptotic Population Dynamics

Under Assumptions 2.1, 2.2, and 3.1, we let $P_t = \iota'\mathbf{n}_t$ be the total population size at time t, and

$$\mathbf{y}_t \equiv \frac{\mathbf{n}_t}{P_t} = \left(\frac{n_T^{f_1}}{\sum_g n_T^g}, \cdots, \frac{n_T^{f_{K+1}}}{\sum_g n_T^g} \right)' \tag{3.2}$$

be the normalized population vector in generation t. Here ι denotes a vector of ones with the same length as $\mathbf{n}_t$. Because of the dynamics between two consecutive generations in Equation (3.1), $\{\mathbf{y}_t\}_{t=0}^\infty$ is a vector-valued Markov process, with a compact state space:

$$\mathcal{Y} \equiv \left\{ \mathbf{y} = (y_1, \cdots, y_{K+1})' \,\middle|\, \mathbf{y} \geq 0, \sum_{i=1}^{K+1} y_i = 1 \right\}.$$

The one-step transition probability for $\mathbf{y} \in \mathcal{Y}$ and $B \subseteq \mathcal{Y}$ is:

$$p_1(\mathbf{y}, B) \equiv \mathrm{Prob}_\Phi \left(\frac{\mathbf{A}\mathbf{y}}{||\mathbf{A}\mathbf{y}||} \in B \right). \tag{3.3}$$

Because different behaviours grow at different exponential rates without mutation, $\mathbf{y}_t$ converges almost surely to a basis vector, $\mathbf{e}_i = (0, \cdots, 1, \cdots, 0)'$ as $T \to \infty$. In the case of populations with positive mutation rates, however, a similar result exists only for non-random matrices $\mathbf{F}_t$ in Equation (3.1), in which case the long-run proportion vector converges to the eigenvector of $\mathbf{F}_t$ (see the models in Robson (1996a) and Gaal, Pitchford, and Wood (2010) for examples). In the case of positive mutation rates when $\mathbf{F}_t$ is a random matrix, environmental uncertainty implies that $\mathbf{y}_t$ is typically stochastic even in the long run. However, we have the following ergodic theorem (Tuljapurkar, 1990) to characterize the asymptotic behaviour of $\mathbf{y}_t$:

Proposition 3.3 (stochastic ergodic theorem) *Under Assumptions 2.1, 2.2, and 3.1, let $\mathscr{L}_t(\cdot)$ be the distribution of $\mathbf{y}_t$, then $\mathscr{L}_t(\cdot)$ converges to a stationary distribution $\mathscr{L}(\cdot)$ pointwisely as T increases without bound:*

$$\lim_{T \to \infty} \mathscr{L}_T = \mathscr{L}.$$

Proposition 3.3 asserts that the proportion vector, $\mathbf{y}_t$, converges weakly as $T \to \infty$. In addition, by the basic properties of Markov chains, the stationary distribution, $\mathscr{L}$, satisfies the following equation:

$$\mathscr{L}(B) = \int_{\mathscr{Y}} p_1(\mathbf{y}, B)\mathscr{L}(d\mathbf{y})$$

for any $B \subseteq \mathscr{Y}$. An important application of Proposition 3.3 is that it provides a formula to estimate the exponential growth rate, α_ε. Note that the total population size,

$$P_t = \iota'\mathbf{n}_t = \iota'\mathbf{M}\mathbf{F}_t\mathbf{n}_{t-1} = \iota'\mathbf{F}_t\mathbf{n}_{t-1} = P_{t-1}\iota'\mathbf{F}_t\mathbf{y}_{t-1},$$

so the log-geometric-average growth rate, α_ε, can be expressed as

$$\alpha_\varepsilon = \mathbb{E}\left[\log(\iota'\mathbf{F}_t\mathbf{y}_{t-1})\right], \tag{3.4}$$

where the expectation is taken over the joint stationary distribution of $(\mathbf{F}_t, \mathbf{y}_{t-1})$.

Corollary 3.1 (bounds of growth rate) *Let f^* be the optimal behaviour without mutation (see Proposition 2.1). Under Assumptions 2.1, 2.2, and 3.1, if the type space is dense enough such that $f^* \in \{f_1, f_2, \cdots, f_{K+1}\}$, then:*

$$\alpha(f^*) - |\log(1-\epsilon)| \leq \alpha_\epsilon \leq \alpha(f^*). \tag{3.5}$$

Corollary 3.1 asserts that the growth rate, α_ϵ, is slightly less than the optimal growth rate of the population without mutation. We will identify cases where mutation does speed up growth in nonstationary environments in Section 3.2.[2]

3.1.2 Extinction Probability

When a population becomes extinct in evolution, the stochastic processes $\mathbf{n}_t$ and $\mathbf{y}_t$ become degenerate. Therefore, all results so far are implicitly conditional on non-extinction sample paths. However, extinction is important in evolution, and it is particularly of interest with mutation. In this section, we investigate the probability of extinction of different behaviours f in different environments $\Phi(x_a, x_b)$.[3]

Consider a specific behaviour $f \in \{f_1, f_2, \cdots, f_{K+1}\}$ starting with an initial population $n_0^f > 0$. We define that the type f is *extinct* if $n_T^f = 0$ for some $T > 0$, and *surviving* otherwise. There are two scenarios for extinction when the number of generation T increases without bound:

(i) $\lim_{T\to\infty} \mathrm{Prob}\left(n_T^f > 0\right) = 0$: the population is extinct with probability 1;
(ii) $\lim_{T\to\infty} \mathrm{Prob}\left(n_T^f > 0\right) > 0$: the population survives with some positive probability.

Note that in case (ii), if $\lim_{T\to\infty} \mathrm{Prob}\left(n_T^f > 0\right) < 1$, then the extinction probability depends on the initial population, n_0. However, when n_0 is relatively large, the survival probability is close to 1. We define that the type

---

[2] Appendix B.2 gives additional results for the dynamics of populations with mutation, in particular, the asymptotic distribution of total population size, P_t, and the rate of convergence for the limit distribution, $\mathscr{L}(\cdot)$.
[3] The finite-moment condition for $\log(fx_a + (1-f)x_b)$ in Assumption 2.1 guarantees that the population does not go extinct for any $f \in [0, 1]$. However, our results from the binary choice model are not affected as long as we adopt the convention that $\log(0) = -\infty$ and, as a result, the population growth rate (Equation (2.7)) of any behaviour that can result in zero offspring becomes $-\infty$. In other words, extinction is possible for certain behaviours. See our discussion of probability matching in Section 2.2) for such an example.

f is *immortal* if the extinction probability is strictly less than 1 as $T \to \infty$, and the extinction probability goes to 0 as the initial number of individuals, n_0, increases without bound. Mathematically, a type f is immortal if $\text{Prob}(n_T^f = 0) < 1$ as $T \to \infty$, and $\text{Prob}(n_T^f = 0) \to 0$ as $T \to \infty$ and $n_0 \to \infty$.

For an immortal population, case (ii) can be treated as an almost sure survival with a large initial population. Propositions 3.1–3.3 are implicitly conditional on non-extinction sample paths. The probability of non-extinction in these results is close to 1 for a large initial population, according to the next proposition:

Proposition 3.4 (immortality with mutation) *Suppose that the initial population of any behaviour $f \in \{f_1, f_2, \cdots, f_{K+1}\}$ is n_0.*

    (i) Consider the model without mutation. Under Assumptions 2.1 and 2.2, any behaviour f with $\alpha(f) < 0$ is extinct with probability 1, and any behaviour f with $\alpha(f) > 0$ is immortal.

    (ii) Consider the model with mutation rate $\varepsilon > 0$. Under Assumptions 2.1, 2.2, and 3.1, all behaviours $f \in \{f_1, f_2, \ldots, f_{K+1}\}$ are immortal if α_ε in Proposition 3.2 is positive. In particular, if there exists a behaviour $f \in \{f_1, f_2, \cdots, f_{K+1}\}$ such that $\alpha(f) > |\log(1 - \varepsilon)|$ without mutation, then all behaviours are immortal.

Proposition 3.4 asserts that positive mutation rates make all behaviours in the population immortal, and help preserve all behaviours, even if some of them are inferior in the current environment. In other words, mutation provides robustness to evolution by avoiding extinction.

So far we have considered stationary environments generating independent and identically distributed (IID) fecundities across time. In this case, mutation does not help increase the speed of population growth (Corollary 3.1). This brings us to the next topic, where nonstationary environments are considered, and mutation can, indeed, speed up growth.

3.2 The Optimal Degree of Irrationality

The binary choice model with mutation provides a framework for the evolution of behaviour. Given a particular environment $\Phi(x_a, x_b)$, we have shown that the growth-optimal behaviour is not necessarily the same as the individually 'rational' behaviour, implying that seemingly 'irrational' behaviours could emerge purely from adaptation under certain environments.

Even if the the growth-optimal behaviour happens to be the individu-ally rational behaviour, however, it does not necessarily dominate the entire population in the presence of mutation. In fact, the very notion of opti-mality is ill defined in isolation, and must be interpreted with respect to a given environment. In stochastic environments, mutation provides the link between seemingly rational and irrational behaviours. Positive mutation rates and 'irrational' behaviours in a population are necessary because envi-ronmental shocks may happen unexpectedly. In this sense, a population with irrational behaviours is favoured in order to maintain robust growth under possible environmental shocks. We further elaborate this idea by considering regime-switching environments.

Following the binary choice model with mutation, we suppose that the environment switches randomly between two regimes, in which the fecun-dities are specified by $\Phi^1(x_a, x_b)$ and $\Phi^2(x_a, x_b)$, respectively. The lengths of regime 1 and regime 2 are positive integer random variables T^1 and T^2 spec-ified by some well-behaved probability distribution function $F(T^1, T^2)$. We draw IID samples from $F(T^1, T^2)$ to generate lengths of consecutive regimes $T_1^1, T_1^2, T_2^1, T_2^2, \cdots$. Note that the superscript denotes the regime number and the subscript indicates the number of cycles, where a cycle is defined as two consecutive changes of regime:

$$0 \xrightarrow{\Phi^1} T_1^1 \xrightarrow{\Phi^2} T_1^2 \xrightarrow{\Phi^1} T_2^1 \xrightarrow{\Phi^2} T_2^2 \cdots.$$

We would like to emphasize that the environment within each regime is still stochastic. This is in important distinction from the existing literature, where the environment is usually assumed to be approximately constant between changes, or within a period (Ishii et al., 1989; Kussell and Leibler, 2005; Acar, Mettetal, and van Oudenaarden, 2008; Gaal, Pitchford, and Wood, 2010). We use a simple example to illustrate the idea of the optimal degree of irrationality in the population.

3.2.1 An Example with Two Behaviours

For simplicity, we consider a world with only two behaviours, $f = 0$ or 1. Suppose that the fecundities in the two regimes are given by $\Phi^1(x_a, x_b)$ and $\Phi^2(x_a, x_b)$, which satisfy the following condition:

$$\text{Prob}_{\Phi^1}(x_b = 0) = \text{Prob}_{\Phi^2}(x_a = 0) = 1.$$

That is, one choice in each regime will certainly result in no offspring. Note that in regime 1, x_a is still a random variable, and in regime 2, x_b is still a random variable. In this world, during regime 1, only action a generates positive offspring; during regime 2, only action b generates positive offspring. Therefore, both behaviours will die out without the presence of mutation after a few regime switches.

A positive mutation rate ε helps preserve irrational behaviours in the current environment in anticipation of possible environmental shocks, at the cost of slowing down the growth of the rational behaviour. In other words, a positive mutation rate implies that there is always a fixed positive fraction of new entrants into the population in each generation, even if their behaviour may be suboptimal with respect to the current environment.

Proposition 3.5 *With a positive mutation rate, $\varepsilon > 0$, let $n_k^{\varepsilon,Total}$ be the total number of individuals in the entire population at the end of the k-th cycle. Under Assumptions 2.1, 2.2, and 3.1 and the regime-switching model described above, where the fecundities $\Phi^1(x_a, x_b)$ and $\Phi^2(x_a, x_b)$ satisfy*

$$\mathrm{Prob}_{\Phi^1}(x_b = 0) = \mathrm{Prob}_{\Phi^2}(x_a = 0) = 1,$$

as k increases without bound, $k^{-1} \log n_k^{\varepsilon,Total}$ converges almost surely to

$$\pi(\varepsilon) \equiv 2\log\frac{\varepsilon}{1-\varepsilon} + \mathbb{E}[T^1 + T^2]\log(1-\varepsilon) + \mathbb{E}[T^1]\mathbb{E}_{\Phi^1}[\log x_a] + \mathbb{E}[T^2]\mathbb{E}_{\Phi^2}[\log x_b]$$

(3.6)

for $0 < \varepsilon < 1$. The growth-optimal mutation rate, ε^*, that maximizes Equation (3.6) is

$$\varepsilon^* = \frac{2}{\mathbb{E}[T^1 + T^2]}.$$

As a special case of Proposition 3.5, we have the following result when the lengths of each regime are all IID.

Corollary 3.2 *Under the assumptions of Proposition 3.5, if in addition the lengths of both regime 1 and regime 2 are drawn IID from a single distribution F(T), then the growth-optimal behaviour that maximizes Equation (3.6) is*

$$\varepsilon^* = \frac{1}{\mathbb{E}[T]}.$$

By Proposition 3.5 and Corollary 3.2, the optimal mutation rate is simply the reciprocal of the expected length of a regime. In the long run, the more stable the environment is, the fewer irrational behaviours are present in the population; likewise, the more frequent environmental change is, the greater the number of irrational behaviours that prevail in the population. The mutation rate and the level of irrationality are not exogenous variables imposed by nature. Rather, they are necessary and important quantities that are selected by evolution to match the degree of environmental instability. In this sense, natural selection shapes the degree of irrationality in the population.

This also implies that the optimal amount of new entrants into the population is determined by the degree of environmental stability. For example, one would expect relatively few new entrants in areas with relatively stable market conditions, such as the automobile industry, and relatively high turnover rates in areas with relatively volatile market conditions, such as the hedge fund industry.

3.3 Generalization and Simulation

The implications we can draw from the above example with two behaviours and a special fecundity structure can be generalized to any number of types and any structure of fecundity. We use simulation techniques to demonstrate the generality of the optimal degree of mutation and irrationality. In this section, we consider eight different pairs of environments and lengths of regimes, and calculate the optimal degree of mutation for each of them.

In the following experiments, the lengths of regimes T^1 and T^2 are independent random variables with expectations $\mathbb{E}[T^1]$ and $\mathbb{E}[T^2]$, respectively, ranging from 10 to 37. For a given expectation $\mathbb{E}[T^1]$, T^1 is uniformly distributed in the interval $\left[0.8 \times \mathbb{E}[T^1], 1.2 \times \mathbb{E}[T^1]\right]$, rounding to the nearest integer. T^2 is distributed in the same way.

For a given pair of $(\mathbb{E}[T^1], \mathbb{E}[T^2])$, we begin with 11 types of behaviour, from $\{0, \frac{1}{10}, \frac{2}{10}, \cdots, 1\}$, each starting with one individual and allowed to evolve for 700 to 1,000 generations. The optimal degree of mutation in each pair of environments is calculated by taking the average over 200 to 500 simulation paths.

Table 3.1 shows eight different environmental conditions, for which we plot the optimal degree of mutation and the optimal log-geometric-average growth rate as a function of $\mathbb{E}[T^1]$ and $\mathbb{E}[T^2]$ in Fig. 3.1. In these figures, the coloured plane with the colour bar shows the optimal mutation rates; the height of the transparent surface is indicated by the z-axis, showing the optimal log-geometric-average growth rate associated with that optimal mutation rate.

Table 3.1 Probability table for the simulation of optimal mutation rates: environments 1–8.

(a) Environment 1

	Regime 1			Regime 2		
Prob.	$\frac{1}{3}$	$\frac{1}{3}$	$\frac{1}{3}$	$\frac{1}{3}$	$\frac{1}{3}$	$\frac{1}{3}$
x_a	3	2	1	0	0	0
x_b	0	0	0	3	2	1

(b) Environment 2

	Regime 1			Regime 2		
Prob.	$\frac{1}{3}$	$\frac{1}{3}$	$\frac{1}{3}$	$\frac{1}{3}$	$\frac{1}{3}$	$\frac{1}{3}$
x_a	3	2	1	1	1	1
x_b	1	1	1	3	2	1

(c) Environment 3

	Regime 1		Regime 2	
Prob.	0.8	0.2	0.8	0.2
x_a	3	0	0	3
x_b	0	3	3	0

(d) Environment 4

	Regime 1		Regime 2	
Prob.	0.8	0.2	0.8	0.2
x_a	3	1	1	3
x_b	1	3	3	1

(e) Environment 5

	Regime 1		Regime 2	
Prob.	0.8	0.2	0.8	0.2
x_a	3	0	1	3
x_b	0	3	3	1

(f) Environment 6

	Regime 1		Regime 2		
Prob.	0.8	0.2	$\frac{1}{3}$	$\frac{1}{3}$	$\frac{1}{3}$
x_a	3	1	1	1	0
x_b	1	3	3	2	1

(g) Environment 7

	Regime 1		Regime 2	
Prob.	0.8	0.2	0.8	0.2
x_a	3	0	3	1
x_b	0	3	1	3

(h) Environment 8

	Regime 1		Regime 2		
Prob.	0.8	0.2	$\frac{1}{3}$	$\frac{1}{3}$	$\frac{1}{3}$
x_a	3	1	3	2	1
x_b	1	3	1	1	0

3.3.1 Symmetric Regimes

Environment 1 assumes that one of the actions in each regime leads to no offspring. These results are consistent with the two-behaviour example: The optimal degree of mutation is inversely proportional to $\mathbb{E}[T^1] + \mathbb{E}[T^2]$. However, the growth rate is proportional to $\mathbb{E}[T^1]$ and $\mathbb{E}[T^2]$: The longer the length of a regime is, the faster the population grows.

Environment 2 considers the case where both actions a and b produce a positive number of offspring. As expected, the growth rates are much higher than those in environment 1. The optimal degree of mutation is inversely proportional to the length of a regime, except for two regions where the length of one regime is much larger than that of the other (the region $\mathbb{E}[T^1] > 25, \mathbb{E}[T^2] < 12$, and the region $\mathbb{E}[T^1] < 12, \mathbb{E}[T^2] > 25$). In these two regions, the optimal degree of mutation drops to nearly 0, because one regime is significantly shorter than the other; therefore, it is not worth sacrificing growth in one regime for the other by mutation.

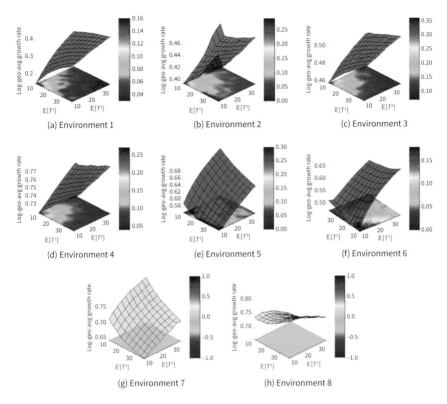

Fig. 3.1 The optimal degree of mutation and optimal log-geometric-average growth rate as a function of regime lengths $\mathbb{E}[T^1]$ and $\mathbb{E}[T^2]$. The eight subfigures show the simulation results of the eight different environments described in Table 3.1. The coloured plane with the colour bar shows the optimal mutation rates; the height of the transparent surface is indicated by the z-axis, which shows the optimal log-geometric-average growth rate associated with that optimal mutation rate.

Environments 3 and 4 add a dependency between x_a and x_b in each regime. In those two cases, the simulation results are similar to those of environment 1.

3.3.2 Asymmetric Regimes

The four experiments considered so far have all been symmetric in terms of their regimes. In other words, the second regime is simply a copy of the first regime with x_a and x_b reversed. As a consequence, the results are expected to be symmetric with respect to the line $\mathbb{E}[T^1] = \mathbb{E}[T^2]$. In this part, we consider asymmetric regimes, and investigate how this changes the optimal mutation and growth rates.

Environment 5 is a mixture of environments 3 and 4 from the symmetric regime case: regime 1 is taken from environment 3, and regime 2 is taken from environment 4. In this case, the optimal behaviour is $f_1^* = 0.8$ in regime 1 and $f_2^* = 0$ in regime 2. Several interesting observations can be made about this situation. Firstly, both the optimal degree of mutation and the growth rate are no longer symmetric with respect to $\mathbb{E}[T^1]$ and $\mathbb{E}[T^2]$. Secondly, the growth rate increases as $\mathbb{E}[T^2]$ increases and decreases as $\mathbb{E}[T^1]$ increases. This takes place because regime 2 has a larger geometric-mean fitness than regime 1, so the growth rate increases as the proportion of generations in regime 2 increases. Thirdly, as in environment 2, there is a region where the optimal degree of mutation drops to nearly 0, when $\mathbb{E}[T^1]$ is large and $\mathbb{E}[T^2]$ is small.

Environment 6 makes the two regimes even more asymmetric than in environment 5. The optimal behaviour is $f_1^* = 1$ in regime 1, and $f_2^* = 0$ in regime 2. The results are similar to those from environment 5.

3.3.3 When Mutation Is Undesirable

Mutations are desirable when the environment is nonstationary and the two regimes favour different actions. When these conditions change, mutation is no longer desirable. We see this in the results of our final two environments.

Environment 7 reverses actions a and b in the second regime of environment 5. The shape of the surface indicating growth rates is still similar to environment 5. However, the optimal degree of mutation is 0 for any combination of $\mathbb{E}[T^1]$ and $\mathbb{E}[T^2]$. This is because the optimal behaviour is $f_1^* = 0.8$ in regime 1 and $f_2^* = 1$ in regime 2. These values are close to each other, and both grow relatively fast in either regime. Likewise, environment 8 reverses actions a and b in the second regime of environment 6. The optimal behaviour is $f^* = 1$ in both regimes, and therefore the optimal mutation rate is 0.

3.3.4 Optimal Degree of Irrationality

It is clear that there exists a balance between growth without mutation and robustness with mutation. Our simulations confirm the inverse relationship between the optimal degree of mutation and expected lengths of regimes that was derived analytically in our simple two-behaviour model with special fecundity structure (Proposition 3.5 and Corollary 3.2). This relationship is robust across a variety of environmental conditions.

For symmetric regimes, the optimal degree of mutation is inversely proportional to $\mathbb{E}[T^1] + \mathbb{E}[T^2]$, and the growth rate is proportional to both $\mathbb{E}[T^1]$ and $\mathbb{E}[T^2]$. For asymmetric regimes, the growth rate increases with the proportion of the regime that has a larger geometric-mean fitness. The relative magnitude of the two regimes matters under these conditions.

The optimal degree of mutation has the possibility of being zero, if the length of one regime is significantly shorter than the other. In this case, it is not worth sacrificing growth in one regime for the other, as long as the other behaviour does not die out in the shorter regime.

The length of regime, or equivalently the frequency of change, is one important aspect of the nature of environmental change. The intensity of each change, however, is another aspect. In our framework, the intensity of environmental change is reflected by the absolute difference in optimal behaviours in the two regimes: $|f_1^* - f_2^*|$. When the optimal behaviours in the two regimes are similar to each other, the optimal degree of mutation is relatively low; when the optimal behaviours in the two regimes are wildly different, the optimal degree of mutation must be high in order to compensate for the slow growth of suboptimal behaviours in each regime.

In general, the evolutionarily optimal degree of irrationality in a population is influenced by both the frequency and intensity of environmental change. A higher frequency or intensity of change would imply a higher degree of irrationality. Practically speaking, this implies that markets and industries with more volatile environments should attract more entrants over time.

3.4 Discussion

Evolutionary models of behaviour are important for understanding the conflicts between individual rationality and actual human behaviour. The binary choice framework described in Chapter 2 provides an explanation for the deviations from neoclassical utility-based economic theory. Building on the binary choice framework, we investigate the evolution of irrational behaviours in this chapter. Mutation is key in our analysis because it provides a link between rational and irrational behaviours in an evolutionary context. Because the definition of rationality depends on a particular environment, rational behaviours may change when the environment changes. As a result, irrational behaviour is necessary to provide robustness to environmental conditions for population growth. Furthermore, we have shown that there is an evolutionarily optimal degree of irrationality in the population as a whole. More unstable environments imply a greater amount of irrational behaviour in the population and more new entrants over time.

The model considered in this chapter does not require any strategic interactions between individuals. Individual decision-making is deliberately modelled to be mindless, allowing us to determine the most primitive and fundamental links between stochastic environments and adaptive behaviour. Even in such a simple setting, we find a range of behaviours that do not conform to common economic intuition about rationality are able to arise and persist via natural selection.

Our model can be extended in several ways. The evolutionary origins of strategic behaviour have also been considered in the literature (Robson, 1996b; Skyrms, 2000, 2014), and natural selection can produce sophisticated behaviours such as overconfidence (Johnson and Fowler, 2011), altruism and self-deception (Trivers, 1971; Becker, 1976), and state-dependent strategies like the hawk–dove game (Maynard Smith, 1979), which emerge as a result of complex environmental conditions. In our framework, if we assume that one individual's action is correlated with the reproductive success of another individual, those individuals who engage in strategic behaviour will reproduce more quickly than those with simpler behaviours, such as probability matching. If the actions of individuals in the current generation are able to affect the reproductive success of individuals in future generations, even more complex dynamics are likely to emerge, as in the well-known overlapping generations model (Samuelson, 1958). In a resource-constrained environment in which one individual's choice can affect another individual's reproductive success, strategic interactions such as reciprocity and cooperation will likely emerge within and across generations (Trivers, 1971; Nowak and Highfield, 2011).

We have modelled mutation in a simple way in this chapter. There are more complicated forms of mutation one can introduce to this evolutionary framework, including mutation rates that are correlated with the environment. This has a correspondence to individual intelligence, arising when individuals have memory and are therefore able to adapt to the environment given past events.

From an applied perspective, our results underscore the importance of addressing different human behaviours in different environments. For example, financial markets are considered to be efficient most of the time (Samuelson, 1965; Fama, 1970), and participants with irrational beliefs constitute a minimal part of them. However, during periods of economic turbulence and financial crisis, which change the financial environment, irrational behaviours are much more prevalent than usual. Irrational traders persist, and behaviours such as herding prevail. These behaviours can and will affect asset prices, creating the potential for bubbles and crashes.

From the perspective of corporate finance, both the economic and regulatory environments can affect managerial behaviour. Our results suggest that behaviours normally regarded as irrational—such as overconfidence—may simply be the result of adaptation in certain market environments. From this perspective, a stable environment would help to reduce the amount of irrational behaviour, yielding higher economic growth, but at the cost of slowing the rate of change in managerial behaviour.

Our results also highlight the importance of entry of new actors into the market, even if they may appear suboptimal in the current context. Our model suggests that the optimal number of new entrants depends on the degree of environmental stability. On the one hand, volatile environments may lead to increases in the degree of irrationality, implying higher social costs and lower economic growth without proper management. On the other hand, our results also highlight the potential dangers of sustained government intervention, which can become a source of systematic risk, causing volatile environments in its own right (Acharya et al., 2011; Lucas, 2011).

4
Group Selection

Many species (including humans) have a social structure in which individuals form groups, and the aggregation of individuals promotes the reproductive fitness of group members.[1] In evolutionary biology, when selection for a biological trait in such populations depends on the difference between groups rather than individual differences within a group, it is described as 'group selection'. Since the publication of the pathbreaking work of Wynne-Edwards (1963) and Hamilton (1963, 1964) in the 1960s, the theory of evolution has been applied to much broader contexts than the individual organism or self-replicating genes. By appealing to notions of inclusive fitness and kin and group selection, there are now compelling evolutionary explanations for previously inexplicable behaviours such as altruism and cooperation. This approach has generated a number of additional intellectual insights such as the theory of reciprocity (Trivers, 1971), the Price equation (Price, 1970), the field of sociobiology (Wilson, 1975b, 2005), and the theory of multi-level selection (Wilson and Sober, 1994). Moreover, empirical studies have lent further support to the theory of group and kin selection, including social behaviour in bacteria (Ben-Jacob et al., 1994, 2004; Ingham and Ben-Jacob, 2008), sterility in social insects (Hamilton, 1964; Queller and Strassmann, 1998), and the avoidance of cannibalism in salamanders (Pfennig, Collins, and Ziemba, 1999).

Nevertheless, despite its many compelling applications in economics, sociobiology, and evolutionary psychology, group selection is still one of the most hotly contested ideas in evolutionary biology. An enormous body of research has been dedicated to understanding the relationship between genetic, organismic, and group selection (Wilson, 1975a; Wright, 1980; Williams, 1996), and the relationship between group and kin selection (Maynard Smith, 1964; Queller, 1992; Wild, Gardner, and West, 2009; Nowak, Tarnita, and Wilson, 2010; Wade et al., 2010; Frank, 2013). Critics over the last few decades have argued forcefully against group selection as a

---

[1] This chapter, including the table and figures, is adapted from Zhang, R., Brennan, T. J., and Lo, A. W. (2014). Group selection as behavioral adaptation to systematic risk. *PLoS ONE* 9(10): e110848. https://doi.org/10.1371/journal.pone.0110848.

The Adaptive Markets Hypothesis. Andrew W. Lo and Ruixun Zhang, Oxford University Press. © Andrew W. Lo and Ruixun Zhang (2024). DOI: 10.1093/oso/9780199681143.003.0004

major mechanism of evolution, while more contemporary attempts to revive it (Wilson and Wilson, 2008; Nowak, Tarnita, and Wilson, 2010; Wilson, 2013) have been met with swift and broad rebuke (Abbot et al., 2011; Pinker, 2012).

Using the binary choice framework, we propose a reconciliation of these two opposing perspectives. We show that what appears to be group selection may, in fact, simply be the consequence of natural selection occurring in stochastic environments with reproductive risks that are correlated across individuals. Those individuals with highly correlated risks will appear to form groups, even if their actions are, in fact, totally autonomous, mindless, and, prior to natural selection, uniformly randomly distributed in the population.

The key to this outcome is the fact that the reproductive risk facing all individuals in the 'group' population is perfectly correlated, which we refer to as systematic risk. If we had assumed instead that reproductive risk was idiosyncratic—that the state of nature is independent and identically distributed (IID) for each individual—then the evolutionarily dominant strategy would be the purely 'selfish' one in which a single choice is always made. This highlights the key difference between individual and group rationality from the evolutionary perspective.

Our results imply that a separate theory of group selection is not strictly necessary to explain observed phenomena such as altruism and cooperation. At the same time, it shows that the notion of group selection does capture a unique aspect of evolution—selection with correlated reproductive risk—that may be sufficiently widespread to warrant a separate term for the phenomenon. There is no controversy around the fact that selection occurs at the genetic level because of the basic biology of reproduction. However, we show that selection can also appear to operate at coarser levels, provided that environmental forces affect a particular subset of individuals in a similar fashion (i.e. if their reproductive risks are highly correlated). We use the term 'appear' here intentionally, because in our framework, selection does not occur at the level of the group; however, the behaviour that is evolutionarily dominant is consistent with some of the empirical implications of group selection.

By studying the impact of selection on behaviour rather than on genes, we are able to derive broad evolutionary implications that cut across different species, physiologies, and genetic origins. In the same way that different magnifications of a microscope reveal the different details of a specimen, applying evolutionary principles to behavioural variation leads to different insights that may yield more relevance for economics, psychology, or behavioural ecology, depending on the lens. Because evolution is essentially a process of elimination (Mayr, 2001), selection and adaptation operate at all levels, from genes to populations, depending on the nature of the corresponding environmental challenges. Our focus on behaviour as the object of selection is a different lens through which the effects of evolution may be studied.

After a necessarily brief review of the literature, Sections 4.1 through 4.4 demonstrate our key results in the context of the binary choice model with two systematic environmental factors. We provide a generalization of the binary choice model to the multinomial case with multiple factors in Section 4.3.

Related Literature

The literature on evolution and group selection is overwhelming, spanning multiple disciplines, including evolutionary and social psychology, evolutionary biology, ecology, and economics. Here we attempt to provide only a representative sampling of the many strands that are most relevant to our focus.

The role of stochastic environments in evolution has been investigated extensively by biologists and ecologists. Stochastic environments cause high genetic variation, and in extreme cases, extinction (Lynch and Lande, 1993; Burger and Lynch, 1995; Pekalski, 1998, 1999, 2002; De Blasio, 1999; Burger and Gimelfarb, 2002). Environmental uncertainty associated with stochasticity over time (Cohen, 1966; Oster and Wilson, 1979; Bergstrom, 2014) or heterogeneity across space (Levins, 1968) can cause natural selection to favour a gene that randomizes its phenotypic expression. Gillespie and Guess (1978) describe a heuristic method to study selection in random environments. Frank (2011a,b, 2012a) analyses how variability in reproductive success affects fitness and relates it to the geometric mean principle. Geometric-mean fitness also appears in a financial context as the Kelly criterion for maximizing the geometric growth rate of a portfolio, as mentioned in Chapter 2, Equation (2.1) (see also Chapter 15).

In addition to the evolutionary biology and behavioural ecology literature discussed in Chapter 2, the literature on risk-spreading behaviour and kin selection is highly relevant to our model in this chapter. Yoshimura and Clark (1991) show that a risk-spreading polymorphism, in which a given genotype consists of a mixture of two or more forms, each employing different behavioural strategies (Levins, 1968; Cooper and Kaplan, 1982), makes sense only for groups. Yoshimura and Jansen (1996) argue that a risk-spreading adaptation is a form of kin selection (Cooper and Kaplan, 1982), in which the strategies of kin can be very important in stochastic environments even if there are no interactions at all. McNamara (1995) introduces the profile of a strategy and relates the geometric-mean fitness to a deterministic game.

In the economics literature, evolutionary principles were first introduced in order to understand cooperation and altruism conceptually (Alexander, 1974; Hirshleifer, 1977, 1978), while evolutionary game theory is considered a foundation for altruistic behaviour (Samuelson, 2001; Bergstrom, 2002). Evolutionary models of behaviour are especially important to economists in order to resolve theoretical conflicts between individual rationality and human behaviour (Robson, 2001b; Brennan and Lo, 2011), including attitudes towards risk and utility functions (Waldman, 1994; Robson, 1996a,b, 2001a; Samuelson, 2001), time preference (Rogers, 1994; Robson and Samuelson, 2007; Robson and Szentes, 2008; Robson and Samuelson, 2009; Burnham, 2013), financial markets and firm selection (Blume and Easley, 1992; Luo, 1995, 1998; Kogan et al., 2006), and the economic analysis of social institutions (Herrmann-Pillath, 1991; van den Bergh and Gowdy, 2009; Safarzyńska and van den Bergh, 2010).

4.1 Environments with Factor Structure

We begin by extending the binary choice framework to include explicitly environmental factors. Consider again a population of individuals that live for one period, produce a random number of offspring asexually, and then die. During their lives, individuals make only one decision: they choose from two actions, a and b, and this results in one of two corresponding random numbers of offspring, x_a and x_b. Suppose that each individual chooses action a with some probability $p \in [0, 1]$ and action b with probability $1 - p$, denoted by the Bernoulli variable I^p. The number of offspring of an individual is thus given by the random variable

$$x^p = I^p x_a + (1 - I^p)x_b,$$

where

$$I^p = \begin{cases} 1 & \text{with probability } p \\ 0 & \text{with probability } 1 - p \end{cases}.$$

We shall henceforth refer to p as the individual's *behaviour* since it completely determines how the individual chooses between actions a and b. (Note that we have used the notation p to denote the individual's behaviour, and reserved our usual notation f for what we call the individual's *type*, for reasons that will become clear below.)

Now suppose that there are two independent environmental factors, λ_1 and λ_2, that determine reproductive success, and that x_a and x_b are both linear combinations of these two factors:

$$\begin{cases} x_a = \beta_1\lambda_1 + (1-\beta_1)\lambda_2 \\ x_b = \beta_2\lambda_1 + (1-\beta_2)\lambda_2 \end{cases},$$

where $\lambda_i \geq 0, 0 \leq \beta_i \leq 1, i = 1, 2$. Examples of such factors are weather conditions, the availability of food, or the number of predators in the environment. Because these factors affect the fecundity of all individuals in the population, we refer to them as *systematic*, and we assume that:

Assumption 4.1 λ_1 and λ_2 are independent random variables with some well-behaved distribution functions, such that (x_a, x_b) and $\log(px_a + (1-p)x_b)$ have finite moments up to order 2 for all $p \in [0,1], \beta_1 \in [0,1], \beta_2 \in [0,1]$, and

Assumption 4.2 (λ_1, λ_2) is IID over time and identical for all individuals in a given generation.

We shall henceforth refer to (β_1, β_2) as an individual's *characteristics*. For each action, individuals are faced with a trade-off between two positive environmental factors because of limited resources.

Under this framework, an individual is completely determined by its behaviour p and its characteristics (β_1, β_2). We shall henceforth refer to $f \equiv (p, \beta_1, \beta_2)$ as an individual's *type*. We assume that any offspring will behave in a manner identical to their parents (i.e. they will have the same characteristics (β_1, β_2), and choose between a and b according to the same p). Thus, the population may be viewed as being composed of different types that are indexed by the triplet f. In other words, offspring from a type-f individual will also be of the same type f. We assume perfect genetic transmission from one generation to the next; that is, once a type f, always a type f. We also assume that the initial population will contain an equal number of all types, which we normalize to be 1 each without loss of generality. In summary, an individual i of type $f = (p, \beta_1, \beta_2)$ produces a random number of offspring:

$$x_i^{p,\beta_1,\beta_2} = I_i^p x_{a,i}^{\beta_1} + (1 - I_i^p)x_{b,i}^{\beta_2}, \tag{4.1}$$

where

$$\begin{cases} x_{a,i}^{\beta_1} = \beta_1\lambda_1 + (1-\beta_1)\lambda_2 \\ x_{b,i}^{\beta_2} = \beta_2\lambda_1 + (1-\beta_2)\lambda_2 \end{cases}. \tag{4.2}$$

Now consider an initial population of individuals with different types. Suppose the total number of type $f = (p, \beta_1, \beta_2)$ individuals in generation T is n_T^f. Under Assumptions 4.1 and 4.2, it is easy to show that $T^{-1} \log n_T^f$ converges in probability to the log-geometric-average growth rate:

$$\alpha(p, \beta_1, \beta_2) = \mathbb{E}\left[\log\left(px_a^{\beta_1} + (1-p)x_b^{\beta_2}\right)\right], \qquad (4.3)$$

as the number of generations and the number of individuals in each generation increase without bound. We define

$$\begin{cases} \psi_1 = p\beta_1 + (1-p)\beta_2 \\ \psi_2 = p(1-\beta_1) + (1-p)(1-\beta_2) \end{cases},$$

then $\psi_1 + \psi_2 = 1$, and Equation (4.3) can be equivalently written as

$$\alpha(p, \beta_1, \beta_2) = \mathbb{E}\left[\log\left(\psi_1\lambda_1 + (1-\psi_1)\lambda_2\right)\right]. \qquad (4.4)$$

We shall refer to (ψ_1, ψ_2) as the *factor loadings* of type-f individuals, where Equations (4.3) and (4.4) characterize the log-geometric-average growth rate of individuals as a function of their type f in terms of both their behaviour p and their characteristics (β_1, β_2).

Over time, individuals with the largest growth rate will dominate the population geometrically fast (see Section 2.1.4).

Proposition 4.1 *Under Assumptions 4.1 and 4.2, the optimal factor loading, ψ_1^*, that maximizes Equation (4.4) is given by*

$$\psi_1^* = \begin{cases} 1 & \text{if } \mathbb{E}\left[\lambda_1/\lambda_2\right] > 1 \text{ and } \mathbb{E}\left[\lambda_2/\lambda_1\right] < 1 \\ \text{solution to Equation (4.6)} & \text{if } \mathbb{E}\left[\lambda_1/\lambda_2\right] \geq 1 \text{ and } \mathbb{E}\left[\lambda_2/\lambda_1\right] \geq 1, \\ 0 & \text{if } \mathbb{E}\left[\lambda_1/\lambda_2\right] < 1 \text{ and } \mathbb{E}\left[\lambda_2/\lambda_1\right] > 1 \end{cases} \qquad (4.5)$$

where ψ_1^* is defined implicitly in the second case of Equation (4.5) by

$$\mathbb{E}\left[\frac{\lambda_1}{\psi_1^*\lambda_1 + (1-\psi_1^*)\lambda_2}\right] = \mathbb{E}\left[\frac{\lambda_2}{\psi_1^*\lambda_1 + (1-\psi_1^*)\lambda_2}\right]. \qquad (4.6)$$

As a result, the growth-optimal type is $f^* = (p^*, \beta_1^*, \beta_2^*)$, which is given explicitly in Table 4.1.

The optimal characteristics and their associated optimal behaviours in Table 4.1 show that when ψ_1^* is 0 or 1, one of the factors, λ_1 or λ_2, is significantly more important than the other, and the optimal strategy places

Table 4.1 Optimal type $f^* = (p^*, \beta_1^*, \beta_2^*)$ for the binary choice model with factors.

	Optimal characteristics (β_1, β_2) pairs such that	Optimal behaviour p^*
If $\psi_1^* = 1$	$\beta_1 = 1$ or $\beta_2 = 1$	$\begin{cases} \frac{\psi_1^* - \beta_2^*}{\beta_1^* - \beta_2^*} = 1 & \text{if } \beta_1^* = 1, \beta_2^* \ne 1 \\ \frac{\psi_1^* - \beta_2^*}{\beta_1^* - \beta_2^*} = 0 & \text{if } \beta_1^* \ne 1, \beta_2^* = 1 \\ \text{arbitrary} & \text{if } \beta_1^* = \beta_2^* = 1 \end{cases}$
If $\psi_1^* = 0$	$\beta_1 = 0$ or $\beta_2 = 0$	$\begin{cases} \frac{\psi_1^* - \beta_2^*}{\beta_1^* - \beta_2^*} = 1 & \text{if } \beta_1^* = 0, \beta_2^* \ne 0 \\ \frac{\psi_1^* - \beta_2^*}{\beta_1^* - \beta_2^*} = 0 & \text{if } \beta_1^* \ne 0, \beta_2^* = 0 \\ \text{arbitrary} & \text{if } \beta_1^* = \beta_2^* = 0 \end{cases}$
If $0 < \psi_1^* < 1$	$(\beta_1 - \psi_1^*)(\beta_2 - \psi_1^*) \le 0$	$\begin{cases} \frac{\psi_1^* - \beta_2^*}{\beta_1^* - \beta_2^*} & \text{if } \beta_1^* \ne \beta_2^* \\ \text{arbitrary} & \text{if } \beta_1^* = \beta_2^* \end{cases}$

all the weight on the more important factor. However, when ψ_1^* is strictly between 0 and 1, a combination of factors λ_1 and λ_2 is necessary to achieve the maximum growth rate. The individual characteristics, (β_1^*, β_2^*), need to be distributed in such a way that one of the two choices of action puts more weight on one factor, while the other choice puts more weight on the other factor. Eventually, the behaviour, p^*, randomizes between the two choices, and therefore achieves the optimal combination of factors.

This result may be viewed as a primitive form of herding behaviour, where all individuals in the population choose to act in the same manner, especially if the relative environmental factors, $\mathbb{E}[\lambda_1/\lambda_2]$ and $\mathbb{E}[\lambda_2/\lambda_1]$, shift suddenly due to rapid environmental changes. To an outside observer, behaviours among individuals in this population will seem heterogeneous before the shift, but will become increasingly similar after the shift, creating the appearance (but not the reality) of intentional coordination, communication, and synchronization. If the reproductive cycle is sufficiently short, this change in population-wide behaviour may seem highly responsive to environmental changes, giving the impression that individuals are learning about their environment. This is, indeed, a form of learning, but it occurs at the level of the population, not at the individual level, and not within an individual's lifespan.

The results in Table 4.1 also highlight the fact that evolution can lead to multiple coexisting types of individuals. It is mathematically possible that types with different characteristics (β_1 and β_2) and different behaviours (p) will lead to the same factor loading (ψ_1^*). They may superficially appear to be doing very different things, but each group of individuals will balance these two actions in its own way, based on its own characteristics. The environmental factor plays an important role in this process, since the ultimate reason that these groups are able to coexist is because they have the same factor loadings. Just as 'All roads lead to Rome', our results show that, in evolution, 'All sustainable behaviours lead to survival', (i.e. those behaviours satisfying the growth-optimality condition in Table 4.1).

4.2 Individual versus Group Optimality

It is instructive to compare the optimal characteristics and behaviours in Table 4.1, which maximize growth, with the behaviours that maximize an individual's reproductive success. According to Equations (4.1) and (4.2), an individually optimal behaviour will maximize

$$\mathbb{E}\left[x^{p,\beta_1,\beta_2}\right] = \mathbb{E}\left[I^p x_a^{\beta_1} + (1 - I^p)x_b^{\beta_2}\right] = \psi_1 \mathbb{E}[\lambda_1] + \psi_2 \mathbb{E}[\lambda_2]$$

over p, β_1, β_2. Therefore, the individually optimal factor loading, denoted by $\tilde{\psi}_1$, is simply:

$$\tilde{\psi}_1 = \begin{cases} 1 & \text{if } \mathbb{E}[\lambda_1] > \mathbb{E}[\lambda_2] \\ 0 & \text{if } \mathbb{E}[\lambda_1] < \mathbb{E}[\lambda_2] . \\ \text{arbitrary} & \text{if } \mathbb{E}[\lambda_1] = \mathbb{E}[\lambda_2] \end{cases}$$

Given a particular environment (λ_1, λ_2), the individually optimal behaviour depends only on the expectation of two factors, and this selfish behaviour is generally suboptimal for the group.

In contrast, individuals of type $f^* = (p^*, \beta_1^*, \beta_2^*)$ described in Table 4.1 are optimal in the group sense, attaining the maximum growth rate as a group by behaving differently than the individually optimal behaviour. Henceforth, we shall refer to f^* as the *growth-optimal* behaviour, in order to underscore the fact that it is optimal from the perspective of the population but not necessarily from the individual's perspective. This gives us a prototype of group selection derived as a consequence of stochastic environments with systematic risk. We thus define a *group* to be a set of individuals with the same characteristics. More precisely, in our model, individuals with the same (β_1, β_2) are considered a group. Natural selection favours the groups with optimal characteristics (β_1^*, β_2^*), and p^* is a reflection of different behaviours for each group.

Like altruism, cooperation, trust, and other behaviours that do not immediately benefit the individual, these growth-optimal characteristics and behaviours derived in our framework flourish because they allow individuals to pass through the filter of natural selection. However, unlike theories of group selection that are based on sexual reproduction and genetic distance, our version of group selection is based on behaviour itself. Individuals with types other than f^* will not reproduce as quickly as those with the optimal type. Hence, from an evolutionary biologist's perspective, it appears that group selection is operating at the level of those individuals with characteristics (β_1^*, β_2^*) and behaving according to p^*. Of course, we cannot measure all of an organism's characteristics and behaviour as readily as we can measure its genetic makeup, but in the case of our binary choice model, it is clear that selection can and does occur according to groups defined by their characteristics and behaviour.

Section 4.3 provides a generalization of the binary choice model to multinomial choices with multiple environmental factors. It must be noted that within our model, it is possible for the optimal growth rate, α^*, to correspond to multiple groups, and for each group to correspond to multiple optimal behaviours. In terms of group selection, this means that several different groups—each defined by a specific combination of characteristics—could simultaneously be optimal from an evolutionary perspective. Within each group, natural selection will determine the behaviour that achieves the optimal growth rate. In other words, the optimal behaviour is not necessarily unique for each group. In addition, the optimal behaviours for different groups might overlap.

4.3 Multinomial Choice with Multiple Factors

We generalize our two-factor, binary choice model to multinomial choice with multiple factors in this section. Consider a population of individuals that live for one period, produce a random number of offspring asexually, and then die. During their lives, individuals make only one decision: they choose from m actions $\{1, \cdots, m\}$, and this results in one of m corresponding random numbers of offspring $(x_1, \cdots, x_m)$. Suppose each individual chooses action i with probability p_i, for $i = 1, 2, \cdots, m$. Let $\mathbf{p} = (p_1, \cdots, p_m)$ be the probability vector that characterizes an individual's behaviour. $\mathbf{p}$ satisfies the following conditions:

$$0 \leq p_i \leq 1, \quad \forall i = 1, \cdots, m,$$

$$\sum_{i=1}^{m} p_i = 1.$$

The environment is described by k factors $\boldsymbol{\lambda} = (\lambda_1, \cdots, \lambda_k)$. Let $\mathbf{B} = (\beta_{ij})_{m \times k}$ be the matrix of an individual's characteristics that satisfies the following conditions:

$$0 \leq \beta_{ij} \leq 1, \quad \forall i = 1, \cdots, m; j = 1, \cdots, k,$$

$$\sum_{j=1}^{k} \beta_{ij} = 1, \quad \forall i = 1, \cdots, m.$$

Note that the second condition is a direct generalization of the binary choice model, which means that each row of $\mathbf{B}$ sums to 1. This reflects the trade-off between k environmental factors for each action.

In the multinomial choice model, an individual is characterized by both $\mathbf{p}$ and $\mathbf{B}$. The number of offspring for individual i of type $f = (\mathbf{p}, \mathbf{B})$ is:

$$x_i^{\mathbf{p},\mathbf{B}} = I_{1,i}^{\mathbf{p}} x_{1,i}^{\mathbf{B}} + \cdots + I_{m,i}^{\mathbf{p}} x_{m,i}^{\mathbf{B}},$$

where $(I_{1,i}^{\mathbf{p}}, \cdots, I_{m,i}^{\mathbf{p}})$ is the multinomial indicator variable with probability $\mathbf{p} = (p_1, \cdots, p_m)$:

$$(I_{1,i}^{\mathbf{p}}, \cdots, I_{m,i}^{\mathbf{p}}) = \begin{cases} (1, 0, \cdots, 0) & \text{with probability } p_1 \\ (0, 1, \cdots, 0) & \text{with probability } p_2 \\ \cdots \\ (0, 0, \cdots, 1) & \text{with probability } p_m \end{cases},$$

and the number of offspring produced by taking each action is given by:

$$\begin{cases} x_{1,i}^{\mathbf{B}} = \beta_{11}\lambda_1 + \cdots + \beta_{1k}\lambda_k \\ \cdots \\ x_{m,i}^{\mathbf{B}} = \beta_{m1}\lambda_1 + \cdots + \beta_{mk}\lambda_k \end{cases}.$$

We assume that

Assumption 4.3 $\lambda_1, \cdots, \lambda_k$ *are independent random variables with some well-behaved distribution functions, such that* $(x_1, \cdots, x_m)$ *and* $\log(p_1 x_1 + \cdots + p_m x_m)$ *have finite moments up to order 2 for all* $\mathbf{p} = (p_1, \cdots, p_m)$ *and* $\mathbf{B} = (\beta_{ij})_{m \times k}$, *and*

Assumption 4.4 $(\lambda_1, \cdots, \lambda_k)$ *is IID over time and identical for all individuals in a given generation.*

Like the binary choice model, it is convenient to define factor loadings of type $f = (\mathbf{p}, \mathbf{B})$ individuals. Define $\boldsymbol{\psi} = (\psi_1, \cdots, \psi_k) = \mathbf{pB}$:

$$(\psi_1, \cdots, \psi_k) = (p_1, \cdots, p_m) \begin{pmatrix} \beta_{11} & \cdots & \beta_{1k} \\ \vdots & \ddots & \vdots \\ \beta_{m1} & \cdots & \beta_{mk} \end{pmatrix}. \tag{4.7}$$

Note that $\psi_1 + \cdots + \psi_k = 1$ by definition.

Suppose that the total number of type-f individuals in generation T is n_T^f. The following proposition gives us the log-geometric-average growth rate of type f in the general m-choice k-factor setting.

Proposition 4.2 *Under Assumptions 4.3 and 4.4, as the number of generations and the number of individuals in each generation increases without bound, $T^{-1} \log n_T^f$ converges in probability to the log-geometric-average growth rate*

$$\alpha(\mathbf{p}, \mathbf{B}) = \mathbb{E}\left[\log\left(\mathbf{pB}\boldsymbol{\lambda}'\right)\right] = \mathbb{E}\left[\log\left(\boldsymbol{\psi}\boldsymbol{\lambda}'\right)\right]. \tag{4.8}$$

Proposition 4.2 characterizes the log-geometric-average growth rate as a function of type f. The next proposition gives the optimal type f^* that maximizes Equation (4.8).

Proposition 4.3 *Under Assumptions 4.3 and 4.4, the optimal factor loading, $\boldsymbol{\psi}^* = (\psi_1^*, \cdots, \psi_k^*)$, that maximizes Equation (4.8) is given by*

$$\boldsymbol{\psi}^* = \begin{cases} (1, 0, \cdots, 0) & \text{if } \mathbb{E}\left[\frac{\lambda_2}{\lambda_1}\right] < 1, \mathbb{E}\left[\frac{\lambda_3}{\lambda_1}\right] < 1, \cdots, \mathbb{E}\left[\frac{\lambda_k}{\lambda_1}\right] < 1 \\ (0, 1, \cdots, 0) & \text{if } \mathbb{E}\left[\frac{\lambda_1}{\lambda_2}\right] < 1, \mathbb{E}\left[\frac{\lambda_3}{\lambda_2}\right] < 1, \cdots, \mathbb{E}\left[\frac{\lambda_k}{\lambda_2}\right] < 1 \\ \cdots & \\ (0, 0, \cdots, 1) & \text{if } \mathbb{E}\left[\frac{\lambda_1}{\lambda_k}\right] < 1, \mathbb{E}\left[\frac{\lambda_2}{\lambda_k}\right] < 1, \cdots, \mathbb{E}\left[\frac{\lambda_{k-1}}{\lambda_k}\right] < 1 \\ \text{solution to Equation (4.10)} & \text{otherwise} \end{cases}$$

$$\tag{4.9}$$

In the last case, assume without loss of generality $\boldsymbol{\psi}^* = (\psi_1^*, \cdots, \psi_l^*, 0, \cdots, 0)$. That is, $\psi_1, \cdots, \psi_l$ are nonzero, and $\psi_{l+1}, \cdots, \psi_k$ are zero. Then $\boldsymbol{\psi}^*$ in the last case of Equation (4.9) is defined implicitly by

$$\mathbb{E}\left[\frac{\lambda_1}{\psi_1^*\lambda_1 + \cdots + \psi_l^*\lambda_l}\right] = \cdots = \mathbb{E}\left[\frac{\lambda_l}{\psi_1^*\lambda_1 + \cdots + \psi_l^*\lambda_l}\right] = 1, \tag{4.10}$$

and ψ^* satisfies:

$$
\begin{cases}
\mathbb{E}\left[\dfrac{\lambda_{l+1}}{\psi_1^*\lambda_1 + \cdots + \psi_l^*\lambda_l}\right] < 1 \\
\cdots \\
\mathbb{F}\left[\dfrac{\lambda_k}{\psi_1^*\lambda_1 + \cdots + \psi_l^*\lambda_l}\right] < 1
\end{cases}
. \tag{4.11}
$$

As a result, the growth-optimal type is $f^* = (\mathbf{p}^*, \mathbf{B}^*)$, given by

$$\mathbf{p}^*\mathbf{B}^* = \boldsymbol{\psi}^*.$$

Note that in Proposition 4.3, it is not possible to characterize fully ψ^* simply by the ratios $\mathbb{E}\left[\lambda_i/\lambda_j\right]$. However, there is still a natural analogue to the binary choice model through Equations (4.10) and (4.11). Thus, $\psi^* = (\psi_1^*, \cdots, \psi_l^*, 0, \cdots, 0)$ is optimal if and only if the expectation of any irrelevant factor divided by the optimal combination of factors is less than 1, and any factor in the optimal combination divided by the optimal combination is equal to 1. Intuitively, this means that any factor in the optimal combination is adding a useful degree of freedom.

When the number of factors is no more than the number of choices (i.e. $k \le m$), the maximization takes place in the k-dimensional space, $(\psi_1, \cdots, \psi_k)$. Put another way, there may be multiple solutions for the original probabilities $(p_1, \cdots, p_m)$ that correspond to the same factor combinations $(\psi_1, \cdots, \psi_k)$ and, therefore, the same growth rates.

If the dimension of the optimization problem is very large, then in practice a population will not be large enough for there to be a reasonable initial representation of all possible types. This underscores the importance of the factor model, which reduces dimensionality and facilitates the selection of characteristics that respond to all the lower-dimensional ranges of environmental uncertainty.

4.4 A Numerical Example

Consider an island that is isolated from the rest of the world. Suppose factor λ_1 is a measure of weather conditions of the local environment, and factor λ_2 is a measure of the local environment's topography. (Without loss of generality, we will assume that larger values of each factor are more conducive to reproductive success.) Moreover, λ_1 and λ_2 are independent random variables described by:

$$\lambda_1 = \begin{cases} 1 & \text{with probability } \frac{1}{2} \\ 2 & \text{with probability } \frac{1}{2} \end{cases},$$

$$\lambda_2 = \begin{cases} 1 & \text{with probability } \frac{1}{2} \\ 2 & \text{with probability } \frac{1}{2} \end{cases}.$$

An individual on this island lives for one period, has one opportunity to choose one of two actions—farming (action a) or mining (action b)—which determines its reproductive success, and then dies immediately after reproduction. The number of offspring is given by $x_a^{\beta_1}$ if action a is chosen, and $x_b^{\beta_2}$ if b is chosen, where $x_a^{\beta_1}$ and $x_b^{\beta_2}$ are given by:

$$\begin{cases} x_a^{\beta_1} = \beta_1 \lambda_1 + (1 - \beta_1)\lambda_2 \\ x_b^{\beta_2} = \beta_2 \lambda_1 + (1 - \beta_2)\lambda_2 \end{cases}.$$

Here, β_1 captures an individual's farming ability as determined by the two factors, weather and topography; β_2 captures an individual's mining ability as determined by the same two factors. According to Table 4.1, the optimal factor loadings will be $\psi_1^* = \psi_2^* = 1/2$, indicating that individuals should have a balanced exposure to both weather and topography. The optimal characteristics are

$$\left\{ (\beta_1^*, \beta_2^*) \middle| \left(\beta_1^* - \frac{1}{2}\right)\left(\beta_2^* - \frac{1}{2}\right) \le 0 \right\}, \tag{4.12}$$

and each group is associated with the optimal behaviour:

$$p^* = \begin{cases} \frac{\frac{1}{2} - \beta_2^*}{\beta_1^* - \beta_2^*} & \text{if } \beta_1^* \ne \beta_2^* \\ \text{arbitrary} & \text{if } \beta_1^* = \beta_2^* = \frac{1}{2} \end{cases}. \tag{4.13}$$

For example, $\left\{ (\beta_1^*, \beta_2^*) \middle| \beta_1^* = \frac{1}{2} \right\}$ is an optimal group associated with $p^* = 1$. These are individuals who can perfectly balance the output of farming with respect to weather and topography. Therefore, they will choose farming with probability 1, and appear as a group of farmers.

Another optimal group is $\left\{(\beta_1^*, \beta_2^*) \middle| \beta_2^* = \frac{1}{2}\right\}$ and it is associated with the optimal behaviour $p^* = 0$. These individuals can perfectly balance the output of mining with respect to weather and topography. Therefore, they will choose mining with probability 1, and appear as a group of miners.

There are also other optimal groups, described by Equation (4.12) in general, in which individuals randomize their choices between farming and mining according to Equation (4.13) to achieve the optimal exposure to weather and topography.

Figure 4.1a shows the optimal behaviour for each group. The optimal groups described by Equation (4.12) correspond to the upper-left and lower-right blocks. Randomized behaviours are optimal for these groups. Interestingly, all the suboptimal groups (upper-right and lower-left blocks) correspond to deterministic behaviours ($p^* = 0$ or 1) except when $\beta_1 = \beta_2$. Figure 4.1b shows the optimal log-geometric-average growth rate for each group. It is clear that all groups described by Equation (4.12) have the largest growth rate.

We can see that multiple optimal groups are able to coexist through natural selection, and, within each group, individuals share the same characteristics. A particular behaviour must be paired with a particular set of characteristics to achieve the optimal growth rate. Note that the individuals in Equation (4.12) are optimal only in the group sense. As a single entity, a group possesses survival benefits above and beyond an individual. In our framework, these benefits arise purely from stochastic environments with systematic risk.

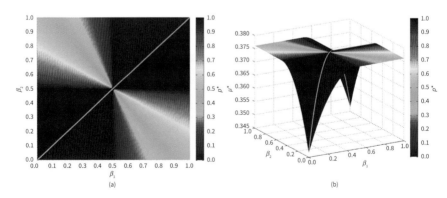

Fig. 4.1 (a) The optimal behaviour for each group in the numerical example of group selection. (b) The optimal log-geometric-average growth rate for each group in the numerical example of group selection.

The usual notion of group selection in the evolutionary biology literature is that natural selection acts at the level of the group instead of at the more conventional level of the individual, with the corollary that interaction among members within each group is much more frequent than interaction among individuals across groups. In such a case, similar individuals are usually clustered geographically. In our model, however, individuals do not interact at all. Nevertheless, the fact that individuals with the same behaviour also generate offspring with the same behaviour makes them more likely to cluster geographically and appear as a group. As a thought experiment, imagine that the environment, (λ_1, λ_2), experiences a sudden shift in circumstance. To an outside observer, behaviours among individuals in this population will become increasingly similar after the shift. Once again, this will create the appearance—but not the reality—of intentional coordination, communication, and synchronization between individuals with no interactions at all.

We have used the phrase 'appear as a group' because our derived behaviour is not strictly the same as group selection as it is defined in the evolutionary biology literature. Instead, we show that a behaviour that is evolutionarily dominant through the traditional mechanism of natural selection is consistent with the implications of group selection. We purposefully model individuals in our population as mindless creatures engaging in random choices in order to demonstrate that group-like selection can arise purely through common factors in reproductive success. If we include more complex features such as sexual reproduction, limited resources, and competitive or cooperative interactions among individuals, we are able to generate even more sophisticated group dynamics.

4.5 Discussion

The debate surrounding genetic, kin, and group selection began over four decades ago, but it has garnered renewed interest thanks to Nowak, Tarnita, and Wilson (2010), who challenged inclusive fitness theory (and its implication of kin selection) in the study of social evolution by arguing that it is not a constructive theory that allows a useful mathematical analysis of evolutionary processes. They concluded that inclusive fitness is neither useful nor necessary to explain the evolution of eusociality or other cooperative phenomena. However, this view was sharply criticized in a flurry of responses by many leading evolutionary biologists (Abbot et al., 2011; Boomsma et al., 2011; Ferriere and Michod, 2011; Herre and Wcislo,

2011; Strassmann et al., 2011), who observed that inclusive fitness theory has stimulated an extensive empirical literature in behavioural and evolutionary ecology over the past forty years (Abbot et al., 2011), and that kin selection is a strong, vibrant theory that forms the basis for our understanding of the evolution of social behaviour (Strassmann et al., 2011).

However, a significant amount of research suggests that group selection and kin selection (and thus inclusive fitness) are essentially one process (Queller, 1992; Lehmann et al., 2007; Wild, Gardner, and West, 2009; Wade et al., 2010; Lion, Jansen, and Day, 2011; Marshall, 2011), with both theories seeking to characterize the genetic structure of a population, but in different ways. These authors argue that it is now time to step back from the details of the specific arguments, and consider the more general question of how evolution works in structured populations. This line of inquiry has the potential to generate insights beyond its traditional areas of application (Lion, Jansen, and Day, 2011).

Instead of entering into this debate, we propose to reconcile these opposing perspectives by studying the impact of selection on behaviour, deriving evolutionary implications that cut across species, physiology, and genetic origin. As a direct consequence of this behavioural approach, we have shown that what appears to be group selection may, in fact, simply be the consequence of natural selection occurring in stochastic environments with reproductive risks that are correlated across individuals. In particular, we provide an evolutionary model with population dynamics for the simplest form of behaviour, a binary choice, and derive the implications of selection on the behaviour of individuals with certain shared characteristics. Unsurprisingly, individuals with similar characteristics experience similar selective pressures. As a result, evolution in stochastic environments with systematic risk can generate empirical phenomena that are consistent with group selection. In fact, nature is able to select for 'groups' of individuals with optimal characteristics, where the optimal behaviour within selected groups is simply a reflection of the optimality of that group's characteristics with respect to the given environment. Moreover, it is possible that multiple groups achieve the same optimal growth rate, but through different means (i.e. many combinations of behaviour and characteristics can be optimal), leading to considerable variation in the types of behaviour and characteristics in the population.

W.D. Hamilton's great insight into behavioural evolution was that individual fitness is not maximized by social evolution; inclusive fitness is (Hamilton, 1963, 1964). The idea that something other than the individual organism could be the fitness-maximizing unit was completely revolutionary at the time, and opened new research areas that are still being explored (Ferriere and Michod, 2011). We have shown that, in addition to Hamilton's insight, individuals with highly correlated risks will appear to form groups in evolution, even if their actions are totally autonomous, mindless, and (prior to natural selection) uniformly randomly distributed in the population. Although this result seems to eliminate the need for a separate theory of group selection, the unique and important evolutionary implications of multiple sources of correlated systematic risk suggest that a separate term for this phenomenon may still be worthwhile.

PART II

BEHAVIOUR

5
Probability Matching

In Chapter 2 we described an evolutionary explanation for probability matching, a behaviour that has long puzzled economists and psychologists because of its apparent inconsistency with basic self-interest.[1] In this chapter, we present the first experimental test of this explanation using monetary payoffs to measure the degree of probability matching among individuals, its variation, and the key factors affecting this behaviour in a real-world decision-making context.

For this test, we recruited a sample of eighty-two volunteers from the MIT Behavioural Research Laboratory to participate in our experiment. Each participant played a computer game consisting of 200 trials of a binary choice decision. In each trial, an image of either Angelina Jolie or Brad Pitt was displayed with a certain probability, and subjects were paid according to the number of trials in which they correctly guessed which image would appear.

By varying the payoff structure of the game, we were able to test whether subjects showed probability matching behaviour, and whether deviations occurred as predicted by the model described in Chapter 2. Specifically, we designed several payoffs where the evolutionarily dominant behaviour was either to maximize (i.e. always choose one option) or to randomize (i.e. choose randomly between two options).

We found strong evidence for a behavioural difference between theoretical maximizers and theoretical randomizers, as predicted by Brennan and Lo (2011). After controlling for a wide range of demographic and socioeconomic variables, theoretical randomizers still engaged in randomizing behaviour more often than theoretical maximizers. When facing different environments (i.e. payoffs in the experiment), our subjects responded differently by adapting to the new conditions and showing different stable behaviours.

We were also able to study individual differences in the tendency to maximize or randomize by collecting basic demographic and socio-economic information from the anonymous participants. We found that subjects with

[1] This chapter, including the tables and figures, is adapted from Lo, A. W., Marlowe, K. P., and Zhang, R. (2021). To maximize or randomize? An experimental study of probability matching in financial decision making. *PLoS ONE* 16(8): e0252540. https://doi.org/10.1371/journal.pone.0252540.

The Adaptive Markets Hypothesis. Andrew W. Lo and Ruixun Zhang, Oxford University Press. © Andrew W. Lo and Ruixun Zhang (2024). DOI: 10.1093/oso/9780199681143.003.0005

a higher level of financial assets tended to randomize less often, while subjects with children tended to randomize more often. Moreover, subjects who had taken probability and statistics classes, and those who self-reported finding a pattern in the game (although none existed), also tended to randomize more often, contrary to our prior expectation that those participants with a better understanding of probability might be more likely to adopt the economically maximizing behaviour. In fact, we found that those subjects would engage in exactly the opposite behaviour. This may be due to an attempt to 'beat the game', based on the qualitative answers to our post-trial survey by participants.

From the evolutionary perspective, the key to understanding these different predictive behaviours lies in the assumption of systematic reproductive risk (Brennan and Lo, 2011; Zhang, Brennan, and Lo, 2014b). The experiment we describe in this chapter involves a binary choice in which the risks to the population are idiosyncratic, that is, the outcomes of one individual's choice are independent of those of another. However, when individuals with preferences formed in response to systematic risks are placed in the different environment, there is the potential for probability matching to occur, creating what appears to be irrational behaviours for those environments.

Our results contribute to the growing literature on rationalizing the existence of probability matching. As far back as the 1950s, researchers (Estes, 1950; Burke, Estes, and Hellyer, 1954; Estes and Strughan, 1954) have developed statistical models that attempt to explain and predict matching behaviour. Since then, several behavioural reasons have been offered, including its emergence as a consequence of pattern searching (Wolford et al., 2004), the greater utility gained from guessing the rarer event correctly (Siegel, 1960), and the role of diversification to avoid boredom (Rubinstein, 2002). Explanations of probability matching from an evolutionary point of view have also been proposed. Wolford, Miller, and Gazzaniga (2000) argue that early human beings looked for explanatory causal relationships as a survival strategy. Wozny, Beierholm, and Shams (2010) have shown that humans match probabilities not only in cognitive tasks, but also in perceptual tasks. This implies that the human nervous system has a built-in function that samples from a distribution of hypotheses, and updates its belief after each observation.

The results of our experiment provide validation for the predictions of Chapter 2, as well as additional evidence that individuals engage in randomized behaviour and probability matching, even with prior experience in probability and investing. More important, our results may provide an explanation for several notable departures from exact probability matching (Baum, 1974; Horne and Lowe, 1993; Kogler and Kühberger, 2007). Randomizing behaviour that matches environmental probabilities depends on the relative reproductive success of the outcomes, and the evolutionary framework proposed in Chapter 2 offers a simple and specific set of conditions for understanding and predicting such behaviour.

5.1 The Binary Choice Game

In Chapter 2 we proposed an evolutionary framework for the origin of several behaviours that are considered anomalous in economic theories based on the assumption of rational behaviour. In particular, probability matching—the tendency of the relative frequency of guesses regarding the outcomes of a sequence of independent random events to match the underlying probability distribution of events—can be explained when the uncertainty in an environment is systematic across all individuals, demonstrating that natural selection is able to yield behaviours that may be individually suboptimal but are optimal for the population.

To test the predictions discussed in Section 2.2.2, we conducted an experiment, presenting live human subjects with a binary choice game in which the risks to the population were idiosyncratic, that is, the outcomes of one individual's game were independent of those of another. We then observed whether participants showed behaviours predicted by our model (or equivalently, behaviours indicated by different colours in Fig. 2.1).

For the experiment, we recruited a sample of eighty-two volunteers with varied personal and socio-economic characteristics through MIT's Behavioural Research Lab (see Section 5.2 for a summary of their characteristics). The full experimental session typically lasted forty-five to sixty minutes for a given participant. Each participant used a computer program that completed 200 iterations of a binary choice trial, in essence playing a lottery. In each iteration of the trial, subjects were shown an image of one of two popular film stars—Angelina Jolie or Brad Pitt—with specific fixed probabilities that were unknown to the subjects. Each participant was randomly assigned to one of four experimental designs (see Table 5.1). In designs 1 and 2, Angelina Jolie appeared 70% of the time and Brad Pitt 30% of the time. Designs 3 and 4 used the opposite probabilities. The participant guessed which image would appear before it was revealed, and received a certain amount of virtual dollars if their guess was correct. Figure 5.1 shows a screenshot of the computer interface used in the experiment.

Fig. 5.1 Example of the experimental program as seen by study participants. The left image shows the screen before the user submitted their guess, and the right image shows the screen displaying the result of a correct guess. Screenshots here are for illustrative purposes only; different images of Angelina Jolie and Brad Pitt were used in the study.

Image Source: Photos of Angelina Jolie and Brad Pitt adapted from UK Foreign, Commonwealth & Development Office, https://www.flickr.com/photos/foreignoffice/14217374639/, under a CC BY 2.0 Deed license (https://creativecommons.org/licenses/by/2.0/).

Table 5.1 Experimental design.

Design	Image Probability	Payoff	Utility Maximizing Behaviour	Evolutionarily Dominant Behaviour (Brennan and Lo, 2011)
1	Prob(Angelina) = 0.7 Prob(Brad) = 0.3	Correct: v$2 Incorrect: v$0	Always Guess Angelina	$f^* =$ Prob(Guess Angelina) = 0.7
2	Prob(Angelina) = 0.7 Prob(Brad) = 0.3	Correct: v$2 Incorrect: v$1	Always Guess Angelina	$f^* =$ Prob(Guess Angelina) = 1.0
3	Prob(Brad) = 0.7 Prob(Angelina) = 0.3	Correct: v$2 Incorrect: v$1	Always Guess Brad	$f^* =$ Prob(Guess Brad) = 1.0
4	Prob(Brad) = 0.7 Prob(Angelina) = 0.3	Correct: v$2 Incorrect: v$0	Always Guess Brad	$f^* =$ Prob(Guess Brad) = 0.7

The different payoff structures were created by varying the parameters in Equation (2.14) and corresponded to the four different evolutionarily dominant behaviours shown in Fig. 2.1 (see also Brennan and Lo (2011)). In designs 1 and 4, subjects received two virtual dollars when they guessed correctly, and zero virtual dollars when they guessed incorrectly. In designs 2 and 3, subjects received two virtual dollars when they guessed correctly, and one virtual dollar when they guessed incorrectly.

Designs 1 and 4 were meant to yield randomized behaviour, while designs 2 and 3 were meant to yield deterministic behaviour. In terms of parameters in Fig. 2.1—using $p = 0.7$—design 1 corresponds to $r_1 = \infty$ and $r_2 = 0$, which yields the dominant behaviour, $f^* = 0.7$. Design 2 corresponds to $r_1 = 2$ and $r_2 = \frac{1}{2}$, which yields the dominant behaviour, $f^* = 1$. Design 3 corresponds to $r_1 = \frac{1}{2}$ and $r_2 = 2$, which yields the dominant behaviour, $f^* = 0$. Lastly, design 4 corresponds to $r_1 = 0$ and $r_2 = \infty$, which yields the dominant behaviour, $f^* = 0.3$.

Figure 5.2 shows the trial-by-trial outcome of two representative subjects. The subject in Fig. 5.2a had a mix of guesses of Angelina Jolie and Brad Pitt throughout the duration of the experiment. We refer to this class of subjects as 'randomizers'. In contrast, the subject in Fig. 5.2b guessed Angelina Jolie for almost the entire duration of the experiment; their only Brad Pitt guesses occurred within the first few attempts, when it is likely that they were still determining the pattern. We refer to this class of subjects as 'maximizers'.

We provided an extensive explanation of the game for all participants, and answered any questions they had before its start. In order to ensure the subjects' comprehension of the mechanics of the game, we conducted fifty iterations of a control game for each subject, either before or after the

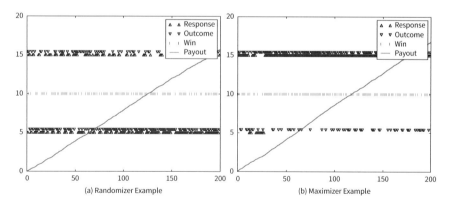

(a) Randomizer Example   (b) Maximizer Example

Fig. 5.2 Experimental outcomes for (a) a representative randomizer and (b) a representative maximizer. The highest row of triangles displays the randomly generated appearances of Angelina Jolie for each trial. The second row of triangles displays the instances when the subject's response was Angelina Jolie. The bottom two rows of triangles represent the same information for Brad Pitt appearances and Brad Pitt responses. The middle row of red ticks represents trials that the subject guessed correctly. The diagonal line shows the cumulative payout to the subject over time.

real experiment. The control game still showed the two images of Angelina Jolie and Brad Pitt at random, but the subjects were explicitly told that they only would earn a reward by always guessing one of the images, randomized between Angelina Jolie and Brad Pitt, but fixed for any one subject. Subjects who understood the payoff structure should always guess the subject with the reward. This was a trivial game, used to test the participant's understanding of the main lottery game.

The majority of our subjects passed the control, demonstrating a clear understanding of the payoff. However, seven subjects guessed the image with zero payoff in the control game more than 40% of the time, and we concluded that they were not paying proper attention to the task, and discarded their data in our subsequent analysis. This left us with valid data from seventy-five subjects.

5.2 Summary Statistics

After participating in the experiment, all participants completed a personal information survey. Table 5.2 contains summary statistics from these surveys, including the subjects' personal and socio-economic characteristics, as well as their game responses. Although our sample was fairly balanced in terms of sex, age, working status, income, wealth, and investment experience, it was skewed towards single (77.3%) subjects and those without children (86.7%). In addition, 64% of our subjects reported taking some probability and statistics classes, an unsurprising finding, given that the experiment took place at MIT.

Each subject received $5 in base pay for showing up and $0.05 for each virtual dollar they earned. Their total dollar earnings ranged from $14.80 to $22.20. Table 5.2 reports the total number of correct guesses for all subjects. The best performer guessed 154 (77%) trials correctly, while the worst performer guessed only ninety-eight (49%) trials correctly. The median subject guessed 129 (64.5%) of the 200 trials correctly, slightly less than the expected number of correct guesses for a perfect maximizer, who would always guess the dominant image.

The post-game survey also asked participants about their perceptions of the binary choice game. Forty-four per cent of subjects reported that they found a pattern in the game. It is clear that many participants were looking for patterns throughout the game, despite its completely random nature. This is consistent with the representativeness heuristic first documented by Tversky and Kahneman (1971); Kahneman and Tversky (1972). We include quotes from two representative subjects.

Table 5.2 Participant demographics and summary statistics.

Variable	Distribution (%)				
Personal Characteristics					
Sex	Male 53.3	Female 45.3			
Has Children	Yes 12.0	No 86.7			
Age	≤ 23 Years 33.3	24–46 Years 34.7	> 46 Years 30.7		
Marital Status	Single 77.3	Partnered 9.3	Married 8.0	Other 4.0	
Socio-economic Characteristics					
Taken Probability and Statistics Class	Yes 64.0	No 34.7			
Gambling Experience	Yes 33.3	No 65.3			
Housing Status	Rent 88.0	Own 10.7			
Working Status	Student 40.0	Currently Working 38.7	Unemployed and Other 20.0		
Annual Family Income	<$25,000 30.7	$25,000–$50,000 24.0	$50,001–$100,000 28.0	>$100,000 16.0	
Total Financial Assets	<$25,000 62.7	$25,000–$50,000 9.3	$50,001–$100,000 14.7	>$100,000 12.0	
Investment Horizon	I don't invest 52.0	Less than 1 year 9.3	Over 1 year 37.3		
Game-related Questions (self-reported)					
Found Pattern in Game	Yes 44.0	No 48.0	I don't remember 6.7		
Had Strategy in Game	Yes 74.7	No 22.7	I don't remember 1.3		
Game Outcome Percentiles					
Correct Guesses (Out of 200 Total)	Min 98	5% 108	50% 129	95% 143	Max 154
Total Earnings ($) (Inc. $5 Base)	Min 14.80	5% 15.80	50% 20.30	95% 22.00	Max 22.20

We received valid responses from seventy-five subjects in the binary choice game, of whom seventy-four provided demographic information.

'I kept losing count, but clearly the ratio of appearance of Jolie's picture to Pitts's kept going up until it was something 7:1, then it went down (not always in increments of one, I think) until it was 1:1, and then it went back up again.'

'Seventy per cent Angelina. If we picked her too many times, Brad was introduced as a counter-pick.'

In addition, 74.7% of subjects reported that they had a specific strategy in the game. By reading the post-study surveys, we realized that our subjects exhibited a wide range of heterogeneous strategies for the game. Here we provide a few representative quotes from the two extremes of these strategies, where some subjects indicated clearly that they were always choosing one image:

'Always pick Angie.'

'Choosing Brad Pitt all the time. His image appeared more frequently and even if the probability was 50% it would not have mattered who I choose, so why not choose him all the time[?] Also minimizes thinking effort and time to click.'

Other subjects seemed to engage in more complicated strategies:

'Chose Brad Pitt the majority of the time—if Brad Pitt appeared at least 6 times in a row, chose Angelina Jolie.'

'…I was switching between one and another until I noticed some sort of pattern and then I favoured Angelina Jolie's picture for the higher number and Brad Pitt for the lower number in the pattern of 5-1-3-1-2.'

These self-reported strategies are also reflected in the wide heterogeneity in behaviour when we analyse participant choices.

5.3 A Model of Individual Behaviour

Since designs 1 and 4 were constructed according to Brennan and Lo (2011) to yield randomizing behaviour, we refer to subjects in these designs as 'theoretical randomizers', and, accordingly, we refer to subjects in designs 2 and 3 to be 'theoretical maximizers' (see Table 5.1). In this section, we test whether theoretical randomizers did, in fact, randomize more often than theoretical maximizers.

We begin by describing a simple model of individual behaviour. We define D to be the dominant option in the game. In our experiment, D represents Angelina Jolie in designs 1 and 2, and Brad Pitt in designs 3 and 4.

Each individual, i, chooses the dominant option D with probability f, where f represents the individual's (unobserved) behaviour. In other words, the individual's decision in each trial is generated by a Bernoulli random variable:

$$I_t = \begin{cases} 1, \text{with probability } f \\ 0, \text{with probability } 1 - f \end{cases}, \tag{5.1}$$

where $I_t = 1$ represents choosing the dominant option D, and $t = 1, ..., 200$. Suppose in T trials, an individual chooses the dominant option

$$N := \sum_{t=1}^{T} I_t \tag{5.2}$$

times. From observed data T and N, our goal is to estimate and understand the factors that determine individual behaviour f in different payoff structures. The sample average proportion,

$$\hat{f} := N/T, \tag{5.3}$$

is the obvious choice as the point estimate of behaviour f.

If an individual's decisions are independent over time, it follows from Equations (5.1) and (5.2) that $N \sim \text{Binomial}(T, f)$, and $\hat{f}$ is approximately normally distributed with mean f and variance $f(1 - f)/T$. More generally, if an individual's decisions are not independent over time, $\hat{f}$ still has a mean f, but its variance may be different. In Section 5.5, we estimate whether an individual's decisions are independent, and in Section 5.6 we discuss its implications for the variance of $\hat{f}$ and the hypothesis tests we carry out.

5.4 Initial Learning

During the experiment, subjects required a number of trials to estimate the frequency of each image. This means that their first few guesses tended to show unstable behaviour. To account for this, we divided each individual's total number of trials into eight consecutive segments of twenty-five trials each, and estimated the aggregate behaviour f for each segment across individuals within the same trial design. Individual behaviour was too noisy for

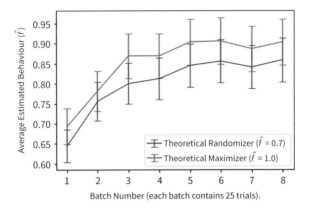

Fig. 5.3 Estimated aggregate behaviour for batches of twenty-five-trial segments.

successful functional estimates over the initial trials, so we used the aggregate pattern across individuals to better understand the speed of participant learning.

Figure 5.3 shows the estimated aggregate behaviour for theoretical maximizers (designs 2 and 3, $f^* = 1.0$) and theoretical randomizers (designs 1 and 4, $f^* = 0.7$), segmented into eight consecutive batches. We used the sample average proportions, $\hat{f}$, in Equation (5.3) as the point estimate of behaviour f, and the normal approximation for binomial distributions to estimate its confidence interval: $\hat{f} \sim \mathcal{N}(f, f(1-f)/T)$. More specifically, for a given confidence level $1 - \alpha$ (e.g. $\alpha = 0.05$, or 95% confidence), the $(1 - \alpha)$-confidence interval is given by:

$$\left(\hat{f} - z\sqrt{\frac{\hat{f}(1 - \hat{f})}{T}}, \ \hat{f} + z\sqrt{\frac{\hat{f}(1 - \hat{f})}{T}} \right),$$

where z is the $1 - \frac{\alpha}{2}$ quantile of a standard normal distribution corresponding to the target error rate, α. For a 95% confidence level, $\alpha = 1 - 0.95 = 0.05$, so $1 - \frac{\alpha}{2} = 0.975$ and $z = 1.96$. There are other approximations for confidence intervals of binomial random variables, such as the Wilson score interval and the Jeffreys interval (Newcombe, 1998; Brown, Goetzmann, and Park, 2001). We use the normal approximation for simplicity.

We see that the estimated behaviours in the first two batches (the first fifty trials) are lower than in the remaining batches, starting to stabilize around batch 3. Therefore, for consistency across all individuals, we consider the responses starting from trial fifty-one as stable, and do not include the first fifty trials in our subsequent analysis. Our main conclusions in this chapter are not sensitive to this choice.

5.5 Decision Autocorrelation

In general, the distribution of our estimated behaviour, $\hat{f}$, depends on the covariance structure of an individual's decisions over time: $\{I_t\}_{t=1}^{T}$. For an individual's stable trials (from trials 51 to 200), we do find evidence for auto-correlation in individual decision-making. In fact, applying the Ljung–Box Q test to each individual's sequence of choices yields thirty-eight p-values that are smaller than 0.05 (thirty-four after the Benjamini–Hochberg procedure to control for the false discovery rate in multiple testing), out of seventy-five subjects. This indicates that roughly half of the subjects show significant autocorrelation.

To incorporate correlation into the variance estimate of $\hat{f}$ in Equation (5.3), we compute an autocorrelation function based on the stable trials of all individuals. Specifically, the lag-l autocorrelation, ACF(l), is estimated using the sample correlation of the following pairs:

$$\left\{\left(I_t^{(i)}, I_{t+l}^{(i)}\right)\right\}_{t=51,\cdots,T-l, \text{ and } i=1,\cdots,n} , \tag{5.4}$$

where the superscripts (i) denote the i-th subject, which we normally omit for simplicity elsewhere in this chapter.

Figure 5.4 shows the autocorrelation function up to a lag of 120. The auto-correlation is 32.4% at lag 1, and quickly stabilizes to around 8%–12%. We also pool together the autocorrelations at all lags to yield an equicorrelation estimate of 10.8%, which we use in the next section to test the hypothesis whether the behaviour for theoretical maximizers is different from the behaviour for theoretical randomizers.

5.6 Probability Matching

By design, the theoretical maximizers of designs 2 and 3 should satisfy $f_{maximizer} = 1.0$ and the theoretical randomizers in designs 1 and 4 should satisfy $f_{randomizer} = 0.7$ under the hypothetical condition that the only determinant of an individual's reproductive success is the payoff from the game. This is obviously an extreme simplification of reality. However, the model

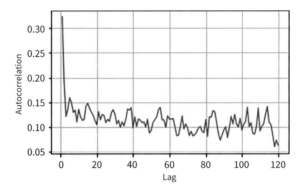

Fig. 5.4 Autocorrelation function estimated from all individuals' stable trials.

still provides the important insight that the presence and degree of probability matching should be determined by the environment, which we can test directly in our experimental design.

In particular, we are able to test the hypothesis that

$$H_0 : f_{maximizer} \leq f_{randomizer}, \quad H_a : f_{maximizer} > f_{randomizer} \qquad (5.5)$$

as predicted by Brennan and Lo (2011), where $f_{maximizer}$ is the behaviour of individuals in designs 2 and 3, and $f_{randomizer}$ is the behaviour of individuals in designs 1 and 4. As specified in Equation (5.1), we observe repeated individual decisions that in our model are determined by the unobserved behaviour, $f_{maximizer}$ and $f_{randomizer}$. We can pool together the data from all theoretical maximizers and compare it against the data from all theoretical randomizers. This is a standard two-sample proportion test, except that decisions for the same individual might be correlated, as shown in Section 5.5.

Given a particular individual, we use vector $\mathbf{y} := (I_1, \cdots, I_T)'$ to denote their sequence of T random Bernoulli trials. For simplicity and analytical tractability, we assume the sequence has an equicorrelation of ρ (estimated as 10.8% in our data set). In other words, the covariance matrix of $\mathbf{y}$ is given by

$$\text{Cov}(\mathbf{y}) = \text{Var}(I_1) \cdot \text{Corr}(\mathbf{y}) = f(1-f) \cdot \begin{pmatrix} 1 & \rho & \cdots & \rho \\ \rho & 1 & \cdots & \rho \\ \vdots & \vdots & \ddots & \vdots \\ \rho & \rho & \cdots & 1 \end{pmatrix}, \qquad (5.6)$$

where the first equation follows from the fact that $I_1, \cdots, I_T$ are identically distributed, as specified in Equation (5.1).

Therefore, the variance of the estimated behaviour, $\hat{f}$, for individual i, as defined in Equation (5.3), is given by

$$\mathrm{Var}\left(\hat{f}^{(i)}\right) = \mathrm{Var}\left(\frac{\sum_{t=1}^{T} I_t}{T}\right) = \frac{\mathrm{Var}\left(\iota'\mathbf{y}\right)}{T^2} = \frac{\iota'\,\mathrm{Cov}\,(\mathbf{y})\,\iota}{T^2}$$

$$= \frac{f(1-f)T(1+(T-1)\rho)}{T^2}$$

$$= \frac{f(1-f)}{T}\cdot(1+(T-1)\rho), \tag{5.7}$$

where ι is a vector of all ones, and we have omitted the superscript i in our derivation for notational simplicity.

Note that the first term in Equation (5.7), $\frac{f(1-f)}{T}$, is simply the variance of $\hat{f}^{(i)}$ if individual decisions are independent Bernoulli random variables. Therefore, the second term in Equation (5.7), $(1+(T-1)\rho)$, can be treated as an adjustment factor of $\hat{f}^{(i)}$'s variance when individual decisions are correlated.

For a set of n independent individuals with T trials each, the overall estimated behaviour is simply the average estimated behaviour of each individual. Therefore, the variance for their overall behaviour is:

$$\mathrm{Var}\left(\hat{f}\right) = \mathrm{Var}\left(\frac{\sum_{i=1}^{n} \hat{f}^{(i)}}{n}\right) = \frac{\mathrm{Var}\left(\hat{f}^{(1)}\right)}{n} = \frac{f(1-f)}{nT}\cdot(1+(T-1)\rho).$$

As a result, for an unpaired two-sample proportion test between two groups of subjects with n_1 and n_2 individuals, we have the test statistic:

$$z = \frac{(\hat{f}_1 - \hat{f}_2) - 0}{\sqrt{f^*(1-f^*)\left(\frac{1}{n_1 T} + \frac{1}{n_2 T}\right)}} \cdot \frac{1}{\sqrt{1+(T-1)\rho}}, \tag{5.8}$$

where $\hat{f}_1$, $\hat{f}_2$, and f^* are the average behaviour for individuals from group 1, group 2, and all pooled together, respectively, and they do not depend on $\mathbf{y}$'s covariance structure. The first term in Equation (5.8) is simply the standard z-score for the two-sample proportion test, and the second term in Equation (5.8) can be treated as the adjustment factor for correlation, which in our case is:

$$\frac{1}{\sqrt{1+(T-1)\rho}} = \frac{1}{\sqrt{1+(150-1)\cdot 10.8\%}} \approx 0.24$$

for stable trials.

With this correlation adjustment, the null hypothesis in Equation (5.5) is rejected with a z-statistic of 2.014 (or a p-value of 0.022), providing evidence for a difference in behaviour between theoretical maximizers and theoretical randomizers. As predicted, when facing different environments (i.e. different payoffs in the experiment), theoretical randomizers do, indeed, randomize more often than theoretical maximizers. In other words, our subjects responded differently by adapting to the environment and showing different stable behaviours.

We performed the same hypothesis test in Equation (5.5) for subjects who answered 'Yes' when asked whether they employed a specific strategy (74.7%) and those who reported 'No' separately. We found that the effect holds strongly for individuals who reported that they used a specific strategy (adjusted z-statistic of 2.489, adjusted p-value of 0.006) but not for those who did not (adjusted z-statistic of −0.058, adjusted p-value of 0.523). This serves as another robustness check that this effect is driven by intentional behaviour on the part of the subjects, not purely noise. This also provides additional empirical evidence for those theories that attempt to explain probability matching through pattern seeking (Wolford et al., 2004) or through searching for causal relationships (Wolford, Miller, and Gazzaniga, 2000).

In principle, one could also perform the same test for different slices of the subjects across demographic, socio-economic, and game-specific dimensions shown in Table 5.2. This would help to build greater intuition on whether the same effect holds true universally, and which types of individuals experience stronger effects. However, we acknowledge that the power of our study is rather limited due to its sample size of only seventy-five subjects, particularly after adjustments for multiple testing, and we leave this to future studies.

5.7 Individual Differences

To study jointly the individual differences in decision-making relative to the variables considered in Table 5.2, we consider a logistic regression model at the level of each guess by the individual subject. Specifically, for individual i, at the t-th trial in the game,

$$I_t^{(i)} \sim \text{Bernoulli}(f^{(i)}),$$

where $I_t^{(i)} = 1$ is a binary random variable that represents whether individual i chooses the dominant option at trial t, similar to the formulation in Equation (5.1). Individual i's behaviour, the probability of choosing the dominant option, is modelled by

$$
\begin{aligned}
f^{(i)} &= \text{Prob}(I_t^{(i)} = 1) \\
&= \text{Logistic}(\text{IsTheoryMaximizer}_i + \text{IsMale}_i + \text{HasChild}_i + \text{AgeBucket}_i \\
&\quad + \text{HasProbClassExp}_i + \text{HasGamblingExp}_i + \text{HasInvestExperience}_i \\
&\quad + \text{IsStudent}_i + \text{IsOwn}_i + \text{IncomeBucket}_i + \text{TotalAssetBucket}_i \\
&\quad + \text{HasPattern}_i),
\end{aligned} \tag{5.9}
$$

where $\text{Logistic}(x) = (1 + \exp(-x))^{-1}$.

We have seen in Section 5.5 that individual decisions are correlated over time. Therefore, the errors for regression in Equation (5.9) may be autocorrelated. We group the trials from the same individuals together, and order their decisions chronologically. In particular, the response variable is organized as

$$
(\underbrace{I_1^{(1)}, I_2^{(1)}, \cdots, I_T^{(1)}}_{\text{1st subject's } T \text{ trials}}, \underbrace{I_1^{(2)}, I_2^{(2)}, \cdots, I_T^{(2)}}_{\text{2nd subject's } T \text{ trials}}, \cdots, \underbrace{I_1^{(n)}, I_2^{(n)}, \cdots, I_T^{(n)}}_{n\text{-th subject's } T \text{ trials}}),
$$

and we apply the Newey-West heteroskedasticity and autocorrelation consistent (HAC) estimator for the variance of the coefficients in the following results. We adopt Newey and West's (1987) suggestion to choose the truncation parameter to be the integer part of $4(nT/100)^{2/9}$, which is 11 in our case. This, indeed, increases the variance estimate of our coefficients compared to the case of independent errors, and our results are not materially different with respect to the choice of the truncation parameter. In fact, we have even used an estimate with a truncation parameter of 150, the number of total valid decisions for one individual. In this extreme case, the main variable, IsTheoryMaximizer, still remains statistically significant at 5%.

Table 5.3 summarizes the independent variables in Equation (5.9). These variables correspond to the collected personal information of the subjects (see Table 5.2), categorized to make them proper binary or ordinal variables. We have dropped several variables that are highly collinear with the covariates in Equation (5.9). The p-value of the log-likelihood ratio test of the full model is 4×10^{-54}, implying a high degree of significance.

The first variable, IsTheoryMaximizer, encodes whether the individual is a theoretical maximizer (i.e. placed in design 2 or 3). The effect is both positive and strongly significant after controlling for all other socio-economic and game-related variables, implying that theoretical maximizers tend to choose the dominant option more often. This is consistent with our analysis in Section 5.6.

Table 5.3 Variables and coefficients for logistic regression.

Variable	Type	Coefficient	HAC Standard Error	z Statistic
IsTheoryMaximizer	Dummy	0.4180	0.106	**3.959*****
IsMale	Dummy	0.1906	0.100	1.901
HasChild	Dummy	−0.5497	0.126	**−4.378*****
AgeBucket	Ordinal	−0.0747	0.078	−0.962
HasProbClassExp	Dummy	−0.2832	0.116	**−2.445***
HasGamblingExp	Dummy	0.0120	0.106	0.113
HasInvestExperience	Dummy	0.0393	0.108	0.365
IsStudent	Dummy	−0.1001	0.128	−0.78
IsOwn	Dummy	−0.2603	0.206	−1.266
IncomeBucket	Ordinal	0.0246	0.038	0.642
TotalAssetBucket	Ordinal	0.0965	0.048	**2.022***
HasPattern	Dummy	−0.5497	0.101	**−5.467*****
Intercept		2.1051	0.160	**13.126*****

Statistics in bold are significant at the 0.1% (***), 1% (**), or 5% (*) level.

Continuing down the table, a significantly positive coefficient corresponds to a dimension along which individuals tend to be a maximizer (i.e. they randomize less often). Our results show that subjects with more financial assets tend to be maximizers more often than subjects with fewer financial assets.

A significantly negative coefficient, however, corresponds to a dimension along which individuals tend to be a randomizer (i.e. they switch between two options more often). Our results show that subjects with children tend to be randomizers.

In addition, subjects who have taken probability and statistics classes, or who self-reported finding a pattern in the game, tend to randomize more. This is contrary to our expectation that those who understand probability might be more likely to always choose the dominant option, the economically maximizing behaviour. In fact, they behave in exactly the opposite manner, perhaps in an attempt to 'beat the game'. This is consistent with our observations of subject narratives in the post-study survey in Section 5.2.

5.8 Discussion

We designed an experiment that used a simple lottery game to test the occurrence of probability matching behaviour in financial decision-making. Our study specifically used a choice between two images rather than more financially related tasks (such as guessing the outcome of asset price movements) in the hopes of triggering a more primitive form of decision-making in our subjects, because financial tasks may be more likely to trigger economically optimizing behaviours. Traditional utility-based theories would yield the same maximizing behaviour for all four designs in our experiment. Nevertheless, despite a large degree of heterogeneity among individual behaviours, we found that different levels of probability matching occur in different environments characterized by the payoff structure. Specifically, individuals in environments with less balanced payoffs between the two random outcomes (designs 1 and 4 in Table 5.1) show a greater degree of randomizing behaviour, consistent with the behavioural predictions of Brennan and Lo (2011).

However, we did not observe individuals behave in exactly the way the simple theoretical model would suggest, most likely because the real effects on the reproductive success of each individual were unlikely to be affected by the payoffs provided in the game, but instead were affected by a number of heterogeneous socio-economic factors such as income and wealth, among others. It is difficult, and perhaps impossible, to specify a single model that predicts behaviour for every participant under all circumstances. However, we observed that at the population level, the effect that theoretical randomizers randomize more than theoretical maximizers is real and robust, after controlling for a wide range of personal and socio-economic variables.

We also find significant evidence of different levels of probability matching behaviour when we alter the payoff structure in the game. However, our study is constrained by the limited magnitude of payoffs (around $20) offered to subjects, as well as the limitations of our sample size (eighty-two subjects in total). It is therefore difficult to perform additional statistical tests on finer slices of the data to study whether the same behavioural mechanism applies to different demographic categories. It is also difficult to conclude that any demographic dimension that appears neutral to individual decision-making would remain neutral in a larger-scale study. It remains a question for future research to confirm whether our experimental conclusions carry over across demographic groups, to other financial and non-financial contexts, and at different magnitudes of payoffs.

In addition to testing the evolutionary model of Chapter 2, our experimental results suggest that it is valuable to derive behavioural predictions and implications through an evolutionary lens. More generally, financial markets—a collection of individual decision makers—can also be studied using the same principles, leading to the adaptive markets hypothesis (Lo, 2004, 2017) and its many empirical implications (Neely, Weller, and Ulrich, 2009; Kim, Shamsuddin, and Lim, 2011; Khuntia and Pattanayak, 2018). In the same way that micro-level individual decisions can be better understood through an evolutionary lens, markets and societies at the macroscopic and system-wide levels can also benefit from an adaptive perspective. We find evidence for such differences in behaviour in reality, and our evolutionary framework offers a potential explanation and prediction for these behaviours—the environment matters. In the next chapter, we develop similar theoretical foundations and empirical implications for an even more fundamental behaviour: risk aversion.

6

Risk Aversion

Risk aversion is one of the most basic assumptions of all of economics, and one of the most widely observed behaviours in the animal kingdom.[1] Although the desire to avoid risk hardly seems to need defining, a formal definition is fairly simple: an individual is risk averse if they have a concave utility function. A risk-averse individual would not accept an actuarially fair bet, and would require some amount of compensation—a risk premium—to do so.

Despite the ubiquity and importance of this fundamental concept, few economists have asked the most basic questions about it: What is the origin of risk aversion and why does it persist? Its prevalence implies that risk aversion must confer significant evolutionary advantages, but many hedge fund managers and Wall Street traders would argue that risk neutrality is far more valuable for long-term financial success. In this chapter, we show that both arguments have some merit in certain environments, but do not hold in others.

In this chapter, we propose an evolutionary explanation for the origin of risk aversion by applying the binary choice framework presented in Chapter 2 to risky and riskless choices. We show that risk aversion emerges via natural selection if reproductive risk is systematic, that is, correlated across individuals in a given generation. In contrast, risk neutrality emerges if reproductive risk is idiosyncratic, or uncorrelated across each given generation. More generally, our framework implies that the degree of risk aversion is determined by the stochastic nature of reproductive rates, and we show that their different statistical properties lead to different utility functions. This is true regardless of species, and without the need for any biological production function, concave or otherwise.

This approach provides an alternate and more fundamental explanation of risk aversion. The fact that our results do not depend on any exogenous production function suggests that risk aversion is a primitive feature of all organisms. Moreover, the simplicity of our framework and the direct

---

[1] This chapter, including Figs 6.1 and 6.2, is adapted from Zhang, R., Brennan, T. J., and Lo, A. W. (2014). The origin of risk aversion. *Proceedings of the National Academy of Sciences* 111(50): 17777–17782.

The Adaptive Markets Hypothesis. Andrew W. Lo and Ruixun Zhang, Oxford University Press. © Andrew W. Lo and Ruixun Zhang (2024). DOI: 10.1093/oso/9780199681143.003.0006

relationship between reproductive success and risk aversion provide an equally simple explanation for the large amount of heterogeneity in risk aversion observed in empirical studies (Szpiro, 1986; Holt and Laury, 2002; Chetty, 2006; Cohen and Einav, 2007; Guiso and Paiella, 2008): variation in the amount of systematic risk in reproductive success.

When applied to economic contexts, our results imply a link between the expected returns of risky assets such as equities and systematic reproductive risk, which, in turn, is correlated with aggregate financial risk. This relationship is consistent with the well-known equilibrium risk–reward trade-off first proposed by Sharpe (1964). However, our theoretical derivation of this relationship does not depend on preferences or general equilibrium. It is solely a consequence of natural selection under systematic reproductive risk.

From a practical perspective, our results underscore the importance of addressing systematic risk through insurance markets, capital markets, and government policy. However, our results also highlight the potential dangers of sustained government intervention, which can become a source of systematic risk in its own right.

Related Literature

Several measures of risk aversion have been developed over time, including curvature measures of utility functions (Pratt, 1964; Arrow, 1971), human-subject experiments and surveys (Rabin and Thaler, 2001; Holt and Laury, 2002), portfolio choice among financial investors (Guiso and Paiella, 2008), labour supply behaviour (Chetty, 2006), deductible choices in insurance contracts (Szpiro, 1986; Cohen and Einav, 2007), contestant behaviour on game shows (Post et al., 2008), option prices (Aït-Sahalia and Lo, 2000), and auction behaviour (Lu and Perrigne, 2008).

Biologists and ecologists have also documented risk aversion in the form of risk-sensitive foraging behaviour in many nonhuman animal species ranging from bacteria to primates (Deneubourg et al., 1987; Harder and Real, 1987; Pasteels, Deneubourg, and Goss, 1987; Hölldobler and Wilson, 1990; Kirman, 1993; Thuijsman et al., 1995; Smallwood, 1996; Keasar et al., 2002; Ben-Jacob, 2008). The neural basis of risk aversion has received greater attention since researchers discovered that the activity of a specific brain region correlates with risk-taking and risk-averse behaviour (Knoch et al., 2006; Fecteau et al., 2007; Tom et al., 2007).

One particular example of evolutionary principles applied to risk by economists is Robson (1996a), which proposes an evolutionary model of risk preferences, assuming an increasing concave relation between an individual's number of offspring and the amount of resources available to that individual. Given this concave 'biological production function', he shows that expected utility arises from idiosyncratic environmental risk, and nonexpected utility arises from systematic risk. Our framework generalizes these results in several respects, and yields new testable implications involving both biological systems (such as foraging behaviour) and economic institutions (such as equity risk premia and insurance markets).

6.1 Environments with Mixed Risks

We again briefly describe the binary choice framework, with an emphasis on the extensions made in this chapter. Consider a population of individuals that live for one period, produce a random number of offspring asexually, and then die. During its life, this individual i will make only one decision: choose one of two possible actions, a or b, which results in one of two corresponding random numbers of offspring, $x_{a,i}$ and $x_{b,i}$, respectively. These two random variables summarize the impact of the environment on the reproductive success of the individual, and they are assumed to be the weighted sum of two components:

$$\begin{cases} x_{a,i} = \omega z_a + (1 - \omega)y_{a,i} \\ x_{b,i} = \omega z_b + (1 - \omega)y_{b,i} \end{cases} . \tag{6.1}$$

The first component of the weighted sum, (z_a, z_b), is assumed to be independent and identically distributed (IID) over time and identical for all individuals in a given generation. We refer to it as systematic risk, since one individual experiences the same reproductive outcome as the others that choose the same action. The second component, $(y_{a,i}, y_{b,i})$, is assumed to be IID both over time and across individuals i in a given generation; we refer to it as idiosyncratic risk. Both components are described by some well-behaved probability distributions,[2] and ω is a real number between 0 and 1.

Each individual will choose a with some probability $f \in [0, 1]$ and b with probability $1 - f$. We again refer to f as the individual's behaviour, since it completely determines how the individual chooses between a and b. We denote by x_i^f the random number of offspring produced by individual i of type f, then $x_i^f = I_i^f x_{a,i} + \left(1 - I_i^f\right) x_{b,i}$, where I_i^f is the Bernoulli random variable that

---

[2] See the supplementary materials of Zhang, Brennan, and Lo (2014b).

equals 1 with probability f and 0 otherwise. These offspring behave in a manner identical to their parents (i.e. they will choose between a and b according to the same f). As a result, the population may be viewed as being segmented into groups of distinct types f. This assumption is tantamount to assuming perfect genetic transmission of traits from one generation to the next, and provides a clearer analysis of the interaction between natural selection and the stochastic properties of reproduction implicit in the environment. As we have seen, mutation can easily be incorporated into this framework, although at the expense of analytical simplicity (see Chapter 3). We also assume that the initial population contains an equal number of all types, and we normalize this common initial population to be 1 for each type without loss of generality.

We wish to emphasize the difference between reproductive success with systematic risk, (z_a, z_b), and idiosyncratic risk, $(y_{a,i}, y_{b,i})$, which points to the central role that systematic risk plays in shaping the evolution of behaviour and preferences. In the case of systematic risk, the number of offspring is given by the same two random variables, (z_a, z_b), for all individuals. If two individuals choose the same action a, both will generate the same number of random offspring, z_a (i.e. their reproductive success is perfectly correlated). It is in this sense that fecundity is systematic. However, for $(y_{a,i}, y_{b,i})$, the randomness in the number of offspring is strictly idiosyncratic, in the sense that the correlation between the number of offspring for two individuals, i and j, is 0, even if both individuals choose the same course of action. Idiosyncratic fecundity implies that even if all individuals in a given population choose the same action, there will still be considerable cross-sectional variability in the number of offspring produced in any generation.

Using Equation (6.1), we can rewrite x_i^f as a combination of systematic and idiosyncratic risk:

$$x_i^f = \omega z_i^f + (1-\omega)y_i^f,$$

where

$$\begin{cases} z_i^f = I_i^f z_a + \left(1 - I_i^f\right)z_b \\ y_i^f = I_i^f y_{a,i} + \left(1 - I_i^f\right)y_{b,i} \end{cases}.$$

The coefficient $\omega \in [0, 1]$ indicates the proportion of systematic risk in the environment. When $\omega = 1$, all reproductive risk is systematic; when $\omega = 0$, all reproductive risk is idiosyncratic; and when $0 < \omega < 1$, both types of risk are present. In a particular environment described by ω, denote by n_T^f the total number of offspring of type f in generation T. It is easy to show that the average of the log-population, $T^{-1} \log n_T^f$, converges in probability to the log-geometric-average growth rate:

$$\alpha_\omega(f) = \mathbb{E}_z\left[\log\left(\omega z^f + (1 - \omega)\, \mathbb{L}_y[y^f]\right)\right], \qquad (6.2)$$

where $\mathbb{E}_z$ denotes the expectation taken with respect to z^f and $\mathbb{E}_y$ denotes the expectation taken with respect to y^f. Equation (6.2) can also be written as

$$\alpha_\omega(f) = \mathbb{E}_z\left[\log\left(f\xi_a^\omega + (1-f)\xi_b^\omega\right)\right], \qquad (6.3)$$

where

$$\begin{cases} \xi_a^\omega = \omega z_a + (1 - \omega)\,\mathbb{E}_y[y_a] \\ \xi_b^\omega = \omega z_b + (1 - \omega)\,\mathbb{E}_y[y_b] \end{cases}.$$

Maximizing Equation (6.3) yields the evolutionarily dominant behaviour in environment ω, that is, the growth-optimal behaviour (see also Section 2.3 of Chapter 2):

$$f_\omega^* = \begin{cases} 1 & \text{if } \mathbb{E}_z[\xi_a^\omega/\xi_b^\omega] > 1 \text{ and } \mathbb{E}_z[\xi_b^\omega/\xi_a^\omega] < 1 \\ \text{solution to Equation (6.5)} & \text{if } \mathbb{E}_z[\xi_a^\omega/\xi_b^\omega] \geq 1 \text{ and } \mathbb{E}_z[\xi_b^\omega/\xi_a^\omega] \geq 1 \\ 0 & \text{if } \mathbb{E}_z[\xi_a^\omega/\xi_b^\omega] < 1 \text{ and } \mathbb{E}_z[\xi_b^\omega/\xi_a^\omega] > 1 \end{cases}, \qquad (6.4)$$

where f_ω^* is defined implicitly in the second case of Equation (6.4) by:

$$0 = \mathbb{E}_z\left[\frac{\xi_a^\omega - \xi_b^\omega}{f\xi_a^\omega + (1-f)\xi_b^\omega}\right]. \qquad (6.5)$$

The three possible behaviours described in Equation (6.4) reflect the relative reproductive success of the two choices. Choosing a deterministically will be optimal if choice a exhibits unambiguously higher expected relative fecundity, while choosing b deterministically will be optimal if the opposite is true, and randomizing between a and b will be optimal if neither choice has a clear-cut reproductive advantage. We saw in Chapter 2 that the last outcome is the most counterintuitive, since it is suboptimal from an individual's perspective.

When $\omega = 0$, that is, the case of pure idiosyncratic risk, the optimal behaviour, f^*, can only be 0 or 1, corresponding to a purely deterministic choice. In this case, the individually optimal choice, to select the action that yields the highest expected number of offspring, coincides with the evolutionarily dominant strategy (see Section 6.4 for further discussion and examples). However, when $\omega > 0$, that is, when a portion of reproductive risk is systematic, the evolutionarily dominant behaviour, f^*, can be between 0 and 1, in which case individuals exhibit randomizing behaviour. Although mixed strategies are well known in the evolutionary game theory literature (Maynard Smith, 1982), those strategies emerge from sophisticated strategic interactions between rational optimizing players. In our framework, randomization is mindless behaviour produced solely through natural selection. Section 6.4 provides several examples for common distributions of relative fecundity $\xi_a^\omega / \xi_b^\omega$.

Imagine a large population with individuals who are exposed to different reproductive risks. Some individuals are exposed only to idiosyncratic risk ($\omega = 0$), some individuals are exposed only to systematic risk ($\omega = 1$), and some individuals are exposed to a mix of both. The same parameters apply to their offspring. These different groups of individuals have different behaviours in terms of Equation (6.4), as well as different growth rates. We examine this further in the next section to derive individual preferences for populations exposed to different natures of risk.

6.2 Individual Preferences

We assume there exists an objective function $V_\omega(z, y)$ that describes an individual's preference, where z represents systematic risk and y represents idiosyncratic risk, in the sense that (z_1, y_1) is favoured over (z_2, y_2) if and only if $V_\omega(z_1, y_1) > V_\omega(z_2, y_2)$. In other words, the individual maximizes $V_\omega(z, y)$ to determine its choice over random outcomes.

The objective function $V_\omega(z, y)$ can take any form. For example,

$$V_\omega(z, y) = \max_{z+y} \mathbb{E}\left[U(z + y)\right]$$

corresponds to an expected utility that does not distinguish between systematic and idiosyncratic risk. However, some functions will give individuals an evolutionary advantage over others in the population. We will thus derive the evolutionarily dominant function in environments with varying proportions of systematic risk.

When $\omega = 1$, the individual faces only systematic risk. The evolutionarily dominant behaviour is given by $f^* = \text{argmax}_f \mathbb{E}_z\left[\log(z^f)\right]$; hence, the evolutionarily implied individual maximization criterion is:

$$V_{\omega=1}(z, y) = \mathbb{E}_z\left[\log(z)\right].$$

This is simply the expected log-utility of the total number of offspring, which Bernoulli proposed in 1738 to resolve the St Petersburg Paradox, in which participants assign a small value to a repeated gambling game with a theoretically infinite expected payoff.

When $\omega = 0$, the individual faces only idiosyncratic risk. The dominant behaviour in this case is given by $f^* = \text{argmax}_f \log\left(\mathbb{E}_y[y^f]\right)$. Therefore, the evolutionarily implied individual maximization criterion is

$$V_{\omega=0}(z, y) = \mathbb{E}_y[y].$$

This is the expected linear utility of the total number of offspring. In other words, the optimal criterion for an individual is simply the expected value. To put it even more simply, individuals are risk-neutral in this environment.

In the general case in which $0 < \omega < 1$, reproductive risk contains both systematic and idiosyncratic components. The implied individual maximization criterion from the evolutionary perspective is therefore:

$$V_\omega(z, y) = \mathbb{E}_z\left[\log\left(\omega z + (1 - \omega)\,\mathbb{E}_y[y]\right)\right]. \qquad (6.6)$$

This objective function does not conform to the traditional expected utility framework in which the individual's behaviour can be represented as the outcome of a constrained optimization of the expected value of a concave function of the total number of offspring, $\omega z + (1 - \omega)y$. The idiosyncratic component gives rise to a linear expectation in y, and the systematic component gives rise to a logarithmic function of z and the expectation in y. Risk aversion emerges as a consequence of systematic risk, and risk neutrality emerges as a consequence of idiosyncratic risk, regardless of species. This is a novel implication of natural selection that has not appeared in prior studies of human or animal risk preferences. We explore this further in the next section.

6.3 Risk Aversion and Systematic Risk

From Equation (6.6), it is clear that the level of risk aversion is determined by natural selection as a function of the level of systematic risk in the environment. Suppose an individual is faced with a random number of offspring, $\omega z + (1 - \omega)y$, and $(1 - \omega)\mu = \mathbb{E}_y[(1 - \omega)y]$ is the expectation of the idiosyncratic component. As a function of z, Equation (6.6) can be written as the expected utility function, $V_\omega(z, y) = \mathbb{E}_z[U_{\omega,\mu}(z)]$, where

$$U_{\omega,\mu}(z) = \log\left(\omega z + (1 - \omega)\mu\right). \qquad (6.7)$$

This expression defines a class of utility functions in which the utility is measured as a function of the number of offspring arising from its systematic component. Different amounts of systematic risk in the environment correspond to different evolutionarily dominant utility functions. Figure 6.1 shows nine example utility functions where $\omega = 0.1, 0.5, 0.9$ and $\mu = 1, 2, 3$. All nine utility functions are normalized by an affine transformation that sets $U_{\omega,\mu}(0) = 0$ and $U_{\omega,\mu}(10) = 10$.

We can see from Fig. 6.1 that variation in the proportion of systematic risk, ω, drives the concavity of the utility functions, while variation in the level of idiosyncratic risk, μ, plays a role in determining the level of risk aversion. More specifically, we consider the Arrow–Pratt measure of absolute risk aversion (ARA) of $U_{\omega,\mu}(\cdot)$:

$$A_{\omega,\mu}(z) = -\frac{U''_{\omega,\mu}(z)}{U'_{\omega,\mu}(z)} = \frac{1}{z + \left(\frac{1}{\omega} - 1\right)\mu}, \tag{6.8}$$

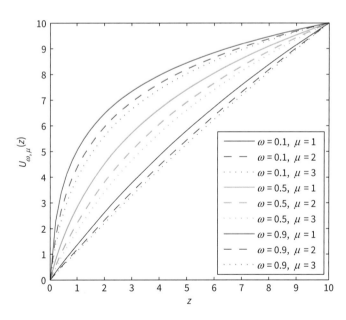

Fig. 6.1 Utility functions implied by environments with different proportions of systematic risk and different levels of idiosyncratic risk. $\omega = 0.1$ represents a low level of systematic risk; $\omega = 0.9$ represents a high level of systematic risk. $\mu = 1$ represents a low level of idiosyncratic risk; $\mu = 3$ represents a high level of idiosyncratic risk. All nine utility functions are normalized by setting $U_{\omega,\mu}(0) = 0$ and $U_{\omega,\mu}(10) = 10$.

and the Arrow–Pratt–De Finetti measure of relative risk aversion (RRA) of $U_{\omega,\mu}(\cdot)$:

$$R_{\omega,\mu}(z) = zA_{\omega,\mu}(z) = \frac{1}{1 + \left(\frac{1}{\omega} - 1\right)\frac{\mu}{z}} . \qquad (6.9)$$

As the number of offspring gets larger, the ARA becomes smaller, while the RRA becomes larger:

$$\begin{cases} A_{\omega,\mu}(z_1) \geq A_{\omega,\mu}(z_2) & \text{if} \quad z_1 \leq z_2 \\ R_{\omega,\mu}(z_1) \leq R_{\omega,\mu}(z_2) & \text{if} \quad z_1 \leq z_2 \end{cases}.$$

Moreover, both measures of risk aversion are increasing functions of the proportion of systematic risk, ω:

$$\begin{cases} A_{\omega_1,\mu}(z) \leq A_{\omega_2,\mu}(z) & \text{if} \quad \omega_1 \leq \omega_2 \\ R_{\omega_1,\mu}(z) \leq R_{\omega_2,\mu}(z) & \text{if} \quad \omega_1 \leq \omega_2 \end{cases},$$

and decreasing functions of the level of idiosyncratic risk, μ:

$$\begin{cases} A_{\omega,\mu_1}(z) \geq A_{\omega,\mu_2}(z) & \text{if} \quad \mu_1 \leq \mu_2 \\ R_{\omega,\mu_1}(z) \geq R_{\omega,\mu_2}(z) & \text{if} \quad \mu_1 \leq \mu_2 \end{cases}.$$

In other words, risk aversion arises from natural selection in environments with systematic risk. More generally, the degree of risk aversion is determined by the stochastic nature of the environment: the more systematic risk there is in the environment, the more risk-averse are the evolutionarily dominant utility functions.

6.4 Common Distributions of Relative Fecundity

We define $R \equiv \xi_a^\omega / \xi_b^\omega$ to be the relative fecundity of two actions of the individual. The growth-optimal behaviour, f^*, depends on the stochastic properties of R, and can be analytically derived for a number of commonly used distribution functions. Figure 6.2 displays f^* as a function of the parameters of five specific distributions: the lognormal, gamma, Pareto, beta prime, and Weibull.

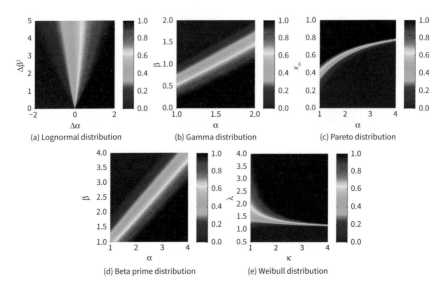

Fig. 6.2 Optimal behaviour, f^*, for several distributions of relative fecundity, $R = \xi_a^\omega / \xi_b^\omega$. (a–e) The different colours correspond to deterministic behaviour ($f^* = 0$ or 1) or randomizing behaviour ($0 < f^* < 1$), given the particular parameters of the distribution.

Lognormal
If R follows a lognormal distribution, $\log N(\Delta\alpha, \Delta\beta^2)$, the expectation of y and $1/y$ is:

$$\mathbb{E}[y] = \exp\left(\Delta\alpha + \frac{\Delta\beta^2}{2}\right),$$

$$\mathbb{E}[1/y] = \exp\left(-\Delta\alpha + \frac{\Delta\beta^2}{2}\right).$$

Therefore, the optimal behaviour, f^*, is given by:

$$f^* = \begin{cases} 1 & \text{if } \frac{\Delta\beta^2}{2} < \Delta\alpha \\ \text{between 0 and 1} & \text{if } \frac{\Delta\beta^2}{2} \geq |\Delta\alpha| \\ 0 & \text{if } \frac{\Delta\beta^2}{2} < -\Delta\alpha \end{cases}.$$

Gamma
If R follows a gamma distribution, $\text{Gamma}(\alpha, \beta)$, where $\alpha > 0, \beta > 0$, the expectation of $1/y$ exists only for $\alpha > 1$, so the parameter space is restricted to $\alpha > 1, \beta > 0$:

$$\mathbb{E}[y] = \frac{\alpha}{\beta},$$

$$\mathbb{E}[1/y] = \frac{\beta}{\alpha - 1}.$$

Therefore, the optimal behaviour, f^*, is given by:

$$f^* = \begin{cases} 1 & \text{if } \beta < \alpha - 1 \\ \text{between 0 and 1} & \text{if } \alpha - 1 \le \beta \le \alpha. \\ 0 & \text{if } \beta > \alpha \end{cases}$$

As special cases of the gamma distribution, we automatically have the results for the exponential, chi-squared, and Erlang distributions.

Pareto

If R follows a Pareto distribution, $\text{Pareto}(x_m, \alpha)$, where $x_m > 0, \alpha > 0$, the expectation of y exists only for $\alpha > 1$, so the parameter space is restricted to $x_m > 0, \alpha > 1$:

$$\mathbb{E}[y] = \frac{\alpha x_m}{\alpha - 1},$$

$$\mathbb{E}[1/y] = \frac{\alpha}{(\alpha + 1)x_m}.$$

Therefore, the optimal behaviour, f^*, is given by:

$$f^* = \begin{cases} 1 & \text{if } x_m > 1 - \frac{1}{\alpha+1} \\ \text{between 0 and 1} & \text{if } 1 - \frac{1}{\alpha} \le x_m \le 1 - \frac{1}{\alpha+1}. \\ 0 & \text{if } x_m < 1 - \frac{1}{\alpha} \end{cases}$$

Beta Prime

If R follows a beta prime distribution, $\text{BetaPrime}(\alpha, \beta)$, where $\alpha > 0, \beta > 0$, the expectation of y exists only for $\beta > 1$, and the expectation of $1/y$ exists only for $\alpha > 1$, so the parameter space is restricted to $\alpha > 1, \beta > 1$:

$$\mathbb{E}[y] = \frac{\alpha}{\beta - 1},$$

$$\mathbb{E}[1/y] = \frac{\beta}{\alpha - 1}.$$

Therefore, the optimal behaviour, f^*, is given by:

$$f^* = \begin{cases} 1 & \text{if } \beta < \alpha - 1 \\ \text{between 0 and 1} & \text{if } \alpha - 1 \leq \beta \leq \alpha + 1. \\ 0 & \text{if } \beta > \alpha + 1 \end{cases}$$

Weibull

If R follows a Weibull distribution, Weibull(k, ω), where $k > 0, \omega > 0$, the expectation of $1/y$ exists only for $k > 1$, so the parameter space is restricted to $k > 1, \omega > 0$:

$$\mathbb{E}[y] = \omega\Gamma\left(1 + \frac{1}{k}\right),$$

$$\mathbb{E}[1/y] = \frac{1}{\omega}\Gamma\left(1 - \frac{1}{k}\right),$$

where $\Gamma(\cdot)$ is the gamma function. Therefore, the optimal behaviour, f^*, is given by:

$$f^* = \begin{cases} 1 & \text{if } \omega > \Gamma\left(1 - \frac{1}{k}\right) \\ \text{between 0 and 1} & \text{if } \frac{1}{\Gamma\left(1+\frac{1}{k}\right)} \leq \omega \leq \Gamma\left(1 - \frac{1}{k}\right). \\ 0 & \text{if } \omega < \frac{1}{\Gamma\left(1+\frac{1}{k}\right)} \end{cases}$$

6.5 Testable Implications

Although our theory of the evolutionary origin of risk aversion is a highly simplified mathematical caricature of reality, its implications should be empirically verifiable if the theory has captured the most relevant features of decision-making under uncertainty, as we claim. While formal tests of these claims are beyond the scope of this study, in this section we describe several methods for conducting such tests to illustrate the potential practical relevance of the theory.

6.5.1 Biology and Behavioural Ecology

Because the individuals in our theory are not assumed to be intelligent beings—they need not even possess a central nervous system—the implications of the theory should apply to the full cross-section of the animal kingdom for which risk-sensitive foraging behaviour has been observed. Therefore, one direct test of our theory would be to perform controlled experiments on nonhuman animal species in which the amount of systematic and idiosyncratic reproductive risk is varied, and the impact of these variations on behaviour is documented and compared to the theory's predictions (Equation (6.4)).

A particularly promising group with which to conduct such experiments is bacteria, which engage in remarkably varied and sophisticated behaviours (Ben-Jacob et al., 1994, 2004; Shapiro and Dworkin, 1997; Ben-Jacob, 2008; Dunny, Brickman, and Dworkin, 2008; Ingham and Ben-Jacob, 2008; Be'er et al., 2009; Sirota-Madi et al., 2010; Kenett et al., 2011). Although an individual bacterium is clearly mindless, colonies of bacteria such as *Paenibacillus vortex* have been observed to engage in seemingly coordinated behaviour such as competition, collaborative foraging, and cell-to-cell chemotactic and physical communication (Ben-Jacob, 2008). Moreover, this setting most closely matches two key assumptions of our theory: asexual reproduction, since bacteria typically reproduce via binary fission and other forms of cellular division; and no environmental resource constraints, unless purposely imposed by the experimenter.

A direct test of our theory may be constructed by focusing on a simple behaviour such as chemotaxis, cell movement in response to gradients in the concentration of a specific chemical agent, usually a food source. The environment can then be manipulated to generate systematic or idiosyncratic risk. Given the speed with which bacteria reproduce, the growth-optimal chemotactic behaviour should be observable within a short time span. Although such behaviour can ultimately be traced to genetic structures (Sirota-Madi et al., 2010), our complementary approach of linking behaviour directly to reproductive outcomes may yield additional insights into the common evolutionary origins of risk preferences.

6.5.2 Financial Economics

A less direct test of our theory may be performed by applying statistical inference to retrospective data on human behaviour. Although these outcomes are likely to be considerably noisier and more difficult to interpret than for bacteria because of the complexity of human cognitive abilities, the simplicity of our evolutionary framework suggests that risk aversion is an extremely primitive adaptation possessed by most animal species, even ones with very complex behaviours. Nevertheless, human evolutionary biology is at odds with several of our theory's assumptions, including asexual semelparous reproduction and a lack of resource constraints. Moreover, current human lifespans make controlled experiments with human subjects impractical. However, growth-optimal behaviour in our theory may be a reasonable approximation to the human decision-making process over long time spans, in which case statistical hypothesis testing of the theory could be conducted using historical data involving financial risk and reward. The challenge is to identify scenarios in which human decision-making is driven primarily by this adaptation, and no other human cognitive mechanisms such as strategy, cooperation, altruism, or ethics might confound the results, and to distinguish between systematic and idiosyncratic reproductive risk in these scenarios.

One possible context might be found in the stock markets of developed economies, which reflect the decisions of many investors facing both systematic and idiosyncratic risk. Although we are using these terms in a different sense than Sharpe (1964), who focused on systematic and idiosyncratic financial risk, it is not hard to see how this type of risk might be related to reproductive risk over long time frames. The impact of economy-wide shocks such as natural disasters, technological hazards, and financial crises can proxy for systematic risk (World Bank, 2013), and low-frequency, high-impact events have already been used in the financial economics literature to explain a variety of asset-pricing anomalies, including high equity risk premia, low risk-free rates, and excess volatility in stock returns (Barro, 2006, 2009), all of which yield a high level of implied risk aversion in rational expectations equilibrium models of expected utility. Examples of idiosyncratic reproductive risk can be found in rates of infant mortality due to accidental suffocation (Shapiro-Mendoza et al., 2009), premature birth (Kramer et al., 2000; Mac-Dorman and Mathews, 2008), and congenital malformations (Rosano et al., 2000). While each of these risks may contain a systematic component, for example birth defects due to environmental pollutants in a given geographical region, this component should be less influential in country-level data.

An indirect hypothesis test of our theory might then be performed by comparing the estimated risk aversion of populations with varying exposures to systematic risk. Those populations with greater exposure to systematic risk should be more risk averse. Measures of risk aversion can be obtained from several sources, including those experimental measures mentioned in the literature review at the beginning of this chapter. By comparing the aggregate risk aversion across countries with high and low amounts of systematic reproductive risk, an indirect econometric test of the evolutionary origin of risk aversion may be constructed. We explore this preliminarily using the equity premium in the next section

6.5.3 The Equity Premium and Systematic Risk

Here we provide an example of how one might test our theory in the context of financial markets, using the equity risk premium as a proxy for country-level risk aversion.

We estimate the systematic risk for each country using the number of individuals affected in natural and technological disasters in that country's history.[3] We estimate the idiosyncratic risk for each country using their infant mortality rates.[4] Finally, we construct an index of the systematic risk proportion of total environmental risk, $Syst_i \in [0, 1]$, for each country:

$$Syst_i = \frac{D_i}{D_i + c \cdot M_i},$$

where D_i is the percentage of the disaster-affected population in country i averaged over time, M_i is the infant mortality in country i's population averaged over time, and c is a fixed constant that allows the constructed index, $Syst_i$, for all countries to spread roughly over $[0, 1]$.[5]

Dimson, Marsh, and Staunton (2002, 2013) review the risk and performance of the principal asset categories in twenty-two countries over the past 100 years. Our study drops four countries from this group,[6] resulting in a sample of eighteen countries summarized in Table 6.1. We estimate a simple linear regression between the country-level equity premium (relative to US Treasury bills) and the systematic risk index, $Syst_i$:

$$EquityPremium_i \sim \alpha + \beta \cdot Syst_i. \tag{6.10}$$

Figure 6.3 gives the scatterplot of these eighteen countries and the ordinary least squares estimation of linear regression. The R^2 of the regression is 39%, and the p-value of the model is 0.0052. Although this is a deliberately naive way to test the relationship between risk aversion and systematic risk without controlling for other known factors that might explain the cross-country risk premium, this still suggests that such a relationship can be empirically validated and is worth further investigation.

---

[3] The Centre for Research on the Epidemiology of Disasters maintains the Emergency Events Database (EM-DAT) (www.emdat.be), which provides detailed information of historical disasters across countries.
[4] The United Nations maintains infant mortality data across countries.
[5] The Maddison Project (Bolt and van Zanden, 2013) documents the total population through time of virtually all countries in the world.
[6] We drop Austria and Finland due to insufficient data on disasters before 1950 from EM-DAT, while Germany and Russia are dropped because of political events in their history.

Table 6.1 Country list and data coverage for the equity premium versus systematic risk.

Country	Code	Equity Premium	Disaster Data	Infant Mortality
Australia	AUS	1900–2012	1934–2012	1950–2010
Belgium	BEL	1900–2012	1901–2012	1950–2010
Canada	CAN	1900–2012	1903–2012	1950–2010
China	CHN	2000–2012	1906–2012	1950–2010
Denmark	DNK	1900–2012	1917–2012	1950–2010
France	FRA	1900–2012	1903–2012	1950–2010
Ireland	IRL	1900–2012	1943–2012	1950–2010
Italy	ITA	1900–2012	1905–2012	1950–2010
Japan	JPN	1900–2012	1900–2012	1950–2010
Netherlands	NLD	1900–2012	1917–2012	1950–2010
New Zealand	NZL	1900–2012	1918–2012	1950–2010
Norway	NOR	1900–2012	1936–2012	1950–2010
South Africa	ZAF	1900–2012	1920–2012	1950–2010
Spain	ESP	1900–2012	1912–2012	1950–2010
Sweden	SWE	1900–2012	1943–2012	1950–2010
Switzerland	CHE	1900–2012	1935–2012	1950–2010
United Kingdom	GBR	1900–2012	1906–2012	1950–2010
United States	USA	1900–2012	1900–2012	1950–2010

Data source: Dimson, Marsh, and Staunton (2013).

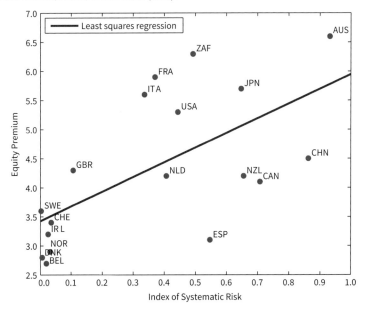

Fig. 6.3 Scatterplot of the historical equity premium (%) and systematic risk for eighteen countries. The blue line is the ordinary least squares estimation of regression for Equation (6.10).

Data source: Dimson, Marsh, and Staunton (2013) and authors' calculations.

6.6 Discussion

The ubiquity of risk aversion in both theory and reality suggests that it must confer certain evolutionary advantages. This intuition is confirmed in our simple but general binary choice model of behaviour, in which risk aversion emerges among mindless organisms as the evolutionarily dominant behaviour in stochastic environments with correlated reproductive risk across the population. Our evolutionary framework shows how the stochastic properties of the environment shape preferences, yielding specific utility functions that depend on the nature of reproductive risk. For example, logarithmic and linear functional forms of utility arise as special cases of the two extremes of pure systematic and idiosyncratic risk, respectively. However, for environments containing a mix of both types of risk, there is a continuum of evolutionarily dominant behaviours that does not conform to expected utility theory. The simplicity of our framework suggests that our results are likely to apply across species, contexts, and time, and that the degree of risk aversion in animal behaviour is significantly influenced by the stochastic properties of the environment as it affects fecundity.

These results are closely related to (but distinct from) those in the extant literature on evolution and economic behaviour (Robson, 1996a; Dekel and Scotchmer, 1999; Samuelson, 2001; Robson and Samuelson, 2009; Robatto and Szentes, 2013). In particular, Robson's (1996a) seminal paper on the evolutionary origins of utility functions specifies an increasing concave relation between the number of offspring and the amount of resources available to a given individual, from which the relationship between expected versus nonexpected utility and systematic versus idiosyncratic risk follows naturally. Robson shows that 'properties of risk aversion or risk preference for gambles over commodities derive from a biological production function relating expected offspring to commodities' (Robson, 1996a, p. 405), where this 'biological production function' is exogenously specified to be increasing and concave (the 'concavity hypothesis').

Our model highlights a different and simpler origin of risk aversion, based on the stochastic nature of the environment, without reference to any biological production function. By developing a formal theory of the evolution of preferences in stochastic environments in the context of the simplest possible nontrivial choice problem, a binary choice, we show that the origin of risk aversion is considerably more primitive than previously thought. Moreover, we derive a class of utility functions that emerges from natural selection as the proportion of systematic risk, ω, in the environment is varied (Equations (6.7)–(6.9)), which may explain the large amount of heterogeneity in risk preferences observed in empirical studies, as mentioned above (Szpiro, 1986; Holt and Laury, 2002; Chetty, 2006; Cohen and Einav, 2007; Guiso and Paiella, 2008).

Other studies have also used the concavity hypothesis to generate risk aversion (Robson, 1996b; Dekel and Scotchmer, 1999), and this specification can be incorporated into our binary choice framework to yield similar results (see Section 2.3 of Chapter 2). There is no doubt that the concavity hypothesis provides one explanation for risk aversion, simply because decreasing marginal returns is a common pattern found in nature. However, the economics literature is also replete with examples of nondecreasing marginal returns both in consumption and production. For example, early research on nonconvex preferences, which imply nonconcave utility functions (Farrell, 1959; Rothenberg, 1960; Bator, 1961; Koopmans, 1961), have motivated a large and diverse literature on general equilibrium with nonconvexities (e.g. the Shapley–Folkman lemma (Starr, 1969) that guarantees the existence of 'approximate' general equilibria with many consumers). From the perspective of producers, nondecreasing marginal returns have been considered since Sraffa (1926), giving rise to an extensive literature on monopolies, oligopolies, externalities, and regulatory policy designed to correct such market failures. In fact, the concavity hypothesis is necessarily restrictive in 'hardwiring' a degree of risk aversion (i.e. curvature, once a particular concave function is specified). No single function can explain the large degree of heterogeneity observed in human risk preferences, or the state-dependent nature of risk aversion, unless these features are also exogenously specified in multiple time-varying state-dependent biological production functions.

We have purposely avoided the use of any such production function, because we wish to highlight the more fundamental role that stochastic environments play in generating risk aversion. Our simple binary choice framework shows that a concave biological production function is unnecessary for generating risk aversion, which in our setting is simply a consequence of natural selection operating in stochastic environments with systematic risk, irrespective of any additional functional transformations. Moreover, a by-product of our simpler framework is a natural explanation for the large heterogeneity in risk preferences observed in empirical studies: natural variation in the proportion of systematic risk across a geographically diverse population. Because our binary choice model is based on such a minimal set of assumptions, its implications are likely to apply much more broadly.

The evolutionary origins of strategic behaviour have also been considered (Robson, 1996b; Dekel and Scotchmer, 1999), and it has been shown that natural selection can also produce overconfidence (Johnson and Fowler, 2011) and altruism (Becker, 1976), both of which emerge as a result of more complex environmental conditions. In contrast, our framework does not require any strategic interactions, while individual decision-making is deliberately mindless, allowing us to determine the most fundamental links between stochastic environments and adaptive behaviour.

Our results have several broader implications for financial economics and public policy. The role of systematic risk in shaping individual and aggregate behaviour provides a more fundamental channel through which Sharpe's (1964) relationship between systematic financial risk and expected asset returns can arise, as long as systematic reproductive risk is positively correlated with systematic financial risk, which is implied by Robson's (1996a) concave reproduction function. However, unlike the fixed preferences assumed in Sharpe's capital asset pricing model, our framework implies that preferences vary over time and across environmental conditions. Consequently, large systematic financial shocks can lead to more risk aversion over time, and vice versa.

From a policy perspective, our results underscore the importance of addressing systematic risk to allow individuals to transfer or mitigate such risks through insurance markets, capital markets, and government policy. If not properly managed, systematic risk can lead to increases in risk aversion, leading to higher risk premia and borrowing costs, and lower economic growth. However, our results also highlight the potential dangers of sustained government intervention, which can become a source of systematic risk in its own right (Acharya et al., 2011; Lucas, 2011).

Having shown in Chapters 5 and 6 that our evolutionary model is capable of generating well-known individual human behaviours such as probability matching and risk aversion, in the next chapter we consider more complex behaviour involving multiple individuals—cooperation.

7
Cooperation

Cooperation is one of the most powerful adaptations of any species, and a key feature of human evolution that has allowed us to occupy virtually every ecological niche on and off the planet.[1] Many theories have been developed to explain its existence, typically involving auxiliary concepts to reconcile the apparent conflict between natural selection—which is assumed to select for selfish offspring-maximizing behaviour—and unselfish cooperation. These concepts include inclusive fitness (Hamilton, 1963, 1964), kin selection (Price, 1970), group selection (Wynne-Edwards, 1963; Hauert and Doebeli, 2004; Nowak et al., 2004; Nowak, 2006; Wilson and Wilson, 2008; Nowak, Tarnita, and Wilson, 2010; Wilson, 2013), multi-level selection (Wilson and Sober, 1994), and reciprocal altruism (Trivers, 1971). Indeed, these auxiliary concepts are all designed to make cooperation selfish in some way.

In this chapter, we develop an alternate theory of the evolution of cooperation. In a simple extension of Chapter 2's binary choice framework, and without making any auxiliary assumptions about the nature of the individuals or their interactions, we show that natural selection does more than select for selfish offspring-maximizing behaviour. It also selects for behaviour that minimizes the correlation in the number of random offspring of different types of individuals.

In particular, we show, both theoretically and computationally, that behaviours that decrease the correlation between the number of offspring (i.e. moving it closer to −1) cause exponential increases in population size. We argue that correlation is an avenue by which evolution can select for cooperation without the implicit assumption that cooperation is selfish. In this respect, cooperation emerges even in the most primitive settings, without the need for intelligence, strategic planning ability, or even sentience. Based on our framework, even a population of bacteria is capable of exhibiting cooperation.

This chapter is also a contribution to the mathematical biology literature. Previous mathematical theories of evolution and interaction have their

[1] This chapter, including the tables and figures, is adapted from Koduri, N., and Lo, A. W. (2021). The origin of cooperation. *Proceedings of the National Academy of Sciences* 118(26): e2015572118.

The Adaptive Markets Hypothesis. Andrew W. Lo and Ruixun Zhang, Oxford University Press. © Andrew W. Lo and Ruixun Zhang (2024). DOI: 10.1093/oso/9780199681143.003.0007

origins in evolutionary game theory (Maynard Smith, 1982, 1984; Nowak and May, 1992), which rely heavily on the concept of evolutionary stability rather than natural selection. They are also tailored to specific interactions. Similarly, economists have used evolutionary models to explain how humans interact with one another, and in specific economic settings (Blume and Easley, 1992; Samuelson, 2001; Robson, 2001b; Kogan et al., 2006). Our framework provides a key step towards a general theory of evolution when replicating units interact with one another and mutually affect one another's reproductive success, assuming nothing more than the principle of natural selection.

7.1 Environments with Interactions

Our starting point is similar to that of Chapters 2 and 4: a population of individuals reproduces asexually and only once in their lifetimes, giving rise to offspring that inherit the behaviour of their parent, where the behaviour is modelled abstractly as a random variable representing the number of offspring in different states of the world. The evolutionarily dominant behaviour is then determined as the one under which the population grows the fastest. However, while Chapters 2 and 4 assume that every individual in the population has the same distribution of offspring, this chapter allows for two types of individuals with different but correlated distributions of offspring, which we argue is necessary and sufficient to capture interaction between individuals.

7.1.1 Assumptions

We assume the existence of two types of individuals, A and B, that have different distributions of random offspring. In generation t, each individual of type A produces a random number of offspring, $x_{A,t}$, and each individual of type B produces a random number of offspring, $x_{B,t}$. The vector $(x_{A,t}, x_{B,t})$ has some well-defined but arbitrary joint distribution function. (Note that we have used the notation A and B to denote two types of individuals, to distinguish from our usual notation, a and b, which represent two possible actions by the same individual in previous chapters.)

The only assumptions we impose on vectors $(x_{A,t}, x_{B,t})$ are that, across generations t, they are independent and identically distributed (IID), and all first and second moments of $(\log x_{A,t}, \log x_{B,t})$ exist and are given by:

$$\mu_A \equiv \mathbb{E}[\log x_{A,t}], \quad \mu_B \equiv \mathbb{E}[\log x_{B,t}],$$

$$\sigma_A^2 \equiv \text{Var}(\log x_{A,t}), \quad \sigma_B^2 \equiv \text{Var}(\log x_{B,t}),$$

$$\rho_{AB} \equiv \text{Corr}(\log x_{A,t}, \log x_{B,t}). \tag{7.1}$$

Because individuals reproduce only once, the total population sizes at generation T of types A and B are given by the products:

$$P_{A,T} \equiv \prod_{t=1}^{T} x_{A,t}, \quad P_{B,T} \equiv \prod_{t=1}^{T} x_{B,t}. \tag{7.2}$$

Note that, because the joint distribution of $(x_{A,t}, x_{B,t})$ is arbitrary, the reproduction of type A and the reproduction of type B are generally dependent. This dependence is both the simplest and most general way to capture interaction between reproducing individuals.

We can appreciate how general the model is by considering the following interpretation. Denote by Ω the set of all possible states of nature in our environment for a given generation. In the simplest case, Ω might contain just two outcomes representing the possibility of rain or shine, each having a probability of, say, $\frac{1}{2}$. The randomness of $x_{A,t}$ and $x_{B,t}$ then represents different reproductive possibilities in different states of nature. For example, suppose that when it rains, type A individuals become predators of type B individuals, but in the absence of rain, the two types do not interact. Therefore, in the rain state, $x_{A,t}$ is large and $x_{B,t}$ is small (say, 3 and 1), and in the sunshine state, $x_{A,t}$ is small and $x_{B,t}$ is large (say, 1 and 3). Since the probability of rain is assumed to be $\frac{1}{2}$, the joint distribution of the vector of random offspring is:

$$(x_{A,t}, x_{B,t}) = \begin{cases} (3,1) & \text{with probability } \frac{1}{2} \\ (1,3) & \text{with probability } \frac{1}{2} \end{cases}.$$

Considering that the states of nature can include not just rain or shine, but outcomes representing all kinds of environmental constraints, physiological occurrences for each type, and actions of other species, this framework can capture very rich varieties of behaviour for both types and very rich varieties of interactions between them. But, as we show in the next section, despite the complexity of behaviours that this specification can generate, the results depend only on the five parameters $(\mu_A, \mu_B, \sigma_A^2, \sigma_B^2,$ and $\rho_{AB})$ of the joint distribution of $x_{A,t}$ and $x_{B,t}$.

Lastly, we emphasize that particular behaviours of individuals of types A and B will induce a particular random vector $(x_{A,t}, x_{B,t})$.[2] For example, in our rain or shine example, if type B individuals manage in the rain state to evade type A individuals, then $x_{A,t}$ may be smaller and $x_{B,t}$ may be larger in that state (say, 2 and 2), in which case the joint distribution of $(x_{A,t}, x_{B,t})$ becomes:

$$(x_{A,t}, x_{B,t}) = \begin{cases} (2, 2) & \text{with probability } \frac{1}{2} \\ (1, 3) & \text{with probability } \frac{1}{2} \end{cases}.$$

Therefore, analysing a particular behaviour of type A and type B individuals amounts to analysing the properties of a particular random vector $(x_{A,t}, x_{B,t})$.

7.1.2 Results

For our purposes, we consider a behaviour to be evolutionarily optimal if under its offspring vector the total population, $P_{A,T} + P_{B,T}$, grows exponentially faster than under that of any other behaviour. To see why this is the correct notion of evolutionary optimality that follows from natural selection, suppose types A and B follow a behaviour that induces offspring vector V_1. Suppose some subset of individuals of these types (by agreement, chance, or some other mechanism) engages in behaviour that induces some other offspring vector V_2, and suppose that the sum of populations under V_2 grows exponentially faster than under V_1. After a few generations, the individuals following V_2 will exponentially outnumber those following V_1, and vector V_2 will win out. This is the principle of natural selection. Note that this notion of evolutionary optimality is not incompatible with competition between types A and B. The evolutionarily optimal behaviour may have one type growing faster than another type, in which case one type will dominate the population.

We proceed to characterize the growth rate of $P_{A,T} + P_{B,T}$ in full generality for an arbitrary offspring vector $(x_{A,t}, x_{B,t})$. To determine which vector among feasible offspring vectors is evolutionarily optimal, one can simply compare the growth rate of $P_{A,T} + P_{B,T}$ under each of them. The following two theorems show that

$$P_{A,T} + P_{B,T} \approx e^{\alpha T + \beta \sqrt{T}} \tag{7.3}$$

for some scalars α and β.

---

[2] The same can be said replacing 'behaviour' with 'trait'.

Proposition 7.1 (characterization of α) *Let the vector* $(\log x_{A,t}, \log x_{B,t})$ *be IID across t with finite first and second moments denoted as in Equation (7.1). Let $P_{A,T}$ and $P_{B,T}$ be defined as in Equation (7.2). Then, as T increases without bound, we have:*

$$\frac{\log(P_{A,T} + P_{B,T})}{T} \overset{a.s.}{\to} \max(\mu_A, \mu_B). \tag{7.4}$$

Proposition 7.2 (characterization of β) *Let the vector* $(\log x_{A,t}, \log x_{B,t})$ *be IID across t with finite first and second moments denoted as in Equation (7.1). Let $P_{A,T}$ and $P_{B,T}$ be defined as in Equation (7.2). Assume that $\mu_A = \mu_B = \mu$. Then as T increases without bound, we have:*

$$\frac{\log(P_{A,T} + P_{B,T}) - T\mu}{\sqrt{T}} \overset{d}{\to} \max(N_A, N_B), \tag{7.5}$$

where N_A and N_B are normally distributed random variables with means 0, variances σ_A^2 and σ_B^2, respectively, and correlation ρ_{AB}.

Proposition 7.1 affirms that the key parameters in determining the growth rate of the combined population are μ_A and μ_B. That is, the behaviours (or traits) that increase the number of offspring of type A and B individuals separately also increase the growth rate of the total population. To find which behaviours win out evolutionarily, we can analyse the effects of the behaviours on the fitness of types A and B separately. This is already well known to evolutionary biologists. Proposition 7.2, however, suggests something new about evolution. Not only does the number of offspring of each type matter, but the correlation, ρ_{AB}, between the two types of offspring also matters. This correlation is determined by the nature of the interaction between the two types.

The main message from Propositions 7.1 and 7.2 is that evolutionarily optimal behaviours are those that maximize μ and minimize ρ_{AB}. Section 7.1.3 contains additional propositions that formalize this, but, intuitively, it is clear from Proposition 7.1 that increasing μ will increase α, and hence increase the growth rate of the total population. From Proposition 7.2, increasing $\max(N_A, N_B)$ will increase β, and thus also increase the growth rate. The parameter ρ_{AB} comes into play because decreasing the correlation between two normal random variables increases their maximum, so decreasing ρ_{AB} will also increase the exponential growth rate. Figure 7.1 depicts the computational confirmation of this.

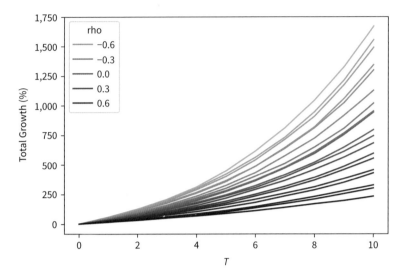

Fig. 7.1 Total population growth vs time. Values of ρ_{AB} range from −0.6 (lightest) to 0.6 (darkest). The number of offspring for both types follows a lognormal distribution with $\mu = 0.1$ and $\sigma = 1.0$.

An important caveat to the results of Propositions 7.1 and 7.2 is that, because of the IID assumption, they apply only to behaviours that are sustainable over time. For example, one cannot use Proposition 7.1 to conclude that a purely altruistic behaviour on the part of type A that decreases μ_A and increases μ_B is evolutionarily optimal through its increase of $\max(\mu_A, \mu_B)$. This is because such a behaviour would lead to type B growing exponentially faster than type A, and the behaviour would not be able to continue when type B exponentially outnumbers type A. In general, a behaviour is sustainable if $\mu_A = \mu_B$, so that both types are growing at the same rate, or if $\mu_A \neq \mu_B$, but the difference is not due to the nature of the interaction, but rather due to better utilization of environmental resources. In this chapter, we are more interested in the case when $\mu_A = \mu_B$, and there can be sustained meaningful interaction.

Although Propositions 7.1 and 7.2 show that the effect of ρ_{AB} on the asymptotic growth rate is second order compared to μ, Monte Carlo simulations show that ρ_{AB} is often more important than μ in its effect on finite-time growth rates.[3] For example, Table 7.1 shows that, after ten generations,

---

[3] For all simulations in this chapter, we compute the expectations as an average over 10,000 samples, and we generate paths of stochastic processes using the Euler method with a time increment of 0.001. All populations start with $P_{A,0} = 1$ and $P_{B,0} = 1$.

Table 7.1 Simulated population growth rate ($\sigma = 1.0$).

μ \ ρ_{AB}	-0.9	-0.8	-0.7	-0.6	-0.5	-0.4	-0.3	-0.2	-0.1	0.0	0.1	0.2	0.3	0.4	0.5	0.6	0.7	0.8	0.9
0.00	21%	20%	19%	18%	18%	17%	16%	15%	15%	13%	12%	11%	10%	9%	8%	7%	5%	4%	2%
0.01	22%	21%	20%	20%	18%	18%	17%	16%	15%	14%	13%	12%	11%	10%	9%	8%	7%	5%	3%
0.02	23%	22%	21%	21%	20%	19%	18%	17%	16%	16%	15%	14%	12%	12%	10%	8%	8%	6%	5%
0.03	24%	24%	23%	22%	21%	20%	19%	19%	18%	17%	16%	15%	14%	13%	11%	10%	9%	7%	5%
0.04	26%	25%	24%	23%	22%	22%	20%	20%	19%	17%	16%	16%	14%	13%	12%	11%	10%	8%	7%
0.05	26%	26%	25%	24%	23%	23%	22%	21%	19%	19%	18%	17%	16%	15%	13%	12%	11%	9%	7%
0.06	28%	27%	26%	26%	24%	24%	23%	22%	21%	20%	19%	18%	16%	16%	15%	14%	12%	10%	8%
0.07	29%	29%	27%	27%	26%	25%	24%	23%	22%	21%	20%	19%	18%	16%	16%	15%	13%	11%	9%
0.08	31%	30%	29%	28%	27%	26%	25%	25%	24%	23%	21%	20%	19%	18%	17%	15%	14%	13%	11%
0.09	32%	31%	30%	29%	28%	28%	27%	26%	25%	24%	22%	22%	21%	20%	18%	17%	15%	13%	12%
0.10	34%	32%	31%	30%	30%	29%	28%	27%	26%	25%	24%	23%	22%	21%	19%	18%	16%	15%	13%
0.11	34%	33%	33%	32%	31%	30%	29%	29%	27%	26%	25%	24%	23%	22%	19%	19%	18%	16%	14%
0.12	36%	35%	34%	34%	32%	31%	30%	29%	28%	28%	27%	26%	23%	23%	22%	20%	20%	17%	15%
0.13	37%	36%	36%	35%	34%	33%	32%	31%	30%	29%	28%	27%	25%	25%	23%	21%	20%	19%	16%
0.14	39%	38%	37%	36%	35%	34%	33%	32%	31%	30%	29%	28%	27%	25%	25%	23%	21%	19%	17%
0.15	40%	39%	39%	38%	37%	36%	35%	33%	33%	31%	30%	29%	27%	27%	25%	24%	22%	21%	19%
0.16	41%	41%	40%	39%	38%	37%	36%	35%	34%	33%	31%	31%	30%	27%	27%	25%	23%	22%	20%
0.17	43%	42%	41%	40%	39%	39%	37%	37%	36%	34%	33%	32%	31%	29%	28%	26%	25%	23%	21%
0.18	44%	43%	42%	42%	41%	39%	39%	39%	36%	36%	34%	33%	32%	30%	29%	28%	26%	24%	22%
0.19	46%	45%	44%	43%	42%	41%	39%	39%	38%	37%	35%	35%	33%	32%	31%	28%	27%	25%	23%
0.20	47%	46%	45%	45%	44%	42%	42%	40%	39%	38%	37%	36%	35%	33%	32%	30%	29%	26%	26%

The number of offspring for both types follows a lognormal distribution with the stated μ and ρ_{AB}, and with $\sigma = 1.0$. Quantities shown represent population growth rate per generation after ten generations, computed as $e^{E[\log(P_{10}/P_0)]/10}$, where $P_T = P_{A,T} + P_{B,T}$.

decreasing ρ_{AB} from 0.5 to −0.5 has approximately the same effect as increasing μ by about 0.09. More concretely, going from $(\mu = 0.05, \rho_{AB} = 0.5)$ to $(\mu = 0.0, \rho_{AB} = -0.5)$ increases the growth rate, despite μ being lower. (Additional simulation results are reported in Appendix B.5.8.) In the same way that the function $y = \sqrt{x}$ grows faster than $y = x$ for some time before its growth rate becomes sublinear, an offspring vector with better ρ_{AB} and worse μ can grow exponentially faster than one with worse ρ_{AB} and better μ for many generations before being overtaken.

Although one might be interested in finite-time growth rates simply to analyse the impact of behaviours over finite time horizons, the next theorem provides another reason to care about the finite-time growth rate. If the proportion of types in the population is rebalanced every T_0 generations (which may be expected if dealing with intraspecies interaction), the finite-time growth rate for T_0 generations becomes the asymptotic growth rate.

Proposition 7.3 *Let T_0 be a positive integer. Let the vector $(\log x_{A,t}, \log x_{B,t})$ be IID across t with finite first and second moments denoted as in Equation (7.1). Let $P_0 > 0$, $P_{A,T}$ and $P_{B,T}$ be defined as*

$$P_{A,nT_0+i} \equiv \frac{P_{nT_0}}{2} \prod_{t=nT_0+1}^{nT_0+i} x_{A,t}, \quad i = 1, \ldots, T_0, \quad n = 0, \ldots, \infty, \tag{7.6}$$

and

$$P_{B,nT_0+i} \equiv \frac{P_{nT_0}}{2} \prod_{t=nT_0+1}^{nT_0+i} x_{B,t}, \quad i = 1, \ldots, T_0, \quad n = 0, \ldots, \infty, \tag{7.7}$$

and let P_T be defined for multiples of T_0 as

$$P_{nT_0} = P_{A,nT_0} + P_{B,nT_0}, \quad n = 1, \ldots, \infty. \tag{7.8}$$

Then, as n increases without bound, we have:

$$\frac{\log(P_{nT_0})}{nT_0} \xrightarrow{\text{a.s.}} \frac{\mathbb{E}\left[\log\left(P_{T_0}/P_0\right)\right]}{T_0}. \tag{7.9}$$

Returning to Table 7.1, this means that if types are rebalanced every ten generations, then a behaviour with $(\mu = 0.0, \rho_{AB} = -0.5)$ would asymptotically grow faster than a behaviour with $(\mu = 0.05, \rho_{AB} = 0.5)$.

Even though we did not assume group selection as a primitive, the fact that, even asymptotically, ρ_{AB} can be more important than μ illustrates the circumstances under which group selection can seem to occur. When a behaviour decreases ρ_{AB} enough to offset a decrease in μ, it can appear that selection is happening at a level other than that of the individual.

7.1.3 Evolutionary Optimality

We use the growth rate results in Propositions 7.1 and 7.2 to characterize an evolutionarily optimal random offspring vector. That is, we find under what conditions and in what sense $P_{A,T} + P_{B,T}$ under one random offspring vector dominates $P_{A,T} + P_{B,T}$ under another. To formalize this, we introduce two sets of types with different random offspring vectors.

Let our two sets of types be (A, B) and $(\tilde{A}, \tilde{B})$. The first set has a random offspring vector $(x_{A,t}, x_{B,t})$ at time t, and the second set has a random offspring vector $(\tilde{x}_{A,t}, \tilde{x}_{B,t})$ at time t. We assume that $(x_{A,t}, x_{B,t})$ is IID across t and that $(\tilde{x}_{A,t}, \tilde{x}_{B,t})$ is IID across t. We do not assume anything about the joint distribution of $(x_{A,t}, x_{B,t})$ and $(\tilde{x}_{A,t}, \tilde{x}_{B,t})$. In particular, $(x_{A,t}, x_{B,t})$ and $(\tilde{x}_{A,t}, \tilde{x}_{B,t})$ can be correlated.

We assume additionally that all first and second moments exist of $(x_{A,t}, x_{B,t})$ and $(\tilde{x}_{A,t}, \tilde{x}_{B,t})$, and are denoted as follows.

$$\mathbb{E}[\log x_{A,t}] = \mu_A, \qquad \mathbb{E}[\log \tilde{x}_{A,t}] = \tilde{\mu}_A,$$
$$\mathbb{E}[\log x_{B,t}] = \mu_B, \qquad \mathbb{E}[\log \tilde{x}_{B,t}] = \tilde{\mu}_B,$$
$$\mathrm{Var}(\log x_{A,t}) = (\sigma_A)^2, \qquad \mathrm{Var}(\log \tilde{x}_{A,t}) = (\tilde{\sigma}_A)^2,$$
$$\mathrm{Var}(\log x_{B,t}) = (\sigma_B)^2, \qquad \mathrm{Var}(\log \tilde{x}_{B,t}) = (\tilde{\sigma}_B)^2,$$
$$\mathrm{Corr}(\log x_{A,t}, \log x_{B,t}) = \rho_{AB}, \quad \mathrm{Corr}(\log \tilde{x}_{A,t}, \log \tilde{x}_{B,t}) = \tilde{\rho}_{AB}.$$

The population sizes at generation T are

$$P_{A,T} = \prod_{t=1}^{T} x_{A,t}, \quad \tilde{P}_{A,T} = \prod_{t=1}^{T} \tilde{x}_{A,t},$$
$$P_{B,T} = \prod_{t=1}^{T} x_{B,t}, \quad \tilde{P}_{B,T} = \prod_{t=1}^{T} \tilde{x}_{B,t}.$$

For simplicity, we introduce names for our random offspring vectors: $V \equiv (x_A, x_B)$ and $\tilde{V} \equiv (\tilde{x}_A, \tilde{x}_B)$. Our first result says that the total population grows exponentially faster under V than under $\tilde{V}$ if $\max(\mu_A, \mu_B) > \max(\tilde{\mu}_A, \tilde{\mu}_B)$.

Proposition 7.4 *Suppose* $\max(\mu_A, \mu_B) > \max(\tilde{\mu}_A, \tilde{\mu}_B)$. *Then, almost surely,*

$$\lim_{T \to \infty} \frac{\log\big((P_{A,T} + P_{B,T})/(\tilde{P}_{A,T} + \tilde{P}_{B,T})\big)}{T} = \max(\mu_A, \mu_B) - \max(\tilde{\mu}_A, \tilde{\mu}_B).$$

This means that if $\max(\mu_A, \mu_B) > \max(\bar{\mu}_A, \bar{\mu}_B)$, then $(P_{A,T} + P_{B,T})/(\bar{P}_{A,T} + \bar{P}_{B,T})$ grows like $e^{\gamma_{AB}T}$ for some $\gamma_{AB} > 0$. Regardless of any other aspects of these distributions, if $\max(\mu_A, \mu_B) > \max(\bar{\mu}_A, \bar{\mu}_B)$, the ratio of the populations of the two sets grows exponentially fast. Thus, the evolutionarily optimal random offspring vector is one that maximizes μ for each type separately.

Now let us restrict ourselves to random offspring vectors that maximize μ for each type separately. The next result characterizes the evolutionarily optimal vector among this set.

Proposition 7.5 *Suppose $\mu_A = \mu_B = \bar{\mu}_A = \bar{\mu}_B = \mu$. Let (N_A, N_B) be normally distributed with mean $(0,0)$, variances $(\sigma_A)^2$ and $(\sigma_B)^2$, and correlation ρ_{AB}. Let $(\bar{N}_A, \bar{N}_B)$ be normally distributed with means 0, variances $(\bar{\sigma}_A)^2$ and $(\bar{\sigma}_B)^2$, and correlation $\bar{\rho}_{AB}$. Suppose $\mathbb{E}[\max(N_A, N_B)] > \mathbb{E}[\max(\bar{N}_A, \bar{N}_B)]$. Then*

$$\liminf_{T \to \infty} \frac{\log\left(\mathbb{E}\left[(P_{A,T} + P_{B,T})/(\bar{P}_{A,T} + \bar{P}_{B,T})\right]\right)}{\sqrt{T}} \geq \mathbb{E}[\max(N_A, N_B)]$$

$$- \mathbb{E}[\max(\bar{N}_A, \bar{N}_B)].$$

Thus, among the behaviours that achieve the highest possible μ, no matter the other aspects of these distributions, if $\mathbb{E}[\max(N_A, N_B)] > \mathbb{E}[\max(\bar{N}_A, \bar{N}_B)]$, then $P_{A,T} + P_{B,T}$ grows exponentially faster under V than under $\bar{V}$. Note that the correlations ρ_{AB} and $\bar{\rho}_{AB}$ affect $\mathbb{E}[\max(N_A, N_B)]$ and $\mathbb{E}[\max(\bar{N}_A, \bar{N}_B)]$. In fact, the correlations are the only things that matter if the variances are fixed. Thus, we next specialize our result to correlation.

Corollary 7.1 *Suppose $\mu_A = \mu_B = \bar{\mu}_A = \bar{\mu}_B = \mu$ and $\sigma_A = \sigma_B = \bar{\sigma}_a = \bar{\sigma}_b = \sigma$. Suppose $\rho_{AB} < \bar{\rho}_{AB}$. Then*

$$\liminf_{T \to \infty} \frac{\log\left(\mathbb{E}\left[(P_{A,T} + P_{B,T})/(\bar{P}_{A,T} + \bar{P}_{B,T})\right]\right)}{\sqrt{T}} \geq \frac{1}{\sqrt{\pi}}\left(\sqrt{1 - \rho_{AB}} - \sqrt{1 - \bar{\rho}_{AB}}\right).$$

Finally, we reach our most interesting result. If $\rho_{AB} < \bar{\rho}_{AB}$, then $\mathbb{E}[(P_{A,T} + P_{B,T})/(\bar{P}_{A,T} + \bar{P}_{B,T})]$ grows like $e^{\gamma_{AB}\sqrt{T}}$ for some $\gamma_{AB} > 0$. In other words, decreases in correlation cause an exponential increase in population size.

7.1.4 Idiosyncratic Risk

So far, we have assumed that all risk in our model is systematic, meaning that all individuals of a certain type have the same number of offspring in a given state of the world. Next, we see what happens when we allow for idiosyncratic risk, meaning that individuals of a certain type potentially have differing numbers of offspring in a given state of the world. Namely, we allow for the offspring of individual i of type A (and analogously for type B) at time t to be the sum of $x_{A,t}$ and $\tilde{x}_{A,i,t}$, where $\tilde{x}_{A,i,t}$ are independent across i. In this setting, populations of type A and B at time T can be written

$$P_{A,T} \equiv \sum_{i=1}^{P_{A,T-1}} x_{A,T} + \tilde{x}_{A,i,T}, \qquad (7.10)$$

$$P_{B,T} \equiv \sum_{i=1}^{P_{B,T-1}} x_{B,T} + \tilde{x}_{B,i,T}. \qquad (7.11)$$

The analogue of Proposition 7.1 in this setting is the next theorem.

Proposition 7.6 *Assume the following:*

1. *For $z = A, B$, the random variable $x_{z,t}$ is IID across t.*
2. *For $z = A, B$, for some $C_l > 0$ and $C_u > C_l$, $C_l \le x_{z,t} \le C_u$.*
3. *For $z = A, B$, the random variable $\tilde{x}_{z,i,t} \ge 0$ is IID across i and t.*
4. *For $z = A, B$, the expectations $\mathbb{E}[\tilde{x}_{z,i,t}]$ and $\mathbb{E}[\log(\mathbb{E}[\tilde{x}_{z,i,t}] + x_{z,t})]$ exist.*
5. *For $z = A, B$, $\mathbb{E}[\log x_{z,t}] > 0$.*

Let $P_{A,T}$ and $P_{B,T}$ be defined as in Equations (7.10) and (7.11). Then as T increases without bound, we have:

$$\frac{\log(P_{A,T} + P_{B,T})}{T} \xrightarrow{\text{a.s.}} \max\left(\mathbb{E}[\log(\mathbb{E}[\tilde{x}_{A,i,t}] + x_{A,t})], \quad \mathbb{E}[\log(\mathbb{E}[\tilde{x}_{B,i,t}] + x_{B,t})]\right).$$
$$(7.12)$$

We see that the idiosyncratic risk is averaged out over time. Any idiosyncratic component to the number of offspring of a type modifies the growth rate identically to adding a constant number of offspring. It is important to keep in mind that, by definition, idiosyncratic risk cannot be correlated, so when we refer to correlation of offspring throughout the chapter, we mean correlation of systematic risk. In Appendix B.5.8, we repeat the simulation of population growth rate discussed earlier (the results of which are displayed in Table 7.1) adding idiosyncratic risk. Adding enough idiosyncratic risk to make the growth rate at ($\mu = 0.0, \rho_{AB} = -0.5$) equal to 131% decreases the impact of correlation such that decreasing ρ_{AB} from 0.5 to -0.5 is equivalent to increasing μ by 0.07 (instead of 0.09 as in the original simulation results shown in Table 7.1).

7.1.5 Random Matching

We can also modify the model to use random matching, a more specific mechanism of interaction that explicitly allows the intermixing of individuals with different behaviours and for different behaviours to exist in the same environment. We show that even with this modification, correlation still plays a key role in determining the evolutionarily dominant behaviour.

Instead of types A and B, let there be new types, 1 and 2. Each generation, all individuals in the population are randomly paired with each other. If a type 1 is paired with a type 1, the offspring vector of the pair will be $(x_{A,1,t}, x_{B,1,t})$. Otherwise, the offspring vector of the pair will be $(x_{A,2,t}, x_{B,2,t})$. We see that, as suggested by the notation, the random pairings determine which individuals play the role of type A and type B from the original model. The new types 1 and 2 represent different behaviours. We use the variable q to denote the pair for each individual. For example, in generation T, if individual i of type 1 is matched with type 1 as the left component of the pairing, then $q_{1,i,T} = A1$. The population sizes at generation T of types 1 and 2 are defined recursively:

$$P_{1,T} \equiv \sum_{i=1}^{P_{1,T-1}} 1_{\{q_{1,i,T-1} = A1\}} x_{A,1,T} + 1_{\{q_{1,i,T-1} = B1\}} x_{B,1,T} + 1_{\{q_{1,i,T-1} = A2\}} x_{A,2,T}$$

$$+ 1_{\{q_{1,i,T-1} = B2\}} x_{B,2,T}, \tag{7.13}$$

$$P_{2,T} \equiv \sum_{i=1}^{P_{2,T-1}} 1_{\{q_{2,i,T-1} = A2\}} x_{A,2,T} + 1_{\{q_{2,i,T-1} = B2\}} x_{B,2,T}. \tag{7.14}$$

The next theorem provides a sufficient condition for type 1 individuals to outnumber exponentially type 2 individuals in the limit. We assume a law of large numbers for random matching. As noted by Duffie and Sun (2007), such laws of large numbers are nontrivial to prove but have been assumed without proof by evolutionary biologists dating back to Hardy (1908) and Weinberg (1908).

Proposition 7.7 *Assume the following:*

1. *For $z = A, B$ and $i = 1, 2$, the random variable $x_{z,i,t}$ is IID across t.*
2. *For $z = A, B$ and $i = 1, 2$, for some $C_l > 0$ and $C_u > C_l$, $C_l \leq x_{z,i,t} \leq C_u$.*
3. *For $i = 1, 2$, the expectations $\mathbb{E}\left[\log\left(\frac{1}{2}x_{A,i,t} + \frac{1}{2}x_{B,i,t}\right)\right]$ exist.*
4. *(Law of large numbers for random matching.) As $T \to \infty$, $P_{1,T} \overset{a.s.}{\to} \infty$,*
   $P_{2,T} \overset{a.s.}{\to} \infty$, and

$$\frac{\sum_{i=1}^{P_{1,T}} 1_{\{q_{1,i,T} = A2\}}}{\sum_{i=1}^{P_{1,T}} 1_{\{q_{1,i,T} = A2\}} + 1_{\{q_{1,i,T} = B2\}}} \overset{a.s.}{\to} \frac{1}{2}.$$

In other words, the proportion of type 1 individuals matched with type 2 in the left side of the pairing converges almost surely to 1/2.

Let $P_{1,T}$ and $P_{2,T}$ be defined as in Equations (7.13) and (7.14). Then if

$$\mathbb{E}\left[\log\left(\frac{1}{2}x_{A,1,t} + \frac{1}{2}x_{B,1,t}\right)\right] > \mathbb{E}\left[\log\left(\frac{1}{2}x_{A,2,t} + \frac{1}{2}x_{B,2,t}\right)\right], \qquad (7.15)$$

as T increases without bound, we have:

$$\frac{\log(P_{1,T}/P_{2,T})}{T} \overset{a.s.}{\to} \mathbb{E}\left[\log\left(\frac{1}{2}x_{A,1,t} + \frac{1}{2}x_{B,1,t}\right)\right] - \mathbb{E}\left[\log\left(\frac{1}{2}x_{A,2,t} + \frac{1}{2}x_{B,2,t}\right)\right].$$
$$(7.16)$$

Condition (7.15) has a close connection to the correlation. Decreasing the correlation of $x_{A,i,t}$ and $x_{B,i,t}$ decreases the second-order Taylor approximation of $\mathbb{E}\left[\log\left(\frac{1}{2}x_{A,i,t} + \frac{1}{2}x_{B,i,t}\right)\right]$. Thus, in general, unless the distributions are highly skewed, if $x_{A,1,t}$ and $x_{B,1,t}$ have the same mean but a lower correlation than $x_{A,2,t}$ and $x_{B,2,t}$, then type 1 will grow exponentially faster than type 2. In other words, in the model with random matching (as in the original model), behaviours that result in a lower correlation in the number of offspring will dominate the population. It is also significant that in the random matching model, correlation is a first-order effect, affecting the coefficient of T in the growth rate, not only $\sqrt{T}$.

7.1.6 Density Dependence

In this section, we study the effect of correlation on population growth when the population growth is density dependent. We do this by taking standard biological models of density-dependent population growth, in which the population at any point in time is the solution to a system of ordinary differential equations (ODEs), and adding stochasticity to them, so that the population becomes a solution to a system of stochastic differential equations (SDEs).

To see the analogy between ODEs and SDEs more clearly, we first consider a model of population growth with no density dependence. Given types A and B, the standard biological model would be

$$dP_{A,t} = r_A P_{A,t}\, dt, \tag{7.17}$$

$$dP_{B,t} = r_B P_{B,t}\, dt. \tag{7.18}$$

We add stochasticity by introducing (potentially correlated) Wiener processes, $W_{A,t}$ and $W_{B,t}$, and converting the standard model to an SDE:

$$dP_{A,t} = r_A P_{A,t}\, dt + s_A P_{A,t}\, dW_{A,t}, \tag{7.19}$$

$$dP_{B,t} = r_B P_{B,t}\, dt + s_B P_{B,t}\, dW_{B,t}. \tag{7.20}$$

Whereas an equation of the type of Equation (7.17) says that for small Δ,

$$P_{A,t+\Delta} - P_{A,t} = r_A P_{A,t}\Delta,$$

an equation of the type of Equation (7.19) says that

$$P_{A,t+\Delta} - P_{A,t} = r_A P_{A,t}\Delta + s_A P_{A,t}(W_{A,t+\Delta} - W_{A,t}),$$

where $W_{A,t+\Delta} - W_{A,t}$ is normally distributed with mean 0 and variance Δ. Equations (7.19) and (7.20) have closed-form solutions from which we can derive continuous-time versions of Propositions 7.1 and 7.2, namely that

$$\frac{\log(P_{A,T} + P_{B,T})}{T} \overset{a.s.}{\to} \max\left(r_A - \frac{1}{2}s_A^2, r_B - \frac{1}{2}s_B^2\right), \tag{7.21}$$

and when $r \equiv r_A = r_B$ and $s \equiv s_A = s_B$

$$\frac{\log(P_{A,T} + P_{B,T}) - \left(r - \frac{1}{2}s^2\right)}{\sqrt{T}} \overset{d}{\to} \max(N_A, N_B), \tag{7.22}$$

where N_A and N_B are normally distributed random variables with means 0, variances s^2, and the same correlation as the Wiener processes, $W_{A,t}$ and $W_{B,t}$.

With density dependence, the standard biological model of population growth would be

$$dP_{A,t} = r_A P_{A,t} \left(1 - \frac{P_{A,t}}{K_A} - \frac{P_{B,t}}{L_A}\right) dt,\tag{7.23}$$

$$dP_{B,t} = r_B P_{B,t} \left(1 - \frac{P_{B,t}}{K_B} - \frac{P_{A,t}}{L_B}\right) dt.\tag{7.24}$$

The stochastic version would be

$$dP_{A,t} = r_A P_{A,t} \left(1 - \frac{P_{A,t}}{K_A} - \frac{P_{B,t}}{L_A}\right) dt + s_A P_{A,t}\, dW_{A,t},\tag{7.25}$$

$$dP_{B,t} = r_B P_{B,t} \left(1 - \frac{P_{B,t}}{K_B} - \frac{P_{A,t}}{L_B}\right) dt + s_B P_{B,t}\, dW_{B,t}.\tag{7.26}$$

The impact of ρ_{AB} as it changes with K is the key thing to determine in this setting. (We assume L is fixed to K.) Tables 7.2, 7.3, and 7.4 show the population growth rate after ten generations for different values of K and ρ_{AB},

Table 7.2 Simulated density-dependent population growth rate ($r = 0.5$).

K \ ρ_{AB}	−0.9	−0.7	−0.5	−0.3	−0.1	0.1	0.3	0.5	0.7	0.9
5.0	−5.4%	−6.3%	−7.3%	−8.1%	−9.1%	−9.8%	−11.3%	−12.6%	−13.8%	−15.5%
10.0	−0.0%	−1.1%	−2.2%	−3.0%	−4.4%	−5.6%	−6.6%	−8.3%	−9.4%	−11.3%
20.0	5.0%	3.6%	2.7%	1.4%	−0.1%	−1.2%	−2.6%	−3.7%	−6.1%	−7.9%
40.0	9.2%	8.1%	6.9%	5.4%	3.9%	2.8%	0.9%	−0.8%	−3.2%	−5.6%
80.0	12.4%	11.1%	10.0%	8.5%	7.1%	5.2%	4.1%	1.4%	−0.6%	−3.3%

The number of offspring for both types follows Equations (7.25) and (7.26) with the stated K and ρ_{AB}, and with $r = 0.5$, $s = 1.0$, and $L = K$. Quantities shown represent the population growth rate per generation after ten generations, computed as $e^{\mathbb{E}[\log(P_{10}/P_0)]/10}$, where $P_T = P_{A,T} + P_{B,T}$.

Table 7.3 Simulated density-dependent population growth rate ($r = 0.6$).

K \ ρ_{AB}	−0.9	−0.7	−0.5	−0.3	−0.1	0.1	0.3	0.5	0.7	0.9
5.0	−3.1%	−3.9%	−4.5%	−5.4%	−6.0%	−7.0%	−8.0%	−8.9%	−10.4%	−11.7%
10.0	3.1%	2.3%	1.4%	0.4%	−0.5%	−1.7%	−2.7%	−4.2%	−5.4%	−7.5%
20.0	9.2%	8.2%	7.0%	5.9%	4.9%	3.6%	2.4%	0.8%	−1.0%	−2.7%
40.0	15.0%	13.7%	12.4%	11.2%	9.7%	8.1%	6.8%	5.1%	3.1%	0.7%
80.0	19.8%	18.3%	16.6%	15.5%	13.8%	12.4%	10.8%	9.1%	6.9%	4.1%

The number of offspring for both types follows Equations (7.25) and (7.26) with the stated K and ρ_{AB}, and with $r = 0.6$, $s = 1.0$, and $L = K$. Quantities shown represent population growth rate per generation after ten generations, computed as $e^{\mathbb{E}[\log(P_{10}/P_0)]/10}$, where $P_T = P_{A,T} + P_{B,T}$.

Table 7.4 Simulated density-dependent population growth rate ($r = 0.7$).

ρ_{AB} / K	−0.9	−0.7	−0.5	−0.3	−0.1	0.1	0.3	0.5	0.7	0.9
5.0	−1.3%	−1.9%	−2.4%	−2.9%	−3.7%	−4.6%	−5.3%	−6.0%	−7.5%	−9.0%
10.0	5.5%	4.8%	3.9%	3.1%	2.4%	1.8%	0.7%	−0.5%	−2.1%	−3.4%
20.0	12.2%	11.4%	10.4%	9.5%	8.5%	7.5%	6.6%	5.0%	3.5%	1.6%
40.0	19.2%	17.9%	17.1%	16.0%	14.5%	13.3%	11.5%	10.8%	8.6%	5.8%
80.0	25.2%	24.0%	22.7%	21.5%	20.1%	18.4%	16.8%	15.3%	13.1%	10.4%

The number of offspring for both types follows Equations (7.25) and (7.26) with the stated K and ρ_{AB}, and with $r = 0.7$, $s = 1.0$, and $L = K$. Quantities shown represent population growth rate per generation after ten generations, computed as $e^{\mathbb{E}[\log(P_{10}/P_0)]/10}$, where $P_T = P_{A,T} + P_{B,T}$.

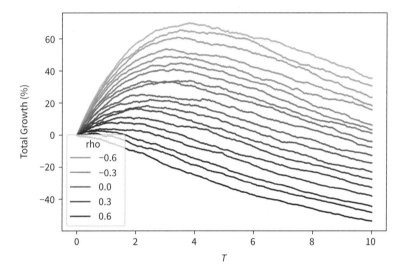

Fig. 7.2 Total density-dependent population growth vs time ($K = 10$). Values of ρ_{AB} range from −0.6 (lightest) to 0.6 (darkest). The number of offspring for both types follows Equations (7.25) and (7.26) with $r = 0.6$, $K = 10$, $L = 10$, and $s = 1.0$.

when $r = 0.5$, $r = 0.6$, and $r = 0.7$, respectively. As K increases without bound, the results reported in Tables 7.2, 7.3, and 7.4 become continuous-time versions of those reported in Table 7.1 with $\mu = 0.0$, $\mu = 0.1$, and $\mu = 0.2$, respectively. It is apparent that the correlation has a significant impact on growth rate even with a level of density dependence extreme enough to induce the population to decline over time. In an absolute sense, the impact of correlation appears to decrease with density dependence. In a relative sense, however, it appears to increase. For example, to have the same impact on growth as increasing r from 0.5 to 0.6, one needs to decrease ρ_{AB} from 0.5 to −0.3 when $K = 80$, but only from 0.5 to −0.1 when $K = 5$. Figures 7.2 and 7.3 show that when the density dependence increases, correlation matters more for earlier time horizons and less for later time horizons.

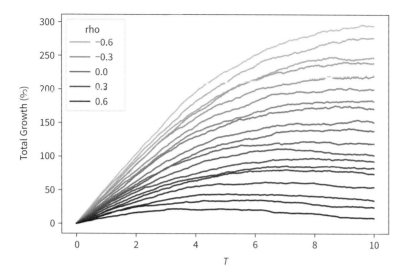

Fig. 7.3 Total density-dependent population growth vs time ($K = 40$). Values of ρ_{AB} range from −0.6 (lightest) to 0.6 (darkest). The number of offspring for both types follows Equations (7.25) and (7.26) with $r = 0.6$, $K = 40$, $L = 40$, and $s = 1.0$.

7.2 Behavioural Implications

Having shown that evolutionarily optimal behaviours will minimize the correlation between the number of offspring (ρ_{AB}) and maximize the number of offspring (μ), we now give three examples of generic behaviours that can decrease ρ_{AB}. The first behaviour involves making the positive outcomes for the two types of offspring occur in different states, what we call 'specialization'. The second method involves decreasing the number of offspring for one type in one state while increasing the number of offspring for the other type. We call behaviours that do this 'sacrifice'. The third example is more abstract, what we call 'coordination'. All these behaviours can be considered forms of cooperation.

7.2.1 Specialization

Let there be two states of the world, ω_r and ω_s, representing rain and shine. Consider the two behaviours in Fig. 7.4. Behaviour 1 implies no specialization, since the positive outcomes for types A and B occur in the rain state. Behaviour 2 implies specialization, because the positive outcomes occur in different states. Since $\max(\mu_A, \mu_B)$ is the same under both behaviours, according to Propositions 7.1 and 7.2, ρ_{AB} determines which action is evolutionarily optimal. It is clear that ρ_{AB} is smaller under behaviour

Let $v > w$ and $y > z$.
Behaviour 1 (no specialization):

	ω_r	ω_s
A	v	w
B	y	z

Behaviour 2 (specialization):

	ω_r	ω_s
A	v	w
B	z	y

Behaviour 2 is evolutionarily optimal.

Fig. 7.4 Specialization.

2; hence, behaviour 2 will be evolutionarily optimal. It is worth noting that although Propositions 7.1 and 7.2 suggest that a behaviour can only be evolutionarily optimal on the basis of ρ_{AB} if it is not dominated on the basis of μ, our finite-time results and Proposition 7.3 suggest a behaviour may be evolutionarily optimal on the basis of ρ_{AB} even if it is dominated on the basis of μ. In other words, a δ could be subtracted from v, w, z, and y in behaviour 2, and behaviour 2 could still be evolutionarily optimal, provided δ is small enough.

7.2.2 Sacrifice

We continue to use two states of the world, ω_r and ω_s, representing rain and shine, each with probability $\frac{1}{2}$ of occurring. Consider the two behaviours in Figure 7.5. Under behaviour 2, type B individuals will sacrifice themselves for type A individuals in the state ω_r, and type A individuals will sacrifice themselves for type B individuals in the state ω_s. Under behaviour 1, however, both types will have the same number of offspring in both states.

We claim that the sacrificial behaviour is the evolutionarily optimal choice according to Propositions 7.1 and 7.2 when $\gamma_{AB} \geq \frac{v^2}{v-\epsilon} - v$. When $\gamma_{AB} > \frac{v^2}{v-\epsilon} - v$, $\max(\mu_A, \mu_B)$ under behaviour 2 is larger than under behaviour 1, which means that behaviour 2 is evolutionarily optimal. However, we are particularly interested in the case when $\gamma_{AB} = \frac{v^2}{v-\epsilon} - v$. In this case, neither type benefits from the sacrifice, which is to say that μ_A is the same under both behaviour 1 and behaviour 2, and likewise μ_B is the same under both behaviours. However, simply by inducing a negative correlation, behaviour 2 becomes evolutionarily optimal. Moreover, as we argued in the case of specialization, if we expand our definition of evolutionary optimality by considering finite-time results and Proposition 7.3, behaviour 2 could become evolutionarily optimal if $\gamma_{AB} < \frac{v^2}{v-\epsilon}$, in which case μ_A and μ_B would, in

Let $\gamma_{AB} \geq \frac{v^2}{v-\varepsilon} - v.$
Behaviour 1 (no sacrifice):

	ω_r	ω_s
A	v	v
B	v	v

Behaviour 2 (sacrifice):

	ω_r	ω_s
A	$v + \gamma_{AB}$	$v - \varepsilon$
B	$v - \varepsilon$	$v + \gamma_{AB}$

Behaviour 2 is evolutionarily optimal.

Fig. 7.5 Sacrifice.

fact, be smaller under behaviour 2 than behaviour 1, and both types would individually be harmed by the sacrifice.

7.2.3 Coordination

In the case of coordination, we assume that both types each have two possible actions, which we label 0 and 1. The variable $x_{z,i}$ is the random offspring of type z choosing action i, for $z = A, B$ and $i = 0, 1$. In general, the random offspring of type A can be written

$$x_A = (x_{A,0})^{1-I_A}(x_{A,1})^{I_A}$$

and the random offspring of type B can be written

$$x_B = (x_{B,0})^{1-I_B}(x_{B,1})^{I_B},$$

where the indicator functions, I_z, denote the action of type z, $z = A, B$.

We assume that the $x_{z,i}$'s and I_z's are both random, and that the $x_{z,i}$'s are independent of the I_z's. The assumption of independence in this case implies that the individual's choice of action is independent of the consequence of the action, which has the interpretation that the individuals have no intelligence. We denote the means, variances, and covariances of the actions, x, by:

$$\mu_{z,i} \equiv \mathbb{E}[\log x_{z,i}] \quad , \quad (\sigma_{z,i})^2 \equiv \mathrm{Var}(\log x_{z,i}) \quad , \quad \varsigma_{ij} \equiv \mathrm{Cov}[\log x_{A,i}, \log x_{B,j}].$$
$$(7.27)$$

Observe the distinction between, for example, μ_A and $\mu_{A,0}$ and $\mu_{A,1}$; μ_A is a function of $\mu_{A,0}$, $\mu_{A,1}$, and I_A. Assume that

$$\mu_{A,0} = \mu_{A,1} = \mu_{B,0} = \mu_{B,1} \equiv \mu, \tag{7.28}$$

so that no action dominates on the basis of μ.

Note that the choice of I_A and I_B completely determines the random offspring vector, (x_A, x_B). We now apply Propositions 7.4 and 7.5 from Section 7.1.3 to characterize the evolutionarily optimal behaviours, I_A and I_B. By design, $\max(\mu_A, \mu_B)$ will be the same for any I_A and I_B. Thus, the evolutionarily optimal I_A and I_B will be a maximizer of $\mathbb{E}[\max(N_A, N_B)]$.

We can compute

$$\mathbb{E}[\max(N_A, N_B)] = \mu + \frac{1}{\sqrt{2\pi}} \sqrt{\sum_{i,j \in \{0,1\}} p_{ij}((\sigma_{A,i})^2 + (\sigma_{B,j})^2 - 2\varsigma_{ij})},$$

where p_{ij} is the probability that $I_A = i$ and $I_B = j$ are jointly chosen. The evolutionarily optimal I_A and I_B will then have all of their probability mass on combinations $(I_A = i, I_B = j)$ that maximize $((\sigma_{A,i})^2 + (\sigma_{B,j})^2 - 2\varsigma_{ij})$. In other words, even if there is uncertainty in I_A and I_B marginally, their probabilities are certain jointly.

For example, suppose that $\sigma_{A,0} = \sigma_{A,1} = \sigma_{B,0} = \sigma_{B,1}$ and $\varsigma_{00} = \varsigma_{11} > \varsigma_{01}$. Then $(i = 1, j = 1)$ and $(i = 0, j = 0)$ would both maximize $((\sigma_{A,i})^2 + (\sigma_{B,j})^2 - 2\varsigma_{ij})$. Thus, at an evolutionarily optimal I_A and I_B, I_A could be uncertain, meaning that type A individuals chose action 0 some of the time and 1 some of the time, and I_B could be uncertain, meaning that type B individuals chose action 0 some of the time and 1 some of the time. However, at any evolutionarily optimal I_A and I_B, type A individuals would only choose 0 when type B individuals chose 0, and type A individuals would only choose 1 when type B individuals chose 1. This behaviour is what we call 'coordination'.

7.3 Discussion

In this chapter, we have attempted to resolve the apparent conflict between selfish natural selection and unselfish cooperation by showing that natural selection is not necessarily selfish. Instead, we show that it gives rise to behaviours that not only increase the number of offspring, but also to behaviours that decrease the correlation between offspring. We use a simple model of evolutionary dynamics without strategic consideration, which assumes nothing about the knowledge or intelligence of the individuals involved. Our principal theoretical result shows that, in a population with two types of individuals, a decrease in the correlation of offspring of the two types increases the exponential growth rate of the population. Thus, correlation has a second-order effect on the growth rate compared to the number of offspring. However, we also show that correlation has a first-order effect in certain situations, including those with a periodic rebalancing of the proportions of type, and in a random matching setting. Our simulation results suggest that correlation matters more relative to the number of offspring over finite time horizons, and if the population growth is density dependent.

Our results have some limitations. Firstly, our most general model assumes that offspring vectors are IID over time. This means it cannot say anything about behaviours that are not sustainable over time, such as purely altruistic behaviours that may result in one type of individual growing exponentially faster than another type for a short period of time, until one type too strongly outnumbers the other for the behaviour to continue. Secondly, although our results show that the correlation of offspring can play a significant role in determining the growth rate, we have not attempted to quantify how much correlation exists in real-world settings (or systematic risk in general), and whether this would be enough to drive natural selection. Finally, while our framework implies that a separate theory of group selection is not strictly necessary to explain cooperation, our results showing that correlation can confer a selective advantage demonstrate why it remains so tempting to identify group selection within a given population, and there may still be conceptual benefits from viewing selection as operating at multiple levels. We shall see just how powerful the selection operating on correlation can be when we consider the evolutionary origin of intelligence in the next chapter.

8
Bounded Rationality and Intelligence

Most economic theories are based on the premises that individuals maximize their own self-interest and correctly incorporate the structure of their environment into all their decisions, a triumph of human intelligence whose personification is known to economists as *Homo economicus*.[1] This framework of economic intelligence has led to numerous breakthroughs in the economic sciences, including expected utility theory, the axiomatic formulation of rational behaviour under uncertainty (von Neumann and Morgenstern, 1944); rational expectations, the notion that individual expectations are formed to be mutually consistent with those arising from economic equilibria (Lucas, 1972); and the efficient markets hypothesis, the concept that market prices fully reflect all available information (Samuelson, 1965; Fama, 1970). The vast majority of current economic models still assume we are all *Homo economicus*, and the influence of this paradigm goes far beyond academia. It underlies current macroeconomic and monetary policies, and has also become an integral part of the rules and regulations that govern financial markets today (Kocherlakota, 2010; Hu, 2012).

However, there is mounting empirical and experimental evidence, including the experience of the 2008 financial crisis, that suggests that humans do not always behave rationally or intelligently, but often make seemingly random and suboptimal decisions (Kahneman, Slovic, and Tversky, 1982). These behavioural anomalies are especially pronounced when elements of risk and probability are involved.

We propose to reconcile these contradictory perspectives by extending Chapter 2's binary choice framework, considering the evolutionary consequences of decisions, as well as the role of intelligence. By 'intelligence', however, we have in mind a very specific meaning that may not agree with how the term is used by psychologists and other cognitive and social scientists. In our context, we define intelligence as any ability of an individual to increase its genetic success. When these abilities are present

---

[1] This chapter, including the figures, is adapted from Brennan, T. J., and Lo, A. W. (2012). An evolutionary model of bounded rationality and intelligence. *PLoS ONE* 7(11): e50310. https://doi.org/10.1371/journal.pone.0050310.

The Adaptive Markets Hypothesis. Andrew W. Lo and Ruixun Zhang, Oxford University Press.
© Andrew W. Lo and Ruixun Zhang (2024). DOI: 10.1093/oso/9780199681143.003.0008

in stochastic environments, natural selection interacts with reproductive success in rather surprising ways. In fact, we derive an implicit formula that shows how intelligence can emerge via selection, why it may be 'bounded' in its capacities, and how such bounds imply the coexistence of multiple levels and types of intelligence as a reflection of varying environmental conditions. To preview some of the logic underlying our results, it is useful to briefly review the groundbreaking ideas of Herbert Simon, which motivated our work.

In the 1950s, in an effort to formalize the process of how people functionally make decisions (as opposed to how economists hypothesize that they make decisions), Simon (1955, 1957) proposed the twin ideas of heuristic approximation ('satisficing') and bounded rationality. Herbert Simon's view was that humans do not maximize or optimize in their decision-making process. Rather, they simply engage in heuristics that are good enough for the task at hand. This groundbreaking view was part of a contentious body of work that nevertheless won Simon the Nobel Prize in Economics. However, despite his Nobel, Simon felt isolated in economics, and ultimately moved into psychology, a shift that highlights the controversy that Simon generated with his ideas.

One controversy about bounded rationality in Simon's time centred on the question, 'If we engage in heuristics that are simply good enough, how do we know when we reach the point that is good enough?' In particular, suppose an individual spends time trying to come up with a better solution than the heuristic; wouldn't that necessarily require that the individual knows how to equalize costs and benefits? And if individuals are able to do that, why can't they reach the rational expectations equilibrium hypothesized by the economists? Simon did not have a compelling retort at the time of the controversy, but we think that the answer is simpler than previously thought. The heuristic approximation hypothesized by Simon is simply evolution at work! In fact, we do not know when 'good enough' has arrived. We simply behave in a way that we develop through trial and error, based upon the environment and the feedback we are given in those environmental conditions.

Our evolutionary framework thus provides us with a natural definition of 'intelligence': it is any behaviour that is positively correlated with reproductive success. If achieving such a correlation imposes biological costs on an individual, for example, because it requires attention, memory, planning, and other cognitive faculties, these costs imply that there is an upper bound on the degree of intelligence that emerges through selection. This yields an evolutionary foundation for Simon's 'bounded rationality' (Simon, 1955), his heuristics-based model of behaviour, as well as a reconciliation between rational economic models and their behavioural violations.

Rational economic behaviour in which individuals maximize their own self-interest is only one of many possible types of behaviour that may arise from natural selection. The key to understanding which types of behaviour are more likely to survive is understanding the effect of such behaviours on reproductive success in a given population's environment. From this perspective, intelligence is naturally defined as behaviour that increases the probability of reproductive success, and bounds on rationality are determined by physiological and environmental constraints.

8.1 Environments with Intelligence

In this section, we extend the binary choice framework introduced in Chapter 2 to encompass the possibility of variation in outcomes across individuals within a generation and across generations, and also the possibility of intelligent behaviour. In the following sections, we consider several special cases giving rise to various results related to intelligence and bounded rationality. Here, natural definitions of intelligence and bounded rationality follow directly from our results.

Recall that in our model each individual in a population is faced with a single decision in its lifetime, choosing action a or b, and this choice results in a certain number of offspring, x_a or x_b, respectively. The quantities x_a and x_b are random variables with a joint distribution $\Phi(x_a, x_b)$. The behaviour of individual i is represented by a 0/1 Bernoulli trial, I, with probability f (i.e. a is chosen with probability f, in which case $I = 1$, and b is chosen with probability $1 - f$, in which case $I = 0$). When we wish to specify the outcomes applicable to a particular individual, i, for any of these variables, we add a subscript i (see also Equation (2.2) in Chapter 2). Similarly, when we wish to specify a particular generation, t, we add the subscript t.

We assume that an individual with a choice function I has offspring with the identical choice function I. We are interested in the growth of the population of individuals with a specific choice function over time, and we write n_t for the number of such individuals in generation t. In general, we have

$$n_t = \sum_{i=1}^{n_{i-1}} \left(I_{i,t} x_{a,i,t} + (1 - I_{i,t}) x_{b,i,t} \right),$$

where the sum runs over all individuals in generation $t - 1$. We assume that although all individuals have the same function I, the random variable for each individual is independent of all the others. We also assume that $(x_{a,i,t}, x_{b,i,t})$ are independent and identically distributed across individuals i and times t.

The individuals in our original model in Chapter 2 are 'mindless', in the sense that their behaviours are assumed to be statistically independent of all other variables. Suppose we relax this assumption, by allowing individual decisions to be correlated with other variables, such as x_a and x_b:

Assumption 8.1 *Let $I_{i,t}$ be correlated with $x_{a,i,t}$ and $x_{b,i,t}$, and define $\rho_t \equiv$ Corr$[I_{i,t}, (x_{a,i,t} - x_{b,i,t})]$.*

The correlation between actions and reproductive success is the essence of what we mean by 'intelligent behaviour'.

Under these assumptions, the value of n_t can be expressed as

$$\frac{n_t}{n_{t-1}} \overset{p}{=} (\mathbb{E}\left[I_t x_{a,t}\right] + \mathbb{E}\left[(1 - I_t) x_{b,t}\right])$$

$$\overset{p}{=} (\mathbb{E}\left[I_t\right] \mathbb{E}\left[x_{a,t}\right] + \mathbb{E}\left[1 - I_t\right] \mathbb{E}\left[x_{b,t}\right] + \text{Cov}\,(I_t, x_{a,t}) + \text{Cov}\,(1 - I_t, x_{b,t})), \tag{8.1}$$

where the expectations and covariances in Equation (8.1) are calculated for a typical individual having offspring at time t. Here, no subscript i is needed to index these individuals, since all members of the population have the same expectation of outcomes and the same choice function I_t. The symbol $\overset{p}{=}$ denotes equivalence in probability, and the equivalence in Equation (8.1) follows from the law of large numbers.[2] Introducing some new notation, we can rewrite Equation (8.1) as

$$\frac{n_t}{n_{t-1}} \overset{p}{=} \left(f\mu_{a,t} + (1 - f)\mu_{b,t} + \sqrt{f(1-f)}\,(\sigma_{a,t}\rho_{a,t} + \sigma_{b,t}\rho_{b,t}) \right), \tag{8.2}$$

where $\mu_{a,t}$ and $\mu_{b,t}$ represent the common expected values for $x_{a,i,t}$ and $x_{b,i,t}$ for each individual i at time t, $\sigma_{a,t}$ and $\sigma_{b,t}$ represent the corresponding standard deviations, and $\rho_{a,t}$ and $\rho_{b,t}$ represent the common correlations at time t of each $x_{a,i,t}$ and $x_{b,i,t}$ with $I_{i,t}$ and $1 - I_{i,t}$, respectively. Because all of these values are the same across all individuals having offspring at time t, the subscript i is not necessary in any of the terms in Equation (8.2). It is also convenient to write

$$\frac{n_t}{n_{t-1}} \overset{p}{=} \left(f\mu_{a,t} + (1 - f)\mu_{b,t} + \sigma_t \rho_t \sqrt{f(1-f)} \right), \tag{8.3}$$

---

[2] In particular, the sums over the sample population converge almost surely to the unrestricted means and covariances. This occurs because the variance of each relevant random variable must be bounded, provided that there is an upper bound on the possible number of offspring a single individual may have.

where ρ_t is the common correlation of $I_{i,t}$ with $y_{i,t} = x_{a,i,t} - x_{b,i,t}$ for each individual i having offspring at time t, and where σ_t is the common standard deviation of $y_{i,t}$ for such individuals.

We use backward recursion to find that

$$\frac{n_T}{n_0} \overset{p}{=} \prod_{t=1}^{T} \left(f\mu_{a,t} + (1-f)\mu_{b,t} + \sigma_t\rho_t\sqrt{f(1-f)} \right),$$

where n_0 is the number of individuals in the population at time $t = 0$. From this we deduce that

$$\frac{1}{T}\log n_T \overset{p}{\to} \mathbb{E}\left[\log\left(f\mu_{a,t} + (1-f)\mu_{b,t} + \sigma_t\rho_t\sqrt{f(1-f)} \right) \right], \qquad (8.4)$$

where the expectation is taken with respect to the continuous limit of the distribution of the random variable values over times t.[3]

It is convenient to introduce a new notation for the right-hand side of Equation (8.4), namely

$$\alpha = \mathbb{E}\left[\log\left(f\mu_{a,t} + (1-f)\mu_{b,t} + \sigma_t\rho_t\sqrt{f(1-f)} \right) \right]. \qquad (8.5)$$

In what follows, we seek to identify the values of I that give rise to the maximum value for α, since individuals with such values will dominate the population over time in a sense made precise by the following proposition.

Proposition 8.1 *Suppose that two different choice functions, I_1 and I_2, give rise to values α_1 and α_2, with the property that $\alpha_1 > \alpha_2$. Individuals with the choice function I_1 will become exponentially more numerous over time, since*

$$\lim_{T\to\infty} \frac{n_T(I_2)}{n_T(I_1)} \overset{p}{\to} \lim_{T\to\infty} e^{T(\alpha_2 - \alpha_1)} = 0.$$

In the following sections, we consider the parameters that give rise to maximal values for α under various specific assumptions about the nature of the distributions, $\Phi_{i,t}$.

[3] Note that to apply the law of large numbers here, we assume that the terms $\log(f\mu_{a,t} + (1-f)\mu_{b,t} + \sigma_t\rho_t\sqrt{f(1-f)})$ have bounded variance. This assumption is valid, provided that the distribution of the argument of the logarithm does not have positive mass in arbitrarily small neighbourhoods of zero.

8.2 An Evolutionary Definition of Intelligence

We first consider the case where ρ is fixed over time, and present our main results in this section as well as Section 8.3. We then analyse the general case where ρ_t potentially varies over time in Section 8.4.

We say that a member of the population exhibits intelligence if its behaviour correlates positively with outcomes (i.e. if $\rho > 0$). If $\rho = 0$, however, then we can say that no intelligence is present. (The case $\rho < 0$ would correspond to a form of intelligence that leads to a less favourable outcome than no intelligence.) If no intelligence is present, the model reduces to what we considered in Chapter 2. In general, the growth rate for individuals of type f with correlations is

$$\alpha(f,\rho) \;=\; \log\!\big(f\mu_a + (1-f)\mu_b + \rho\sigma\sqrt{f(1-f)}\,\big), \qquad (8.6)$$

where σ is the standard deviation of $x_a - x_b$. In this case, the growth rate is equal to the growth rate of the mindless population, plus an extra term $\rho\sigma\sqrt{f(1-f)}$ that reflects the impact of correlation between an individual's decision and the number of offspring. Several implications follow immediately from this expression.

Subpopulations with negative correlation between behaviour and $x_a - x_b$ clearly cannot survive in the long run; their growth rates are less than in the case of no correlation, corresponding to counterproductive behaviour in which decisions coincide with lower-than-average reproductive outcomes more often than not (i.e. choosing a when $x_a - x_b$ is lower than average, and choosing b when the reverse is true). By the same logic, subpopulations with positive correlation will grow faster, and individuals with the highest correlations, ρ^*, will dominate the population. We suggest that these cases may be considered primitive forms of intelligence, that is, behaviour yielding improved fitness.

The subpopulation with the largest ρ will grow the fastest and come to dominate the population. By optimizing $\alpha(f,\rho)$ with respect to f and ρ to yield f^* and ρ^*, we arrive at the growth-optimal levels of intelligence and behaviour that emerge from the population (see Section 8.6 for further details):

$$\rho^* = 1 \quad , \quad f^* = \mathrm{Prob}(x_a > x_b)\,. \qquad (8.7)$$

Perfect positive correlation always dominates imperfect correlation. Despite the presence of idiosyncratic reproductive risk, the growth-optimal behaviour involves probability matching, albeit a different kind than what we discussed in Section 2.2 and Chapter 5, in which f^* matches the probability of x_a exceeding x_b.

8.3 Bounded Rationality

If there is no biological cost to attaining $\rho^* = 1$, then perfect correlation will quickly take over the entire population. Since we have assumed no mutational change from one generation to the next, all individuals will eventually possess this trait. However, it seems plausible that a positive correlation would be associated with a positive cost. For example, potential prey animals may be able to fend off predators by using assorted defence mechanisms, such as chemical repellents or physical force. This behaviour increases their expected number of offspring, but the physiological cost of defence may decrease this expectation. Thus, the evolutionary success of such behaviour depends on the *net* impact to fitness. If we define a cost function $c(\rho)$, then we can express the net impact of correlation by deducting this cost from the correlation itself to yield the following asymptotic growth rate of type-f individuals:

$$\alpha(f, \rho) \quad = \quad \log\!\big(f\mu_a + (1-f)\mu_b + [\rho - c(\rho)]\sigma\sqrt{f(1-f)}\big). \qquad (8.8)$$

With plausible conditions on $c(\cdot)$ and $\Phi(x_{a,i,t}, x_{b,i,t})$, there is a unique solution (f^*, ρ^*) to $\alpha^* = \max_{\{f,\rho\}} \alpha(f, \rho)$. Because ρ is subject to a nonlinear constraint that depends on f, explicit expressions for (f^*, ρ^*) are not as simple as the no intelligence case (see Section 8.6 for those details and an example). However, the structure of the solution is qualitatively identical to earlier solutions, and intuitive to grasp: f^* reduces to three possibilities, either 0 or 1 if the correlation is too 'expensive' to achieve, or the probability-matching solution, $f^* = \mathrm{Prob}(x_a > x_b)$, if the cost function, $c(\rho)$, is not too extreme. This growth-optimal solution is an example of bounded rationality—bounded in the sense that higher levels of ρ might be achievable, but at too high a cost, $c(\rho)$. The behaviour that eventually dominates the population is good enough, where 'good enough' now has a precise meaning: the maximum growth rate, α^*, is attained. In other words, f^* is an example of satisficing, to use Simon's terminology.

If the cost of intelligence is influenced by other biological and environmental factors, $\mathbf{z} = [\, z_1 \cdots z_n \,]$, then the multivariate cost function $c(\rho, \mathbf{z})$ will almost certainly induce a multiplicity of solutions to the growth-optimization problem. This implies a multitude of behaviours and levels of intelligence that can coexist because they yield the same maximum population growth rate, α^*. The set of behaviours, $f^*(\mathbf{z})$, and intelligence, $\rho^*(\mathbf{z})$, that emerge from the population will be a function of $\mathbf{z}$, and given implicitly by the solution to $\alpha^* = \max_{\{f,\rho\}} \alpha(f,\rho)$. This provides a direct link between adaptive behaviour and the environment, which is the basis for many models of social evolution and evolutionary psychology (Hamilton, 1964; Wilson, 1975b; Trivers, 2002; Buss, 2004).

8.4 A Universal Measure of Intelligence and its Cost

As we have noted, the case of no intelligence corresponds to no correlation between behaviour and outcome (i.e. $\rho_t = 0$), while the case of intelligence corresponds to a positive correlation (i.e. $\rho_t > 0$), with higher values representing more intelligence. The correlation, ρ_t, cannot necessarily assume any value in the range $[0, 1]$, however, and it is, in fact, constrained by the choice of f. More specifically, ρ_t can assume all values in the range $[0, \rho_{t,\max}(f)]$, but no values outside this range, where $\rho_{t,\max}(f)$ is a function dependent on f and $\Phi_{i,t}$. A precise value for $\rho_{t,\max}$ is calculated in Proposition 8.2 (see Section 8.5). Because the upper bound for ρ_t depends on f, the measure ρ_t is difficult to use as a universal representation of underlying intelligence. We therefore introduce the additional variable γ, defined as

$$\gamma = \frac{\rho_t}{\rho_{t,\max}(f)}. \tag{8.9}$$

This is a universal representation of intelligence, at least in the sense that it represents the fraction of the maximum achievable correlation. This fraction will remain constant, even as the maximum possible correlation varies with f.

In the case in which there is no variation in $\Phi_{i,t}$ across time, then the values of ρ_t and $\rho_{t,\max}(f)$ are the same for all t. We write these common values as ρ and $\rho_{\max}(f)$. This is the case considered in Sections 8.2 and 8.3, where we simply used ρ as the measure of intelligence instead of γ, since the two measures are the same up to a constant rescaling factor that is common to all generations. Beginning in this section, however, we work with a more general situation in which we use γ instead of ρ as the universal measure of intelligence.

We suppose that a member of a population has a particular value of $f \in [0, 1]$ and a particular value of $\gamma \in [0, 1]$, and that these attributes are passed on to all offspring of an individual. In terms of f and γ, the expression for α in Equation (8.5) can be rewritten as

$$\alpha = \mathbb{E}\left[\log\left(f\mu_{a,t} + (1-f)\mu_{b,t} + \sigma_t\gamma\rho_{t,\max}(f)\sqrt{f(1-f)}\right)\right]. \tag{8.10}$$

We also consider the possibility that γ has a cost associated with it, $c(\gamma)$. Once this cost is factored in, the expression for α becomes

$$\alpha = \mathbb{E}\left[\log\left(f\mu_{a,t} + (1-f)\mu_{b,t} + \sigma_t\left(\gamma - c(\gamma)\right)\rho_{t,\max}(f)\sqrt{f(1-f)}\right)\right]. \tag{8.11}$$

We assume that $c(0) = 0$ and $c(\gamma) > 0$ for $\gamma > 0$. We also assume that $\gamma - c(\gamma)$ > 0 for sufficiently small values of γ and that $\gamma - c(\gamma) < 0$ for values of γ sufficiently close to 1. Thus, at least some small amount of intelligence is beneficial, but high costs make the choice of $\gamma = 1$ prohibitively expensive. We make the further assumption that c is twice continuously differentiable and that $c'(\gamma) > 0$ and $c''(\gamma) > 0$. Because of this assumption, there is a unique value of γ^* that maximizes $\gamma - c(\gamma)$.

$$\gamma^* = \text{unique } \gamma \text{ such that } c'(\gamma) = 1. \tag{8.12}$$

It is convenient to introduce some additional notation related to the distribution of the $y_{i,t}$, which is given by the function $\Phi_{i,t}$. We write φ_t for the probability that $y_{i,t} > 0$ for individuals in generation t, that is,

$$\varphi_t = \text{Prob}(y_{i,t} > 0). \tag{8.13}$$

This value is thus the probability that choice a is superior to choice b in generation t. In addition, we write δ_t^+ and δ_t^- for the expected value of $y_{i,t}$ conditional on either $y_{i,t} > 0$ or $y_{i,t} \leq 0$, respectively. That is,

$$\delta_t^+ = \mathbb{E}[y_{i,t}|y_{i,t} > 0] \quad \text{and} \quad \delta_t^- = \mathbb{E}[y_{i,t}|y_{i,t} \leq 0]. \tag{8.14}$$

The values of φ_t, δ_t^+, and δ_t^- are constant across all individuals in generation t because the functions $\Phi_{i,t}$ are independent and identical across individuals in generation t. In much of what follows, we also find it convenient to make the following assumption about the independence of $y_{i,t}$ and $I_{i,t}$, conditional on the sign of $y_{i,t}$. This assumption may be violated in the fully general case, but it allows us to simplify our analysis and obtain more tractable formulas, while still retaining a rich framework in which to operate.

Assumption 8.2 *For all i and t, conditional on the sign of $y_{i,t}$, the distribution of $y_{i,t}$ and the distribution of $I_{i,t}$ are independent. Thus,*

$$\mathbb{E}[I_{i,t}y_{i,t}|y_{i,t} > 0] = \delta_t^+ \mathbb{E}[I_{i,t}|y_{i,t} > 0] \quad \text{and} \quad \mathbb{E}[I_{i,t}y_{i,t}|y_{i,t} \le 0] = \delta_t^- \mathbb{E}[I_{i,t}|y_{i,t} \le 0].$$

In other words, the value of $I_{i,t}$ can only depend on the sign of $y_{i,t}$, and thus on the question of whether a or b is the superior choice, and not on additional information about the degree of the superiority of one choice over the other.

Under Assumption 8.2, and using Propositions 8.2 and 8.3 (provided in Section 8.5), we can rewrite (8.11) as

$$\alpha = \mathbb{E}\left[\log\left(f\mu_{a,t} + (1-f)\mu_{b,t} + (\delta_t^+ - \delta_t^-)(\gamma - c(\gamma))(\min(f, \varphi_t) - f\varphi_t)\right)\right]. \tag{8.15}$$

We seek the values of f and γ that maximize α, as defined in Equation (8.15). If the optimal value occurs when $f = 0$ or $f = 1$, then the amount of intelligence is clearly irrelevant, since the term involving intelligence vanishes, and the behaviour is simply deterministic. If the optimal value occurs when $f \in (0, 1)$, then the optimal amount of intelligence is clearly $\gamma = \gamma^*$, as defined above. The nature of the optimal choice of f is derived in Propositions 8.4 and 8.5, in the case of no systematic variation across generations, and in Proposition 8.6, in the general case.

8.5 Upper Bound on Correlation

In this section, we consider restrictions on the possible values for ρ_t, which is subject to constraints that depend upon the nature of the distributions, $\Phi_{i,t}(x_a, x_b)$, as well as on the value of f for the population. The next proposition makes this dependence clear, when Assumption 8.2 holds.

Proposition 8.2 *Under Assumption 8.2, the value of ρ_t is given by*

$$\rho_t = \text{Corr}\,(I_{i,t}, y_{i,t}) = \text{Corr}\,(I_{i,t}, H(y_{i,t}))\left(\frac{\delta_t^+ - \delta_t^-}{\sigma_t/\sqrt{\varphi_t(1 - \varphi_t)}}\right), \tag{8.16}$$

where $H(y_{i,t})$ is the Heaviside function, which is 1 when $y_{i,t} > 0$ and 0 otherwise. The values of δ_t^+, δ_t^-, and φ_t are as defined in Equations (8.13) and (8.14). The correlation between $I_{i,t}$ and $H(y_{i,t})$ may also be written as

$$r_t \equiv \text{Corr}\left(I_{i,t}, H\left(y_{i,t}\right)\right) = \frac{\left(\pi_t - \varphi_t f\right)}{\sqrt{\varphi_t(1 - \varphi_t)}\sqrt{f(1 - f)}}, \tag{8.17}$$

where

$$\pi_t = \text{Prob}\left(I_{i,t} = 1 \text{ and } y_{i,t} > 0\right). \tag{8.18}$$

The values of r_t and π_t are the same for each individual i in a given generation t.

An implication of the formula in Equation (8.16) is that the possible values for ρ_t cannot necessarily be made arbitrarily close to 1. The range of possible values for ρ_t is made more precise by the following proposition.

Proposition 8.3 *Under Assumption 8.2, the range of possible values for π_t when intelligence is present is*

$$f\varphi_t < \pi_t \leq \min\left(f, \varphi_t\right). \tag{8.19}$$

The corresponding range of possible values for r_t is

$$0 < r_t \leq r_{t,\max}, \quad where \quad r_{t,\max} = \frac{\max\left(f, \varphi_t\right) - \varphi_t f}{\sqrt{f(1 - f)}\sqrt{\varphi_t(1 - \varphi_t)}}. \tag{8.20}$$

The inequality $r_t < 1$ holds whenever $f \neq \varphi_t$. The corresponding range of possible values for ρ_t is

$$0 < \rho_t \leq \rho_{t,\max}, \quad where \quad \rho_{t,\max} = r_{t,\max} \frac{\delta_t^+ - \delta_t^-}{\sigma_t / \sqrt{\varphi_t(1 - \varphi_t)}}. \tag{8.21}$$

The inequality $\rho_{t,\max} < 1$ holds unless $r_t = 1$ and both $\mathbb{E}\left[y_{i,t}^2 | y_{i,t} > 0\right] = \left(\mathbb{E}\left[y_{i,t}^2 | y_{i,t} > 0\right]\right)^2$ and $\mathbb{E}\left[y_{i,t}^2 | y_{i,t} \leq 0\right] = \left(\mathbb{E}\left[y_{i,t}^2 | y_{i,t} \leq 0\right]\right)^2$.

8.6 Intelligence across Generations

We now consider the case in which there may be intelligence—so that it is possible to have $y > 0$—which can be separated into two subcases: one in which there is no variation in the distribution of possible outcomes across generations, and the other where there is variation.

8.6.1 No Inter-Generational Variation

In the case of no inter-generational variation, we have $\mu_{a,t} = \mu_a$, $\mu_{b,t} = \mu_b$, $\delta_t^+ = \delta^+$, $\delta_t^- = \delta^-$, and $\varphi_t = \varphi$. In this case, we can rewrite the expression for α from Equation (8.10) as

$$\alpha = \log\left(f\mu_a + (1-f)\mu_b + (\gamma - c(\gamma))\left(\min(\varphi, f) - \varphi f\right)(\delta^+ - \delta^-)\right). \quad (8.22)$$

Note that we do not take the expectation of the logarithm in this expression for α, since the value of the logarithm is constant across generations under these assumptions. The values of f and γ that maximize α in the case in which intelligence is costless (so that $c(\gamma) \equiv 0$) are characterized by the following proposition.

Proposition 8.4 *Under Assumption 8.2, and the further assumptions that intelligence has no cost and that there is no variation in outcome possibilities across generations, the values of f and γ at which α is maximized are f = φ and $\gamma = 1$, provided that $\varphi \in (0, 1)$. If φ is either 0 or 1, then α is maximized when f = φ, and the value of γ is irrelevant.*

Proposition 8.4 shows that, when $c(\gamma) \equiv 0$, more intelligence (i.e. a higher γ value) is always desirable, except in situations in which behaviour is completely deterministic (i.e. f is equal to 0 or 1). This result makes sense when intelligence is costless, but to make the situation more realistic, we also consider the case in which an intelligence level of γ is associated with a cost $c(\gamma) \not\equiv 0$ of the type described in Section 8.4. Proposition 8.5 characterizes the values of f and γ that maximize α when there is no variation across generations and when there is such a cost to intelligence.

Proposition 8.5 *Under Assumption 8.2, and the further assumptions that there is no variation in outcome possibilities across generations and that there is a cost c(γ) of intelligence of the type described in Section 8.4, the values of f and γ that maximize α are characterized in the following way. If $\mu_b > \mu_a$ and $\varphi \in (0, 1)$, then*

$$f^* = \begin{cases} \varphi & \text{if } \gamma^* - c(\gamma^*) > \frac{\mu_b - \mu_a}{\delta^+ + \mu_b - \mu_a} \\ [0, \varphi] & \text{if } \gamma^* - c(\gamma^*) = \frac{\mu_b - \mu_a}{\delta^+ + \mu_b - \mu_a} \\ 0 & \text{if } \gamma^* - c(\gamma^*) < \frac{\mu_b - \mu_a}{\delta^+ + \mu_b - \mu_a} \end{cases} \quad (8.23)$$

Here y^* is as defined in Equation (8.12). If $\mu_b < \mu_a$ and $\varphi \in (0, 1)$, then

$$f^* = \begin{cases} \varphi & \text{if } y^* - c(y^*) > \frac{\mu_a - \mu_b}{\mu_a - \mu_b - \delta^-} \\ [\varphi, 1] & \text{if } y^* - c(y^*) = \frac{\mu_a - \mu_b}{\mu_a - \mu_b - \delta^-} \\ 1 & \text{if } y^* - c(y^*) < \frac{\mu_a - \mu_b}{\mu_a - \mu_b - \delta^-} \end{cases} . \tag{8.24}$$

If $\mu_a = \mu_b$ then $f^* = \varphi$, and if $\varphi \in \{0, 1\}$, then $f^* = \varphi$. In all cases for which $f^* \notin \{0, 1\}$, the optimal choice of y is y^*. If, however, $f^* \in \{0, 1\}$, then intelligence is unimportant, and the choice of y does not matter.

For an example of how the benefits of intelligence are traded off against the costs of intelligence, suppose that those costs are given by the following function:

$$c(y) = \kappa \frac{y^2}{1 - y},$$

where $\kappa > 0$ is a parameter that can be set higher to indicate a greater cost to intelligence, or lower to indicate the reverse situation. This function $c(y)$ can also be written

$$c(y) = \kappa \left(-y - 1 + \frac{1}{1 - y} \right). \tag{8.25}$$

It is straightforward to check that this satisfies all of our requirements for a cost function for $y \in [0, 1]$. Specifically, $y - c(y) > 0$ for small values of y, and $y - c(y) < 0$ for values of y sufficiently close to 1. In addition, $c(y)$ is twice continuously differentiable, increasing, and convex. For this cost function, the value of y^* defined in Equation (8.12) can be rewritten as

$$y^* = 1 - \sqrt{\frac{\kappa}{1 + \kappa}}.$$

Also, the value of $y^* - c(y^*)$, which is needed to determine the cases specified in Proposition 8.5, can be written as

$$y^* - c(y^*) = 1 + 2\left(\kappa - \sqrt{\kappa(1 + \kappa)} \right).$$

The values of y^* and $y^* - c(y^*)$ are plotted as functions of κ in Fig. 8.1.

The result of Proposition 8.5 is illustrated in Fig. 8.2. We assume that $\mu_b > \mu_a$, and use the horizontal axis to indicate the size of the ratio $r = \delta^+/(\mu_b - \mu_a)$ and the vertical axis to indicate the value of κ. For any r and κ values, Proposition 8.5 can be used to determine the optimal f value,

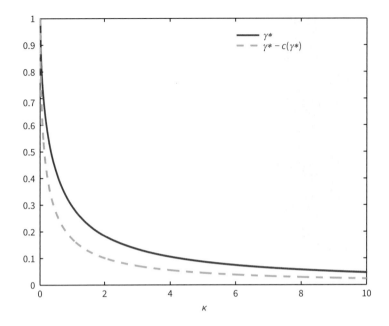

Fig. 8.1 Values of γ^* and $\gamma^* - c(\gamma^*)$ as functions of κ, the cost of intelligence parameter in Equation (8.25).

namely f^*. The value of f^* is either 0 or φ, except when $\gamma^* - c(\gamma^*) = 1/(1+r)$, and in this special case the value of f^* may be anywhere between 0 and φ. The deterministic value 0 is possible, while the deterministic value 1 is not, simply because we have assumed that $\mu_b > \mu_a$. As the figure indicates, a sufficiently high cost of intelligence, as indicated by a high κ value, corresponds to the deterministic choice, $f^* = 0$, where there is no use of intelligence. When intelligence has a low enough cost for a given ratio value, however, the optimal choice is $f^* = \varphi$, which is the same frequency for f that occurs in probability matching (see Section 2.2.1).

8.6.2 Inter-Generational Variation

The following proposition describes the nature of the optimal choice of f and γ when there is intelligence, as well as variation in outcomes across generations.

Proposition 8.6 *Under Assumption 8.2, and the further assumptions that the distribution of φ_t is smooth and intelligence has a cost of the type described in*

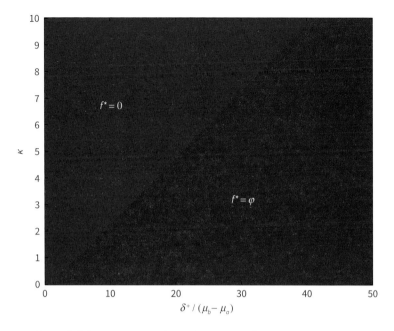

Fig. 8.2   Values of f^* for particular values of κ and $r = \delta^+/(\mu_b - \mu_a)$. The region towards the upper left corresponds to relatively costly intelligence and deterministic behaviour of the form $f^* = 0$. The region towards the lower right corresponds to relatively cheap intelligence and probability matching of the form $f^* = \varphi$. On the line between the two large regions, any value for f^* between 0 and φ is optimal.

Section 8.4, the maximal value of α occurs when $\gamma = \gamma^*$. In addition, if the optimal choice of f is in the interior of the interval $[0, 1]$, then this choice is defined implicitly by the equation

$$\mathbb{E}\left[\frac{\mu_{a,t} - \mu_{b,t} + (\gamma^* - c(\gamma^*))\left(\delta_t^+ - \delta_t^-\right)\left(H(\varphi_t - f) - \varphi_t\right)}{f^*\mu_{a,t} + (1 - f^*)\mu_{b,t} + (\gamma^* - c(\gamma^*))\left(\delta_t^+ - \delta_t^-\right)\left(\min(\varphi_t, f) - \varphi_t f\right)}\right] = 0,$$

where H is the Heaviside function, and where the expectations are taken with respect to the joint distributions across time t for $\mu_{a,t}$ and $\mu_{b,t}$, as these distributions are implied by the $\Phi_{i,t}$.

8.7 Discussion

The simplicity and generality of our framework suggest that the behaviours we have derived from our basic binary choice model are likely to be primitive on an evolutionary timescale, and that most species will have developed the necessarily biological apparatus to engage in such behaviour under the right environmental conditions.

However, evolution can also produce more sophisticated behaviours, such as overconfidence (Johnson and Fowler, 2011), altruism and self-deception (Trivers, 2002), and state-dependent strategies like the hawk–dove game (Maynard Smith, 1979), which emerge as a result of more complex environmental conditions. For example, if we assume that one individual's action can affect the reproductive success of another individual (e.g. i's fecundity is influenced by j's selection of a or b), individuals engaging in strategic behaviour will reproduce more quickly than those with simpler behaviours such as probability matching or loss aversion. If the actions of individuals in the current generation can affect the reproductive success of individuals in future generations, even more complex dynamics are likely to emerge, as in the well-known overlapping generations model (Samuelson, 1958). In a resource-constrained environment in which one individual's choice can affect another individual's reproductive success, strategic interactions such as reciprocity and cooperation will likely emerge within and across generations (Trivers, 1971; Nowak and Highfield, 2011). Other extensions of the binary choice framework include time-varying environmental conditions $\Phi_t(\cdot, \cdot)$, mutation through sexual reproduction, and multiple reproductive cycles within a single lifetime (iteroparity). Each of these extensions captures more realistic aspects of human behaviour. Taken together, they may provide aggregate measures of systemic risk, and even of the likelihood of a financial crisis (Kenett et al., 2011).

In this chapter, we have purposefully assumed a much simpler structure, including an unconstrained stable stochastic environment with no strategic considerations, in order to determine what types of behaviour are truly primitive. Even in such a simple setting, we find a surprisingly complex and subtle range of behaviours—behaviours that do not always conform to common economic intuition about rationality—can arise and persist via natural selection. Simon (1981) illustrated this principle vividly with the example of a single ant traversing a mixed terrain of sand, rocks, and grass. The ant's path seems highly complex, but the complexity may be due more to the environment than the ant's navigational algorithm. The perspective that complex behaviours can be generated from much simpler structures has also received support from the discovery of remarkably sophisticated social behaviour among bacteria (see the discussion in Section 6.5.1).

While it is nearly self-evident that the critical determinant of which behaviour emerges from a given population is the interaction between the biological features of the individuals and the nature of the environment, our simple framework shows just how powerful environmental forces can be in shaping fundamental aspects of decision-making. If we seek to understand the origin of intelligence and the limits of rational behaviour, we may find useful answers by studying current and past environments in addition to studying our genes. In the next two chapters, we will see how evolution can generate two behavioural extremes: highly intelligent behaviour in the form of Bayesian inference in Chapter 9, and highly irrational behaviour in the form of bias, discrimination, and polarization in Chapter 10. Both are feasible outcomes under specific conditions, underscoring the fact that evolution is not a monotonic process of improvement, but rather an adaptive process in which the population is shaped by the particular environment at hand.

9

Learning to be Bayesian

One of the most impressive recent feats of human intelligence is Bayes' rule, a disarmingly compact and cut-and-dried statement about the probability of an arbitrary event A, conditional on another arbitrary event B:[1]

$$\text{Prob}(A|B) \;=\; \frac{\text{Prob}(B|A)\text{Prob}(A)}{\text{Prob}(B)}\;. \tag{9.1}$$

At first blush, this relationship seems like more of an accounting identity than the revered fundamental mathematical principle it is today. To understand its importance, suppose that B is an event in the past and A is an event that has yet to occur. Through this simple mathematical expression, Bayes' rule offers us a glimpse into our unknown future. The very essence of inductive inference, learning, and prediction is given by this formula, which has been applied across virtually every scientific discipline.[2]

However, despite all of this success and impact, two fundamental questions about the origin of Bayes' rule remain unanswered: how did humans acquire the cognitive capabilities for making Bayesian inferences, and why do these capabilities differ so much from one individual to the next? It is difficult to reconcile the perfection of a fully Bayesian strategy with known deviations in actual human behaviour. For example, human subjects will follow Bayesian strategies on average but not individually (Goodman et al., 2008; Vul et al., 2014), while human subjects have also been shown to make decisions based on a small number of samples instead of computing the fully Bayesian solution (Griffiths and Tenenbaum, 2006; Sanborn and Griffiths, 2008; Vul and Pashler, 2008).

---

[1] This chapter, including the figures, is adapted from Lo, A. W., and Zhang, R. (2021). The evolutionary origin of Bayesian heuristics and finite memory. *iScience* 24(8): 102853.

[2] In particular, cognitive scientists have applied Bayesian models to understand human inductive learning and generalization (Tenenbaum, Griffiths, and Kemp, 2006), visual scene perception and concepts (Lake, Salakhutdinov, and Tenenbaum, 2015), language processing and acquisition (Chater and Manning, 2006; Xu and Tenenbaum, 2007), and causal learning and inference (Steyvers et al., 2003; Griffiths and Tenenbaum, 2005), among other topics (Griffiths, Kemp, and Tenenbaum, 2008). Financial economists have applied Bayes' rule to portfolio analysis (Black and Litterman, 1992; Pástor and Stambaugh, 2000; Avramov and Zhou, 2010), while evolutionary biologists and behavioural ecologists have studied the role of Bayes' theorem in biological evolution (Greaves and Wallace, 2006; Leitgeb and Pettigrew, 2010a,b; Okasha, 2013; Castellano, 2014; Campbell, 2016).

The Adaptive Markets Hypothesis. Andrew W. Lo and Ruixun Zhang, Oxford University Press. © Andrew W. Lo and Ruixun Zhang (2024). DOI: 10.1093/oso/9780199681143.003.0009

In this chapter, we provide an evolutionary explanation for behaviours consistent with Bayesian inference, which shows that such inferences are, in fact, an emergent product of natural selection. Such behaviour emerges purely through the forces of evolution, despite the fact that our model population again consists of mindless individuals without any ability to reason, act strategically, or accurately encode or infer environmental states probabilistically. Using our workhorse binary choice model from Chapter 2, in which individuals make decisions based on observed data, we first show that decision-making emerges based on the posterior distribution of environmental states, implying that behaviours and heuristics that resemble Bayesian inferences are a natural outcome of evolution. Here we use the term 'resemble' intentionally, because the Bayesian heuristics we derive are conditional on an evolutionarily endogenous utility function, and do not include an explicit probabilistic representation of the environment. In other words, evolution leads to behaviours and heuristics with the appearance—but not necessarily the reality, in the strict mathematical sense—of Bayesian inference.

In one sense, the connection between Bayes and evolution is quite natural. After all, the choice of an organism's behaviour that maximizes its conditional expected reproductive output—a Bayes 'policy'—is evolutionarily optimal under a simple model of deterministic strategy when individuals face risks independent of each other (Okasha, 2013). More generally, Suchow, Bourgin, and Griffiths (2017) have pointed out the deep correspondence between certain evolutionary dynamics and Bayesian inference, leading to the reinterpretation of evolutionary processes as Bayesian inference algorithms.

In our framework, we identify three factors that constitute intelligence from an evolutionary perspective, including the ability to increase average fitness, to correlate positively with variations in fitness, and to reduce risk when fitness has high variance. The Bayesian heuristics we derive combine all three of these characteristics.

Finally, we demonstrate that a finite memory naturally emerges in certain environments, including Markov environments, nonstationary environments, and environments where sampling contains too little or too much information about local conditions. This provides an evolutionary justification for decision-making with small sample sizes, and offers a new rationale for limitations on memory that go beyond biological resource constraints (Anderson and Milson, 1989; Lieder and Griffiths, 2020).

9.1 Environments with States

As in previous chapters, we assume an initial population of individuals that live for one period of unspecified length and engage in a single binary decision—a choice between one of two possible actions, a and b—that yields one of two corresponding random numbers of offspring, x_a and x_b, respectively. We use s_t to denote the state of its environment in period t. It determines the joint distribution of x_a and x_b. The state, s_t, is observable to individuals *after* period t. We use $S_t = \{s_{t-1}, s_{t-2}, \cdots\}$ to denote the information available to individuals in period t.

We make the following two assumptions.

Assumption 9.1 s_t *has finite moments up to order 2 for all t.* (x_a, x_b) *and* $\log(fx_a + (1 - f)x_b)$ *have finite moments up to order 2 for all* $f \in [0, 1]$*, both marginally and conditioned on any state* s_t*.*

Assumption 9.2 *Conditioned on state* s_t*,* (x_a, x_b) *are independent and identically distributed (IID) over time and identical for all individuals in a given generation.*

In other words, if two individuals choose the same action a, both will produce the same number of random offspring x_a. The environment is jointly determined by both s_t and (x_a, x_b), which are described by a well-behaved probability distribution function, $\Phi(\cdot)$.

After observing all available information, S, each individual chooses action a with a probability $f(S) \in [0, 1]$, and b with a probability $1 - f(S)$, where $f(\cdot)$ is a function that maps information into a probability. We assume that:

Assumption 9.3 $f(\cdot)$ *is a function bounded between 0 and 1 (inclusive).*[3]

We shall henceforth refer to $f(\cdot)$ as an individual's 'behaviour', since it completely determines the individual choice between a and b given the available information, S.[4] Offspring will behave in a manner identical to their parents (i.e. they will choose between a and b according to the same function $f(\cdot)$). Therefore, the population may be viewed as being segmented into groups of distinct types $f(\cdot)$.

The role of Φ is critical in our framework, as it represents the entirety of the implied consequences of an individual's actions towards reproductive success. If action a leads to higher fecundity than action b for individuals in a given population, the particular set of genes that predispose individuals to select a over b will be favoured by natural selection, in which case these genes will survive and flourish, thus implying that the behaviour

---

[3] Strictly speaking, we require $f(\cdot)$ to be an $\mathcal{F}$-measurable function where $(\Omega, \mathcal{F}, P)$ is the same probability measure space on which S is defined. For simplicity, we omit the measure-theoretic definitions.

[4] We drop the subscript t for notational convenience. Since $f(S)$ can be 0 or 1, we do not require individuals to randomize. Instead, that will be derived as a population-wide consequence of selection under certain conditions.

'choose *a* over *b*' will also flourish. This abstraction defines two equivalent classes of actions with different consequences for reproduction (i.e. all actions yielding the same reproductive fitness are considered equivalent in our framework).[5]

Our binary choice model can be more easily understood through a simple concrete environment that we will use throughout this chapter. Consider an environment where the weather can either be sunny or rainy, and individuals will need to decide whether to build shelter by the river or on the plateau. The reproductive success of each action is specified by:

Action	Sunny	Rainy
a (river)	$x_a = c$	$x_a = 0$
b (plateau)	$x_b = 0$	$x_b = c$

This is a special case of the general environment in our model. At time t, with some probability p_t, the environment is sunny, and choice a yields $c > 0$ offspring, while choice b yields none. With probability $1 - p_t$, however, the environment is rainy, in which case the reproductive outcome is reversed. The probability of a sunny day, p_t, summarizes the impact on the environment in the state, s_t. We can think of s_t as any variable that affects weather, such as season or temperature.

In this chapter, we impose various assumptions on the state, s_t, and determine the type of behaviour that emerges in each environment.

9.2 Bayesian Behaviours in Stationary Environments

We first consider the case in which the state, s_t, is stationary.

Assumption 9.4 *The set of environmental states, $\{s_t\}$, is stationary and ergodic. In particular, s_t is ergodic if $\{s_t\}$ is stationary with a finite second moment, and its covariance $\operatorname{cov}(s_0, s_t) \to 0$ as $t \to \infty$.*

In this case, we can explicitly characterize how fast the population grows as a function of the behaviour. We denote by $n_t^{f(\cdot)}$ the total number of offspring of

---

[5] The specification of Φ also captures the fundamental distinction between traditional models of population genetics and more contemporary applications of evolution to behaviour; the former focuses on the natural selection of traits, determined by genetics, whereas the latter focuses on the natural selection of behaviour. Although behaviour is obviously linked to genetics, the specific genes involved, their loci, and the mechanisms by which they are transmitted from one generation to the next are much less relevant to economic analysis than the ultimate consequences of behaviour for reproduction, which is captured by Φ.

type $f(\cdot)$ in generation t. It is easy to show that $T^{-1} \log n_t^{f(\cdot)}$, the log population divided by time, converges to the log geometric average growth rate:

$$\alpha(f(\cdot)) \equiv \mathbb{F}_{(x_a,x_b,S)}[\log(f(S)x_a + (1 - f(S))x_b)] \tag{9.2}$$

as time T increases without bound, where $\mathbb{E}_{(x_a,x_b,S)}$ is the expected value taken over the joint distribution of the environment. Maximizing Equation (9.2) yields the following result:

Proposition 9.1 *Under Assumptions 9.1–9.4, the growth-optimal behaviour, $f^*(\cdot)$, that maximizes Equation (9.2) is:*

$$f^*(S) = \begin{cases} 1 & \text{if } \mathbb{E}_{(x_a,x_b|S)}[x_b/x_a] < 1 \\ \text{solution to Equation (9.4)} & \text{if } \mathbb{E}_{(x_a,x_b|S)}[x_a/x_b] \geq 1 \text{ and } \mathbb{E}_{(x_a,x_b|S)}[x_b/x_a] \geq 1, \\ 0 & \text{if } \mathbb{E}_{(x_a,x_b|S)}[x_a/x_b] < 1 \end{cases} \tag{9.3}$$

where $f^*(S)$ is defined implicitly in the second case of Equation (9.3) by:

$$\mathbb{E}_{(x_a,x_b|S)}\left[\frac{x_a - x_b}{f^*(S)x_a + (1 - f^*(S))x_b}\right] = 0. \tag{9.4}$$

The expected values in Equations (9.3) and (9.4) are with respect to the joint distribution of (x_a, x_b), given all available information, S.

This growth-optimal behaviour is, in fact, what is implied by Bayesian inference. We can see this from two different perspectives. Firstly, the population dynamic between two generations in evolution, called the 'replicator equation' in evolutionary biology, is given by

$$l_t^{f(\cdot)} \overset{a.s.}{\equiv} \frac{l_{t-1}^{f(\cdot)} \cdot Fitness_t^{f(\cdot)}}{\sum_{g(\cdot)} l_{t-1}^{g(\cdot)} \cdot Fitness_t^{g(\cdot)}}, \tag{9.5}$$

where $l_t^{f(\cdot)}$ is the relative frequency of behaviour $f(\cdot)$ in the population in generation t, $Fitness_t^{f(\cdot)} = (f(S_t)x_{a,t} + (1 - f(S_t))x_{b,t})$ represents the fitness (that is, the random reproductive success) of behaviour $f(\cdot)$ in generation t, and the summation in the denominator is over a finite set of all possible behaviours, $g(\cdot)$, in the population. This is identical to the Bayes formula, where we treat

$l_t^{f(\cdot)}$ as the posterior, $l_{t-1}^{f(\cdot)}$ as the prior, and *Fitness*$_t^{f(\cdot)}$ as the likelihood (see further details in Appendix B.7), an observation also shared by the cognitive neuroscience literature (Suchow, Bourgin, and Griffiths, 2017; Czégel et al., 2020).

Secondly, we can view the population growth rate for behaviour $f(\cdot)$ in Equation (9.2) as the expected value of a logarithmic utility function, where the utility is with respect to the reproductive success of this particular behaviour: $f(S)x_a + (1 - f(S))x_b$. We would like to emphasize that the log utility is endogenous in our model, resulting from systematic reproductive risks in the environment, since all individuals share the same risk (see also the formal definitions in Lo and Zhang (2021)). More generally, different forms of utility functions, and different levels of risk aversion, emerge from evolution in environments with different compositions of systematic and idiosyncratic reproductive risks (see Chapter 6).

From this perspective, the dominant behaviour in Equation (9.3) corresponds to maximizing the endogenous expected utility, where the expected value is taken over the posterior distribution of the environment, conditioned on all available information, S.[6] This phenomenon is known as 'conditionalization' in the evolutionary biology literature (Okasha, 2013). This behaviour is what Bayesian inference with a particular utility function would imply, because individuals will appear to behave in a manner in which decisions are made in each generation to maximize the growth rate based on all available information at the time. Note that if the environment is independent over time, there is no benefit from information about past realized states. As a result, intelligent behaviours will not be useful, and $f^*(\cdot)$ will simply be a constant (see Chapter 2).

We use the phrase 'appear to behave' in the previous paragraph quite deliberately, because our evolutionary framework does not require individuals to possess any Bayesian reasoning ability. As in previous chapters, we do not require individuals to be sentient, much less have the ability to encode the environment probabilistically or manipulate those probabilities according to Bayes' rule. In this sense, the dominant behaviour may well be a heuristic rather than deliberate Bayesian inference. Nonetheless, our framework shows that even purely mindless individuals can adapt to show behaviours that are identical to Bayesian inference through the forces of natural selection. The claim that human minds learn and reason according to Bayesian principles is not a claim that the human mind can implement any Bayesian inference,

---

[6] We impose no regularity conditions on the behaviour $f^*(\cdot)$ other than it being bounded between 0 and 1. In fact, $f^*(\cdot)$ does not even need to be continuous.

because this can be computationally costly and intractable (Gigerenzer, 2008; Mozer, Pashler, and Homaei, 2008; Gershman, Horvitz, and Tenenbaum, 2015). Rather, Bayesian inference gives individuals a rational framework for updating beliefs about latent variables in generative models given the observed data (Tenenbaum et al., 2011).

In addition, in our framework, Bayesian inferential behaviour occurs with respect to the environment only to the extent that it matters for reproductive success. It does not necessarily track the true underlying probabilities of states of the world. In fact, as Hoffman's (2016) interface theory of perception argues, our perceptions of the world are not 'veridical', meaning that they do not necessarily represent the world accurately.[7] The perceptual systems with which we have been endowed by natural selection are a species-specific interface that allows us to interact adaptively and successfully with objective reality, while remaining blissfully ignorant of the complexity of that objective reality (Hoffman, 2016). This is consistent with our abstraction of the environment that matters for reproductive success: the joint distribution of (x_a, x_b, S). In this sense, the dominant behaviour that resembles Bayesian inference is with respect to the fitness for individuals to reproduce—not necessarily to the actual underlying environment. The problem is not that veridical perceptions are necessarily counter-adaptive, but rather that veridicality is irrelevant to adaptation (Hoffman, 2016).

The three possible behaviours described in Equation (9.3) reflect the relative reproductive success of the two choices. Choosing a deterministically will be optimal if choice a exhibits an unambiguously higher expected relative reproductive success, while choosing b deterministically will be optimal if the opposite is true. Randomizing between a and b, however, will be optimal if neither choice has a clear-cut reproductive advantage. This last outcome is perhaps the most counterintuitive, because it is suboptimal from an individual's perspective (see Section 2.2.1).

Because the dominant behaviour is non-deterministic in the general case, $f^*(\cdot)$ cannot be observed for each individual based on one instance of the binary choice proper. It will therefore be difficult, if not impossible, to tell if any given individual exhibits perfect Bayesian behaviour. However, at the population level, $f^*(\cdot)$ can be interpreted as the proportion of individuals that take action a, which can be easily observed. This is consistent with the observation described earlier that perfectly Bayesian behaviour is only

[7] Hoffman (2016) provides a metaphor of a computer interface in which files and folders are merely icons and abstractions of the true underlying transistors, voltages, magnetic fields, and megabytes of a system. In our model, the abstraction of the environment—the joint distribution of (x_a, x_b, S)—precisely defines such an interface.

present as an average behaviour among humans, not in individual people or in individual trials (Goodman et al., 2008; Vul et al., 2014).

9.3 What is Intelligence? Revisited

Our results also allow us to revisit intelligence from an evolutionary perspective. Recall from Chapter 8 that intelligent behaviour is defined as any behaviour that accelerates population growth, increasing the odds of survival. The dominant behaviour described in Equation (9.3) is determined by the environment through the relative fitness of the two available choices. With $R \equiv x_a/x_b - 1$ denoting relative fitness, we have the following result:

Proposition 9.2 *Under Assumptions 9.1–9.4, the population growth rate in Equation (9.2), $\alpha(f(\cdot))$, can be rewritten as*

$$\alpha(f(\cdot)) \approx \mathbb{E}[f(S)]\mathbb{E}[R] + \mathrm{Cov}(f(S), R) - \frac{1}{2}\mathbb{E}\left[(f(S)R)^2\right] + constant \qquad (9.6)$$

using a second-order Taylor approximation and additional regularity conditions specified in Appendix B.7.3. In this notation, intelligent behaviour $f(\cdot)$ increases the population growth rate given a particular environment as described by the relative fitness, R.

Each of the three terms in Equation (9.6) highlights a different factor in determining intelligence. The first term in Equation (9.6) is the average relative fitness, $\mathbb{E}[R]$. This states that intelligent behaviour amplifies the average relative fitness. The second term in Equation (9.6) is the covariance of the behaviour, $f(S)$, with the relative fitness, R. In other words, intelligent behaviour is correlated with the environment, moving in the same direction as relative fitness. The third term is the second moment of $f(S)R$, its variance; thus, intelligent behaviour reduces risk the most when the relative fitness has high variability.

The Bayesian heuristics we derived are precisely the combination of these three characteristics, which, in turn, define intelligence within our model's evolutionary framework. This is consistent with Chapter 8's behaviour that is correlated with reproductive success across populations in environments with idiosyncratic risks. In this chapter, we see that the definition of intelligence also includes behaviour correlated with reproductive success over time.

9.4 Finite Memory in Nonstationary Environments

Our analysis has so far focused on stationary environments. In nonstationary environments, however, there is a trade-off between collecting more information and waiting too long to make a decision, as the past becomes increasingly irrelevant to the future. A balance between continuous learning and forgetting is thus necessary to cope with such environments (Lughofer and Sayed-Mouchaweh, 2015). By extending our model to nonstationary environments, we show that the degree of nonstationarity of the environment plays a critical role in the emergence of finite memory as an adaptive trait.

In nonstationary environments, we assume that:

Assumption 9.5 *The environmental states, $\{s_t\}$, form an α-mixing sequence.*

In general, $\{s_t\}$ can be nonstationary. White (2001, Definition 3.42) provides a formal definition for mixing stochastic processes. In this chapter, we use a simple necessary condition for α-mixing to illustrate the intuition behind the concept. α-mixing stochastic processes are always *asymptotically uncorrelated*: there exist constants $\{\rho_\tau\}$ such that $0 \leq \rho_\tau \leq 1$, $\sum_{\tau=0}^{\infty} \rho_\tau < \infty$, and $\mathrm{corr}(s_t, s_{t+\tau}) \leq \rho_\tau$ for all $\tau > 0$. In other words, Assumption 9.5 asserts that the environment forgets about the past asymptotically.

Proposition 9.3 *Under Assumptions 9.1–9.3 and 9.5, $T^{-1} \log n_t^{f(\cdot)}$, the log population divided by time, still converges:*

$$
\begin{aligned}
\alpha(f(\cdot)) &= \overline{\mathbb{E}_{(x_{a,t}, x_{b,t}, S_t)}[\log\left(f(S_t)x_{a,t} + (1 - f(S_t))x_{b,t}\right)]}^{\infty}_{t=1} \\
&\equiv \lim_{T \to \infty} \frac{1}{T} \sum_{t=1}^{T} \mathbb{E}_{(x_{a,t}, x_{b,t}, S_t)}[\log\left(f(S_t)x_{a,t} + (1 - f(S_t))x_{b,t}\right)],
\end{aligned}
\tag{9.7}
$$

where we use $\overline{}^{\infty}_{t=1}$ to denote the average over t. Compared to the growth rate in stationary environments in Equation (9.2), the expected log fitness is replaced by its average over time.[8]

We can now ask what is the dominant behaviour in the population, and what amount of information should $f^*(\cdot)$ use in nonstationary environments? For intelligent behaviours that use past information, there is no explicit solution for the optimal behaviour, $f^*(\cdot)$, in the general case of nonstationary

---

[8] In nonstationary environments that are independent over time, the dominant behaviour is a constant. In terms of our sunny/rainy example, the dominant behaviour, $f^* = \overline{\mathbb{E}[p_t]}^{\infty}_{t-1}$, is the average expected value of a sunny day over time, which corresponds to probability matching in the average sense.

environments. Continuing with our sunny/rainy example, consider an environment where the states follow a linear combination of a simple random walk (SRW) and an autoregressive (AR) process: $s_t = \lambda \cdot SRW_t + (1 - \lambda) \cdot AR_t^{(k)}$. Here, λ is a constant between 0 and 1, SRW_t is an SRW defined by $SRW_0 = 0$ and $SRW_t = SRW_{t-1} + z_t$, and $AR_t^{(k)}$ is an AR process of order k defined by $AR_0 = 0$ and $AR_t^{(k)} = 0.9 \cdot k^{-1} \sum_{i=1}^{k} AR_{t-i}^{(k)} + \epsilon_t$.[9] The probability of a sunny day is the logistic transformation of the states that bound it between 0 and 1: $p_t = \text{logistic}(s_t) = (1 + \exp(-s_t))^{-1}$. There are two important parameters that determine this environment: the order of the AR process (k), which determines its degree of memory over time, and the weight of the SRW (λ), which determines the degree of nonstationarity in the environment. Figure 9.1a shows two simulated paths of p_t in environments with different degrees of nonstationarity.

Individuals observe only the state of the environment, s_t, not the realization of the subprocesses, SRW_t and $AR_t^{(k)}$. We assume that individuals use the average of the previous m observed states as their best estimate of the next state, and behave accordingly: $f^m(S_t) = \text{logistic}\left(m^{-1} \sum_{i=1}^{m} s_{t-i}\right)$, where logistic

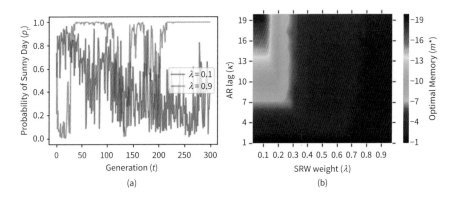

Fig. 9.1 The adaptation of the optimal amount of memory as a function of environmental conditions. (a) Two sample paths of p_t (y-axis) from a simulation of 300 generations (x-axis) in environments with different degrees of nonstationarity. The blue path is generated from $\lambda = 0.1$ (low nonstationarity), and the orange path is generated from $\lambda = 0.9$ (high nonstationarity), both with an autoregressive lag of $k = 10$. (b) The optimal amount of individual memory (shown in the colour bar) in environments with a degree of memory as parameterized by the autoregressive lag, k (y-axis), and a degree of nonstationarity as parameterized by the simple random walk (SRW) weight, λ (x-axis).

[9] z_t is an IID Bernoulli random variable with an equal probability of being -1 or 1, and ϵ_t is an IID standard normal random variable following $\mathcal{N}(0, 1)$.

is the logistic function. Strictly speaking, individuals do not have to follow this functional form. However, this behaviour is a good approximation of a simple heuristic, and it is sufficient to illustrate our main point. Figure 9.1b shows the optimal amount of memory, m^*, that an individual should use in a given environment to maximize the population growth rate as functions of k and λ, based on an evolutionary simulation of 30,000 generations.[10]

Unsurprisingly, given a fixed degree of stationarity in the environment (λ), the optimal amount of memory, m^*, increases with the order of the AR process. In other words, the greater the degree of memory exhibited by the environment, the more memory individuals should adapt to use. In particular, when the environment is mostly driven by the AR process (i.e. when λ is very low), the optimal amount of memory, m^*, equals the maximum AR lag—that is, individuals adapt to the environment to match its memory.

Conversely, given a fixed amount of memory in the AR process, the optimal amount of memory, m^*, decreases as the degree of stationarity (λ) increases. This highlights another reason for finite memory, and more generally, for decision-making based on limited samples: the nonstationarity of the environment. When the environment is nonstationary and its distribution changes over time, it becomes costly for individuals to use outdated data.

Finally, it should be observed that only an environment with high stationarity *and* high memory (the upper left quadrant of Fig. 9.1b) warrants that an individual possess a large memory, highlighting the fact that finite memory can emerge in environments with either low memory *or* high nonstationarity. Indeed, in the vast majority of the area in Fig. 9.1b, the optimal behaviour uses only one or two observed states from the past.

This result is consistent with the well-documented phenomenon in cognitive science that human subjects tend to make decisions based on only a small number of data points instead of computing the fully Bayesian answer (Griffiths and Tenenbaum, 2006; Sanborn and Griffiths, 2008; Vul and Pashler, 2008; Vul et al., 2014). The small-sample phenomenon is often explained as the consequence of costly data acquisition and Bayesian inference, whereas our model provides an alternate and arguably more fundamental explanation. Nonstationary environments induce adaptation to rapid generalization and decision-making based on a short memory, even if there is no cost for using an infinite amount of data.

This result also provides an explanation for the recency effect documented in a wide range of disciplines (Kahneman, 2011), which is often considered to be a bias relative to a fully rational agent. However, our results show

---

[10] To reduce noise, we run the simulation fifty times and take the median values of m^* in each environment.

that in nonstationary environments, the recency effect is, in fact, desirable, highlighting the key role of the environment in shaping behaviour.

9.5 Sampling with Limited Information

We now turn to the context of cognition with limited computational resources (Lieder and Griffiths, 2020). We show that if obtaining and using data for inference is costly, the information contained in each data point also determines the optimal number of data points to use. Either too much or too little information can lead to inferences based on a small number of data points.

Continuing with our sunny/rainy day example, we assume that the probability of a sunny day, p_t, is either 80% or 20%, with an equal probability in each period. Once again, there are only two states in this environment. In each period, individuals receive imperfect information about their state. The information comes in the form of samples, $D = \{d_1, d_2, \cdots\}$. Each sample, d_j, tells an individual its state with an accuracy $q > 0.5$: $\text{Prob}(d_j = \text{correct state}) = q$. We can think of D as a weather forecast, and individuals are able to use data from D for their decisions. We assume that the cost of obtaining m samples is $C(m) = 1 + \eta m$, where $\eta \geq 0$ determines the magnitude of the cost. The cost is used as a multiplicative factor in reproductive success.[11]

We can now calculate the optimal number of data points that individuals should use to determine their behaviour $f(\cdot)$. Given m samples, if an individual follows a simple majority rule, the probability that the majority indicates the correct state is: $\beta = 1 - CDF(m/2; m, q)$, where $CDF(m/2; m, p)$ is the cumulative binomial distribution function with m total draws and probability p, evaluated at $m/2$.[12] Figure 9.2a shows β as a function of m and q. When the accuracy, q, of the information in each sample is high, the confidence of the aggregate prediction of multiple samples quickly approaches 1 as the sample size increases, indicating that the marginal benefit of an extra sample quickly diminishes.

We now demonstrate that the optimal sample size depends on the amount of information contained in one sample.[13] Figure 9.2b shows the optimal sample size as a function of the information contained in each sample (q),

---

[11] Appendix B.7.5 provides further details about the incorporation of the cost of obtaining samples into the growth rate. The cost is multiplicative to the number of offspring of an individual. For example, when $\eta = 0$, there is no cost; when $\eta = 1$, $C(1) = 2$, which means that one sample cuts the reproductive success by half; when $\eta = 0.1$, $C(10) = 2$, which means that ten samples also cut the reproductive success by half.

[12] When the data indicate a tie between the two states, we assume individuals choose randomly.

[13] Appendix B.7.5 provides the analytical solution of the optimal behaviour given m samples, and its corresponding population growth rate. The optimal number of samples, m^*, can be obtained by maximizing the growth rate over m.

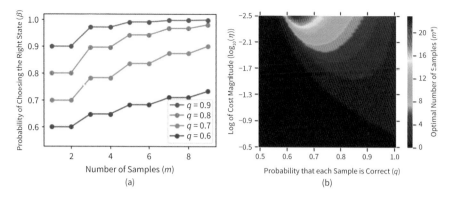

Fig. 9.2 The optimal sample size as a function of the information contained in each sample. (a) Probability, β, that the majority of samples predict the correct state (y-axis) as a function of the number of samples, m (x-axis), and the probability that each sample is correct, q. (b) Optimal sample sizes (shown in the colour bar) given different levels of information contained in one sample (x-axis), and the magnitude of the cost, $\log_{10}(\eta)$ (y-axis). Greater absolute values of $\log_{10}(\eta)$ indicate a lower magnitude of cost.

and the magnitude of the cost (η in log scale). Given a fixed cost, finite memory appears when the information contained in each sample is either too low or too high. When the amount of information in each sample is low (i.e. the q is close to 0.5), there is little to gain from each sample. As a result, it is not worth paying the cost for any sample. However, when the amount of information in each sample is very high (i.e. the q is close to 1), one sample is sufficient to infer the state reliably. As a result, it is not worth paying the cost beyond just one sample.

This provides an additional reason for the emergence of finite memory beyond nonstationary environments. It is only desirable to obtain a large number of samples when there is partial information. Otherwise, we adapt to generalize from a small number of samples.[14]

9.6 Discussion

In the simple binary choice model of Chapter 2, Bayesian inference emerges quite naturally as an adaptive behaviour under certain stochastic environments. Despite the fact that our population consists of mindless individuals without any ability to reason, act strategically, or accurately encode or infer environmental states probabilistically, the forces of natural

---

[14] Vul et al. (2014) considered a similar model, which also showed that individuals should make guesses based on very few samples.

selection are sufficient to yield one of the most powerful inferential tools at our disposal. In addition, we have identified three specific environments that favour the emergence of finite memory—those that are Markov, nonstationary, and where sampling contains too little or too much information about local conditions. These results provide an explanation for several known phenomena in human cognition, including deviations from the optimal Bayesian strategy, as well as the benefits of finite memory apart from the existence of resource constraints.

Given its evolutionary foundations, our framework has implications that can be tested through controlled laboratory experiments, such as those described for experimental evolution (Burnham, Dunlap, and Stephens, 2015). Central to this idea is the creation of test and control environments that vary in payoffs, or, in a biological context, fitness. Various species, ranging from bacteria to *Drosophila* (fruit flies), have been used to design experiments to better understand decision-making under uncertainty (Mery and Kawecki, 2002; Yang et al., 2008; Beaumont et al., 2009; Dunlap and Stephens, 2014).

Finite memory emerges as an evolutionary adaptation to Markov environments, nonstationary environments, and environments in which samples contain either too little or too much information. We therefore conclude that we are hardwired to make quick decisions based on limited information precisely because evolution taught us to do so. From a policy perspective, our conclusion also highlights the importance of maintaining stability in public policy and financial markets. Otherwise, critical information about the past is doomed to be quickly forgotten.

Bayes' rule is now widely used in the field of machine learning, from the classical Bayes optimal classifier and the multi-arm bandit problem to applications in deep learning (Kendall and Gal, 2017; Wang and Yeung, 2020; Wilson and Izmailov, 2020) and reinforcement learning (Strens, 2000; Ghavamzadeh et al., 2015). Understanding the evolutionary and cognitive origins of Bayesian heuristics can illuminate a more natural derivation of machine learning algorithms from human intelligence, and the kinds of inference (or algorithms) that are more suitable for varying environmental conditions in terms of their stochastic nature. Like the 'learning machine' Alan Turing proposed over seven decades ago as a parallel to the principles of evolution (Turing, 1950), the fact that machine learning can benefit from nature's bounty in both inspiration and mechanism is highly relevant today in the quest for artificial general intelligence (Goertzel and Pennachin, 2007).

We now turn to an application of our evolutionary framework that generates the polar opposite result: the failure of the wisdom of crowds.

10
The Madness of Mobs

Collective intelligence—a term for shared or group knowledge and wisdom that emerges from the collaboration and competition of many individuals—has been studied in many disciplines over decades.[1] Despite its power and prevalence, however, collective intelligence can also fail, sometimes repeatedly. One example is the prevalence of bubbles and bursts in financial markets, such as the dot-com bubble in 1990s, the financial crisis of 2008, and, most recently, the financial turmoil experienced during the COVID-19 pandemic. No matter how different the latest financial frenzy or crisis appears to be, there are almost always parallels in history (Reinhart and Rogoff, 2009).

Two of the most hotly debated issues today—political polarization and discrimination—are also examples of the failure of collective intelligence. Since the 2010s, we have witnessed the rise of populism and nationalism as part of a reaction against the global policies of the last thirty years in Western democracies and beyond, not to mention gender, religious, and other types of bias. Although some of these movements may be rooted in rational self-interest, they often do more harm than good to their proponents. These examples raise the natural question of why the wisdom of crowds falters in these cases but succeeds in so many other contexts.

In this chapter, we apply the binary choice framework of Chapters 2 and 4 to understand *failures* of collective intelligence by answering the following questions: In what environments are discrimination likely to emerge? What are the drivers behind them? And, more importantly, how can we avoid collective ignorance and promote collective intelligence instead? Sceptics may question the feasibility of analysing qualitative phenomena such as polarization, bias, and discrimination within a quantitative framework. We shared such scepticism at the outset of this research programme. However, we quickly realized that when any behaviour has consequences for reproductive success, it is subject to the laws of evolution.

---

[1] This chapter, including the figures, is adapted with permission of SAGE Publications Inc. from Lo, A. W., and Zhang, R. (2022). The wisdom of crowds vs. the madness of mobs: an evolutionary model of bias, polarization, and other challenges to collective intelligence. *Collective Intelligence* 1(1). https://doi.org/10.1177/26339137221104785.

The Adaptive Markets Hypothesis. Andrew W. Lo and Ruixun Zhang, Oxford University Press. © Andrew W. Lo and Ruixun Zhang (2024). DOI: 10.1093/oso/9780199681143.003.0010

In particular, we apply Chapter 4's framework to model the emergence of coordinated groups and the rise of extreme political views by allowing the reproductive success of individuals to share several common factors. The implications of this one feature—which is the evolutionary instantiation of the adage 'the enemy of my enemy is my friend'—are enormous, giving rise to seemingly coordinated behaviour among subsets of individuals, or groups. If we extend the binary choice model to the case in which reproductive success depends on two factors, a globalization factor and an opposing populist factor that is negatively correlated with globalization, two distinct groups of individuals naturally emerge.[2] The fact that the two groups have different exposures to the two factors implies that they will evolve to hold different political views which, in turn, will affect the reproductive success of individuals in the two groups differently.[3] This represents a primitive form of polarization. When the average degree of globalization is either very low or very high, two opposing political views emerge in response to the distinct economic exposures (or, in an evolutionary context, biological exposure) of individuals to globalization. Given a continuous spectrum of individuals in a population who benefit or are harmed by globalization to varying degrees, the ultimate political composition of the population will be determined by the specific distribution of economic exposures. Our framework may serve as a way to understand and predict the evolution and adaptation of these political views.

Our second focus is on discrimination, including, but not limited to, racial discrimination. A key observation with respect to racial discrimination is the fact that, in certain cases, an individual's race is plainly observable by others and difficult to hide or alter. As argued by the neurocognitive memory/prediction framework of intelligence (Hawkins and Blakeslee, 2004), we store memory patterns and use them to make predictions about future events. When individuals experience a random adverse event (such as a crime) during an encounter with a member of a specific race, they tend to attribute causality to the race of that individual because it is the most easily observable feature, leading to discrimination against that group, even in cases where there are other root causes for the adverse event that have nothing to do with race. In other words, it is easy to confuse correlation with causation. By further extending the binary choice model to include path-dependent feedback loops, we derive even stronger results by showing that discrimination still

---

[2] By globalization, we mean the growing interaction and integration among individuals, institutions, and economies worldwide.

[3] Individuals with the same behaviour share the same reproductive success and therefore rise and fall together in evolution. Although it appears that groups of individuals emerge, natural selection operates on the behaviours or strategies of these individuals.

emerges when the under-represented group has an equal or even diminished probability of adverse events. The fact that natural selection with a simple feedback mechanism alone can generate such bias is striking. In reality, these negative feedback loops are ubiquitous for every minority group. With the growing reach of social media over the last decade, news travels faster than ever, and it is therefore now easier for negative feedback to reinforce itself.[4] Our results demonstrate how powerful negative feedback can be in generating widespread bias and discriminatory tendencies in the population.

We also introduce the notion of a locally evolutionarily stable strategy (L-ESS)—which extends the definition of an evolutionarily stable strategy first introduced by Maynard Smith and Price (1973) (see also Maynard Smith (1982))—and show that with path dependence, only L-ESS behaviours are able to survive in the long run. In fact, with negative feedback, such behaviours are more discriminatory than non-L-ESS strategies, and, strikingly, they always lead to a lower population growth rate than their non-L-ESS counterpart, but non-L-ESS behaviours (i.e. no discrimination), are not stable strategies in stochastic environments with negative feedback loops, because individuals can increase their reproductive success by discriminating. Therefore, path dependency can lead to evolutionary outcomes with slower growth rates than would otherwise take place, and the entire population ends up in a suboptimal state, which we call 'collective ignorance'.[5] More broadly, this result implies that a multiplicity of viewpoints is an important and inevitable consequence of evolution with multiple environmental factors.

Finally, our framework yields several practical policy implications for reducing or preventing bias and discrimination. The key idea is to foster environments under which the desired behaviour—collective intelligence—will emerge naturally through natural selection, instead of simply regulating against the undesired outcome which could create selective pressures that make matters worse. In our example of globalization, the fundamental cause of the emergence of polarization is the sharp difference in personal outcomes that comes with global integration: some individuals benefit, while others suffer. Constructing the right tools for those who are harmed by the polarizing factor—options such as (re)-education and providing employment opportunities in the new industrial landscape—is likely to be more effective than simply 'shutting down' globalization. More generally, proactively

---

[4] For example, engagement-based recommendations on news and social media platforms have the potential to reinforce negative feedback (Cho et al., 2020).

[5] Here we use 'collective ignorance' to refer to either lack of knowledge or bad judgement.

providing educational, social, and economic opportunities to counteract negative feedback loops, encouraging more accurate beliefs among current and future generations through early exposure, and shaping the environment to favour collective intelligence are likely to be more successful policies than attempting to outlaw undesirable behaviours. As long as the environmental factors giving rise to these behaviours are still in force, the banned behaviours will re-emerge in one form or another.

Related Literature

Given the breadth of engagement in this chapter's topic, several distinct literatures are related to our contributions. With respect to polarization, Flew and Iosifidis (2020), Pastor and Veronesi (2020), Swank and Betz (2003), and Rodrik (2018, 2020) provide compelling evidence that globalization policies and shocks have played an important role in driving support for populist movements and nationalism.

The literature on racism and discrimination is even more multidisciplinary, complex, and vast. Roberts and Rizzo (2020) provide one pertinent example, outlining seven factors that contribute to American racism. Several studies have documented the fact that black individuals are more likely to be searched by the police, charged with a serious crime, detained before trial, convicted of an offense, and incarcerated than observably similar white individuals (Arnold, Dobbie, and Hull, 2021; Vomfell and Stewart, 2021). Similar studies have documented Asian and Hispanic discrimination, including the Colfax massacre in 1873, the Mexican repatriations between 1929 and 1936, the Chinese Exclusion Act of 1882, the internment of Japanese Americans during World War II, and centuries of enslavement and exploitation. The surge in anti-Asian crimes during the COVID-19 pandemic (Lu et al., 2021) is just the most recent example of discrimination in societies around the globe.

There is also an extensive economics-based literature on why bias and stereotyping might emerge, including through statistical discrimination based on stereotypes (Phelps, 1972; Arrow, 1973; Coate and Loury, 1993), taste-based discrimination based on the personal prejudices of individuals (Becker, 1957), scarce cognitive resources leading to biased representations of the world (Schneider, 2005; Bordalo et al., 2016), motivated reasoning (Fuligni, 2007; Gorski, 2008; Bohren et al., 2019), and the strategic benefits of distorted beliefs (Brocas and Carrillo, 2000; Carrillo and Mariotti, 2000; Bénabou and Tirole, 2002; Compte and Postlewaite, 2004; Charness, Rustichini, and Van de Ven, 2018; Heller and Winter, 2020). People can discriminate against certain groups implicitly (Lai and Banaji, 2020), and in the context of economic decisions, even at the expense of their own financial gain (Kubota et al., 2013).

Our work is also related to the collective intelligence literature, which spans several disciplines, including sociology (Merton, 1960), engineering and computer science (Leimeister, 2010), and economics and finance (Samuelson, 1965; Fama, 1970). Strong empirical evidence of a collective-intelligence factor has been documented in groups performing various problem-solving tasks (Woolley et al., 2010; Riedl et al., 2021), and the degree of collective intelligence has been related to both group composition and group interaction (Woolley, Aggarwal, and Malone, 2015). Malone (2018) coined the term *superminds* to describe this phenomenon, and these ideas now have widespread applications in business (Malone, Laubacher, and Dellarocas, 2010), healthcare (Jean et al., 2020), education (Gregg, 2009; Ilon, 2012), human/computer interaction (Segaran, 2007; Gregg, 2010), and many other fields.

In financial markets, the primary example of collective intelligence is the efficient markets hypothesis (Samuelson, 1965; Fama, 1970), which maintains that market prices fully reflect all publicly available information. It is remarkable that a single number, price, contains the collective wisdom of all market participants. Surowiecki (2005) aptly describes such phenomena as the 'wisdom of crowds': a random group of investors can, under certain conditions, achieve better results than any individual within the group. More broadly, collective intelligence forms the basis for voting and collective decision-making, the foundations of democracy in modern society. By appealing to the principles of evolution, the adaptive markets hypothesis (AMH) provides a natural and internally consistent reconciliation of the apparent contradiction between the wisdom of crowds in normal times and the 'madness of mobs' during times of financial turmoil (Lo, 2004, 2005, 2012, 2017).

The framework we propose in this chapter is most closely related to the notion of group selection—a hypothesized and controversial evolutionary mechanism in which natural selection acts at the level of the group, instead of at the level of the individual or the gene—which we covered in Chapter 4. In contrast to Wynne-Edwards (1963), Hamilton (1963), and Wilson (1975b), we follow the work of Zhang, Brennan, and Lo (2014a) in which this phenomenon is simply the consequence of natural selection occurring in stochastic environments with reproductive risks that are correlated across individuals. As we showed in Chapter 4, to an outside observer, individuals in this population will become increasingly similar after the shift, creating the appearance—but not necessarily the reality—of intentional coordination, communication, and synchronization. Frank and Slatkin (1990) and Frank (2011a,b, 2012a) provide a more detailed analysis of the impact of correlation between individuals in evolutionary biology.

Finally, the surprising impact of negative feedback loops in reinforcing bias is similar to how health recommendations can generate spurious empirical patterns in public health data due to behavioural changes by certain subpopulations. For example, Oster (2020) documented that when new research claims to have found a link between a specific behaviour and positive health outcomes, the widespread adoption of this behaviour by more health-conscious individuals can yield an empirical relation between such behaviour and improved health, even though the improvement is due to selection bias and not a causal link between that behaviour and health.

10.1 Political Polarization

The starting point for the basic evolutionary framework to explain the emergence of coordinated groups and biases is the binary choice model with factor structure developed in Chapter 4. Coordinated groups are groups whose individual members appear to act with a single purpose, such as unions, military alliances, and patient advocacy groups, among others. Here we focus on extreme political views as an example to illustrate the emergence of polarization.

Consider an island that is isolated from the rest of the world. There are two factors that determine the reproductive success of any individual on this hypothetical island. The first factor, λ_{glob}, represents the degree of globalization where, without loss of generality, we assume that larger values represent higher degrees of globalization. The second factor, λ_{other}, represents everything else that may be relevant to an individual's reproductive success. This is obviously an oversimplification, but more general specifications will become obvious once we present the analysis for this simpler setting.[6] We follow Assumptions 4.1 and 4.2 from Chapter 4, and use $(\beta_{anti}, \beta_{pro})$ to represent an individual's *characteristics*, which determines an individual's reproductive success as a trade-off between exposure to these two factors.

---

[6] See Rodrik (2018, 2020) for more extensive discussions about globalization and the emergence of populism. As Rodrik states, 'Globalization is probably not the only force at play in the rise of extreme political views. Changes in technology, rise of winner-take-all markets, erosion of labour-market protections, and decline of norms restricting pay differentials all have played their part. These developments are not entirely independent from globalization, insofar as they both fostered globalization and were reinforced by it.' With that awareness, we use globalization as a single factor in our model to illustrate its role in shaping political views, using it to develop the intuition to apply our model to other factors.

10.1.1 A Simple Example

To develop intuition about the model, we first consider the special case in which the factors are specified by the following Bernoulli distribution:

$$\lambda_{glob} = \begin{cases} 4 & \text{with probability } q \\ 1 & \text{with probability } 1 - q \end{cases}, \quad \lambda_{other} \equiv 2. \qquad (10.1)$$

In each period, the degree of globalization is either 4 or 1, and the higher values of the probability, q, represent a higher average degree of globalization. However, we may simply assume that all other factors are represented by a constant factor λ_{other} without loss of generality.

An individual on this island lives for one period, has one opportunity to choose one of two political attitudes (actions)—pro-globalization or anti-globalization—that determines its reproductive success, and then dies immediately after reproduction. The number of offspring is given by x_{anti} if the individual chooses to be anti-globalization, and x_{pro} if the individual chooses to be pro-globalization:

$$\begin{aligned} x_{anti} &= \beta_{anti}\lambda_{glob} + (1 - \beta_{anti})\lambda_{other} \\ x_{pro} &= \beta_{pro}\lambda_{glob} + (1 - \beta_{pro})\lambda_{other} \end{aligned}. \qquad (10.2)$$

The characteristics β_{anti} and β_{pro} determine how an individual's chosen action affects its reproductive success through the two factors. Different individuals may possess different characteristics. Here we focus on two specific kinds of individuals: those who benefit from globalization, and those who are harmed by it. Higher values of λ_{glob} are more conducive to reproductive success for those who benefit from globalization, yielding a positive characteristic if the individual chooses to be pro-globalization. We use $\beta_{pro}^{benefit} = 1$ to represent this characteristic. However, if the individual chooses to be anti-globalization, they do not benefit from it, and their reproductive success is purely determined by other factors. We use $\beta_{anti}^{benefit} = 0$ to represent this characteristic.

For those who are harmed by globalization, choosing to be anti-globalization and supporting policies that limit it can promote their reproductive success when the level of globalization is high. Therefore, they have a positive characteristic, $\beta_{anti}^{harm} = 1$. In contrast, when they choose to be pro-globalization, their reproductive success is purely determined by other factors: $\beta_{pro}^{harm} = 0$.

To summarize, we use the superscript 'benefit' or 'harm' to represent these two kinds of individuals, and their reproductive success is determined by:

$$
\begin{aligned}
x_{\text{anti}}^{\text{benefit}} &= \lambda_{\text{other}}, & x_{\text{anti}}^{\text{harm}} &= \lambda_{\text{glob}} \\
x_{\text{pro}}^{\text{benefit}} &= \lambda_{\text{glob}}, & x_{\text{pro}}^{\text{harm}} &= \lambda_{\text{other}}
\end{aligned}
. \tag{10.3}
$$

An individual's behaviour is characterized by their probability, p, to choose action 'anti-globalization' (see Chapter 4 for formal definitions). We have the following result characterizing the growth-optimal behaviour in this example:

Proposition 10.1 *Under Assumptions 4.1 and 4.2 and the environment specified by Equations (10.1) and (10.2), the population growth rate in Equation (4.3) can be evaluated explicitly as*

$$
\begin{aligned}
\alpha^{\text{benefit}}(p) &= q\log(4-2p)+(1-q)\log(1+p) \\
\alpha^{\text{harm}}(p) &= q\log(2+2p)+(1-q)\log(2-p)
\end{aligned}
, \tag{10.4}
$$

and the behaviour (value of p) that maximizes this growth rate is:

$$
p^{\text{benefit}} = \begin{cases} 1 & \text{if } q \le \frac{1}{3} \\ 2-3q & \text{if } \frac{1}{3} < q < \frac{2}{3}, \\ 0 & \text{if } q \ge \frac{2}{3} \end{cases} \tag{10.5}
$$

$$
p^{\text{harm}} = \begin{cases} 0 & \text{if } q \le \frac{1}{3} \\ 3q-1 & \text{if } \frac{1}{3} < q < \frac{2}{3}. \\ 1 & \text{if } q \ge \frac{2}{3} \end{cases} \tag{10.6}
$$

We plot p^{benefit} and p^{harm} in Fig. 10.1. As the average degree of globalization (q) increases, the growth-optimal behaviour for individuals who benefit from globalization (p^{benefit}) (i.e. lean pro-globalization) decreases, while the the growth-optimal behaviour for individuals who are harmed by globalization (p^{harm}) (i.e. lean anti-globalization) increases. This is due to the fact that as selection pressure on the globalization factor increases, these two groups of individuals are forced by the environment to choose the political views that benefit their respective interests (i.e. reproductive success).

This example illustrates a primitive form of polarization. When the average degree of globalization is either too low or too high, two distinct groups of individuals emerge. They coexist through the evolutionary process, but within each group, individuals share the same characteristics. A particular behaviour must be paired with a particular set of characteristics to achieve the optimal growth rate. Note that the individuals in Equations (10.5) and (10.6) are optimal only in the group sense. In fact, from any individual's perspective, the survival-maximizing behaviour is to always choose the action with higher average reproductive success ($p = 0$ or 1). The continuous spectrum of growth-optimal behaviours in Fig. 10.1 only emerges because a group possesses survival benefits above and beyond an individual. In our framework, these benefits arise purely from stochastic environments with systematic risk.[7]

The usual conception of group selection in the evolutionary biology literature is that natural selection acts at the level of the group, instead of at the more conventional level of the individual (or the gene), and that interaction between members within each group is much more frequent than interaction among individuals across groups. In this case, similar individuals are usually clustered geographically. However, in our model, individuals do not interact at all. Nevertheless, the fact that individuals with the same behaviour generate offspring with like behaviour makes them more likely to cluster geographically and *appear* as a group, as described in Chapter 4.

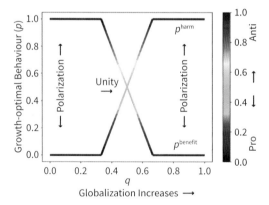

Fig. 10.1 Growth-optimal behaviour for individuals who benefit from globalization ($p^{benefit}$), and for individuals who are harmed by globalization (p^{harm}). The horizontal axis shows the probability q in Equation (10.1). The vertical axis and the colour bar show the growth-optimal behaviour, p^*, in different environments parameterized by q. Blue indicates the pro-globalization action, while brown indicates the anti-globalization action.

---

[7] See Chapters 2 and 6 for more discussions about individual versus group optimality, where the stochastic nature of the environment is key.

In reality, the environment is generally nonstationary. Factor distributions change over time, and old factors fade while new ones emerge. In fact, the change in the environment can itself be a consequence of previous adaptations. We see this in the history of globalization itself. From the Silk Road dating back to the second century BCE, to the World Trade Organization established in 1995, the course of globalization has always been fuelled by a number of historical factors, such as the desire to trade local goods for exotic products, or to gain access to cheap labour. Imagine that the environment, $(\lambda_{glob}, \lambda_{other})$, experiences a sudden shift. To an outside observer, behaviours among individuals in this population will become increasingly similar after the shift, creating the appearance—but not necessarily the reality—of intentional coordination, communication, and synchronization. If the reproductive cycle is sufficiently short, this change in population-wide behaviour may seem highly responsive to environmental changes, giving the impression that individuals are learning about their environment. This is, indeed, a form of learning, but it occurs at the population level—a form of collective learning—not at the individual level, and not within an individual's lifespan.

10.1.2 The General Case

The factor distribution in Equation (10.1) can be easily generalized to any arbitrary number of offspring:

$$\lambda_{glob} = \begin{cases} C_1 & \text{with probability } q \\ 1 & \text{with probability } 1 - q \end{cases}, \quad \lambda_{other} = \begin{cases} C_2 & \text{with probability } r \\ 1 & \text{with probability } 1 - r \end{cases}.$$

$$(10.7)$$

We assume, without loss of generality, that one of the outcomes for each factor yields exactly one offspring while the other is parameterized by C_1 and C_2, since it is the relative reproductive success between these two outcomes that matters. In addition, probabilities q and r parameterize the average level of the two factors. In Fig. 10.2 we show the growth-optimal behaviour for both the 'benefit' group and the 'harm' group, $f^{benefit}$ and f^{harm}, as functions of these environmental parameters.

Figure 10.2a shows the case with a moderate level of globalization over time ($q = 0.5$). The plot in the top row shows the growth-optimal behaviour for those who benefit from globalization ($f^{benefit}$). As the reproductive success for the globalization factor (C_1) increases, individuals tend to be pro

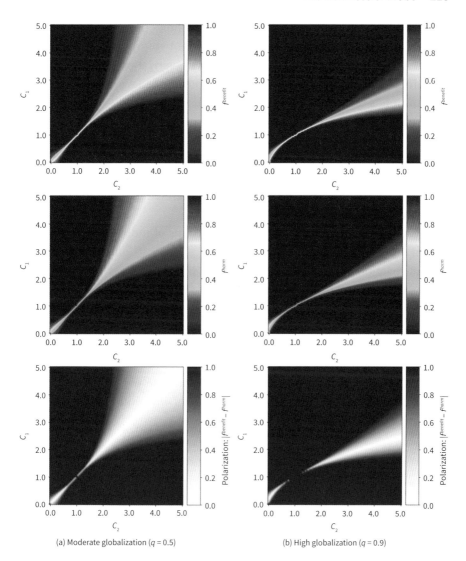

Fig. 10.2 Growth-optimal behaviours for both the 'benefit' group and the 'harm' group, $f^{benefit}$ and f^{harm}, as functions of environmental parameters. (a) Moderate globalization with $q = 0.5$. (b) High globalization with $q = 0.9$. The top row shows $f^{benefit}$; the middle row shows f^{harm}; the bottom row shows the absolute difference (i.e. polarization): $|f^{benefit} - f^{harm}|$.

(blue), but as the reproductive success for the other factor (C_2) increases, individuals tend to be anti (brown). The plot in the middle row shows the growth-optimal behaviour for those who are harmed by globalization (f^{harm}), which is the opposite of the behaviour for the 'benefit' group, in the sense that

$f^{\text{harm}} = 1 - f^{\text{benefit}}$. The plot in the bottom row shows the absolute difference between the growth-optimal behaviours of the two groups of individuals, $|f^{\text{benefit}} - f^{\text{harm}}|$, which is a simple measure of polarization. When the 'benefit' group and the 'harm' group show opposing behaviours, the level of polarization is high (dark blue).

Figure 10.2b shows the same set of growth-optimal behaviours when the average level of globalization is high ($q = 0.9$). Compared to the behaviours in Fig. 10.2a, when the average globalization shifts towards a higher level, behaviours also shift accordingly. As a result, the same environmental conditions (the region of the (C_1, C_2)-plane) that generated unity before may lead to polarization in this environment.

The simple example here considers two groups of individuals: those who benefit from globalization ($\beta^{\text{benefit}}_{\text{pro}} = 1, \beta^{\text{benefit}}_{\text{anti}} = 0$) and those harmed by globalization ($\beta^{\text{harm}}_{\text{pro}} = 0, \beta^{\text{harm}}_{\text{anti}} = 1$). In this stylized example, both groups coexist while different political views emerge. In reality, there is a spectrum—individuals in the population benefit from or are harmed by globalization to varying degrees. This corresponds to a continuum of characteristics (β) associated with globalization and 'other' factors. As a result, the population will consist of a more diverse set of political views, spanning the entire range from pro to anti. The ultimate political composition in the population is determined by the mix of individuals with different characteristics.

10.2 Bias and Discrimination

Our framework can also be used to understand the emergence of bias and discrimination, as well as to determine their underlying causes and what can be done to counteract these causes. We use racial discrimination as the main example of bias in this section, but the same principles apply more broadly to other kinds of bias and discrimination, including gender, sexual orientation, religion, socio-economic strata, and so on.

10.2.1 A Simple Example

We consider a hypothetical world with a population composed of two racial groups: a majority group, which we refer to as the 'Andorians', and a minority group, which we refer to as the 'Tellarians'. Group membership is unambiguous, mutually exclusive (an individual is a member of one and only one group), immutable, and observable by all.[8] Two factors determine each individual's reproductive success: λ_A and λ_T. They represent social interactions with Andorian and Tellarian individuals, respectively. An individual who interacts with Andorian individuals is subject to the Andorian factor, λ_A, whereas an individual who interacts with Tellarian individuals is subject to the Tellarian factor, λ_T. λ_A and λ_T are independent random variables with the following distributions:

$$\lambda_A = \begin{cases} 1 & \text{with probability } q \\ 2 & \text{with probability } 1 - q \end{cases}, \quad \lambda_T = \begin{cases} 1 & \text{with probability } r \\ 2 & \text{with probability } 1 - r \end{cases}.$$

$$(10.8)$$

Without loss of generality, we have assumed that each factor takes only two possible values: a low reproductive success of 1, which happens in the context of an adverse event related to that group,[9] and a high reproductive success of 2, which represents the normal case. Here, we use q and r to represent the probability of the adverse event for the Andorian and the Tellarian groups, respectively, which we refer to as the 'adverse probability' for simplicity. For example, with a (small) probability r, if an adverse event happens in an interaction with the Tellarian individual, anyone with an interaction with that individual will experience low reproductive success in that period.

Historically, the Tellarian community has been politically underrepresented, with less access to education and economic opportunity. As a result, this greater inequality has led to a higher crime rate for the Tellarian community compared to the average population. Note that the higher crime rate is not *because* of race, but the result of a complicated set of determinants, including less access to resources historically. However, in this model, individuals observe only each other's race, modelled here as group membership, which they use as a marker in the absence of any other information. The true underlying causes of higher crime rates, such as a lack of educational opportunity or socio-economic status, are assumed to be unobservable, a key assumption.

We now focus on the perspective of an Andorian, who faces a decision between one of two actions—whether or not to discriminate against a Tellarian—which determines their reproductive success. We assume that

---

[8] We have deliberately chosen to use fictitious races borrowed from science fiction to lower the tension that accompanies a discussion of these highly emotionally charged issues, and also to illustrate the generality of our analysis. In particular, our framework can be applied to any marginalized group.
[9] Examples of adverse events might include crimes, disease, or economic hardship, among others, as long as the adverse event represents a systematic factor for the particular group in consideration.

an Andorian's number of offspring is given by $x_{\text{discriminate}}$ if the individual chooses to discriminate, and $x_{\text{not discriminate}}$ if the individual chooses not to discriminate:

$$
\begin{aligned}
x_{\text{discriminate}} &= \lambda_A \\
x_{\text{not discriminate}} &= \beta\lambda_T + (1-\beta)\lambda_A
\end{aligned}. \tag{10.9}
$$

If an Andorian chooses to discriminate against a Tellarian, it avoids any interactions with that individual, and therefore its reproductive success will be subject only to λ_A. However, if an Andorian does not discriminate, its reproductive success is subject to both λ_T and λ_A. Here, β represents the percentage of Tellarians in the population, hence the weight on the factor λ_T.[10]

For a particular behaviour p (the probability to discriminate against a Tellarian), the population growth rate in Equation (4.3) is a function of the environment (i.e. the adverse probabilities, q and r) and the characteristic (β). In this simple case, as in the example of political polarization in the previous section, we can characterize the growth-optimal behaviour explicitly:

Proposition 10.2 *Under Assumptions 4.1 and 4.2 and the environment specified by Equations (10.8) and (10.9), the population growth rate can be evaluated explicitly as:*

$$\alpha(p) = q(1-r)\log(1+\beta-p\beta)+(1-q)r\log(1-\beta+p\beta)+(1-q)(1-r)\log(2-p), \tag{10.10}$$

and the behaviour (i.e. the value of p) that maximizes this growth rate is:

$$
p^* = \begin{cases}
1 & \text{if } r \geq \frac{2q}{1+q} \\
1 - \frac{qr-2q+r}{(2qr-q-r)\beta} & \text{if } \frac{(2-\beta)q}{(1-2\beta)q+(1+\beta)} < r < \frac{2q}{1+q} \\
0 & \text{if } r \leq \frac{(2-\beta)q}{(1-2\beta)q+(1+\beta)}
\end{cases}. \tag{10.11}
$$

Equation (10.11) is the behaviour that yields the highest growth rate and therefore characterizes the behaviour favoured by natural selection. Based on the definition in Equation (10.9), higher values of p^* correspond to more discriminatory behaviour. We plot p^* in Fig. 10.3 with two different population group percentages. Figure 10.3a shows a world with an equal number of Andorian and Tellarian individuals ($\beta = 0.5$), and Fig. 10.3b shows a world with only 20% Tellarians ($\beta = 0.2$).

---

[10] β is exogenous in our framework. However, one can consider extensions where the weights on the two factors, λ_T and λ_A, are, in turn, determined by the percentage of Tellarians in the population. This may generate time-varying patterns and cycles of discrimination levels in the population. We thank an anonymous reviewer for this point.

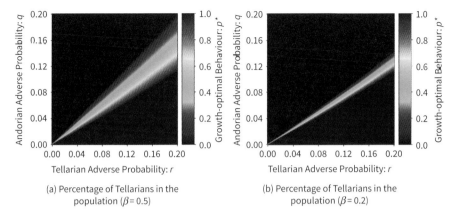

Fig. 10.3 Growth-optimal behaviours, p^*, as a function of environmental parameters. (a) Percentage of Tellarians in the population $\beta = 0.5$. (b) Percentage of Tellarians in the population $\beta = 0.2$.

In both cases, when the adverse probability associated with Tellarians (r) is low compared to the adverse probability associated with Andorians (q), no discrimination emerges. As r increases relative to the adverse probability for Andorians (q), discrimination emerges, that is, p^* increases from 0 to 1. This is because individuals who choose to avoid interactions with Tellarians gain an evolutionary advantage by reducing their exposure to the factor λ_T and the higher adverse probability, r, on average. This effect emerges from the fact that, in our model, race is the only observable marker of the individuals in the population and the true underlying causes of the higher adverse probability are not observable. This phenomenon is also referred to as statistical discrimination (Phelps, 1972; Arrow, 1973).

In addition, we can observe from the first case of Equation (10.11) that the environment leading to full discrimination ($p^* = 1$) does not depend on the percentage of Tellarians in the population (β). It is only a function of the adverse probability, q and r. This is also clear by comparing Fig. 10.3a to Fig. 10.3b. In both cases, when the adverse probability associated with Tellarians is high compared to that for Andorians ($r \geq \frac{2q}{1+q}$), full discrimination emerges.

However, when Tellarians are the minority ($\beta = 0.2$), the region where individuals have partially discriminatory behaviour shrinks (given by the middle case in Equation (10.11), where p^* is strictly between 0 and 1). This implies that when the group in consideration consists of a small fraction of the entire population, the boundary of the environmental conditions leading to no discrimination and full discrimination is sharper.

In our simple example, the key to the emergence of discrimination is the fact that race is the only observable feature of individuals. However, these implications will likely remain true even if other attributes of the individuals are partially observable, given the insight of the memory/prediction framework by Hawkins and Blakeslee (2004), who argue that we store memory patterns and use them to predict what will happen in the future. When individuals experience a random adverse event in association with a Tellarian, they tend to attribute it to the Tellarian's race, because it is the most easily observable marker, leading to discrimination against Tellarians. Based on a similar hypothesis, Bordalo et al. (2016) develop a model of stereotyping based on the representativeness heuristic (Tversky and Kahneman, 1983): agents overweight the prevalence of a trait in a group when that trait appears to be highly representative of the group in question. This is, however, not the root cause of the adverse event. In other words, it is much too easy to confuse correlation with causation.

We have seen that the difference in relative adverse probabilities, q and r, can lead to serious biases and discriminatory practices. Next, we are able to strengthen our results by showing that even when the two groups have equal probabilities of adverse events, or in certain cases when Tellarian individuals have a lower probability of adverse events than their Andorian counterparts, discrimination can still emerge.

10.2.2 Feedback Loops

Discrimination against Tellarians in the general population affects the Tellarian community adversely. For example, those individuals who participate in discriminatory behaviour against Tellarians may contact law enforcement more often, leading to a higher incidence of false accusations against the Tellarian community. They may develop more hostile behaviours towards the Tellarian community, reducing educational and economic opportunities for the Tellarian community, which further increases the probability of an adverse event associated with Tellarians.

Another less obvious type of feedback comes from the increasing popularity and prevalence of engagement-based recommender systems on news and social media platforms. When presented with new information (which may be a news broadcast or a social media post), humans tend to anchor towards what they originally believe (Tversky and Kahneman, 1974). As a result, even a small initial bias acquired randomly can be reinforced and amplified through feedback based on a recommender algorithm.

To incorporate this feedback loop into our model, we make the following assumption:

Assumption 10.1 *Factor λ_T's distribution in generation T is given by:*

$$\lambda_T = \begin{cases} 1 & \text{with probability } \tilde{r} \equiv r(1 + \tau \bar{p}_{T-1}), \\ 2 & \text{with probability } 1 - \tilde{r} \end{cases} \tag{10.12}$$

where $\bar{p}_{T-1}$ represents the average behaviour in the population in the previous generation, $T - 1$.

When the level of bias is higher in the population (i.e. when $\bar{p}_{T-1}$ is higher), the adverse probability associated with Tellarians ($\tilde{r}$) is higher. Here, τ represents the intensity of the feedback effect. For example, when $\tau = 1$, the adverse probability is, at most, twice when everyone discriminates against Tellarians, compared to when no one discriminates. A higher value of τ implies higher multiples of this effect.

Note that the factors in Equation (10.8) are identically distributed over time. In other words, they do not depend on time or on realizations of the past evolution of results. In contrast, the factor in Equation (10.12) introduces path dependency into the evolutionary process, because it depends on the past realizations of population behaviour. As a result, λ_T is no longer stationary over time. This simple change generates a surprisingly rich set of new implications.

We first use simulation methods to develop an intuition for the effect of different intensities of negative feedback. We consider a world that starts from an equal number of individuals in the population with eleven different behaviours: $p \in \{0, 1/10, 2/10, \cdots, 1\}$. Figure 10.4 shows the evolution of the relative frequency of these behaviours over 10,000 generations, given different environmental conditions.

Figures 10.4a–10.4c depict simulations of an environment with equal adverse probabilities for Tellarians and Andorians ($q = r = 0.2$), with the feedback intensity, τ, increasing from 0 (no feedback) to 1 (the adverse probability is doubled with full discrimination in the population).[11] Figure 10.4a corresponds to an environment with no feedback, and the behaviour $p^* = 0$ (no discrimination) quickly dominates the population. This also corresponds to the growth-optimal behaviour in the upper right corner of Fig. 10.3a. As the feedback intensity increases to $\tau = 0.6$, as shown in Fig. 10.4b, positive p^*

---

[11] For this set of simulations, we fix the fraction of the Tellarian population at $\beta = 0.5$.

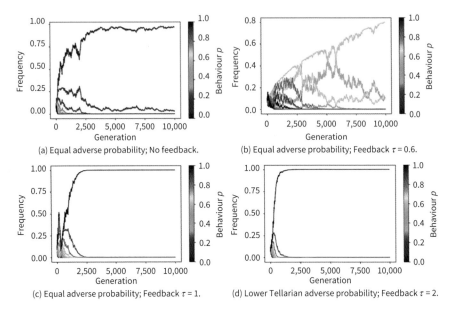

(a) Equal adverse probability; No feedback.
(b) Equal adverse probability; Feedback $\tau = 0.6$.
(c) Equal adverse probability; Feedback $\tau = 1$.
(d) Lower Tellarian adverse probability; Feedback $\tau = 2$.

Fig. 10.4 The evolution of eleven behaviours, $p \in \{0, 1/10, 2/10, \cdots, 1\}$, over 10,000 generations. The vertical axis represents the relative frequency of each behaviour, and the horizontal axis represents time. (a) Equal adverse probability ($q = r = 0.2$), no feedback $\tau = 0$; (b) equal adverse probability ($q = r = 0.2$), mild feedback ($\tau = 0.6$); (c) equal adverse probability ($q = r = 0.2$), more feedback ($\tau = 1$); (d) lower Tellarian adverse probability ($q = 0.2, r = 0.15$), even more feedback ($\tau = 2$).

(partial discrimination) emerges. Finally, as the feedback intensity increases to $\tau = 1$, as shown in Fig. 10.4c, $p^* = 1$ (full discrimination) quickly dominates the population.

In addition, Fig. 10.4d illustrates an environment in which Tellarians have a lower probability of an adverse event than Andorians ($r < q$). Given conditions of strong feedback ($\tau = 2$), fully discriminatory behaviour ($p^* = 1$) still dominates the population. This is because the feedback intensity is so high that discrimination quickly worsens the adverse probability for the Tellarian population, leading to severe discrimination against the population, despite the fact that the Tellarian population starts with a more favourable adverse probability.[12]

More generally, despite the challenging complexities of a nonstationary and path-dependent environment created by the feedback mechanism, we can analytically quantify the growth-optimal behaviour, p^*, implicitly. The factor with feedback in Equation (10.12) is mathematically equivalent to the simple environment we considered in Equation (10.8), except that the adverse

---

[12] Readers may wonder why the nondiscriminatory behaviour ($p^* = 0$) cannot persist in this case, which will become clear as we discuss the notion of locally evolutionarily stable strategies below.

probability associated with Tellarians, r, is replaced by the feedback-adjusted adverse probability, $\tilde{r}$. Therefore, a behaviour can survive in the long run only when it satisfies the growth-optimal condition in Equation (10.11), with r replaced by the feedback-adjusted $\tilde{r}$. Thus, we have:

Proposition 10.3 *Under Assumptions 4.1, 4.2, and 10.1, and the environment specified by Equation (10.9), the growth-optimal behaviour, p^*, with feedback must satisfy the following fixed-point condition:*

$$p^* = \text{Bound}_0^1\left(1 - \frac{q\tilde{r} - 2q + \tilde{r}}{(2q\tilde{r} - q - \tilde{r})\beta}\right) = \text{Bound}_0^1\left(1 - \frac{(q+1)r(1 + \tau p^*) - 2q}{[(2q-1)r(1+\tau p^*) - q]\beta}\right),$$

(10.13)

where $\text{Bound}_0^1(x) = \max(0, \min(1, x))$ *represents a function that bounds the behaviour to lie within the closed unit interval.*

Equation (10.13) is a necessary, but insufficient, condition for any behaviour to survive in the long run. Due to its nonlinearity, the growth-optimal behaviour, p^*, implied by Equation (10.13) may not be unique for some environments. However, without intervention, only one behaviour is stable and able to persist in each environment, for which we need to define the new notion of a L-ESS.

10.2.3 Locally Evolutionarily Stable Strategies

An evolutionarily stable strategy (ESS), first introduced by Maynard Smith and Price (1973),[13] is a strategy that is impermeable to other strategies when adopted by a population in adaptation to a specific environment. In other words, it cannot be displaced by an alternative strategy, which may be novel or initially rare. In game-theoretical terms, an ESS is an equilibrium refinement of the Nash equilibrium concept, given that a Nash equilibrium is also 'evolutionarily stable'. Once fixed in a population, natural selection alone is sufficient to prevent alternative (or mutant) strategies from replacing it.

We define a L-ESS to be one that is stable locally. In other words, it is a strategy that cannot be displaced by any local perturbation of that strategy.[14]

---

[13] See also Maynard Smith (1982).

[14] There is also a large literature in evolutionary biology on the local properties and stability for ESSs, including convergence stability (Christiansen, 1991), neighbourhood invader strategy (Apaloo, 1997), frequency-dependent ESS (Pohley and Thomas, 1983), evolutionarily singular strategies (Geritz et al., 1998), and sets of equilibrium strategies (Thomas, 1985). See Apaloo, Brown, and Vincent (2009) for a comparison of these concepts. We thank Steve A. Frank for bringing this to our attention.

Definition 10.1 *A L-ESS behaviour, p^*, is one for which any local perturbation in the average population behaviour $\{\bar{p}: \bar{p} = p^* + \epsilon\}$ leads to a growth-optimal behaviour, p', as given by Equation (10.11), that is closer to p^* than $\bar{p}: |p' - p^*| < |\epsilon|$.*

In other words, when randomness in the environment causes the average behaviour of the population, $\bar{p}$, to change around the growth-optimal behaviour, p^*, the perturbed $\bar{p}$ will lead to a new behaviour that is very close to the original growth-optimal behaviour. As a result, natural selection itself will always bring the population back to the original growth-optimal behaviour, p^*. In this sense, such behaviours are locally stable from an evolutionary perspective.

The L-ESS is an additional requirement to the growth-optimal behaviour, p^*, implied by the fixed-point condition in Equation (10.13). Without intervention, only L-ESS behaviours can persist in the long run. When there is no or little feedback in the environment (i.e. when τ is small), behaviours implied by Equation (10.13) are always L-ESS. However, as the feedback intensity increases, non-L-ESS behaviours can emerge.

Figure 10.5 shows an environment with strong feedback intensity ($\tau = 2$). Recall that the nonlinearity of the fixed-point condition in Equation (10.13) can lead to multiple solutions of p^*, and we compare the L-ESS (Figure 10.5a) and non-L-ESS behaviours (Figure 10.5b). The dashed triangular regions[15] represent the set of environments where the fixed-point condition in Equation (10.13) leads to one L-ESS and one non-L-ESS behaviour. In this region, the non-L-ESS behaviours are less discriminatory, and the strong feedback intensity nudges the population to evolve towards fully discriminatory behaviours.

In addition, Fig. 10.5c shows the differences in population growth rates between the L-ESS behaviour and the non-L-ESS behaviour. We refer to this as the 'L-ESS excess growth rate':

L-ESS excess growth rate

$$= \begin{cases} \alpha\left(p^*_{\text{L-ESS}}\right) - \alpha\left(p^*_{\text{non-L-ESS}}\right) & \text{if Equation (10.13) yields multiple solutions} \\ 0 & \text{otherwise} \end{cases}.$$

$$(10.14)$$

---

[15] The left boundary is not, strictly speaking, linear, but we refer to the region as triangular for simplicity.

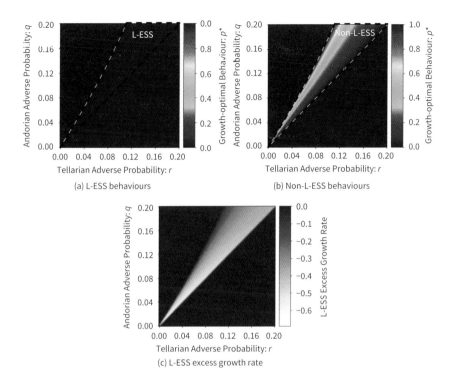

Fig. 10.5 Comparison of L-ESS and non-L-ESS behaviours for an environment with strong feedback intensity ($\tau = 2$). (a) L-ESS growth-optimal behaviours implied by the fixed-point Equation (10.13); (b) non-L-ESS growth-optimal behaviours if the fixed-point Equation (10.13) yields multiple solutions, otherwise we plot the unique solution from Equation (10.13) which is L-ESS; (c) L-ESS excess growth rate as defined in Equation (10.14), which is the difference in growth rates between the L-ESS behaviour and the non-L-ESS behaviour.

Proposition 10.4 *Under Assumptions 4.1, 4.2, and 10.1, and the environment specified by Equation (10.9), if Equation (10.13) yields multiple solutions where the L-ESS behaviour is more discriminatory than the non-L-ESS behaviour ($p^*_{\text{L-ESS}} > p^*_{\text{non-L-ESS}}$), the L-ESS excess growth rate is always negative, which means that the L-ESS behaviour will always yield a lower growth rate than non-L-ESS behaviour.*

This example demonstrates that path dependency can lead to evolutionary outcomes with slower growth rates than otherwise achievable, and the population ends up with a suboptimal growth rate compared to a world without feedback.

In the context of our model, L-ESS behaviour implies that the Andorian individual will always avoid any interaction with the Tellarian individual, a state of collective ignorance that could otherwise be improved with greater diversity in the population.[16]

10.2.4   Feedback Can Lead to Greater Bias

With our understanding of L-ESS behaviour, we can now finally show the variation in growth-optimal behaviour in environments with different feedback intensities. We have the following intuitive but important result:

Proposition 10.5 *Under Assumptions 4.1, 4.2, and 10.1, and the environment specified by Equation (10.9), as the feedback intensity, τ, increases, discriminatory behaviours are more likely to emerge, in the sense that they dominate the population for increasingly larger regions of environmental conditions, as parameterized by the adverse probabilities, q and r, for the Andorian and Tellarian groups, respectively.*

Figure 10.6 shows L-ESS behaviours for different levels of feedback intensity and demonstrates Proposition 10.5. As τ increases from 0 (Fig. 10.6a) to 2 (Fig. 10.6d), discriminatory behaviours dominate the population for increasingly larger regions of environmental conditions. When feedback is absent from these evolutionary dynamics (Fig. 10.6a), discrimination only emerges when Tellarians have a higher probability of adverse events than Andorians. However, when the feedback intensity is high (Figs 10.6c and 10.6d), full discrimination prevails, even in environments where the adverse probability for Tellarians is lower than that for Andorians.

These results emphasize the central role feedback plays in the emergence of bias and discrimination. By combining the observation that individuals tend to associate the occurrence of random adverse events to the only observable characteristic, race, along with the negative feedback from those random adverse events, our model has demonstrated the power of these forces in generating widespread bias and discrimination in the population.

These results also shed light on the evolutionary dynamics behind the emergence of biases not only towards the Tellarian community (which is, of course, fictional), but also other forms of bias and discrimination. From

---

[16] For example, Jones, Dovidio, and Vietze (2013) document that sharing varied perspectives, talents, and worldviews is beneficial to human interaction and institutional performance. They also demonstrate the resistance elicited in response to diversity, and the benefits that arise when it is overcome.

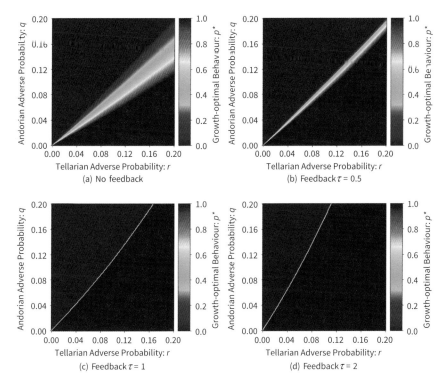

Fig. 10.6 L-ESS behaviours, p^*, as a function of environmental parameters, when there is feedback. The feedback intensity, τ, increases from 0 in (a) to 2 in (d).

the policy perspective, these results emphasize the importance of preventing the effects of negative feedback in the greater population. For example, by proactively providing more educational and economic opportunities among disadvantaged groups. This does not directly eliminate the negative feedback, but will indirectly help to reduce its impact by elevating their socio-economic status and reducing their adverse probabilities. Another example is to enforce regulations that cut through such (sometimes unconscious) negative feedback mechanisms. These actions together will create more favourable environments for collective intelligence to emerge rather than allowing collective ignorance to propagate, and can potentially reduce, and eventually reverse, selection pressure behind the emergence of bias and discrimination.

10.2.5 Path-Dependent Evolution

When feedback loops exist in the environment, evolution may become path dependent. Therefore, the dominant behaviour that emerges in a given population will sometimes depend on the initial composition of that population. We consider evolution in populations that begin with nonuniform initial distributions of behaviours in this section.

Figure 10.7 demonstrates that different initial populations can lead to different growth-optimal behaviours. Like the simulations illustrated in Fig. 10.4, we simulate the evolution of eleven behaviours, $p \in \{0, 1/10, 2/10, \cdots, 1\}$, for an environment with equal adverse probabilities for the Tellarian and Andorian populations ($q = r = 0.2$), and with a feedback intensity $\tau = 1$.

We use n_0 to denote the frequency of different behaviours in the initial population. Figure 10.7a shows the evolution for an initial population with little bias: $n_0 = (0.8, 0.02, 0.02, \cdots, 0.02)$. In other words, 80% of the initial population starts with no discrimination ($p = 0$). In contrast, Fig. 10.7b shows the evolution for an initial population with a substantial amount of bias: $n_0 = (0.02, 0.02, \cdots, 0.02, 0.8)$; hence, 80% of the initial population starts

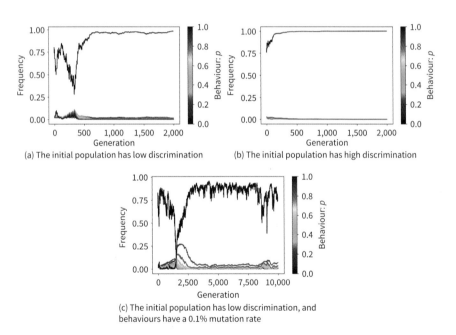

(a) The initial population has low discrimination

(b) The initial population has high discrimination

(c) The initial population has low discrimination, and
behaviours have a 0.1% mutation rate

Fig. 10.7 Path dependency of evolution in an environment with equal adverse probability ($q = r = 0.2$) and feedback $\tau = 1$. We show the evolution of behaviours $p \in \{0, 1/10, 2/10, \cdots, 1\}$ over time, with different starting populations. The vertical axis represents the relative frequency of each behaviour, and the horizontal axis represents time. (a) The initial population has low discrimination, $n_0 = (0.8, 0.02, 0.02, \cdots, 0.02)$; (b) the initial population has high discrimination, $n_0 = (0.02, 0.02, \cdots, 0.02, 0.8)$; (c) the initial population has low discrimination, $n_0 = (0.8, 0.02, 0.02, \cdots, 0.02)$, and behaviours have a 0.1% mutation rate.

with fully discriminatory behaviour ($p = 1$). Unsurprisingly, $p = 0$ dominates the population in the former case, whereas $p = 1$ dominates in the latter.

When the initial population is nonuniform, some behaviours may quickly become extinct before they have a chance to spread. In fact, if we allow a small amount of mutation in each generation—modelled as in Chapter 3 (i.e. with some small probability e.g. 0.1%, that offspring of type-p parents will be, in fact, type $p' \neq p$ where p' is uniformly distributed in $[0, 1] - \{p\}$)— discrimination will again dominate, even if the initial population begins with very little bias. Figure 10.7c shows such an example.[17]

This result underscores the fact that public policy may be able to guide a society towards different outcomes by purposefully imposing a strong prior belief onto the population. This may be achievable by encouraging fairer beliefs through early education, and by providing more accurate portrayals of other cultures to counteract inaccurate stereotypes. From the perspective of our binary choice model, these policies would nudge the initial population such that its subsequent evolution may lead to a less discriminatory society collectively.

10.3 Practical Implications

The key to preventing the failures of collective intelligence lies in the environment. Our results imply that potential policy interventions should focus on environmental changes that will facilitate adaptation towards collective intelligence rather than collective ignorance. These potential interventions include reducing the gap of economic success between groups for people with different exposures to these broadly considered environmental factors, in order to encourage harmony and reduce the chances of polarization, and to equalize reproductive success in the evolutionary sense. Concrete examples include (re)-education, providing employment opportunities when macroeconomic factors shift industry landscapes, and encouraging more accurate beliefs among current and future generations through early education to nudge the initial beliefs in the population.

Our results on bias and discrimination also imply that incentives (and, if necessary, regulations) should focus on preventing negative feedback loops, whether caused by our natural cognitive tendencies or as an unintended consequence of the development of recommender-systems-based social media

---

[17] See Chapter 3 for a more detailed discussion of the role mutation plays in the context of the binary choice model.

and information technology. Proactively providing educational and economic opportunities among disadvantaged groups can also counteract negative feedback loops by elevating their socio-economic status and reducing their adverse probabilities. These policies will create more favourable environments for collective intelligence to emerge, and can potentially reduce, and eventually reverse, selection pressure behind the emergence of collective ignorance.

However, simply regulating against the undesired outcome is likely to be less effective. Continuing with our example of Andorians and Tellarians, if bias and discrimination already exist against the Tellarians, an obvious policy may be simply to criminalize such discrimination. This can lead to more forced interactions between the Andorians and the Tellarians, which, in turn, causes everyone to have a higher factor exposure to the Tellarians. However, as bias already exists in the population (since the Tellarians will have a higher probability of adverse events either initially or through negative feedback loops), this will lead to more Andorians experiencing adverse events from their interactions with Tellarians, inevitably leading to even stronger negative feedback (and even higher adverse probabilities) for the Tellarians— a cognitive tendency that is difficult to change, as Hawkins and Blakeslee's (2004) framework shows. As a result, direct attempts to outlaw bias and discrimination against the Tellarians may actually make matters worse.

A similar situation can happen in the context of political polarization due to unequal exposure to globalization. It is tempting to simply condemn or even ban particular groups with certain political views. However, this does not solve the fundamental cause of the emergence of such groups, and may even create more negative feedback for these individuals because of a similar mechanism that generates bias. Another, more extreme, policy response would be to shut down globalization altogether, which is also unlikely to be constructive because it merely shifts who benefits and who is harmed. Groups of individuals will likely emerge again in the new environment with strongly polarized beliefs if policy does not proactively help those who are harmed by the new environment.

These simple examples illustrate how seemingly well-intended policies can create more selective pressure for collective ignorance to emerge. The fundamental reason is that they are addressing the symptoms, not the root cause, of these failures of collective intelligence. We do not model the objective function policymakers should use for managing societal issues such as polarization and discrimination, but implicit in our framework is the reproductive success of different types of individuals that determines their survival. Therefore, as representatives of a given group of constituents, policymakers can reasonably be expected to focus on what improves the long-term reproductive success (in the economic sense) of those constituents. Our evolutionary framework provides a lens through which the underlying causes—the environment in which these failures emerge—can be identified so as to construct more productive policies.

Using history as a mirror, these implications are even more relevant now as we begin to experience the artificial intelligence (AI) revolution we believe is currently in progress (Makridakis, 2017; Diamandis and Kotler, 2020). Just as in the Industrial Revolution 200 years ago, and modern globalization over the last fifty years, the AI revolution will increase productivity in aggregate, while inevitably leading to another major shift in the industrial landscape and composition of the labour market. In this process, some individuals will benefit, while others may be harmed. The policy suggestions outlined in this chapter, including re-education for those whose jobs have been replaced by AI, and providing children with equal access to education, particularly in STEM (science, technology, engineering, and mathematics) and AI-related subjects, are more pressing than ever.

10.4 Discussion

Our binary choice model is able to yield collective intelligence in the form of sophisticated rational behaviours that emerge out of an initially uniform set of behaviours (Chapters 2 and 8). At the same time, within the same model, we can also specify conditions under which this collective intelligence breaks down, especially under conditions where agents face correlated reproductive success, or there is path-dependent feedback. This helps us understand the emergence of political polarization, bias, and racial discrimination, all of which exemplify the failure of collective intelligence.

More broadly, these evolutionary principles have the potential to offer fundamental insights into the behavioural primitives of many complex adaptive systems. This includes economic and financial systems, as described by the AMH (Lo, 2004, 2005, 2012, 2017). The 'animal spirits' of our economy that Keynes (1936) singled out eight decades ago as a factor affecting the macroeconomy are still highly relevant today, and our evolutionary framework offers a formal description that extends this idea to broader contexts.

Some of the biggest challenges facing humanity will only be solved through a collective and global effort. They include not only political polarization and discrimination, but also climate change, economic and social inequality, and the spread of disinformation. The model developed here is by no means a complete description of reality. Even a partial description would involve the interplay between sophisticated human behaviour and highly complex nonstationary environments with multiple unknown factors. However, our framework offers a starting point for describing and understanding the fundamental principles behind the emergence of these failures of collective intelligence.

The insight that negative feedback leads to bias and discrimination applies to any group whose members are identifiable by an observable marker that cannot easily be changed or hidden (e.g. race, gender, family history, etc.). The simple idea that 'the enemy of an enemy is a friend' implies that we humans tend to form groups based on antipathies, sometimes unconsciously, through the force of natural selection, and such alliances can often reduce our collective intelligence even as they increase the chances that the group survives.

Another example of the failure of collective intelligence that our model may help to explain is the spread of disinformation and belief polarization (Haghtalab, Jackson, and Procaccia, 2021). This is closely related to political polarization and racial discrimination because the spread of disinformation facilitates the formation of these biases. With the advent and popularity of engagement-based recommender systems on news and social media platforms, disinformation has a much greater chance of propagating across the population. One of the great insights of Tversky and Kahneman (1974) is that humans tend to anchor towards their original beliefs. When first presented with new information, either through a news service, or simply a tweet, regardless of its authenticity, there will always be a group of people who happen to share a similar belief, even if that belief is false. Regardless of the initially small size of this group, through engagement-based recommendations, their beliefs can be reinforced rapidly throughout the population. This effect, in turn, will cause recommender algorithms to serve up similar information more frequently, reinforcing these false beliefs in a vicious cycle.

The COVID-19 pandemic has accelerated the adoption of collective online decision-making across geographical locations. Consequently, it is now more important than ever to make sure we have the right tools and the right environment in which the wisdom of crowds can emerge naturally and forestall the madness of mobs.

Having shown how evolutionary forces can easily give rise to a variety of behaviours—both rational and otherwise—we now turn to how these behaviours are encoded in our biology. Part III, entitled 'Neurons', explores the neurophysiology of financial decision-making. We begin with an overview in Chapter 11 of how the human brain works and what its architecture implies for financial crises. We then narrow our focus to financial decisions at the level of individual traders in Chapters 12 and 13 using psychophysiological and survey tools. These results provide a more complex, but more complete, map of human decision-making, and a deeper understanding of the role that selection and adaption play, even within a single decision maker.

PART III

NEURONS

11

Fear, Greed, and Financial Crises

In March 1933, unemployment in the US was at an all-time high.[1] Over 4,000 banks had failed during the previous two months. Bread lines stretched around entire blocks in the largest cities. The country was in the grip of the Great Depression. This was the context in which Franklin Delano Roosevelt (FDR) delivered his first inaugural address to the American people as the thirty-second president of the US. He began his address not by discussing economic conditions, or by laying out his proposal for the 'New Deal', but with a powerful observation that still resonates today: 'So, first of all, let me assert my firm belief that the only thing we have to fear is fear itself— nameless, unreasoning, unjustified terror which paralyzes needed efforts to convert retreat into advance.' Nearly a century later, these words are still more relevant than FDR could ever have imagined, given the financial crisis of 2008, the recurring US debt ceiling showdowns and associated political stale-mates, and the gyrations of financial markets in response to the COVID-19 pandemic.

Even a cursory review of expansive histories of past crises such as Kindle-berger's (1978) classic and Reinhart and Rogoff's (2009) more recent defini-tive treatise suggests a common origin for all financial bubbles and busts: fear and greed. A period of unchecked greed leads to unsustainable asset price lev-els, while the inevitable price decline ushers in a period of unbridled fear. The broader the participation in the growth of the bubble, the deeper the impact on the real economy, due to the number of households affected by the bubble bursting. In this chapter, we focus squarely on this boom-and-bust cycle by examining the behavioural underpinnings of financial crisis.

The importance of human behaviour to financial markets and economic affairs is not a new idea. Keynes (1936) observed over eight decades ago that economic decisions were due more to 'animal spirits' than carefully weighed probabilities, and that financial markets operated more like beauty contests than efficient price discovery platforms. However, despite the early successes of Keynesian macroeconomics, the dominance of the rational expectations school of thought has left little room for animal spirits in the policymaker's

---

[1] This chapter is adapted from Lo (2013).

The Adaptive Markets Hypothesis. Andrew W. Lo and Ruixun Zhang, Oxford University Press.
© Andrew W. Lo and Ruixun Zhang (2024). DOI: 10.1093/oso/9780199681143.003.0011

toolkit. One of the few positive consequences of the financial crisis of 2008 is the realization that the current approach to measuring and managing systemic risk in the financial system is inadequate, and that policymakers need a broader intellectual framework.

We propose to provide such a framework by exploring the neuroscientific underpinnings of human behaviour, particularly those behaviours most relevant to financial stability. If fear and greed are the key drivers of all financial crises, then a better understanding of how the brain produces these behaviours may eventually allow us to formulate more effective policies to manage their consequences. For example, neuroscientists have shown that monetary gain stimulates the same reward circuitry as cocaine—in both cases, dopamine is released into the nucleus accumbens. Similarly, the threat of financial loss apparently activates the same fight-or-flight response as a physical attack, releasing adrenaline and cortisol into the bloodstream, resulting in elevated heart rate, blood pressure, and alertness. These reactions are hardwired into human physiology, and while we are often able to overcome our biology through education, experience, or genetic good luck during normal market conditions, under more emotionally charged circumstances, the vast majority of the human population will behave in largely predictable ways. This neurophysiological basis for Keynes's animal spirits has important implications for regulatory reform, including the need for path-dependent and adaptive capital requirements and leverage constraints, more accurate and timely measures of systemic risk so regulators and market participants can respond appropriately, and more direct feedback loops between policies and outcomes that will enhance our collective intelligence through reinforcement learning.

To develop this cognitive neurosciences perspective of financial crises, we begin in Section 11.1 with a brief history of our understanding of the brain, which was surprisingly primitive until quite recently. Of course, the brain is extraordinarily complex, so, by necessity, we have to narrow our focus to just those components that are most relevant for our purposes: fear, greed (or its close complement, pleasure), risk preferences, rationality, and the various combinations of these elements. In Section 11.2, we describe fear learning and the amygdala, one of the most important neural components of financial crises. In Section 11.3, we turn to the neural mechanisms most closely associated with the build up of bubbles—pleasure and greed—and show how the adaptiveness of neural systems for reward and punishment makes crises virtually unavoidable. This tendency is spelled out more clearly in Section 11.4, which is devoted to the effects of risk on decision-making, which are predictable and, in the case of rogue traders, often disastrous. Too much emotion can trigger irrational behaviour, but so can too little emotion, and in Section 11.5 we describe a definition of rationality from the perspective of the neurosciences that is radically different from the economic notion of rational expectations, the difference hinging critically on the unique role of emotion. The mechanisms described in Sections 11.2–11.5 all refer to individual behaviour, but in Section 11.6, we explore the impact of social interactions through the neurophysiology of mirror neurons, brain cells dedicated to allowing others to 'feel your pain'. All of these neural components interact to produce intentions and actions, and, in Section 11.7, we describe some properties of the 'executive brain' in orchestrating the complexity of what we observe as human behaviour. This orchestration is unique to *Homo sapiens* and we place it in proper evolutionary context in Section 11.8. We consider the public policy implications of the neurosciences perspective in Section 11.9, and argue that one of the most important aspects of government and regulation is to protect ourselves from our own behavioural patterns by moderating the extremes of fear and greed. Section 11.10 concludes with some thoughts on the potential role that the cognitive neurosciences can play in financial economics.

11.1 A Brief History of the Brain

It seems obvious that a better understanding of the brain should lead to a better understanding of economic decision-making. Our subjective experience as human beings strongly suggests that we do not always act rationally or in our own self-interest. Under the influence of strong emotion or stress, or for no reason we can consciously pinpoint, we have all made decisions that we later regret. In the twenty-first century, we now know that thought takes place in the brain, through the interconnections of nerves, mediated by chemicals and electricity, even if we are unsure of the exact details. It seems eminently logical, then, that a better understanding of the brain would necessarily lead to a better understanding of how humans make economic decisions, just as a better understanding of the heart led William Harvey to discover how blood flows through the human body.

However, this understanding of the brain is a very new development in science. For decades, if not centuries, the study of economics has been more highly advanced than the study of the brain. Adam Smith sought to explain human behaviour in terms of our inner psychology, yet there was no way he could measure the moral sentiments he so eloquently described. As late as 1871, the British economist William Stanley Jevons could write (Jevons, 1871, pp. 13–14):

> I hesitate to say that men will ever have the means of measuring directly the feelings of the human heart. A unit of pleasure or of pain is difficult even to conceive; but it is the amount of these feelings which is continually prompting us to buying and selling, borrowing and lending, labouring and resting, producing and consuming; and *it is from the quantitative effects of the feelings that we must estimate their comparative amounts.*

Modern economics emerged under the assumption that the internal processes leading to an economic decision could *never* be directly measured. This assumption led to the ideas of revealed preference and utility theory, which still form the bedrock of modern microeconomics today.

In comparison, the scientific study of the brain would remain backwards. During Jevons's time, even the idea that nerves were composed of independent cells was still in doubt. This is surprising to us today, when children's books and prescription drug commercials routinely contain illustrations of neurons, admittedly sometimes fanciful, and how they work. It took the laboratory advances of the Italian pathologist Camillo Golgi and the close observations of the Spanish pathologist Santiago Ramón y Cajal to demonstrate the validity of the 'neuron theory', using state-of-the-art microscopic techniques for their time. Golgi and Ramón y Cajal were quickly honoured for their work, jointly winning the Nobel Prize in Physiology or Medicine in 1906. (Although Golgi himself was not a believer in neuron theory!)

In the same way, most scientists were sceptical that the brain contained specialized regions for different purposes until remarkably late in the scientific era. Today, we refer casually to 'speech centres' or 'visual centres', and it is natural for us to speculate if there is a particular part of the brain that assesses economic value or financial risk, but for much of the modern era, this would have sounded like nonsense to an educated person. This can be explained, in part, by the sociology of science. In the mid-eighteenth century, the Swedish philosopher Emanuel Swedenborg correctly described the specialized nature of the cerebral cortex, linking its structures of nerve fibres to their function, but Swedenborg was also known for his religious writings about dreams and angels (there is still a Swedenborg Chapel on the Harvard campus), and his hypothesis was ignored for decades (Finger, 1994). Meanwhile, the physiologist Franz Joseph Gall also believed that different parts of the brain had different functions; however, he believed that these were reflected in the external shape of the skull. This led to the pseudoscience of phrenology, through which one's personality could be determined by examining the bumps on one's head, a theory which was quite popular in the first half of the nineteenth century. Eventually, this discipline came into disrepute, creating a degree of scepticism by association for the heterogeneous nature of the brain.

This scepticism was slowly overturned in the nineteenth century, principally through the study of individuals with brain tumours, lesions, or other head injuries. One of the most famous cases was of a young New Hampshire man named Phineas Gage, who had an iron rod pass under his upper jaw and through the top of his head during a rock-blasting accident in the construction of the Rutland & Burlington Railroad in 1848. Gage survived and recovered from this horrific accident—well enough to later become a stagecoach driver in Chile—but his personality and habits changed markedly. Gage's case is especially interesting from an economic point of view. In the words of his doctor, writing several years after Gage's death, 'The equilibrium or balance, so to speak, between his intellectual faculties and animal propensities, seems to have been destroyed.' Before the accident, Gage was 'a shrewd, smart businessman, very energetic and persistent in executing all his plans of operation'. After the accident, however, Gage was 'impatient of restraint or advice when it conflicts with his desires, at times pertinaciously obstinate, yet capricious and vacillating, devising many plans of future operations, which are no sooner arranged than they are abandoned in turn for others appearing more feasible' (Harlow, 1868, 1974). It was as though an important component of Gage's ability to plan ahead *rationally* had been removed along with part of his brain.

As interesting as these hints to the brain's function were to medical researchers, they made very little impact on the field of economics. Even John Maynard Keynes, with his interest in medical psychology and psychiatry, could only invoke 'animal spirits' as a characteristic of human nature in 1936: 'a spontaneous urge to action rather than inaction, and not as the outcome of a weighted average of quantitative benefits multiplied by quantitative probabilities' (Keynes, 1936). While Keynes's animal spirits are an evocative metaphor against the concept of *Homo economicus*—rational economic man—they sound far too shaman-like to be satisfying as an explanation for human behaviour today.[2]

At the same time that neuroscience was developing a more detailed understanding of how the brain works, economic theory was becoming more

---

[2] Keynes himself took this term from the Scottish Enlightenment philosopher David Hume's *Enquiry Concerning Human Understanding*.

narrowly focused on models of perfectly rational behaviour, so much so that despite the intellectual merits of alternatives such as Herbert Simon's 'satisficing' theory of bounded rationality discussed in Chapter 8, the more mathematically sophisticated rational expectations school of thought pioneered by Muth (1961) and Lucas (1972) quickly became the dominant perspective of the economics profession in the 1960s and 1970s. The more empirical, foundational approach of the neurosciences had little appeal in that climate, and, despite the subsequent explosion of discoveries in the brain sciences, the two fields would have little to say to each other until the 1990s.

11.2 Fear

Several years ago, Robert Thompson, an airline pilot, stopped at a convenience store to pick up a few magazines, but he turned around and walked right out of the store that he had just entered because he felt afraid, even though, at the time, he could not understand why (de Becker, 1997). It turned out the store was being robbed at gunpoint, and, shortly after Thompson left, a police officer entered the store and was shot and killed. Only afterwards—with some thoughtful debriefing by Gavin de Becker, a public safety expert—did Thompson realize some of the things that may have triggered his discomfort: a customer wearing a heavy jacket despite the hot weather, the clerk's intense focus on that customer, and a single car with the engine running in the parking lot. But Thompson's decision to leave the store came almost instantaneously, long before he was even aware that he had observed anything unusual.

Fear of the unknown—FDR's 'nameless, unreasoning, unjustified terror'— is one of the most powerful motivating forces of our conscious and subconscious minds. Neuroscientists have demonstrated with remarkable detail that our fear circuitry is highly refined, in some cases reacting much faster than we can perceive. The fight-or-flight response, hardwired in all mammals, is just one example of the evolutionary mechanisms that have kept our species alive for the last 100,000 years.

To develop a deeper understanding of how fear works, we have to look inside the human brain, perhaps the most complicated structure known to science. Most estimates put the number of neurons in the brain at around 100 billion, not counting the many other important cell types found there.[3] Each neuron can have several thousand synapses sending signals to other

---

[3] See Williams and Herrup (1988). Of course, this is only an 'order of magnitude' estimate: the total number has never been physically counted.

cells, forming a dense network of interconnections between neurons. In comparison, the number of human beings that have ever lived is estimated to be substantially less than 100 billion. If the average person throughout history only made a few hundred personal connections in their lifetime (as seems likely), the extended social network of everyone who has ever lived is still much less complex than a single human brain.

The brain is not only complicated, but it is also extremely difficult to examine while functioning. It is, in effect, what the mathematician Norbert Wiener called a 'black box', an opaque system in which one can only examine the inputs and the outputs. For many years, information on how the black box functioned internally was scarce. Brain researchers could only rely on evidence from post-mortem neuroanatomy case studies after brain surgery or other head injuries like Phineas Gage, and ablation experiments, in which regions of the brain on rats, monkeys, and other model organisms are selectively destroyed surgically to see their impact, under the assumption that brain functions are similar in evolutionarily related species.

One such experiment took place in 1937, the year after Keynes made his pronouncement about animal spirits. Two researchers, the German émigré psychologist Heinrich Klüver and the American neurosurgeon Paul Bucy, were attempting to discover which areas of the brain were involved in the visual hallucinations caused by mescaline, the active chemical compound in peyote cactus. In one set of experiments, Bucy removed the temporal lobes of the lateral cerebral cortex of rhesus monkeys (in humans, this part of the brain is slightly above and behind the ears). Klüver and Bucy discovered something startling: the monkeys' ability to see was not impaired, but their ability to recognize objects was. 'The hungry animal, if confronted with a variety of objects, will, for example, indiscriminately pick up a comb, a Bakelite knob, a sunflower seed, a screw, a stick, a piece of apple, a live snake, a piece of banana, and a live rat. Each object is transferred to the mouth and then discarded if not edible' (Klüver and Bucy, 1937, p. 353). At the same time, the monkeys also lost their sense of fear, behaving calmly in the presence of humans and snakes. Klüver and Bucy called this behaviour 'psychic blindness'.[4] The monkeys apparently suffered no loss of visual acuity, but what they saw had lost the set of emotional and physical associations they previously conveyed.

This was a remarkable result—a particular part of the brain was responsible for mediating the emotional response to recognizing an object. We live in a world where image recognition by computers is becoming more common by the day, and we tend to think of it as an unemotional, purely

---

[4] Klüver and Bucy (1937). Klüver–Bucy syndrome was later found in humans, although it is very rare.

rational act. It would be disconcerting, to say the least, to discover that the software processing photographs of license plate numbers in speed traps triggered emotion-like responses based on the numbers it recognized—but this is what occurs in the brain. In fact, the brain appears to have several pathways that mediate emotion. Klüver and Bucy had fortuitously removed the part of the brain essential for linking memories to fear: the amygdala.

The amygdala is a small but distinct structure located deep within the brain. In humans, it is located roughly where a line entering one's eye and a line entering one's ear would intersect. Like most brain structures, the amygdala is paired. Early anatomists thought it resembled an almond, hence its name, *amygdala* (the Latinized form of the Greek word for 'almond'). Researchers following in Klüver and Bucy's footsteps suspected that it was involved in how the brain learned fear. It was not until the late 1970s, however, when the first neurophysiological studies used the technique of fear conditioning to examine the function of the amygdala.

Many people know the century-old story of Pavlov and his dogs: the Russian scientist would ring a bell while feeding his dogs, and the dogs became so conditioned to the sound of the bell that they would still salivate when Pavlov rang his bell, even when unfed. Fear conditioning involves replacing the unconditioned stimulus—in Pavlov's experiments, food—with a negative stimulus such as an electric shock. Conditioned fear learning is much faster than other forms of learning. It can take place even in a single session of linked stimuli, and, compared to other forms of learning, it is nearly indelible. There are sound evolutionary reasons for this asymmetry, and the same kind of fear conditioning has been found throughout the animal kingdom, not merely in mammals.

In 1979, Bruce Kapp and his team at the University of Vermont first published evidence that lesions on the central nucleus of the amygdala disrupted fear conditioning in rabbits (Kapp et al., 1979). Inspired by this work, Joseph LeDoux set out to trace exactly how a fear-conditioned stimulus was processed by the brain. In his book *The Emotional Brain*, LeDoux recounts how he discovered that pathway, or, as he puts it, 'the road map of fear' (LeDoux, 1996, p. 152). LeDoux made lesions in the brains of rats conditioned to fear a specific sound, working backwards along the known pathways for auditory processing. LeDoux writes, 'My approach was to let the natural flow of information be my guide. ... I reasoned that damaging the ear would be uninteresting, since a deaf animal is obviously not going to be able to learn anything about a sound. So, instead, I started by damaging the highest parts of the auditory pathway.' It turned out that damaging the higher auditory functions in the cortex—the 'rind' of the brain—had no effect on fear conditioning. Damaging the auditory thalamus further in did. This posed a puzzle for LeDoux: Where did the road map of fear lead, if not along the standard auditory pathway?

To find the answer, LeDoux injected a special chemical tracer into the auditory thalamus. The neurons there absorbed the tracer and sent the chemical down the long thin connections of the axons to the next stage of the pathway. The brains were then sectioned and stained to determine where the tracer ended up: 'Bright orange particles formed streams and speckles against a dark-blue background. It was like looking into a strange world of inner space.' LeDoux found four regions that contained the tracer. Three of those regions, when damaged, showed no change in response in fear conditioning. The fourth region was the amygdala. The amygdala, it turned out, was the final destination of the road map of fear.

There are several important implications of LeDoux's research for financial crises. Fear is the hardwired fire alarm of the brain, setting off sprinkler systems and calling the fire department automatically, sometimes even faster than we know. In his book, *The Gift of Fear*, public safety expert Gavin de Becker points out that we can detect and process subtle cues of impending danger far faster than our conscious minds realize. For example, when the hairs on the back of one's neck stand up, that is the fear instinct at work. The amygdala has direct connections to the brainstem, the central switchboard for all the muscles of our body. This neural shortcut from fear to physical movement is what allows us to react to a threat before our conscious awareness of it. It is what caused Robert Thompson to exit that convenience store quickly before he understood why. These automatic behaviours are extremely useful for survival, particularly in the face of physical threats.

But physical threats are not the same as financial threats. While high blood pressure, dilated blood vessels in our muscles, and a rush of adrenaline may protect us from the former, they do little to shield us from the latter. In fact, sustained emotional stress has been shown to impair rational decision-making abilities, leading to some well-known behavioural biases such as 'doubling down' rather than cutting losses, selling at the bottom and buying back at the top, and other financial traps that have confounded most retail investors and not a few professional traders.

When taken out of its proper context, our fear circuitry can be counter-productive, and, in some cases, downright deadly. For example, the natural instincts that saved Thompson's life in that convenience store would have killed him long ago in the context of flying an airplane. This is why earning a pilot's license requires hundreds of hours of training, designed to overcome human physical instinct. A common mistake among inexperienced pilots is the tendency to pull back on an airplane's control wheel to prevent the plane from crashing during a stall. Pulling back on the wheel causes the airplane to point upwards—towards the sky and away from the ground—which is a totally intuitive and instinctive reaction to a life-threatening situation.

Unfortunately, in this context our instinct is exactly wrong: pointing the plane upwards reduces its air speed, making a stall all but certain. The correct but counterintuitive behaviour is to push the control wheel forward, pointing the plane down—towards the ground and a loss of altitude—which has the effect of increasing the plane's airspeed, decreasing the 'angle of attack' that increases lift to its wings, and allowing the pilot to recover from the stall and regain altitude.[5] This manouevre involves first losing altitude, so the pilot must make sure that the angle and speed of descent are not too steep, or else the plane will hit the ground before generating enough lift to pull out of the dive. This balancing act is played out in a matter of seconds, the reason why so many hours of training are required for pilot certification.

The same logic applies to financial investment, risk management, economic policy and regulation, and crisis response. In each of these contexts, fear can play a productive role, provided it is properly balanced against other considerations. The fear of losing money will rationally cause investors to manage their risks actively and in proportion to their expected reward. Extreme fear, however, can cause investors to sell their risky assets at fire-sale prices in favour of government bonds and cash, which may not serve their longer-term objectives should they maintain these holdings for too long. On a broader scale, if we allow our instinctive fears to drive our reaction to financial crises, we may regret the policy responses produced by our amygdalas. This applies not only to investors, but also to regulators and policymakers, whose response to fear may have considerably larger consequences.

The work of Kapp, LeDoux, and many others showed that the pathway for fear response in the brain sidesteps the higher brain functions, including the ones we usually associate with rationality. This pathway leads instead to a specific centre that processes the *emotional* significance of stimuli. We fear things for reasons outside our conscious, rational mind, and we do this because we have no choice; we are physiologically hardwired to do so. More broadly, we behave, think, reach conclusions, and make decisions with the

---

[5] One of the industry's standard textbooks, *Jeppesen's Guided Flight Discovery: Private Pilot* (Willits, 2007, pp. 3–38), lists three key steps to recover from a stall, of which the first is this: 'Decrease the angle of attack. Depending on the type of aircraft, you may find that a different amount of forward pressure on the control wheel is required. Too little forward movement may not be enough to regain lift; too much may impose a negative load on the wing, hindering recovery.'

effects of the emotional brain always running in the background. This has clear implications for economic behaviour.

11.3 Greed

Neuroscience has shown that fear and its emotional response are intimately linked to decision-making in the human brain. But what about more positive emotions such as happiness, joy, a sense of accomplishment, or pleasure? Surely most economic decisions are made for nonaverse reasons. William Stanley Jevons spoke of a 'double coincidence of wants', not a 'double coincidence of fears'. It turns out that neuroscience also has something to say about the pleasurable emotions.

In 1954, two researchers at Montreal's McGill University, James Olds and Peter Milner, implanted electrodes into the septal area of the brains of rats. These rats were placed in Skinner boxes with a lever which, when pressed, would deliver a low voltage of 60-cycle alternating current to the rat's brain. These rats then did something remarkable: they would *choose* to have their brains electrically stimulated by repeatedly pressing the lever—on one occasion, almost 2,000 times an hour. Olds and Milner were careful to rule out that the voltage was reducing the pain of implantation (Olds and Milner, 1954).

This strongly suggested to neuroscientists that there was a 'pleasure centre' in the brain. In fact, many electrode studies were performed across a variety of animals to find the pleasure centre, including several (of dubious ethics) on humans. As with most things involving the brain, however, it was more complicated than it first appeared. Instead of a pleasure centre, the brain seems to have a 'reward' system. In psychology, a reward is anything positive that makes a behaviour more likely. Rewards can be as basic and fundamental as food, or as abstract and intangible as intellectual satisfaction. Surprisingly, all these different rewards—food, sex, love, money, music, beauty—appear to use the same neurological system. Moreover, the pathways of this system all transmit the same chemical signal: dopamine.

Dopamine is a comparatively simple compound that was once thought to have very little neurological significance. It was best known as a chemical precursor to the hormone adrenaline in the body, until in 1957 the Swedish researcher Arvid Carlsson showed that it was, in fact, a neurotransmitter, a discovery for which he won the Nobel Prize for Physiology or Medicine in 2000 (Carlsson, Lindqvist, and Magnusson, 1957). Carlsson had given reserpine, a drug known to deplete neurotransmitters, to rabbits, which then fell into a catatonic state. Carlsson theorized that the rabbits' catatonia was caused by a lack of an as-yet-undiscovered neurotransmitter. By injecting the rabbits with L-DOPA, a chemical that converts to dopamine in the brain, Carlsson was able to revive the rabbits—leading the Greek-American neurologist George Cotzias only a few years later to successfully treat patients with Parkinson's disease, and the neurologist Oliver Sacks to treat paralyzed patients with sleeping sickness, as celebrated in his famous book *Awakenings* (Sacks, 1974).

However, one peculiarity of patients treated with L-DOPA was that they often became addicted to gambling. This was one of the first clues that dopamine was involved in the brain's reward system. Other researchers discovered that addictive drugs such as cocaine and methamphetamine flooded the brain with dopamine through the mesolimbic pathway, releasing it into the nucleus accumbens, located not very far from the septal area where Olds and Milner had implanted their electrodes. Neuroanatomists have since discovered eight separate dopamine pathways in the brain, including ones associated with attention and learning. While the full picture of how dopamine and the reward system interact is still far from clear, there is growing consensus among neuroscientists that the broad outlines have been established.[6] The implications for financial crises are clear: an imbalance in an individual's dopamine system can easily lead to greater risk-taking, and if risk-taking activities are, on average, associated with financial gain, a potentially destructive positive feedback loop can easily emerge.

In another study of the brain's reward system, a team led by Hans Breiter at Harvard Medical School and Massachusetts General Hospital, and including the participation of psychologist Daniel Kahneman, used functional magnetic resonance imaging (fMRI) to determine which areas of the brain were activated when an individual experienced monetary gains and losses (Breiter et al., 2001).

What does fMRI actually measure? This is an important question in all imaging studies, and indeed in all physiological studies of the human brain. The common denominator for all such studies is to find physical 'correlates' to internal mental processes within the black box of the brain, the minute physiological changes that correlate to subjective experience. In the most commonly used form of fMRI, blood oxygenation level-dependent contrast fMRI (BOLD fMRI), the oxygenation levels of the blood throughout the brain are measurable because haemoglobin molecules without oxygen respond more strongly to a magnetic field than those with oxygen. Neuroscientists

---

[6] It is tempting to speculate that because of the multiplicity of uses and pathways of dopamine in the brain, we have many ways to feel pleasure, while we have only one way to feel fear. There is some support for this asymmetry from purely evolutionary grounds.

reason that, in an active region of the brain, the neurons will use more oxygen than average, implying that the level of deoxygenated haemoglobin in that area will increase relative to other areas. In deactivated regions of the brain, in comparison, the neurons will use less oxygen than average. In this way, fMRI data can show which regions of the brain become more active (or less active) in response to a given task.

In Breiter's study, subjects were given a $50 stake in real money. While in the fMRI machine, they were asked to play a simple gambling game. One of three computer-animated spinners was displayed to the subject. Each spinner was divided equally into three possible outcomes: the 'good' spinner with $10, $2.50, and $0; the 'intermediate' spinner with $2.50, $0, and –$1.50; and the 'bad' spinner with $0, –$1.50, and –$6.[7] Unknown to the test subjects, the outcomes of the spinners only appeared to be random. In fact, the spinners went through a preprogrammed sequence such that each subject earned $78.50 by the end of the experiment.

Breiter, Kahneman, and their colleagues found that as the monetary rewards increased, so did the activation in several key parts of the brain's anatomy: the nucleus accumbens, part of the reward system; the sublenticular extended amygdala, associated with emotional reaction; the hypothalamus, a part of the brain closely linked to the endocrine hormonal system; and the ventral tegmental area, which releases dopamine into the reward system. These were direct neurological correlates to monetary reward.

The pattern of activations following a monetary reward was extremely familiar to Breiter. He had found the same pattern in another study he conducted with cocaine addicts and first-time morphine users. In the human brain, monetary gain stimulates the same reward circuitry as cocaine; in both cases, dopamine is released into the nucleus accumbens, reinforcing the behaviour. In the case of cocaine, we call this addiction. In the case of monetary gain, we call this capitalism. Our most fundamental reactions to monetary gain are hardwired into human physiology.

Neuroscientists have also attempted to link the results of fMRI research directly to economic theory. For example, Read Montague at Baylor Medical Center and Gregory Berns at Emory University School of Medicine have tried to discover how the brain's different reactions to financial reward translate into an internal mental 'currency'. They suspect that the brain uses a common scale of valuation to compare different outcomes. In their view, due to the vast multiplicity of possible human behaviours, the brain needs a

---

[7] As the experimenters noted, 'The gains were made larger than the losses to compensate for the well-established tendency of subjects to assign greater weight to a loss than to a gain of equal magnitude', a psychological result that comes directly from Kahneman and Tversky's research.

single internal scale of representing value to choose a proper course of action, although this course of action might not be rational from the standpoint of *Homo economicus* (Montague and Berns, 2002).

Other researchers have tried to use fMRI research to *predict* economic behaviour. Since many brain regions are activated before a specific type of behaviour—for example the nucleus accumbens and risk-seeking—Brian Knutson and Peter Bossaerts at Stanford University have theorized that these anticipations could be used to create a 'physiologically constrained' theory of decision-making (Knutson and Bossaerts, 2007). This is reminiscent of Herbert Simon's attempt to emulate the psychology of the human decision-making process in a computer program. Here, however, the neurological correlates could be directly measured by fMRI and other brain imaging techniques, and the resulting behaviours compared to the results of the theoretical model.

However, the fMRI method has limitations. Its spatial resolution can detect volumes the size of a grain of sand or the head of a pin, but it is much too coarse to detect the activity of a single neuron, or even of a small group of neurons. Its resolution in time is even coarser, taking several seconds to build up a single image.[8] Some researchers are sceptical of the chain of logic that links deoxygenated blood to local brain activity; at best, they argue, it is imperfectly correlated. Moreover, even under the most favourable conditions, fMRI only provides the researcher with brain activity data. It is a little as though someone were attempting to study how New York City worked, but the only information they had about the city was the power company's meter readings block by city block. It would take a truly skilled researcher to discover the purpose of the Financial District or Broadway from that data, and events as memorable as the Thanksgiving Day parade would effectively be invisible to the researcher.

Nevertheless, fMRI has been revolutionary in allowing researchers to see inside the black box of the brain as never before. Entirely new areas of research linking neuroscience to economics and finance have emerged thanks to the use of fMRI, barely scratching the surface of potential insights from this tool. In particular, higher brain functions such as logical reasoning, numerical computation, and long-term planning are all intimately involved in the economic and financial decision-making process. We are still in a state of deep ignorance about the brain, even if our knowledge is growing exponentially each day.

---

[8] In comparison, the old-fashioned electroencephalograph could record changes in the brain's surface electrical activity in milliseconds.

11.4 Risk

If our reactions to monetary gain are hardwired, what about our reactions to monetary risk? Aversion to risk seems nearly universal among all living organisms, most likely a close corollary of the survival instinct. In our simple evolutionary model of behaviour, we have shown in Chapters 2 and 6 that when there are systematic environmental risks to fertility, the forces of natural selection will favour those individuals that are risk averse. The reason is simple: if one course of action leads to three offspring with certainty, and a second course of action leads to a 50/50 gamble of two or four offspring, it can be shown that the first course of action leads to much faster population growth.[9]

But human responses to risk are more subtle than simple risk aversion, as the Peltzman effect described in Chapter 1 illustrated. In the same way that automobile safety improvements are *perceived* to be more effective than they are—leading drivers to take more risk than intended—what if financial securities are perceived to be *less* risky than they really are? This was obviously a critical factor in the 2008 financial crisis. Given the AAA ratings of collateralized debt obligations (CDOs) and their relatively short history of growth and profitability, certain investors may have thought they were safer than, in fact, they were. This adaptive nature of human risk preferences is one of the most important reasons for producing accurate and timely risk analytics in a financial context.

However, even when risk is accurately measured, human behaviour shows some very interesting biases in how losses and gains are weighed, as illustrated in Chapter 2's slightly modified version of Kahneman and Tversky's (1979) loss-aversion experiment in which subjects are asked to choose between investments A vs B and C vs D (see Section 2.3.3). The fact that individuals tend to be risk averse in the face of gains (A vs B) and risk seeking in the face of losses (C vs D)—which Kahneman and Tversky (1979) more accurately called 'aversion to sure loss'—can lead to poor financial decisions.

A common response to this thought experiment by chagrined MBA students that fall into this behavioural pattern is 'this isn't fair, since the pairs of investment opportunities were presented sequentially, not simultaneously'. However, all of us have been put in the situation where we must make decisions about risky choices sequentially, without the luxury of contemplating the cumulative effects of those decisions before we make them. Moreover,

---

[9] This is a consequence of Jensen's inequality, which, in this simple example, is illustrated by the fact that the safe choice yields $3 \times 3 = 9$ individuals after two generations, while the risky choice yields only $2 \times 4 = 8$, on average. See Chapter 2 for a more formal derivation.

imagine a multinational organization in which a London-based trader is faced with choices A and B and a Tokyo-based trader is faced with choices C and D. From the local perspective, it does not seem like there is a right or wrong choice, but the globally consolidated portfolio will clearly show suboptimal risk-taking behaviour.

In fact, aversion to sure loss is a very real problem that lies at the heart of one of the biggest potential exposures of every major financial institution: the rogue trader. The cases of Nick Leeson (Barings, 1995, £827 million loss), Yasuo Hamanaka (Sumitomo, 1996, $2.6 billion loss), John Rusnak (Allied Irish Banks, 2002, $691 million loss), Chen Jiulin (China Aviation Oil, 2005, $550 million loss), Jérôme Kerviel (Société Générale, 2006–2008, €4.9 billion loss), Boris Picano-Nacci (Caisse d'Epargne, 2008, €751 million loss), and Kweku Adoboli (UBS, 2011, $2.3 billion loss) are all too familiar: a trader loses more than they expected, but rather than owning up to the loss and moving on, they hide it and increase their bet, hoping to make it up on the next trade, after which all might be forgiven. Of course, this rarely happens, and the 'doubling down' process continues, usually until the losses become so large as to be impossible to hide. It is no wonder that the first piece of advice given to novice traders by more seasoned professionals is to 'cut your losses and ride your gains'. It is an attempt to train the novice not to be overly averse to sure losses, in the same way that professional pilots must learn not to pull back on their controls to recover from a stall.

This advice applies not only to traders and investors, but also to regulators. Some economists claim that regulatory forbearance—the tacit or active cooperation of regulators in overvaluing bank assets to avoid violating minimum capital requirements—in the years leading up to the financial crisis of 2008 was partly responsible for the crisis (Huizinga and Laeven, 2010; Brown and Dinç, 2011). Although there are elaborate explanations for why regulatory forbearance might occur, including global competition among regulatory agencies and the political economy of regulation (Espinosa-Vega et al., 2011), a more mundane explanation is aversion to sure loss. When a bank supervisor first identifies an undercapitalized bank, they must decide whether to require the bank to raise additional capital, or to wait and see whether the bank's assets will rebound. Requiring a bank to raise capital is costly to the supervisor in terms of the bank's invariably negative response, as well as the potential risk that this action may cause a loss of confidence among the bank's customer base, possibly triggering a bank run. Even worse, the regulatory action may, in retrospect, seem unwarranted, causing a loss of confidence in the regulator's competence. Waiting to see whether the bank's assets will increase in value—thereby eliminating the need for such costly regulatory action—is a form of doubling down with similar consequences.

Unsurprisingly, the asymmetry between our reactions to monetary gains and losses has a neurophysiological explanation. Camelia M. Kuhnen and Brian Knutson at Stanford University followed up Breiter's findings about the similarities between monetary gain and addiction with another fMRI study (Kuhnen and Knutson, 2005). Experimental subjects played a computer game Kuhnen and Knutson developed—the Behavioural Investment Allocation Strategy (BIAS) task—while undergoing MRI. The players had a choice between three investment options: a 'safe' bond or one of two stocks, which moved randomly. Unknown to the players, one of the stocks was a 'good' stock that gained in the long run, and the other a 'bad' stock that declined in the long run. Additionally, the good stock gave a larger long-run reward than the bond, on average $2.50 per turn versus a consistent $1.

Kuhnen and Knutson discovered a very interesting pattern. When players made a risk-seeking mistake—for example choosing the bad stock over the good stock—their nucleus accumbens was activated before they made their decision. The nucleus accumbens is the same part of the reward circuit activated in response to cocaine and monetary gain. In contrast, before players made a risk-averse mistake—for example choosing the safe bond over the good stock—a completely different part of the brain was activated, the anterior insula. This part of the brain is not associated with any reward pathways at all; rather, it seems to be associated with disgust, whether due to an unpleasant odour, expressions of someone reacting to an unpleasant odour, or seeing graphic pictures of contamination or bodily mutilation (Wicker et al., 2003; Wright et al., 2004). It seems that risk-averse investors process the risk of monetary loss along the same circuit they contemplate viscerally disgusting things, while risk-seeking investors process the risky potential gain along the same reward circuits as cocaine.

11.5 Rationality

In the mid-1970s, a successful 35-year-old businessman began suffering from intense headaches and a lack of concentration, enough to disrupt his personal and professional life. He was diagnosed with a brain tumour, a meningioma the size of a small orange that was pressing at his frontal lobes from below. His surgery to remove the tumour was successful, although some frontal lobe tissue was also removed. His intelligence, his motor skills, and his ability to use language were undamaged in his recovery, but his personality was drastically altered. He lost all sense of proportion at his place of employment, spending the day obsessing over unimportant details while ignoring the most pressing tasks. Deciding what clothes to wear in the morning or what restaurant to dine in at night consumed an inordinate amount of time. He soon lost his job, quickly running through a series of bad business ventures, and then his wife left him. He remarried and then quickly divorced. By the time the neurologist Antonio Damasio encountered him, this man was attempting to get his disability benefits restored; they had been cancelled since his mental and physical abilities were, in the opinion of other doctors, still intact. The man was, to all external appearances, a 'malingerer' (Eslinger and Damasio, 1985; Damasio, 1994, pp. 34–37).

Damasio was doubtful. The imaging techniques of the time—computed tomography (CT), MRI, and single-photon emission CT (SPECT)—were used to scan the patient's brain. They revealed very localized lesions on the left and right frontal lobes of his cortex. The man—referred to as 'patient E.V.R.' in the neurological literature and given the pseudonym 'Elliot' by Damasio in his book *Descartes' Error*—had a only small portion of his brain damaged, the ventromedial prefrontal cortex, located a few centimetres behind the lower forehead. Damasio theorized that this small section of the brain was involved in the higher function of decision-making.

Unlike other patients with frontal lobe damage, Elliot performed normally on specialized psychological and personality tests. After extensive conversations with him, however, Damasio began to believe there was something else missing besides his ability to make good decisions. Although a pleasant, even witty conversationalist, Elliot showed very little emotional affect talking about his misfortunes. As Damasio probed further, he found that Elliot was almost always on a seemingly even emotional keel: never sad, never anxious, never impatient, and only very briefly angry. Psychological tests measuring physiological reactions to violent imagery confirmed this deficit. After one series of tests, Elliot himself confirmed this change to Damasio: 'topics that had once evoked a strong emotion no longer caused any reaction, positive or negative'. Damasio tentatively called this set of conditions 'acquired sociopathy' (Damasio, Tranel, and Damasio, 1991, 1998; Saver and Damasio, 1991; Damasio, 1994, pp. 41–45). Apparently, this loss of emotional faculties had a surprisingly profound effect on Elliot's day-to-day activities, as Damasio (1994, p. 36) describes:

> When the job called for interrupting an activity and turning to another, he might persist nonetheless, seemingly losing sight of his main goal. Or he might interrupt the activity he had engaged, to turn to something he found more captivating at that

particular moment.... The flow of work was stopped. One might say that the particular step of the task at which Elliot balked was actually being carried out too well,
and at the expense of the overall purpose. One might say that Elliot had become
irrational concerning the larger frame of behaviour...

Elliot's inability to feel—his lack of emotional response—somehow caused
him to make irrational choices in his daily decisions.

This conclusion surprises many economists, because of the common association between emotion and irrationality. After all, is it not fear and greed,
or animal spirits as Keynes suggested, that cause prices to deviate irrationally
from their fundamentals? In fact, a more sophisticated view of the role of
emotions in human cognition is that they are central to rationality.[10] Emotions are the basis for a reward-and-punishment system that facilitates the
selection of advantageous behaviour, providing a numeraire for animals to
engage in a 'cost–benefit analysis' of the various actions open to them (Rolls,
1999, Chapter 10.3). Even fear and greed—the two most common culprits
in the downfall of rational thinking, according to most behaviouralists—are
the product of evolutionary forces, adaptive traits that increase the probability of survival. From an evolutionary perspective, emotion is a powerful
tool for improving the efficiency with which animals learn from their environment and their past. When an individual's ability to experience emotion is
eliminated, an important feedback loop is severed and their decision-making
process is impaired.

What, then, is the source of irrationality, if not emotion? The perspective
of the neurosciences provides a hint, from which we can craft a conjecture.
Neuroscientists have shown that emotion—especially fear and the fight-or-
flight response—is the 'first response', in the sense that we exhibit emotional
reactions to objects and events far more quickly than we can articulate
what those objects and events are, as in Robert Thompson's case.[11] In fact,
extreme emotional reactions can 'short-circuit' rational deliberation altogether (Baumeister, Heatherton, and Tice, 1994). That is, a strong stimulus to

[10] See, for example, Rolls (1990, 1992, 1994, 1999) and Damasio (1994). Cognitive neuroscientists and
economists have suggested that rationality in decision-making and emotion are not antithetical, but, in
fact, complementary (Grossberg and Gutowski, 1987; Damasio, 1994; Elster, 1998; Lo, 1999; Loewenstein,
2000; Peters and Slovic, 2000; Lo and Repin, 2002). For example, contrary to the common belief that
emotions have no place in rational financial decision-making processes, Lo and Repin (2002) present
evidence that physiological variables associated with the autonomic nervous system are highly correlated
with market events, even for highly experienced professional securities traders, discussed in more detail
in Chapter 12. They argue that emotional responses are a significant factor in the real-time processing
of financial risks, and that an important component of a professional trader's skills lies in their ability to
channel emotion, consciously or unconsciously, in specific ways during certain market conditions.
[11] See Section 11.2, de Becker (1997), and Zajonc (1980, 1984).

the amygdala seems to inhibit activity in the prefrontal cortex, the region of the brain associated with logical deliberation and reasoning ability. From an evolutionary standpoint, this seems quite sensible. Emotional reactions are a call to arms that should be heeded immediately because individual survival may depend on it, and higher brain functions such as language and logical reasoning are suppressed until the threat is over (i.e. until the emotional reaction subsides).

However, in our current environment, many 'threats' identified by the amygdala are not in fact life threatening, yet our physiological reactions may still be the same. In such cases, the suppression of our prefrontal cortex may be unnecessary, and possibly counterproductive. This is implicit in the common advice to refrain from making any significant decisions after experiencing the death of a loved one, or after a similar emotional trauma. This is sage advice, for the ability to 'think straight' is physiologically hampered by extreme emotional reactions.[12]

The complexity of the interactions among the distinct components of the brain can be illustrated by two complementary examples. The first involves the difference between a natural smile and a forced one (Damasio, 1994, pp. 141–143 and Figure 7-3), which is easily detected by most of us. Why is this the case? A natural smile is generated by one region of the brain—the anterior cingulate—and involves certain involuntary facial muscles that are not under the control of the motor cortex. The forced smile, however, is a purely voluntary behaviour emanating from the motor cortex, and does not look exactly the same because involuntary muscles do not participate in this action. It takes great effort and skill to generate particular facial expressions on cue, as actors trained in the 'Method' school can attest. Only by conjuring up emotionally charged experiences in their past are they able to produce the kind of genuine emotional reactions needed in a given scene. Anything less authentic is recognized as bad acting.

The second example is taken from Eisenberger, Lieberman, and Williams (2003). This study deliberately induced feelings of social rejection among a group of subjects, then identified the regions of the brain that were most activated during the stimulus. They discovered that two components were involved, the anterior cingulate and the insula, both of which are also known to process physical pain. In other words, emotional trauma—hurt feelings, emotional loss, embarrassment, and shame—can generate the same kind of

---

[12] Other familiar manifestations of the antagonistic effect of emotion on the prefrontal cortex include being so angry that one cannot see ('blinded by one's anger', both physically and metaphorically), and becoming tongue-tied and disoriented in the presence of someone one finds unusually attractive. Both vision and speech are mediated by the prefrontal cortex.

neural response that a broken bone does. Many who have experienced the death of a loved one have commented that they felt *physical* pain from their loss, despite the fact that no physical trauma was involved. We are now beginning to develop a neuroscientific basis for this phenomenon. Eisenberger, Lieberman, and Williams (2003, p. 292) conclude that '…social pain is analogous in its neurocognitive function to physical pain, alerting us when we have sustained injury to our social connections, allowing restorative measures to be taken'.

These examples illustrate some of the many ways in which specialized components in the brain can interact to produce behaviour. The first example shows that two different components of the brain are capable of producing the same outcome: a smile. The second example shows that the same components can be involved in producing two different outcomes: physical and emotional pain. The point of specialization in brain function is increased fitness in the evolutionary sense. Each specialized component may be viewed as an evolutionary adaptation designed to increase the chances of survival in response to a particular environmental condition. As environmental conditions change, so too does the relative importance of each component. *Homo sapiens* has the ability to adapt to new situations by learning and implementing more advantageous behaviour, which is accomplished by several components of the brain acting together. As a result, what economists call 'preferences' are often complicated, context-dependent interactions among various components of the brain.

The neuroscientific perspective thus implies that preferences may not be stable through time, but are likely to be shaped by a number of factors, both internal and external to the individual (i.e. factors related to the individual's personality), and factors related to specific environmental conditions in which the individual is currently situated. When the environmental conditions shift, we should expect behaviour to change in response, both through learning and through changes in preferences via the forces of natural selection over time. These evolutionary foundations are more than speculation in the context of financial markets. The extraordinary degree of competitiveness in global financial markets and the outsized rewards that accrue to the 'fittest' traders suggest that a form of Darwinian selection is at work in determining the typical profile of the successful investor, where unsuccessful market participants are eventually eliminated from the population after a certain level of loss.

What we consider to be 'rational' behaviour is, in fact, a complex balancing act between a number of components of the brain, some hardwired, others more adaptive, and if these components become imbalanced—either too much fear or too little greed—we observe 'maladaptive' behaviour. The definition of rationality and its opposite are therefore inextricably tied to an individual's environment. The great white shark moves through the water with fearsome grace and efficiency, thanks to 400 million years of natural selection, but take that shark out of water and onto a sandy beach, and its flailing undulations will seem irrational. The origins of human behaviour are similar, differing only in the length of time we have had to adapt to our environment, and the speed with which that environment is now changing, thanks to our technology. The evolutionarily advantageous responses of *Homo sapiens* to threats on the plains of the African savannah 50,000 years ago may not be as effective in dealing with threats on the New York Stock Exchange today.

Consequently, it should not be surprising to discover that the lack of sunlight during winter months tends to depress stock market prices (Kamstra, Kramer, and Levi, 2003), that traders who exhibit too little or too much emotional response tend to be less profitable than those with mid-range sensitivity (see Chapters 12 and 13), or that traders tend to make more money on days when their levels of testosterone are higher than average (Coates and Herbert, 2008). These are just a few examples from the neuroeconomics literature, in which economic behaviour is reinterpreted from a neurophysiological perspective, providing a deeper and richer basis for understanding rationality and irrationality.

11.6 Sentience

While neuroscience clearly shows that the human decision-making process is very far from the hyper-rationality of *Homo economicus*, the internal logic of the efficient markets hypothesis (EMH) suggests that this might not matter very much. Consider a modern financial market with many traders. If one trader makes a poor decision in the heat of emotion, another trader acting more rationally should see this as an arbitrage opportunity and make an easy profit. Of course, we know that this ideal depiction of the wisdom of the market does not always happen, since entire markets can be infected with what the nineteenth-century journalist Charles Mackay called 'the madness of crowds', but it happens far more often than not. But what if there were biological limits to human rationality itself?

It is a truism in freshman economics that price is determined by supply and demand. Every economic transaction has a buyer and a seller, each trying to come to a mutually satisfying agreement via Jevons's 'double coincidence of wants'. If a seller refuses to lower the asking price to a level a buyer wishes to bid, no transaction will take place. That might be a rational decision on the seller's part. Alternatively, it might reflect a lack of awareness of what the buyer is willing to offer. A well-functioning market's price discovery process requires participants to engage in a certain degree of causal reasoning: 'If I do this, then others will do that, which means I should …'. This chain of logic presumes that individuals have what psychologists call a 'theory of mind'—the ability to understand another person's mental state. To understand why, consider the most basic form of bilateral negotiation between a buyer and a seller. Even the simplest back-and-forth process of price discovery requires that the buyer understand the motives of the seller, and vice versa. In fact, to compute the equilibrium price as hypothesized by rational expectations and efficient markets theory requires an unending recursive chain of reasoning, as if buyer and seller were trapped in a hall of mirrors: the seller knows that the buyer knows that the seller knows that the buyer knows that the bid is too high, etc. In other words, market equilibrium requires a rather *sophisticated* theory of mind, and presumably a high level of abstract thought.

In the early 1990s, a chance discovery by a group of researchers at the University of Parma led by Giacomo Rizzolatti showed that perhaps the theory of mind was not very abstract at all, but hardwired into the structure of the brain itself (Di Pellegrino et al., 1992). Using recording microelectrodes, Rizzolatti and his group found there were specific neurons in the macaque monkey brain that responded to 'mirrored' motions in others. For instance, a certain neuron in the premotor cortex would fire when a macaque grasped an object, as well as when an experimenter grasped an object. This was direct physical evidence that the macaque could understand the actions of others in terms of its own experience, even across species. In short, the macaque had a basic theory of mind hardwired into its neurophysiology.

This discovery of mirror neurons was entirely unexpected. While some neuroscientists had jokingly spoken of 'grandmother neurons', neurons that would fire when individuals saw their grandmothers, no neurologist expected a basic system in the brain for understanding the behaviour of others in terms of one's own physical actions. The discovery was so unexpected that the scientific journal *Nature* declined to publish Rizzolatti's manuscript because its editors believed it lacked general interest (Rizzolatti and Fabbri-Destro, 2010). This rejection notwithstanding, in a short time Rizzolatti and his team also detected mirror neurons in humans, through the use of positron emission tomography (PET), which showed neural activity in the analogous areas of the human brain as in the macaque in response to mirrored behaviour. Like our evolutionary cousins, we humans have neurons that automatically 'light up' in sympathy to the actions of others.

In contrast to the common neuroscientific approach of determining the function of parts of the brain by studying the behaviour of individuals in whom such parts are damaged, in the case of mirror neurons, the approach has been reversed. We believe we know what the neurons do, but we do not know how they might affect behaviour. One hypothesis, proposed by Rizzolatti and others, is that a deficit in the brain's mirror mechanism may be involved in autism spectrum disorder, the complex syndrome of learning, social, communicative, and emotional deficits. People with autism often have difficulty understanding other people's motives, and therefore connecting socially, suggesting they have an undeveloped theory of mind, as the British neuroscientist Baron-Cohen (1989) believes. However, we do not have to look for specific neurological case studies to understand this phenomenon. Every one of us has, as a child, passed through life stages where our own theory of mind was undeveloped.

It is strange to think that, at some point before the age of four years, we were not able to understand that another person, perhaps a parent, could believe something that we ourselves knew was not true. As adults, of course, most of us are comfortable with the idea that other people might be mistaken. For those of us who are parents, the knowledge that a child under the age of four is mentally incapable of understanding this is vaguely comforting, particularly when we are faced with what looks like otherwise unreasonable behaviour. However, by the time most children reach the age of four, they are able to deal with what psychologists call 'first-order false belief'. At that age, our brains have developed to the point where we can understand that other people can be fallible, an important step on the pathway to a more fully formed theory of mind.

A four-year-old might be able to understand a statement like, 'Alan thinks his Christmas present is in red wrapping, but the present is really in the green wrapping'. However, a typical four-year-old would not understand a statement like, 'Bethany thinks Alan thinks his Christmas present is blue, and Alan thinks his Christmas present is red, but it's really green'. The ability to understand a second-order false belief, instead of following naturally and recursively from the ability to understand a first-order false belief, takes a few more years to develop. In general, a seven-year-old can understand a story with a second-order false belief. This means their theory of mind is rich enough not only to model another person's mental state, but also to model another person's model of a person's mental state. A four-year-old can see one mirror deep into the hall of mirrors of intention, while a seven-year-old can see two mirrors deep (Perner and Wimmer, 1985).

How far does this hall of mirrors extend? We might suspect, on purely theoretical grounds, that the potential for infinite regress is present in humans, even if rarely used. After all, the English language can support infinite levels of clauses in its grammar, as in the nursery rhyme 'This is the cat that killed the rat that ate the malt that lay in the house that Jack built', and so on. However, we might try to construct a mental experiment about a third-order false belief—Clayton thinks that Bethany thinks that Alan thinks etc.—and come to the conclusion that this mental task is rather difficult. In fact, psychological tests have shown that normal adults start making significant errors when answering questions about the fifth-order theory of mind (Kinderman, Dunbar, and Bentall, 1998).

This has consequences for the assumption of human rationality in the EMH. It is not difficult to construct a scenario where correct knowledge regarding another individual's intentions five layers removed from a given transaction has economic implications, whether in a complicated mergers-and-acquisitions deal, in terms of an exotic financial derivative, or even in the picks and trades of the NFL draft. However, if it is impossible for all but a very few chess grandmasters to hold such a chain of intentions as a single thought—impossible in the same way that a young child literally cannot understand that their parent does not know where their blanket is—how can an investor always act rationally to maximize their profit? Alternatively, if the investor fails to act rationally, how can other investors know they are taking successful advantage of the failure? This might involve a sixth-order theory of mind. While the arbitrage mechanism can correct misjudgements, it relies on the ability of investors in the market to recognize when a correct judgement by the market has taken place. In some cases, this expectation is simply unrealistic.

11.7 Interactions Among Components

Although there have been many breakthroughs in neuroscience in recent years, one of the most important questions about human cognition has yet to be answered: How do the individual components of the brain interact to produce observed human behaviour? We now know a great deal more about how fear and greed are physiologically generated, but what can we say about how an individual will respond to a 20% decline in their retirement portfolio? Despite the fact that the fight-or-flight response may be triggered by such an event, not all individuals will react in the same manner; some may panic and switch their portfolio to cash immediately, while others may not react at all.

Can neuroscience provide any insight into these individual differences and the underlying mechanisms by which such heterogeneity arises? From the economist's point of view, these kinds of questions are the most relevant. They are also the most difficult to answer from the neuroscientific perspective.

While no complete theory of how the brain works yet exists, there are a few observations that hint at how the various components of the brain interact. The first observation is that not all neural components are created equal. From an evolutionary perspective, certain components are much older than others and are found in many species in addition to *Homo sapiens*. Therefore, these common components are more likely to engage in functions that are critical for basic survival across all species. For example, pain receptors exist in virtually all mammals and reptiles; hence, pain avoidance and fear conditioning is obviously critical for survival, since it is equally ubiquitous among all species descended from the common ancestor of reptiles and mammals over 200 million years ago. This universality implies a priority in its impact on behaviour: pain avoidance and fear trump all other neural components under sufficiently threatening circumstances, as they should. While a 20% decline in one's retirement portfolio might not lead to the same response across a diverse population of investors, a raging fire in a crowded theater will.

However, the behaviour of *Homo sapiens* can be considerably more subtle, as illustrated by the remarkable story of the mountain climber Aron Lee Ralston, whose ordeal was chronicled in the gripping film *127 Hours*. On 26 April 2003, Ralston, then 27 years old, was climbing a three-foot wide crevasse in Bluejohn Canyon in a remote region of southeastern Utah when an 800-pound boulder slipped and pinned his arm to the wall of the crevasse. He was trapped in the crevasse for five days, and he finally escaped by amputating his right arm below the elbow with a dull knife. This story is incredible because we recognize that Ralston voluntarily inflicted extraordinary pain on himself, in direct contradiction to our most basic instinct of pain avoidance. To fully appreciate the magnitude of the pain Ralston underwent, the following is a short summary of his self-amputation written by a mountain-climbing blogger, Shane Burrows (http://climb-utah.com/Roost/bluejohn2.htm). WARNING: Squeamish readers should read no further:[13]

> Ralston prepared to amputate his right arm below the elbow using the knife blade on his multi-tool. Realizing that the blade was not sharp enough to cut through the bone he forced his arm against the boulder and broke the bones so he would

---

[13] For those interested in all the gory details, an even more graphic description is provided by Ralston (2004, pp. 281–285).

be able to cut through the tissue. First he broke the radius bone, which connects the elbow to the thumb. Within a few minutes he cracked the ulna, the bone on the outside of the forearm. Next he applied a tourniquet to his arm. He [then] used his knife blade to amputate his right arm below the elbow. The entire procedure required approximately one hour.

How was Ralston able to accomplish this feat? Presumably, he was able to over-ride his pain-avoidance circuitry by creating an alternate scenario in his mind that was considerably more rewarding—despite the fact that it included the painful amputation—than dying alone in the crevasse on that day.

Our capacity to create complex scenarios, pure figments of our substantial imaginations, is one of the most important evolutionary advantages the human species has developed, and it seems to be unique to our species. The portion of the brain responsible for these complex thoughts is known as the prefrontal cortex. While similar structures exist in other mammals, *Homo sapiens* seems to have the largest and most highly connected version (Schoenemann, Sheehan, and Glotzer, 2005; Smaers et al., 2011). Neuroscientists have shown that many of the uniquely human traits such as language, mathematical reasoning, complex planning, self-control, and delayed gratification originate in the prefrontal cortex. For this reason, the region is sometimes referred to as the 'executive brain'. Like the chief executive officer (CEO) of a well-run company, the prefrontal cortex is responsible for developing a vision for the organization, monitoring the performance of the various divisions and subordinates, and making resource-allocation decisions that weigh the costs and benefits of each competing division's goals in order to maximize the chances of achieving the overall objectives of the organization while protecting it from current and potential threats. This corporate hierarchy is not simply a useful analogy, but part of our neurophysiology (Botvinick, 2008). This 'command-and-control centre' was the region of the brain destroyed in Phineas Gage's unfortunate accident, with predictable consequences.

The executive functions of the human brain allow us to engage in far more complex behaviours than other species. A simple manifestation of this difference is the fact that we can more easily predict the behaviour of other animals than those of humans. Great white sharks circle their prey before striking, Canadian geese migrate south during the winter, and ocean-dwelling Pacific salmon return to freshwater rivers to lay their eggs. While humans also exhibit certain predictable traits, the number of possible behaviours generated by the prefrontal cortex is exponentially greater, simply because of our ability to imagine and choose from a multitude of hypothetical realities. Many of these alternate realities are highly elaborate 'what-if' scenarios that can move us to do extraordinary things. According to Aron Ralston, it was the following hypothetical reality that allowed him to do the unthinkable (Ralston, 2004, p. 248):

> A blond three-year-old boy in a red polo shirt comes running across a sunlit hardwood floor in what I somehow know is my future home. By the same intuitive perception, I know the boy is my own. I bend to scoop him into my left arm, using my handless right arm to balance him, and we laugh together as I swing him up to my shoulder…. Then, with a shock, the vision blinks out. I'm back in the canyon, echoes of his joyful sounds resonating in my mind, creating a subconscious reassurance that somehow I will survive this entrapment. Despite having already come to accept that I will die where I stand before help arrives, now I believe I will live.
> That belief, that boy, changes everything for me.

Remarkably, Ralston was not married or engaged at the time, and had no children. In August 2009, he married Jessica Trusty, and their first child, Leo, was born in January 2010, nearly seven years after his fateful vision in Bluejohn Canyon.

The prefrontal cortex is a remarkable piece of neural machinery that, in the blink of an eye on an evolutionary time scale, has allowed humans to dominate their world and spread to virtually every type of environment on this planet and its moon. The prefrontal cortex is the closest thing to rational expectations and *Homo economicus* that the brain has to offer to economists. If agents maximize expected utility subject to budget constraints, or optimize portfolios via quadratic programming, or engage in strategic subterfuge in a dynamic bargaining context, they will be using the prefrontal cortex to do so.

Like any organ of any living being, however, there are limits to its capabilities. As impressive and unique as the human prefrontal cortex is, it is not able to operate instantaneously or indefinitely. In certain circumstances, it is not able to operate at all. For example, individuals who faint when confronted with shocking news do so through a sudden loss of blood pressure that shuts down the prefrontal cortex, causing them to lose consciousness. A less extreme illustration of the limitations of the prefrontal cortex is decision fatigue, a phenomenon that has been documented among a group of judges presiding over parole hearings for Israeli prisoners. During each day of hearings, there were two food breaks that divided the day into three distinct sessions, and researchers found a striking pattern over these sessions: the judges rendered favourable parole decisions about 65% of the time at the start of these sessions, but the percentage would systematically decline to nearly

0% by the end of each session (Danziger, Levav, and Avnaim-Pesso, 2011). It appears that difficult decisions can be mentally taxing in some manner, so as these sessions wore on, the Judges became more inclined to avoid such decisions by denying parole. However, after the food breaks (a late-morning snack and then a lunch break), the judges were refreshed and ready to resume their complex deliberations; hence, parole rates at the beginning of the following session were considerably higher. The fact that the increased parole rates followed food breaks is consistent with well-known findings that glucose can reverse the effects of decision fatigue (Tierney, 2011).

As with corporate CEOs who lead their companies astray, there are many paths to failure. Early behavioural models of economic choice recognized these pathologies and modelled their effects explicitly to produce more realistic consumer saving and spending patterns, such as the behavioural life-cycle model of Shefrin and Thaler (1988). These insights led to a significant innovation in retirement savings plans, pioneered by Thaler and Benartzi (2004): the idea of allowing participants to opt out instead of asking them to opt in, while reducing the number of choices so that participants do not over-diversify into investments that they do not understand or truly want. These seemingly superficial changes can have a large positive impact on the participation rate of 401(k) plans. In one empirical study, participation rates for the standard opt-in plan were around 20% after three months of employment, increasing gradually to 65% after thirty-six months. With automatic enrollment, the participation rate of new employees jumped immediately to 90%. That participation increased to 98% after thirty-six months suggests that few individuals opted out (Madrian and Shea, 2001). Not only did this simple change increase the participation rate, but it also caused employees to join more quickly, with obvious benefits to long-term wealth creation.

These examples highlight the complexity and subtlety of *Homo sapiens*, and they also offer hope that we can one day develop a more complete understanding of human behaviour that integrates economics, psychology, and neuroscience in mutually beneficial ways. This is the goal of the adaptive markets hypothesis (AMH) and this volume.

11.8 Evolution at the Speed of Thought

In 2008, Ian Tattersall, an anthropologist and former curator of the American Museum of Natural History, published a study on the acquisition of symbolic cognition by *Homo sapiens* (Tattersall, 2008). Tattersall's very simple yet earth-shattering idea is that there exists a puzzle in the fossil record for humans. Two hundred thousand years ago, our species had evolved to the point where we were essentially anatomically identical to where we are today, yet evidence of abstract thought and symbolic thought does not seem to appear in the fossil record until 80,000 years ago. Looking at the artefacts, for example, certain kinds of stone tools have abstract patterns that did not happen by accident—they are far too regular—dated to 77,000 years ago.

How do we explain this strange gap in fossil history? Tattersall's conjecture, which seems to be borne out by further evidence, is that somewhere between 80,000 and 60,000 years ago, humans developed the ability for abstract thought. This ability to engage in symbolic thought and symbolic computation changed everything in human experience. It allowed us to think about things *before* they happened, to make predictions about them, and to affect those predictions. In other words, it allowed forward-looking behaviour, and, ultimately, rational expectations. Of course, there was an explosion of accelerating cognition that followed: cave art, the Pyramids, writing, and other wonderful developments.

Why is symbolic thought so powerful? It allows us to fine-tune our abilities via natural selection. Not individual by individual or species by species, as in Darwinian evolution, but evolution at the speed of thought. Imagine if each of the individuals of the binary choice model of Part I was, in fact, an idea rather than an organism. We can conjure up twenty-five ideas, determine that twenty-four of them are not likely to succeed, and then take the twenty-fifth and turn it into reality: a bronze spear tip, a wheel, or a DNA sequencer. This ability to generate ideas, and *select* among them, has given us a tremendous advantage over other creatures on this planet. As far as we know, no other animal on this planet is able to engage in the evolution of ideas via abstract cognitive selection.

The AMH is an application of this framework to financial contexts. Behaviours are produced by multiple neural components, and evolution shapes these components across time and circumstances. Evolution occurs at the speed of thought, via narratives. We generate a number of different hypothetical scenarios, and we pick the one that we think will be the most important to us. Ultimately, rational behaviour emerges from the proper balance of these components, but irrational behaviour emerges when these components have an improper balance, where 'proper' and 'improper' are a function of the environment and the forces of selection on that environment.

One example of this form of selection from finance is the evolution of strategies that begin as uniquely proprietary and ultimately become commoditized: investment alpha turning to market beta. An excellent example of this process can be found in the hedge fund industry. John Paulson was one of the few hedge fund managers who made large bets against US residential real estate in the midst of the housing market boom, starting around 2004 and 2005. He ultimately made tens of billions of dollars for his investors, and billions of dollars for himself in fees, because of that bet. It is fair to argue that, in 2004 and 2005, Paulson & Company (John Paulson's hedge fund) had unique alpha and unique investment expertise. At the beginning of 2009, Paulson's right-hand man, Paolo Pellegrini, decided to leave Paulson & Company to start his own firm, Pellegrini & Associates. Pellegrini raised a billion dollars in a matter of weeks. However, Pellegrini's investors did not take money away from Paulson. They left money with Paulson, and they gave more money to Pellegrini. What started out as absolutely unique investment alpha, became less singular. Today, there are Paulson and Pellegrini and many others; Zuckerman (2010) describes this dynamic in the hedge fund industry during the mortgage crisis (see, also, Chapter 16). We provide even more explicit examples in Parts IV and V, including the the Quant Meltdown of August 2007 (Chapter 17), and in discussing the co-evolution of regulations and financial technology over time (Chapter 18).

11.9 Practical Implications

Although the perspective outlined in this chapter has been largely qualitative, it nevertheless offers several practical implications for policymakers focusing on financial reform and systemic risk (see Chapter 20 for a deeper dive on the AMH and regulation).

Individual behaviour is a complicated and dynamic medley of several decision-making neural components, including primitive hardwired responses such as fight-or-flight, and more refined processes such as logical deliberation and strategic planning. One immediate implication is that assuming that individuals or populations always behave in only one manner is too simplistic, and may lead to ineffective or counterproductive policies. Financial markets and their participants are not always rational, and they are not always emotional. Instead, they engage in both types of mental processes, constantly adapting and evolving to new sets of circumstances. Under the AMH, many of the tenets of market efficiency and rational expectations may not hold at all times, but they do serve as useful benchmarks that reality may eventually approximate under certain conditions (Lo, 1999, 2004, 2005). In particular, if environmental conditions are relatively stable, then the process of natural selection will eventually allow market participants to adapt successfully to such conditions, after which the market will appear to be quite efficient. However, if the environment is unstable, then market dynamics will be considerably less predictable as some 'species' lose their competitive edge to others, and the market may appear to be quite inefficient. Indeed, the evolutionary theory of punctuated equilibrium—in which periods of seeming evolutionary stasis are punctuated by bursts of new species, like an exclamation point—may be as relevant to economic contexts as it is to biology.

If punctuated equilibria also characterize financial markets, then the policies designed under the assumptions of rationality will be inappropriate during periods of financial distress, and policies designed to deal with periods of distress will be inappropriate during periods of calm. The AMH suggests that the most durable form of regulation is one that adapts to changing environments and populations. Countercyclical capital requirements are one example, but there are many other possibilities for revamping existing regulations to be more responsive to current systemic exposures.

Another implication of the neuroscientific perspective is that the biological hierarchy of the components of the brain should be respected. Fear, particularly fear of the unknown, over-rides most other decision-making components. Once triggered, this circuit can be very difficult to interrupt. Central bankers are no strangers to this concept, which lies at the very core of a bank run and of the raison d'être of the central bank as lender of last resort, but it applies much more broadly. Policymakers would do well to focus more on clear, accurate, timely, and regular communication with the public throughout periods of significant turmoil, irrespective of the cause. Only through such trusted communication can fear be successfully managed, and ultimately, eliminated.

If the active management of fear involves greater communication and transparency, a prerequisite is the collection and dissemination of information regarding systemic risk. It is a truism that one cannot manage what one does not measure. Therefore, the starting point for any serious discussion of macroprudential policymaking and systemic risk management must be the raw data on which risk measures are based. Financial data are often quite sensitive, and individual and institutional privacy must be guaranteed. Fortunately, specific measures of systemic risk can be derived without infringing on privacy by aggregating information over all financial institutions. The very meaning of systemic risk involves the entire financial system; hence, aggregation should serve to protect the privacy of individuals under most circumstances.[14] These measures could be as significant to public interest as the

---

[14] In addition, more sophisticated methods of preserving privacy, such as the encryption algorithms of Abbe, Khandani, and Lo (2012), may be implemented in situations involving particularly sensitive information.

air-quality measures published by the US Environmental Protection Agency or the hurricane warnings issued by the National Weather Service. In both cases, only through the constant feedback of these published indicators can we know how to change our behaviour accordingly (e.g. by imposing more stringent auto emission standards or ordering evacuations of areas in the path of a hurricane).

The importance of measurement goes hand-in-hand with the executive functions of delayed gratification and pain avoidance. An individual or insti-tution can be expected to voluntarily reduce or discontinue an otherwise currently pleasurable or profitable activity under only two conditions: the change may result in even greater pleasure or profit later, or the change may reduce the likelihood of pain in the future. Absent both of these conditions, the neural incentives to reduce risk are also absent; hence, the role of publi-cizing risk measures is to provide all parties with the appropriate information by which they can weigh the fear of future losses against the pleasure of cur-rent gains. As Damasio's explication of rationality shows, only through the proper balance of fear, greed, and other emotional debits and credits can we make good decisions.

The behavioural feedback loop created by accurate measures of systemic risk is a relatively simple example of how we adapt to changing environments. A more sophisticated version involves definitive forensic analyses of prior events that lead us to change our behaviour. Perhaps the best illustration of this type of learning behaviour is the National Transportation Safety Board (NTSB), the independent US investigatory agency charged with the respon-sibility of analysing all transportation accidents (see Section 20.6 for more background on the NTSB). In the event of an aeroplane crash, the NTSB assembles a seasoned team of engineers and flight-safety experts who are immediately dispatched to the crash site to conduct a thorough investigation, including interviewing witnesses, poring over flight logs and maintenance records, sifting through the wreckage to recover the flight recorder or 'black box', and, if necessary, literally reassembling the aircraft from its parts to determine the ultimate cause of the crash. Once its work is completed, the NTSB publishes a report summarizing the team's investigation, concluding with specific recommendations for avoiding future occurrences of this type of accident. The report is entered into a searchable database that is available to the general public,[15] and this has been one of the major factors underlying the remarkable safety record of commercial air travel in the US.

---

[15] See http://www.ntsb.gov/ntsb/query.asp.

Financial blow-ups are less immediately dire than plane crashes, generally involving no loss of life. However, as the financial crisis of 2008 amply illustrated, the disruption to economic life can be devastating in its own right, with far broader and longer-lasting impact than a plane crash. For these reasons, an independent organization dedicated to investigating, reporting, and archiving the 'accidents' of the financial industry may yield significant social benefits in much the same way that the NTSB has improved transportation safety enormously for all air travellers. By maintaining teams of experienced professionals—forensic accountants, financial engineers from industry and academia, and securities and tax attorneys—that work together on a regular basis to investigate the collapse of every major financial institution, a 'Capital Markets Safety Board' would be able to determine quickly and accurately how each collapse came about, and the resulting reports would be an invaluable source of ideas for improving financial markets and avoiding similar debacles in the future. We discuss this proposal in more detail in Section 20.6.

It is unrealistic to expect that market crashes, panics, collapses, and fraud will ever be completely eliminated from our capital markets, but we should avoid compounding our mistakes by failing to learn from them. A better-informed investing public will be the only means of conquering our fears and re-establishing the level of faith and trust that has made US financial markets among the most liquid and efficient in the world.

11.10 Discussion

One of the most significant consequences of the financial crisis of 2008 was the realization that the intellectual framework of economics and finance is incomplete. While the crisis exposed some of the limitations of neoclassical economics, critiques of traditional economic theory have been accumulating from within the profession for quite some time. The conflict between the rational expectations paradigm of economics and the many behavioural biases documented by psychologists, behavioural economists, sociologists, and neuroscientists has been hotly debated for decades. Rational expectations and its close cousin, the EMH, have come under fire because of their apparent failure in predicting and explaining the financial crisis.

Some of this criticism is undoubtedly misplaced populist anger at the life-altering economic consequences of the bursting of the housing bubble in 2006, and its knock-on effects on the financial system, employment, and real economic growth in its aftermath. In such an emotionally charged atmosphere, it is easy to forget the many genuine breakthroughs that have occurred in economics over the last half-century, such as general equilibrium theory, game theory, growth theory, econometrics, portfolio theory, and option-pricing models. But any virtue can become a vice when taken to an extreme. The fact that the 2,319-page Dodd–Frank financial reform bill was signed into law on 21 July 2010—six months before the Financial Crisis Inquiry Commission submitted its 27 January 2011 report, and well before economists developed any consensus on the crisis—underscores the relatively minor scientific role that economics has played in responding to the crisis. Imagine the US Food and Drug Administration approving a drug before its clinical trials are concluded, or the Federal Aviation Administration adopting new regulations in response to an airplane crash before the NTSB has completed its accident investigation.

There are legitimate arguments that the rigorous and internally consistent economic models of rational self-interest—the models used implicitly and explicitly by policymakers, central bankers, and regulators to formulate policy, manage leverage, and rein in risk-taking in the economy—are deficient. Even the most sophisticated stochastic dynamic general equilibrium models did not account for the US housing market boom and bust, and they were not rich enough to capture the consequences of securitization, credit default insurance, financial globalization, or the political dynamics underlying Fannie Mae and Freddie Mac.

However, we should not be too quick to dismiss the positive role that markets have played, even during the build-up to the crisis. In an April 2006 publication by the *Financial Times*, reporter Christine Senior filed a story on the enormous growth of the CDO market in Europe, quoting Nomura's estimate of $175 billion of CDOs issued in 2005. When asked by Senior to comment on this remarkable growth, Cian O'Carroll, European head of structured products at Fortis Investments, replied, 'You buy a AA-rated corporate bond you get paid LIBOR plus 20 basis points; you buy a AA-rated CDO and you get LIBOR plus 110 basis points' (Senior, 2006). Did investors ever ask why bonds with the identical rating were offering ninety basis points of additional yield, and where that yield might have been coming from? Even at the height of the CDO market, it seems that the crowd was still quite wise. It may not have been the disciples of the EMH who were misled during those frothy times, but, more likely, it was those investors who were convinced they had discovered a free lunch.

Rather than discarding rationality altogether, a more productive response may be to confront the inconsistencies between economic models of behaviour and those from other disciplines, and attempt to reconcile them and improve our models in the process. While frustrating, these contradictions often present opportunities for developing a deeper under-standing of the phenomena in question. In particular, neuroscience, psy-chology, anthropology, sociology, and economics all intersect with respect to human behaviour. When these disparate fields share the same object of study, their respective theories must be mutually consistent in their implications. For example, the neurophysiological mechanisms of risk processing must be consistent with psychological experiments involving human subjects choos-ing among risky alternatives; otherwise, flaws exist in one or both of these bodies of knowledge.[16] By reconciling the inconsistencies and contradictions between disciplines, we can develop a broader and deeper understanding of *Homo sapiens*.

This approach highlights the value of 'consilience', a term reintroduced into the lexicon by the great evolutionary biologist E.O. Wilson (1998). Wilson himself attributes its first use to William Whewell's 1840 treatise *The Philos-ophy of the Inductive Sciences*, in which Whewell wrote: 'The Consilience of Inductions takes place when an Induction, obtained from one class of facts, coincides with an Induction, obtained from another different class. This Con-silience is a test of the truth of the Theory in which it occurs.' In this book, and particularly this chapter, we hope to have facilitated the consilience between financial economics and the neurosciences.

From the perspective of the neurosciences, it is not surprising that there have been seventeen national-level banking-related crises around the globe since 1974, the majority of which were preceded by periods of rising real estate and stock prices, large capital inflows, and financial liberalization. Extended periods of prosperity act as an anaesthetic in the human brain, lulling investors, business leaders, and policymakers into a state of compla-cency, a drug-induced stupor that causes us to take risks that we know we should avoid. In the case of the über-fraudster Bernard Madoff, seasoned investors were apparently sucked into the fraud despite their better judge-ment because they found his returns too tempting to pass up.[17] In the case of subprime mortgages, homeowners who knew they could not afford certain homes proceeded to buy nonetheless, because the prospect of 'living large' through home price appreciation was too tempting to pass up. Investors in

---

[16] Of course, in many cases, these implications may not overlap. The particular biochemical structure of the neurotransmitters involved in fear learning has no direct bearing on the behavioural origins of time-varying stock market volatility, so checking for consistency between the former and the latter is unlikely to yield new insights. For those areas involving fundamental drivers and mechanisms of human behaviour, however, opportunities for consistency checks will often arise, and we should take advantage of them whenever possible.

[17] See Section 19.4 for a more detailed discussion of the Madoff Ponzi scheme and how US Securities and Exchange Commission (SEC) culture changed in the aftermath of the scheme's collapse in 2008.

mortgage-backed securities, who knew that AAA ratings were too optimistic given the riskiness of the underlying collateral, purchased these securities anyway, because they found the promised yields and past returns too tempting to pass up. If we add to these temptations a period of financial gain that anaesthetizes the general population—including CEOs, chief risk officers, investors, regulators, and politicians—it is easy to see how tulip bulbs, Internet stocks, gold, real estate, securitized debt, and fraudulent hedge funds could develop into bubbles. Such gains are unsustainable, and once the losses start mounting, our fear circuitry kicks in and panic ensues, a flight-to-safety leading to a market crash.

Like hurricanes, financial crises are a force of nature that cannot be legislated away, but we can greatly reduce the damage they do with proper preparation. In the long run, more transparency, more education—for investors, policymakers, and business leaders alike—and more behaviourally oriented and adaptive regulation will allow us to weather any type of financial crisis. Regulation enables us to restrain our behaviour during periods when we know that misbehaviour will reign; regulation is most useful during periods of collective fear or greed, and should be designed accordingly. Corporate governance should also be revisited from this perspective; if we truly value naysayers and whistle-blowers during periods of corporate excess, then we should institute changes in management to protect and reward their independence (see Chapter 19 for a more detailed discussion of the culture of finance and how to change certain negative aspects).

With respect to the future of economics, (Wilson 1998, p. 182) makes a thought-provoking observation in comparing the rate of progress in the medical sciences vs the social sciences:

> There is also progress in the social sciences, but it is much slower, and not at all animated by the same information flow and optimistic spirit….
>
> The crucial difference between the two domains is consilience: the medical sciences have it and the social sciences do not. Medical scientists build upon a coherent foundation of molecular and cell biology. They pursue elements of health and illness all the way down to the level of biophysical chemistry….
>
> Social scientists by and large spurn the idea of the hierarchical ordering of knowledge that unites and drives the natural sciences. Split into independent cadres, they stress precision in words within their specialty but seldom speak the same technical language from one specialty to the next.

This is a bitter pill for economists to swallow, but it provides a clear directive for improving the status quo.

Although economics occupies an enviable position among the social sciences because of its axiomatic consistency and uniformity, *Homo economicus* is a fiction that can no longer be maintained in light of mounting evidence to the contrary from allied fields like psychology and the cognitive neurosciences. For disciplines in which controlled experimentation is possible, consilience may be less critical to progress, because inconsistencies can be generated and resolved within the discipline through clever experimental design. For disciplines such as financial economics, however, in which controlled experimentation is more challenging, consilience is an essential means for moving the field forward. Even in fields where experiments are routine, consilience can speed up progress dramatically. The revolution in psychology that transformed the field from a loosely organized collection of interesting and suggestive experiments and hypotheses to a bona fide science occurred only within the last three decades, thanks to synergistic advances in neuroscience, medicine, computer science, and even evolutionary biology. This could be the future of economics.

If there is any truth to the adage that 'a crisis is a terrible thing to waste', we may have already missed our window of opportunity to reform our regulatory infrastructure for the better. The fact that time heals all wounds may be good for our mental health, but it may not help maintain our financial wealth or physical health. Having developed effective vaccines and treatments to deal with COVID-19 may mean the immediate crisis is over, but what about preparing for the next pandemic? Do we still have the political will to do so?

Policymakers should consider the parallels between Aron Ralston's predicament in Bluejohn Canyon and the current challenges we face such as cancer, Alzheimer's disease, future pandemics, climate change, and so on. When caught between a rock and a hard place, no one wants to do what Ralston eventually did; in fact, it took him five days to come to his terrible, life-saving decision. The only way to achieve such an extraordinary outcome is to develop a vision of an alternate reality so compelling that it can justify the magnitude of short-term pain required to achieve it. In the end, this is the essence of leadership—to unite the population in a shared vision that is far greater than what individuals could achieve left to their own devices.

12
The Psychophysiology of Trading

Critics of the efficient markets hypothesis argue that investors are often (if not always) irrational, exhibiting such predictable and financially ruinous biases as overconfidence (Fischoff and Slovic, 1980; Barber and Odean, 2001; Gervais and Odean, 2001), over-reaction (De Bondt and Thaler, 1985), loss aversion (Kahneman and Tversky, 1979; Shefrin and Statman, 1985; Odean, 1998), herding (Huberman and Regev, 2001), psychological accounting (Tversky and Kahneman, 1981), miscalibration of probabilities (Lichtenstein, Fischhoff, and Phillips, 1982), and regret (Bell, 1983; Clarke, Krase, and Statman, 1994).[1] The sources of these irrationalities are often attributed to psychological factors such as fear and greed, or other emotional responses to large price fluctuations and other dramatic changes in an individual's wealth. From this perspective, either the run-up to the financial crisis of 2008 was driven by unbridled greed and optimism, or the precipitous drop in value of a significant portion of the US economy must have been due to irrational fears and pessimism, or both.

However, as we saw in Chapter 11, research at the intersection of the cognitive sciences and financial economics suggests that there is an important link between rationality in decision-making and emotion (Grossberg and Gutowski, 1987; Damasio, 1994; Elster, 1998; Lo, 1999; Loewenstein, 2000; Peters and Slovic, 2000), implying that the two notions are not antithetical, but, in fact, complementary.

In this chapter, we apply this insight to a very specific financial decision-making context: trading. Financial securities traders are ideal subjects in which to study the link between emotion and rational decision-making in the face of uncertainty. Because the basic functions of securities trading involve frequent decisions concerning risk–reward trade-offs, traders are almost continuously engaged in the activity we wish to study. They are typically provided with significant economic incentives to avoid many of the biases that are often associated with irrational investment practices. Moreover, they have undergone a variety of training exercises, apprenticeships, and trial periods

---

[1] This chapter, including the tables and figure, is adapted from Lo, A. W., and Repin, D. V. (2002). The psychophysiology of real-time financial risk processing. *Journal of Cognitive Neuroscience* 14(3): 323–339.

The Adaptive Markets Hypothesis. Andrew W. Lo and Ruixun Zhang, Oxford University Press. © Andrew W. Lo and Ruixun Zhang (2024). DOI: 10.1093/oso/9780199681143.003.0012

through which their skills have been finely honed. Therefore, they are likely to be among the most rational decision-makers in the general population. Finally, due to the real-time nature of most professional trading operations, it is possible to construct accurate records of the environment in which traders make their decisions (i.e. the fluctuations of market prices of the securities they trade). With such real-time records, we are able to match market events such as periods of high price volatility to synchronous real-time measurements of physiological characteristics.

To study the role of emotion in their decision-making process, we conducted an experiment that involved measuring the traders' physiological characteristics—skin conductance (also referred to as electrodermal response or galvanic skin response), blood volume pulse (BVP), heart rate (HR), muscle response, respiration, and body temperature—in real-time, during live trading sessions. Using portable biofeedback equipment, we were able to measure these physiological characteristics in each trader's natural environment without disrupting their workflow while simultaneously capturing real-time financial pricing data from which market events could be defined. This allowed us to conduct our study *in vivo* with minimal interference, and therefore minimal contamination of the subjects' natural motives and behaviour. And by matching the market events against the traders' physiological responses, we are able to determine the relation between measures of financial risk and the dynamics of emotional states.

In a pilot sample of ten traders, we found statistically significant differences in mean electrodermal responses during transient market events compared to a control baseline with no events, and statistically significant mean changes in cardiovascular variables during periods of heightened market volatility compared to a control baseline with normal volatility. We also observed significant differences in mean physiological responses among the ten traders that may be systematically related to the amount of trading experience.

12.1 Measuring Emotional Response

To measure the emotional responses of our subjects during their trading activities, we focus on their indirect physiological manifestations, which are largely controlled by the autonomic nervous system (ANS) (Cacioppo, Tassinary, and Berntson, 2000). The ANS is one of the body's control systems that regulates basic bodily functions, those that work automatically without conscious effort like the beating of the heart, sweating, breathing, and blood pressure. It is the system responsible for the fight-or-flight response discussed in previous chapters, which means it is also related to emotional and cognitive processes. ANS responses are relatively easy to measure—many of them can be measured non-invasively without interfering with cognitive tasks performed by the subject. ANS responses occur on a time scale of seconds, which is essential for the investigation of real-time risk-processing.

Previous studies have focused primarily on time-averaged levels of autonomic activity (over hours or tens of minutes) as a function of task complexity or mental strain. For example, some experiments have considered the link between autonomic activity and driving conditions and road familiarity in non-professional drivers (Brown and Huffman, 1972), and between autonomic activity and the stage of flight (take-off, steady flight, landing) in a jet fighter flight simulator (Lindholm and Cheatham, 1983). The focus of subsequent research shifted towards finer temporal scales of autonomic responses associated with cognitive and emotional processes, on the order of seconds. Perhaps the most influential set of experiments in this area was conducted in the context of an investigation of the role of emotion in decision-making processes (Damasio, 1994). In one such experiment, skin conductance responses were measured in subjects involved in a gambling task (Bechara et al., 1997). The results indicated that the anticipation of the more risky outcomes led to more skin conductance responses than anticipation of the less risky ones. As discussed in Chapter 11, Breiter et al. (2001) localized the brain circuitry involved in anticipating monetary rewards via functional magnetic resonance imaging (fMRI), which turned out to be the exact same circuitry involved in cocaine addiction. Fredrikson et al. (1998) reported neuroanatomical correlates of skin conductance activity with the brain regions that also support anticipation, affect, and cognitively or emotionally mediated motor preparation. A subsequent set of experiments conducted by Critchley et al. (1999) supports the significance of autonomic responses during risk-taking and reward-related behaviour. The authors provide more details on brain activation correlates of peripheral autonomic responses, claiming it is possible to discriminate between activity patterns related to changing versus continuing the behaviour based on the history of immediate gains or losses in a gambling task.

In our study, we focus on five physiological characteristics related to the ANS—skin conductance, cardiovascular data (BVP and HR), respiration rate, and body temperature–as well as muscle response as measured through electromyography (EMG). We discuss each of these components next before turning to our experimental design and results.

The skin conductance response (SCR) is measured by the voltage drop between two electrodes placed a few centimetres apart on the surface of the skin. Changes in skin conductance occur when the eccrine sweat glands that are innervated by the sympathetic ANS fibres receive a signal from a certain part of the brain. Three distinct 'brain–information systems' can potentially elicit SCR signals (Boucsein, 1992). The affect arousal system is capable of generating a phasic response (a response that lasts temporarily—in this case on the scale of seconds—even in the continued presence of stimuli) that is associated directly with sensory input, indicating an attention-focusing or defence response. The amygdala is the primary brain region involved; the emotional response to a novel or highly complex task is an example of affect arousal. Another system that can initiate a phasic SCR is centred on the basal ganglia, and is related to preparatory activation, mediated by internal cognitive processes. The body exhibits increased perceptual and motor readiness and high attention levels. The expectation of an event, or preparation for an important action, illustrates the operation of this system. The third system, often called the 'effort system', produces a tonic change (a sustained response in the presence of sustained stimuli) in the level of skin conductance, and is related to the long-term changes in the general emotional (i.e. 'hedonic') state or attitude, indicating a nonspecific increase in attention or arousal. Information processing in the hippocampus is believed to be behind this system, which is associated with a higher degree of conscious awareness, whereas the first two systems have been attributed mostly to subconscious processes.

The cardiovascular system consists of the heart and all the blood vessels. Here, the variables of particular interest are BVP and HR. BVP is the rate of flow of blood through a particular blood vessel, related to both blood pressure and the diameter of the blood vessel. The constriction or dilation of blood vessels is controlled by the sympathetic branch of the ANS. Along with electrodermal activity, it has been shown to be related to information processing and decision-making (Papillo and Shapiro, 1990). HR refers to the frequency of the contractions of the heart muscle, or myocardium. Specialized neurons—the so-called 'pacemaker' cells—initiate the contraction of the myocardium. The output of the pacemaker cells is controlled by both the parasympathetic and sympathetic branches of the ANS, the former leading to a decrease in HR, and the latter to an increase. BVP and HR track each other closely—a deceleration in HR usually causes an increase in BVP. Unlike indications of SCR arousal, which refer mostly to cognitive processes, changes in cardiovascular variables register higher levels of arousal that are often somatically mediated. These variables provide supplemental information for interpreting high SCR signals; for example, an elevated SCR accompanied by an increase in HR may be an indication of extreme significance of the task or stimulus; alternatively, it may simply indicate that some physical activity is being performed simultaneously (Boucsein, 1992).

Respiration influences HR through vascular receptors (Lorig and Schwartz, 1990). Although this variable is not usually of primary psychological importance, it is a reliable indicator of physically demanding activities undertaken by the subject (e.g. speaking or coughing), which can often yield anomalous sensor readings if not properly accounted for. Respiration can be measured by placing a sensor that monitors chest expansion and compression.

Body temperature regulation involves the integration of autonomic, motor, and endocrine responses. Several studies have related the temperatures of different parts of the body to certain cognitive and emotional contents of the task or stimuli. For example, the forehead temperature (used as a proxy for brain temperature) increases while experiencing negative emotions; cooling enhances a positive affect, while warming depresses it (McIntosh et al., 1997). Another study reports that skin temperature of the hand increases with positive affect, and decreases with threatening and unpleasant tasks (Rimm-Kaufman and Kagan, 1996).

Finally, EMG measurements are based on the electrical signals generated by the contraction process of striated muscles. Muscle action potentials travel along muscle fibres, but some portion of this electrical activity leaks to the skin surface, where it can be detected with the help of surface electrodes. The activation of particular muscles reflects different types of actions. For example, the activation of the masseter muscle, a facial muscle that helps the jaw close, may indicate ongoing speech; the activation of the forearm muscle group (i.e. the flexor digitorum group) corresponds to finger movements, such as typing on a keyboard. In addition to their role in motor activity, certain muscle groups exhibit strong correlations with emotional states. Most of the research in this literature has focused on facial muscles, since facial expressions have been linked to emotional states (Ekman, 1982). For example, an increase in EMG activity along the forehead is associated with anxiety and tension, and an increase in activity along the brow accompanied by a slight decrease in activity along the cheek often corresponds to unpleasant sensory stimuli (Cacioppo, Tassinary, and Berntson, 2000). EMG measurements can capture very subtle changes in muscle activity that are able to differentiate otherwise indistinguishable response patterns. However, in our current implementation, the role of EMG measurements is limited to identifying and eliminating anomalous sensor readings caused by certain physical movements of a subject.

12.2 Experimental Design

Here, we briefly describe our experiment and data collection process, before turning to the main findings in Section 12.4. We provide the full details of our subjects, data collection, feature extraction, and statistical tests for interested readers in Appendix C.

Our sample of subjects consisted of ten professional traders employed by the foreign-exchange and interest-rate derivatives business unit of a major global financial institution based in Boston, Massachusetts. This institution provides banking and other financial services to clients ranging from small regional start-ups to Fortune 500 multinational corporations. At the time of our study, the foreign exchange and interest rate derivatives business unit employed approximately ninety professionals, of whom two-thirds specialized in the trading of foreign exchange and related instruments, and one-third specialized in the trading of interest rate derivative securities. In a typical day, this business unit would engage in 1,000–1,200 trades, with an average size of $3–$5 million per trade. Approximately 80% of the trades were executed on behalf of the clients of the financial institution, with the remaining 20% motivated by the financial institution's market-making activities.

For each of the ten subjects, five physiological variables were monitored in real time during the entire duration of each session, while the subjects sat at their trading consoles (Fig. 12.1). Six sensors were used to capture SCR, BVP, body temperature, respiration, and facial and forearm EMG.

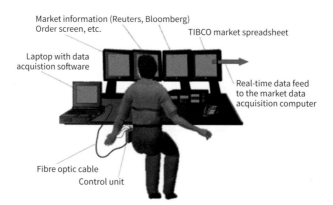

Fig. 12.1 Typical set-up for the measurement of real-time physiological responses of financial traders during live trading sessions. Real-time market data used by the traders were recorded synchronously and subsequently analysed with the physiological response data.

The benefits of acquiring real-time physiological measurements *in vivo* must be balanced against the cost of measurement error, spurious signals, and other statistical artefacts, which, if left untreated, can obscure and confound genuine signals in the data. To eliminate as many artefacts as possible while maximizing the informational content of the data, each of the five physiological variables were preprocessed with filters calibrated to each variable individually, and adaptive time windows were used in place of fixed-length windows in order to match the event-driven nature of the market variables.

After pre-processing, the following seven features were extracted from the SCR, BVP, temperature, and respiration signals:

1. Time of onset of SCRs.
2. Amplitude of SCRs.
3. Average HR (at three-second intervals).
4. BVP signal amplitude.
5. Respiration rate (at five-second intervals).
6. Respiration amplitude.
7. Temperature change (with a ten-second lag).

These features were selected to reflect the different properties and information contained in the raw physiological variables. SCRs were characterized by smooth 'bumps' with a relatively fast onset and slow decay. Consequently, the number of such bumps and their relative strength are excellent summary measures of the SCR signal. The three- and five-second intervals for heart and respiration rates, respectively, were chosen as a compromise between the need for finer time slices to distinguish the onset and completion of physiological and market events, and the necessity of a sufficient number of heartbeats and respiration cycles within each interval to compute an average. Under normal conditions, a typical subject will exhibit an average of 3–4 heartbeats per three-second interval and approximately three breaths per five-second interval. The temperature was the most slow-varying physiological signal, and the ten-second interval to register its change reflected the maximum possible interval in our analysis.

For each session, the real-time market data for key financial instruments actively traded or monitored by the subject was collected synchronously with the physiological data. In particular, across the ten subjects, a total of fifteen instruments were considered—thirteen foreign currencies and two futures contracts: the euro (EUR), the Japanese yen (JPY), the British pound (GBP), the Canadian dollar (CAD), the Swiss franc (CHF), the Australian dollar

(AUD), the New Zealand dollar (NZD), the Mexican peso (MXP), the Brazilian real (BRL), the Argentinian peso (ARS), the Colombian peso (COP), the Venezuelan bolivar (VEB), the Chilean peso (CLP), S&P 500 futures (SPU), and eurodollar futures (EDU). For each security, four time series were monitored: (1) the bid price, P_t^b; (2) the ask price, P_t^a; (3) the bid/ask spread, $S_t \equiv P_t^b - P_t^a$; and (4) the net return, $R_t \equiv (P_t - P_{t-1})/P_{t-1}$, where P_t denotes the price at time t. All prices were sampled every second.

For each of the financial time series, we identified three classes of market events: deviations, trend reversals, and volatility events. These events are often cited by traders as significant developments requiring heightened attention, potentially signalling a shift in market dynamics and risk exposure. With these definitions and calibrations in hand, we implemented an automatic procedure for detecting deviations, trend reversals, and volatility events for all the relevant time series in each session. Table 12.1 reports the event counts for the financial time series monitored in each subject. Feature vectors were then constructed for all detected market events in all time series for all subjects, and a set of control feature vectors was generated by applying the same feature extraction process to randomly selected windows containing no events of any kind. One set of control feature vectors were constructed for deviation and trend reversal events (at ten-second intervals), and a second set was constructed for volatility-type events (at five-minute intervals). A two-sided t-test was applied to each component of the feature vector and the corresponding control vector to test the null hypothesis that the feature vectors were statistically indistinguishable from the control feature vectors.

For volatility events, which occurred in five-minute intervals by definition ('event windows'), we constructed feature vectors containing the following information for the duration of the event window:

1. Number of SCRs.
2. Mean SCR amplitude.
3. Mean HR.
4. Mean ratio of BVP amplitude to local baseline.
5. Mean ratio of BVP amplitude to global baseline.
6. Number of temperature changes exceeding 0.1°F.
7. Mean respiration rate.
8. Mean respiration amplitude.

The local baseline for the BVP signal was the average level during the event window and the global baseline was the average over the entire recording

Table 12.1 Number of deviation (DEV), trend reversal (TRV), and volatility (VOL) events detected in real-time market data for each trader over the course of each trading session.

Trader ID	EUR			JPY			Other Major Currencies[a]			Latin American Currencies[b]			Derivatives[c]		
	DEV	TRV	VOL	DEV	TRV	VOL	DEV	TRV	VOL	DEV	TRV	VOL	DEV	TRV	VOL
B32	21	16	15	25	17	15	–	–	–	–	–	–	–	–	–
B34	18	10	14	17	17	14	–	–	–	–	–	–	–	–	–
B35	20	16	14	13	17	15	21	9	15	24	16	13	–	–	–
B36	–	–	–	–	–	–	–	–	–	–	–	–	28	23	31
B37	19	19	14	18	18	12	18	18	14	105	86	63	–	–	–
B38	21	20	12	22	18	13	23	20	15	96	61	56	–	–	–
B39	–	–	–	–	–	–	–	–	–	–	–	–	40	37	23
B310	10	17	10	18	16	14	116	59	61	–	–	–	–	–	–
B311	17	15	15	17	16	15	94	61	67	–	–	–	–	–	–
B312	19	17	15	16	19	13	107	83	71	–	–	–	–	–	–

[a]GBP, CAD, CHF, AUD, NZD.
[b]MXP, BRL, ARS, COP, VEB, CLP.
[c]EDU, SPU.

session for each trader. The control feature vectors were constructed by applying the feature extraction process to randomly selected five-minute windows containing no events of any kind. For the other two types of market events, deviations and trend reversals, 'pre-event' and 'post-event' feature vectors were constructed before and after each market event using the same variables, where the features were aggregated over ten-second windows immediately preceding and following the event. Control feature vectors were also generated for these cases.

The motivation for the post-event feature vector was to capture the subject's reaction to the event, with the pre-event feature vector as a benchmark from which to measure the magnitude of the reaction. A comparison between the pre-event feature vector and a control feature vector may provide an indication of a subject's anticipation of the event. The latency of the autonomic responses reported in previous studies was on the time scale of 1–10 seconds (Cacioppo, Tassinary, and Berntson, 2000); hence, ten-second event windows were judged to be long enough for event-related autonomic responses to occur, and short enough to minimize the likelihood of overlaps with other events or anomalies. Five-minute windows were used for volatility events because ten-second intervals were insufficient for meaningful volatility calculations. For all the financial time series used in this study, and for most financial time series in general, there are few volatility events that occur in any ten-second interval, except under extreme conditions (e.g. the stock market crash of 19 October 1987). No such conditions prevailed during any of our sessions.

12.3 Results

The statistical analysis of our physiology and market data was motivated by four objectives: (1) to identify particular classes of events with statistically significant differences in mean autonomic responses before or after an event, compared to the control baseline with no events; (2) to identify particular traders or groups of traders based on their experience or other personal characteristics who demonstrated significant mean autonomic responses during market events; (3) to identify particular physiological variables demonstrating significant mean response levels immediately following the event, or during the event anticipation period, as compared to a control baseline with no events; and (4) to identify particular financial instruments or groups of instruments that were associated with significant mean autonomic responses.

To address the first objective, a total of eight types of events were used for each of the time series:

1. Price deviations.
2. Spread deviations.
3. Return deviations.
4. Price trend reversals.
5. Spread trend reversals.
6. Maximum volatility.
7. Price volatility.
8. Return volatility.

For each type of event, a two-sided t-test was performed for the pooled sample of all subjects and all time series, in which the mean autonomic responses during event periods were compared to the mean autonomic responses during control periods with no events.

The t-statistics corresponding to the two-sided hypothesis test are given in the left sub-panel of Table 12.2, labelled 'All Traders'. Statistics that are significant at the 5% level, based on the t-distribution with the appropriate degrees of freedom for each entry, are in bold. For deviations and trend reversals, both the number of SCRs and the number of jumps in temperature reached statistically significant levels for three out of the six event types. BVP amplitude-related features were highly significant for volatility events; significance levels less than 1% were obtained for both BVP amplitude features for all three types of volatility events. Because the results were so similar across the three types of volatility events (maximum volatility, price volatility, and return volatility), we report the results for only one in Table 12.2: maximum volatility. Such patterns of autonomic responses may indicate the presence of transient emotional responses to deviations and trend reversal events that occurred within ten-second windows, while volatility events, defined in five-minute windows, elicited a tonic response in BVP.

To explore the potential differences between experienced and less experienced traders, our sample of ten traders was divided into two groups, each consisting of five traders, the first containing highly experienced traders and the second containing traders with low or moderate experience, where the levels of experience were determined through interviews with the traders' supervisors. The results for each of the two groups are reported in the two right subpanels of Table 12.2, labelled 'High Experience' and 'Low or Moderate Experience'. Traders with high experience generally exhibited low responses to deviations and trend reversal events, with only two types of

Table 12.2 *t*-statistics for two-sided hypothesis tests of the difference in mean autonomic responses during market events versus no-event controls for each of the eight components of the physiology feature vectors (rows) for each type of market event (columns).

Physiology Features	All Traders						High Experience						Low or Moderate Experience					
	DEV, Price	DEV, Spread	DEV, Return	TRV, Price	TRV, Spread	VOL, Maximum	DEV, Price	DEV, Spread	DEV, Return	TRV, Price	TRV, Spread	VOL, Maximum	DEV, Price	DEV, Spread	DEV, Return	TRV, Price	TRV, Spread	VOL, Maximum
Number of SCRs	**2.872**	0.604	**2.088**	**1.664**	0.636	0.579	0.561	1.228	-0.221	-1.261	0.184	**2.081**	**2.696**	0.123	**2.752**	**2.170**	-0.665	-0.688
Average SCR amplitude	-0.695	0.887	0.186	-2.478	1.136	0.880	0.030	0.344	0.744	-1.340	1.149	0.904	0.756	1.578	-1.265	-1.947	-0.012	-0.615
Average HR	0.905	-0.588	-0.596	-0.617	1.032	-0.270	0.449	**1.886**	-1.797	-1.635	**1.836**	-2.018	1.310	0.051	-0.382	-1.106	-0.311	1.283
Average BVP amplitude relative to local baseline	0.128	-0.855	0.688	1.408	-0.523	**3.619**	-0.061	-0.747	0.334	0.015	0.164	**2.623**	-0.204	-1.775	0.875	**1.796**	-1.289	**2.708**
Average BVP amplitude relative to global baseline	1.417	-2.726	**2.324**	1.417	-2.211	**2.886**	-2.529	-1.367	1.590	1.110	-1.165	**2.301**	**1.917**	-2.664	**1.884**	**2.082**	-1.759	**2.758**
Number of temperature jumps	0.988	**2.820**	0.650	**1.777**	**4.868**	-2.482	-1.010	-1.435	NA	NA	NA	1.644	0.837	**2.902**	1.145	**2.445**	**2.633**	-3.213
Average respiration rate	0.729	-1.173	0.671	1.155	-1.628	-0.064	-1.556	1.109	0.121	0.866	-0.102	0.093	0.079	-0.552	0.323	-0.631	-2.170	-1.528
Average respiration amplitude	-1.646	-0.250	0.136	0.034	-1.487	-3.499	1.087	0.265	-1.777	-0.657	0.121	-0.607	-2.749	-1.319	**2.142**	0.055	-2.832	-4.533

Statistics significant at the 5% level are in bold.

The left panel gives aggregate results for all traders. Similar *t*-tests for traders with high experience and low or moderate experience are shown in the middle and right panels, respectively. Entries marked 'NA' indicate that no valid data were present in either the event or control feature vector for the particular market-event type. DEV = deviation; HR = heart rate; SCR = skin conductance response; TRV = trend reversal; VOL = volatility. BVP = blood volume pulse.

market events eliciting significant mean autonomic responses (spread deviations and spread trend reversals on their average HR). However, even for experienced traders, volatility events induced statistically significant mean responses for both number of SCRs and BVP amplitude. Less experienced traders showed a much higher number of significant mean responses in the number of SCRs, BVP amplitude, and the number of temperature increases for deviations and trend reversal events. Table 12.2 shows that sessions with low and moderately experienced traders yielded thirteen t-statistics significant at the 5% level, while sessions with high-experience traders yielded only five t-statistics significant at the 5% level. For both sets of traders, volatility events were associated with significant BVP amplitude. The observed differences in response to deviations and trend reversals indicate that less experienced traders may be more sensitive to short-term changes in the market variables than their more experienced colleagues.

To address the third objective, identifying particular physiological variables demonstrating significant mean autonomic responses before and after an event, the ten-second intervals immediately preceding and immediately following each deviation and trend reversal event were compared to the control time intervals with no event. Two separate t-tests were conducted, one for pre-event time intervals and another for post-event intervals, for each of the three types of deviations and two types of trend reversals. Because the objective was to detect differences in how pre- and post-event feature vectors differed from the control, we used the same control feature vectors for both sets of t-tests. In all cases, the t-tests were designed to test the null hypothesis that both pre- and post-event feature vectors were statistically indistinguishable from the control feature vector. Surprisingly, these two sets of t-tests yielded very similar results, reported in Table 12.3, implying that none of the physiological variables were predictors of anticipatory emotional responses. These findings may be at least partly explained by how the events were defined. In particular, the definitions of deviation and trend reversal are instances where the time series achieved a prespecified deviation from the time-series mean and its moving average, respectively. In the absence of large jumps, the values of the time series near an event defined in this way are likely to be comparable to the event itself. Therefore, the traders may be responding to market conditions occurring throughout the pre- and post-event period, not only at the exact time of the event, hence the similarity between the two periods. More complex definitions of events may allow us to discriminate between pre- and post-event physiological responses.

Table 12.3 *t*-statistics for two-sided hypothesis tests of the difference in mean autonomic responses during pre- and post-event time intervals versus no-event controls for each of the eight components of the physiology feature vectors (rows) for each type of market event (columns).

	Market Events											
	Pre-event Interval						Post-event Interval					
Physiology Features	DEV, Price	DEV, Spread	DEV, Return	TRV, Price	TRV, Spread	VOL, Maximum	DEV, Price	DEV, Spread	DEV, Return	TRV, Price	TRV, Spread	VOL, Maximum
Number of SCRs	**3.756**	1.543	**2.540**	**2.118**	**2.401**	0.579	**2.872**	0.604	**2.088**	**1.664**	0.636	0.579
Average SCR amplitude	0.700	-0.454	-1.793	0.511	1.068	0.880	-0.695	0.887	0.186	-2.478	1.136	0.880
Average HR	0.968	-0.205	-0.552	-0.663	-0.386	-0.270	0.905	-0.588	-0.596	-0.617	1.032	-0.270
Average BVP amplitude relative to local baseline	0.043	-0.895	0.060	0.814	-0.045	**3.619**	0.128	-0.855	0.688	1.408	-0.523	**3.619**
Average BVP amplitude relative to global baseline	1.183	-2.794	**2.397**	1.317	-2.256	**2.886**	1.417	-2.726	**2.324**	1.417	-2.211	**2.886**
Number of temperature jumps	1.110	**2.767**	0.505	**2.158**	**3.925**	-2.482	0.988	**2.820**	0.650	**1.777**	**4.868**	-2.482
Average respiration rate	1.261	-1.650	-0.254	1.303	-1.999	-0.064	0.729	-1.173	0.671	1.155	-1.628	-0.064
Average respiration amplitude	-1.620	-0.067	0.561	0.068	-1.807	-3.499	-1.646	-0.250	0.136	0.034	-1.487	-3.499

Statistics significant at the 5% level are in bold.

The left panel contains *t*-statistics for pre-event feature vectors and the right panel contains *t*-statistics for post-event feature vectors, both tested against the same set of controls.

BVP = blood volume pulse; DEV = deviation; HR = heart rate; SCR = skin conductance response; TRV = trend reversal; VOL = volatility.

Finally, to address the fourth objective, the following four groups of financial instruments were formed on the basis of similarity in their statistical characteristics:

- Group 1: EUR, JPY.
- Group 2: GBP, CAD, CHF, AUD, NZD (other major currencies).
- Group 3: MXP, BRL, ARS, COP, VEB, CLP (Latin American currencies).
- Group 4: SPU, EDU (derivatives).

Group 1 was by far the most actively traded set of financial instruments, accounting for most of the trading activities of the ten traders in our sample. Therefore, it is unsurprising that the pattern of statistical significance for Group 1, as seen in Table 12.4, is almost identical to the pattern for all traders in Table 12.2 (the left panel). SCR is significant for price and return deviations, while temperature jumps are significant for spread deviations and price trend reversals, and both measures of BVP are significant for volatility events. For Group 2, none of the eight physiological variables were significant for price or spread deviations, although temperature changes and respiration rates were significant for return deviations, and both BVP measures were significant for price trend reversals and volatility events. The financial instruments in Group 2 were not the primary focus of any of the traders in our sample, which may explain the different patterns of significance compared to Group 1. Group 4 contains the fewest significant responses, consistent with the fact that these securities were traded by two of the most experienced traders in our sample. Derivative securities are considerably more complex instruments than spot currencies, requiring more skill and training. However, SCR was significant for both price and return deviations in Group 4, which was not the case for the sample of high-experience traders (see Table 12.2). SCR was also significant for volatility events in Group 4, which is consistent with the central role that volatility plays in the pricing and hedging of derivative securities (Black and Scholes, 1973; Merton, 1973). Volatility is a sophisticated aspect of the trading milieu, requiring a greater degree of training to appreciate fully its implications for market trends and profit-and-loss probabilities. This may explain the fact that SCR is significant for volatility events only among the high-experience traders (see Table 12.2) and the derivatives traders (see Table 12.4).

Table 12.4 t-statistics for two-sided hypothesis tests of the difference in mean autonomic responses during market events versus no-event controls for each of the eight components of the physiology feature vectors (rows) for each type of market event (columns), grouped into four distinct sets of financial instruments.

Physiology Features	Group 1: EUR and JPY						Group 2: Other Major Currencies[a]						Group 3: Latin American Currencies[b]						Group 4: Derivatives[c]					
	DEV, Price	DEV, Spread	DEV, Return	TRV, Price	TRV, Spread	VOL, Maximum	DEV, Price	DEV, Spread	DEV, Return	TRV, Price	TRV, Spread	VOL, Maximum	DEV, Price	DEV, Spread	DEV, Return	TRV, Price	TRV, Spread	VOL, Maximum	DEV, Price	DEV, Spread	DEV, Return	TRV, Price	TRV, Spread	VOL, Maximum
Number of SCRs	1.653	-1.902	**1.964**	-0.554	**-2.286**	-0.940	0.332	0.112	0.544	-1.795	**-2.417**	-1.108	**2.498**	**2.188**	-0.397	**2.995**	-0.405	0.898	**2.682**	1.094	1.669	1.594	-0.239	**2.236**
Average SCR amplitude	-1.639	0.623	0.279	-1.756	1.098	-1.112	-0.503	0.540	1.138	**-2.190**	-0.106	0.896	1.116	1.279	-1.525	-1.802	**2.220**	-0.986	-0.610	1.236	0.930	-1.513	0.242	-1.510
Average HR	0.731	-0.004	-1.268	-1.815	-0.698	-1.612	-0.991	-1.452	-1.034	-1.326	-0.308	-1.089	**2.921**	-1.432	-1.070	-1.002	-1.416	1.183	0.816	-0.322	0.577	0.492	0.515	-0.169
Average BVP amplitude relative to local baseline	0.562	-1.368	-0.805	1.273	0.885	**2.587**	-0.922	0.220	1.457	**2.323**	-1.275	**2.308**	-0.982	-0.001	**2.828**	1.454	0.598	**2.192**	-0.592	**-3.032**	**-3.953**	-0.894	-1.904	-1.433
Average BVP amplitude relative to global baseline	0.597	**-3.010**	1.714	0.375	-0.252	**2.592**	0.521	1.448	0.972	**3.087**	-1.499	**2.633**	-1.925	-0.849	1.482	0.259	-0.351	-0.129	-0.660	-1.501	**-3.274**	-1.626	**-2.004**	**-2.411**
Number of temperature jumps	0.688	**4.141**	-1.444	**2.283**	0.295	**-2.043**	1.073	-1.557	**2.404**	1.248	**3.726**	-1.564	-1.603	-1.275	-1.922	-0.512	-1.128	-1.540	-1.367	-1.349	-1.362	-1.367	-1.053	NA
Average respiration rate	0.525	-1.741	-0.797	0.163	-1.884	-0.004	0.756	-0.560	**2.023**	-1.095	-1.784	-0.116	0.037	0.446	-1.124	0.643	-1.392	0.125	-1.946	-0.291	0.361	0.416	-1.105	-1.725
Average respiration amplitude	-2.120	-0.692	0.345	-0.509	-0.935	-2.079	-0.746	0.560	0.470	0.905	0.893	**-3.839**	0.280	-0.207	1.426	-0.360	-0.534	-0.437	0.920	-0.955	-1.915	1.257	1.593	-0.039

Statistics significant at the 5% level are in bold.

[a] GBP, CAD, CHF, AUD, NZD.

[b] MXP, BRL, ARS, COP, VEB, CLP.

[c] EDU, SPU.

Entries marked 'NA' indicate that no valid data were present in either the event or control feature vector for the particular market-event type.

BVP = blood volume pulse; DEV = deviation; HR = heart rate; SCR = skin conductance response; TRV = trend reversal; VOL = volatility.

12.4 Discussion

Our findings suggest that emotional responses are a significant factor in the real-time processing of financial risks. Contrary to the common belief that emotions have no place in the rational financial decision-making process, the physiological variables associated with the ANS are highly correlated with market events even for highly experienced professional traders. Moreover, the response patterns among variables and events differed in important ways for less experienced traders—for example the mean autonomic responses were significantly higher—suggesting the possibility of relating trading skills to certain measurable physiological characteristics.

More generally, our experiments demonstrate the feasibility of relating real-time quantitative changes in cognitive inputs (in our case, financial information) to the corresponding quantitative changes in physiological responses in a complex field environment. Despite the challenges of such measurements, a wealth of information can be obtained regarding high-pressure decision-making under uncertainty. Financial traders operate in a controlled environment where the inputs and outputs of their decisions are carefully recorded, and where the subjects are highly trained, with substantial economic incentives to make rational trading decisions. Therefore, *in vivo* experiments in the securities trading context are likely to become an important part of the empirical analysis of individual risk preferences and the decision-making process. In particular, there is considerable anecdotal evidence that subjects involved in professional trading activities perform very differently depending on whether real financial capital is at risk, or if they are trading with 'play' money. Such distinctions have been documented in other contexts; for example, as discussed in Chapter 11, it has been shown that different brain regions are activated during a subject's naturally occurring smile and a forced smile (Damasio, 1994). For this reason, measuring subjects while they are making decisions in their natural environment is essential for any truly unbiased study of the financial decision-making process.

In capturing the often subconscious relationships between cognitive inputs and affective reactions, of which our subjects may not be fully aware, our findings may be viewed more broadly as a study of cognitive–emotional interactions and the genesis of intuition. Decision-making processes based on intuition are characterized by low levels of cognitive control and conscious awareness, rapid processing rates, and a lack of clear organizing principles. When intuitive judgements are formed, a large number of cues are processed simultaneously, and the task is not decomposed into subtasks (Hammond et al., 1987). Expert judgement is often based on intuition, not on explicit analytical processing, making it almost impossible to fully explain or replicate the process of how that judgement has been formed. This is particularly germane to financial traders. As a group, they are unusually heterogeneous with respect to educational background and formal analytical skills, yet the most successful traders seem to trade on their intuition about price swings and market dynamics, often without the ability (or the need) to articulate a precise quantitative algorithm for making these complex decisions (Schwager, 1989, 1992; Niederhoffer, 1997). Their intuitive trading 'rules' are based on the associations and relationships between various informational tokens that are formed on a subconscious level. Our findings, like those in the extant cognitive sciences literature, suggest that decisions based on intuitive judgements require not only cognitive mechanisms, but also emotional ones. A natural conjecture is that such emotional mechanisms are at least partly responsible for the ability to form intuitive judgements, and for those judgements to be incorporated into a rational decision-making process.

Our results may surprise some financial economists because of the apparent inconsistency with market rationality, but a more sophisticated view of the role of emotion in human cognition—see Chapter 11 and Rolls (1990, 1994, 1999), for example—can reconcile any contradiction in a complete and intellectually satisfying manner. Emotion is the basis for a reward-and-punishment system that facilitates the selection of advantageous behavioural actions, providing the numeraire for animals to engage in a cost–benefit analysis of the various actions open to them (Rolls, 1999, Chapter 10.3). From an evolutionary perspective, emotion is a powerful adaptation that dramatically improves the efficiency with which animals learn from their environment and their past.

These evolutionary underpinnings are more than simple speculation in the context of financial traders. The extraordinary degree of competitiveness of global financial markets and the outsized rewards that accrue to the 'fittest' traders suggest that a form of Darwinian selection—financial selection, to be specific—is at work in determining the typical profile of the successful trader. Unsuccessful traders are generally 'eliminated' from the population after suffering a certain level of losses. Our results indicate that emotion is a significant determinant of the evolutionary fitness of financial traders. The binary choice model of Part I can be extended to this context as well, along the lines of earlier evolutionary models of traders and trading strategies such as Blume and Easley (1992), Farmer (2001, 2002), Farmer and Lo (1999), Luo (1995, 1998, 2001, 2003), and Kogan et al. (2006).

We hope to investigate this conjecture more formally in the future in several ways: a comparison between traders and a control group of subjects without trading experience or with unsuccessful trading experiences; an analysis of the psychophysiological responses of traders in a laboratory environment; a more direct analysis of the correlation between autonomic responses and trading performance; a more fundamental analysis of the neural basis of emotion in traders, aimed at the function of the amygdala and the orbitofrontal cortex (Rolls, 1992, 1999, Chapters 4.4–4.5); and a direct mapping of the neural centres for trading activity through fMRI (Breiter et al., 2001).

A number of caveats must be kept in mind in interpreting our findings. Firstly, because of the small sample size of ten subjects, our results are, at best, suggestive and promising, not conclusive. A more comprehensive study with a larger and more diverse sample of traders, a more refined set of market events, and a broader set of controls is necessary before coming to any firm conclusions regarding the precise mechanisms of the psychophysiology of financial risk processing and the role of emotion in market efficiency.

Secondly, while we have documented the statistical significance of autonomic responses during market events relative to control baselines, we have not established specific causal factors for such responses. Many cognitive tasks generate autonomic effects; hence, a marked change in any one psychophysiological index may be due to changes in cognitive processing (e.g. complex numerical computations), rather than more fundamental affective responses. For example, more experienced traders in our sample may have displayed lower autonomic response levels because they required less cognitive effort to perform the same functions as less experienced traders, which may have nothing to do with emotion. Without a more targeted set of tasks or additional data on the characteristics of the subjects, it is difficult to distinguish between the two. One way to address this issue is to correlate a subject's autonomic responses with their trading performance, in order to develop a more complete profile of the relationship between psychophysiological indices and the dynamics of the trading process. However, because trading performance is generally summarized by multiple characteristics, such as the total profit and loss, volatility, the maximum drawdown, the Sharpe ratio, and so on, estimating a relationship between autonomic responses and these characteristics may require significantly larger sample sizes and longer observation windows due to the 'curse of dimensionality'. It may be possible to overcome this challenge to some degree through a more carefully crafted experimental design in which specific emotional responses can be paired with specific trading performance measures (e.g. anxiety levels during consecutive sequences of losing trades). With a larger sample size, we can also begin to track groups of traders over a period of time and through varying market conditions. By measuring their autonomic response profiles at different stages of their careers, it may be possible to determine more directly the role of emotion in financial risk-processing.

Finally, a much larger set of controls should accompany a larger sample of traders. These controls should include psychophysiological measurements for professional traders taken *outside* their natural trading environment, ideally in a laboratory setting that is identical for all traders, as well as corresponding measurements for subjects with little or no trading experience, in both trading and non-trading environments. Along with the psychophysiological data, more traditional personality inventory data (e.g. Minnesota Multiphasic Personality Inventory (MMPI) or Myers-Briggs testing) may provide additional insights into the psychology of trading.

We plan to address each of these issues in our ongoing research programme to better understand the cognitive processes underlying financial risk-processing. For example, in a more recent study using a more compact and less invasive smart-watch device to measure physiological traits such as HR, BVP, and electrodermal activity, Singh et al. (2022) documented the relationship between the real-time psychophysiological activity of a much larger sample of fifty-five professional traders, their financial transactions, and market fluctuations. The less cumbersome device allowed us to collect real-time data during normal working hours over a five-day observation window, yielding an enormous amount of data to which machine-learning techniques could be applied. Using this data, we implemented a novel metric of trader 'psychophysiological activation' to capture affect such as excitement, stress, and irritation, and documented statistically significant relations between traders' psychophysiological activation levels and their financial transactions, market fluctuations, the type of financial products they traded, and their trading experience. Post-measurement interviews with traders who participated in the study were conducted to obtain additional insights in the key factors driving their psychophysiological activation during financial risk processing. This larger study confirms and expands the findings described in this chapter, that psychophysiological activation plays a prominent role in financial risk processing for professional traders, and has the potential to be incorporated directly into the human trading process and risk management protocols.

In the next chapter, we describe another study, conducted by Lo, Repin, and Steenbarger (2005), with a larger sample of subjects (eighty anonymous day traders) that used a different method for gauging emotional response (including personality inventory data), which confirms several results from the smaller study described in this chapter and highlights new factors that separate profitable traders from unprofitable ones.

13
What Makes a Good Day Trader?

In Chapter 12 we considered the role of emotion in real-time financial decision-making and established a clear link using psychophysiological measurements—skin conductance, breathing rate, heart rate, blood volume pulse, and body temperature—for ten professional traders during live trading sessions (see also Lo and Repin (2002)).[1] However, an important limitation of that analysis was the lack of any information about the traders' financial gains and losses because of confidentiality requirements at the participating financial institution. Therefore, we were unable to relate psychophysiological responses directly to trading profits and losses, and had to settle for indirect inferences using price data for the instruments being traded by the subjects. We remedy this shortcoming in this chapter by describing a study in which subjects provided their daily profits and losses, as well as the number of trades executed.

We recruited eighty volunteers from a five-week online training programme for day traders offered by Linda Bradford Raschke, a well-known professional futures trader (see Schwager (1992)). These subjects were asked to complete surveys that recorded their psychological profiles before and after their training programme. During the course of the programme, which involved live trading through their own personal accounts, the subjects were also asked to complete surveys at the end of each trading day that were designed to measure their emotional state and their trading performance for that day.

The results from this experiment confirm and extend those described in Chapter 12. We find there is a clear link between emotional reactivity and trading performance as measured by profits and losses (normalized by the standard deviation of daily profits and losses). Specifically, the survey data indicate that those subjects whose emotional reactions to monetary gains and losses were more intense, positively or negatively, exhibited

---

[1] This chapter, including the tables and figure, is adapted from Lo, A. W., Repin, D. V., and Steenbarger, B. N. (2005). Fear and greed in financial markets: a clinical study of day traders. *American Economic Review* 95(2): 352–359.

significantly worse trading performance, implying that there is a negative correlation between successful trading behaviour and emotional reactivity. Also, contrary to the common intuition regarding typical personality traits of professional traders, the psychological traits derived from a standardized personality inventory survey instrument do not reveal any specific 'trader personality type' in our sample. This raises the possibility that different personality types may be able to function equally well as traders after proper instruction and practice. Alternatively, it may be the case that individual differences pertinent to trading success lie outside the domain of behaviour that can be assessed through personality questionnaires, only becoming visible at deeper physiological and neuropsychological levels, or with a larger or more homogeneous sample of traders. In statistical terms, our psychological instruments may not have sufficient power to distinguish between successful and unsuccessful trading personality types, and a larger sample size or a more refined alternative hypothesis may yield a more powerful test.

13.1 Risk-Taking and Emotion

Risk-taking as an attribute or a characteristic of personal preferences has been investigated extensively from both the psychological and the economic perspective. Psychologists have asked whether risk propensity exists as a stable personality trait, and how the tendency to take risks manifests itself across different domains of social and personal life. They have also attempted to ascertain the presence of a persistent connection between the biological basis of personality and risk-taking (Zuckerman and Kuhlman, 2000). Similarly, economists have advanced the concept of risk aversion, as discussed in Chapter 6 (see also Sections 2.3 and 11.4), and considerable research has been devoted to parameterizing and estimating its value for individuals and for various demographic, social, and age groups.

Unfortunately, neither psychologists nor economists have been particularly successful in these respective endeavours. In particular, no single psychological questionnaire predicts risk-taking behaviour across multiple domains, or explains why someone highly risk-averse in financial decision-making contexts would pursue extremely dangerous sports (Nicholson et al., 2005). Similarly, the scant differences in risk aversion coefficients that financial advisors are able to collect from their clients seem to lose much of their value in the face of the naive asset-allocation rules—for example dividing wealth equally among all available assets, or the so-called '$1/n$' heuristic—that Benartzi and Thaler (2001) have documented among individual investors. Moreover, there has been little direct evidence of correlation between hypothetical financial decisions made on paper versus real financial decisions involving live market transactions.

These limitations suggest that risk-taking may be context dependent, and that characterizing the context along some standardized dimensions may be a more productive line of inquiry. We propose that the emotional or affective state of the decision-maker and certain affective properties of the environment are plausible candidates for such a characterization. In various studies, risk preferences have been linked to the affective state of the subject or the affective characteristics of the task. For example, more risk-taking is reported for negatively framed situations than for positively framed ones (Sitkin and Weingart, 1995; Mittal and Ross Jr, 1998). When in a positive mood, people tend to be more risk-averse (Isen and Geva, 1987; Isen, Nygren, and Ashby, 1988). When a positive mood is induced, people report losses to be worse than when no affect is induced (Isen, Nygren, and Ashby, 1988). When the affective state is manipulated through artificially generated outcomes—for example in gambling experiments (Thaler and Johnson, 1990) or assumed-role decision experiments (Sitkin and Weingart, 1995)—a history of success has been found to lead to higher risk-taking.

Mano (1992, 1994) suggests that a two-dimensional representation of affect—valence (positive or negative emotion) and arousal (the strength of an emotional response)—leads to a better understanding of the interaction between affect and risk-taking (see Section 13.1.2 for further details). In particular, Mano (1994) demonstrates that higher arousal is correlated with greater risk-taking in the willingness to pay for lotteries and insurance experiments. Lerner and Keltner (2001) observe that most of the previous risk studies (e.g. Johnson and Tversky (1983) and Wright and Bower (1992)) have taken a valence-based approach, focusing exclusively on positive versus negative affective states. They propose a more subtle differentiation regarding negative affect, arguing, for example, that fear and anger influence judgements of risk in opposite ways: whereas fearful individuals make pessimistic judgements about future events, angry individuals seem to make optimistic judgements.

The specific emotional context of an individual is often influenced by external factors such as market events, family history, and even weather and other environmental conditions. In particular, the nonspecific influence on the emotional states of market participants, as reflected in the systematic depression of stock prices, has been documented with respect to the amount of sunshine (Hirshleifer and Shumway, 2003), the duration of daylight (Kamstra, Kramer, and Levi, 2003), and even geomagnetic activity (Krivelyova and

Robotti, 2003). These findings suggest there is the possibility of gauging the aggregate affective state of the market through indirect means, which may provide yet another motivation for multifactor asset-pricing models where certain common factors are affect-related.

13.1.1 Emotion, Personality, and Preferences

There is substantial evidence from the personality and social psychology literature that preferences are fairly heterogeneous across the general population. Several studies have established links between specific personality traits and performance in experimental economics. For example, higher extraversion and emotional stability—the opposite of neuroticism—appear to be related to a higher level of stability in intertemporal consumption patterns (Brandstätter and Güth, 2000). In dictator and ultimatum games, commonly used in experimental economics and social psychology, higher benevolence as a personality trait facilitated more equitable choices in offers to powerless opponents, and reciprocity orientation induced powerful recipients to set higher acceptance thresholds (Brandstätter and Güth, 2002). A greater internal locus of control, better self-monitoring ability, and a higher level of sensation-seeking have all been linked to higher levels of cooperative behaviour in prisoner's dilemma experiments (Boone, De Brabander, and Van Witteloostuijn, 1999).

In securities trading, the heterogeneity of preferences implies potential differences in attitudes towards risk-taking across individuals. Various personality assessment methods developed by social psychologists have been used to examine the relationships between specific personality traits and risk-taking in different domains. In particular, Nicholson et al. (2005) examine the relationship between personality dimensions from a five-factor personality model and risk propensity in recreational, health, career, finance, safety, and social domains. In a study with over 1,600 subjects, they use the NEO PI-R personality inventory (McCrae and Costa, 1996),[2] and find that sensation-seeking, a subscale of the Extraversion dimension, was highly correlated with most risk-taking domains, while the overall risk propensity was higher for

---

[2] The NEO PI-R consists of 240 items, each rated on a five-point scale, and can usually be completed within forty minutes. The five dimensions or factors of personality captured by this instrument are Neuroticism, Extraversion, Openness to Experience, Agreeableness, and Conscientiousness (see Costa and McCrae (1992) for details). A shorter version containing 120 items has also been developed and calibrated; in the study described in this chapter, we used the public domain version of this shorter survey. See Goldberg (1999), Goldberg et al. (2006), and the International Personality Item Pool (IPIP) website http://ipip.ori.org/ for further details.

subjects with higher Extraversion and Openness scores and lower for subjects with higher Neuroticism, Agreeableness, and Conscientiousness scores.[3] The five-factor model has been independently developed by several investigators (e.g. Goldberg (1990) and Costa and McCrae (1992)), and, despite its age, is still one of the most widely used frameworks for measuring personality traits. Meta-analytic studies by Barrick and Mount (1991), Tett, Jackson, and Rothstein (1991), and Hurtz and Donovan (2000) suggest that the personality dimensions from the five-factor model may provide some utility for selecting employees. Barrick and Mount (1991) aggregate the results from 117 studies using meta-analysis and find that Conscientiousness exhibits consistent relationships with all job performance criteria for five occupational groups, while the other dimensions were related to job performance for certain types of occupations. In a cross-cultural study, Salgado (1997) conducted a similar meta-analysis using European data; his findings indicate that Conscientiousness and Emotional Stability were valid predictors across job criteria and occupational groups.

13.1.2 Emotional Response Metrics

Historically, emotion has been one of the most intriguing and challenging psychological concepts to define and study. Emotion became a bona fide subject of investigation among psychologists after the seminal work of James (1884) and Wundt (1897). Measuring emotion is an inherently complicated task for a number of reasons. By its nature, emotion is a highly subjective experience, and imposing a common scale across individuals is likely to yield a fair amount of estimation error. Moreover, if an introspective or instantaneous report is used to assess an individual's emotional state, the very act of asking the individual about their feelings may change those feelings in some way.

As we saw in Chapter 12, one way to gauge emotional state is by measuring its physiological manifestations. A related set of techniques is to employ some method of facial expression recognition by an independent observer or through facial electromyography sensors. However, none of these approaches has been shown to work reliably for an arbitrary emotional expression except for cases where a well-defined, finite set of specific emotions is experienced by the subject during the course of an experiment (Ekman and Davidson,

---

[3] In their study, 'risk propensity' is defined as in Sitkin and Pablo (1992) (i.e. as 'the tendency of a decision-maker either to take or avoid risks').

1994; Collet et al., 1997; Cacioppo, Tassinary, and Berntson, 2000). Moreover, although generally non-invasive, physiological measurements are still fairly difficult to obtain and properly calibrate—even with the development of new technologies like the Apple Watch—and collecting such data may not be feasible for many larger-scale field studies such as the online training programme that is the focus of this chapter.

A more traditional method for measuring emotional response is the University of Wales Institute of Science and Technology (UWIST) Mood Adjective Checklist (MACL), a survey instrument developed by Matthews, Jones, and Chamberlain (1990) consisting of forty-two adjectives that a subject must rate on a seven-point scale (1 = not at all true to 7 = very true) as to how well each describes their mood at that moment (see Table 13.1). The UWIST MACL measures the emotional state of the subject using a two-dimensional representation of affect, the affect circumplex model of Russell (1980). In this model, each specific emotion is characterized along two dimensions: its 'valence', which indicates how pleasant or unpleasant the emotional state is, and its 'arousal', which characterizes how activated or deactivated the person experiencing the emotion feels Mano (1992, 1994). For example, feeling bored would imply a low activation unpleasant emotional state, whereas feeling excited would imply a highly activated pleasant emotional state. The scores for eight categories that compose different sectors in the affect circumplex, summarized in Table 13.1, are calculated based on the UWIST MACL responses: (1) pleasant, (2) unpleasant, (3) activated, (4) deactivated, (5) pleasant activated, (6) pleasant deactivated, (7) unpleasant activated, and (8) unpleasant deactivated.

Table 13.1 UWIST Mood Adjectives Checklist, grouped into eight categories of emotional state.

State	Mood Adjectives
Pleasant	Happy, pleased, content
Unpleasant	Miserable, troubled, unhappy
Activated	Aroused, alert, hyperactivated
Deactivated	Sleepy, still, quiet
Unpleasant Activated	Distressed, upset, guilty, scared, hostile, irritable, ashamed, nervous, jittery, afraid
Pleasant Deactivated	Relaxed, at rest, serene, calm, at ease
Pleasant Activated	Interested, excited, strong, enthusiastic, proud, inspired, determined, attentive, active
Unpleasant Deactivated	Tired, sluggish, droopy, dull, drowsy, bored

The accuracy of the valence/arousal affect representation is not universally accepted in the psychological literature (Ekman and Davidson, 1994). Moreover, factors such as the specific process for eliciting emotion, an insufficient emotional intensity in a laboratory setting, and the purity of emotional experience (i.e. experiencing only one emotion at a time) all contribute to the challenges of distinguishing individual emotions (Parkinson, 1995). However, distinguishing specific emotions is significantly more difficult than identifying valence and arousal (for a discussion see Levenson (1994); Davidson and Irwin (1999)). As a result, the UWIST MACL often serves as a useful first-order approximation.

13.2 Experimental Design

For this study, we recruited participants from Linda Bradford Raschke's (LBR's) five-week online training programme for day traders. This program me was centred around the Observe–Orient–Decide–Act (OODA) paradigm developed by Col. John R. Boyd as an efficient framework for aiding the decision-making process in a combat environment (Steenbarger, 2002). The notable aspects of this paradigm are the emphasis on the speed of information processing by the trader and frequent drills of the OODA loop applied to a given trading context multiple times during the trading day. The LBR training programme was conducted through a series of online lessons and chat sessions conducted by Raschke and her colleagues. Each participant was expected to complete a daily set of specific paper trades (i.e. hypothetical trades), but participants were also free to engage in actual trades through their personal accounts. The programme was completely anonymous: all communication was done through anonymous e-mail addresses of the type tr1234@yahoo.com, where 'tr1234' served as a unique identifier for each trader.

Volunteers for our study were recruited through an online announcement during one of the initial LBR training programme sessions. The subjects were told that a study independent of the LBR training would be conducted by the MIT Laboratory for Financial Engineering. All interested traders then received an e-mail inviting them to participate in the 'Emotions and Personality in Trading' study, and were promised personalized results after the completion of the study; no other incentives were provided. The timeline of the study and subject consent form were provided in the invitation e-mail. The study began on 7 July 2002 and was completed on 9 August 2002, for a total of twenty-five trading days.

Because subjects were geographically dispersed throughout the US, and the duration of the study was several weeks, the most practical method for assessing the emotional state and psychological profile of participants was through online questionnaires. Therefore, we asked the participants to complete several survey instruments prior to, during each day of, and after the training programme. Subjects filled out all questionnaires online using a dedicated website and their trading identifiers to obtain authorized access.

At the start of the training programme, all study participants were asked to complete the following three questionnaires:

A1 **Zung Self-Rating Anxiety Scale (SAS) and Self-Rating Depression Scale (SDS).** The SDS and SAS instruments are widely used twenty-item depression and anxiety scales, respectively (Zung, 1965, 1971). The aim of the SDS is to assess 'psychic-active', physiological, psychomotor, and psychological manifestations of depression, and is useful for discriminating between depressed and non-depressed individuals (Shaver and Brennan, 1991). The SAS measures the affective and somatic symptoms of anxiety disorders; scores above a cut-off value suggest the presence of clinically meaningful anxiety. These instruments were used only to screen out subjects with clinical levels of depression or anxiety, and none was eliminated by this filter.

A2 **International Personality Item Pool (IPIP) NEO.** The shorter (120-item), public-domain version of McCrae and Costa's (1996) NEO IP-R five-factor personality inventory instrument, which can typically be completed within 15–25 minutes. Responses from over 20,000 individuals have been used to calibrate this questionnaire. See Goldberg (1999) and the IPIP website, http://ipip.ori.org/, for further details.

A3 **Demographics and Strengths and Weaknesses.** The demographics component of this questionnaire included basic background information for each subject such as age, trading experience, account size, and educational background. Each subject was also asked to report, as free-form text, their trading-related strengths and weaknesses. These reports were then analysed by the experimenters and similar strengths and weaknesses were grouped into categories with a single common underlying theme. Each subject could report several or no strengths and weaknesses. See Table 13.3 for a summary.

Then, at the end of each trading day for the duration of the training programme, each subject was asked to provide the following information:

B1 **UWIST MACL**. A forty-two-item questionnaire, with each item rated on a seven-point scale, that is meant to capture the emotional state of the subject at the end of the trading day. The responses were then converted into Russell's (1980) eight-category emotional circumplex model to reduce the estimation error (see Section 13.1.2 and Table 13.1). The score for each of the eight emotion categories was calculated as the sum of raw scores for individual mood adjectives in that category.

B2 **Daily Trading Information**. Each subject was asked to report: (1) the total profit or loss on paper trades for the day; (2) the total profit or loss on actual trades for the day; and (3) the number of actual trades for the day.

In their daily routine, the subjects first reported their trading results followed by the emotional state questionnaire. During the course of the study, the subjects were reminded several times that they had to fill out their daily emotion and trading reports. The web interface allowed users to complete daily reports only for the current day or the day before, which facilitated late-night reporting and accommodated subjects living in different time zones, but ensured timely responses.

Finally, at the conclusion of the five-week programme, subjects were asked to complete the following questionnaires:

C1 **Internality, Powerful Others, and Chance (IPC)**. The IPC questionnaire (Levenson, 1972) measures personality traits related to the locus of control, which is a term from social psychology that reflects 'a generalized expectancy pertaining to the connection between personal characteristics and/or actions and experienced outcomes' (Lefcourt, 1991). This twenty-four-item questionnaire consists of three subscales consisting of eight questions each, rated on a six-point scale. The Internality Scale (I) measures how much of the control over their lives subjects attribute to themselves; the Powerful Others Scale (P) measures the extent to which subjects believe that their lives are controlled by other people; and the Chance Scale (C) is related to how much they believe that pure chance influences their experiences and outcomes.

C2 **Zung SAS and SDS**. We asked participants to complete these questionnaires again to check for any changes in their levels of anxiety and
depression. No subject's score on this or survey (A1) reached clinically
relevant thresholds.

13.3 Results

During the period of study, the US stock market experienced a significant
decline of over 20%.[4] Therefore, it was unsurprising that a number of traders
dropped out of the study, expressing their frustration with trading in general. Of the eighty participants that initially enrolled, sixty-nine actually
participated and only thirty-three provided valid responses to the final questionnaires. The latter's responses to survey (A3) clearly indicated that their
primary motivation for participating in the LBR programme was to eliminate
trading mistakes and improve their weaknesses. We assume that a similar
motivation applied to their participation in our study. Moreover, many of
the subjects did not explicitly distinguish between our study and the LBR
programme, often asking us questions that pertained exclusively to the LBR
programme.

Table 13.2 provides a summary of the demographic characteristics and personality traits of the sixty-nine participants, each of whom acknowledged that
they were engaged in high-frequency securities trading (i.e. day trading) for
their own personal account. The personality profile data reflect the raw scores
for the five main scales of the IPIP NEO five-factor model (survey (A2)), and
the IPC scores reflect the raw scores assessed through survey (C1). Figure 13.1
contains histograms of each of the five IPIP NEO personality dimensions for
the entire sample of subjects.

Table 13.2 shows that the account sizes of the subjects varied from $0 to
$1,800,000, with a mean of about $118,000 and a median of $30,000. The
subjects' reported trading experience varied from virtually none to forty-
four years, with an average of 5.9 years and a median of three years. More
than half of the subjects indicated that trading was their full-time occupation.
When asked to rate their own trading performance, twenty subjects indicated
that they 'mostly break even'; for sixteen, trading was 'mostly profitable'; for
fourteen, 'mostly unprofitable'; for ten, 'consistently profitable'; and for four
subjects, trading was 'consistently unprofitable'. Among the sixty-four subjects who provided their personal demographic characteristics, fifty-seven

---

[4] For example, from 20 June to 23 July 2002, the S&P 500 Index dropped from 1006.29 to 797.70.

Table 13.2 Summary statistics for demographic profiles and personality traits of sixty-nine subjects (sixty-four valid responses).

| Variable | Mean | SD | Percentiles | | | | |
			Min	5%	50%	95%	Max
			Entire Sample				
Extraversion	47.0	25.3	1.0	5.5	45.0	91.7	98.0
Agreeableness	35.0	31.1	0.0	0.0	26.0	89.0	93.0
Conscientiousness	44.6	29.3	1.0	2.0	41.0	93.9	99.0
Neuroticism	34.5	24.9	0.0	2.2	33.0	81.6	99.0
Openness	34.3	25.3	0.0	0.2	28.0	84.8	99.0
IPC-Internality	36.5	6.2	21.0	26.1	38.0	46.0	48.0
IPC-PowerfulOthers	8.7	5.7	0.0	0.1	8.0	19.8	26.0
IPC-Chance	8.5	5.7	0.0	0.0	8.0	17.9	21.0
Age	46.0	12.9	0.0	28.3	45.0	65.0	70.0
Experience (Years)	5.9	8.1	0.1	0.5	3.0	23.0	44.0
Account Size ($)	$118,004	$269,748	$0	$50	$30,000	$500,000	$1,800,000
			Three Years or Less of Experience				
Extraversion	46.4	24.5	1.0	4.4	50.0	87.8	92.0
Agreeableness	21.8	24.5	0.0	0.0	11.0	68.5	77.0
Conscientiousness	40.7	26.7	1.0	1.0	40.0	87.3	89.0
Neuroticism	36.8	28.6	0.0	0.9	34.0	99.0	99.0
Openness	35.6	27.8	0.0	0.9	27.0	91.4	99.0
			More Than Three Years of Experience				
Extraversion	47.5	26.5	2.0	6.8	44.0	94.8	98.0
Agreeableness	48.7	31.7	0.0	0.0	54.5	91.4	93.0
Conscientiousness	48.7	31.7	2.0	2.0	43.5	96.6	99.0
Neuroticism	32.2	20.7	4.0	5.6	30.5	75.6	82.0
Openness	33.0	22.8	0.0	0.0	29.5	71.6	78.0

Note: There were 33 valid responses to the IPC questionnaire (survey (C1)).

were male and seven were female, with ages ranging from 24 to 70 years, and a mean age of 46. Thirty-four subjects were college educated, seventeen held graduate degrees, and thirteen completed high school only.

Figure 13.1 contains a few interesting patterns. Our sample of subjects scored quite low in the Agreeableness dimension, and the histograms for Neuroticism and Openness are also skewed to the left, though not nearly to the same degree. These patterns may seem to suggest a certain 'personality type' for traders, but such a conclusion is unwarranted for several reasons. Firstly, our sample of day traders was quite heterogeneous, even with respect to trading experience, as indicated in Table 13.2. Secondly, these histograms are 'point estimates' of the true distribution of personality traits in the population, and the estimation error is likely to be quite significant in

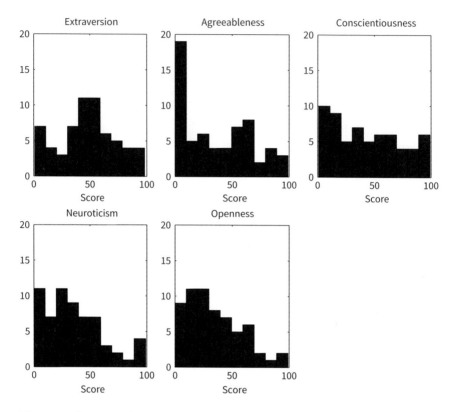

Fig. 13.1 Histogram of IPIP NEO personality traits for sixty-nine subjects.

such a small sample. Finally, we do not have a benchmark distribution for the general population that is matched by age, sex, and education to compare with the personality score distribution in our sample of traders. Hence, there is no way to determine whether the histograms in Fig. 13.1, even if measured perfectly, are distinct from those of non-traders.

Table 13.3 contains a summary of the self-reported strengths and weaknesses of the subjects, stratified by account size and trading performance. A number of common traits and behavioural patterns emerge from these strengths and weaknesses. Good technical analysis or 'tape reading' skills were common among eighteen subjects; persistence, tenacity, perseverance, and commitment among sixteen subjects; enthusiasm or desire to succeed among thirteen subjects; focus or concentration among nine subjects; discipline among six subjects; intuition or market 'feel' among five subjects; and ability to cut losses among three subjects. Among the most common weaknesses reported were lack of discipline, overtrading, or unplanned trades (twelve subjects); exiting a winning trade too early (fifteen subjects); being too emotional or impulsive (fourteen subjects); not exiting losing trades soon

Table 13.3 Trading results of sixty-nine subjects, stratified by self-reported strengths and weaknesses.

Characteristics	Number of Subjects	Account Size ($)			Average Daily P&L ($)			SD(|ΔV|)/Mean(|ΔV|)		
		Mean	Median	SD	Mean	Median	SD	Mean	Median	SD
Strengths:										
Persistence/tenacity/perseverance /commitment/patience as related to trading	16	34,000	15,000	46,921	96	85	155	1.63	1.25	0.92
Technical analysis/tape reading	18	100,333	32,500	173,906	90	30	207	1.40	1.38	0.43
Enthusiasm/desire to succeed	13	24,385	25,000	17,149	27	25	105	2.00	1.53	1.15
Discipline	6	265,000	225,000	195,832	2,306	1,792	2,125	0.82	0.92	0.44
Intuition/market 'feel'	5	24,000	25,000	12,942	150	43	254	1.31	1.33	0.24
Ability to cut losses	3	41,667	40,000	7,638	479	163	640	1.14	1.11	0.25
Concentration/focus	9	269,444	50,000	578,362	412	280	421	1.23	1.23	0.14
Weaknesses:										
Lack of discipline/overtrading/unplanned trades	23	69,174	35,000	109,929	279	157	433	1.39	1.23	0.77
Too emotional/impulsivity	14	189,571	17,500	482,063	176	27	377	1.42	1.28	0.41
Too cautious/cannot pull the trigger /not enough confidence/procrastination	7	121,571	40,000	178,906	1,591	619	2,279	1.42	0.90	1.36
Not exiting losing trades soon enough	10	159,600	45,000	219,029	389	67	747	1.47	1.40	0.45
Exiting winning trade too early	15	153,067	30,000	457,298	183	48	346	1.56	1.39	0.93
Lack of experience/lack of knowledge	8	15,250	14,500	11,081	68	42	135	2.20	1.54	1.18
Lack of patience	5	63,000	50,000	31,145	66	0	225	1.48	1.48	1.03
Unwillingness to accept losses/fear of losses	7	75,000	50,000	81,803	150	104	195	1.32	1.24	0.42

enough (ten subjects); lack of knowledge or experience (eight subjects); lack of confidence, procrastination, or inability to 'pull the trigger' (seven subjects); unwillingness to accept or fear of losses (seven subjects); and lack of patience (five subjects).

We next consider the links between personality traits and trading performance in our sample, followed by the relationship between emotional state and trading performance.

13.3.1 Personality Traits and Trading Performance

A correlation analysis of trading performance and personality traits revealed that four out of the five major personality dimensions exhibited a small negative correlation with self-reported performance and actual trading performance, with Extraversion exhibiting a small positive correlation. However, none of these correlations was statistically significant. Older subjects tended to perform more poorly, or at least more of them reported mostly or consistently unprofitable trading (-34%, $p < 1\%$). Account size was positively correlated with better trading performance (31%, $p < 5\%$). Women tended to trade less than men, while older subjects tended to trade less than younger subjects (all $p < 10\%$).

13.3.2 Emotional States and Trading Performance

Table 13.4 contains summary statistics for the emotional scores of the sixty-nine subjects who completed daily UWIST and trading performance questionnaires, yielding a total of 755 usable individual daily reports over the five-week period. For each individual daily report, the score for each emotional category was calculated as the sum of raw scores for the individual

Table 13.4 Summary statistics for daily emotional state scores of sixty-nine subjects.

Variable	Mean	SD	Min	5%	50%	95%	Max
Pleasant	7.86	2.71	3	3	8	12	15
Unpleasant	4.60	2.24	3	3	4	9	15
Activated	6.85	2.05	3	4	6	11	15
Deactivated	6.27	2.08	3	3	6	10	13
Unpleasant Activated	14.65	5.52	10	10	13	26	50
Pleasant Deactivated	12.84	4.30	5	5	13	20	25
Pleasant Activated	27.47	7.04	9	16	28	40	45
Unpleasant Deactivated	8.24	3.29	6	6	7	15	24

Table 13.5 Correlation matrix of emotional state categories (percentage) derived from aggregate emotional state scores for sixty-nine subjects over twenty-five trading days.

Correlation Matrix for Emotional State Categories (%)	Pleasant	Unpleasant	Activated	Deactivated	Unpleasant Activated	Pleasant Deactivated	Pleasant Activated	Unpleasant Deactivated
Pleasant	100.0							
Unpleasant	−45.0	100.0						
p-value (%)	< 0.01							
Activated	48.4	8.0	100.0					
p-value (%)	< 0.01	2.7						
Deactivated	37.6	6.1	29.6	100.0				
p-value (%)	< 0.01	9.7	< 0.01					
Unpleasant Activated	−36.1	78.3	14.4	4.7	100.0			
p-value (%)	< 0.01	< 0.01	< 0.01	20.0				
Pleasant Deactivated	72.8	−29.9	41.8	57.4	−33.4	100.0		
p-value (%)	< 0.01	< 0.01	< 0.01	< 0.01	< 0.01			
Pleasant Activated	73.4	−30.5	59.5	32.0	−24.6	64.0	100.0	
p-value (%)	< 0.01	< 0.01	< 0.01	< 0.01	< 0.01	< 0.01		
Unpleasant Deactivated	−9.5	36.1	5.3	37.9	39.8	−4.8	−13.0	100.0
p-value (%)	0.9	< 0.01	14.2	< 0.01	< 0.01	18.5	0.0	

UWIST mood adjectives in that category. Table 13.5 contains the correlation matrix for emotional categories, calculated using the raw scores for each emotional category across all days and all individuals. For those subjects who completed meaningful daily reports for three or more days, we computed the correlation coefficients between each emotion category and daily trading performance normalized by the standard deviation of daily profits and losses, reported in Table 13.6.

The correlations in Table 13.5 show that valence and arousal of the affect circumplex model—which decomposes emotional responses into two distinct and possibly independent dimensions, activation level and pleasant/unpleasant—are related, but they do capture some independent characteristics of emotion. The highest correlations are between the Unpleasant Activated and Unpleasant categories (78.3%) and the Pleasant

Table 13.6 Correlation between profits and losses and eight emotional state category scores for sixty-nine subjects, and those in the top and bottom cumulative profits-and-losses terciles (percentage).

Sample	Pleasant	Unpleasant	Activated	Deactivated	Pleasant Activated	Unpleasant Activated	Pleasant Deactivated	Unpleasant Deactivated
All traders	37.5	−31.7	9.5	4.7	30.0	−27.5	25.8	−13.9
p-value	< 0.01	< 0.01	1.4	22.6	< 0.01	< 0.01	< 0.01	0.0
Top 1/3	32.4	−39.3	10.5	−0.2	19.1	−25.2	22.1	−17.4
p-value	< 0.01	< 0.01	19.7	98.1	1.8	0.2	0.6	3.2
Bottom 1/3	52.0	−46.2	4.5	9.8	36.0	−44.4	42.5	−13.9
p-value	< 0.01	< 0.01	50.8	15.0	< 0.01	< 0.01	< 0.01	4.0

Activated and Pleasant categories (73.4%), not only underscoring the importance of valence as a common factor, but also demonstrating the fact that the correlation is not perfect; thus, arousal is responsible for some additional variation. As expected, the Unpleasant and Pleasant categories are negatively correlated (−45.0%), and the only other correlations greater than 50.0% in absolute value are between the Pleasant Activated and Pleasant Deactivated categories (64.0%), the Pleasant Activated and Activated categories (59.5%), and the Pleasant Deactivated and Deactivated categories (57.4%).

Unsurprisingly, we see from Table 13.6 that normalized daily performance is highly positively correlated with Pleasant emotional states (37.5, $p < 0.01\%$) and highly negatively correlated with Unpleasant emotional states (−31.7, $p < 0.01\%$) but not as highly correlated with the Activated or Deactivated categories. When viewed from the valence/arousal standpoint, trading performance exhibits correlation with all four combinations of the Pleasant/Unpleasant and Activated/Deactivated categories. Given the low correlations for the arousal categories, the higher correlations for the interacting categories may be attributed primarily to valence. A substantially smaller but still statistically significant correlation is observed for the trading performance of paper trades for the Pleasant category, suggesting that paper trading provides some of the same emotional stimuli of live trading, but is not a perfect simulacrum.

Table 13.6 also shows that for traders in the top trading performance tercile, the correlations between profits and losses and the Pleasant and Unpleasant categories are lower than for the bottom tercile. This suggests that emotional reactivity may be counterproductive for trading performance, but the differences are not large enough to render this conjecture conclusive. However, the subjects whose emotional states exhibited higher correlations with their normalized daily profits and losses (Pleasant with gains, Unpleasant with

losses) did tend to have worse overall profits-and-losses records, supporting the common wisdom that traders too emotionally affected by their daily
profits and losses are, on average, less successful.

13.4 Discussion

The results of this chapter underscore the importance of the emotional state
for real-time trading decisions, extending previous findings in several significant ways. In particular, although Lo and Repin (2002) documented a
significant emotional response among the most experienced traders (see
Chapter 12), these results show that extreme emotional responses are apparently counterproductive from the perspective of trading performance.

Contrary to the common folk wisdom that financial traders share a certain
set of personality traits (e.g. aggressiveness or extraversion), we found there
was little correlation between measured traits and trading performance. Of
course, this may be due to a lack of statistical power because of our small
sample size and the heterogeneity of our subject pool. In a larger sample,
or perhaps in a more homogeneous sample of professional traders, certain
personality traits may become more pronounced. For example, in a study by
Fenton-O'Creevy et al. (2005) of 118 professional traders employed at investment banking institutions, they found that successful traders tended to be
emotionally stable introverts who were open to new experiences.

These findings suggest that the typical emotional responses may be too
crude an evolutionary adaptation for purposes of 'financial fitness'. As a
result, one component of successful trading may be a reduced level of emotional reactivity. Given that trading is likely to involve higher brain functions
such as logical reasoning, numerical computation, and long-term planning, our results are consistent with the current neuroscientific evidence
that automatic emotional responses such as fear and greed (e.g. responses
mediated by the amygdala) often trump the more controlled or 'higher-
level' responses (e.g. the responses mediated by the prefrontal cortex).[5] To
the extent that emotional reactions 'short-circuit' more complex decision-
making faculties—for example, those involved in the active management of a
portfolio of securities—it should come as no surprise that the result is poorer
trading performance.

---

[5] See Chapter 11, as well as Camerer, Loewenstein, and Prelec (2005) for a review of the neurosciences
literature most relevant to economics and finance.

A number of open research questions remain to be addressed. The lack of correlation between personality traits and trading performance begs for additional data and a more refined analysis, particularly in light of the tantalizing results of Fenton-O'Creevy et al. (2005). The specific interaction between emotional state and trading performance also deserves further investigation, particularly the dynamic aspects that involve the *sequence* of emotional and financial states. Finally, the large body of neuroimaging research provides a wealth of information about where certain types of decisions and actions originate in the brain. A more detailed analysis of the neuroanatomical origins of financial risk-processing may yield significant insights into the individual and aggregate behaviour of market participants and market rationality. Ultimately, armed with the tools from Chapter 12 and this chapter, we hope to provide a solid scientific basis for the kind of recommendations for trading success made by Gilbert (2004) in his summary of Fenton-O'Creevy et al. (2005):

> Be an introvert. Keep your emotions stable. Stay open to new experiences. Oh, and try not to be misled by randomness, stop thinking you are in control of the situation, and don't expect any help from your boss.

PART IV
FINANCIAL MARKET DYNAMICS

14

A Computational View of Market Efficiency

Having introduced the theoretical framework for studying the evolution of behaviour in Part I, derived specific behaviours such as risk aversion, cooperation, and intelligence in Part II, and explored the neurophysiological basis of these behaviours in individuals in Part III, we are now ready to expand our focus in Part IV to interactions among individuals (i.e. financial market dynamics).[1]

We begin in this chapter by revisiting the concept of market efficiency, the idea that 'prices fully reflect all available information'. Recall that efficiency is not simply an assumption, but rather the direct result of many active market participants attempting to profit from their information. Driven by greed, legions of investors will pounce on even the smallest informational advantages at their disposal and, in doing so, they will incorporate their information into market prices. This competitive process quickly eliminates the profit opportunities that first motivated their trades. And if it occurs instantaneously, as in an idealized world of 'frictionless' markets and costless trading, then prices will, indeed, fully reflect all available information. As an additional consequence, no profits can be garnered from information-based trading, because such profits must have already been captured.

This theory contrasts sharply with those finance practitioners who attempt to forecast future prices based on the prices of the past. Surprisingly, some of them do appear to make consistent profits that cannot only be attributed to chance.

In the first part of this chapter (Sections 14.1–14.3), we propose that a reinterpretation of market efficiency in computational terms may be key to reconciling theory with practice. We argue that it does not make sense to talk about market efficiency without taking into account that market participants

---

[1] This chapter, including the tables and figure, is adapted from Hasanhodzic, J., Lo, A. W., and Viola, E. (2019). What do humans perceive in asset returns? *The Journal of Portfolio Management* 45(4): 49–60, with permission from the publisher, IPR Journals; and Hasanhodzic, J., Lo, A. W., and Viola, E. (2011). A computational view of market efficiency. *Quantitative Finance* 11(7): 1043–1050, with permission from the publisher, Taylor & Francis Ltd., http://www.tandfonline.com.

The Adaptive Markets Hypothesis. Andrew W. Lo and Ruixun Zhang, Oxford University Press.
© Andrew W. Lo and Ruixun Zhang (2024). DOI: 10.1093/oso/9780199681143.003.0014

have bounded resources, as discussed in Chapters 2 and 8. Instead of claiming that a given market is 'efficient' or 'inefficient', we should instead be borrowing from theoretical computer science and stating that a market is *efficient with respect to a given set of resources, S* (e.g. time, memory, and computing resources) *if no strategy using S resources can generate a substantial profit.* Similarly, we should not state that investors act optimally given all available information, but rather that they act optimally *within the limits of their resources.*

This change in perspective allows for markets to be efficient for some investors but not for others. For example, a large and computationally sophisticated hedge fund may extract profits from a market that looks very efficient from the point of view of an individual day-trader who has less resources at their disposal.

In the second part of this chapter (Sections 14.4–14.6), we provide experimental evidence of a very primitive test of weak-form efficiency in which human subjects were asked to distinguish between real and synthetic financial time series. The surprising results shed considerable light on both the efficient markets hypothesis (EMH) and how it can be revised to capture a broader spectrum of human financial decision-making.

Related Literature

Many prior studies have explored limits to market rationality. For example, Simon (1955) argued that agents are not rational, but *boundedly rational*, which can be interpreted in modern terms as bounded in computational resources.[2] While most previous work in this line of research uses sophisticated continuous-time models that explicitly address the market-making mechanism (which then sets the price, given the agents' actions), the model we describe in this chapter differs in that it is simple and discrete, abstracted from the market-making mechanism.

Since the publication of the landmark studies of Samuelson (1965) and Fama (1965, 1970), many others have extended their original framework, yielding a 'neoclassical' version of the EMH in which price changes, properly weighted by aggregate marginal utilities, are unforecastable (LeRoy, 1973; Rubinstein, 1976; Lucas, 1978). In markets where, according to Lucas (1978), all investors have 'rational expectations', prices do fully reflect all available information and prices weighted by marginal utility follow martingales. Market efficiency has since been extended in many other directions, but the

---

[2] See Chapter 8 for a discussion of the evolutionary origin of bounded rationality.

general thrust has been the same: individual investors form expectations rationally, markets aggregate information efficiently, and equilibrium prices incorporate all available information instantaneously. See Lo (1997, 2008a) for a more detailed summary of the market efficiency literature in economics and finance.

There are two branches of the market efficiency literature that are particularly relevant for this chapter: the asymmetric information literature, and the literature on asset bubbles and crashes. In Black's (1986) presidential address to the American Finance Association, he argued that financial market prices were subject to noise, which could temporarily create inefficiencies that would ultimately be eliminated through intelligent investors competing against each other to generate profitable trades. Since then, many researchers have modelled financial markets by hypothesizing two types of traders—the informed and the uninformed—where informed traders have private information regarding the true economic value of a security, and uninformed traders have no information at all but trade merely for liquidity needs (Grossman and Stiglitz, 1980; Diamond and Verrecchia, 1981; Admati, 1985; Kyle, 1985; Campbell and Kyle, 1993)). In this context, Grossman and Stiglitz (1980) argued that market efficiency is impossible, because if markets were truly efficient, there would be no incentive for investors to gather private information and trade. De Long et al. (1990, 1991) provide a more detailed analysis in which certain types of uninformed traders can destabilize market prices for periods of time, even in the presence of informed traders. Studies by Luo (1995, 1998, 2001, 2003), Hirshleifer and Luo (2001), and Kogan et al. (2006) focus on the long-term viability of noise traders when competing for survival against informed traders; while noise traders are exploited by informed traders as expected, certain conditions do allow them to persist, at least in limited numbers.

The second relevant offshoot of the market efficiency literature involves 'rational bubbles', in which financial asset prices can become arbitrarily large even when all agents are acting rationally, similar to our market spikes (Blanchard and Watson, 1982; Allen, Morris, and Postlewaite, 1993; Santos and Woodford, 1997; Abreu and Brunnermeier, 2003). LeRoy (2004) provides a comprehensive review of this literature.

Market efficiency has yet to be addressed explicitly in the computer science literature. However, a number of studies have touched upon this concept tangentially. For example, computational learning methods have been applied to the pricing and trading of financial securities by Hutchinson, Lo, and Poggio (1994). Evolutionary approaches in the dynamical systems and complexity literature have also been applied to financial markets by Farmer and Lo (1999), Farmer (2002), Farmer and Joshi (2002), Lo (2004, 2005); Farmer,

Patelli, and Zovko (2005), and Bouchaud, Farmer, and Lillo (2009). Simulations of market dynamics using autonomous agents have coalesced into a distinct literature on the 'agent-based modelling' of financial markets by Arthur (1994), Palmer et al. (1994), Arthur et al. (1997), LeBaron, Arthur, and Palmer (1999), Farmer (2001), LeBaron (2001a,b,c, 2002, 2006), and Challet, Marsili, and Zhang (2004). Our model has features that are similar to the 'El Farol' model of Arthur (1994) and the 'minority game' model of Challet, Marsili, and Zhang (2004). However, the mathematical understanding of those models requires familiarity with the sophisticated techniques of statistical physics, while our techniques are elementary.

Another part of this literature is devoted to the analytical study of game theory with computationally bounded agents (e.g. Axelrod (1984), Gode and Sunder (1993), and Halpern and Pass (2015)). Here, typically, computationally bounded agents are modelled via finite automata; however, their focus is not directly market efficiency, but rather on the nature of the strategies that emerge. While none of the publications in these distinct strands of the computational markets literature focuses on a new definition of market efficiency, they nevertheless all touch upon different characteristics of this aspect of financial markets.

With respect to the experiments described in this chapter on whether humans can distinguish real versus synthetic price series, although this question is of interest in its own right as a 'financial Turing test' of sorts, it also has implications for the EMH. A strong form of this hypothesis presumes asset returns to be independent and identically distributed (Fama, 1970), in which case it would be impossible to distinguish actual asset returns from a random permutation of them. Lo and MacKinlay (1988, 1999) and Lo, Mamaysky, and Wang (2000) have already established that stock market prices do not follow random walks, and they show that returns are statistically significantly autocorrelated. But their analysis relies solely on *computer*-based, not *human*-based, calculations, leaving open the question of whether markets look efficient *to human beings*. The experiments of Hasanhodzic, Lo, and Viola (2019) described in Sections 14.4–14.6 provide the answer, and further show that humans do, in fact, have the capacity to distinguish between actual and synthetic financial time series data.

The idea of testing the ability of human subjects to distinguish random vs real data using graphical representations is not new. Indeed, this has been studied in depth in the information visualization literature (see, e.g., Heer, Kong, and Agrawala (2009) and Wickham et al. (2010), and the references therein). However, we are unaware of any previous work where this idea has been used in a financial setting.

14.1 The Model

We consider an economy where there exists only one asset. The daily returns of this asset (given as price differences) follow a pattern, for example:

$$(-1, 1, -1, 1, -1, 1, 2, -1, 1, -1, 1, -1, 1, 2, -1, 1, -1, 1, -1, 1, 2, \ldots),$$

which we write as $[-1, 1, -1, 1, -1, 1, 2]$ (Fig. 14.1). Such patterns may arise from a variety of causes ranging from the biological to the political; think of seasonal cycles for commodities, or the four-year presidential cycle. Although one can consider more complicated dependencies, working with these finite patterns keeps the mathematics simple, and is sufficient for our purposes in this chapter.

We then consider a new agent A who is allowed to trade the asset daily, with no transaction costs. Intuitively, agent A can profit whenever they can predict the sign of the next return. However, the key point is that A is computationally bounded: their prediction can only depend on the previous m returns. Continuing the above example, and setting the memory, $m = 2$, we see that upon seeing returns $(-1, 1)$, A's best strategy is to guess that the next return will be negative: this will be correct for two out of the three occurrences of $(-1, 1)$, in each occurrence of the pattern.

Next, we consider a model of market evolution where A's strategy affects the market by pushing the return closer to 0 when the sign of the return is

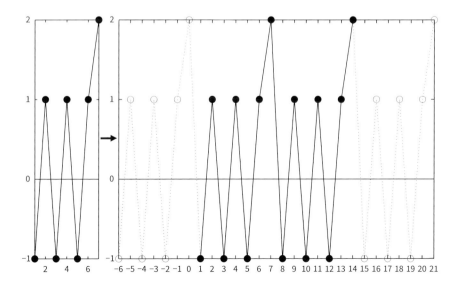

Fig. 14.1 The market corresponding to a market pattern.

correctly forecast, thereby exploiting the existing possibility of profit, or by pushing the return away from 0 when the forecast is incorrect, thereby creating a new possibility for profit. In other words, the evolved market is the difference between the original market and the guess made by the strategy (we think of the guess in $\{-1, 0, 1\}$). For example, Fig. 14.2 shows how the most profitable strategy using a memory $m = 2$ evolves the market given by the pattern $[-2, 2, -2, 2, -2, 2, 3]$, similar to the previous example.

The main question addressed in this chapter is: *What do the markets evolved by memory-bounded strategies look like?*

We show that the effect of optimal strategies using a memory m can lead to 'market conditions' that were not present initially, such as (1) market spikes and (2) the possibility that a strategy using a memory $m' > m$ will be able to make larger profits than previously possible. By 'market spikes' in point (1) we mean that some returns will grow much higher than in the case without these strategies, an effect already anticipated in Fig. 14.2. For point (2), we consider a new agent B that has memory m' that is larger than that of A. We let B trade on the market evolved by A. We show that, for some initial market, B may make more profit than what would have been possible if A had not evolved the market, or even if another agent with a large memory m' had evolved the market instead of A. Thus, it is precisely the presence of low-memory agents (A) that allows high-memory agents (B) to make large profits.

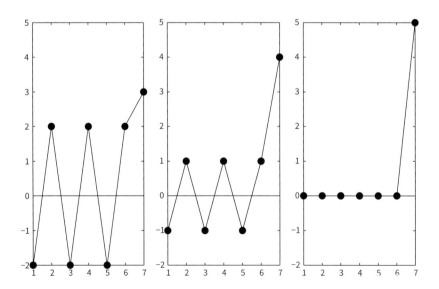

Fig. 14.2 Optimal memory-2 strategy evolves the market, creating a spike.

Regarding the framework for point (2), we stress that we only consider agents trading sequentially, not simultaneously; after A evolves the market, it is incorporated into a new market, on which B may trade. While a natural extension of our model is to include simultaneous agents, we argue that an assumption of sequentiality is not unrealistic. For example, some popular strategies A are updated only once a month. Within any such month, a higher-frequency strategy B can, indeed, trade in the market evolved by A without A making any adjustment.

Motivated by the computational definition of market efficiency, in the second part of this chapter (Sections 14.4–14.7), we describe several experiments we ran that test whether and how human subjects can differentiate between time series of actual asset returns and time series that are generated 'synthetically' via various processes, including the common autoregressive (AR) process, AR(1). In contrast with previous anecdotal evidence, we found that subjects were able to distinguish between the two. These results show that temporal charts of asset prices convey to investors information that cannot be reproduced by summary statistics. They also provide a first refutation based on human perception of a strong form of the EMH.

14.2 A Computational Definition of Market Efficiency

We model a market by an infinite sequence of random variables $R_1, R_2, \ldots$, where $R_t \in \mathbb{R}$ is the *return* at time t. For the points made in this chapter, it is enough to consider markets that are obtained by the repetition of a pattern. This has the added benefit of keeping the mathematics to a minimum level of sophistication.

Definition 14.1 (market) *A market pattern of length p is a sequence of p random variables $[R_1, \ldots, R_p]$, where each $R_i \in \mathbb{R}$.*

A market pattern $[R_1, \ldots, R_p]$ gives rise to a market obtained by the *independent* repetition of the patterns: $R_1^1, \ldots, R_p^1, R_1^2, \ldots, R_p^2, R_1^3, \ldots, R_p^3, \ldots$, where each block of random variables $R_1^i, \ldots, R_p^i$ is distributed like $R_1, \ldots, R_p$ and independent from $R_1^j, \ldots, R_p^j$ for $j \neq i$. Figure 14.1 shows an example for a market pattern in which the random variables are constant.

We now define strategies. A memory-m strategy takes as its input the previous m observations of market returns, and outputs 1 if it thinks that the next return will be positive. We can think of this '1' as corresponding to a buy-and-sell order (which will be profitable if the next return is, indeed, positive).

Similarly, a strategy output of −1 corresponds to a sell-and-buy order, while 0 corresponds to no order.

Definition 14.2 *A memory-m strategy is a map, $s : \mathbb{R}^m \to \{-1, 0, 1\}$.*

We now define the gain of a strategy over a market. At every market observation, the gain of the strategy is the sign of the product of the strategy output and the market return: the strategy gains a profit when it correctly predicts whether the next return will be positive or negative, and loses a profit otherwise. A more sophisticated definition could take into account the magnitude of the return, but, for simplicity, we only consider its sign here. Since we think of markets as defined by the repetition of a pattern, it is enough to define the gain of the strategy over this pattern.

Definition 14.3 (gain of a strategy) *The gain of a memory-m strategy $s : \mathbb{R}^m \to \{-1, 0, 1\}$ over market pattern $[R_1, ..., R_p]$ is:*

$$\sum_{i=1}^{p} \mathbb{E}_{R_1,...,R_p} \left[\text{sign} \left(s(R_{i-m}, R_{i-m+1}, ..., R_{i-1}) \cdot R_i \right) \right],$$

where for any k, the random variable $(R_{1-k \cdot p}, ..., R_{p-k \cdot p})$ is independent from all the others and distributed like $(R_1, ..., R_p)$.

A memory-m strategy s is optimal over a market pattern if no memory-m strategy has a bigger gain than s over that market pattern.

The gain of an optimal memory-1 strategy over a certain market is intuitively related to the first-order *autocorrelation* of the market (i.e. the correlation between the return at time t and the return at time $t + 1$ (for random t)), a well-studied measure of market efficiency (Lo, 2005, Fig. 2). This analogy can be made exact up to a normalization for markets that are given by balanced sequences of $+1, -1$. In this case, higher memory can be thought of as an extension of autocorrelation.

Given a deterministic market pattern (a sequence of numbers such as $[2, -1, 5, ...]$), its optimal strategies can be easily computed. It is easy to see that an optimal strategy outputs $+1$ on an input $x \in \mathbb{R}^m$ if more than half the occurrences of x in the market pattern are followed by a positive value.

We are now ready to give our definition of market efficiency.

Definition 14.4 (market efficiency) *A market pattern $[R_1, ..., R_p]$ is efficient with respect to memory-m strategies if no such strategy has strictly positive gain over $[R_1, ..., R_p]$.*

For example, let R_1 be a $\{-1, 1\}$ random variable that is -1 with probability 1/2. Then the market pattern $[R_1]$ is efficient with respect to memory-m strategies for every m.

A standard parity argument gives the following hierarchy, which we provide for the sake of completeness.

Proposition 14.1 *For every m, there is a market pattern that is efficient for memory-m strategies but is not efficient for memory-$(m + 1)$ strategies.*

14.3 Market Evolution

In this section, we describe the dynamics of our market model. We consider a simple model of evolution in which the strategies enter the market sequentially. After a strategy enters, its impact on the market is recorded by the market, and produces a new evolved market. The way in which a strategy impacts the market is by subtracting the strategy's output from the market data.

Definition 14.5 (Market evolution) *We say that a memory-m strategy $s : \mathbb{R}^m \to \{-1, 0, 1\}$ evolves a market pattern $[R_1, R_2, ..., R_p]$ into the market pattern*

$$[R_1 - s(R_{1-m}, ..., R_{1-1}), R_2 - s(R_{2-m}, ..., R_{2-1}), ..., R_p - s(R_{p-m}, ..., R_{p-1})].$$

Figure 14.2 shows the evolution of a market pattern. Definition 14.5 can be readily extended to multiple strategies acting simultaneously, by subtracting all the impacts of the strategies on the market, but for the points made in this framework the above definition is sufficient. We next discuss two consequences of the market evolution definition.

14.3.1 Market Spikes

We show that an optimal low-memory strategy can evolve a market pattern into another pattern with values that are much larger than those of the original market pattern in absolute value (i.e. that low-memory strategies can give rise to *market bubbles*). Consider, for example, the market pattern $[-2, 2, -2, 2, -2, 2, 3]$ in Fig. 14.2. An *optimal* memory-2 strategy will profit on most time instances of this pattern, but not all. In particular, on input $(-2, 2)$, its best output is -1, which agrees with the sign of the market in two out of three occurrences of $(-2, 2)$. This shrinks the returns towards 0 on most time instances, but will make the last return in the pattern rise. The optimal memory-2 strategy evolves the original market pattern into $[-1, 1, -1, 1, -1, 1, 4]$. The situation then repeats, and an optimal memory-2 strategy evolves the latter pattern into $[0, 0, 0, 0, 0, 0, 5]$. This is an example of how an optimal strategy creates market conditions that were not initially present. We point out that the market spike does not form with memory 3 (Fig. 14.3).

The formation of such spikes is not an isolated phenomenon or specific to memory 2: we have generated several random markets and plotted their evolution, and spikes often arise with various memories. We report one such example in Fig. 14.4, where a random pattern of length 20 is evolved by optimal memory-3 strategies into a spike after sixteen iterations. In fact, the framework proposed here gives rise to a 'game' in the spirit of Conway's famous Game of Life, demonstrating how simple trading rules can lead to apparently chaotic market dynamics. Perhaps the main difference between our game and Conway's is that, in ours, strategies perform optimally within their resources.

14.3.2 High-Memory Strategies Feed off Low-Memory Strategies

The next example shows a pattern by which a high-memory strategy can make a larger profit after a low-memory strategy has acted and modified

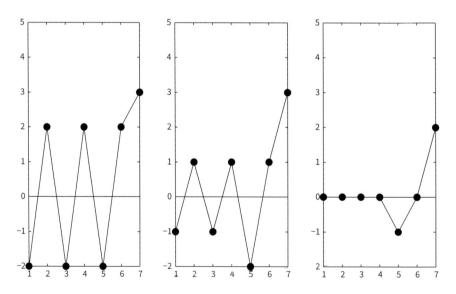

Fig. 14.3 Optimal memory-3 strategy evolves the market without creating a spike.

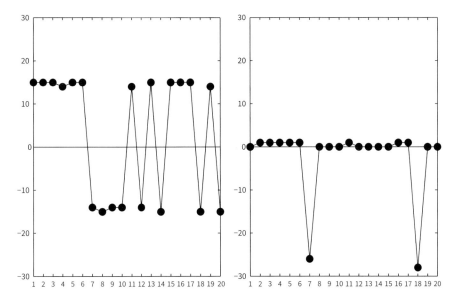

Fig. 14.4 Random market pattern (on the left) evolved by an optimal memory-3 strategy into a spike after sixteen iterations (on the right).

the existing market pattern. This profit is larger than the profit that can be obtained with a high-memory strategy in the case in which no strategy acts beforehand, and in the case in which another high-memory strategy acts beforehand. It is precisely the presence of low-memory strategies that creates opportunities for high-memory strategies that were not present initially. This example provides an explanation for the real-life status quo, which sees a growing quantitative sophistication among asset managers.

Informally, the proof of this claim exhibits a certain symmetry in the market. For high-memory strategies, the best choice is to maintain this symmetry by profiting at multiple points, something a low-memory strategy will be unable to do. Its optimal choice will be to 'break the symmetry', creating new profit opportunities for high-memory strategies.

Proposition 14.2 *For every $m < m'$ there is a market pattern $\mathcal{P} = [R_1, ..., R_p]$, an optimal memory-m strategy, s_m, that evolves $\mathcal{P}$ into $\mathcal{P}_m$, and an optimal memory-m' strategy, $s_{m'}$, that evolves $\mathcal{P}$ into $\mathcal{P}_{m'}$ such that the gain of an optimal memory-m' strategy over $\mathcal{P}_m$ is bigger than any of the following:*

- *the gain of $s_{m'}$ over $\mathcal{P}$;*
- *the gain of any memory-m strategy over $\mathcal{P}_m$;*
- *the gain of any memory-m' strategy over $\mathcal{P}_{m'}$.*

Regarding Proposition 14.2, a similar claim can be made for deterministic market patterns by considering the exponentially longer market pattern where the random variables take all possible combinations. However, the randomized example is easier to describe. Also, although in Proposition 14.2 we talk about *an* optimal strategy, the particular strategies considered are natural in that they are those that minimize the number of $\{-1, 1\}$ outputs (i.e., the amount of trading). We could have forced this to be the case by adding to our definition of gain a negligible transaction cost, in which case our claim would talk about *the* optimal strategy, but we preferred a simpler definition of gain.

14.4 A Financial Turing Test

When we redefined market efficiency from the computational perspective of Sections 14.2–14.3, we saw that a simple constraint on memory is capable of capturing realistic market dynamics such as the formation of market bubbles and crashes, and creates the possibility for high-memory strategies to 'feed off' low-memory ones. Given that human cognition is certainly limited in many dimensions, including memory, a natural corollary of our computational interpretation of the EMH is that markets exhibit inefficiencies that reflect the cognitive and technological capabilities of market participants.

To gauge the extent of these capabilities, in the remaining sections of this chapter we take a more empirical approach by considering Hasanhodzic, Lo, and Viola's (2019) experimental evidence on whether human subjects are capable of distinguishing between real and artificially generated financial price series.

It has often been noted that when it comes to investing, individuals are not well positioned to make sound decisions. Several reasons for this deficit have been proposed in the literature, including an overload of information about the choice of investment products, marketing strategies designed to mislead, behavioural biases, and financial illiteracy (e.g. see Bazerman (2001), Bodie (2007), Choi, Laibson, and Madrian (2011), and the references therein). The challenges of individual investment decision-making are especially acute in the case of retirement savings, where the shift from defined-benefit pension plans to privatized defined-contribution 401(k) plans has forced individuals to become their own portfolio managers. As a result, there has been much debate among policymakers and academics about improving the quality and presentation of data available to investors. For example, Bazerman (2001) and

Kozup, Howlett, and Pagano (2008) call for research on investor perception of investment products and methods to make information about those products more easily accessible and comprehensible.

An example of work in this direction is by Hung, Heinberg, and Yoong (2010). The authors evaluated versions of the Department of Labor's proposed Model Comparative Chart, which provides a standard simplified disclosure format for investment information. They conducted an online experiment in which subjects were asked to allocate $10,000 among different funds based on the funds' performance disclosure. In one version of the disclosure, past returns were presented as a numerical table. In another version, in addition to the numerical table, the disclosure gave a graphical representation of returns over a ten-year period, as a bar chart. Surprisingly, the authors found that the two disclosures had a statistically significant effect on retirement investment allocation, although the effect may not have practical significance in terms of investment outcomes.

Together with the prevalence of temporal charts of asset returns in the financial media and their widespread use by both casual and professional investors, the above issues bring a fundamental question to the forefront of this research: Just what information can human beings extract from charts of financial returns? This question has several ramifications. For example, are there any patterns in financial asset returns that humans can extract by looking at such charts? Is seeing a chart more informative than describing a few statistical parameters such as average and variance? Could popular market websites that display charts save space by getting rid of them altogether, with no harm to investors? And in Hung, Heinberg, and Yoong's (2010) experiment, is the mere *presence* of a chart biasing the subjects, or are subjects actually gathering information from the contents of the chart? We provide some answers in the next sections.

14.5 Experimental Design

We developed a simple, web-based video game in which subjects were shown two dynamic price series (i.e. moving charts) one above the other, both of which displayed price graphs evolving in real time—similar to graphs that appear in live trading-platform displays—plotting the new price at roughly one-second intervals, as well as the trailing prices over a fixed time window over the recent past. Of the two moving charts, only one corresponded to a sequence of actual market prices from the historical data set; we call this graph the 'real' chart. The other was a synthetic sequence of prices, as described in Section 14.6. We call this graph the 'synthetic chart'. The computer chose at random which of the two graphs was placed at the top or the bottom (see Figs 14.5 and 14.6).

The subject was asked to decide which of the two moving charts was the real one by clicking on it. The game registered the subject's choice, and informed the subject immediately whether their guess was correct or incorrect (see Figs 14.7 and 14.8, which are snapshots from the video game), after which the next pair of price series would be displayed. Since the charts were moving, at any point in time there were only a certain number of observations present on the screen for each time series, which was a subset of the total number of observations the subjects saw on a moving chart before having to make a guess (these parameters are reported for each data set later in this chapter).

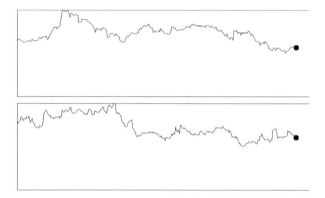

Fig. 14.5 Snapshot of reindeer contest in online game (real data in top panel).

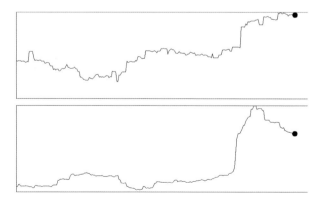

Fig. 14.6 Snapshot of bear contest in online game (real data in bottom panel).

Fig. 14.7 Wrong choice in beaver contest.

Fig. 14.8 Correct choice in elk contest.

Subjects did not have to wait until the entire moving chart was displayed and could make their guess at any time prior to its completion. An omnipresent counter informed them of the time left. The game was fast-paced: subjects could observe the charts for 10–25 seconds (depending on the data set) before having to make a guess.

For the historical time series, we used eight data sets consisting of returns of commonly traded financial assets. These data sets were arbitrarily named after animals, so that users had no knowledge of the specific financial assets used in the experiment. Table 14.1 summarizes the data used. It also reports the number of charts shown to each subject, the number of data points per chart, and, since the charts were moving, the number of data points that fit onto the screen at any given time. Subjects were given eleven seconds to guess in the bull contest, fifteen in the bear, elk, and reindeer contests, twenty in the lynx and mandrill contests, twenty-two in the seal contest, and twenty-four in the beaver contest. The Dow Jones Corporate Bond Price Index was obtained

Table 14.1 The correspondence between contest names and data sets and parameters used in the presentation of data to the subjects during the game.

Contest	Data	Points on Screen	Charts per Subject	Points per Chart
Mandrill	S&P GSCI Corn Index Spot daily data June 1982–October 2009	38	50	125
Bear	Nasdaq Composite Index tick data (about 1 sec.) May–July 2009	250	37	400
Lynx	Canada/US Foreign Exchange Rate daily data August 1978–April 2009	90	35	190
Reindeer	Gold Spot Price tick data (1–60 sec.) June–October 2009	350	40	500
Beaver	Dow Jones Industrial Average daily data September 1926–May 2009	300	36	500
Bull	Russell 2000 Index tick data (about 10 sec.) May–December 2009	110	31	153
Seal	Dow Jones Corporate Bond Price Index daily data January 1941–April 2009	250	39	400

from the Global Financial Database, while all other data series were obtained from Bloomberg. Several statistics of the data sets are presented in Table 14.6, which shed light on the differences in performance between our random permutation and AR(1) experiments.

Subjects were recruited via the Amazon Mechanical Turk platform.[3] After registration, a subject was able to participate in eight different contests, each consisting of the same game applied to different data sets.[4] For each data set, the user was shown approximately thirty-five pairs of moving charts and asked to make as many choices. The subject was also free to refrain from

---

[3] The advertisement read: 'The game you are about to play is part of a research project which studies how humans see random data. The game has been designed to be fun to play: we are going to show you pairs of charts; in each pair, one chart is based on real data (such as price fluctuations) and one is randomly generated. You are required to indicate which one you think is real by clicking on it.'

[4] In the first iterations, subjects completed a short demographic questionnaire upon registration, which included a question about financial literacy. We found no correlation between their answers and their performance in our experiment, so we discontinued the questionnaire.

making a selection. This happened only rarely; erring on the conservative side, we recorded the absence of a guess as an incorrect choice for that trial. To provide the participants with an incentive for making correct choices, we paid each participant as follows: we counted the number of correct guesses made by the participant and subtracted the number of wrong guesses to calculate v. If v was larger than 0, then we paid the participant v multiples of ten cents.

To evaluate the robustness of our experimental design, we varied the parameters of the experiment across data sets, as indicated in Table 14.1. In addition, we presented the subjects with data charts in two different ways. For half of the data sets corresponding to transaction-by-transaction (or 'tick') data, each subject was shown a fresh set of charts, based on a sequence of returns disjoint from the sequences shown to any other subjects. For the other half of the data, corresponding to daily data, the charts shown to each subject were based on the same sequence of returns.[5]

Finally, for each data set, before entering the contest, subjects were required to train on a disjoint set of data.

14.6 Synthetic Processes and Results

In this section, we describe the various synthetic processes we considered and their corresponding results. In each case, we began with a time series of actual historical prices, $\{P_0, P_1, P_2, \ldots, P_T\}$, and generated from it a synthetic series, $\{P_0^*, P_1^*, P_2^*, \ldots, P_T^*\}$. When displayed during the game, each series was scaled so that its maximum and minimum lay on the borders of the window on the computer screen.

14.6.1 Random Permutation

Initially, we wanted to test the null hypothesis, H, that human subjects cannot distinguish between actual historical time series and a time series that is obtained by permuting at random the entries of the historical one.

We began with a time series of actual historical prices, $\{P_0, P_1, P_2, \ldots, P_T\}$, and computed the logarithmic returns, $\{R_t\}$,

$$R_t \equiv \log(P_t) - \log(P_{t-1}).$$

---

[5] The data, however, were shifted by a random amount for security reasons, to avoid the possibility that two subjects could coordinate their guesses, for example by simultaneously playing the same charts on two nearby machines.

From this, we constructed a randomly generated price series, $\{P_0^*, P_1^*, ..., P_T^*\}$, by accumulating randomly permuted returns:

$$P_{t+1}^* \equiv P_t^* \cdot e^{R_{\pi(t+1)}}, \quad P_0^* \equiv 1,$$

$$\pi(k) : \{1, ..., T\} \rightarrow \{1, ..., T\},$$

where $\pi(k)$ is a uniform permutation of the set of time indexes, $\{1, ..., T\}$. A random permutation of the actual historical returns does not alter the marginal distribution of the returns, but it does destroy the time-series structure of the original series, including any temporal patterns contained in the data. Therefore, the randomly permuted returns had the same mean, standard deviation, and moments of higher order as the actual return series but did not contain any time-series patterns that could be used for prediction. This construction allowed us to test specifically for the ability of human subjects to detect temporal dependencies in financial data.

The results are reported in Table 14.2. In particular, for each contest we report the p-value of the two-sided t-test of the null hypothesis, according to which the average number of correct guesses across subjects equals the total number of guesses in the contest divided by 2.[6] We also report the correct guesses per subject as a percentage of total guesses. The table shows that the null hypothesis is refuted for all eight data sets: the p-value is always less than 1%.

14.6.2 A Variant

To evaluate the robustness of these results, we also considered the following variant of the process, in which returns were obtained via simple price differences:

$$R_t \equiv P_t - P_{t-1}.$$

From this, we constructed a randomly generated price series, $\{P_0^*, P_1^*, ..., P_T^*\}$, by accumulating randomly permuted returns:

$$P_t^* \equiv \sum_{k=1}^{t} R_{\pi(k)}, \quad P_0^* \equiv P_0,$$

$$\pi(k) : \{1, ..., T\} \rightarrow \{1, ..., T\}.$$

---

[6] We also used this test for our other synthetic processes, considered below.

Table 14.2 Results for distinguishing price charts from their permutations.

Contest	Subjects	p-value	Correct Guesses per Subject as Percentage of Total Guesses
Mandrill	56	0.00972	50 70 48 54 58 48 64 46 34 54 38 40 50 48 50 60 56 50 54 64 62 40 48 64 46 62 48 46 68 56 52 56 62 56 52 38 54 58 36 58 64 40 62 46 54 56 68 46 52 50 54 66 60 42 56 60
Bear	55	0.00000	78 81 86 73 76 65 76 92 78 43 57 76 76 78 89 46 95 86 54 57 76 46 59 73 81 86 65 86 73 84 46 84 62 78 46 81 86 59 68 65 89 81 92 81 43 92 97 65 51 49 43 97 51 57 68
Lynx	56	0.00045	31 57 60 49 60 57 60 57 54 49 60 43 49 54 66 51 49 60 49 49 46 51 49 69 54 51 60 49 54 63 57 54 54 46 60 51 57 69 54 29 54 66 60 54 63 57 66 37 57 54 66 51 49 46 49 57
Reindeer	56	0.00000	53 63 75 93 95 45 65 85 63 85 78 38 63 65 68 35 48 53 70 45 63 55 73 78 60 70 78 48 60 70 93 70 50 70 45 63 73 65 63 60 80 75 53 60 60 73 43 43 63 43 58 95 70 53 60 55
Beaver	58	0.00013	58 58 64 53 72 47 67 53 42 44 42 61 42 64 56 53 36 61 42 67 64 53 56 44 56 72 53 72 50 72 50 56 53 64 56 47 50 47 56 75 44 50 75 78 75 53 58 61 44 50 50 56 69 39 58 39 69 42
Bull	57	0.00000	81 97 84 97 100 81 84 100 65 61 90 100 90 84 100 100 100 74 39 55 97 48 94 100 29 52 97 61 55 100 97 97 100 100 100 81 97 100 90 71 100 100 94 97 100 68 100 97 35 52 39 61 90 74 29 100 97
Elk	58	0.00000	85 73 68 70 68 68 60 83 48 90 78 83 80 53 85 45 95 40 35 83 30 80 93 48 75 80 70 45 73 60 83 65 83 83 88 45 83 95 100 93 75 78 90 95 78 83 80 80 60 53 50 55 93 73 68 35 85 83
Seal	55	0.00000	77 72 85 54 82 64 64 85 85 62 64 79 38 85 92 59 54 62 77 38 44 85 85 64 87 87 46 74 72 54 79 85 82 69 90 90 85 67 82 74 85 79 79 64 85 85 69 51 51 56 85 64 59 72 90

For each contest, the p-value is for a two-sided t-test of the null hypothesis such that the average number of correct guesses across subjects will equal the total number of guesses in the contest divided by 2.

For this variant, we also changed the recruitment and incentive mechanisms. To recruit subjects, an announcement was e-mailed to members of several groups: Northeastern computer science students, MIT Sloan MBA students in the fall section of 15.970, the American Association of Individual Investors mailing list, the Market Technicians Association mailing list, the MTA Educational Foundation mailing list, and the staff and Twitter followers of TraderPsyches. As an incentive, we offered a $100 Amazon gift certificate to the top scorer in each contest.

Results for this variant are reported in Table 14.3. The p-value is less than 5% for all but one data set. We attribute the slightly less decisive outcome for this variant to the smaller number of subjects.

Table 14.3 Results for distinguishing price charts from their permutation using a variant of the random process for permuting the actual time series.

Contest	Subjects	p-value	Correct Guesses per Subject as Percentage of Total Guesses
Mandrill	17	0.05770	38 42 46 46 48 50 50 52 54 58 58 60 60 64 64 66 70
Bear	29	0.00000	100 70 78 100 92 16 89 86 95 78 100 86 97 84 81 95 100 81 70 73 54 73 73 92 78 89 89 51 57
Lynx	26	0.00156	43 43 46 46 46 46 49 49 51 51 54 54 57 57 57 60 60 63 63 63 63 63 63 63 66 71
Reindeer	22	0.00000	100 40 68 95 75 73 80 68 78 95 78 63 75 68 75 53 63 73 78 85 53 38
Beaver	23	0.00332	33 36 42 50 50 53 53 53 53 56 56 58 64 64 64 64 64 64 67 67 69 81 83
Bull	32	0.00000	100 94 94 100 81 100 97 97 84 94 97 90 100 100 94 97 100 100 100 84 97 97 100 94 97 100 94 100 100 100 97 45
Elk	25	0.00000	100 45 78 88 90 88 55 75 93 90 83 100 83 90 90 88 100 90 95 90 88 93 100 85 53
Seal	38	0.00000	41 44 46 49 54 59 59 59 62 62 64 64 64 67 67 69 69 72 74 74 74 77 77 79 79 79 79 82 82 82 82 85 85 87 90 90 92 100

For each contest, the p-value is for the two-sided t-test of the null hypothesis such that the average number of correct guesses across subjects will equal the total number of guesses in the contest divided by 2.

14.6.3 AR(1)

Next, we wanted to test the null hypothesis, H, that human subjects cannot distinguish between an actual time series, S, and a time series that is generated by an AR(1) process calibrated to match the mean, variance, and first-order autocovariance of S. (We refer to Hamilton (1994, Section 3.4) for background on AR(1) processes.)

Again, we began with a time series of actual historical prices, $\{P_0, P_1, P_2, ..., P_T\}$, and computed its logarithmic returns, $\{R_t\}$,

$$R_t \equiv \log(P_t) - \log(P_{t-1}).$$

We then computed the sample mean, μ, variance, v, and first-order autocovariance, α, of the series, R. This defines an AR(1) process

$$y_t \equiv c + \phi \cdot y_{t-1} + \epsilon_t,$$

where ϵ_t are independent and identically distributed normal distributions with mean 0 and variance σ^2 as follows:

$$\phi = \alpha/\nu,$$

$$c = \mu(1 - \phi), \text{and}$$

$$\sigma^2 = \nu(1 - \phi^2).$$

The starting point, y_0, of the AR(1) process is taken to be R_h for an index h chosen uniformly at random.

Finally, we set

$$P^*_{t+1} \equiv P^*_t \cdot e^{y_{t+1}}, \quad P^*_0 \equiv 1.$$

The results are reported in Table 14.4. We obtain a p-value less than 0.505% for five of our eight data sets, and higher for the remaining three.

14.6.4 Comparison of Random Permutation and AR(1) Results

In this section, we investigate whether subjects did better when presented with the permutation process than with an AR(1) process. As a first step, in Table 14.5 we present the results of a one-sided, independent samples

Table 14.4 Results for distinguishing price charts from AR(1).

Contest	Subjects	p-value	Correct Guesses per Subject as Percentage of Total Guesses
Mandrill	36	0.55792	52 46 40 44 48 54 58 36 58 64 48 56 60 44 36 50 42 56 50 58 52 56 50 50 46 60 44 56 48 54 48 58 50 44 54 54
Bear	40	0.00000	100 59 86 97 49 62 100 54 27 73 54 89 73 92 49 78 59 78 89 89 95 70 62 92 73 97 95 43 86 95 54 100 76 57 92 89 76 92 97 100
Lynx	38	0.14392	54 60 51 43 31 46 40 57 46 63 57 54 51 57 40 60 57 66 60 57 49 66 37 43 37 57 37 51 54 69 60 63 51 54 51 51 46 54
Reindeer	39	0.00033	58 48 90 58 63 55 43 58 53 63 70 45 40 43 48 45 45 43 45 68 48 45 90 58 70 55 43 58 90 43 70 78 83 73 70 55 80 70 65
Beaver	37	0.10729	50 58 39 72 47 64 69 69 58 47 56 56 44 42 56 56 61 44 53 58 44 47 47 69 53 53 50 58 28 44 53 33 33 58 56 67 61
Bull	37	0.00000	77 65 65 77 77 55 81 58 42 77 81 97 81 87 55 61 97 97 87 48 90 74 61 87 58 90 71 55 77 65 55 71 71 87 84 81 87
Elk	36	0.00505	53 55 63 45 40 63 48 43 63 48 48 63 45 48 48 68 48 63 88 60 45 58 63 70 48 65 58 55 60 38 50 55 48 53 75 58
Seal	38	0.00000	67 51 59 67 59 69 64 46 59 67 85 69 79 56 56 49 69 82 59 79 62 33 82 44 79 74 62 77 67 49 62 56 79 69 77 74 59 79

For each contest, the p-value is for the two-sided t-test of the null hypothesis that the average across number of correct guesses across subjects will equal the total number of guesses in the contest, divided by 2.

Table 14.5 One-sided, independent samples t-test for success rate decline between the random permutation and AR(1) experiments.

Contest	p-value
Mandrill	0.067
Bear	0.949
Lynx	0.156
Reindeer	0.084
Beaver	0.096
Bull	0.014
Elk	0.000
Seal	0.009

For each contest, the null hypothesis is that the average success rate across subjects is equal for the two experiments. The alternative hypothesis is that the average success rate in the AR(1) experiment is lower than the average success rate in the random permutation experiment. The success rate of a particular subject is defined as the number of their correct guesses divided by the number of charts in the contest.

t-test for a decline in success rate between the random permutation and AR(1) experiments, reported in Tables 14.2 and 14.4, respectively. For each contest, the null hypothesis was that the average success rate across subjects is equal for the two experiments. The alternative hypothesis was that the average success rate in the AR(1) experiment is lower than the average success rate in the random permutation experiment. The success rate of a particular subject is defined as the number of their correct guesses divided by the number of charts in the contest. For six of the eight data sets, the null hypothesis was rejected at least at the 10% level.

To gain further insight into the differences in performance between the two experiments, in Table 14.6, we present the first five autocorrelations and the Ljung–Box Q statistic, computed using twenty lagged terms of the actual and synthetic data. The Q statistic tests the null hypothesis that autocorrelations up to lag 20 will equal zero—that is, it tests for the 'overall' randomness in returns. For the actual data (the top panel of Table 14.6), we are able to reject the null hypothesis of overall randomness in each of the eight data sets with high confidence (the p-values of the Q statistic are 0.000). Under random permutation, we fail to reject the null (the middle panel of Table 14.6). The fact that overall randomness of the shuffled data is so different from that of the actual data helps explain why subjects performed so well in the permutation experiment.

However, for the AR(1) process, we do reject the null hypothesis of overall randomness (the bottom panel of Table 14.6). In fact, for six of the eight contests, the p-value of the Q statistic is the same as that of the actual data up to three decimal places. For the remaining two contests, we reject the null

Table 14.6 Autocorrelations and the Ljung–Box Q statistic, computed using twenty lagged terms.

Contest	ρ_1	ρ_2	ρ_3	ρ_4	ρ_5	Ljung–Box Q_{20}	p-value (Q_{20})
				Actual Data			
Mandrill	8.0	1.7	0.4	1.6	−3.0	99	0.000
Bear	11.2	6.5	4.4	4.1	3.8	18845	0.000
Lynx	2.9	−0.3	1.4	1.1	−3.2	66	0.000
Reindeer	−34.8	11.0	−4.0	4.0	−2.4	137260	0.000
Beaver	1.4	−3.0	1.6	1.3	1.1	99	0.000
Elk	31.0	20.2	15.9	13.0	10.6	52615	0.000
Bull	−12.3	1.2	1.2	0.3	0.1	15227	0.000
Seal	8.4	6.2	7.4	4.9	5.5	710	0.000
				Random Permutation			
Mandrill	−2.1	3.1	−2.5	−1.1	−0.5	25	0.189
Bear	−0.2	0.0	−0.1	0.0	0.0	18	0.611
Lynx	0.7	0.9	−0.4	−0.7	0.5	15	0.753
Reindeer	0.1	0.0	0.0	0.1	0.0	10	0.966
Beaver	−0.4	1.7	0.1	−0.8	1.1	20	0.474
Elk	0.1	0.1	0.3	0.0	0.2	16	0.687
Bull	0.1	0.0	0.0	−0.1	−0.1	13	0.868
Seal	0.6	0.8	1.5	0.2	0.1	21	0.420
				AR(1)			
Mandrill	10.1	1.1	0.7	−1.9	−0.8	80	0.000
Bear	11.2	1.5	0.1	0.0	−0.1	9354	0.000
Lynx	4.3	−1.0	0.6	0.3	−0.9	39	0.006
Reindeer	−35.0	12.2	−4.2	1.4	−0.5	138450	0.000
Beaver	0.9	−0.4	0.1	−0.1	−0.6	29	0.092
Elk	30.8	9.2	2.6	0.9	0.3	24274	0.000
Bull	−12.4	1.7	−0.4	0.0	0.0	15425	0.000
Seal	8.2	0.4	−0.5	−1.6	0.2	137	0.000

The Q statistic tests the null hypothesis that autocorrelations up to lag 20 equal zero (i.e. that returns are random and independent). The corresponding p-values are also presented. These statistics are reported for the actual data, as well as for the synthetic processes constructed using random permutation or an AR(1) process calibrated to the data. The synthetic processes are constructed using the entire data sample.

hypothesis at the 1% level in one case, and at the 10% level in the other case. This similarity in the overall randomness between the actual and AR(1) data helps explain why the subjects had a somewhat harder time in the AR(1) test. Interestingly, this similarity appears especially pronounced in the three contests in which subjects had the hardest time distinguishing the AR(1) process from the actual data: Mandrill, Lynx, and Beaver.

14.6.5 Learning

Because the game provided feedback to participants, we investigated whether subjects improved their performance while playing. To do so, we compared the subjects' performance in the first and last parts of each contest. Specifically, for each contest, we considered the subset consisting of the first one-fifth of guesses and that consisting of the last one-fifth.[7] For each subset, we added up the number of correct guesses across subjects and divided that sum by the total number of guesses in the subset multiplied by the number of subjects. We call this the fraction of correct guesses made by the combined pool of subjects. We refer to this fraction in the first and last part of each contest as *correct first* and *correct last*, respectively. In addition, our experimental subjects were required to practice before entering a contest. This makes the results in this section less prone to influence from extraneous factors, such as becoming comfortable with the game interface.

Table 14.7 reports the results for the random permutation and AR(1) processes. For the random permutation process (presented in the left-hand panel

Table 14.7 Performance improvement with the random permutation and AR(1) processes.

Contest	Random Permutation			AR(1)		
	Num. Guesses	Correct First	Correct Last	Num. Guesses	Correct First	Correct Last
Mandrill	557	0.506	0.589	359	0.496	0.482
Bear	384	0.693	0.734	280	0.739	0.832
Lynx	391	0.573	0.588	265	0.525	0.536
Reindeer	445	0.620	0.656	312	0.510	0.635
Beaver	406	0.559	0.594	258	0.543	0.500
Bull	342	0.798	0.825	221	0.674	0.819
Elk	461	0.690	0.755	287	0.544	0.568
Seal	385	0.787	0.592	266	0.677	0.519

p-values of One-Sided Signed Rank Test

	Random Permutation	AR(1)
All contests	0.098	0.320

For each contest, the column 'correct first' reports the fraction of correct guesses made by the combined pool of subjects in the first one-fifth of guesses. The column 'correct last' reports the corresponding value for the last one-fifth of guesses. The column 'Num. guesses' is the denominator in the calculation of these fractions of correct guesses. For each synthetic process, the table also reports the *p*-values of the one-sided Wilcoxon signed rank test, which tests the null hypothesis that 'correct first' minus 'correct last' comes from a distribution with zero median against the alternative hypothesis that the median of the 'correct first' column is less than the median of the 'correct last' column.

---

[7] Noninteger numbers are rounded down to the nearest integer.

of the table), in all but one contest the average number of correct guesses increases. To check whether this increase is statistically significant across contests, we conducted a one-sided Wilcoxon signed rank test on the results presented in the table. In particular, we tested the null hypothesis that 'correct first' minus 'correct last' comes from a distribution with zero median, against the alternative hypothesis that the median of the 'correct first' column is less than the median of the 'correct last' column.[8] Table 14.7 shows that the increase in correct guesses is significant at the 10% level.

The right-hand panel of Table 14.7 reports the results for the AR(1) process. Across all contests, we cannot reject the null hypothesis that the median success rate is the same in the first and the last fraction of guesses. In some cases, like in the reindeer or bull contest, the difference in the average success rates seems significant. Indeed, Table 14.8 shows that if we conduct a significance test contest by contest (rather than across contests as in Table 14.7), we find there is evidence of learning in three of the eight contests under either random permutation or AR(1). Here, for each subject in a given contest, we take the fraction of correct guesses in the first one-fifth of guesses and the fraction of correct guesses in the last one-fifth of guesses. For each contest, we then report the p-value of the one-sided t-test of the null hypothesis that, subject by subject, 'correct first' minus 'correct last' comes from a distribution with zero mean, against the alternative hypothesis that the mean of the subject-by-subject 'correct first' data is less than that of the corresponding

Table 14.8 Performance improvement contest by contest.

Contest	Random Permutation	AR(1)
	p-values of One-Sided t-test	
Mandrill	0.006	0.654
Bear	0.095	0.011
Lynx	0.344	0.399
Reindeer	0.158	0.006
Beaver	0.164	0.801
Bull	0.134	0.001
Elk	0.020	0.317
Seal	1.000	0.998

For each subject in each contest, we take the fraction of correct guesses in the first one-fifth of guesses and the fraction of correct guesses in the last one-fifth of guesses. For each contest, we then report the p-value of the one-sided t-test of the null hypothesis that, subject by subject, 'correct first' minus 'correct last' comes from a distribution with zero mean. The alternative hypothesis is that the mean of the 'correct first' column is less than the mean of the 'correct last' column.

[8] We use the signed rank test rather than the t-test because of the small sample size.

'correct last' data. The table shows that for the random permutation process learning is statistically significant for mandrill, bear, and elk at least at the 10% level, while for the AR(1) process, it is significant for bear, reindeer, and bull at least at the 5% level.

14.7 Discussion

We began this chapter by borrowing from theoretical computer science to define an efficient market with respect to a given set of resources, S, as a market in which no strategy using S can generate a profit. In a simple model of market evolution, where strategies enter sequentially and impact the market by their decision to buy or sell, we showed that the effect of optimal strategies using S can lead to 'market conditions' that were not present initially, such as the possibility for a strategy using resources $S' \gg S$ to make a bigger profit than was initially possible. These results may explain the increasing quantitative sophistication of real-world asset managers. Moreover, when we implement our model as a game, in the spirit of Conway's 'Game of Life', we find that computationally simple trading rules can lead to apparently chaotic market dynamics.

In our experimental analysis of human cognitive abilities, we find that humans are able to distinguish actual financial time series from synthetic ones, and that they improve over time. An interesting future research direction would be to compare human performance against the performance of computers, following a vast literature (Lawrence et al., 2006). In our experimental setting, the human eye may have an advantage over computer algorithms. It is well known that computers still struggle with many image-recognition and classification tasks that are trivial for humans. The same may be the case for distinguishing asset returns from synthetic processes. However, given the remarkable progress of machine-learning algorithms over the past decade—especially deep-learning networks—it may not be long before computers are able to out-compete humans even in this domain.

Our findings contradict previous anecdotal evidence that humans cannot tell price charts from 'random' charts, such as charts generated by a random walk. For example, in an experiment by Malkiel (1973) students were asked to generate returns (i.e. price differences) by tossing fair coins, and it was argued that those yielded observations were indistinguishable from market returns to human subjects observing corresponding price charts. Similar arguments in the finance literature include Roberts (1959), Kroll, Levy, and Rapoport (1988), De Bondt (1993), Wäneryd (2001), and Swedroe (2005).

Such anecdotal evidence has also been collected in the computer science literature. Keogh and Kasetty (2003) asked twelve professors at the University of California at Riverside's Anderson Graduate School of Management to view a series of numerical sequences and determine which three sequences were random walks, and which three were real S&P 500 stocks. They found that subjects achieved an accuracy rate of 55.6%, which was not statistically different from random guesses.

In the next chapter, we consider the related question of how an investor *should* behave in order to optimize their wealth and whether such behaviours are, in fact, sustainable over time.

15
Maximizing Relative versus Absolute Wealth

How to invest one's wealth is among the most important decisions anyone will have to face.[1] The groundbreaking approach of Markowitz (1952), using mean-variance theory to solve this problem, has remained the cornerstone of modern investment theory. This body of work has led to numerous break-throughs in financial economics, including the famous capital asset pricing model (Sharpe, 1964; Lintner, 1965a,b; Treynor, 1965; Mossin, 1966). More-over, the influence of this paradigm goes far beyond academia, thanks to practitioners like Vanguard's John C. Bogle, who applied these ideas to create the passive index funds that now comprise a multi-trillion-dollar industry (Lo, 2022).

Traditional applications of portfolio theory to maximize wealth have focused on absolute or total wealth, as in the Kelly criterion of Chapter 2, Equation (2.1) (Kelly, 1956; Samuelson, 1971; Thorp, 1971, 2006; Cover and Thomas, 1991). However, in this chapter, we will consider *relative* wealth, in the spirit of Orr (2017), an evolutionary biologist who argues that, from a population genetics point of view, relative success is more important than absolute success.

Relative wealth or income has been discussed in a number of studies (Rob-son, 1992; Bakshi and Chen, 1996; Corneo and Jeanne, 1997; Hens and Schenk-Hoppé, 2005; Frank, 2011a), and the behavioural economics liter-ature provides voluminous evidence that investors sometimes assess their performance relative to a reference group (Frank, 1985; Clark and Oswald, 1996; Clark, Frijters, and Shields, 2008). It is particularly important to under-stand the consequences of investment decisions in a setting where relative wealth, not absolute wealth, is the standard. As Burnham, Dunlap, and Stephens (2015, p. 1) point out, 'if people are envious by caring about relative wealth, then free trade may make all parties richer, but may cause envious

---

[1] This chapter, including the figures, is adapted with permission of Springer Nature Customer Service Centre GmbH: Springer Nature from Lo, A. W., Orr, H. A., and Zhang, R. (2018). The growth of relative wealth and the Kelly criterion. *Journal of Bioeconomics* 20(1): 49–67.

The Adaptive Markets Hypothesis. Andrew W. Lo and Ruixun Zhang, Oxford University Press. © Andrew W. Lo and Ruixun Zhang (2024). DOI: 10.1093/oso/9780199681143.003.0015

people to be less happy. If economics misunderstands human nature, then free trade may simultaneously increase wealth and unhappiness.'

In this chapter, we compare the consequences of maximizing relative wealth to maximizing absolute wealth over both short-term and long-term investment horizons. In particular, we compare the results obtained by Orr (2017) to those of an extension of the binary choice model of Chapter 2, in the context of an investor who allocates their wealth between two assets over time. Rather than maximizing their absolute wealth, the investor maximizes their wealth relative to another investor with a fixed behaviour. We consider the cases of a single time period, multiple periods, and an infinite time horizon. We then ask the question: What is the optimal behaviour for an investor as a function of the environment, given that the environment consists of the asset returns and the behaviour of the other participants? In our framework, relative wealth is defined as a proportion of total wealth, which corresponds closely to the allele frequency in population genetics. This analogy acts as a bridge to the earlier literature on the relevance of relative wealth to behaviour. While some of our results will be familiar to population geneticists, they do not appear to be widely known in a financial context. For completeness, we derive them from first principles here.

Our approach leads to several interesting conclusions about the Kelly criterion. We show that the Kelly criterion is the optimal behaviour provided an investor intends to maximize their absolute wealth in the case of an infinite horizon. However, if the investor decides to maximize their relative wealth instead, we identify the conditions under which the Kelly criterion is optimal, and those under which the investor should deviate from it. The investor's initial relative wealth—which represents the investor's market power—plays a critical role in determining the deviation of optimal behaviour from the Kelly criterion regardless of whether the investor is myopic across a single time period, or maximizing wealth over an infinite horizon. Moreover, the dominant investor's optimal behaviour is different from other investors' optimal behaviour.

In the remainder of this chapter, we will first consider a two-asset model in which investors maximize their absolute wealth. It is shown that the long-run optimal behaviour is equivalent to the behaviour implied by the Kelly criterion. We then extend the binary choice model, and consider in a non-game theoretic framework the case of two investors who maximize their wealth relative to the population, given the other investor's behaviour. The Kelly criterion emerges as a special case under certain environmental conditions. We also provide a numerical example to illustrate our theoretical results, and discuss several implications that can be tested through experimental evolutionary techniques.

Related Literature

Applying evolutionary principles to investing is clearly motivated by the many strands of the literature described in Parts I and II, which reconcile the behavioural inconsistencies between *Homo economicus* and *Homo sapiens*. These applications are also closely related to optimal portfolio growth theory, as explored by Kelly (1956), Hakansson (1970), Thorp (1971), Algoet and Cover (1988), Browne and Whitt (1996), and Aurell et al. (2000), among others. While the evolutionary framework tends to focus on the long-term performance of a strategy, investors are also concerned with the short to medium term (Browne, 1999). Myopic investor behaviour has been documented in both theoretical and empirical studies (Strotz, 1955; Stroyan, 1983; Thaler et al., 1997; Bushee, 1998). Since much of the field of population genetics focuses on short-term competition between different types of individuals, population geneticists have applied their ideas to portfolio theory (Frank, 1990, 2011a; Orr, 2017), in some cases considering the maximization of one-period expected wealth.

The market dynamics of investment strategies under evolutionary selection have been explored under the assumption that investors will try to maximize absolute wealth (Evstigneev, Hens, and Schenk-Hoppé, 2002, 2006; Amir et al., 2005; Hens and Schenk-Hoppé, 2005). Some studies have found that individual investors with more accurate beliefs will accumulate more wealth, and thus dominate the economy (Sandroni, 2000, 2005), while others have argued that wealth dynamics need not lead to rules that maximize expected utility using rational expectations (Blume and Easley, 1992), and that investors with incorrect beliefs may drive out those with correct beliefs (Blume and Easley, 2006). Research on the performance of rational versus irrational traders has also adopted evolutionary ideas; for example, it has been shown that irrational traders can survive in the long run, resulting in prices that diverge from fundamental values (De Long et al., 1990, 1991; Biais and Shadur, 2000; Hirshleifer and Luo, 2001; Hirshleifer, Subrahmanyam, and Titman, 2006; Kogan et al., 2006; Yan, 2008).

15.1 The Kelly Criterion

Reinterpreting the basic binary choice model of Chapter 2 to apply to wealth rather than to population growth yields the classical Kelly criterion. In particular, consider two assets, a and b, in a discrete-time model, each generating gross returns $x_a \in (0, \infty)$ and $x_b \in (0, \infty)$ in one period. For example, asset a can be a risky asset, whereas asset b can be the riskless asset. In this case, $x_a \in (0, \infty)$ and $x_b = 1+r$, where r is the risk-free interest rate. In general, $(x_{a,t}, x_{b,t})$ are independent and identically distributed over time $t = 1, 2, \cdots$, and are described by the probability distribution function, $\Phi(x_a, x_b)$.

Consider an investor who allocates $f \in [0,1]$ of their wealth in asset a and $1-f$ in asset b. Henceforth, we refer to f as the investor's behaviour. Assumption 2.1 in Chapter 2 guarantees that the gross return of any investment portfolio is positive. In other words, the investor cannot lose more than what they have. This is made possible by assuming that x_a and x_b are positive, and f is between 0 and 1. In other words, the investor only allocates their money between two assets, and no short-selling or leverage is allowed.[2]

Let n_t^f be the total wealth of investor f in period t. To simplify our notation, let $\omega_t^f = fx_{a,t}+(1-f)x_{b,t}$ be the gross return of investor f's portfolio in period t. With these notational conventions in mind, we can follow the same analysis as in Section 2.1 of Chapter 2 to derive the following result:

Proposition 15.1 *The optimal allocation, f^{Kelly}, that maximizes investor f's absolute wealth as T increases without bound is*

$$
f^{Kelly} = \begin{cases} 1 & \text{if } \mathbb{E}[x_a/x_b] > 1 \quad \text{and} \quad \mathbb{E}[x_b/x_a] < 1 \\ \text{solution to Equation (15.2)} & \text{if } \mathbb{E}[x_a/x_b] \geq 1 \quad \text{and} \quad \mathbb{E}[x_b/x_a] \geq 1, \\ 0 & \text{if } \mathbb{E}[x_a/x_b] < 1 \quad \text{and} \quad \mathbb{E}[x_b/x_a] > 1 \end{cases}
$$

$$(15.1)$$

where f^{Kelly} is defined implicitly in the second case of Equation (15.1) by:

$$
\mathbb{E}\left[\frac{x_a - x_b}{f^{Kelly}x_a + (1 - f^{Kelly})x_b}\right] = 0.
$$

$$(15.2)$$

The optimal allocation given in Proposition 15.1 coincides with the Kelly criterion (Kelly, 1956; Thorp, 1971) in probability theory and the portfolio choice literature. To emphasize this connection, we will henceforth refer to this optimal allocation as the Kelly criterion. As we will see, in the case of maximizing an individual's relative wealth, the Kelly criterion plays a key role as a reference strategy.

In portfolio theory, the Kelly criterion is used to determine the optimal size of a series of bets for the long run. Although this strategy's promise of doing better than any other strategy in the long run seems compelling, some researchers have argued against it, principally because the specific

---

[2] One could relax this assumption by allowing short selling and leverage, which correspond to $f < 0$ or $f > 0$. However, f would still need to be restricted such that $fx_a + (1 - f)x_b$ is always positive. This does not change our results in any essential way, but it would complicate the presentation of some results mathematically. Therefore, we stick to the simple assumption that $f \in [0, 1]$ as in Chapter 2.

investing constraints of an individual may over-ride the desire for an optimal growth rate. In other words, different investors might have different utility functions. In fact, to an individual with a logarithmic utility function, the Kelly criterion will maximize the expected utility, so the Kelly criterion can be considered as the optimal strategy under expected utility theory with a specific utility function.

15.2 Maximizing Relative Wealth

In this section, we consider two investors. The first investor allocates $f \in [0, 1]$ of their wealth in asset a and $1 - f$ in asset b. The second investor allocates $g \in [0, 1]$ of their wealth in asset a and $1 - g$ in asset b. Investor f's objective is to maximize the proportion of their wealth relative to the total wealth in the population, which we define as investor f's relative wealth. Note that we use f and g to mean both the proportion of wealth and as a label for the investor, to simplify our notation.

Here we introduce a concept taken from evolutionary theory. In population genetics, the metric for natural selection is the expected reproduction of a genotype divided by the average reproduction of the population (i.e. the relative reproduction), analogous to investor f's relative wealth. Our use of relative wealth rather than absolute wealth naturally unlocks existing tools and ideas from population genetics for us.

In the case of maximizing relative wealth, initial wealth plays an important role in the optimal allocation. Let $\eta \in (0, 1)$ be the relative initial wealth of investor f:

$$\eta = \frac{n_0^f}{n_0^f + n_0^g}.$$

Let l_t^f be the relative wealth of investor f in subsequent periods $t = 1, 2, \cdots. l_t^f$ and l_t^g are defined similarly:

$$l_t^f = \frac{n_t^f}{n_t^f + n_t^g} = \frac{1}{1 + n_t^g/n_t^f},$$

$$l_t^g = 1 - l_t^f.$$

It is obvious that the ratio n_t^g/n_t^f is sufficient to determine the relative wealth, l_t^f. Let W_T^f be the T-period average log-relative-growth:

$$W_T^f = \frac{1}{T} \log \frac{\prod_{t=1}^T \omega_t^g}{\prod_{t=1}^T \omega_t^f} = \frac{1}{T} \sum_{t=1}^T \log \frac{\omega_t^g}{\omega_t^f}. \tag{15.3}$$

Then we can write the relative wealth in period T as:

$$l_T^f = \frac{1}{1 + \frac{n_T^g}{n_T^f}} = \frac{1}{1 + \frac{(1-\eta)\prod_{t=1}^{T}\omega_t^g}{\eta\prod_{t=1}^{T}\omega_t^f}} = \frac{1}{1 + \frac{1-\eta}{\eta}\exp\left(TW_T^f\right)}. \tag{15.4}$$

Analogues to Equations (15.3) and (15.4) are well known in the population genetics literature, used when the fitnesses of genotypes are assumed to vary randomly through time. (For reviews of this literature, see Felsenstein (1976) and Gillespie (1991, Chapter 4).)

15.2.1 One-Period Results

We first consider a myopic investor, who maximizes their expected relative wealth in the first period. By Equation (15.4), the expectation of l_1^f is:

$$\mathbb{E}[l_1^f] = \mathbb{E}\left[\frac{1}{1 + \frac{1-\eta}{\eta}\frac{\omega^g}{\omega^f}}\right].$$

Here we have dropped the subscripts in ω_1^f and ω_1^g, and instead simply use ω^f and ω^g, because there is only one period to consider.

Given investor g, we denote f_1^* as investor f's optimal allocation that maximizes $\mathbb{E}[l_1^f]$. There is no general formula to compute $\mathbb{E}[l_1^f]$ because it involves the expectation of the ratio of random variables. Population geneticists sometimes use diffusion approximations to estimate similar quantities, for example, the change in allele frequency (Gillespie, 1977; Frank and Slatkin, 1990; Frank, 2011a), which are essentially linear approximations of the non-linear quantity using the Taylor series. The diffusion approximation is also used by Orr (2017) in a similar model for relative wealth.

Without the diffusion approximation, one can still characterize f_1^* to a certain degree:

Proposition 15.2 *The optimal behaviour of investor f that maximizes expected relative wealth in the first period is given by:*

$$f_1^*$$

$$= \begin{cases} 1 & \text{if } \mathbb{E}\left[\frac{(x_a-x_b)\omega^g}{(\eta x_a+(1-\eta)\omega^g)^2}\right] > 0 \\ \text{solution to Equation (15.6)} & \text{if } \mathbb{E}\left[\frac{(x_a-x_b)\omega^g}{(\eta x_a+(1-\eta)\omega^g)^2}\right] \leq 0 \ \text{and } \mathbb{E}\left[\frac{(x_a-x_b)\omega^g}{(\eta x_b+(1-\eta)\omega^g)^2}\right] \geq 0, \\ 0 & \text{if } \mathbb{E}\left[\frac{(x_a-x_b)\omega^g}{(\eta x_b+(1-\eta)\omega^g)^2}\right] < 0 \end{cases}$$

$$\tag{15.5}$$

where f_1^* is defined implicitly in the second case of Equation (15.5) by:

$$\mathbb{E}\left[\frac{(x_a - x_b)\omega^g}{\left(\eta\omega^f + (1-\eta)\omega^g\right)^2}\right] = 0. \tag{15.6}$$

In general, the optimal behaviour, f_1^*, is a function of g. The next proposition asserts that f_1^* is always 'bounded' by g.

Proposition 15.3 *To maximize the expected relative wealth in period 1, investor f should never deviate more from the Kelly criterion, f^{Kelly}, than investor g in the same direction:*

- *If $g = f^{Kelly}$, then $f_1^* = f^{Kelly}$.*
- *If $g < f^{Kelly}$, then $f_1^* > g$.*
- *If $g > f^{Kelly}$, then $f_1^* < g$.*

The conclusion in Proposition 15.3 makes intuitive sense. When investor g takes a position that is riskier than the Kelly criterion, investor f should never be even riskier than investor g. Similarly, when investor g takes a position that is more conservative than the Kelly criterion, investor f should never be even more conservative than investor g.

It is interesting to compare the optimal behaviour, f_1^*, with the Kelly criterion, f^{Kelly}, which is provided in the next proposition. It shows that when g is not far from the Kelly criterion, the relationship between f_1^* and f^{Kelly} depends on the initial relative wealth of investor f.

Proposition 15.4 *If investor f is the dominant investor ($\eta > \frac{1}{2}$), then they should be locally more/less risky than the Kelly criterion in the same way as investor g: for small $\varepsilon > 0$,*

$$g = f^{Kelly} - \varepsilon \Rightarrow f_1^* < f^{Kelly},$$
$$g = f^{Kelly} + \varepsilon \Rightarrow f_1^* > f^{Kelly}.$$

If investor f is the minorant investor ($\eta < \frac{1}{2}$), then they should be locally more/less risky than the Kelly criterion in the opposite way as investor g: for small $\varepsilon > 0$,

$$g = f^{Kelly} - \varepsilon \Rightarrow f_1^* > f^{Kelly},$$
$$g = f^{Kelly} + \varepsilon \Rightarrow f_1^* < f^{Kelly}.$$

If investor f starts with the same amount of wealth as investor g ($\eta = \frac{1}{2}$), then they should be locally Kelly:

$$g \approx f^{Kelly} \Rightarrow f_1^* \approx f^{Kelly}.$$

Note that when g is far from the Kelly criterion, the conclusions in Proposition 15.4 may not necessarily hold. Section 15.3 provides a numerical example (Fig. 15.1b) in which investor f is the minorant investor ($\eta < \frac{1}{2}$) and $g \ll f^{Kelly}$ but $f_1^* < f^{Kelly}$. However, Orr (2017) has shown that these results are still approximately true for any g up to a diffusion approximation, which is consistent with the numerical results for maximizing one-period relative wealth shown in Fig. 15.1a. We will provide more discussion on this point in Section 15.3.

15.2.2 Multi-Period Results

The previous results are based on maximizing the expected relative wealth in period 1: $\mathbb{E}[l_1^f]$. To generalize these results to maximizing expected relative wealth in period T: $\mathbb{E}[l_T^f]$, we have:

Proposition 15.5 *The optimal behaviour of investor f that maximizes expected relative wealth in the T-th period is given by:*

$$f_T^* = \begin{cases} 1 & \text{if } \mathbb{E}\left[\dfrac{\exp(TW_T^1)\left(T-\sum_{t=1}^T \frac{x_{b,t}}{x_{a,t}}\right)}{\left(1+\frac{1-\eta}{\eta}\exp(TW_T^1)\right)^2}\right] > 0 \\[4ex] \text{solution to Equation (15.8)} & \text{if } \mathbb{E}\left[\dfrac{\exp(TW_T^1)\left(T-\sum_{t=1}^T \frac{x_{b,t}}{x_{a,t}}\right)}{\left(1+\frac{1-\eta}{\eta}\exp(TW_T^1)\right)^2}\right] \leq 0 \\[4ex] & \text{and } \mathbb{E}\left[\dfrac{\exp(TW_T^0)\left(\sum_{t=1}^T \frac{x_{a,t}}{x_{b,t}}-T\right)}{\left(1+\frac{1-\eta}{\eta}\exp(TW_T^0)\right)^2}\right] \geq 0 \\[4ex] 0 & \text{if } \mathbb{E}\left[\dfrac{\exp(TW_T^0)\left(\sum_{t=1}^T \frac{x_{a,t}}{x_{b,t}}-T\right)}{\left(1+\frac{1-\eta}{\eta}\exp(TW_T^0)\right)^2}\right] < 0 \end{cases} , \quad (15.7)$$

where f_T^* is defined implicitly in the second case of Equation (15.7) by:

$$\mathbb{E}\left[\frac{\exp\left(TW_T^f\right)\sum_{t=1}^T \frac{x_{a,t}-x_{b,t}}{fx_{a,t}+(1-f)x_{b,t}}}{\left(1+\frac{1-\eta}{\eta}\exp\left(TW_T^f\right)\right)^2}\right] = 0. \quad (15.8)$$

We have assumed that f is constant through time, which implies that the investor does not dynamically change their position from period to period. This passive strategy is of interest for two reasons: the information about each investor's relative wealth may be difficult to obtain in each period, and it may also be costly to rebalance the portfolio after each period.

If the investor is, indeed, able to adjust f dynamically at each new period as a function of their current relative wealth, it is clear the expected growth of their relative wealth can be increased. This is studied numerically in a similar model in Orr (2017).

Similarly, one can 'bound' f_T^* by g, and compare f_T^* with f^{Kelly} when g is near the Kelly criterion.

Proposition 15.6 *The conclusions in Propositions 15.3 and 15.4 hold for f_T^* in multi-period, $T = 2, 3, \cdots$.*

Simply put, when investor g takes a position that is riskier than the Kelly criterion, investor f should never be even riskier than investor g, no matter how many horizons forward they are looking. Similarly, when investor g takes a position that is more conservative than the Kelly criterion, investor f should never be even more conservative than investor g, no matter how many horizons forward they are looking. However, if investor g deviates from the Kelly criterion only slightly, then investor f should deviate from the Kelly criterion in the opposite direction than investor g, provided that investor f has less initial wealth than investor g, but in the same direction, provided that investor f has more initial wealth than investor g.

As a special case, if investor g is playing the Kelly criterion strategy, then investor f should also play Kelly; if investor g is not playing Kelly, however, investor f should also not play Kelly. This implies that the Kelly criterion is a Nash equilibrium when investors maximize their relative wealth. This is consistent with the existing literature of evolutionary portfolio theory (Evstigneev, Hens, and Schenk-Hoppé, 2002, 2006) when absolute wealth is maximized.

Note that, in the multi-period case, one does not have analogous results to a diffusion approximation as in the one-period case (Orr, 2017). The numerical results of Section 15.3 show that the condition that g is near the Kelly criterion is essential (Fig. 15.2a).

15.2.3 Infinite Horizon

Recall from Equation (15.3) that the T-period average log-relative-growth, W_T^f, is given by:

$$W_T^f = \frac{1}{T}\sum_{t=1}^{T}\log \omega_t^g - \frac{1}{T}\sum_{t=1}^{T}\log \omega_t^f \xrightarrow{p} \alpha(g) - \alpha(f) \tag{15.9}$$

as T increases without bound. It is therefore easy to see from Equation (15.4) that:

Proposition 15.7 *As T increases without bound, the relative wealth of investor f converges in probability to a constant:*

$$l_T^f \xrightarrow{p} \begin{cases} 0 & \text{if } \alpha(f) < \alpha(g) \\ \eta & \text{if } \alpha(f) = \alpha(g). \\ 1 & \text{if } \alpha(f) > \alpha(g) \end{cases} \tag{15.10}$$

Proposition 15.7 is consistent with well-known results in the population genetics literature (see, e.g., Gillespie (1973)), as well as in the behavioural finance literature cited in Parts I and II. It asserts that investor f's relative wealth will converge to 1 as long as its log-geometric-average growth rate, $\alpha(f)$, is greater than investor g's. This implies that when T increases without bound, there are multiple behaviours that are all optimal in the following sense:

$$\operatorname*{argmax}_{f} \lim_{T\to\infty} l_T^f = \operatorname*{argmax}_{f} \mathbb{E}\left[\lim_{T\to\infty} l_T^f\right] = \operatorname*{argmax}_{f} \lim_{T\to\infty} \mathbb{E}\left[l_T^f\right]$$

$$= \{f : \alpha(f) > \alpha(g)\}.$$

Note that the above equality uses the dominant convergence theorem (l_T^f is always bounded) to switch the limit and the expectation operator.

However, this is not equivalent to the limit of the optimal behaviour, f_T^*, as T increases without bound, because one cannot switch the operator 'argmax' and 'lim' in general, and

$$\operatorname*{argmax}_{f} \lim_{T\to\infty} \mathbb{E}\left[l_T^f\right] \neq \lim_{T\to\infty} \operatorname*{argmax}_{f} \mathbb{E}\left[l_T^f\right].$$

Section 15.3 provides such an example.

15.3 A Numerical Example

We construct a numerical example in this section to illustrate the results of Sections 15.1 and 15.2. Consider the following two simple assets:

$$x_a = \begin{cases} \alpha & \text{with probability} \quad p \\ \beta & \text{with probability} \quad 1-p \end{cases}, \qquad x_b = \gamma \quad \text{with probability} \quad 1.$$

In this case, asset a is risky and asset b is riskless. The expected relative wealth of investor f in period T is explicitly given by:

$$\mathbb{E}\left[l_T^f\right] - \sum_{k=0}^{T} \frac{\binom{T}{k}p^k(1-p)^{T-k}}{1 + \frac{1-\eta}{\eta}\exp\left(k\log\frac{g\alpha+(1-g)\gamma}{f\alpha+(1-f)\gamma} + (T-k)\log\frac{g\beta+(1-g)\gamma}{f\beta+(1-f)\gamma}\right)}. \tag{15.11}$$

It is easy to numerically solve from Equation (15.11) the optimal behaviour, f_T^*, for any given environment α, β, γ, p.

For simplicity, we focus on one particular environment henceforth:

$$x_a = \begin{cases} 2 & \text{with probability} \quad 0.5 \\ 0.5 & \text{with probability} \quad 0.5 \end{cases}, \qquad x_b = 1 \quad \text{with probability} \quad 1.$$

It is easy to show by Proposition 15.1 that $f^{Kelly} = \frac{1}{2}$ in this case. In order to guarantee that the gross return for any investment portfolio is positive, f can take values between -1 and 2. For simplicity and consistency with our theoretical results, we will restrict f to be between 0 and 1, which does not affect the comparisons below in any essential way.

15.3.1 Maximizing One-Period Relative Wealth

We first consider the case of maximizing one's relative wealth in one period. Figure 15.1a shows f_1^* for several different cases of investor f's relative wealth, η. We can see that investor f's optimal behaviour is always 'bounded' by g, and the more dominant that investor f is, the closer f_1^* will be to g. These observations are consistent with Propositions 15.3 and 15.4.

Figure 15.1b zooms into one particular case of $\eta = 0.49$, with the f-axis from 0.495 to 0.505. It emphasizes the fact that the comparison between f_1^* and f^{Kelly} is only valid when g is close to the Kelly criterion, as asserted in Proposition 15.4. However, except for this particular case, the conclusions in Proposition 15.4 are true for any g. This provides numerical evidence that the diffusion approximation in Orr (2017) is relatively accurate for one-period results.

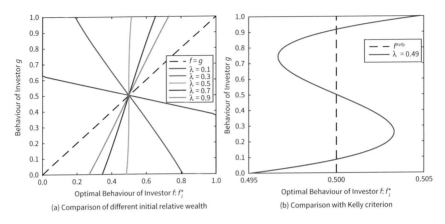

Fig. 15.1 Optimal behaviour of investor f as a function of g: f_1^*. Different values of η correspond to different initial levels of relative wealth. (a) Investor f's optimal behaviour is always 'bounded' by g, and the more dominant investor f is, the closer f_1^* is to g; (b) one particular example that the comparison between f_1^* and f^{Kelly} in Proposition 15.4 is only valid when g is close to the Kelly criterion.

15.3.2 Maximizing Multi-Period Relative Wealth

Next, we consider maximizing relative wealth over multiple periods. Figure 15.2 shows the evolution of f_T^* for three different initial values of relative wealth, $\eta = 0.2, 0.5, 0.8$. It is clear that investor f's optimal behaviour is always 'bounded' by g as T increases. In this example, it is also clear that f_T^* does not converge to f^{Kelly} as T increases without bound.

When investor f is the minorant investor (Fig. 15.2a, $\eta = 0.2$), their optimal behaviour deviates from the Kelly criterion in the opposite direction of investor g near $g = 0.5$. When investor f is the dominant investor (Fig. 15.2c, $\eta = 0.8$), their optimal behaviour deviates from the Kelly criterion in the same direction as investor g near $g = 0.5$. When investor f has the same initial wealth as investor g (Fig. 15.2b, $\eta = 0.5$), their optimal behaviour is approximately equal to the Kelly criterion near $g = 0.5$.

It is interesting to note that when investor f is the minorant investor (Fig. 15.2a, $\eta = 0.2$), the comparison between f_T^* and f^{Kelly} is only true when g is close to the Kelly criterion. This becomes more pronounced as the number of periods, T, increases. In this case, the fact that g must be close to the Kelly criterion is critical.

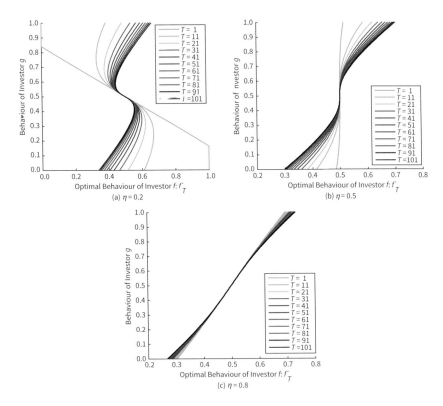

Fig. 15.2 Evolution of the optimal behaviour of investor f: f_T^*, $T = 1, 11, \cdots, 101$. Different values of η in (a)–(c) correspond to different initial levels of relative wealth.

15.4 Testable Implications

Given the similarities between biological evolution and our financial model, it should be possible to design experimental evolutionary studies to test our model's implications biologically, through studying organisms raised in different environments. As Burnham, Dunlap, and Stephens (2015) have pointed out, experimental evolution allows for the empirical investigation of decision-making under uncertainty. Central to this idea is the creation of test and control environments that vary in payoffs—or, in a biological context, fitness. Various species, ranging from bacteria to *Drosophila* (fruit flies), have been used to design experiments to understand decision-making under uncertainty (Mery and Kawecki, 2002; Beaumont et al., 2009; Dunlap and Stephens, 2014).

To test our model, it should be possible to create an environment in which *Drosophila* individuals must choose between two places to lay their eggs (media A or B). Different media would be associated with fruits with different odours, like orange and pineapple, as a signal to individual *Drosophila*. Competing 'investment' payoffs would be implemented as different rules for harvesting *Drosophila* eggs from the two media.[3]

In principle, one could create any possible payoff through different harvesting rules. For instance, to test our numerical example, let one of the media be the safe asset, and the other the risky one. One could harvest 100 eggs every generation from the safe asset (e.g. the orange-scented medium), and then 0 or 200 eggs every generation with equal probability from the risky asset (e.g. the pineapple-scented medium). Over many generations, one would measure the percentage of eggs laid by *Drosophila* on the pineapple-scented medium, which one would treat as a proxy for the allocation to the risky asset (behaviour f in our model).

The above procedure creates an 'investor', and tracks the evolution of its 'investing' behaviour given the environment. One might use two or more distinct groups of *Drosophila* and expose them to the same reproductive environment. By varying the initial relative proportion of the two groups of *Drosophila*, one would measure the investing behaviour (the percentage of eggs laid on the pineapple-scented medium) over many generations, as a function of the initial relative wealth, and the different payoffs of the safe and risky assets, and compare that to the predictions from the theory.

Even simpler experiments could be conducted with bacteria along the lines of Ben-Jacob et al. (1994, 2004) and Ben-Jacob (2008). For example, bacterial colonies could be confronted with a riskless outcome (i.e. constant fitness, corresponding to a fixed payoff) and a risky outcome (i.e. variable fitness, corresponding to different payoffs), much like the numerical example in Section 15.3.

15.5 Discussion

Unlike the traditional approach to maximizing an investor's expected wealth, this chapter imports ideas from evolutionary biology and population genetics to focus on an investor's relative wealth rather than their absolute wealth.

[3] We thank Terence C. Burnham for suggesting this design.

Relative wealth is financially important because success and satisfaction are sometimes measured by investors relative to the success of others despite their absolute success (Frank, 1990, 2011a; Robson, 1992; Bakshi and Chen, 1996; Clark and Oswald, 1996; Corneo and Jeanne, 1997; Clark, Frijters, and Shields, 2008). Our model considers the case of two investors in a non-game theoretic framework. We show how the optimal behaviour of one investor is dependent on the other investor's behaviour, which might be far from the Kelly criterion. While some of our results are already known in the finance literature, and other results are known in the population genetics literature, our framework brings both sets of results together in a single paradigm.

For myopic investors who maximize their expected relative wealth, their optimal investment strategies often deviate from those associated with the Kelly criterion. In particular, when one investor is wealthier than the other, that investor should roughly mimic the other's behaviour in being more or less aggressive than the Kelly criterion. Conversely, when one investor is poorer than the other, that investor should roughly act in the opposite manner of the other investor (Orr, 2017).

These implications may explain certain anomalous behaviours of investors—many of whom clearly do not invest according to the Kelly criterion—and warrant further empirical testing. In the next chapter, we shall provide a detailed review of the hedge fund industry in which multiple investment styles exist and interact in a highly dynamic and adaptive fashion.

16

Hedge Funds: The Galápagos Islands of Finance

In this chapter, we bring together the various ideas presented so far in this book into something practical—an analysis of the hedge fund industry.[1] We refer to this industry as the Galápagos Islands of finance, for reasons that will become clear. The standard efficient markets hypothesis (EMH) seems to fail when it comes to hedge fund managers, what they do, how they do it, and the track records that they produce. The only way to understand the hedge fund industry is through the lens of adaptive markets.

The growth of the hedge fund industry over the last three decades has been nothing short of miraculous. In 1990, hedge funds managed approximately $39 billion in assets, but despite multiple industry-wide crises—including the Asian contagion (1997), Long-Term Capital Management (1998), the bursting of the technology bubble (2001–2002), the subprime mortgage crisis (2006–2008), the European debt crisis (2009–2014), and the COVID-19 shock (2019 to the time of writing)—current estimates put hedge fund assets at $4.3 trillion. This astonishing rate of growth is not accidental. It reflects a broad and abiding demand for what hedge funds offer: higher risk-adjusted expected returns; greater diversification across assets, markets, and styles; and fewer constraints on portfolio managers who are incentivized to generate unique sources of excess expected returns (i.e. alpha).

However, along with these advantages, hedge funds also offer more complex risk exposures that vary according to style and market circumstances—risks such as tail events, illiquidity, and valuation uncertainty. In addition, because hedge funds enjoy greater latitude in their investment mandate and typically provide little transparency to their investors because of the proprietary nature of their strategies, the possibility of fraud and operational risks is of much greater concern to their investors. If typical hedge fund investors are considered 'hot money', there may be good reason.

---

[1] This chapter, including the tables and figures, is adapted from Getmansky, M., Lee, P. A., and Lo, A. W. (2015). Hedge funds: a dynamic industry in transition. *Annual Review of Financial Economics* 7: 483–577.

The Adaptive Markets Hypothesis. Andrew W. Lo and Ruixun Zhang, Oxford University Press.
© Andrew W. Lo and Ruixun Zhang (2024). DOI: 10.1093/oso/9780199681143.003.0016

These conflicting characteristics may explain why investors have a love/hate relationship with alternative investments. According to Hedge Fund Research (2013), in Q4 of 2013, 63% of funds of funds experienced fund outflows; however, only 45% of single-manager funds did. This is consistent with the general decline in the number of funds of funds, which is attributable to their fees, competition from multi-strategy funds, and their general inability to avoid losses during the 2008 financial crisis. The relative value, equity hedge, and event driven categories each encompass about 27% of total hedge fund assets under management. The rest (about 19%) is invested with global macro funds. This situation changed dramatically from the situation in Q4 of 1990, when 40% was invested with global macro funds, and the event driven category comprised only 10% of total hedge fund assets. About half (47%) of all hedge funds never reach their fifth anniversary. However, 40% of funds survive for seven years or longer.

It is now apparent that hedge funds are not simply a fad that will disappear. The industry has matured considerably over the last three decades, now providing critical functions in the global financial system such as liquidity provision, risk transfer, price discovery, credit, and insurance. For all these reasons, a critical survey of the hedge fund literature is worthwhile, and is undertaken later in this chapter. In addition to providing a review of academic studies on hedge funds, we report empirical results on their performance and risk characteristics.

To appreciate fully the relevance of evolutionary dynamics in the hedge fund industry, we must consider four distinct stakeholders or, in the language of ecology, 'species'. Investors are most concerned with the risk–reward profile offered by hedge fund strategies, especially compared to more traditional investment vehicles. Managers are focused on generating profitable trading strategies while managing the risks of the investments, as well as the business. Regulators are focused on the degree to which hedge fund blowups may spill over to the rest of the financial system and harm the real economy. Finally, financial academics focus on the many ramifications of hedge fund profitability for the EMH, passive investing, linear factor models, and the traditional quantitative investment paradigm. Rather than choosing one of these groups, we hope to broaden the usefulness of this survey by attempting to cover all four to some degree.

We begin by summarizing the basic characteristics of hedge funds in Section 16.1, and then review the various sources of hedge fund data—a prerequisite for any serious study of the industry—in Section 16.2. We then provide an overview of the basic investment performance statistics for hedge funds in Section 16.3. One of the most important factors driving hedge fund performance is illiquidity, and we focus squarely on this issue in Section 16.4. Of course, hedge funds exhibit many sources of risk beyond illiquidity, and in Section 16.5 we explore these risks, and examine the corresponding linear and nonlinear factor models to measure and manage such risks. No survey of hedge funds would be complete without some discussion of how the industry fared during and after the 2008 financial crisis, and we provide such a post-mortem in Section 16.6. Finally, in Section 16.7, we turn to some practical considerations for today's hedge fund investors.

16.1 Hedge Fund Characteristics

Hedge funds generally have more complex structural and risk characteristics than mutual funds or other traditional investment vehicles. In this section, we highlight four of the most important of these characteristics from an investor's perspective: fees, leverage, the restrictions on entering and exiting a hedge fund, and the dynamic nature of assets under management.

16.1.1 Fees

Most hedge funds charge annual fees consisting of two components: a fixed percentage of assets under management (typically 1%–2%), and an incentive fee that is a percentage (typically 20%) of the fund's annual net profits, often defined as the fund's total earnings above and beyond some minimum threshold such as the LIBOR or SOFR return, and net of previous cumulative losses (often called a 'high-water mark').[2] The usual justification for such a fee structure is that the fixed fee covers the basic operating expenses of the fund, while the incentive fee aligns the interests of the manager with the investor, in that the manager is paid an incentive if and only if the manager has made money for the investor, not only in the current year, but since inception.

Of course, the same logic should apply to portfolio managers of other types of investment vehicles, such as mutual funds, exchange-traded funds (ETFs), and pension funds, yet none of them earns incentive fees. The practical answer to why hedge funds charge an incentive fee in addition to a fixed fee is 'because they can'. In other words, hedge funds claim to offer unique sources of investment return (i.e. alpha), and they are willing to share some

---

[2] A high-water mark is a contractual provision that requires losses in any given year to be carried forward for purposes of incentive-fee computations, so that incentive fees are paid only on net profits (i.e. profits net of any previous cumulative losses).

of this alpha with investors for a price. That price is the fee structure that hedge funds charge. Is it justified?

Titman and Tiu (2011) argue that better-informed hedge funds have less exposure to common-factor risks, and show that funds with fewer factor exposures, as measured by the R^2 of a regression of their monthly returns on various factors, tend to have higher Sharpe ratios, something investors will gladly pay for. As a result, funds in the lowest R^2 quartile, on average, charge twelve basis points more in management fees, and 385 basis points more in incentive fees, compared to hedge funds in the highest R^2 quartile. Goetzmann, Ingersoll, and Ross (2003) conjecture that the option-like fees commanded by hedge funds exist because hedge fund strategies have limited capacity; hence, good recent performance cannot be rewarded with fees that scale linearly with the assets under management. They estimate that the present value of fees and other costs could be as high as 33% of the amount invested. However, Ibbotson, Chen, and Zhu (2011) decompose their estimated pre-fee average hedge fund return from 1995 to 2008 of 11.13% into 3.43% of fees, 3.00% of alpha, and 4.70% of beta.

Feng, Getmansky, and Kapadia (2013) develop an algorithm to estimate empirically the monthly fees, fund flows, and gross asset values of individual hedge funds. They find that management fees represent a major component in the dollar amount of total hedge fund fees (62% equally weighted and 54% value-weighted). Anson (2001) shows that incentive fees resemble a call option at maturity, and that hedge fund managers can increase the value of this option by increasing the volatility of their assets. Aragon and Qian (2010) examine the role of high-water mark provisions in hedge fund compensation contracts. The authors suggest that compensation contracts in hedge funds help alleviate the inefficiencies created by asymmetric information.

Fees may be relevant to investors not only because of their direct impact on returns, but also because they impact manager behaviour. Using the Zurich hedge fund database, Kouwenberg and Ziemba (2007) find that hedge funds with incentive fees have significantly lower mean returns (net of fees), while the downside risk is positively related to the incentive fee level. Agarwal, Daniel, and Naik (2009) propose using the 'delta' of the hedge fund manager (defined as the expected dollar increase in the manager's compensation for a 1% increase in the fund's net asset value), the hurdle rate, and the high-water mark provision to proxy for managerial incentives. The authors find that hedge funds that have higher delta and a high-water mark perform better.

Fees are especially relevant for funds of funds, as Brown, Goetzmann, and Liang (2004) conclude. They find that individual funds dominate funds of funds in terms of net-of-fee returns and Sharpe ratios, which they attribute to the double fees implicit in fund-of-funds compensation structures. This consists of the fees charged by all the constituent funds, as well as a second layer of fees charged by the fund of funds, typically a 1% fixed fee and a 10% incentive fee. Table 16.1 provides a simple illustration of this effect for a hypothetical fund of funds charging 1% and 10% and investing an equal amount of its assets in two funds, A and B, each charging 2% and 20%. If both of the underlying hedge fund managers generate gross returns of 20%, the net-of-fee return for the fund-of-funds investor is a reasonably attractive 11.70%,

Table 16.1 Net-of-fee returns for a hypothetical fund of funds charging a 1% fixed fee and a 10% incentive fee, and investing an equal amount of capital in two funds, A and B, with both funds charging a 2% fixed fee and a 20% incentive fee, for various realized annual gross-of-fee returns for A and B.

Net Returns of Fund of Funds as a Function of Underlying Managers' Investment Returns

Manager A Return	Manager B Return													
	-15%	-10%	-5%	0%	5%	10%	15%	20%	25%	30%	35%	40%	45%	50%
-15%	-18.00%	-15.50%	-13.00%	-10.50%	-8.50%	-6.50%	-4.50%	-2.50%	-0.50%	1.35%	3.15%	4.95%	6.75%	8.55%
-10%	-15.50%	-13.00%	-10.50%	-8.00%	-6.00%	-4.00%	-2.00%	0.00%	1.80%	3.60%	5.40%	7.20%	9.00%	10.80%
-5%	-13.00%	-10.50%	-8.00%	-5.50%	-3.50%	-1.50%	0.45%	2.25%	4.05%	5.85%	7.65%	9.45%	11.25%	13.05%
0%	-10.50%	-8.00%	-5.50%	-3.00%	-1.00%	0.90%	2.70%	4.50%	6.30%	8.10%	9.90%	11.70%	13.50%	15.30%
5%	-8.50%	-6.00%	-3.50%	-1.00%	0.90%	2.70%	4.50%	6.30%	8.10%	9.90%	11.70%	13.50%	15.30%	17.10%
10%	-6.50%	-4.00%	-1.50%	0.90%	2.70%	4.50%	6.30%	8.10%	9.90%	11.70%	13.50%	15.30%	17.10%	18.90%
15%	-4.50%	-2.00%	0.45%	2.70%	4.50%	6.30%	8.10%	9.90%	11.70%	13.50%	15.30%	17.10%	18.90%	20.70%
20%	-2.50%	0.00%	2.25%	4.50%	6.30%	8.10%	9.90%	11.70%	13.50%	15.30%	17.10%	18.90%	20.70%	22.50%
25%	-0.50%	1.80%	4.05%	6.30%	8.10%	9.90%	11.70%	13.50%	15.30%	17.10%	18.90%	20.70%	22.50%	24.30%
30%	1.35%	3.60%	5.85%	8.10%	9.90%	11.70%	13.50%	15.30%	17.10%	18.90%	20.70%	22.50%	24.30%	26.10%
35%	3.15%	5.40%	7.65%	9.90%	11.70%	13.50%	15.30%	17.10%	18.90%	20.70%	22.50%	24.30%	26.10%	27.90%
40%	4.95%	7.20%	9.45%	11.70%	13.50%	15.30%	17.10%	18.90%	20.70%	22.50%	24.30%	26.10%	27.90%	29.70%
45%	6.75%	9.00%	11.25%	13.50%	15.30%	17.10%	18.90%	20.70%	22.50%	24.30%	26.10%	27.90%	29.70%	31.50%
50%	8.55%	10.80%	13.05%	15.30%	17.10%	18.90%	20.70%	22.50%	24.30%	26.10%	27.90%	29.70%	31.50%	33.30%

Fees as a Percentage of Net Profits of Underlying Investments

Manager A Return	Manager B Return													
	-15%	-10%	-5%	0%	5%	10%	15%	20%	25%	30%	35%	40%	45%	50%
-15%	NA	NA	NA	NA	NA	NA	NA	200.00%	110.00%	82.00%	68.50%	60.40%	55.00%	51.14%
-10%	NA	NA	NA	NA	NA	NA	180.00%	100.00%	76.00%	64.00%	56.80%	52.00%	48.57%	46.00%
-5%	NA	NA	NA	NA	NA	160.00%	91.00%	70.00%	59.50%	53.20%	49.00%	46.00%	43.75%	42.00%
0%	NA	NA	NA	NA	140.00%	82.00%	64.00%	55.00%	49.60%	46.00%	43.43%	41.50%	40.00%	38.80%
5%	NA	NA	NA	140.00%	82.00%	64.00%	55.00%	49.60%	46.00%	43.43%	41.50%	40.00%	38.80%	37.82%
10%	NA	NA	160.00%	82.00%	64.00%	55.00%	49.60%	46.00%	43.43%	41.50%	40.00%	38.80%	37.82%	37.00%
15%	NA	180.00%	91.00%	64.00%	55.00%	49.60%	46.00%	43.43%	41.50%	40.00%	38.80%	37.82%	37.00%	36.31%
20%	200.00%	100.00%	70.00%	55.00%	49.60%	46.00%	43.43%	41.50%	40.00%	38.80%	37.82%	37.00%	36.31%	35.71%
25%	110.00%	76.00%	59.50%	49.60%	46.00%	43.43%	41.50%	40.00%	38.80%	37.82%	37.00%	36.31%	35.71%	35.20%
30%	82.00%	64.00%	53.20%	46.00%	43.43%	41.50%	40.00%	38.80%	37.82%	37.00%	36.31%	35.71%	35.20%	34.75%
35%	68.50%	56.80%	49.00%	43.43%	41.50%	40.00%	38.80%	37.82%	37.00%	36.31%	35.71%	35.20%	34.75%	34.35%
40%	60.40%	52.00%	46.00%	41.50%	40.00%	38.80%	37.82%	37.00%	36.31%	35.71%	35.20%	34.75%	34.35%	34.00%
45%	55.00%	48.57%	43.75%	40.00%	38.80%	37.82%	37.00%	36.31%	35.71%	35.20%	34.75%	34.35%	34.00%	33.68%
50%	51.14%	46.00%	42.00%	38.80%	37.82%	37.00%	36.31%	35.71%	35.20%	34.75%	34.35%	34.00%	33.68%	33.40%

The top panel reports net-of-fee returns as a percentage of assets under management. The bottom panel reports fees as a percentage of net profits of the total gross investment returns generated by A and B. No high-water mark or clawback provisions are assumed.

with fees composing 41.50% of the total gross investment returns and the rest going to the investor. However, if manager A earns a gross return of 20% and manager B loses 5%, the net-of-fee return for the fund-of-funds investor is only 2.25%; in this case, the vast majority of the total gross investment return (70%) is paid to the individual managers and the fund-of-funds manager as fees. More importantly, a double layer of fees implies certain incentives to take on higher risk investments, as well as high Sharpe ratio strategies that can be leveraged at the fund of funds level in order to generate incentive fees on the portfolio of hedge funds.

16.1.2 Leverage

Hedge funds often employ leverage in their strategies to boost returns. Leverage involves borrowing capital, usually from banks or broker-dealers, which is used to increase a fund's investment in its strategies, thereby magnifying its gains and its losses.[3] In particular, leverage increases both the expected return and the volatility of any strategy. Accordingly, it is most relevant for strategies that have low volatility because they can afford to be leveraged without generating unacceptable levels of risk. However, return volatility is not the only type of risk that is relevant for leveraged investments. Illiquidity risk often accompanies low volatility investments, which we shall consider in more detail in Section 16.4. The amount of leverage varies considerably across hedge funds and over time, from none to a large multiple of assets under management. Margin calls are quite common during financial crises, after which many hedge funds are forced to shut down because of the extreme losses stemming from excessive leverage (see Section 16.6).

Several authors have identified key drivers in determining how hedge funds adjust their leverage over time. Ang, Gorovyy, and Van Inwegen (2011) find that economy-wide factors tend to predict changes in hedge fund leverage better than fund-specific characteristics. Decreases in funding costs and fund return volatilities, and increases in market values all predict increases in hedge fund leverage. The authors conclude that hedge fund leverage decreased in 2007, prior to the start of the financial crisis, and was at its lowest in early 2009 when the leverage of investment banks was the highest. In a related study, Cao et al. (2013) show that hedge funds are able to adjust their portfolios' market exposure as aggregate market liquidity

---

[3] Leverage is typically measured by the ratio of the total gross investments, both long and short, to the assets under management. For example, a $100 million portfolio consisting of $100 million of long positions and $100 million of short positions has a total gross investment of $200 million; hence, its leverage ratio is 2-to-1.

conditions change. Using a large sample of equity-oriented hedge funds from 1994 to 2009, they find there is strong evidence for liquidity timing ability, and, in out-of-sample tests, they find that the top liquidity-timing funds outperform the bottom liquidity-timing funds by 4.0% to 5.5% annually on a risk-adjusted basis (see Section 16.3.3 for further discussion).

16.1.3 Share Restrictions

The ability to invest or withdraw money from a hedge fund is often subject to various share restrictions. For example, new investors have to undergo a subscription process before their funds are invested in a hedge fund. Also, because of the capacity constraints of a given strategy, hedge fund managers might decide to close a fund to new investors. Restrictions are also often imposed on fund withdrawals. For example, new investors (and new deposits) are often subject to a one-year lock-up period, during which investors cannot withdraw their funds. In addition, all withdrawals are subject to advance notice (typically 30 days, but sometimes as long as one year) and redemption periods (usually quarterly or annually). During periods of financial distress, hedge fund managers sometimes impose gates, temporary restrictions on how much of an investor's capital can be redeemed within a given period of time. Such restrictions are meant to protect against fire-sale liquidations that can generate extreme losses for the fund's remaining investors.

Ang and Bollen (2010) model the investor's decision to withdraw capital as a real option, and treat lock-ups and notice periods as exercise restrictions. They estimate that a two-year lock-up with a three-month notice period for redemptions is worth approximately 1% of the investment capital of an investor with a constant relative risk aversion utility and a risk aversion coefficient of 3. They also find that a manager's discretion to impose gates during times of especially high illiquidity, as many managers did during the 12–18-month period following the 2008 stock market decline, can cost investors much more.

Aragon (2007) studies the relationship between hedge fund returns and lock-up restrictions, and concludes that hedge funds with lock-up restrictions have 4% to 7% higher excess returns per year than those of non-lock-up funds. Aragon, Hertzel, and Shi (2013) find that onshore hedge funds impose stronger share restrictions (e.g. a lock-up provision) than offshore hedge funds but hold more liquid assets. Aragon and Qian (2010) find that high-water marks are commonly used by funds that restrict investor redemptions.

Among the hedge funds that imposed gates during the 2008 financial crisis, Aiken, Clifford, and Ellis (2013) observe that the use of these restrictions was more common among funds with lock-up provisions. This suggests that the 4%–7% in excess returns reflects illiquidity risk from both lock-ups and discretionary liquidity restrictions such as gates. Ramadorai (2012) documents that funds that are gated can be traded on secondary markets for hedge funds, often at substantial discounts, but sometimes at premiums. This means that we can measure the monetary impact of share restrictions on funds. Discounts and premiums at which these shares are traded bear an intriguing resemblance to closed-end mutual fund discounts and premiums, and are related to measures of fund illiquidity and performance.

16.1.4 Fund Flows and Capital Formation

A number of studies have documented a positive empirical relationship between fund flows and recent performance, suggesting that hedge fund investors chase positive returns and flee from negative returns (Goetzmann, Ingersoll, and Ross, 2003; Baquero and Verbeek, 2009; Liang et al., 2019). However, the particular relation between fund flows and investment performance is often nonlinear, and depends on a combination of factors, including manager alpha, investor perceptions, market conditions, fund restrictions (Section 16.1.3), and other hedge fund characteristics.

Aragon, Hertzel, and Shi (2013) find that capital flows are less sensitive to past performance in onshore funds than they are in offshore funds due to regulation on advertising for onshore hedge funds. Goetzmann, Ingersoll, and Ross (2003) conjecture that the unwillingness of successful funds to accept new money may be indicative of diminishing returns in the industry as a whole as investments flow in. Aragon and Qian (2010) find that high-water marks are associated with a greater sensitivity of investor flows to past performance but less so following poor performance.

Teo (2011) evaluates a group of liquid hedge funds and concludes that, for this group, funds with high net inflows subsequently outperform funds with low net inflows by 4.79% per year after adjusting for risk. He defines liquid funds as those allowing monthly or less-than-monthly redemptions. The return impact of fund flows is stronger when funds embrace liquidity risk, when the market liquidity is low, and when funding liquidity (as measured by the Treasury–Eurodollar spread, aggregate hedge fund flows, and prime broker stock returns) is tight.

Agarwal, Aragon, and Shi (2019) concentrate on fund flows in funds of funds. They find that funds of funds experiencing large outflows tend to liquidate holdings in funds with relatively few redemptions (i.e. liquid funds), even when these funds perform well. The authors conjecture that the best-performing hedge funds are unlikely to accept capital from funds of funds that are subject to greater liquidity mismatches because hedge funds are likely to face significant redemption requests in the case of large outflows from funds of funds. Fung et al. (2008) find that alpha-producing funds of funds experience far greater and steadier capital inflows than non-alpha producers.

Liang et al. (2019) study the effect of share restrictions on the relationship between a fund's capital inflows and outflows and its performance, and document a convex flow–performance relationship in the absence of share restrictions (similar to mutual funds), but a concave relation in the presence of restrictions. Further, they find that live funds are subject to stricter restrictions than defunct funds.

Baquero and Verbeek (2009) explore the flow–performance relationship by separating inflows and outflows using a regime-switching model. They find a weak positive response of fund inflows to past performance at quarterly horizons but a very pronounced positive response of fund outflows to past performance. However, this pattern is reversed at an annual horizon. Baquero and Verbeek (2021) find that the lengths of winning and losing streaks (the number of subsequent quarters a fund performs above or below a given benchmark) has a significant impact on future fund flows. However, the authors conclude that such a simple heuristic is suboptimal, and that investors would have performed better by simply using recursive out-of-sample forecasts from basic linear regressions. Baquero and Verbeek (2009) do not find evidence that hedge fund flows can predict future returns (i.e. the 'smart money' effect).

16.2 An Overview of Hedge Fund Return Data

Hedge funds are under no obligation to report their monthly returns to any parties other than their investors and the US Securities and Exchange Commission (SEC).[4] However, these data are not publicly available. Because

---

[4] On 26 October 2011, the SEC voted unanimously to adopt Rule 204(b)-1 (the 'Rule') under the Investment Advisers Act of 1940, as amended (the 'Advisers Act'), which implements Sections 404 and 406 of the Dodd–Frank Act. The Rule requires certain SEC registered investment advisers to make periodic informational filings on Form PF detailing certain information with respect to private funds that they manage. Under the rule, as of 2012, all SEC-registered investment advisers that have at least $150 million in regulatory assets under management in one or more private funds have to file Form PF. However, Form PF is currently not publicly disclosed.

investment strategies are currently not patentable, hedge funds protect their intellectual property—which includes their historical returns—through trade secrecy. Some of the most successful hedge funds do not provide their returns to any third party, and we can only speculate as to their performance.

Offsetting this reluctance, however, is the need for most hedge funds to attract new capital from investors. SEC Rule 502(c) of the Securities Act of 1933 bars hedge fund advisers from general advertising, including any form of communication published in newspapers or magazines, or broadcast over television or radio. Therefore, many hedge fund advisers choose to self-report to commercial databases in order to market their funds and attract new clients.[5] A cottage industry of hedge fund data vendors has grown to accommodate this need, and now many hedge funds share their return information with one or more of the companies listed in Section 16.2.1 that maintain databases of historical hedge fund returns. Although these data are not free, potential investors and academics can purchase access through monthly or annual subscription fees. Much of what we know about hedge funds, and most of the empirical research on this industry, depends upon such archival data.

Many researchers have pointed out that the voluntary reporting of these returns yields a number of selection biases (e.g. survivorship and backfill biases) that can affect statistical inference in various ways, and we consider their potential impact in Section 16.2.2. Although biases can arise in any data set, they are likely to be more severe when there is greater filtering of the entries, either deliberately or through the nature of the industry. In Section 16.2.3, we attempt to quantify one aspect of this filtering process by exploring the dynamics of hedge fund entries and exits each year. Any financial decision based on hedge fund data should take these biases and dynamics into account in some manner.

We conclude our survey of basic hedge fund data by describing the properties of hedge fund indexes in Section 16.2.4. Despite the use of the term 'index', no hedge fund index is currently investable to the same extent as traditional indexes such as the S&P 500. Nevertheless, as indicators of broad industry performance, these indexes serve a useful purpose, and their statistical characteristics highlight some interesting differences between alternative and traditional investments.

[5] See Ackermann, McEnally, and Ravenscraft (1999), Aiken, Clifford, and Ellis (2013), and Agarwal, Fos, and Jiang (2014).

16.2.1 Data Sources

Some of the most widely used hedge fund databases include Refinitiv Lipper (formerly Lipper TASS), which we will refer to as Lipper, Morningstar CISDM, Hedge Fund Research (HFR), Barclay Hedge, Albourne, Eurekahedge, eVestment, HedgeCo.net, Mercer, US Offshore Funds Directory, and Wilshire (Odyssey). The type of data provided for each hedge fund may include its net monthly returns, assets under management, style category, reporting currency, the names of the principals, its fund managers and brokers, share restrictions, audit company information, the geography and composition of its investments, and other information. When comparing hedge fund databases, some key considerations are the number of funds in the database, whether a graveyard database is available, and how long ago the database was established.

It can also be useful to compare the coverage of different databases; for example, do they cover complementary portions of the hedge fund universe, or are they redundant? With access to both the Lipper and Morningstar CISDM databases, we found that many of the funds are redundant even within a single database. This duplication is due to the fact that funds often have multiple legal entities employing the same investment strategy but in different jurisdictions to accommodate onshore versus offshore investors. For both the Lipper and Morningstar CISDM databases, roughly one-third of the funds within each of the databases is redundant. We identified redundant funds by searching for similarly named funds with highly correlated returns. We then checked how many incremental unique funds are present in the Morningstar CISDM database relative to Lipper, and found that roughly half the funds in the Morningstar CISDM database are also present in the Lipper database.

Schneeweis, Kazemi, and Szado (2011) compare the Lipper and Morningstar CISDM hedge fund databases further, and find some differences in return and risk between the two databases at the portfolio and average manager levels. However, these differences are often relatively small. Liang (2000) compares hedge funds in the Lipper and HFR databases. He finds that for identical funds tracked by both databases, the returns, assets, fees, and investment style classifications can differ. He suggests that the Lipper database should be used for academic research because of its relative completeness and accuracy. Much academic research does rely on the Lipper database; however, a combination of databases is also used by Fung and Hsieh (1997), Ackermann, McEnally, and Ravenscraft (1999), Agarwal, Daniel, and Naik (2011), and others.

In this chapter, we use monthly returns data from the Lipper database, subject to minor cleaning to reduce the incidence of bad data, described in the appendix of Getmansky, Lee, and Lo (2015). For completeness and to mitigate survivorship bias, we combine the Lipper live and graveyard hedge fund databases.

16.2.2 Biases

When a hedge fund manager reports returns to any database, it is a purely voluntary decision—managers are not required to disclose their returns to any data provider or regulator, and are free to stop reporting at any time. Therefore, a number of biases may arise among hedge fund returns databases that are not present in other asset-pricing databases in which all securities of a given type are included (e.g. the University of Chicago's Center for Research in Security Prices (CRSP) stock returns database).

Firstly, given that the primary motivation for participating in a database is for marketing purposes, funds generally appear to begin contributing their returns to a database after a period of outperformance. Because such funds are allowed to include prior returns upon their entry into the database, this practice leads to backfill bias or instant history bias, further boosting the average returns of funds in the database, which are already inflated from the selection bias associated with the decision to be listed. Fung and Hsieh (2000) estimate a backfill bias of 1.4% per year for the Lipper database from 1994 to 1998. Using the Managed Account Reports database (subsequently subsumed by Morningstar CISDM) from January 1990 to August 1998, Edwards and Caglayan (2001) estimate a backfill bias of 1.2% per year.

Secondly, funds can choose to delist from the database at any time, and typically do so for one of two reasons: (1) fund managers decide to close their funds to new investments because they no longer have sufficient capacity; or (2) they shut down because of poor performance. These two motivations impart a considerably different set of biases on the data, collectively known as extinction bias, the latter being more common and yielding a spurious favourable bias on the average investment returns.

Thirdly, some databases do not include extinct funds. This introduces survivorship bias, and generally increases the average fund's returns, since the vast majority of funds that leave the database do so because they have underperformed and are shutting down.[6] Survivorship bias affects the

---

[6] However, survivorship bias is mitigated to some degree by the fact that some of the largest and most successful funds are also not included because they have no need to raise additional assets, and prefer to

estimated mean and volatility of hedge fund returns, as many authors have pointed out.[7] The estimated magnitude of this bias ranges from 0.16% (Ackermann, McEnally, and Ravenscraft, 1999) to 2% (Liang, 2000; Amin and Kat, 2003), or up to 3% for offshore hedge funds (Brown, Goetzmann, and Ibbotson, 1999).

Aggarwal and Jorion (2010a) introduce the notion of a hidden survivorship bias, which they attribute to a merger between the Lipper and Tremont databases: 60% of the funds added to the Lipper database between April 1999 and November 2001 are likely to be survivors (i.e. funds that were alive as of 31 March 1999). This hidden survivorship bias boosts average returns by more than 5% a year. The authors propose a sorting algorithm to exclude these funds' histories. Aggarwal and Jorion (2009, 2010b) also find that both the performance and risk of emerging hedge funds and managers are biased. Emerging funds and managers have particularly strong financial incentives to create positive investment performance and to take on greater risk. Liang (2003) finds that data quality is directly related to auditing effectiveness; funds with more reputable auditors and more updated auditing reveal less data inconsistency.

Aggarwal and Jorion (2009) document that typical hedge fund volatilities tend to be higher in the early years of the funds, but this result is driven entirely by the sample of dead funds. Aggarwal and Jorion (2010b) find strong evidence of outperformance during the first 2–3 years of existence. Joenväärä et al. (2020) show that variations in database coverage with respect to defunct funds, small funds, fund characteristics, assets under management, and backfill bias can lead to different performance results. In conducting fund performance analysis, the authors recommend using an aggregate database, adjusting for the attrition rate, and 'filling in' the missing observations of assets under management rather than dropping such observations from the analysis.

Fourthly, most funds report their investment results net of management fees, which consist of fixed and incentive fees (see Section 16.1.1). While the fixed fee affects the first moment of the distribution of returns, the variable incentive fee can affect higher moments, and induce nonlinearities and discontinuities into standard risk–reward relationships such as linear factor

keep their performance strictly confidential. Nevertheless, because there are considerably more underperforming funds than outperforming ones, the net effect of survivorship bias is to impart an upward bias on average returns.

[7] See, for example, Brown et al. (1992), Schneeweis, Spurgin, and McCarthy (1996), Fung and Hsieh (1997, 2000), Hendricks, Patel, and Zeckhauser (1997), Ackermann, McEnally, and Ravenscraft (1999), Brown, Goetzmann, and Ibbotson (1999), Carpenter and Lynch (1999), Brown, Goetzmann, and Park (2001), Malkiel and Saha (2005), Baquero, Horst, and Verbeek (2005), and Horst and Verbeek (2007).

models (see Section 16.5.2). Furthermore, it is hard to reverse engineer the gross returns with precision, because the incentive fees may be different for each individual investor and subject to additional considerations such as hurdle rates, high-water marks, and clawbacks. The impact of these fees makes it harder to gauge the profitability of hedge fund strategies.

Fifthly, many funds, especially those larger and well-known funds that do not need any additional advertisement, are more likely to refrain from reporting to commercial databases. This missing return bias was first noted by Ackermann, McEnally, and Ravenscraft (1999). Edelman, Fung, and Hsieh (2013) try to capture this bias by comparing nonreporting mega-hedge funds to large funds in the database. They collected information on mega-hedge funds from two industry surveys: Hedge Fund 100 and the Billion Dollar Club. They find that both sets of funds have similar behaviours. However, some return differences emerge during large moves in the credit market: mega-hedge funds apparently load up on the credit factor more than other funds. The authors' overall conclusion is that an index of reporting large firms is a reasonable proxy for the performance of nonreporting mega firms.

Patton, Ramadorai, and Streatfield (2015) find that hedge fund returns change substantially depending on the vintage of the data that are provided by commonly available databases. The authors explore numerous reasons for this empirical fact, and document systematic variation that suggests this is a product of the voluntary disclosure regime for hedge fund data.

Finally, Aragon and Nanda (2017) find that monthly returns are sometimes strategically delayed in reporting to the Lipper database. Specifically, they observe delays of three weeks, on average, but document longer delays when performance is worse, the public market news is better, and fund investors are restricted from redeeming their shares. Returns also tend to be reported simultaneously in clusters. Strategic listing decisions and issues related to misreporting to hedge fund databases have been further studied by Jorion and Schwarz (2014a,b), who find that hedge fund managers strategically list their small, best-performing funds in multiple databases immediately, while delaying listing for other funds.

In the remainder of this chapter, we adjust all results for survivorship and backfill biases. We address survivorship bias by including the Lipper graveyard database in our analysis, and we address backfill bias by deleting any returns that appear to have been backfilled. We identify and delete backfilled returns based primarily on a list of fund-inclusion dates provided by Lipper. We also have access to a number of monthly database snapshots from

Table 16.2 Summary statistics for cross-sectionally averaged returns from the Lipper database with no bias adjustments, adjusted for survivorship bias, adjusted for backfill bias, and adjusted for both biases during the sample period from January 1996 to December 2014.

	# Fund-Months	Annualized Mean	Annualized Volatility	Annualized Skewness	Skewness	Kurtosis	Maximum DD	ac(1)	Box-Q(3) p-value
Naive Estimate	351,364	12.6%	5.9%	−0.25	4.41	−14.9%	0.28	0.00003
Remove Survivorship Bias	927,690	9.7%	5.6%	−0.22	4.96	−15.0%	0.26	0.00009
Remove Backfill Bias	195,816	11.5%	8.1%	−0.54	9.02	−19.9%	0.32	0.00000
Remove Both Biases	505,844	6.3%	6.3%	−0.50	5.72	−20.5%	0.25	0.00056

For each database sample, the number of fund-months, annualized mean, annualized volatility, skewness, kurtosis, maximum drawdown, first-order autocorrelation, and the *p*-value of the Ljung–Box test statistic with three lags are reported.

previous years, and based on the date of a fund's first appearance in these snapshots, we are able to delete some additional backfilled returns.

Table 16.2 presents the annualized mean, annualized volatility, skewness, kurtosis, maximum drawdown, first-order autocorrelation, and *p*-value of the Ljung–Box test statistic with three lags for the Lipper database without any bias adjustments and with adjustments for survivorship bias, for backfill bias, and for both biases during the sample period from January 1996 to December 2014. For this illustrative analysis, we constructed a time series of cross-sectionally averaged hedge fund returns. While not an investable hedge fund proxy, this average clearly shows the general impact of these biases, which is relevant for both hedge fund research and practical hedge fund investment decisions. These biases make hedge funds look misleadingly attractive in average return, volatility, skewness, kurtosis, and maximum drawdown. For example, the annualized mean return across all funds using the unadjusted data is 12.6%, which is halved to 6.3% when survivorship and backfill biases are addressed. Skewness, kurtosis, and maximum drawdowns increase significantly after both bias adjustments. The volatility increases slightly, and the first-order autocorrelation stays almost the same.

16.2.3 Entries and Exits

The hedge fund industry saw a prolonged boom that lasted through 2007 (see Table 16.3). In each of the years from 1996 to 2006, more than twice as many new funds entered than exited the Lipper database. This growth arised despite the funds' high single-digit attrition rates. However, during the five-year period from 2010 to 2014, the process reversed and the number of

Table 16.3 Statistics for entries and exits of single-manager hedge funds, including the number of entries, exits, and funds at the start and end of a given year, attrition rate, average return, and percentage of funds that performed negatively, are reported for each year from January 1996 to December 2014.

	# Funds at Start	# Newly Reporting	# Stopped Reporting	# Funds at End	Attrition Rate	Average Return	% Neg Perf
1996	1,117	354	107	1,364	10%	13.5%	15%
1997	1,364	371	83	1,652	6%	14.0%	17%
1998	1,652	368	137	1,883	8%	−2.6%	42%
1999	1,883	453	157	2,179	8%	25.4%	16%
2000	2,179	479	186	2,472	9%	1.4%	38%
2001	2,472	616	212	2,876	9%	2.4%	32%
2002	2,876	676	246	3,306	9%	0.6%	45%
2003	3,306	862	246	3,922	7%	17.2%	10%
2004	3,922	1,042	311	4,653	8%	7.4%	18%
2005	4,653	1,109	433	5,329	9%	8.6%	17%
2006	5,329	1,135	522	5,942	10%	11.3%	13%
2007	5,942	1,217	865	6,294	15%	8.7%	19%
2008	6,294	997	1,347	5,944	21%	−18.4%	71%
2009	5,944	953	855	6,042	14%	16.6%	21%
2010	6,042	848	878	6,012	15%	9.1%	17%
2011	6,012	657	971	5,698	16%	−3.7%	55%
2012	5,698	487	1,058	5,127	19%	6.0%	23%
2013	5,127	288	1,057	4,358	21%	7.0%	21%
2014	4,358	129	1,128	3,359	26%	3.2%	29%

exits greatly exceeded the number of entries. The number of funds peaked in 2007–2008, coinciding with the financial crisis. In 2008, the attrition rate jumped to 21% and, during that year, the average return was the lowest of any year (−18.4%), with 71% of all hedge funds experiencing negative performance.

In the years following the crisis, rather than rebounding to pre-crisis levels, the number of hedge funds reporting to the Lipper database declined markedly, particularly in the last part of the sample: 2012, 2013, and 2014. In 2014, for example, the attrition rate rose to an unprecedented 26%, suggesting a decline in the number of hedge funds or that fewer hedge funds chose to report their returns to the Lipper commercial database.

These industry-wide statistics obscure interesting variations within the highly heterogeneous hedge fund industry. For example, emerging market funds saw a spike in fund exits associated with the Asian and Russian crises: ten exits in 1997 and eleven in 1999, but thirty exits in 1998. Fixed income arbitrage funds, presumably investing in a manner similar to Long-Term Capital Management (LTCM),[8] saw a similar pattern: four exits in 1997 and six in 1999, but thirteen in 1998.

---

[8] LTCM is *not* in the Lipper database.

One final striking feature of the Lipper data involves funds of funds: these investment vehicles proliferated rapidly through 2007, with the number of funds growing by more than 20% every year. By the end of 2007, there were 4,506 in Lipper, and, during this period (1996–2007), the attrition rate averaged 5%, lower than that of single-manager funds. However, the fund formation rate in 2008–2014 was, on average, only 8% per year, and the attrition rate leapt to 19% per year, implying a significant decline in this sector.[9]

The survival rates of hedge funds have been estimated by a number of authors. Brown, Goetzmann, and Park (2001) show that the probability of liquidation increases with increasing risk, and that funds with negative returns for two consecutive years have a higher risk of shutting down. Liang (2000) finds that the annual hedge fund attrition rate is 8.3% for the 1994–1998 sample period using Lipper data, and Horst and Verbeek (2007) find a slightly higher rate of 8.6% for the 1994–2000 sample period. Horst and Verbeek (2007) also find that surviving funds outperform nonsurviving funds by approximately 2.1% per year, which is similar to the findings of Fung and Hsieh (2000, 2002) and Liang (2000), and that investment style, size, and past performance are significant factors in explaining survival rates. Many of these patterns are also documented by Liang (2000). In analysing the life cycle of hedge funds, Getmansky (2012) finds that the liquidation probabilities of individual hedge funds depend on fund-specific characteristics such as past returns, asset flows, age, and assets under management, as well as category-specific variables such as competition and favourable positioning within the industry. Further, Liang and Park (2010) demonstrate that traditional risk measures like standard deviation cannot easily predict fund attrition, while downside risk measures, including fat tails, are more effective.

Brown, Goetzmann, and Park (2001) find that the half-life of the typical Lipper hedge fund is thirty months, while Brooks and Kat (2002) estimate that approximately 30% of new hedge funds do not make it past thirty-six months due to poor performance, and Amin and Kat (2003) find that 40% of their hedge funds do not make it to the fifth year. Howell (2001) observes that the probability of hedge funds failing in their first year is 7.4%, only to increase to 20.3% in their second year. Younger funds with poor performance drop out of databases at a faster rate than older funds (Jen, Heasman, and Boyatt, 2001; Getmansky, 2012), presumably because younger funds are more likely to take additional risks to obtain good performance, which they can use to attract new investors, whereas older funds that have survived already have track records with which to attract and retain capital.

---

[9] Results for formation and attrition rates for funds of funds are not reported, but are available from the authors upon request.

Ineichen (2001), Getmansky, Lo, and Mei (2004), and Kundro and Feffer (2004) study the reasons for hedge fund liquidations. Hedge funds are categorized as 'liquidated' due to failure, fraud, no longer reporting to the database, being closed to new investment, or a merger into another entity. Kramer (2001) focuses on fraud, providing detailed accounts of six of history's most egregious cases. Kundro and Feffer (2004) conclude that 'half of all failures could be attributed to operational risk alone', of which fraud is one example.

Aragon and Qian (2010) find that funds with high-water marks in their fee structures can reduce inefficient liquidation by raising after-fee returns following poor performance. Studying funds of funds, Fung et al. (2008) find that alpha-producing funds are not as likely to liquidate as those that do not deliver alpha.

Finally, Liang and Park (2010) find that funds with a larger downside risk have a higher hazard rate, after controlling for style, performance, fund age, size, lock-up, high-water mark, and leverage. The authors show that the real failure rate of hedge funds is 3.1% compared to the attrition rate of 8.7% on an annual basis using 1995–2004 data. This implies that hedge fund liquidation does not necessarily mean failure in the hedge fund industry.

16.2.4 Hedge Fund Indexes

Just as investors find it useful to have a data vendor calculate and disseminate equity indexes such as the S&P 500, the Dow Jones Industrial Average, the Russell 2000, and the MSCI World Index, hedge fund investors find it useful to be able to see a measure of the average performance of the hedge fund industry. Accordingly, several firms calculate and disseminate such aggregates. Because the industry is so heterogeneous, these firms generally also publish category indexes, some of which were launched over three decades ago. A more recent phenomenon is daily hedge fund indexes, which are typically based on the returns of a much smaller number of hedge funds—those that are willing to share daily performance data.

Before turning to the properties of some commonly cited hedge fund indexes in Section 16.3, it is important to qualify these results with the observation that such indexes are not investable in the same way that popular equity and fixed-income indexes are investable. This qualification is significant because many institutional investors such as pension funds base their investment decisions on the properties of indexes. They have come to depend on indexes because, as mostly passive investors, they concentrate on keeping costs to a minimum and earning expected returns through buy-and-hold investments in assets that offer reasonable long-term risk premia from beta or common risk exposures. Accordingly, such investors focus more on asset allocation decisions across asset classes (e.g. equities, fixed income, and commodities). Within each asset class, the majority of the returns are generated through low-cost passive vehicles that track the corresponding benchmarks to within basis points of their monthly returns. These benchmarks are almost always indexes like the S&P 500, which have liquid investment vehicles like pooled funds and separately managed accounts that invest directly in the underlying securities, futures and swap contracts on such indexes, ETFs, and more customized over-the-counter (OTC) derivatives contracts. The combined effect of these offerings is to allow large institutional investors to realize the stated performance of indexes even when investing billions of dollars at a time.

The same cannot be said for any existing hedge fund index. While some indexes include funds still open to new investors, it is not yet possible to invest a billion dollars of assets within a thirty-day period in a hedge fund index and expect to achieve nearly the same return realized by that index during the same period. In contrast, the investment returns of a $1 billion investment in the S&P 500 can be achieved by purchasing 4,541 E-mini S&P 500 futures contracts on the Chicago Mercantile Exchange.[10] This kind of passive, liquid, and near-perfect index tracking is not yet possible for any existing hedge fund index. Hence, hedge fund index performance results should be interpreted with this caveat in mind.

Billio, Getmansky, and Pelizzon (2009) examine four daily hedge fund return indexes (MSCI, FTSE, Dow Jones, and HFRX), all based on investable hedge funds, and three monthly hedge fund return indexes (CSFB Tremont, CISDM, and HFR), which are composed of both investable and non-investable hedge funds. They find that key variables like fund selection, asset liquidity, data frequency, sample period, and index construction methodologies have significant explanatory power for a number of statistical properties of hedge fund indexes. One of the most important of these key variables is investability.

A new group of indexes is built around the idea of factor replication. These indexes generally aim to answer the following question: If a portfolio of liquid instruments is formed to match the performance of the investable liquid-beta portion of a typical hedge fund's portfolio, what would its returns be? These indexes can be used in determining whether a fund of funds

---

[10] As of Friday 28 January 2022, the E-mini S&P 500 futures closing price for the March 2022 contract was 4,405.00, and, given a contract unit of $50 times the futures price, yielding a notional value of $220,250 per contract, 4,541 contracts would generate a notional exposure of $1,000,155,250.00. On that day, the total volume was 2,251,268 contracts and the end-of-day open interest was 2,321,171 contracts, so 4,541 contracts would be a trivial position to establish over the course of a few trading days.

Table 16.4 Information about hedge fund index providers, index family, and the availability of total industry and category indexes for commonly used monthly, daily, and replication hedge fund indexes.

Index Type	Index Provider	Includes Total Industry Index	Includes Category Indexes
Monthly	Credit Suisse/Dow Jones	Yes	Yes
	Hedge Fund Research	Yes	Yes
	Eurekahedge	Yes	Yes
	Hennessee	Yes	Yes
	Barclay Hedge	Yes	Yes
	MSCI	Yes	Yes
	Morningstar	Yes	Yes
	CISDM	Yes	Yes
Daily	Hedge Fund Research	Yes	Yes
	Credit Suisse/Dow Jones	Yes	Yes
	Barclay Hedge	No	CTAs Only
Replication	Credit Suisse/Dow Jones	Yes	Yes

CTAs: commodity trading advisors.

is delivering alpha or beta, or as a basis for hedge fund beta replication products (see Section 16.5.6). This group consists of two subgroups: (a) the daily replication indexes published by data vendors, who seem to have begun calculating them as an extension of their existing index business, and (b) the indexes published by asset-management firms, whose motivation appears to be the support of hedge fund beta replication funds launched by the same firms. We include only the former subgroup in our summary.

In Table 16.4 we report information about index providers, index families, and the availability of the total industry and category indexes for commonly used hedge fund indexes. Monthly indexes reflect the returns of hedge funds that report to databases at a monthly frequency. Daily indexes reflect the returns of hedge funds that are willing to report their returns daily. Replication indexes are daily indexes that show the hypothetical profit and loss for a factor model-based hedge fund beta replication strategy. The total industry index represents the aggregate performance of the entire hedge fund industry. A category index is designed to represent the performance of funds within a specific category.

16.3 Investment Performance

Despite the heterogeneity and uniqueness of individual hedge funds, most hedge funds share common characteristics with other hedge funds that deploy similar strategies or invest in similar financial markets and securities.

Based on these commonalities, hedge funds may be clustered into styles or categories. One popular categorization is that provided by the Lipper database, which contains eleven main groupings: convertible arbitrage, dedicated short bias, emerging markets, equity market neutral, event driven, fixed income arbitrage, global macro, long/short equity hedge, managed futures, multi-strategy, and fund of funds (see the appendix of Getmansky, Lee, and Lo (2015) for definitions of these categories). While these categories provide a useful nomenclature for interpreting the investment performance of hedge funds, it should be emphasized that the heterogeneity within any single category is considerably greater than that of traditional investment categories, such as large-cap growth or small-cap value funds. We will illustrate both the commonalities and the heterogeneity of hedge fund styles through the statistical properties of their investment returns.

We begin in Section 16.3.1 with a summary of the hedge fund performance literature, in which the risks and rewards of hedge funds are linked to attributes such as managerial incentive structures, managers' ability to hedge, strategy distinctiveness, connections with political lobbyists, education and career concerns, confidential holdings, delayed reporting, managerial skills, and capacity constraints. While several of these links are intuitive, a more important question is whether or not they imply persistence in performance, which we consider in Section 16.3.2, and whether hedge fund managers can actively change their positions and leverage in response to changes in market conditions, which we consider in Section 16.3.3. In Section 16.3.4, we show that hedge funds are not all alike by comparing the investment performance of funds across different style categories, and we also show that hedge funds are not all unique by identifying a number of common factors among hedge funds that may reduce their diversification properties. We explore the investment implications of these empirical findings in Section 16.7.3.

16.3.1 Basic Performance Studies

The empirical properties of hedge fund performance have been documented by many authors using several of the databases cited in Section 16.2.[11] Unlike the literature on mutual fund performance, a number of these studies document positive risk-adjusted returns in the hedge fund industry

---

[11] See, for example, Liang (1999, 2001, 2003), Ackermann, McEnally, and Ravenscraft (1999), Agarwal and Naik (2000a,c), Fung and Hsieh (2000, 2001), Edwards and Caglayan (2001), Kao (2002), and Kosowski, Naik, and Teo (2007). More detailed performance attribution and style analysis for hedge funds has been considered by Fung and Hsieh (1997, 2002), Brown, Goetzmann, and Ibbotson (1999), Brown, Goetzmann, and Park (2000, 2001), Agarwal and Naik (2000a,c), Lochoff (2002), and Brown and Goetzmann (2003).

(i.e. positive alphas).[12] In fact, using data from 1995 to 2009, Ibbotson, Chen, and Zhu (2011) find that alphas were positive every year of the first decade of the 2000s, even during the 2008 financial crisis. More specifically, using a sample of 4,750 stock swap mergers, cash mergers, and cash tender offers from 1963 to 1998, Mitchell and Pulvino (2001) find that risk-arbitrage strategies generate excess returns of 4% per year.

Fung et al. (2008) investigate performance, risk, and capital formation in the hedge fund industry from 1995 to 2004. Over their 120-month sample, they find that the average fund of funds delivered positive and statistically significant alpha only in the eighteen-month subperiod between October 1998 and March 2000. However, Malkiel and Saha (2005) report that, after adjusting for various hedge fund database biases, hedge funds significantly underperform their benchmarks, on average, and our results confirm these findings. In a sample of 7,000 hedge funds, Billio, Frattarolo, and Pelizzon (2014) find that alpha changes dramatically through time and across categories, related to the level of competition among hedge funds.

Several studies link hedge fund performance to various hedge fund and strategy characteristics such as managerial incentive structures, geography, career concerns, strategy capacity, strategy distinctiveness, political connections, and even manager SAT scores. Agarwal, Daniel, and Naik (2009) find that hedge funds with greater managerial incentives (proxied by the delta of option-like incentive fee contracts), higher levels of managerial ownership, and the inclusion of high-water mark provisions in the incentive contracts are associated with superior performance. Getmansky (2012) documents a concave relationship between size and performance for illiquid and capacity-constrained hedge funds, which connects strategy capacity with fund performance. Ramadorai (2013) defines capacity constraints based on past flows, fund size, and a novel indicator variable that indicates whether the fund's management company launched a new fund or a new share class. Consistent with other results in the literature, he finds that capacity constraints lead to a reduction in future returns.

Sun, Wang, and Zheng (2012) show that hedge fund strategy distinctiveness is associated with higher performance, and Titman and Tiu (2011) find that managers' ability to hedge is directly related to hedge fund performance. Gao and Huang (2016) conclude that hedge fund managers gain an informational advantage in securities trading through their connections with political lobbyists. They identify politically sensitive companies as those with

---

[12] See Ackermann, McEnally, and Ravenscraft (1999), Brown, Goetzmann, and Ibbotson (1999), Liang (1999), Agarwal and Naik (2000a,b,c); Fung and Hsieh (2004), Kosowski, Naik, and Teo (2007), and Fung et al. (2008).

high lobbying expenditures relative to their operating cash flows, and find that politically connected hedge funds outperform nonconnected funds by 1.6% to 2.5% per month on their holdings of politically sensitive stocks compared to their less politically sensitive holdings. Tco (2009) shows that hedge funds with headquarters or a research office in their investment region outperform those without a presence in the particular region, suggesting that local funds possess an informational advantage. Liang and Park (2007) show that downside risk measures incorporating higher return moments can effectively predict future fund performance. Finally, Li, Zhang, and Zhao (2011) conclude that education and career concerns can positively impact hedge fund performance; managers from undergraduate institutions with higher average SAT scores apparently have higher raw and risk-adjusted returns.

Hedge fund performance has also been linked to macroeconomic factors. For example, Avramov et al. (2011) show that conditioning on macroeconomic variables such as the VIX index and default spreads is important in detecting managerial skill, and this information can be exploited in forming optimal portfolios of hedge funds. These results can be interpreted in at least two ways: managerial alpha is, in fact, 'exotic beta'; or hedge fund managers generate alpha when macro conditions are conducive. We shall have more to say about factors driving hedge fund returns in Section 16.5.

An important focus of research on hedge fund performance is managerial ability to perform during periods of market distress. Gao, Gao, and Song (2018) show that hedge fund managers with better skills in exploiting the market's *ex ante* disaster concerns deliver superior returns. Jiang and Kelly (2012) find that hedge funds are exposed to downside tail risk, so that a one-standard deviation positive shock to tail risk is associated with a contemporaneous decline of 2.88% per year in the value of the aggregate hedge fund portfolio.

There is a growing literature using 13F data in hedge fund research. Standard databases (e.g. Thomson-Reuters Institutional Holdings) systematically exclude certain positions that are 13F-reportable, like call and put option positions (Aragon and Martin, 2012), and confidentially held stock positions (Agarwal et al., 2013; Aragon, Hertzel, and Shi, 2013). Brunnermeier and Nagel (2004) examine long stock holdings of hedge funds during the period of the technology bubble in 2000, and find that hedge funds reduced their exposure to technology stocks before prices collapsed, and their technology stock holdings outperformed characteristic-matched benchmarks. Griffin and Xu (2009) show that hedge fund managers are only marginally better than mutual fund managers in stock picking, and also find weak evidence of differential ability among hedge funds.

Agarwal et al. (2013) study quarter-end equity holdings of hedge funds that are disclosed with a delay through amendments to their 13F filings. Hedge fund managers delay reporting their positions owing to concerns about private information and price impact. Hedge funds that manage large and concentrated portfolios, adopt nonstandard investment strategies with higher idiosyncratic risk, and hold stocks associated with information-sensitive events such as mergers and acquisitions seek confidentiality more frequently. The authors find that confidential holdings exhibit superior performance up to twelve months, and take longer to build. Aragon, Hertzel, and Shi (2013) find that managers seek confidential treatment of some of their 13F-reportable positions in order to hide confidential information from the public. These hedge fund managers are also more likely to seek confidential treatment of illiquid positions that are more susceptible to front-running. Thus, 13F public filings are likely to attract informed hedge fund traders and investors. However, there are some significant challenges in the detection of informed trading by hedge funds, because they pertain to a narrow scope of reportable securities, exclude short positions, and are only observable at a low (quarterly) frequency.

16.3.2 Performance Persistence

The evidence regarding performance persistence is mixed. Agarwal and Naik (2000b) and Chen (2007) find that monthly hedge fund performance persists for short periods but disappears at an annual horizon. Using annual offshore hedge fund data, Brown, Goetzmann, and Ibbotson (1999) find no evidence of performance persistence. Edwards and Caglayan (2001) use both parametric and nonparametric procedures to study persistence over one- and two-year horizons, and also find no persistence, although they do observe considerable variation across style categories. Boyson (2008) does not find any performance persistence over short or long intervals when funds are selected based purely on past performance, but when manager tenure is taken into consideration, hedge funds do seem to exhibit performance persistence over quarterly intervals.

However, Bares, Gibson, and Gyger (2003) do find short-term performance persistence, and Baquero, Horst, and Verbeek (2005) find positive persistence in hedge funds at the quarterly level after correcting for investment styles, but annual persistence is statistically insignificant. Kat and Menexe (2003) find weak persistence in mean returns but strong persistence in hedge fund standard deviations and their correlations with the stock market. Fung et al.

(2008) find that there is a greater chance for a fund to deliver alpha in the subsequent two-year period if it has a positive estimated alpha in the previous two-year period. In particular, they show that the overall average transition probability for a positive-alpha fund into the subsequent positive-alpha group is 28%, while the transition probability for a no-alpha fund is only 14%. More-over, the year-by-year alpha transition probability for a positive-alpha fund is always higher than that for a no-alpha fund, implying greater alpha persistence among members of the positive-alpha group. Consistent with these findings, Jagannathan, Malakhov, and Novikov (2010) document significant performance persistence among superior hedge funds, while they find little evidence of persistence among inferior funds.

Persistence in hedge fund performance challenges the no-persistence equilibrium result of the Berk and Green (2004) model for mutual funds. Extending the model to deliver persistence in a hedge fund setting may be an interesting direction for future research (e.g. Glode and Green (2011)).

16.3.3 Timing Ability

Among the entire population of professional investment managers, hedge funds should be the most likely to display timing skills of some form, given that they are less constrained and more active. In fact, because of their broader investment mandates and greater flexibility to exploit investment opportunities as they emerge, hedge funds can engage in several forms of timing such as market timing, volatility timing, and liquidity timing. The empirical evidence generally seems to support this intuition.

Fung, Xu, and Yau (2002) examine global hedge fund managers and conclude that they do not show positive market timing ability, but have superior security-selection ability. Aragon (2005) finds that funds of funds do not exhibit timing ability, but that market-timing ability is positive for the funds holding the most liquid portfolios and negative for the funds holding the most illiquid portfolios. However, Chen (2007) extends the timing measures in Treynor and Mazuy (1966) and Henriksson and Merton (1981) and finds significant market-timing ability for individual hedge funds and funds of funds in the bond, currency, and equity markets. Chen and Liang (2007) propose a new market-timing measure by relating fund returns to the squared Sharpe ratio of the market portfolio. Using a sample of 221 market-timing funds from January 1994 to June 2005, they find economically and statistically significant evidence of return timing, volatility timing, and joint timing, both at the aggregate and individual-fund levels.

Kazemi and Li (2009) consider the market- and volatility-timing ability of commodity trading advisors (CTAs), and observe that CTAs display a negative relationship between market-timing and security-selection ability. They also find that systematic CTAs are, in general, better at market timing than discretionary CTAs. Cave, Hubner, and Sougne (2012) identify 'positive', 'mixed', and 'negative' market timers, and study their performance during the financial crisis of 2008. Aragon and Martin (2012) study volatility timing ability and selectivity skill revealed by the use of calls, puts, and equity positions by hedge fund investment advisers. They find that hedge funds successfully use derivatives to profit from private information about stock fundamentals. For example, hedge funds greatly increased their use of puts in the aftermath of the technology bubble, and there is a strong positive (negative) relationship between call (put) holdings and subsequent abnormal stock returns. Chen (2011) finds that 71% of hedge funds trade derivatives. After controlling for fund strategies and characteristics, derivatives users, on average, exhibit lower market, downside, and event risk.

Cao et al. (2013) examine the liquidity timing ability for hedge funds, and find strong evidence at both the strategic and individual-fund levels. Specifically, they show that hedge fund managers increase (decrease) their portfolios' market exposure when equity market liquidity is high (low), and liquidity timing is the most pronounced when market liquidity is very low.

16.3.4 Hedge Fund Styles

Despite the heterogeneity among hedge funds and their myriad strategies, they fall into several broad groupings or categories of investment styles. Fung and Hsieh (1997) study hedge fund styles and find that the strategies are highly dynamic, and behave very differently from those used by mutual funds. To develop some intuition for these styles and how they are related, we report in Table 16.5 the correlations of monthly average returns of hedge funds in each Lipper style category from January 1996 to December 2014. These estimates show that the correlations between some categories' average returns are as high as 0.80 (between the event driven and long/short equity hedge categories), but the long/short equity hedge and dedicated short bias categories are negatively correlated at −0.74, and the managed futures category has virtually no correlation with any other category except for global macro. The fixed income arbitrage and convertible arbitrage categories have much in common, and the event driven category is highly correlated with several categories. Meanwhile, the equity market neutral and global macro categories have, at most, moderate correlations with other styles.

To develop further insight into these correlations, we consider a simple factor model based on principal component analysis (PCA). From the PCA perspective, correlated hedge fund investment styles can be decomposed into a linear combination of uncorrelated 'eigen-strategies'. PCA is able to tell us how many uncorrelated eigen-strategies underpin the majority of the performance of the ten hedge fund categories listed in Table 16.5. We find that 78% of the strategies' volatility-equalized variances is explained by only three factors, suggesting that a large fraction of hedge fund returns are generated by a very small universe of uncorrelated strategies. The fraction of variance explained by each of the first six eigenvalues is as follows:

$$\{\lambda_1 : 52.3\%, \lambda_2 : 15.0\%, \lambda_3 : 11.0\%, \lambda_4 : 6.3\%, \lambda_5 : 3.7\%, \lambda_6 : 3.5\%\}.$$

To put the magnitude of these eigenvalues in context, we simulated one million correlation matrices, each based on 216 independent and identically distributed (IID) Gaussian returns of ten simulated time series, from which we computed an empirical distribution of the matrices' largest eigenvalues. The mean of this distribution is 13.51%, while the minimum and maximum are 11.59% and 17.18%, respectively—all much smaller than the estimated λ_1.[13] This suggests that the first principal component accounts for significantly more variability than in the case of purely random returns, and hedge fund category returns do have factors in common.

As with any PCA decomposition, the principal components may not be easily interpretable, and we caution against reading too much into their significance. However, the distribution of the corresponding eigenvalues provides some insight into how many genuinely unique investment strategies are reflected in category returns. In this respect, the PCA results are informative: the ten categories' returns are certainly not unique, but neither are they all explained by a single factor. On the one hand, hedge fund investors should be mindful that the returns of any two hedge fund styles may be driven by completely uncorrelated factors and that, far from any two hedge fund investments being interchangeable, the choice of hedge fund style may be as significant as the choice between stocks and bonds. On the other hand, because nearly 80% of hedge fund category returns are implicitly driven by three factors, hedge fund investors should also recognize that the benefits of diversification are limited; the returns of, say, twenty hedge funds are unlikely to be completely uncorrelated.

[13] For robustness, we repeated the million-sample simulation using a fat-tailed distribution (the t distribution with one degree of freedom) and reached the same conclusion. The mean proportion of variance explained by the largest eigenvalue is 13.57%, while the minimum and maximum were 10.24% and 37.23%, respectively. Even with a fat-tailed distribution, it is very unlikely that λ_1 could be as large as 52.3% by chance.

Table 16.5 Monthly correlations of the average returns of funds in each hedge fund style category.

	Convertible Arbitrage	Dedicated Short Bias	Emerging Markets	Equity Market Neutral	Event Driven	Fixed Income Arbitrage	Global Macro	Long/Short Equity Hedge	Managed Futures	Multi-Strategy	Funds of Funds	All Single Manager Funds
Convertible Arbitrage	1.00	-0.41	0.63	0.55	0.77	0.69	0.23	0.61	-0.08	0.66	0.63	0.69
Dedicated Short Bias	-0.41	1.00	-0.57	-0.25	-0.60	-0.17	-0.15	-0.74	0.03	-0.53	-0.55	-0.66
Emerging Markets	0.63	-0.57	1.00	0.41	0.78	0.47	0.40	0.78	0.05	0.71	0.85	0.88
Equity Market Neutral	0.55	-0.25	0.41	1.00	0.59	0.46	0.18	0.49	0.04	0.54	0.46	0.52
Event Driven	0.77	-0.60	0.78	0.59	1.00	0.58	0.32	0.80	0.01	0.75	0.81	0.86
Fixed Income Arbitrage	0.69	-0.17	0.47	0.46	0.58	1.00	0.32	0.37	0.03	0.49	0.50	0.50
Global Macro	0.23	-0.15	0.40	0.18	0.32	0.32	1.00	0.33	0.55	0.43	0.54	0.51
Long/Short Equity Hedge	0.61	-0.74	0.78	0.49	0.80	0.37	0.33	1.00	0.09	0.74	0.84	0.94
Managed Futures	-0.08	0.03	0.05	0.04	0.01	0.03	0.55	0.09	1.00	0.23	0.29	0.24
Multi-Strategy	0.66	-0.53	0.71	0.54	0.75	0.49	0.43	0.74	0.23	1.00	0.83	0.83
Funds of Funds	0.63	-0.55	0.85	0.46	0.81	0.50	0.54	0.84	0.29	0.83	1.00	0.94
All Single Manager Funds	0.69	-0.66	0.88	0.52	0.86	0.50	0.51	0.94	0.24	0.83	0.94	1.00

Correlations for the ten main Lipper hedge fund categories, funds of funds, and all single manager funds found in the Lipper database from January 1996 to December 2014 are reported. The 'all single manager funds' category includes the funds in all ten main Lipper categories and any other single manager funds present in the database (relatively few) while excluding funds of funds.

A more intuitive illustration of the heterogeneity and commonality among hedge fund styles is presented in Table 16.6, in which a variety of summary statistics such as average return, volatility, Sharpe ratio, and higher-order moments are reported for hedge fund category returns. The top panel reports the summary statistics for the average fund (averaged across all available funds in the Lipper database for each month), and the bottom panel reports the same summary statistics for the Credit Suisse/Dow Jones Hedge-Fund Category Index.

We observe new patterns of similarities and differences among hedge fund categories in Table 16.6. During the period from January 1996 to December 2014, the dedicated short bias category underperformed compared to all other categories, which is unsurprising given that equities performed well during a significant portion of the sample period. Consistent with Agarwal and Kale (2007), we find that multi-strategy hedge funds outperformed funds of funds. The average managed futures fund's returns appear roughly IID and Gaussian, while the returns of the average convertible arbitrage fund are autocorrelated and have fat tails. Although some categories are uncorrelated or negatively correlated with stocks, the long/short equity hedge, event driven, and emerging markets funds have correlations with the S&P 500 total return index of 0.74, 0.65, and 0.64, respectively. A high correlation with a traditional equities-based portfolio can undermine a hedge fund's diversification advantage.

The return volatility also differs considerably across categories. For example, the volatility of the average emerging markets fund is three times greater than that of the average fixed income arbitrage fund. Intriguingly, a lower volatility does not unambiguously imply lower risk: the managed futures category has a high volatility but low maximum drawdown, while fixed income arbitrage and multi-strategy hedge funds have roughly half the volatility but a higher maximum drawdown. These last two categories also have a history of negative skewness and large kurtosis (i.e. their returns have fat left tails). Heuson, Hutchinson, and Kumar (2019) show that traditional performance measures systematically underestimate (overestimate) managerial performance when returns exhibit positive (negative) skewness, and propose a new measure to account for skewness in performance measurement.

Figure 16.1 suggests that categories that exhibit higher autocorrelation generally also exhibit kurtosis and negative skewness (we show in Section 16.4 that positive autocorrelation is a proxy for illiquidity risk). This cluster of traits should give investors cause for concern, so it is worth listing the hedge fund styles that most clearly exhibit them: convertible arbitrage, fixed income arbitrage, event driven, emerging markets, and multi-strategy. These

Table 16.6 Summary statistics for the returns of the average fund in each Lipper style category and summary statistics for the corresponding Credit Suisse/Dow Jones Index.

		# Fund-Months	Annualized Mean	Annualized Volatility	Sharpe Ratio	Sortino Ratio	Skewness	Kurtosis	Maximum DD	S&P 500 Corr.	ac(1)	Box–Q(3) p-value
Database Estimate	Convertible Arbitrage	14,231	5.4%	7.3%	0.38	0.51	-3.37	28.94	-34.4%	0.51	0.48	0.00
	Dedicated Short Bias	2,503	-1.1%	15.6%	-0.23	-0.41	0.62	5.23	-47.3%	-0.72	0.10	0.08
	Emerging Markets	47,054	6.8%	14.2%	0.29	0.42	-1.43	9.94	-49.3%	0.64	0.31	0.00
	Equity Market Neutral	27,459	4.7%	3.3%	0.61	0.99	-0.25	12.86	-14.6%	0.32	0.20	0.00
	Event Driven	39,227	6.8%	5.9%	0.70	1.05	-1.64	8.97	-24.8%	0.65	0.42	0.00
	Fixed Income Arbitrage	18,834	5.1%	4.4%	0.56	0.68	-4.35	32.93	-20.7%	0.29	0.37	0.00
	Global Macro	32,034	4.9%	5.2%	0.44	0.81	0.48	4.93	-14.2%	0.28	0.01	0.48
	Long/Short Equity Hedge	178,926	7.7%	9.0%	0.56	0.98	0.00	5.47	-24.7%	0.74	0.22	0.00
	Managed Futures	46,204	4.8%	9.4%	0.23	0.44	0.26	3.13	-16.3%	-0.05	-0.02	0.29
	Multi-Strategy	76,233	5.8%	5.2%	0.62	0.93	-1.18	7.16	-21.5%	0.57	0.22	0.00
	Funds of Funds	270,369	3.8%	6.0%	0.20	0.31	-0.57	6.80	-21.9%	0.58	0.28	0.00
	All Single Manager Funds	505,844	6.3%	6.3%	0.58	0.97	-0.50	5.72	-20.5%	0.71	0.25	0.00
Credit Suisse/Dow Jones Index	Convertible Arbitrage	228	7.3%	6.8%	0.69	0.95	-2.75	20.03	-32.9%	0.37	0.55	0.00
	Dedicated Short Bias	228	-6.4%	16.7%	-0.53	-0.95	0.78	4.65	-76.3%	-0.77	0.08	0.53
	Emerging Markets	228	8.4%	13.1%	0.44	0.65	-1.28	10.74	-45.1%	0.60	0.26	0.00
	Equity Market Neutral	228	4.8%	10.2%	0.21	0.23	-11.88	165.26	-45.1%	0.31	0.07	0.06
	Event Driven	228	9.2%	6.3%	1.03	1.52	-2.25	13.60	-19.1%	0.63	0.36	0.00
	Fixed Income Arbitrage	228	5.3%	5.6%	0.48	0.58	-4.64	36.20	-29.0%	0.32	0.53	0.00
	Global Macro	228	10.9%	8.9%	0.92	1.60	-0.06	8.01	-26.8%	0.24	0.05	0.30
	Long/Short Equity Hedge	228	9.7%	9.6%	0.72	1.29	-0.03	6.63	-22.0%	0.67	0.18	0.04
	Managed Futures	228	6.1%	11.4%	0.30	0.57	0.06	2.69	-17.4%	-0.05	0.03	0.21
	Multi-Strategy	228	8.4%	4.9%	1.16	1.77	-1.99	11.52	-24.7%	0.43	0.44	0.00
	All Single Manager Funds	228	8.6%	7.1%	0.82	1.44	-0.20	6.27	-19.7%	0.59	0.17	0.01

Number of fund months, annualized mean, annualized volatility, Sharpe ratio, Sortino ratio, skewness, kurtosis, maximum drawdown, correlation coefficient with the S&P 500, first-order autocorrelation, and p-value of the Ljung–Box test statistic with three lags for the ten main Lipper hedge fund categories, funds of funds, and all single manager funds found in the Lipper database from January 1996 to December 2014 are reported. The Sharpe and Sortino ratios are adjusted for the three-month US Treasury bill rate. The 'all single manager funds' category includes the funds in all ten main Lipper categories and any other single manager funds present in the database (relatively few) while excluding funds of funds.

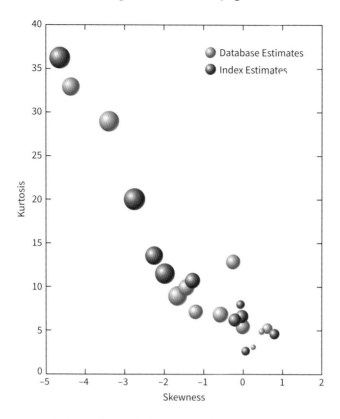

Fig. 16.1 Autocorrelation and fat-tailed returns for funds in the Lipper database and in the Credit Suisse/Dow Jones hedge fund indexes. The location of each bubble reflects the skewness (x-axis) and kurtosis (y-axis) of a hedge fund category. The size of each bubble reflects the corresponding category returns' autocorrelation. Results are provided for each category based on the average returns of funds in the Lipper database and also based on the widely used Credit Suisse/Dow Jones hedge fund indexes.

strategies have the highest autocorrelations and the most fat-tailed return distributions. When investing in a fund with positively autocorrelated returns, investors may want to consider the increased likelihood that a simple analysis based on the volatility of these returns will understate the actual downside risk.

The extremely high autocorrelation of the returns for several categories demands further study; hence, in Fig. 16.2, we display the thirty-six-month rolling autocorrelation for each category. Some categories exhibit consistently high autocorrelation, while others exhibit little or negative autocorrelation. Curiously, some categories' autocorrelations increased sharply during the financial crisis, while others were unaffected. For example, Fig. 16.2a

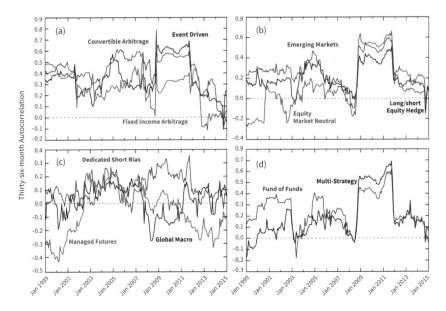

Fig. 16.2 One-month lag autocorrelations over rolling thirty-six-month windows of (a) convertible arbitrage, event driven, and fixed income arbitrage; (b) emerging markets, long/short equity hedge, and equity market neutral; (c) dedicated short bias, global macro, and managed futures; and (d) fund of funds and multi-strategy category returns from January 1996 to December 2014.

depicts, among others, the rolling thirty-six-month autocorrelation of the convertible arbitrage strategy from January 1996 to December 2014. A comparison with subsequent figures shows that over nineteen years, the average returns of funds in the convertible arbitrage category have generally been more autocorrelated than those of any other category. Based on a thirty-six-month rolling-window estimate, the autocorrelation has typically ranged between 0.3 and 0.6. It fluctuated sharply during the 2008 financial crisis, and dropped to zero in 2014 for the first time in the whole sample period.[14] We shall return to the subject of autocorrelation when we focus on measures of illiquidity risk in Section 16.4.

16.4 Illiquidity

Illiquidity is one of the most important characteristics of certain hedge fund investments, and one that has only recently begun to receive the attention it

[14] We further show in Fig. 16.4 that, in the end of the sample, the equity exposure of the convertible arbitrage strategy shifted from positive to negative.

deserves. Not only is illiquidity at the heart of most financial crises (see, e.g., the discussion in Section 16.6), but it is also central to how many financial investments generate their returns. Taking on illiquidity risk is one of the most effective ways for long-horizon investors to build wealth, but it can also be the downfall of investors who are unaware of their illiquidity exposure and attempt to liquidate certain investments at the wrong time.

One of the biggest challenges to measuring illiquidity is the fact that there is currently no single definition of liquidity. The reason is simple: liquidity is not a one-dimensional characteristic, but has at least three distinct aspects. An asset is considered liquid if (1) it can be bought or sold quickly; (2) the amount that can be bought or sold is large; and (3) buying or selling such large amounts will not adversely impact the market price. Certain assets may have one or two of these properties, but only truly liquid assets will have all three. For example, residential real estate can be sold quickly, but usually not without significant price concessions; hence, this asset would not be considered liquid. What makes liquidity even harder to define is that these three characteristics are time- and context-dependent; what is liquid today may be highly illiquid tomorrow. A clear illustration of just how dynamic liquidity can be is the Quant Meltdown of August 2007, described in more detail in Section 16.6.1 and Chapter 17.

In Section 16.4.1, we review several measures of illiquidity that are specifically designed with hedge funds in mind. We consider the impact of illiquidity on statistical measures of hedge fund performance such as volatilities, Sharpe ratios, and betas, and how to correct for it in Section 16.4.2. Based on these and other measures of illiquidity, the magnitude of illiquidity risk premia in hedge fund returns can be quantified, which we describe in Section 16.4.3. Finally, in Section 16.4.4, we show how to incorporate measures of illiquidity into the traditional mean-variance portfolio optimization framework.

16.4.1 Measures of Illiquidity and Return Smoothing

The finance literature offers a number of theoretical and empirical measures of illiquidity, including percentage bid–offer spreads (Tinic, 1972; Glosten and Milgrom, 1985; Amihud and Mendelson, 1986), price impact (Kraus and Stoll, 1972; Kyle, 1985; Hasbrouck and Schwartz, 1988; Lillo, Farmer, and Mantegna, 2003), and volume-based statistics (Pástor and Stambaugh, 2003; Lo, Mamaysky, and Wang, 2004; Lo and Wang, 2006). However, these measures all assume the existence of a centralized exchange in which price discovery occurs regularly, designated market makers who post bids and offers, and a trading volume that can be measured. As a result, none of these measures is applicable to investments in hedge funds, of which the vast majority are structured as privately placed securities.

Lo (2002b) and Getmansky, Lo, and Makarov (2004) propose an alternate measure of illiquidity that requires only asset returns: return autocorrelation, ρ_k, where

$$\rho_k = \frac{\text{Cov}[R_t, R_{t-k}]}{\text{Var}[R_t]}, \ k > 0, \tag{16.1}$$

$$\hat{\rho}_k = \frac{(T - k + 1)^{-1} \sum_{t=k-1}^{T} (R_t - \hat{\mu})(R_{t-k} - \hat{\mu})}{(T - 1)^{-1} \sum_{t=1}^{T} (R_t - \hat{\mu})^2}, \ \hat{\mu} = T^{-1} \sum_{t=1}^{T} R_t. \tag{16.2}$$

In an efficient market, asset returns should be approximately serially uncorrelated, hence, $\rho_k = 0$ for all $k > 0$—that is, past returns should contain very little information about future returns, otherwise the information could be exploited via trading strategies that buy (short-sell) securities with positive (negative) return forecasts. The very process of exploiting this information will tend to reduce, if not eliminate entirely, any return autocorrelation. The only two reasons such information cannot be exploited, and therefore cannot be eliminated, are (1) if the autocorrelation is due to time-varying equilibrium expected returns; or (2) if the autocorrelation cannot be exploited due to trading frictions (i.e. illiquidity). The first possibility is less likely for shorter-horizon holding periods such as monthly or daily returns, given the definition of equilibrium expected returns; thus, the second possibility is the more likely explanation for significant return autocorrelation. In other words, returns may be autocorrelated because information about the underlying asset diffuses over time, but investors with early access to this information cannot exploit it because the asset cannot be traded quickly, in large size, or without moving the price significantly.

Getmansky, Lo, and Makarov (2004) construct a simple econometric model to estimate the degree of autocorrelation in hedge fund returns by assuming that the true but unobservable economic return, R_t, of a hedge fund in period t satisfies a linear single-factor model:

$$R_t = \mu + \beta \Lambda_t + \epsilon_t, \ \mathbb{E}[\Lambda_t] = \mathbb{E}[\epsilon_t] = 0, \ \epsilon_t, \Lambda_t \ \sim \ \text{IID}, \tag{16.3a}$$

$$\text{Var}[R_t] \equiv \sigma^2, \tag{16.3b}$$

whereas the reported return, R_t^o, is:

$$R_t^o = \theta_0 R_t + \theta_1 R_{t-1} + \cdots + \theta_k R_{t-k} \tag{16.4}$$

$$\theta_j \in [0, 1], j = 0, \ldots, k \tag{16.5}$$

$$1 = \theta_0 + \theta_1 + \cdots + \theta_k \tag{16.6}$$

which is a weighted average of the fund's true returns over the most recent $k + 1$ periods, including the current period. True returns represent the flow of information that would determine the equilibrium value of the fund's securities in a frictionless market, and the observed returns represent the results that the fund reports each month. Using the maximum likelihood to estimate the smoothing parameters, $\{\theta_j\}$, Getmansky, Lo, and Makarov (2004) confirm that funds with higher autocorrelation tend to be the more illiquid funds (e.g. emerging market debt and fixed income arbitrage).

More generally, Khandani and Lo (2011a) establish a link between illiquidity and positive autocorrelation in asset returns among a sample of hedge funds, mutual funds, and various equity portfolios. For hedge funds, this link can be confirmed by comparing the return autocorrelations of funds with shorter versus longer redemption notice periods. They also document significant positive return autocorrelation in portfolios of securities that are generally considered less liquid (e.g. small-cap stocks, corporate bonds, mortgage-backed securities, and emerging market investments).

Getmansky, Lo, and Makarov (2004) and Bollen and Pool (2008) also observe that return autocorrelation may be evidence of return smoothing, the unsavoury practice of reporting only part of the gains in the months when a fund has positive returns partially to offset potential future losses, thereby reducing the volatility and improving risk-adjusted performance measures such as the Sharpe ratio (see Section 16.4.2). However, while large positive return autocorrelations should raise concerns regarding the potential for deliberate return-smoothing behaviour, Getmansky, Lo, and Makarov (2004) emphasize that it is impossible to determine whether a fund is intentionally smoothing returns only from its return autocorrelations.

Bollen and Pool (2009) and Jylha (2011) show that hedge funds often push otherwise small negative returns above zero. Agarwal, Daniel, and Naik (2011) find evidence of manipulating reported returns upward in the month of December. Cici, Kempf, and Puetz (2016) use 13F filings to show that hedge fund advisers strategically employ mismarking in stock positions to smooth their reported returns and also push otherwise small negative returns above zero.

Aragon and Nanda (2017) link reporting delays to return smoothing, through reporting returns in clusters. Patton, Ramadorai, and Streatfield (2015) find that hedge fund performance is lower among funds that have restated their return history to a database, especially among funds that show a high degree of monthly return autocorrelation. Ben-David et al. (2013) provide evidence that suggests some hedge funds manipulate stock prices on critical reporting dates. They find that the stocks in the top quartile of hedge fund holdings exhibit abnormal returns of 0.30% on the last day of the quarter, and a reversal of 0.25% on the following day. A significant part of the return is earned during the last minutes of trading. Kruttli, Patton, and Ramadorai (2015) use an aggregate version of the liquidity measure of Getmansky, Lo, and Makarov (2004), estimated across a large set of hedge funds, and find that the measure has the ability to predict a large range of asset returns (commodities, currencies, bonds, and equities). The authors relate this finding to the role of hedge funds in liquidity provision in capital markets.

16.4.2 Illiquidity and Statistical Biases

Illiquidity can lead to a number of biases in the statistical properties of hedge fund returns. For example, using a linear moving average time series model for illiquid hedge fund returns, Getmansky, Lo, and Makarov (2004) show that standard estimators of volatility are biased downward, Sharpe ratios are biased upward, and the betas of regressions of hedge fund returns on lagged market factors are nonzero. The authors find that, after correcting for the effects of smoothed returns, some of the most successful types of funds tend to have considerably less attractive performance characteristics. Lo (2002b) provides the appropriate correction term for computing volatilities and Sharpe ratios in these cases, and shows that corrected annualized Sharpe ratios based on monthly data can differ from the standard Sharpe ratio estimator by as much as 70%. Asness, Krail, and Liew (2001) show that in some cases where hedge funds purport to be market neutral (i.e. relatively small market betas calculated with only contemporaneous returns as regressors), their market exposures are considerably higher when measured by summing the beta coefficients of both contemporaneous and lagged market returns. Large differences between these two methods of measuring market neutrality can be a sign of illiquidity in the funds' underlying positions, with potentially significant implications for assessing the risks and expected returns of hedge fund investments, including potential fraud detection.

16.4.3 Measuring Illiquidity Risk Premia

Suppose investors are given the choice between two assets that are identical in all respects but one: while one asset can be traded around the clock, the other can only be traded on the first Tuesday of months starting with the letter 'J'. Most investors would choose the first, more liquid asset. But, when enough investors do this, the supply of the first asset may dwindle, and its price would rise relative to the second asset. At some point, investors will feel that the discount on the second asset—which will yield a higher expected return today, assuming that its future expected payoff is unchanged—is sufficiently large to compensate them for the infrequency with which it can be traded, leading them to buy the second asset. The investors buying the second asset will obtain a higher expected return than investors in the first asset, in exchange for accepting the risk, that, at the moment they want to sell their asset, it may not be possible to do so. This incremental return is called the illiquidity premium.

Unfortunately, paired with the illiquidity premium is the illiquidity penalty: the periods when many owners want to sell are typically the times during which few investors want to buy, so the asset's price may plummet beyond reason. In these circumstances, it may be impossible to sell at a price near what an owner considers fair.

Liang (1999) and Aragon (2007) study the relationship between hedge fund returns and a very specific form of illiquidity—lock-up restrictions—and document a positive relationship between lock-ups and fund performance. Aragon (2007) finds that hedge funds with lock-ups have 4%–7% per year higher excess returns than those of non-lock-up funds (see Section 16.1.3 for a further discussion of lock-ups and other share restrictions). Sadka (2010, 2012) shows that the liquidity risk is an important determinant of the cross-sectional differences in hedge fund returns, and concludes that hedge funds with significant liquidity risk subsequently outperform low liquidity-risk funds by an average of 6% annually. Consistent with Brunnermeier and Pedersen (2009), Teo (2011) finds that hedge funds with strong incentives to raise capital, low manager option deltas, and no manager capital co-invested are more likely to take on excessive liquidity risk.

Using a sample of 2,927 hedge funds, 15,654 mutual funds, and 100 size- and book-to-market-sorted portfolios of US common stocks, Khandani and Lo (2011a) construct autocorrelation-sorted long/short portfolios, and conclude that illiquidity premia are generally positive and significant, ranging from 2.74% to 9.91% per year among various hedge funds and fixed-income mutual funds. They do not find evidence for this premium among equity and asset-allocation mutual funds, or among the 100 US equity portfolios studied.

The time variation in their aggregated illiquidity premium shows that, while 1998 was a difficult year for most funds with large illiquidity exposure, the following four years yielded significantly higher illiquidity premia that led to greater competition in credit markets, contributing to much lower illiquidity premia in the years leading up to the financial crisis of 2008.

16.4.4 The Mean-Variance–Illiquidity Frontier

Modern portfolio theory implies that, to earn higher expected returns, an investor must bear higher systematic risk. While the historical time series evidence suggests that this is a good general guide (Ibbotson, 2013), we believe that this model is too narrowly interpreted. Risk is generally thought of as the distribution of magnitudes of possible losses over a given time period. In a well-functioning market, this characterization should be conceptually adequate, even if, as a practical matter, obtaining a good estimate of risk is nontrivial. However, when markets break down, some assets cease to have a meaningful price. For a period of time, there may be no transactions at all, and, if there are any sales, they will generally be made by investors desperate for cash and willing to sell at fire-sale prices. The possibility of such temporary market failures is not captured very well by traditional risk measures. Nevertheless, it is a type of risk, and it stands to reason that investors willing to assume it should earn higher returns. Viewed this way, the illiquidity premium exists because illiquid assets carry extra risk, albeit of a unique sort.

We test this hypothesis by using data for the nineteen-year period from January 1996 to December 2014, and creating portfolios made up of three-month T-bills, stocks, bonds, and any blend of our eleven average hedge fund-style return series. Traditional mean-variance optimization would produce an efficient frontier that shows the best return one could have obtained for the indicated level of risk. In such an analysis, risk is typically proxied by the annualized standard deviation of the portfolio's returns. We generalize this framework to include a second nonlinear constraint: autocorrelation. The resulting three-dimensional surface based on volatility, return, and autocorrelation is depicted in Fig. 16.3. Since return autocorrelation is often associated with portfolio illiquidity (see Section 16.4.1), constraining a portfolio to have low autocorrelation is likely to limit the illiquidity risk and, consequently, the amount of the illiquidity premium in the portfolio. Figure 16.3 shows that this is exactly the case: to earn high returns in the period from 1996 to 2014, an investor would have had to bear the risk of ordinary market fluctuations (volatility), the risk of temporary market

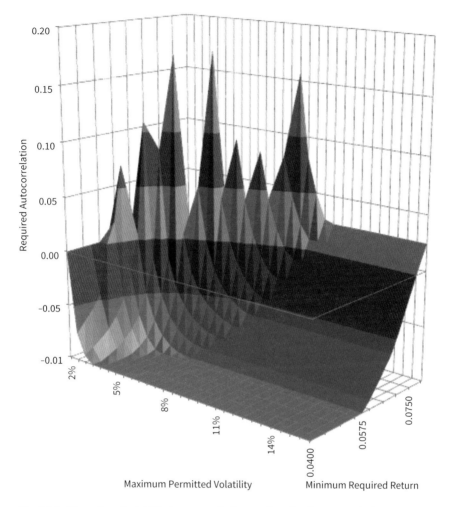

Fig. 16.3 The return/volatility/autocorrelation surface for the optimal allocation among three-month T-bills, stocks, bonds, and hedge fund categories, using data from January 1996 to December 2014.

failure (illiquidity/autocorrelation), or a combination of both. The extra return that corresponds to the increased autocorrelation is as much as 2%, which is broadly consistent with other estimates of the illiquidity premium (Aragon, 2007; Sadka, 2010, 2012).

This analysis of the relationship between illiquidity and returns over nineteen years suggests that investors may benefit from determining their tolerance for illiquidity alongside their tolerance for traditional risk, and choosing their asset allocation accordingly. Table 16.6 shows the striking differences in autocorrelation among hedge fund categories; it is possible that the highly autocorrelated categories present investors with a greater opportunity to earn the illiquidity premium, while less autocorrelated categories present investors with more protection against the downside surprises due to market failures.

16.5 Hedge Fund Risks

What risks do hedge funds take and do they earn expected returns commensurate with those risks? Understanding the answers to these two questions is crucial for any investor seeking to determine whether a hedge fund investment would be a prudent addition to their portfolio. The traditional investment framework of the Sharpe–Lintner capital asset pricing model (CAPM) provides a natural starting point. Do hedge fund expected returns exhibit any alpha? That is, do they exceed their risk-adjusted cost of capital where the risk adjustment is with respect to their equity beta?

In many cases, the answer to this narrow question is yes, but there is a concern among academics and hedge fund investment professionals that a portion of this alpha may be attributed to exposures to factors other than the stock market (e.g. other asset classes such as commodities, currencies, and real estate). Moreover, many once-unique investment strategies pioneered by the hedge fund industry have become commoditized. For example, the carry trade, the size spread, and trend-following strategies are now so well understood that retail investors can invest in them through ETFs and mutual funds that use mechanical trading strategies.[15] Exposures to all these well-understood drivers of returns may now be thought of as 'alternative' or 'exotic' betas. Therefore, hedge fund expected returns are inextricably intertwined with the risk exposures associated with hedge fund strategies. Measuring and managing these exposures is the focus of this section.

In Section 16.5.1 we review how risk is measured and how hedge fund managers adjust their risk-taking in response to incentives. In Section 16.5.2 we discuss the use of linear factor models, a common risk-analysis tool that enables the user to estimate not only how much risk is being taken, but also what kind of risk is being taken, even in the absence of portfolio transparency. As useful as these models are, they have important limitations, and, in Section 16.5.3, we provide a specific example of how they can yield misleading results if used improperly.

In Section 16.5.4, we continue our focus on hedge fund risks, turning from market-based risks to operational risks; in Section 16.5.5, we describe

---

[15] For a comprehensive guide to ETFs, refer to Hill, Nadig, and Hougan (2015).

how investors and hedge fund managers manage the risks associated with hedge fund investing. In Section 16.5.6, we conclude our discussion of hedge fund risks with the natural follow-on topic of hedge fund replication. As some aspects of hedge fund investing have become well-understood, investor demand has grown for cheaper access to alternative betas. Hedge fund replication strategies built to meet this demand now invest billions of dollars around the world.[16]

16.5.1 Value at Risk and Risk Shifting

Because of the heterogeneity and inherent nonlinearities of hedge fund strategies, a natural starting point for risk management in the hedge fund industry is value at risk (VaR), a concept that originated in the derivatives industry. Instead of adopting the traditional mean-variance framework of the investment management industry, derivatives traders and their risk managers focus instead on estimating the likelihood of extreme losses over a given investment horizon. If the daily change in the value of a portfolio is given by the random variable X_t, then the 5% one-day VaR of this portfolio is defined to be value $K > 0$ such that

$$\text{Prob}(X_t \le -K) \ = \ 5\%. \tag{16.7}$$

By specifying a limit on K, investors and managers can control the amount of risk in their portfolios. Of course, doing so requires the distribution of X_t, which involves statistical inference, as well as considerable knowledge of the underlying strategies that generate X_t.

Jorion (2007) illustrates how VaR methods can be used to measure and control the market risk of hedge funds. Gupta and Liang (2005) examine the risk characteristics and capital adequacy through the VaR approach. They find that, as of March 2003, 3.7% of live funds and 10.9% of defunct funds were under-capitalized. Jorion (2008) develops methods to measure the forward-looking risk of portfolios exposed to corporate events such as restructurings, bankruptcies, mergers, acquisitions, or other special situations. Using both Lipper and HFR data at the individual and portfolio levels, Bali, Gokcan, and Liang (2007) find that live funds with high VaR

---

[16] In the interest of full disclosure, two of the authors of the article Getmansky, Lee, and Lo (2015) on which this chapter is based—P. Lee and A. Lo—had commercial interests in a hedge fund beta replication mutual fund at the time the article was published in 2015. Lo's affiliation formally ended as of 1 January 2022.

outperform those with low VaR by 9% annually. However, the relationship between downside risk and expected returns is negative for defunct funds. Using the Lipper database, Liang and Park (2007) describe the shortcomings of VaR, and find that other left-tail risk measures such as expected shortfall and tail risk can be superior in explaining the cross-sectional variation in hedge fund returns.

Brown, Goetzmann, and Park (2001) investigate risk-shifting in hedge funds, and find evidence of tournament behaviour among hedge funds. Specifically, good performers in the first half of the year reduce the volatility of their portfolios, and poor performers increase portfolio volatility. Agarwal, Daniel, and Naik (2002) also report this finding for hedge funds, using an alternative method in high-water mark estimation. Hodder and Jackwerth (2007) analyse the effect of incentive fees, high-water marks, and managerial ownership of shares on hedge fund risk-taking. In a related study, Panageas and Westerfield (2009) challenge the basic intuition that convex compensation schemes, in which managers are rewarded for gains but not punished for losses, increase risk-taking. Convex payoffs are common in hedge fund contracts, and the authors show that in an infinite-horizon setting, even a risk-neutral manager will not take unbounded risks. As a result, the incentive to take greater risk depends on the interaction between convexity and finite horizons, and not just on convex compensation structures.

Using the Zurich hedge fund universe, Kouwenberg and Ziemba (2007) test the relationship between risk-taking and incentive fees. They find that loss-averse managers increase the risk of the fund's investment strategy with higher incentive fees. However, risk-taking is greatly reduced if a substantial amount of the manager's own money (at least 30%) is in the fund. Aragon and Nanda (2012) find that when hedge funds are likely to be liquidated, and therefore managers do not expect to operate the funds for many periods, high-water marks are far less effective in moderating risk-shifting following poor performance. Goetzmann, Ingersoll, and Ross (2003) provide a closed-form solution to the high-water mark contract under certain conditions. This solution shows that managers have an incentive to take risks.

16.5.2 Linear Factor Models

A more refined approach to risk management for hedge funds is to approximate a fund's return, R_{pt}, by a linear factor model:

$$R_{pt} = \alpha_p + \beta_{p1}F_{1t} + \cdots + \beta_{pK}F_{Kt} + \epsilon_{pt}, \qquad (16.8)$$

where the factors $\{F_{it}\}$ are observable explanatory variables such as stock and bond indexes or the returns of well-defined algorithmic strategies such as trend-following, mean reversion, or carry trade strategies. Such factor models are especially useful for answering questions about the likely impact of various scenarios on a hedge fund's returns (e.g. How will a specific hedge fund's return be affected if the stock market declines by 10%? How sensitive is it to interest-rate fluctuations? Does the hedge fund employ momentum strategies?).

The unexplained components of Equation (16.8) are attributable to three sources: alpha (the unique investment skills of the hedge fund manager), omitted factors, and idiosyncratic returns. The portion of the returns explained by the factors is generally referred to as beta(s), which comes from the traditional Sharpe–Lintner CAPM investment framework.

Linear factor models can provide insight into the intrinsic characteristics and risks of a hedge fund's investments and how they vary across time and circumstances. For example, Titman and Tiu (2011) regress individual hedge fund returns on several risk factors, and show that hedge funds with low R^2 with respect to these factors tend to have higher Sharpe ratios. However, Asness, Krail, and Liew (2001) use linear factor models to show that certain hedge funds that claim to be market neutral are not, containing highly significant lagged exposure to the S&P 500, which is a symptom of illiquidity (see Section 16.4).

The usefulness of linear factor models is determined largely by the choice of factors, and many studies have contributed to our understanding of the types of factors that are most relevant for hedge fund applications.[17] As a result, many linear factor models have been proposed for hedge funds, and the sheer number of published studies on this topic is a reflection of the heterogeneity of the hedge fund industry, as well as the complexity and nonlinearity of the returns that are being approximated by linear models.[18] Several authors have suggested using more easily interpretable factors such as fund characteristics and simple indexes.[19] The sensitivity of a fund's value to a broad-based gauge of asset-class returns in a well-known category such as stocks is sometimes called traditional beta, while the sensitivities of a fund's returns to more

---

[17] Examples of linear factor models for hedge funds include Fung and Hsieh (1997, 2002, 2004), Liang (1999, 2005), Chan et al. (2004, 2005, 2006), Agarwal and Naik (2004), Bondarenko (2004), Bali, Brown, and Caglayan (2011, 2012), and Buraschi, Kosowski, and Trojani (2014).

[18] For example, Fung and Hsieh (2001), Mitchell and Pulvino (2001), and Agarwal and Naik (2004) have empirically documented nonlinear relationships between hedge fund and market returns, and Lo (1999) provides a simple analytical example of a nonlinear hedge fund strategy consisting of shorting out-of-the-money put options on S&P 500 index futures.

[19] See Schneeweis and Spurgin (1998), Liang (1999), Edwards and Caglayan (2001), and Capocci and Hübner (2004).

poorly known factors such as the returns on lookback straddles or mechanical carry trade strategies are often called exotic betas or alternative betas (Roncalli and Teiletche, 2008). In the past two decades, a number of ETFs and mutual funds have launched with the aim of providing investors access to some of these alternative betas (see Section 16.5.6).

These methods for selecting easily interpretable factors exhibit varying degrees of success depending on the nature of the hedge fund strategies to which they are applied, but they are generally preferred to purely statistical approaches such as Fung and Hsieh's (1997) use of PCA to extract factors from the covariance matrix of their sample of 409 hedge funds and CTAs.

To develop some intuition for linear factor models applied to hedge funds, consider Fung and Hsieh's (2001) seven-factor model consisting of bond-trend, currency-trend, commodity-trend, equity-market, size-spread, bond-market, and credit-spread factors.[20] The first three factors are the returns of lookback straddles that capture the idea that trend-following funds find profit opportunities in large market moves in several asset classes. The equity-market factor is simply the return of the S&P 500 total return index, while the size-spread factor is the outperformance of small-cap stocks relative to large cap ones (Russell 2000 vs S&P 500). The bond-market factor is the change in yield of the US ten-year bond, and is thus inversely related to returns on an investment in the same. The credit-spread factor is the difference between the changes in the yield on Baa-rated debt and the yield on US Treasuries. Roughly speaking, this factor is inversely related to the return on a strategy of buying high-yield debt while shorting US Treasuries.

To illustrate how linear factor models might be used in practice, we regress our set of average hedge fund category returns on the Fung and Hsieh (2001) seven factors over two time periods: January 1996–December 2014 (Table 16.7) and January 2006–December 2014 (see Table 16.10).[21] The results in Table 16.7 suggest that the equity-market, size-spread, and credit-spread factors are linked to the returns of many hedge fund categories. For example, the 'all single manager funds' row suggests that over the years 1996–2014, the average hedge fund portfolio included investments that behaved like stocks (especially small cap stocks) and high-yield debt. The results in Table 16.7 also suggest that some funds behaved more idiosyncratically. For example, managed futures and global macro funds are associated with investment strategies that rely on currency and commodity straddles, and equity

---

[20] The data for Fung and Hsieh's (2001) seven factors are located at https://people.duke.edu/~dah7/HFData.htm.

[21] We use bond data from the Federal Reserve and stock data from Bloomberg (SPTR Index and RU30INTR Index).

Table 16.7 Conditional exposures of average hedge fund category returns to the seven Fung and Hsieh (2001) factors.

Annualized Factor Volatility	Annualized Category Volatility	R^2	Monthly Alpha	Bond Trend Following Factor 51.4%	Currency Trend Following Factor 63.4%	Commodity Trend Following Factor 50.1%	Equity Market Factor 15.4%	Size Spread Factor 11.8%	Bond Market Factor 92.6%	Credit Spread Factor 76.9%
	NA	NA	NA							
Convertible Arbitrage	7.3%	0.58	0.332%*	-0.014*	-0.003	-0.010	0.114*	0.055	-0.020*	-0.061*
Dedicated Short Bias	15.6%	0.62	0.557%*	-0.022	0.000	-0.006	-0.722*	-0.410*	-0.013	-0.009
Emerging Markets	14.2%	0.52	0.181%	-0.041*	0.015	-0.006	0.468*	0.210*	-0.010	-0.047*
Equity Market Neutral	3.3%	0.24	0.333%*	-0.012*	0.002	-0.002	0.037*	0.054*	-0.001	-0.010*
Event Driven	5.9%	0.67	0.391%*	-0.020*	0.003	-0.008	0.167*	0.120*	-0.004	-0.029*
Fixed Income Arbitrage	4.4%	0.43	0.374%*	-0.010*	-0.007	0.000	0.009	0.019	-0.018*	-0.039*
Global Macro	5.2%	0.24	0.310%*	-0.008	0.024*	0.015*	0.100*	0.009	-0.015*	-0.017*
Long/Short Equity Hedge	9.0%	0.72	0.322%*	-0.003	0.009	0.003	0.388*	0.300*	-0.002	-0.014*
Managed Futures	9.4%	0.23	0.389%*	0.016	0.033*	0.048*	0.051	0.070	-0.019*	-0.003
Multi-Strategy	5.2%	0.43	0.339%*	-0.003	-0.003	0.006	0.156*	0.100*	-0.006	-0.016*
Funds of Funds	6.0%	0.46	0.147%	-0.011	0.010	0.007	0.185*	0.113*	-0.008*	-0.022*
All Single Manager Funds	6.3%	0.66	0.304%*	-0.008	0.010*	0.007	0.246*	0.161*	-0.008*	-0.022*
Corr. w/ Equity Factor	NA	NA	NA	-0.23	-0.21	-0.17	1.00	0.08	0.22	-0.44

The exposures for the ten main hedge fund categories, funds of funds, and all single manager funds found in the Lipper database are based on a multivariate regression with a constant term. Regression outputs that are significant with 95% confidence are indicated by '*' and shown in colour. Monthly correlations between hedge fund returns and all seven factors are presented. This analysis spans January 1996–December 2014.

market neutral funds are associated with a relative value strategy (long small caps, short large caps).

Although linear factor models such as Fung and Hsieh's (2001) are able to capture historical relationships between hedge funds and risk factors, they may not be ideal for practical purposes such as risk management. In particular, four of the seven factors in Fung and Hsieh (2001) do not have liquid futures contracts associated with them (the three lookback straddles and the credit spread); hence, if an investor wishes to reduce exposure to one of these factors, it would be difficult to do so. Additionally, the large number of factors increases the potential for overfitting, and therefore implies less effective out-of-sample performance.

In contrast, consider a more parsimonious four-factor model that is very nearly investable. Two factors are the same as in Fung and Hsieh (2001)— the equity-market and size-spread factors—and one is similar: a bond-market factor (we use the Barclays US Aggregate Bond Index). We also include an additional factor, 2–3-month lagged returns of the S&P 500, to capture illiquidity exposure, as documented by Asness, Krail, and Liew (2001).[22] The estimates are presented in Table 16.8. For the average hedge fund, this model has about the same in-sample R^2 as Fung and Hsieh's (2001) model, despite its greater parsimony, although for specific categories it often falls slightly short for lack of some of the noninvestable factors present in Fung and Hsieh (2001).

For practical purposes, investors and managers are the most interested in forecasting a fund's future risks. Accordingly, we also evaluate the funds' out-of-sample fit for each linear factor model using a twenty-four-month rolling window and one-month-ahead predictions. The results are reported in Table 16.9, which shows that, in the out-of-sample period, the simpler model does a better job for seven of the ten hedge fund categories. This suggests that, except where specialized factors dominate a fund's returns (e.g. the credit spread), the best linear factor model forecast of a hedge fund's future risk may be obtained from simpler, investable factors.

Table 16.10 contains the conditional risk-adjusted exposures of average hedge fund category returns to the seven Fung and Hsieh (2001) factors during the period from January 2006 to December 2014. These exposures suggest an interesting difference between the latter nine years and the preceding period: hedge funds no longer have a positive exposure to the size-spread factor. This implies that, while hedge funds generally maintained

---

[22] While lagged exposure to stocks is not traditionally considered an investable factor, one could simply add a corresponding exposure to the S&P 500 to obtain a substantively similar portfolio.

Table 16.8 Conditional exposures of average hedge fund category returns to four investable factors.

	Annualized Category Volatility	R^2	Monthly Alpha	Equity Market Factor	Lagged Equity Market Factor	Size Spread Factor	Bond Market Factor
Annualized Factor Volatility	NA	NA	NA	15.4%	11.4%	11.8%	3.5%
Convertible Arbitrage	7.3%	0.34	0.01%	0.23*	0.13*	0.12*	0.33*
Dedicated Short Bias	15.6%	0.62	0.38%	−0.70*	0.05	−0.39*	0.38*
Emerging Markets	14.2%	0.47	0.01%	0.57*	0.14*	0.27*	0.10
Equity Market Neutral	3.3%	0.25	0.25%*	0.06*	0.08*	0.07*	0.02
Event Driven	5.9%	0.61	0.21%*	0.24*	0.16*	0.15*	0.07
Fixed Income Arbitrage	4.4%	0.22	0.11%	0.08*	0.11*	0.05*	0.35*
Global Macro	5.2%	0.16	0.10%	0.09*	0.08*	0.02	0.38*
Long/Short Equity Hedge	9.0%	0.72	0.20%	0.41*	0.09*	0.31*	0.07
Managed Futures	9.4%	0.05	0.17%	−0.03	0.02	0.05	0.58*
Multi-Strategy	5.2%	0.42	0.20%*	0.18*	0.08*	0.11*	0.14
Funds of Funds	6.0%	0.45	−0.03%	0.21*	0.12*	0.13*	0.19*
All Single Manager Funds	6.3%	0.64	0.14%	0.27*	0.09*	0.18*	0.17*
Corr. w/ Equity Factor	NA	NA	NA	1.00	0.04	0.08	−0.01

The exposures for the ten main hedge fund categories, funds of funds, and all single manager funds found in the Lipper database are based on a multivariate regression with a constant term. Regression outputs that are significant with 95% confidence are indicated by '*' and shown in colour. Monthly correlations between hedge fund returns and all four factors are presented. This analysis spans January 1996–December 2014.

Table 16.9 Out-of-sample analysis for the period 1998–2014.

Out-of-sample R^2	Fung and Hsieh's Seven Factor Model	Investable Four-Factor Model
Convertible Arbitrage	0.49	0.31
Dedicated Short Bias	0.57	0.66
Emerging Markets	0.36	0.45
Equity Market Neutral	−0.06	0.14
Event Driven	0.52	0.56
Fixed Income Arbitrage	0.14	0.13
Global Macro	−0.39	−0.20
Long/Short Equity Hedge	0.62	0.71
Managed Futures	−0.13	−0.22
Multi-Strategy	0.28	0.44
Funds of Funds	0.26	0.33
All Single Manager Funds	0.54	0.62

Comparison between the four-factor investable model and the seven-factor Fung and Hsieh (2001) model. For each category, the better-performing model is marked in blue.

their exposure to stocks and the credit spread, on average, they stopped holding long small-cap/short large-cap relative-value positions. Given these funds' historical preference for small-cap stocks, this change may reflect a

Table 16.10 Conditional risk-adjusted exposures of average hedge fund category returns to the seven Fung and Hsieh (2001) factors.

Annualized Factor Volatility	Annualized Category Volatility	R^2	Monthly Alpha	Bond Trend Following Factor	Currency Trend Following Factor	Commodity Trend Following Factor	Equity Market Factor	Size Spread Factor	Bond Market Factor	Credit Spread Factor
	NA	NA	NA	52.7%	67.6%	54.3%	15.3%	8.6%	90.1%	95.3%
Convertible Arbitrage	9.5%	0.70	0.132%	-0.013	-0.004	-0.021	0.150*	-0.031	-0.021*	-0.069*
Dedicated Short Bias	9.9%	0.59	0.209%	-0.004	0.009	-0.009	-0.347*	-0.281*	-0.012	0.009
Emerging Markets	11.6%	0.67	-0.069%	-0.030	0.017	-0.017	0.426*	-0.070	-0.011	-0.046*
Equity Market Neutral	3.5%	0.56	0.154%*	-0.008	-0.003	-0.005	0.094*	-0.050	0.005	-0.011*
Event Driven	6.4%	0.76	0.238%*	-0.015*	0.002	-0.018*	0.189*	0.009	0.005	-0.026*
Fixed Income Arbitrage	4.9%	0.69	0.183%*	-0.006	-0.008	-0.010	0.090*	-0.080*	-0.016*	-0.034*
Global Macro	3.7%	0.28	0.373%*	0.007	0.006	0.009	0.121*	-0.050	0.004	-0.005
Long/Short Equity Hedge	7.4%	0.77	0.140%	-0.009	0.007	-0.007	0.305*	0.068	0.004	-0.021*
Managed Futures	8.6%	0.21	0.425%	0.025	0.016	0.048*	0.148*	-0.104	0.008	0.011
Multi-Strategy	4.8%	0.60	0.146%	-0.003	-0.003	0.000	0.152*	-0.052	0.001	-0.020*
Funds of Funds	5.2%	0.54	-0.016%	-0.007	0.004	-0.001	0.166*	-0.053	0.002	-0.019*
All Single Manager Funds	5.8%	0.70	0.179%	-0.005	0.005	-0.001	0.225*	-0.019	0.000	-0.022*
Corr. w/ Equity Factor	NA	NA	NA	-0.36	-0.31	-0.23	1.00	0.40	0.29	-0.55

The exposures for the ten main hedge fund categories, funds of funds, and all single manager funds found in the Lipper database are based on a multivariate regression with a constant term. Regression outputs that are significant with 95% confidence are indicated by '*' and shown in colour. Monthly correlations between hedge fund returns and all seven factors are presented. This analysis spans January 2006–December 2014.

significant change within the industry, and could be a direction for further research. This result is supported by Table 16.11 where, in the context of the four-factor investable model, the exposure of hedge funds to the size-spread factor again is seen to have dwindled to insignificance or become negative.

16.5.3 Limitations of Hedge Fund Factor Models

As useful as linear factor models are for capturing the risks and rewards of hedge fund returns, these models have their limitations and there are reasons to be cautious in their use:

1. **Correlation versus causation.** The fact that a combination of well-understood factors may have similar patterns of gains and losses to a given hedge fund does not necessarily mean that the hedge fund's strategy is based on those factors. Correlation need not imply causation, but could be the result of chance, overfitting, or some common latent factor.
2. **Approximate fit.** A factor model usually explains only part of hedge fund returns, and even that part is typically overfit because of a mismatch between the explanatory factors and the true contents of the hedge fund portfolio.
3. **Nonstationarity.** Even if a factor model accurately explains a fund's returns, the risks associated with every hedge fund change over time, albeit often slowly. A factor model rarely predicts the future as well as it explains the past.
4. **Noninvestability.** In general, a researcher cannot consider the returns of every combination of well-understood factors to be an alternative to investing in the indicated hedge fund, as the factors may not be investable. A combination of factors might not be investable for many reasons. For example, one cannot invest $1 billion in the Case–Shiller Atlanta housing index, even though using the index in a factor model might provide insight into the intrinsic properties of the hedge fund's portfolio. Even simple factors like stock market indexes are not entirely investable (although they are very nearly so) because accessing them incurs commissions, management fees, and/or tracking error.

Several of these weaknesses are manifest in the following example, which involves two categories of hedge funds that focus on relative value bets, often using illiquid fixed income instruments: the fixed income arbitrage and convertible arbitrage categories. With a twelve-month window, we use a

Table 16.11 Factor analysis based on the four-factor investable model over the period from January 2006 to December 2014.

Annualized Factor Volatility	Annualized Category Volatility	R^2	Monthly Alpha	Equity Market Factor	Lagged Equity Market Factor	Size Spread Factor	Bond Market Factor
	NA	NA	NA	15.3%	11.8%	8.6%	3.2%
Convertible Arbitrage	9.5%	0.43	-0.36%	0.35*	0.16*	0.04	0.62*
Dedicated Short Bias	9.9%	0.57	0.17%	-0.40*	-0.02	-0.29*	0.28
Emerging Markets	11.6%	0.60	-0.40%	0.56*	0.16*	-0.02	0.38
Equity Market Neutral	3.5%	0.52	0.08%	0.15*	0.09*	-0.03	-0.07
Event Driven	6.4%	0.67	0.04%	0.29*	0.17*	0.05	0.00
Fixed Income Arbitrage	4.9%	0.45	-0.11%	0.18*	0.11*	-0.04	0.43*
Global Macro	3.7%	0.22	0.36%*	0.12*	-0.01	-0.05	-0.03
Long/Short Equity Hedge	7.4%	0.72	0.04%	0.38*	0.07*	0.09	-0.05
Managed Futures	8.6%	0.02	0.47%	0.04	-0.01	-0.15	-0.11
Multi-Strategy	4.8%	0.55	-0.01%	0.21*	0.12*	-0.03	0.06
Funds of Funds	5.2%	0.52	-0.16%	0.22*	0.12*	-0.03	0.02
All Single Manager Funds	5.8%	0.65	0.02%	0.29*	0.09*	0.00	0.08
Corr. w/ Equity Factor	NA	NA	NA	1.00	0.11	0.40	0.06

univariate factor model to estimate the exposure of each category to the S&P 500 index (see Fig. 16.4). At first this is low, as one would expect in strategies like these. But, in the fall of 2008, the estimated sensitivity of these funds' returns to those of the S&P 500 spikes dramatically. A naive interpretation of the results might be that the average fund manager in both of these categories decided to buy a large quantity of equities. However, it seems unlikely that so many managers of low-volatility relative-value strategies would suddenly boost risk and take directional bets. A more plausible alternative is that, although the assets in the funds' portfolios usually exhibit a relatively placid return profile, during the financial crisis, their prices swung sharply as plunging equity prices forced synchronous fire sales of illiquid assets (Khandani and Lo, 2007). This type of synchronized behaviour seems to be a more plausible driver of the covariation reported in Fig. 16.4.

The most common approach to addressing nonlinearities in hedge fund returns is to use factors that exhibit similar kinds of nonlinearities. For example, Fung and Hsieh (2001) create 'style factors' that embed option-like characteristics of hedge funds. Similarly, Agarwal and Naik (2004) propose option-based risk factors consisting of highly liquid at-the-money and out-of-the-money call and put options for analysing the dynamic risk exposures of hedge funds. Agarwal and Naik (2004) suggest using piecewise linear

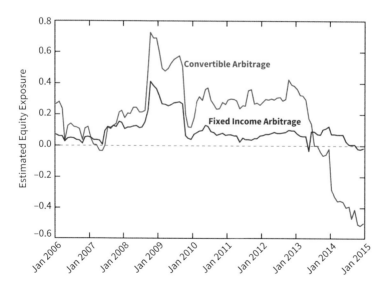

Fig. 16.4 Time-varying exposures to the S&P 500 for convertible arbitrage and fixed income arbitrage styles from January 2006 to December 2014. Trailing twelve-month S&P 500 betas from a univariate factor model are graphed.

models to study the market risk for hedge fund returns. Fung and Hsieh (1997, 2001, 2004) introduce nonlinearity in factor returns by dividing the monthly returns of each asset class (excluding cash) into five 'states' to capture the trading dynamics of hedge fund styles. Billio, Getmansky, and Pelizzon (2012) propose a regime-switching beta model to measure the dynamic risk exposures of hedge funds to various risk factors during different market volatility conditions. Bondarenko (2004) and Buraschi, Kosowski, and Trojani (2014) introduce and analyse variance and correlation risk factors for hedge funds. Roncalli and Weisang (2010) apply advanced Bayesian filter algorithms known as particle filters to capture the nonlinearities documented in hedge fund returns (see Section 16.5.6 for a more detailed discussion in the context of hedge fund beta replication). Patton and Ramadorai (2013) introduce a new econometric methodology to capture nonlinearities and time-series variation in hedge fund exposures to risk factors using high-frequency data, and find that these exposures vary significantly across months. Diez De Los Rios and Garcia (2011) show that nonlinearities are important for some strategies but not for the entire hedge fund industry. Cai and Liang (2012a,b) use rolling-window ordinary least squares and Kalman filtering/smoothing to study nonlinearities in hedge fund returns.

16.5.4 Operational Risks

Owing to the complexities of proprietary trading, lack of transparency, and lack of regulatory oversight, hedge funds are especially exposed to operational risk, defined by the Basel Committee on Banking Supervision as 'the risk of loss resulting from inadequate or failed internal processes, people and systems, or from external events'. Kundro and Feffer (2004) were perhaps the first to call attention to this important source of risk, noting that half of all hedge fund failures can be attributed to operational risk alone. They observe that 'the most common operational issue related to hedge fund losses have been misrepresentation of fund investments, misappropriation of investor funds, unauthorized trading, and inadequate resources' (Kundro and Feffer, 2004, p. 5). They report that only 6% of their sample involved inadequate resources, whereas 41% involved misrepresentation of investments, 30% involved misappropriation of funds, and 14% involved unauthorized trading.

Since then, a number of studies have focused on operational risk. For example, Gupta and Kazemi (2007) study the failure of the $9 billion hedge fund Amaranth Advisors, and conclude that operational issues were a key factor in the fund's demise. In a series of publications, Brown et al. (2008,

2009, 2012) develop several quantitative models for measuring operational risk in managed funds. Using a complete and unique SEC Form ADV filing data set, they find that operational risk (represented by past legal or regulatory problems) is significantly related to the usage of leverage, fund ownership structure, and conflict-of-interest issues. Funds with higher operational risk tend to have relatively low leverage because of strict scrutiny from lenders, more concentrated ownership, and severe conflict-of-interest problems. Through a canonical correlation analysis, they map the ADV information to regular fund information such as assets, returns, volatility, fees, leverage, and share restrictions, which, in turn, they use to construct an omega-score model to predict future fund performance and attrition. Consistent with the Basel definition, they find that the higher the omega score, the lower the future performance is, and the higher the fund attrition is.

Brown et al. (2012) use more fine-grained information on the individual funds to quantify operational risk. Based on 444 proprietary due diligence reports, they are able to show that operational risk is directly related to inadequate or failed internal processes, represented by the internal pricing of the portfolio, a lack of reliability of reputable auditors and institutional quality signatures, and frequent misrepresentation of past problems or fund characteristics. The quantitative model based on these variables sharply predicts future fund performance and fund disappearance. However, the risk-flow analysis indicates that investors either ignore the operational risk issues or are ignorant of them, which further validates the importance of mandatory disclosure on fund information and information verification.

They also find that hedge funds that have experienced legal problems are less likely to use independent pricing agents and are more likely to have switched pricing agents within the past year, allowing these hedge funds greater pricing discretion. Cassar and Gerakos (2011) highlight this discretion as a potential concern, showing that hedge funds with less verifiable pricing sources and greater pricing discretion for their managers report smoother returns, which results in misleading volatility and Sharpe ratio estimates (see Section 16.4.1). Bollen and Pool (2012) link the incidence of SEC lawsuits to suspicious patterns in reported returns. They find that the discontinuity in a fund's return distribution (some funds pushing returns above zero) is a reliable predictor of subsequent charges of misreporting brought by the SEC.

Ozik and Sadka (2015) argue that hedge funds offer informational advantages to managers over their clients through fund flows. They demonstrate that fund flows predict returns and find evidence that managers front-run their clients using this information.

On a more positive note, Brown, Fraser, and Liang (2008) argue that due diligence is an important source of alpha for diversified hedge fund portfolios. Effective due diligence can eliminate or reduce problematic funds and avoid future losses resulting from operational risk. However, due diligence is an expensive process; there is a strong competitive advantage to those sufficiently large funds of funds that are able to absorb this fixed and necessary cost. In contrast to hedge funds, the authors find significant economies of scale for funds of funds—the larger the fund of funds, the better its performance.

16.5.5 Risk Management

The discussions in previous sections highlight the fact that hedge funds have more complex and dynamic risk exposures than traditional investments. Therefore, proper risk management protocols are essential from both the investor and the managerial perspectives. The old adage 'a good way to make money is not to lose it in the first place' is particularly relevant for hedge funds, given the active bets they make and the critical role that risk management plays in generating their returns. Moreover, with reliable estimates of risk exposures from a linear factor model, it is possible for investors to hedge certain risks that they wish to reduce, and accentuate other risks that they are especially keen to take on.

This is the motivation for Healy and Lo's (2009) proposal for hedge fund investors to use an overlay strategy consisting of futures contracts on major asset-class indexes such as stocks, bonds, interest rates, currencies, and commodities to manage actively the factor exposures of their hedge fund investments.[23] By using these 'beta blockers' in concert with properly estimated linear factor models, Healy and Lo (2009) argue that investors can reduce or eliminate exposures that they do not wish to have, while increasing exposures they believe are more rewarding, and this can be accomplished in a cost-effective manner thanks to the liquidity and capital efficiency of futures contracts and markets. Black (2006) finds that adding a small VIX position to an investment portfolio significantly reduces the portfolio volatility due to the negative correlation of VIX to the S&P 500 and most hedge fund styles. Even in cases where certain risks simply cannot be managed due to the nature of the investment (e.g. illiquidity risk in a real estate portfolio), a clear understanding of the risks will at least allow those exposed to them to prepare accordingly.

---

[23] Please see footnote 16 for a conflict disclosure with respect to the article on which this chapter is based.

Beyond these overlay strategies, risk management is, of course, a well-developed discipline with a broad and deep literature that goes well beyond hedge funds, and is impossible to summarize in a single chapter, much less a section. However, Lo (2002b) focuses on at least three unique aspects of hedge fund returns with implications for risk management that are worth reviewing here. The first is the nonlinear nature of hedge fund risk exposures, a feature that is not captured by linear factor models unless specific accommodations are made in defining the factors. A case in point is the relationship between the trend-following strategies of CTAs and the S&P 500 index. A regression of the monthly returns of the Credit Suisse/Tremont Managed Futures Index on those of the S&P 500 Total Return Index from January 1994 to December 2014 yields the following estimated equation (standard errors in parentheses):

$$R_{MF,t} = \underset{(0.0021)}{0.0056} - \underset{(0.0486)}{0.0546}\ R_{SP500,t} + \epsilon_t,\ R^2 = 0.0050 \qquad (16.9)$$

which shows that the Managed Futures Index has a positive and statistically significant alpha of 0.56% per month or 6.8% per year, and a slightly negative and insignificant beta of -0.0546 with respect to the S&P 500. Decomposing the S&P 500 return into its positive and negative components, $R^+_{SP500,t}$ and $R^-_{SP500,t}$, we have:

$$R^+_{SP500,t} = \begin{cases} R_{SP500,t} & \text{if } R_{SP500,t} > 0 \\ 0 & \text{otherwise} \end{cases}, \qquad (16.10a)$$

$$R^-_{SP500,t} = \begin{cases} R_{SP500,t} & \text{if } R_{SP500,t} \leq 0 \\ 0 & \text{otherwise} \end{cases}, \qquad (16.10b)$$

$$R_{SP500,t} = R^+_{SP500,t} + R^-_{SP500,t}. \qquad (16.10c)$$

A regression of the returns of the Managed Futures Index on these two components yields the estimate:

$$R_{MF,t} = \underset{(0.0035)}{-0.0012} + \underset{(0.0937)}{0.1454}\ R^+_{SP500,t} - \underset{(0.0891)}{0.2411}\ R^-_{SP500,t}$$
$$+ \epsilon_t,\ R^2 = 0.0291, \qquad (16.11)$$

which tells a very different story about the dynamics of the Managed Futures Index. The estimated alpha is now insignificant and negative, and the positive and negative betas are quite different, implying very different behaviour in a bull versus bear market. The beta coefficient for the positive S&P 500 returns is +0.1454 and statistically indistinguishable from 0, whereas the beta coefficient for the negative S&P 500 returns is −0.2411 and statistically significant at the 5% level. This asymmetry implies that when the stock market does well, the Managed Futures Index bears little relationship to stocks, but when the stock market does poorly, the Managed Futures Index tends to do well, and there is little excess performance beyond these two components. In the context of the Merton (1981) timing model, this result seems to suggest that the Managed Futures Index resembles a put-plus-cash strategy. If the risk-free rate is zero, then the insignificant intercept implies that the manager can deliver this put at zero cost to investors.

Experienced investors in managed futures funds are familiar with this countercyclical pattern of trend followers, which Kaminski (2011) describes as 'crisis alpha'. However, during extended periods of positive equity-market performance, trend followers may underperform relative to their long-term average. For example, in 2012 the compound annual return of the S&P 500 was 16.0%, whereas the return of the Managed Futures Index was −2.9%. These periods of underperformance can cause inexperienced investors to panic and liquidate, largely eliminating the diversification benefits of such countercyclical investments.

The second unique aspect of hedge fund returns is the risk of rare events (i.e. tail risk). A classic example is liquidity provision among strategies that sell more liquid assets and buy less liquid assets of similar payoffs, a common feature of fixed-income arbitrage funds. Such strategies generate positive cash flows most of the time, since liquid assets are priced higher than their less liquid counterparts (e.g. on-the-run versus off-the-run US Treasury securities with identical coupons, call provisions, and other terms). During normal market conditions, these strategies yield very steady returns, implying high Sharpe ratios, but during periods of market distress, they can suffer tremendous losses in the face of flights to safety. This pattern of mostly positive small returns punctuated by the occasional large loss characterizes a number of hedge fund strategies besides fixed-income arbitrage, including equity market neutral strategies, convertible bond arbitrage, high-frequency trading, and catastrophe reinsurance.

Seasoned hedge fund investors are fully aware of this pattern, and are able to withstand periodic losses so as to capture the full benefits of these strategies. However, less experienced investors may not be as well prepared, and if they respond by reducing or liquidating their investments during periods of market distress, they will compound their losses and fail to profit from the risk premia associated with tail risk exposures.

However, perhaps the biggest concern with respect to such strategies is that standard risk measures will not fully reflect their risks. Lo (2002b) provides a simple illustration of a hypothetical hedge fund strategy consisting of selling out-of-the-money put options on the S&P 500 index, which generates a very attractive risk–reward profile, as long as the stock market does not decline by more than the amount that the put option is out of the money. Sharpe ratios do not reflect tail risk unless a significant loss has occurred within a given fund's track record, and when it has, the Sharpe ratio is likely to be misleadingly conservative.

This leads to the third unique aspect of hedge fund returns, which is their tendency to become highly correlated during times of market distress. To develop an intuition for this aspect of hedge fund returns, consider the heat map of the empirical distribution of trailing twelve-month returns of all single-manager hedge funds in the Lipper database from 1997 to 2014 in Fig. 16.5. The downward plume of density during the financial crisis of 2008 is in stark contrast to the relatively consistent returns of the previous years. Red and yellow indicate higher density, while turquoise and blue indicate lower density. For example, the deep red area during the mid-2000s reflects tightly clustered performance among hedge funds, and the subsequent downward plume shows the negative skewness in hedge fund returns during the crisis

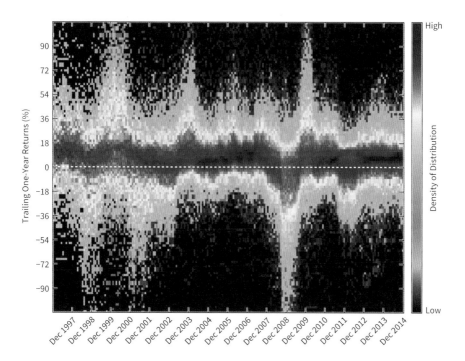

Fig. 16.5 Empirical distribution of the trailing twelve-month returns of single-manager hedge funds from 1997 to 2014, where red and yellow indicate higher density, and turquoise and blue indicate lower density.

period. This is followed by another plume, this time upward, that reflects positive skewness in the cross-sectional distribution of the post-crisis hedge fund returns, when some funds profited handsomely as fears abated.

A simple way to capture this phenomenon is offered by Lo's (2002b) discrete-time model of 'phase-locking' behaviour, in which hedge fund i's returns are given by the following factor model:

$$R_{it} = \alpha_i + \beta_i \Lambda_t + I_t Z_t + \epsilon_{it}, \tag{16.12}$$

where Λ_t, I_t, Z_t, and ϵ_{it} are mutually IID with the following moments:

$$
\begin{aligned}
\mathbb{E}[\Lambda_t] &= \mu_\lambda, & \mathrm{Var}[\Lambda_t] &= \sigma_\lambda^2, \\
\mathbb{E}[Z_t] &= 0, & \mathrm{Var}[Z_t] &= \sigma_z^2, \\
\mathbb{E}[\epsilon_{it}] &= 0, & \mathrm{Var}[\epsilon_{it}] &= \sigma_{\epsilon_i}^2,
\end{aligned}
\tag{16.13}
$$

and the phase-locking event indicator, I_t, is defined as:

$$
I_t = \begin{cases} 1 & \text{with probability } p \\ 0 & \text{with probability } p_0 = 1 - p \end{cases}. \tag{16.14}
$$

According to Equation (16.12), expected returns are driven by three components: the fund's alpha, α_i, a 'market' component, Λ_t, to which each fund has its own individual sensitivity, β_i, and a phase-locking component that is identical across all funds at all times, taking only one of two possible values, either 0 (with probability p) or Z_t (with probability $1-p$).

If we assume that p is small, say 0.001, then, most of the time, the expected returns of fund i will be determined by $\alpha_i + \beta_i \Lambda_t$, but, every once in a while, an additional term Z_t appears. If the volatility, σ_z, of Z_t is much larger than the volatilities of the market factor, Λ_t, and the idiosyncratic risk, ϵ_{it}, then the common factor Z_t will dominate the expected returns of all stocks when $I_t = 1$ (i.e. phase-locking behaviour is present).

Now consider the *conditional* correlation coefficient of two funds, i and j, defined as the ratio of the conditional covariance divided by the square root of the product of the conditional variances, conditioned on $I_t = 0$:

$$
\mathrm{Corr}[R_{it}, R_{jt} \mid I_t = 0] = \frac{\beta_i \beta_j \sigma_\lambda^2}{\sqrt{\beta_i^2 \sigma_\lambda^2 + \sigma_{\epsilon_i}^2}\sqrt{\beta_j^2 \sigma_\lambda^2 + \sigma_{\epsilon_j}^2}} \approx 0, \quad \text{for } \beta_i \approx \beta_j \approx 0,
$$

$$\tag{16.15}$$

where we have assumed that $\beta_i \approx \beta_j \approx 0$ to capture the market neutral characteristic that many hedge fund investors desire. The conditional correlation, conditioned on $I_t = 1$, will be:

$$\text{Corr}\left[R_{it}, R_{jt} \mid I_t = 1\right] = \frac{\beta_i \beta_j \sigma_\lambda^2 + \sigma_z^2}{\sqrt{\beta_i^2 \sigma_\lambda^2 + \sigma_z^2 + \sigma_{\varepsilon_i}^2}\sqrt{\beta_j^2 \sigma_\lambda^2 + \sigma_z^2 + \sigma_{\varepsilon_j}^2}} \qquad (16.16)$$

$$\approx \frac{1}{\sqrt{1 + \sigma_{\varepsilon_i}^2/\sigma_z^2}\sqrt{1 + \sigma_{\varepsilon_j}^2/\sigma_z^2}}, \quad \text{for } \beta_i \approx \beta_j \approx 0. \qquad (16.17)$$

If σ_z^2 is large relative to $\sigma_{\varepsilon_i}^2$ and $\sigma_{\varepsilon_j}^2$ (i.e. if the variability of the market-distress component dominates the variability of the residuals of both funds, a plausible condition that follows from the very definition of market distress), then Equation (16.17) will be approximately equal to 1! When phase-locking occurs, the correlation between funds i and j, which is close to 0 during normal times, can become arbitrarily close to 1.

But the most dangerous feature of Equation (16.12) is the fact that it implies a very small value for the *unconditional* correlation, which is the quantity most readily estimated and the one most commonly used in risk reports, VaR calculations, and portfolio decisions. To see why, recall that the unconditional correlation coefficient is simply the unconditional covariance divided by the product of the square roots of the unconditional variances. Hence, the unconditional correlation coefficient under Equation (16.12) is given by:

$$\text{Corr}\left[R_{it}, R_{jt}\right] = \frac{\beta_i \beta_j \sigma_\lambda^2 + p\sigma_z^2}{\sqrt{\beta_i^2 \sigma_\lambda^2 + p\sigma_z^2 + \sigma_{\varepsilon_i}^2}\sqrt{\beta_j^2 \sigma_\lambda^2 + p\sigma_z^2 + \sigma_{\varepsilon_j}^2}} \qquad (16.18)$$

$$\approx \frac{p}{\sqrt{p + \sigma_{\varepsilon_i}^2/\sigma_z^2}\sqrt{p + \sigma_{\varepsilon_j}^2/\sigma_z^2}}, \quad \text{for } \beta_i \approx \beta_j \approx 0. \qquad (16.19)$$

If we let $p = 0.001$, and assume that the variability of the phase-locking component is ten times the variability of the residuals, ε_i and ε_j, this implies an unconditional correlation of

$$\text{Corr}\left[R_{it}, R_{jt}\right] \approx \frac{p}{\sqrt{p + 0.1}\sqrt{p + 0.1}} = 0.001/.101 = 0.0099,$$

or less than 1%. As the variance, σ_z^2, of the phase-locking component increases, the unconditional correlation in Equation (16.19) also increases, so that eventually the existence of Z_t will have an impact. However, to achieve an unconditional correlation coefficient of, say, 10%, σ_z^2 would have to be about 100 times larger than σ_ε^2. Without the benefit of an explicit risk model such as Equation (16.12), it is virtually impossible to detect the existence of a phase-locking component from standard correlation coefficients.

These considerations suggest that risk management for hedge funds cannot be approached in the same manner as for traditional investments. Measuring and managing the risk exposures of hedge funds require not only more sophisticated risk analytics, but also a deeper understanding of the nature of the strategies being managed.

16.5.6 Hedge Fund Beta Replication

Our discussion of factor modelling suggests that a portion of hedge fund returns may be attributable to simple investments that do not require the high fees or expensive trading infrastructure of hedge funds. The insights of a handful of researchers have encouraged asset managers to develop strategies that generate the 'simple' portion of fund returns while charging low fees and providing greater transparency and liquidity. Today, hundreds of billions of dollars are managed in these strategies. In the interest of full disclosure, two of the authors of the original article by Getmansky, Lee, and Lo (2015) on which this chapter is based—P. Lee and A. Lo—were affiliated with an asset-management company offering a hedge fund beta replication mutual fund at the time the article was written.[24] While every effort was undertaken to avoid bias, readers should be aware of this potential conflict of interest, and interpret the discussion in this section accordingly.

Current replication methods fall into three categories: linear factor model replication, the replication of strategies, and the replication of payoff functions or return distributions. In the linear factor model approach, a linear factor model with investable factors is used to construct a portfolio with the same betas and corresponding risk premia of the aggregate hedge fund industry or sector being replicated. Successful linear factor model replication depends on the explanatory power of the factors and the timeliness of the beta estimates. In the strategy replication approach, a manager employs a rules-based strategy that aims to make the same sort of trades that a hedge fund would make and thereby generate similar returns. One challenge faced by this approach is that a fund that trades in a manner similar to a hedge fund

---

[24] Lo is no longer affiliated with that company or product.

may effectively become a hedge fund itself, not a replicator at all. Finally, the distributional approach aims to replicate the characteristics of the probability distribution of hedge fund returns. The challenge with this approach is that matching payoff distributions can sometimes be more complex and costly than implementing the hedge fund strategy itself.

Given the many linear factor models that have been estimated with hedge fund returns (see Section 16.5.2), a natural starting point for hedge fund beta replication is to use these models to construct portfolios with alternative beta exposures. This is the approach proposed by Hasanhodzic and Lo (2006, 2007), who constructed 'linear clones' of individual hedge funds in the Lipper hedge fund database using six factors: the US Dollar Index return; the return on the Lehman Corporate AA intermediate Bond Index; the spread between the Lehman BAA Corporate Bond Index and the Lehman Treasury Index; the S&P 500 total returns; the Goldman Sachs Commodity Index total return; and the first-difference of the end-of-month value of the CBOE Volatility Index.

Based on these findings, they proposed using liquid futures contracts to construct replication portfolios. This proposal was subsequently implemented by the investment advisory firm AlphaSimplex Group, LLC, in 2008, using just over two dozen futures contracts; the resulting strategy was one of the first, and eventually one of the largest, hedge fund beta replication mutual funds (see Lee and Lo (2014) for further discussion). However, Goldman Sachs was the first to market with a hedge fund beta replication mutual fund designed to track the Goldman Sachs Absolute Return Tracker Index. Other large banks and some asset managers have followed suit, with their own versions of hedge fund beta replication indexes or funds, including Barclays, Credit Suisse, Deutsche Bank, Index IQ, Merrill Lynch, and Société Générale.

Amenc et al. (2010) extend Hasanhodzic and Lo (2007) by assessing the out-of-sample performance of various nonlinear and conditional hedge fund replication models. They find that going beyond the linear case does not necessarily enhance the replication power. However, the authors find that selecting factors on the basis of an economic analysis allows for a substantial improvement of the out-of-sample replication quality, whatever the underlying form of the factor model. Overall, the authors confirm the findings in Hasanhodzic and Lo (2007) that the performance of replicating strategies is systematically inferior to that of the actual hedge funds, but still attractive enough to warrant consideration by investors seeking additional sources of risk premia.

With respect to the replication of hedge fund payoff distributions, Kat and Palaro (2005, 2006a,b) argue that sophisticated dynamic trading strategies involving liquid futures contracts can replicate many of the statistical properties of hedge fund returns. The authors propose several models for the replication of return distribution. More generally, Bertsimas, Kogan, and Lo (2001) show that securities with very general payoff functions (like hedge funds or complex derivatives) can be synthetically replicated to an arbitrary degree of accuracy by dynamic trading strategies—called 'epsilon-arbitrage' strategies—involving more liquid instruments. Although these algorithmic strategies can replicate virtually any payoff distribution, their complexity makes this form of replication less attractive to investors that do not have the necessary trading and risk-management infrastructure.

A less complex approach to hedge fund beta replication is to implement 'plain vanilla' versions of certain hedge fund strategies, specifically those that can be fully described by mechanical trading rules. Examples include the currency carry-trade strategy, trend-following managed futures, risk arbitrage, and a 130/30 long/short equity strategy.[25] Investment products based on these algorithms acknowledge that no managerial alpha is contained in their funds; instead, they seek to provide the corresponding risk premia associated with these strategies at a lower cost and with greater liquidity than their hedge fund counterparts.

Kazemi, Tu, and Li (2008) develop a replication methodology suited for hedge fund performance evaluation. This methodology develops two replicating portfolios such that the distribution properties of the target are matched. The first portfolio delivers the statistical properties at the lowest possible cost, while the other is more expensive, but delivers the same properties as the target. Azlen (2011) combines a core holding of single managers and a secondary holding of a blend of synthetic replication products to reduce the cost and increase liquidity.

Using Bayesian filters, Roncalli and Weisang (2010) propose solutions for a tracking problem in hedge fund replication. They find that hedge fund trackers have smaller Sharpe ratios than their respective indexes, even though they generally exhibit lower volatilities. The trackers also exhibit a smaller maximum drawdown and kurtosis of the returns. Many illiquid strategies (e.g. distressed securities), strategies with small betas (e.g. relative value), and strategies based on stock picking (e.g. merger arbitrage and equity market neutral) have a low correlation with their respective trackers, and are thus hard to replicate. Interestingly, for funds of funds the authors

---

[25] A number of carry-trade and trend-following managed futures mutual funds and ETFs already exist. See Mitchell and Pulvino (2001) for a mechanical risk-arbitrage strategy, and Lo and Patel (2008) and Hasanhodzic, Lo, and Patel (2009) for a mechanical 130/30 long/short equity strategy.

find that a replicating portfolio does not have a high correlation with its respective index but still exhibits similar performance.

Finally, Wallerstein, Tuchschmid, and Zaker (2009) survey twenty-one replication funds and indexes from April 2008 to May 2009. They find that these replication products are sold at a far lower fee level than hedge funds, and that many of them seem to live up to their promise of low correlation with market indexes. All of them underperformed during the financial crisis of 2008, but so did hedge funds over this period. As a result, the authors conclude that, benchmarked against hedge fund indexes, many replication products perform well.

16.6 The Financial Crisis

No review of the hedge fund literature would be complete without some discussion of the impact of the financial crisis of 2008 on the hedge fund industry, as well as the industry's role in the crisis, issues that are both nuanced and important from all stakeholders' perspectives. If hedge funds are the 'tip of the spear' in exploiting profitable opportunities during good times, they are also the 'canary in the coal mine' that suffers first during bad times. We provide an in-depth case study in the next chapter about how one specific hedge-fund sector—equity market neutral funds—was among the first canaries to be hit by the incipient financial crisis (in 2007), but in this section we focus more generally on the entire industry.

Figure 16.5 shows that the 2008 financial crisis had an unprecedented effect on the industry. While some funds were able to profit handsomely from these adverse market conditions, about 70% of the funds in our sample experienced negative returns in 2008. Losses suffered by funds invested in illiquid assets such as credit were particularly disproportionate to the typical volatility levels of those funds. As the crisis began, reports of '10-sigma' or '20-sigma' events were commonplace, until a sort of ennui set in, and it became understood that models designed to characterize the behaviour of asset prices during normal market conditions had little relevance in a crisis so extreme that the need to survive trumped many financial institutions' normal profit-seeking behaviours.

In the face of heavy losses and investor redemptions, a record number of funds shut down, and, for the first time in the industry's modern history, the number of funds began to decline (see Table 16.3). Moreover, these losses led many investors to re-evaluate the significance of supposedly well-understood concepts such as diversification and absolute return strategies. Hedge fund managers rushing to exit from crowded trades found that once diversified positions were now highly correlated, and many suffered acute losses. However, Sias, Turtle, and Zykaj (2016) find that hedge fund trades are not very crowded, subject to the limitations of 13F data. Managers whose portfolios survived the mayhem were often more agile, more liquid, more tactical, and more contrarian (e.g., those in managed futures, global macro, dedicated short bias funds, and funds with less autocorrelated returns).

Although many hedge funds were unsuspecting victims of the financial crisis of 2008, several studies have considered the possibility that hedge funds played a significant role in causing the crisis. Ever since the demise of LTCM in 1998, hedge funds have become inextricably linked to systemic risk, although the links are still not yet well defined. From a survey of more than 170 hedge funds encompassing over $1.1 trillion in assets as of early 2010, the Financial Crisis Inquiry Commission found that hedge funds were one of the largest purchasers of the riskiest equity tranches of collateralized debt obligation (CDO) securities. More than half of the equity tranches were purchased by hedge funds that simultaneously shorted other tranches, thus engaging in a correlation trade. However, many hedge funds also used credit default swaps (CDSs) to take offsetting positions in different tranches of the same CDO security. Therefore, hedge funds would profit if the CDOs performed but stood to earn even more if the entire market crashed (Financial Crisis Inquiry Commission, 2011). By being positioned to benefit from financial instability, hedge funds had an incentive to increase systemic risk.

The crisis underscored the need for regulators to obtain greater transparency from hedge funds to gauge the potential systemic risks posed by certain strategies such as the correlation trade, keep track of crowded trades (which could be vulnerable to runs, such as the August 2007 Quant Meltdown, or the more opaque runs on mortgage-linked products), evaluate liquidity risks, and the like. In 2012, the SEC began collecting confidential hedge fund data via Form PF. Regulators now have access to limited aggregate results about hedge fund positions, exposures, leverage, the use of derivatives, and different types of risks.

Moreover, because hedge funds do lie outside the purview of banking supervision, despite the fact that they now engage in many of the same businesses as banks, they could pose unique risks to financial stability that are more difficult to measure and manage in the current regulatory framework. Although several industry leaders have argued that the hedge fund industry is simply not large enough to have an impact on financial stability, the experience of LTCM—a hedge fund with only $4.7 billion in assets immediately prior to August 1998—seems to suggest otherwise. But even if the hedge fund industry played only a supporting role in the 2008 financial crisis, as the empirical evidence suggests, its unconstrained and dynamic investment strategies can certainly facilitate both the build up of systemic risk during periods of market exuberance and the propagation of systemic shocks during periods of market dislocation.

In fact, contributions to systemic risk may be an unavoidable consequence of the provision of market liquidity and price discovery during normal market conditions. Although often criticized as being part of the opaque 'shadow banking system', hedge funds also played a critical role in supporting the economy when the official banking system ground to a halt in 2007–2008. For example, of the eight investment funds created jointly by the private sector and the US Treasury as part of its Public–Private Investment Program (PPIP) to purchase 'troubled assets' (i.e. mortgage-backed securities) from banks to allow them to start lending again, two were co-sponsored by hedge funds (Angelo, Gordon & Co. and Oaktree),[26] and many of the investors in all eight funds were hedge fund investors. Hedge funds and their investors are central to the financial ecosystem in providing much-needed capital, particularly during times when typical investors are fleeing to safety.

Whether it is possible to keep the benefits that hedge funds offer while eliminating the potential risks they pose is still an open question. But even if this is not possible, monitoring the hedge fund industry is essential for developing an accurate map of risk-taking activity in the economy, and may also yield early warning signs of impending financial distress. This latter objective is the focus of Section 16.6.1, which contains a summary of the literature on early indications of the financial crisis of 2008 among a subset of hedge funds. We then turn to a more systematic accounting of the hedge fund winners and losers during the crisis period in Section 16.6.2, and summarize the post-crisis performance of hedge funds in Section 16.6.3. Finally, in Section 16.6.4 we review the subset of the systemic risk literature that involves the hedge fund industry.

16.6.1 Early Warning Signs of the Crisis

Most of the public first became aware of the financial crisis during the fourth quarter of 2008 when Lehman Brothers filed for bankruptcy and the Reserve Primary Fund 'broke the buck'. However, well before 2008, early

---

[26] Incidentally, these two funds earned the highest net internal rates of return for their investors among the eight: 26.3% for the Oaktree PPIP Fund, L.P. and 24.8% for the AG GECC PPIF Master Fund, L.P. from inception to end (US Treasury, 2013).

warning signs of the crisis emerged in three distinct but interrelated sectors—US residential real estate, banking, and hedge funds—and were highlighted by several academics. In January 2005, Shiller (2005b) published excerpts from his new edition of *Irrational Exuberance* in *Money Magazine* in which he warned of an asset bubble in the US housing market. In August 2005, Rajan (2006) presented research showing that recent financial innovations had increased risk in the banking sector. Even earlier, at an October 2004 conference on systemic risk organized by the National Bureau of Economic Research, Chan et al. (2004) first presented their empirical findings of an increased probability of a systemic shock in the hedge fund industry due to significant losses among large, leveraged, hedge funds investing in illiquid securities (see also their published versions, Chan et al. (2006, 2007)).

Chan et al. (2004) based their inferences on several indirect measures, including asset-weighted return autocorrelations that pointed to greater reliance on illiquid assets (see Section 16.4); regime-switching models that pointed to lower expected returns, higher volatility, and therefore a greater use of leverage; and increasing common-factor exposures in individual hedge fund returns, implying higher conditional correlations when market indexes crash (see Section 16.5). In September 2005, *The New York Times* published a story about this research and concluded that 'The nightmare script ... would be a series of collapses of highly leveraged hedge funds that bring down the major banks or brokerage firms that lend to them' (Gimein, 2005). Such an outcome seemed absurd at the time, but the losses that brought down Bear Stearns, a company founded in 1923 with assets of $350 billion, over 13,500 employees, and record net revenues of $9.2 billion in 2006, began with their two subprime mortgage hedge funds: the Bear Stearns High-Grade Structured Credit Fund and the Bear Stearns High-Grade Structured Credit Enhanced Leveraged Fund.

With the benefit of hindsight, these three different warning signs, generated by three very different sources, were manifestations of the same forces at play in the economy. Real estate prices were being driven to unprecedented levels by tremendous inflows of assets from around the world via both the banking system and capital markets, thanks to financial innovations such as securitization and CDSs. Because hedge funds are largely unconstrained in their investment mandates and trading style, stress fractures in the financial system are more likely to show up first in the hedge fund industry. Their aggressive risk appetite and incentive to generate absolute return cause them to be first to take advantage of emerging investment opportunities, and also the first to take losses when a crisis hits. In fact, signs of credit problems were visible in the hedge fund industry as early as May 2005, when convertible arbitrage funds suffered extraordinary losses in the aftermath of the down-grading of General Motors and Ford corporate debt to non-investment-grade status by the rating agencies. The two automakers had over $450 billion of debt outstanding, all of which turned to junk bonds overnight.

These downgrades were emblematic of a broader deterioration of credit quality throughout the debt markets, wreaking havoc with highly leveraged financial institutions and many of their counterparties. Like a pandemic in the age of international air travel, the credit crisis spread quickly around the globe, occasionally erupting in unexpected venues. One of the most unex-pected venues was a little-known corner of the hedge fund industry called equity market neutral or statistical arbitrage funds. During the first four days of the second week of August 2007, these highly quantitative equity trad-ing funds all experienced significant losses at the same time, for no apparent reason, and then, on the last day of that week, they experienced dramatic reversals. The press dubbed this episode the 'Quant Meltdown of August 2007' but offered no explanation for what had happened—since hedge funds do not talk to the press. As a harbinger of the 2008 financial crisis, this event is worthy of a much more detailed exposition; hence, we devote the entirety of the next chapter to it.

16.6.2 Winners and Losers

During periods of financial distress, hedge funds have often suffered larger losses than traditional risk-assessment methods have predicted. A number of authors have investigated this curious phenomenon, and pointed to the potential impact of latent factors, with illiquidity being the most signifi-cant (see Sections 16.4 and 16.5). The prices of illiquid assets often plummet during market dislocations in response to forced liquidations that result in fire-sales, generating losses for all entities invested in illiquid assets. As can be seen in Fig. 16.6, funds with the highest autocorrelated returns, an indi-cation of illiquidity (see Section 16.4.1), underperform during periods of market stress. More directly, Billio, Getmansky, and Pelizzon (2013) esti-mate the latent factor present in hedge fund returns during the 1998 and 2008 financial crises, and find that this factor is connected to funding and asset liq-uidity. Cao et al. (2018) conclude that hedge fund trading increases market efficiency in general. However, during crises, hedge funds face leverage-induced margin calls and liquidity squeezes; hence, their trading leads to

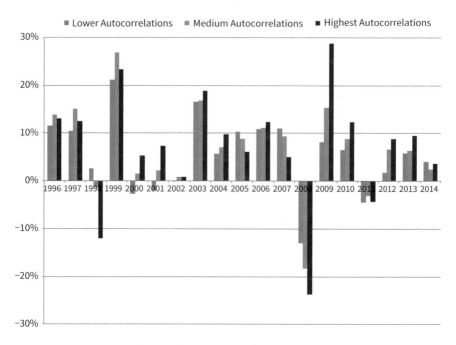

Fig. 16.6 Average hedge fund performance for individual hedge funds in three liquidity groups from the Lipper database: the most liquid (lowest autocorrelation), medium-liquid (medium autocorrelation), and the least liquid (highest autocorrelation). Returns are calculated yearly for each liquidity group from January 1996 to December 2014.

greater price deviations from fundamentals during these episodes. Therefore, the positive role of hedge funds in improving market efficiency critically depends on funding liquidity. Figure 16.6 highlights three crises: the Russian debt default and LTCM's collapse (1998), the automakers' bond downgrade (2005), and the financial crisis (2007–2008). During each of these periods of stress, highly autocorrelated funds underperformed their more liquid peers. In 'normal' years, however, illiquid funds generally appear to be the out-performers (Aragon, 2007; Sadka, 2010, 2012). In fact, the less liquid funds outperformed others in 2009, perhaps driven by a rebound in the prices of illiquid assets.

In 2008, the financial crisis was at its most intense, although equity markets continued to decline until mid-March of 2009. Although hedge funds earned positive returns in 2007 and 2009, on average, the combination of plunging equity markets and evaporating liquidity in 2008 proved toxic—and in many cases fatal—for them, leading to the industry's worst-ever annual return and the shutdown of over 2,000 hedge funds, as documented in Table 16.3. In 2008, the attrition rate was 21%, while the average hedge fund return was –18.4%, and the proportion of hedge fund managers reporting negative returns for the year was 71%. Critics of the industry have asked why these absolute-return funds failed to generate positive returns, while supporters note that an investor would have fared far better in the average hedge fund than in, for example, a stock index fund.

Lehman Brothers acted as one of the major prime brokers to the hedge fund industry prior to its bankruptcy on 15 September 2008. Aragon and Strahan (2012) study Lehman and the hedge funds that used it as a prime broker as an example of the propagation of illiquidity during the financial crisis. They document that the failure rate of Lehman's hedge fund clients doubled after the bankruptcy, relative to funds with similar performance characteristics using other brokers. The authors also show that stocks held by Lehman's hedge fund clients prior to the bankruptcy experienced unexpectedly large declines in liquidity after the bankruptcy. Ben-David, Franzoni, and Moussawi (2012) show that in Q3–Q4 of 2008, hedge funds sold about 29% of their aggregate portfolio. Redemptions and margin calls were the primary drivers of the sell-offs. In comparison, fund outflows and stock sales for mutual funds were not as severe.

The remainder of 2009 was marked by the sharp appreciation of depressed asset prices as governments flooded the markets with liquidity. In 2010, we saw a continued (albeit uneven) recovery and the development of the European sovereign debt crisis. Hedge fund attrition, although still in the double digits, decreased to 15% in 2009 and 2010. Hedge fund returns were positive for both 2009 and 2010.

Although hedge funds in most categories experienced losses during 2008, those in three categories did not (see Table 16.12). As one would expect in a declining equity market, the dedicated short bias category produced handsome returns. The managed futures category, an investment style that makes heavy use of trend-following, also performed well. Indeed, one of the primary motivations for investing in managed futures funds is their performance during and after crises, what Kaminski (2011) dubbed 'crisis alpha'. However, the global macro category, the more discretionary counterpart to managed futures that does not have as much crisis alpha, finished the year roughly flat. Table 16.13 shows that funds belonging to these three categories exhibited the lowest autocorrelation and the lowest correlation with the S&P 500 during this period, which supports the narrative that the evaporation of liquidity and the decline in the prices of equities or equity-like investments played important roles in the losses of hedge funds.

Table 16.12 Average annual returns of convertible arbitrage, dedicated short bias, emerging markets, equity market neutral, event driven, fixed income arbitrage, global macro, long/short equity hedge, managed futures, and multi-strategy funds from January 2004 to December 2014.

	Convertible Arbitrage	Dedicated Short Bias	Emerging Markets	Equity Market Neutral	Event Driven	Fixed Income Arbitrage	Global Macro	Long/Short Equity Hedge	Managed Futures	Multi-Strategy
2004	1.2%	−9.8%	16.8%	3.9%	12.3%	5.5%	2.6%	8.5%	2.5%	4.5%
2005	−1.7%	−0.2%	21.5%	5.2%	8.0%	4.3%	7.6%	10.7%	4.0%	8.1%
2006	11.9%	−13.2%	23.2%	6.7%	13.8%	7.1%	5.0%	12.1%	8.5%	8.7%
2007	2.0%	3.7%	22.3%	5.7%	6.5%	−0.3%	10.5%	8.5%	10.3%	7.3%
2008	−32.2%	31.2%	−38.2%	−12.9%	−23.2%	−18.7%	0.8%	−20.8%	19.6%	−21.1%
2009	43.8%	−17.1%	34.7%	6.7%	24.7%	20.3%	11.3%	19.0%	−5.9%	9.4%
2010	12.7%	−3.0%	11.2%	4.3%	10.4%	5.0%	6.2%	9.4%	12.4%	6.3%
2011	−7.1%	5.1%	−14.3%	−0.6%	−2.6%	5.1%	1.1%	−7.5%	−4.8%	2.2%
2012	11.0%	−13.7%	5.8%	4.1%	9.4%	7.4%	5.8%	7.1%	−3.4%	7.7%
2013	1.7%	−0.4%	2.7%	7.6%	11.2%	4.6%	3.1%	14.5%	−1.5%	5.8%
2014	−2.0%	6.0%	−1.6%	4.5%	−2.3%	3.3%	2.5%	1.3%	12.7%	4.1%

16.6.3 Post-Crisis Performance

In the years following the financial crisis, some industry analysts expressed disappointment with hedge funds in light of their underperformance relative to public equities. As a result, the ever-present interest of investors in gauging manager alpha has a new and urgent form: in the post-crisis era, have hedge funds lost their ability to generate attractive returns?

In Table 16.14, we report summary statistics for the returns of the average hedge fund during pre- and post-crisis periods, where the pre-crisis period is from January 1996 to December 2006, and the post-crisis period is from January 2010 to December 2014. In each period, we calculate the bias-adjusted average monthly returns for single fund managers in the Lipper database, along with the other standard measures of investment performance. The entries confirm the popular perception that the absolute returns of hedge funds were higher, on average, during the pre-crisis period: 8.7% pre-crisis versus 4.2% post-crisis. Moreover, this inequality holds for every single category.

Table 16.13 Summary statistics for the returns of the average fund in each Lipper style category from January 2004 to December 2014.

	# Fund-Months	Annualized Mean	Annualized Volatility	Sharpe Ratio	Sortino Ratio	Skewness	Kurtosis	Maximum DD	S&P 500 Corr.	ac(1)	Box–Q(3) p-value
Convertible Arbitrage	10,133	2.3%	8.8%	0.09	0.12	-3.08	23.06	-34.4%	0.60	0.48	0.00
Dedicated Short Bias	1,648	-1.8%	10.1%	-0.32	-0.56	0.41	3.12	-34.1%	-0.71	0.16	0.27
Emerging Markets	39,670	5.6%	11.2%	0.36	0.55	-1.17	6.62	-40.6%	0.73	0.36	0.00
Equity Market Neutral	22,129	3.0%	3.2%	0.49	0.66	-2.20	10.50	-14.6%	0.63	0.45	0.00
Event Driven	30,113	5.5%	6.0%	0.66	1.00	-1.40	6.90	-24.8%	0.76	0.48	0.00
Fixed Income Arbitrage	15,191	3.6%	4.5%	0.47	0.55	-5.16	41.74	-20.7%	0.57	0.32	0.00
Global Macro	27,845	5.1%	3.7%	0.96	1.94	0.21	3.85	-4.7%	0.45	0.00	1.00
Long/Short Equity Hedge	144,706	5.1%	7.2%	0.50	0.81	-0.82	4.23	-24.7%	0.82	0.26	0.00
Managed Futures	39,056	4.6%	8.8%	0.36	0.70	0.28	3.22	-14.5%	0.07	0.02	0.33
Multi-Strategy	72,889	3.5%	4.6%	0.45	0.62	-1.95	10.19	-21.5%	0.68	0.44	0.00
Funds of Funds	247,483	2.1%	5.0%	0.13	0.18	-1.36	6.66	-21.9%	0.66	0.35	0.00
All Single Manager Funds	425,222	4.7%	5.6%	0.57	0.89	-1.05	5.86	-20.5%	0.77	0.32	0.00

Number of fund months, annualized mean, annualized volatility, Sharpe ratio, Sortino ratio, skewness, kurtosis, maximum drawdown, correlation coefficient with the S&P 500, first-order autocorrelation, and p-value of the Ljung–Box test statistic with three lags for the ten main hedge fund categories, funds of funds, and all single manager funds found in the Lipper database are reported. Sharpe and Sortino ratios are adjusted for the three-month US Treasury bill rate. The 'all single manager funds' category includes the funds in all ten main Lipper categories and any other single manager funds present in the database (relatively few) while excluding funds of funds.

Table 16.14 Summary statistics for the pre- and post-crisis returns of the average hedge fund in each Lipper style category.

Category	# Fund-Months	Ann. Mean (%)	Ann. SD (%)	Sharpe Ratio	Sortino Ratio	Skew.	Kurt.	MaxDD (%)	Corr. to S&P 500 (%)	ρ_1 (%)	Box-Q(3) p-value (%)
					January 1996–December 2006						
Convertible Arbitrage	7,827	8.1	4.3	0.95	1.53	-1.25	8.63	-8.70	42.9	45.9	0.0
Dedicated Short Bias	1,384	-2.3	18.8	-0.31	-0.58	0.59	4.17	-42.29	-76.8	8.9	19.1
Emerging Markets	12,673	11.6	15.7	0.47	0.69	-1.61	10.51	-49.26	58.5	28.0	0.8
Equity Market Neutral	11,537	6.5	3.0	0.82	1.82	2.05	16.06	-2.21	3.0	-11.7	22.4
Event Driven	18,565	9.4	5.2	1.02	1.55	-2.02	13.89	-12.56	54.7	32.3	0.2
Fixed Income Arbitrage	7,749	6.8	3.7	0.75	0.95	-3.56	24.53	-13.69	-1.0	42.7	0.0
Global Macro	8,948	4.7	6.1	0.14	0.26	0.46	4.17	-14.24	21.7	2.5	41.6
Long/Short Equity Hedge	69,160	11.1	9.8	0.71	1.33	0.15	5.31	-18.52	68.8	18.7	16.7
Managed Futures	13,761	5.0	9.8	0.11	0.20	0.14	2.97	-16.34	-8.7	0.0	72.9
Multi-Strategy	8,100	8.5	5.2	0.85	1.43	-0.73	5.16	-6.67	49.1	0.1	65.1
Funds of Funds	55,507	6.6	6.4	0.41	0.68	-0.33	6.51	-12.97	53.3	22.2	5.0
All Single Manager Funds	163,702	8.7	6.5	0.72	1.28	-0.26	5.46	-10.95	65.2	19.2	13.1

The pre-crisis period is from January 1996 to December 2006 and the post-crisis period is from January 2010 to December 2014. Number of fund months, annualized mean, annualized volatility, Sharpe ratio, Sortino ratio, Skewness, kurtosis, maximum drawdown, correlation coefficient with the S&P 500, first-order autocorrelation, and p-value of the Ljung–Box test statistic with three lags for the ten main hedge fund categories, funds of funds, and all single manager funds found in the Lipper database are reported. Sharpe and Sortino ratios are adjusted for the three-month US Treasury bill rate. The 'all single manager funds' category includes the funds in all ten main Lipper categories and any other single manager funds present in the database (relatively few) while excluding funds of funds

January 2010–December 2013

Convertible Arbitrage	3,940	3.0	5.7	0.52	0.96	-0.07	2.67	-10.20	50.4	10.6	63.6
Dedicated Short Bias	571	-1.5	7.3	-0.21	-0.33	-0.40	2.94	-22.56	-59.1	10.2	66.5
Emerging Markets	22,401	0.4	8.5	0.04	0.06	-0.67	3.84	-16.10	78.6	7.9	41.9
Equity Market Neutral	8,930	3.9	2.4	1.59	2.97	-0.69	4.00	-3.35	81.6	22.4	25.1
Event Driven	11,465	5.0	4.9	1.01	1.78	-0.70	3.04	-7.66	77.1	20.1	20.2
Fixed Income Arbitrage	7,202	5.0	1.7	2.90	6.29	-0.94	4.23	-1.03	54.1	-10.0	68.3
Global Macro	16,824	3.7	2.5	1.46	3.29	0.12	3.54	-2.03	63.2	9.7	68.7
Long/Short Equity Hedge	66,758	4.7	6.2	0.73	1.27	-0.54	3.42	-10.67	89.0	11.1	64.2
Managed Futures	23,471	2.8	7.5	0.36	0.71	0.11	2.28	-14.48	25.4	-12.4	78.4
Multi-Strategy	57,505	5.2	2.5	2.06	4.06	-0.87	5.52	-3.20	80.9	16.3	23.2
Funds of Funds	139,161	1.7	3.5	0.46	0.78	-0.55	2.73	-7.42	79.3	11.6	59.1
All Single Manager Funds	233,194	4.2	4.2	1.00	1.84	-0.39	3.63	-6.36	85.3	11.7	46.8

However, Table 16.14 also shows that the Sharpe ratios of hedge funds were generally as high or higher in the post-crisis period as they were in the pre-crisis period, suggesting that managers are no less skilled at generating returns than they were before the crisis. Specifically, across all categories, the average Sharpe ratio is 0.72 in the pre-crisis period and 1.00 in the post-crisis period. As a check, we calculated the Sharpe ratio of the Credit Suisse/Dow Jones hedge fund index for the same periods, and found that, if anything, the Sharpe ratio had increased: 0.97 in the pre-crisis period and 1.29 in the post-crisis period. This result is hardly definitive, as the length of the post-crisis period analysed is rather short, and many authors have proposed more elaborate measures of hedge fund skill. Nonetheless, it suggests that any reports of the disappearance of hedge fund manager skill may be exaggerated.[27]

This surprising result also suggests a somewhat different narrative regarding the source of hedge fund underperformance. The most obvious explanation is that the average volatility of hedge funds' returns was lower in the post-crisis period, damping the absolute returns even as risk-adjusted returns remained strong. We estimate that the annualized volatility of the cross-sectionally averaged hedge fund returns in the Lipper database dropped from 6.5% to 4.2% between the two periods, and that, among the individual categories, only convertible arbitrage funds had higher average volatilities in the post-crisis period. This decline in volatility is likely due to the lower amounts of leverage being deployed in the hedge fund industry for several reasons: a decrease in risk appetite among investors in the aftermath of the financial crisis, more stringent capital requirements on the part of regulators, and fewer market opportunities due to central banking interventions that have changed the traditional risk–reward relations among assets.

This potential decrease in leverage is related to the second possible source of apparent underperformance of post-crisis hedge funds: a lower risk-free rate. We estimate that the average risk-free rate declined from 3.80% in the pre-crisis period to 0.07% in the post-crisis period. If hedge funds earn a portion of their return from cash holdings (e.g. as collateral in margin accounts), it makes logical sense that their post-crisis returns would be affected by the low interest rate policies of the world's major central banks, irrespective of manager skill.

Finally, a third explanation is that hedge fund database biases are much stronger for older data (see Section 16.2.2). A researcher who naively averaged the pre-crisis returns in the Lipper database might introduce an upward

---

[27] From January 2015 to January 2022, the geometrically compounded annual return of the Credit Suisse Hedge Fund Index was 4.71% with an annualized standard deviation of 4.45% for a Sharpe ratio of 1.05.

bias of 8.6%, whereas post-crisis average returns may be subject to only a 1.9% bias. Unless these biases are corrected before averaging (as we do in this chapter), they will tend to exaggerate the difference between pre- and post-crisis hedge fund returns.

These three factors are sufficient to explain the entirety of the post-crisis underperformance of hedge funds.

16.6.4 Hedge Funds and Systemic Risk

In the aftermath of the financial crisis of 2008, the concept of 'systemic risk' emerged as an important phenomenon that goes far beyond its original domain of macroeconomics and central banking policy. Although a review of the systemic risk literature is beyond the scope of this chapter, the extent to which the hedge fund industry can offer insights into systemic risk is clearly within our purview.

A natural starting point for developing such insights is to first define and then measure systemic risk. The adage that 'one cannot manage what one does not measure' is particularly relevant in this context. Remarkably, years after one of the worst financial crises since the Great Depression of 1929, we still do not have a consensus definition for systemic risk, much less a standardized measure for it. In fact, the review article on systemic risk measures published by Bisias et al. (2012) lists thirty-one distinct measures, none of which has been universally endorsed as a canonical measure of systemic risk that could be regularly computed and released by the government. Even after reviewing eight centuries of financial crises, Reinhart and Rogoff's (2009) definitive treatise offers no single barometer with which financial stability can be reliably gauged.

Billio et al. (2012) define systemic risk as the risk of a systemic event, which is any set of circumstances that threatens the stability of, or public confidence in, the financial system. This is consistent with the 'four L's' of financial crisis—liquidity, leverage, linkages, and losses—that appear repeatedly in various narratives of 2007–2008. All of these L's touch the hedge fund industry to some extent. Under this definition, there is little doubt that LTCM's decline in August and September of 1998 was a systemic event, and that the private sector bailout facilitated by the Federal Reserve Bank of New York (New York Fed) was a reasonable, if somewhat hastily arranged, response. However, in September 2006, when the much larger ($9 billion vs $4.7 billion in assets under management) hedge fund Amaranth Advisors shut down because of extreme trading losses, there was no Fed-facilitated bailout, and financial markets hardly noticed. Clearly, this event was not systemic. This comparison to LTCM underscores the heterogeneity and complexity of the hedge fund industry, and the need for more refined analytics to determine how hedge funds may or may not affect systemic risk.

In a series of publications, Chan et al. (2004, 2006, 2007) propose using the hedge fund industry as a Geiger counter to construct measures of systemic risk. Employing aggregate measures of volatility, illiquidity, and financial distress for hedge funds based on statistical regime-switching models, autocorrelation, and linear factor exposures, they show that periods of market dislocation can be predicted to some degree by certain trends in the hedge fund industry such as regime switches to lower mean/higher volatility returns, and increases in illiquidity as measured by asset-weighted autocorrelations.[28]

Billio et al. (2012) have proposed measures of interconnectedness among four types of financial institutions that figured prominently in the 2008 financial crisis: banks, broker-dealers, insurance companies, and hedge funds. Using monthly returns for the top twenty-five institutions in each of these four categories, they estimate common factor exposures using PCA, and estimate pairwise connections using Granger causality tests. The former technique captures concentrated sources of risk and return across the four sectors, and the latter is used to construct Granger causality networks, directed graphs that capture both the direction and statistical significance of pairwise relations among financial institutions over time. By applying standard measures of connectivity from social network analysis such as the eigenvector centrality parameter, they conclude that the banking and insurance sectors are particularly important sources of interconnectedness and, therefore, key channels through which systemic events are propagated. Hedge funds are also important nodes in this financial web, but they do not play as large a role in transmitting systemic shocks as banks.[29] A distinct literature focusing on the reverse question—How does systemic risk affect hedge funds?—developed in parallel. Brunnermeier (2009) argues that hedge funds could be affected by financial crises through many mechanisms: direct exposure, funding liquidity, market liquidity, loss and margin spirals, runs on hedge funds, and aversion to Knightian uncertainty. Some of these mechanisms, like direct exposure and market liquidity, can be captured by hedge fund exposures to market risk factors.

---

[28] Regime-switching models are commonly used in the broader financial economics literature (e.g. Bekaert and Harvey (1995), Ang and Bekaert (2002) and Guidolin and Timmermann (2008), among others).
[29] The role of hedge funds in financial crises has been documented in several studies, including Eichengreen et al. (1998), Brown, Goetzmann, and Park (2000), Fung, Hsieh, and Tsatsaronis (2000), Brunnermeier and Nagel (2004), and Chen and Liang (2007). Hedge fund failures and liquidations, and their underlying causes, have also been studied (e.g. Getmansky, Lo, and Mei (2004) and Liang and Park (2010)). See also the discussion of hedge-fund entries and exits in Section 16.2.3.

Billio, Getmansky, and Pelizzon (2013) find that liquidity, credit, equities, and equity-market volatility are common risk factors during crises for various hedge fund strategies. They apply a novel methodology to identify the presence of a common latent risk-factor exposure across all hedge fund strategies, and find that this latent factor is related to asset and funding liquidity. If this latent risk factor is omitted in risk modelling, the resulting effect of financial crises on hedge fund risk is greatly underestimated. These results support the conclusions of Boyson, Stahel, and Stulz (2010), who document significant contagion from lagged bank and broker returns to hedge fund returns.

Other factors such as funding liquidity, margin spirals, runs on hedge funds, and aversion to Knightian uncertainty are hedge fund-specific, and affect the residual volatility of hedge fund returns (Krishnamurthy, 2010). For example, Khandani and Lo (2007, 2011b) argue that a forced liquidation of a given strategy should increase the strategy volatility through the increase in the residual volatility of hedge fund returns. Billio, Getmansky, and Pelizzon (2013) investigate the residual volatility of hedge fund strategies, and show that the increase in this volatility is common among all hedge fund strategies they consider during the LTCM crisis of 1998 and the financial crisis of 2008.

Chan et al. (2004, 2006, 2007), Adrian (2007), and Khandani and Lo (2007, 2011b) show that the risk profile of hedge funds during the LTCM crisis was drastically different from other financial crises. Khandani and Lo (2007, 2011b) find an increased correlation among hedge fund styles in this period, and conjecture that this was due to the increase in systematic linkages with market factors, liquidity, and credit proxies (e.g. the Quant Meltdown of August 2007; see Section 16.6.1 and also Chapter 17). Boyson, Stahel, and Stulz (2010) study potential explanations for clustering of the worst returns of hedge funds and find that adverse shocks to asset and funding liquidity, as well as contagion, may potentially explain this tail risk.

Despite the fact that dislocation in the hedge fund industry often presages broader financial crises, it is easy to miss or ignore these early warning signs. Although academic studies raised the possibility of crisis as early as 2004 and 2005 (see Chan et al. (2004), Rajan (2006), and Shiller (2005b), and Section 16.6.1), these were outliers with respect to the financial industry's perspective at the time. A sense for the magnitude of the gulf between academia and industry can be obtained from the views of the Counterparty Risk Management Policy Group II (CRMPG-II), a nonprofit industry consortium with the following mandate: 'The primary purpose of CRMPG II—building on the 1999 report of CRMPG I—is to examine what additional steps should be taken by the private sector to promote the efficiency, effectiveness and stability of the global financial system.' The CRMPG-II was chaired by Gerald Corrigan, then a managing director at Goldman Sachs, and the two vice chairs were Don Wilson, then Chief Risk Officer of JP Morgan, and David Bushnell, then senior risk officer of Citigroup. The other members of the policy group included senior representatives from top financial institutions and their law firms: Bear Stearns, Cleary Gottlieb Steen & Hamilton, Deutsche Bank, General Motors Asset Management, HSBC, Lehman Brothers, Merrill Lynch, Morgan Stanley, TIAA-CREF, and Tudor Investment Corporation. On 25 July 2005, this body of industry experts published their report, which began with the following summary assessment (Counterparty Risk Management Policy Group II, 2005, p. 1):

> In approaching its task, the Policy Group shared a broad consensus that the already low statistical probabilities of the occurrence of truly systemic financial shocks had further declined over time.

While this statement may seem naive with the benefit of hindsight, it must be emphasized that business was booming during this period, with many of the firms represented in the CRMPG-II earning record profits that year and the following year. However, even in this context, the CRMPG-II report contains some prescient warnings that the members both documented and then dismissed with their blanket assessment. Recommendations 12, 21, and 22 of the report called for industry-wide efforts to: (1) cope with serious 'back-office' and potential settlement problems in the CDS market; and (2) stop the practice whereby some market participants 'assign' their side of a trade to another institution without the consent of the original counterparty to the trade (Counterparty Risk Managment Policy Group II, 2005, p. iv). The first recommendation referred to the fact that the largest institutions engaging in CDSs had, at one point, a one-year backlog in entering into their record-keeping and therefore into their risk-management systems, the terms of various CDS contracts they had consummated and to which they were legally bound. The second point referred to the fact that a number of CDS contracts could legally be reassigned to other counterparties without prior approval or notification, making it virtually impossible to determine the counterparty credit risk of such contracts.[30] These recommendations seem grossly inconsistent with the CRMPG-II's conclusion that the risk of a systemic shock had declined.

This example highlights the challenges that the financial industry faces in identifying threats to financial stability; such threats are often forged in the crucible of highly profitable, rapidly growing lines of business. Unless

---

[30] Both problems were not isolated issues, but were so widespread that eventually Timothy Geithner, then president of the New York Fed, was motivated to intervene through moral suasion to get the financial industry to address them.

corporate executives have perfect timing, it is unrealistic to expect them to reduce risk as their businesses are expanding and shareholders will not support such behaviour. While the concept of countercyclical capital buffers seems sensible, it is virtually impossible for them to be self-imposed by the industry. Therefore, macroprudential regulation can play a positive role in creating a more stable and robust financial system (see Chapter 20 for discussions on regulatory reforms in the wake of the financial crisis in more detail).

16.7 Implementation Issues for Hedge Fund Investing

Having reviewed much of the academic hedge fund literature in Sections 16.1–16.6, we now turn to four implementation issues facing hedge fund investors. In Section 16.7.1, we consider the potential dangers of mindlessly applying traditional mean-variance portfolio analysis to hedge fund returns. The multifaceted nature of hedge fund risk exposures, the smoothness of certain hedge fund returns due to illiquidity, and the nonstationarity of their return distributions imply that standard mean-variance analysis can yield highly misleading portfolio allocations, especially at the asset-class level.

A related problem is discussed in Section 16.7.2 involving the potential over-diversification of hedge fund portfolios, which can lead to lower expected returns and, surprisingly, greater risks. The consequences of adding hedge funds to a portfolio of traditional assets are discussed in Section 16.7.3. Given the potential pitfalls in hedge fund investing, the need for a more systematic framework for making alternative investment decisions is clear, and in Section 16.7.4 we present such a framework.

From a broader perspective, investing in hedge funds seems at odds with much of the academic investment literature, which emphasizes passive risk premia and dismisses the possibility of consistent sources of alpha. However, the popularity of hedge funds among large institutional investors who also invest passively suggests a troubling contradiction between theory and practice. In Section 16.7.5, we discuss the adaptive markets hypothesis (AMH) as an alternative that reconciles this contradiction in an intellectually satisfying manner.

16.7.1 The Limits of Mean-Variance Optimization

A common question facing investors, advisers, and institutional money managers is how much they should allocate to hedge funds. Many turn to mathematical optimization tools, only to discover that their optimizer recommends a 200% allocation to hedge funds and −100% allocation to other assets. Such results are usually disregarded, and rightly so. While hedge funds may be desirable investments for some investors, biases in hedge fund reporting can artificially boost the historical estimates of expected returns, while autocorrelation due to illiquid portfolios artificially dampens the estimated variances and covariances. Furthermore, optimizers may produce recommendations that are fine-tuned for a previous period, but poorly suited for the future, and the resulting portfolios may have unsuitable risk characteristics.

In Table 16.15 we show that a (nearly) unconstrained optimizer can produce a portfolio that would have earned an amazing 40.4% per year between 1996 and 2014. However, the investments required for such a portfolio are not even feasible: the optimizer calls for short exposure to certain hedge fund categories. Nevertheless, mathematical optimizers can be a useful guide for investors, calling attention to assets that have historically had desirable average returns, low correlation, or other characteristics. It is usually helpful to constrain the set of solutions from which the optimizer may choose, pre-emptively eliminating solutions that are too risky or too illiquid, involve too much leverage, or are outside the feasible investment universe. In Table 16.15, we show a number of mean-variance-optimized portfolio weights subject to such constraints. Results towards the top of the table are generally more constrained, and are probably a better guide to the sorts of choices a prudent investor might have made during that nineteen-year period.

In addition to the traditional constraint on the portfolio's standard deviation, we employ a more novel constraint on portfolio autocorrelation in an effort to avoid portfolios that are likely to be too illiquid. While some endowments may be able to tolerate an illiquid portfolio because their investment horizon is presumably unbounded, individual investors often need to access their assets sooner, and may choose to be more cautious about illiquidity. See Section 16.4.4 for further discussion about mean-variance–illiquidity optimization.

16.7.2 Over Diversification

The proliferation of multi-strategy funds and funds of funds over the past three decades has given investors an unprecedented amount of diversification within the hedge fund industry (Lhabitant and Learned, 2002; Amo, Harasty, and Hillion, 2007). However, the financial crisis of 2008 called into question the view that hedge funds are really hedged, and that diversification

Table 16.15 Results of Markowitz mean-variance optimization over the period January 1996 to December 2014.

Maximum Volatility	Maximum Auto-correlation	Shorting Constraints	Optimized Annualized Return	Optimized Annualized Volatility	Optimized Auto-correlation	3 Month US Treasury Bills	S&P 500 Total Return Index	Barclays US Aggregate Bond Index	Convertible Arbitrage	Dedicated Short Bias	Emerging Markets	Equity Market Neutral	Event Driven	Fixed Income Arbitrage	Global Macro	Long/Short Equity Hedge	Managed Futures	Multi-Strategy	Funds of Funds
0.05	0.10	Long Only	6.8%	5.0%	0.10	0.00	0.15	0.54	0.00	0.00	0.00	0.00	0.01	0.00	0.00	0.30	0.00	0.00	0.00
0.05	0.25	Long Only	6.8%	5.0%	0.17	0.00	0.12	0.43	0.00	0.00	0.00	0.00	0.17	0.00	0.00	0.27	0.00	0.00	0.00
0.05	0.40	Long Only	6.8%	5.0%	0.17	0.00	0.12	0.43	0.00	0.00	0.00	0.00	0.17	0.00	0.00	0.27	0.00	0.00	0.00
0.10	0.10	Long Only	8.2%	10.0%	0.10	0.00	0.54	0.22	0.00	0.00	0.00	0.00	0.00	0.00	0.00	0.24	0.00	0.00	0.00
0.10	0.25	Long Only	8.3%	10.0%	0.16	0.00	0.34	0.05	0.00	0.00	0.00	0.00	0.00	0.00	0.00	0.62	0.00	0.00	0.00
0.10	0.40	Long Only	8.3%	10.0%	0.16	0.00	0.34	0.05	0.00	0.00	0.00	0.00	0.00	0.00	0.00	0.62	0.00	0.00	0.00
0.15	0.25	Long Only	9.4%	15.0%	0.09	0.00	0.95	0.00	0.00	0.00	0.00	0.00	0.00	0.00	0.00	0.05	0.00	0.00	0.00
0.15	0.40	Long Only	9.4%	15.0%	0.09	0.00	0.95	0.00	0.00	0.00	0.00	0.00	0.00	0.00	0.00	0.05	0.00	0.00	0.00
0.20	0.25	Long Only	9.4%	15.4%	0.08	0.00	1.00	0.00	0.00	0.00	0.00	0.00	0.00	0.00	0.00	0.00	0.00	0.00	0.00
0.20	0.40	Long Only	9.4%	15.4%	0.08	0.00	1.00	0.00	0.00	0.00	0.00	0.00	0.00	0.00	0.00	0.00	0.00	0.00	0.00
0.05	0.10	Can Short T-bills	8.6%	5.0%	0.10	-1.06	0.03	1.12	0.00	0.13	0.00	0.27	0.24	0.00	0.01	0.22	0.04	0.00	0.00
0.05	0.25	Can Short T-bills	8.8%	5.0%	0.17	-1.11	0.02	1.03	0.00	0.12	0.00	0.37	0.42	0.00	0.00	0.14	0.02	0.00	0.00
0.05	0.40	Can Short T-bills	8.8%	5.0%	0.16	-1.12	0.02	1.03	0.00	0.12	0.00	0.39	0.40	0.00	0.00	0.14	0.02	0.00	0.00
0.10	0.10	Can Short T-bills	14.8%	10.0%	0.10	-3.09	0.06	2.22	0.00	0.26	0.00	0.49	0.50	0.00	0.00	0.47	0.09	0.00	0.00
0.10	0.25	Can Short T-bills	15.0%	10.0%	0.16	-3.25	0.04	2.05	0.00	0.25	0.00	0.78	0.79	0.00	0.00	0.30	0.03	0.00	0.00
0.10	0.40	Can Short T-bills	15.0%	10.0%	0.17	-3.23	0.04	2.05	0.00	0.25	0.00	0.74	0.83	0.00	0.00	0.29	0.03	0.00	0.00
0.15	0.10	Can Short T-bills	20.8%	15.0%	0.10	-5.16	0.08	3.33	0.00	0.39	0.00	0.81	0.67	0.00	0.00	0.74	0.13	0.00	0.00
0.15	0.25	Can Short T-bills	21.2%	15.0%	0.17	-5.36	0.06	3.08	0.00	0.37	0.00	1.16	1.21	0.00	0.00	0.43	0.05	0.00	0.00
0.15	0.40	Can Short T-bills	21.2%	15.0%	0.17	-5.36	0.06	3.07	0.00	0.37	0.00	1.16	1.19	0.00	0.00	0.45	0.17	0.00	0.00
0.20	0.10	Can Short T-bills	26.9%	20.0%	0.10	-7.20	0.11	4.43	0.00	0.53	0.00	1.06	0.88	0.00	0.00	1.01	0.06	0.00	0.00
0.20	0.25	Can Short T-bills	27.4%	20.0%	0.17	-7.51	0.08	4.10	0.00	0.48	0.00	1.56	1.55	0.00	0.00	0.55	0.06	0.00	0.00
0.20	0.40	Can Short T-bills	27.4%	20.0%	0.17	-7.49	0.08	4.09	0.00	0.50	0.00	1.57	1.57	0.00	0.00	0.61	0.06	0.00	0.00
0.05	0.10	Can Short Anything	12.0%	5.0%	0.10	-0.60	-0.06	0.75	-0.46	0.16	0.11	0.03	0.86	0.25	0.21	0.72	0.09	0.76	-1.82
0.05	0.25	Can Short Anything	12.1%	5.0%	0.14	-0.55	-0.06	0.76	-0.40	0.15	0.12	0.01	0.92	0.19	0.20	0.69	0.10	0.74	-1.88
0.05	0.40	Can Short Anything	12.1%	5.0%	0.14	-0.54	-0.06	0.76	-0.40	0.15	0.12	0.01	0.92	0.20	0.21	0.69	0.10	0.73	-1.89
0.10	0.10	Can Short Anything	21.4%	10.0%	0.10	-2.27	-0.12	1.50	-0.96	0.33	0.20	0.09	1.77	0.49	0.38	1.42	0.19	1.48	-3.50
0.10	0.25	Can Short Anything	21.5%	10.0%	0.14	-2.15	-0.11	1.51	-0.80	0.32	0.20	0.07	1.87	0.35	0.37	1.37	0.21	1.46	-3.66
0.10	0.40	Can Short Anything	21.5%	10.0%	0.14	-2.14	-0.11	1.51	-0.80	0.31	0.21	0.06	1.87	0.36	0.37	1.36	0.21	1.46	-3.68
0.15	0.10	Can Short Anything	30.8%	15.0%	0.10	-3.91	-0.18	2.23	-1.43	0.50	0.29	0.15	2.61	0.71	0.56	2.17	0.28	2.25	-5.23
0.15	0.25	Can Short Anything	31.0%	15.0%	0.14	-3.71	-0.16	2.25	-1.21	0.48	0.31	0.11	2.79	0.50	0.53	2.07	0.31	2.22	-5.49
0.15	0.40	Can Short Anything	31.0%	15.0%	0.15	-3.71	-0.17	2.26	-1.20	0.47	0.31	0.09	2.80	0.54	0.55	2.05	0.31	2.19	-5.50
0.20	0.10	Can Short Anything	40.2%	20.0%	0.10	-5.54	-0.24	2.98	-1.92	0.66	0.38	0.21	3.45	0.94	0.74	2.90	0.36	3.02	-6.95
0.20	0.25	Can Short Anything	40.4%	20.0%	0.14	-5.26	-0.22	3.03	-1.64	0.64	0.42	0.14	3.70	0.66	0.69	2.79	0.41	2.94	-7.30
0.20	0.40	Can Short Anything	40.4%	20.0%	0.14	-5.27	-0.22	3.01	-1.62	0.64	0.41	0.15	3.71	0.66	0.70	2.77	0.41	2.95	-7.30

The variably coloured columns show the optimal portfolio weights and the adjacent blue columns show the optimized portfolio's expected arithmetic rate of return, volatility, and autocorrelation. Each row corresponds to a different set of constraints on volatility, liquidity (using autocorrelation as an indicator), and shorting.

across hedge fund styles is beneficial. Billio, Getmansky, and Pelizzon (2013) find that the average correlation among hedge fund strategies jumped from 0.32 in August 2008 to 0.52 in September 2008, a 64% increase. At the same time, the average returns of most hedge funds declined significantly (see Section 16.6.3), which left investors wondering whether hedge fund investing would still be worthwhile. With the benefit of over a decade of returns since the crisis, this question has since been resolved in the affirmative.

Shawky, Dai, and Cumming (2012) show that on a risk-adjusted basis, hedge funds that diversify across sectors and asset classes outperform other funds by an average of 1.6% per year. However, diversification across styles is found to exhibit a significant negative association with hedge fund returns. Nevertheless, for funds of funds, the authors find there is a significant positive relationship between performance and diversification across sectors, styles, and geographies.

In documenting the performance of the hedge fund industry from 1995 to 2004, Fung et al. (2008) find that, on average, funds of funds delivered alpha only in the period between October 1998 and March 2000, although a subset of funds of funds do seem to have consistent alpha.

Furthermore, Brown, Gregoriou, and Pascalau (2012) find that the variance-reducing effects of diversification become insignificant once a fund of funds holds more than twenty underlying hedge funds. However, the majority of funds of funds are more diversified than this. They find that over-diversification by funds of funds can increase left-tail risk exposure and lower expected returns, especially when hedge fund returns are smoothed. This increase in tail risk is accompanied by lower returns, which they attribute to the cost of necessary due diligence, a drag on performance that increases with the number of underlying hedge funds in the portfolio.

16.7.3 Investment Implications

Reviewing the performance characteristics of hedge funds has provided ample evidence to support the view that investors selecting their strategic asset allocations should not consider hedge funds to be a monolithic category. The decision to allocate assets to a hedge fund strategy should involve the consideration of a number of factors. Chief among them is a strategy's potential for contributing positive returns; determining this factor we leave solely to the investor. However, just as important is the investor's consideration as to which hedge fund risks they can best afford to add to their portfolio. Are occasional large losses acceptable? Is an investment uncorrelated with

Table 16.16 Summary statistics for the stock, bond, and 60/40 stocks/bonds portfolios from January 1996 to December 2014.

	# Fund-Months	annualized Mean	Annualized Volatility	Sharpe Ratio	Sortino Ratio	Skewness	Kurtosis	Maximum DD	S&P 500 Corr.	ac(1)	Box–Q(3) p-value
S&P 500 Total Return Index	228	8.6%	15.4%	0.38	0.61	−0.67	4.00	−50.9%	1.00	0.08	0.27
Barclays US Aggregate Index	228	5.6%	3.5%	0.85	1.56	−0.32	4.00	−3.8%	−0.01	0.07	0.02
60/40 Stocks/Bonds	228	7.7%	9.3%	0.54	0.88	−0.67	4.30	−32.5%	0.99	0.06	0.25

The number of months, annualized mean, annualized volatility, Sharpe ratio, Sortino ratio, skewness, kurtosis, maximum drawdown, correlation coefficient with the S&P 500, first-order autocorrelation, and p-value of the Ljung–Box test statistic with three lags are calculated for the S&P 500 Total Return Index (stock portfolio), Barclays US Aggregate Index (bond portfolio), and 60/40 stocks/bonds portfolio.

equities preferable? What volatility is acceptable? Are correlated strategies already in their portfolio? Our results suggest that while many hedge fund categories have similar characteristics, they are different enough that an investor in alternatives should pause and determine which investment styles are most consistent with their risk preferences.

If an investor simply sought to maximize expected returns without regard for risk, their investment procedure would be simple: forecast the returns of each candidate investment and allocate 100% of their assets to the investment associated with the highest expected return. However, most investors are concerned about the risk of large losses. To limit the potential for large losses, investors tend to exploit at least one of two strategies. Firstly, they generally spread their capital across a number of investments that they expect to produce good returns in the hope that not all of the investments will simultaneously decline in value (diversification). Secondly, they may choose to allocate more of their assets to investments that they deem less likely to experience large price decreases. The implementation of these two risk-mitigation strategies is often based on forecasts of volatility and correlation. While a good starting place, this approach falls short when one contemplates investments with distributions that are likely to have nonzero higher moments. Of particular concern is the combination of positive excess kurtosis and negative skewness, which reflects a history of large sudden losses. Unfortunately, this encompasses nearly all of the investments considered thus far to a degree, including stocks and bonds (see Table 16.16).

Investor confidence in the traditional 60% stocks, 40% bonds portfolio seems to have declined in recent years. The brutal stock market slumps book-ending the first decade of the 2000s seem to have erased the investing euphoria of the 1990s, while the expectation that interest rates may reverse their decades-long trend and plateau and rise tempers interest in bonds. Thus, ever more investors are asking whether they should allocate a portion of their portfolios to 'alternatives', generally defined as anything other than stocks, bonds, and cash. For many investors, especially high-net-worth investors, pension funds, and endowments, investing in alternatives may include an allocation to hedge funds.

Table 16.16 reports the performance statistics for the S&P 500 Total Return Index (a representative stock portfolio), the Barclays US Aggregate Index (a representative bond portfolio), and a 60/40 stocks/bonds portfolio for the period January 1996–December 2014. Over these nineteen years, both stock and bond asset classes produced attractive returns, albeit at strikingly different volatilities. Because US interest rates declined over this period, some argue that the extremely attractive risk/reward ratio of bonds should be viewed with an extra dose of scepticism when making decisions about future asset allocations. Although the returns of stocks and bonds are hardly IID normal, in comparison to the returns of most hedge fund investment styles they look well behaved, having relatively modest kurtosis, negative skewness, and autocorrelation. Interestingly enough, the average return (and Sharpe ratio) of hedge funds over this period falls between that of stocks and bonds (see Table 16.6). In Table 16.16 we also summarize the simulated performance of a prototypical 60% stocks, 40% bonds portfolio (with free monthly rebalancing) based on these two indexes. Note that the resulting two-asset portfolio, while less volatile, is still highly correlated with equities. Geczy (2014) finds similar results—over the fifteen-year period 1999–2013, the correlation of returns between a 60/40 portfolio and a 100% equity portfolio was 0.98. Even if an investor invested 30% in stocks and 70% in bonds, the resulting correlation with a 100% stock portfolio would be 0.85. As a result, a long-only stock and bond portfolio is not particularly well diversified.

Table 16.17 shows that reallocating 5%, 10%, 20%, or 50% from a 60/40 portfolio into the (noninvestable) 'average' hedge fund would have decreased a traditional portfolio's volatility more than its returns. The combined effect is to increase the risk-adjusted excess return by roughly 13%. The experience of actual investors, of course, would have varied based on how similar their investment choices were to this average (and monthly rebalanced) measure of hedge fund returns, fees, and the tracking error associated with their stock and bond investments. It is worth noting that many investors seeking a diverse exposure to hedge funds choose to invest through a fund of funds, which, on average, would have resulted in inferior returns (see Table 16.18).

Returning briefly to our earlier theme of hedge fund style heterogeneity, we also simulated the performance of a 48/32/20 stock/bond/hedge fund portfolio in which 20% of the assets were allocated to one specific hedge fund style

Table 16.17 Summary statistics for the 60%/40%/0%, 57%/38%/5%, 54%/36%/10%, 48%/32%/20%, and 30%/20%/50% stock/bond/hedge fund (HF) portfolios from January 1996 to December 2014.

	# Fund-Months	Annualized Mean	Annualized Volatility	Sharpe Ratio	Sortino Ratio	Skewness	Kurtosis	Maximum DD	S&P 500 Corr.	ac(1)	Box–Q(3) p-value
60% Stocks, 40% Bonds, 0% HF	228	7.7%	9.3%	0.54	0.88	−0.67	4.30	−32.5%	0.99	0.06	0.25
57% Stocks, 38% Bonds, 5% HF	228	7.6%	9.1%	0.54	0.90	−0.70	4.35	−32.0%	0.99	0.07	0.25
54% Stocks, 36% Bonds, 10% HF	228	7.6%	8.9%	0.55	0.91	−0.72	4.40	−31.4%	0.99	0.07	0.25
48% Stocks, 32% Bonds, 20% HF	228	7.5%	8.4%	0.57	0.93	−0.77	4.52	−30.2%	0.99	0.09	0.23
30% Stocks, 20% Bonds, 50% HF	228	7.1%	7.2%	0.61	0.99	−0.86	4.95	−26.6%	0.95	0.14	0.10

The number of months, annualized mean, annualized volatility, Sharpe ratio, Sortino ratio, skewness, kurtosis, maximum drawdown, correlation coefficient with the S&P 500, first-order autocorrelation, and p-value of the Ljung–Box test statistic with three lags are calculated for each portfolio.

(see Table 16.18). In some cases, this would have resulted in returns similar to those of the 60/40 stocks/bonds portfolio, earned a lower volatility, and had a smaller maximum drawdown (e.g. in the event driven and long/short equity hedge categories). In other cases, it would result in similar levels of volatility and returns (emerging markets). The impact on the return distribution kurtosis is particularly varied, as some portfolios have nearly no kurtosis, while others have heavy tails.

As before, these simulations are based on the average return of funds within a category and on portfolios rebalanced monthly. Both assumptions are likely to make the simulated results look more attractive. It is interesting that, even with this advantage, adding a 20% average hedge fund allocation to a 60/40 portfolio would not have increased the portfolio's average (non-risk-adjusted) rate of return, despite the popular conception that hedge funds regularly earn outsized returns. We note that many hedge fund index calculators, following a different methodology than the simple de-biased monthly average used here, report more attractive returns for the industry. For example, Geczy (2014) shows that adding a 15% allocation to alternatives and 5% each to alternative equity and alternative fixed-income investments decreases the total portfolio risk and increases the expected returns.

In summary, the historical data show that hedge funds have not, on average, meaningfully outperformed traditional portfolios of stocks and bonds after fees. On average, once biases have been corrected, hedge funds do not routinely generate double-digit returns. However, the ride for hedge fund investors has generally been smoother: as a group, hedge funds have exhibited lower volatility than traditional stock/bond portfolios. In addition, there

Table 16.18 Summary statistics for the 60%/40%/0% and 48%/32%/20% stock/bond/hedge fund (HF) portfolios from January 1996 to December 2014.

	# Fund-Months	Annualized Mean	Annualized Volatility	Sharpe Ratio	Sortino Ratio	Skewness	Kurtosis	Maximum DD	S&P 500 Corr.	ac(1)	Box–Q(3) p-value
60% Stocks, 40% Bonds, 0% HF	228	7.7%	9.3%	0.54	0.88	-0.67	4.30	-32.5%	0.99	0.06	0.25
48% Stocks, 32% Bonds, 20% Convertible Arbitrage	228	7.3%	8.3%	0.55	0.89	-1.00	6.51	-32.0%	0.98	0.14	0.06
48% Stocks, 32% Bonds, 20% Dedicated Short Bias	228	6.3%	5.8%	0.64	1.09	-0.67	5.18	-20.5%	0.89	0.02	0.34
48% Stocks, 32% Bonds, 20% Emerging Markets	228	7.6%	9.5%	0.52	0.82	-0.96	5.49	-34.1%	0.97	0.10	0.22
48% Stocks, 32% Bonds, 20% Equity Market Neutral	228	7.1%	7.7%	0.58	0.95	-0.80	4.80	-28.8%	0.99	0.10	0.13
48% Stocks, 32% Bonds, 20% Event Driven	228	7.6%	8.3%	0.59	0.96	-0.86	4.95	-31.0%	0.99	0.11	0.14
48% Stocks, 32% Bonds, 20% Fixed Income Arbitrage	228	7.2%	7.8%	0.58	0.95	-0.92	5.70	-29.8%	0.98	0.09	0.15
48% Stocks, 32% Bonds, 20% Global Macro	228	7.2%	7.9%	0.58	0.97	-0.59	3.90	-26.7%	0.98	0.06	0.35
48% Stocks, 32% Bonds, 20% Long/Short Equity Hedge	228	7.7%	8.9%	0.57	0.94	-0.73	4.26	-31.0%	0.98	0.09	0.23
48% Stocks, 32% Bonds, 20% Managed Futures	228	7.3%	7.7%	0.60	1.05	-0.44	3.24	-23.9%	0.95	0.02	0.57
48% Stocks, 32% Bonds, 20% Multi-Strategy	228	7.4%	8.1%	0.58	0.95	-0.80	4.71	-30.4%	0.98	0.08	0.24
48% Stocks, 32% Bonds, 20% Funds of Funds	228	6.9%	8.2%	0.52	0.84	-0.80	4.63	-30.4%	0.98	0.08	0.26
48% Stocks, 32% Bonds, 20% All Single Manager Funds	228	7.5%	8.4%	0.57	0.93	-0.77	4.52	-30.2%	0.99	0.09	0.23

The number of months, annualized mean, annualized volatility, Sharpe ratio, Sortino ratio, skewness, kurtosis, maximum drawdown, correlation coefficient with the S&P 500, first-order autocorrelation, and p-value of the Ljung–Box test statistic with three lags are calculated for each portfolio. The ten main hedge fund categories, funds of funds, and all single manager funds found in the Lipper database are considered in the hedge fund allocation.

are a number of styles of hedge fund investing. While many are correlated and have much in common, on the whole they are a heterogeneous lot: some are as dissimilar as stocks and bonds. This is consistent with Brown and Goetzmann (2003) who find that hedge funds are a reasonably heterogeneous group and present distinct styles. Based on historical data, some styles of hedge fund investing result in higher volatility, and some lower; some are correlated with equities, and some not; and some have a high propensity to occasionally experience large losses, while others experience this to a lesser extent (see Section 16.3.4). Liang (2005) studies asset allocation among hedge funds, funds of funds, and CTAs. He shows that CTAs are a natural hedging tool for equity especially during market declines; CTAs have relatively low correlations with hedge funds and funds of funds, and they have very different fund characteristics from hedge funds. We propose a more systematic approach to alternative investing in the next section.

16.7.4 An Integrated Hedge Fund Investment Process

Investing in hedge funds has changed considerably over the last three decades as the population of investors has grown beyond family offices, foundations, endowments, and high-net-worth investors to include more traditional institutional investors such as pension funds, sovereign wealth funds, and investment consultants. This shift in the investor base has brought new tools, policies, and procedures to the hedge fund industry because today's institutional investors require an unprecedented degree of transparency, accountability, and repeatability (i.e. they require an *investment process*, not just the ability to select a portfolio of hedge funds). Although, historically, many institutional investors have relied primarily on the qualitative judgements that fund of funds managers offer, institutional investors today often prefer a more systematic approach to making manager-selection decisions, as well as broader asset-allocation decisions among various hedge fund style categories.

Several systematic approaches have been proposed, largely led by practitioners from the hedge fund and fund of funds industry. These approaches fall loosely into two groups: top-down (in which broad strategy-level investment decisions are the focus) and bottom-up (in which the focus is selecting individual funds) investment processes.

Goldman Sachs & Co. and Financial Risk Management Ltd. (1999) suggest an absolute return fund analysis in which different sources of returns and stable and low (or negative) correlations of returns between sectors, and, in many cases, between funds within the same sector, improve hedge fund port-folio characteristics. They suggest diversifying across and within hedge fund strategies, with the primary constraint being the investor's ability to monitor multiple managers. Bein and Wander (2002) propose a top-down risk-allocation framework that allows investors explicitly to integrate active man-agement decisions and hedge fund risks into a traditional overall asset allo-cation process. Chung, Rosenberg, and Tomeo (2004) provide another top-down hedge fund asset-allocation process by dividing hedge fund strategies into two classes: convergent strategies that benefit from small temporary mis-pricings, which are short volatility, and divergent strategies that exploit larger and longer-horizon market inefficiencies, which are long volatility. Given that divergent strategies tend to be profitable during periods of heightened volatility and economic uncertainty, the authors argue that allocating assets to both types of strategies can improve expected returns and reduce risk.

In contrast, several other studies propose a bottom-up approach to constructing hedge fund portfolios. Zask (2000) describes a method for hedge fund valuation based on management fees, performance fees, and discounted cash flows analysis. Stemme and Slattery (2002) outline the practical considerations involved in selecting individual hedge funds, hiring a consultant, or investing in a fund of funds, including costs, control, track record, and capacity issues. Clark and Winkelmann (2004) develop a framework where all hedge funds are analysed based on how much of the projected performance is due to market movements or manager skill, and whether an investor is confident in the manager's (or strategy's) ability to continue to deliver performance.

A hybrid approach proposed by Lo (2008b) combines qualitative judge-ment with quantitative methods, a particularly important feature for invest-ing in complex, multifaceted, and highly heterogeneous assets such as hedge funds. This combination is achieved through a two-stage investment process in which a top-down asset allocation decision in broad hedge fund categories is coupled with bottom-up manager-selection decisions within each category. Although a two-stage investment process is generally suboptimal relative to a single-stage optimization, the complexities and qualitative aspects of hedge fund investing make a two-stage approach more robust and easier to imple-ment. This investment process is based on a set of six basic design principles:

- The target expected return for each strategy should be commensurate with the risks of that strategy: higher-risk strategies should have higher target expected returns.
- The uses of funds should determine the target expected return and not the sources of capital.

- In evaluating the risk/reward ratio for each strategy, return autocorrelation and illiquidity exposure should be explicitly considered. In particular, the Sharpe ratios of strategies with large positively serially correlated returns should be deflated (see Lo (2002b), Getmansky, Lo, and Makarov (2004), and Section 16.4 for details).
- Qualitative judgements about managers, strategies, and market conditions are valuable inputs into the capital allocation process that no quantitative models can replace, but those judgements should be integrated with quantitative methods in a systematic and consistent fashion.
- Risk and performance attribution should be performed on a regular basis for and by each manager, as well as for the entire portfolio.
- Risk limits and related guidelines for each manager should be consistent across time and across managers, and should be communicated clearly to all managers on a regular basis.

These design principles, coupled with insights from traditional portfolio management theory and practice, imply a portfolio optimization component in which required or target expected returns and variances are determined in advance by investor mandates and market conditions, covariances are estimated via econometric methods and modified by qualitative judgement, and then asset-class allocations are determined by minimizing the variance subject to an expected-return constraint. Within each asset class, manager-specific allocations would be determined by incorporating qualitative information into the investment process through a scoring process. The seven components of this quantitative/qualitative investment process (or 'QQIP' for convenience) are depicted in Figure 16.7 and given by:

1. Define asset classes by strategy.
2. Set target portfolio expected return, μ_o, and desired volatility, σ_o.
3. Set target expected returns and risks for asset classes.
4. Determine correlations via econometric analysis.
5. Compute minimum-variance asset-class allocations subject to μ_o constraint.
6. Allocate capital to managers within each asset class.
7. Monitor performance and risk budgets, and reoptimize as needed.

Although Lo (2008b) provides detailed discussions for each of these steps, he emphasizes that this framework is meant to serve only as a starting point for designing a suitable alternative investment process. Because of the heterogeneity of the hedge fund industry and the variability of investment

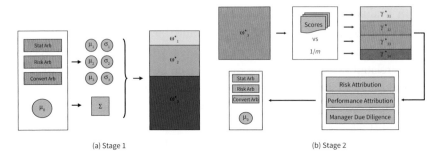

Fig. 16.7 Two-stage hybrid quantitative/qualitative investment process (QQIP) for alternative investments where, (a) in the first stage, asset classes are defined and optimal asset-class weights are determined as a function of target expected returns and risk levels, and an estimated covariance matrix; and, (b) in the second stage, capital is allocated to managers within an asset class according to a scoring procedure that incorporates qualitative as well as quantitative information.

objectives and constraints among investors, there is no single investment process that fits all investors.

The first step in QQIP is to define the universe of all hedge funds into a smaller set of categories in which managers in each category pursue relatively homogeneous styles of investing. An example of such categories is the Lipper classification, but finer stratifications may be appropriate, depending on the investment objectives of the investor and the size of the assets to be deployed.

The second step is to set a target expected return, a desired level of risk, and acceptable loss limits or maximum drawdown for the entire portfolio. While these parameters are, by nature, rather ambiguous quantities when discussed among investment committee members and officers, such discussions are invaluable in setting realistic expectations for what a portfolio of hedge funds can offer.

Once these high-level parameters (or ranges of parameters) have been specified, the third step is to do the same for the categories specified in the first step. This requires more specialized knowledge of both the historical performance of individual categories of hedge funds and how the categories are currently positioned. One way to develop target expected returns and volatilities for hedge fund categories is to estimate linear factor models for category indexes (see Section 16.5), and then to develop target expected returns and volatilities for the factors. In many cases, it is easier to develop a prospective intuition for the likely behaviour of factors such as liquidity, credit, the business cycle, and exchange ratios than for hedge fund category index returns.

Given the target expected returns and volatilities of the hedge fund categories in the investment universe, the next step in QQIP is to estimate the correlation matrix among the index returns of the hedge fund categories. This may seem straightforward from a statistical perspective; one might use the standard estimator with historical data or a linear factor model estimator that requires fewer estimated parameters (see Section 16.5.2). However, the fact that correlations can change in response to market conditions makes this step more challenging, requiring qualitative input to adjust the correlations to reflect current market conditions that might not yet be reflected in historical time series estimators.[31] In such cases, qualitative adjustments to the correlation matrix of category-index returns may be necessary, but it must be kept in mind that arbitrary changes to entries in a correlation matrix could violate the positive semi-definiteness of the matrix. If such violations are ignored, the outcome of a portfolio optimization using such a matrix could yield non-sensical results, such as negative variances. To avoid these pathologies, it is possible to compute the positive semi-definite correlation matrix that is 'closest' to the qualitatively adjusted correlation matrix using methods developed by Higham (2002) and Qi and Sun (2006).

Once the target expected returns, volatilities, and correlations among the hedge fund categories have been determined, the next step in QQIP is to construct an optimal portfolio. There are several methods for doing so (see, e.g., Brennan, Lo, and Nguyen (2015)), but a natural starting point is to find the asset allocation over hedge fund categories that minimizes the portfolio variance subject to the target portfolio expected return constraint specified in step 1. For most fund-of-funds and multi-manager applications, it is also necessary to impose non-negativity constraints on the portfolio weights, since it is typically impossible to establish a 'short' position in a manager. However, as long as the target expected returns are realistic and the covariance matrix is well behaved, the solution of the optimization problem:

$$\text{Min}_{\boldsymbol{\omega}} \frac{1}{2} \boldsymbol{\omega}' \Sigma \boldsymbol{\omega} \text{ subject to } \boldsymbol{\omega}' \boldsymbol{\mu} \geq \mu_o \text{ and } \boldsymbol{\omega}' \boldsymbol{\iota} = 1, \tag{16.20}$$

given by (see Lo (2008b)):

$$\boldsymbol{\omega}^* = \lambda \Sigma^{-1} \boldsymbol{\mu} + \xi \Sigma^{-1} \boldsymbol{\iota}, \tag{16.21}$$

---

[31] For example, during periods of macroeconomic stress, US equities become more highly correlated with foreign currency movements; hence, the correlations between long/short equity managers and foreign currency traders may be higher than historical estimates would imply if economic conditions were to deteriorate.

where λ and ξ are constants defined in Lo (2008b), should yield non-negative portfolio weights.[32] As a consistency check, it is useful to compute the volatility, σ, of the entire portfolio implied by $\boldsymbol{w}^*$:

$$\sigma = \sqrt{\boldsymbol{w}^{*\prime}\Sigma\boldsymbol{w}^*} . \tag{16.22}$$

If σ is higher than σ_o, this implies an inconsistency with the following set of objectives:

- target expected return (μ_o);
- desired risk level (σ_o);
- target expected returns and risks of asset classes (μ_i, σ_i).

At least one of these three objectives must be modified to restore consistency. If the total investment capital is K, the optimal dollar-allocation to each asset class is simply K_i^*, where:

$$K_i^* = \omega_i^* K. \tag{16.23}$$

Once the category asset allocations, $\{K_i^*\}$, have been determined, the next step is to decide how to allocate each K_i^* across individual managers within each category i. Although a similar mean-variance optimization may be performed at this stage, the target expected returns, variances, and correlations among individual managers are much harder to estimate precisely. Therefore, the impact of estimation error may outweigh the gains from optimization methods at this level.

An alternative is to begin with identical allocations, K_i^*/m_i, across all m_i managers in category i that satisfy certain minimum conditions (e.g. assets under management, years of experience, and track record). Then, for each manager, construct a score, S_{ik}, by evaluating the manager against the following criteria, perhaps using a numerical score from 1 to 5 for each criterion:

- anticipated alpha;
- anticipated risk;
- anticipated capacity;

[32] If not, this may be a sign of model mis-specification that can serve as a useful diagnostic for identifying potential problems with the portfolio construction process. Alternatively, innovations in structured products do allow the synthetic shorting of certain hedge fund strategies, in which case, more efficient fund-of-funds portfolios may be possible. However, given the complexities of OTC derivatives on hedge funds and the significant risks they can generate, shorting hedge funds should be contemplated only by the most sophisticated and well-capitalized investors.

- anticipated correlation with other managers and asset classes;
- trading experience and past performance;
- back-test performance attribution;
- tracking error;
- risk controls;
- risk transparency;
- alpha transparency;
- operational risks;
- social impact;
- other qualitative characteristics.

For example, a manager with a high anticipated alpha (as determined through the largely qualitative manager-selection and due diligence processes) would receive a score of 5, and a manager with a low anticipated alpha would receive a score of 1. Similarly, a high-risk manager (relative to the asset-class volatility, σ_i) would receive a score of 1 and a moderate-risk manager would receive a score of 3. The sum of each of these ratings yields the manager's score, S_{ik}. Then define the relative score, s_{ik}, as:

$$s_{ik} = \frac{S_{ik}}{S_{i1} + \cdots + S_{im_i}}. \tag{16.24}$$

These scores are given equal weighting in Equation (16.24), but they can easily be assigned unique weights to over- or under-emphasize specific attributes. The manager's allocation can then be defined as:

$$\gamma_{ik} = (1 - \delta) \times \frac{1}{m_i} + \delta \times s_{ik}, \tag{16.25}$$

where δ is a parameter that determines the weight placed on the relative score in Equation (16.24) versus equal-weighting.

For a given set of manager allocations $\boldsymbol{\gamma}_i \equiv [\, \gamma_{i1} \cdots \gamma_{im_i} \,]'$ in asset class i, the implied expected return and volatility of the asset class is given by:

$$\tilde{\mu}_i = \boldsymbol{\gamma}_i' \boldsymbol{v}_i, \qquad \tilde{\sigma}_i = \sqrt{\boldsymbol{\gamma}_i' \Sigma_i \boldsymbol{\gamma}_i}, \tag{16.26}$$

where $\boldsymbol{v}_i$ is the vector of expected returns of each manager in asset class i (as determined either by back-tests or historical performance), and Σ_i is the covariance matrix of the managers in asset class i. Before implementing the allocation, $\boldsymbol{\gamma}_i$, it is important to check whether the implied expected return and risk of $\boldsymbol{\gamma}_i$ given in Equation (16.26) is consistent with the target expected return and risk, μ_i and σ_i, for sector i. If not, then the allocations in $\mathbf{y}_i$ may need to be adjusted, or the target expected return and risk must be adjusted to reduce the discrepancy.

Given an allocation $\mathbf{y}_i$, each manager's dollar allocation is then:

$$K_{ik}^* \;=\; K_i^* \times \gamma_{ik}. \tag{16.27}$$

These scores should be recomputed at least quarterly, and possibly more frequently as changes in market conditions might dictate. Each manager should be given their score so they are aware of the link between performance (as determined by the many dimensions of the score) and capital allocation. Moreover, such scores can be used as a hurdle for evaluating new managers, so that the process of managerial selection is less arbitrary over time and across individual fund analysts.

The last step in QQIP is to monitor the performance of each manager regularly to ensure that risk budgets and investment mandates are being maintained. For example, if the target risk of asset class i is σ_i, then the realized volatility, $\hat{\sigma}_i$, of the asset class can be compared to σ_i to determine any discrepancies that require further investigation, where

$$\hat{\sigma}_i \;\equiv\; \sqrt{\gamma_i' \Sigma_i \gamma_i}, \tag{16.28}$$

and Σ_i is the estimated covariance matrix of the m_i managers in asset class i. Those managers that contribute more than proportionally to the asset-class volatility, $\hat{\sigma}_i$, may be required to accept lower capital allocations, and vice versa, all else being equal. As performance varies and as parameters change, the allocations across asset classes and across managers will require periodic updating. These allocations should be recomputed monthly, although no action is needed unless the updated allocations are significantly different from the current allocations.

The scope of QQIP can be broadened to include other alternative investments such as venture capital, private equity, and impact investments. However, in such cases, a mean-variance objective function is likely to be inadequate for capturing the investment characteristics of these asset classes. In particular, both venture capital and private equity contain significant illiquidity premia given the nature of those investments, and also involve longer holding periods; hence, the mean-variance–liquidity objective function described in Section 16.4.4 and depicted in Fig. 16.3 may be more appropriate. For impact investments such as environment-related technologies, socially responsible companies, and venture philanthropy, additional metrics that measure impact must be incorporated into the objective function along with the risk and expected return. Once such metrics are constructed, the framework of QQIP can be applied to the augmented objective function.

QQIP is considerably more intricate than the straightforward construction of a typical long-only large-cap US equity portfolio, but its intricacies are a manifestation of the greater complexities of alternative investments and the fact that qualitative judgement still plays a significant role in this endeavour. Nevertheless, the industry is changing rapidly, and the hedge fund investment process is becoming more systematic across all investors. Supporting this trend are various innovations in academic research, new and improved hedge fund data sources, more sophisticated software applications for hedge fund portfolio construction and risk management, and professional organizations such as the Alternative Investment Management Association (AIMA), the Managed Funds Association (MFA), and the Chartered Alternative Investment Analysts (CAIA) Association and CAIA certification. These innovations parallel the shift in the mutual fund industry during the 1970s and 1980s towards greater transparency, lower fees, and a more disciplined investment framework, all of which has contributed to the growth and success of the entire industry.

16.7.5 Implications for Adaptive Markets

One of the most enduring challenges to the very existence of the hedge fund industry is the EMH, the idea that market prices fully reflect all available information. If the EMH holds, how can hedge funds earn 'excess' expected returns over time? The answer to this question is not just of academic interest; it has consequences for how investors should allocate their capital across traditional and alternative assets, and how they and regulators should respond to the rapid growth of the hedge fund industry.

One possible answer is that the EMH is false, and hedge funds routinely exploit the departures from efficiency. However, this explanation does not account for the high failure rate in the hedge fund industry, the capacity constraints that the most successful funds face, and the occasional periods of significant underperformance experienced by the entire industry in comparison to passive buy-and-hold investments. By all accounts, it is very difficult to produce excess risk-adjusted returns consistently and for large pools of assets.

The other extreme is that the EMH is true, and hedge funds are simply taking on additional sources of risk that have positive risk premia associated with them. There is some empirical evidence for this view based on estimates of linear factor models for hedge fund returns in which liquidity, credit, and volatility are statistically significant factors driving industry returns (see Section 16.5). However, there are a number of inordinately successful managers that earn positive risk-adjusted returns even after controlling for such factors, including industry icons such as Warren Buffett, Paul Tudor Jones, Julian Robertson, David Shaw, James Simons, and George Soros. It is difficult to dismiss all of these individuals as statistical flukes.

The theoretical foundations of the hedge fund industry can be found in the work of Sandy Grossman, a successful hedge fund manager in his own right. In Grossman (1976) and Grossman and Stiglitz (1980), he and Nobel Prize-winning economist Joseph Stiglitz argue convincingly that perfectly informationally efficient markets are an *impossibility*. If markets are perfectly efficient, there is no profit to gathering information, in which case there would be little reason to trade, and markets would not exhibit the volume they currently do. Alternatively, market efficiency is not a binary state, but rather a continuum; the *degree* of market inefficiency determines the effort investors will expend to gather and trade on information. Therefore, a non-degenerate market equilibrium occurs only when there are sufficient profit opportunities (i.e. inefficiencies) to compensate investors for the costs of trading and information-gathering. The profits earned by these industrious investors are not free lunches, but the 'economic rents' that accrue to those willing to engage in such activities.

Who are the providers of these rents? Black (1986) provides a compelling answer: noise traders, individuals who trade for non-informational reasons such as liquidity needs, portfolio rebalancing trades, or random misinformation.

More broadly, the conflict between the EMH and the hedge fund industry can be reconciled by acknowledging that, like any other industry, value-added is created through innovation, and eventually commoditized and depleted through competition. For example, the first mobile device that allowed users to exchange emails remotely—the Blackberry—generated enormous shareholder value for its owners. The returns that accrued to Blackberry's original investors are unlikely to be explained by any set of risk factors, especially since the mobile communications industry was just emerging, thanks in no small part to the market that this company created. Since then, this industry has matured, and competitors have captured the dominant market share, including the Apple iPhone and other Android smartphones. The subsequent returns to Blackberry investors were disappointing, not because of changes in factor risk premia, but because competition reduced its customer base. On 4 January 2022, Blackberry announced the expected but still-momentous extinction event that it would no longer support the original Blackberry Classic device.

The dynamics of industrial organization, innovation, and competition can easily explain the rise and fall of corporations. The same principles apply to hedge fund strategies and funds. The waxing and waning and re-emergence of various hedge fund styles are simply manifestations of Schumpeter's (1939) 'creative destruction', an observation that led Lo (2012) to call the hedge fund industry the 'Galápagos Islands of the financial sector'.[33] By appealing to the principles of evolution described in Parts I and II—innovation, adaptation, competition, and natural selection—the AMH offers a natural and internally consistent reconciliation of the apparent contradiction between the EMH and the existence and profitability of hedge funds. From the AMH perspective, the EMH is not wrong; it is simply incomplete. Prices reflect as much information as available from the combination of environmental conditions and the number and nature of 'species' in the economy or, to use the appropriate biological term, the market *ecology*. By species, we are referring to distinct groups of market participants, each behaving in a common manner. For example, pension funds may be considered one species; mutual funds, another; broker-dealers, a third; and hedge fund managers, a fourth. If multiple species (or the members of a single highly populous species) are competing for scarce resources within a single market, that market is likely to become highly efficient (e.g. the market for S&P 500 futures contracts). If, however, a small number of species are competing for rather abundant resources in a given market, that market is likely to be less efficient (e.g. the market for pre-Columbian artefacts). Market efficiency is highly context-dependent and dynamic, in much the same way that animal populations advance and decline as a function of the seasons, the number of predators and prey they face, and their abilities to adapt to an ever-changing environment.

The profit opportunities in any given market are akin to the amount of food and water in a particular local ecology: the more resources present, the less fierce the competition. As the competition increases, either because of dwindling food supplies or an increase in the animal population, resources are depleted, which, in turn, causes an eventual population decline, decreasing the level of competition and starting the cycle again. In some cases, cycles

---

[33] Other evolutionary models of financial markets and, in particular, arbitrage opportunities, include Blume and Easley (1992), Luo (1995, 1998, 2001, 2003), Farmer and Lo (1999), Hirshleifer and Luo (2001), Farmer (2002), Kogan et al. (2006), and Brennan and Lo (2011). See Parts I and II for more details.

converge to corner solutions—certain species become extinct, food sources are permanently exhausted, or environmental conditions shift dramatically. By viewing economic profits as the ultimate food source on which market participants depend for their survival, the dynamics of market interactions and financial innovation can be readily derived. From this perspective, the hedge fund industry is, indeed, the Galápagos Islands of the financial system, a place where the evolutionary dynamics can be seen by the naked eye through the waxing and waning of investment strategies and the birth and death of hedge funds across the various categories. Likewise, in the same way that an extinction event for one species can generate ripple effects that have devastating consequences for many other species, extreme losses in the hedge fund industry can serve as early warning signs of far greater dislocation in the financial ecosystem (see Section 16.6.1).

Under the AMH, there is no contradiction between the competitiveness of the financial industry and the possibility that market dislocation can occur, and, as a result, certain hedge funds can earn extraordinary profits. During the fall of 1998, the desire for liquidity and safety by a certain population of investors overwhelmed the population of hedge funds attempting to arbitrage such preferences, causing those arbitrage relations to break down. However, in the years prior to August 1998, fixed-income relative-value traders profited handsomely from these activities, presumably at the expense of individuals with seemingly 'irrational' preferences. In fact, such preferences were shaped by a certain set of evolutionary forces, and might be quite rational in other contexts like Chapter 11's great white shark in its natural habit.

Therefore, under the AMH, investment strategies undergo cycles of profitability and loss in response to changing business conditions, the number of competitors entering and exiting the industry, and the type and magnitude of profit opportunities available. As opportunities shift, so too will the affected populations. For example, after 1998, the number of fixed-income relative-value hedge funds declined dramatically—because of outright failures, investor redemptions, and fewer start-ups in this sector—but many reappeared in subsequent years as performance for this type of investment strategy improved, until the financial crisis of 2008.

Empirical support for the AMH as it applies to the hedge fund industry can be found in the dynamics of hedge fund births and deaths, documented in Section 16.2.3. Hedge fund strategies and funds wax and wane in response to risk and reward, as Table 16.3 clearly shows. A more specific illustration is contained in Fig. 16.8, which depicts the entries, exits, and average annual returns for funds in two particularly dynamic hedge fund categories, fixed income arbitrage and equity market neutral. Figure 16.8a shows that the 1998 rout in fixed income arbitrage caused a slight increase in the number of funds exiting this category, but its annual returns recovered quickly, and the total number of fixed income arbitrage funds continued to climb until the 2008 financial crisis. However, even before the crisis, as the average annual return of fixed income arbitrage trended downward from 2001 to 2006, the number of exits climbed. Beginning in 2007, the widespread liquidity problems of the crisis caused returns to drop precipitously, along with an unprecedented exodus of capital and hedge funds from fixed income arbitrage, after which returns improved once more.

Figure 16.8b offers a somewhat different narrative for equity market neutral hedge funds, whose pre-crisis annual returns were more stable than those of fixed income arbitrage. This stability contributed to the popularity of this category, also known as statistical arbitrage, which grew rapidly until its peak in 2007. However, the Quant Meltdown of August 2007 caught many investors and managers by surprise (see Section 16.6.1 and Chapter 17), leading to a large number of hedge fund exits and capital flight from this category post-crisis. Returns recovered a few years later, partly due to changes in the financial environment, and also because managers in this space adapted and innovated. However, the changing technological and regulatory landscape of equity markets have greatly increased the complexity of the environment in which equity market neutral hedge funds operate, creating winners and losers among existing funds and causing new entries and exits as discussed in Section 16.2.3.

The AMH has a number of concrete implications for the hedge fund industry. The first implication is that, contrary to the classical EMH, arbitrage opportunities do exist from time to time in the AMH, as Grossman and Stiglitz (1980) have argued. From an evolutionary perspective, the existence of active liquid financial markets implies that profit opportunities must be present. As they are exploited, they disappear. But new opportunities are also continually being created as certain species die out and others are born, and as institutions and business conditions change. Rather than the inexorable trend towards higher efficiency predicted by the EMH, the AMH implies considerably more complex market dynamics, with cycles, as well as trends, and panics, manias, bubbles, crashes, and the other phenomena that are routinely witnessed in natural market ecologies. These dynamics provide the motivation for active management as Bernstein (1998) suggests, also giving rise to Niederhoffer's (1997) 'carnivores' and 'decomposers' cited in Chapter 2.

A second implication—highlighted by the entry-and-exit dynamics noted in Section 16.2.3 and Fig. 16.8—is that investment strategies will also wax and wane, performing well in certain environments and performing poorly in other environments. Contrary to the classical EMH in which arbitrage opportunities are competed away, eventually eliminating the profitability of

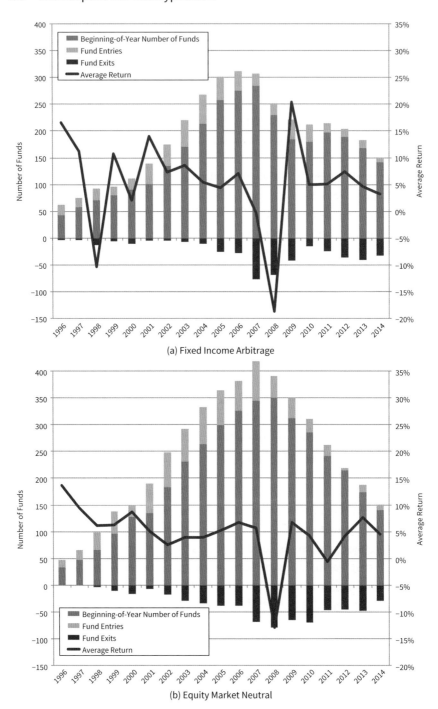

Fig. 16.8 Fund entries, exits, and average annual returns for single manager funds in the Credit Suisse/Tremont database from 1996 to 2014 for two categories: (a) fixed income arbitrage and (b) equity market neutral.

the strategy designed to exploit the arbitrage, the AMH implies that such strategies may decline for a time, and then return to profitability when environmental conditions become more conducive to such trades. An obvious example is risk arbitrage, which has been unprofitable for several years because of the decline in investment banking activity since 2001. However, as M&A activity begins to pick up again, risk arbitrage will start to regain its popularity among both investors and portfolio managers, as it has over the past decade.

A more striking example is autocorrelation in US stock returns. As a measure of market efficiency (recall that the random walk hypothesis implies that returns are serially uncorrelated), autocorrelations of the CRSP value-weighted equity returns index might be expected to take on larger values during the early part of the sample, and become progressively smaller during the latter part of the sample as the US equity market becomes more competitive. Figure 16.9 displays the statistical significance of the first five autocorrelations of 500-day rolling windows of daily CRSP value-weighted returns according to the Ljung–Box statistic.[34] There are clearly extended periods during which autocorrelation is statistically significant, such as the 1950s, the 1970s, and the last five-year period in the figure. The *degree* of efficiency—as measured by the first five autocorrelations—varies through time in a cyclical fashion; for example, there are periods in the 1960s where the market was apparently more efficient than today.

Such cycles are not ruled out by the EMH in theory, but, in practice, none of its existing empirical implementations has incorporated these dynamics, assuming instead a stationary world in which markets are perpetually in equilibrium. This widening gulf between the stationary EMH and obvious shifts in market conditions have no doubt contributed to the recent spate of new investment offerings, including risk-parity funds, tactical asset allocation funds, environmental, social, and governance (ESG) and social-impact products, and various active ETFs.

A third implication is that innovation is the key to survival. The classical EMH suggests that certain levels of expected returns can be achieved simply

---

[34] To obtain a summary measure of the overall statistical significance of the autocorrelations, Ljung and Box (1978) propose the following statistic:

$$Q \; = \; T(T+2) \sum_{k=1}^{p} \hat{\rho}_k^2 / (T-k), \qquad (16.27)$$

which is asymptotically χ_p^2 under the null hypothesis of no autocorrelation (Kendall, Stuart, and Ord, 1983, Chapter 50.13). By forming the sum of squared autocorrelations, Q reflects the absolute magnitudes of the $\hat{\rho}_k$'s irrespective of their signs; hence, time series with large positive or negative autocorrelation coefficients will exhibit large Q-statistics.

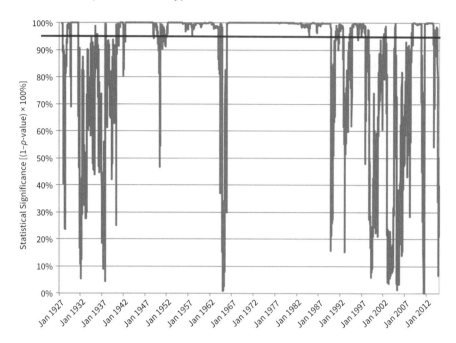

Fig. 16.9 Five-hundred-day rolling-window statistical significance (1−p-value) of the Ljung–Box Q statistic for autocorrelation in daily CRSP Value-Weighted Index returns using the first five autocorrelation coefficients, from 31 August 1927 to 31 December 2014. The red line denotes 95% significance; hence, all realizations above this line are significant at the 5% level.

by bearing a sufficient degree of risk. The AMH implies that the risk–reward relationship varies through time, and that a better way of achieving a consistent level of expected returns is to adapt to changing market conditions. By evolving a multiplicity of capabilities that are suited to a variety of environmental conditions, investment managers are less likely to become extinct as a result of rapid changes in business conditions (see also Chapter 3). Consider the current theory of the demise of the dinosaurs (Alvarez, 1997), and ask where the next financial asteroid might come from.

Finally, the AMH has a clear implication for all financial market participants: survival is the *only* objective that matters in the long run. While profit maximization, utility maximization, and general equilibrium are certainly relevant aspects of market ecology, the organizing principle in determining the evolution of markets and financial technology is simply survival.

These evolutionary underpinnings are more than simple speculation in the context of the hedge fund industry. The extraordinary degree of competitiveness of global financial markets, the outsized rewards that accrue to the 'fittest' managers, and the relatively low barriers to entry and minimal fixed costs of setup suggest that Darwinian selection—the 'survival of the richest', to be precise—is at work in determining the typical profile of the successful hedge fund. After all, unsuccessful managers are rather quickly eliminated from the population after suffering a certain level of losses, only to be replaced by many eager professionals hoping to make their own name in this dynamic industry. In the same spirit in which the evolutionary biologist Theodosius Dobzhansky observed that 'nothing in biology makes sense except in the light of evolution', none of the dynamics of the hedge fund industry makes sense except in the light of adaptive markets.

16.8 Discussion

Two dangerous myths about hedge funds can mislead investors, portfolios, regulators, and policymakers into making inappropriate decisions. The first myth is that all hedge funds are alike, implying that alternative investments comprise a homogeneous asset class that have similar investment character-istics with returns that move in concert. The second myth is that all hedge funds are unique, implying no commonalities, and therefore have no impli-cations for diversification or systemic risk. In this chapter, we hope to have dispelled both these myths by reviewing various aspects of the hedge fund literature and their implications for all stakeholders in this important and dynamic industry.

The freedom with which hedge funds are allowed to invest their capital gives them a unique breadth of coverage as an industry and a unique depth of expertise at the level of the individual fund. However, their unconstrained and varied investment strategies contain non-standard forms of risk includ-ing phase-locking behaviour, illiquidity, nonlinearities, and operational risks that are poorly captured by conventional metrics. More sophisticated risk models are available, but they require much greater training and experience.

The highly competitive nature of this industry implies rapid innovation and attrition, which can greatly benefit the nimble and risk-tolerant investor, but which can be a source of great stress and financial loss for the naive and inattentive investor. By considering the suitability of the various risk dimensions associated with each hedge fund investment style, however, along with the potential for generating attractive returns, investors should be able to construct a systematic investment process that incorporates hedge fund investments into more traditional portfolios.

The adaptability of the hedge fund industry also implies that hedge funds can serve as an invaluable monitoring system for identifying trouble spots throughout the financial system. The financial crisis of 2008 left a significant mark on the industry, ending an era of excessive optimism about hedge fund returns, and starting a new era in which the industry is retrenching and re-emphasizing its core competencies under heavier investor scrutiny and regulatory oversight.

Because the hedge fund industry will continue to evolve rapidly in response to new challenges and opportunities, continuous monitoring and research will be necessary for investors, regulators, and hedge fund managers to keep up with these changes, and we hope this survey, and the AMH framework provided in this volume, provide a useful perspective for this task.

17

What Happened to the Quants
in August 2007?

During the first half of 2007, events in the subprime mortgage markets in the US affected many parts of the financial industry, setting the stage for more turmoil in the fixed-income and credit world.[1] But few investment professionals expected this turmoil to spill over to equity markets, which is exactly what happened during July and August 2007. We touched upon this issue in Chapter 16's discussion of the Quant Meltdown, but because of the importance of the event for understanding the nature of systemic risk, we will take a deeper dive in this chapter.

Apart from stocks in the financial sector, equity markets were largely unaffected by these troubles prior to July 2007. With the benefit of hindsight, however, signs of macro stress and shifting expectations of future economic conditions were apparent in equity prices during this period. In July, the performance of certain well-known equity-valuation factors such as Fama and French's small-minus-big (SMB) market-cap and high-minus-low (HML) book-to-market factors began a downward trend. While this fact is unremarkable in and of itself, the events that transpired during the second week of August 2007 have made it much more meaningful in retrospect.

Starting on Monday 6 August, and continuing through Thursday 9 August, some of the most successful equity hedge funds in the history of the industry reported record losses.[2] But what made these losses even more extraordinary

---

[1] This chapter, including the tables and figures, is adapted from Khandani, A. E., and Lo, A. W. (2011). What happened to the quants in August 2007? Evidence from factors and transactions data. *Journal of Financial Markets* 14(1): 1–46.

[2] For example, *The Wall Street Journal* reported on 10 August 2007 that 'After the close of trading, Renaissance Technologies Corp., a hedge fund company with one of the best records in recent years, told investors that a key fund has lost 8.7% so far in August and is down 7.4% in 2007. Another big fund company, Highbridge Capital Management, told investors its Highbridge Statistical Opportunities Fund was down 18% as of the 8th of the month, and was down 16% for the year. The $1.8 billion publicly traded Highbridge Statistical Market Neutral Fund was down 5.2% for the month as of Wednesday…Tykhe Capital, LLC—a New York-based quantitative, or computer-driven, hedge fund firm that manages about $1.8 billion—has suffered losses of about 20% in its largest hedge fund so far this month…' (Zuckerman, Hagerty, and Gauthier-Villars, 2007), and on 14 August, *The Wall Street Journal* reported that the Goldman Sachs Global Equity Opportunities Fund '…lost more than 30% of its value last week…' (Sender, Kelly, and Zuckerman, 2007).

The Adaptive Markets Hypothesis. Andrew W. Lo and Ruixun Zhang, Oxford University Press. © Andrew W. Lo and Ruixun Zhang (2024). DOI: 10.1093/oso/9780199681143.003.0017

was the fact that they seemed to be concentrated among quantitatively managed equity market neutral or 'statistical arbitrage' hedge funds, giving rise to the monikers 'Quant Meltdown' and 'Quant Quake' of 2007.

In an attempt to piece together this puzzling sequence of events, Khandani and Lo (2007) combined inferences from Lipper hedge fund data and simulations of the returns of a specific equity market neutral strategy, the contrarian trading strategy of Lehmann (1990) and Lo and MacKinlay (1990), and reproduced the huge losses in August 2007. They proposed the 'unwind hypothesis' to explain the empirical facts (see also Goldman Sachs Asset Management (2007), and Rothman (2007a,b,c)), which conjectures that the initial losses during the second week of August 2007 were due to the forced liquidation of one or more large equity market neutral portfolios, primarily to raise cash or reduce leverage, and the subsequent price impact of this massive and sudden unwinding caused other similarly constructed portfolios to experience losses. In turn, these losses caused other funds to deleverage their portfolios, yielding an additional price impact that led to further losses, more deleveraging, and so on.[3] This is one of the clearest examples of Brunnermeier's (2009) margin and deleveraging spirals.[4] As with LTCM and other fixed income arbitrage funds in August 1998, the deadly feedback loop of coordinated forced liquidations leading to deterioration of collateral value took hold during the second week of August 2007, ultimately resulting in the collapse of a number of quantitative equity market neutral managers, and double-digit losses for many others.

A significant rebound of these strategies occurred on 10 August, presumably in response to an announced injection of capital into one of the hardest-hit funds, Goldman Sachs's Global Equity Opportunities Fund. But another factor that may have contributed to the reversal on the tenth was the overnight liquidity injection by the major central banks into short-term interbank lending markets in response to the so-called 'run on repo' on 9 August (Gorton and Metrick, 2012).

The unwind hypothesis underscores the apparent commonality among quantitative equity market neutral hedge funds and the importance of liquidity in determining market dynamics. We focus on these twin issues in this chapter by simulating the performance of typical mean-reversion and

---

[3] In particular, Khandani and Lo (2011b) simulate simple equity market neutral strategies using five factors commonly used in quantitative equity trading strategies, three value-factors similar to those in Lakonishok, Shleifer, and Vishny (1994), and two momentum factors as in Chan, Jegadeesh, and Lakonishok (1996), and show that funds began unwinding portfolios constructed with these factors as early as the beginning of July 2007.

[4] Although Brunnermeier's (2009) focus was on mortgage-related losses, his argument applies verbatim to the Quant Meltdown. In both cases, the amplification mechanism is key: the deteriorating balance sheets of borrowers generate liquidity spirals from relatively small shocks, and, once started, these spirals continue as lower asset prices and higher volatility raise the margin levels and lower the available leverage.

valuation-factor-based long/short equity portfolios, and by using transactions data during the months surrounding August 2007 to measure the market liquidity and price impact before, during, and after the Quant Meltdown. With respect to the former simulations, we find that during the month of July 2007, long/short portfolios constructed based on traditional equity characteristics (such as book-to-market, earnings-to-price, and cashflow-to-market) steadily declined, while portfolios constructed based on momentum metrics (price momentum and earnings momentum) increased. With respect to the latter simulations, we find that intradaily liquidity in US equity markets declined significantly during the second week of August, and that the expected return of a simpler mean-reversion strategy increased monotonically with the holding period during this time (i.e. those market-makers that were able to hold their positions longer received higher premiums). The shorter-term losses also imply that market-makers reduced their risk capital during this period. In particular, we identify two unwinds—one on 1 August starting at 10:45am ET and ending at 11:30am ET, and a second at the open on 6 August, ending at 1:00pm ET—that began with stocks that were in the financial sector, long book-to-market, and short earnings momentum.

Together, these results suggest that the Quant Meltdown of August 2007 began in July with the steady unwinding of one or more factor-driven portfolios, and this unwinding caused significant dislocation in August, because the pace of liquidation increased, and because liquidity providers decreased their risk capital during the second week of August.

If correct, these conjectures highlight additional risks faced by investors in long/short equity funds, namely, the tail risk due to occasional liquidations and deleveraging that may be motivated by events completely unrelated to equity markets. Such risks also imply that long/short equity strategies may contribute to systemic risk because of their ubiquity, their importance to market liquidity and price continuity, and their impact on market dynamics when capital is suddenly withdrawn.

As in Khandani and Lo (2007), we wish to acknowledge at the outset that the hypotheses advanced in this chapter are speculative, tentative, and based solely on indirect evidence. Because the events surrounding the Quant Meltdown involve hedge funds, proprietary trading desks, and their prime brokers and credit counterparties, primary sources are virtually impossible to access. Such sources are not at liberty to disclose any information about their positions, strategies, or risk exposures; hence, the only means for obtaining insight into these events are indirect. However, in contrast to Khandani and Lo's (2007) earlier claim that '…the answer to the question of what happened to the quants in August 2007 is indeed known, at least to a number of industry professionals who were directly involved', Khandani and Lo (2011b) argue instead that industry participants directly involved in the Quant Meltdown may not have been fully aware of the broader milieu in which they were operating. Accordingly, there is, indeed, a role for academic studies that attempt to piece together the various components of the market dislocation of August 2007 by analysing the simulated performance of specific investment strategies like the strategies considered in this chapter and in Khandani and Lo (2007).

Nevertheless, we recognize the challenges that outsiders face in attempting to understand such complex issues without the benefit of hard data, and emphasize that our educated guesses may be off the mark, given the limited data we have to work with. We caution readers to be appropriately sceptical of our hypotheses, as are we.

Related Literature

Although the focus of this chapter is the Quant Meltdown of August 2007, several studies have considered the causes and inner workings of the broader liquidity and credit crunch of 2007–2008. For example, Gorton (2008) discusses the details of security design and securitization of subprime mortgages and argues that lack of transparency arising from the interconnected links of securitization is at the heart of the problem. Brunnermeier (2009) argues that the mortgage-related losses are relatively small. For example, he indicates that the total expected losses are about the same amount of wealth lost in a not uncommon 2% to 3% drop in the US stock market. Starting from this observation, he emphasizes the importance of the amplification mechanism at play, and argues that borrowers' deteriorating balance sheets generate liquidity spirals from relatively small shocks. Once started, these spirals continue as lower asset prices and higher volatility raise margin levels and lower the available leverage. Adrian and Shin (2008) document a pro-cyclical relationship between the leverage of US investment banks and the sizes of their balance sheets, and explore the aggregate effects that such a relationship can have on asset prices and the volatility risk premium. This empirical observation increases the likelihood of Brunnermeier's (2009) margin and deleveraging spiral. Allen and Carletti (2008) provide a more detailed analysis of the role of liquidity in the financial crisis, and consider the source of the 'cash-in-the-market' pricing (i.e. market prices that are significantly below what plausible fundamentals would suggest).

Following the onset of the credit crunch in July 2007, beginning on 6 August, many equity hedge funds reported significant losses, and much of the blame was placed on quantitative factors, or the 'Quants', as the most severe losses appear to have been concentrated among quantitative hedge funds.

The research departments of the major investment banks also produced analyses (e.g. Goldman Sachs Asset Management (2007) and Rothman (2007a,b,c)), citing coordinated losses among portfolios constructed according to several well-known quant factors, arguing that simultaneous deleveraging and a lack of liquidity were responsible for these losses. For example, the study by Rothman (2007b), which was first released on 9 August 2007, reports the performance of a number of quant factors and attributes the simultaneous bad performance to 'a liquidity based deleveraging phenomena'. Goldman Sachs Asset Management (2007) provides additional evidence from foreign equity markets (Japan, the UK, and Europe-ex-UK), indicating that the unwinds involved more than US securities alone. In a follow-up study, Rothman (2007c) called attention to the perils of endogenous risk; in referring to the breakdown of the risk models during that period, he concluded that: 'By and large, they understated the risks as they were not calibrated for quant managers/models becoming our own asset class, creating our own contagion.'[5] Litterman (2013) provides a fascinating personal account of these events as he witnessed them firsthand as a partner at Goldman Sachs during August 2007.[6] His analysis of the Quant Meltdown is both riveting and intellectually stimulating, and should be required viewing for all hedge fund managers, investors, and financial regulators.

In its conclusion, the Goldman Sachs Asset Management (2007) study suggests that '…it is not clear that there were any obvious early warning signs…. No one, however, could possibly have forecasted the extent of deleveraging or the magnitude of last week's factor returns.' Our analysis suggests that the dislocation was exacerbated by the withdrawal of market-making risk capital—possibly by high-frequency hedge funds—starting on 8 August. This highlights the endogenous nature of liquidity risk and the degree of interdependence among market participants, or 'species' in the terminology of Farmer and Lo (1999). The fact that the ultimate origins of this dislocation were apparently outside the long/short equity sector—most likely in a completely unrelated set of markets and instruments—suggests that systemic risk in the hedge fund industry increased significantly during this period.

In this chapter, we turn our attention to the impact of specific quant factors before, during, and after the Quant Meltdown, using a set of the most well-known factors from the academic 'anomalies' literature such

---

[5] See also Montier (2007).
[6] See https://youtu.be/oIKbWTdKfHs.

as Banz (1981), Basu (1981), Bhandari (1988), and Jegadeesh and Titman (1993). Although the evidence for some of these anomalies is subject to debate,[7] they have nevertheless resulted in various multifactor pricing models such as the widely cited Fama and French (1993) three-factor model. We limit our attention to five factors—three value factors similar to those in Lakonishok, Shleifer, and Vishny (1994), and two momentum factors as in Chan, Jegadeesh, and Lakonishok (1996)—and describe their construction in Sections 17.1 and 17.2.

17.1 The Data

We use three sources of data for our analysis. All of our analysis focuses on the members of S&P Composite 1500, which includes all stocks in the S&P 500 (large-cap), S&P 400 (mid-cap), and S&P 600 (small-cap) indexes. Annual and quarterly balance-sheet information from Standard & Poor's Compustat database is used to calculate the relevant characteristics for the members of the S&P 1500 index in 2007. To study market microstructure effects, we use the Trades and Quotes (TAQ) data set from the New York Stock Exchange (NYSE). In addition, we use daily stock returns and volume from the University of Chicago's Center for Research in Security Prices (CRSP) to calculate the daily returns of various long/short portfolios and their trading volumes. Sections 17.1.1 and 17.1.2 contain brief overviews of the Compustat and TAQ data sets, respectively, and we provide details for the CRSP data set throughout the chapter as needed.

17.1.1 Compustat Data

Balance sheet information is obtained from Standard & Poor's Compustat database via the Wharton Research Data Services (WRDS) platform. We use the 'CRSP/Compustat Merged Database' to map the balance sheet information to CRSP historical stock returns data. From the annual Compustat database, we use:

- *Book Value Per Share* (item code BKVLPS);
- *Basic Earnings Per Share Excluding Extraordinary Items* (item code EPSPX);

---

[7] See, for example, Fama and French (2006), Lewellen and Nagel (2006), and Ang and Chen (2007).

- *Net Cashflow of Operating Activities* (item code OANCF);
- *Fiscal Cumulative Adjustment Factor* (item code ADJEX_F).

We also use the following variables from the quarterly Compustat database:

- *Quarterly Basic Earnings Per Share Excluding Extraordinary Items* (item code EPSPXQ);
- *Cumulative Adjustment Factor by Ex-Date* (item code ADJEX);
- *Report Date of Quarterly Earnings* (item code RDQ).

There is usually a gap between the end of the fiscal year or quarter and the date that the information is available to the public. We implement the following rules to make sure any information used in creating the factors is, in fact, available on the date that the factor is calculated. For the annual data, a gap of at least four months is enforced (e.g. an entry dated December 2005 is first used starting in April 2006) and, to avoid using old data, we exclude data that are more than one year and four months old (i.e. if a security does not have another annual data point after December 2005, that security is dropped from the sample in April 2007). For the quarterly data, we rely on the date given in Compustat for the actual reporting date (item code RDQ, *Report Date of Quarterly Earnings*) to ensure that the data are available on the portfolio construction date. For the handful of cases in which RDQ is not available, we employ an approach similar to that taken for the annual data. In those cases, to ensure that the quarterly data are available on the construction date and not stale, the quarterly data are used with a forty-five-day gap, and any data older than 135 days are not used (e.g. to construct the portfolio in April 2007, we use data from December 2006, and January or February 2007, and do not use data from April or March 2007).

17.1.2 TAQ Transactions Data

The NYSE's TAQ database contains intraday transactions and quotes data for all securities listed on the NYSE, the American Stock Exchange, the NASDAQ National Market System, and SmallCap issues. The data set consists of the Daily National Best Bids and Offers (NBBO) File, the Daily Quotes File, the Daily TAQ Master File, and the Daily Trades File. For the purposes of this study, we only use actual trades as reported in the Daily Trades File. This file includes information such as the security symbol, trade time, size, and exchange on which the trade took place, as well as a few condition and correction flags. We only use trades that occur during normal trading hours (9:30am–4:00pm ET). We also discarded all records that have *Trade Correction Indicator* field entries other than '00'[8] and removed all trades that were reported late or reported out of sequence, according to the *Sale Condition* field.[9] During the sixty-three trading days of our sample of TAQ data from 2 July 2007 to 28 September 2007, the stocks within the universe of our study (the S&P 1500) yielded a total of approximately 805 million trades, ranging from a low of 4.9 million trades on 3 July 2007 to a high of 23.7 million trades on 16 August 2007. The cross-sectional variation of the number of trades was quite large; for example, there were approximately 11 million trades in Apple (AAPL) during our sample period, while Lawson Products (LAWS) was traded only 6,830 times during the same period. On average, we analysed approximately 11.3 million trades per day to develop our liquidity measures.

Using transactions prices in the Daily Trades File, we construct five minute returns within each trading day (no overnight returns are allowed) based on the most recent transactions price within each five minute interval, subject to the filters described above. These returns are the inputs to the various strategy simulations reported in Sections 17.2 and 17.3. For the estimation of price-impact coefficients in Section 17.3.3, transactions prices are used, again subject to the same filters described above.

17.2 Factor Portfolios

To study the Quant Meltdown of August 2007, we use the returns of several long/short equity market neutral portfolios based on the kinds of quantitative processes and characteristic-based security rankings that might be used by quant funds. For example, it is believed that the value premium is a proxy for a market-wide distress factor (Fama and French, 1992).[10] Fama and French (1995) note that the typical value stock has a price that has been driven down due to financial distress. This observation suggests a direct explanation of the

[8] According to the TAQ documentation, a Trade Correction Indicator value of '00' signifies a regular trade that was not corrected, changed or canceled. This field is used to indicate trades that were later signified as errors (code '07' or '08') or cancelled records (code '10'), as well as several other possibilities. Please see the TAQ documentation for more detail.
[9] These filters have been used in other studies based on TAQ data; see, for example, Christie, Harris, and Schultz (1994) or Chordia, Roll, and Subrahmanyam (2001). See the TAQ documentation for further details.
[10] Kao and Shumaker (1999) document some intuitive links between macro factors and the return for value stocks. Of course, the problem can be turned on its head, and stock returns can be used to predict future macro events, as in Liew and Vassalou (2000) and Vassalou (2003). Behavioural arguments are also used to explain the apparent premium for value factors (Lakonishok, Shleifer, and Vishny, 1994).

value premium: in the event of a credit crunch, stocks in financial distress will do poorly, and this is precisely when investors are least willing to put money at risk.[11]

By simulating the returns of a portfolio formed to highlight such factors, we may be able to trace out the dynamics of other portfolios with similar exposures to these factors. An example of this approach is given in Fig. 17.1, which contains the cumulative returns of the Fama and French SMB and HML portfolios, as well as a price-momentum factor portfolio during 2007.[12] The trading volume during this period also shows some unusual patterns, giving some support to the unwind hypothesis. During the week of 23 July 2007, the volume began building to levels well above normal.[13] The average volume during the weeks of 23 July, 30 July, 6 August and 13 August reached record levels of 2.9, 3.0, 3.6, and 3.1 billion shares, respectively, before finally returning to a more normal level of 1.9 billion shares during the week of 20 August.

Figure 17.1 also displays the cumulative return of Lehmann's (1990) and Lo and MacKinlay's (1990) short-term mean-reversion or contrarian strategy, which was used by Khandani and Lo (2007) to illustrate the Quant Meltdown of 2007.[14] The sudden drop and recovery of this strategy during the week of 6 August, following several weeks of lower-than-expected performance, captures much of the dislocation during this period.

To develop some intuition for this dislocation, consider the underlying economic motivation for the contrarian strategy. By taking long positions in stocks that have declined and short positions in stocks that have advanced over the previous trading day, the strategy actively provides liquidity to the marketplace.[15] By implicitly making a bet on daily mean reversion among a large universe of stocks, the strategy is exposed to any continuation or

---

[11] One should note that the 'distress' of an individual firm cannot always be treated as a risk factor, since such distress is often idiosyncratic and can, therefore, be diversified away. Only aggregate events that a significant portion of the population of investors care about will result in a risk premium.

[12] Data obtained from the data library section of Kenneth French's website: http://mba.tuck.dartmouth.edu/pages/faculty/ken.french/. Refer to the documentation available from that site for further details.

[13] The first day with extremely high volume is 22 June 2007, which was the rebalancing day for all Russell indexes, and a spike in volume was expected on this day because of the amount of assets invested in funds tracking these indexes.

[14] Components of the S&P 1500 as of 3 January 2007 are used. Strategy holdings are constructed and the daily returns are calculated based on the holding period return from the CRSP daily returns file. See Khandani and Lo (2007) for further details.

[15] By definition, losers are stocks that have underperformed relative to some market average, implying a supply-and-demand imbalance in the direction of excess supply that has caused the prices of those securities to drop, and vice versa for the winners. By buying losers and selling winners, the contrarians are adding to the demand for losers and increasing the supply of winners, thereby stabilizing the imbalances in supply and demand.

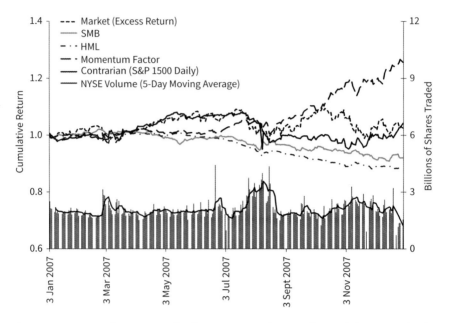

Fig. 17.1 Factor performance and volume in 2007. The cumulative daily returns for the market, small-minus-big (SMB), high-minus-low (HML), and momentum factors, as well as the contrarian strategy of Lehmann (1990) and Lo and MacKinlay (1990) for 3 January 2007 to 31 December 2007. Data for market, SMB, HML, and momentum factors were obtained from Kenneth French's website (see footnote 12 for details). The contrarian strategy was implemented as in Khandani and Lo (2007) using daily returns for stocks listed in the S&P 1500 on 3 January 2007. Volume represents the Daily NYSE Group Volume in NYSE-listed securities obtained from the NYSE Euronext website.

persistence in the daily returns (i.e. price trends or momentum).[16] Broad-based momentum across a group of stocks can arise from a large-scale liquidation of a portfolio that may take several days to complete, depending on the size of the portfolio and the urgency of the liquidation. In short, the contrarian strategy underperforms when the usual mean reversion in stock prices is replaced by momentum, possibly due to a sizeable and rapid liquidation. We will elaborate on this theme in Section 17.3.1.

In Section 17.2.1, we describe the five specific factors that we propose to capture the events of August 2007, and in Section 17.2.2 we present the simulations for these factor portfolios before, during, and after the Quant Meltdown.

---

[16] Note that positive profits for the contrarian strategy may arise from sources other than mean reversion. For example, positive lead–lag relations across stocks can yield contrarian profits (see Lo and MacKinlay (1990) for details).

17.2.1 Factor Construction

We focus our analysis on five of the most studied and highly cited quantitative equity valuation factors: three value measures, price momentum, and earnings momentum. The three value measures, book-to-market, earnings-to-price, and cashflow-to-market, are similar to the factors discussed in Lakonishok, Shleifer, and Vishny (1994). These factors are based on the most recent annual balance sheet data from Compustat and constructed according to the procedure described below. The two remaining factors, price momentum and earnings momentum, have been studied extensively in connection with momentum strategies (e.g. see Chan, Jegadeesh, and Lakonishok (1996)). The earnings momentum factor is based on quarterly earnings from Compustat, while the price momentum factor is based on the reported monthly returns from the CRSP database. At the end of each month, each of these five factors is computed for each stock in the S&P 1500 index using the following procedure.

1. The book-to-market factor is calculated as the ratio of the book value per share (item code BKVLPS in Compustat) reported in the most recent annual report (subject to the availability rules outlined in Section 17.1.1) divided by the closing price on the last day of the month. The share adjustment factor from CRSP and Compustat is used to reflect any changes in the number of outstanding common shares.

2. The earnings-to-price factor is calculated from the basic earnings per share excluding extraordinary items (item code EPSPX in Compustat) reported in the most recent annual report (subject to the availability rules outlined in Section 17.1.1) divided by the closing price on the last day of the month. The share adjustment factor available in CRSP and Compustat is used to reflect stock splits and other changes in the number of outstanding common shares.

3. The cashflow-to-market factor is calculated using the net cashflow of operating activities (item code OANCF in Compustat) reported in the most recent annual data (subject to the availability rules outlined in Section 17.1.1) divided by the total market cap of common equity on the last day of the month. The number of shares outstanding and the closing price reported in CRSP files are used to calculate the total market value of common equity.

4. The price momentum factor is the stock's cumulative total return (calculated using the holding period return from CRSP files, which

includes dividends) over the period spanning the previous two to twelve months.[17]

5. The earnings momentum factor is constructed using the quarterly basic earnings per share excluding extraordinary items (item code EPSPXQ in Compustat), and the standardized unexpected earnings (SUE). The SUE factor is calculated as the ratio of the earnings growth in the most recent quarter (subject to the availability rules outlined in Section 17.1.1) relative to the year earlier, divided by the standard deviation of the same factor calculated over the prior eight quarters (see Chan, Jegadeesh, and Lakonishok (1996) for a more detailed discussion of this factor).

At the end of each month during our sample period, we divide the S&P 1500 universe into deciles according to each factor. Decile 1 contains the group of companies with the lowest value of the factor; for example, companies whose stocks have performed poorly in the last 2–12 months will be in the first decile of the price momentum factor. Deciles 1–9 have the same number of stocks, while decile 10 may have more if the original number of stocks was not divisible by ten. We do not require a company to have data for all five factors or to be a US common stock to be used in each ranking. However, we use only those stocks that are listed as US common shares (CRSP Share Code '10' or '11') to construct portfolios and analyse returns.[18] For example, if a company does not have eight quarters of earnings data, it cannot be ranked according to the earnings momentum factor, but it will still be ranked according to other measures if the information required for calculating those measures is available.

This process yields decile rankings for each of these factors for each month of our sample. In most months, we have the data to construct deciles for more than 1,400 companies. However, at the time we obtained the Compustat data for this analysis, the Compustat database was still not fully populated with the 2007 quarterly data; in particular, the data for the quarter ending September 2007 (2007Q3) was very sparse. Given the forty-five-day lag we employ for quarterly data, the lack of data for 2007Q3 means that the deciles can be formed for only about 370 companies at the end of November 2007 (the comparable count was 1,381 in October 2007 and 1,405 at the end of September

---

[17] The most recent month is not included, as in the price momentum factor available on Kenneth French's data library (see footnote 12).

[18] This procedure should not impact our analysis materially, as there are only 50–60 stocks in the S&P indexes without these share codes, and these are typically securities with share code '12', indicating companies incorporated outside the US.

2007). Since any analysis of factor models for December 2007 is affected by this issue, we will limit our study to the first eleven months of 2007.

Given the decile rankings of the five factors, we can simulate the returns of portfolios based on each of these factors. In particular, for each of the five factors, at the end of each month in our sample period, we construct a long/short portfolio by investing \$1 long in the stocks in the tenth decile and investing \$1 short in the stocks in the first decile of that month. Each \$1 investment is distributed using equal weights among stocks in the respective decile, and each portfolio is purchased at the closing price on the last trading day of the previous month. For the daily analysis, the cumulative return is calculated using daily returns based on the holding period return available from CRSP daily returns files. For the intraday return analysis, we compute the value of long/short portfolios using the most recent transactions price in each five minute interval based on TAQ Daily Trades File (see Section 17.1.2 for details). We use the cumulative factor to adjust price (CFACPR) from the CRSP daily files to adjust for stock splits but do not adjust for dividend payments.[19] Each portfolio is rebalanced on the last trading day of each month, and a new portfolio is constructed. For a few rare cases where a stock stops trading during the month, we assume that the final value of the initial investment in that stock is kept in cash for the remainder of the month.

17.2.2 Market Behaviour in 2007

Figure 17.2 contains the daily cumulative returns for each of the five factors in 2007 until the end of November. The results are consistent with the patterns in Fig. 17.1—the three value factors began their downward drift at the start of July 2007, consistent with the HML factor-portfolio returns in Fig. 17.1. However, the two momentum factors were the two best performers over the second half of 2007, again consistent with Fig. 17.1. Also, the two momentum factors and the cashflow-to-market portfolio experienced very large drops and subsequent reversals during the second week of August 2007.

Of course, secular declines and advances of factor portfolios need not have anything to do with deleveraging or unwinding; they may simply reflect the changing market valuations of value stocks, or trends and reversals that

---

[19] Our intraday returns are unaffected by dividend payments; hence, our analysis of market-making profits and price-impact coefficients should be largely unaffected by omitting this information. However, when we compute the cumulative returns for certain strategies that involve holding overnight positions, small approximation errors may arise from the fact that we do not take dividends into account when using transactions data.

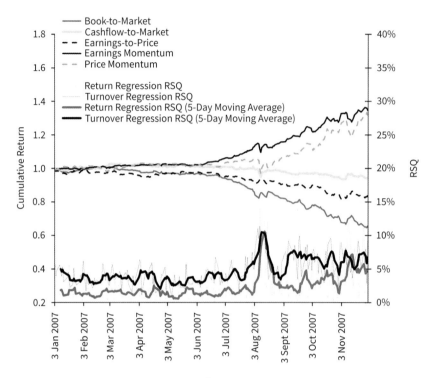

Fig. 17.2 Cumulative performance and R^2 (RSQ) of cross-sectional regressions for quant factors. Cumulative performance of five long/short equity market neutral portfolios constructed from commonly used equity-valuation factors, from 3 January 2007 to 31 December 2007. Also plotted are daily RSQs and their five-day moving averages of the following cross-sectional regressions of returns and turnover: $R_{i,t} = \alpha_t + \sum_{f=1}^{5} \beta_{f,t} D_{i,f} + \epsilon_{i,t}$, and $TO_{i,t} = \gamma_t + \sum_{f=1}^{5} \delta_{f,t} |D_{i,f} - 5.5| + \eta_{i,t}$, where $R_{i,t}$ is the return for security i on day t, $D_{i,f}$ is the decile ranking of security i according to factor f, and $TO_{i,t}$, the turnover for security i on day t, is defined as the ratio of the number of shares traded to the shares outstanding.

arise from typical market fluctuations. To establish a link between the movements of the five factor portfolios during July and August 2007 and the unwind hypothesis, we perform two cross-sectional regressions each day from January to November 2007 using daily stock returns and turnover as the dependent variables:

$$R_{i,t} = \alpha_t + \sum_{f=1}^{5} \beta_{f,t} D_{i,f} + \epsilon_{i,t}, \tag{17.1a}$$

$$TO_{i,t} - \gamma_t + \sum_{f=1}^{5} \delta_{f,t} |D_{i,f} - 5.5| + \eta_{i,t}, \tag{17.1b}$$

where $R_{i,t}$ is the return for security i on day t, $D_{i,f}$ is the decile ranking of security i according to factor f,[20] and $TO_{i,t}$, the turnover for security i on day t, is defined as:[21]

$$TO_{i,t} \equiv \frac{\text{Number of Shares Traded for Security } i \text{ on Day } t}{\text{Number of Shares Outstanding for Security } i \text{ on Day } t}. \qquad (17.2)$$

If, as we hypothesize, there was a significant unwinding of factor-based portfolios in July and August 2007, the explanatory power of these two cross-sectional regressions should spike up during those months because of the overwhelming price impact and concentrated volume of the unwind. If, however, it was business as usual, then the factors should not have any additional explanatory power during that period than any other period.

The lower part of Fig. 17.2 displays the R^2 for the regressions in Equation (17.1) each day during the sample period. To smooth the sampling variation of these R^2, we also display their five-day moving average. These plots confirm that, starting in late July, the turnover regression's R^2 increased significantly, exceeding 10% in early August. Moreover, the turnover-regression R^2 continued to exceed 5% for the last three months of our sample, a threshold that was not passed at any point prior to July 2007.

As expected, the daily return regressions typically have lower R^2, but, at the same point in August 2007, the explanatory power of this regression also spiked above 10%, adding further support to the unwind hypothesis.

17.2.3 Evidence from Transactions Data

To develop a better sense of market dynamics during August 2007, we construct the intraday returns of long/short market neutral portfolios based on the factors described in Section 17.2.1 for the two weeks before and after 6 August. Figure 17.3 displays the cumulative returns of these portfolios from 9:30am ET on 23 July to 4:00pm ET on 17 August. These patterns suggest that on 2 and 3 August, long/short portfolios based on book-to-market,

---

[20] Note the decile rankings change each month, and are time-dependent, but we have suppressed the time subscript for notational simplicity.

[21] Turnover is the appropriate measure for trading activity in each security because it normalizes the number of shares traded by the number of shares outstanding (Lo and Wang, 2000, 2006). The values of the decile rankings are reflected around the 'neutral' level for the turnover regressions, because the stocks that belong to either of the extreme deciles—deciles 1 and 10—are equally 'attractive' to each of the five factors (but in opposite directions), and thus should exhibit 'abnormal' trading during those days on which portfolios based on such factors were unwound.

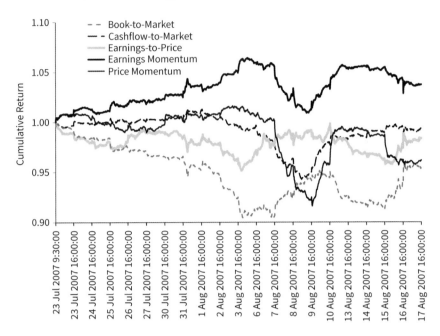

Fig. 17.3 Intraday cumulative return of representative quant long/short portfolios in August 2007. Cumulative returns for long/short portfolios based on five equity-valuation factors from 9:30am ET 23 July 2007 to 4:00pm ET 17 August 2007 computed from five-minute returns using TAQ transactions data. Portfolios were rebalanced at the end of July 2007 to reflect the new factors rankings. Note that these returns are constructed under the assumption that only Reg-T leverage is used (see Khandani and Lo (2007) for further details).

cashflow-to-market, and earnings-to-price were being unwound, while portfolios based on price momentum and earnings momentum were unaffected until 8 and 9 August, when they also experienced sharp losses. However, on Friday 10 August, sharp reversals in all five strategies erased nearly all of the losses of the previous four days, returning portfolio values back to their levels on the morning of 6 August.

Of course, this assumes that portfolio leverage did not change during this tumultuous week, which is an unlikely assumption given the enormous losses during the first few days. If, for example, a portfolio manager had employed a leverage ratio of 8:1 for the book-to-market portfolio on the morning of 1 August, they would have experienced a cumulative loss of 24% by the close of 7 August, which is likely to have triggered a reduction in leverage at that time, if not before. With reduced leverage, the book-to-market portfolio would not have been able to recoup all of its losses, despite the fact that prices did revert back to their beginning-of-week levels by the close of 10 August.

To obtain a more precise view of the trading volume during this period, we turn to the cross-sectional regression in Equation (17.1) of individual turnover data described in Section 17.2.2 on exposures to decile rankings of the five factors. The estimated impact is measured in basis points (bps) of turnover for a unit of difference in the decile ranking; for example, an estimated coefficient of twenty-five basis points for a given factor implies that *ceteris paribus*, stocks in the tenth decile of that factor had a 1% (4×25 bps) higher turnover than stocks in the sixth decile.

Figure 17.4 displays the estimated turnover impact, $\hat{\delta}_{f,t}$, and R^2 of the daily cross-sectional regressions, which clearly shows the change in the trading activity and R^2 among stocks with extreme exposure to these five factors. The estimated coefficients are always positive, implying that the securities ranked as 'attractive' or 'unattractive' according to each of these measures

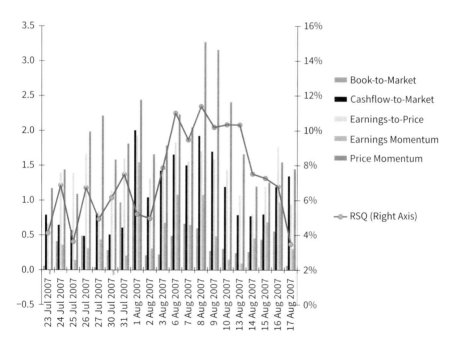

Fig. 17.4 Cross-sectional regression of daily turnover on decile rankings according to quant factors for S&P 1500. Estimated coefficients, $\hat{\delta}_{f,t}$ and R^2, of the cross-sectional regression of daily individual stock turnover on absolute excess decile rankings for five valuation factors from 23 July 2007 to 17 August 2007: $TO_{i,t} = \hat{\gamma}_t + \sum_{f=1}^{5} |D_{i,f} - 5.5|\hat{\delta}_{f,t} + \hat{\varepsilon}_{i,t}$, where $TO_{i,t}$ is the turnover for stock i on day t and $D_{i,f}$ is the decile assignment for stock i based on factor f, and where the five factors are book-to-market, cashflow-to-market, earnings-to-price, price momentum, and earnings momentum.

(i.e. deciles 10 and 1, respectively) tend to have a higher turnover than the securities that are ranked 'neutral' (deciles 5 or 6). These coefficients are both economically and statistically significant. For example, the median estimated coefficient during the period of 23 July–12 August 2007 for the constant term and the five factors was 5.19 (constant term), 0.29 (book-to-market), 0.93 (cashflow-to-market), 1.42 (earnings-to-price), 0.40 (earnings momentum), and 1.73 (price momentum), all measured in basis points. This implies, for example, that the securities in the first or the tenth decile of the price momentum factor had an expected turnover of $5.19 + 1.73 \times 4.5 = 12.98$ bps, which is 2.5 times higher than the average turnover of 5.19 bps. The statistical significance of the estimated coefficients is also high. The median t-stat for the estimated coefficients during the period of 23 July–12 August 2007 for these factors was 3.77 (constant term), 1.25 (book-to-market), 3.20 (cashflow-to-market), 4.40 (earnings-to-price), 1.32 (earnings momentum), and 6.07 (price momentum).

Figure 17.4 shows that there was a substantial jump in the price momentum coefficient on 8 August, which coincides with the start of the steep losses shown in Fig. 17.3. The coefficients for the other factors also exhibit increases during this period, along with the R^2 of the cross-sectional regressions, consistent with the unwind hypothesis. However, the explanatory power of these regressions and the estimated impact of the factors (other than price momentum) on 8 and 9 August were not markedly different than earlier in the same week. What changed on 8, 9, and 10 August that yielded the volatility spike in Fig. 17.2? We argue in the next section that a sudden withdrawal of liquidity may be one explanation.

17.3 Measures of Market Liquidity

In Section 17.2, we provided suggestive but indirect evidence supporting the unwind hypothesis for factor-based portfolios during the months of July and August 2007, but this still leaves unanswered the question of what happened during the second week of August. To address this issue head on, in this section we focus on changes in market liquidity during 2007, and find evidence of a sharp temporary decline in liquidity during the second week of August 2007.

To measure equity market liquidity, we begin in Section 17.3.1 by analysing the contrarian trading strategy of Lehmann (1990) and Lo and MacKinlay (1990) from a market-making perspective (i.e. the provision of *immediacy*).

Using analytical and empirical arguments, we conclude that market-making profits declined substantially over the decade leading up to 2007, which is consistent with the common wisdom that increased competition, driven by a combination of technological and institutional innovations, has resulted in greater liquidity and a lower premium for liquidity provision services. We confirm this conjecture in Section 17.3.2 by estimating the price impact of equity trades using daily returns from 1995 to 2007, which shows there was a substantial increase in market depth (i.e. a reduction in the price impact of trades). Markets were, indeed, much more liquid at the beginning of 2007 compared to only five years earlier. However, using transactions data for the months of July, August, and September 2007, in Section 17.3.3 we document a sudden and significant decrease in market liquidity in August 2007. Finally, in Section 17.3.4, we use these tools to detect the exact date and time that the meltdown started, and even the initial groups of securities that were involved.

17.3.1 Market-making and Contrarian Profits

The motivation behind the empirical analysis of this section can be understood in the context of Grossman and Miller's (1988) model. In that framework, there are two types of market participants, market-makers and outside customers, and the provision of liquidity and immediacy by the market-makers to randomly arriving outside customers generates mean-reverting prices. However, as observed by Campbell, Grossman, and Wang (1993), when the price of a security changes, the change in price is partly due to new fundamental information about the security's value, and partly due to temporary imbalances in supply and demand. Although the latter yields mean-reverting prices, the former is typically modelled as a random walk where shocks are 'permanent' in terms of the impulse-response function. To understand the role of liquidity in the Quant Meltdown of 2007, we need to separate these components.

Because the nature of liquidity provision is inherently based on mean reversion (i.e. buying losers and selling winners), the contrarian strategy of Lehmann (1990) and Lo and MacKinlay (1990) is ideally suited for this purpose. As Khandani and Lo (2007) showed, a contrarian trading strategy applied to daily US stock returns is able to trace out the market dislocation in August 2007, and, in this section, we provide an explicit analytical explanation of their results in the context of market-making and liquidity provision.

This contrarian strategy consists of an equal dollar amount of long and short positions across N stocks, where at each rebalancing interval, the long positions consist of 'losers' (past underperforming stocks, relative to some market average) and the short positions consist of 'winners' (past outperforming stocks, relative to the same market average). Specifically, if $\omega_{i,t}$ is the portfolio weight of security i at date t, then:

$$\omega_{i,t} = -\frac{1}{N}(R_{i,t-k} - R_{m,t-k}) \,, \quad R_{m,t-k} \equiv \frac{1}{N}\sum_{i=1}^{N} R_{i,t-k}, \qquad (17.3)$$

for some $k > 0$. Observe that the portfolio weights are the negative of the degree of outperformance k periods ago, so each value of k yields a somewhat different strategy. As in Khandani and Lo (2007), we set $k = 1$ day. By buying yesterday's losers and selling yesterday's winners at each date, such a strategy actively bets on one-day mean reversion across all N stocks, profiting from reversals that occur within the rebalancing interval. For this reason, Equation (17.3) has been called a 'contrarian' trading strategy that benefits from market over-reaction (i.e. when underperformance is followed by positive returns and vice versa for outperformance; see Khandani and Lo (2007) for further details). A more ubiquitous source of profitability for this strategy is the fact that liquidity is being provided to the marketplace, and investors are implicitly paying a fee for this service, both through the bid–offer spread and from price reversals, as in the Grossman and Miller (1988) model. Historically, designated market-makers such as the NYSE/AMEX specialists and NASDAQ dealers have played this role, but, in recent years, hedge funds and proprietary trading desks have begun to compete with traditional market-makers, adding enormous amounts of liquidity to US stock markets and earning attractive returns for themselves and their investors in the process.

One additional subtlety in interpreting the profitability of the contrarian strategy of Equation (17.3) is the role of the time horizon over which the strategy's profits are defined. Because the demand for immediacy arises at different horizons, disentangling liquidity shocks and informed trades can be challenging. All else being equal, if market-makers reduce the amount of capital they are willing to deploy, the price impact of a liquidity trade will be larger, and the time it takes for prices to revert back to their fundamental levels after such a trade will increase. To capture this phenomenon, we propose to study the expected profits of the contrarian trading strategy for various holding periods. In particular, consider a strategy based on the portfolio weights in Equation (17.3), but where the positions are held fixed for q periods. The profits for such a q-period contrarian strategy are given by:[22]

$$\pi_t(q) \equiv \sum_{i=1}^{N} \left(\omega_{i,t} \sum_{l=1}^{q} R_{i,t+l} \right). \tag{17.4}$$

The properties of $\mathbb{E}[\pi_t(q)]$ under general covariance-stationary return-generating processes are summarized in the following proposition (see Appendix B.11 for the derivations):

Proposition 17.1 *Consider a collection of N securities and denote by* $\mathbf{R}_t$ *the* $(N \times 1)$-*vector of their period t returns,* $[R_{1,t} \cdots R_{N,t}]'$. *Assume that* $\mathbf{R}_t$ *is a jointly covariance-stationary stochastic process with expectation* $\mathbb{E}[\mathbf{R}_t] \equiv \boldsymbol{\mu} \equiv [\mu_1 \cdots \mu_N]'$ *and autocovariance matrices* $\mathbb{E}[(\mathbf{R}_{t-l} - \boldsymbol{\mu})(\mathbf{R}_t - \boldsymbol{\mu})'] \equiv \boldsymbol{\Gamma}_l \equiv [\gamma_{i,j}(l)]$. *Consider a zero net-investment strategy that invests* $\omega_{i,t}$ *dollars given by Equation (17.3) in security i. The expected profits over q periods,* $\mathbb{E}[\pi_t(q)]$, *is given by:*

$$\mathbb{E}[\pi_t(q)] = \mathcal{M}(\boldsymbol{\Gamma}_1) + \cdots + \mathcal{M}(\boldsymbol{\Gamma}_q) - q\,\sigma^2(\boldsymbol{\mu}), \tag{17.5}$$

where

$$\mathcal{M}(A) \equiv \frac{1}{N^2} \boldsymbol{\iota}' A \boldsymbol{\iota} - \frac{1}{N} \mathrm{tr}(A),$$

$$\sigma^2(\boldsymbol{\mu}) \equiv \frac{1}{N} \sum_{i=1}^{N} (\mu_i - \mu_m)^2 \quad and \quad \mu_m \equiv \frac{1}{N} \sum_{i=1}^{N} \mu_i, \tag{17.6}$$

and $\boldsymbol{\iota}$ *is an* $(N \times 1)$-*vector of ones.*

If mean reversion implies that contrarian trading strategies will be profitable, then price momentum implies the reverse. In the presence of return persistence (i.e. positively autocorrelated returns), Lo and MacKinlay (1990) show that the contrarian trading strategy of Equation (17.3) will exhibit negative profits. As with other market-making strategies, the contrarian strategy loses when prices exhibit trends, either because of private information, which the market microstructure literature calls 'adverse selection', or through a sustained liquidation in which the market-maker bears the losses by taking the other side and losing value as prices move in response to the liquidation.

---

[22] This expression is an approximation, since the return of security i in period t, $R_{i,t}$, is defined to be a simple return, and the log of the sum is not equal to the sum of the logs. The approximation error is typically small, especially for short holding periods of just a few days.

We argue below that this can explain the anomalous pattern of losses during the second week of August 2007.

To develop this argument further, suppose that stock returns satisfy the following simple linear multivariate factor model:

$$R_{i,t} = \mu_i + \beta_i v_t + \lambda_{i,t} + \eta_{i,t}, \tag{17.7a}$$

$$\lambda_{i,t} = \theta_i \lambda_{i,t-1} - \epsilon_{i,t} + \epsilon_{i,t-1} , \quad \theta_i \in (0,1), \tag{17.7b}$$

$$v_t = \rho v_{t-1} + \zeta_t , \quad \rho \in (-1,1), \tag{17.7c}$$

where $\epsilon_{i,t}$, ζ_t, and $\eta_{i,t}$ are white-noise random variables that are uncorrelated at all leads and lags.

The impact of random idiosyncratic supply and demand shocks are represented by $\epsilon_{i,t}$, and $\lambda_{i,t}$ is the reduced-form expression of the interaction between public orders and market-makers over the cumulative history of $\epsilon_{i,t}$. In particular, the reduced form in Equation (17.7) is an ARMA(1,1) process that exhibits negative autocorrelation to capture the mean reversion generated by market-making activity (e.g. a bid–ask bounce, as in Roll (1984)). To develop a better sense of its time-series properties, we can express $\lambda_{i,t}$ as the following infinite-order moving average process:

$$\lambda_{i,t} = -\epsilon_{i,t} + \left(\frac{1-\theta_i}{\theta_i}\right)\theta_i \epsilon_{i,t-1} + \left(\frac{1-\theta_i}{\theta_i}\right)\theta_i^2 \epsilon_{i,t-2} + \cdots , \quad \theta_i \in (0,1). \tag{17.8}$$

Note that the coefficients in Equation (17.8) sum to zero, so that the impact of each $\epsilon_{i,t}$ is temporary, and the parameter θ_i controls the speed of mean reversion.

Market information is represented by the common factor v_t, which can capture mean reversion, noise, or momentum, if ρ is less than, equal to, or greater than zero, respectively. The error term, $\eta_{i,t}$, represents idiosyncratic fluctuations in security i's returns that are unrelated to liquidity or common factors. Appendix B.11 provides additional motivation and intuition for this specification.

By varying the parameters of the return-generating process of Equation (17.7), we can change the relative importance of fundamental shocks and market-making activity in determining security i's returns. For example, if we assume parameters that cause v_t to dominate $R_{i,t}$, this corresponds to a set of market conditions in which liquidity traders are of minor importance, and the common factor is the main driver of returns. If, however, the variability of v_t is small in comparison to $\lambda_{i,t}$, this corresponds to a market in which the liquidity traders are the main drivers of returns. We shall see in the following subsections that these two cases lead to very different patterns for the profitability of the contrarian strategy of Equation (17.3), which raises the possibility of inferring the relative importance of these two components by studying the empirical properties of contrarian trading profits. We perform this study below.

We now consider a few special cases of Equation (17.7) to build our intuition and set the stage for the empirical analysis.

Uncorrelated Returns

Let $\beta_i \equiv 0$ and $\lambda_{i,t} \equiv 0$ in Equation (17.7), implying that R_t is driven only by firm-specific idiosyncratic shocks, $\eta_{i,t}$, which are both serially and cross-sectionally uncorrelated. In this case, $\Gamma_l = 0$ for all nonzero l; hence,

$$\mathbb{E}[\pi_t(q)] = -q\sigma^2(\mu) < 0. \tag{17.9}$$

Returns are both serially and cross-sectionally uncorrelated, and the expected profit is negative as long as there is some cross-sectional variation in the expected returns. In this special case, the contrarian strategy involves shorting stocks with higher expected return and buying stocks with lower expected return, which yields a negative expected return that is linear in the holding period, q, and in the cross-sectional variance of the individual securities' expected returns.

Idiosyncratic Liquidity Shocks

Let $\rho \equiv 0$ in Equation (17.7), so that the common factor is serially uncorrelated. The expected q-period profit is then given by (see Appendix B.11 for the derivation):

$$\mathbb{E}[\pi_t(q)] = \frac{N-1}{N^2} \sum_{i=1}^{N} \frac{1-\theta_i^q}{2}\sigma_{\lambda_i}^2 - q\sigma^2(\mu). \tag{17.10}$$

In this case, the strategy benefits from correctly betting on mean reversion in $\lambda_{i,t}$, but again loses a small amount due to the cross-sectional dispersion of expected returns. For a fixed holding period q, the expected profit is an increasing function of the volatility of the liquidity component, $\sigma_{\lambda_i}^2$, and a decreasing function of the speed of mean reversion, θ_i, which is consistent with our intuition for the returns to market-making. Moreover, as long as the cross-sectional dispersion of expected returns, $\sigma^2(\mu)$, is not too large, the expected profit will be an increasing and concave function of the length of the holding period, q.

Common-Factor and Idiosyncratic Liquidity Shocks

Now suppose that $\rho \neq 0$ in Equation (17.7), so that the common factor is auto-correlated. In this case, the expected q-period profit is given by (see Appendix B.11 for the derivation):

$$\mathbb{E}[\pi_t(q)] = \frac{N-1}{N^2} \sum_{i=1}^{N} \frac{1 - \theta_i^q}{2} \sigma_{\lambda_i}^2 - \rho \frac{1 - \rho^q}{1 - \rho} \sigma_v^2 \sigma^2(\boldsymbol{\beta}) - q\sigma^2(\boldsymbol{\mu}). \qquad (17.11)$$

In contrast to Equation (17.10), when $\rho \neq 0$ the contrarian strategy can profit or lose from the common factor (depending on the sign of ρ), provided there is any cross-sectional dispersion in the common-factor betas, β_i. If the common factor is negatively serially correlated (i.e. $\rho < 0$), then the first two terms of Equation (17.11) are unambiguously positive. In this case, mean reversion in both the common and liquidity components contribute positively to expected profits.

If, however, the common-factor component exhibits momentum (i.e. $\rho > 0$), then the first two terms in Equation (17.11) are of opposite sign. By buying losers and selling winners, the contrarian strategy of Equation (17.3) profits from mean-reverting liquidity shocks, $\lambda_{i,t}$, but suffers losses from momentum in the common factor. For sufficiently large ρ and large cross-sectional variability in the β_i, the second term of Equation (17.11) can dominate the first, yielding negative expected profits for the contrarian strategy over all holding periods q.

However, if ρ is small and positive, Equation (17.11) yields an interesting relationship between the expected profits and the holding period, q—the contrarian strategy can exhibit negative expected profits over short holding periods due to momentum in the common factor, and yield positive expected profits over longer holding periods as the influence of the common factor decays, and as the liquidity term grows with q.[23] To see this possibility more directly, consider the following simplifications: let $\theta_i = \theta$ and $\sigma_{\lambda_i}^2 = \sigma_\lambda^2$ for all i, $\sigma^2(\boldsymbol{\mu}) \approx 0$, and assume that N is large. Then the expected profit under Equation (17.7), normalized by the variance of the liquidity component, σ_λ^2, reduces to:

$$\frac{\mathbb{E}[\pi_t(q)]}{\sigma_\lambda^2} \approx \frac{1 - \theta^q}{2} - \rho \frac{1 - \rho^q}{1 - \rho} \frac{\sigma_v^2}{\sigma_\lambda^2} \sigma^2(\boldsymbol{\beta}). \qquad (17.12)$$

---

[23] Of course, for (17.11) to be positive, the liquidity term must dominate both the common-factor term and the cross-sectional variability in expected returns. However, since this latter component is independent of the parameters of the liquidity and common-factor components, our comparisons centre on the first two terms of Equation (17.11).

Figure 17.5 plots the normalized expected profit (Equation (17.12)) as a function of the common factor's autocorrelation coefficient, ρ, and the holding
period, q, assuming the following values for the remaining parameters:[24]

$$\theta = \frac{1}{2} \ , \ \frac{\sigma_v^2}{\sigma_\lambda^2} = 50 \ , \ \sigma^2(\beta) = \left(\frac{1}{4}\right)^2.$$

Figure 17.5 shows that the expected profits are always increasing and concave in the holding period, q. While mean reversion in the common factor
increases the expected profits of the strategy, for sufficiently large momentum
(i.e. positive ρ), the expected profits become negative for all holding periods.
The more interesting intermediate region is one in which expected profits are
negative for short holding periods but become positive if positions are held

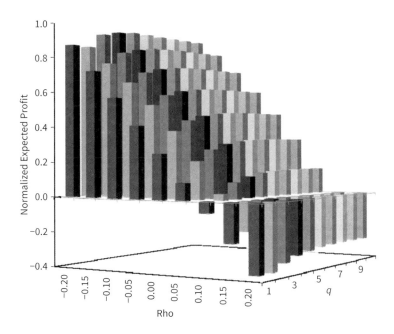

Fig. 17.5 Normalized expected profit of the contrarian strategy under benchmark
return generating processes. Plot of the normalized expected profit of the contrarian
strategy, $\frac{1-\theta^q}{2} - \rho\frac{1-\rho^q}{1-\rho}\frac{\sigma_v^2}{\sigma_\lambda^2}\sigma^2(\beta)$, for parameter values $\frac{\sigma_v^2}{\sigma_\lambda^2} = 50$, $\sigma^2(\beta) = 1/16$, and $\theta = 1/2$, as a
function of the serial correlation coefficient of the common factor, ρ, and the holding
period, q.

[24] These calibrations are arbitrary, but the motivation for the value of $\sigma_v^2/\sigma_\lambda^2$ is the importance of the
common factor during the Quant Meltdown, and the motivation for the value of $\sigma^2(\beta)$, is that 95% of the
betas will fall between plus and minus 0.5 of its mean if they are normally distributed with a variance of
1/16.

for a sufficiently long period of time. This pattern will be particularly relevant in light of the events of August 2007, as we will see in the results that follow.

Empirical Results

We now apply the contrarian strategy of Equation (17.3) to historical US stock returns from 3 January 1995 to 31 December 2007. As in Lehmann (1990), Lo and MacKinlay (1990), and Khandani and Lo (2007), we expect to find positive expected profits for short-term holding periods (i.e. small values of q), and the expected profits should be increasing in q but at a decreasing rate, given the timed decay implicit in liquidity provision and its implied mean reversion.[25] By construction, the weights for the contrarian strategy of Equation (17.3) sum to zero; hence, the *return* of the strategy is ill-defined. We follow Lo and MacKinlay (1990) and the practice of most equity market neutral managers in computing the return of this strategy, $R_{p,t}$, each period t by dividing each period's dollar profit or loss by the total capital, J_t, required to generate that profit or loss, hence:

$$R_t(q) \equiv \pi_t(q)/J_t \ , \ J_t \equiv \frac{1}{2}\sum_{i=1}^{N}|\omega_{i,t}|, \qquad (17.13)$$

where $\pi_t(q)$ is given by Equation (17.4).[26]

Figure 17.6 displays the average return of the contrarian strategy when applied to components of the S&P 1500 index between January 1995 and December 2007.[27] When averaged over the entire sample, the results confirm that the average return increases in the holding period, q, and, as predicted, increases at a decreasing rate.[28] Even though the average return remains generally an increasing function of the holding period, its absolute level has decreased over time. For example, the average returns in the years prior to 2002 are all above the full-sample average in Fig. 17.6, but, in the years 2002

[25] Note that, as a matter of convention, we date the multi-holding period return, $R_t(q)$, as of the date, t, on which the positions are established and not the date on which the positions are closed out and the return is realized, which is date $t+q$.
[26] This expression for $R_t(q)$ implicitly assumes that the portfolio satisfies Regulation T leverage restrictions, which are $1 long and $1 short for every $1 of capital. However, most equity market neutral managers used considerably greater leverage just prior to August 2007, and returns should be multiplied by the appropriate leverage factor when comparing properties of this strategy between 2007 and earlier years. See Khandani and Lo (2007) for further discussion.
[27] The S&P indexes are based on the last day of the previous month and not changed throughout each month. Plots based on strategy profits, $\pi_t(q)$, are qualitatively the same, but the values are more difficult to interpret, since they are not scaled by the amount of capital used.
[28] Clearly, the actual returns calculated here are not achievable due to market microstructure issues such as order book competition and non-synchronous trading. For our argument in this chapter, however, we focus only on the pattern of profitability for different holding periods.

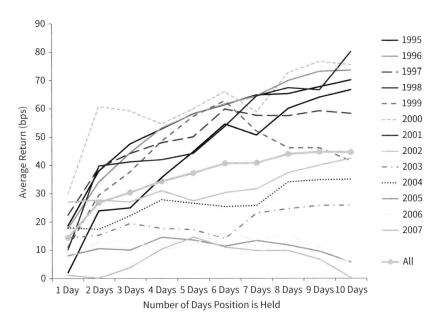

Fig. 17.6 Average return of daily contrarian strategy across different holding periods. Average return of the contrarian strategy when portfolios are constructed based on one-day lagged returns and positions are held for 1–10 days for 3 January 1995–31 December 2007. A return is assigned to the year in which the position was established and averages are then calculated for different holding periods. Components of the S&P 1500 are based on memberships as of the last day of the previous month.

and after, they are below the full-sample average. This pattern is consistent with the common intuition that increased competition and technological innovation in the equity markets have reduced the profitability of such market-making activity. The decline in profitability also suggests that US equity markets may have been more liquid in 2007 than a decade prior, and we will confirm this conjecture in the next section by studying the link between trading volume and price changes.

17.3.2 Market Liquidity: 1995–2007

Many methods have been suggested for measuring liquidity in financial markets. For example, volume is used in Brennan, Chordia, and Subrahmanyam (1998), quoted bid–ask spreads and depths are used in Chordia, Roll, and Subrahmanyam (2000), and the ratio of absolute stock returns to dollar volume is proposed by Amihud (2002).[29] Because the days leading up to August 2007 exhibited unusually high volume (Fig. 17.1), any volume-based measure is not likely to capture the full extent of illiquidity during that time. Instead, we take an approach motivated by Kyle's (1985) model, in which liquidity is measured by a linear regression estimate of the volume required to move the price by one dollar.[30] Sometimes referred to as 'Kyle's lambda', this measure is an inverse proxy of liquidity, with higher values of lambda implying lower liquidity and market depth. From an empirical perspective, this is a better measure of liquidity than the quoted depth, since it captures undisclosed liquidity not reflected in the best available quotes, and correctly reflects lower available depth if narrower spreads come at the expense of smaller quantities available at the best bid and offer prices.

We estimate this measure using daily returns for individual stocks each month from January 1995 to December 2007. To be included in our sample, the stock must be in the corresponding S&P index as of the last day of the previous month and have at least fifteen days of returns in that month. Given the sequence of daily returns, $\{R_{i,1}, R_{i,2}, \cdots, R_{i,T}\}$, closing prices, $\{P_{i,1}, P_{i,2}, \cdots, P_{i,T}\}$, and volumes, $\{V_{i,1}, V_{i,2}, \cdots, V_{i,T}\}$, for security i during a specific month, we estimate the following regression:

$$R_{i,t} = \hat{c}_i + \hat{\lambda}_i \cdot \text{Sgn}(t)\log(V_{i,t}P_{i,t}) + \epsilon_{i,t}, \tag{17.14}$$

where $\text{Sgn}(t) \equiv \{+1 \text{ or } -1\}$ depending on the direction of the trade (i.e. buy or sell), as determined according to the following rule: if $R_{i,t}$ is positive, we assign the value $a+1$ to that entire day (to indicate net buying), and if $R_{i,t}$ is negative, we assign the value $a-1$ to the entire day (to indicate net selling).[31] Any day with zero return receives the same sign as that of the most recent prior day with a nonzero return (using returns from the prior month, if necessary). Because of evidence that the impact of trade size on price adjustment is concave (Hasbrouck, 1991; Dufour and Engle, 2000; Bouchaud, Farmer, and Lillo, 2009), we use the natural logarithm of trade size in our analysis.[32]

---

[29] See Amihud, Mendelson, and Pedersen (2006) and Hasbrouck (2007) for a comprehensive discussion of different theoretical and empirical aspects of liquidity with an overview of most relevant studies in this area.

[30] For examples of prior empirical work based on a similar measure, see Brennan and Subrahmanyam (1996) and Anand and Weaver (2006), or Pástor and Stambaugh (2003) for a closely related measure.

[31] This approach is similar to the so-called 'tick test' used in many studies of transactions data for signing trades (e.g. see Cohen et al. (1986)). We adopt this method since it can be applied easily to daily returns. Some studies such as Finucane (2000) suggest that this method is the most reliable method for determining whether a trade is buyer- or seller-initiated.

[32] We conducted a similar analysis using a square root transformation of the trade size. The results for both the daily analysis given in Fig. 17.7 and the intraday analysis given in Fig. 17.9 were similar, so our analysis is relatively robust to the functional form used.

Days with zero volume were dropped from the sample.[33] The monthly cross-sectional average of the estimated price-impact coefficients, $\sum_i \hat{\lambda}_i / N$, then yields an aggregate measure of market liquidity. This approach is similar to the aggregate liquidity measure of Pástor and Stambaugh (2003).

Figure 17.7 graphs the time series of our aggregate price-impact measure, showing that equity markets were more liquid at the end of 2007 than they were a decade prior, and became progressively more liquid over the last five years of the period studied. The spikes in price impact correspond with well known periods of uncertainty and illiquidity: the first large spike starts in August 1998 and reaches its highest level in October 1998 (the LTCM crisis), another spike occurs in March 2000 (the end of the technology bubble),

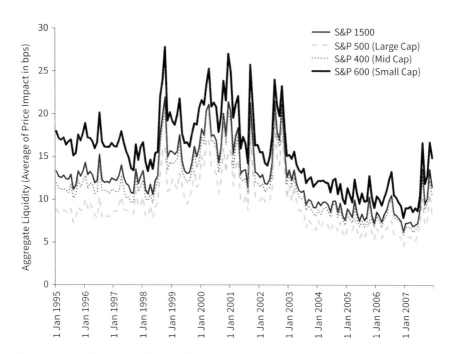

Fig. 17.7 Price-impact coefficients for S&P 1500 index estimated using daily data. Monthly cross-sectional averages of price-impact coefficients $\hat{\lambda}_i$ of stocks in the S&P 1500 and sub-components between January 1995 and December 2007, based on daily time series regressions for each stock i within each month: $R_{i,t} = \hat{c}_i + \hat{\lambda}_i \cdot \mathrm{Sgn}(t)$ $\log(V_{i,t}P_{i,t}) + \epsilon_{i,t}$, where $\mathrm{Sgn}(t)\log(V_{i,t}P_{i,t})$ is the signed volume of security i on date t and the sign is determined by the 'tick test' applied to daily returns. Components of these indexes are based on the memberships on the last day of the previous month.

---

[33] Zero-volume days are rare in general, and extremely rare among S&P 500 stocks.

a third occurs in September 2001 (the September 11 terrorist attacks), and the last spike in our sample occurs in August 2007 (the Quant Meltdown).

Kyle's (1985) framework yields a market depth function that is decreasing in the level of informed trading; hence, it is no surprise that spikes in this measure coincide with periods of elevated uncertainty about economic fundamentals, during which trading activity is more likely to be attributed to informed trading. However, for our purposes, the importance of the patterns in Fig. 17.7 involves the systematic nature of liquidity. Studies such as Chordia, Roll, and Subrahmanyam (2000, 2001), Hasbrouck and Seppi (2001), and Huberman and Halka (2001) have documented a commonality in liquidity using different measures and techniques. Chordia, Sarkar, and Subrahmanyam (2005) observe liquidity shocks in common between equity and bond markets. Perhaps motivated by these studies, Pástor and Stambaugh (2003) propose the sensitivity to a common liquidity factor as a risk measure in an asset-pricing framework. But how does such commonality in liquidity arise?

Chordia, Roll, and Subrahmanyam (2000) argue that a common liquidity factor can emerge from co-movements in the optimal inventory levels of market-makers, inventory carrying costs, commonality in private information, and common investing styles shared by large institutional investors (see also Comerton-Forde et al. (2010)). Carrying costs are considered explicitly in Chordia, Sarkar, and Subrahmanyam (2005), and are modelled by Brunnermeier and Pedersen (2009). These studies suggest that the availability of credit and low carrying costs may have contributed to the very low price-impact levels observed between 2003 and August 2007 (see also Brunnermeier (2009)). Institutional changes such as decimalization and technological advances are also likely contributors to the overall trend of increasing liquidity over the past decade.

17.3.3 Market Liquidity in 2007

Having documented the historical behaviour of market-making profits and liquidity in Sections 17.3.1 and 17.3.2, we now turn our attention to the events of August 2007 by applying similar measures to transactions data from July to September 2007 for the stocks in the S&P 1500 universe.

For computational simplicity, we use a simpler mean-reversion strategy than the contrarian strategy in Equation (17.3) to proxy for market-making profits. This high-frequency mean-reversion strategy is based on buying losers and selling winners over lagged m-minute returns, which we vary from 5 to 60 minutes. Specifically, each trading day is broken into nonoverlapping m-minute intervals. During each m-minute interval, we construct a long/short dollar-neutral portfolio that is long those stocks in the decile with the lowest return over the previous m-minute interval, and short those stocks in the decile with the highest return over the previous m-minute interval.[34] The value of the portfolio is then calculated for the next m-minute holding period, and this procedure is repeated for each of the nonoverlapping m-minute intervals during the day.[35]

Figure 17.8 plots the cumulative returns of this mean-reversion strategy from 2 July to 28 September 2007 for various values of m. For $m = 60$ minutes,

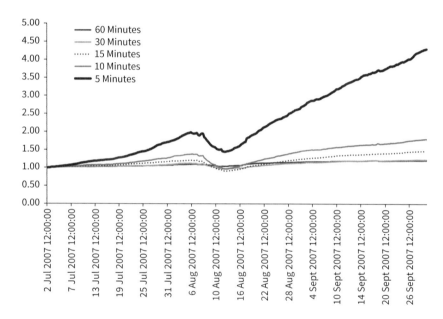

Fig. 17.8 Cumulative return of intraday mean-reversion strategy applied to S&P 1500 in 2007. Cumulative return of m-minute mean-reversion strategy applied to stocks in the S&P 1500 universe from 2 July 2007 to 28 September 2007, for $m = 5$, 10, 15, 30, and 60 minutes. No overnight positions are allowed, initial positions are established at 9:30am ET plus $2m$ minutes each day, and all positions are closed at 4:00pm ET. Components of the S&P 1500 are based on memberships as of the last day of the previous month.

[34] Stocks are equal-weighted. In case there is a tie between returns in several securities that crosses the decile threshold, we ignore all securities with equal returns to focus on the supply–demand imbalance and to enhance the reproducibility of our numerical results. No overnight positions are allowed.
[35] We always use the last traded price in each m-minute interval to calculate returns; hence, the first set of prices for each day are based on the prices of trades just before 9:30am ET plus m minutes, and the first set of positions are established at 9:30am ET plus $2m$ minutes.

the cumulative return is fairly flat over the three-month period, but as the horizon shortens, the slope increases, implying increasingly larger expected returns. This reflects the fact that shorter-horizon mean-reversion strategies are closer approximations to market-making, with correspondingly more consistent profits. As noted before (see footnote 28), the level of returns reported in Fig. 17.8 are probably not achievable. However, for our argument in this chapter, we only focus on the pattern of profit and loss for different holding periods and across different time periods from July to September of 2007. As shown in Fig. 17.8, for all values of m, we observe the same dip in profits during the second week of August. Consider, in particular, the case where $m = 5$ minutes—on 6 August the cumulative profit levels off, and then declines from 7 August to 13 August, after which it resumes its growth path at nearly the same rate. This inflection period suggests that there was a substantial change in the price dynamics, and potentially in the activity of market-makers, starting in the second week of August.

To obtain a more concrete measure of changes in liquidity during this period, we estimate a price-impact model according to Equation (17.14) but using transactions volume and prices.[36] To focus on the change in market liquidity during this period, in Fig. 17.9 we display the relative increase in our price-impact measure as compared to its value on 2 July 2007 (the first day of our sample of transactions data). The empirical evidence suggests that relative increases in price impact were common to all market-cap groups and not limited to the smaller stocks. Note that the specification given in Equation (17.14) uses the natural logarithm of transactions dollar volume as a regressor; hence, a relative increase of 1.5, first occurring on 26 July 2007 indicates a very large increase in trading costs. This implies that trading 100 shares of a stock at a price of $50/share on 26 July—a total dollar volume of $5,000— would have had the same price impact as trading approximately $353,000 of stock on 2 July.

Although Fig. 17.8 shows that short-term market-making profits did not turn negative until the second week of August, the pattern of price impact displayed in Fig. 17.9 documents a substantial drop in liquidity in the days leading up to 6 August 2007.[37] Given the increased trading activity in factor-based portfolios as documented in Fig. 17.2, sustained pressure on market-maker

---

[36] We use only those transactions that occur during normal trading hours and discard all trades that are reported late, out of sequence, or have a nonzero correction field (see Section 17.1.2 for further details).

[37] Our analysis also shows a sudden change in liquidity on 18 September, which was the day the US Federal Open Market Committee lowered the target for the federal funds rate by 50 bps, and the CBOE Volatility Index dropped by more than 6 points to close at about 20. Based on cumulative intraday returns (which we have omitted to conserve space), the market values of our factor-based portfolios dropped and subsequently recovered over the following two days, similar to the pattern observed in Fig. 17.3.

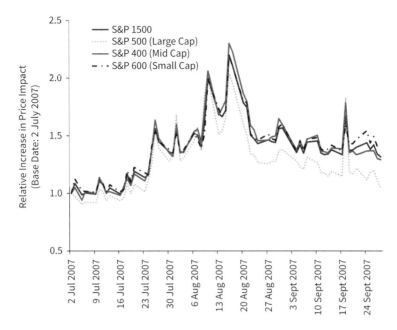

Fig. 17.9 Price-impact coefficients for the S&P 1500 index estimated using transactions data. The relative increase in the estimated price impact, $\hat{\lambda}_i$, based on transactions data regression estimates for each day from 2 July 2007 to 28 September 2007. Using all transactions data for each security on each day, the following price-impact equation is estimated: $R_{i,t} = \hat{c}_i + \hat{\lambda}_i \cdot \mathrm{Sgn}(t) \log(V_{i,t}P_{i,t}) + \varepsilon_{i,t}$, where $\mathrm{Sgn}(t) \log(V_{i,t}P_{i,t})$ is the signed volume of trade t in security i and the sign is determined by the 'tick test'. The relative increase in the average of all $\hat{\lambda}_i$ for each day, using 2 July 2007 (the first day of our sample) as the base, is then calculated as a measure of the relative decrease in market depth. Components of various S&P indexes as of the last day of the previous month are used.

inventory levels due to the unwinding of correlated investment portfolios seems to be the most likely explanation for such a large increase in the price impact of trades during this time.[38] Furthermore, this measure of liquidity was at its lowest level in the week after the week of 6 August (i.e. its price impact was at its highest level). This pattern suggests that perhaps some market-makers, hurt by the turn of events in the week of 6 August, reduced their market-making capital in the following days, and, in turn, caused the price impact to rise substantially beginning on 10 August, and remaining high for the following week. Although NYSE/AMEX specialists and

---

[38] See also Comerton-Forde et al. (2010) for an analysis of the effect of market-makers' inventory on liquidity.

NASDAQ dealers have an affirmative obligation to maintain orderly markets and to stand ready to deal with the public, in recent years, hedge funds and proprietary trading desks have become de facto market-makers by engaging in high-frequency trading strategies that exploit mean reversion in intradaily stock prices.[39] In contrast to exchange-designated market-makers, however, such traders are under no obligation to make markets, and can cease trading without notice.

To further explore the profitability and behaviour of market-makers during this period, we use lagged five-minute returns to establish the positions of the mean-reversion strategy, and hold those positions for m minutes, where m varies from 5 to 60 minutes, after which new positions are established based on the most recent lagged five-minute returns. This procedure is applied to each day, and average returns are computed for each week and each holding period, the results of which are displayed in Fig. 17.10. With the notable exception of the week of 6 August, the average return is generally increasing in length of holding period, consistent with the patterns in the daily strategy in Section 17.3.1 and Fig. 17.6.

To interpret the observed patterns in Fig. 17.10, recall that this mean-reversion strategy provides immediacy by buying losers and selling winners every 5 minutes. As quantitative factor portfolios were being deleveraged and unwound during the last two weeks of July 2007, the price for immediacy presumably increased, implying higher profits for market-making strategies. This is confirmed in Fig. 17.10. However, during the week of 6 August 2007, the average return to our simplified mean-reversion strategy turned sharply negative, with larger losses for longer holding periods that week. This pattern is consistent with the third special case of Proposition 17.1 in Section 17.3.1 — a trending common factor and mean reversion in the idiosyncratic liquidity factor. In particular, the pattern of losses in Fig. 17.10 supports the unwind hypothesis, in which sustained liquidation pressure for a sufficiently large subset of securities created enough price pressure to overcome the profitability of our short-term mean-reversion strategy, resulting in negative returns for holding periods from 5 minutes to 60 minutes. Figure 17.10 also shows a higher premium for the immediacy service provided by market-makers during the two-week period after the week of 6 August. This is consistent with our conjecture that some market-makers may have reduced their exposure after observing massive unwinding pressure in the week of 6 August, thus

---

[39] The advent of decimalization in 2001 was a significant factor in the growth of market-making strategies by hedge funds because of the ability of such funds to 'step in front' of designated market-makers to achieve price priority in posted bids and offers at a much lower cost after decimalization (e.g. a penny versus 12.5 cents).

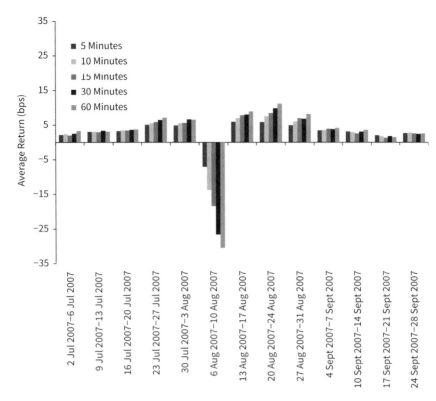

Fig. 17.10 Average return of intraday mean-reversion strategy applied to the S&P 1500 in 2007. The average return for the contrarian strategy applied to five-minute returns from 2 July 2007 to 28 September 2007. Each day is divided into nonoverlapping five-minute intervals, and positions are established based on lagged five-minute returns and then held for 5, 10, 15, 30, or 60 minutes. The average return for each holding period is calculated for each week during this sample. No overnight positions are allowed, initial positions are established at 9:40am ET each day, and all positions are closed at 4:00pm ET. Components of the S&P 1500 are based on memberships as of the last day of the previous month.

reducing the supply of immediacy service during that period and increasing the premium for this service. This evidence is also consistent with the pattern of price impacts shown in Fig. 17.9.

   If the losses observed in Fig. 17.10 were, indeed, due to pressure to unwind during the week of 6 August and a short-term demand for immediacy, these losses should have reverted back for those market-makers who had the ability to hold on to their position for longer periods. To test this hypothesis, in Table 17.1 we compute the performance of the short-term market-making strategy based on five-minute returns for holding periods from 5 minutes to

Table 17.1 Performance of contrarian strategy at intraday and daily frequencies.

Panel (a): High-Frequency Contrarian Strategy

Date	\multicolumn{5}{c}{Average Return (bps)}				
	5 Minutes	10 Minutes	15 Minutes	30 Minutes	60 Minutes
1/8/2007	5.06	6.81	5.15	8.02	7.37
2/8/2007	6.74	6.97	8.47	9.48	9.02
3/8/2007	4.28	2.93	1.77	1.47	−0.62
6/8/2007	−1.30	−2.57	−3.57	−8.75	−5.30
7/8/2007	−1.12	−6.32	−10.14	−14.55	−15.43
8/8/2007	−18.69	−31.60	−40.99	−56.82	−62.49
9/8/2007	−9.82	−16.86	−20.87	−27.65	−26.06
10/8/2007	−4.38	−11.41	−16.25	−25.15	−42.97
13/8/2007	−4.90	−10.29	−15.17	−23.18	−28.69
14/8/2007	5.39	7.72	8.30	10.12	10.28
15/8/2007	6.79	8.96	9.63	8.46	8.35
July Sigma	1.58	1.96	2.15	2.58	3.53

Panel (b): Daily Contrarian Strategy

Construction Date	1 Day	2 Days	3 Days	4 Days	5 Days
1/8/2007	0.14	−1.03	−2.69	−2.57	−0.34
2/8/2007	−0.76	−1.62	−2.57	−2.63	−2.79
3/8/2007	−0.30	−0.57	0.65	0.29	2.04
6/8/2007	−1.47	−1.79	−1.75	1.24	3.44
7/8/2007	−2.88	−4.49	1.38	4.00	4.52
8/8/2007	−3.99	3.79	7.81	8.31	8.20
9/8/2007	6.85	10.12	9.83	9.47	8.96
10/8/2007	−1.46	−1.71	−1.48	−1.84	−1.49
13/8/2007	0.19	0.82	3.79	4.61	3.77
14/8/2007	−0.95	−0.83	0.22	0.34	0.56
15/8/2007	−1.34	−0.58	0.31	0.76	1.69
January to July 2007 Sigma	0.36	0.49	0.59	0.66	0.69

Return (%) header spans over 1-5 Days.

Performance of the contrarian strategy applied to five-minute and daily returns from 1 August to 15 August 2007. Each entry in panel (a) shows the average return over the specified day for the contrarian strategy applied to five-minute returns when positions are held for 5, 10, 15, 30, or 60 minutes. Panel (b) shows the performance of the contrarian strategy based on daily returns, with positions established based on stock returns on the 'Construction Date', and positions are held for 1–5 days afterwards.

60 minutes (a) and daily returns for holding periods from 1 to 5 days (b). Recall that this strategy can be viewed as providing immediacy to the market at regular intervals (every five minutes or every day). Accordingly, the strategy will suffer losses if information flows generate price trends over intervals that match or exceed the typical holding period of the market-maker.

Panel (a) of Table 17.1 indicates that even as early as Monday 6 August, the deleveraging that began earlier (Fig. 17.2) seems to have overwhelmed the amount of market-making capital available, and prices began exhibiting momentum during the day. This situation became more severe on 8 and 9 August. However, the entries in panel (b) of Table 17.1 show that the premiums collected on the eighth and ninth by those market-makers who were intrepid (and well-capitalized) enough to hold their positions for five days would have earned unleveraged returns of 8.20% and 8.96% from positions established on those two days, respectively. Although these returns were probably not achievable (see footnote 28), even a simple comparison with the historical standard deviation of five-day cumulative returns, given in the last row of Table 17.1, shows just how extraordinary these returns were compared to the historical norms. These returns are yet another indication of just how much dislocation occurred during that fateful week.

By 10 August, it seems that imbalances in supply and demand returned to more normal levels, as the daily contrarian strategies started to recover on that day (Table 17.1, panel (b)), presumably as new capital flowed into the market to take advantage of the opportunities created by the previous days' dislocation. For example, a daily contrarian portfolio based on stock returns on 6 August suffered a 1.47% loss by the close of the market the next day, and these losses continued for the next two days. However, there was a reversal on 10 August that continued through 13 August, resulting in a cumulative profit of 3.44% over the five-day period. We should again emphasize that although this level of return was probably not achievable (see footnote 28), our argument mainly relies on the sign and magnitude of these returns relative to the historical standard deviation, as reported in Table 17.1. Daily contrarian portfolios constructed on 7 and 8 August suffered for two days and one day, respectively, but both recovered on 10 August. In short, while prices trended intraday (panel (a)) and even over multiple days (panel (b)) during this week, they eventually reverted back to their beginning-of-the-week levels by 10 August. While the managers who had the ability to stay fully invested for the duration of this dislocation recovered most, if not all, of their losses by Monday 13 August (Fig. 17.3), those market-makers with sufficient capital and fortitude to hold their positions throughout this period would have profited handsomely. Unsurprisingly, during periods of extreme dislocation, liquidity becomes scarce and highly valued; thus, those who are able to provide liquidity during those periods stand to earn outsized returns.

It should also be emphasized that the returns reported in these tables and figures are all *unleveraged* (2:1 or Regulation T leverage) returns. The volatility and drawdowns would have been substantially higher for leveraged portfolios (e.g. a portfolio with 8:1 leverage and constructed based on the price momentum factor would have lost about 31% of its value over the two-day period from 8 to 9 August). As argued by Khandani and Lo (2007), the use of leverage ratios ranging from 4:1 to 10:1 was quite common among quantitative equity market neutral strategies, where the higher leverage ratios were used by those managers engaged in high-frequency mean-reversion strategies, because those strategies exhibited the lowest volatilities and highest Sharpe ratios.

17.3.4 Determining the Epicentre of the Quake

When applied to transactions data, the contrarian strategy can be used to pinpoint the origins of the Quant Meltdown even more precisely. In particular, we apply the contrarian strategy to the following subsets of stocks: three market-cap based subsets (small-, mid-, and large-cap subsets representing the bottom 30%, middle 40%, and top 30% of stocks by market capitalization), five factor-based subsets (each subset consisting of stocks in either the top or bottom decile of each of the five quantitative factors discussed in Section 17.2), and six industry-based subsets, based on the twelve-industry classification codes available from Kenneth French's website.[40] To each of these subsets, we apply the simpler version of the contrarian strategy described in Section 17.3.3.

Table 17.2 and Fig. 17.11 contain the returns of these portfolios from 23 July to 17 August, the two weeks before and after 6 August. Each entry in Table 17.2 is the average return of the five-minute contrarian strategy applied to a particular subset of securities over the specified day. As discussed in Section 17.3.1, days with negative average returns in Table 17.2 correspond to those days when price pressure due to a trending common factor overwhelmed mean-reverting idiosyncratic liquidity shocks. This interpretation, coupled with the cumulative returns of various factor-based portfolios in Fig. 17.11, allows us to detect visually the intraday emergence of price pressure, and determine when the liquidation began and in which factor-based portfolios it was concentrated. Based on these results, we have developed the following set of hypotheses regarding the epicentre of the Quant Quake of August 2007:

1. The first wave of deleveraging began as early as 1 August around 10:45am ET, with the activity apparently concentrated among factor-based subsets of stocks. One can visually detect the sudden abnormal behaviour of the long/short portfolios at the exact

---

[40] See footnote 12. Note that industries with fewer than 100 stocks are included in the 'Other Industries' subset.

Table 17.2 Performance of contrarian strategy among different subsets of stocks.

Date	By Size			By Factor				
	Small-Cap (Bottom 30%)	Mid-Cap (Middle 40%)	Large-Cap (Top 30%)	Book-to-Market (Deciles 1&10)	Cashflow-to-Market (Deciles 1&10)	Earnings-to-Price (Deciles 1&10)	Price Momentum (Deciles 1&10)	Earnings Momentum (Deciles 1&10)
23/7/2007	6.19	3.45	1.04	5.43	5.97	5.89	6.38	3.09
24/7/2007	8.98	3.61	1.08	5.93	6.30	6.38	5.39	3.71
25/7/2007	7.98	1.51	0.63	5.98	5.19	7.22	6.53	1.38
26/7/2007	13.56	4.20	2.78	7.42	10.62	8.85	9.13	8.43
27/7/2007	9.63	4.83	2.04	6.81	10.49	8.52	7.58	4.72
30/7/2007	7.72	2.99	2.40	4.94	6.33	6.16	6.61	4.53
31/7/2007	7.40	2.52	0.53	2.77	3.71	1.43	2.74	3.19
1/8/2007	7.63	3.94	3.72	-0.83	0.56	0.44	0.42	-2.27
2/8/2007	9.28	7.69	1.64	4.80	6.63	7.34	7.84	6.30
3/8/2007	7.01	2.53	2.99	4.45	4.64	5.44	5.71	2.72
6/8/2007	-1.55	-1.02	-1.21	-6.52	-3.32	-3.33	-5.41	-8.11
7/8/2007	-1.02	-2.24	1.20	-0.68	0.10	-1.34	-1.04	-3.50
8/8/2007	-26.30	-18.07	-5.54	-16.16	-15.21	-18.81	-23.27	-20.08
9/8/2007	-7.93	-14.97	-2.57	-5.36	-7.93	-5.72	-9.31	-11.08
10/8/2007	-3.02	-8.89	2.54	-1.82	-0.25	2.02	-3.87	-1.58
13/8/2007	-8.10	-3.24	0.41	-7.22	-3.35	-5.05	-4.92	-4.49
14/8/2007	5.94	6.20	4.99	6.00	5.59	6.66	7.32	5.39
15/8/2007	9.31	6.42	4.62	9.25	11.12	10.98	11.09	5.57
16/8/2007	12.97	8.64	7.61	9.42	8.50	10.18	11.85	8.05
17/8/2007	18.17	14.11	6.22	16.86	16.82	17.86	17.71	15.61

Date	By Industry						All Stocks
	Computer, Software & Electronics	Money & Finance	Wholesale & Retail	Manufacturing	Health Care, Medical Equipment, Drugs	Other Industries	
23/7/2007	7.58	4.38	3.18	4.07	3.98	4.09	4.09
24/7/2007	8.41	5.38	3.84	4.96	5.87	4.90	4.90
25/7/2007	7.07	1.93	2.41	2.03	4.63	3.56	3.56
26/7/2007	10.81	6.44	5.74	7.55	7.60	7.07	7.07
27/7/2007	9.53	3.64	6.53	7.29	5.43	5.88	5.88
30/7/2007	6.10	3.82	3.86	5.40	6.70	4.72	4.72
31/7/2007	8.02	2.30	3.60	3.18	7.94	3.74	3.74
1/8/2007	9.18	3.27	11.13	9.11	3.98	5.06	5.06
2/8/2007	9.53	5.30	9.42	6.00	10.09	6.74	6.74
3/8/2007	10.23	2.62	3.31	5.49	6.14	4.28	4.28
6/8/2007	3.01	-0.60	-1.57	-0.16	4.04	-1.30	-1.30
7/8/2007	0.48	-1.20	-2.20	2.40	5.58	-1.12	-1.12
8/8/2007	-20.89	-12.16	-24.57	-18.78	-16.36	-18.69	-18.69
9/8/2007	-4.37	-3.92	-11.69	-17.36	-7.01	-9.82	-9.82
10/8/2007	0.56	1.15	-10.56	-5.27	0.12	-4.38	-4.38
13/8/2007	-3.78	-1.88	-8.20	2.82	-1.07	-4.90	-4.90
14/8/2007	6.36	7.65	5.36	7.45	4.34	5.39	5.39
15/8/2007	8.32	6.78	5.59	11.63	5.30	6.79	6.79
16/8/2007	8.69	8.94	9.89	12.02	12.96	9.46	9.46
17/8/2007	14.67	15.66	11.58	17.94	13.71	13.03	13.03

The average return for the contrarian strategy applied to various subsets of the S&P 1500 index using five-minute returns for 23 July 2007–17 August 2007. Each day is divided into nonoverlapping five-minute intervals, and positions are established based on lagged five-minute returns and held for the subsequent five-minute interval. The average return for each subset of stocks over each day of this period is then calculated. No overnight positions are allowed, initial positions are established at 9:40am ET each day, and all positions are closed at 4:00pm ET. All entries are in units of basis points.

same time in Fig. 17.3. Portfolios based on book-to-market and earnings-to-price dropped in value, while portfolios based on the other three factors—cashflow-to-market, earnings momentum, and price momentum—gained a little, suggesting that portfolios being deleveraged or unwound during this time were probably long book-to-market and earnings-to-price factors and short the other three. This wave of activity was short-lived, and by approximately 11:30am ET that day, markets returned to normal. By the end of the day, the

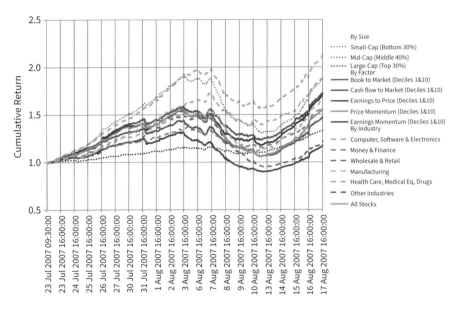

Fig. 17.11 Cumulative returns for the contrarian strategy applied to various subsets of the S&P 1500 index. The cumulative returns for the contrarian strategy applied to various subsets of the S&P 1500 index using five-minute returns for 23 July 2007–17 August 2007. Each day is divided into nonoverlapping five-minute intervals, and positions are established based on lagged five-minute returns and held for the subsequent five-minute interval. The average return for each subset of stocks over each day of this period is then calculated. No overnight positions are allowed, initial positions are established at 9:40am ET each day, and all positions are closed at 4:00pm ET.

contrarian strategy applied to all subsets except for earnings momentum and book-to-market yielded positive average returns for the day (Table 17.2), implying that the liquidation may have been more heavily concentrated on portfolios formed according to these two factors.

2. The second wave started on 6 August at the market open, and lasted until approximately 1:00pm ET. Once again, the action was concentrated among factor-based subsets. This time, the price pressure due to the hypothesized forced liquidation was strong enough to overcome the idiosyncratic liquidity shocks, and, as such, the contrarian strategy applied to all factor-based subsets of stocks yielded negative returns for the entire day. The earnings momentum and book-to-market portfolios within the financial sector suffered the largest losses, implying that the deleveraging was strongest among these groups of stocks. The patterns in Fig. 17.3 suggest that the portfolios being deleveraged were probably

long book-to-market, price momentum, and cashflow-to-market, and short earnings momentum and earnings-to-price. The appendix of Khandani and Lo (2011b) contains a more detailed analysis of the specific stocks that were affected. The day of 6 August was remarkable in another respect—for the first time in our sample, the contrarian strategy applied to all stocks also registered a loss for the day (Table 17.2), implying widespread and strong price pressure due to a forced liquidation on this day.

3. On 7 August, portfolios based on price momentum and cashflow-to-market continued to drift downward, as Fig. 17.3 shows, suggesting continued deleveraging among portfolios based on these two factors. Furthermore, the contrarian strategy applied to all stocks yielded a second day of negative returns, suggesting that the forced liquidation carried over to this day.

4. The start of the so-called 'Meltdown' happened on 8 August. On this day, the contrarian strategy suffered losses when applied to *any* subset of stocks (factor-based, industry, and market-cap). The sudden drop and subsequent reversal is clearly visible in Fig. 17.3.

5. Starting on Friday 10 August, the long/short factor-based portfolios sharply reversed their losing trend, and, by the closing bell on Monday 13 August, all five long/short portfolios were within 2% of their values on the morning of 8 August. We conjecture that this reversal was due to two possible things: new capital that came into the market to take advantage of buying and selling opportunities created by the price impact of the previous days' deleveraging, and the absence of further deleveraging pressure, because the unwind that caused the initial losses was completed.

6. As seen in Fig. 17.9, the price impact of trades suddenly increased as of Friday 10 August—above and beyond the already elevated levels of the prior weeks—and stayed high until the end of the following week, implying reduced market depth and lower liquidity during that period. We conjecture that this stemmed from a reduction in market-making activity, most likely from certain hedge funds engaged in high-frequency market-making activities. We conjecture that the motivation for the reduction in market-making capital is due to the unusual trends in returns that started on 6 and 7 August. This claim is supported by the negative average returns for the all-stocks contrarian strategy, as shown in Table 17.2. The situation only became worse over the subsequent four days (Table 17.2). This revealed a much larger pending unwind than market-makers could handle. Unlike NYSE

specialists and other designated market-makers that are required to provide liquidity, even in the face of strong price trends, hedge funds have no such obligation. However, in more recent years, such funds have injected considerable liquidity into US equity markets by their high-frequency trading activities. Such de facto market-makers probably reduced their exposure starting on 10 August, causing the price impact to increase substantially, as shown in Fig. 17.9. This reduction in the supply of immediacy caused the premium for immediacy to rise substantially in the following two weeks, as shown in Fig. 17.10.

The appendix of Khandani and Lo (2011b) shows how the contrarian strategy can be used to identify with even greater precision the specific stocks and sectors that were involved at the start of the Quant Meltdown of August 2007.

17.4 Discussion

The events of August 2007 in US equity markets provide a living laboratory for developing insights into the dynamics of portfolio liquidity and market-making activity. By simulating the performance of simple trading strategies that proxy for factor bets like book-to-market and cashflow-to-market, we find indirect evidence of the unwinding of factor-based portfolios starting in July 2007, and continuing through August and September 2007. By simulating the performance of a high-frequency (five-minute return) mean-reversion strategy that proxies for market-making activity, we find indirect evidence that liquidity declined sharply during the second week of August 2007, raising the possibility that market-makers reduced their risk capital in the face of mounting losses from the onslaught of portfolio liquidations by long/short equity managers.

If these conjectures are well-founded, they point to a new financial order in which the 'crowded trade' phenomenon now applies to entire classes of hedge fund strategies, not only to a collection of overly popular securities. In much the same way that a passing speedboat can generate a wake with significant consequences for other ships in a crowded harbour, the scaling up and down of portfolios can have significant consequences for all other portfolios and investors. Managers and investors involved in long/short equity strategies must now incorporate this characteristic in designing their portfolios and implementing their risk-management protocols. The Quant Meltdown of 2007 is another piece of evidence supporting the claim by Chan et al. (2007) that systemic risk in the hedge fund industry has risen.

The hypothesized interplay between long/short equity managers and market-makers is consistent with the ecological view of financial markets in Farmer and Lo (1999) and Farmer (2002), and the adaptive markets hypothesis (AMH) of Lo (2004, 2005, 2017). In that framework, market participants are not infinitely rational, but they do learn over time and adapt to changing market conditions. As the size of one 'species' grows (as measured by assets under management or risk capital), the population dynamics change to reflect the impact of its dominance. In the case of the hedge fund industry, we can observe these changes in real time given how quickly managers and investors adapt and evolve. Although the fallout from August 2007 was severe for many market participants, this narrow slice of time and industry has nevertheless been a boon to academics interested in market dynamics.

Yet another interpretation of the Quant Meltdown of August 2007 is a case study in how betas are born. The fact that the entire class of long/short equity strategies moved together so tightly during August 2007 implies the existence of certain common factors within that class. The analysis in this chapter confirms the identities of several such factors, but more refined simulations may uncover others. In any case, there should be little doubt now about the existence of 'alternative betas' (see Section 16.5.6), the next step in the natural progression from long-only investing to indexation to long/short investing to the nascent hedge fund beta replication industry. To the extent that the demand for alternative investments continues to grow as Chapter 16 predicts, the increasing amounts of assets devoted to such endeavours will create their own common factors that can be measured, benchmarked, managed, and, ultimately, passively replicated, as proposed in Hasanhodzic and Lo (2007).

However, our conclusions must be circumscribed by the warning that we began with in the beginning of this chapter: all of our inferences are indirect, tentative, and speculative. We have no inside information about the workings of the hedge funds that were affected in August 2007, and we do not have any access to proprietary prime brokerage records, trading histories, or other confidential industry data. Therefore, our academic perspective of the events during the week of 6–10 August should be interpreted with some caution and a healthy dose of scepticism. These qualifications were highlighted in Khandani and Lo (2007), and we repeat them here for completeness.

Our empirical findings are based on very simple strategies applied to US stocks, which may be representative of certain short-term market neutral mean-reversion strategies, but are unlikely to be as good a proxy for the broader set of quantitative long/short equity products that involve both US and international equities, as well as other securities. A more refined analysis using more sophisticated strategies and a broader set of assets will no doubt yield a more complex and accurate picture of the same events.

More importantly, even if our hypothesis is correct—that an unwind initiated the losses during the second week of August 2007—we cannot say much about the ultimate causes of such an unwind. It is tempting to conclude that a multi-strategy proprietary trading desk's exposure to subprime mortgage portfolios caused it to reduce leverage by liquidating a portion of its most liquid positions (e.g. a statistical arbitrage portfolio). However, another possible scenario is that several quantitative equity market neutral managers decided at the beginning of August that it would be prudent to reduce leverage in the wake of so many problems facing credit-related portfolios. They could have deleveraged accordingly, not realizing that this strategy was so crowded and that the price impact of their liquidation would be so severe. Once this price impact had been realized, other funds employing similar strategies may have decided to cut their risks in response to their losses, which then led to the kind of 'death spiral' that we witnessed in August 1998, as managers attempted to unwind their fixed income arbitrage positions to meet margin calls.

Finally, we conjecture that the liquidations of a number of strategies and asset classes may have started earlier. For example, other liquid investment categories such as global macro, managed futures, and currency strategies seem to have experienced similar unwinds earlier in 2007, as problems in the subprime mortgage markets became more prominent in the minds of managers and investors. The so-called carry trade among currencies was supposedly unwound to some extent in July and August 2007, generating losses for a number of global macro and currency-trading funds. Obviously, our long/short equity strategies are incapable of detecting dislocation among currency strategies, but a simple carry-trade simulation—similar to our simulation of the contrarian trading strategy—could shed considerable light on the dynamics of the foreign exchange markets. Indeed, a collection of simulated strategies across all hedge fund categories could serve as a kind of multi-resolution microscope, one with many lenses and magnifications, with which to examine the full range of financial market activity and vulnerabilities. It is only by deconstructing every market dislocation that we will eventually learn how to minimize their disruptive impact on market participants, and we hope that the insights drawn from our simulations will encourage others to take up this important challenge.

This completes Part IV's objective of applying the AMH to specific financial market contexts, including individual and institutional investment processes and the hedge fund industry. In Part V, we conclude by examining the relevance of the AMH to financial institutions, culture, and regulation. Although necessarily more qualitative than quantitative, these final three chapters are no less rigorous in applying the principles of evolution to these human adaptations, and no less important to our understanding of financial market dynamics.

PART V

FINANCIAL INSTITUTIONS AND ADAPTATION

18
The Co-Evolution of Financial Markets and Technology

In Part V, we consider the evolutionary dynamics of three aspects of financial institutions: technology, culture, and regulation.

This chapter begins our focus on technology by noting that 2020 marked the seventy-fifth anniversary of the *Financial Analysts Journal*, one of the most highly cited practitioner journals in the financial industry. The history of this journal's publications reflects the impact of technological advances on financial institutions, and, by reviewing it, we can discern distinct evolutionary shifts in the industry predicted by the adaptive markets hypothesis (AMH).

18.1 Historical Context

In 1937, a small group of security analysts decided over a luncheon that 'the benefit of their discussions could be multiplied by organizing a formal group and holding meetings regularly' (Tatham Jr, 1945, p. 3).[1] Thus began the New York Society of Security Analysts, with an initial membership of twenty analysts. The *Financial Analysts Journal* was launched eight years later, in 1945. Today, CFA Institute has roughly 180,000 investment professionals, of which over 175,000 hold the chartered financial analyst (CFA) designation. In 2019, more than 350,000 participants took the CFA Program examination. With 161 local societies globally, the CFA Institute is the most widely recognized professional organization in the world for financial analysts, and its flagship publication, the *Financial Analysts Journal*, reflects the diversity and creativity that such an organization has fostered over more than three-quarters of a century.

---

[1] This chapter is adapted from Lo, A. W. (2021). The financial system red in tooth and claw: 75 years of co-evolving markets and technology. *Financial Analysts Journal* 77(3): 5–33, with permission from the publisher, Taylor & Francis Ltd., http://www.tandfonline.com.

The Adaptive Markets Hypothesis. Andrew W. Lo and Ruixun Zhang, Oxford University Press.
© Andrew W. Lo and Ruixun Zhang (2024). DOI: 10.1093/oso/9780199681143.003.0018

Through seismic historical shifts and spectacular technological developments, the *Financial Analysts Journal* has continued to advance the theory and practice of financial analysis into a very different world from the one in which it originated. It is now a richer and more participatory world—a development made possible in no small part by the journal's efforts—but it is still a world with the same recognizable functions and objectives that existed in the 1940s.

At one level, this functional constancy makes intuitive sense. We are all human—buyers and sellers, practitioners and academics, regulators and the regulated—and there are fundamental commonalities in what we seek to accomplish. The means may differ over time, in the different kinds of technologies and the different ways and extents to which they are used, but the goals remain very much the same.

However, there is a deeper reason for this constancy amidst the current explosion of financial diversity. The financial system is subject to evolutionary pressures that shape its ability to survive through different economic environments, which is what we refer to as the AMH (Lo, 2004, 2005, 2012, 2017). According to this hypothesis, the story of financial markets is one of competition, innovation, adaptation, and selection. This is no analogy; the financial system is as much a product of literal human evolution as the opposable thumb and our prefrontal cortex.

Underlying this narrative of financial market dynamics is the remarkable success of *Homo sapiens*, as shown in Fig. 1.4 in Chapter 1, which documents the growth in our numbers from 10,000 BC to the present. Over the course of the past twelve millennia, humans have reproduced virtually unimpeded and with no natural predators—other than ourselves! Because the vertical axis is scaled logarithmically, the growth rate is simply the slope of the curve, which tells a fascinating story. Based on the changes in slope, we can discern at least four distinct periods of human evolution. The flattest part of the curve, from 10,000 BC to 4,000 BC, is the Stone Age. The sharp increase in growth between 4,000 BC and 3,000 BC signalled the beginning of the Bronze Age, followed by the Iron Age, when those metals became commonplace. This curve continues in a nearly straight line until the 1800s, when another increase in slope occurs. This marks the beginning of the Industrial Age, which spans about a century before the curve steepens once more. This last inflection point, which occurred at the start of the twentieth century, is where we are today, a period that some have called the 'Digital Age'. In 1900, the world population is estimated to have been approximately 1.5 billion; as of 2019, the corresponding estimate is 7.7 billion. Within a century—a blink of an eye on an evolutionary timescale—we managed to increase our numbers fivefold.

How did *Homo sapiens* come to dominate its environment so completely, populating virtually every ecological niche on the planet, even including short stays beneath the oceans, at both poles, atop the highest mountains, and in outer space?

The answer, of course, is technology. Technologies of all kinds—agricultural, biomedical, manufacturing, transportation, computational, telecommunications, and so on—are key drivers of our success. Underlying each of these technological advances, however, is a common denominator: financial technology. The reason is simple: theory can only be put into practice with financing. Here, 'financing' refers not only to money, but also to the particular terms by which money is provided to stakeholders to foster innovation. It is no coincidence that technological innovation is almost always accompanied by financial innovation. 'Necessity is the mother of all invention', but invention necessarily requires financing. Nevertheless, as Robert C. Merton—the economist, not the sociologist—observed, individual institutions change much more quickly than the core functions of finance. Merton enumerates six such functions:[2]

1. To provide ways to transfer economic resources through time, across borders, and among industries.
2. To provide ways of managing risk.
3. To provide ways of clearing and settling payments to facilitate trade.
4. To provide a mechanism for the pooling of resources and for the subdividing of ownership in various enterprises.
5. To provide price information to help coordinate decentralized decision-making in various sectors of the economy.
6. To provide ways of dealing with the incentive problems created when one party to a transaction has information that the other party does not or when one party acts as agent for another.

By focusing on functions rather than institutions, we can develop a deeper understanding of how financial technology co-evolves with other technologies and can even anticipate to some degree how institutions will adapt as the environment changes. This is the theme of this chapter. In honour of the recent seventy-fifth anniversary of the founding of the *Financial Analysts Journal*, we take readers on a guided tour of the evolution of financial markets

---

[2] Merton (1993, 1995a, 1995b). See also Merton and Bodie (2006).

across the journal's lifespan, highlighting the interconnected and dynamic roles that theory, practice, and regulation played along the way.

18.2 The Evolution of Technology and Finance

In 1965, three years before he co-founded Intel, now the largest semiconductor chip manufacturer in the world, Gordon Moore published an article in *Electronics* magazine in which he observed that the number of transistors that could be placed onto a microchip seemed to double every year (Moore, 1965). This simple observation, implying not merely constant growth, but a constant rate of growth, led Moore to extrapolate an increase in computing potential from sixty transistors per chip in 1965 to 60,000 in 1975. This number seemed absurd at the time, but it was realized on schedule a decade later. Later revised by Moore to a doubling every two years, 'Moore's Law' has been a remarkably prescient forecast of the growth of the semiconductor industry over the last forty years, as Fig. 18.1a confirms.

Moore's Law now influences a broad spectrum of modern life. It affects everything from household appliances to biomedicine to national defence, and its impact is no less evident in the financial industry. As computing has become faster, cheaper, and better at automating a variety of tasks, financial institutions have been able to increase greatly the scale and sophistication of their services. Automated algorithmic trading, online brokerage, mobile banking, crowdfunding, financial robo-advisers, and cryptocurrencies (such as bitcoin) are all consequences of Moore's Law.

Therefore, it should come as no surprise that there are financial analogues of Moore's Law, one of which is depicted in Fig. 18.1b. This graph of average daily trading volume of exchange-listed options and futures from the Options Clearing Corporation from 1973 to 2014 shows that volume doubles approximately every five years.

In fact, technological innovation has always been intimately interconnected with financial innovation.[3] New stamping and printing processes, used to prevent clipping, counterfeiting, and other forms of financial fraud, directly led to the modern system of paper banknotes and token coinage. To take another example, New York City's Wall Street in its earliest days was not far removed from the Dutch coffee shops where the first modern business of financial trading took place, and the light of a candle was used to

---

[3] See, for example, Bodie (1999) and the other contributions in Litan and Santomero (1999).

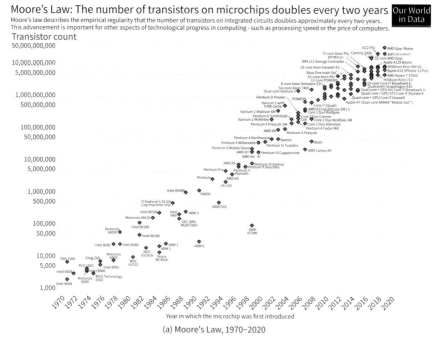

(a) Moore's Law, 1970–2020

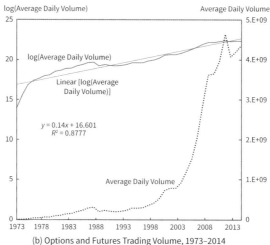

(b) Options and Futures Trading Volume, 1973–2014

Fig. 18.1   (a) Moore's Law and (b) its financial counterpart.

(a) Before   (b) After

Fig. 18.2 Photographs of Wall Street before and after the invention of the telegraph.
Sources: (a) Wallach Division Picture Collection, The New York Public Library. (b) Milstein Division, The New York Public Library.

time the length of an auction. After the invention of the telegraph, however, Wall Street quickly found itself wired, and its physical appearance changed in short order (see Fig. 18.2), sparking a continent-spanning communications revolution that led to the creation of the modern futures market in the new nineteenth-century city of Chicago. And improvements to the ticker tape machine—symbolic of Wall Street for over a century—made Thomas Edison his early fortune.

The current financial system has survived world wars, trade wars, shifts in ideology large and small, the collapse of governments, and multiple financial crises. In the process, it has catalysed the rise of most of the world out of grinding poverty. Its development has been disorderly, the product of trillions of individual decisions in response to ever-changing social, economic, and technological trends. Nevertheless, the financial system has become a highly complex and finely tuned machine for the allocation of finite financial resources. In short, the financial system has evolved into its current central role in much the way we ourselves as a species have evolved biologically over the ages. The six functions of the financial system that Merton described are precisely the ones that facilitated our survival and growth over eons.

However, there is one important difference between financial evolution and its biological counterpart. Thanks to the uniquely human abilities of engaging in abstract thought, high-level communication, and expansive methods of collaboration, our financial institutions and technologies evolve not generation by generation over geological timescales, but within a single generation and at the speed of thought. If we can imagine it, with sufficient time and resources, we can almost always make it so. Even the sixteenth-century alchemist's dream of turning lead into gold is now a reality, albeit a rather impractical one.[4] In fact, on the one hand, the market may immediately adopt an innovation that previously existed only on paper if the financial environment is thought to be ripe for it. On the other hand, an idea may lie fallow for years, if not decades, until the proper mix of demand, technology, and environment allows it to flourish.

Despite its important role, technological invention is far from the only source of evolutionary change in the financial industry. Academia is another important engine of innovation. Advances in research are analogous to mutations in biological systems, a source of evolutionary surprise rather than an intensification of earlier trends. Academics develop and refine new ideas for the pure joy of learning, without necessarily attempting to profit from them. This difference in goals separates them from the practitioner, who may be equally knowledgeable, but whose intentions are often far more practical. As a consequence, academic research plays a critical role in driving financial evolution, as underscored by the seventy-five-year history of the *Financial Analysts Journal* and the specific journal publications cited in this chapter.

The evolutionary lens also helps explain otherwise difficult-to-interpret trends about the adoption and diffusion of these innovations. For example, rather than an innovation always occurring in a large, dominant market and spreading to smaller ones, at times, a useful innovation will occur in a smaller market, where its success as a proof of concept will allow it to expand to larger ones, such as the index future, originally developed in Kansas City, or the exchange-traded fund, first implemented in Toronto. These have exact analogues in population genetics, which describe how a favourable rare mutation can first become fixed in a small isolated population and, from there, proceed to become the most frequent variant in the population as a whole.

In addition, the role of the economic and regulatory environment in shaping financial innovation cannot be overlooked. To take a well-documented example, the switch from a gold-dollar standard and fixed exchange rates in the Bretton Woods international monetary system to a world of independently managed currencies and floating exchange rates in 1971 inspired an enormous wave of financial innovation. In that same period, the emergence of stagflation precipitated by oil shortages created the need

---

[4] See, for example, Matson (2014). Unfortunately, the current cost of this transformation far exceeds the market price of gold.

for risk-management tools, such as exchange-traded and over-the-counter (OTC) derivative securities. Other shifts in the environment are far subtler, such as May Day in 1975, when commissions for trades switched from a fixed rate, no matter the size of the trade, to a negotiable commission. A more recent example is decimalization, when, in 2001, price movements on all US stocks switched over to decimals from eighths or sixteenths of a dollar. Not only did these changes shift trading terms more favourably towards the retail investor, but they allowed discount brokerages to proliferate and automated trading strategies to become much more than curiosities.

Innovation has thus transformed the financial system in the last seventy-five years in unforeseen and unforeseeable ways. However, institutional form follows financial function, and the evolutionary process of innovation, competition, and selection in performing Merton's six functions expedites a convergence in form.

18.3 Timetable of Financial Evolution

Expanding on Merton's insight, we classify financial innovation over time into six practical categories of implementation based on their broad functions: communication, computation, security, commercial use, accessibility, and cost. Communication in this schema is the transmission of financial information, while computation is the transformation of financial information and security is the protection of that information. Similarly, considering a financial innovation's interaction with the human environment, commercial use is the application of an innovation in a business setting, accessibility is a widening of its potential user base, and cost is a reduction in price.

These categories encompass the specific implementations of these broad functions to incorporate the timelessness of Merton's functional perspective. For example, take communication speed in trading. In 1920, the highest speeds would involve a seat on an exchange and a physical presence on the trading floor. In 2020, it involved high-frequency trading (HFT) servers competing for microsecond advantages in latency. Similarly, a wire transfer is still a wire transfer, whether it uses a telegraph and a codebook or a fibre-optic line and advanced cryptographic techniques. As with the six functions of finance, it is useful to make a distinction between the timeless implementation of these concepts and their time-bound manifestations.

Looking through the evolutionary lens reveals that different financial environments will benefit different sets of stakeholders. They can be considered analogous to distinct species within the financial ecosystem. For example, an inflationary environment favours debtors, while a deflationary environment favours creditors. High transaction costs will favour large institutional investors and financial intermediaries over retail investors and ordinary consumers. A shift in interest rates relative to stock market performance will shift the position of banking relative to trading. And two groups—academics and regulators—will often respond to a rapidly changing financial environment with innovations of their own.

We can use Merton's six functions of the financial system, the six corresponding conceptual categories of implementation, and the intellectual history of academic finance to organize the long post-World War II (WWII) period of financial innovation into a series of eight distinct periods—analogous to the major eras in the timetable of evolution[5]—each with its particular defining characteristics. When the natural history of the financial industry is viewed in a sequential narrative, the functional perspective of finance and how it relates to the AMH comes into sharper focus. Also, by recognizing how environmental changes can help or harm a given species, we can use the adaptive markets framework to increase our chances of survival in the face of extinction-level events. Table 18.1 presents a birds-eye view of these eight eras, spanning the years from 1944 to 2021.

The first era, dating from the establishment of the Bretton Woods monetary system in 1944, we call the 'Classical Financial Era'. The Bretton Woods agreement established the US dollar, backed by gold, as the basis for the global postwar economy, which was dominated by the US—unlike any other era before or since.

The Classical Financial Era ended with Harry Markowitz's first definitive publication on modern portfolio theory in 1952. Although it would take time for Markowitz's ideas to be digested by the financial community, his publication introduced the theoretical basis for portfolio diversification into risk management, at a time when the US economy was beginning to diversify from the heavy industry that made the country a superpower. For this reason, it seems appropriate to characterize this next period as the 'Modern Portfolio Theory Era'.

The Modern Portfolio Theory Era ended with William Sharpe's first publication on the capital asset pricing model (CAPM), in 1964, although, of course, Jack Treynor's private work foreshadowed it, and John Lintner and Jan Mossin nearly simultaneously developed it (Treynor, 1961, 1962; Sharpe,

---

[5] See, for example, Knoll and Nowak (2017).

Table 18.1 Timeline of eight eras of financial evolution from 1944 to 2021 and key technology, financial, and regulatory milestones during those eras.

Classical Financial	Modern Portfolio Theory	Alpha Beta	Derivatives	Automation	Financial Globalization	Algorithmic Trading	Digital Assets
Tech Milestones: • Transistor • Information theory • ENIAC	*Tech Milestones:* • IBM 650 • Sputnik • Integrated circuits • Mass-market TV sets	*Tech Milestones:* • Moore's Law • NASDAQ • Instinet	*Tech Milestones:* • Cboe • DOT • TI SR-52 calculator	*Tech Milestones:* • Bloomberg Terminal • SuperDOT/SOES • Practical cryptosystems • eCash	*Tech Milestones:* • WWW • RSA cryptosystem • Smartphones • Dot-com boom	*Tech Milestones:* • Bitcoin, blockchain • Dot-com bust • Fintech • Facebook, social media	*Tech Milestones:* • Coinbase • Fintech • mRNA vaccines
Financial Milestones: • Breton Woods • Hedge funds • Diners Club card • *Financial Analysts Journal*	*Financial Milestones:* • Mean-variance analysis • Portfolio optimization	*Financial Milestones:* • CAPM • Efficient Markets Hypothesis • GNMA, FHLMC • Floating exchange rates	*Financial Milestones:* • Cboe • Black–Scholes/ Merton • Vanguard • BARRA	*Financial Milestones:* • Program trading • Portfolio insurance • Statistical arbitrage • 1987 crash	*Financial Milestones:* • Credit derivatives • Global portfolio optimization • 1997 Asian crisis • LTCM	*Financial Milestones:* • HFT • Securitization • 2008 financial crisis • Fintech	*Financial Milestones:* • Coinbase • Fintech • GameStop • COVID-19 policy responses
Regulatory Milestones: • Multiple acts from previous decade (Glass–Steagall, Securities Exchange, Investment Company, etc.)	*Regulatory Milestones:* • Bank Holding Company Act	*Regulatory Milestones:* • Fair Credit Reporting Act • FASB	*Regulatory Milestones:* • Negotiable commissions • Equal Credit Opportunity • CFTC	*Regulatory Milestones:* • Circuit breakers	*Regulatory Milestones:* • Office of Thrift Supervision • Glass–Steagall repeal	*Regulatory Milestones:* • Sarbanes-Oxley Act • Decimalization	*Regulatory Milestones:* • Dodd–Frank Act • CFPB • OFR
1944–1951	1952–1963	1964–1972	1973–1981	1982–1988	1989–1999	2000–2009	2010–2021

Source: Lo, A. W. (2021). The financial system red in tooth and claw: 75 years of co-evolving markets and technology. *Financial Analysts Journal* 77(3): 5–33. Reprinted with permission from the publisher, Taylor & Francis Ltd., http://www.tandfonline.com.

1964; Lintner, 1965b; Mossin, 1966). This new financial model was applied not only to the first technology boom, which John Brooks called the 'go-go years', but also to the bust that followed. Overall, this era can be called the 'Alpha Beta Era'.

The Alpha Beta Era came to an end with the opening of the Chicago Board Options Exchange (Cboe) in 1973 and, in the same year, Black and Scholes's (1973) publication of their study on option pricing, as well as Robert C. Merton's nearly simultaneous development of the idea (Merton, 1973). This tumultuous period can only be named the 'Derivatives Era' for the explosive growth of these instruments that followed.

The Derivatives Era ended with a technological development, the advent of the first Bloomberg Terminal at the end of 1982. This phase in financial history was characterized by the adoption of consumer electronics in financial practice, from specialized terminals to home spreadsheets to program trading. The 'Automation Era' captures the essence of these years.

The Automation Era ended with another technological milestone, the development of the World Wide Web (WWW) in 1989 by Sir Timothy Berners-Lee, then a young computer scientist working at a CERN research facility outside Geneva. This event coincided with major geopolitical changes that led to the reintegration of the global economy, supplying an apposite name, the 'Financial Globalization Era'.

The next dividing line may appear arbitrary, but many computer professionals were worried about the systemic failures that might have taken place because of obsolescent code on the date of 31 December 1999, the infamous 'Y2K' problem. It is also a convenient milestone for the establishment of HFT in global markets. For this reason, the following period is named the 'Algorithmic Trading Era'. At the end of the Algorithmic Trading Era, the seeds for the next era were planted with the self-publication in 2008 of the bitcoin protocol by the mysterious figure known as Satoshi Nakamoto. Still in their infancy, cryptocurrencies and their related technologies form an entirely new evolutionary branch in our financial history that will no doubt create a series of offshoot technologies and financial institutions in the coming years. Therefore, this last period is called the 'Digital Assets Era'.

To set the stage for the next section's detailed review of the eight eras, we begin with a short retrospective of the period just prior to the first era. Although the financial system was quite extensive in the prewar era, in comparison to contemporary developments, this was a 'prehistoric' period when it comes to financial technology.

Consider, for example, the role of communication. Even the simplest forms of barter and exchange include a transfer of information, often weighted with symbolic meaning. By the modern era, market participants often vied to be the first to acquire information that could move markets—for example, in the apocryphal legend of Nathan Rothschild, the founder of the banking dynasty, who made his fortune when he learned of the British victory over Napoleon at Waterloo by carrier pigeon and, armed with that information, bought British government bonds on the cheap before news of the victory could reach London. (In fact, Rothschild seems to have learned of the news via fast couriers, although the family did employ a pigeon network as well.)

The speed of communication has a fundamental limit set by the laws of physics: the speed of light. This limit was reached as early as 1838, with the invention of the telegraph by Samuel F. B. Morse, for whom Morse code is named. The telegraph revolutionized the markets, allowing information about commodities in distant regions to reach financial centres nearly instantaneously. In the US, former frontier settlements became enormous hubs organized around the buying and selling of commodities, none of the hubs bigger than the new city of Chicago, which spawned the modern futures market. Market information could be sent over the wire to the first stock tickers, as could encrypted financial information, such as the first wire transfers, using printed codebooks as an early form of cryptographic security for the transaction.

By current criteria, financial activity in this period moved at a snail's pace. The financial system's reliance on a metallic standard was intended to limit activity that might lead to inflationary pressures, creating an environment that broadly favoured creditors over debtors. Membership in the financial professions was often limited by social strictures and laws that would seem grotesque today. Despite these restrictions on use and accessibility, the financial system was also prone to systemic crises, the larger ones leading to regulatory innovation, structural changes, and reforms, such as the formation of the Federal Reserve System following the Panic of 1907 and the creation of the Securities and Exchange Commission (SEC's), the Federal Deposit Insurance Company, and much of the regulatory framework of the entire financial industry—the Banking (also known as Glass–Steagall) Act of 1933, the Securities Act of 1933, the Securities Exchange Act of 1934, and the Investment Advisers Act of 1940—during and after the Great Depression. But perhaps the greatest innovation in financial analysis to emerge from this primordial period was Graham and Dodd's (1934) now classic tome *Security Analysis*, which would dominate the financial world—and the pages of the *Financial Analysts Journal*—until the Modern Portfolio Theory Era.

18.4 The Eight Eras of Financial Evolution

In this section, we describe each of the eight eras in more detail from an evolutionary perspective, with particular attention paid to the complementary roles of financial theory and practice and how they interact with technological innovation and the changing environment. To highlight the role of research in these evolutionary dynamics, we draw on the rich fossil record of all past publications of the *Financial Analysts Journal* in its seventy-five-year history.[6]

Also, in keeping with our theme of technology, we use a bit of data science by tabulating the top twenty authors (ranked by number of *Financial Analysts Journal* articles) and the top twenty words in article titles during each of the eight eras. The results, given in Table 18.2, offer a fascinating glimpse of the changing list of personalities and topics that have graced the pages of this venerable journal over time.[7] In subsequent references to this table, we will use Jacobs and Levy's (2022) updated values so those references may not agree with the author numbers displayed in Table 18.2 (the word counts are unaffected).

18.4.1 1944–1951: Classical Financial Era

The political and economic pressures of WWII transformed the financial landscape into that of the Classical Financial Era. By 1944, it was clear that a postwar order would emerge with the US as the dominant capitalist power. A blueprint for the financial underpinnings of this new order was put together in July 1944 at Bretton Woods, New Hampshire: a gold-dollar standard designed to finance the reconstruction of the damaged economies of the postwar period. The demobilization of millions of Americans in the armed forces taking place so quickly after the mass unemployment of the Great Depression caused legislators to pursue policies to improve the lives of returning

---

[6] Please note that citations to specific publications are not meant to represent the 'greatest hits' of the journal (which the editors already highlight periodically in special issues, such as issue 1, volume 51 in 1995) but are highly idiosyncratic references to particular topics and authors that are particularly relevant for the evolutionary narrative of this book.

[7] We are grateful to Manish Singh for assistance in preparing Table 18.2. Subsequent to the publication of Lo (2021), Bruce Jacobs and Ken Levy pointed out several inaccuracies in this table due, in part, to missing data from the *Financial Analysts Journal* online database, and also to methodological shortcomings such as using only author surnames rather than entire names (which led to over-counting common surnames such as Smith or Wang), and not considering tied rankings (which led to the omission of authors with surnames beginning with letters in the latter part of the alphabet, since only the top twenty authors were listed, irrespective of ties). See Jacobs and Levy (2022) for a corrected version of Table 18.2's author counts.

Table 18.2 Top twenty authors and words in the titles of all articles published in the *Financial Analysts Journal* within each of eight distinct eras from 1944 to 2021.

Rank	Classical Financial Era: 1944–1951				MPT Era: 1952–1963				Alpha Beta Era: 1964–1972				Derivatives Era: 1973–1981			
	Author	AuthFreq	Word	WordFreq	Author	AuthFreq	Word	WordFreq	Author	AuthFreq	Word	WordFreq	Author	AuthFreq	Word	WordFreq
1	Slade	9	industry	32	Molodovsky	13	industry	108	Packer	11	investment	80	Weil	12	investment	45
2	Hooper	6	outlook	24	Griffith	12	stock	87	Smith	11	stock	70	Treynor	7	market	43
3	Graham	5	investment	20	Storer	12	investment	73	Spigelman	10	industry	66	Davidson	6	stock	38
4	Bretey	5	utility	19	Bretey	11	market	62	Stern	9	market	54	Black	6	inflation	33
5	Gutman	5	market	19	Greene	9	growth	61	Milne	9	earnings	49	Baylis	5	accounting	29
6	Tatham Jr.	4	stock	16	Davis	8	outlook	51	Gumperz	8	financial	43	Smith	5	financial	24
7	Young	4	security	16	Smith	8	stocks	49	Bretey	7	growth	40	Rosenberg	5	risk	23
8	Davis	4	analysis	16	Graham	8	new	39	Molodovsky Jr.	7	performance	37	Ferguson	5	management	21
9	Kerr Jr.	4	railroad	15	Bolton	8	analysis	38	Murphy Jr.	7	new	37	Jahnke	4	new	17
10	Tucker	3	stocks	14	Mennis	7	future	35	Johnson	7	management	35	Good	4	portfolio	17
11	Naess	3	securities	13	Conklin	7	business	34	Block	6	price	32	Barrett	4	industry	16
12	Boulton	3	public	11	Collins	6	common	33	Neil Jr.	6	analysis	30	Leibowitz	4	analysis	14
13	Cogitator	3	earnings	10	Poole	6	security	32	Ellis	6	corporate	30	Ellis	4	corporate	13
14	Laufer	3	new	9	Lambourne	5	economic	31	Hayes	6	portfolio	29	Williams	4	earnings	13
15	Jenks	3	oil	9	Morehouse	5	financial	30	Mennis	6	accounting	28	Gutmann	4	long	12
16	Sterling	2	method	8	Murray	5	price	27	Levy	6	policy	28	Reilly	3	policy	12
17	Miller	2	factors	8	Peterson	5	research	24	Renshaw	6	capital	24	Jones	3	securities	12
18	Pastoriza	2	corporate	8	Kahn	5	oil	24	Reilly	6	money	23	Fisher	3	pension	12
19	Dunn	2	forum	8	Naess	4	earnings	23	Bauman	5	outlook	23	Norr	3	prices	11
20	Stevenson	2	growth	7	Brown	4	economy	22	Biggs	5	stocks	22	Sharpe	3	stocks	11

Rank	Automation Era: 1982–1988				Globalization Era: 1989–1999				Algorithmic Trading Era: 2000–2009				Digital Assets Era: 2010–2021			
	Author	AuthFreq	Word	WordFreq	Author	AuthFreq	Word	WordFreq	Author	AuthFreq	Word	WordFreq	Author	AuthFreq	Word	WordFreq
1	Leibowitz	8	stock	44	Fridson	50	risk	70	Fridson	101	risk	57	Sullivan	15	risk	38
2	Levy	7	market	34	Kritzman	26	market	66	Arnott	34	stock	49	Li	12	financial	32
3	Ferguson	5	portfolio	31	Treynor	17	stock	62	Rzepczynski	18	market	44	Wang	12	asset	30
4	Treynor	5	investment	24	Leibowitz	16	performance	45	Ennis	15	investment	35	Siegel	9	market	27
5	Canto	5	futures	22	Johnson	11	returns	40	Antia	13	financial	33	Ellis	9	investing	26
6	Chua	5	returns	20	Morris	11	asset	39	Statman	12	performance	31	Ibbotson	8	equity	23
7	Peavy III	5	bond	20	Black	9	equity	38	Bernstein	10	value	31	Kritzman	8	stock	22
8	Arnott	5	pension	18	Statman	9	investment	34	Leibowitz	8	markets	30	Asness	8	investment	22
9	Rol	4	performance	18	Kogelman	9	management	32	Siegel	8	returns	29	Chen	7	management	21
10	Siegel	3	asset	17	Ferguson	8	value	31	Hirschey	7	pension	28	Xiong	7	returns	20
11	Ibbotson	3	risk	17	Altman	8	financial	30	Morris	7	fund	25	Litterman	7	allocation	20
12	Curnmin	3	bonds	14	Harvey	8	bonds	29	Xu	7	portfolio	25	CIPM	7	performance	20
13	Bierman Jr.	3	financial	14	Brown	8	bond	28	Smith	7	asset	24	Pedersen	7	markets	19
14	Tosini	3	management	13	Arnott	7	stocks	28	Treynor	7	allocation	24	Goldberg	7	long	19
15	Ferris	3	index	13	Levy	7	know	28	Sullivan	7	equity	23	Bernstein	6	portfolio	18
16	Herbst	3	model	13	Kawaller	7	portfolio	27	Brown	6	management	23	Zhou	6	volatility	15
17	Beaver	3	duration	13	Bernstein	7	need	27	Johnson	6	investor	22	Leibowitz	6	active	15
18	Sorensen	3	price	12	Renshaw	6	allocation	26	Markowitz	6	corporate	21	Idzorek	6	trading	15
19	Good	3	analysis	12	Gastineau	6	practitioners	26	Moy	6	capital	20	Page	6	investors	14
20	Hunter	3	allocation	12	Taylor	5	international	25	Waring	6	funds	19	Hsu	6	fund	14

Source: Lo, A. W. (2021). The financial system red in tooth and claw: 75 years of co-evolving markets and technology. *Financial Analysts Journal* 77(3): 5–33. Reprinted with permission from the publisher, Taylor & Francis Ltd, http://www.tandfonline.com

veterans. The GI Bill provided financing for their college education, while the newly founded Veterans Administration insured home mortgages, which catalysed a postwar wave of home ownership and shifted the residential patterns of Americans from central cities to suburbs for generations.

This business environment set the stage for increased growth in commercial finance focused on the needs of its newly prosperous clients. After almost two decades of the Great Depression and wartime dearth, US society became strongly consumerist, and this pent up demand found new outlets. The first modern hedge fund, started by Alfred Winslow Jones in 1949, was the harbinger of new fund types and trading strategies, while the first general-purpose charge card, Diners Club, would become the forerunner to an enormous expansion of consumer credit.

The war effort also brought about enormous advances in computation. The first programmable digital computer, ENIAC, created in 1945 for the needs of war, performed the numerical calculations necessary in weapons development and in the hybrid field of operations research. The invention in 1947 of a new type of electronic component, the transistor, by three scientists at Bell Labs in New Jersey, opened up new possibilities for the miniaturization of these room-sized devices. In 1948, Claude Shannon, also working at Bell Labs, published the basic concepts of information theory, which was to revolutionize communications (Shannon, 1948).

Similarly, the young science of economics was given a boost by two important events: the publication of Samuelson's (1947) *Foundations of Economic Analysis* and, just one year later, the publication of Samuelson's principles-based textbook, *Economics*, which became the best-selling economics textbook for decades and is currently in its nineteenth edition (Samuelson, 1948).

The *Financial Analysts Journal* was launched in this intellectual milieu. From Table 18.2, we see that the focus of articles during this era was on the financial outlook for various industries—utilities and railroads—and general investment and security analysis. Benjamin Graham is among the top twenty authors in this time period, with eight articles to his credit. Based on the most frequently used words appearing in *Financial Analysts Journal* titles during this era, the origins of value investing and security analysis and the canonization of Graham and Dodd become self-evident.

18.4.2 1952–1963: The Modern Portfolio Theory Era

Under these conditions, it is no coincidence that the Classical Financial Era is also the precursor to a golden age of academic finance. With a background in operations research and frustrated with the lack of treatment of risk in the financial models of the time, Markowitz (1952) developed the mean-variance theory of portfolio selection. He incorporated the trade-off between risk and return into a systematic analysis for the first time and almost incidentally set into motion the development of a new academic field and a multi-trillion-dollar industry.

This body of work gave rise to the Modern Portfolio Theory Era, a development that we now take for granted as an obvious intellectual advance. In the heyday of Graham and Dodd's (1934) *Security Analysis*, however, the thought of abandoning the company-specific analysis of financial ratios, earnings multiples, and discounted cash flows in favour of return expectations, standard deviations, and covariances must have been considered absurd by most finance professionals. Even decades later, Benjamin Graham's most famous disciple, Warren Buffett, famously quipped that, rather than not putting all his eggs in one basket, as modern portfolio theory recommends, he preferred to do just that and then watch that basket very carefully.

Of course, such a strategy is highly effective if you happen to have Buffett's considerable basket-watching skills. Markowitz offered an alternative that required a different set of skills, one more easily acquired than Buffett's stock-picking ability. Markowitz's alternative quietly marked the beginning of two important trends that would continue for decades: the democratization of finance and the 'revenge of the nerds'. We shall return to both in subsequent eras.

During the Modern Portfolio Theory Era, the US had an expanding and confident economy marked by short recessions and stable prices. Americans, believing (rather inaccurately) that these years were a high point of American prosperity and stability, would later become nostalgic for this period. Below the surface, however, this seeming stability concealed a subterranean current of technological innovation, and sometimes even technological panic. It was the first decade when every household had to have a television set, which prefigured our age of ubiquitous screen technology. The first integrated circuit was invented in this decade, as was the first metal oxide semiconductor field-effect transistor, the basis for the modern computer chip. It was the decade in which the US first realized that it might fall technologically behind its competitors, after the Soviet Union successfully launched Sputnik 1, the first artificial Earth satellite, in 1957.

It was also the decade when the first mass-produced electronic computer, the IBM 650, went to market. It was becoming clear that the electronic computer, far from being a niche product for a select group of scientists, engineers, and military professionals, was a general-purpose technology, one that could be applied to any field that generated a large amount of data, including financial markets. With this greater computing power, it became possible to apply statistical methods to financial data in greater depth and with greater rigour, in addition to performing humbler tasks, such as calculating values for bonds and mortgages that were unlisted in standard financial tables.

The *Financial Analysts Journal* during this time continued to focus on industry outlooks and security analysis, with six articles from Graham in this era, including his highly influential 1952 contribution, 'Toward a Science of Security Analysis' (Graham, 1952). For the first time, however, 'economic' and 'economy' appear in the list of top twenty title words, perhaps reflecting the growing impact of economics on business analysis, thanks to Samuelson's (1948) best-selling textbook from the previous era.

18.4.3 1964–1972: The Alpha Beta Era

The popular memory of the 1960s is one of a politically tumultuous and, at times, violent era, but it was also the time of the first long technology stock bull market, the 'go-go years', and, not coincidentally, also the time of the first tech stock bust.

Underlying the technology stock boom was the realization that there was something new in the technological world, as Gordon Moore presciently observed in 1965. In this intellectual environment, four financial researchers proposed the tenets of the CAPM almost simultaneously: Treynor (1961, 1962), Sharpe (1964), Lintner (1965b), and Mossin (1966). These four individuals with varying backgrounds—three Americans and one Norwegian, three born in the 1930s and one in the 1910s, three academics and one practitioner—converged on the same fundamental concepts of a quantifiable trade-off between risk and reward, where risk is measured by the correlation of an asset's return with the return of the market portfolio.

The CAPM was the final brick in the theoretical foundation of passive investing that began with Markowitz and his development of modern portfolio theory. The CAPM gave investors a framework that distinguished unique investment skill, alpha, from commoditized risk premium, beta. In doing so, the CAPM catalysed the development of an array of financial innovations, including index products and benchmarking, portable-alpha and hedging strategies, performance attribution, risk budgeting, and many more. But, most important of all, the CAPM framework and lexicon provided a systematic method through which institutional portfolio managers could discharge their fiduciary duties, thereby unleashing trillions of dollars of investable assets for those seeking prudent investment opportunities. It is only fitting that the Alpha Beta Era is bookended by Sharpe's (1964) academic publication on the CAPM at its start and his very first *Financial Analysts Journal* publication, the practitioner version entitled 'Risk, Market Sensitivity and Diversification' (Sharpe, 1972), at its end.

Ironically, at the same time that the seeds of passive investing were being planted and watered, the age of the 'gunslinger' portfolio manager had arrived. The finance profession elevated a new generation of managers and analysts, such as the charismatic financier Gerry Tsai of Fidelity and subsequently the Manhattan Fund, who entered it during a period of financial euphoria, and propelled the popularity of retail mutual funds to a new level, only to see the market falter and plunge by the end of the decade. It was an extinction-level event among hedge funds, since those that failed to hedge, a forgotten skill, failed entirely. While the market was increasingly accessible, transaction costs were still high, making it difficult for the retail investor to diversify.

Moore's Law, first announced in 1965, was originally a statement about computing power, but the same discoveries in electronics that created a revolution in computing also made possible a less heralded revolution in financial communications. The Alpha Beta Era saw the emergence of electronic clearinghouse operations between banks; the opening of Instinet, the first off-exchange trading system; and the opening of NASDAQ, the first electronic exchange, although initially it only served as an electronic quotation system for the 'pink sheets' of the OTC market.

At the same time, analyses of return data making use of new computing technologies showed that professional managers often experienced worse performance than simple strategies and portfolios. By current standards, this quantity of big data was absurdly small, but computing power, and thus the ability to crunch these numbers, was increasing at an exponential rate. In this informationally richer environment, Samuelson (1965) and Fama (1970) first formulated the radical idea that asset prices reflect all available information—the efficient markets hypothesis. Further empirical work testing the CAPM and its application to measure the alphas of mutual fund managers added more weight to the academic conviction that active management did not justify its fees, setting the stage for the passive-investment revolt in the subsequent era.

Underneath these technologically driven innovations was a slower trend, dating back to the wave of postwar home ownership, but now vastly accelerated thanks to the Housing and Urban Development Act of 1968. The Government National Mortgage Association, known as Ginnie Mae, which guaranteed many federally issued residential mortgages, developed a new financial process, securitization, aggregating a pool of mortgages into a new type of financial instrument, the mortgage-backed security For decades, this financial innovation would allow lenders to provide loans to prospective homebuyers at a lower cost by providing a market for the risk. The process of securitization would eventually be applied to other assets, such as credit card receivables, auto loans, student loans, and music royalties.

In this era, the *Financial Analysts Journal* debuted three articles in 1971 by a 32-year-old practitioner who had launched his consulting practice, called Associates in Finance, only two years earlier. His first article in the journal was titled 'Implications of the Random Walk Hypothesis for Portfolio Management', while his second and third were Parts I and II of 'Toward a Fully Automated Stock Exchange' (see the cover illustration in Fig. 18.3b).[8] These contributions presaged the central role that academic finance and technology were to play in the next decades, particularly the ideas of market efficiency and the growing importance of artificial intelligence and algorithmic trading. This young financial analyst was named Fischer Black.

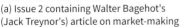
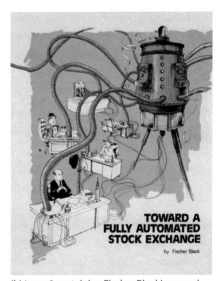

(a) Issue 2 containing Walter Bagehot's (Jack Treynor's) article on market-making

(b) Issue 6 containing Fischer Black's second article on automated stock exchanges

Fig. 18.3 Illustrations for volume 27 of the *Financial Analysts Journal*.
Source: CFA Institute.

[8] Black (1971a,b,c).

This same volume of the *Financial Analysts Journal* also included Bage-hot's (1971) article 'The Only Game in Town', a landmark contribution on the role of the market-maker in providing liquidity in exchange for the bid-offer spread. This penetrating analysis-by an author adopting the name of a long-departed financial writer of the Victorian Era as a pseudonym-was the acorn that sprouted into the mighty oak of the market microstructure literature, one of the earliest examples of a practitioner and *Financial Analysts Journal* author having a substantial impact on academic finance rather than the other way around. In fact, this article was cited by both of the academic publications often considered to be the theoretical cornerstones of microstructure theory: Glosten and Milgrom (1985) and Kyle (1985). It was subsequently revealed that Walter Bagehot was, in fact, Jack Treynor, and his article was republished in 1995 in the *Financial Analysts Journal*'s special fiftieth anniversary issue under Treynor's own name (Treynor, 1995).

During the Alpha Beta Era, several new words appeared in the *Financial Analysts Journal*'s list of top twenty title words, as can be seen in Table 18.2: 'portfolio', 'accounting', and 'policy'. As a testament to the durable impact of academic finance on practice, 'portfolio' also appears in the top twenty list for all future eras. Meanwhile, the growing importance of accounting and policy to financial analysis is consistent with the introduction of government-sponsored enterprises and their impact on mortgage markets in particular, and fixed-income markets more generally.

18.4.4   1973–1981: The Derivatives Era

In addition to the aforementioned banner articles, the year 1971 saw the suspension of convertibility of the dollar into gold and the formation of a floating-currency exchange rate regime to replace the fixed exchange rates of the Bretton Woods monetary system. This monetary crisis was a foreseeable one. As the world's economies regained their former strength, imbalances in the system made the US' central role increasingly untenable. The US left this system at a time of increasing inflation and increasing debt. Over the next several years, it would be struck by a shock in the price of meat, lead-ing to price ceilings set by the president, and by two oil shocks, causing local shortages in gasoline and escalating energy prices, while the price of gold, now disconnected from the dollar, reached a record high. Standard macroe-conomic policy did not gain any traction. These were the years of stagflation, a combination of low growth, high unemployment, high interest rates, and high inflation.

This economic environment of risk and uncertainty was the ideal setting for the growth in financial derivatives to better manage these challenges. For this reason, this period is named the 'Derivatives Era'. There is a recurring pattern of development between necessity and technology in this era, most famously between the founding of the Cboe in 1973; Black, Scholes, and Merton devising the option pricing formula that bears their name in that same year;[9] and the release in 1975 of the Texas Instruments SR-52, the first programmable handheld calculator capable of handling the logarithmic and exponential functions of the Black–Scholes/Merton formula.[10]

This turning point not only sparked a blossoming of the derivatives markets, but also cemented the connection between academia and the financial industry, started by Markowitz and fuelled by Sharpe and his CAPM co-creators years before, by giving practitioners a formal and systematic framework for understanding the behaviour of increasingly complex financial instruments. Finance professionals began to think of their field as a form of engineering rather than deal making, part of a longer sociological trend in which the broader economic sciences would take their primary inspiration from physics and mathematics (see Lo and Mueller (2010)).

Meanwhile, the change to floating exchange rates was a perfect environment for the creation of entirely new categories of derivatives. Although currency futures and forward contracts were developed in anticipation of the abandonment of fixed exchange rates, they became actively traded only afterwards. These were followed by currency swaps, developed in order to avoid capital controls, and then interest rate swaps. Salomon Brothers brokered the first such deal in 1981, between IBM and the World Bank, with IBM swapping its Swiss francs and German marks for the World Bank's US dollars. These derivatives would grow exponentially in popularity.

Nevertheless, other markets were in the doldrums. Brokerages had urged the SEC for years to increase the rate of commissions in response to a long-term decline in retail investors. On May Day 1975, however, the SEC abolished fixed rates entirely, signalling a new wave of financial competition and innovation centred on the drop in trading cost, resulting in the growth of index and mutual funds, as well as electronic and automated trading

---

[9] Black and Scholes (1973); Merton (1973).

[10] In fact, Lo (2017, p. 357) noted that 'shortly after the SR-52 debuted, one of the founders of the Cboe, a savvy options trader named Irwin Guttag, bought one for his teenage son John and asked him to program the Black–Scholes/Merton formula for it. Within a year, many Cboe floor traders were sporting SR-52's of their own. By 1977, Texas Instruments introduced a new programmable TI-59 with a "Securities Analysis Module" that would automatically calculate prices using the Black–Scholes/Merton formula. (When Myron Scholes himself confronted Texas Instruments about their unauthorized use of the formula, they replied that it was in the public domain. When he asked for a calculator instead, Texas Instruments replied that he should go buy one)'.

technologies. The First Index Investment Trust, later to become the Vanguard 500 Index Fund, implementing John C. Bogle's at-cost philosophy, was incorporated on 31 December 1975.

Thus began the decades-long trend towards passive investment strategies and products, built on the firm academic foundations of the two previous eras. This trend was hastened by attractive equity returns, declining trading costs, and technological advances in trade execution, order processing, and telecommunications, such as the Designated Order Turnaround (DOT) routing system at the New York Stock Exchange (NYSE) and the realization of NASDAQ into a fully electronic financial exchange. Moore's Law continued to accelerate the infrastructure of the financial system, and even consumers with no direct connection to the financial markets experienced this acceleration firsthand through the birth of direct deposit for their paychecks.

This era also included a key milestone for the co-evolution of technology and finance theory: the founding of Barr Rosenberg Associates, or BARRA, in 1974 by its eponymous University of California, Berkeley, finance professor. A consulting firm that eventually became a technology company, BARRA provided the entire financial industry with the tools to implement the theories of Markowitz, Sharpe, and others, becoming a pioneer in translating finance theory into practice. The legacy of Rosenberg still stands to this day through Morgan Stanley Capital International (MSCI), which acquired BARRA in 2004 and now offers a greatly expanded set of portfolio construction tools under the MSCI/BARRA brand.

With the arrival of BARRA, the practical infrastructure needed to accelerate the trend from active to passive investment was now complete. The elitism of unique investment opportunities was beginning to give way to the democratization of finance. Access to the old-boy network began losing ground to those with knowledge of computer networks. Graduates of Harvard and Yale began losing ground to the graduates of Caltech and MIT. Meanwhile, the cult of the star portfolio manager was giving way to the science and engineering practice of portfolio management and the rise of the Wall Street quant.

This was the revenge of the nerds, the trend first initiated by Markowitz in 1952, whose thesis adviser, Milton Friedman, jokingly threatened to withhold Markowitz's PhD in economics because his dissertation was not 'economics'. Markowitz (1991, p. 476) acknowledged that 'at the time I defended my dissertation, portfolio theory was not part of economics. But now it is'. In the same vein, alpha, beta, and the Black–Scholes/Merton option-pricing formula were not part of financial analysis at the birth of the *Financial Analysts Journal*—but now they are.

During the Derivatives Era, the word 'risk' made its first appearance in the top twenty *Financial Analysts Journal* title words list, right on cue in this financially tumultuous period, and it has remained in the top twenty ever since. Given the double-digit levels of inflation during this era, it is no surprise that 'inflation' also joined the top twenty, but it has not appeared on the top twenty lists of subsequent eras.

In this era, Fischer Black, no stranger to the *Financial Analysts Journal*, joined the list of top twenty authors for the first time, as did Barr Rosenberg and future Nobel Laureate William Sharpe. The many *Financial Analysts Journal* publications by top academics, alongside such profoundly insightful practitioner articles as Treynor's 'The Only Game in Town' (Bagehot, 1971) and Black's (1975) 'Fact and Fantasy in the Use of Options', transformed the journal's reputation among finance academics from an industry trade magazine to a highly respected research forum for those academics interested in the practice of finance. As a result, in this era and beyond, finance academics began publishing some of their best work in the *Financial Analysts Journal*. The list includes Rosenberg and Guy's (1976a; 1976b) articles on estimating linear multifactor models; Jensen and Meckling's (1978) foray into the political economy of the theory of the firm; Modigliani and Cohn's (1979) argument that the stock market was significantly undervalued because it did not properly account for inflation; Reinganum's (1981) empirical documentation of the small-firm premium; and Rubinstein and Leland's (1981) recipe for constructing portfolio insurance.

18.4.5   1982–1988: The Automation Era

The next several years saw the US economy return to a period marked by the absence of macroeconomic shocks and an environment of low inflation and low unemployment. Internationally, Japan was going through a long boom and was viewed by many Americans as the US' primary economic competitor, while the Soviet Union remained its primary military competitor. The personal computer became a common household item, and the home spreadsheet program one of its most popular forms of software, while the US stock market began another long bull run. Therefore, almost inescapably, this period must be named the 'Automation Era'.

In this newly wired environment, necessity drove mathematicians and computer scientists to develop new cryptographic security concepts to cope with the possible violation of trust in an increasingly networked world, while new cryptographic systems were implemented to protect everyday transactions from interference (Chaum, 1982, 1983; Lamport, Shostak, and Pease, 1982). The first major financial hack took place against the First National Bank of Chicago in 1988; it was an attempted electronic transfer of $70 million from United Airlines and Merrill Lynch to banks in Austria, and was considered at the time an exotic form of embezzlement.

At the same time, the financial exchanges continued to modernize, with the NYSE installing its SuperDOT electronic order-routing system and NAS-DAQ its Small Order Execution System (SOES), and, in December 1982, the first Bloomberg Terminal (with its colour-coded 'chiclet' keyboard) debuted. New types of trading took advantage of these new electronic interconnections. For example, the pairs trading strategy developed at Morgan Stanley and then at D.E. Shaw used statistical analysis to identify pairs of correlated stocks for automated trading systems to buy and sell.[11] Other forms of statistical arbitrage quickly followed, and the term 'SOES bandits' became both a despised moniker used by unsuspecting institutional investors and a badge of honour among those with the technological savvy to profit from their ability to exploit this system.

This newly interconnected financial environment may have contributed to the wholly unexpected Black Monday stock market crash of 19 October 1987. Others cast blame on portfolio insurance, particularly on strategies implemented by Leland O'Brien Rubinstein Associates, as first outlined in the *Financial Analysts Journal* article by Rubinstein and Leland (1981). While its causes are still unknown, the Black Monday crash introduced the important financial innovation of the 'circuit breaker' trading curb, now mandatory in US financial exchanges, which halts trades should prices fall below a set threshold, to reduce volatility and prevent panic sell-offs.

In the Automation Era, three important new additions appeared in the *Financial Analysts Journal*'s top twenty title words for the first time: 'bond', 'pension', and 'index'. The journal's history until this point was dominated by topics related to equities, understandable given its roots in the New York Society of Security Analysts. However, the increasing sophistication of fixed-income markets and investors, including pension funds, motivated an equally sophisticated financial analysis. In the jargon of ecology, pension funds are a 'keystone species', a group of stakeholders that are central to the health and robustness of an ecosystem, without which the functioning of

---

[11] See Lo (2017, pp. 236–240) for a more detailed history of how a young computer scientist managed to revolutionize the hedge fund industry through technology and became a billionaire along the way.

that system would be radically impaired. In a pair of articles, mathematician-cum-bond-guru Leibowitz (1986a,b)—a top twenty *Financial Analysts Journal* author across five eras—introduced the notion of a dedicated bond portfolio for pension plans, forever changing the way institutional investors manage interest rate risk in their massive portfolios.

Indexing also came of age during the Automation Era, hence the term's popularity in *Financial Analysts Journal* titles, but the rise of the index fund is also related to the innovation of stock index futures in this period. It is difficult to imagine financial life without S&P 500 Index futures, especially from the perspective of risk management. Figlewski and Kon (1982) first described the benefits and applications of this important contract in the journal prior to the creation of futures contracts in April 1982, when the Chicago Mercantile Exchange first launched its S&P 500 futures contract. There is little debate that pension funds contributed significantly to the popularity of this contract and other financial futures.

Finally, during this era, we see the seeds of algorithmic trading being planted through articles by Burns (1982) on electronic trading in futures markets and Hill and Jones (1988) on what was then called 'program trading', as well as from academics, such as Amihud and Mendelson (1982), who were pioneers of the empirical market microstructure literature.

18.4.6 1989–1999: The Financial Globalization Era

With the benefit of hindsight, the most important financial innovation during the Automation Era was taking place outside the financial world entirely, at CERN, the European Organization for Nuclear Research, located outside Geneva. A young physicist employed by the world's largest particle accelerator was creating a software platform to share data and coordinate experimental design efforts among fellow physicists hailing from multiple universities around the world. In 1989, this platform—known as the World Wide Web—was launched by Timothy Berners-Lee, ushering in the Financial Globalization Era.

At the time, the fall of the Berlin Wall and the later dissolution of the Soviet Union seemed to over-shadow any mere technological innovation. The US became the world's first hyperpower, while the diminished geopolitical tensions allowed Germany to reunify and the European Union as we know it today to form. However, Moore's Law continued to operate, making computing and communication devices cheaper and more powerful with every passing year. Cellphones became common in the US, and the first smartphone, combining the power of the computer with the function of a telephone, was invented, becoming popular first in Japan.

The internet and the WWW were becoming commonplace in US households, but their economic potential would not be realized until the development of cryptographically secure transactions for payment over the internet, to keep financial transactions safe and to prevent fraudulent transactions from taking place. Although RSA Security was founded in the previous era (1982) by the three MIT computer scientists who developed this technology (see Rivest, Shamir, and Adleman (1978)), it was in the mid-1990s that the company's encryption technology became the de facto standard of the computer industry and, by extension, the standard of most companies that conducted business through computers.

This single innovation brings into sharp focus the deep interdependencies between technology and the financial system. By ensuring the security and privacy of data transmission, RSA established trust in all online transactions, and trust is at the very core of finance and commerce. It is no exaggeration to say that RSA encryption facilitated not just the entire e-commerce industry, but also the spectacular globalization of the financial industry, which depends on encrypted telecommunications.

Almost immediately following this innovation came what is known as the dot-com boom. An enormous wave of speculative investment funded prospective internet retailers, technology and telecommunications companies, and providers of other internet services, including entirely new categories of enterprise, such as the search engine and the internet auction.

The dot-com boom helped fund the rise of mass accessibility and the further democratization of finance, including the online brokerage and the online payment processor, the cornerstones of current fintech. It specifically made itself felt on NASDAQ, whose composite index rose fourfold from 1995 to its peak in 2000. But other financial innovations were being made at this time, too, including the development of the modern credit derivative and the credit default swap, and the creation of the first exchange-traded funds.

An important factor behind these innovations was the low-interest rate environment leading up to this era. In contrast to the stagflation of the Derivatives Era, during which the US federal funds rate reached an all-time peak of 22% in December 1980, interest rates declined precipitously, to below 3% by December 1992 (Fig. 18.4). If return on investment is viewed as the foodstuff of the financial ecosystem, a low-yield environment is tantamount to widespread famine, with all its attendant consequences for investor behaviour, including a 'reach for yield' by such financial species

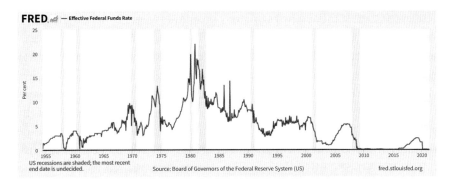

Fig. 18.4 Effective Federal Funds Rate, 1 July 1954–6 May 2021.

Source: FRED Graph courtesy of Federal Reserve Bank of St. Louis, with data provided by Board of Governors of the Federal Reserve System (US).

as pension funds, insurance companies, and other large institutional fixed-income investors.[12] In this milieu of heightened competition, financial intermediaries created and expanded for these yield-starved financial institutions a smorgasbord of higher-yielding investments, such as junk bonds, collateralized debt obligations, and mortgage-backed securities, and a host of exotic hedge fund strategies, such as statistical arbitrage, convertible bond arbitrage, and emerging market debt. Because higher yields are linked to higher risk, however, reaching for yield inevitably implies the prospect of greater financial losses. It is no coincidence that this era was associated with financial crisis and contagion.

The Japanese asset bubble popped in the early 1990s, leading to decades of stagnation in Japan. The Asian financial crisis of 1997 transmitted itself across nations as different as South Korea and Indonesia. Finally, the Russian financial crisis of 1998 caused Russia to devalue the ruble and default on its debt, almost incidentally bringing down LTCM, whose central connection to many US financial firms led to fears that it would precipitate a chain reaction of failure in the US financial system. Is there any better illustration of the butterfly effect and the complex interconnections of the global financial system than the default of a sovereign debt issue (held by relatively few investors) triggering a major global financial crisis four weeks later?[13] Despite

---

[12] Reaching for yield is widely accepted by practitioners as a behavioural reality, but it is not easy to document because it requires a measure of 'fair' prices. However, Becker and Ivashina (2015) provided compelling evidence for the phenomenon in the case of insurance companies, the largest holders of corporate bonds.

[13] The butterfly effect—a popular shorthand for the branch of mathematics known as chaos theory—is often used to illustrate the complexity of nonlinear dynamic systems in which the flapping of a butterfly's wings in Beijing can trigger a tornado in Kansas City two weeks later.

these events, substantial new regulatory proposals were dismissed. In fact, it was during this era that the famous firewall between commercial and investment banking, put in place by the Glass–Steagall Act six decades earlier, was deliberately and systematically dismantled.

During the Financial Globalization Era, the most frequently used word in the titles of *Financial Analysts Journal* articles was 'risk'—almost as if the authors sensed they were heading into challenging financial waters. For the first time in the journal's history, 'international' entered the top twenty list, underscoring the fact that the previous Automation Era led inexorably to a more globally connected financial world. Hedging international exposures was the concern at the start of the Financial Globalization Era, as illustrated by the hedging strategies of Black (1989), Kritzman (1989), and many others. But attention eventually turned towards constructing a globally optimal portfolio, as in the highly cited publication of Black and Litterman (1992), and the empirical properties of globally diversified portfolios, as documented by Capaul, Rowley, and Sharpe (1993), Odier and Solnik (1993), and Sinquefield (1996). The US financial industry had finally awakened to the rest of the world.

18.4.7   2000–2009: The Algorithmic Trading Era

The dot-com boom, peaking in March 2000, failed to last. Ready to feed on its downturn, however, was HFT, a form of algorithmic trading that places, revises, and cancels buy-and-sell orders at ultra-fast speeds to generate profits. At the turn of the millennium, this speed could still be measured in seconds—fast but not exceptionally so. However, the frequency of trading rose exponentially in less than a decade to microsecond levels, a pace of innovation so quick that HFT practitioners discovered that their results (and sometimes their systems infrastructure) would become obsolete in a matter of months (Loveless, 2013). HFT became rapid enough that traders were actually running up against the speed of light and other pesky laws of physics as a practical limitation of their algorithms, causing HFT firms to vie for coveted locations for their computers, in specific shelves on the metal racks of giant server farms that were closest in physical proximity to the servers of major stock exchanges. Thanks to Moore's Law and RSA encryption algorithms, HFT became a significant percentage of the daily trading volume on most electronic exchanges.

But another change in the financial ecosystem facilitated the rise of high-frequency traders: decimalization, the SEC-mandated shift of all US stock market price movements from fractions of a dollar (eighths and, for larger trades, sixteenths) to cents on 9 April 2001. On the surface, such a shift seemed a long time coming. After all, denominating heavily traded assets such as the equities of Fortune 500 companies in increments of 0.125 and 0.0625 during the age of programmable calculators, computers, and automated trading systems seems completely incongruous. The fact that this practice originated in the 1600s in Spain—because traders once used gold doubloons that could be easily cut in half, quarters, and eighths—added even more motivation to modernize the system. The final push came from institutional investors, such as pension fund managers, who argued that bid-offer spreads were artificially inflated because of the use of fractional dollars and that decimalization would result in lower trading costs for all market participants. However, as with many well-intentioned proposals, there were unintended consequences.

Bagehot (1971) and Treynor (1995) recognized that the existence of the bid–offer spread was meant to compensate designated market-makers or 'specialists', individuals charged with the responsibility of 'maintaining fair and orderly markets' by quoting bid-and-offer prices at which they were willing to transact at any time with any counterparty that sought to buy or sell. This responsibility makes the market a market; specialists provide the liquidity to maintain it. In doing so, however, specialists are often trading against parties that possess more information about the asset than they do, hence the existence of a bid-offer spread to compensate the specialist for having an informational disadvantage (known as adverse selection in the market microstructure literature).

What would be the consequences if spreads were allowed to move more freely, a penny at a time instead of at 12.5 cent intervals? The immediate consequences were as expected: Spreads declined, in some cases, to just a penny, benefiting retail and institutional investors as trading costs also fell. However, the decline in spreads reduced the profitability of specialists, causing a mass exodus of these designated market-makers.[14] In the wake of their departure, hedge funds, proprietary trading desks, and HFT shops stepped in, providing the liquidity that specialists had previously offered. As Merton (1993) taught, the need for liquidity services did not change in response

---

[14] A Government Accountability Office (2005, p. 2) study of the impact of decimalization concluded the following: 'Although conditions in the securities industry overall have improved recently, market intermediaries, particularly exchange specialists and NASDAQ market-makers, have faced more challenging operating conditions since 2001. From 2000 to 2004, the revenues of the broker-dealers acting as New York Stock Exchange specialists declined over 50 percent, revenues for firms making markets on NASDAQ fell over 70 percent, and the number of firms conducting such activities shrank from almost 500 to about 260.'

to a seemingly minor regulatory shift from eighths to decimals, but the institutions providing that liquidity changed dramatically.

However, unlike the designated market-makers of the NYSE and NAS-DAQ, these new liquidity providers were not under any exchange-mandated obligations to provide liquidity regardless of market conditions. By dynamically deploying capital only when it suited them while getting up from the poker table when the odds were against them, these sophisticated algorithmic traders were able to generate remarkably consistent profits. A rare glimpse of this consistency was afforded by the 2014 initial public offering of the HFT firm Virtu Financial. Its S-1 filing disclosed that between 1 January 2009 and 28 February 2014, a period of 1,278 consecutive trading days, it experienced only one losing day.[15]

The 'fair-weather friend' nature of liquidity provision during this era was made painfully clear during the 'Quant Meltdown' of August 2007, when a large statistical arbitrage portfolio was apparently liquidated abruptly, causing losses in that entire strategy class for many hedge fund portfolios.[16] In the midst of heavy trading, liquidity dried up much more quickly than expected, presumably because the new liquidity providers, such as high-frequency traders, experienced losses at the start of the liquidation process and decided not to participate during this rout.

Since decimalization began, institutional investors have observed and complained about the fact that, although spreads are indeed lower, the size of the trades that can be transacted at these lower spreads has also declined and the sensitivity of spreads to changes in market conditions and imbalances between supply and demand is much higher. This episode illustrates the subtle, complex, and dynamic nature of adaptive markets and how new species quickly emerge to occupy ecological niches relinquished by less adaptive competitors.

But the main story of the Algorithmic Trading Era was, of course, the dot-com bust followed by the tragedy of the 11 September 2001 attacks and their military sequels. In response, the Federal Open Market Committee lowered the federal funds rate from 6.5% at the peak of the boom to only 1.0% three years later. At the same time, US politicians told US consumers to spend to prevent an economic downturn and actively promoted the 'ownership society' in which home ownership played a significant part. House prices were appreciating, and bipartisan policies were implemented to extend more

[15] www.sec.gov/Archives/edgar/data/1592386/000104746914003044/a2219101zs-1a.htm#dm16701_business (accessed 8 May 2021).
[16] See Chapter 17 and Khandani and Lo (2007, 2011b) for details of the Quant Meltdown of August 2007.

credit to potential homeowners, while mortgage originators expanded their business. Financial innovations such as adjustable-rate and teaser-rate mortgages, automated mortgage approvals, and NINJA ('no income, no job, no assets') loans expedited this process. In this environment, more homeowners began to use home ownership as a speculative asset. Meanwhile, these mortgages were packaged into a newly popular form of asset-backed security known as the collateralized debt obligation, which pooled the mortgages and divided them into tranches based on the probability of default. Some of these tranches were insured against default through credit default swaps.

In the meantime, the global economy had begun to shift. The entry of the People's Republic of China into the World Trade Organization in 2001 marked the beginning of the largest economic expansion in human history. Chinese-manufactured goods became staple items in global commerce, while the Chinese population solidly entered the global middle class, some of its members entering into the ranks of the ultra-rich. In the US, the technology companies that survived the dot-com bust began to consolidate, as many of their functions expanded to fill the role of natural monopolies. A new form of communication, social media, began to displace the role of older sources of information, while the ease of copying digital media displaced traditional recorded media, such as music.

The story of the downturn in the US housing market, and the financial chain reaction that led to the global financial crisis, has been told and retold, so there is little need to do so again here. By most accounts, the global financial system very nearly collapsed in 2008, as two major US investment banks failed and others were poised to follow. For our adaptive narrative, however, these events had at least three important consequences. The first was the realization that there was no single financial innovation or regulatory failure that was responsible for the crisis. It was a system-wide crisis, with system-wide causes. In fact, Khandani, Lo, and Merton (2013) showed that the combined effect of rising home prices, declining interest rates, and near-frictionless refinancing opportunities—none of which by itself is considered dysfunctional or deleterious—can create an unintentional synchronization of homeowner leverage leading to a 'ratchet' effect, because homes are indivisible and their owner-occupants cannot raise equity to reduce their leverage when home prices fall. A simulation of this refinancing ratchet effect in the US housing market yields potential losses of $1.7 trillion from June 2006 to December 2008, which is comparable in order of magnitude to the actual losses during this period.

The second consequence of the financial crisis of 2008 was that, as with any ecological system experiencing major disruption, there would be new winners and losers in its aftermath, when an 'adaptive radiation' of species often occurs in newly unoccupied ecological niches.[17] In the case of the financial crisis, this adaptive radiation involved two closely related trends: the continuing consolidation of financial institutions within each financial subsector into more capital-efficient behemoths (e.g. mutual fund complexes, investment and commercial banks, hedge funds, and private equity funds), and the emergence of smaller, more nimble financial technologies, or 'fintech', to compete with these behemoths. The same innovative energy that gave rise to e-commerce, search engines, and social media now turned its focus to reinventing the financial system in its own disruptive image. New payment systems, lending institutions, brokerages, and asset-management services were launched, not from Wall Street, but from Silicon Valley. One of the most unlikely and most innovative of these new businesses was cryptocurrencies.

Many people distrusted the measures taken to preserve the global financial system, which they saw as rewarding the malefactors who caused it. One of these people may have been an anonymous computer scientist using the name Satoshi Nakamoto. This person's invention, bitcoin, used cryptographically secure principles to create a distributed system of electronic transactions that did not rely on a central authority or trust of any kind to transfer digital assets. It is believed that Nakamoto was influenced by hard-money theorists who favoured the historically unfounded stability of a metallic currency standard, since the ultimate supply of bitcoin, although the result of a digital process, is inherently limited and progressively more difficult to generate. This new wave of cutting-edge technologists effectively wanted a return to the gold standard but on their terms.

The third consequence of the financial crisis of 2008 was to refocus attention on financial ethics, the importance of corporate governance, and the broader environmental, social, and governance (ESG) investment trend that will become even more mainstream in the next era. None of these issues was new to the financial industry, but they gathered considerably more urgency thanks to the financial excesses and malfeasance of this era, topped off in December 2008 with the unravelling of the $50 billion Bernie Madoff Ponzi scheme.

All of these developments were reflected in the concerns of *Financial Analysts Journal* authors and, in some cases, anticipated by them. At the start of the Algorithmic Trading Era, several articles were published on the risk–reward characteristics of hedge fund strategies—including day trading,

[17] See, in particular, the notion of punctuated equilibrium proposed by Eldredge and Gould (1972).

statistical arbitrage, commodity futures, and HFT—and how they differed from more traditional investments.[18] The title of Leibowitz's (2005) contribution to this literature, 'Alpha Hunters and Beta Grazers', provides a pithy summary of the ecological dynamics involved in the financial industry during this era.

The growing importance of credit markets and the unique risks they contain were reflected in two articles by Kealhofer (2003a, 2003b), the co-founder of the eponymous KMV, a leading credit risk analytics company acquired by Moody's Corporation in 2002. Meanwhile, the rapid development of structured finance, including the alphabet soup of mortgage-related financial instruments, was covered by Fabozzi (2005), near the peak of the US residential real estate market.

Finally, in the aftermath of the 2008 crisis, the *Financial Analysts Journal* played an important role in sifting through the wreckage, with articles on regulatory and policy reforms by Markowitz (2009), Reinganum (2009), Statman (2009), and Roll (2011).

With respect to ethics, the 2008 crisis highlighted an important new ethical concern to the profession—the over-reliance on quantitative methods and models, encouraged by the false precision that these tools exhibit. This concern was well expressed by McAlmond's (2008, p. 10) letter to the editor, entitled 'Too Much Emphasis on Quantitative Methods Instead of Ethics?':

In my most recent [*Financial Analysts Journal* issue], I find not one article on ethics. The articles are full of probability graphs; they cover relative earnings forecasts, buy-side versus sell-side arguments, and the benefits of short extensions. But what of the benefits of making the best ethical decisions and keeping our clients' trust? And how can we understand these issues? Our business is more than a hard science. The most important quality we bring to our clients is not our ability to calculate numbers or create graphs.

The most recent credit crisis is full of ethical dimensions that could be discussed. Was it ethical to push people into buying homes that they could not afford? Was it ethical to package these products that did not live up to their credit ratings? Was it ethical to sell these packages to investors, foreign banks, and others? Analysis of the ethical issues of our products and services can be just as important as, if not more important than, the mathematical analysis.

I hope to see many more articles in [the *Financial Analysts Journal*] that discuss the ethical dimensions of investment products and services.

---

[18] See, for example, Liang (2001), Fung and Hsieh (2002), Jordan and Diltz (2003), Leibowitz 2005), Malkiel and Saha (2005), Gorton and Rouwenhorst (2006), and Fernholz and Maguire Jr (2007).

18.4.8 2010–2021: The Digital Assets Era

Following the financial crisis, the US led the long recovery among the advanced economies through financial sector reforms, bailouts of systemically important institutions, and the largest overhaul of the financial regulatory system since the 1930s, culminating in the Dodd–Frank Wall Street Reform and Consumer Protection Act of 2010. This piece of legislation called for a number of new regulations—some of which have yet to be implemented—but one of the signature components was the establishment of the Office of Financial Research (OFR), perhaps the first time the federal government has so explicitly acknowledged the importance of financial research and data collection since Alexander Hamilton's establishment of the Treasury Department (in which the OFR resides).

This era also saw expansive monetary policy, including several rounds of quantitative easing that seemed extraordinarily aggressive at the time, but turned out to be only the dress rehearsal for the multi-trillion dollar US stimulus amidst the COVID-19 pandemic in 2020–2021. The overhang of accumulated debt, however, exerted a drag on the US economy, while greater fiscal stimulus was politically constrained. Other nations had poorer outcomes, especially those on the periphery of the eurozone, the unified currency area established by the European Union in 1999. Despite fears of inflation, deflationary pressures dominated the recovery. With lower yields and lower amounts of leverage available to hedge funds, their returns suffered, hastening the already sizeable flow of capital from actively managed financial products and services to passive index products and causing even greater consolidation across all categories of financial institutions.

Nevertheless, Moore's Law continued to operate, although signs began to appear that it was finally slowing down. After a significant delay, smartphones became popular and then nearly ubiquitous in the US. Another technology boom began, centred on applications for these phones. Many previously overlooked services were transformed through these 'apps', such as taxi and ridesharing services and short-term rentals, while banking, trading, and financial advisory apps were quickly developed. These allowed financial services to become portable, accessible, and available at low cost to a much broader population of potential clients.

During this time, regulators began to discuss the problem of large technology-based companies exerting effective monopoly power over their industries. Web-based analytics made analysing the behavioural effects of advertising more practical and at a lower cost than ever before, a catastrophe for many traditional industries supported by advertising revenue, including most forms of journalism. Paired with the rise of social media as an alternate source of information, these technological advances led to a rise in misinformation and deliberate disinformation. Rumours, gossip, and 'memes' transmitted through alternate forms of media became commonplace, fuelling the rise of nativist and populist politics around the world.

This trend had an exact parallel in the financial sector, with the rise of meme stocks and meme trading strategies transmitted on message boards and trading apps, and through short videos shared for public consumption. New financial apps allowed consumers to make financially sophisticated trades at little or no cost but at high risk to themselves. This trend culminated in January 2021 in the meteoric rise of GameStop, the heavily shorted bricks-and-mortar videogame retailer that started the year at $20 per share and reached a peak of $483 thanks to the coordinated efforts of participants on the WallStreetBets channel of the popular internet forum Reddit.

Cryptocurrencies, developed in the wake of bitcoin, were also beneficiaries of this movement, as their idiosyncratic features resonated with a populist audience. While there is still considerable scepticism regarding the long-term viability of these 'assets', their proponents were validated by the successful initial public offering of Coinbase, the largest US cryptocurrency exchange platform, with a market capitalization of $60 billion as of 21 April 2021.

Such an auspicious launch may seem to bode well for this emerging asset class. However, three observations should give potential investors pause, at least until the dust settles on whether these digital assets are, indeed, long-term investment vehicles. The first observation is the extraordinary volatility of bitcoin and other cryptocurrencies, often multiples of the volatility of the S&P 500, as illustrated in Fig. 18.5. The second observation is the fact that the success of the Coinbase initial public offering was followed by the collapse of two Turkish cryptocurrency exchanges, Thodex and Vebitcoin, highlighting the 'Wild West' aspect of this emerging asset class. The third observation is that, even if cryptocurrencies are here to stay, significant market dislocations might be in store for any given cryptocurrency, especially if a large sovereign entity were to issue its own cryptocurrency. In particular, the impact of a hypothetical US-issued 'Fedcoin' on other cryptocurrencies might not be that dissimilar to the experience of the 'wildcat banks' of the American frontier during the nineteenth century. The collapse of a number of state-chartered banks that issued their own currencies—some legendarily printed with images of wildcats on the notes, hence the nickname—finally motivated the creation of a single national currency through the National Bank Act of 1863, effectively ending the wildcat banking era.

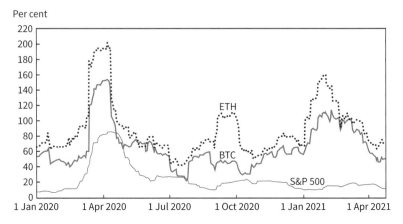

Fig. 18.5 Thirty-day rolling-window volatility of daily log returns of Bitcoin (BTC), Etherium (ETH), and the S&P 500, 1 January 2020–25 April 2021.

Source: Moore, G., and Acheson, N. (2021). Crypto long & short: the pattern in Bitcoin's volatility, CoinDesk, April 25. www.coindesk.com/bitcoin-volatility-pattern (accessed 26 July 2022).

The Digital Assets Era also saw another shift in the fitness landscape of the financial ecosystem. As in every other industry, advances in technology create new winners and losers, and the ability to store and process massive data sets has changed the relative value of training in quantitative finance versus computer science. In the same way that the financial quants of the Derivatives and Algorithmic Trading Eras displaced the fundamental security analysts that came before them, data scientists—software engineers with strong data-wrangling skills and experience with Python, TensorFlow, and deep learning networks—have begun displacing the quants during this era.

Despite these technological advances, or perhaps in reaction to them, the decidedly nontechnological trend of ESG and impact investing also blossomed during this era, as did the study of the financial consequences of climate change. ESG investing began as a grassroots movement arising largely from Millennials (the generation born in the Automation and Financial Globalization Eras), who led the charge for greater meaning from their investments during the previous era. Given the enormous amount of investable wealth represented by this demographic, the financial industry has listened carefully to their concerns, producing an array of products and services to satisfy these demands.

This seventy-five-year narrative ends with the global COVID-19 pandemic, emerging from the new economic powerhouse of China at the end of 2019, but striking the economies of Europe and North America the hardest.

As the full weight of the pandemic made itself known, March 2020 saw a spectacular drop in the financial markets, and perhaps a narrowly averted financial catastrophe as liquidity problems reached US Treasury bills, one of the most liquid markets in the world.

Two years later, the world is emerging from its pandemic-induced recession after frantic social and technological shifts to maintain its economic functions while biomedical researchers developed vaccines and treatments for this lethal disease. Undoubtedly, there will be financial adaptations to this new status quo, which likely marks the beginning of a new financial era. Like the 2008 financial crisis, COVID-19 was a watershed event that caused massive systemic disruption. However, unlike 2008, the pandemic was not a financial crisis; it was a public health crisis, albeit one with significant financial consequences. In contrast to the lengthier recovery period of the 2008 financial crisis (which, in some respects, we are still dealing with today), the financial system and the broader macroeconomy appear to be bouncing back much more quickly from the COVID-19 pandemic.

From the perspective of the AMH, the selective pressures imposed by the two-year lockdown, during which economies around the world were deliberately put into the equivalent of a medically induced coma, imply that less profitable businesses have been eliminated, leaving stronger and more adaptable businesses in the aftermath. This process of financial selection and the extra boost from pent up demand will likely propel the global economy forward over the next few years, creating a period of substantial economic growth and prosperity.

If the last truly global pandemic, the influenza pandemic of 1918, offers any guidance to our current situation, the decade known as the Roaring Twenties was so named because a surging economy and stock market followed that even deadlier disease.[19] Nietzsche's adage that 'what does not kill me makes me stronger' apparently applies to economies, but with an important caveat. The Roaring Twenties also gave rise to financial excesses, such as unsustainable leverage in retail equity margin accounts, which ultimately resulted in Black Monday, 28 October 1929, when the Dow Jones Industrial Average dropped nearly 13%, followed by Black Tuesday, when the market dropped another 12%, and the Great Depression. Given the unprecedented magnitude of US government stimulus applied to the economy in response to COVID-19 and the low-interest-rate environment we are facing today, we must be particularly vigilant about reducing and reversing these policies in due course, lest we create the new Roaring Twenties and next financial crisis.

---

[19] See, for example, Garrett (2008).

The trends of the Digital Assets Era are well represented by *Financial Analysts Journal* publications throughout this period. In 'Adaptive Asset Allocation Policies', Sharpe's (2010) reconsideration of the age-old problem of asset allocation underscores the relevance of evolutionary principles in the context of a rapidly changing market ecology. Growing concerns about two particular species in that ecology, high-frequency traders and cryptocurrencies, were voiced in Harris (2013), Edwards et al. (2019), and Krückeberg and Scholz (2020). Meanwhile, the benefits of the emerging field of data science and its impact on the much older field of artificial intelligence (AI) were illustrated in articles on sentiment analysis via natural language processing by Heston and Sinha (2017) and stock selection via machine learning by Rasekhschaffe and Jones (2019). The financial consequences of climate change and ESG investing have been considered by a number of *Financial Analysts Journal* authors, including Litterman (2011), Andersson, Bolton, and Samama (2016), Brown (2016), de Jong and Nguyen (2016), and Madhavan, Sobczyk, and Ang (2021).

Finally, with respect to the top twenty title words, it is a curious fact that the most frequently used word in *Financial Analysts Journal* titles during this era and the previous two is 'risk'. We have been warned.

18.5 Discussion

What can be learned from the evolutionary rhythms of financial innovation? There are several interesting clusters of developments, each following a shift in the financial environment, defining a characteristic financial ecology of innovation. For example, the needs of WWII almost simultaneously generated the first digital computers (for cryptanalysis, operations analysis, and computations for the practical implementation of nuclear fission) and the postwar global financial order of Bretton Woods. These two developments interacted to produce a generation of financial stability and slow but steady innovation. Likewise, the impact of the transistor and the integrated circuit had accelerating effects on the cost and efficiency of computation and communication. The circle of innovation began to feed on itself, with advances in computing leading to advances in communication, making financial services more accessible and less costly to the client—at this point, one might speak of the financial consumer—which could, in turn, be used to fund further innovation. Ultimately, financial services that were available only to a select few thirty years ago have become today's latest popular freemium app.

A parallel trend, and one often overlooked, is accessibility. Consider the credit card, today a mundane consumer item available to nearly everyone with an address and phone number, increasingly used as a substitute for cash. In the 1930s, however, the credit card was a luxury service available only to elite travellers to purchase airline tickets. The automated teller machine, now ubiquitous, allows people to have access to banking services around the clock, seven days a week, when, in recent memory, it was almost impossible to withdraw money from an account except during banking hours, and only on certain days of the week. There was also a discriminatory dimension to this access; for example, credit cards were not generally available to women before 1974. The combination of low cost and high accessibility has created an unusual and unprecedented financial environment, one whose future effects are, at present, unknown.

Behind this ever-increasing crescendo of financial innovation has been the hard work and scholarship of academic finance. Modern portfolio theory and the CAPM are two cornerstones of this edifice, leading to a better understanding of performance attribution and the risk–reward trade-off. However, these ideas would have languished in a theoretical vacuum without the intensive empirical studies of real-world financial data that have been the hallmark of financial analysis from its beginning. The collection, measurement, and statistical study of these data have led, in a surprisingly straight line, to financial innovations such as option pricing, index funds, and cryptocurrencies. Financial analysis continues to drive financial innovation as today's academics use new tools to study the mysteries of liquidity, volatility, systemic risk, and market structure.

What does the future hold for financial analysis? As the plumbing of the financial system converges with other systems of information technology, one should naturally expect the materials and methods from those related fields to impinge on financial academic research—for example, in machine-learning and natural-language-processing techniques for the analysis of big data (still accelerating exponentially), in network analysis of the world's increasingly fragmented financial markets, and in applications of cryptographic methods to create structures for exchanging and processing sensitive or proprietary financial data.

While it is impossible to predict evolutionary trends with certainty, two innovations appear to have the potential to shift the financial landscape as much as the earlier computing and communications revolution. The first is in the category of security—the use of cryptographic principles in finance, including the secure distributed ledger technology known as blockchain (but not limited to it). These innovations have expanded the range of financial products to include not only new forms of currency and other financial instruments, but also such items as nonfungible tokens, which attempt to create scarcity in digital goods in an age of perfect digital reproducibility.

However, perhaps the most important innovation at the current time is the long-awaited fruition of a development dating back to WWII, the mathematical study of neural networks, emulating the behaviour of biological nervous systems (McCulloch and Pitts, 1943). Neural networks were a road not taken compared with conventional digital technologies, due to their difficulty in implementation and prevailing theoretical beliefs about their lack of capacity. These networks, however, along with other machine-learning techniques, may turn out to be a forerunner of the next wave of general-purpose technologies, fulfilling the goals of the decades-long research programme of AI. These networks have already been able to master games that had been resistant to older AI techniques, such as the classic board game Go. Even more impressively, prototype language models using deep neural networks have been able to compose lengthy pieces of text on impromptu topics that are indistinguishable from those written by humans. As a general-purpose technology, it is possible that these neural networks will reshape the financial markets as deeply as electricity and the computer have done in decades past.

Marvin Minsky, one of the founding fathers of AI, once shared with an interviewer his life goal, which was not to build a computer that he could be proud of, but to build a computer that could be proud of him. If we are close to this goal, as a growing number of AI experts now believe, then perhaps one day we will have financial technology that will be proud of the role that financial analysts and their esteemed journal have played in getting us there.

19

The Role of Culture in Finance

Culture is a potent force in shaping individual and group behaviour, yet it has received scant attention in the context of financial risk management or in addressing such financial events as the 2008 crisis.[1] We present a brief overview of the role of culture according to psychologists, sociologists, and economists, and then describe a specific framework for analysing culture in the context of financial practices and institutions, a framework in which three questions are addressed: (1) What is culture? (2) Does it matter? and (3) Can it be changed? We illustrate the utility of this framework by applying it to five concrete situations—the collapse of LTCM, the fall of AIG Financial Products, the use by Lehman Brothers of 'Repo 105', Société Générale's rogue trader, and the US Securities and Exchange Commission's (SEC's) handling of the Madoff Ponzi scheme—and conclude with a proposal to change culture via 'behavioural risk management'.

In the 1987 Oliver Stone film *Wall Street*, Michael Douglas delivered an Oscar-winning performance as financial 'Master of the Universe' Gordon Gekko. An unabashedly greedy corporate raider, Gekko delivered a famous, frequently quoted monologue in which he described the culture that has since become a caricature of the financial industry:

> The point is, ladies and gentleman, that greed, for lack of a better word, is good. Greed is right, greed works. Greed clarifies, cuts through, and captures the essence of the evolutionary spirit. Greed, in all of its forms, greed for life, for money, for love, knowledge, has marked the upward surge of mankind. And greed, you mark my words, will not only save Teldar Paper, but that other malfunctioning corporation called the USA.

Despite the notoriety of this encomium to enlightened self-interest, few people know that these words are based on an actual commencement speech delivered in 1986 at what is now the Haas School of Business of the

---

[1] This chapter is adapted from Lo (2016).

The Adaptive Markets Hypothesis. Andrew W. Lo and Ruixun Zhang, Oxford University Press. © Andrew W. Lo and Ruixun Zhang (2024). DOI: 10.1093/oso/9780199681143.003.0019

University of California at Berkeley. The speaker was Ivan Boesky, who would be convicted just eighteen months later in an insider trading scandal.[2]

Millions of people saw *Wall Street*, and Gekko's monologue became part of popular culture. Hundreds, perhaps thousands, of young people were inspired to go into finance as a result of Douglas's performance. This dismayed Stanley Weiser, the co-writer of the screenplay, who met many of these young people for himself. As Weiser wrote in 2008, at the height of the financial crisis

> A typical example would be a business executive or a younger studio development person spouting something that goes like this: 'The movie changed my life. Once I saw it I knew that I wanted to get into such and such business. I wanted to be like Gordon Gekko.' … After so many encounters with Gekko admirers or wannabes, I wish I could go back and rewrite the greed line to this: 'Greed is good. But I've never seen a Brinks truck pull up to a cemetery.'[3]

What makes this phenomenon truly astonishing is that Gekko is not the hero of *Wall Street*—he is, in fact, the villain. Moreover, Gekko fails in his villainous plot, thanks to his young protégé-turned-hero, Bud Fox. The man whose words Weiser put into Gekko's mouth, Ivan Boesky, later served several years in a federal penitentiary for his wrongdoings. Nevertheless, many young people decided to base their career choices on the screen depiction of a fictional villain whose most famous lines were taken from the words of a convict. Culture matters.

This is a prime example of what Lo (2016) proposed to call 'the Gordon Gekko effect'. It is known that some cultural values are positively correlated to better economic outcomes, perhaps through the channel of mutual trust.[4] Firms with stronger corporate cultures, as self-reported in surveys, appear to perform better than those with weaker cultures, through the channel of behavioural consistency, although this effect is diminished in a volatile environment (Gordon and DiTomaso, 1992; Sørensen, 2002). However, not all strong values are positive ones. The Gekko effect highlights the fact that some corporate cultures may transmit negative values to their members in ways that make financial malfeasance significantly more probable. To understand these channels and formulate remedies, we have to start by asking what culture is, how it emerges, and how it is shaped and transmitted over time and across individuals and institutions.

---

[2] Bob Greene, 'A $100 Million Idea: Use Greed for Good', *Chicago Tribune*, 15 December 1986; James Sterngold, 'Boesky Sentenced to 3 Years in Jail in Insider Scandal', *The New York Times*, 19 December 1987.
[3] Stanley Weiser, 'Repeat after Me: Greed Is Not Good', *Los Angeles Times*, 5 October 2008.
[4] For example, see Guiso, Sapienza, and Zingales (2006).

19.1 What is Culture?

What do we mean when we talk about corporate culture? There are, quite literally, hundreds of definitions of culture. In 1952, the anthropologists A.L. Kroeber and Clyde Kluckhohn listed 164 definitions that had been used in the field up to that time, and, to this day, we still do not have a singular definition of culture. We do not propose to solve that problem, but merely to find a working definition to describe a phenomenon. Kroeber and Kluckhohn (1952, p. 35) settled on the following: 'Culture consists of patterns, explicit and implicit, of and for behavior acquired and transmitted by symbols, constituting the distinctive achievements of human groups, including their embodiments in artifacts'. Embedded in this seemingly straightforward and intuitive definition is an important assumption that we shall revisit and challenge later in this chapter—that culture is transmitted rather than innate—but that we will adopt temporarily for the sake of exposition and argument.

A corporate culture exists as a subset of a larger culture, with variations found specifically in that corporate entity. Again, there are multiple definitions. The organizational theorists O'Reilly and Chatman (1996, p. 166) define corporate culture as 'a system of shared values that define what is important, and norms that define appropriate attitudes and behaviors for organizational members', while Schein (2004, p. 17) defines it in his classic text as 'a pattern of shared basic assumptions that was learned by a group… that has worked well enough to be considered valid and, therefore, to be taught to new members as the correct way to perceive, think, and feel in relationship to [the group's] problems'.

The key point here is that the distinctive assumptions and values of a corporate or organizational culture define the group. These assumptions and values will be shared within the culture, and they will be taught to newcomers to the culture as the correct norms of behaviour. People who lack these values and norms will not be members of the shared culture, even though they may occupy the appropriate position on the organizational chart. In fact, these outsiders may even be viewed as hostile to the values of the culture, a point to which we will return.

It is clear from these definitions that corporate culture propagates itself less like an economic phenomenon, with individuals attempting to maximize some quantity through their behaviour, and more like a biological phenomenon, such as the spread of an epidemic through a population. Gordon Gekko, then, can be considered the 'patient zero' of an epidemic of shared values (most of which are considered repugnant by the larger society, including Gekko's creator).

This biologically inspired model of corporate culture can be generalized further. Three factors will affect the transmission of a corporate culture through a group: the group's leadership, analogous to the primary source of an infection; the group's composition, analogous to a population at risk; and the group's environment, which shapes its response. The next sections will explore how the transmission of values conducive to corporate failure might occur, how such values emerge, and what can be done to change them.

19.2 What Determines Corporate Values?

Who maintains the values of a corporate culture? Economics tells us that individuals respond to incentives: monetary rewards and penalties. From this mercenary perspective, corporate culture is almost irrelevant to the financial realities of risk and expected return. However, the other social sciences offer a different perspective. In this section we consider the determinants of corporate values from the top down, bottom up, the environment, incentives, and evolutionary forces. Contrary to current economic thinking, values are shaped via a multifactorial process that does not always involve pecuniary considerations.

19.2.1 Values from the Top Down: Authority and Leadership

A corporate culture directs its employees through authority—sometimes called 'leadership' in the corporate world—as much as through financial incentives, if not more so. The great German sociologist Max Weber broke down authority into three ideal types: the charismatic, who maintains legitimacy through force of personality; the traditional, who maintains legitimacy through established custom; and the legal-rational, whose legitimacy comes from shared agreement in the law (Kronman, 1983, pp. 43–50). We can see that Gordon Gekko is almost a pure example of Weber's charismatic authority; however, at this point in our discussion, the style of authority is less important than the fact of authority.

According to Herbert A. Simon's classic analysis of administrative behaviour, a person in authority establishes the proper conduct for subordinates through positive and negative social sanctions (Simon, 1997, pp. 184–185). These sanctions, in the form of social approval or disapproval, praise or embarrassment, may be the most important factor in inducing the acceptance of authority. Also important is the sense of shared purpose, which in the military is sometimes called *esprit de corps*. People with a sense of purpose are more likely to subordinate themselves to authority in the belief that their subordination will aid in achieving the goals of the group.

How much economic incentive is needed for an authority figure to influence the members of a culture into bad behaviours? Experimental social psychology gives us a rather disturbing answer. In the infamous Milgram experiment, originally conducted by the psychologist Stanley Milgram at Yale University in 1961, volunteers administered what they believed were high-voltage electric shocks to a human experimental subject, simply because a temporary authority figure made verbal suggestions to continue (Milgram, 1963). Of these scripted suggestions, 'You have no other choice, you must go on', was the most forceful. If a volunteer still refused after this suggestion was given, the experiment was stopped. Ultimately, twenty-six out of forty people administered what they believed was a dangerous, perhaps fatal, 450-volt shock to a fellow human being, even though all expressed doubts verbally and many exhibited obvious physiological manifestations of stress; three even experienced what appeared to be seizures. One businessman volunteer 'was reduced to a twitching, stuttering wreck, who was rapidly approaching a point of nervous collapse … yet he continued to respond to every word of the experimenter, and obeyed to the end'. Milgram's volunteers were paid $4 plus carfare, worth about $60 in 2022.

Even more notorious is the Stanford prison experiment, conducted by the Stanford University psychologist Philip Zimbardo in 1971. In the two-week experiment conducted in the basement of the Stanford psychology department, Zimbardo randomly assigned volunteers to the roles of guards and prisoners (Haney, Banks, and Zimbardo, 1973a,b). Almost immediately after the experiment began, the 'guards' started to behave in a dehumanizing way towards the 'prisoners', subjecting them to verbal harassment, forced exercise, manipulation of sleeping conditions, manipulation of bathroom privileges (some of it physically filthy), and the use of nudity to humiliate the 'prisoners'. Zimbardo, who played the role of prison superintendent, terminated the experiment after only six days, at the urging of his future wife, Christina Maslach, whom he had brought in as an outsider to conduct interviews with the subjects.[5] Zimbardo paid his subjects $15 a day, roughly $108 a day in 2022 dollars.

It should be obvious that monetary incentives are a completely insufficient explanation for the behaviour of the volunteers in these two experiments. In Milgram's experiment, the majority of subjects submitted themselves to

---

[5] Additional details from the Stanford Prison Experiment are available at http://www.prisonexp.org.

the verbal demands of an authority, despite the severe mental stress inflicted by these tasks. In Zimbardo's experiment, volunteers threw themselves into the role of guards with gusto, with Zimbardo himself playing the role of the superintendent willing to overlook systemic abuses. In each case, the volunteers fulfilled the roles that they believed were expected of them by the authority.

Leadership is important in harnessing the behaviour of a corporation's employees to become more productive and competitive. Unfortunately, as Milgram and Zimbardo demonstrated, the same factors that allow leadership to manifest itself through performance and teamwork also allow it to promote goals that lack a moral, ethical, legal, profitable, or even rational basis. Remember that the 65 per cent of Milgram's experimental subjects who continued to administer electric shocks were compelled to do so merely by verbal expressions of disapproval by the authority figure.

In corporate cultures that lack the capacity to assimilate an outside opinion, the primary check on behaviour is the authority. From within a corporate culture, an authority may see their role as similar to that of the conductor of an orchestra, managing a group of highly trained professionals in pursuit of a lofty goal. From a viewpoint outside the culture, however, the authority may be cultivating the moral equivalent of a gang of brutes, as did Zimbardo himself in his role as mock prison superintendent. It took a trusted outsider to see the Stanford prison experiment with clear eyes and to convince Zimbardo that his experiment was, in fact, an unethical degradation of his test subjects.

Finally, even if the authority has an excellent track record, a subtle form of moral hazard is associated with this excellence, as has been pointed out by Robert Shiller: 'people have learned that when experts tell them something is all right, it probably is, even if it does not seem so ... thus the results of Milgram's experiment can also be interpreted as springing from people's past learning about the reliability of authorities' (Shiller, 2005a, p. 159).

19.2.2 Values from the Bottom Up: Composition

Not all of corporate culture is created from the top down. A culture is also composed of the behaviour of the people within it, from the bottom up. Corporate culture is subject to compositional effects, based on the values and behaviours of the people the organization hires, even as corporate authority attempts to inculcate its preferred values and behaviours into employees.

The pool of possible corporate employees today is wide and diverse. Firms and industries draw from this pool with a particular employee profile in mind, often filtering out other qualified candidates. However, this filter may shape the corporate culture in unexpected ways. In the late 1990s, the anthropologist Karen Ho conducted an ethnographic survey of Wall Street investment banks. Beginning in the 1980s, the era of Oliver Stone's *Wall Street*, these firms deliberately targeted recent graduates of elite schools, in particular Harvard and Princeton, appealing to their intellectual vanity: 'the best and the brightest'. These fresh recruits brought their social norms and values with them to Wall Street (Ho, 2009, pp. 39–66). As they were promoted, and older members departed, a new norm of behaviour developed within investment bank culture through population change. Knowledge of the older Wall Street culture faded and became secondhand, while *Liar's Poker*, Michael Lewis's memoir about graduating from Princeton and going to work at Salomon Brothers, became a manifesto for the new elite (Ho, 2009, p. 337). Even the drawbacks of a Wall Street job could confirm the values of an elite worldview. Ho found that her informants rationalized Wall Street job insecurity as normative, since the insecurity revealed 'who is flexible and who can accept change' (Ho, 2009, p. 274). The historically high levels of Wall Street compensation were, in her informants' view, the natural reward for members of the elite assuming the personal risk of losing their jobs.

Corporations deliberately choose employees with attributes that corporate leadership believes are useful to the corporation. To borrow another biological metaphor, the hiring process is a form of artificial selection from a population with a great deal of variation in personality type, worldview, and other individual traits. All else being equal, employees with traits that more closely fit the corporate culture will do better in the corporation, since they are already adapted to that particular environment. This leads to a feedback loop reinforcing the corporate culture's values. Employees who do not fit this profile find themselves under social pressure to adapt or leave the organization. This process of selection and adaptation leads to stronger corporate cultures, which are correlated with stronger performance. However, there are times when a corporation benefits from a diversity of viewpoints to prevent groupthink (Janis, 1982). The innovator, the whistleblower, the contrarian, and the devil's advocate all have necessary roles in the modern corporation, especially in a shifting economic environment. A human resources manager, then, faces much the same dilemma as a portfolio manager—how to pick winners, shed losers, and manage risk so as to increase the value of the overall portfolio.

Many corporations deliberately hire 'self-starters' or 'go-getters', people with aggressive or risk-taking personalities who are thought to have a competitive nature and whose presence (so goes the belief) will lead to higher profits for the firm. This personality type is drawn to what the sociologist Stephen Lyng has described as 'edgework' (Lyng, 1990). Borrowing the term from the writings of journalist Hunter S. Thompson, Lyng uses it to describe the pleasurable form of voluntary risk-taking sometimes found in adventure sports such as skydiving or in hazardous occupations such as test piloting. In these fields, the individual is put at severe risk, but the risk is made pleasurable through a sense of satisfaction in one's superior ability to navigate such dangerous waters. This dynamic naturally extends to the financial industry, and, in fact, sociologist Charles W. Smith used the concept of edgework to compare the financial market trader to the sea kayaker (Smith, 2005).

Edgeworkers normally think of themselves as ferociously independent. Nevertheless, Lyng has found that success in the face of risk reinforces among edgeworkers a sense of group solidarity and belonging to an elite culture, even across professions. But this sense of solidarity extends only to fellow edgeworkers, which puts these individuals at odds with the larger culture. In a corporation, this can lead to a split between a trading desk, or even upper management, and the rest of the corporate culture. For example, the organizational theorist Zur Shapira conducted surveys of fifty American and Israeli executives and found that, even though many urged their subordinates to maintain risk-averse behaviour, they themselves took greater risks, deriving active enjoyment in succeeding in the face of those risks. One company president still viewed himself as an edgeworker, telling Shapira, 'Satisfaction from success is directly related to the degree of risk taken' (Shapira, 1995, p. 58). For a new hire who patterns their job behaviour on an authority figure within the firm, this may be a case of 'Do as I say, not as I do'.

Group composition may lead to differences that cannot be explained by culture alone. An individual's temperament and personality are largely internal in origin and difficult to change. Some traits, such as the propensity for risk-taking, may have deeper causes. For example, it has long been documented that younger men are more prone to dangerous activities than older men or women of the same age, with behaviours ranging from reckless driving to homicide (Wilson and Daly, 1985). There may be a neuroscientific reason for this difference in the development of the adolescent brain.[6] These differences are by definition not cultural: they can neither be learned noɪ transmitted symbolically. Yet these differences affect the highest levels of human behaviour.

Nevertheless, culture is still powerful, even in the face of intrinsic behavioural variation. To take the most dramatic example, consider risk-taking behaviour, which has known physiological and neurological correlates (see Part III). Insurance companies use automobile fatalities as a proxy to measure risk-taking behaviour among groups. However, there has been an absolute decline in automobile fatalities in the US over the last forty years, despite a vast increase in the number of drivers and miles travelled. This decline was caused by changes in culture: in material culture, such as advances in the design of automobiles and highways; in regulatory culture, such as the enforcement of appropriate speed limits; and in social culture, such as the stigmatization of driving under the influence of alcohol. The same propensity for risk is as present today as it was in 1975, but the culture, at large, has changed to limit its negative effects on the highway.

19.2.3 Values from the Environment: Risk and Regulation

The third factor influencing corporate culture is the environment. Competition, the economic climate, regulatory requirements—the list of possible environmental factors that affect corporate culture may seem bewilderingly complex. However, anthropologist Mary Douglas made the elegant observation that a culture's values are reflected in how it manages risk, which, in turn, reflects how the culture perceives its environment (Douglas and Wildavsky, 1983). No culture has the resources to eliminate all risk; therefore, a culture ranks its dangers according to what it finds most important, both positively and negatively. This prioritization acts as a snapshot of the culture's operating environment, just as an insurance portfolio might act as a snapshot of the policyholder's day-to-day environment. It is important to note that a culture's ranking of danger may have little to do with the mathematical probability of an event. As a modern example, Douglas looked at the expansion of legal liability in the US and its role in the insurance crisis of the 1970s. The underlying probability of medical malpractice or illness from toxic waste changed very little over that decade. In Douglas's analysis, what changed was how society chose to respond to those dangers, owing to a change in cultural values.

---

[6] For example, see Steinberg (2008).

Cultures warn against some dangers but downplay others in order to reinforce internal cultural values. For example, sociologist Sudhir Venkatesh finds that in 'Maquis Park', his pseudonym for a poor African American neighbourhood in Chicago, it is a risk-taking behaviour to leave the established network of formal and informal business relationships that define the community and experience the impossible-to-measure Knightian uncertainty of establishing new connections with few resources in the hostile environment of greater Chicago (Venkatesh, 2006, pp. 148–150). Despite the neighbourhood's high crime rate, the culture of Maquis Park is risk-averse. Criminal behaviour there is often an application of economic rationalism and cost–benefit analysis in the face of limited options, rather than an expression of a higher tendency to take risks.

Douglas's idea that the values of a culture are reflected in how it prioritizes risk has immediate application in understanding differences in corporate behaviour. For example, compare risk-taking in the insurance industry with that of the banking industry. The insurance industry is culturally more conservative precisely because a significant portion of insurers' revenue is determined by state regulation. As a result, insurers make money by protecting their downside—in other words, by carefully managing risk. In the banking industry, however, revenue is variable and, in many cases, directly related to bank size and leverage; therefore, risk-taking is much more flexible and encouraged.

According to Douglas, modern cultures fall into one of three ideal types: the hierarchical, including the bureaucratic tendencies not only of government, but also of the large corporation; the individualistic, the world of the market, the entrepreneur, and classic utility theory; and the sectarian, the world of the outsider, the interest group, and the religious sect. These cultures interact with one another in predictable ways. The US is obviously multicultural, but its central institutions are largely hierarchical or individualistic, while its population is largely sectarian. Each type of culture has a distinctive response to danger—a re-emphasis of the importance of the hierarchy, the individual, or the sect—which it uses to reinforce the values of the culture, often at the expense of competing views. Thus, for individualistic cultures, as the late German sociologist Ulrich Beck said, 'community is dissolved in the acid bath of competition' (Beck, 1992, p. 94).

This cultural defence mechanism has important consequences, not only for managers, but also for regulators. To borrow Douglas's distinction, the central cultures of the financial world find it very easy to ignore voices from the border, whether they are radicalized protestors in the streets, regulators from a government agency, or a dissenting opinion from within the financial community. Regulators are not immune to this defence mechanism, whether they are federal agencies, professional standards organizations, or law enforcement. In fact, the sanctions taken against a whistleblower in a regulatory organization may be much harsher than those taken against a corporate whistleblower because the regulatory whistleblower diminishes the regulator's legitimacy, the source of its legal-rational authority over others.

A corporate culture may defend itself so strongly that, despite almost everyone's dissatisfaction with the status quo, the organization may find itself unable to change its norms of behaviour. This statement is not an exaggeration. In the 1990s, the organizational theorist John Weeks conducted an ethnographic survey of a large British bank, 'British Armstrong', in which he found precisely this pattern of behaviour (Weeks, 2004). Prevailing corporate cultural values in 'BritArm' were used to diminish or discount criticism. For example, BritArm prided itself on its discretion, which meant that complaints had to be made obliquely, and these complaints were therefore easily ignored. However, employees who made blunt or outspoken criticisms were viewed as outsiders who lacked BritArm's cultural values, and their complaints were also ignored as part of the culture's immune response. An acceptable level of complaint, in fact, became a new norm among BritArm's employees, part of their corporate cultural identity. As Weeks explains, 'Complaining about a culture in the culturally acceptable ways should not be seen as an act of opposition to that culture. Rather, it is a cultural form that … has the effect of enacting the very culture that it ostensibly criticizes' (Weeks, 2004, p. 12).

Culture is also subject to the social trends and undercurrents in the environment, creating a unique and palpable set of ideals, customs, and values that broadly influence societal behaviour. From a sociological perspective, we might call these instances the 'collective consciousness' of society, a term first proposed by the late nineteenth-century French sociologist Émile Durkheim (Durkheim, 1893). Twentieth-century examples might include the giddy dynamism of the Roaring Twenties, the mid-century flirtation with Marxism and socialism, and the countercultural movement of the 1960s. From an economic perspective, examples might include recessions, depressions, hyperinflation, and asset bubbles—periods when macroeconomic factors overwhelm industry- or institution-specific factors in determining behaviour throughout the economy.

During such periods, it is easy to see how entrepreneurs, investors, corporate executives, and regulators are all shaped by the cultural milieu. In good times, greed is, indeed, good and regulation seems unnecessary or counterproductive; in bad times, especially in the aftermath of a financial crisis, greed is the root of all evil and regulation must be strengthened to combat such evil.

19.2.4 Values from Economists: Responding to Incentives

Economists have traditionally looked at theories of cultural values with scepticism, whether such theories have come from psychology, anthropology, ethnography, sociology, or management science. Part of this scepticism stems from the culture of economics, which prizes the narrative of rational economic self-interest above all else. Given two competing explanations for a particular market anomaly, a behavioural theory and a rational expectations model, the vast majority of economists will choose the latter—even if rationality requires unrealistically complex inferences about everyone's preferences, information, and expectations. The mathematical elegance of a rational expectations equilibrium usually trumps the messy and imprecise narrative of corporate culture. For example, Schein (2004) breaks down an organizational culture into its observable artefacts, espoused values, and unspoken assumptions. In the pure economist's view, this is much too touchy-feely. An economist will measure observables but look askance at self-reported values, and ignore unspoken assumptions in favour of revealed preferences. Gordon Gekko's motivation—and his appeal to moviegoers—is simple: wealth and power. He is *Homo economicus*—the financial equivalent of John Galt in Ayn Rand's *Atlas Shrugged*—optimizing his expected utility, subject to constraints. From the economist's perspective, Gekko's only fault is optimizing with fewer constraints than those imposed by the legal system.

However, the economist's view of rational self-interest is not simply axiomatic: economic self-interest is a learned and symbolically transmitted behaviour. We do not expect children or the mentally impaired to pursue their rational self-interest, and we do not expect the financially misinformed to be able to maximize their self-interest correctly. Therefore, this view of economic behaviour fulfills the textbook definition of a cultural trait, albeit one that economists believe is universal and all-encompassing, as the term *Homo economicus* suggests.

Through the cultural lens of an economist, individuals are good if they have an incentive to be good. The same motivation of self-interest that drives a manager to excel at measurable tasks in the Wall Street bonus culture may also induce the manager to shirk the less observable components of job performance, such as following ethical guidelines (Bénabou and Tirole, 2016). Yet, the same manager might behave impeccably under different circumstances—in other words, when faced with different incentives.

There are a few notable exceptions to this cultural bias against culture in economics. Hermalin (2001) presents an excellent overview of economic models of corporate culture, citing the work of several researchers who have modelled culture as:

1. Game-theoretic interactions involving incomplete contracts, coordination, reputation, unforeseen contingencies, and multiple equilibria (Kreps, 1990).
2. A store of common knowledge that provides efficiencies in communication within the firm (Crémer, 1993).
3. An evolutionary process in which preferences are genetically transmitted to descendants and shaped by senior management, like horse breeders seeking to produce championship thoroughbreds (Lazear, 1995).
4. The impact of situations on agents' perceptions and preferences (Hodgson, 1996).

Despite these early efforts, and Hermalin's compelling illustrations of the potential intellectual gains from trade between economics and culture, the study of culture by economists is still the exception rather than the rule. One reason is that the notion of rational self-interest, and its rich quantitative implications for behaviour, has made economics the most analytically powerful of the social sciences. The assumption that individuals respond to incentives according to their self-interest leads to concrete predictions about behaviour, rendering other cultural explanations unnecessary. In this framework, phenomena such as tournament salaries and Wall Street bonuses are a natural and efficient way to increase a firm's productivity, especially in a high-risk/high-reward industry in which it is nearly impossible to infer performance differences between individuals in advance.[7] If a corporate culture appears greedy to the outside world, it is because the world does not understand the economic environment in which the culture operates. The economist's view of culture, reducing differences in behaviour to different structures of incentives, can even be made to fit group phenomena that do not appear guided by rational self-interest, such as self-deception, over-optimism, willful blindness, and other forms of groupthink (Bénabou, 2013). Greed is not only good, it is efficient and predictive. Therefore, individual misbehaviour and corporate malfeasance are simply incentive problems that can be corrected by an intelligently designed system of financial rewards and punishments.

---

[7] However, see Burns, Minnick, and Starks (2017) for links between culture and compensation in a tournament framework.

This description is, of course, a caricature of the economist's perspective, but it is no exaggeration that the first line of inquiry in any economic analysis of misbehaviour is to investigate incentives. A case in point is the rise in mortgage defaults by US homeowners during the financial crisis of 2007–2009. Debt default has been a common occurrence since the beginning of debt markets, but after the peak of the US housing market in 2006, a growing number of homeowners engaged in *strategic defaults*, defaults driven by rational economic considerations rather than the inability to pay. The rationale is simple. As housing prices decline, a homeowner's equity declines in lockstep. When a homeowner's equity becomes negative, there is a much larger economic incentive to default, irrespective of income or wealth. This tendency to default under conditions of negative home equity has been confirmed empirically.[8] In a sample of homeowners holding mortgages in 2006 and 2007, Cohen-Cole and Morse (2010) find that 74 per cent of those households that became delinquent on their mortgage payments were nevertheless current on their credit card payments, behaviour consistent with strategic default. Moreover, homeowners with negative equity are found to be more likely to re-default, even when offered a mortgage modification that initially lowered their monthly payments (Quercia and Ding, 2009). As Geanakoplos and Koniak observe in the aftermath of the bursting of the housing bubble:

> Every month, another 8 percent of the subprime homeowners whose mortgages … are 160 percent of the estimated value of their houses become seriously delinquent. On the other hand, subprime homeowners whose loans are worth 60 percent of the current value of their house become delinquent at a rate of only 1 percent per month. Despite all the job losses and economic uncertainty, almost all owners with real equity in their homes are finding a way to pay off their loans. It is those 'underwater' on their mortgages—with homes worth less than their loans—who are defaulting, but who, given equity in their homes, will find a way to pay. They are not evil or irresponsible; they are defaulting because … it is the economically prudent thing to do.[9]

Economists can confidently point to these facts when debating the relative importance of culture versus incentives in determining consumer behaviour.

However, the narrative becomes more complex the further we dig into the determinants of strategic default. In survey data of 1,000 US households from December 2008 to September 2010, Guiso, Sapienza, and Zingales (2013, Table VI) show that respondents who know someone who strategically

---

[8] See, for example, Deng, Quigley, and Van Order (2000) and Elul et al. (2010).
[9] John Geanakoplos and Susan Koniak, 'Matters of Principal', *The New York Times*, 5 March 2009.

defaulted are 51 per cent more likely to declare their willingness to default strategically. This contagion effect is confirmed in a sample of more than 30 million mortgages originated between 2000 and 2008 that were observed from 2005 to 2009 by Goodstein et al. (2017), who find that mortgage defaults are influenced by the delinquency rates in surrounding ZIP codes, even after controlling for income-related factors. The authors' estimates suggest that a 1 per cent increase in the surrounding delinquency rate increases the probability of a strategic default by up to 16.5 per cent.

These results show that there is no simple dichotomy between incentives and culture. Neither explanation is complete, because the two factors are inextricably intertwined and jointly affect human behaviour in complex ways. Reacting to a change in incentives follows naturally from the unspoken assumptions of the economist. Economic incentives certainly influence human decisions, but they do not explain all behaviour in all contexts. They cannot do so, because humans are incentivized by a number of forces that are nonpecuniary and difficult to measure quantitatively. As Hill and Painter (2015) observe, these forces may include status, pride, mystique, and excitement. In addition, 'what confers status is contingent, and may change over time' (Hill and Painter, 2015, p. 111). These cultural forces often vary over time and across circumstances, causing individual and group behaviour to adapt in response to such changes (as in Chapter 4's analysis of group selection, Chapter 7's model of cooperation, and Chapter 10's discussion of bias and political polarization).

However, economists rarely focus on the adaptation of economic behaviour to time-varying, nonstationary environments. Our discipline is far more comfortable with comparative statics and general equilibria than it is with dynamics and phase transitions. Yet changes in the economic, political, and social environment have important consequences for the behaviour of individual employees and corporations alike, as Hermalin (2001) and Chapter 10 underscore. To resolve this problem, we need a broader theory, one capable of reconciling the analytical precision of *Homo economicus* with the cultural tendencies of *Homo sapiens*.

19.2.5 Values from Evolution: The Adaptive Markets Hypothesis

If corporate culture is shaped from the top down, from the bottom up, and through incentives in a given environment, the natural follow-on question to ask is, how? A corporation's leadership may exert its authority to establish norms of behaviour within the firm, but a corporation's employees also bring their pre-existing values to the workplace, and all of the actors in this drama have some resistance to cultural sway for noncultural, internal reasons. None of them is a perfectly malleable individual waiting to be moulded by external forces. This resistance has never stopped corporate authority from trying, however. In one notorious case, Henry Ford employed hundreds of investigators in his company's Sociological Department to monitor the private lives of his employees in order to ensure that they followed his preferred standard of behaviour inside the factory and out (Snow, 2013). The success or failure of such efforts depends critically on understanding the broader framework in which culture emerges and evolves over time and across circumstances.

Determining the origin of culture, ethics, and morality may seem to be a hopeless task, one more suited to philosophers than economists. However, there has been substantial progress in the fields of anthropology, evolutionary biology, psychology, and the cognitive neurosciences that has important implications for economic theories of culture. For example, evolutionary biologists have shown that cultural norms such as altruism, fairness, reciprocity, charity, and cooperation can lead to advantages in survival and reproductive success among individuals in certain settings.[10] E.O. Wilson argued even more forcefully that social conventions and interactions are the product of evolution, coining the term 'sociobiology' in the 1970s. More recent observational and experimental evidence from other animal species, such as our close cousins the chimpanzees, has confirmed the commonality of certain cultural norms, suggesting that they are adaptive traits passed down across many generations and species. A concrete illustration is the notion of fairness, a seemingly innate moral compass that exists in children as young as fifteen months old, as well as in chimpanzees.[11]

This evolutionary perspective of culture arises naturally in financial economics as part of the adaptive markets hypothesis (AMH) (Lo, 2004, 2005, 2012, 2017). Financial market dynamics are the result of a population of individuals competing for scarce resources and adapting to past and current environments. This hypothesis recognizes that competition, adaptation, and selection occur at multiple levels—from the subtle methylation of sequences in an individual's DNA to the transmission of cultural traits from one generation to the next—and they can occur simultaneously, each level operating at speeds dictated by specific environmental forces. To understand what

[10] See, for example, Hamilton (1964), Trivers (1971), Nowak and Highfield (2011), and the discussion in Chapters 2, 4, and 7.
[11] See Burns and Sommerville (2014) for experimental evidence of fairness with fifteen-month-old infants, and De Waal, Macedo, and Ober (2006) for similar experimental evidence for capuchin monkeys and chimpanzees.

individuals value, and how they will behave in various contexts, we have to understand how they interacted with the environments of their past.

The AMH explains why analogies to biological reasoning are often effective in the social sciences. Darwinian evolution is not the same process as cultural evolution, but the two processes occur under similar constraints of selection and differential survival. As a result, one can fruitfully use biological analogies, as well as biology itself, to explain aspects of culture—even of corporate culture, a concept that did not exist until the late nineteenth and early twentieth centuries. These explanations fall into two categories: explanations of individual behaviour by itself, and explanations of the interactions between individuals that lead to group dynamics.

Viewing behaviour at the level of the individual, current research in the cognitive neurosciences has refined our insights into the nature of moral and ethical judgements. These judgements arise from one of two possible neural mechanisms: one instinctive, immediate, and based on emotion; and the other more deliberative, measured, and based on logic and reasoning (Greene, 2015). The former is fast, virtually impossible to over-ride, and relatively inflexible, while the latter is slow, much more nuanced, and highly adaptive. This dual-process theory of moral and ethical decision-making—which is supported by a growing body of evidence from detailed, experimental neuroimaging studies—speaks directly to the question at hand of the origin of culture. At this level of examination, culture is the combination of hardwired responses embedded in our neural circuitry, many innate and not easily reprogrammed, and more detailed complex analytic behaviours that are path-dependent on life history, which *can* be reprogrammed (slowly) and are more in tune with our social environment.

Apart from its pure scientific value, the dual-process theory has several important practical implications. Current efforts to shape culture may be placing too much emphasis on the analytical process, while ignoring the less malleable and, therefore, more persistent innate process. A deeper understanding of this innate process is essential to answering questions about whether and how culture can be changed. One starting point is the work of social psychologist Jonathan Haidt, who proposed five moral dimensions that are innately determined and whose relative weightings yield distinct cultural mores and value systems: harm versus care, fairness versus cheating, loyalty versus betrayal, authority versus subversion, and purity versus degradation.[12] Since the relative importance of these moral dimensions is innately determined, their presence in the population naturally varies along with hair colour, height, and other traits.

---

[12] Haidt (2007). In subsequent writings, Haidt added a sixth dimension, liberty versus oppression.

Haidt and his colleagues discovered that, far from being distributed across the population in a uniformly random way, these traits had strong correlations to political beliefs (Fig. 19.1) (Graham, Haidt, and Nosek, 2009; Iyer et al., 2012). For example, people in the US who identified themselves as liberal believed that questions of harm/care and fairness/cheating were almost always relevant to making moral decisions. The other three moral foundations Haidt identified—loyalty/betrayal, authority/subversion, and purity/degradation—were much less important to liberals. However, those who identified themselves as conservative believed that all five moral foundations were equally important, although conservatives did not place as high an importance on any of the factors as liberals placed on fairness/cheating or harm/care. These traits had predisposed people to sort themselves into different political factions.

It takes little imagination to see this sorting process at work across professions. People who believe that fairness is the highest moral value will want

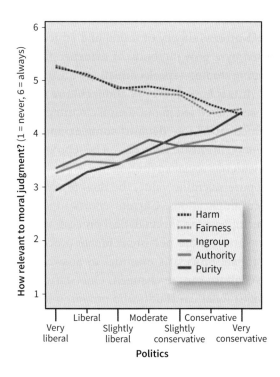

Fig. 19.1 The importance of Haidt's five moral dimensions among individuals of various political views.

Source: Haidt, J. (2007). The new synthesis in moral psychology. *Science* 316: 998–1002. Reprinted with permission from AAAS.

to choose a vocation in which they can exert this value, perhaps as a public defender, a teacher of underprivileged children, or a sports referee. Those who believe, instead, that fairness is less important than other values might find themselves drawn to high-pressure sales, or indeed, Gordon Gekko's caricature of predatory finance. This is not to say that everyone in those professions shares those values, of course, but rather that individuals with those values may find such professions more congenial—a form of natural selection bias—and will, therefore, eventually be statistically over-represented in that subpopulation.

At the same time that evolution shapes individual behaviour, it also acts on how individuals relate to one another. We call the collective behaviour that ultimately emerges from these interactions 'culture'. It has been conceptually difficult for classical evolutionary theory to explain many forms of collective and group behaviour, because evolutionary theory is primarily centred on the reproductive success of the individual or, even more reductively, of the gene. However, Nowak, Tarnita, and Wilson (2010) have revived the controversial notion of group selection, in which groups, not just individuals or genes, are the targets of natural selection. Although many evolutionary biologists have rejected this idea (Abbot et al., 2011), arguing that selection can occur only at the level of the gene, an application of the AMH can reconcile this controversy and also provide an explanation for the origins of culture.

The key insight is that individual behaviour that appears to be coordinated is simply the result of certain common factors in the environment—'systematic risk' in the terminology of financial economics—that impose a common threat to a particular subset of individuals. Within specific groups under systematic risk, natural selection on individuals can sometimes produce group-like behaviour. In such cases, a standard application of natural selection to individuals can produce behaviours that may seem like the result of group selection but that are, in fact, merely a reflection of systematic risk in the environment (see Chapter 4 and Zhang, Brennan, and Lo (2014a)).

For example, consider the extraordinary behaviour of Specialist Ross A. McGinnis, a nineteen-year-old machine-gunner in the US Army who, during the Iraq war, sacrificed himself when a fragmentation grenade was tossed into a Humvee during a routine patrol in Baghdad on 4 December 2006. McGinnis reacted immediately by yelling 'grenade' to alert the others in the vehicle, and then pushed his back onto the grenade, pinning it to the Humvee's radio mount and absorbing the impact of the explosion with his body. His actions saved the lives of his four crewmates.[13]

---

[13] http://www.army.mil/medalofhonor/mcginnis/profile/ (accessed 20 March 2015).

Although this was a remarkable act of bravery and sacrifice, it is not an isolated incident. Acts of bravery and sacrifice have always been part of the military tradition, as documented by the medals and other honours awarded to military heroes. Part of the explanation may be selection bias—the military may simply attract a larger proportion of altruistic individuals, people who sincerely believe that 'the needs of the many outweigh the needs of the few'.

A more direct explanation, however, may be that altruistic behaviour is produced by natural selection operating in the face of military conflict. Put another way, selfish behaviour on the battlefield is a recipe for defeat. Military conflict is an extreme form of systematic risk, and, over time and across many similar circumstances, the military has learned this lesson. Altruistic behaviour confers survival benefits for the population on the battlefield, even if it does not benefit the individual. Accordingly, military training instills these values in individuals—through bonding exercises like boot camp, stories of heroism passed down from seasoned veterans to new recruits, and medals and honours for courageous acts—so as to increase the likelihood of success for the entire troop. Military culture is the evolutionary product of the environment of war.

Now consider an entirely different environment: imagine a live grenade being tossed into a New York City subway car. Would we expect any of the passengers to behave in a manner similar to Specialist McGinnis in Baghdad? Context matters, and culture is shaped by context, as Milgram and Zimbardo discovered in their experiments with ordinary subjects placed in extraordinary circumstances (see Section 19.2.1).

Context matters not only on the battlefield, but also in the financial industry. Cohn, Fehr, and Maréchal (2014) document the impact of context on financial culture in an experiment involving 128 human subjects recruited from a large international bank. These subjects were asked to engage in a task that measured their honesty, using a simple coin-tossing exercise in which self-reported outcomes determined whether they would receive a cash prize. Prior to this exercise, subjects were split into two groups. In one group, participants were asked seven questions pertaining to their banking jobs; in the other, participants were asked seven non-banking related questions. By bringing the banking industry to the forefront of the subjects' minds just prior to the exercise, the authors induced the subjects to apply the cultural standards of that industry to the task at hand. The subjects in the former group showed significantly more dishonest behaviour than the subjects in the latter group, who exhibited the same level of honesty as participants from non-banking industries. The authors concluded that 'the prevailing business culture in the banking industry weakens and undermines the honesty norm,

implying that measures to reestablish an honest culture are very important'
(Cohn, Fehr, and Maréchal, 2014, p. 86).

However, innate variation determines how much the individual is influenced by context. Gibson, Tanner, and Wagner (2015) show that even in
cultures where there has been a crowding-out of honest behaviour by situational norms, individuals with strong intrinsic preferences to honesty as a
'protected' value resist the bad norm, and may potentially be able to form the
nucleus of a good norm in an altered situation.

Two empirical studies of fraud provide additional support for the impact of
context on financial culture. Dyck, Morse, and Zingales (2013) use historical
data on securities class action lawsuits to estimate the incidence of fraud from
1996 to 2004 in US publicly traded companies with at least $750 million in
market capitalization. They document an increasing amount of fraud as the
stock market rose in the first five or six years of the period, but find that the
fraud eventually declined in the wake of the bursting of the internet bubble
in 2001–2002 (Fig. 19.2). This interesting pattern suggests that the business

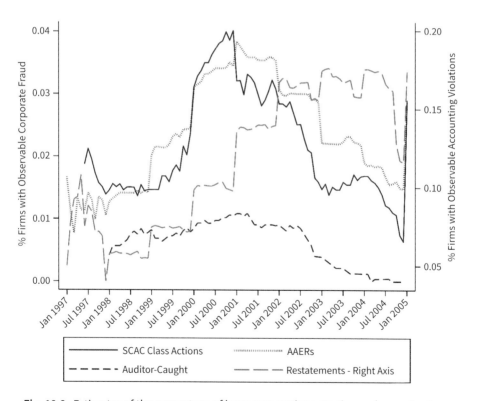

Fig. 19.2 Estimates of the percentage of large corporations starting and engaging in
fraud, from 1996 to 2004.

Source: Dyck, Morse, and Zingales (2013, Figure 1). Reprinted with permission of authors.

environment may be related to changes in corporate culture that involve fraudulent activity and corporate risk-taking behaviour. Deason, Rajgopal, and Waymire (2015) find a similar pattern in the number of Ponzi schemes prosecuted by the SEC between 1988 and 2012 (Fig. 19.3). The number of schemes shows an upwards trend during the bull market of the late 1990s, a decrease in the aftermath of the internet bust of 2001–2002, and another increase as the market climbed until the financial crisis in 2007–2009, after which the number of Ponzi schemes fell sharply. In fact, Deason, Rajgopal, and Waymire (2015) estimate a correlation of 47.9 per cent between the quarterly return on the S&P 500 index and the number of SEC-prosecuted Ponzi schemes per quarter, which they attribute to several factors: Ponzi schemes are harder to sustain in declining markets, and SEC enforcement budgets tend to increase after bubbles burst, due to more demand for enforcement by politicians and the public. The authors also find that Ponzi schemes are more likely when there is some affinity link between the perpetrator and the victim, such as a common religious background or shared membership in an ethnic group, or when the victim group tends to place more trust in others (e.g. senior citizens)—reminding us that culture can also be exploited maliciously.

These two studies confirm what many already knew instinctively: Culture is very much a product of the environment, and as environments change, so, too, does culture. Therefore, if we wish to change culture, we must first understand the forces that shape it over time and across circumstances. This broader contextual, environmental framework—informed by psychology, evolutionary theory, and neuroscience, and quantified through empirical

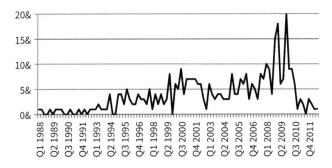

Fig. 19.3 Frequency of SEC-prosecuted Ponzi schemes by calendar quarter from 1988 to 2012.

Source: Deason, Rajgopal, and Waymire (2015, Figure 1). Reprinted with permission of authors.

measurement—will play a key role in Section 19.6, where we consider what can be done about culture from a practical perspective.

19.3 Examples from the Financial Industry

Moving from the general to the specific, we now explore several financial debacles that demonstrate the role of corporate culture in financial failure. Let us start with a control case, the fall of LTCM. In organizational theorist Charles Perrow's terminology, LTCM's collapse was a 'normal accident' (Perrow, 1999). That is, it was caused by a combination of tight coupling in the engineering sense—in which the execution of one process depends critically on the successful completion of another—and complex interactions within the financial system. To summarize a well-known story very briefly, LTCM's sophisticated models were caught off guard by the aftermath of Russia's default on its short-term government bonds, or GKOs, on 17 August 1998, triggering a short and vicious cycle of losses and flights to liquidity and ultimately leading to LTCM's bailout on 23 September 1998.[14]

On paper, LTCM's corporate culture was excellent. The firm's composition was elite, as LTCM was founded by John Meriwether, the former head of bond trading at Salomon Brothers, and future Nobel Prize winners Robert C. Merton and Myron Scholes. Its culture was individualistic, as the cultures of many trading groups are, but the firm derived its authority from a legal-rational basis—the superiority of its mathematics. Its corporate culture played little direct role in its failure. In fact, with much of their personal fortunes invested in the business, LTCM's managing partners were perfectly aligned with their investors. Not a single client has sued them for inappropriate behaviour. Not a single regulator has cited them for violations of any sort.

Because of this excellence, however, the general culture of Wall Street was caught off guard by LTCM's predicament. LTCM's counterparties perceived the impressive firm to be a paragon of the industry's highest values—a combination of intelligence, market savvy, and ambition that was sure to succeed—when a more accurate assessment of LTCM might have been as an experimental engineering firm, working daringly (or hubristically, as some have argued) on the cutting edge. LTCM's creditors notoriously gave it virtually no haircut on loans, on the assumption that its trades were essentially risk-free. In addition to these very low, or even zero, margin requirements,

---

[14] See, for example, General Accounting Office (1999, pp. 38–45).

LTCM was able to negotiate other favourable credit enhancements with its counterparties, including two-way collateral requirements, rehypothecation rights, and high thresholds for loss (General Accounting Office, 1999, p. 42). These were often made on the strength of the firm's reputation rather than on a detailed examination of its methods. Daniel Napoli, Merrill Lynch's head of risk management at the time, was quoted as saying, 'We had no idea they would have trouble—these people were known for risk management. They had taught it; they *designed* it [emphasis in original]' (Lowenstein, 2000, p. 179). (Napoli himself lost his position shortly after LTCM's collapse.) And so, while LTCM's failure may be viewed as akin to the failure of a bridge whose experimental materials were exposed to an unfamiliar stress, the behaviour of LTCM's creditors is more likely a failure of their own corporate cultures.

Corporate cultures can be overconfident in their abilities to assess risk. This overconfidence can be seen in the fall of the large multinational insurer American International Group (AIG) in 2008. Under its original chairman, Maurice 'Hank' Greenberg, AIG was run not merely hierarchically, but almost feudally, with reciprocal chains of loyalty and obligation centred on Greenberg.[15] In fact, Greenberg had deliberately structured AIG's compensation plan to promote lifetime loyalty to the firm. Greenberg was, in Weberian terms, a charismatic authority, overseeing each division of his large, multinational organization personally. In regular questioning sessions, Greenberg demanded to know exactly what risks each unit of AIG was taking and what measures were being used to reduce them. Many observers ascribed AIG's continued growth to the firm's excellent practice in insurance underwriting, closely monitored by Greenberg.

However, the 'headline risk' of Greenberg's possible role in financial irregularities caused AIG's board of directors to replace him with Martin Sullivan in early 2005. Sullivan had risen through the ranks of AIG, originally starting as a teenage office assistant. Sullivan assumed that AIG's vigorous culture of risk management would maintain itself without Greenberg at the helm. Meanwhile, Joseph Cassano, the head of AIG's Financial Products (AIGFP) unit, had a working relationship with Greenberg that did not transfer to Sullivan. Cassano's conduct grew more aggressive without Greenberg's check on his behaviour (Boyd, 2011, p. 161).

AIGFP's portfolio contained billions of dollars of credit default swaps (CDSs) on 'toxic' collateralized debt obligations (CDOs). These CDSs were not the only toxic items on AIG's balance sheet, which also reflected significant problems in the company's securities lending programme, but they

---

[15] Boyd (2011) and Shelp and Ehrbar (2009) provide two viewpoints of AIG's culture from which a triangulation can be made.

were the largest, and they created the most visible effects during the financially dangerous autumn of 2008. While AIGFP's first sales of CDSs on CDOs began in 2004, during Greenberg's tenure, they accelerated into 2005, before executives within AIGFP convinced Cassano about declining standards in the subprime mortgage market. AIGFP's final sale of CDSs took place in early 2006, leaving a multi-billion-dollar time bomb on AIG's balance sheet, which the prolonged downturn in the housing market started ticking. Cassano defended his actions in an increasingly adverse environment until his ouster from AIG in early 2008 (Boyd, 2011, pp. 258–262).

It is probably too easy to ascribe AIGFP's extended period of CDS sales to Greenberg's departure. As noted, Cassano's unit began selling CDSs well before Greenberg's exit. However, Robert Shiller's insight into the Milgram experiment is pertinent here. Greenberg's culture of risk management, which was accompanied by consistently high growth in the traditionally low-growth insurance industry, led Cassano and Sullivan to believe that AIG's risk-management procedures were consistently reliable under conditions when they were not. Paradoxically, the moral hazard of past success may have led AIG to make much riskier investments than a company with a poorer track record of risk management would have made.

Some corporate cultures actively conceal their flaws and irregularities, not only from the public or from regulators, but also from others within the corporation itself because of the risk that wider knowledge of these issues might undermine the firm's position. For example, let us look at Lehman Brothers' use of the 'Repo 105' accounting trick.[16] Briefly, this was a repo, or repurchase agreement, valued at $1.05 for every dollar, that was designed to look like a sale. Lehman Brothers paid more than five cents on the dollar temporarily to pay down the liabilities on its balance sheet before it repurchased the asset. The firm used this accounting trick in amounts totalling $50 billion in late 2007 and 2008 to give itself the appearance of greater financial health—which, of course, was ultimately a failure.

Was this tactic legal? No American law firm would agree to endorse it, so Lehman Brothers engaged in regulatory arbitrage, and found a distinguished British law firm, Linklaters, willing to give the practice its imprimatur. Linklaters' endorsement of Repo 105 was kept secret from the outside world (except for Lehman's auditors, Ernst and Young, who also allowed the practice to pass[17]) and also from Lehman's board members.[18] Lehman Brothers

---

[16] Valukas (2010).

[17] Valukas (2010, pp. 782–786 and pp. 948–951). See also Nolder and Riley (2014) for the impact of cultural differences on auditors.

[18] Valukas (2010, pp. 945–947).

omitted its use of Repo 105 in its quarterly disclosures to the SEC, and also neglected to tell its outside disclosure counsel.[19]

In contrast to LTCM, the corporate culture at Lehman Brothers less resembled a cutting-edge engineering firm experiencing an unforeseen design failure than it did Zimbardo's Stanford experiment. An internal hierarchy within Lehman's management deliberately withheld information about the firm's misleading accounting practices from outsiders who might have objected, as well as from those within the firm, because this internal hierarchy believed that was its proper role. When Lehman's global financial controller reported to two consecutive chief financial officers his misgivings that Repo 105 might be a significant reputational risk to the company, his concerns were ignored.[20] Lehman's hierarchical culture defended its values against voices from its border, even though these voices occupied central positions on its organizational chart. Instead of taking measures to avoid headline risk, the firm buried its practices in secrecy.

The case of rogue trader Jérôme Kerviel illustrates another possible type of failure of corporate culture, that of neglect. Unauthorized or rogue trading is necessarily a form of fraud, since it deliberately evades the legal responsibilities of proper financial management. In January 2008, Kerviel, a trader in the corporate and investment banking division of the French bank Société Générale, built up a €49 billion long position on index futures before his trades were detected (Société Générale, 2008, p. 2). For comparison purposes, Société Générale's total capital at the time was only €26 billion. Unwinding his unauthorized position cost Société Générale €6.4 billion, an immense loss that threatened to take down the bank. Kerviel has stated that Société Générale turned a blind eye to his activities when they were making money—and Société Générale's own internal investigation reports that he made €1.5 billion for the bank on his unauthorized trades in 2007.

However, the internal investigation paints a very different, if equally unflattering, picture of Société Générale's corporate culture. Kerviel's first supervisor did not notice his early fraudulent trades or the cover-up of those trades but, in fact, allowed Kerviel to make intraday trades, a privilege well above Kerviel's status as a junior trader. In January 2007, Kerviel's supervisor quit, and his trading desk was left effectively unsupervised for three months. During this time, Kerviel built up a futures position of €5.5 billion, his first very large position. His new desk manager, hired in April 2007, had no prior knowledge of Kerviel's trading activities and did not use the monitoring programs that would have detected his trades. Moreover,

---

[19] Valukas (2010, pp. 853–856).
[20] Valukas (2010, pp. 884–887).

Kerviel's new manager was not supported by his own supervisor in assisting or supervising Kerviel's new activities. The Société Générale report found that a culture of inattention and managerial neglect existed up to four levels above Kerviel's position, to the head of Société Générale's arbitrage activities (Société Générale, 2008, pp. 3–8). Ultimately, it was the attention and perseverance of a monitor in Société Générale's accounting and regulatory reporting division that caught Kerviel, after the monitor noticed an unhedged €1.5 billion position while calculating the Cooke ratio for Société Générale's Basel compliance requirements (Société Générale, 2008, pp. 31–34).

This is Douglas's individualistic culture taken to a point of absurdity. Mark Hunter and N. Craig Smith believe that the roots of Société Générale's Corporate and Investment Banking division's inept management culture can be found in the firm's complex corporate history (Hunter and Smith, 2011). Société Générale was a private retail bank nationalized after World War II, and then privatized again in 1986. Throughout its postwar history, however, the bank was a proving ground for elite French graduates, similar to the way Wall Street investment banks recruit from Ivy League universities in the US. The key difference is that the elite focused its oversight on Société Générale's retail banking business, because of its close connection to French policymakers in the public and private sectors, rather than its proprietary trading desks. Société Générale's corporate culture viewed the Corporate and Investment Banking division as a 'cash machine', not central to its elite outcomes. Kerviel, a graduate of provincial universities, was not expected to rise in the elite hierarchy. Therefore, little attention was paid to his activities, even when he made surprisingly large amounts of money.

19.4 Regulatory Culture

Regulatory culture is not immune to these challenges. Consider the unravelling of the mother of all Ponzi schemes: Bernard Madoff's. The SEC formally charged Madoff with securities fraud on 11 December 2008, the day after Madoff's sons turned him in to the Federal Bureau of Investigation. Justice was swift in this case; on 12 March 2009, Madoff pleaded guilty to all charges.[21] However, although justice was swift, the SEC's internal Office of Investigations discovered that the SEC was not. The Office of Investigations learned that the SEC had received six 'red flag' complaints about Madoff's hedge fund operations, dating as far back as 1992, and had been presented

---

[21] Securities and Exchange Commission (2009, p. 1).

with two reputable articles in the trade and financial press from 2001 that questioned Madoff's abnormally consistent returns.[22]

It is instructive to consider how the SEC's culture dealt with these claims. A portfolio manager named Harry Markopolos submitted the earliest of the analytical complaints about Madoff's performance to the SEC. Markopolos, originally with Rampart Investment Management, found he could not replicate Madoff's returns without making impossible assumptions. Markopolos submitted his findings to the SEC several times to no avail: in 2000, through its Boston office, a complaint that was never recorded as reaching the SEC's Northeast Regional Office (NERO);[23] in 2001, a submission that NERO decided not to pursue after one day's analysis;[24] in 2005, which we will discuss in further detail below; in 2007 via a significant follow-up e-mail that was 'ignored', in the words of the Office of Investigations report;[25] and in April 2008, which failed to arrive owing to an incorrect e-mail address.[26]

Two similar analyses were brought to the SEC's attention, one directly and one indirectly. In May 2003, an unnamed hedge fund manager contacted the SEC's Office of Compliance Inspections and Examinations (OCIE) with a parallel analysis.[27] In November 2003, upper management at the hedge fund Renaissance Technologies became concerned that Madoff's returns were 'highly unusual' and that 'none of it seems to add up'. In April 2004, this Renaissance correspondence was flagged for attention by a compliance examiner at NERO during a routine examination.[28]

OCIE and NERO conducted two separate, independent examinations of Madoff. Each examination was unaware of the other, until Madoff himself informed examiners of their mutual existence. (OCIE had not used the SEC's tracking system to update the status of its examination; however, NERO had not checked the system, rendering the point moot.)[29] OCIE passed its unresolved examination documents to NERO and made no further communication with NERO about the case.[30] Although NERO examiners still had important questions about Madoff's actions, NERO closed the examination before they were answered because of cultural time constraints.

---

[22] Securities and Exchange Commission (2009, pp. 21–22); Michael Ocrant, 'Madoff Tops Charts; Skeptics Ask How', *MARHedge*, May 2001; Erin Arvedlund, 'Don't Ask, Don't Tell', *Barron's*, 7 May 2001.
[23] Securities and Exchange Commission (2009, pp. 61–67).
[24] Securities and Exchange Commission (2009, pp. 67–74).
[25] Securities and Exchange Commission (2009, p. 61 and p. 354).
[26] Securities and Exchange Commission (2009, pp. 361–363).
[27] Securities and Exchange Commission (2009, pp. 77–80).
[28] Securities and Exchange Commission (2009, pp. 145–149).
[29] Securities and Exchange Commission (2009, pp. 195–197).
[30] Securities and Exchange Commission (2009, pp. 136–138).

'There's no hard and fast rule about field work but ... field work cannot go on indefinitely because people have a hunch', one NERO assistant director later testified.[31]

Markopolos' 2005 complaint reached NERO with the strong endorsement of the SEC's Boston office.[32] However, the previous fruitless examination of claims against Madoff biased the NERO examiners against Markopolos' claim.[33] The examiners quickly discounted Markopolos' idea that Madoff was running a Ponzi scheme. The staff attorney involved with the examination wrote at the beginning of the investigation that there wasn't 'any *real* reason to suspect some kind of wrongdoing ... all we suspect is disclosure problems [emphasis in original]'.[34] The Office of Investigations was harsh in its verdict: 'As a result of this initial failure, the Enforcement staff never really conducted an adequate and thorough investigation of Markopolos' claim that Madoff was operating a Ponzi scheme'.[35]

The Madoff failure, summarized above in a necessarily streamlined account, was only one of many events that caused the internal culture of the SEC to fall under scrutiny. An extensive study of the SEC by the Government Accountability Office (GAO) in 2012 and 2013 found systemic problems throughout its organizational culture:[36]

Based on analysis of views from Securities and Exchange Commission (SEC) employees and previous studies from GAO, SEC, and third parties, GAO determined that SEC's organizational culture is not constructive and could hinder its ability to effectively fulfill its mission. Organizations with constructive cultures are more effective and employees also exhibit a stronger commitment to mission focus. In describing SEC's culture, many current and former SEC employees cited low morale, a distrust of management, and the compartmentalized, hierarchical, and risk-averse nature of the organization. According to an Office of Personnel Management (OPM) survey of federal employees, SEC currently ranks 19th of 22 similarly sized federal agencies based on employee satisfaction and commitment. GAO's past work on managing for results indicates that an effective personnel management system will be critical for transforming SEC's organizational culture.

Apparently, the SEC's hierarchical culture was hardened into silos, which not only prevented the flow of information from one division to another,

[31] Securities and Exchange Commission (2009, p. 223).
[32] Securities and Exchange Commission (2009, pp. 240–244).
[33] Securities and Exchange Commission (2009, pp. 255–259).
[34] Securities and Exchange Commission (2009, pp. 266–268).
[35] Securities and Exchange Commission (2009, p. 368).
[36] Government Accountability Office (2013).

but also hindered the flow of information between management and staff.[37] Morale, the sense of shared purpose, was low among staff, but management believed it was much higher.[38] Despite earlier initiatives, the SEC's culture had grown more risk-averse over time, and a majority of both staff and senior officers explicitly agreed that this was due to the fear of public scandal. Some staff members anonymously reported that 'managers have been afraid to close cases or make decisions because senior officers want to minimize the chances that they would be criticized later'.[39]

The GAO concluded its report with seven specific recommendations for changing the SEC's culture. These included improvements in coordination and communication across internal departments and other agencies—presumably to prevent future cases like Madoff's from slipping through the cracks—and changes in personnel management practices to better align job performance with compensation and promotions. The SEC agreed with all seven recommendations. By its own account, it has made significant progress in addressing each of them since then. For example:[40]

> Based on GAO's recommendations, SEC made significant efforts to improve communication and collaboration. In an effort to optimize communications and collaboration, the SEC benchmarked and implemented a variety of best practices used both within the public and private sector, including cross-agency working groups, an agency-wide culture change initiative, and a more robust internal communication strategy. Work continues in this area to ensure that employees across the SEC are sharing critical information … The purpose of OPM's audit was to determine SEC's adherence to merit system principles, laws, and regulations, and to assess the efficiency and effectiveness in administering human resources programs under the Talent Management System of the Human Capital Framework. OHR is currently in the process of addressing all of the required and recommended actions identified in the OPM audit and anticipates that all recommendations will be resolved by the end of FY 2015.

These changes seem to be having an impact. The SEC's score on the Office of Personnel Management's (OPM) Global Satisfaction Index—based on the same survey (Office of Personnel Management, 2019) cited in the GAO's earlier report—improved from 59 in 2012 to 75 in 2019. For comparison, the National Aeronautics and Space Administration, which is typically among

---

[37] Government Accountability Office (2013, pp. 33–38).
[38] Government Accountability Office (2013, p. 11). To be clear, low morale was not an issue at the SEC in 2008, but emerged in the wake of the unravelling of the Madoff Ponzi scheme and the realization that the SEC had failed to prevent it.
[39] Government Accountability Office (2013, pp. 16–17).
[40] Securities and Exchange Commission (2014, p. 132).

the highest satisfaction agencies, was rated 81, and the government-wide index value was 65.

19.5 The Importance of Feedback Loops

Although the SEC's improvements may seem too little too late to those swindled by Madoff, the process by which these changes were proposed and implemented is a significant mechanism through which culture can be modified. By conducting a thorough, nonpartisan analysis of what happened, how it happened, why it happened, and what can be done to reduce the likelihood of it happening again in the future, the GAO provided important feedback that led to improvements at the SEC, including improvements in its organizational culture. This is not the only institutional feedback mechanism now in place at the SEC. The SEC Office of the Inspector General—an independent office within the SEC that conducts periodic audits and investigations within the agency—provides ongoing feedback to the SEC's leadership to '…promote the integrity, efficiency, and effectiveness of the critical programs and operations of the U.S. Securities and Exchange Commission.'[41] Meanwhile, regular employee surveys conducted by the OPM and the SEC provide objective metrics by which to measure progress and identify problems with morale and culture as they emerge. The well-known adage that 'one cannot manage what one does not measure' encapsulates the critical role that metrics and feedback play in managing culture.

Perhaps the best example of the impact that negative feedback can have is the work of the National Transportation Safety Board (NTSB), which we describe in Chapters 11 and 20. By investigating accidents, providing careful and conclusive forensic analysis, and making recommendations for avoiding such accidents in the future, the NTSB has been one of the major factors underlying the stunning improvement in the safety record of modern air transportation. We provide a specific example of one of these investigations in Section 20.6 of Chapter 20.

Financial crashes are, of course, far less deadly, generally involving no immediate loss of life. However, the financial crisis and its impact on people's lives should be enough motivation to create a Capital Markets Safety Board (CMSB)—the financial equivalent of the NTSB proposed in Chapters 11 and 20—dedicated to investigating, reporting, and archiving the 'accidents' of the financial industry.

---

[41] https://www.sec.gov/oig (accessed 15 March 2022).

A case in point is the Madoff Ponzi scheme. While several reports have been written on the SEC's failure to recognize and stop this massive fraud, the forensic analysis on how Bernard Madoff—a highly respected and successful businessman who accumulated a huge fortune long before he began conning investors—came to commit such a crime has yet to be written. What was the cultural milieu that gave rise to Madoff? How did someone with so many genuine accomplishments come to defraud friends and family, not to mention legions of admiring and (in not a few cases) worshipful investors? Is this an isolated incident that can be forgotten now that the perpetrator has been caught and punished (and since passed away), or should it serve as a cautionary tale because we each have the capacity for similar crimes within us? What were the factors that allowed even sophisticated institutional investors to be duped and seduced by Madoff? Greed? Exclusivity? Competitive pressures from a low-yield environment and gyrating stock markets? Madoff's power and wealth? Unless we begin conducting forensic analyses of cultures gone wrong so we can learn what and how to change, we will be condemned to repeat the mistakes of our past. This is why we need a CMSB, making the case for such an agency in more detail in Chapter 20.

As an aside, consider the cultural features that have led to the NTSB's success. The NTSB's culture of definitive expertise and teamwork has earned the public's trust, and the agency is widely regarded as 'the best in the business', not only in the US, but throughout the world (Lebow et al., 1999, p. 2). If we apply the classification scheme discussed earlier in this chapter, the NTSB has an individualistic culture with an elite composition and a legal-rational basis for its authority, but with a twist: small teams are the cohesive, accountable unit in the organization, rather than individuals per se. This organizational structure increases the sense of shared purpose during an investigation, while allowing flexibility of assignments at other times. Unlike at other regulatory agencies, a job at the NTSB is considered the capstone of a career, rather than a stepping stone. As a result, the NTSB is that rarest of government agencies: a highly focused, effective organization with strong morale (Fielding, Lo, and Yang, 2011, pp. 29–33).

19.6 Behavioural Risk Management

Corporate culture is clearly a relevant factor in financial failure, error, and malfeasance. As we have seen, risk priorities mirror a corporate culture's values, since no corporation has the resources to manage risk perfectly. Société Générale put very little priority on managing its trading desks, which reflected the low value it placed on its traders. Lehman Brothers spent more

time concealing the flaws in its balance sheet than it spent remedying them—
the risk of disclosure was more important than the risk of bankruptcy. AIG
felt so secure in its practice of risk management that it allowed billions of
dollars of toxic assets to appear on its balance sheet not once, but twice, the
second in its much less publicized but comparably vulnerable securities lending programme. These generalizations contain grains of truth, but they offer
little guidance on what to change and how to change it.

So what is the best way to immunize against the Gordon Gekko effect?
The psychologist Philip Zimbardo put it succinctly enough: resist situational
influences (Zimbardo, 2007, pp. 451–456). Zimbardo was lucky enough to
have a dissenting opinion that he implicitly trusted before his prison experiment spiralled out of control. Since that time, Zimbardo has investigated how
the surrounding culture can influence good people to do evil things, much as
the character Bud Fox was seduced by Gordon Gekko's culture in *Wall Street*.
Zimbardo offers ten key behaviours that he believes will minimize the effectiveness of a destructive culture in spreading its values, whether corporate or
otherwise. Among them are the willingness to admit mistakes, the refusal
to respect unjust authority, the ability to consider the future rather than
the immediate present, and the individual values of honesty, responsibility, and independence of thought. These behaviours may sound hackneyed,
but they are no more hackneyed than the instructions to cover one's mouth
while coughing or to wash one's hands regularly to prevent the spread of
communicable diseases.

Sceptics would argue that, like fighting city hall or trying to cheat death,
attempting to change a large organization's culture is a Sisyphean task. How
can any single agent expect to change attitudes and behavioural patterns that
can span years and tens of thousands of current and former employees? While
we believe such scepticism is misplaced, the dual-process theory of moral
and ethical decision-making does explain one source of this scepticism: it is,
indeed, hard to change innate behaviour, by definition. But the dual-process
theory also implies a path by which culture *can* be changed. More practically,
the AMH provides a framework in which we can think systematically about
taking on this challenge.

The first step is a subtle but important semantic shift. Instead of seeking
to 'change culture', which seems naive and hopelessly ambitious, suppose
our objective is to engage in 'behavioural risk management'.[42] Despite the
fact that we are referring to essentially the same goal, the latter phrase is
more concrete, actionable, and unassailable from the perspective of corporate
governance. Human behaviour is a factor in virtually every type of corporate malfeasance; hence, it is only prudent to take steps to manage those

---

[42] We thank Hamid Mehran for suggesting this terminology.

behaviours most likely to harm the business. Once this semantic leap has been made, it is remarkable how readily more practical implications follow. By drawing on traditional risk-management protocols used at all major financial institutions, we can develop a parallel process for managing behavioural risk.

Consider, for example, the typical process used to manage the risk of a financial portfolio (Lo, 1999), which can be summarized by the mnemonic SIMON (Select, Identify, Measure, Optimize, Notice). Firstly, select the major risk factors driving portfolio returns; secondly, identify the objective function to be optimized, along with any constraints that must be satisfied; thirdly, measure the statistical laws of motion governing portfolio-return dynamics; fourthly, optimize the objection function subject to the return dynamics and any constraints, which yields the optimal portfolio weights and hedging positions; and, finally, notice any change in the system and repeat the previous four steps, as needed. Any systematic financial risk-management protocol must have every element of SIMON represented in some fashion. For example, an emerging market debt fund might select exchange rates and interest rates as the major risk factors affecting the fund; identify the information ratio as the objective to be optimized; measure exchange rate and interest rate dynamics using statistical time series and mathematical term structure models; optimize the information ratio subject to these dynamics and a volatility or tracking-error constraint; and notice when the optimal weights for futures and forward contracts require rebalancing, and start the process all over again. SIMON says 'manage your risk'!

Now consider applying SIMON to the management of behavioural risks. Firstly, select the major behavioural risks facing the firm—for example, a lack of appreciation and respect for compliance procedures, senior management's intolerance for opposing views, the cutting of corners with respect to operational policies and procedures to achieve growth and profitability targets, and so on. Secondly, identify the objective function and constraints—for example, corporate values, short- and long-run goals, and the firm's mission statement. Thirdly, measure the statistical 'laws of motion' governing behaviour—for example, the dual-process theory of moral reasoning, Haidt's five-factor model, and the OPM's Global Satisfaction Index. Fourthly, optimize the objective function subject to constraints, which yields the optimal compensation structures and hedging instruments—that is to say, compliance procedures, reporting requirements, and supervisory relationship—for aligning the culture with the objectives. Finally, and most importantly, notice any changes in the system to ensure that the behavioural risk-management protocol is achieving the desired result, and repeat the previous four steps as often as needed.

The weakest link in this analogical chain is the third: measuring the behavioural laws of motion. Our quantitative understanding of human behaviour is still in its infancy, and without reasonably accurate predictive analytics, behavioural risk management is more aspirational than operational. In the case of financial risk management, the laws of motion of asset returns are readily available from a multitude of risk management software platforms and real-time data vendors in the form of linear factor models, credit scores, and value-at-risk and loss-probability models. Nothing comparable exists to support behavioural risk managers. Psychological profiles, social network maps, and job satisfaction surveys such as those conducted by the OPM are currently relegated to human resources departments, not risk committees or corporate boards.

However, the starting point for any scientific endeavour is measurement. Psychological profiles, social networks, and human resources data can serve as the basis for constructing behavioural risk models, perhaps along the lines implied by the work of social psychologists such as Haidt (2007), and empirically based models of the systematic and idiosyncratic factors underlying fraud, malfeasance, and excessive risk-taking behaviour, as described in Dyck, Morse, and Zingales (2013) and Deason, Rajgopal, and Waymire (2015). But even before attempting to construct such models, we can learn a great deal by simply documenting the reward structure for individuals within an organization so as to develop an integrated view of the corporate ecosystem. For example, if a financial institution's chief risk officer (CRO) is compensated through bonuses tied only to the firm's profitability and not to its stability, it should be obvious that risk may not be the CRO's primary focus.

From a quantitative perspective, the ultimate achievement would be an empirically based methodology for predicting individual and group behaviour to some degree as a function of observable systematic and idiosyncratic factors. For example, imagine being able to quantify the risk appetite of financial executive i by the linear factor model

$$\text{Risk Appetite}_i = \alpha_i + \beta_{i1}(\text{Reward}) + \beta_{i2}(\text{Potential Loss}) + \beta_{i3}(\text{Career Risk})$$
$$+ \beta_{i4}(\text{Competitive Pressure}) + \beta_{i5}(\text{Peer Pressure})$$
$$+ \beta_{i6}(\text{Self-Image}) + \beta_{i7}(\text{Regulatory Environment}) + \epsilon_i,$$

where the coefficients measure how important each factor is to the executive's risk appetite, and the factors vary across time, circumstances, and institutions. If we could estimate such a behavioural risk model for each executive, then we would be able to define culture quantitatively as a preponderance of individuals with numerically similar factor loadings. A culture of excessive risk-taking and blatant disregard for rules and regulations might consist of an entire division of individuals who share very high loadings for the 'Reward' and 'Competitive Pressure' factors, and very low loadings for the 'Potential Loss' and 'Regulatory Environment' factors. If such a risk model could be empirically estimated, we would begin to understand the Gordon Gekko effect at a more granular level, and to develop ways to address it. Moreover, since this framework implicitly acknowledges that the factors driving behaviour are time-varying and context-dependent, as competitive pressures increase owing to low yields and increased competition, regulators can expect behaviour to change and should adapt accordingly.

Such a framework may seem more like science fiction than science at this point, but its development has already begun. In 2009, in the aftermath of the financial crisis, De Nederlandsche Bank (DNB), the Dutch central bank, proposed a new approach to supervising banks. In a memorandum titled 'The Seven Elements of Ethical Culture' (De Nederlandsche Bank, 2009), the bank said:

> This document presents DNB's strategy on the issue of behaviour and culture. It describes the background and reasons why it is important to include ethical behaviour and culture in supervision, sets out the legal framework for doing so, and explains what the current situation is, both within institutions and in the exercise of supervision by DNB. In presenting these elements for an ethical culture and sound conduct, this document describes the supervisory model that DNB wishes to follow in determining its supervisory efforts and, in a general sense, the plan of action for 2010–2014.

To support this effort, DNB has created the Expert Centre on Culture, Organisation, and Integrity, hired organizational psychologists and change experts, and launched several internal research projects to develop new supervisory methods specific to corporate culture.[43] Researchers at the Federal Reserve Bank of New York (New York Fed) undertook an important empirical first step in creating a behavioural risk model: they conducted and published a survey about the New York Fed's supervisory activities for large financial institutions, describing how these activities are staffed, organized, and implemented by the New York Fed on a day-to-day basis (Eisenbach et al., 2017).

---

[43] See Conley et al. (2019) for an in-depth third-party study of DNB's groundbreaking efforts to supervise bank culture.

This survey provides an unprecedented level of transparency into bank supervision for the many stakeholders not privy to these policies and procedures. As observed by the authors of the survey, 'Understanding how prudential supervision works is a critical precursor to determining how to measure its impact and effectiveness'.

Pan, Siegel, and Wang (2017) provide another example of a new breed of empirical analysis of culture by economists. They define and measure corporate risk culture by determining the risk preferences among corporate founders, executives, and board members at more than 6,000 US public firms from 1996 to 2012, using surnames to infer cultural heritage, then linking this heritage to the risk attitude of the country of origin. Although surely imperfect and subject to the obvious critiques of overgeneralization and cultural stereotyping, this intriguing method of inferring risk culture is worthy of study and, with time and collective effort, can be refined as a better understanding of its strengths and weaknesses is developed. As Knight (1940, p. 16) instructed, ' … when you can't measure, measure anyhow'.

Once the specific behaviours, objectives, and value systems in a corporate culture are identified and quantified, the alignment of corporate values and mission with behaviour can be facilitated in a number of ways. Economic incentives are the most direct approach, and the one favoured by economists and the private sector (see Section 19.2.4). However, other tools are available to the behavioural risk manager, including changes in corporate governance, the use of social networks and peer review, and public recognition or embarrassment.

If, for example, an organization is concerned about insufficient controls owing to a culture that equates risk-taking with power and prestige, consider the following three measures: Firstly, the organization can appoint a CRO who (1) reports directly to the company's board of directors, (2) can only be removed by a vote of the board, and (3) has the authority and the responsibility to temporarily relieve the CEO of their responsibilities if the CRO determines that the firm's risk levels are unacceptably high and the CEO has not responded to the CRO's request to reduce risk. A second, more radical measure to change the risk-taking culture of an organization is to make all employees who are compensated above some threshold (e.g. $1 million) jointly and severally liable for all lawsuits against the firm. Such a measure would greatly increase the scrutiny that these well-paid individuals place on their firm's activities, reducing the chances of misbehaviour. A third, even more extreme, measure is Kane's (2015) proposal to hold individual executives criminally liable for not fulfilling a fiduciary duty to the public, which would no doubt change the corporate culture of important financial institutions.

Of course, such measures would also greatly decrease the amount of risk that the firm is willing to take, which may not sit well with shareholders. Balancing the trade-offs between various incentives and governance mechanisms will ultimately determine the kind of culture that emerges and whether this culture is consistent with the corporation's core values and mission.

A similar behavioural risk model can be estimated for regulators. The reforms at the SEC provide an opportunity to consider how quantitative metrics, such as those produced by the OPM survey, can be combined with empirical patterns of corporate fraud and malfeasance to produce more adaptive regulation. For example, rising markets should be accompanied by increasing surveillance for potential Ponzi schemes among the most vulnerable affinity groups, and regulatory examinations should target those institutions with cultures most likely—as defined by their behavioural risk models—to violate key regulations.

In addition, the potential exists for regulators to pick up elements of culture from the corporations they regulate that can render them less effective, much like public health workers becoming infected with the disease they are fighting. In some cases, this leads to fully fledged regulatory capture, while in others it merely leads to an inaccurate bill of good health. It is essential to the goal of regulatory efficacy that regulators remain immune to the values of other corporate cultures while maintaining a sufficiently deep working knowledge of them. This is easier said than done, but the measurement of regulatory culture may be a starting point for identifying potential problems before they turn into more serious lapses.

19.7 Discussion

These hypothetical examples show that culture can be a choice, not a fixed constraint. The emerging discipline of behavioural risk management can be the means by which a corporation's culture is measured and managed. And, thanks to advances in the behavioural and social sciences, big data, and human resources management, for the first time in regulatory history, we have the intellectual means to construct behavioural risk models. We just need the will to do so. To paraphrase Reinhold Niebuhr's well-known serenity prayer, the behavioural risk manager must seek the serenity to accept those parts of culture that cannot be changed, the courage and the means to change those parts of culture that can and should be changed, and the behavioural risk models and forensic studies required to distinguish one from the other.

20
Regulation and Adaptive Markets

Precipitated by credit problems in the US residential housing market, the financial crisis of 2008 was one of the most far-reaching dislocations in global markets in recorded history, with shockwaves that affected every major country and market centre in the world.[1] Accordingly, the focus on regulatory reform in its aftermath has been intense, with diverse proposals for new laws and agencies from all major stakeholders. In this respect, there is a positive side to a crisis—it provides us with the opportunity and the modus operandi to make major changes in our regulatory infrastructure that would otherwise be impossible because of the ever-present conflicts among multiple constituencies. Crisis can temporarily align conflicting interests to achieve a greater good.

However, crisis can also bring danger, in the form of unreasoned emotional responses to the crisis as we saw in Chapters 11 and 17. Therefore, we must approach each crisis with a sense of both urgency and caution. While the need for regulatory reform may seem clear, the underlying causes of most financial crises are complex, multifaceted, and not fully understood until after we have sifted through all the wreckage. Accordingly, we must resist the temptation to react too hastily to market events, and instead deliberate thoughtfully and broadly in crafting new regulations for the financial system of the twenty-first century. Financial markets do not need more regulation; they need smarter and more effective regulation.

This chapter proposes a framework for regulatory reform that begins with the observation that financial manias and panics cannot be legislated away, and may be an unavoidable aspect of modern capitalism—a consequence of the interactions between hardwired human behaviour and the unfettered ability to innovate, compete, and evolve. However, the truly disruptive systemic effects of bubbles and crashes arise not from financial loss, but rather from certain groups of investors being unprepared for such losses. For example, hedge fund investors lost hundreds of billions of dollars of wealth in 2007 and 2008, but these losses were not at the heart of the subsequent credit

---

[1] This chapter is adapted from Lo (2009).

The Adaptive Markets Hypothesis. Andrew W. Lo and Ruixun Zhang, Oxford University Press. © Andrew W. Lo and Ruixun Zhang (2024). DOI: 10.1093/oso/9780199681143.003.0020

crisis that developed (see Chapters 16 and 17). Instead, the consequences of losses by banks, insurance companies, and money market funds—entities that were undercapitalized relative to the magnitude of their losses—were far more serious for the global financial system.

The most disruptive effects of financial crises can therefore be reduced significantly by ensuring that the appropriate parties are bearing the appropriate risks, and this, in turn, is best achieved through greater transparency, particularly risk transparency, and the necessary expertise to make use of it (i.e. education). With sufficient transparency and knowledge, many of the problems posed by financial excess can be solved by market forces and private enterprise, and such solutions are often more efficient and more effective than government intervention. Facilitating access to information and education should be one of the two primary objectives of regulation.

The second primary objective of regulation should be to address the undesirable consequences of human behaviour that are not adequately addressed by private markets and normal economic activity. Economists usually attribute such consequences to externalities, public goods, and incomplete markets (see Section 19.2.4), but there is an additional motivation for regulation: human behaviour that is driven not by logic and rationality, but by emotion (see also Chapters 11–13). For example, fear and greed are among the most powerful of human emotions, and the deep roots of most financial calamities can be traced to these twin forces—greed, which inflates asset bubbles to unsustainable levels, and the fear that ultimately causes the bubble to burst via panic selling. These are the 'animal spirits' that Keynes cited as a key driver of business cycle fluctuations, and also one of the reasons that he concluded, 'the market can stay irrational longer than you can stay solvent'.

If we acknowledge that the two main purposes of regulation are to facilitate access to information and education, and to address market failures and human behaviour, then a number of implications for regulatory reform follow naturally:

1. Before we can hope to manage the risks of financial crises effectively, we must be able to define and measure those risks explicitly. Therefore, the first order of business for designing new regulations is to develop a formal definition of systemic risk, and to construct specific measures that are sufficiently practical and encompassing to be used by policymakers and the public. Such measures may require hedge funds and other parts of the shadow banking system to provide more transparency on a confidential basis to regulators (see item 10 below).
2. The most pressing regulatory change with respect to the financial system is to provide the public with information regarding those

institutions that have 'blown up' (i.e. failed in one sense or another). This could be accomplished by establishing an independent investigatory agency, a Capital Markets Safety Board (CMSB) along the lines of the National Transportation Safety Board (NTSB), which we touched upon in Chapters 11 and 19, and describe in more detail in Section 20.6.

3. To the average American, the financial crisis of 2008 is still a mystery even after more than a decade, and concepts like subprime mortgages, collateralized debt obligations (CDOs), credit default swaps (CDSs), and the 'seizing up' of credit markets only creates more confusion and fear. A critical part of any crisis management protocol is to establish clear and regular lines of communication with the public, and a dedicated interagency team of public relations professionals should be formed for this express purpose, possibly within the CMSB. In addition, the CMSB should be charged with the following additional mandates:

   • maintain a historical record of financial blow-ups;
   • measure and monitor systemic risks using a variety of analytics;
   • engage in active research on issues involving systemic risk.

4. Current GAAP (Generally Accepted Accounting Principles) accounting methods are backward-looking by definition, and not ideally suited to providing risk transparency, yet accounting measures are the primary inputs to corporate decisions and regulatory requirements. A new branch of accounting—risk accounting—must be developed and widely implemented before we can truly measure and manage systemic risk on a global scale.

5. The most significant dislocation stemming from the financial crisis of 2008 was due to the 'shadow hedge fund system', the banks, insurance companies, and money market funds that took on greater risks than for which they were prepared. A major overhaul of the regulatory infrastructure for these entities is needed to simplify compliance, re-align capital requirements with accounting rules and liquidity risk, and implement counter-cyclical leverage constraints. Also, current bankruptcy laws should be revised to allow 'pre-packaged' bankruptcies for banks, insurance companies, broker-dealers, and other financial institutions facing unusually high costs of financial distress. Finally, as we have done with utilities and other natural monopolies, any financial companies that are 'too big to fail' should be broken up into smaller entities that are no longer too big to fail.

6. All technology-focused industries run the risk of technological innovations which temporarily exceed our ability to use those technologies

wisely. In the same way that government grants currently support the majority of PhD programmes in science and engineering, new funding should be allocated to major universities to greatly expand degree programmes in financial technology. A portion of these funds could be raised by imposing a small fee on derivatives transactions.

7. To the extent that the financial crisis was fuelled by corporate leaders and directors who did not fully understand the risks of the securities in which they were investing, minimum educational standards with periodic certification checks should be required for the senior management and directors of institutions involved in securitized debt, derivatives, and other complex financial instruments.

8. The complexity of financial markets is straining the capacity of regulators to keep up with its innovations, many of which were not contemplated when the existing regulatory bodies were first formed. New regulations should be adaptive and focused on financial functions rather than institutions, making them more flexible and dynamic. An example of an adaptive regulation is a requirement to standardize an over-the-counter (OTC) contract and create an organized exchange for it (with standardized contracts, a clearing corporation, and daily mark-to-market and settlement) whenever its size—as measured by open interest, trading volume, or notional exposure—exceeds a certain threshold. The CDS market should be among the first to be transformed into an exchange.

9. Human behaviour is a factor in the dynamics of all organizations, both public and private. Therefore, regulations should be designed to counterbalance the unavoidable and predictable tendencies of both sectors during periods of prosperity, when businesses tend to over-extend their activities, and regulators and policymakers are less likely to rein them in because of their apparent success, and during periods of decline, when businesses tend to contract, and regulators and policymakers over-react to the excesses that preceded the contraction. Also, corporate governance structures need to be revised to allow more independence for the risk-management function, for example by appointing a chief risk officer (CRO) who reports directly to the board of directors and whose compensation is tied to the stability of the company and not to last year's profits (see Section 19.6).

10. While the most significant fall-out from the financial crisis of 2008 was due to banks, insurance companies, and money market funds, the 'shadow banking system'—hedge funds and proprietary trading operations—nevertheless contributed to systemic risk, and may be a valuable source of early warning signals for broader dislocation in

financial markets (see, e.g., Section 16.6.1). Therefore, hedge funds and other proprietary trading entities with assets above $1 billion should be required to satisfy certain capital adequacy requirements as dictated by the Federal Reserve ('the Fed'), and also required to provide monthly disclosures to the Fed regarding the following information: (1) assets under management; (2) leverage; (3) securities held; (4) illiquidity exposure; (5) investor base; and (6) other risk analytics, as needed, to measure systemic risk exposures.

11. Legislative inertia and the cost of regulatory reform suggest that whenever possible, we should make use of existing structures to deal with the financial crisis of 2008. Two clear examples include Robert C. Merton's proposal to require money market funds with net asset values fixed at $1 per share to purchase explicit insurance contracts that will allow them to make good on this implicit guarantee of principal (which is covered by existing truth-in-advertising laws), and Macey et al.'s (2008) proposal to enforce suitability requirements for mortgage-broker advice (which is covered under the 1940 Investment Adviser's Act).

12. The ultimate protection against financial excess and crisis is a more sophisticated population of consumers and investors. To that end, basic economic and financial reasoning and the principles of risk management should be taught to high-school students in the ninth or tenth grade.

Before turning to the details of these proposals and their motivation, it should be noted that although much of the material in this chapter is based on and informed by academic research, a significant portion of the inferences surrounding systemic risk is indirect and circumstantial, due to the lack of transparency of certain parts of the financial industry. Without more comprehensive data on characteristics such as assets under management, leverage, counterparty relationships, and portfolio holdings, it is virtually impossible to draw conclusive inferences about the level of systemic risk in the financial sector. We will attempt to point out the most fragile of our claims below, but readers are cautioned to bear in mind the tentative and potentially controversial nature of some of the conclusions and recommendations.

Also, it should be emphasized that this chapter is intended for a broader audience of policymakers and regulators. In particular, academic readers may be alarmed by the lack of comprehensive citations and literature review, the imprecise and qualitative nature of certain arguments, and the abundance of illustrative examples, analogies, and metaphors. Accordingly, such readers are hereby forewarned—this chapter is *not* research, but is instead a summary of the policy implications that we have drawn from our interpretation of that research.

20.1 Measures of Systemic Risk

Despite the length of time since the 2008 financial crisis, and the fact that 'systemic risk' has come into common usage, there is still no commonly agreed-upon definition or quantification of this important but elusive concept. Like Justice Potter Stewart's definition of the obscene, systemic risk has historically been defined in a similar fashion, mainly by central bankers who know it when they see it. Systemic risk is usually taken to mean the risk of a broad-based breakdown in the financial system, often realized as a series of correlated defaults among financial institutions, typically banks, that occurs over a short period of time, and typically is caused by a single major event. The classic example is a banking panic in which large groups of depositors decide to withdraw their funds simultaneously, creating a 'run' on bank assets that can ultimately lead to multiple bank failures. Banking panics were not uncommon in the US during the nineteenth and early twentieth centuries, culminating in 1930–1933, a period of time with an average of 2,000 bank failures per year (Mishkin, 1997), which prompted the Glass–Steagall Act of 1933 and the establishment of the Federal Deposit Insurance Corporation (FDIC) in 1934.

Although banking panics are virtually nonexistent today, thanks to the FDIC and related central banking policies, systemic risk exposures have taken shape in other forms. In particular, many financial institutions now provide some of the same services that banks have traditionally provided but are outside of the banking system. For example, securitization has opened up new sources of capital to finance various types of borrowing that used to be the exclusive province of banks, including credit card debt, trade credit, auto and student loans, mortgages, small business loans, and revolving credit agreements. This so-called shadow banking system—consisting of investment banks, hedge funds, mutual funds, insurance companies, pension funds, endowments and foundations, and various broker-dealers and related intermediaries—has provided a significant fraction of the liquidity needs of the global economy over the past half century, supporting the growth and prosperity that we have enjoyed. After the repeal of the Glass–Steagall Act in 1999, the shadow banking system grew even more rapidly in size and importance. However, as its name suggests, the shadow banking system is neither observable nor controlled by the regulatory bodies that were created to manage the risks of potential liquidity disruptions. Therefore, it is not surprising that we were unprepared for a financial crisis in 2008, and lacked the proper tools to manage it effectively.

The starting point for regulatory reform is to develop a formal definition of systemic risk, one that captures the linkages and vulnerabilities of the entire financial system, not just those of the banking system. From such a definition, several quantitative measures of systemic risk should follow, with which we can monitor and manage the overall level of risk to the financial system. Even the most conservative central banker would agree that attempting to eliminate all systemic risk is neither feasible nor desirable—risk is an unavoidable by-product of financial innovation. But, unless we are able to measure this type of risk objectively and quantitatively, it is impossible to determine the appropriate trade-off between such risk and its rewards.

Given the complexity of the global financial system, it is unrealistic to expect that a single measure of systemic risk will suffice. A more plausible alternative is a collection of measures, each designed to capture a specific risk exposure. For example, any comprehensive collection of risk measures should capture the following characteristics of the entire financial system:

- leverage;
- liquidity;
- correlation;
- concentration;
- sensitivities;
- connectedness.

Leverage refers to the aggregate amount of credit that has been extended in the financial system, and liquidity refers to the ease with which investments may be liquidated to raise cash. The precise mechanism by which these two characteristics combine to produce systemic risk is now well understood. Because many investors make use of leverage, their positions are often considerably larger than the amount of collateral posted to support those positions. Leverage has the effect of a magnifying glass, expanding small profit opportunities into larger ones, and also expanding small losses into larger losses. When adverse changes in market prices reduce the market value of collateral, credit is withdrawn quickly, and the subsequent forced liquidation of large positions over short periods of time can lead to widespread financial panic, as we witnessed over the financial crisis of 2008. The more illiquid the portfolio, the larger the price impact of a forced liquidation, which erodes the investor's risk capital that much more quickly. If many investors face the same 'death spiral' at the same time (i.e. if they become more highly correlated during times of distress), and if those investors are obligors of a small number of major financial institutions, then small market movements can cascade quickly into a global financial crisis (see, in particular, the Quant Meltdown described in Chapter 17). This is systemic risk. However, the likelihood of a major dislocation also depends on the degree of correlation among the holdings of financial institutions, how sensitive they are to changes in market prices and economic conditions, how concentrated the risks are among those financial institutions, and how closely connected those institutions are with each other and with the rest of the economy.

Although these six characteristics are simple to state, developing quantitative measures that can be applied to the global financial system may be more challenging. By looking at the financial system as a single portfolio, several useful measures of systemic risk can be derived by applying the standard tools of modern portfolio analysis. For example, Gray, Merton, and Bodie (2010) and Gray and Malone (2008) apply the well-known framework of contingent claims analysis to the macroeconomy, which yields several potentially valuable early warning indicators of systemic risk, including aggregate asset-liability mismatches, nonlinearities in the risk–return profile of the financial sector, and default probabilities for sovereign debt. Getmansky, Lo, and Makarov (2004) propose simple measures of illiquidity risk exposures that can also be applied to the financial system. Chan et al. (2006, 2007) and Lo (2008) contain other risk analytics that are designed to measure sensitivities, correlations, and concentration in traditional and alternative investments, and these measures did provide early warning signs of potential dislocation in the hedge fund industry in 2004 and 2005 (Gimein, 2005). See Chapter 16 for a more detailed discussion of these measures.

Finally, a number of tools from the theory of networks (Watts and Strogatz, 1998; Watts, 1999) may be applicable to analysing vulnerabilities in the financial network. A simple example of this new perspective is contained in Fig. 20.1, which displays the absolute values of correlations among hedge fund indexes over two periods, April 1994–December 2000 and January 2001–June 2007, where thick lines represent absolute correlations greater than 50%, thinner lines represent absolute correlations between 25% and 50%, and no lines represent absolute correlations below 25%. A comparison of the two sub-periods shows a significant increase in the absolute correlations in the more recent sample—the hedge fund industry has clearly become more closely connected. Soramäki et al. (2007) adopted this network perspective by mapping the topology of the Fedwire inter-bank

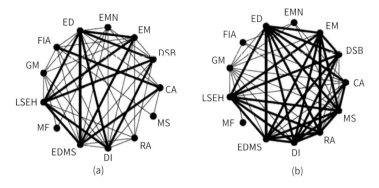

Fig. 20.1 Network diagrams of correlations among thirteen Credit Suisse/Tremont hedge fund indexes over two periods: (a) April 1994–December 2000 (excluding the month of August 1998), and (b) January 2001–June 2007. Thicker lines represent absolute correlations greater than 50%, thinner lines represent absolute correlations between 25% and 50%, and no connecting lines corresponds to correlations less than 25%. CA: convertible arbitrage, DSB: dedicated short bias, EM: emerging markets, EMN: equity market neutral, ED: event driven, FIA: fixed income arbitrage, GM: global macro, LSEH: long/short equity hedge, MF: managed futures, EDMS: event driven multi-strategy, DI: distressed index, RA: risk arbitrage; MS: multi-strategy.

Source: Khandani and Lo (2007). Reprinted with permission from the *Journal of Investment Management.*

payment system, which has generated a number of new insights about the risk exposures of this important network, including the location of the most significant vulnerabilities (Fig. 20.2). Billio et al. (2012) provide a more sophisticated analysis of the network of hedge funds, banks, broker-dealers, and insurance companies using the concept of Granger causality and highlight several interesting properties of such networks and how they can be used to predict threats to financial stability.

Although a number of indirect measures of systemic risk can be computed from existing data, the biggest obstacle is the lack of sufficient transparency with which to implement these measures directly. While banks and other regulated financial institutions already provide such information, the shadow banking system does not (although certain bank assets are not marked to market, which is another form of lack of transparency; see Section 20.7). Without access to primary sources of data—data from hedge funds, their brokers, and other counterparties— it is simply not possible to derive truly actionable measures of systemic risk. Therefore, the need for additional data from all parts of the shadow banking system is a prerequisite for regulatory reform in the hedge fund industry. In particular, we propose that hedge funds with more than $1 billion in gross notional exposures be required to provide regulatory authorities such as the Federal Reserve or the US Securities and

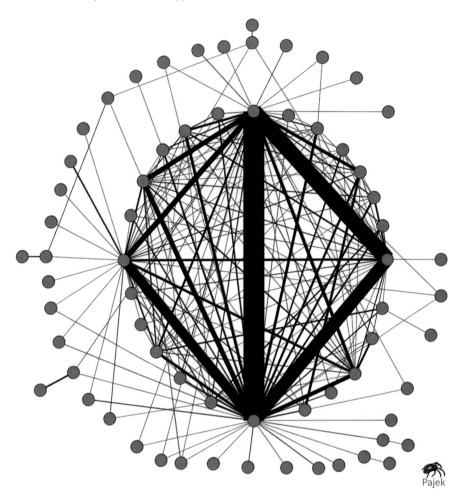

Fig. 20.2 Core of the Fedwire Interbank Payment Network.

Source: Reprinted from Soramäki, K., Bech, M. L., Arnold, J., Glass, R. J., and Beyeler, W. E. (2007). The topology of interbank payment flows. *Physica A: Statistical Mechanics and its Applications* 379: 317–333, with permission from Elsevier.

Exchange Commission (SEC) with the following information on a regular, timely, and confidential basis:

- assets under management;
- leverage;
- mark-to-market portfolio holdings;
- list of credit counterparties;
- list of investors.

Given the large number of hedge funds versus the much smaller number of prime brokers (i.e. brokers that have hedge funds as clients), it may be more efficient for regulatory authorities to obtain these data directly from the prime brokers, or even to ask prime brokers to compute certain risk analytics specified by regulators, and provide them electronically on an automated basis to regulators to preserve confidentiality and streamline the reporting process.

However, it is important to balance the desire for transparency against the necessity of preserving the intellectual property that hedge funds possess. Unlike other technology-based industries, the vast majority of financial innovations are protected through trade secrecy, not patents.[2] Hedge funds are among the most secretive of financial institutions because their franchise value is almost entirely based on the performance of their investment strategies, and this type of intellectual property is perhaps the most difficult to patent. Therefore, hedge funds have an affirmative obligation to their investors to protect the confidentiality of their investment products and processes. If hedge funds are forced to reveal their strategies, the most intellectually innovative ones will simply cease to exist, or move to other less intrusive regulatory jurisdictions. This would be a major loss to US capital markets and the US economy.

Therefore, it is imperative that regulators tread carefully with respect to this issue. One compromise is for regulators to obtain aggregated, redacted, and coded hedge fund information—possibly pre-computed risk analytics described above—from the prime brokers that service hedge funds. This approach is operationally more efficient (there are only a few prime brokers, and they service the majority of hedge funds), and by assigning anonymous codes to every fund, so that the identities of the hedge funds are not divulged, but their information is stored in a consistent fashion across multiple prime brokers, or by transmitting pre-computed risk analytics, the proprietary aspects of the hedge funds' portfolios and strategies are protected. A more sophisticated approach is to use cryptographic methods such as secure multi-party computation to encrypt data of individual financial institutions in such a way as to allow regulators the ability to compute aggregate risk statistics without being able to reverse-engineer the data of any individual institution. See Abbe, Khandani, and Lo (2012) and de Castro et al. (2020) for examples of this technology applied to financial data.

20.2 The Shadow Banking System

As Chapter 16 showed, one of the most vibrant parts of the financial sector over the last several decades has been the hedge fund industry. Relatively unconstrained by regulatory oversight, motivated by profit-sharing incentive

---

[2] See Lerner (2002) for a review of financial patents.

fees, and drawn to far-flung corners of the investment universe, hedge funds have taken on a broad array of risks that would have otherwise been borne by less willing market participants. The increased risk-sharing capacity and liquidity provided by hedge funds over the last decade has contributed significantly to the growth and prosperity that the global economy has enjoyed. For example, hedge funds and private equity firms have raised tens of billions of dollars over the past several years for infrastructure investments (e.g. highways, bridges, power plants, and waste treatment and water purification facilities in India, Africa, and the Middle East). In their quest for greater profitability, hedge funds now provide liquidity in every major market, taking on the role of banks in fixed-income and money markets, and market-makers and broker-dealers in equities and derivatives markets. During times of prosperity, hedge funds are the 'tip of the spear' of the investment industry, the first to take advantage of lucrative and unique investment opportunities. However, during times of distress, hedge funds are the 'canary in the coal mine', the first to suffer losses and show signs of market dislocation, as in the Quant Meltdown of 2007 (see Chapter 17). Therefore, hedge funds play critical roles not only in capital formation and economic growth, but also as early warning signs of impending systemic shocks.

As part of the shadow banking system, hedge funds lie outside the purview of the Federal Reserve, the Office of the Comptroller of the Currency (OCC), the SEC, the Commodity Futures Trading Commission (CFTC), and the Treasury. Therefore, it is impossible to determine definitively their contribution to systemic risk. As early as 2004, Chan et al. (2004) presented indirect evidence that the level of systemic risk in the hedge fund industry had increased; in particular, they conclude with the following summary:

- The hedge fund industry has grown tremendously over the last few years, fuelled by the demand for higher returns in the face of stock market declines and mounting pension fund liabilities. These massive fund inflows have had a material impact on hedge fund returns and risks in recent years, as evidenced by changes in correlations, reduced performance, increased illiquidity as measured by the weighted autocorrelation, ρ_t^*, and the large number of hedge funds launched and closed.
- The banking sector is exposed to hedge fund risks, especially smaller institutions, but the largest banks are also exposed through proprietary trading activities, credit arrangements and structured products, and prime brokerage services.
- The risks facing hedge funds are nonlinear and more complex than those facing traditional asset classes. Because of the dynamic nature of hedge fund investment strategies, and the impact of fund flows

on leverage and performance, hedge fund risk models require more sophisticated analytics, and more sophisticated users.

- The sum of regime-switching models' high-volatility or low mean state probabilities can measure the aggregate level of distress in the hedge fund sector. Recent measurements suggest that we may be entering a challenging period. This, coupled with the recent uptrend in the weighted autocorrelation, ρ_t^*, implies that systemic risk is increasing.

Although based on indirect technical research findings, these conclusions were not hard to justify from casual empirical observation of general economic conditions over several decades. The low interest rate and low credit spread environment of the 1990s created greater competition for yield among investors, causing large sums of money from retail and institutional investors to flow into virtually every type of higher-yielding investment opportunity available, including hedge funds, mutual funds, residential real estate, mortgages, and, of course, CDOs, CDSs, and other exotic securities. This push for yield also manifested itself in significant legislative pressure to relax certain constraints, resulting in the repeal of the Glass–Steagall Act and the growth of government-sponsored enterprises such as Fannie Mae and Freddie Mac. The overall impact of these conditions was to create an over-extended financial system—part of which was invisible to regulators and outside their direct control—that could not be sustained indefinitely. Moreover, the financial system became so crowded in terms of the extraordinary amounts of capital deployed in every corner of every investable market, that the overall liquidity of those markets declined significantly.

The consequences of this crowdedness are simple: the first sign of trouble in one part of the financial system will cause nervous investors to rush for the exits, but—as the analogy suggests—it is impossible for everyone to get out at once, and this panic can quickly spread to other parts of the financial system. To develop a sense for the potential scale of such a panic, consider the growth of hedge fund assets from 1990 to 2008 plotted in Fig. 20.3, and note the sharp decline in assets and leverage in 2008 (with Q4 of 2008 estimated by Credit Suisse). The responsiveness of hedge fund investors to underperformance is well known, and these relatively rapid changes in risk capital can lead to the kind of wild market gyrations we experienced in 2007–2008 (see also Chapter 17 and an analysis of the August 2007 Quant Meltdown by Khandani and Lo (2007, 2011b)).

In 2006 and 2007, Chan et al. (2006, 2007) extended these tentative conclusions with additional data and analytics, and, with each iteration, they uncovered more indirect evidence for increasing levels of systemic risk. As

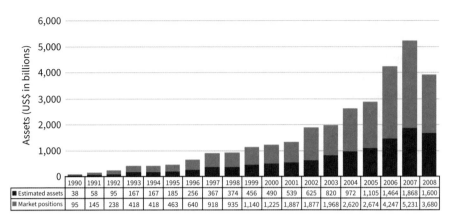

	1990	1991	1992	1993	1994	1995	1996	1997	1998	1999	2000	2001	2002	2003	2004	2005	2006	2007	2008
■ Estimated assets	38	58	95	167	167	185	256	367	374	456	490	539	625	820	972	1,105	1,464	1,868	1,600
■ Market positions	95	145	238	418	418	463	640	918	935	1,140	1,225	1,887	1,877	1,968	2,620	2,674	4,247	5,231	3,680

Fig. 20.3 Growth of assets and leverage in the hedge fund industry from 1990 to 2008. *Source:* Lo (2009, Figure 3).

Chapter 16 described, the recurring themes from their analysis were increasing assets flowing into all parts of the hedge fund industry; correspondingly lower returns, presumably as a result of these increased asset levels; greater illiquidity risk and leverage as hedge funds undertook more exotic investments using greater leverage to boost their returns; and, finally, greater correlation among different hedge fund strategies, particularly with respect to losses. These themes built to a crescendo in the first half of 2007, with the demise of several prominent multi-billion-dollar hedge funds involved in mortgage-backed securities (MBSs) and credit-related strategies, and apparently caused significant dislocation in August 2007 in a completely unrelated part of the hedge fund industry—long/short equity market neutral funds—because of desperate attempts by investors to reduce risk and raise cash to meet margin calls (see Chapter 17 and Khandani and Lo (2007, 2011b)).

But why should we be concerned about the fortunes of private partnerships or wealthy investors? The reason is that, over the last several decades, these investors and funds have become central to the global financial system, providing loans, liquidity, insurance, risk-sharing, and other importance services that used to be the exclusive domain of banks. But, unlike banks—which are highly regulated entities (although less so since the repeal of the Glass–Steagall Act in 1999), with specific capital adequacy requirements and leverage and risk constraints—hedge funds and their investors are relatively unconstrained. This freedom is important. By giving managers a broad investment mandate, hedge fund investors are able to garner higher returns on their investments in various economic environments, including market downturns and recessions. The dynamic and highly competitive nature of hedge funds also implies that such investors will shift their assets tactically and quickly, moving into markets when profit opportunities arise, and moving out when those opportunities have been depleted. Although such tactics benefit hedge fund investors, they can also cause market dislocation in crowded markets with participants that are not fully aware of or prepared for the crowdedness of their investments.

Beyond the proposal of Section 20.1 requiring hedge funds to provide additional data to regulators, it may be necessary to expand the scope of the Fed to include direct oversight for the very largest hedge funds, their prime brokers, and other related financial institutions such as certain insurance companies engaged in bank-like activities (e.g. highly leveraged loans, credit guarantees, and retail liquidity provision). If the Fed is expected to serve as lender of last resort to nonbank financial institutions during times of distress, such institutions should be part of the Fed's permanent regulatory mandate during times of calm, which includes capital adequacy requirements, leverage restrictions, and periodic on-site examinations.

20.3 The Shadow Hedge Fund System

While the shadow banking system has no doubt contributed to systemic risk in the financial industry, hedge funds played only a minor role in the 2008 financial crisis, as evidenced by the lack of attention they received in the government's crisis bailout response. Instead, the main focus of the government's rescue packages centred on the 'shadow hedge fund system', the banks, insurance companies, money market funds, and other financial institutions that were engaged—in some cases unknowingly—in hedge fund-like investments, and who were unprepared for the magnitude of losses in their portfolios caused by the decline of the US residential real estate market in 2007 and 2008. Unlike hedge fund investors, who are typically high net-worth individuals, funds of funds, or other institutional investors, who can withstand large losses and illiquidity in their hedge fund investments, bank depositors and money market fund investors expect neither from their deposits and money market accounts. Moreover, money market funds actively promote the belief that there is instant liquidity and no risk to principal by maintaining a constant net asset value of $1 and daily liquidity. When faced with an unexpected loss of principal and restrictions on redemptions, it is no surprise that the reaction is panic, massive attempted withdrawals, and a flight to US Treasuries and cash. Similar reactions have stalled other important credit markets, including markets for commercial paper, auction rate securities, and corporate bonds.

Perhaps the most significant casualty of the financial crisis of 2008 was the banking sector, which became undercapitalized due to large losses from MBSs, CDOs, and other so-called toxic assets that were previously considered high-quality and traded close to par prior to 2007. In response to these losses, banks decreased their lending, both to preserve capital in case of further deterioration of their assets, and to avoid lending to financial institutions with toxic assets of their own. The lack of transparency of these assets, coupled with their illiquidity, greatly reduced the availability of credit in the banking sector, with predictable effects on real economic activity.

But the pejorative term 'toxic asset' is misleading, implying some intrinsic properties of these bonds might contaminate all who come into contact with them. In fact, when priced properly (i.e. marked to market), these securities are like any other and, in the aftermath of the 2008 financial crisis, many of these much-maligned instruments have become quite attractive. Their supposed toxicity stemmed from two sources: their illiquidity and the fact that, with the benefit of hindsight, many of them were assigned overly optimistic credit ratings and therefore priced incorrectly when issued. But these two issues are intimately related; the illiquidity of the CDO market was largely driven by the fact that holders of CDOs were unwilling to sell at fire-sale prices given their subjective valuations of these securities' cashflows and credit risks, and potential buyers were unwilling to pay anything close to the original prices of these securities given the decline in the real estate market and deterioration of their credit quality.

Ordinarily, a failure of a 'meeting of the minds' between buyer and seller does not turn into a financial crisis. However, when such an event involves a bank, which is required to maintain a certain level of capital relative to its assets (the capital ratio), the consequences of so-called toxic assets on the bank's balance sheet are significant. Banks with such assets will reduce their lending activities, opting instead to preserve capital so as to avoid breaching their required capital ratio threshold. If the largest banks all reduce their lending simultaneously, this yields an industry-wide credit crunch, which, in turn, can lead to a contraction of real economic activity and a recession.

The underlying causes of the challenges faced by the banking industry will no doubt be the subject of many studies for years to come, and with the benefit of time and sufficient hindsight, a clearer picture will emerge. But even in the midst of the crisis, several obvious themes could be identified. Heightened competition over the previous decade—from investment banks and, thanks to securitization, global capital markets—drove banks to broaden their business scope to include non-traditional businesses and assets. The low-yield investment climate during this time also contributed to greater risk-taking and leverage to enhance returns. The rapid pace of financial innovation placed even more pressure on banks and other financial institutions to work harder and faster to keep up with their competition. Finally, the highly regulated environment of the banking industry created unintended risk exposures by allowing persistent mismatches between book and market values of certain bank assets, which were exacerbated by apparently inaccurate credit ratings for those assets and non-performing default insurance contracts on those assets.

The fact that several insurance companies also defaulted on their credit-default insurance contracts may seem surprising, given that insurance companies are in the business of assessing such risks and diversifying them across large uncorrelated populations of policyholders. Their extraordinary losses suggest one or more of the following:

- they underestimated the correlations;
- they were misled by the credit ratings of the bonds they insured;
- they were too aggressive in providing such insurance at rates that were unsustainably low, due to competition from non-traditional insurance providers that entered the industry through the CDS market;
- they did not maintain adequate reserves to prepare for such risks because CDSs fell outside the regulatory oversight of traditional insurance markets.

These dislocations among banks, insurance companies, and money market funds—among the most heavily regulated entities of the US economy—suggest that regulatory reform has particular urgency in these critical industries, more so than in any other part of the financial services industry. The reason is clear—all three types of entities interact directly with the public and provide services that are essential to basic business and consumer activity: credit, liquidity, and transactional efficiency. Apart from the direct benefits that these businesses provide, there are many well-known positive externalities that affect consumer confidence, spending patterns, employment levels, and real investment activity. Therefore, the systemic risk is considerably higher in these industries than in any others. Without a stable and robust financial services sector, economic recovery and growth are simply not possible.

Regulatory reform in such highly regulated industries is not a simple matter, and much of the focus of the government's rescue plans in the wake of the 2008 crisis centred on these issues. Despite the many new regulations and organizations that were created, more can be done to address future crises.

- As we have done with utilities and other business entities, banks and insurance companies that are 'too big to fail' should be broken up into smaller units that are not too big to fail.
- The CDS market should be converted to an organized exchange with standardized contracts, a clearing corporation, and daily mark-to-market and settlement.
- Robert C. Merton has proposed that money market funds with net asset values fixed at \$1 per share should be required to purchase explicit insurance contracts that will allow them to make good on this implicit guarantee of principal.
- The regulatory infrastructure for banks and insurance companies needs a major overhaul because it was originally designed to cover a much narrower and simpler set of business activities and instruments than those confronting today's banks and insurance companies. A major focus should be to reconsider how required capital ratio rules interact with mark-to-market accounting rules for computing such ratios (Section 20.7).

20.4 Behavioural Foundations of Systemic Risk

Apart from the obvious and indisputable need to develop measures of systemic risk and to require financial institutions to provide additional data to regulators, more specific regulatory reforms require a deeper understanding of the underlying causes of the crisis. There is, of course, no shortage of culprits on which the crisis can be pinned. The following is a partial list of participants who were complicit in the rise and fall of the real-estate market and the financial side-bets that went along with the bubble:

- homeowners;
- commercial banks and savings and loan associations;
- investment banks and other issuers of MBSs, CDOs, and CDSs;
- mortgage lenders, brokers, servicers, and trustees;
- credit rating agencies;
- insurance companies;
- investors (hedge funds, pension funds, sovereign wealth funds, mutual funds, endowments, and other investment institutions);
- regulators (SEC, OCC, CFTC, the Fed, etc.);

- government-sponsored enterprises;
- politicians and their constituents.

Unsurprisingly, with a crisis of this magnitude, all of us played a part in its care and feeding, and there is plenty of blame to go around. However, a more productive line of inquiry is to identify causal factors that can *only* be addressed through regulatory oversight. To that end, there are two observations that may be useful in identifying such factors.

The first observation is that the crisis of 2008 was not unique. Despite the number of seemingly unprecedented events that transpired in 2007 and 2008, from a longer and global historical perspective, credit crises occur with some regularity. Consider, for example, the following set of concerns regarding the strength of the banking system expressed by a US central banker:

> …first, the attenuation of the banking systems' base of equity capital; second, greater reliance on funds of a potentially volatile character; third, heavy loan commitments in relation to resources; fourth, some deterioration in the quality of assets; and, fifth, increased exposure to the larger banks to risks entailed in foreign exchange transactions and other foreign operations.

This seems as relevant today as it was in 1974 when Federal Reserve chairman Arthur Burns spoke before the American Bankers Association about the soundness of the banking system (Minsky, 2008, p. 57). In his conclusion, Burns observed that 'our regulatory system failed to keep pace with the need', and 'a substantial reorganization [of the regulatory machinery] will be required to overcome the problems inherent in the existing structural arrangement'.

Reinhart and Rogoff (2009) provide a more systematic analysis of the uniqueness of the subprime mortgage meltdown of 2007–2008 by identifying eighteen bank-centred financial crises that have occurred around the world since 1974,[3] and come to the following conclusion after comparing them to the financial crisis of 2008:

> Our examination of the longer historical record, which is part of a larger effort on currency and debt crises, finds stunning qualitative and quantitative parallels across a number of standard financial crisis indicators. To name a few, the run-up in U.S. equity and housing prices that Graciela L. Kaminsky and Carmen

---

[3] In particular, Reinhart and Rogoff (2009) identify five 'big' crises (with the year in which the crisis started in parentheses)—Spain (1977), Norway (1987), Finland (1991), Sweden (1991), and Japan (1992)—and thirteen other banking and financial crises—the UK (1974, 1991, 1995), Germany (1977), Canada (1983), the US (1984), Iceland (1985), Denmark (1987), New Zealand (1987), Australia (1989), Italy (1990), Greece (1991), and France (1994).

M. Reinhart (1999) find to be the best leading indicators of crisis in countries experiencing large capital inflows closely tracks the average of the previous eighteen post-World War II banking crises in industrial countries. So, too, does the inverted V-shape of real growth in the years prior to the crisis. Despite widespread concern about the effects on national debt of the early 2000s tax cuts, the run-up in U.S. public debt is actually somewhat below the average of other crisis episodes.

Figure 20.4 shows four graphs from Reinhart and Rogoff (2009) that highlight the remarkable parallels in real housing prices, real equity prices, real gross domestic product (GDP) growth per capita, and public debt as a fraction of GDP between the financial crisis of 2008 and the eighteen other financial crises that have occurred in various countries since 1974.

The second observation is that the common theme in the majority of these crises is a period of great financial liberalization and prosperity that preceded the crisis (Kaminsky and Reinhart, 1999; Reinhart and Rogoff, 2008). While this boom–bust pattern is familiar to macroeconomists, who

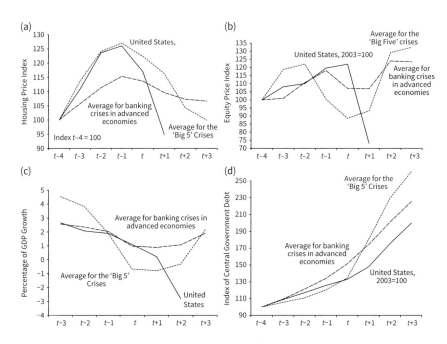

Fig. 20.4 Comparison of (a) real housing prices; (b) real equity prices; (c) real GDP growth per capita; and (d) public debt as a fraction of GDP to those of other countries before, during, and after eighteen financial crises between 1974 and 2009.

Source: Republished with permission of Princeton University Press, from *This Time Is Different: Eight Centuries of Financial Folly*, Carmen M. Reinhart and Kenneth S. Rogoff, 2009. Permission conveyed through Copyright Clearance Center, Inc.

have developed complex models for generating business cycles, there may be a simpler explanation based on human behaviour. During extended periods of prosperity, market participants become complacent about the risk of loss—either through systematic underestimation of those risks because of recent history, or a decline in their risk aversion due to increasing wealth, or both (see Chapter 9 for discussions on the evolutionary origin of short memory). In fact, there is mounting evidence from cognitive neuroscientists that financial gain affects the same 'pleasure centres' of the brain that are activated by certain narcotics (see also Chapter 11).[4] This suggests that prolonged periods of economic growth and prosperity can induce a collective sense of euphoria and complacency among investors that is not unlike the drug-induced stupor of a cocaine addict. Moreover, the financial liberalization that typically accompanies this prosperity implies a greater availability of risk capital, greater competition for new sources of excess expected returns, more highly correlated risk-taking behaviour because of the 'crowded trade' phenomenon, and a false sense of security derived from peers who engage in the same behaviour and with apparent success.

Consider, for example, the case of a CRO of a major investment bank XYZ, a firm actively engaged in issuing and trading CDOs in 2004. Suppose this CRO was convinced that US residential real estate was a bubble that was about to burst and, based on a simple scenario analysis, realized there would be devastating consequences for their firm. What possible actions could they have taken to protect their shareholders? They might ask the firm to exit the CDO business, to which their superiors would respond that the CDO business was one of the most profitable over the past decade with considerable growth potential, other competitors are getting into the business, not leaving, and the historical data suggest that real estate values would be unlikely to fall by more than 1 or 2 per cent per year, so why should XYZ consider exiting and giving up its precious market share? Unable to convince senior management of the likelihood of a real estate downturn, the CRO suggests a compromise—reduce the firm's CDO exposure by half. Senior management's likely response would be that such a reduction in XYZ's CDO business will decrease the group's profits by half, causing the most talented members of the group to leave the firm, either to join XYZ's competitors, or to launch a hedge fund. Given the cost of assembling and training these professionals, and the fact that they have generated sizeable profits over the recent past,

---

[4] In particular, the same neural circuitry that responds to cocaine, food, and sex—the mesolimbic dopamine reward system that releases dopamine in the nucleus accumbens—has also been shown to be activated by monetary gain (Delgado et al., 2000; Breiter et al., 2001; Montague and Berns, 2002; Schultz, 2002; Knutson and Peterson, 2005).

scaling down their business is also difficult to justify. Finally, suppose the CRO takes matters into their own hands and implements a hedging strategy using OTC derivatives to bet against the CDO market.[5] From 2004 to 2006, such a hedging strategy would likely have yielded significant losses, and the reduction in XYZ's earnings due to this hedge, coupled with the strong performance of the CDO business for XYZ and its competitors, would be sufficient grounds for dismissing the CRO.

In this simple thought experiment, all parties are acting in good faith, and from their individual perspectives, acting in the best interests of the shareholders. Yet the most likely outcome is the financial crisis of 2008. This suggests that the ultimate origin of the crisis may be human behaviour—the profit motive, the intoxicating and anaesthetic effects of success, and the panic sell-off that inevitably brings that success to an end.

Economists do not naturally gravitate towards behavioural explanations of economic phenomena, preferring instead the framework of rational deliberation by optimizing agents in a free-market context as described in Section 19.2.4. The inexorable logic of neoclassical economics is difficult to challenge. However, research in the cognitive neurosciences has provided equally compelling experimental evidence that human decision-making consists of a complex blend of logical calculation and emotional response (see Part III). Under normal circumstances, that blend typically leads to decisions that work well in free markets. However, under extreme conditions, the balance between logic and emotion can shift, leading to extreme behaviour such as the gyrations in stock markets around the world in September and October 2008 and during the initial phases of the COVID-19 pandemic in 2020.

This perspective implies that preferences may not be stable through time or over circumstances, but are likely to be shaped by a number of factors, both internal and external to the individual (i.e. factors related to the individual's personality, and factors related to specific environmental conditions in which the individual is currently situated). As we established in Parts I and II, when environmental conditions shift, we should expect behaviour to change in response, both through learning and, over time, through changes in preferences via the forces of natural selection. These evolutionary underpinnings are more than simple speculation in the context of financial market participants. The extraordinary degree of competitiveness of global financial

---

[5] In fact, most CROs do not have unilateral authority to engage in such hedging strategies, but let us endow them with such powers just to illustrate how difficult it would be for any single individual to rein in the risk budgets of firms profiting from subprime-related activities in the most recent years leading up to the crisis.

markets and the winner-take-all nature of the competition suggest that Darwinian selection is at work in determining the typical profile of the successful investor. After all, unsuccessful market participants are eventually eliminated from the population after suffering a certain level of losses. This is why we called the hedge fund industry the Galápagos Islands of the financial system in Chapter 16—the forces of competition, innovation, and natural selection are visible to the naked eye in that industry.

This perspective also yields a broader interpretation of free-market economics (Lo, 2004, 2005), and presents a new rationale for regulatory oversight. Left to their own devices, market forces generally yield economically efficient outcomes under normal market conditions, and regulatory intervention is not only unnecessary, but often counterproductive. However, under atypical market conditions, whether prolonged periods of prosperity or episodes of great uncertainty, market forces cannot be trusted to yield the most desirable outcomes, which motivates the need for regulation. Of course, the traditional motivation for regulation—market failures due to externalities, natural monopolies, and public goods characteristics—is no less compelling, and the desire to prevent suboptimal behaviour under these conditions provides yet another role for government intervention.

A simple example of this dynamic is the existence of fire codes enacted by federal, state, and local governments requiring all public buildings to have a minimum number of exits, well-lit exit signs, a maximum occupancy, and certain types of sprinklers, smoke detectors, and fire alarms. Why are fire codes necessary? In particular, given the costs associated with compliance, why not let markets determine the appropriate level of fire protection demanded by the public? Those seeking safer buildings should be willing to pay more to occupy them, and those willing to take the risk need not pay for what they deem to be unnecessary fire protection. A perfectly satisfactory outcome of this free-market approach should be a world with two types of buildings, those with fire protection and those without it, leaving the public free to choose between the two according to their risk preferences.

But this is not the outcome that society has chosen. Instead, we require all new buildings to have extensive fire protection, and the simplest explanation for this state of affairs is the recognition—after years of experience and many lost lives—that we systematically underestimate the likelihood of a fire.[6] In fact, assuming that improbable events are impossible is a universal human

---

[6] This phenomenon is a special case of the more general behavioural bias of underestimating the likelihood of negative outcomes, and the heuristic of assigning zero probability to low-probability events (see, e.g., Plous (1993, Chapter 12) and Slovic (2000)).

trait (Plous, 1993; Slovic, 2000). Hence, the typical builder will not voluntarily spend significant sums to prepare for an event that most individuals will not value because they judge the likelihood of such an event to be nil. Of course, experience has shown that fires do occur, and, when they do, it is much too late to add fire protection. What free-market economists interpret as interference with Adam Smith's invisible hand may, instead, be a mechanism for protecting ourselves from our own behavioural blind spots. Just as Odysseus asked his shipmates to tie him to the mast as they sailed past the three Sirens of Circe's islands so he could hear the Sirens' song without being bewitched, we often use regulation as a tool to protect ourselves from our most self-destructive tendencies (e.g. Fed-mandated leverage constraints, speed limits, seat belt laws, and bans on smoking advertisements).[7]

Beyond the natural predilection of human behaviour to excess, there is yet another reason to suspect that financial crises are inevitable. In studying accidents across many industries and professions—including nuclear meltdowns, chemical plant explosions, power grid failures, and airplane crashes—Perrow (1984) identifies two common elements that routinely lead to disaster: complexity and tight coupling. The former concept is clear. The latter is defined by Perrow (1984, pp. 89–90) as 'a mechanical term meaning there is no slack or buffer or give between two items [in a system]. What happens to one directly affects what happens in the other…'. Perrow concludes that accidents are normal and to be expected in complex systems that are tightly coupled. The current financial system certainly satisfies the complexity criterion (see Figs 20.6 and 20.7, and the discussion in Section 20.8), and the credit relationships between various counterparties—and the legal, accounting, and regulatory constraints on collateral and liquidity—have created tight coupling among many parts of the financial system. Financial crises are normal accidents.

20.5 A Process for Regulatory Design and Reform

With respect to regulatory reform, we acknowledge that an academic may not be in the best position to make recommendations—legislation is, perhaps, best left to professional legislators. However, we do think that academic research can inform the process of regulatory reform, and may provide useful

---

[7] Externalities also play an important role in the motivation for regulation. For example, fires can spread easily from one building to the next, yet there is no way for the market to properly compensate developers for the public benefits that would accrue to the installation of fire prevention in their individual buildings. Hence, regulation is desirable in this case. However, if this were the only motivation for fire prevention, far more economical and localized means for addressing these externalities than state-wide fire codes would have arisen (e.g. block associations for pooling resources to pay for fire prevention).

input in considering priorities, structure, and even implementation. This is the spirit in which we propose a somewhat different perspective to financial regulation in this section.

The behavioural and traditional rationales for regulation lead naturally to a broader approach for formulating policy and regulatory reform, an approach first advocated by Merton and Bodie (1993) for deposit insurance reform that focuses on financial functions, not financial institutions (see also Merton, 1993, 1995a,b; Crane et al., 1995; Hogan and Sharpe, 1997; Merton and Bodie, 2006). The functional approach to studying financial institutions and regulation begins with the observation that there are six functions of the financial system—a payments system, a pooling mechanism for undertaking large-scale investments, resource transfer across time and space, risk management, information provision for coordinating decisions, and a means of contracting and managing agency problems. Because functions tend to be more stable than institutions, regulations designed around functional specifications are less likely to generate unintended consequences.

From a functional perspective, the standard economic approach to determining the need for regulatory oversight (i.e. identifying market failures) may be applied to various functions of the financial system. Among the possible sources of market failures are:

- *Public goods.* Commodities like national defence that benefit everyone, but where no one has an incentive to pay for it because it is not possible to exclude anyone from its benefits once it is produced.
- *Externalities.* Unintended costs or benefits of an activity that are not incorporated into the market price of that activity (e.g. pollution from a factory or live music from a neighbourhood bar).
- *Incomplete markets.* The absence of certain markets because there are insufficient suppliers or demanders of that product or service (e.g. unemployment insurance).
- *Behavioural biases.* Certain patterns of human behaviour that are recognized as undesirable and counterproductive but are likely to occur under particular circumstances (e.g. over-eating, driving while intoxicated, and panic selling investments).

Systemic risk is a public good (or, more accurately, a public 'bad'); hence, government can play a positive role in addressing this market failure. To see this more clearly, consider the converse of systemic risk (i.e. systemic safety). Everyone in the global economy benefits from systemic safety—the assurance that financial markets are stable, liquid, and reliable—but no single individual is willing to pay for this public good (in fact, it is unclear whether most individuals were even aware of the importance of this public good in their own lives until the financial crisis of 2008). The public goods aspect of liquidity in the banking system was clearly recognized by the public and private sectors at the turn of the twentieth century in the US, which led to the development of the Federal Reserve System. However, the growth in importance of the shadow banking system (Section 20.2), as well as the emergence of the shadow hedge fund system (Section 20.3), have significantly reduced the ability of the Federal Reserve to maintain the same level of systemic safety as before. Several new regulations for addressing this issue are proposed in Sections 20.6 and 20.7.

Once a particular market failure is identified, the appropriate regulatory tools needed to address the failure will follow naturally (e.g. subsidies or taxes, proper disclosure of private information, government provision, or new securities regulation). In the case of systemic risk in the financial system, all four characteristics apply to some degree. The government is the natural provider of systemic safety because of the public goods nature of liquidity, stability and reliability, the positive externalities of a well-functioning financial system, the inability of the private sector to credibly provide systemic safety, and because individual behaviour is not reliably rational during just those times when systemic safety is in jeopardy.

The functional perspective can also be applied to the organization of regulatory agencies. In the aftermath of the terrorist attacks of 11 September 2001, the need for better coordination among the US Federal Bureau of Investigation, Central Intelligence Agency, and National Security Agency, and other government agencies became painfully obvious. A similar case can be made for financial regulation, which is currently distributed among several agencies and offices, including the SEC, CFTC, OCC, Office of Thrift Supervision (OTS), Treasury, and the Federal Reserve. Rather than creating a new super-agency to coordinate among existing regulators, it may be more cost-effective to reorganize regulatory responsibilities according to functional lines. For example, the SEC has traditionally focused on protecting investors and ensuring fair and orderly markets, whereas the focus of the Federal Reserve has been to provide liquidity to the banking system as lender of last resort. This suggests a natural division of new regulatory responsibilities, in which the management of systemic risk falls within the Federal Reserve's mandate, and the creation of new exchanges continues to be part of the SEC's mandate. By focusing on functions rather than institutions, a more efficient regulatory infrastructure may be achieved.

The multifaceted nature of systemic risk implies that several approaches to regulatory reform are necessary. Moreover, because of the competitive and adaptive nature of financial markets, the most effective regulations are those that can adapt to changing market conditions. From an archaeological perspective, the body of securities laws may be viewed as the fossil record of the unbounded creativity of unscrupulous financiers in devising new ways to separate individuals from their money, and the multitude of strata of securities regulations trace out the co-evolution of financial misdeeds and the corresponding static regulatory responses. The most durable regulations are those that recognize the adaptive nature of markets and their participants, and are allowed to adapt accordingly.

To illustrate how adaptive regulations may be formulated, consider the CDS market. The magnitude and importance of this OTC market led to the very sensible proposal to establish a CDS exchange with standardized contracts, daily mark-to-market and settlement, and a clearing corporation. An adaptive version of this proposal would be to require the establishment of a similar organized exchange and clearing corporation for any set of OTC contracts that exceeds certain thresholds in volume, open interest, and notional exposure, where such thresholds should be defined in terms of percentages of those quantities in existing markets (e.g. 5% of the combined dollar volume of all organized futures markets). Such an adaptive regulation would promote the orderly and organic creation of new exchanges as the need arises, and reduce the likelihood of systemic shocks emanating from the failure of a small number of too-big-to-fail institutions. Of course, exemptive relief can always be provided under certain conditions, but the benefit of an adaptive regulation is that an orderly transition from small heterogeneous OTC trading to a market that has become vital to global financial system is permanently institutionalized.

20.6 The Capital Markets Safety Board

With any form of technological innovation, there is always the risk that the technology outpaces our ability to use it properly, bringing unintended consequences. The current threat of global warming is, perhaps, the most dramatic example of this common pattern of human progress. But, in the face of space shuttle explosions, nuclear meltdowns, bridge collapses, and airplane crashes, we rarely blame the technology itself, but, instead, seek to understand how our possibly inappropriate use of the technology may have caused the accident. The outcome of that evaluation process may yield improvements in both the technology and how it is used, and this is how progress is made. Technological innovation of any form entails risk, but, as long as we learn from our mistakes, we reduce the risk of future disasters.

In this respect, the financial industry can take a lesson from other technology-based professions. In the medical, chemical engineering, and semiconductor industries, for example, failures are routinely documented, catalogued, analysed, internalized, and used to develop new and improved processes and controls. Each failure is viewed as a valuable lesson, to be studied and reviewed until all the wisdom has been gleaned from it, which is understandable given the typical cost of each lesson.

One of the most successful models for conducting such reviews is the NTSB, briefly described in Chapters 11 and 19. The NTSB is an independent government agency whose primary mission is to investigate transportation-related accidents, provide careful and conclusive forensic analysis, and make recommendations for avoiding such accidents in the future. In the event of an airplane crash, the NTSB assembles a team of engineers and flight-safety experts who are immediately dispatched to the crash site to conduct a thorough investigation, including interviewing witnesses, poring over historical flight logs and maintenance records, and sifting through the wreckage to recover the flight recorder or 'black box' and, if necessary, reassembling the aircraft from its parts so as to determine the ultimate cause of the crash. Once its work is completed, the NTSB publishes a report summarizing the team's investigation, concluding with specific recommendations for avoiding future occurrences of this type of accident. The report is entered into a searchable database that is available to the general public (https://data.ntsb.gov/carol-main-public/landing-page), and this has been one of the major factors underlying the remarkable safety record of commercial air travel.

For example, it is now current practice to spray airplanes with de-icing fluid just prior to take-off when the temperature is near freezing and it is raining or snowing. This procedure was instituted in the aftermath of USAir flight 405's crash on 22 March 1992. Flight 405 stalled just after becoming airborne because of ice on its wings, despite the fact that de-icing fluid was applied before it left its gate. Apparently, flight 405's take-off was delayed because of air traffic and ice re-accumulated on its wings while it waited for a departure slot on the runway in the freezing rain. NTSB Aircraft Accident Report AAR-93/02—published on 17 February 1993, and available through several internet sites—contains a sobering summary of the NTSB's findings (Report AAR–93/02, p. vi):

> The National Transportation Safety Board determines that the probable cause of this accident were the failure of the airline industry and the Federal Aviation Administration to provide flightcrews with procedures, requirements, and criteria

compatible with departure delays in conditions conducive to airframe icing and the decision by the flightcrew to take off without positive assurance that the airplane's wings were free of ice accumulation after 35 minutes of exposure to precipitation following de-icing. The ice contamination on the wings resulted in an aerodynamic stall and loss of control after liftoff. Contributing to the cause of the accident were the inappropriate procedures used by, and inadequate coordination between, the flightcrew that led to a takeoff rotation at a lower than prescribed air speed.

Rather than placing blame on the technology, or on human error, alone the NTSB conducted a thorough forensic examination and concluded that an incorrect application of the technology—waiting too long after de-icing and not checking for ice build-up just before take-off—caused the crash. Current de-icing procedures have no doubt saved many lives thanks to NTSB Report AAR–93/02, but this particular innovation did not come cheaply; it was paid for by the lives of the twenty-seven individuals who did not survive the crash of flight 405. Imagine the waste if the NTSB did not investigate this tragedy and produce concrete recommendations to prevent such an accident from happening again.

Financial crashes are, of course, considerably less dire, generally involving no loss of life. However, the financial crisis of 2008, and the eventual cost of the bailout, should be sufficient motivation to create a 'Capital Markets Safety Board' (CMSB) dedicated to investigating, reporting, and archiving the 'accidents' of the financial industry. By maintaining teams of experienced professionals—forensic accountants, financial engineers from industry and academia, and securities and tax attorneys—who work together on a regular basis over the course of many cases to investigate every single financial disaster, a number of new insights, common threads, and key issues would emerge from their analysis. The publicly available reports from the CMSB would yield invaluable insights to investors seeking to protect their future investments from similar fates, and, in the hands of investors, this information would eventually drive financial institutions to improve their 'safety records'.

In addition to collecting, analysing, and archiving data from financial blow-ups, the CMSB should also be tasked with the responsibility of obtaining and maintaining information from the shadow banking system—hedge funds, private partnerships, sovereign wealth funds, etc.—and integrating this information with that of other regulatory agencies (see Section 20.1 for further discussion). By having a single agency responsible for managing data related to systemic risk, and creating high-level risk analytics such as a network map of the financial system and estimates of illiquidity exposure, leverage, and asset flows, the repository of data will be far easier to access and analyse.

This function is now being addressed by one of the key innovations of the Dodd–Frank Wall Street Reform and Consumer Protection Act, the creation of the Office of Financial Research (see https://financialresearch.gov).

The NTSB provides an additional valuable service that the CMSB should also take on: At the very start of its investigative process, the NTSB establishes itself as the clearinghouse for all information related to the accident, and communicates frequently and regularly with the press to provide as much transparency as possible to an undoubtedly anxious public. Specifically, the NTSB describes their standard operating procedure in the following way:[8]

> While the exact scope and extent of any specific investigation depends on the nature of the accident being investigated, every NTSB investigation goes through the same general process, which involves:
>
> - the initial notification and decision to investigate;
> - on-site fact gathering;
> - analysis of facts and determination of probable cause;
> - acceptance of a final report; and
> - advocating for the acceptance of safety recommendations arising from the investigation.

By taking such an active role in providing information to the public immediately and continuously throughout its investigations, the NTSB reduces the likelihood of panic and over-reaction, and, over the years, this policy has earned the NTSB the public's trust and confidence. Compare this approach to the sporadic and inconsistent messages that were communicated to the public regarding the financial crisis of 2008, which may well have magnified the dislocation that ensued in the stock market and money market funds during September and October 2008. Of course, the Treasury and Federal Reserve can hardly be faulted for not providing polished presentations of every aspect of their deliberations—public relations has never been a significant component of their mandate. But, in times of crisis, when emotions run high, it is particularly important to communicate directly, truthfully, and continuously with all stakeholders no matter how bad the news, as any experienced emergency-room doctor will acknowledge.

Of course, formal government investigations of major financial events do occur from time to time, as in the April 1999 *Report of the President's Working Group in Financial Markets on Hedge Funds, Leverage, and the Lessons of*

---

[8] See https://www.ntsb.gov/investigations/process/Pages/default.aspx, accessed 15 March 2022.

Long-Term Capital Management. However, this inter-agency report was put together on an *ad hoc* basis, with committee members that had not worked together previously or regularly on forensic investigations of this kind. With multiple agencies involved, and none in charge of the investigation, the administrative overhead becomes more significant. Although any thorough investigation of the financial services sector is likely to involve the SEC, the OCC, the CFTC, the US Treasury, and the Federal Reserve—and inter-agency cooperation should be promoted—there are important operational advantages in tasking a single office with the responsibility for coordinating all such investigations and serving as a repository for the expertise in conducting forensic examinations of financial incidents.

The establishment of a CMSB will not be inexpensive. The lure of the private sector poses a formidable challenge to government agencies to attract and retain individuals with expertise in these highly employable fields. Individuals trained in forensic accounting, financial engineering, and securities law now command substantial premiums on Wall Street over government pay scales. Although the typical government employee is likely to be motivated more by civic duty than financial gain, it would be unrealistic to build an organization on altruism alone. However, the cost of a CMSB is trivial in comparison to the losses that it may prevent. For example, if regulators had fully appreciated the impact of the demise of Lehman Brothers—which a fully operational CMSB with the proper network map would have been able to forecast—the savings from this one incident would be sufficient to fund the CMSB for half a century. Moreover, the benefits provided by the CMSB would accrue not only to the wealthy, but would also flow to pension funds, mutual funds, and retail investors in the form of more stable financial markets, greater liquidity, reduced borrowing and lending costs as a result of decreased systemic risk exposures, and a wider variety of investment choices available to a larger segment of the population because of increased transparency, oversight, and ultimately, financial security.

It is unrealistic to expect that market crashes, manias, panics, collapses, and fraud will ever be completely eliminated from our capital markets, but we should avoid compounding our mistakes by failing to learn from them.

20.7 Transparency and Fair Value Accounting

A common theme among the issues and proposals throughout this chapter has been the importance of transparency for managing systemic risk. Financial markets are highly competitive and adaptive, and—apart from the occasional dislocations due to overwhelming behavioural reactions—are extremely effective in aggregating, parsing, internalizing, and disseminating information, the quintessential illustration of the wisdom of crowds. As a general principle, the more transparency is provided to the market, the more efficient are the prices it produces, and the more effective will the market allocate capital and other limited resources. When the market is denied critical information, its participants will infer what they can from existing information, in which case rumours, fears, and wishful thinking will play a much bigger role in how the market determines prices and quantities. Therefore, from a systemic risk perspective, as well as a social welfare perspective, it is difficult to justify any regulatory change that interferes with or otherwise reduces transparency.

One example of such a change is the proposal to suspend fair value accounting (FASB Statement No. 157) that emerged during the 2008 financial crisis. Fair value, or mark-to-market, accounting requires firms to value their assets and liabilities at fair market prices, not on a historical-cost basis, and this practice has been blamed for the financial crisis of 2008 because it forced many firms to write down their assets, thereby triggering defaults and insolvencies. At first blush, this proposal seems ill-conceived, because it calls for less transparency. After all, in the credit crisis of 2008, banks reduced their lending activities partly because they had no idea what the other banks' assets were worth, and suspending fair value accounting would not have improved the state of affairs. Imagine a doctor advising the parents of a feverish child to discontinue hourly temperature readings because the frequent readings only serve to alarm them. Instead, the doctor suggests that the parents either wait until the child is feeling better before taking the next reading, or that they construct an estimate of the child's temperature based on readings taken last week when the child was feeling better.

Nevertheless, the proposal is worth more serious consideration, because it involves several subtle issues surrounding the economic nature of markets, prices, and the importance of transparency. There is no doubt that suspending fair value accounting in the immediate aftermath of the financial crisis of 2008 would have reduced pressures on a number of potentially insolvent financial institutions, but not without a cost, which would depend on whether the suspension were temporary or permanent. If it were permanent, market participants would lose a significant degree of transparency regarding corporate assets and liabilities, and price securities accordingly. Borrowing costs would likely increase across the board, and because firms with higher-quality assets may not have any mechanism to convince the market of this fact, such firms may refrain from participating in capital markets, thereby reducing market liquidity and also creating adverse selection (in which only firms with lower quality assets remain in the market), which raises borrowing costs even more. Moreover, on an ongoing basis, firms would have to maintain larger reserves to achieve the same credit quality because of the increased risk of their less transparent portfolios, further reducing liquidity and increasing borrowing costs.

If, however, the suspension of fair value accounting were temporary, then there would come a day of reckoning when firms would have to mark their assets and liabilities to market, and the suspension would be merely a postponement of that eventuality. A postponement would be reasonable under two conditions:

1. The existence of extraordinary circumstances that cause market prices of the firm's assets and liabilities to deviate significantly from economic value.
2. The extraordinary circumstances are temporary and unrelated to the economic value of the firm's assets and liabilities.

For example, suppose a terrorist attack on US soil creates a massive but temporary flight-to-quality, during which time the value of an insurance company's assets, which are largely invested in AAA-rated corporate debt, falls precipitously. In this scenario, the flight-to-quality is temporary, and the decline in the insurance company's assets is largely (although not completely) unrelated to its economic value. Hence, a temporary suspension of fair value accounting may be defensible since the insurance company is likely to be solvent once the flight-to-quality passes.

However, this argument implicitly assumes that the flight-to-quality is a form of temporary insanity that should be dismissed, or at the very least, discounted. But if the flight-to-quality is not a temporary phenomenon, but rather a change in regime that is likely to last for years (e.g. because the terrorist event portends ongoing threats that cannot easily be eliminated), then the suspension of fair value accounting is only delaying the inevitable, and interfering with the appropriate re-pricing of business enterprises under a new economic regime.

Also, the temporariness of impairments to economic value is insufficient justification for suspending fair value accounting. The condition that the impairment be unrelated to the economic value of the impaired asset is also critical. The reason is simple: even if an asset's market value is only temporarily impaired, if the impairment is directly related to the nature of that asset, then it *should* be taken into account and marked to market. For example, suppose a bank holds part of its assets in a hurricane insurance company. During an unusually active hurricane season, the value of these holdings may be temporarily impaired, but this impairment is directly related to the economic value of the insurance company, and suspension of fair value accounting only interferes with the price discovery process.

A more subtle argument for suspending fair value accounting was put forward by Plantin, Sapra, and Shin (2008), who observe that during periods where liquidity is very low, a forced liquidation of an asset by firm A can depress the market price of that asset, which affects the value of firm B if it also holds that same asset and is required to mark that asset to market. In such situations, fair value accounting inadvertently creates correlation among the assets of many firms, even those that are not attempting liquidations, and this increased correlation can lead to the kind of death spiral discussed in Section 20.1, where liquidations cause deterioration of collateral that leads to more liquidations, further deterioration of collateral, and so on. They consider this spillover effect a negative externality, a negative consequence of the liquidation that is not part of the economic value of the asset being liquidated, and argue that in some cases (e.g. long-lived and illiquid assets), it is socially optimal to use historical cost accounting instead of fair value accounting.

However, their conclusion rests heavily on the interpretation of the spillover effect as a negative externality. Another interpretation is that such spillover effects are, in fact, part of the economic value of an asset. In particular, if the asset in question were short-term US Treasury bills, then, presumably, the spillover effects of a liquidation would be minimal. However, then the price of T-bills should reflect this property, and the price of less liquid assets should reflect the potential spillover effects as well. Therefore, the potential for spillover effects is a characteristic that can be known in advance and priced accordingly, in which case the welfare implications of switching from fair value to historical cost accounting is unclear. In any case, Plantin, Sapra, and Shin (2008) do not consider the case where fair value accounting is temporarily suspended, and the impact of moving from one regime to another in their framework is an open question. The answer likely depends on whether the two conditions described above would hold for the fair value postponement.

Other studies have argued that during liquidity crises, market prices are not as meaningful as they are during normal times; hence, marking to market may not always yield the same informational content (Allen and Carletti, 2008; Sapra, 2008; Easley and O'Hara, 2010). While no consensus has yet emerged regarding which alternative to mark-to-market pricing is best, the fact that the distinction between 'liquidity pricing' and 'normal pricing' is being drawn more frequently by accountants and economists suggests that neither historical cost accounting nor fair value accounting can be appropriate for all circumstances. This implies that neither approach is the correct one, but that a more flexible mechanism for pricing assets and liabilities is needed, one that can accommodate both normal and distressed market conditions.

A more general observation about accounting methods is that they are designed to yield information about value, not about risk, a point made by Merton and Bodie (1995) as part of their call for a separate branch of accounting focusing exclusively on risk. They use the example of a simple fixed/floating interest-rate swap contract which has zero value at the start, and thus is considered neither an asset nor a liability, but an 'off-balance sheet' item. We have learned from experience that off-balance sheet items can have enormous impact on a firm's bottom line, hence it is remarkable that our accounting practices have yet to incorporate them more directly in valuation. In fairness to the accounting profession, accounting methods are designed to be *backward-looking*, involving the allocation of revenues and costs that have already occurred to various categories. Accountants tell us what *has* happened, leaving the future to corporate strategists and fortunetellers. However, this exclusive focus on realized results implies that risk is not part of the accountant's lexicon (i.e. there is no natural way to capture risk from the current GAAP accounting perspective). Yet accounting concepts like capital ratios and asset–liability gaps are used to formulate and implement regulatory requirements and constraints.

A modest beginning for developing risk accounting methods is to define the concept of a 'risk balance sheet', which is simply the risk decomposition of a firm's mark-to-market balance sheet where both assets and liabilities are considered to be random variables (i.e. unknown quantities with certain statistical properties). Since assets must always equal liabilities, the variance of assets must always equal the variance of liabilities; hence, the risk balance sheet is just the variance decomposition of both sides (Fig. 20.5). Note that the variance of both total assets and total liabilities is given by the sum of the variances of the individual assets and liabilities, plus their pairwise covariances. These are the terms that have created so much controversy with respect to subprime MBSs: they swelled to unprecedented levels in 2007, as subprime mortgage defaults became highly correlated throughout the country. Risk accounting standards—which have yet to be developed—must address both the proper methods for estimating the variances and covariances of assets and liabilities, and the potential instabilities in these estimates across different economic environments.

Assets	Liabilities
A_1	L_1
A_2	L_2
...	...
A_N	L_M
V	V

$\Rightarrow$

Assets	Liabilities
$\text{Var}[A_1]$	$\text{Var}[L_1]$
$\text{Var}[A_2]$	$\text{Var}[L_2]$
...	...
$\text{Var}[A_N]$	$\text{Var}[L_M]$
$\text{Cov}[A_i,A_j], i \neq j$	$\text{Cov}[L_i,L_j], i \neq j$
$\text{Var}[V]$	$\text{Var}[V]$

Fig. 20.5 The 'risk balance sheet', defined as the risk decomposition of a firm's market-value balance sheet.

Source: Lo (2009, Figure 7).

This challenge is not just a regulatory one, but requires regulators to collaborate with accountants and financial experts to develop a completely new set of accounting principles focused exclusively on risk budgeting. This new branch of risk accounting may be one of the most critical pieces of the financial and regulatory infrastructures of the twenty-first century.

20.8 The Role of Technology and Education

Given the complexity of the financial structures involved in the financial crisis of 2008—MBSs, CDOs, CDSs, special purpose vehicles (SPVs), and other exotic entities and securities—a natural question is whether the crisis was due to financial technology (e.g. derivative securities, structured products, and the mathematical methods involved in pricing and hedging them). If, as Warren Buffett claims, derivatives are financial weapons of mass destruction, should we consider outlawing derivatives altogether?

There is no doubt that financial technology has had an indelible impact on the financial system over the last century, as Chapter 18, and especially Table 18.2, highlighted. However, that technology has been used to reduce risk as often as it has to augment it. For example, as of the first half of 2021, the notional amount outstanding of interest rate derivatives, one of the most popular instruments among non-financial corporations for *hedging* interest rate risk, was $488 trillion, according to the Bank of International Settlements.[9] In contrast to that market, the comparable notional amount for CDSs over the same period was $8.8 trillion, and only $7.5 trillion for equity-linked

---

[9] https://stats.bis.org/statx/srs/table/d7?f=pdf, accessed on 15 March 2022.

derivatives.[10] These figures suggest that the most common use of derivatives today is not as financial weapons of mass destruction, but as hedging vehicles for transferring interest rate risk from part of the global economy to other parts that are better equipped to bear that risk. Therefore, limiting the use of such important risk-management tools would be counterproductive and highly disruptive.

However, Mr Buffett may be half-right in that financial technology has become more complex over the last several decades. Because the derivatives and structured finance businesses have grown so rapidly, the expertise required to grasp fully the risk and return profiles of many new financial instruments and vehicles has increased just as rapidly. In some cases, even large financial institutions may not have had sufficient time to develop such expertise among their senior management and board members, and hiring the necessary expertise in booming business lines involving new technologies is always difficult, by definition. To appreciate fully the intellectual challenges of financial innovation, consider the case of the hybrid CDO first issued by HVB Asset Management in 2003, described by Bluhm (2003) in the following passage:

HVB Asset Management Asia (HVBAM) has brought to market the first ever hybrid collateralized debt obligation (CDO) managed by an Asian collateral manager. The deal, on which HVB Asia (formerly known as HypoVereinsbank Asia) acted as lead manager and underwriter, is backed by 120 million of asset-backed securitization bonds and 880 million of credit default swaps…Under the structure of the transaction, Artemus Strategic Asian Credit Fund Limited—a special purpose vehicle registered in the Cayman Islands—issued 200 million of bonds to purchase the 120 million of cash bonds and deposit 80 million into the guaranteed investment contract, provided by AIG Financial Products. In addition, the issuer enters into credit default swap agreements with three counterparties (BNP Paribas, Deutsche Bank and JPMorgan) with a notional value of 880 million. On each interest payment date, the issuer, after payments of certain senior fees and expenses and the super senior swap premium, will use the remaining interest collections from the GIC accounts, the cash ABS bonds, the hedge agreements, and the CDS premiums from the CDS to pay investors in the CDO transaction… The transaction was split into five tranches, including an unrated 20 million junior piece to be retained by HVBAM. The 127 million of A-class notes have triple-A ratings from Fitch, Moody's

[10] https://stats.bis.org/statx/srs/table/d10.1?f=pdf for CDS and https://stats.bis.org/statx/srs/table/d8?f=pdf for equity-linked derivatives, both accessed on 15 March 2022.

and S&P, the 20 million B-notes were rated AA/Aa2/AA, the 20 million C bonds were rated A/A2/A, while the 13 million of D notes have ratings of BBB/Baa2 and BBB.

This new financial security is a claim on the ARTEMUS Strategic Asian Credit Fund, a Cayman Islands SPV structured according to Fig. 20.6. Note that this diagram is just an outline of the legal structure of the instrument! How many boards of directors of institutions managing these types of funds—of which there are many—truly understood the complexities of these investments?

Pricing such instruments is even more complex, involving a blend of mathematical, statistical, and financial models and computations, all of which are typically done under simplistic assumptions that rarely hold in practice, such as constant means, variances, and correlations that are assumed to be without measurement error. To develop an appreciation for the mathematical complexity of some of these pricing models, Fig. 20.7 contains a technical appendix from Bluhm and Overbeck (2007) in which they describe one aspect of their proposed model for default probabilities, a critical element in evaluating the price of credit-sensitive instruments like CDSs. Models such as these are central to the current financial crisis, and their miscalibration is

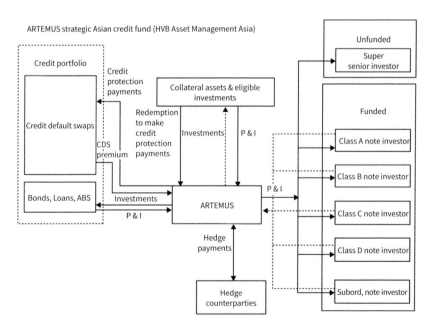

Fig. 20.6 Structure of the ARTEMUS Strategic Asian Credit Fund, a Cayman Islands special purpose vehicle.

Source: Bluhm, C. (2003). CDO modeling: techniques, examples and applications, Unpublished working paper, https://citeseerx.ist.psu.edu/viewdoc/summary?doi=10.1.1.139.4129 (accessed 25 July 2022).

Appendix I: stochastic rationale of the NHCTMC approach

In this appendix, we briefly comment on the stochastic rationale of our approach. For the sake of convenient notation, let us denote by $\Psi(t)$ the diagonal matrix with diagonal elements:

$$\psi_{ii}(t) = t\varphi_{\alpha_i,\beta_i}(t) \quad (i = 1,...,8; t \geq 0)$$

The transition matrix M_t in (5) for the time period $[0, t]$ can then be written as:

$$M_t = \exp(\Psi(t) \times Q) \quad (t \geq 0) \qquad (6)$$

Writing the exponential matrix as a power series and using the typical Markov kernel notation $P_{0,t} = M_t$ term-by-term differentiation yields:

$$\frac{\partial}{\partial t}P_{0,t} = \sum_{k=0}^{\infty}\frac{\partial}{\partial t}\frac{(\Psi(t)\times Q)^k}{k!}$$

$$= \sum_{k=1}^{\infty}\left(\frac{\partial}{\partial t}\Psi(t)\times Q\right)\times\frac{(\Psi(t)\times Q)^{(k-1)}}{(k-1)!} \qquad (7)$$

$$= \left(\frac{\partial}{\partial t}\Psi(t)\times Q\right)\times P_{0,t}$$

Because $\Psi(t)$ is a diagonal matrix:

$$\frac{\partial\Psi(t)}{\partial t}$$

is the diagonal matrix with entries $\psi'_{ii}(t)$. Therefore, the matrix:

$$\frac{\partial\Psi(t)}{\partial t}\times Q$$

is a Q-matrix, arguing in the same way as above where we said that $\Psi(t) \times Q$ is a Q-matrix and taking into account that $\psi'_{ii}(t) \geq 0$ at all times[1] t. As a consequence of general Markov theory (see Ethier & Kurtz, 2005, theorem 7.3 in chapter 4, Lando & Skodeberg, 2002, and Schoenbucher, 2005), equation (7) is part of the forward equation of a non-homogeneous Markov chain $(X_t)_{t\geq0}$ with state space $\{1, 2, ... , 8\}$ corresponding to a semigroup $\{P_{s,t} \mid 0 \leq s \leq t\}$ satisfying the Kolmogorov backward and forward equations associated with the family:

$$\left\{\frac{\partial\Psi(t)}{\partial t}\times Q \mid t \geq 0\right\}$$

defining the infinitesimal generator of the Markov process. Equation (7) shows that the non-homogeneous continuous-time Markov chain $(X_t)_{t\geq0}$ induces the PD term structures illustrated in figure 2 via the default column of kernel-based transition matrices $P_{0,t} = M_t = \exp(\Psi(t) \times Q)$.

[1] We have $(1 - \exp(-\alpha t))\psi'_{ii}(t) = \alpha\exp(-\alpha t)t^\beta + (1 - \exp(-\alpha t))\beta t^{\beta-1} \geq 0$ for all $t \geq 0$

Fig. 20.7 Appendix I from Bluhm and Overbeck (2007) providing details of their Markov default probability model.

one possible explanation for how so many firms underestimated the risks of subprime-related securities so significantly. Unless senior management has the technical expertise to evaluate and challenge the calibrations of these models, they cannot manage their risks effectively.

We often take it for granted that large financial institutions capable of hiring dozens of 'quants' each year must have the technical expertise to advise senior management, and senior management has the necessary business and markets expertise to guide the quantitative research process. However, in fast-growing businesses, the realities of day-to-day market pressures make this idealized relationship between senior management and research a fantasy. Senior management typically has little time to review the research, much less guide it, and quants are often hired from technically sophisticated disciplines such as mathematics, physics, and computer science without any formal training in finance or economics. While some on-the-job training is inevitable, the broad-based failure of the financial industry to appreciate fully the magnitude of the risk exposures in the CDO and CDS markets suggests that the problem was not too much knowledge of financial technology, but rather too little knowledge.

A case in point is the credit-rating agencies, which have been roundly criticized for their apparently overly optimistic ratings of the MBSs and related instruments that were at the epicentre of the 2008 financial crisis. Some have argued that the inherent conflict of interest in the ratings business led to upward-biased ratings, while others claim that the mathematical models on which ratings were based were too simplistic and static, and yet another set of critics blames the limited history that the rating agencies used to calibrate their models. Although we may never uncover the origins of the breakdown in these credit ratings, one fact has emerged that seems uncontroversial: the clients of the rating agencies—hedge funds, commercial banks, investment banks, and mortgage companies—routinely hired away the raters' most talented analysts. Given the business model of rating agencies, this was not difficult to do, and the rating agencies did not object, because it was both a compliment to the quality of their staff, and also a means for developing closer ties to their clients. However, it did result in a continuous 'brain drain' from the rating agencies to their clients, and, even then, the demand for such talent continued to grow until the financial crisis hit.

Indirect evidence for an excess demand of finance expertise may also be found in Philippon and Reshef's (2012) comparison of the annual incomes of US engineers and finance-trained graduates from 1967 to 2005. The comparison between finance and engineering students is a useful one, since both are technical disciplines. Over the last thirty years, engineers have made significant inroads into the finance labour market. Figure 20.8 shows that until the mid-1980s, college graduates in engineering enjoyed higher incomes than college graduates in finance, and postgraduates in engineering had about the

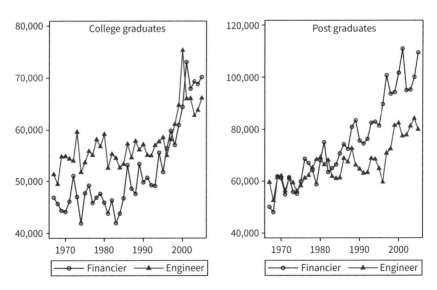

Fig. 20.8 Comparison of finance and engineering graduates from 1967 to 2005, in 2001 US dollars.

Source: Philippon and Reshef (2009). Reprinted with permission from authors.

same compensation as postgraduates in finance. However, since the 1980s, finance-trained college graduates have caught up to their engineering counterparts, surpassing them in 2000 and every year thereafter. But the more impressive comparison is for postgraduates: since 1982, the annual income of finance postgraduates has exceeded that of engineers every year, and the gap has widened steadily over these two decades. This pattern suggests that the demand for financial expertise has grown considerably during this time.[11]

Table 20.1, which reports the number of MIT engineering and finance degrees awarded from 1999 to 2007 (just prior to the financial crisis), provides another perspective on the dearth of financial expertise. In 2007, MIT's School of Engineering graduated 337 PhDs in engineering; in contrast, the MIT Sloan School of Management produced only four finance PhDs. These figures are not unique to MIT, but are, in fact, typical among the top engineering and business schools. Now, it can be argued that the main focus of the Sloan School is its MBA programme, which graduates approximately 450 students each year, but most MBA students at Sloan and other top business schools do not have the technical background to implement models such as the one described in Fig. 20.7, and the standard MBA curriculum does not include courses that cover such models in any depth. Such material—which requires advanced training in arcane subjects such as stochastic processes, stochastic calculus, and partial differential equations—is usually geared towards PhD students. However, due to the growth of

Table 20.1 Number of MIT degrees awarded in engineering and in finance from 1999 to 2007.

Year	Bachelor's	MIT School of Engineering Master's and MEng	PhD and ScD	MIT Sloan Finance PhD
2007	578	710	337	4
2006	578	735	298	2
2005	593	798	286	1
2004	645	876	217	5
2003	679	817	210	7
2002	667	803	239	3
2001	660	860	248	1
2000	715	739	237	2
1999	684	811	208	4

Source: Lo (2009, Table I).

[11] The increase in income can also be explained by a decline in the supply of finance graduates, but Philippon and Reshef (2012) show that the number of employees in this sector increased significantly since the 1980s, which suggests that a supply shock is not the source of the growth in income.

the derivatives business over the last decade, a number of universities have begun to offer specialized Master's-level degree programmes in financial engineering and mathematical finance to meet the growing demand for more technically advanced students trained in finance. Whether or not such students are sufficiently prepared to fill the current knowledge gap in financial technology remains to be seen. In 2021, MIT awarded 295 doctorates in engineering and five in finance.

The disparity between the number of PhDs awarded in engineering and finance in Table 20.1 raises the question of why such a difference exists. One possible explanation may be the sources of funding. MIT engineering PhD students are funded largely through government grants (Defense Advanced Research Projects Agency (DARPA), Department of Energy (DOE), National Institutes of Health (NIH), and the National Science Foundation (NSF)), whereas MIT Sloan PhD students are funded exclusively through internal MIT funds. Given the importance of finance expertise, one proposal for regulatory reform is to provide comparable levels of government funding to support finance PhD students, perhaps in conjunction with the research activities of the CMSB (see Section 20.6). Alternatively, funding for finance PhD students might be raised by imposing a small surcharge on certain types of derivatives contracts (e.g. those that are particularly complex or illiquid and, therefore, contribute to systemic risk). This surcharge may be viewed as a means of correcting some of the externalities associated with the impact of derivatives on systemic risk. A minuscule surcharge on, say, CDSs, could support enough finance PhD students at every major university to have a noticeable and permanent impact on the level of financial expertise in both industry and government.

In addition to providing support for finance PhD students, another potential new role for government oversight is to mandate minimum levels of disclosure, 'truth-in-labelling' laws, and financial expertise for those market participants involved in creating and selling complex financial securities to the public, much like the requirements imposed by the Food and Drug Administration on accurate and complete labelling of pharmaceuticals, and the educational and licensing requirements for pharmacists dispensing those products. Currently, a licensed pharmacist must earn a PharmD degree from an accredited college or school of pharmacy, and then pass a series of examinations, including the North American Pharmacist Licensure Exam (which tests for pharmacy skills and knowledge) and, in most states, the Multi-state Pharmacy Jurisprudence Exam (which tests for knowledge of pharmacy law). The SEC already performs this function to some degree, but its focus is limited to a much narrower and simpler set of financial products than those at the centre of the financial crisis of 2008.[12] Rather than setting up new infrastructure for administering such educational and licensing requirements, the government can partner with existing industry organizations such as the CFA Institute, the International Association of Financial Engineers, or the Global Association of Risk Professionals, and have these organizations provide the certification, subject to government approval. If the senior management and directors of financial institutions dealing with complex financial instruments were subject to periodic certification standards in financial engineering, many more questions might have been asked before such institutions plunged head-first into the depths of the subprime mortgage market and their derivatives.

Of course, education begins much earlier than in graduate school, and subtle concepts like opportunity cost, supply and demand, present value, default risk, and risk–reward trade-offs require repeated exposure and reinforcement before they become part of an individual's cognitive framework. For this reason, one of the most important changes we can make to produce a more educated population of consumers and investors is to teach basic economic and financial reasoning, as well as the fundamentals of risk management, to high-school students, preferably in the ninth and tenth grades so that they have sufficient time to incorporate these ideas fully into other parts of their curriculum. Without early training in such concepts as loss probabilities, standard deviation, and mean reversion, it is unlikely that a non-specialist will be able truly to understand the basic risks of their personal financial transactions.

Education is the ultimate weapon that humans wield against their baser instincts.

20.9 The Role of Corporate Governance

Throughout the aftermath of the financial crisis of 2008, politicians and the media zeroed in on the apparently excessive levels of executive compensation among the various troubled financial institutions. Whether or not such compensation is, in fact, excessive depends, of course, on the supply and demand of corporate executives with comparable skills, and a large literature has emerged around this issue (Murphy, 1999). However, with respect to the

---

[12] However, Macey et al. (2008) make the following two bold claims: 'First, we argue that the current subprime mortgage and credit crisis would have been avoided, or at least greatly mitigated, if existing securities laws had been properly applied to subprime mortgage brokers and originators. Second, we argue that under either of what we regard as two extremely reasonable interpretations of the securities laws, many of the problematic mortgages are actually under the SEC's jurisdiction.'

financial crisis of 2008, the focus on compensation levels seems misplaced— the more relevant concern is the lack of independence between risk and reward in the corporate governance structure.

The example of the CRO of Company XYZ in Section 20.4 provides a clear illustration of the impact of this obvious conflict of interest. If, as with most senior managers, the CRO is compensated according to a combination of salary, cash bonus, and stock or option incentives, then the CRO has much the same risk-taking incentives as the chief executive officer (CEO) and other senior managers. It is a well-known fact that the common stock of a leveraged corporation is a call option on the firm's assets; hence, one way to maximize shareholder wealth is to increase the risks of the assets. But, apart from these agency problems, which are especially significant for financial institutions in which risk plays a central role in corporate strategy, the fact that the CRO has much the same perspective as the rest of senior management necessarily reduces their ability to counterbalance the emotional overload of their colleagues. Under current corporate governance structures, the CRO (when the position exists) has taken on more of a public relations and marketing function rather than serving as a genuine risk watchdog for the shareholders' benefit.

This conflict of interest can be addressed in a straightforward manner by changing the corporate governance structure as it relates to enterprise risk management. Firstly, require each corporation's senior management and board of directors to develop an enterprise risk mandate document that describes specific measures for measuring enterprise risks and acceptable limits and current targets for each of those risks. This document should be updated at least annually, and whenever there is a material change in enterprise risks or market conditions. Secondly, appoint a CRO—a senior-management-level appointment—who will report directly to the board of directors, not the CEO, and structure their compensation so that they are rewarded for maintaining corporate stability (via its enterprise risk mandates), not for corporate profitability or growth. Then give the CRO the necessary authority to carry out their responsibilities (i.e. require all material changes in enterprise risk levels to be approved in advance in writing by the CRO). To focus sufficient attention on these enterprise risk levels, require the CRO to provide senior management and the board with monthly risk estimates, to be certified in writing by the CRO. Finally, add a clause in the CRO's employment contract that if any enterprise risk measure breaches its risk mandate, the CRO may be terminated for cause.

By creating a clear separation in both responsibility and compensation between business development and enterprise risk management, a healthy tension is created between the natural inclination for corporations to take on new risks and the countervailing objective of self-preservation during more turbulent business conditions. In much the same way that an individual's decision-making process is best served by the proper balance between logical analysis and emotional response—where too much weight on either set of faculties can lead to disaster (Damasio, 1994)—the same is likely to hold for the modern corporation. For most situations, the conflict between business growth and risk should be easy to adjudicate, particularly given the prespecified enterprise risk mandate that will guide both the CEO and CRO. However, on occasion, an impasse will emerge that cannot be resolved by senior management, but these situations are precisely those which corporate strategy requires guidance from the board of directors. Therefore, the independence of the CRO serves as a self-regulating mechanism by which only the most significant conflicts become issues involving the directors, where significance will be measured either in terms of the magnitude of business opportunities forgone, or the magnitude of enterprise risk that may be created, or both.

Although this proposed change in corporate governance structure may seem intuitive and desirable given the spectacular losses reported by some of the largest corporations in the world, there are at least two objections to it that must be addressed.

The first objection is an old saw among proprietary traders and seasoned portfolio managers: risk and reward go hand in hand, so how can risk management be delegated to other parts of an organization, especially when those parts are far removed from the specific business lines most familiar with their own risk–reward trade-offs? This objection has considerable merit, particularly in the financial industry where risk is virtually synonymous with reward, so closely tied are earnings to a trader's risk-bearing capacity. However, the risk of a particular corporate division may not be justified by its reward in the larger context of the enterprise, as shareholders of Bear Stearns and Lehman Brothers can now attest. While the risk–reward profile of each division is important in determining the amount of resources allocated to that activity, other factors must be considered by senior management in maximizing the enterprise value of the business, including the enterprise risk exposures of the business and how to allocate its risk budget across its activities.

The second objection is the fact that corporate risk management flies in the face of academic financial orthodoxy. In particular, in an idealized world of frictionless efficient markets, corporate risk management is unnecessary because shareholders can manage their own risks using various market mechanisms—for example, portfolio diversification, T-bills, options, and swaps—and expect corporate managers to focus solely on maximizing shareholder wealth, not on balancing shareholder wealth against shareholder risks. Using the standard arbitrage arguments that Modigliani and Miller (1958) pioneered to demonstrate the irrelevance of capital structure in frictionless efficient markets, it can be shown that corporate risk management is also irrelevant because it can be 'undone' by investors through a combination of trades in the corporation's debt and equity securities.

But, like the capital structure irrelevance proposition, the irrelevance of corporate risk management rests heavily on the assumption of frictionless efficient markets, which sweeps a number of important practical considerations aside, any one of which can cause the proposition to fail, including:

- taxes;
- transaction costs;
- illiquid or non-traded corporate assets;
- credit constraints;
- costs of financial distress (e.g. goodwill, reputation, and franchise value);
- departures from market efficiency.

Therefore, from a practical perspective, an independent CRO with both the authority and responsibility to manage enterprise risks may be viewed as an attempt to deal with market frictions and institutional rigidities of the type listed above.

Corporate governance is also inextricably tied to technological advances, as well as corporate culture. Therefore, the ideas discussed in this chapter must be integrated with the co-evolution of technology described in Chapter 18 and the non-economic aspects of culture described in Chapter 19. Only by viewing corporate behaviour through these multiple lenses will we be able to create the rules, regulations, processes, and institutions necessary to safeguard us from the worst consequences of future financial crises.

20.10 Discussion

While the financial crisis of 2008 was one of the most significant challenges in our lifetime, it was not unprecedented from a global historical perspective, and the magnitude was not unexpected given the excesses, growth, and financial liberalization of the last two decades. While there were many factors that contributed to the crisis, ultimately we may conclude that the boom–bust pattern of economies is a natural consequence of human evolution and adaptation to a complex and dynamic economy. Research in the cognitive neurosciences confirms that fear and greed are hardwired into our decision-making processes, and the cyclical nature of economic growth is merely one manifestation of that hardwiring. Financial crises are an unfortunate but normal consequence of modern capitalism.

Although financial crises may be difficult to avoid, their devastating impact can be dramatically reduced with proper preparation. Financial losses are inevitable—in fact, they are a necessary consequence of innovation—but disruptions and dislocations are greatly magnified when risks have been incorrectly assessed and incorrectly assigned. For example, a money market fund investing in AAA-rated securities is not prepared for situations in which those securities exhibit one-year default rates of 5%, but a hedge fund investing in B-rated securities is prepared for considerably higher default rates. The most effective means for reducing the impact of any financial crisis is providing the public with greater transparency into the underlying risks of their investments.

The years after the crisis were without a doubt extremely challenging for the US economy. However, the economic contraction, rise in unemployment, and regulatory reforms can be viewed as the necessary restructuring costs for transitioning from the existing economy to an even more robust one, a globally integrated economy in which labour and capital have become more mobile, production more efficient, and information more central to profitability and survival. By implementing adaptive and functional regulatory changes, we will be creating the new infrastructure to support that growth and prosperity.

Epilogue

We have travelled a considerable intellectual distance over the last twenty chapters, and we thank you, the patient and persistent reader, for having reached this point. Despite the many applications of evolutionary ideas to financial markets and institutions that we—and many other authors before us—have developed, we are still at the very beginnings of this emerging discipline. Although we believe that the framework and tools described in this volume serve as a rigorous basis for the adaptive markets hypothesis, only time and additional research will tell whether the data and their empirical testing will confirm or refute our paradigm. Our hope in writing this book is to motivate the next generation of scholars to take up the challenge of these next steps, and the 2021 special issue of the *Proceedings of the National Academy of Sciences* on evolutionary models of financial markets (Levin and Lo, 2021) may be the beginning of a trend.

But changing the status quo in mainstream economics and finance will not be easy. The very data we decide to collect are determined by our worldview. A molecular biologist studying marine life in a coral reef will focus on entirely different features of that ecosystem than an ecologist, whose perceptions will differ again from those of a geologist. We will need academics to shift their paradigm first, and then decide how best to conduct their empirical tests and applications. By approaching the study of finance as an ecologist or evolutionary biologist would—by understanding the flora and fauna first, before developing theories for how they ought to behave—many new insights will naturally emerge and flourish.

We submitted this manuscript as we enter the third (and we hope, final) year of the COVID-19 pandemic. We could not have imagined a more pertinent illustration of how the financial system adapts to stochastic environments. Many of the traditional financial paradigms faltered during this period, but the principles of evolution continued to operate throughout the turmoil. By studying and applying those principles, we are convinced it is possible to improve our response to crises and create a more robust and resilient society. By definition, it is virtually impossible to forecast the unanticipated future challenges to our survival. But two things are certain: meeting those challenges will require financial markets and institutions, and the most successful stakeholders are those who can adapt to shifting environments.

Andrew W. Lo
Ruixun Zhang
March 2022

Notational Glossary

Table A.1 Glossary of main notations used, including brief descriptions and chapters in which they are used.

Notation	Meaning	Chapter(s)
x_a and x_b	Numbers of offspring produced by action a and b, respectively, in the binary choice model.	2, 3, 4, 5, 6, 8, 9, 10, 15
$\Phi(x_a, x_b)$	Joint probability distribution function of x_a and x_b.	2, 3, 4, 5, 6, 8, 9, 10, 15
f	Individual types in the binary choice model.	2, 3, 4, 5, 6, 8, 9, 10, 15
$f(\cdot)$	Individual behaviour as a function of the environment.	9
f^*	The growth-optimal type in the binary choice model.	2, 3, 4, 5, 6, 8, 9, 10, 15
$\tilde{f}$	The behaviour that maximizes an individual's reproductive success.	2
$\hat{f}$	Estimated individual types from the data.	5
I^f	A Bernoulli random variable that takes value 1 with probability f, representing individual decisions.	2, 3, 4, 5, 6, 8, 9, 10, 15
x^f	The number of offspring for an individual that chooses action a with probability f.	2, 3, 4, 6, 8, 9, 10, 15
n_t^f	Total number of individuals of type f in generation t.	2, 3, 4, 6, 8, 9, 10, 15
$\alpha(f)$	Log-geometric average growth rate of the population of type-f.	2, 3, 4, 6, 8, 9, 10, 15
r_j	Relative fecundity for each of the two possible states of the world, $j = 1, 2$.	2, 5
z_a and z_b	Numbers of offspring subject to systematic reproductive risks.	2, 6
$y_{a,i}$ and $y_{b,i}$	Numbers of offspring subject to idiosyncratic reproductive risks.	2, 6
$r(w)$	A reproduction function that yields the number of offspring produced by an individual with wealth w.	2
ϵ	Mutation rate.	3
ϵ^*	The growth-optimal mutation rate.	3
$\mathbf{M}$	Mutation matrix that describes the population relationship between two generations.	3

Continued

Table A.1 *Continued*

Notation	Meaning	Chapter(s)
$\mathbf{F}_t$	Fecundity matrix that describes the population relationship between two generations.	3
$\mathbf{n}_t$	Vector of number of individuals of all types in generation t.	3
$\mathbf{y}_t$	Normalized population proportion vector in generation t.	3
$\mathscr{L}_t(\cdot)$	Distribution of $\mathbf{y}_t$.	3
$n_k^{\varepsilon,\text{Total}}$	Total number of individuals in the entire population at the end of k-th cycle for mutation rate ε.	3
$\pi(\varepsilon)$	Log-geometric average growth rate of the total population with mutation rate ε.	3
p	Probability to choose action a. (The same as f in Chapters 2 and 3.).	4, 10
λ_i	Factors in the binary choice model.	4, 10
β_i	Individual characteristics with respect to factor values.	4, 10
ψ_i	Factor loadings in the binary choice model.	4, 10
ψ_i^*	The growth-optimal factor loadings.	4, 10
$\mathbf{p}$	Probability vector to characterize a multinomial-choice individual.	4
$\mathbf{B}$	Matrix of individual characteristics in the multinomial-choice model.	4
N	The number of times an individual chooses the dominant option out of a total of T trials.	5
ρ	Correlation between sequential decisions for each subject.	5
ω	Proportion of systematic reproductive risks over total risk.	6
ξ_a^ω and ξ_b^ω	Numbers of offspring in environments where the weight for systematic risk is ω.	6
R	Relative reproductive success of action a over action b for an individual.	6, 9
$V_\omega(z, y)$	Each individual's objective function which is maximized in the binary choice model.	6
$U_{\omega,\mu}(z)$	Each individual's derived utility function from the binary choice model.	6
$A_{\omega,\mu}(z)$	Arrow–Pratt measure of absolute risk aversion (ARA) of $U_{\omega,\mu}(z)$.	6
$R_{\omega,\mu}(z)$	Arrow–Pratt–De Finetti measure of relative risk aversion (RRA) of $U_{\omega,\mu}(z)$.	6
$Syst_i$	An empirical index of the proportion of systematic risk in total environmental risk for each country.	6
D_i	Percentage of the disaster-affected population in country i.	6
M_i	Infant mortality in country i's population.	6
ρ_{AB}	Correlation between the number of offspring from individuals of type A and B.	7
x_A and x_B	Numbers of offspring for individuals (rather than actions) of type A and B, respectively. Similarly, $x_{A,t}$ and $x_{B,t}$ represent the same quantities in generation t.	7
μ_A and μ_B	Expected values of $\log x_A$ and $\log x_B$, respectively.	7
σ_A^2 and σ_B^2	Variances of $\log x_A$ and $\log x_B$, respectively.	7
ρ	Correlation between $\log x_A$ and $\log x_B$.	7
$P_{A,T}$ and $P_{B,T}$	Total population size at generation T of types A and B, respectively.	7

Notation	Meaning	Chapter(s)
ς_{ij}	Covariances of random offspring of type z choosing action l, for $z = A, B$ and $i = 0, 1$.	7
$\mu_{a,t}$ and $\mu_{b,t}$	Common expected values for $x_{a,i,t}$ and $x_{b,i,t}$ for each individual i at time t.	8
$\sigma_{a,t}$ and $\sigma_{b,t}$	Corresponding standard deviations for the above quantities.	8
$\rho_{a,t}$ and $\rho_{b,t}$	Common correlations at time t of each $x_{a,i,t}$ and $x_{b,i,t}$ with $I_{i,t}$ and $1 - I_{i,t}$.	8
ρ_t	Correlation between individual decisions and reproductive success $(x_{a,i,t} - x_{b,i,t})$ at time t.	8
σ_t	Common standard deviation of y_{it} for the above individuals.	8
γ	A universal representation of intelligence: $\frac{\rho_t}{\rho_{t,max}(f)}$.	8
$c(\rho)$ and $c(\gamma)$	Cost function for intelligence.	8
s_t	Environmental state at generation t.	9
S_t	Set of environmental states up to generation t.	9
l_t^f	Relative frequency of behaviour f in the population in generation t.	9, 15
$p^{benefit}$ and p^{harm}	Optimal behaviours for individuals who benefit from or are harmed by globalization, respectively.	10
q and r	Probability of adverse events.	10
$\tilde{p}_{T-1}$	The average behaviour in the population in generation $T - 1$.	10
$\mathrm{Bound}_0^1(x)$	A function that truncates the value of x to be between 0 and 1.	10
τ	Intensity for feedback effect.	10
P_t	Stock price at time t.	12, 14, 17
P_t^b and P_t^a	Bid price and ask price at time t.	12
R_t	The net return at time t: $R_t \equiv (P_t - P_{t-1})/P_{t-1}$. In some chapters we also use R_t to denote the log return, $\log(P_t) - \log(P_{t-1})$, or the simple return, $P_t - P_{t-1}$, with a slight abuse of notation.	2, 12, 14, 17
$\mathbb{R}$	The set of real numbers.	14
$\mathcal{P}$	A market pattern of returns $\mathcal{P} \equiv [R_1, ..., R_p]$.	14
$s : \mathbb{R}^m \to \{-1, 0, 1\}$	Memory-m strategy.	14
$\pi(k)$	A uniform permutation of the set of time indexes $\{1, ..., T\}$.	14
ω_t^f	Gross return of investor f's portfolio in period t: $f x_{a,t} + (1 - f)x_{b,t}$.	15
W_T^f	Average log-relative-growth in period T.	15
η	Initial relative wealth of investor f over the total wealth in the population.	15
β_a and β_b	Sensitivity of investment style returns to the common return component.	15
$D_{i,f}$	Decile ranking of security i according to factor f.	17
$TO_{i,t}$	Turnover for security i on day t.	17
v_t	Common factor that represents market information.	17

Continued

Table A.1 *Continued*

Notation	Meaning	Chapter(s)
$\epsilon_{i,t}$, ζ_t, and $\eta_{i,t}$	White-noise random variables.	17
$\lambda_{i,t}$	Interaction between public orders and market-makers over the cumulative history of $\epsilon_{i,t}$'s.	17
$\omega_{i,t}$	Portfolio weight of security i at date t.	17
$V_{i,t}$	Volume for security i during a specific month t.	17
$\pi_t(q)$	The profits for a q-period contrarian strategy.	17
$\mathbf{R}_t$	A $(N \times 1)$-vector of period t returns.	17
μ	Expectation of $\mathbf{R}_t$.	17
Γ_l	Lag-l autocovariance of $\mathbf{R}_t$.	17

Please see the relevant chapter for formal definitions.

Proofs and Additional Results

In this appendix, we provide proofs for all the key results contained in this volume, as well as some additional results, organized by chapter. These proofs are taken from the publications on which each chapter is based.

B.1 Chapter 2: The Binary Choice Model

These proofs are drawn from Brennan and Lo (2011). We first provide a brief summary of the basic properties of stochastic convergence that are used throughout our analysis; see Serfling (1980) for further details.

We begin with formal definitions of convergence in probability and distribution:

Definition B.1 *A sequence of random variables $\{X_n\}$ is said to converge in probability to X if and only if for any $\epsilon > 0$:*

$$\lim_{n \to \infty} \mathrm{Prob}(|X_n - X| > \epsilon) \ = \ 0, \tag{B.1}$$

and we denote this type of convergence by the expressions:

$$\mathrm{plim}_{n \to \infty} X_n \ = \ X \ \ or \ \ X_n \overset{p}{\to} X. \tag{B.2}$$

If two sequences of random variables $\{X_n\}$ and $\{Y_n\}$ satisfy the relation $X_n - Y_n \overset{p}{\to} 0$, they are said to be 'equal in probability' and we denote this relation as $X_n \overset{p}{=} Y_n$. Under this definition, we can write $\mathrm{plim}_{n \to \infty} X_n = X$ as $X_n \overset{p}{=} X$.

Definition B.2 *A sequence of random variables $\{X_n\}$ with distribution functions $\{F_n(x)\}$ is said to converge in distribution to X with distribution function $F(x)$ if and only if:*

$$\lim_{n \to \infty} F_n(x) \ = \ F(x) \tag{B.3}$$

for each continuity point x of $F(\cdot)$, and we denote this type of convergence by the expression:

$$X_n \overset{d}{\to} X. \tag{B.4}$$

These notions of convergence satisfy the following properties:

Proposition B.1 *If $X_n \overset{p}{\to} X$, $Y_n \overset{p}{\to} Y$, and $Z_n \overset{d}{\to} Z$, then:*

$$X_n + Y_n \overset{p}{\to} X + Y, \tag{B.5}$$

$$X_n Y_n \overset{p}{\to} XY, \tag{B.6}$$

$$g(X_n) \overset{p}{\to} g(X), \text{ for any } g(\cdot) \text{ continuous at } X. \tag{B.7}$$

If X is a finite constant, then:

$$X_n + Z_n \overset{d}{\to} X + Z, \tag{B.8}$$

$$X_n Z_n \overset{d}{\to} XZ, \tag{B.9}$$

$$Z_n / X_n \overset{d}{\to} Z/X, \text{ if } X \neq 0. \tag{B.10}$$

B.1.1 Proof of Proposition 2.1

This follows from the first and second derivatives of Equation (2.7). Because the second derivative is strictly negative, there is exactly one maximum value obtained in the interval $[0, 1]$. The values of the first derivative of $\alpha(f)$ at the endpoints are given by:

$$I'(0) = \mathbb{E}[x_a/x_b] - 1, \quad I'(1) = 1 - \mathbb{E}[x_b/x_a]. \tag{B.11}$$

If $I'(0)$ and $I'(1)$ are both positive or both negative, then $\alpha(f)$ increases or decreases, respectively, throughout the interval and the maximum value is attained at $f=1$ or $f=0$, respectively. Otherwise, $f=f^*$ is the unique point in the interval for which $\alpha'(f)=0$, where f^* is defined in Equation (2.9), and it is at this point that $\alpha(f)$ attains its maximum value. The expression in Equation (2.8) summarizes the results of these observations for the various possible values of $\mathbb{E}[x_a/x_b]$ and $\mathbb{E}[x_b/x_a]$. Note that the case $\mathbb{E}[x_a/x_b] \leq 1$ and $\mathbb{E}[x_b/x_a] \leq 1$ is not considered because this set of inequalities implies that $I'(0) \leq 0$ and $I'(1) \geq 0$, which is impossible since $I''(f)$ is strictly negative.

B.1.2 Proof of Corollary 2.1

Kolmogorov's law of large numbers (Serfling 1980, Chapter 1.8) implies that $T^{-1} \log n_T^f$ converges almost surely to its expectation $\alpha(f)$, hence the exponential of the former converges almost surely to the exponential of the latter (see White (2001, Proposition 2.11)). Note that almost-sure convergence is stronger than convergence in probability, but we use the latter concept in this and later results in anticipation of generalizations in which $\{x_{a,t}, x_{b,t}\}$ are not necessarily independent and identically distributed (IID) over time. As long as $\{x_{a,t}, x_{b,t}\}$ is stationary and ergodic, a weak law of large numbers applies, implying convergence in probability White (2001, Chapter 5).

The second part of the corollary follows from the fact that

$$\left(n_T^f\right)^{1/T} = \exp\left(T^{-1} \sum_{t=1}^{T} \log(fx_{a,t} + (1-f)x_{b,t})\right) \overset{p}{=} \exp(\alpha(f)), \tag{B.12}$$

$$\left(\frac{n_T^{f'}}{n_T^{f^*}}\right)^{1/T} \stackrel{p}{=} \exp\Big((\alpha(f') - \alpha(f^*))\Big) \;\to\; 0, \tag{B.13}$$

where the equality in probability in Equation (B.12) follows from Kolmogorov's law of large numbers and the continuity of the exponential function, and Equation (B.13) follows from applying Proposition B.1 to the ratio $(n_T^{f'})^{1/T}/(n_T^{f^*})^{1/T}$ and the fact that $\alpha(f') < \alpha(f^*)$ for any $f' \neq f^*$ due to the optimality of f^*.

B.1.3 Proof of Proposition 2.2

This result follows directly from the Lindeberg–Levy central limit theory applied to $T^{-1} \log n_T^{f}$ (Serfling 1980, Chapter 1.9).

B.1.4 Proof of Proposition 2.3

This result follows from the fact that the expectation in Equation (2.7) is given by

$$\alpha(f) \;=\; p \log\big(fc_{a1} + (1 - f)c_{b1}\big) + q \log\big(fc_{a2} + (1 - f)c_{b2}\big), \tag{B.14}$$

and taking the derivative of this function and solving for $\alpha'(f) = 0$ yields the unique solution $f = f^*$, where f^* is as defined in the second case of Equation (2.15). Whenever this value of f^* lies in the interval $[0, 1]$, it is the optimal value of f. Otherwise, analysis of the sign of the first derivative of $\alpha(f)$ at each endpoint of the interval $[0, 1]$ shows that the optimal value, f^*, is either 0 or 1 as described in the first and third cases of Equation (2.15).

B.1.5 Proof of Corollary 2.2

Observe that the intermediate expression for f^* in Equation (2.15) can be rewritten as:

$$f^* \;=\; p + p\left(\frac{r_2}{1 - r_2}\right) + q\left(\frac{1}{1 - r_1}\right).$$

The second term on the right is $O(r_2)$, and the third term on the right is $O(1/r_1)$.

B.1.6 Proof of Proposition 2.4

In particular, because an individual's expected number of offspring,

$$\mathbb{E}[x_i] \;=\; p\big(fc_{a1} + (1 - f)c_{b1}\big) + q\big(fc_{a2} + (1 - f)c_{b2}\big), \tag{B.15}$$

is a monotone function of f, an individual seeking to maximize $\mathbb{E}[x_i]$ will select f to be 0 or 1, depending on which of these two extremes yields a higher expectation, as specified in Equation (2.18).

B.1.7 Proof of Proposition 2.5

If $r(w)$ is twice continuously differentiable, then the derivative of $r(w)$ is everywhere non-negative because of Assumption 2.3, and tends towards zero as w becomes sufficiently large or sufficiently small because of Assumptions 2.4 and 2.5. It must also be positive in some region so that $r(w)$ increases from 0 to a positive number. As a result, the derivative of $r(w)$ is increasing for sufficiently small values of w and decreasing for sufficiently large values, which, in turn, implies that $\tilde{r}(w)$ is concave for sufficiently large w and convex for sufficiently small w.

If $r(w)$ is not continuously differentiable, then pick any two values w_1' and w_2' such that $r(w_1') < r(w_2')$ and such that $r(w)$ is not linear and increasing in a neighbourhood of either point. (It must be possible to pick such points, because, if not, $r(w)$ would always be linear and increasing as w becomes small or large without bound, and so either Assumption 2.4 or 2.5 would necessarily be violated.) Consider the segment connecting the point on the graph of $r(w)$ at $w = w_1'$ to the point at $w = w_2'$, and let w_1 be the smallest value of w greater than w_1' at which the segment intersects the graph, and let w_2 be the largest value of w less than w_2' at which the segment intersects the graph. By construction, $w_1' < w_1 \leq w_2 < w_2'$, and w_1 satisfies Equation (2.26) for all $w \leq w_1'$, and w_2 satisfies Equation (2.27) for all $w \geq w_2'$.

B.1.8 Proof of Corollary 2.4

It was shown in Section 2.3.1 that the growth-optimal behaviour is to take the risky bet, to randomize, or to take the safe bet, according to whether c_b is in $[c_{a1}, c_0]$, $[c_0, c_p]$, or $[c_p, c_{a2}]$, respectively. The corollary follows if these c values are transformed into w values via the function $c^{-1}(\cdot)$, and the fact that $c^{-1}(c_p) < w_p$ follows because $r(w)$ is concave throughout the interval $[w_{a1}, w_{a2}]$.

B.1.9 Proof of Corollary 2.5

As with the proof of Corollary 2.4, we note that the growth-optimal behaviour is to take the risky bet, to randomize, or to take the safe bet, according to whether c_b' is in $[c_{a1}', c_0']$, $[c_0', c_p']$, or $[c_p', c_{a2}']$, respectively. These values can be transformed into w values via the function $c^{-1}(\cdot)$, and the fact that $c^{-1}(c_p') > w_p'$ follows because $r(w)$ is concave throughout the interval $[w_{a1}', w_{a2}']$. If $r(w)$ is invertible in this region, and if $1/r(w)$ is concave throughout this region as well, then

$$\frac{1}{c_0'} = \frac{p}{c_{a1}'} + \frac{q}{c_{a2}'} \leq \frac{1}{r(w_p')} .$$

Taking reciprocals of this inequality and applying the function c^{-1}, we have $c^{-1}(c_0') \geq w_p'$. Therefore, the interval $[w_{a1}', c^{-1}(c_0')]$, which is the interval for which the risky choice B' is always optimal, contains the point w_p'. As a result, the final assertion of the corollary follows.

B.2 Chapter 3: Mutation

These proofs are drawn from Brennan, Lo, and Zhang (2018). We first provide additional technical details for our analysis, followed by proofs for the main results.

The definition and properties of Birkhoff's contraction coefficient can be found in (Caswell 2001, pp. 370–372) or (Ipsen and Selee 2011, p.159). Let $\mathbf{x}$ and $\mathbf{y}$ be positive vectors. The Hilbert pseudo-metric distance between $\mathbf{x}$ and $\mathbf{y}$ is defined as:

$$d(\mathbf{x}, \mathbf{y}) \equiv \log\left(\frac{\max_i \frac{x_i}{y_i}}{\min_i \frac{x_i}{y_i}}\right) = \max_{i,j} \log\left(\frac{x_i y_j}{x_j y_i}\right).$$

It measures the distance between two vectors in a way that depends only on their proportional composition, independent of their absolute size. It satisfies the following conditions:

$$d(\mathbf{x}, \mathbf{y}) \geq 0,$$

$$d(\mathbf{x}, \mathbf{y}) = d(\mathbf{y}, \mathbf{x}),$$

$$d(\mathbf{x}, \mathbf{y}) \leq d(\mathbf{x}, \mathbf{z}) + d(\mathbf{z}, \mathbf{y}),$$

$$d(\mathbf{x}, \mathbf{y}) = 0 \quad \text{iff} \quad \mathbf{x} = a\mathbf{y},$$

$$d(\mathbf{x}, \mathbf{y}) = d(a\mathbf{x}, b\mathbf{y}) \quad \text{for} \quad a, b > 0.$$

Birkhoff's contraction coefficient of a non-negative matrix $\mathbf{A}$ is defined as:

$$\tau(\mathbf{A}) = \sup \frac{d(\mathbf{A}\mathbf{x}, \mathbf{A}\mathbf{y})}{d(\mathbf{x}, \mathbf{y})}, \tag{B.16}$$

where the supremum is taken over all vectors $\mathbf{x} > 0$ and $\mathbf{y} > 0$ that are not multiples of each other. Note that because d is invariant with respect to the absolute magnitude of vectors, the supremum can be taken over a compact subset equivalently, say $||\mathbf{x}||_1 = ||\mathbf{y}||_1 = 1$.

If $\mathbf{A}$ is a strictly positive matrix, then $\tau(\mathbf{A}) < 1$ (see Caswell (2001, p. 372)). Under Assumptions 2.1, 2.2, and 3.1, the matrix $\mathbf{A}_t$ might not be strictly positive. However, there is at least one positive entry in each row of $\mathbf{A}_t$, so $\tau(\mathbf{A}_t) \leq 1$ (see Hajnal (1976) discussion on 'row allowable' matrices). We will prove in Lemma B.1 that $\tau(\mathbf{A}_t)$ is, indeed, strictly less than 1.

Lemma B.1 (Contraction properties of A_t) *Under Assumptions 2.1, 2.2, and 3.1, Birkhoff's contraction coefficient τ of $\mathbf{A}_t$ is strictly less than 1 almost surely:*

$$\text{Prob}\,(\tau(\mathbf{A}_t) < 1) = 1.$$

Because of Assumption 2.1, there are only finitely many possible random matrices $\mathbf{A}_t$ if x_a and x_b are integers. Therefore, Birkhoff's contraction coefficient, $\tau(\mathbf{A}_t)$, is uniformly less than some positive constant $\delta < 1$. But Lemma B.1 is enough for the analysis henceforth.

Proposition B.2 (asymptotic population distribution) *Under Assumptions 2.1, 2.2, and 3.1, there exists some σ such that the total population size, $P_t = \iota'\mathbf{n}_t$, at time t satisfies:*

$$\frac{\log P_t - t\alpha_\varepsilon}{\sigma\sqrt{t}} \implies Normal(0, 1)$$

in distribution as $t \to \infty$.

By Proposition B.2, the asymptotic distribution of total population is lognormal, and the mean and variance of $\log P_t$ both increase linearly with time.

Proposition B.3 (rate of convergence) *Under Assumptions 2.1, 2.2, and 3.1, the Markov chain* $\{y_t\}_{t=0}^{\infty}$ *is uniformly ergodic if the support of* $\mathscr{L}(\cdot)$ *has a non-empty interior.*[1] *By uniformly ergodic we mean that* $\mathscr{L}_T$ *converges to the stationary distribution* $\mathscr{L}$ *geometrically fast:*

$$||\mathscr{L}_T(\cdot) - \mathscr{L}(\cdot)||_{TV} \le M\rho^T, T = 1, 2, 3, \cdots$$

for some $\rho < 1$ *and* $M < \infty$, *where* $||\cdot||_{TV}$ *is the total variation distance between two probability measures.*

Proposition B.3 asserts that the rate of convergence in Proposition 3.3 is exponential. Therefore, one would expect that the convergence of $\mathscr{L}_T(\cdot)$ to the stationary distribution $\mathscr{L}(\cdot)$ is very fast in evolution.

B.2.1 Proof of Lemma B.1

The proof generalizes the discussion in Caswell (2001, pp. 371–372). Let $\mathbf{A} = (a_{ij})_{(K+1)\times(K+1)}$ be any matrix drawn under Assumptions 2.1, 2.2, and 3.1. If $\mathbf{A}$ is strictly positive, then $\tau(\mathbf{A}) < 1$. If $\mathbf{A}$ is not strictly positive, because $\mathbf{P}(x_a > 0 \text{ or } x_b > 0) = 1$, $\mathbf{A}$ must be a strictly positive matrix except for the first column or the $(K + 1)$-th column (but not both). Suppose without loss of generality that the first column of $\mathbf{A}$ is 0 and the rest is strictly positive, and it suffices to prove $\tau(\mathbf{A}) < 1$ in this case.

Now let $\mathbf{x}(t) = (x_i(t + 1))_{i=1}^{K+1}$ and $\mathbf{y}(t) = (y_i(t + 1))_{i=1}^{K+1}$ be positive vectors that are not proportional to each other, and $\mathbf{x}(t + 1) = \mathbf{A} \cdot \mathbf{x}(t)$ and $\mathbf{y}(t + 1) = \mathbf{A} \cdot \mathbf{y}(t)$. Then

$$\frac{x_i(t + 1)}{y_i(t + 1)} = \frac{\sum_j a_{ij}x_j(t)}{\sum_k a_{ik}y_k(t)} = \sum_j \left(\frac{a_{ij}y_j(t)}{\sum_k a_{ik}y_k(t)} \right) \frac{x_j(t)}{y_j(t)} = \sum_j p_{ij} \frac{x_j(t)}{y_j(t)},$$

where $\sum_j p_{ij} = 1$. A careful examination of p_{ij} yields that for any i,

$$p_{i1} = 0, \quad \text{and} \quad p_{ij} > 0 \text{ for } j = 2, 3, \cdots, K + 1.$$

Therefore, $\frac{x_i(t+1)}{y_i(t+1)}$ is a positive weighted average of $\{\frac{x_j(t)}{y_j(t)}\}_{j=2}^{K+1}$, and this is true for all i. Because $\mathbf{x}(t)$ and $\mathbf{y}(t)$ are not proportional to each other, there are two possibilities:

(1) The ratios in $\{\frac{x_j(t)}{y_j(t)}\}_{j=2}^{K+1}$ are all the same, but different from $\frac{x_1(t)}{y_1(t)}$. In this case exactly one of the following must be true:

$$\min_j \frac{x_j(t)}{y_j(t)} < \frac{x_i(t + 1)}{y_i(t + 1)} \le \max_j \frac{x_j(t)}{y_j(t)}, \quad \text{for all } i,$$

or

$$\min_j \frac{x_j(t)}{y_j(t)} \le \frac{x_i(t + 1)}{y_i(t + 1)} < \max_j \frac{x_j(t)}{y_j(t)}, \quad \text{for all } i.$$

---

[1] The support of $\mathscr{L}(\cdot)$ is defined to be the set of all points $\mathbf{y} \in \mathscr{Y}$ for which every open neighbourhood of $\mathbf{y}$ has positive measure.

(2) The ratios in $\{\frac{x_j(t)}{y_j(t)}\}_{j=2}^{K+1}$ are not all the same. In this case we have

$$\min_j \frac{x_j(t)}{y_j(t)} < \frac{x_i(t+1)}{y_i(t+1)} < \max_j \frac{x_j(t)}{y_j(t)}, \quad \text{for all } i,$$

In both (1) and (2) we have:

$$d\left(\mathbf{x}(t+1), \mathbf{y}(t+1)\right) < d\left(\mathbf{x}(t), \mathbf{y}(t)\right).$$

That is, each multiplication by $\mathbf{A}$ contracts the distance between the two vectors. Because the supremum in Birkhoff's contraction coefficient in Equation (B.16) can be taken over a compact set, we have $\tau(\mathbf{A}) < 1$ with probability 1.

B.2.2 Proof of Proposition 3.1

Let I^f be a Bernoulli variable that equals 1 with probability f and 0 otherwise. Define 'not mutation' indicator N and 'mutation from g to f' indicator $M^{g \to f}$:

$$N = \begin{cases} 1 & \text{with prob } 1 - \epsilon \\ 0 & \text{with prob } \epsilon \end{cases}, \quad M^{g \to f} = \begin{cases} 1 & \text{with prob } \frac{\epsilon}{K} \\ 0 & \text{with prob } 1 - \frac{\epsilon}{K} \end{cases}.$$

In generation t, type f individuals come from type f individuals without mutation and type $g(\neq f)$ individuals with mutation in generation $t-1$. Consider them separately. From type f:

$$\sum_{i=1}^{n_{t-1}^f} x_{i,t}^{f \to f} = \left(\sum_{i=1}^{n_{t-1}^f} N_{i,t} I_{i,t}^f\right) x_{a,t} + \left(\sum_{i=1}^{n_{t-1}^f} N_{i,t}(1 - I_{i,t}^f)\right) x_{b,t}$$

$$\overset{\text{a.s.}}{=} (1 - \epsilon) n_{t-1}^f \left(f x_{a,t} + (1 - f) x_{b,t}\right)$$

as n_{t-1}^f increases without bound. From type $g(\neq f)$:

$$\sum_{g \neq f} \sum_{i=1}^{n_{t-1}^g} x_{i,t}^{g \to f} = \sum_{g \neq f} \left[\left(\sum_{i=1}^{n_{t-1}^g} M_{i,t}^{g \to f} I_{i,t}^g\right) x_{a,t} + \left(\sum_{i=1}^{n_{t-1}^g} M_{i,t}^{g \to f}(1 - I_{i,t}^g)\right) x_{b,t}\right]$$

$$\overset{\text{a.s.}}{=} \frac{\epsilon}{K} \sum_{g \neq f} n_{t-1}^g \left(g x_{a,t} + (1 - g) x_{b,t}\right)$$

as n_{t-1}^g increases without bound. Note that

$$n_t^f = \sum_{i=1}^{n_{t-1}^f} x_{i,t}^{f \to f} + \sum_{g \neq f} \sum_{i=1}^{n_{t-1}^g} x_{i,t}^{g \to f}$$

$$\overset{\text{a.s.}}{=} (1 - \epsilon) n_{t-1}^f \left(f x_{a,t} + (1 - f) x_{b,t}\right) + \frac{\epsilon}{K} \sum_{g \neq f} n_{t-1}^g \left(g x_{a,t} + (1 - g) x_{b,t}\right).$$

Equation (3.1) simply rewrites the above equation in matrix form.

B.2.3 Proof of Proposition 3.2

By Lemma B.1 and Caswell (2001, p. 386, 14.22), demographic weak ergodicity[2] holds. In addition, $\mathbb{E}\log_+ \|\mathbf{A}_1\| < \infty$ because x_a and x_b are bounded, where $\log_+ \|\mathbf{A}_1\| = \max\{0, \log\|\mathbf{A}_1\|\}$. Therefore, assumption 4.2.1 in Tuljapurkar (1990) is satisfied, and Proposition 3.2 follows from Tuljapurkar (1990, p. 26 (A)).

B.2.4 Proof of Proposition 3.3

Because the random matrices $\mathbf{A}_t$ are IID, Assumptions 4.2.1, 4.2.3, and 4.2.6 in Tuljapurkar (1990) are satisfied, and the conclusion follows directly from Tuljapurkar (1990, p. 29 (J)).

B.2.5 Proof of Proposition 3.4

Part (i) is a standard result for single type branching process in random environments (see Smith and Wilkinson (1969, Theorem 3.1), for example). Part (ii) follows from Proposition 3.2 and Corollary 3.1.

B.2.6 Proof of Proposition 3.5

Let $x^1_{a,j}$ be the number of offspring generated by Φ^1 for action a in the j-th generation, and $x^2_{b,j}$ the number of offspring generated by Φ^2 for action b in the j-th generation. Table B.1 calculates the number of individuals of both behaviours along evolution, starting with one individual of each type. From the last line of Table B.1 we have:

$$n_k^{\epsilon,\text{Total}} = \epsilon^{2k-1}(1-\epsilon)^{\sum_{i=1}^{k}(T_i^1+T_i^2)-2k} \prod_{j=1}^{\sum_{i=1}^{k}T_i^1} x_{a,j}^1 \prod_{j=1}^{\sum_{i=1}^{k}T_i^2} x_{b,j}^2.$$

Therefore,

$$\frac{1}{k}\log n_k^{\epsilon,\text{Total}} = \frac{2k-1}{k}\log\epsilon + \left(\frac{1}{k}\sum_{i=1}^{k}(T_i^1+T_i^2)-2\right)\log(1-\epsilon)$$

$$+ \frac{1}{k}\sum_{j=1}^{\sum_{i=1}^{k}T_i^1}\log x_{a,j}^1 + \frac{1}{k}\sum_{j=1}^{\sum_{i=1}^{k}T_i^2}\log x_{b,j}^2$$

$$\overset{\text{a.s.}}{\to} 2\log\epsilon + \left(\mathbb{E}[T^1+T^2]-2\right)\log(1-\epsilon) + \mathbb{E}[T^1]\mathbb{E}[\log x_a^1] + \mathbb{E}[T^2]\mathbb{E}[\log x_b^2]$$

$$= 2\log\frac{\epsilon}{1-\epsilon} + \mathbb{E}[T^1+T^2]\log(1-\epsilon) + \mathbb{E}[T^1]\mathbb{E}[\log x_a^1] + \mathbb{E}[T^2]\mathbb{E}[\log x_b^2],$$

where '$\overset{\text{a.s.}}{\to}$' denotes almost sure convergence and follows from the strong law of large numbers as k increases without bound. Since the value of ϵ that maximizes the population size $n_k^{\epsilon,\text{Total}}$ is

---

[2] The definition of demographic weak ergodicity is given in Caswell (2001, p. 383) and Tuljapurkar (1990, p. 17). Essentially, it means that the difference between the probability distributions of normalized population vectors resulting from any two initial populations, exposed to independent sample paths of the stochastic environment, decays to zero.

Table B.1 Population dynamics for the two-behaviour regime-switching model.

Cycle	Regime	Generation	# of individuals $f = 0$	# of individuals $f = 1$
			1	1
1	Φ^1	1	$q \cdot x_{a,1}^1$	$\epsilon \cdot x_{a,1}^1$
		$\vdots$	$\vdots$	$\vdots$
		T_1^1	$q^{T_1^1} \prod_{j=1}^{T_1^1} x_{a,j}^1$	$\epsilon q^{T_1^1-1} \prod_{j=1}^{T_1^1} x_{a,j}^1$
1	Φ^2	$T_1^1 + 1$	$\epsilon^2 q^{T_1^1-1} \prod_{j=1}^{T_1^1} x_{a,j}^1 \cdot x_{b,1}^2$	$\epsilon q^{T_1^1} \prod_{j=1}^{T_1^1} x_{a,j}^1 \cdot x_{b,1}^2$
		$\vdots$	$\vdots$	$\vdots$
		$T_1^1 + T_1^2$	$\epsilon^2 q^{T_1^1+T_1^2-2} \prod_{j=1}^{T_1^1} x_{a,j}^1 \prod_{j=1}^{T_1^2} x_{b,j}^2$	$\epsilon q^{T_1^1+T_1^2-1} \prod_{j=1}^{T_1^1} x_{a,j}^1 \prod_{j=1}^{T_1^2} x_{b,j}^2$
2	Φ^1	$T_1^1 + T_1^2 + 1$	$\epsilon^2 q^{T_1^1+T_1^2-1} \prod_{j=1}^{T_1^1} x_{a,j}^1 \prod_{j=1}^{T_1^2} x_{b,j}^2 \cdot x_{a,T_1^1+1}^1$	$\epsilon^3 q^{T_1^1+T_1^2-2} \prod_{j=1}^{T_1^1} x_{a,j}^1 \prod_{j=1}^{T_1^2} x_{b,j}^2 \cdot x_{a,T_1^1+1}^1$
		$\vdots$	$\vdots$	$\vdots$
		$T_1^1 + T_1^2 + T_2^1$	$\epsilon^2 q^{T_1^1+T_1^2+T_2^1-2} \prod_{j=1}^{T_1^1+T_2^1} x_{a,j}^1 \prod_{j=1}^{T_1^2} x_{b,j}^2$	$\epsilon^3 q^{T_1^1+T_1^2+T_2^1-3} \prod_{j=1}^{T_1^1+T_2^1} x_{a,j}^1 \prod_{j=1}^{T_1^2} x_{b,j}^2$
2	Φ^2	$T_1^1 + T_1^2 + T_2^1 + 1$	$\epsilon^4 q^{T_1^1+T_1^2+T_2^1-3} \prod_{j=1}^{T_1^1+T_2^1} x_{a,j}^1 \prod_{j=1}^{T_1^2} x_{b,j}^2 \cdot x_{b,T_1^2+1}^2$	$\epsilon^3 q^{T_1^1+T_1^2+T_2^1-2} \prod_{j=1}^{T_1^1+T_2^1} x_{a,j}^1 \prod_{j=1}^{T_1^2} x_{b,j}^2 \cdot x_{b,T_1^2+1}^2$
		$\vdots$	$\vdots$	$\vdots$
		$T_1^1 + T_1^2 + T_2^1 + T_2^2$	$\epsilon^4 q^{T_1^1+T_1^2+T_2^1+T_2^2-4} \prod_{j=1}^{T_1^1+T_2^1} x_{a,j}^1 \prod_{j=1}^{T_1^2+T_2^2} x_{b,j}^2$	$\epsilon^3 q^{T_1^1+T_1^2+T_2^1+T_2^2-3} \prod_{j=1}^{T_1^1+T_2^1} x_{a,j}^1 \prod_{j=1}^{T_1^2+T_2^2} x_{b,j}^2$
$\vdots$	$\vdots$	$\vdots$	$\vdots$	$\vdots$
k	Φ^2	$\sum_{i=1}^{k} (T_i^1 + T_i^2)$	$\epsilon^{2k} q^{\sum_{i=1}^{k}(T_i^1+T_i^2)-2k} \prod_{j=1}^{\sum_{i=1}^{k} T_i^1} x_{a,j}^1 \prod_{j=1}^{\sum_{i=1}^{k} T_i^2} x_{b,j}^2$	$\epsilon^{2k-1} q^{\sum_{i=1}^{k}(T_i^1+T_i^2)-(2k-1)} \prod_{j=1}^{\sum_{i=1}^{k} T_i^1} x_{a,j}^1 \prod_{j=1}^{\sum_{i=1}^{k} T_i^2} x_{b,j}^2$
$\vdots$	$\vdots$	$\vdots$	$\vdots$	$\vdots$

Source: Brennan, T. J., Lo, A. W., and Zhang, R. (2018). Variety is the spice of life: irrational behavior as adaptation to stochastic environments. *Quarterly Journal of Finance* 8(03): 1850009, with permission of World Scientific Publishing Co., Inc.; permission conveyed through Copyright Clearance Center, Inc.

also the value of ε that maximizes $k^{-1} \log n_k^{\varepsilon,\text{Total}}$, the above analysis implies that this maximum converges in probability to the maximum of

$$\pi(\varepsilon) = 2 \log \frac{\varepsilon}{1-\varepsilon} + \mathbb{E}[T^1 + T^2] \log(1-\varepsilon) + \mathbb{E}[T^1]\mathbb{E}_{\Phi^1}[\log x_a] + \mathbb{E}[T^2]\mathbb{E}_{\Phi^2}[\log x_b],$$

where $0 < \varepsilon < 1$. Take the first and second derivatives of the above equation:

$$\pi'(\varepsilon) = \frac{2}{\varepsilon} - \frac{\mathbb{E}[T^1 + T^2] - 2}{1-\varepsilon},$$

$$\pi''(\varepsilon) = -\frac{2}{\varepsilon^2} - \frac{\mathbb{E}[T^1 + T^2] - 2}{(1-\varepsilon)^2}.$$

Note that T^1 and T^2 are positive integers, so $\mathbb{E}[T^1 + T^2] \geq 2$. Therefore, the second derivative is always negative for $0 < \varepsilon < 1$. In addition, $\pi'(0^+) > 0, \pi'(1^-) < 0$, which implies that $\pi(\varepsilon)$ has a unique maximum in $(0,1)$ at $\pi'(\varepsilon) = 0$. Solving for ε, we get the desired result.

B.2.7 Proof of Proposition B.2

Because the random matrices $\mathbf{A}_t$ are IID, Assumptions 4.2.1 and 4.2.3 in Tuljapurkar (1990) are satisfied, and the conclusion follows directly from Tuljapurkar (1990, p. 27, (F)).

B.2.8 Proof of Proposition B.3

We utilize Meyn and Tweedie (2009, p. 411, Theorem 16.2.5):

> If $\{\mathbf{y}_t\}_{t=0}^\infty$ is a ψ-irreducible[3] and aperiodic T-chain[4], and if the state space $\mathcal{Y}$ is compact, then $\{\mathbf{y}_t\}_{t=0}^\infty$ is uniformly ergodic.

The uniqueness of the stationary distribution $\mathcal{L}$ in Proposition 3.3 implies that $\{\mathbf{y}_t\}_{t=0}^\infty$ is aperiodic, so it suffices to prove that $\{\mathbf{y}_t\}_{t=0}^\infty$ is a ψ-irreducible T-chain.

Take $\psi = \mathcal{L}$ to be the stationary distribution of $\{\mathbf{y}_t\}_{t=0}^\infty$, then for all $\mathbf{y} \in \mathcal{Y}$ and $B \subseteq \mathcal{Y}$, whenever $\psi(B) > 0$, there exists some $n > 0$, possibly depending on both $\mathbf{y}$ and B, such that the n-step transition probability $p_n(\mathbf{y}, B) > 0$. It follows from Meyn and Tweedie (2009, p. 82, Proposition 4.2.1(ii)) that $\{\mathbf{y}_t\}_{t=0}^\infty$ is ψ-irreducible.

Furthermore, the one-step transition probability, $p_1(\cdot, O)$, is a lower semi-continuous function for any open set $O \subseteq \mathcal{Y}$. Remember that the support of ψ is assumed to have a non-empty interior. It follows from Meyn and Tweedie (2009, p. 124, Theorem 6.0.1(iii)) that $\{\mathbf{y}_t\}_{t=0}^\infty$ is a T-chain.

Finally, the uniform ergodicity of the Markov chain $\{\mathbf{y}_t\}_{t=0}^\infty$ follows from Meyn and Tweedie (2009, p. 411, Theorem 16.2.5).

---

[3] The definition of ψ-irreducibility can be found in Meyn and Tweedie (2009, p. 82).
[4] The definition of T-chains can be found in Meyn and Tweedie (2009, p. 124).

B.2.9 Proof of Corollary 3.1

The lower bound is obvious by simply considering the growth of non-mutated type f^* individuals. To prove the upper bound, first note that

$$\iota' \mathbf{F}_t \mathbf{y}_{t-1} = \iota' \begin{pmatrix} f_1 x_{a,t} + (1-f_1) x_{b,t} & \cdots & 0 \\ \vdots & \ddots & \vdots \\ 0 & \cdots & f_{K+1} x_{a,t} + (1-f_{K+1}) x_{b,t} \end{pmatrix} \begin{pmatrix} y_{t-1}(1) \\ \vdots \\ y_{t-1}(K+1) \end{pmatrix}$$

$$= \sum_{i=1}^{K+1} y_{t-1}(i) \left(f_i x_{a,t} + (1 - f_i) x_{b,t} \right) = (\alpha_{t-1} x_{a,t} + \beta_{t-1} x_{b,t}),$$

where

$$\alpha_{t-1} = \sum_{i=1}^{K+1} y_{t-1}(i) f_i, \quad \beta_{t-1} = \sum_{i=1}^{K+1} y_{t-1}(i)(1 - f_i),$$

and $\alpha_{t-1} + \beta_{t-1} = 1$. Note that $\mathbf{F}_t$ and $\mathbf{y}_{t-1}$ are independent in Equation (3.4), and α_{t-1} and β_{t-1} are constants conditioning on $\mathbf{y}_{t-1}$, so one has:

$$\alpha_\epsilon = \mathbb{E}_{\mathscr{L}} \left\{ \mathbb{E}_\Phi \left[\log(\iota' \mathbf{F}_t \mathbf{y}_{t-1}) \right] \Big| \mathbf{y}_{t-1} \right\} = \mathbb{E}_{\mathscr{L}} \left\{ \mathbb{E}_\Phi \left[\log\left(\alpha_{t-1} x_{a,t} + \beta_{t-1} x_{b,t} \right) \right] \Big| \mathbf{y}_{t-1} \right\}$$

$$\leq \mathbb{E}_{\mathscr{L}} \left\{ \mathbb{E}_\Phi \left[\log\left(f^* x_{a,t} + (1 - f^*) x_{b,t} \right) \right] \Big| \mathbf{y}_{t-1} \right\} = \mathbb{E}_{\mathscr{L}} \left\{ \alpha(f^*) \Big| \mathbf{y}_{t-1} \right\} = \alpha(f^*),$$

where the following fact is used for the inequality:

$$f^* = \mathrm{argmax}_{0 \leq f \leq 1} \mathbb{E}_\Phi \left[\log\left(f x_{a,t} + (1 - f) x_{b,t} \right) \right].$$

B.2.10 Proof of Corollary 3.2

The conclusion follows immediately from Proposition 3.5 by replacing $\mathbb{E}[T^1 + T^2]$ by $2 \cdot \mathbb{E}[T]$.

B.3 Chapter 4: Group Selection

These proofs are drawn from Zhang, Brennan, and Lo (2014a).

B.3.1 Proof of Proposition 4.1

Note that, by definition, $\psi_1^* = p^* \beta_1^* + (1 - p^*) \beta_2^*$, so ψ_1^* is a convex combination of β_1^* and β_2^*. If $\psi_1^* = 1$, at least one of β_1^* and β_2^* must be 1. If $\psi_1^* = 0$, at least one of β_1^* and β_2^* must be 0. If $0 < \psi_1^* < 1$, β_1^* and β_2^* cannot be both greater than or both smaller than ψ_1^*. p^* can be solved accordingly given ψ_1^*, β_1^*, and β_2^*.

B.3.2 Proof of Proposition 4.2

The total number of type $f = (\mathbf{p}, \mathbf{B})$ individuals in generation T is

$$
n_T^f = \sum_{i=1}^{n_{T-1}^f} x_i^{\mathbf{p},\mathbf{B}} = \sum_{i=1}^{n_{T-1}^f} I_{1,i}^{\mathbf{p}} x_1^{\mathbf{B}} + \cdots + I_{m,i}^{\mathbf{p}} x_m^{\mathbf{B}} = n_{T-1}^f \left(\frac{1}{n_{T-1}^f} \sum_{i=1}^{n_{T-1}^f} I_{1,i}^{\mathbf{p}} x_1^{\mathbf{B}} + \cdots + I_{m,i}^{\mathbf{p}} x_m^{\mathbf{B}} \right).
$$

As n_{T-1}^f increases without bound, by the law of large numbers, it converges in probability to

$$
n_{T-1}^f \left(p_1 x_1^{\mathbf{B}} + \cdots + p_m x_m^{\mathbf{B}} \right) = n_{T-1}^f \cdot \mathbf{p} \mathbf{B} \lambda_T'.
$$

Through backward recursion, the total number of type $f = (\mathbf{p}, \mathbf{B})$ individuals in generation T is

$$
n_T^f \overset{p}{=} n_0^f \cdot \prod_{t=1}^{T} \mathbf{p} \mathbf{B} \lambda_t' = \exp \left(\sum_{t=1}^{T} \log \left(\mathbf{p} \mathbf{B} \lambda_t' \right) \right).
$$

Therefore,

$$
\frac{1}{T} \log n_T^f \overset{p}{=} \frac{1}{T} \sum_{t=1}^{T} \log \left(\mathbf{p} \mathbf{B} \lambda_t' \right) \overset{p}{\to} \mathbb{E} \left[\log \left(\mathbf{p} \mathbf{B} \lambda_t' \right) \right]
$$

as T increases without bound. Here '$\overset{p}{=}$' denotes equality in probability and '$\overset{p}{\to}$' denotes convergence in probability.

B.3.3 Proof of Proposition 4.3

We first prove the following lemma and then prove Proposition 4.3.

Lemma B.2 $(\psi_1^*, \cdots, \psi_k^*)$ *maximizes Equation (4.8) if and only if*

$$
\mathbb{E} \left[\frac{\psi_1 \lambda_1 + \cdots + \psi_k \lambda_k}{\psi_1^* \lambda_1 + \cdots + \psi_k^* \lambda_k} \right] \leq 1, \quad \forall (\psi_1, \cdots, \psi_k). \tag{B.17}
$$

Proof of Lemma B.2 Note that Equation (4.8) is a concave function with respect to $\psi_1, \cdots, \psi_k$, so a local maximum is the global maximum. Now suppose $\psi^* = (\psi_1^*, \cdots, \psi_k^*)$ is a local maximum, then a necessary and sufficient condition is that if we move ψ^* towards a direction of any $\psi = (\psi_1, \cdots, \psi_k)$, the growth rate decreases. Formally, let

$$
\psi^\delta = (1 - \delta) \psi^* + \delta \psi,
$$

where ψ is arbitrary and $0 \leq \delta \leq 1$, and

$$
\alpha(\psi^\delta) = \mathbb{E} \left[\log \left(\left((1 - \delta) \psi_1^* + \delta \psi_1 \right) \lambda_1 + \cdots + \left((1 - \delta) \psi_k^* + \delta \psi_k \right) \lambda_k \right) \right].
$$

Then,

$$\boldsymbol{\psi}^* = (\psi_1^*, \cdots, \psi_k^*) \text{ maximizes Equation (4.8)}$$

$$\Longleftrightarrow \frac{\partial \alpha(\boldsymbol{\psi}^\delta)}{\partial \delta}\Big|_{\delta=0} \leq 0, \text{for any } \boldsymbol{\psi} = (\psi_1, \cdots, \psi_k)$$

$$\Longleftrightarrow \mathbb{E}\left[\frac{(\psi_1 - \psi_1^*)\lambda_1 + \cdots + (\psi_k - \psi_k^*)\lambda_k}{\psi_1^*\lambda_1 + \cdots + \psi_k^*\lambda_k}\right] \leq 0, \text{for any } \boldsymbol{\psi} = (\psi_1, \cdots, \psi_k)$$

$$\Longleftrightarrow \mathbb{E}\left[\frac{\psi_1\lambda_1 + \cdots + \psi_k\lambda_k}{\psi_1^*\lambda_1 + \cdots + \psi_k^*\lambda_k}\right] \leq 1, \text{for any } \boldsymbol{\psi} = (\psi_1, \cdots, \psi_k),$$

which completes the proof of the lemma.

The first k conditions in Equation (4.9) follow directly from the lemma. As of the last case, note that $\psi_1 = 1 - \psi_2 - \cdots - \psi_k$ and we can write $\alpha(\cdot)$ as a function of $(\psi_2, \cdots, \psi_k)$. Therefore $\boldsymbol{\psi}^*$ is given by the following equations:

$$\begin{cases} \frac{\partial \alpha(\psi_2, \cdots, \psi_k)}{\partial \psi_2}\Big|_{\psi_{l+1}=\cdots=\psi_k=0} = 0 \\ \frac{\partial \alpha(\psi_2, \cdots, \psi_k)}{\partial \psi_3}\Big|_{\psi_{l+1}=\cdots=\psi_k=0} = 0 \\ \cdots \\ \frac{\partial \alpha(\psi_2, \cdots, \psi_k)}{\partial \psi_l}\Big|_{\psi_{l+1}=\cdots=\psi_k=0} = 0 \end{cases} \tag{B.18}$$

Also, the following partial derivatives must be negative:

$$\begin{cases} \frac{\partial \alpha(\psi_2, \cdots, \psi_k)}{\partial \psi_{l+1}}\Big|_{\boldsymbol{\psi}^*} < 0 \\ \cdots \\ \frac{\partial \alpha(\psi_2, \cdots, \psi_k)}{\partial \psi_k}\Big|_{\boldsymbol{\psi}^*} < 0 \end{cases} \tag{B.19}$$

Equation (B.18) yields

$$\mathbb{E}\left[\frac{\lambda_1}{\psi_1\lambda_1 + \cdots + \psi_l\lambda_l}\right] = \cdots = \mathbb{E}\left[\frac{\lambda_l}{\psi_1\lambda_1 + \cdots + \psi_l\lambda_l}\right].$$

Suppose that the above value is C, then

$$1 = \mathbb{E}\left[\frac{\psi_1\lambda_1 + \cdots + \psi_l\lambda_l}{\psi_1\lambda_1 + \cdots + \psi_l\lambda_l}\right] = (\psi_1 + \cdots + \psi_l)C = C.$$

Equation (B.19) yields

$$\mathbb{E}\left[\frac{\lambda_j}{\psi_1\lambda_1 + \cdots + \psi_l\lambda_l}\right] < \mathbb{E}\left[\frac{\lambda_1}{\psi_1\lambda_1 + \cdots + \psi_l\lambda_l}\right] = 1$$

for $j = l + 1, l + 2, \cdots, k$. which completes the proof.

B.4 Chapter 6: Risk Aversion

These proofs are drawn from Zhang, Brennan, and Lo (2014b). Throughout this section, we assume that:

- (z_a, z_b), $(y_{a,i}, y_{b,i})$, $\log(fz_a + (1-f)z_b)$, and $\log(fy_{a,i} + (1-f)y_{b,i})$ have finite moments up to order 2 for all $f \in [0,1]$ and i.

If assuming further that:

- for all $f \in [0,1]$, $\mathbb{E}[fz_a + (1-f)z_b] = \mathbb{E}[fy_{a,i} + (1-f)y_{b,i}]$ for all i,

one can compare population growth rates in different environments. More specifically, the optimal log-geometric-average growth rate increases as the portion of idiosyncratic risk increases:

$$\alpha_{\lambda_1}(f_{\lambda_1}^*) \geq \alpha_{\lambda_2}(f_{\lambda_2}^*) \quad \text{if} \quad 0 \leq \lambda_1 \leq \lambda_2 \leq 1.$$

To prove this, for any given f, take the first derivative of $\alpha_\lambda(f)$ to λ:

$$\frac{\partial \alpha_\lambda(f)}{\partial \lambda} = \mathbb{E}_z \left[\frac{z^f - \mathbb{E}[y^f]}{\lambda z^f + (1-\lambda)\mathbb{E}[y^f]} \right].$$

Evaluate the first derivative at $\lambda = 0, 1$, and note that the additional assumptions above imply that $\mathbb{E}_z[z^f] = \mathbb{E}_y[y^f]$:

$$\frac{\partial \alpha_\lambda(f)}{\partial \lambda} \bigg|_{\lambda=0} = \mathbb{E}_z \left[\frac{z^f - \mathbb{E}_y[y^f]}{\mathbb{E}_y[y^f]} \right] = 0,$$

$$\frac{\partial \alpha_\lambda(f)}{\partial \lambda} \bigg|_{\lambda=1} = \mathbb{E}_z \left[\frac{z^f - \mathbb{E}_y[y^f]}{z^f} \right] = 1 - \mathbb{E}_y[y^f]\mathbb{E}_z\left[\frac{1}{z^f}\right] \leq 0,$$

where the last step uses Jensen's inequality. Now take the second derivative of $\alpha_\lambda(f)$ to λ:

$$\frac{\partial^2 \alpha_\lambda(f)}{\partial \lambda^2} = \mathbb{E}_z \left[\frac{-\left(z^f - \mathbb{E}[y^f]\right)^2}{\left(\lambda z^f + (1-\lambda)\mathbb{E}[y^f]\right)^2} \right] \leq 0.$$

Therefore, for any given f, $\alpha_\lambda(f)$ is a nonincreasing concave function in the interval $0 \leq \lambda \leq 1$. Because $\alpha_\lambda(f_\lambda^*)$ is the maximum of $\alpha_\lambda(f)$ over all f, it follows that $\alpha_{\lambda_1}(f_{\lambda_1}^*) \geq \alpha_{\lambda_2}(f_{\lambda_2}^*)$ whenever $\lambda_1 \leq \lambda_2$, as desired.

B.4.1 Proof of Equations (6.2) and (6.3)

The total number of offspring of type f in generation t is simply the sum of all the offspring from the type-f individuals of the previous generation:

$$n_t^f = \sum_{i=1}^{n_{t-1}^f} x_{i,t}^f = \lambda \sum_{i=1}^{n_{t-1}^f} z_{i,t}^f + (1-\lambda) \sum_{i=1}^{n_{t-1}^f} y_{i,t}^f$$

$$= \lambda \left(z_{a,t} \sum_{i=1}^{n_{t-1}^f} I_{i,t}^f + z_{b,t} \sum_{i=1}^{n_{t-1}^f}(1 - I_{i,t}^f) \right) + (1-\lambda) \left(\sum_{i=1}^{n_{t-1}^f} I_{i,t}^f y_{a,i,t} + \sum_{i=1}^{n_{t-1}^f}(1 - I_{i,t}^f) y_{b,i,t} \right),$$

where we have added time subscripts to the relevant variables to clarify their temporal ordering. As n_{t-1}^f increases without bound, the law of large numbers implies that:

$$\frac{n_t^f}{n_{t-1}^f} \overset{p}{=} \lambda \left(f z_{a,t} + (1-f) z_{b,t} \right) + (1-\lambda) \left(f \mathbb{E}_y[y_a] + (1-f)\mathbb{E}_y[y_b] \right)$$

$$= \lambda \left(f z_{a,t} + (1-f) z_{b,t} \right) + (1-\lambda)\mathbb{E}_y[y^f],$$

where '$\overset{p}{=}$' denotes equality in probability. Through backward recursion and assuming that $n_0^f = 1$ without loss of generality, the population of type-f individuals in generation T is given by:

$$n_T^f \overset{p}{=} \prod_{t=1}^{T} \left(\lambda \left(f z_{a,t} + (1-f) z_{b,t} \right) + (1-\lambda)\mathbb{E}_y[y^f] \right).$$

Taking the logarithm on both sides and again using the law of large numbers, we get:

$$\frac{1}{T} \log n_T^f \overset{p}{=} \frac{1}{T} \sum_{t=1}^{T} \log \left(\lambda \left(f z_{a,t} + (1-f) z_{b,t} \right) + (1-\lambda)\mathbb{E}_y[y^f] \right) \overset{p}{\to} \mathbb{E}_z \left[\log \left(\lambda z^f + (1-\lambda)\mathbb{E}_y[y^f] \right) \right],$$

where '$\overset{p}{\to}$' denotes convergence in probability, which completes the proof of Equation (6.2). Equation (6.3) is a simple re-expression of Equation (6.2) as a function of ξ_a^ω and ξ_b^ω.

B.5 Chapter 7: Cooperation

These proofs and additional simulation results are drawn from Koduri and Lo (2021). We begin with a lemma that is useful throughout this section.

Lemma B.3 (log-sum-exp inequality)

$$\max(x_1, \cdots, x_m) \le \log(\exp(x_1)+\cdots+\exp(x_m)) \le \max(x_1, \cdots, x_m) + \log(m).$$

Proof of Lemma B.3. The left inequality is because

$$\max(x_1, \cdots, x_m) = \log(\max(\exp(x_1), \cdots, \exp(x_m))) \tag{B.20}$$

$$\le \log(\exp(x_1)+\cdots+\exp(x_m)). \tag{B.21}$$

The right inequality is because

$$\exp(x_1)+\cdots+\exp(x_m) \le m \max(\exp(x_1), \cdots, \exp(x_m)). \tag{B.22}$$

B.5.1 Proof of Proposition 7.1

$$\log(P_{A,T} + P_{B,T}) = \log\left(\exp\left(\sum_{t=1}^{T}\log x_{A,t}\right) + \exp\left(\sum_{t=1}^{T}\log x_{B,t}\right)\right). \tag{B.23}$$

Using Lemma B.3 with $m = 2$,

$$\max\left(\sum_{t=1}^{T}\log x_{A,t}, \sum_{t=1}^{T}\log x_{B,t}\right) \le \log(P_{A,T} + P_{B,T}) \le \max\left(\sum_{t=1}^{T}\log x_{A,t}, \sum_{t=1}^{T}\log x_{B,t}\right) + \log(2). \tag{B.24}$$

Dividing by T on all sides and using the strong law of large numbers, we have the desired result.

B.5.2 Proof of Proposition 7.2

Again,

$$\log(P_{A,T} + P_{B,T}) - T\mu = \log\left(\exp\left(\sum_{t=1}^{T}\log x_{A,t}\right) + \exp\left(\sum_{t=1}^{T}\log x_{B,t}\right)\right) - T\mu. \tag{B.25}$$

Using the left hand inequality of Lemma B.3 with $m = 2$,

$$\max\left(\sum_{t=1}^{T}\log x_{A,t}, \sum_{t=1}^{T}\log x_{B,t}\right) - T\mu \le \log(P_{A,T} + P_{B,T}) - T\mu, \tag{B.26}$$

so

$$\max\left(\frac{\sum_{t=1}^{T}\log x_{A,t} - T\mu}{\sqrt{T}}, \frac{\sum_{t=1}^{T}\log x_{B,t} - T\mu}{\sqrt{T}}\right) \le \frac{\log(P_{A,T} + P_{B,T}) - T\mu}{\sqrt{T}}. \tag{B.27}$$

Similarly, using the right hand inequality of Lemma B.3 with $m = 2$,

$$\log(P_{A,T} + P_{B,T}) - T\mu \le \max\left(\sum_{t=1}^{T}\log x_{A,t}, \sum_{t=1}^{T}\log x_{B,t}\right) + \log(2) - T\mu, \tag{B.28}$$

and

$$\frac{\log(P_{A,T} + P_{B,T}) - T\mu}{\sqrt{T}} \le \max\left(\frac{\sum_{t=1}^{T}\log x_{A,t} - T\mu}{\sqrt{T}}, \frac{\sum_{t=1}^{T}\log x_{B,t} - T\mu}{\sqrt{T}}\right) + \frac{\log(2)}{\sqrt{T}}. \tag{B.29}$$

The central limit theorem states that the joint vector $\left(\frac{\sum_{t=1}^{T}\log x_{A,t} - T\mu}{\sqrt{T}}, \frac{\sum_{t=1}^{T}\log x_{B,t} - T\mu}{\sqrt{T}}\right)$ converges in distribution to (N_A, N_B), where N_A and N_B are normally distributed vectors with means 0, variances σ_A^2 and σ_B^2, and correlation ρ. Since max is continuous, the continuous mapping theorem implies that $\max\left(\frac{\sum_{t=1}^{T}\log x_{A,t} - T\mu}{\sqrt{T}}, \frac{\sum_{t=1}^{T}\log x_{B,t} - T\mu}{\sqrt{T}}\right)$ converges to $\max(N_A, N_B)$. Since $\left|\frac{\log(P_{A,T}+P_{B,T})-T\mu}{\sqrt{T}} - \max\left(\frac{\sum_{t=1}^{T}\log x_{A,t} - T\mu}{\sqrt{T}}, \frac{\sum_{t=1}^{T}\log x_{B,t} - T\mu}{\sqrt{T}}\right)\right|$ converges almost surely to 0, $\frac{\log(P_{A,T}+P_{B,T})-T\mu}{\sqrt{T}}$ converges in distribution to $\max(N_A, N_B)$.

B.5.3 Proof of Proposition 7.3

We have that

$$\frac{\log(P_{nT_0})}{nT_0} = \frac{\sum_{i=1}^{n} \log P_{iT_0} - \log P_{(i-1)T_0}}{nT_0}. \tag{B.30}$$

Since

$$\log P_{iT_0} - \log P_{(i-1)T_0} = \log\left(\frac{1}{2} \prod_{t=(i-1)T_0+1}^{iT_0} x_{A,t} + \frac{1}{2} \prod_{t=(i-1)T_0+1}^{iT_0} x_{B,t} \right), \tag{B.31}$$

$\log P_{iT_0} - \log P_{(i-1)T_0}$ is IID over i, and the strong law of large numbers gives the result.

B.5.4 Proof of Proposition 7.4

$$\frac{\log\left((P_{A,T} + P_{B,T})/(\bar{P}_{A,T} + \bar{P}_{B,T})\right)}{T} = \left(\frac{\log(P_{A,T} + P_{B,T})}{T} - \frac{\log(\bar{P}_{A,T} + \bar{P}_{B,T})}{T} \right), \tag{B.32}$$

so by Proposition 7.1,

$$\frac{\log\left((P_{A,T} + P_{B,T})/(\bar{P}_{A,T} + \bar{P}_{B,T})\right)}{T} \to \max(\mu_A, \mu_B) - \max(\bar{\mu}_A, \bar{\mu}_B) \tag{B.33}$$

almost surely.

B.5.5 Proof of Proposition 7.5

The central limit theorem implies that the joint vector,

$$\left(\frac{\sum_{t=1}^{T} \log x_{A,t} - T\mu}{\sqrt{T}}, \frac{\sum_{t=1}^{T} \log x_{B,t} - T\mu}{\sqrt{T}}, \frac{\sum_{t=1}^{T} \log \bar{x}_{A,t} - T\mu}{\sqrt{T}}, \frac{\sum_{t=1}^{T} \log \bar{x}_{B,t} - T\mu}{\sqrt{T}} \right)$$

converges in distribution to

$$(N_A, N_B, \bar{N}_A, \bar{N}_B),$$

where $(N_A, N_B, \bar{N}_A, \bar{N}_B)$ has the same correlation structure as $(x_{A,t}, x_{B,t}, \bar{x}_{A,t}, \bar{x}_{B,t})$. By the continuous mapping theorem,

$$\max\left(\frac{\sum_{t=1}^{T} \log x_{A,t} - T\mu}{\sqrt{T}}, \frac{\sum_{t=1}^{T} \log x_{B,t} - T\mu}{\sqrt{T}} \right) - \max\left(\frac{\sum_{t=1}^{T} \log \bar{x}_{A,t} - T\mu}{\sqrt{T}}, \frac{\sum_{t=1}^{T} \log \bar{x}_{B,t} - T\mu}{\sqrt{T}} \right)$$

converges in distribution to

$$\max(N_A, N_B) - \max(\bar{N}_A, \bar{N}_B).$$

As in the proof of Proposition 7.2,

$$\frac{\log(P_{A,T} + P_{B,T}) - T\mu}{\sqrt{T}} \xrightarrow{\text{a.s.}} \max\left(\frac{\sum_{t=1}^{T} \log x_{A,t} - T\mu}{\sqrt{T}}, \frac{\sum_{t=1}^{T} \log x_{B,t} - T\mu}{\sqrt{T}}\right), \quad \text{(B.34)}$$

and

$$\frac{\log(\tilde{P}_{A,T} + \tilde{P}_{B,T}) - T\mu}{\sqrt{T}} \xrightarrow{\text{a.s.}} \max\left(\frac{\sum_{t=1}^{T} \log \tilde{x}_{A,t} - T\mu}{\sqrt{T}}, \frac{\sum_{t=1}^{T} \log \tilde{x}_{B,t} - T\mu}{\sqrt{T}}\right). \quad \text{(B.35)}$$

If $X_n \to Z$ in distribution and $|X_n - Y_n| \to 0$ almost surely, then $Y_n \to Z$ in distribution. So

$$\frac{\log(P_{A,T} + P_{B,T}) - T\mu}{\sqrt{T}} - \frac{\log(\tilde{P}_{A,T} + \tilde{P}_{B,T}) - T\mu}{\sqrt{T}} \xrightarrow{d} \max(N_A, N_B) - \max(\tilde{N}_A, \tilde{N}_B), \quad \text{(B.36)}$$

and rearranging the left hand side,

$$\frac{\log\left((P_{A,T} + P_{B,T})/(\tilde{P}_{A,T} + \tilde{P}_{B,T})\right)}{\sqrt{T}} \xrightarrow{d} \max(N_A, N_B) - \max(\tilde{N}_A, \tilde{N}_B). \quad \text{(B.37)}$$

By the continuous mapping theorem,

$$\left((P_{A,T} + P_{B,T})/(\tilde{P}_{A,T} + \tilde{P}_{B,T})\right)^{1/\sqrt{T}} \xrightarrow{d} \exp\left(\max(N_A, N_B) - \max(\tilde{N}_A, \tilde{N}_B)\right). \quad \text{(B.38)}$$

Passing to a probability space where the above convergence happens almost surely and using Fatou's lemma,

$$\liminf_{T \to \infty} \mathbb{E}\left[\left((P_{A,T} + P_{B,T})/(\tilde{P}_{A,T} + \tilde{P}_{B,T})\right)^{1/\sqrt{T}}\right] \geq \mathbb{E}\left[\exp\left(\max(N_A, N_B) - \max(\tilde{N}_A, \tilde{N}_B)\right)\right]. \quad \text{(B.39)}$$

Since $\rho < \tilde{\rho}$,

$$\mathbb{E}\left[\max(N_A, N_B) - \max(\tilde{N}_A, \tilde{N}_B)\right] > 0. \quad \text{(B.40)}$$

By Jensen's inequality,

$$\mathbb{E}\left[\exp\left(\max(N_A, N_B) - \max(\tilde{N}_A, \tilde{N}_B)\right)\right] \geq \exp\left(\mathbb{E}[\max(N_A, N_B) - \max(\tilde{N}_A, \tilde{N}_B)]\right), \quad \text{(B.41)}$$

where $c > 1$. Also by Jensen's inequality,

$$\mathbb{E}\left[(P_{A,T} + P_{B,T})/(\tilde{P}_{A,T} + \tilde{P}_{B,T})\right]^{1/\sqrt{T}} \geq \mathbb{E}\left[\left((P_{A,T} + P_{B,T})/(\tilde{P}_{A,T} + \tilde{P}_{B,T})\right)^{1/\sqrt{T}}\right], \quad \text{(B.42)}$$

so

$$\liminf_{T \to \infty} \mathbb{E}\left[(P_{A,T} + P_{B,T})/(\tilde{P}_{A,T} + \tilde{P}_{B,T})\right]^{1/\sqrt{T}} \geq \exp\left(\mathbb{E}[\max(N_A, N_B) - \max(\tilde{N}_A, \tilde{N}_B)]\right). \quad \text{(B.43)}$$

Taking the log of both sides, we have the desired result.

B.5.6 Proof of Proposition 7.6

Using Lemma B.3 with $m = 2$,

$$\max\left(\log P_{A,T}, \log P_{B,T}\right) \leq \log(P_{A,T} + P_{B,T}) \leq \max\left(\log P_{A,T}, \log P_{B,T}\right) + \log(2). \quad \text{(B.44)}$$

Therefore, if we show separately that $\frac{\log P_{A,T}}{T}$ converges almost surely to

$$\mathbb{E}[\log(\mathbb{E}[\tilde{x}_{A,i,t}] + x_{A,t})],$$

and $\frac{\log P_{B,T}}{T}$ converges almost surely to

$$\mathbb{E}[\log(\mathbb{E}[\tilde{x}_{B,i,t}] + x_{B,t})],$$

then the result is proved. We will show the claim for $\frac{\log P_{A,T}}{T}$, and the claim for $\frac{\log P_{B,T}}{T}$, follows by an identical argument replacing A with B.

Firstly, decompose

$$\frac{\log P_{A,T}}{T} = \frac{\log P_{A,0} + \log \frac{P_{A,1}}{P_{A,0}} + \cdots + \log \frac{P_{A,T}}{P_{A,T-1}}}{T}. \quad \text{(B.45)}$$

Since

$$P_{A,T} = \sum_{i=1}^{P_{A,T-1}} x_{A,T} + \tilde{x}_{A,i,T}, \quad \text{(B.46)}$$

$\log \frac{P_{A,T}}{P_{A,T-1}}$ can be written as

$$\log \frac{P_{A,T}}{P_{A,T-1}} = \log \left(x_{A,T} + \frac{\sum_{i=1}^{P_{A,T-1}} \tilde{x}_{A,i,T}}{P_{A,T-1}} \right). \quad \text{(B.47)}$$

Since $\mathbb{E}[\log(x_{A,t})] > 0$, $P_{A,T} \to \infty$ almost surely. Using the strong law of large numbers, and since $x_{A,t}$ is bounded,

$$\left| \log \left(x_{A,T} + \frac{\sum_{i=1}^{P_{A,T-1}} \tilde{x}_{A,i,T}}{P_{A,T-1}} \right) - \log \left(x_{A,T} + \mathbb{E}[\log(\tilde{x}_{A,i,t})] \right) \right| \overset{\text{a.s.}}{\to} 0. \quad \text{(B.48)}$$

Using the strong law of large numbers once more in Equation (B.45), the claim is proved.

B.5.7 Proof of Proposition 7.7

We will show separately that $\frac{\log P_{2,T}}{T}$ converges almost surely to

$$\mathbb{E}\left[\log \left(\frac{1}{2} x_{A,2,T} + \frac{1}{2} x_{B,2,T} \right) \right]$$

and that $\frac{\log P_{1,T}}{T}$ converges almost surely to

$$\mathbb{E}\left[\log \left(\frac{1}{2} x_{A,1,T} + \frac{1}{2} x_{B,1,T} \right) \right].$$

Firstly, observe that

$$\frac{\log P_{2,T}}{T} = \frac{\log P_{2,0} + \log \frac{P_{2,1}}{P_{2,0}} + \cdots + \log \frac{P_{2,T}}{P_{2,T-1}}}{T}. \tag{B.49}$$

Since

$$P_{2,T} = \sum_{i=1}^{P_{2,T-1}} 1_{\{q_{2,i,T-1}=A2\}} x_{A,2,T} + 1_{\{q_{2,i,T-1}=B2\}} x_{B,2,T}, \tag{B.50}$$

$P_{2,T} \overset{a.s.}{\to} \infty$ almost surely (implicit in the assumption of the law of large numbers for random matching), and $x_{A,2,t}$ and $x_{B,2,t}$ are bounded, by the strong law of large numbers,

$$\left| \log\left(\frac{P_{2,T}}{P_{2,T-1}}\right) - \log\left(\frac{1}{2}x_{A,2,T} + \frac{1}{2}x_{B,2,T}\right) \right| \overset{a.s.}{\to} 0. \tag{B.51}$$

Again, by the strong law of large numbers, as T increases without bound,

$$\frac{\log P_{2,0} + \log \frac{P_{2,1}}{P_{2,0}} + \cdots + \log \frac{P_{2,T}}{P_{2,T-1}}}{T} \overset{a.s.}{\to} \mathbb{E}\left[\log\left(\frac{1}{2}x_{A,2,T} + \frac{1}{2}x_{B,2,T}\right)\right]; \tag{B.52}$$

hence, as T increases without bound,

$$\frac{\log P_{2,T}}{T} \overset{a.s.}{\to} \mathbb{E}\left[\log\left(\frac{1}{2}x_{A,2,T} + \frac{1}{2}x_{B,2,T}\right)\right]. \tag{B.53}$$

Similarly,

$$\frac{\log P_{1,T}}{T} = \frac{\log P_{1,0} + \log \frac{P_{1,1}}{P_{1,0}} + \cdots + \log \frac{P_{1,T}}{P_{1,T-1}}}{T}. \tag{B.54}$$

From the relation

$$P_{1,T} = \sum_{i=1}^{P_{1,T-1}} 1_{\{q_{1,i,T-1}=A1\}} x_{A,1,T} + 1_{\{q_{1,i,T-1}=B1\}} x_{B,1,T} + 1_{\{q_{1,i,T-1}=A2\}} x_{A,2,T} + 1_{\{q_{1,i,T-1}=B2\}} x_{B,2,T}, \tag{B.55}$$

we can write

$$P_{1,T} = \left(\sum_{i=1}^{P_{1,T-1}} 1_{\{q_{1,i,T-1}=A1\}} + 1_{\{q_{1,i,T-1}=B1\}}\right)\left(\frac{1}{2}x_{A,1,T} + \frac{1}{2}x_{B,1,T}\right)$$

$$+ \left(\sum_{i=1}^{P_{1,T-1}} 1_{\{q_{1,i,T-1}=A2\}} + 1_{\{q_{1,i,T-1}=B2\}}\right)\left(\frac{1_{\{q_{1,i,T-1}=A2\}}}{\sum_{i=1}^{P_{1,T-1}} 1_{\{q_{1,i,T-1}=A2\}} + 1_{\{q_{1,i,T-1}=B2\}}} x_{A,2,T}\right.$$

$$\left. + \frac{1_{\{q_{1,i,T-1}=B2\}}}{\sum_{i=1}^{P_{1,T-1}} 1_{\{q_{1,i,T-1}=A2\}} + 1_{\{q_{1,i,T-1}=B2\}}} x_{B,2,T}\right). \tag{B.56}$$

Let

$$n_{1,T} = \sum_{i=1}^{P_{1,T-1}} 1_{\{q_{1,i,T-1}=A1\}} + 1_{\{q_{1,i,T-1}=B1\}}, \quad n_{2,T} = \sum_{i=1}^{P_{1,T-1}} 1_{\{q_{1,i,T-1}=A2\}} + 1_{\{q_{1,i,T-1}=B2\}}. \tag{B.57}$$

By the assumption of the law of large numbers for random matching, and since $x_{z,i,t}$ and $n_{i,t}/P_{1,t-1}$ are bounded for $z = A, B$ and $i = 1, 2$, by the strong law of large numbers,

$$\left| \log\left(\frac{P_{2,T}}{P_{2,T-1}}\right) - \log\left(\frac{n_{1,T}}{P_{1,T-1}}\left(\frac{1}{2}x_{A,1,T} + \frac{1}{2}x_{B,1,T}\right) + \frac{n_{2,T}}{P_{1,T-1}}\left(\frac{1}{2}x_{A,2,T} + \frac{1}{2}x_{B,2,T}\right)\right) \right| \overset{\text{a.s.}}{\to} 0. \tag{B.58}$$

Fix an outcome ω. Consider any subsequence of the sequence $\frac{\log P_{1,T}(\omega)}{T}$. From the decomposition (B.54), the fact that $\frac{n_{1,T}}{P_{1,T-1}}$ and $\frac{n_{2,T}}{P_{1,T-1}}$ are bounded, and by the strong law of large numbers, there exists a further subsequence such that

$$\frac{\log P_{1,T}(\omega)}{T} \overset{\text{a.s.}}{\to} \mathbb{E}\left[\log\left(p\left(\frac{1}{2}x_{A,1,T} + \frac{1}{2}x_{B,1,T}\right) + (1-p)\left(\frac{1}{2}x_{A,2,T} + \frac{1}{2}x_{B,2,T}\right)\right)\right] \tag{B.59}$$

for some p. If $p = 0$, it would imply that $P_{1,T}$ and $P_{2,T}$ grow at the same rates, which would make it impossible for p to be 0. Similarly, if $0 < p < 1$, by Jensen's inequality, $P_{1,T}$ would grow exponentially faster than $P_{2,T}$, making it impossible that $p < 1$. Thus, the only possibility is that $p = 1$. Therefore, any subsequence of $\frac{\log P_{1,T}(\omega)}{T}$ has a further subsequence converging to $\mathbb{E}\left[\log\left(\frac{1}{2}x_{A,1,T} + \frac{1}{2}x_{B,1,T}\right)\right]$, proving that $\frac{\log P_{1,T}}{T}$ converges to $\mathbb{E}\left[\log\left(\frac{1}{2}x_{A,1,T} + \frac{1}{2}x_{B,1,T}\right)\right]$ almost surely.

B.5.8 Additional Simulation Results

In this section we present additional simulation results for the cooperation framework of Chapter 7 in which we consider a broader range of growth rates, idiosyncratic risk, and density dependence. As in the simulations of Chapter 7, we compute the expectations as an average over 10,000 samples, and we generate paths of stochastic processes using the Euler method with a time increment of 0.001. All populations start with $P_{A,0} = 1$ and $P_{B,0} = 1$.

Greater Range of Growth Rates μ

Table B.2 is a replication of Table 7.1 but with a larger range of μ values. The trends we found earlier are consistent over this larger range as well. Notably, decreasing ρ from 0.5 to -0.5 is similar to increasing μ by only 0.09. Table B.3 reports results when σ, the standard deviation of the log offspring, is halved, while Table B.4 reports the results when σ is doubled. It is no surprise that increasing σ increases the importance of ρ relative to μ, since σ controls how much variation there is to be correlated.

Idiosyncratic Risk

In this section, we fix the systematic risk at the same level as the simulation discussed in Section 13.3 (Tables 7.1 and B.2 report the results), while adding a component of idiosyncratic risk. Table B.5 reports results from adding a deterministic component of e^{-1} to each individual's offspring, while Table B.6 provides the results from adding a deterministic component of e^0 to each individual's offspring. Table B.7 reports the results of adding a random component to each individual's offspring, one that is lognormally distributed with $\mu_{\text{id}} = -1$ and $\sigma_{\text{id}} = \sqrt{2}$.

Table B.2 Simulated population growth rate ($\sigma = 1.0$).

μ \ ρ	-0.9	-0.8	-0.7	-0.6	-0.5	-0.4	-0.3	-0.2	-0.1	0.0	0.1	0.2	0.3	0.4	0.5	0.6	0.7	0.8	0.9
0.00	20.3%	20.0%	19.1%	18.6%	17.4%	16.2%	15.8%	15.0%	14.1%	13.0%	12.1%	11.2%	10.3%	9.0%	7.8%	7.0%	4.9%	4.3%	1.7%
0.02	22.9%	22.6%	21.6%	21.0%	19.9%	18.9%	18.1%	17.7%	16.3%	15.6%	14.3%	13.6%	12.5%	11.2%	9.9%	8.6%	7.4%	6.2%	4.8%
0.04	25.2%	24.7%	24.1%	23.0%	22.0%	21.5%	20.5%	19.6%	18.4%	18.2%	17.1%	15.7%	14.3%	13.8%	12.8%	10.8%	10.1%	7.8%	6.3%
0.06	28.2%	27.0%	26.3%	25.8%	24.7%	24.3%	22.9%	22.0%	20.8%	20.4%	19.0%	17.7%	16.5%	16.1%	14.4%	13.4%	11.7%	10.0%	8.5%
0.08	30.4%	29.7%	29.1%	28.1%	27.5%	27.1%	25.6%	23.9%	23.9%	22.5%	21.3%	20.5%	19.4%	18.6%	16.8%	14.8%	14.4%	12.8%	11.0%
0.10	33.4%	32.5%	31.0%	30.2%	29.7%	28.9%	27.4%	26.2%	25.9%	24.5%	23.7%	23.4%	21.4%	20.6%	19.2%	17.8%	16.0%	14.7%	12.8%
0.12	36.0%	34.9%	34.1%	33.7%	32.5%	31.5%	30.3%	30.1%	28.4%	27.6%	26.4%	25.9%	24.0%	23.3%	21.8%	20.3%	19.4%	17.3%	15.1%
0.14	38.8%	37.7%	36.7%	35.6%	34.7%	33.7%	33.4%	31.7%	31.1%	30.4%	28.6%	27.3%	27.0%	25.1%	23.9%	23.5%	21.0%	18.9%	17.0%
0.16	41.6%	40.9%	40.0%	39.0%	37.8%	37.1%	35.9%	34.7%	33.8%	32.4%	31.5%	30.1%	28.5%	27.8%	26.2%	25.2%	23.3%	22.1%	20.1%
0.18	44.3%	43.1%	42.4%	41.4%	40.7%	39.5%	38.9%	37.7%	36.2%	35.5%	34.5%	32.6%	31.9%	30.7%	28.8%	27.2%	25.9%	24.7%	22.2%
0.20	47.3%	46.4%	45.6%	44.3%	43.6%	43.0%	42.1%	40.6%	39.2%	37.6%	37.4%	36.3%	34.5%	33.3%	31.9%	30.8%	28.2%	26.9%	25.3%
0.22	50.1%	49.8%	48.6%	46.9%	46.3%	45.2%	44.1%	42.9%	42.2%	41.3%	40.1%	38.6%	37.4%	35.8%	34.7%	32.9%	31.1%	28.7%	27.3%
0.24	53.2%	52.8%	51.0%	50.0%	49.2%	47.9%	47.4%	45.7%	44.8%	43.0%	43.4%	41.1%	40.0%	39.5%	37.3%	35.4%	33.5%	31.9%	29.8%
0.26	56.1%	55.5%	54.0%	53.8%	52.1%	50.5%	50.3%	48.7%	47.8%	47.2%	45.1%	43.6%	42.1%	41.8%	39.8%	38.4%	36.5%	34.8%	32.8%
0.28	60.0%	58.6%	57.4%	56.3%	55.4%	53.9%	53.5%	52.3%	51.7%	50.1%	47.9%	47.3%	45.7%	43.6%	42.8%	41.1%	39.2%	37.0%	35.0%
0.30	62.6%	61.3%	60.8%	59.5%	58.4%	57.3%	56.2%	55.0%	53.9%	52.8%	51.0%	50.1%	48.6%	47.5%	45.8%	44.1%	42.2%	40.6%	37.5%
0.32	66.4%	65.2%	64.3%	63.0%	62.1%	60.6%	59.8%	58.2%	56.9%	55.9%	54.4%	53.2%	51.1%	49.9%	48.9%	46.5%	44.8%	43.3%	41.0%
0.34	69.1%	68.2%	67.5%	66.2%	65.3%	64.3%	62.1%	60.9%	60.6%	58.6%	57.3%	56.3%	54.7%	53.6%	50.8%	49.5%	47.7%	45.8%	43.5%
0.36	72.4%	71.1%	71.3%	69.6%	68.8%	67.4%	65.6%	64.0%	63.1%	62.4%	61.0%	59.3%	58.3%	56.1%	54.9%	52.8%	50.6%	49.2%	47.1%
0.38	75.9%	75.5%	73.9%	72.6%	71.6%	71.0%	69.4%	68.6%	66.8%	65.4%	63.6%	62.6%	60.6%	59.7%	57.6%	55.7%	53.8%	51.0%	49.3%
0.40	79.8%	79.4%	77.2%	76.1%	75.1%	74.0%	72.9%	72.0%	69.7%	68.1%	67.0%	65.4%	63.9%	62.8%	62.2%	59.4%	57.0%	53.9%	52.3%
0.42	83.6%	82.1%	81.7%	80.4%	78.5%	77.6%	76.4%	75.0%	73.6%	72.6%	69.8%	69.4%	67.9%	66.0%	63.9%	62.3%	60.6%	57.4%	55.9%
0.44	87.8%	86.1%	85.7%	84.0%	82.5%	81.1%	79.8%	77.9%	76.2%	75.9%	73.9%	72.0%	71.5%	68.6%	67.4%	65.7%	63.1%	61.0%	58.6%
0.46	90.7%	90.0%	89.0%	87.9%	85.9%	85.0%	82.6%	81.6%	81.0%	78.7%	76.9%	76.0%	73.9%	72.8%	71.4%	67.2%	66.9%	64.6%	61.3%
0.48	94.5%	93.6%	92.5%	90.8%	90.1%	88.8%	87.2%	86.1%	84.6%	82.1%	80.8%	79.7%	77.9%	76.8%	74.4%	72.7%	70.1%	67.3%	65.3%

0.50	98.5%	97.2%	96.1%	94.4%	94.0%	91.7%	90.1%	90.0%	87.2%	86.9%	85.5%	82.6%	81.5%	79.2%	78.0%	75.8%	74.1%	70.9%	68.7%
0.52	103.4%	101.2%	100.1%	99.6%	97.7%	95.1%	93.4%	95.1%	92.2%	90.3%	88.4%	86.7%	85.4%	83.6%	80.5%	79.4%	77.1%	75.1%	72.1%
0.54	106.7%	106.0%	104.4%	103.4%	101.7%	101.1%	96.6%	99.2%	95.5%	94.1%	93.0%	90.1%	89.6%	87.1%	84.9%	83.1%	80.9%	77.3%	75.8%
0.56	110.9%	109.9%	108.2%	107.1%	105.0%	103.9%	100.8%	103.4%	99.9%	97.6%	95.8%	94.9%	92.9%	90.2%	88.8%	87.1%	84.9%	80.4%	78.4%
0.58	116.2%	113.9%	112.3%	111.2%	110.6%	108.2%	105.7%	107.5%	103.5%	101.6%	100.2%	98.3%	96.8%	95.1%	92.7%	90.0%	88.2%	85.5%	82.0%
0.60	120.5%	118.2%	117.1%	115.7%	113.7%	112.6%	108.7%	111.5%	107.7%	105.9%	104.2%	102.4%	100.9%	98.3%	98.0%	94.3%	91.7%	90.0%	86.5%
0.62	124.2%	122.0%	120.9%	120.0%	119.2%	116.3%	114.1%	115.6%	112.0%	109.9%	109.7%	107.0%	104.3%	102.6%	100.4%	98.9%	96.1%	93.1%	90.0%
0.64	128.3%	127.3%	126.1%	124.2%	123.0%	120.7%	117.8%	119.2%	116.6%	114.4%	112.3%	111.4%	108.3%	106.6%	103.7%	101.9%	100.7%	98.6%	93.9%
0.66	133.6%	132.0%	130.5%	128.4%	126.9%	126.3%	122.3%	124.7%	121.6%	118.8%	117.6%	115.5%	112.2%	111.5%	108.6%	106.2%	104.4%	100.3%	98.2%
0.68	137.9%	136.4%	134.7%	133.6%	132.4%	128.8%	126.2%	127.7%	124.4%	122.1%	120.3%	119.9%	117.2%	116.0%	112.1%	110.4%	107.7%	105.6%	102.1%
0.70	143.8%	141.1%	139.9%	137.8%	137.4%	134.8%	131.8%	133.3%	129.1%	127.1%	126.0%	123.4%	122.3%	120.4%	117.1%	114.1%	112.4%	109.6%	106.5%
0.72	147.9%	146.9%	144.4%	143.2%	141.7%	139.6%	135.2%	138.4%	134.5%	131.8%	130.4%	128.6%	126.2%	124.1%	121.3%	119.5%	115.5%	113.5%	109.5%
0.74	152.4%	151.5%	149.9%	147.5%	146.9%	144.1%	141.3%	142.6%	139.5%	136.9%	134.8%	132.6%	130.2%	127.5%	126.5%	123.4%	120.5%	118.5%	113.9%
0.76	157.2%	156.4%	154.4%	153.0%	152.2%	149.4%	145.6%	147.6%	142.7%	142.6%	139.6%	138.6%	135.3%	133.1%	131.9%	128.1%	124.7%	121.6%	119.9%
0.78	164.5%	161.8%	159.8%	158.3%	156.4%	153.5%	150.1%	153.7%	148.7%	148.0%	144.8%	143.1%	140.2%	138.2%	135.7%	131.5%	129.8%	125.8%	123.2%
0.80	168.7%	166.0%	165.6%	162.5%	161.9%	160.3%	156.0%	157.5%	153.8%	152.3%	150.6%	145.8%	145.1%	142.9%	139.9%	137.5%	134.8%	131.5%	127.0%
0.82	172.9%	172.5%	169.9%	168.3%	166.9%	164.5%	160.7%	162.9%	159.1%	156.8%	154.4%	152.6%	149.8%	146.8%	145.5%	142.2%	138.4%	135.8%	132.3%
0.84	179.0%	177.8%	176.5%	174.2%	172.9%	169.4%	165.2%	167.9%	164.5%	161.6%	159.3%	157.0%	154.7%	153.7%	149.9%	146.1%	142.3%	140.8%	137.7%
0.86	185.5%	183.1%	181.6%	180.0%	177.3%	175.4%	170.4%	173.0%	170.3%	166.8%	164.8%	162.8%	159.8%	156.7%	153.6%	150.9%	149.1%	144.6%	140.4%
0.88	191.3%	189.2%	186.4%	184.8%	181.9%	181.6%	176.4%	180.1%	174.4%	172.3%	170.0%	167.1%	164.8%	164.9%	160.9%	156.8%	153.3%	151.2%	145.8%
0.90	196.7%	194.3%	192.3%	190.5%	187.6%	186.2%	182.8%	185.5%	181.9%	179.4%	175.4%	173.7%	170.5%	168.1%	165.1%	163.2%	158.6%	155.1%	150.2%
0.92	202.5%	200.3%	199.0%	195.7%	194.7%	192.2%	186.7%	191.8%	185.4%	184.8%	181.6%	177.3%	175.5%	172.9%	171.6%	167.2%	163.4%	159.6%	155.3%
0.94	208.8%	207.2%	204.6%	203.0%	200.0%	198.8%	193.6%	196.9%	192.0%	188.3%	186.9%	183.9%	183.0%	179.4%	175.3%	171.8%	170.3%	164.2%	161.5%
0.96	215.0%	212.9%	210.0%	209.1%	205.8%	205.0%	199.0%	202.2%	197.4%	195.6%	192.2%	189.8%	186.5%	183.5%	181.3%	178.3%	176.5%	171.7%	167.4%
0.98	222.6%	219.8%	216.4%	214.6%	213.1%	210.6%	206.6%	207.8%	203.6%	203.0%	198.4%	197.5%	193.6%	191.2%	187.0%	184.8%	180.2%	176.2%	171.4%
1.00	227.8%	224.2%	224.8%	221.1%	219.0%	217.9%	213.6%	214.8%	210.2%	207.7%	204.4%	201.9%	199.6%	197.0%	192.4%	189.9%	184.6%	182.5%	176.4%

The number of offspring for both types follows a lognormal distribution with the stated μ and ρ, and with $\sigma = 1.0$. Quantities shown represent population growth rate per generation after ten generations, computed as $e^{\mathbb{E}[\log(P_{10}/P_0)]/10}$, where $P_T = P_{A,T} + P_{B,T}$.

Source: Appendix of Koduri, N., and Lo, A. W. (2021). The origin of cooperation. *Proceedings of the National Academy of Sciences* 118(26): e2015572118.

Table B.3 Simulated population growth rate ($\sigma = 0.5$).

μ \ ρ	-0.9	-0.8	-0.7	-0.6	-0.5	-0.4	-0.3	-0.2	-0.1	0.0	0.1	0.2	0.3	0.4	0.5	0.6	0.7	0.8	0.9
0.00	7.7%	7.2%	6.8%	6.5%	6.4%	6.0%	5.8%	5.2%	5.1%	4.5%	4.2%	3.8%	3.5%	3.3%	2.4%	2.0%	1.7%	1.3%	0.3%
0.02	9.8%	9.3%	9.1%	8.7%	8.5%	8.0%	7.8%	7.4%	7.2%	6.7%	6.2%	6.0%	5.3%	4.9%	4.5%	4.2%	3.7%	3.0%	2.7%
0.04	11.9%	11.5%	11.2%	11.0%	10.6%	10.3%	9.9%	9.5%	9.1%	8.9%	8.3%	8.0%	7.7%	7.2%	6.7%	6.4%	5.9%	5.0%	4.7%
0.06	14.3%	13.8%	13.4%	13.2%	12.9%	12.3%	12.2%	12.0%	11.4%	11.1%	10.6%	10.1%	9.9%	9.4%	8.9%	8.1%	8.1%	7.6%	6.9%
0.08	16.4%	16.3%	15.8%	15.4%	15.0%	15.0%	14.4%	14.1%	13.6%	13.3%	12.9%	12.5%	12.1%	11.7%	11.2%	10.9%	10.1%	9.3%	9.1%
0.10	19.1%	18.6%	18.3%	17.9%	17.5%	17.2%	16.8%	16.3%	16.1%	15.5%	15.0%	14.7%	14.2%	13.6%	13.0%	12.9%	12.6%	11.9%	11.4%
0.12	21.4%	20.9%	20.6%	20.2%	20.1%	19.6%	19.1%	18.6%	18.4%	17.9%	17.2%	17.1%	16.5%	16.2%	15.4%	14.9%	14.7%	14.0%	13.1%
0.14	24.0%	23.3%	22.8%	22.6%	22.1%	22.2%	21.3%	21.1%	20.7%	20.4%	19.9%	19.5%	19.0%	18.6%	17.7%	17.5%	17.1%	16.0%	15.9%
0.16	26.2%	25.7%	25.6%	25.3%	24.9%	24.4%	23.9%	23.7%	23.1%	22.9%	22.5%	21.8%	21.1%	20.5%	20.5%	19.9%	19.2%	18.8%	18.0%
0.18	28.7%	28.4%	28.0%	27.7%	27.1%	27.0%	26.4%	26.1%	25.6%	25.3%	24.5%	24.3%	23.9%	23.1%	22.9%	22.0%	21.8%	20.9%	20.4%
0.20	31.4%	31.1%	30.9%	30.3%	30.1%	29.6%	29.5%	28.7%	27.9%	27.5%	27.4%	27.0%	26.4%	26.1%	25.3%	24.7%	24.3%	23.5%	22.8%
0.22	33.8%	33.5%	33.2%	32.9%	32.5%	32.0%	31.5%	31.2%	31.0%	30.4%	29.8%	29.5%	29.0%	28.6%	27.6%	27.4%	26.7%	26.2%	25.2%
0.24	36.8%	36.3%	35.6%	35.6%	35.2%	34.5%	34.1%	33.7%	33.6%	33.0%	32.3%	32.1%	31.6%	30.8%	30.6%	30.0%	29.3%	28.6%	27.7%
0.26	39.7%	39.1%	38.5%	38.3%	38.1%	37.4%	37.0%	36.6%	36.3%	35.8%	35.5%	34.5%	33.9%	33.5%	33.0%	32.3%	32.0%	31.4%	30.4%
0.28	42.4%	42.0%	41.4%	41.0%	40.7%	40.3%	39.8%	39.4%	38.9%	38.6%	37.8%	37.1%	36.7%	36.2%	35.8%	35.3%	34.6%	33.7%	33.0%
0.30	45.2%	44.7%	44.4%	43.9%	43.8%	42.9%	42.7%	42.4%	41.5%	41.0%	40.5%	39.7%	39.6%	38.8%	38.4%	38.0%	37.1%	36.6%	36.0%
0.32	48.0%	47.5%	47.2%	46.7%	46.4%	45.5%	45.2%	44.8%	44.8%	44.2%	43.7%	43.0%	42.4%	41.9%	40.9%	40.9%	40.5%	39.5%	38.3%
0.34	51.0%	50.6%	50.4%	50.0%	49.1%	48.8%	48.2%	47.9%	47.6%	46.9%	46.6%	46.0%	45.3%	44.7%	44.2%	43.8%	42.9%	42.2%	41.1%
0.36	54.3%	53.7%	53.4%	53.0%	52.4%	51.8%	51.5%	51.3%	50.3%	50.3%	49.2%	48.8%	48.2%	47.8%	46.9%	46.1%	45.8%	45.5%	44.3%
0.38	57.2%	56.9%	56.4%	56.0%	55.5%	54.6%	54.3%	54.0%	53.3%	53.1%	52.5%	51.5%	51.4%	50.7%	50.3%	49.5%	48.9%	47.8%	47.1%
0.40	60.4%	60.0%	59.7%	59.1%	58.6%	58.2%	57.3%	57.1%	56.3%	56.1%	55.4%	54.9%	54.1%	53.8%	53.2%	52.3%	51.9%	50.9%	50.5%
0.42	63.9%	63.3%	62.5%	62.5%	61.6%	61.5%	60.7%	60.4%	59.5%	59.1%	58.5%	58.3%	57.7%	56.7%	56.1%	55.5%	54.4%	54.0%	53.3%
0.44	66.9%	66.5%	65.8%	65.4%	64.8%	64.7%	63.9%	63.6%	62.9%	62.0%	61.8%	61.3%	60.8%	59.9%	59.2%	58.6%	57.7%	57.0%	56.3%
0.46	70.6%	70.0%	69.9%	68.9%	68.6%	68.1%	67.3%	66.6%	66.3%	65.6%	65.0%	64.5%	63.9%	63.0%	62.4%	61.7%	60.6%	60.5%	59.0%
0.48	73.9%	73.3%	73.0%	72.4%	71.8%	71.5%	70.8%	70.0%	69.6%	69.1%	68.6%	67.6%	67.1%	66.4%	65.9%	64.9%	64.3%	63.2%	62.3%

0.50	77.6%	76.9%	76.1%	75.8%	75.0%	74.8%	73.9%	73.7%	73.2%	72.2%	71.8%	71.4%	70.4%	69.5%	69.2%	68.3%	68.0%	66.2%	65.0%
0.52	80.8%	80.3%	80.0%	79.4%	78.5%	78.3%	78.1%	77.2%	76.8%	76.2%	75.3%	74.8%	74.0%	73.1%	72.9%	72.1%	71.0%	70.2%	68.7%
0.54	84.8%	84.1%	83.7%	82.9%	82.4%	82.1%	81.0%	80.7%	80.2%	79.2%	78.8%	78.2%	77.3%	76.4%	76.4%	75.2%	74.4%	73.5%	73.3%
0.56	88.4%	87.8%	87.3%	86.8%	86.0%	85.5%	84.7%	84.6%	83.6%	82.8%	82.5%	81.8%	81.2%	80.1%	80.1%	79.1%	77.6%	77.3%	76.3%
0.58	92.0%	91.7%	91.0%	90.4%	90.0%	89.4%	88.7%	88.2%	87.4%	86.8%	85.7%	85.2%	84.2%	83.8%	83.0%	82.3%	81.9%	80.7%	79.4%
0.60	96.1%	95.2%	94.9%	94.4%	93.9%	93.3%	92.5%	91.7%	91.2%	90.6%	89.7%	88.8%	88.5%	87.7%	87.1%	86.2%	85.0%	84.6%	83.3%
0.62	99.8%	99.6%	99.1%	98.3%	97.7%	96.8%	96.5%	95.7%	95.3%	94.8%	93.8%	92.7%	92.3%	91.7%	90.9%	90.1%	88.8%	88.1%	86.3%
0.64	103.9%	103.5%	102.6%	102.1%	101.7%	101.2%	100.4%	99.6%	99.4%	98.0%	97.2%	96.7%	95.9%	95.2%	94.5%	93.7%	92.6%	92.1%	91.3%
0.66	107.8%	107.5%	107.2%	106.0%	105.4%	105.0%	104.4%	103.7%	102.7%	102.3%	101.4%	101.1%	100.0%	99.1%	98.3%	97.6%	96.6%	95.8%	94.9%
0.68	112.5%	111.7%	111.6%	110.3%	110.0%	109.2%	108.2%	108.1%	106.7%	106.3%	105.9%	105.1%	103.8%	103.1%	102.4%	101.8%	100.7%	100.1%	98.3%
0.70	116.5%	116.4%	115.6%	114.6%	114.1%	113.1%	112.7%	112.2%	111.2%	110.7%	109.8%	109.4%	108.3%	107.5%	106.7%	105.3%	104.4%	104.1%	102.1%
0.72	120.8%	120.3%	119.7%	118.9%	118.3%	117.1%	116.3%	116.3%	115.5%	114.8%	114.0%	113.5%	112.7%	111.9%	110.7%	109.9%	108.6%	107.7%	106.2%
0.74	125.2%	124.5%	124.2%	122.9%	122.9%	122.2%	121.3%	120.4%	119.7%	119.1%	118.3%	117.4%	116.7%	116.1%	115.0%	114.3%	113.0%	112.1%	111.0%
0.76	129.9%	129.6%	129.0%	127.7%	127.8%	126.5%	125.7%	125.5%	124.1%	123.5%	122.4%	122.3%	121.4%	120.5%	119.3%	118.1%	117.8%	115.5%	115.1%
0.78	134.5%	133.8%	133.2%	132.6%	132.1%	131.2%	130.3%	129.7%	128.8%	128.5%	127.1%	126.4%	125.6%	124.5%	123.9%	122.4%	122.4%	120.6%	119.1%
0.80	139.5%	138.7%	138.2%	137.4%	136.8%	136.3%	135.0%	134.5%	134.0%	132.8%	131.5%	131.0%	130.3%	129.3%	127.8%	127.4%	126.4%	125.7%	123.6%
0.82	144.7%	143.2%	143.1%	142.4%	141.3%	140.7%	140.0%	138.5%	138.6%	137.1%	136.6%	136.3%	134.7%	134.2%	133.1%	131.9%	130.8%	129.1%	128.3%
0.84	149.2%	148.2%	147.7%	146.9%	145.7%	145.2%	144.8%	144.0%	142.7%	142.4%	141.3%	140.4%	140.2%	138.7%	137.4%	136.2%	135.5%	134.6%	133.2%
0.86	154.3%	153.6%	152.6%	152.0%	151.4%	150.0%	150.0%	148.6%	147.9%	146.8%	146.7%	145.2%	144.6%	144.0%	142.2%	141.4%	140.3%	139.5%	138.0%
0.88	159.5%	158.5%	158.3%	157.8%	156.4%	155.4%	154.4%	153.6%	153.4%	152.2%	151.1%	150.0%	149.9%	148.7%	147.1%	146.6%	144.8%	143.7%	142.5%
0.90	164.2%	163.9%	163.1%	162.2%	161.4%	160.8%	159.7%	159.1%	158.6%	157.0%	156.6%	155.4%	154.3%	153.3%	152.4%	150.6%	149.2%	148.7%	147.5%
0.92	170.0%	168.9%	168.5%	167.2%	167.2%	165.6%	165.4%	164.1%	163.0%	162.6%	161.4%	160.7%	160.1%	158.4%	157.2%	156.5%	154.9%	154.3%	152.4%
0.94	175.5%	174.7%	173.8%	173.0%	172.4%	171.4%	171.2%	169.9%	168.9%	167.5%	167.0%	165.5%	164.7%	163.4%	162.3%	161.3%	160.1%	158.8%	157.4%
0.96	180.8%	180.6%	179.6%	179.0%	177.3%	176.8%	175.4%	175.0%	174.0%	173.0%	172.1%	171.6%	170.6%	168.8%	167.8%	166.4%	165.2%	164.4%	162.4%
0.98	186.8%	186.2%	184.7%	183.9%	183.1%	182.1%	181.7%	180.2%	179.8%	178.6%	177.6%	176.4%	175.1%	174.0%	173.3%	171.7%	170.2%	170.3%	168.0%
1.00	192.3%	191.6%	190.5%	189.9%	189.3%	187.6%	187.0%	186.6%	185.3%	184.7%	183.7%	181.7%	180.7%	179.8%	179.7%	177.5%	176.7%	175.3%	173.6%

The number of offspring for both types follows a lognormal distribution with the stated μ and ρ, and with $\sigma = 0.5$. Quantities shown represent population growth rate per generation after ten generations, computed as $e^{E[\log^2 P_{10}/P_0)]/10}$, where $P_T = P_{A,T} + P_{B,T}$.

Source: Appendix of Koduri, N., and Lo, A. W. (2021). The origin of cooperation. *Proceedings of the National Academy of Sciences* 118(26): e201557118.

Table B.4 Simulated population growth rate ($\sigma = 2.0$).

μ \ ρ	-0.9	-0.8	-0.7	-0.6	-0.5	-0.4	-0.3	-0.2	-0.1	0.0	0.1	0.2	0.3	0.4	0.5	0.6	0.7	0.8	0.9
0.00	53.1%	51.9%	48.8%	46.9%	45.9%	42.1%	41.5%	38.8%	36.8%	34.0%	31.8%	31.1%	27.0%	23.7%	21.8%	18.7%	16.2%	11.1%	7.2%
0.02	57.0%	53.9%	52.8%	50.4%	46.9%	45.5%	44.2%	42.2%	39.1%	36.9%	34.7%	32.4%	28.0%	26.2%	25.0%	20.1%	16.0%	13.7%	8.8%
0.04	60.0%	57.2%	55.7%	53.2%	51.1%	50.4%	46.7%	44.4%	42.2%	39.9%	36.4%	35.3%	32.8%	28.3%	26.5%	22.8%	19.2%	14.8%	11.3%
0.06	63.9%	60.5%	58.6%	57.2%	52.8%	51.9%	51.3%	48.6%	45.2%	41.4%	39.9%	37.4%	34.7%	33.0%	28.8%	25.1%	22.3%	18.5%	14.6%
0.08	67.4%	63.6%	60.1%	58.7%	58.3%	55.2%	54.6%	51.6%	48.5%	45.8%	42.6%	40.7%	38.5%	34.2%	31.2%	27.1%	25.4%	21.4%	15.2%
0.10	69.7%	66.9%	64.7%	62.8%	60.8%	58.3%	56.0%	53.0%	52.2%	49.0%	45.9%	42.1%	40.4%	39.4%	35.5%	31.3%	27.0%	22.9%	17.1%
0.12	73.3%	71.3%	67.8%	66.2%	63.5%	60.9%	58.2%	55.8%	53.8%	52.4%	47.2%	46.0%	42.1%	40.2%	36.3%	31.7%	28.8%	25.4%	21.4%
0.14	77.0%	74.1%	71.9%	71.1%	65.2%	66.0%	61.1%	59.4%	56.4%	54.5%	53.2%	49.0%	46.9%	42.2%	40.0%	35.8%	31.8%	26.7%	22.1%
0.16	79.8%	77.4%	74.9%	72.7%	71.4%	68.0%	65.3%	63.4%	57.7%	58.1%	53.1%	51.9%	49.6%	43.5%	43.3%	37.4%	34.6%	31.2%	25.4%
0.18	82.7%	81.9%	79.0%	76.9%	73.9%	71.7%	67.9%	66.4%	63.1%	61.3%	58.4%	55.8%	51.8%	48.0%	45.5%	40.4%	38.1%	32.9%	28.4%
0.20	86.2%	84.9%	81.1%	79.0%	77.5%	76.0%	72.4%	69.9%	67.0%	64.0%	60.9%	59.2%	53.8%	51.2%	47.7%	44.8%	40.0%	35.8%	30.0%
0.22	90.7%	88.7%	85.4%	84.5%	81.6%	79.3%	75.3%	74.4%	70.6%	67.8%	64.2%	60.7%	58.4%	54.4%	51.6%	46.6%	43.6%	38.2%	33.8%
0.24	95.5%	93.2%	89.7%	86.4%	84.6%	81.2%	79.2%	74.9%	73.5%	71.1%	66.1%	64.7%	61.5%	57.9%	55.1%	50.6%	46.6%	40.5%	34.8%
0.26	99.3%	95.9%	93.7%	90.9%	88.1%	85.5%	83.4%	79.5%	77.1%	74.7%	69.6%	65.9%	65.3%	59.4%	56.5%	50.8%	50.0%	44.6%	38.0%
0.28	103.0%	99.5%	98.7%	92.7%	93.4%	89.6%	88.2%	83.8%	80.9%	77.5%	74.0%	70.4%	68.5%	64.2%	59.3%	55.3%	50.1%	47.0%	43.3%
0.30	106.0%	104.0%	102.3%	100.3%	96.2%	94.5%	89.4%	88.8%	84.5%	82.0%	78.8%	74.3%	71.5%	66.9%	64.1%	59.5%	54.5%	49.6%	43.3%
0.32	111.5%	109.1%	106.9%	102.8%	98.6%	97.6%	94.8%	90.8%	87.4%	85.2%	82.4%	78.8%	74.6%	70.5%	66.9%	62.9%	57.1%	51.9%	47.8%
0.34	115.2%	111.9%	110.2%	107.1%	104.9%	101.6%	98.5%	95.4%	92.8%	88.7%	85.4%	83.1%	80.1%	74.3%	70.4%	66.4%	61.9%	54.8%	50.1%
0.36	120.9%	118.3%	114.3%	110.9%	108.0%	106.3%	100.1%	98.6%	96.1%	92.8%	88.0%	85.0%	81.1%	77.5%	74.3%	68.7%	64.9%	59.2%	51.0%
0.38	125.1%	122.0%	118.7%	114.9%	113.4%	109.5%	107.5%	103.3%	99.3%	94.3%	94.5%	88.9%	84.8%	81.0%	80.1%	73.2%	66.2%	63.1%	56.1%
0.40	128.8%	126.2%	123.2%	119.4%	117.2%	113.0%	110.9%	108.3%	104.5%	101.2%	97.7%	93.8%	89.8%	85.1%	82.7%	78.1%	72.4%	67.5%	59.1%
0.42	133.7%	131.7%	126.9%	123.1%	121.9%	119.2%	114.6%	110.0%	109.7%	104.1%	100.3%	95.6%	92.6%	89.0%	85.9%	79.4%	75.6%	70.2%	60.7%
0.44	137.7%	135.4%	132.7%	127.7%	126.6%	122.1%	121.3%	114.9%	112.1%	107.8%	104.9%	99.8%	96.5%	92.2%	89.1%	84.8%	76.8%	72.1%	67.5%
0.46	142.1%	140.6%	137.7%	133.6%	130.1%	125.8%	124.3%	117.5%	118.0%	111.2%	107.9%	104.4%	102.1%	96.4%	92.7%	87.3%	82.6%	76.3%	69.5%
0.48	147.8%	144.3%	140.5%	136.7%	136.5%	130.5%	127.6%	124.0%	121.6%	116.5%	113.2%	110.1%	104.2%	100.0%	97.0%	90.0%	84.9%	77.5%	72.2%

0.50	151.8%	145.4%	142.7%	140.1%	137.3%	132.3%	128.7%	125.4%	121.4%	118.0%	114.2%	107.1%	105.1%	99.9%	94.7%	89.0%	83.2%	76.2%		
0.52	158.1%	154.4%	150.7%	146.5%	144.8%	143.2%	135.4%	133.3%	130.7%	125.1%	122.4%	117.5%	112.9%	110.6%	103.3%	98.2%	93.4%	87.3%	79.6%	
0.54	162.1%	160.6%	157.1%	153.9%	150.9%	147.1%	142.5%	137.8%	134.9%	130.3%	125.7%	121.4%	118.5%	111.5%	111.0%	102.6%	96.8%	90.5%	83.6%	
0.56	169.5%	165.3%	161.8%	158.2%	152.7%	150.1%	146.6%	142.2%	140.6%	132.9%	125.8%	125.3%	122.5%	116.4%	112.8%	105.3%	101.9%	94.9%		
0.58	174.7%	171.9%	166.6%	164.1%	158.3%	155.1%	150.5%	148.7%	145.2%	137.4%	135.6%	130.6%	128.7%	121.0%	116.2%	111.6%	104.9%	96.7%	89.2%	
0.60	182.0%	177.1%	172.7%	169.8%	165.2%	160.7%	155.1%	146.7%	145.1%	135.6%	132.8%	130.6%	125.5%	121.9%	115.9%	113.7%	102.0%	93.1%		
0.62	186.0%	183.0%	177.8%	173.3%	172.2%	165.3%	159.0%	155.0%	153.4%	147.7%	142.4%	140.4%	134.3%	129.4%	122.1%	114.2%	107.7%	96.3%		
0.64	191.8%	189.3%	181.9%	179.7%	175.8%	172.1%	161.9%	159.2%	155.0%	148.5%	146.1%	140.5%	136.5%	134.3%	129.4%	124.9%	118.9%	110.9%	103.4%	
0.66	198.8%	194.2%	187.3%	183.9%	177.9%	178.5%	167.4%	162.1%	158.0%	156.4%	150.1%	143.7%	139.8%	132.6%	127.2%	121.6%	114.9%	106.7%		
0.68	204.0%	197.9%	191.4%	187.7%	182.3%	176.8%	170.9%	164.3%	162.0%	156.4%	154.7%	152.1%	144.0%	141.2%	133.6%	128.9%	120.0%	110.3%		
0.70	207.6%	204.3%	202.5%	195.3%	194.3%	190.3%	176.3%	172.6%	167.4%	162.0%	160.5%	155.8%	152.1%	149.9%	144.2%	136.5%	132.6%	123.5%	117.0%	
0.72	218.4%	211.0%	207.4%	202.1%	197.9%	197.5%	174.8%	172.6%	170.6%	167.4%	166.0%	159.1%	155.4%	147.6%	143.2%	136.6%	130.1%	123.5%	116.6%	
0.74	222.9%	219.4%	213.5%	207.8%	206.4%	197.5%	181.0%	178.6%	175.5%	174.4%	170.6%	169.8%	167.3%	161.2%	156.0%	145.6%	138.7%	133.9%	130.1%	123.3%
0.76	230.2%	225.1%	221.3%	213.2%	211.5%	201.9%	195.8%	193.5%	188.2%	181.0%	175.5%	174.1%	172.9%	163.5%	158.7%	152.1%	145.8%	139.7%	133.9%	128.8%
0.78	234.2%	229.6%	224.6%	218.4%	218.8%	207.0%	202.8%	199.1%	194.1%	189.1%	182.1%	177.7%	168.7%	164.8%	158.4%	147.9%	143.9%	133.1%		
0.80	241.8%	238.1%	229.3%	226.3%	226.3%	212.4%	211.3%	207.0%	202.8%	199.6%	195.9%	189.6%	184.0%	176.4%	169.6%	161.0%	154.0%	147.9%	136.2%	
0.82	246.9%	243.0%	234.8%	231.1%	231.1%	220.9%	215.1%	211.9%	206.0%	197.8%	195.1%	188.1%	179.5%	178.2%	169.6%	162.8%	152.6%	143.1%		
0.84	255.3%	249.0%	239.8%	235.6%	235.6%	228.0%	221.2%	214.9%	209.9%	204.7%	198.0%	193.8%	188.0%	181.3%	172.6%	167.3%	157.4%	145.4%		
0.86	262.7%	258.1%	242.6%	246.3%	242.6%	233.9%	229.7%	221.9%	216.6%	213.9%	204.4%	201.1%	195.9%	185.9%	179.2%	171.0%	164.8%	152.6%		
0.88	270.3%	265.8%	259.8%	255.2%	251.0%	240.2%	232.7%	227.1%	224.2%	217.3%	211.9%	209.7%	200.0%	189.8%	188.7%	178.8%	168.3%	156.8%		
0.90	275.8%	272.0%	265.9%	263.2%	254.2%	245.9%	244.4%	238.4%	230.7%	220.9%	220.9%	215.1%	209.2%	199.3%	191.2%	179.0%	169.6%	164.6%		
0.92	286.1%	281.5%	270.1%	266.8%	266.8%	255.0%	249.1%	244.8%	236.7%	228.3%	227.2%	219.2%	209.1%	201.9%	200.7%	190.8%	178.8%	167.3%		
0.94	292.9%	289.8%	280.0%	270.2%	270.2%	260.2%	257.9%	248.6%	246.1%	240.1%	229.4%	224.6%	217.7%	211.2%	202.3%	193.3%	184.9%	174.6%		
0.96	303.6%	291.9%	286.3%	278.7%	278.7%	268.3%	263.1%	258.2%	250.1%	243.7%	234.9%	229.9%	220.1%	221.1%	211.0%	198.9%	187.7%	179.6%		
0.98	308.1%	302.3%	297.6%	293.7%	286.5%	279.6%	276.5%	271.4%	263.3%	256.5%	245.4%	244.5%	240.0%	229.0%	225.0%	214.4%	209.0%	198.9%	185.8%	
1.00	319.3%	311.2%	306.1%	300.3%	295.0%	289.3%	283.3%	276.5%	272.5%	263.4%	255.4%	250.5%	245.3%	234.1%	230.5%	221.3%	213.3%	205.0%	198.9%	187.7%

The number of offspring for both types follows a lognormal distribution with the stated μ and ρ, and with $\sigma = 2.0$. Quantities shown represent population growth rate per generation after ten generations, computed as $e^{\frac{\pi}{6}[\log(P_{10}/P_0)]/10}$, where $P_T = P_{A,T} + P_{B,T}$.

Source: Appendix of Koduri, N., and Lo, A. W. (2021). The origin of cooperation. *Proceedings of the National Academy of Sciences* 118(26): e201557118.

Table B.5 Simulated population growth rate with idiosyncratic risk ($\mu_{id} = -1.0$, $\sigma_{id} = 0.0$).

$\mu \backslash \rho$	-0.9	-0.7	-0.5	-0.3	-0.1	0.1	0.3	0.5	0.7	0.9
0.00	69.1%	67.6%	66.0%	65.0%	63.3%	61.3%	59.3%	57.0%	54.5%	52.7%
0.01	69.5%	69.2%	67.0%	65.9%	63.6%	62.5%	59.6%	57.7%	56.5%	53.0%
0.02	71.2%	69.7%	68.4%	67.0%	65.6%	63.7%	61.6%	59.3%	57.2%	54.6%
0.03	72.3%	71.7%	69.4%	67.6%	65.9%	64.5%	63.0%	60.3%	58.2%	55.1%
0.04	73.7%	72.7%	71.3%	69.3%	67.2%	65.7%	63.9%	61.7%	59.1%	56.2%
0.05	75.3%	74.0%	72.1%	70.5%	69.5%	66.6%	65.1%	62.5%	60.4%	57.8%
0.06	76.8%	75.0%	73.4%	72.2%	70.4%	68.8%	66.1%	64.4%	61.8%	58.3%
0.07	77.5%	76.9%	75.0%	73.4%	71.9%	68.9%	66.8%	65.3%	62.8%	59.1%
0.08	78.8%	77.5%	76.2%	74.9%	72.5%	71.3%	68.5%	66.8%	64.6%	60.0%
0.09	80.1%	79.0%	77.1%	76.3%	74.0%	72.8%	70.2%	68.4%	65.2%	61.8%
0.10	82.2%	80.0%	78.5%	77.1%	75.3%	73.3%	71.6%	68.5%	66.2%	62.7%
0.11	83.4%	81.6%	79.4%	78.6%	75.9%	75.5%	72.4%	70.3%	67.8%	63.4%
0.12	85.2%	83.2%	81.5%	80.0%	77.8%	75.8%	73.8%	71.1%	68.4%	66.1%
0.13	85.8%	84.8%	82.7%	81.1%	79.5%	77.6%	74.5%	72.7%	70.5%	67.6%
0.14 ·	87.0%	85.9%	84.3%	82.7%	80.5%	78.8%	76.7%	74.2%	71.1%	68.4%
0.15	89.0%	87.2%	85.8%	83.5%	82.2%	79.9%	77.6%	75.6%	72.9%	68.7%
0.16	90.6%	88.8%	86.7%	85.2%	83.3%	81.4%	78.9%	77.1%	73.0%	70.5%
0.17	92.3%	90.1%	88.4%	86.5%	84.3%	82.9%	80.3%	78.7%	75.3%	71.2%
0.18	93.1%	91.5%	89.5%	87.7%	86.1%	83.9%	81.1%	78.9%	76.8%	72.8%
0.19	94.5%	92.8%	91.1%	89.3%	87.9%	85.3%	82.7%	80.9%	77.6%	74.0%
0.20	96.1%	94.4%	92.7%	91.3%	88.9%	86.6%	84.7%	82.3%	78.9%	74.9%

The systematic component of number of offspring for both types follows a lognormal distribution with the stated μ and ρ, and with $\sigma = 1.0$. The idiosyncratic component follows a lognormal distribution with $\mu_{id} = -1.0$ and $\sigma_{id} = 0.0$. Quantities shown represent population growth rate per generation after ten generations, computed as $e^{E[\log(P_{10}/P_0)]/10}$, where $P_T = P_{A,T} + P_{B,T}$.

Source: Appendix of Koduri, N., and Lo, A. W. (2021). The origin of cooperation. *Proceedings of the National Academy of Sciences* 118(26): e2015572118.

The mean of this lognormally distributed component is 1, so the results in Table B.7 should be very similar to the results in Table B.6.

In general, this experiment finds that idiosyncratic risk, even large amounts, will decrease the importance of ρ relative to μ, but only by a small amount. For example, comparing the results in Table 7.1 (or Table B.2) to those in Table B.6 or B.7, we see that enough idiosyncratic risk has been added to increase the finite-time growth rate by over 100 percentage points. Nevertheless, decreasing ρ from 0.5 to −0.5 is still comparable to increasing μ by 0.07, compared to 0.09 originally.

Density Dependence

We reproduce Tables 7.2–7.4 with $r = 1.4$ in Table B.8 and $r = 1.5$ in Table B.9 to match the range of μ in Table B.2. At first glance, it seems as though ρ plays a smaller role when r is large. However, this is somewhat deceptive, since all growth rates go zero over time with density dependence, and ρ, in fact, becomes much more important compared to r. To obtain the same effect as increasing r from 1.4 to 1.5, one need only decrease ρ from 0.5 to about 0.2 when $K = 5$, or to about 0.0 when $K = 80$. (In comparison, to obtain the same effect as increasing r from 0.5 to 0.6, one needs to decrease ρ from 0.5 to −0.1 when $K = 5$, or 0.5 to −0.3 when $K = 80$.) Figures B.1 and B.2 show the population growth over time when $r = 1.5$ for $K = 10$ and $K = 40$,

Table B.6 Simulated population growth rate with idiosyncratic risk ($\mu_{\text{id}} = 0.0$, $\sigma_{\text{id}} = 0.0$).

μ \ ρ	-0.9	-0.7	-0.5	-0.3	-0.1	0.1	0.3	0.5	0.7	0.9
0.00	140.9%	139.2%	138.4%	137.0%	135.9%	134.2%	131.9%	130.5%	127.7%	126.2%
0.01	142.4%	141.3%	139.8%	138.4%	137.5%	135.5%	133.6%	131.6%	128.9%	126.7%
0.02	143.8%	142.6%	141.4%	139.7%	139.0%	136.4%	134.5%	133.4%	130.7%	127.6%
0.03	145.3%	143.8%	142.8%	140.9%	139.5%	137.5%	135.5%	134.0%	131.3%	128.7%
0.04	146.0%	145.3%	143.5%	142.5%	140.9%	138.4%	136.8%	135.5%	132.6%	130.5%
0.05	147.8%	146.8%	145.3%	143.7%	142.4%	140.0%	138.4%	136.0%	133.9%	131.9%
0.06	148.8%	147.2%	147.0%	144.4%	143.4%	141.6%	139.5%	138.0%	135.1%	132.7%
0.07	150.5%	149.3%	148.1%	146.1%	145.0%	143.2%	140.6%	138.3%	136.4%	134.2%
0.08	151.9%	150.8%	149.7%	147.6%	146.2%	144.2%	142.3%	139.8%	137.4%	135.4%
0.09	153.5%	151.8%	150.2%	149.4%	147.5%	145.3%	143.6%	141.4%	139.3%	135.7%
0.10	154.8%	153.4%	152.4%	150.7%	148.3%	146.9%	145.1%	142.3%	140.0%	137.7%
0.11	155.9%	154.9%	153.3%	151.8%	150.2%	148.4%	146.1%	144.6%	141.7%	139.3%
0.12	157.6%	156.8%	154.9%	153.7%	151.2%	149.7%	147.8%	144.6%	142.2%	139.0%
0.13	159.0%	157.7%	155.9%	155.2%	152.4%	151.2%	149.8%	147.1%	145.0%	141.7%
0.14	160.6%	159.1%	157.3%	156.0%	154.3%	152.2%	150.5%	148.1%	145.6%	142.4%
0.15	161.7%	160.7%	158.9%	157.8%	155.5%	153.5%	152.2%	149.6%	146.7%	144.7%
0.16	163.7%	162.6%	160.8%	158.5%	157.5%	154.8%	154.1%	151.7%	147.8%	145.0%
0.17	164.8%	164.2%	162.4%	160.7%	158.8%	156.3%	154.2%	151.8%	149.9%	146.2%
0.18	166.3%	165.0%	164.1%	162.4%	160.6%	158.3%	155.9%	153.6%	151.3%	147.5%
0.19	168.6%	166.8%	165.5%	163.0%	161.3%	159.7%	157.1%	155.6%	152.6%	148.8%
0.20	170.1%	168.3%	166.6%	164.3%	163.2%	161.2%	158.8%	155.9%	153.2%	150.3%

The systematic component of number of offspring for both types follows a lognormal distribution with the stated μ and ρ, and with $\sigma = 1.0$. The idiosyncratic component follows a lognormal distribution with $\mu_{\text{id}} = 0.0$ and $\sigma_{\text{id}} = 0.0$. Quantities shown represent population growth rate per generation after ten generations, computed as $e^{\mathbb{E}[\log(P_{10}/P_0)]/10}$, where $P_T = P_{A,T} + P_{B,T}$.

Source: Appendix of Koduri, N., and Lo, A. W. (2021). The origin of cooperation. *Proceedings of the National Academy of Sciences* 118(26): e2015572118.

respectively. The impact of correlation is remarkably consistent over time, even in populations whose growth has plateaued.

B.6 Chapter 8: Bounded Rationality

These proofs are drawn from Brennan and Lo (2012).

B.6.1 Proof of Proposition 8.1

Based on Equations (8.4) and (8.5), and the condition that $\alpha_1 > \alpha_2$, we have:

$$\lim_{T \to \infty} \frac{n_T(I_2)}{n_T(I_1)} \xrightarrow{p} \lim_{T \to \infty} \frac{e^{T\alpha_2}}{e^{T\alpha_1}} = \lim_{T \to \infty} e^{T(\alpha_2 - \alpha_1)} = 0,$$

which proves Proposition 8.1.

Table B.7 Simulated population growth rate with idiosyncratic risk ($\mu_{\text{id}} = -1.0$, $\sigma_{\text{id}} = \sqrt{2}$).

$\mu \backslash \rho$	-0.9	-0.7	-0.5	-0.3	-0.1	0.1	0.3	0.5	0.7	0.9
0.00	131.7%	129.7%	128.2%	127.3%	125.5%	123.1%	121.6%	118.4%	118.0%	114.4%
0.01	132.9%	131.5%	129.5%	127.7%	126.8%	125.0%	123.7%	121.3%	118.6%	116.1%
0.02	133.8%	133.5%	131.3%	129.3%	127.6%	125.8%	124.5%	122.3%	119.7%	117.9%
0.03	135.5%	134.2%	132.5%	132.1%	128.3%	127.4%	125.6%	122.9%	121.1%	117.9%
0.04	137.1%	135.8%	134.1%	132.4%	131.1%	129.2%	127.2%	124.9%	122.6%	119.0%
0.05	138.6%	136.5%	135.6%	133.3%	132.4%	130.2%	128.1%	125.8%	123.3%	121.6%
0.06	139.8%	138.6%	137.5%	135.1%	133.1%	131.3%	130.3%	127.0%	125.6%	121.6%
0.07	141.4%	139.8%	138.1%	137.1%	134.9%	133.0%	131.8%	129.0%	126.2%	123.4%
0.08	142.7%	141.7%	139.4%	138.0%	136.4%	134.5%	131.7%	131.1%	127.6%	125.0%
0.09	143.8%	143.0%	141.5%	139.4%	137.8%	135.9%	133.4%	131.7%	129.1%	126.1%
0.10	146.1%	143.9%	142.4%	141.5%	139.0%	137.7%	134.7%	133.2%	130.3%	128.2%
0.11	147.9%	146.2%	143.7%	142.9%	140.5%	138.3%	136.3%	134.7%	132.3%	128.0%
0.12	149.0%	147.8%	145.6%	144.2%	141.4%	140.1%	137.3%	135.6%	132.6%	130.4%
0.13	150.1%	148.3%	146.8%	145.4%	143.2%	141.9%	139.1%	137.0%	134.1%	131.4%
0.14	151.9%	150.3%	148.8%	147.3%	144.5%	143.0%	141.5%	138.5%	136.3%	133.0%
0.15	153.6%	152.1%	150.2%	148.3%	146.2%	145.6%	142.2%	139.4%	137.0%	133.8%
0.16	154.8%	153.3%	151.5%	149.9%	147.8%	146.1%	144.0%	141.9%	138.2%	135.8%
0.17	156.3%	155.2%	152.9%	151.4%	149.3%	147.5%	145.4%	142.4%	140.3%	136.3%
0.18	157.7%	156.3%	154.8%	152.5%	151.0%	148.5%	146.4%	144.9%	141.0%	138.1%
0.19	159.6%	158.4%	156.2%	154.7%	152.5%	149.9%	148.0%	145.4%	143.1%	139.6%
0.20	161.1%	159.7%	157.7%	154.8%	154.2%	152.3%	149.4%	146.4%	143.5%	141.4%

The systematic component of number of offspring for both types follows a lognormal distribution with the stated μ and ρ, and with $\sigma = 1.0$. The idiosyncratic component follows a lognormal distribution with $\mu_{\text{id}} = -1.0$ and $\sigma_{\text{id}} = \sqrt{2}$. Quantities shown represent population growth rate per generation after ten generations, computed as $e^{\mathbb{E}[\log(P_{10}/P_0)]/10}$, where $P_T = P_{A,T} + P_{B,T}$.

Source: Appendix of Koduri, N., and Lo, A. W. (2021). The origin of cooperation. *Proceedings of the National Academy of Sciences* 118(26): e2015572118.

Table B.8 Simulated density-dependent population growth rate ($r = 1.4$).

$K \backslash \rho$	-0.9	-0.7	-0.5	-0.3	-0.1	0.1	0.3	0.5	0.7	0.9
5.0	4.6%	4.3%	4.2%	4.1%	3.8%	3.6%	3.4%	3.0%	2.8%	2.1%
10.0	12.0%	11.7%	11.6%	11.5%	11.3%	11.0%	10.7%	10.3%	9.8%	9.4%
20.0	20.0%	19.7%	19.6%	19.5%	19.2%	19.0%	18.5%	18.3%	17.9%	17.4%
40.0	28.5%	28.5%	28.2%	28.0%	27.6%	27.3%	27.0%	26.8%	26.2%	25.4%
80.0	38.0%	37.5%	37.4%	37.2%	37.0%	36.5%	36.3%	35.7%	35.1%	34.5%

The number of offspring for both types follows Equations (7.25) and (7.26) with the stated K and ρ, and with $r = 1.4$, $s = 1.0$ and $L = K$. Quantities shown represent population growth rate per generation after ten generations, computed as $e^{\mathbb{E}[\log(P_{10}/P_0)]/10}$, where $P_T = P_{A,T} + P_{B,T}$.

Source: Appendix of Koduri, N., and Lo, A. W. (2021). The origin of cooperation. *Proceedings of the National Academy of Sciences* 118(26): e2015572118.

Table B.9 Simulated density-dependent population growth rate ($r = 1.5$).

$K \backslash \rho$	−0.9	−0.7	−0.5	−0.3	−0.1	0.1	0.3	0.5	0.7	0.9
5.0	4.9%	4.7%	4.5%	4.4%	4.2%	3.9%	3.8%	3.5%	3.2%	2.8%
10.0	12.3%	12.1%	12.1%	11.8%	11.8%	11.5%	11.2%	10.8%	10.7%	10.2%
20.0	20.5%	20.2%	20.2%	20.0%	19.7%	19.5%	19.3%	18.8%	18.5%	18.2%
40.0	29.1%	28.9%	28.7%	28.4%	28.3%	28.1%	27.6%	27.5%	27.2%	26.4%
80.0	38.6%	38.1%	37.9%	37.8%	37.5%	37.4%	37.1%	36.8%	36.1%	35.4%

The number of offspring for both types follows Equations (7.25) and (7.26) with the stated K and ρ, and with $r = 1.5$, $s = 1.0$ and $L = K$. Quantities shown represent population growth rate per generation after ten generations, computed as $e^{\mathbb{E}[\log(P_{10}/P_0)]/10}$, where $P_T = P_{A,T} + P_{B,T}$.

Source: Appendix of Koduri, N., and Lo, A. W. (2021). The origin of cooperation. *Proceedings of the National Academy of Sciences* 118(26): e2015572118.

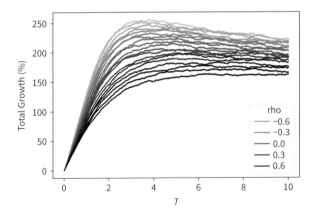

Fig. B.1 Total density-dependent population growth vs time ($K = 10$). Values of ρ range from −0.6 (lightest) to 0.6 (darkest). The number of offspring for both types follows Equations (7.25) and (7.26) with $r = 1.5$, $K = 10$, $L = 10$, and $s = 1.0$.

Source: Appendix of Koduri, N., and Lo, A. W. (2021). The origin of cooperation. *Proceedings of the National Academy of Sciences* 118(26): e2015572118.

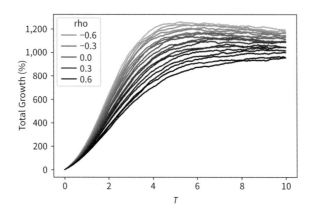

Fig. B.2 Total density-dependent population growth vs time ($K = 40$). Values of ρ range from −0.6 (lightest) to 0.6 (darkest). The number of offspring for both types follows Equations (7.25) and (7.26) with $r = 1.5$, $K = 40$, $L = 40$, and $s = 1.0$.

Source: Appendix of Koduri, N., and Lo, A. W. (2021). The origin of cooperation. *Proceedings of the National Academy of Sciences* 118(26): e2015572118.

B.6.2 Proof of Proposition 8.2

The result follows directly from the definition of correlation. We have

$$
\begin{aligned}
\mathrm{Corr}\,(I_{i,t}, y_{i,t}) &= \frac{\mathbb{E}\,[I_{i,t}y_{i,t}] - \mathbb{E}\,[I_{i,t}]\,\mathbb{E}\,[y_{i,t}]}{\mathrm{Std}\,(y_{i,t})\,\mathrm{Std}\,(I_{i,t})} \\[2mm]
&= \frac{\pi_t \delta_t^+ + (f - \pi_t)\delta_t^- - f(\varphi_t \delta_t^+ + (1 - \varphi_t)\delta_t^-)}{\sigma_t \sqrt{f(1 - f)}} \\[2mm]
&= (\pi_t - \varphi_t f)\,\frac{\delta_t^+ - \delta_t^-}{\sigma_t \sqrt{f(1 - f)}} \\[2mm]
&= \left(\frac{\pi_t - \varphi_t f}{\sqrt{f(1 - f)}\sqrt{\varphi_t(1 - \varphi_t)}}\right)\left(\frac{\delta_t^+ - \delta_t^-}{\sigma_t / \sqrt{\varphi_t(1 - \varphi_t)}}\right) \\[2mm]
&= \mathrm{Corr}\,(I_{i,t}, H\,(y_{i,t}))\left(\frac{\delta_t^+ - \delta_t^-}{\sigma_t / \sqrt{\varphi_t(1 - \varphi_t)}}\right),
\end{aligned}
$$

which proves Equation (8.16).

The value of π_t does not depend upon the choice of individual i, because the functions $\Phi_{i,t}$ and $I_{i,t}$ are IID across individuals in generation t. The lack of dependence of r_t on the choice of individual i within a given generation can be seen by noting that

$$
r_t = \mathrm{Corr}\,(I_{i,t}, H\,(y_{i,t})) = \frac{\pi_t - \varphi_t f}{\sqrt{f(1 - f)}\sqrt{\varphi_t(1 - \varphi_t)}},
$$

and observing that the right-hand side of this equation does not depend upon the choice of individual i.

B.6.3 Proof of Proposition 8.3

From the definition of π_t in Equation (8.18), it is clear that π must be bounded above by $\min(f, \varphi_t)$. Also, because intelligence only occurs when $\rho_t > 0$, the formulas in Equations (8.16) and (8.17) show that it must also be the case that π_t is bounded below by $f\varphi_t$, and this suffices to prove Equation (8.19).

The range of possible values for r_t can be derived by substituting the limits of the possible range for π_t into the expression for r_t in Equation (8.17), and the range of possible values for ρ_t follows from Equation (8.16).

To obtain an upper bound on $\rho_{t,\max}$, it is useful to proceed by first deriving a lower bound for σ_t. Note that Hölder's inequality shows that

$$\sigma_t^2 = \mathbb{E}\left[y_{i,t}^2\right] - (\mathbb{E}\left[y_{i,t}\right])^2 = \varphi_t \mathbb{E}\left[y_{i,t}^2 | y_{i,t} > 0\right] + (1 - \varphi_t)\,\mathbb{E}\left[y_{i,t}^2 | y_{i,t} \le 0\right]$$
$$- (\varphi_t \mathbb{E}\left[y_{i,t} | y_{i,t} > 0\right] + (1 - \varphi_t)\,\mathbb{E}\left[y_{i,t} | y_{i,t} \le 0\right])^2$$
$$\ge \varphi_t\,(\mathbb{E}\left[y_{i,t} | y_{i,t} > 0\right])^2 + (1 - \varphi_t)\left(\mathbb{E}\left[y_{i,t}^2 | y_{i,t} \le 0\right]\right)^2$$
$$- (\varphi_t \mathbb{E}\left[y_{i,t} | y_{i,t} > 0\right] + (1 - \varphi_t)\,\mathbb{E}\left[y_{i,t} | y_{i,t} \le 0\right])^2$$
$$= \varphi_t(1 - \varphi_t)\left(\delta_t^+ - \delta_t^-\right)^2.$$

The expectations are all taken with respect to a particular individual within generation t and are also independent of the specific choice of individual within the generation. Also, the conditions for equality in Hölder's inequality show that equality only holds for our lower bound on σ_t^2, when both $\mathbb{E}\left[y_{i,t}^2 | y_{i,t} > 0\right] = (\mathbb{E}\left[y_{i,t}^2 | y_{i,t} > 0\right])^2$ and $\mathbb{E}\left[y_{i,t}^2 | y_{i,t} \le 0\right] = (\mathbb{E}\left[y_{i,t}^2 | y_{i,t} \le 0\right])^2$. The lower bound on σ_t^2 can be rewritten as

$$\frac{\delta_t^+ - \delta_t^-}{\sigma_t / \sqrt{\varphi_t(1 - \varphi_t)}} \le 1,$$

and this is the upper bound on $\rho_{t,\max}$ described in the proposition.

B.6.4 Proof of Proposition 8.4

The expression for α in Equation (8.22) is maximized when the argument of the logarithm is maximized, and this can be written

$$e^\alpha = f\mu_a + (1 - f)\mu_b + \gamma\left(\min(\varphi, f) - \varphi f\right)\left(\delta^+ - \delta^-\right).$$

The partial derivative of e^α with respect to γ is

$$\frac{\partial e^\alpha}{\partial \gamma} = \left(\min(\varphi, f) - \varphi f\right)\left(\delta^+ - \delta^-\right),$$

and this value is greater than 0 provided that $f \notin \{0, 1\}$, since $\delta^+ - \delta^- > 0$. Thus, if $f \notin \{0, 1\}$, e^α is a strictly increasing function of γ, and the maximum value of e^α for any fixed value of $f \in (0, 1)$ is obtained when $\gamma = 1$.

The partial derivative of e^α with respect to f is

$$\frac{\partial e^\alpha}{\partial f} = \varphi(1-\gamma)\delta^+ + (1-\varphi(1-\gamma))\delta^-,$$

when $f > \varphi$, and

$$\frac{\partial e^\alpha}{\partial f} = (1-(1-\varphi)(1-\gamma))\delta^+ + (1-\varphi)(1-\gamma)\delta^-,$$

when $f < \varphi$. When $\gamma = 1$, the expressions for $\partial e^\alpha/\partial f$ become simply δ^- or δ^+, when $f > \varphi$ and $f < \varphi$, respectively. Because $\delta^- < 0$ and $\delta^+ > 0$, e^α obtains its maximum for $f \in (0,1)$ is at $f = \varphi$ and $\gamma = 1$.

If φ is 0 or 1, then the value of f that maximizes α and e^α is clearly $f = \varphi$, and the value of γ is irrelevant, since intelligence is irrelevant for an optimal outcome in this situation.

B.6.5 Proof of Proposition 8.5

The proof follows from a straightforward analysis of the partial derivatives of e^α with respect to γ and f. The derivative of e^α with respect to γ is

$$\frac{\partial e^\alpha}{\partial \gamma} = (1 - c'(\gamma))(\min(\varphi,f) - \varphi f)(\delta^+ - \delta^-),$$

and for any value of $f \in (0,1)$, this partial derivative is zero exactly when $\gamma = \gamma^*$. Thus, if the optimal value of f is in the interior of the interval $[0,1]$, the optimal value of γ is γ^*.

When $\gamma = \gamma^*$, the partial derivative of e^α with respect to f can be written

$$\frac{\partial e^\alpha}{\partial f} = \mu_a - \mu_b + (\delta^+ - \delta^-)(\gamma^* - c(\gamma^*))(1 - \varphi), \tag{B.60}$$

when $f < \varphi$, and

$$\frac{\partial e^\alpha}{\partial f} = \mu_a - \mu_b + (\delta^+ - \delta^-)(\gamma^* - c(\gamma^*))(-\varphi), \tag{B.61}$$

when $f > \varphi$. When $\mu_b > \mu_a$ and $\varphi \in (0,1)$, the expression in Equation (B.61) is always negative, and so e^α is decreasing in f in the region $f \in [\varphi, 1]$. Also, the sign of Equation (B.60) is positive, zero, or negative, according to whether $\gamma^* - c(\gamma^*)$ is larger than, equal to, or less than, respectively, the value of $\frac{\mu_b - \mu_a}{\delta^+ + \mu_b - \mu_a}$. In these three situations, the function e^α is increasing, constant, or decreasing, respectively, in the region $f \in [0, \varphi]$. These observations lead directly to the results in Equation (8.23).

The remaining results of the proposition follow from similar analysis of the partial derivative of e^α with respect to f in the various cases described.

B.6.6 Proof of Proposition 8.6

The optimality of the choice $\gamma = \gamma^*$ follows from consideration of the derivative of α with respect to γ. The optimality of f described in the proposition follows from the fact that the second derivative of α with respect to f is continuous and strictly negative, since φ_t has a smooth distribution. Also, because the optimal value of f is assumed to occur in the interior of the interval $[0, 1]$, it follows that this value is the unique place at which the derivative with respect to f vanishes, when $\gamma = \gamma^*$.

B.7 Chapter 9: Learning to be Bayesian

These proofs are drawn from Lo and Zhang (2021). We first derive the population analytics of the binary choice model with environmental states, which forms the basis for the main results.

Individuals in a given generation t are indexed by i, and generations are indexed by $t = 1, \cdots, T$. In all cases, we assume IID randomness over time, or, equivalently, over generations. On occasion, we will omit the t subscript, unless we wish to emphasize the temporal ordering of the variables, such as in a recursive relation between two successive generations.

After observing all available information, S, each individual i chooses action a with some probability $f(S) \in [0, 1]$ and b with probability $1 - f(S)$, denoted by the Bernoulli variable $I_i^{f(S)}$. As a result, i's offspring, $x_i^{f(S)}$, is given by:

$$x_i^{f(S)} = I_i^{f(S)} x_a + \left(1 - I_i^{f(S)}\right) x_b, \quad I_i^{f(S)} = \begin{cases} 1 & \text{with prob} \quad f(S) \\ 0 & \text{with prob} \quad 1 - f(S) \end{cases}. \qquad (B.62)$$

We use the superscript $f(\cdot)$ to denote the particular type of individual as defined by the decision rule in Equation (B.62). With this convention in mind, we denote by $n_t^{f(\cdot)}$ the total number of offspring of type $f(\cdot)$ in generation t, which is simply the sum of all the offspring from the type-$f(\cdot)$ individuals of the previous generation:

$$n_t^{f(\cdot)} = \sum_{i=1}^{n_{t-1}^{f(\cdot)}} x_{i,t}^{f(S_t)} = \left(\sum_{i=1}^{n_{t-1}^{f(\cdot)}} I_i^{f(S_t)}\right) x_{a,t} + \left(\sum_{i=1}^{n_{t-1}^{f(\cdot)}} \left(1 - I_i^{f(S_t)}\right)\right) x_{b,t}$$

$$= n_{t-1}^{f(\cdot)} \left(\left(\frac{\sum_{i=1}^{n_{t-1}^{f(\cdot)}} I_i^{f(S_t)}}{n_{t-1}^{f(\cdot)}}\right) x_{a,t} + \left(\frac{\sum_{i=1}^{n_{t-1}^{f(\cdot)}} \left(1 - I_i^{f(S_t)}\right)}{n_{t-1}^{f(\cdot)}}\right) x_{b,t}\right).$$

Applying the law of large numbers, we determine the population dynamics between two generations:

$$\frac{n_t^{f(\cdot)}}{n_{t-1}^{f(\cdot)}} \overset{a.s.}{=} \left(f(S_t) x_{a,t} + (1 - f(S_t)) x_{b,t}\right), \qquad (B.63)$$

where the notation '$\overset{a.s.}{=}$' in Equation (B.63) denotes 'almost sure' convergence as $n_{t-1}^{f(\cdot)}$ increases without bound.

B.7.1 Proof of Equation (9.5)

We can rewrite Equation (B.63) in terms of the relative frequency of each behaviour in the population. Let $l_t^{f(\cdot)}$ be the relative frequency of behaviour $f(\cdot)$ in the population in generation t. We have:

$$l_t^{f(\cdot)} = \frac{n_t^{f(\cdot)}}{\sum_{g(\cdot)} n_t^{g(\cdot)}} \stackrel{a.s.}{=} \frac{n_{t-1}^{f(\cdot)} (f(S_t)x_{a,t} + (1 - f(S_t))x_{b,t})}{\sum_{g(\cdot)} n_{t-1}^{g(\cdot)} (g(S_t)x_{a,t} + (1 - g(S_t))x_{b,t})} = \frac{l_{t-1}^{f(\cdot)} \cdot Fitness_t^{f(\cdot)}}{\sum_{g(\cdot)} l_{t-1}^{g(\cdot)} \cdot Fitness_t^{g(\cdot)}}, \quad (B.64)$$

where $Fitness_t^{f(\cdot)} = (f(S_t)x_{a,t} + (1 - f(S_t))x_{b,t})$ is the fitness (random reproductive success) of behaviour $f(\cdot)$ in generation t, and the summation in the denominator is over a finite set of all possible behaviours, $g(\cdot)$, in the population.

Note that Equation (B.64) has the same mathematical form as the Bayes formula:

$$\text{Prob}(A_i|data) = \frac{\text{Prob}(data|A_i)\text{Prob}(A_i)}{\sum_j \text{Prob}(data|A_j)\text{Prob}(A_j)} \quad (B.65)$$

if we treat $l_t^{f(\cdot)}$ (the frequency in the current generation) as the posterior $\text{Prob}(A_i|data)$, $l_{t-1}^{f(\cdot)}$ (the frequency in the previous generation) as the prior $\text{Prob}(A_i)$, and $Fitness_t^{f(\cdot)}$ (the fitness in the current generation) as the likelihood $\text{Prob}(data|A_i)$.

This completes the proof of Equation (9.5).

B.7.2 Proof of Proposition 9.1

Through backward recursion based on Equation (B.63), the population size of type-$f(\cdot)$ individuals in generation T is given by

$$n_T^{f(\cdot)} \stackrel{a.s.}{=} \prod_{t=1}^{T} (f(S_t)x_{a,t} + (1 - f(S_t))x_{b,t}), \quad (B.66)$$

$$\frac{1}{T} \log n_T^{f(\cdot)} \stackrel{a.s.}{=} \frac{1}{T} \sum_{t=1}^{T} \log (f(S_t)x_{a,t} + (1 - f(S_t))x_{b,t}) \quad (B.67)$$

$$\stackrel{a.s.}{\to} \mathbb{E}_{(x_a,x_b,S)}[\log (f(S)x_a + (1 - f(S))x_b)], \quad (B.68)$$

where '$\stackrel{a.s.}{\to}$' in Equation (B.68) denotes almost sure convergence as T increases without bound. The expected value is taken over the joint distribution of (x_a, x_b, S), and we have assumed that $n_0 = 1$ without loss of generality.

This result follows from the ergodic theorem (see, e.g., White (2001, Theorem 3.34)). Specifically, Assumptions 9.1 and 9.3 together imply that $\log (f(S_t)x_{a,t} + (1 - f(S_t))x_{b,t})$ has finite moments up to order 2. Assumptions 9.2, 9.3, and 9.4 together imply that $\log (f(S_t)x_{a,t} + (1 - f(S_t))x_{b,t})$ is stationary and ergodic (see, e.g., White (2001, Theorem 3.35)).

Since the behaviour, $f(\cdot)$, that maximizes the population size, $n_T^{f(\cdot)}$, is also the $f(\cdot)$ that maximizes $T^{-1} \log n_T^{f(\cdot)}$, Equation (B.68) implies that this value converges almost surely to the maximum of the following expected value:

$$\alpha(f(\cdot)) \equiv \mathbb{E}_{(x_a,x_b,S)}[\log (f(S)x_a + (1 - f(S))x_b)]. \quad (B.69)$$

Expression (B.69) is simply the expected value of the log-geometric-average growth rate of the population, given a particular behaviour $f(\cdot)$. Note that behaviour $f(\cdot)$ is a function of the observed data S. The pertinent evolutionary question is what forms of $f(\cdot)$ maximize growth.

By conditioning on the observed states S (or mathematically, by the law of total expectation), Equation (B.69) can be rewritten as

$$\alpha(f(\cdot)) = \mathbb{E}_S \left[\mathbb{E}_{(x_a, x_b | S)} \left[\log \left(f(S) x_a + (1 - f(S)) x_b \right) \mid S \right] \right]. \tag{B.70}$$

Given observed states S, the behaviour $f(S)$ is fixed, and the growth rate in Equation (B.70) is simply an integration over the distribution of S. It therefore suffices to find the function $f(\cdot)$ that maximizes the conditional expected value $\mathbb{E}_{(x_a, x_b | S)} \left[\log \left(f(S) x_a + (1 - f(S)) x_b \right) \mid S \right]$ for every possible value of S. The rest of the proof follows from a similar derivation to the proof of Proposition 2.1 in Section B.1.1.

B.7.3 Proof of Proposition 9.2

We can rewrite the population growth rate, $\alpha(f(\cdot))$, in Equation (B.69) as

$$\alpha(f(\cdot)) = \mathbb{E}[\log \left(f(S) r + 1 \right)] + \mathbb{E}[\log(x_b)], \tag{B.71}$$

provided that the expected value for both terms in Equation (B.71) exists. This is a more restrictive condition than Assumption 9.1. We do not make this distributional assumption in general except for this result.

The last term, $\mathbb{E}[\log(x_b)]$, does not depend on $f(\cdot)$. Therefore, maximizing $\alpha(f(\cdot))$ over $f(\cdot)$ is equivalent to maximizing the first term in Equation (B.71). We further approximate Equation (B.71) by a Taylor expansion around $r = 0$:[5]

$$\begin{aligned} \alpha(f(\cdot)) &\approx \mathbb{E}[f(S) r] - \frac{1}{2} \mathbb{E} \left[(f(S) r)^2 \right] + constant \\ &= \mathbb{E}[f(S)] \mathbb{E}[r] + \text{Cov}(f(S), r) - \frac{1}{2} \mathbb{E} \left[(f(S) r)^2 \right] + constant \end{aligned} \tag{B.72}$$

up to the second-order Taylor approximation. This expansion is the basis for the three factors pertaining to intelligence in this chapter.

B.7.4 Proof of Proposition 9.3

We return to the fundamental relationship between two generations, Equation (B.63), to derive the population dynamics of nonstationary environments. Through backward recursion based on Equation (B.63), the population size of type-$f(\cdot)$ individuals in generation T is given by

$$n_T^{f(\cdot)} \stackrel{a.s.}{=} \prod_{t=1}^{T} \left(f(S_t) x_{a,t} + (1 - f(S_t)) x_{b,t} \right), \tag{B.73}$$

$$\frac{1}{T} \log n_T^{f(\cdot)} \stackrel{a.s.}{=} \frac{1}{T} \sum_{t=1}^{T} \log \left(f(S_t) x_{a,t} + (1 - f(S_t)) x_{b,t} \right) \tag{B.74}$$

$$\stackrel{a.s.}{\to} \lim_{T \to \infty} \frac{1}{T} \sum_{t=1}^{T} \mathbb{E}_{(x_{a,t}, x_{b,t}, S_t)} [\log \left(f(S_t) x_{a,t} + (1 - f(S_t)) x_{b,t} \right)], \tag{B.75}$$

---

[5] When the fitnesses of the two actions $x_{,a}$, and x_b are similar, r varies around 0. This is another assumption that is specific to this result, and not used in the remainder of this appendix.

where '$\overset{a.s.}{\rightarrow}$' in Equation (B.75) denotes almost sure convergence as T increases without bound. The expected value is taken over the joint distribution of (x_a, x_b, S_t), and we have assumed that $n_0 = 1$ without loss of generality.

This result follows from White (2001, Theorem 3.47). Specifically, Assumptions 9.1 and 9.3 together imply that $\log(f(S_t)x_{a,t} + (1 - f(S_t))x_{b,t})$ has finite moments up to order 2. Assumptions 9.2, 9.3, and 9.5 together imply that $\log(f(S_t)x_{a,t} + (1 - f(S_t))x_{b,t})$ is α-mixing (e.g. see White (2001, Theorem 3.49)).

For behaviours that use past information, there is no explicit solution for the optimal behaviour $f^*(\cdot)$ for the general nonstationary environment. Although each term in the growth rate for the nonstationary environment, Equation (B.75), is mathematically equivalent to the growth rate for the stationary environment, Equation (B.69), the optimal behaviour, $f^*(\cdot)$, that maximizes Equation (B.75) is fundamentally different from $f^*(\cdot)$ in stationary environments (Proposition 9.1). This is because the state in period t is conditioned on information in period t ($s_t|S_t$, or, equivalently, $s_t|s_{t-1}, s_{t-2}, \cdots$). As a result, the conditional distribution $(x_{a,t}, x_{b,t}|S_t)$ depends on t, but individual behaviour $f^*(\cdot)$ is not time-aware (i.e. $f^*(\cdot)$ is not a function of time t). Therefore, it is impossible for $f^*(\cdot)$ to be optimal with respect to the distribution of $(x_{a,t}, x_{b,t}|S_t)$ for any period t.

B.7.5 Additional Technical Details for Section 9.5

We assume that all available information in period t, S_t, contains a large number of data points. There is a cost for each individual to obtain and use this data, $C(m)$, where m is the number of data points used for inferential purposes. Instead of making decisions based on all available information, individuals make decisions based on this limited number of data points, and their behaviour is denoted by $f(S(m))$. When the reproductive risk is systematic, the number of individual i's offspring, $x_i^{f(S(m))}$, is given by:

$$x_i^{f(S(m))} = \frac{I_i^{f(S(m))} x_a + \left(1 - I_i^{f(S(m))}\right) x_b}{C(m)}, \quad I_i^{f(S(m))} = \begin{cases} 1 & \text{with prob} \quad f(S(m)) \\ 0 & \text{with prob} \quad 1 - f(S(m)) \end{cases}, \quad (B.76)$$

where $C(m) > 0$ is an increasing function of m. Equation (B.76) adjusts the individual reproductive success by a factor of $C(m)^{-1}$ relative to Equation (B.62) to reflect this cost.

Through a similar transformation of the population dynamics described in Equations (B.62)–(B.69), it is not hard to see that the population growth rate for individuals using limited samples of data points in stationary environments is:

$$\alpha(f(S(m))) \equiv \mathbb{E}_{(x_a, x_b, S)}[\log(f(S(m))x_a + (1 - f(S(m)))x_b)] - \log C(m). \quad (B.77)$$

Note that in Equation (B.77) the expected value is over the distribution of (x_a, x_b, S), that is, all available information S, but individual behaviour is restricted to only limited samples, $S(m)$.

In this setting, an evolutionarily optimal behaviour is achieved by maximizing the growth rate, $\alpha(f(S(m)))$, over both the number of samples, m, and the specific functional form, $f(\cdot)$. As m increases, the first term in Equation (B.77) increases, while the second term in Equation (B.77) decreases due to the increase in the cognitive cost. The optimal number of samples, m^*, depends on the relative magnitude of the marginal change of an additional sample.

Next, we solve for the optimal behaviour and growth rate in two steps. Firstly, we fix the number of samples, m, and solve for the optimal behaviour, $f^*(D(m))$. We then maximize the growth rate by optimizing over m.

Given m samples, the probability that the majority indicates the correct state is:

$$\beta = 1 - CDF(m/2; m, q),$$

where $CDF(m/2; m, q)$ is the binomial cumulative distribution function. The growth rate for a behaviour using m samples can therefore be written as:

$$
\begin{aligned}
\alpha(f(D(m))) &= \mathbb{E}_D \left[\mathbb{E}_{(x_a, x_b|D)} [\log (f(D(m))x_a + (1 - f(D(m)))x_b)] \right] - \log(C(m)). \\
&= p \left(\beta \log(fc) + (1 - \beta) \log((1 - f)c) \right) \\
&\quad + (1 - p) \left(\beta \log((1 - f)c) + (1 - \beta) \log(fc) \right) - \log(C(m)) \\
&= (1 - p - \beta + 2p\beta) \log(fc) + (p + \beta - 2p\beta) \log((1 - f)c) - \log(C(m)).
\end{aligned}
\tag{B.78}
$$

Given m samples, we can derive the optimal $f^*(D(m))$ by maximizing $\alpha(f(D(m)))$:

$$
f^*(D(m)) = \begin{cases} \beta p + (1 - \beta)(1 - p) & \text{if } D(m) \text{ implies summer} \\ \beta(1 - p) + (1 - \beta)p & \text{if } D(m) \text{ implies winter} \end{cases}.
\tag{B.79}
$$

This is the weighted average of the state probabilities p and $1 - p$, where the probability that the majority indicates the correct state, β, is used as the weight. Equation (B.79) can be treated as an approximation to probability matching, where the approximation is determined by the confidence of the data.

Substituting Equation (B.79) into Equation (B.78), we can determine the optimal growth rate given m samples, $\alpha(f^*(D(m)))$:

$$
\begin{aligned}
\alpha(f^*(D(m))) &= (1 - p - \beta + 2p\beta) \log((\beta p + (1 - \beta)(1 - p)) c) \\
&\quad + (p + \beta - 2p\beta) \log(((1 - p) + (1 - \beta)p) c) - \log(C(m)).
\end{aligned}
\tag{B.80}
$$

The optimal number of samples, m^*, is obtained by maximizing Equation (B.80) over m. Here, β will depend on the cumulative distribution function of the binomial distribution, and therefore m^* does not have an explicit solution.

B.8 Chapter 10: The Madness of Mobs

These proofs are drawn from Lo and Zhang (2022).

B.8.1 Proof of Proposition 10.1

Equation (10.4) follows directly from substituting the definitions of the environment in Equations (10.1) and (10.3) into the population growth rate in Equation (4.3), and p^{benefit} and p^{harm} follow directly from the maximization of $\alpha^{\text{benefit}}(p)$ and $\alpha^{\text{harm}}(p)$ over $p \in [0, 1]$.

B.8.2 Proof of Proposition 10.2

Equation (10.10) follows directly from substituting the definitions of the environment in Equations (10.8) and (10.9) into the population growth rate in Equation (4.3), and p^* follows directly from the maximization of $\alpha(p)$ over $p \in [0, 1]$.

B.8.3 Proof of Proposition 10.3

Proposition 10.2 characterizes the growth-optimal behaviour, p^*, with factors defined by Equation (10.8). The factor with feedback in Equation (10.12) is mathematically equivalent to the environment defined by Equation (10.8), except that the adverse probability associated with Tellarians, r, is replaced by the feedback-adjusted adverse probability, $\tilde{r}$. Therefore, a behaviour can survive in the long run only when it satisfies the growth-optimal behaviour in Proposition 10.2, with r replaced by the feedback-adjusted $\tilde{r}$, which gives us the fixed-point condition of Equation (10.13).

B.8.4 Proof of Proposition 10.4

The key to proving Proposition 10.4 lies in the observation that the population growth rate, $\alpha(p)$, in Equation (10.10) is a decreasing function of the feedback-adjusted Tellarian adverse probability, $\tilde{r}$. To avoid confusion, here we explicitly write the population growth rate as

$$\alpha(p, \tilde{r}(p)) \tag{B.81}$$

because, under Assumption 10.1, $\alpha(p)$ is also a function of $\tilde{r}$ which is, in turn, defined by the growth-optimal behaviour.

When $p^*_{\text{non-L-ESS}}$ is one solution of the fixed-point condition, Equation (10.13), it maximizes the population growth rate, $\alpha(p, \tilde{r}(p^*_{\text{non-L-ESS}}))$, by definition. In other words,

$$\alpha\left(p, \tilde{r}(p^*_{\text{non-L-ESS}})\right) < \alpha\left(p^*_{\text{non-L-ESS}}, \tilde{r}(p^*_{\text{non-L-ESS}})\right) \tag{B.82}$$

for any $p \neq p^*_{\text{non-L-ESS}}$. In particular, this implies that

$$\alpha\left(p^*_{\text{L-ESS}}, \tilde{r}(p^*_{\text{non-L-ESS}})\right) < \alpha\left(p^*_{\text{non-L-ESS}}, \tilde{r}(p^*_{\text{non-L-ESS}})\right), \tag{B.83}$$

where $\tilde{r}$ is defined by $p^*_{\text{non-L-ESS}}$. Because $p^*_{\text{L-ESS}} > p^*_{\text{non-L-ESS}}$ and $\alpha(p)$ is a decreasing function of $\tilde{r}$, the left side of Equation (B.83) becomes even smaller when we substitute $\tilde{r}$ defined by $p^*_{\text{L-ESS}}$. Therefore,

$$\alpha\left(p^*_{\text{L-ESS}}, \tilde{r}(p^*_{\text{L-ESS}})\right) < \alpha\left(p^*_{\text{L-ESS}}, \tilde{r}(p^*_{\text{non-L-ESS}})\right) < \alpha\left(p^*_{\text{non-L-ESS}}, \tilde{r}(p^*_{\text{non-L-ESS}})\right), \tag{B.84}$$

which completes the proof.

B.8.5 Proof of Proposition 10.5

The growth-optimal behaviour, p^*, in Equation (10.11) is an increasing function of r, which follows from the derivative of p^* with respect to r. As the feedback intensity, τ, increases, the feedback-adjusted adverse probability, $\bar{r}$, increases, and therefore p^* also increases (behaviours are more discriminative).

B.9 Chapter 14: A Computational View of Market Efficiency

These proofs are drawn from Hasanhodzic, Lo, and Viola (2011).

B.9.1 Proof of Proposition 14.1

Let $R_1, R_2, \cdots, R_{m+1}$ be IID random variables with range $\{-1, 1\}$ whose probability of being 1 is 1/2. Consider the market pattern

$$\left[R_1, R_2, \cdots, R_{m+1}, R_{m+2} \equiv \prod_{i=1}^{m+1} R_i \right]$$

of length $p = m + 2$. By the definition of the pattern, the distribution of each variable is independent from the previous m, and therefore any memory-m strategy has gain 0.

Then consider the memory-$(m + 1)$ strategy $s(x_1, x_2, \cdots, x_{m+1}) \equiv \prod_{i=1}^{m+1} x_i$. Its gain over the market pattern is

$$\sum_{i=1}^{p} \mathbb{E}_{R_1, \cdots, R_p} \left[\text{sign} \left(R_{i-m-1} \cdot R_{i-m} \cdots R_{i-1} \cdot R_i \right) \right]$$

$$= \mathbb{E}_{R_1, \cdots, R_p} \left[\text{sign} \left(R_1 \cdot R_2 \cdots R_{m+1} \cdot R_{m+2} \right) \right] = 1.$$

B.9.2 Proof of Proposition 14.2

Consider the market pattern

$$\left[R_1, \cdots, R_{m-1}, a \cdot R_m, b \prod_{i=1}^{m} R_i, y_2, \cdots, y_{m'-1}, c \cdot y_{m'}, \prod_{i=1}^{m} R_i \prod_{i=2}^{m'} y_i, \right.$$

$$\left. R_1, \cdots, R_{m'-1}, a' \cdot R_{m'}, b \prod_{i=1}^{m'} R_i, y_2, \cdots, y_{m'-1}, c \cdot y_{m'}, -\prod_{i=1}^{m'} R_i \prod_{i=2}^{m'} y_i \right],$$

where $R_1, \cdots, R_{m'}$ and $y_2, \cdots, y_{m'}$ are independent $\{-1, 1\}$ random variables (note that some of these variables will appear multiple times in the pattern), and $a = 10, a' = 20, b = 30, c = 40$.

We now analyse the gains of various strategies. It is convenient to define the *latest input* of a strategy $s(x_1, \cdots, x_\ell)$ as x_ℓ; this corresponds to the most recent observation the strategy is taking into consideration.

The strategy s_m. We note that there is an optimal strategy s_m on $\mathcal{P}$ that produces an output 0, unless its latest input has absolute value a. This is because in all other instances, the random variable that the strategy is trying to predict is independent of the previous m. Thus, $s_m(x_1, \cdots, x_m)$ equals 0 unless $|x_m| = a$, in which case it outputs the sign of $\prod_{i=1}^{m} x_i$. The gain of this strategy is 1. This strategy evolves the pattern into a similar pattern, except that the *first* occurrence of b is now replaced with $b - 1$:

$$\mathcal{P}_m \equiv \Big[R_1, \cdots, R_{m-1}, a \cdot R_m, (b-1) \prod_{i=1}^{m} R_i, y_2, \cdots, y_{m'-1}, c \cdot y_{m'}, \prod_{i=1}^{m} R_i \prod_{i=2}^{m'} y_i,$$

$$R_1, \cdots, R_{m'-1}, a' \cdot R_{m'}, b \prod_{i=1}^{m'} R_i, y_2, \cdots, y_{m'-1}, c \cdot y_{m'}, - \prod_{i=1}^{m'} R_i \prod_{i=2}^{m'} y_i \Big].$$

The strategy $s_{m'}$. We note that there is an optimal memory-m' strategy over $\mathcal{P}$ that produces an output 0, unless its latest input has absolute value a, a', or c. Again, this occurs because, in all other instances, the strategy is trying to predict a variable that is independent of the previous m'. Moreover, when its latest input has absolute value c, we can also assume that the strategy produces an output of 0. This is because the corresponding contribution is

$$\mathbb{E}\left[\text{sign}\left(s_{m'}(b \cdot \prod_{i=1}^{m} R_i, y_2, \cdots, y_{m'-1}, c \cdot y_{m'}) \cdot \prod_{i=1}^{m} R_i \prod_{i=2}^{m'} y_i \right) \right]$$

$$+ \mathbb{E}\left[\text{sign}\left(s_{m'}(b \cdot \prod_{i=1}^{m'} R_i, y_2, \cdots, y_{m'-1}, c \cdot y_{m'}) \cdot - \prod_{i=1}^{m'} R_i \prod_{i=2}^{m'} y_i \right) \right] = 0.$$

Thus, there is an optimal memory-m' strategy with gain 2 that evolves the market pattern into a pattern $\mathcal{P}_{m'}$ that is similar to $\mathcal{P}$ but with b replaced by $b - 1$ in *both* occurrences, as opposed to $\mathcal{P}_m$, which has b replaced by $b - 1$ only in its first occurrence.

The optimal memory-m' strategy on $\mathcal{P}_{m'}$. Since $\mathcal{P}_{m'}$ is similar to $\mathcal{P}$, only with b replaced by $b - 1$, the gain of the optimal memory-m' strategy on $\mathcal{P}_{m'}$ will be 2.

The optimal memory-m strategy on $\mathcal{P}_m$. Essentially, the same argument for s_m can be applied again to argue that any memory-m strategy on $\mathcal{P}_m$ has, at most, a gain of 1.

The optimal memory-m' strategy on $\mathcal{P}_m$. Finally, note that there is a memory-m' strategy whose gain is 4 on $\mathcal{P}_m$. This is because the replacement of the first occurrence of b in $\mathcal{P}$ with $b - 1$ allows a memory-m' strategy to predict the sign of the market correctly when its latest input has absolute value c.

B.10 Chapter 15: Maximizing Relative versus Absolute Wealth

These proofs are drawn from Lo, Orr, and Zhang (2018).

B.10.1 Proof of Proposition 15.2

The first partial derivative of $\mathbb{E}[l_1^f]$ to f is:

$$\frac{\partial \mathbb{E}[l_1^f]}{\partial f} = \lambda(1 - \lambda)\mathbb{E}\left[\frac{(x_a - x_b)\omega^g}{\left(\lambda\omega^f + (1-\lambda)\omega^g\right)^2} \right].$$

The second partial derivative of $\mathbb{E}[l_1^f]$ to f is:

$$\frac{\partial^2 \mathbb{E}[l_1^f]}{\partial f^2} = -2\lambda^2(1-\lambda)\mathbb{E}\left[\frac{(x_a - x_b)^2 \omega^g}{\left(\lambda\omega^f + (1-\lambda)\omega^g\right)^3}\right] \leq 0,$$

which indicates that $\mathbb{E}[l_1^f]$ is a concave function of f. Therefore, it suffices to consider the value of the first partial derivative at its endpoints 0 and 1.

$$f_1^* = \begin{cases} 1 & \text{if } \dfrac{\partial \mathbb{E}[l_1^f]}{\partial f}\Big|_{f=1} > 0 \\ 0 & \text{if } \dfrac{\partial \mathbb{E}[l_1^f]}{\partial f}\Big|_{f=0} < 0 \ . \\ \text{solution to } \dfrac{\partial \mathbb{E}[l_1^f]}{\partial f} = 0 & \text{otherwise} \end{cases}$$

Proposition 15.2 follows from trivial simplifications of the above equation.

B.10.2 Proof of Proposition 15.3

Consider $\frac{\partial \mathbb{E}[l_1^f]}{\partial f}$ when $f = g$:

$$\frac{\partial \mathbb{E}[l_1^f]}{\partial f}\Big|_{f=g} = \lambda(1-\lambda)\mathbb{E}\left[\frac{x_a - x_b}{fx_a + (1-f)x_b}\right].$$

Note that the right-hand side consists of a factor that also appears in the first-order condition in Equation (15.2) of the Kelly criterion. Therefore, its sign is determined by whether f is larger than f^{Kelly}:

$$\frac{\partial \mathbb{E}[l_1^f]}{\partial f}\Big|_{f=g} \begin{cases} > 0 & \text{if } f = g < f^{Kelly} \\ = 0 & \text{if } f = g = f^{Kelly} \ . \\ < 0 & \text{if } f = g > f^{Kelly} \end{cases} \tag{B.85}$$

Since $\mathbb{E}[l_1^f]$ is concave as a function of f for any g, we know that:

$$f_1^* \begin{cases} > g & \text{if } g < f^{Kelly} \\ = g & \text{if } g = f^{Kelly} \ , \\ < g & \text{if } g > f^{Kelly} \end{cases}$$

which completes the proof.

B.10.3 Proof of Proposition 15.4

The cross partial derivative of $\mathbb{E}[l_1^f]$ is:

$$\frac{\partial^2 \mathbb{E}[l_1^f]}{\partial f \partial g} = \lambda(1-\lambda)\mathbb{E}\left[\frac{(x_a - x_b)^2 \left(\lambda \omega^f - (1-\lambda)\omega^g\right)}{\left(\lambda \omega^f + (1-\lambda)\omega^g\right)^3}\right].$$

Consider $\frac{\partial^2 \mathbb{E}[l_1^f]}{\partial f \partial g}$ when $f = g = f^{Kelly}$:

$$\left.\frac{\partial^2 \mathbb{E}[l_1^f]}{\partial f \partial g}\right|_{f=g} = 2\lambda(1-\lambda)\left(\lambda - \frac{1}{2}\right)\mathbb{E}\left[\left(\frac{x_a - x_b}{f x_a + (1-f)x_b}\right)^2\right]\begin{cases} < 0 & \text{if } \lambda < \frac{1}{2} \\ = 0 & \text{if } \lambda = \frac{1}{2} \\ > 0 & \text{if } \lambda > \frac{1}{2} \end{cases}.$$

The first-order condition of Equation (B.85) is 0 when $f = g = f^{Kelly}$, so when g is near f^{Kelly}, the sign of the first-order condition is determined by whether λ is greater than, equal to, or less than $1/2$. For example, if $\lambda < 1/2$, then the derivative of the first-order condition of Equation (B.85) with respect to g is negative, which implies that the first-order condition is negative when $g = f^{Kelly} + \epsilon$, where ϵ is a small positive quantity. Therefore, when $g = f^{Kelly} + \epsilon$, f_1^* is smaller than f^{Kelly}. The cases when $\lambda > 1/2$ and $\lambda = 1/2$ follow similarly.

B.10.4 Proof of Proposition 15.5

The first partial derivative of $\mathbb{E}[l_T^f]$ to f is:

$$\frac{\partial \mathbb{E}[l_T^f]}{\partial f} = \frac{1-\lambda}{\lambda}\mathbb{E}\left[\frac{\exp\left(TW_T^f\right)\sum_{t=1}^{T}\frac{x_{a,t} - x_{b,t}}{f x_{a,t} + (1-f)x_{b,t}}}{\left(1 + \frac{1-\lambda}{\lambda}\exp\left(TW_T^f\right)\right)^2}\right].$$

$\mathbb{E}[l_T^f]$ is not necessarily concave, but it is unimodal. The rest follows from similar calculations to Proposition 15.2.

B.10.5 Proof of Proposition 15.6

The first partial derivative of $\mathbb{E}[l_T^f]$ to f evaluated at $f = g$ is given by:

$$\left.\frac{\partial \mathbb{E}[l_T^f]}{\partial f}\right|_{f=g} = T\lambda(1-\lambda)\mathbb{E}\left[\frac{(x_a - x_b)}{f x_a + (1-f)x_b}\right].$$

The cross partial derivative of $\mathbb{E}[l_T^f]$ evaluated at $f = g$ is given by:

$$\left.\frac{\partial^2 \mathbb{E}[l_T^f]}{\partial f \partial g}\right|_{f=g} = 2\lambda(1-\lambda)\left(\lambda - \frac{1}{2}\right)\mathbb{E}\left[\left(\sum_{t-1}^{T}\frac{x_{a,t} - x_{b,t}}{f x_{a,t} + (1-f)x_{b,t}}\right)^2\right].$$

The rest follows similarly to the proof of Propositions 15.3 and 15.4.

B.10.6 Proof of Proposition 15.7

It follows directly from Equations (15.4) and (15.9).

B.11 Chapter 17: What Happened to the Quants in August 2007?

These results are drawn from Khandani and Lo (2011b). We first provide the details of the computation of expected profits for the contrarian trading strategy of Lehmann (1990) and Lo and MacKinlay (1990), and its application to transactions data on 6 August 2007. In Section B.11.1, we derive a general expression for the expected profit under the assumption of jointly covariance-stationary returns for individual securities. In Section B.11.2, we derive the expected profit for the special case of the linear factor model (17.7), which incorporates an idiosyncratic market-making component and a common factor that may exhibit either mean reversion or momentum.

B.11.1 Expected Profits for Stationary Returns

Consider the collection of N securities and denote by $\mathbf{R}_t$ the $N \times 1$ vector of their period t returns, $[R_{1,t} \cdots R_{N,t}]'$. Assume that $\mathbf{R}_t$ is a jointly covariance-stationary stochastic process with expectation $\mathbb{E}[\mathbf{R}_t] = \boldsymbol{\mu} = [\mu_1 \cdots \mu_N]'$ and auto covariance matrices:

$$\mathbb{E}[(\mathbf{R}_{t-l} - \boldsymbol{\mu})(\mathbf{R}_t - \boldsymbol{\mu})'] = \Gamma_l = [\gamma_{i,j}(l)].$$

Define $R_{i,t}(q)$ as the q-period return of security i starting at time t:

$$R_{i,t}(q) \equiv \prod_{k=0}^{q-1}(1 + R_{i,t+k}) - 1 \approx \sum_{k=0}^{q-1} R_{i,t+k},$$

where the approximation is needed because period returns, $R_{i,t}$, are simple returns and the logarithm of a sum is not equal to the sum of the logarithms.

We will consider the return of a market neutral strategy that invests an amount $\omega_{i,t}$ in security i at time t, where:

$$\omega_{i,t} \equiv -\frac{1}{N}(R_{i,t-1} - R_{m,t-1}) \ , \ R_{m,t-1} \equiv \frac{1}{N}\sum_{i=1}^{N} R_{i,t-1}.$$

Define $\pi_t(q)$ as the profit for this strategy for a portfolio constructed at date t and held fixed for q periods. Then we have:

$$\begin{aligned}
\pi_t(q) &= \sum_{i=1}^{N} \omega_{i,t} R_{i,t}(q) \approx \sum_{i=1}^{N}\left(\omega_{i,t}\sum_{l=0}^{q-1} R_{i,t+l}\right) \\
&\approx \sum_{i=1}^{N}\left(-\frac{1}{N}(R_{i,t-1} - R_{m,t-1})\sum_{l=0}^{q-1} R_{i,t+l}\right) \\
&\approx -\frac{1}{N}\sum_{i=1}^{N}\left(R_{i,t-1}(R_{i,t}+\cdots+R_{i,t+q-1})\right) + R_{m,t-1}(R_{m,t}+\cdots+R_{m,t+q-1}).
\end{aligned}$$

Now, taking expectations yields:

$$E[\pi_t(q)] \approx -\frac{1}{N}\sum_{i=1}^{N}\left(\gamma_{i,i}(1)+\cdots+\gamma_{i,i}(q) + q\mu_i^2\right) +$$

$$\frac{1}{N^2}\sum_{i=1}^{N}\sum_{j=1}^{N}\left(\gamma_{i,j}(1)+\cdots+\gamma_{i,j}(q) + q\mu_i\mu_j\right). \qquad (B.86)$$

For lag l, the group of terms has the following structure:

$$-\frac{1}{N}\sum_{i=1}^{N}\left(\gamma_{i,i}(l) + \mu_i^2\right) +$$

$$\frac{1}{N^2}\sum_{i=1}^{N}\sum_{j=1}^{N}\left(\gamma_{i,j}(l) + \mu_i\mu_j\right) \quad = \quad \frac{1}{N^2}\sum_{i=1}^{N}\sum_{j=1}^{N}\gamma_{i,j}(l) - \frac{1}{N}\sum_{i=1}^{N}\gamma_{i,i}(l) +$$

$$\frac{1}{N^2}\sum_{i=1}^{N}\sum_{j=1}^{N}\mu_i\mu_j - \frac{1}{N}\sum_{i=1}^{N}\mu_i^2$$

$$= \quad \frac{1}{N^2}\iota'\Gamma_l\iota - \frac{1}{N}\text{tr}(\Gamma_l) +$$

$$\frac{1}{N^2}\iota'(\mu\mu')\iota - \frac{1}{N}\text{tr}(\mu\mu')). \qquad (B.87)$$

To simplify this expression, define the following operator:

$$\mathcal{M}(\mathbf{A}) \equiv \frac{1}{N^2}\iota'\mathbf{A}\iota - \frac{1}{N}\text{tr}(\mathbf{A}). \qquad (B.88)$$

Note that $\mathcal{M}(\cdot)$ is linear, i.e.

$$\mathcal{M}(\mathbf{A} + \mathbf{B}) \quad = \quad \mathcal{M}(\mathbf{A}) + \mathcal{M}(\mathbf{B}). \qquad (B.89)$$

$$\mathcal{M}(\alpha\mathbf{A}) \quad = \quad \alpha\mathcal{M}(\mathbf{A}). \qquad (B.90)$$

Now, for any $(N\times1)$ column-vector $\mathbf{c}$, define $\sigma^2(\mathbf{c})$ as:

$$\sigma^2(\mathbf{c}) \quad \equiv \quad \frac{1}{N}\sum_{i=1}^{N}(c_i - c_m)^2, \quad c_m \equiv \frac{1}{N}\sum_{i=1}^{N}c_i. \qquad (B.91)$$

Note that if $\mathbf{A} = \mathbf{cc}'$, where $\mathbf{c}$ is an $(N\times1)$ column-vector, it is easy to show that:

$$\mathcal{M}(\mathbf{A}) \quad = \quad \frac{1}{N^2}\sum_{i=1}^{N}\sum_{j=1}^{N}c_ic_j - \frac{1}{N}\sum_{i=1}^{N}c_i^2$$

$$= \quad -\sigma^2(\mathbf{c}). \qquad (B.92)$$

Combining these relations and substituting Equation (B.87) into Equation (B.86) yields:

$$\mathbb{E}[\pi_t(q)] \approx \mathcal{M}(\Gamma_1) + \cdots + \mathcal{M}(\Gamma_q) + q\mathcal{M}(\mu\mu')$$

$$\approx \mathcal{M}(\Gamma_1) + \cdots + \mathcal{M}(\Gamma_q) - q\sigma^2(\mu). \tag{B.93}$$

B.11.2 Expected Profits for a Linear Factor Model

Consider the following return-generating process:

$$R_{i,t} = \mu_i + \beta_i \nu_t + \lambda_{i,t} + \eta_{i,t}, \tag{B.94a}$$

$$\lambda_{i,t} = -\epsilon_{i,t} + \left(\frac{1-\theta_i}{\theta_i}\right)\theta_i \epsilon_{i,t-1} + \left(\frac{1-\theta_i}{\theta_i}\right)\theta_i^2 \epsilon_{i,t-2} + \cdots \quad , \quad \theta_i \in (0,1), \tag{B.94b}$$

$$\nu_t = \rho \nu_{t-1} + \zeta_t, \quad \rho \in (-1,1), \tag{B.94c}$$

where $\epsilon_{i,t}$, ζ_t, and $\eta_{i,t}$ are white-noise random variables that are uncorrelated at all leads and lags.

In this specification, $\beta_i \nu_t$ represents a market-wide or common factor, $\eta_{i,t}$ represents firm-specific fundamental shocks, and $\lambda_{i,t}$ represents firm-specific liquidity shocks. The specification of this liquidity component in Equation (B.94b) may seem odd at first, but it has a natural interpretation. It is an infinite-order moving average where each term $\epsilon_{i,t}$ is meant to capture idiosyncratic liquidity shocks to security i at time t; hence, positive realizations represents buying pressure and vice versa for negative realizations. The coefficients for these idiosyncratic shocks are meant to decay at a rate of θ_i to reflect the gradual decline in buying or selling pressure, and they sum to one so as to eliminate any long-term impact of these shocks on prices.

The expressions for expected profits derived in Section B.11.1 are functions of the variance–covariance matrix of returns $R_{i,t}$. Since $\epsilon_{i,t}$ and ζ_t are uncorrelated at all leads and lags, the covariance matrix of the $R_{i,t}$s can be decomposed into two parts: a liquidity component and a common factor component. We will refer to these two parts as $\Gamma_{l,\lambda}$ and $\Gamma_{l,\nu}$, respectively, which are related to the covariance matrix Γ_l by:

$$\Gamma_l = \Gamma_{l,\lambda} + \Gamma_{l,\nu}. \tag{B.95}$$

Because $\mathcal{M}(\cdot)$ is linear, the above decomposition will simplify our derivation of expected profits. We now turn to computing each component of Γ_l.

B.11.3 Derivation of $\Gamma_{l,\nu}$

Observe that ν_t is a simple AR(1) process so its variance and covariances are given by:

$$\sigma_{\nu_t}^2 = \frac{1}{1-\rho^2}\sigma_\zeta^2,$$

$$\gamma_{\nu_t,\nu_{t+l}} = \frac{\rho^l}{1-\rho^2}\sigma_\zeta^2 = \rho^l \sigma_\nu^2.$$

Note that v_t is multiplied by β_i in the $R_{i,t}$, which will cause the covariance terms due to the common factor between different securities to be scaled accordingly. Therefore, we have:

$$\Gamma_{l,v} \quad = \quad \beta\beta^T \rho^l \sigma_v^2, \tag{B.96}$$

where β is a column vector of the β_is. Appealing to the linearity and other properties of $\mathcal{M}(\cdot)$ discussed in Section B.11.1, we have:

$$\mathcal{M}(\Gamma_{l,v}) \quad = \quad \mathcal{M}(\beta\beta^T \rho^l \sigma_v^2) \quad = \quad -\rho^l \sigma_v^2 \sigma^2(\beta). \tag{B.97}$$

B.11.4 Derivation of $\Gamma_{l,\lambda}$

The variance of $\lambda_{i,t}$ is given by:

$$
\begin{aligned}
\sigma_{\lambda_i}^2 \quad &= \quad \left(1 + \left(\frac{1 - \theta_i}{\theta_i}\right)^2 \theta_i^2 + \left(\frac{1 - \theta_i}{\theta_i}\right)^2 \theta_i^4 + \cdots\right) \sigma_{\epsilon_i}^2 \\
&= \quad \left(1 + \left(\frac{1 - \theta_i}{\theta_i}\right)^2 \left(\frac{\theta_i^2}{1 - \theta_i^2}\right)\right) \sigma_{\epsilon_i}^2 \quad = \quad \left(1 + \frac{1 - \theta_i}{1 + \theta_i}\right) \sigma_{\epsilon_i}^2 \\
&= \quad \frac{2}{1 + \theta_i} \sigma_{\epsilon_i}^2.
\end{aligned}
\tag{B.98}
$$

To compute the covariance between $\lambda_{i,t}$ and $\lambda_{i,t+l}$, we need to focus on the common $\epsilon_{i,t}$s in the cross product of the MA coefficients of $\lambda_{i,t}$ and $\lambda_{i,t+l}$. This yields:

$$
\begin{aligned}
\gamma_{\lambda_{i,t}, \lambda_{i,t+l}} \quad &= \quad \left(-\left(\frac{1 - \theta_i}{\theta_i}\right)\theta_i^l + \left(\frac{1 - \theta_i}{\theta_i}\right)^2 \theta_i^{l+2} + \left(\frac{1 - \theta_i}{\theta_i}\right)^2 \theta_i^{l+4} + \cdots\right) \sigma_{\epsilon_i}^2 \\
&= \quad \left(-\left(\frac{1 - \theta_i}{\theta_i}\right)\theta_i^l + \left(\frac{1 - \theta_i}{\theta_i}\right)^2 \theta_i^l \frac{\theta_i^2}{1 - \theta_i^2}\right) \sigma_{\epsilon_i}^2 \\
&= \quad \left(\frac{1 - \theta_i}{\theta_i}\right)\theta_i^l \left(-1 + \frac{1 - \theta_i}{\theta_i}\frac{\theta_i^2}{1 - \theta_i^2}\right) \sigma_{\epsilon_i}^2 \\
&= \quad \left(\frac{1 - \theta_i}{\theta_i}\right)\theta_i^l \left(-1 + \frac{\theta_i}{1 + \theta_i}\right) \sigma_{\epsilon_i}^2 \\
&= \quad -\left(\frac{1 - \theta_i}{\theta_i}\right)\theta_i^l \frac{1}{1 + \theta_i} \sigma_{\epsilon_i}^2 \\
&= \quad -\left(\frac{1 - \theta_i}{2\theta_i}\right)\theta_i^l \sigma_{\lambda_i}^2,
\end{aligned}
\tag{B.99}
$$

where we use our expression for $\sigma_{\lambda_i}^2$ to simplify. Combining these yields the following expression for $\Gamma_{l,\lambda}$:

$$\Gamma_{l,\lambda} \quad = \quad \mathrm{diag}\left(-\frac{1 - \theta_1}{2\theta_1}\theta_1^l \sigma_{\lambda_1}^2, \cdots, -\frac{1 - \theta_N}{2\theta_N}\theta_N^l \sigma_{\lambda_N}^2\right),$$

$$\mathcal{M}(\Gamma_{l,\lambda}) \quad = \quad \frac{N - 1}{N^2} \sum_{i=1}^{N} \frac{1 - \theta_i}{2\theta_i}\theta_i^l \sigma_{\lambda_i}^2. \tag{B.100}$$

B.11.5 Derivation of Expected Profit

We can now combine $\Gamma_{l,v}$ and $\Gamma_{l,\lambda}$ to yield an expression for the expected profit of the contrarian strategy. Recall that the expected profit is given by:

$$\mathbb{E}[\pi_t(q)] \quad \approx \quad \mathcal{M}(\Gamma_1) + \cdots + \mathcal{M}(\Gamma_q) - q\sigma^2(\boldsymbol{\mu}). \qquad (B.101)$$

Due to the linearity of $\mathcal{M}(\cdot)$ and using Equation (B.95), we can rewrite this expression as:

$$\mathbb{E}[\pi_t(q)] \quad \approx \quad \mathcal{M}(\Gamma_{1,\lambda}) + \cdots + \mathcal{M}(\Gamma_{q,\lambda}) +$$

$$\mathcal{M}(\Gamma_{1,v}) + \cdots + \mathcal{M}(\Gamma_{q,v}) - q\sigma^2(\boldsymbol{\mu}). \qquad (B.102)$$

The two parts of this expression can be simplified as follows:

$$\mathcal{M}(\Gamma_{1,\lambda}) + \cdots + \mathcal{M}(\Gamma_{q,\lambda}) \quad = \quad \sum_{l=1}^{q}\left[\frac{N-1}{N^2}\sum_{i=1}^{N}\frac{1-\theta_i}{2\theta_i}\theta_i^l\sigma_{\lambda_i}^2\right]$$

$$= \quad \frac{N-1}{N^2}\sum_{l=1}^{q}\sum_{i=1}^{N}\frac{1-\theta_i}{2\theta_i}\theta_i^l\sigma_{\lambda_i}^2$$

$$= \quad \frac{N-1}{N^2}\sum_{i=1}^{N}\frac{1-\theta_i}{2\theta_i}\theta_i\frac{1-\theta_i^q}{1-\theta_i}\sigma_{\lambda_i}^2$$

$$= \quad \frac{N-1}{N^2}\sum_{i=1}^{N}\frac{1-\theta_i^q}{2}\sigma_{\lambda_i}^2, \qquad (B.103)$$

$$\mathcal{M}(\Gamma_{1,v}) + \cdots + \mathcal{M}(\Gamma_{q,v}) \quad = \quad -\sum_{l=1}^{q}\rho^l\sigma_v^2\sigma^2(\boldsymbol{\beta})$$

$$= \quad -\rho\frac{1-\rho^q}{1-\rho}\sigma_v^2\sigma^2(\boldsymbol{\beta}). \qquad (B.104)$$

Substituting Equations (B.103) and (B.104) into Equation (B.102) yields the final expression for expected profits:

$$\mathbb{E}[\pi_t(q)] \quad \approx \quad \frac{N-1}{N^2}\sum_{i=1}^{N}\frac{1-\theta_i^q}{2}\sigma_{\lambda_i}^2 - \rho\frac{1-\rho^q}{1-\rho}\sigma_v^2\sigma^2(\boldsymbol{\beta}) - q\sigma^2(\boldsymbol{\mu}). \qquad (B.105)$$

Psychophysiological Methodology

These results are drawn from Lo and Repin (2002).

C.1 Subjects

The descriptive characteristics of the ten subjects are summarized in Table C.1. Based on discussions with their supervisors, the traders were categorized into three levels of experience: low, moderate, and high. Five traders specialized in handling client order flow ('Retail'), three specialized in trading foreign exchange ('FX'), and two specialized in interest-rate derivative securities ('Derivatives'). The durations of the sessions ranged from forty-nine minutes to eighty-three minutes, and all sessions were held during live trading hours, typically between 8:00am and 5:00pm ET.

C.2 Physiological Data Collection

A ProComp+ data acquisition unit and Biograph (Version 1.2) biofeedback software from Thought Technologies, Ltd were used to measure physiological data for all subjects. All six sensors were connected to a small control unit with a battery power supply, which was placed on each subject's belt and from which a fibre-optic connection led to a laptop computer equipped with real-time data acquisition software (Fig. C.1). Each sensor was equipped with a built-in notch filter at 60 Hz for automatic elimination of external power line noise, while a standard AgCl triode and single electrodes were used for the skin conductance response (SCR) and electromyography (EMG) sensors, respectively. The sampling rate for all data collection was fixed at 32 Hz. All physiological data except for respiration and facial EMG were collected from each subject's nondominant arm. SCR electrodes were placed on the palmar sites, the blood volume pulse (BVP) photoplesymographic sensor was placed on the inside of the ring or middle finger, the arm EMG triode electrode was placed on the inside surface of the forearm, over the flexor digitorum muscle group, and the temperature sensor was inserted between the elastic band placed around the wrist and the skin surface. The facial EMG electrode was placed on a masseter muscle, which controls jaw movement, and is active during speech or any other activity involving the jaw. The respiration signal was measured by chest expansion using a sensor attached to an elastic band placed around the subject's chest. An example of the real-time physiological data collected over a two-minute interval for one subject is given in Fig. C.2.

The entire procedure of outfitting each subject with sensors and connecting the sensors to the laptop required approximately five minutes, and was often performed either before the trading day began or during relatively calm trading periods. Subjects indicated that presence of the sensors, wires, and a control unit did not compromise or influence their trading in any significant manner, and that their workflow was not impaired in any way. This was verified not only by the subject, but also by their supervisors. Given the magnitudes of the financial transactions that were being processed, and the economic and legal responsibilities that the subjects and their supervisors bore, even the slightest interference with the subjects' workflow

Table C.1 Summary statistics for all subjects: individual trader's characteristics, specialty, type, and number of market time-series collected during the session, session duration, and absolute time (Eastern Time) of the start of the session.

Trader ID	Sex	Experience	Specialty	Market Data Available	Number of Market Time-Series Recorded	Session Duration (min and sec)	Session Start Time
B33	F	High	Retail	Major currencies	2	49'30"	13:20
B34	M	High	FX	Major currencies	3	83'32"	08:56
B35	M	High	Retail	Major currencies	4	66'30"	11:02
B36	M	High	Derivatives	S&P 500 futures, Eurodollar futures	3	79'16"	12:55
B37	M	Moderate	FX	Latin American, Major currencies	9	70'06"	09:17
B38	M	Low	FX	Latin American, Major currencies	3	72'12"	11:02
B39	M	High	Derivatives	S&P 500 futures, Eurodollar futures	9	62'03"	08:19
B310	M	Low	Retail	Major currencies	7	60'08"	09:47
B311	M	Moderate	Retail	Major currencies	7	54'25"	11:32
B312	M	Low	Retail	Major currencies	7	59'00"	09:10

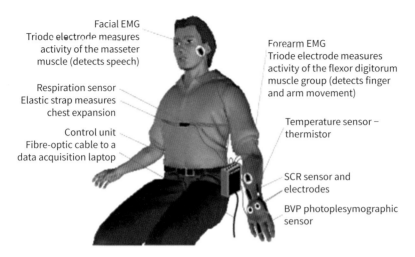

Fig. C.1 Placement of sensors for measuring physiological responses.

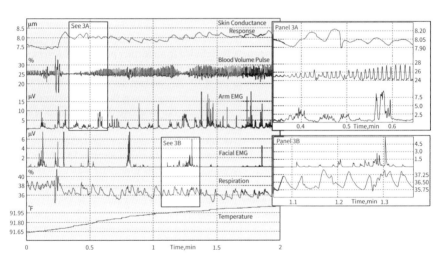

Fig. C.2 Typical physiological response data recorded by six sensors for a single subject over a two-minute time interval.

or performance standards would have caused the supervisors or the subjects to terminate the sessions immediately. None of the sessions was terminated prematurely.

C.3 Physiological Data Feature Extraction

An initial smoothing of the raw EMG signals (sampled at 32 Hz) was performed with a moving-average filter of order 23. If the level of the filtered forearm EMG signal exceeded a threshold of 0.75 mV, both SCR and BVP readings at this time were discarded because of the

Table C.2 Summary statistics of physiological response data for all traders: mean and standard deviation (SD) for each of the six sensors.

Trader ID	Facial EMG (μV) Mean	SD	Forearm EMG (μV) Mean	SD	SCR (μm) Mean	SD	TMP (°C) Mean	SD	BVP (%) Mean	SD	RSP (%) Mean	SD
B32	1.23	1.46	8.84	25.69	3.32	1.38	30.7	0.13	23.34	6.31	34.20	1.69
B34	1.36	3.15	0.88	1.86	11.54	4.55	31.4	0.39	24.93	4.05	33.28	1.15
B35	1.26	1.65	3.31	3.57	2.16	2.71	31.3	0.74	25.00	6.60	35.57	1.65
B36	2.50	4.06	1.04	2.13	10.09	2.16	29.7	0.36	24.87	3.80	33.45	1.57
B37	2.73	18.53	3.66	18.84	3.96	1.73	28.7	0.67	25.06	3.27	31.04	2.43
B38	8.35	20.12	1.51	1.93	12.24	2.21	28.4	0.25	25.09	7.61	29.75	0.61
B39	1.96	2.64	0.36	1.85	25.09	3.40	29.6	0.15	25.10	6.72	36.65	1.08
B310	1.26	0.73	1.75	2.75	1.99	0.47	32.2	0.29	24.87	5.12	36.93	1.53
B311	1.37	8.59	1.85	10.22	28.87	2.10	33.3	0.55	25.21	8.82	33.12	1.61
B312	1.64	1.19	1.08	8.22	3.59	0.71	29.2	0.08	25.10	5.12	31.32	0.79

BVP = blood volume pulse; EMG = electromyographic data; RSP = respiration rate; SCR = skin conductance response; TMP = body temperature.

high probability of artefacts (e.g. typing, grasping telephone handsets, or inadvertent physical disturbances to the sensors). Similarly, if the level of the filtered facial EMG signal exceeded 0.75 mV, the respiration signal at this time was excluded from further processing. A very small spatial displacement of the sensor or the electrode was able to produce a different kind of arte-fact, an abrupt change in the signal of the order of 10–20 standard deviations within 1/32 of a second. Such jumps did not have any physiological meaning; hence, they were excluded from further analysis via adaptive thresholding. Specifically, our adaptive thresholding procedure involved marking all observations that differed by more than ten standard deviations from a local average (with both the standard deviation and local average computed over the most recent thirty seconds of data, which yields 960 observations at a sampling rate of 32 Hz), replac-ing these outliers with the immediately preceding values. This procedure was then repeated until all such artefacts were eliminated. Finally, irrelevant high-frequency signal components and noise were eliminated through a low-pass filter that was individually designed for each of the physiological variables. The relatively smooth nature of the SCR signals permitted the elimination of all harmonics above 1.5 Hz, while the periodic structure of the BVP signals pushed the cut-off frequency to 4.5 Hz. Table C.2 reports the means and standard deviations of the signals measured by the six sensors for each of the ten subjects. After pre-processing, feature vectors were constructed from the SCR, BVP, temperature, and respiration signals.

C.4 Financial Data Collection

At the start of each session, a common time marker was set in the biofeedback unit and in the subject's trading console (a networked PC or workstation with real-time data feeds such as Bloomberg and Reuters) and software installed on the trading console (MarketSheet, by Tibco, Inc.) stored all market data for the key financial instruments in an Excel spreadsheet, time-stamped to the nearest second. The initial time markers and time-stamped spreadsheets allowed us to align the market and physiological data to within 0.5 seconds of accuracy. Figure C.3 displays an example of the real-time financial data—the euro/US dollar exchange rate—collected over a sixty-minute interval.

C.5 Financial Data Feature Extraction

Deviations of a time series $\{Z_t\}$ were defined as those observations that deviated from the series mean by a certain threshold, defined as a multiple k of the standard deviation, σ_z, of the time series. Positive deviations were defined as those observations Z_t such that $Z_t > \overline{Z} + k\sigma_z$, and negative deviations were defined as those observations Z_t such that $Z_t < \overline{Z} - k\sigma_z$. The value of the multiplier, k, varied with the particular series and session, and was calibrated to yield approximately 5–10 events per session. Because the volatility of financial time series can vary across instruments and over time, a single value of k for all subjects and instruments is clearly inappropriate. However, the sole objective in our calibration procedure was to maintain an approximately equal number of events for each time series in each session. Deviation events were defined for prices, spreads, and returns. Table C.3 reports the average values of k for each of the fifteen financial instruments in our study, which ranged from 0.10 for ARS and BRL (the Argentinian peso and Brazilian real) to 2.03 for EUR (the euro) for price deviations, 0.10 for ARS, BRL, and MXP (the Argentinian peso, Brazilian real, and Mexican peso) to 2.85 for GBP (the British pound) for spread deviations, and 0.01 for ARS (the Argentinian peso) to 15.00 for COP and MXP (the Colombian and Mexican pesos) for return deviations.

Trend reversal events were defined as instances when a time series $\{Z_t\}$ intersected its five-minute moving average, $\mathrm{MA}_{5\,\min}(Z_t)$ (e.g. see Fig. C.3 (upper panel)). Positive and negative trend reversals were defined as those observations Z_t such that $Z_t > (1 + \delta) \cdot \mathrm{MA}_{5\,\min}(Z_t)$ and $Z_t < (1 - \delta) \cdot \mathrm{MA}_{5\,\min}(Z_t)$, respectively. The parameter δ also varied with the particular series and session (see Table C.3), ranging from an average of 0.0001 to 0.1 for price series and from 0.005 to 1.575 for spreads. Owing to the high-frequency sampling rate (one second), prices did not vary often from one observation to the next; hence, most of the return values were zero, making it difficult to define trends in returns. Therefore, we defined trend reversals only for prices and spreads, excluding returns from this event category.

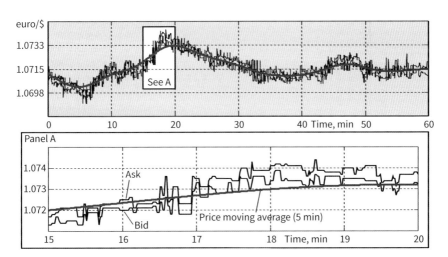

Fig. C.3 Typical real-time market data (euro/US dollar exchange rate) recorded during a sixty-minute time interval and the corresponding five-minute moving average.

Table C.3 Average values of the parameters used to define market events: deviations (k), trend reversals (δ), and volatility events (η).

Security Identifier	Mean k for Price	Mean k for Spread	Mean k for Return	Mean δ for Price	Mean δ for Spread	Mean δ for Return	Mean η for Maximum Volatility	Mean η for Average Price Volatility	Mean η for Average Return Volatility
ARS	0.10	0.10	0.01	0.10000	0.100	–	0.10	0.10	0.10
AUD	1.38	1.47	10.14	0.00090	0.475	–	0.58	0.43	0.58
BRL	0.10	0.10	0.50	0.00010	0.005	–	20.00	10.00	20.00
CAD	1.02	0.84	10.83	0.00058	0.250	–	0.72	0.72	0.63
CHF	1.75	2.12	9.17	0.00053	0.610	–	0.38	0.42	0.38
CLP	0.40	1.00	12.00	0.00020	0.200	–	0.60	0.50	0.50
COP	0.50	0.50	15.00	0.00070	0.200	–	5.00	3.00	3.00
EDU	1.40	2.50	11.00	0.00155	1.575	–	0.75	0.70	0.43
EUR	2.03	2.43	7.06	0.00066	1.274	–	0.45	0.45	0.36
GBP	1.54	2.85	9.24	0.00039	0.472	–	0.46	0.51	0.42
JPY	1.18	1.86	8.56	0.00089	0.803	–	0.54	0.54	0.41
MXP	1.00	0.10	15.00	0.00040	0.010	–	1.00	1.05	0.85
NZD	1.58	1.30	10.00	0.00085	0.288	–	0.73	0.65	0.73
SPU	0.63	0.25	14.09	0.00004	0.002	–	0.68	0.07	0.03
VEB	1.90	2.50	11.00	0.00060	0.500	–	0.30	0.40	0.40

Three types of volatility events were defined for five-minute time intervals, indexed by j, based on the following statistics:

$$\sigma_j^1 = \frac{\max_{t_j-300<\tau\le t_j} P_\tau - \min_{t_j-300<\tau\le t_j} P_\tau}{\frac{1}{2}(\max_{t_j-300<\tau\le t_j} P_\tau + \min_{t_j-300<\tau\le t_j} P_\tau)}, \tag{C.1}$$

$$\sigma_j^2 = \sqrt{\frac{1}{300} \sum_{t_j-300<\tau\le t_j} (P_\tau - \overline{P}_{t_j})^2}, \tag{C.2}$$

$$\sigma_j^3 = \sqrt{\frac{1}{300} \sum_{t_j-300<\tau\le t_j} R_\tau^2}, \tag{C.3}$$

where $\overline{P}_{t_j}$ denotes the average price in the interval t_j-300 to t_j, and R_τ^2 is the squared return between $\tau-1$ and τ. We refer to σ_j^1 as the 'maximum volatility' since it is the difference between the maximum and minimum prices as a fraction of their average, while σ_j^2 and σ_j^3 are the standard deviations of prices and returns, respectively. 'Plus' and 'minus' volatility events are then defined as those instances when

$$\sigma_j^l > (1+\eta)\cdot\sigma_{j-1}^l \quad \text{(Plus Event)}, \tag{C.4}$$

$$\sigma_j^l < (1-\eta)\cdot\sigma_{j-1}^l \quad \text{(Minus Event)} \tag{C.5}$$

for $l = 1, 2, 3$. The parameter η was calibrated to yield five or fewer volatility events per session, and ranged from an average of 0.10 to 20.0 (see Table C.3). For volatility events, we calibrated the threshold to yield five or fewer events to ensure that the combined time intervals containing volatility events comprised less than 50% of the total session time.

C.5.1 Test Statistics

For each of the eight types of events, a sample mean, $\hat{\mu}_j$, was computed for that component X_{jt} of the feature vector, $[\begin{array}{cccc} X_{1t} & X_{2t} & \cdots & X_{8t} \end{array}]$, and, compared to the sample mean, $\hat{\mu}_j^c$ of the corresponding component of the control feature vector, $[\begin{array}{cccc} Y_{1t} & Y_{2t} & \cdots & Y_{8t} \end{array}]$, according to the test statistic:

$$z_j = \frac{\hat{\mu}_j - \hat{\mu}_j^c}{\sqrt{2\hat{\sigma}_j^2/n_j}}, \tag{C.6}$$

where

$$\hat{\mu}_j = \frac{1}{n_j}\sum_{t=1}^{n_j} X_{jt}, \quad \hat{\mu}_j^c = \frac{1}{n_j}\sum_{t=1}^{n_j} Y_{jt}, \tag{C.7}$$

$$\hat{\sigma}_j^2 = \frac{1}{2n_j-2}\left(\sum_{t=1}^{n_j}(X_{jt}-\hat{\mu}_j)^2 + \sum_{t=1}^{n_j}(X_{jt}-\hat{\mu}_j)^2\right). \tag{C.8}$$

Under the null hypothesis that X_{jt} and Y_{jt} are independent and identically distributed normal random variables with mean μ and variance σ^2, the test statistic, z_j, has a t-distribution with

$2n_j-2$ degrees of freedom. In the absence of normality (Riniolo and Porges, 2000), the central limit theorem implies that under certain regularity conditions, z_j is approximately standard normal in large samples (Bickel and Doksum, 1977, Chapter 4.4.B), in which case the 95% critical region is defined by the complement of the interval $[-1.96, 1.96]$.

References

Abbe, E. A., A. E. Khandani, and A. W. Lo, 2012, Privacy-preserving methods for sharing financial risk exposures, *American Economic Review* 102, 65–70.

Abbot, P., J. Abe, J. Alcock, S. Alizon, J. A. C. Alpedrinha, M. Andersson, J.-B. Andre, M. van Baalen, F. Balloux, S. Balshine, N. Barton, L. W. Beukeboom, J. M. Biernaskie, T. Bilde, G. Borgia, M. Breed, S. Brown, R. Bshary, A. Buckling, N. T. Burley, M. N. Burton-Chellew, M. A. Cant, M. Chapuisat, E. L. Charnov, T. Clutton-Brock, A. Cockburn, B. J. Cole, N. Colegrave, L. Cosmides, I. D. Couzin, J. A. Coyne, S. Creel, B. Crespi, R. L. Curry, S. R. X. Dall, T. Day, J. L. Dickinson, L. A. Dugatkin, C. E. Mouden, S. T. Emlen, J. Evans, R. Ferriere, J. Field, S. Foitzik, K. Foster, W. A. Foster, C. W. Fox, J. Gadau, S. Gandon, A. Gardner, M. G. Gardner, T. Getty, M. A. D. Goodisman, A. Grafen, R. Grosberg, C. M. Grozinger, P.-H. Gouyon, D. Gwynne, P. H. Harvey, B. J. Hatchwell, J. Heinze, H. Helantera, K. R. Helms, K. Hill, N. Jiricny, R. A. Johnstone, A. Kacelnik, E. T. Kiers, H. Kokko, J. Komdeur, J. Korb, D. Kronauer, R. Kummerli, L. Lehmann, T. A. Linksvayer, S. Lion, B. Lyon, J. A. R. Marshall, R. McElreath, Y. Michalakis, R. E. Michod, D. Mock, T. Monnin, R. Montgomerie, A. J. Moore, U. G. Mueller, R. Noe, S. Okasha, P. Pamilo, G. A. Parker, J. S. Pedersen, I. Pen, D. Pfennig, D. C. Queller, D. J. Rankin, S. E. Reece, H. K. Reeve, M. Reuter, G. Roberts, S. K. A. Robson, D. Roze, F. Rousset, O. Rueppell, J. L. Sachs, L. Santorelli, P. Schmid-Hempel, M. P. Schwarz, T. Scott-Phillips, J. Shellmann-Sherman, P. W. Sherman, D. M. Shuker, J. Smith, J. C. Spagna, B. Strassmann, A. V. Suarez, L. Sundstrom, M. Taborsky, P. Taylor, G. Thompson, J. Tooby, N. D. Tsutsui, K. Tsuji, S. Turillazzi, F. Ubeda, E. L. Vargo, B. Voelkl, T. Wenseleers, S. A. West, M. J. West-Eberhard, D. F. Westneat, D. C. Wiernasz, G. Wild, R. Wrangham, A. J. Young, D. W. Zeh, J.A. Zeh, and A. Zink, 2011, Inclusive fitness theory and eusociality, *Nature* 471, E1–E4.

Abreu, D., and M. K. Brunnermeier, 2003, Bubbles and crashes, *Econometrica* 71, 173–204.

Acar, M., J. T. Mettetal, and A. van Oudenaarden, 2008, Stochastic switching as a survival strategy in fluctuating environments, *Nature Genetics* 40, 471–475.

Acharya, V. V., M. Richardson, S. Van Nieuwerburgh, and L. J. White, 2011, *Guaranteed to Fail: Fannie Mae, Freddie Mac, and the Debacle of Mortgage Finance* (Princeton University Press, Princeton, NJ).

Ackermann, C., R. McEnally, and D. Ravenscraft, 1999, The performance of hedge funds: risk, return, and incentives, *The Journal of Finance* 54, 833–874.

Admati, A. R., 1985, A noisy rational expectations equilibrium for multi-asset securities markets, *Econometrica* 53, 629–657.

Adrian, T., 2007, Measuring risk in the hedge fund sector, *Current Issues in Economics and Finance* 13, 1–7.

Adrian, T., and H. S. Shin, 2008, Liquidity, monetary policy, and financial cycles, *Current Issues in Economics and Finance* 14, 1–7.

Agarwal, V., G. O. Aragon, and Z. Shi, 2019, Liquidity transformation and financial fragility: evidence from funds of hedge funds, *Journal of Financial and Quantitative Analysis* 54, 2355–2381.

Agarwal, V., N. D. Daniel, and N. Y. Naik, 2002, Determinants of money-flow and risk-taking behavior in the hedge fund industry, Working Paper, Georgia State University.

Agarwal, V., N. D. Daniel, and N. Y. Naik, 2009, Role of managerial incentives and discretion in hedge fund performance, *The Journal of Finance* 64, 2221–2256.

Agarwal, V., N. D. Daniel, and N. Y. Naik, 2011, Do hedge funds manage their reported returns? *Review of Financial Studies* 24, 3281–3320.

Agarwal, V., V. Fos, and W. Jiang, 2014, What happens 'before the birth' and 'after the death' of a hedge fund? *Bankers, Markets & Investors* 129, 17–25.

Agarwal, V., W. Jiang, Y. Tang, and B. Yang, 2013, Uncovering hedge fund skill from the portfolio holdings they hide, *The Journal of Finance* 68, 739–783.

Agarwal, V., and J. Kale, 2007, On the relative performance of multi-strategy and funds of hedge funds, *Journal of Investment Management* 5, 41–63.

Agarwal, V., and N. Y. Naik, 2000a, Generalised style analysis of hedge funds, *Journal of Asset Management* 1, 93–109.

Agarwal, V., and N. Y. Naik, 2000b, Multi-period performance persistence analysis of hedge funds, *Journal of Financial and Quantitative Analysis* 35, 327–342.

Agarwal, V., and N. Y. Naik, 2000c, On taking the "alternative" route: the risks, rewards, and performance persistence of hedge funds, *The Journal of Alternative Investments* 2, 6–23.

Agarwal, V., and N. Y. Naik, 2004, Risks and portfolio decisions involving hedge funds, *Review of Financial Studies* 17, 63–98.

Aggarwal, R. K., and P. Jorion, 2009, The risk of emerging hedge fund managers, *The Journal of Investing* 18, 100–107.

Aggarwal, R. K., and P. Jorion, 2010a, Hidden survivorship in hedge fund returns, *Financial Analysts Journal* 66, 69–74.

Aggarwal, R. K., and P. Jorion, 2010b, The performance of emerging hedge funds and managers, *Journal of Financial Economics* 96, 238–256.

Aiken, A. L., C. P. Clifford, and J. Ellis, 2013, Out of the dark: hedge fund reporting biases and commercial databases, *Review of Financial Studies* 26, 208–243.

Aït-Sahalia, Y., and A. W. Lo, 2000, Nonparametric risk management and implied risk aversion, *Journal of Econometrics* 94, 9–51.

Alexander, R. D., 1974, The evolution of social behavior, *Annual Review of Ecology and Systematics* 5, 325–383.

Algoet, P. H., and T. M. Cover, 1988, Asymptotic optimality and asymptotic equipartition properties of log-optimum investment, *The Annals of Probability* 16, 876–898.

Allen, F., and E. Carletti, 2008, The role of liquidity in financial crises, 2008 Jackson Hole Symposium. Available at SSRN: https://ssrn.com/abstract=1268367.

Allen, F., S. Morris, and A. Postlewaite, 1993, Finite bubbles with short sale constraints and asymmetric information, *Journal of Economic Theory* 61, 206–229.

Alvarez, W., 1997, *T. Rex and the Crater of Doom* (Princeton University Press, Princeton, NJ).

Amenc, N., L. Martellini, J.-C. Meyfredi, and V. Ziemann, 2010, Passive hedge fund replication—beyond the linear case, *European Financial Management* 16, 191–210.

Amihud, Y., 2002, Illiquidity and stock returns: cross-section and time-series effects, *Journal of Financial Markets* 5, 31–56.

Amihud, Y., and H. Mendelson, 1982, Asset price behavior in a dealership market, *Financial Analysts Journal* 38, 50–59.

Amihud, Y., and H. Mendelson, 1986, Asset pricing and the bid-ask spread, *Journal of Financial Economics* 17, 223–249.

Amihud, Y., H. Mendelson, and L. H. Pedersen, 2006, Liquidity and asset prices, *Foundation and Trends in Finance* 1, 269–364.

Amin, G. S., and H. M. Kat, 2003, Hedge fund performance 1990–2000: do the "money machines" really add value? *Journal of Financial and Quantitative Analysis* 38, 251–274.

Amir, R., I. V. Evstigneev, T. Hens, and K. R. Schenk-Hoppé, 2005, Market selection and survival of investment strategies, *Journal of Mathematical Economics* 41, 105–122.

Amo, A.-V., H. Harasty, and P. Hillion, 2007, Diversification benefits of funds of hedge funds: identifying the optimal number of hedge funds, *The Journal of Alternative Investments* 10, 10–21.

Anand, A., and D. G. Weaver, 2006, The value of the specialist: empirical evidence from the CBOE, *Journal of Financial Markets* 9, 100–118.

Anderson, J. R., and R. Milson, 1989, Human memory: an adaptive perspective, *Psychological Review* 96, 703.

Anderson, P., K. Arrow, and D. Pines (eds.), 1988, *The Economy as an Evolving Complex System* (Addison-Wesley, Reading, MA).

Andersson, M., P. Bolton, and F. Samama, 2016, Hedging climate risk, *Financial Analysts Journal* 72, 13–32.

Ang, A., and G. Bekaert, 2002, International asset allocation with regime shifts, *Review of Financial Studies* 15, 1137–1187.

Ang, A., and N. P. Bollen, 2010, Locked up by a lockup: valuing liquidity as a real option, *Financial Management* 39, 1069–1096.

Ang, A., and J. Chen, 2007, CAPM over the long run: 1926–2001, *Journal of Empirical Finance* 14, 1–40.

Ang, A., S. Gorovyy, and G. B. Van Inwegen, 2011, Hedge fund leverage, *Journal of Financial Economics* 102, 102–126.

Anson, M. J., 2001, Hedge fund incentive fees and the "free option", *The Journal of Alternative Investments* 4, 43–48.

Apaloo, J., 1997, Revisiting strategic models of evolution: the concept of neighborhood invader strategies, *Theoretical Population Biology* 52, 71–77.

Apaloo, J., J. S. Brown, and T. L. Vincent, 2009, Evolutionary game theory: ESS, convergence stability, and NIS, *Evolutionary Ecology Research* 11, 489–515.

Apicella, C. L., A. Dreber, B. Campbell, P. B. Gray, M. Hoffman, and A. C. Little, 2008, Testosterone and financial risk preferences, *Evolution and Human Behavior* 29, 384–390.

Aragon, G., 2005, Timing multiple markets: theory and evidence from balanced mutual funds, Working Paper, Arizona State University.

Aragon, G. O., 2007, Share restrictions and asset pricing: evidence from the hedge fund industry, *Journal of Financial Economics* 83, 33–58.

Aragon, G. O., M. Hertzel, and Z. Shi, 2013, Why do hedge funds avoid disclosure? Evidence from confidential 13F filings, *Journal of Financial and Quantitative Analysis* 48, 1499–1518.

Aragon, G. O., and J. S. Martin, 2012, A unique view of hedge fund derivatives usage: safeguard or speculation? *Journal of Financial Economics* 105, 436–456.

Aragon, G. O., and V. Nanda, 2012, Tournament behavior in hedge funds: high-water marks, fund liquidation, and managerial stake, *Review of Financial Studies* 25, 937–974.

Aragon, G. O., and V. Nanda, 2017, Strategic delays and clustering in hedge fund reported returns, *Journal of Financial and Quantitative Analysis* 52, 1–35.

Aragon, G. O., and J. Qian, 2010, High-water marks and hedge fund compensation, Working Paper, Arizona State University. Available at SSRN: https://ssrn.com/abstract=1540205.

Aragon, G. O., and P. E. Strahan, 2012, Hedge funds as liquidity providers: evidence from the Lehman bankruptcy, *Journal of Financial Economics* 103, 570–587.

Arnold, D., W. S. Dobbie, and P. Hull, 2021, Towards a non-discriminatory algorithm in selected data, Technical Report, National Bureau of Economic Research.

Arrow, K., 1971, The theory of risk aversion, *Essays in the Theory of Risk Bearing*, 90–109 (Markham Publishing Co., Chicago, IL).

Arrow, K., 1973, The theory of discrimination, in O. Aschenfelter, and A. Rees, *Discrimination in Labor Markets*, 3–33 (Princeton University Press, Princeton, NJ).

Arrow, K. J., and S. A. Levin, 2009, Intergenerational resource transfers with random offspring numbers, *Proceedings of the National Academy of Sciences* 106, 13702–13706.

Arthur, B., J. Holland, B. LeBaron, R. Palmer, and P. Tayler, 1997, Asset pricing under endogenous expectations in an artificial stock market, in B. Arthur, S. Durlauf, and D. Lane, *The Economy as an Evolving Complex System II* (Addison Wesley, Reading, MA).

Arthur, W. B., 1994, Inductive reasoning and bounded rationality, *American Economic Review* 84, 406–411.

Asness, C. S., R. J. Krail, and J. M. Liew, 2001, Do hedge funds hedge? *The Journal of Portfolio Management* 28, 6–19.

Audretsch, D. B., and T. Mahmood, 1994, Firm selection and industry evolution: the post-entry performance of new firms, *Journal of Evolutionary Economics* 4, 243–260.

Aurell, E., R. Baviera, O. Hammarlid, M. Serva, and A. Vulpiani, 2000, Growth optimal investment and pricing of derivatives, *Physica A: Statistical Mechanics and its Applications* 280, 505–521.

Avramov, D., R. Kosowski, N. Y. Naik, and M. Teo, 2011, Hedge funds, managerial skill, and macroeconomic variables, *Journal of Financial Economics* 99, 672–692.

Avramov, D., and G. Zhou, 2010, Bayesian portfolio analysis, *Annual Review of Financial Economics* 2, 25–47.

Axelrod, R., 1984, *The Evolution of Cooperation* (Basic Books, New York).

Azlen, M., 2011, Hedge funds replication: a blended approach, Working Paper, Frontier Capital Management LLP.

Bagehot, W., 1971, The only game in town, *Financial Analysts Journal* 27, 12–14.

Bakshi, G. S., and Z. Chen, 1996, The spirit of capitalism and stock-market prices, *American Economic Review* 86, 133–157.

Bali, T. G., S. J. Brown, and M. O. Caglayan, 2011, Do hedge funds' exposures to risk factors predict their future returns? *Journal of Financial Economics* 101, 36–68.

Bali, T. G., S. J. Brown, and M. O. Caglayan, 2012, Systematic risk and the cross section of hedge fund returns, *Journal of Financial Economics* 106, 114–131.

Bali, T. G., S. Gokcan, and B. Liang, 2007, Value at risk and the cross-section of hedge fund returns, *Journal of Banking & Finance* 31, 1135–1166.

Banz, R. W., 1981, The relationship between return and market value of common stocks, *Journal of Financial Economics* 9, 3–18.

Baquero, G., J. t. Horst, and M. Verbeek, 2005, Survival, look-ahead bias, and persistence in hedge fund performance, *Journal of Financial and Quantitative Analysis* 40, 493–517.

Baquero, G., and M. Verbeek, 2009, A portrait of hedge fund investors: flows, performance and smart money, Working Paper, Erasmus University.

Baquero, G., and M. Verbeek, 2021, Hedge fund flows and performance streaks: how investors weigh information, *Management Science* 68, 4151–4172.

Barber, B. M., and T. Odean, 2001, Boys will be boys: gender, overconfidence, and common stock investment, *The Quarterly Journal of Economics* 116, 261–292.

Bares, P.-A., R. Gibson, and S. Gyger, 2003, Performance in the hedge funds industry: an analysis of short- and long-term persistence, *The Journal of Alternative Investments* 6, 25–41.

Barkow, J. H., L. Cosmides, and J. Tooby, 1992, *The Adapted Mind: Evolutionary Psychology and the Generation of Culture* (Oxford University Press, New York).

Baron-Cohen, S., 1989, The autistic child's theory of mind: a case of specific developmental delay, *Journal of Child Psychology and Psychiatry* 30, 285–297.

Barrick, M. R., and M. K. Mount, 1991, The big five personality dimensions and job performance: a meta-analysis, *Personnel Psychology* 44, 1–26.

Barro, R. J., 2006, Rare disasters and asset markets in the twentieth century, *Quarterly Journal of Economics* 121, 823–866.

Barro, R. J., 2009, Rare disasters, asset prices, and welfare costs, *American Economic Review* 99, 243–264.

Basu, S., 1981, The relationship between earnings' yield, market value and return for NYSE common stocks: further evidence, *Journal of Financial Economics* 12, 129–156.

Bator, F. M., 1961, On convexity, efficiency, and markets, *Journal of Political Economy* 69, 480–483.

Baum, W. M., 1974, On two types of deviation from the matching law: bias and undermatching, *Journal of the Experimental Analysis of Behavior* 22, 231–242.

Baumeister, R. F., T. F. Heatherton, and D. M. Tice, 1994, *Losing Control: How and Why People Fail at Self-regulation* (Academic Press, San Diego, CA).

Bazerman, M. H., 2001, Consumer research for consumers, *Journal of Consumer Research* 27, 499–504.

Beaumont, H. J., J. Gallie, C. Kost, G. C. Ferguson, and P. B. Rainey, 2009, Experimental evolution of bet hedging, *Nature* 462, 90–93.

Bechara, A., H. Damasio, D. Tranel, and A. R. Damasio, 1997, Deciding advantageously before knowing the advantageous strategy, *Science* 275, 1293–1295.

Beck, U., 1992, *Risk Society: Towards A New Modernity* (Sage Publications, London).

Becker, B., and V. Ivashina, 2015, Reaching for yield in the bond market, *The Journal of Finance* 70, 1863–1902.

Becker, G. S., 1957, *The Economics of Discrimination* (University of Chicago Press, Chicago, IL).

Becker, G. S., 1962, Irrational behavior and economic theory, *Journal of Political Economy* 70, 1–13.

Becker, G. S., 1976, Altruism, egoism, and genetic fitness: economics and sociobiology, *Journal of Economic Literature* 14, 817–826.

Bednar, J., Y. Chen, T. X. Liu, and S. Page, 2012, Behavioral spillovers and cognitive load in multiple games: an experimental study, *Games and Economic Behavior* 74, 12–31.

Be'er, A., H. P. Zhang, E.-L. Florin, S. M. Payne, E. Ben-Jacob, and H. L. Swinney, 2009, Deadly competition between sibling bacterial colonies, *Proceedings of the National Academy of Sciences* 106, 428–433.

Behrend, E. R., and M. E. Bitterman, 1961, Probability-matching in the fish, *American Journal of Psychology* 74, 542–551.

Bein, D. M., and B. H. Wander, 2002, How to incorporate hedge funds and active portfolio management into an asset allocation framework, *The Journal of Wealth Management* 5, 14–19.

Bekaert, G., and C. R. Harvey, 1995, Time-varying world market integration, *The Journal of Finance* 50, 403–444.

Belavkin, R. V., 2006, Acting irrationally to improve performance in stochastic worlds, in M. Bramer, F. Coenen, and T. Allen, *Research and Development in Intelligent Systems XXII*, 305–316 (Springer, London).

Bell, D. E., 1983, Risk premiums for decision regret, *Management Science* 29, 1156–1166.

Ben-David, I., F. Franzoni, A. Landier, and R. Moussawi, 2013, Do hedge funds manipulate stock prices? *The Journal of Finance* 68, 2383–2434.

Ben-David, I., F. Franzoni, and R. Moussawi, 2012, Hedge fund stock trading in the financial crisis of 2007–2009, *Review of Financial Studies* 25, 1–54.

Ben-Jacob, E., 2008, Social behavior of bacteria: from physics to complex organizations, *European Physics Journal B* 65, 315–322.

Ben-Jacob, E., I. Becker, Y. Shapira, and H. Levine, 2004, Bacterial linguistic communication and social intelligence, *Trends in Microbiology* 12, 366–372.

Ben-Jacob, E., O. Schochet, A. Tenenbaum, I. Cohen, A. Czirok, and T. Vicsek, 1994, Generic modelling of cooperative growth patterns in bacterial colonies, *Nature* 368, 46–49.

Bénabou, R., 2013, Groupthink: collective delusions in organizations and markets, *Review of Economic Studies* 80, 429–462.

Bénabou, R., and J. Tirole, 2002, Self-confidence and personal motivation, *The Quarterly Journal of Economics* 117, 871–915.

Bénabou, R., and J. Tirole, 2016, Bonus culture: competitive pay, screening, and multitasking, *Journal of Political Economy* 124, 305–370.

Benartzi, S., and R. Thaler, 2001, Naive diversification strategies in retirement saving plans, *American Economic Review* 91, 475–482.

Bergstrom, T. C., 2002, Evolution of social behavior: individual and group selection, *Journal of Economic Perspectives* 16, 67–88.

Bergstrom, T. C., 2014, On the evolution of hoarding, risk-taking, and wealth distribution in nonhuman and human populations, *Proceedings of the National Academy of Sciences* 111, 10860–10867.

Berk, J. B., and R. C. Green, 2004, Mutual fund flows and performance in rational markets, *Journal of Political Economy* 112, 1269–1295.

Bernheim, B., and A. Rangel, 2009, Beyond revealed preference: theoretic foundations for behavioral economics, *Quarterly Journal of Economics* 124, 51–104.

Bernstein, P. L., 1998, *Against the Gods: The Remarkable Story of Risk* (John Wiley & Sons, New York).

Bertsimas, D., L. Kogan, and A. W. Lo, 2001, Hedging derivative securities and incomplete markets: an ε-arbitrage approach, *Operations Research* 49, 372–397.

Bhandari, L. C., 1988, Debt/equity ratio and expected common stock returns: empirical evidence, *The Journal of Finance* 43, 507–528.

Biais, B., and R. Shadur, 2000, Darwinian selection does not eliminate irrational traders, *European Economic Review* 44, 469–490.

Bickel, P., and K. Doksum, 1977, *Mathematical Statistics: Basic Ideas and Selected Topics* (Holden-Day, Inc, San Francisco, CA).

Billio, M., L. Frattarolo, and L. Pelizzon, 2014, A time-varying performance evaluation of hedge fund strategies through aggregation, *Bankers, Markets & Investors*, 40–58.

Billio, M., M. Getmansky, A. W. Lo, and L. Pelizzon, 2012, Econometric measures of connectedness and systemic risk in the finance and insurance sectors, *Journal of Financial Economics* 104, 535–559.

Billio, M., M. Getmansky, and L. Pelizzon, 2009, Non-parametric analysis of hedge fund returns: new insights from high frequency data, *The Journal of Alternative Investments* 12, 21–38.

Billio, M., M. Getmansky, and L. Pelizzon, 2012, Dynamic risk exposures in hedge funds, *Computational Statistics & Data Analysis* 56, 3517–3532.

Billio, M., M. Getmansky, and L. Pelizzon, 2013, Crises and hedge fund risk, Working Paper, University of Massachusetts, Amherst.

Bisias, D., M. Flood, A. W. Lo, and S. Valavanis, 2012, A survey of systemic risk analytics, *Annual Review of Financial Economics* 4, 255–296.

Bitterman, M. E., J. Wodinsky, and D. K. Candland, 1958, Some comparative psychology, *American Journal of Psychology* 71, 94–110.

Black, F., 1971a, Implications of the random walk hypothesis for portfolio management, *Financial Analysts Journal* 27, 16–22.

Black, F., 1971b, Toward a fully automated stock exchange, part I, *Financial Analysts Journal* 27, 28–35.

Black, F., 1971c, Toward a fully automated stock exchange, part II, *Financial Analysts Journal* 27, 24–28.

Black, F., 1975, Fact and fantasy in the use of options, *Financial Analysts Journal* 31, 36–41.

Black, F., 1976, Studies of stock market volatility changes, *Proceedings of the American Statistical Association (Business and Economic Statistics Section)* 7, 177–181.

Black, F., 1986, Noise, *The Journal of Finance* 41, 528–543.

Black, F., 1989, Universal hedging: optimizing currency risk and reward in international equity portfolios, *Financial Analysts Journal* 45, 16–22.

Black, F., and R. Litterman, 1992, Global portfolio optimization, *Financial Analysts Journal* 48, 28–43.

Black, F., and A. Perold, 1992, Theory of constant proportion portfolio insurance, *Journal of Economic Dynamics and Control* 16, 403–426.

Black, F., and M. Scholes, 1973, The pricing of options and corporate liabilities, *Journal of Political Economy* 81, 637–654.

Black, K. H., 2006, Improving hedge fund risk exposures by hedging equity market volatility, or how the VIX ate my kurtosis, *The Journal of Trading* 1, 6–15.

Blanchard, O. J., and M. W. Watson, 1982, Bubbles, rational expectations and financial markets, in P. Wachtel, *Crisis in the Economic and Financial Structure: Bubbles, Bursts, and Shocks* (Lexington Press, Philadelphia, PA).

Bluhm, C., 2003, CDO modeling: techniques, examples and applications, Unpublished working paper, http://www.defaultrisk.com/pp_crdrv_42.htm.

Bluhm, C., and L. Overbeck, 2007, Calibration of PD term structures: to be Markov or not to be, *Risk* November, 98–103.

Blume, L., and D. Easley, 1992, Evolution and market behavior, *Journal of Economic Theory* 58, 9–40.

Blume, L., and D. Easley, 2006, If you're so smart, why aren't you rich? Belief selection in complete and incomplete markets, *Econometrica* 74, 929–966.

Bodie, Z., 1999, Investment management and technology: past, present, and future, in R. Litan and A. Santomero, *Brookings–Wharton Papers on Financial Services: 1999* (Brookings Institution, Washington, DC).

Bodie, Z., 2007, The challenge of investor education, in Z. Bodie, D. McLeavey, and L. B. Siegel, *The Future of Life-Cycle Saving and Investing*, 169–171 (Research Foundation of the CFA Institute, New York).

Bohren, J. A., K. Haggag, A. Imas, and D. G. Pope, 2019, Inaccurate statistical discrimination, Technical Report, National Bureau of Economic Research.

Bollen, N. P., and V. K. Pool, 2008, Conditional return smoothing in the hedge fund industry, *Journal of Financial and Quantitative Analysis* 43, 267–298.

Bollen, N. P., and V. K. Pool, 2009, Do hedge fund managers misreport returns? Evidence from the pooled distribution, *The Journal of Finance* 64, 2257–2288.

Bollen, N. P., and V. K. Pool, 2012, Suspicious patterns in hedge fund returns and the risk of fraud, *Review of Financial Studies* 25, 2673–2702.

Bolt, J., and J. L. van Zanden, 2013, The first update of the Maddison Project: re-estimating growth before 1820, Working Paper 4, Maddison Project.

Bondarenko, O., 2004, Market price of variance risk and performance of hedge funds, Working Paper, University of Illinois at Chicago.

Boomsma, J. J., M. Beekman, C. K. Cornwallis, A. S. Griffin, L. Holman, W. O. H. Hughes, L. Keller, B. P. Oldroyd, and F. L. W. Ratnieks, 2011, Only full-sibling families evolved eusociality, *Nature* 471, E4–E5.

Boone, C., B. De Brabander, and A. Van Witteloostuijn, 1999, The impact of personality on behavior in five prisoner's dilemma games, *Journal of Economic Psychology* 20, 343–377.

Bordalo, P., K. Coffman, N. Gennaioli, and A. Shleifer, 2016, Stereotypes, *The Quarterly Journal of Economics* 131, 1753–1794.

Bossaerts, P., 2009, What decision neuroscience teaches us about financial decision making, *Annual Review of Financial Economics* 1, 383–404.

Botvinick, M. M., 2008, Hierarchical models of behavior and prefrontal function, *Trends in Cognitive Sciences* 12, 201–208.

Bouchaud, J.-P., J. D. Farmer, and F. Lillo, 2009, How markets slowly digest changes in supply and demand, in T. Hens and K. Schenk-Hoppe, *Handbook of Financial Markets: Dynamics and Evolution*, 57–160 (Elsevier, New York).

Boucsein, W., 1992, *Electrodermal Activity* (Plenum Press, New York).

Bowe, M., and D. Domuta, 2004, Investor herding during financial crisis: a clinical study of the Jakarta stock exchange, *Pacific-Basin Finance Journal* 12, 387–418.

Boyd, R., 2011, *Fatal Risk: A Cautionary Tale of AIG's Corporate Suicide* (John Wiley & Sons, Hoboken, NJ).

Boyson, N. M., 2008, Do hedge funds exhibit performance persistence? A new approach, *Financial Analysts Journal* 64, 15–26.

Boyson, N. M., C. W. Stahel, and R. M. Stulz, 2010, Hedge fund contagion and liquidity shocks, *The Journal of Finance* 65, 1789–1816.

Bradshaw, C. M., E. Szabadi, and P. Bevan, 1976, Behavior of humans in variable-interval schedules of reinforcement, *Journal of the Experimental Analysis of Behavior* 26, 135–141.

Brandstätter, H., and W. Güth, 2000, A psychological approach to individual differences in intertemporal consumption patterns, *Journal of Economic Psychology* 21, 465–479.

Brandstätter, H., and W. Güth, 2002, Personality in dictator and ultimatum games, *Central European Journal of Operations Research* 10, 191–215.

Breiter, H. C., I. Aharon, D. Kahneman, D. Anders, and P. Shizgat, 2001, Functional imaging of neural responses to expectancy and experience of monetary gains and losses, *Neuron* 30, 619–639.

Brennan, M. J., T. Chordia, and A. Subrahmanyam, 1998, Alternative factor specifications, security characteristics, and the cross-section of expected stock returns, *Journal of Financial Economics* 49, 345–373.

Brennan, M. J., and A. Subrahmanyam, 1996, Market microstructure and asset pricing: on the compensation for illiquidity in stock returns, *Journal of Financial Economics* 41, 441–464.

Brennan, T. J., and A. W. Lo, 2011, The origin of behavior, *Quarterly Journal of Finance* 1, 55–108.

Brennan, T. J., and A. W. Lo, 2012, An evolutionary model of bounded rationality and intelligence, *PLoS One* 7, e50310.

Brennan, T. J., A. W. Lo, and T. Nguyen, 2015, Portfolio theory, in N. Higham, *The Princeton Companion to Applied Mathematics* (Princeton University Press, Princeton, NJ).

Brennan, T. J., A. W. Lo, and R. Zhang, 2018, Variety is the spice of life: irrational behavior as adaptation to stochastic environments, *Quarterly Journal of Finance* 8, 1850009.

Brocas, I., and J. D. Carrillo, 2000, The value of information when preferences are dynamically inconsistent, *European Economic Review* 44, 1104–1115.

Brooks, C., and H. M. Kat, 2002, The statistical properties of hedge fund index returns and their implications for investors, *The Journal of Alternative Investments* 5, 26–44.

Brown, C. O., and I. S. Dinç, 2011, Too many to fail? Evidence of regulatory forbearance when the banking sector is weak, *Review of Financial Studies* 24, 1378–1405.

Brown, J. D., and W. J. Huffman, 1972, Psychophysiological measures of drivers under actual driving conditions, *Journal of Safety Research* 4, 172–178.

Brown, S. J., 2016, Climate risk, *Financial Analysts Journal* 72, 9–10.

Brown, S. J., T. L. Fraser, and B. Liang, 2008, Hedge fund due diligence: a source of alpha in a hedge fund portfolio strategy, *Journal of Investment Management* 6, 23–33.

Brown, S. J., and W. N. Goetzmann, 2003, Hedge funds with style, *The Journal of Portfolio Management* 29, 101–112.

Brown, S. J., W. N. Goetzmann, and R. G. Ibbotson, 1999, Offshore hedge funds: survival and performance 1989–1995, *Journal of Business* 72, 91–117.

Brown, S. J., W. N. Goetzmann, R. G. Ibbotson, and S. A. Ross, 1992, Survivorship bias in performance studies, *Review of Financial Studies* 5, 553–580.

Brown, S. J., W. N. Goetzmann, and B. Liang, 2004, Fees on fees in funds of funds, *Journal of Investment Management* 2, 39–56.

Brown, S. J., W. N. Goetzmann, B. Liang, and C. Schwarz, 2008, Mandatory disclosure and operational risk: evidence from hedge fund registration, *The Journal of Finance* 63, 2785–2815.

Brown, S. J., W. N. Goetzmann, B. Liang, and C. Schwarz, 2009, Estimating operational risk for hedge funds: the ω-score, *Financial Analysts Journal* 65, 43–53.

Brown, S. J., W. N. Goetzmann, B. Liang, and C. Schwarz, 2012, Trust and delegation, *Journal of Financial Economics* 103, 221–234.

Brown, S. J., W. N. Goetzmann, and J. M. Park, 2000, Hedge funds and the Asian currency crisis, *The Journal of Portfolio Management* 26, 95–101.

Brown, S. J., W. N. Goetzmann, and J. M. Park, 2001, Careers and survival: competition and risk in the hedge fund and CTA industry, *The Journal of Finance* 56, 1869–1886.

Brown, S. J., G. N. Gregoriou, and R. Pascalau, 2012, Diversification in funds of hedge funds: is it possible to overdiversify? *The Review of Asset Pricing Studies* 2, 89–110.

Browne, S., 1999, Reaching goals by a deadline: digital options and continuous-time active portfolio management, *Advances in Applied Probability* 31, 551–577.

Browne, S., and W. Whitt, 1996, Portfolio choice and the Bayesian Kelly criterion, *Advances in Applied Probability* 28, 1145–1176.

Brunnermeier, M. K., 2009, Deciphering the liquidity and credit crunch 2007–2008, *Journal of Economic Perspectives* 23, 77–100.

Brunnermeier, M. K., and S. Nagel, 2004, Hedge funds and the technology bubble, *The Journal of Finance* 59, 2013–2040.

Brunnermeier, M. K., and L. H. Pedersen, 2009, Market liquidity and funding liquidity, *Review of Financial Studies* 22, 2201–2238.

Buraschi, A., R. Kosowski, and F. Trojani, 2014, When there is no place to hide: correlation risk and the cross-section of hedge fund returns, *Review of Financial Studies* 27, 581–616.

Burger, R., and A. Gimelfarb, 2002, Fluctuating environments and the role of mutation in maintaining quantitative genetic variation, *Genetical Research* 80, 31–46.

Burger, R., and M. Lynch, 1995, Evolution and extinction in a changing environment: a quantitative-genetic analysis, *Evolution* 49, 151–163.

Burke, C. J., W. K. Estes, and S. Hellyer, 1954, Rate of verbal conditioning in relation to stimulus variability, *Journal of Experimental Psychology* 48, 153–161.

Burnham, T. C., 2013, Toward a neo-Darwinian synthesis of neoclassical and behavioral economics, *Journal of Economic Behavior and Organization* 90, S113–S127.

Burnham, T. C., A. Dunlap, and D. W. Stephens, 2015, Experimental evolution and economics, *SAGE Open* 5, 2158244015612524.

Burns, J. M., 1982, Electronic trading in futures markets, *Financial Analysts Journal* 38, 33–41.

Burns, M. P., and J. Sommerville, 2014, "I pick you": the impact of fairness and race on infants' selection of social partners, *Frontiers in Psychology* 5, 93.

Burns, N., K. Minnick, and L. Starks, 2017, CEO tournaments: a cross-country analysis of causes, cultural influences, and consequences, *Journal of Financial and Quantitative Analysis* 52, 519–551.

Bushee, B. J., 1998, The influence of institutional investors on myopic R&D investment behavior, *Accounting Review* 73, 305–333.

Buss, D. M., 2004, *Evolutionary Psychology: The New Science of the Mind* (Pearson, Boston, MA).

Cacioppo, J. T., L. G. Tassinary, and G. Berntson (eds.), 2000, *Handbook of Psychophysiology* (Cambridge University Press, Cambridge).

Cai, L., and B. Liang, 2012a, Asset allocation dynamics in the hedge fund industry, *Journal of Investment Management* 10, 35–59.

Cai, L., and B. Liang, 2012b, On the dynamics of hedge fund strategies, *The Journal of Alternative Investments* 14, 51–68.

Camerer, C., G. Loewenstein, and D. Prelec, 2005, Neuroeconomics: how neuroscience can inform economics, *Journal of Economic Literature* 43, 9–64.

Camerer, C. F., and E. Fehr, 2006, When does "economic man" dominate social behavior? *Science* 311, 47–52.

Campbell, J. R., 1998, Entry, exit, embodied technology, and business cycles, *Review of Economic Dynamics* 1, 371–408.

Campbell, J. O., 2016, Universal Darwinism as a process of Bayesian inference, *Frontiers in Systems Neuroscience* 10, 49.

Campbell, J. Y., S. J. Grossman, and J. Wang, 1993, Trading volume and serial correlation in stock returns, *The Quarterly Journal of Economics* 108, 905–939.

Campbell, J. Y., and A. S. Kyle, 1993, Smart money, noise trading and stock price behaviour, *The Review of Economic Studies* 60, 1–34.

Cao, C., Y. Chen, B. Liang, and A. W. Lo, 2013, Can hedge funds time market liquidity? *Journal of Financial Economics* 109, 493–516.

Cao, C., B. Liang, A. W. Lo, and L. Petrasek, 2018, Hedge fund holdings and stock market efficiency, *The Review of Asset Pricing Studies* 8, 77–116.

Capaul, C., I. Rowley, and W. F. Sharpe, 1993, International value and growth stock returns, *Financial Analysts Journal* 49, 27–36.

Capocci, D., and G. Hübner, 2004, Analysis of hedge fund performance, *Journal of Empirical Finance* 11, 55–89.

Caraco, T., 1980, On foraging time allocation in a stochastic environment, *Ecology* 61, 119–128.

Carlsson, A., M. Lindqvist, and T. Magnusson, 1957, 3, 4-dihydroxyphenylalanine and 5-hydroxytryptophan as reserpine antagonists, *Nature* 180, 1200.

Carpenter, J. N., and A. W. Lynch, 1999, Survivorship bias and attrition effects in measures of performance persistence, *Journal of Financial Economics* 54, 337–374.

Carrillo, J. D., and T. Mariotti, 2000, Strategic ignorance as a self-disciplining device, *The Review of Economic Studies* 67, 529–544.

Cassar, G., and J. Gerakos, 2011, Hedge funds: pricing controls and the smoothing of self-reported returns, *Review of Financial Studies* 24, 1698–1734.

Castellano, S., 2014, Bayes' rule and bias roles in the evolution of decision making, *Behavioral Ecology* 26, 282–292.

Caswell, H., 2001, *Matrix Population Models: Construction, Analysis and Interpretation*, second edition (Sinauer Associates, Sunderland, MA).

Cave, A., G. Hubner, and D. Sougne, 2012, The market timing skills of hedge funds during the financial crisis, *Managerial Finance* 38, 4–26.

Challet, D., M. Marsili, and Y.-C. Zhang, 2004, *Minority Games: Interacting Agents in Financial Markets* (Oxford University Press, Oxford).

Chan, L. K., N. Jegadeesh, and J. Lakonishok, 1996, Momentum strategies, *The Journal of Finance* 51, 1681–1713.

Chan, N., M. Getmansky, S. M. Haas, and A. W. Lo, 2004, Systemic risk and hedge funds, presentation at NBER Conference on the Risks of Financial Institutions, October 22–23.

Chan, N., M. Getmansky, S. M. Haas, and A. W. Lo, 2006, Do hedge funds increase systemic risk? *Federal Reserve Bank of Atlanta Economic Review* 91, 49–80.

Chan, N., M. Getmansky, S. M. Haas, and A. W. Lo, 2007, Systemic risk and hedge funds, in M. Carey and R. Stulz, *The Risks of Financial Institutions and the Financial Sector* (University of Chicago Press, Chicago, IL).

Charness, G., A. Rustichini, and J. Van de Ven, 2018, Self-confidence and strategic behavior, *Experimental Economics* 21, 72–98.

Chater, N., and C. D. Manning, 2006, Probabilistic models of language processing and acquisition, *Trends in Cognitive Sciences* 10, 335–344.

Chaum, D., 1983, Blind signatures for untraceable payments, in D. Chaum, R. L. Rivest, and A. T. Sherman, *Advances in Cryptology*, 199–203 (Springer, New York).

Chaum, D. L., 1982, Computer systems established, maintained and trusted by mutually suspicious groups, PhD thesis granted by the University of California, Berkeley.

Chen, R., and Y. Chen, 2011, The potential of social identity for equilibrium selection, *American Economic Review* 101, 2562–2589.

Chen, Y., 2007, Timing ability in the focus market of hedge funds, *Journal of Investment Management* 5, 66–98.

Chen, Y., 2011, Derivatives use and risk taking: evidence from the hedge fund industry, *Journal of Financial and Quantitative Analysis* 46, 1073–1106.

Chen, Y., and B. Liang, 2007, Do market timing hedge funds time the market? *Journal of Financial and Quantitative Analysis* 42, 827–856.

Chetty, R., 2006, A new method of estimating risk aversion, *American Economic Review* 96, 1821–1834.

Cho, J., S. Ahmed, M. Hilbert, B. Liu, and J. Luu, 2020, Do search algorithms endanger democracy? An experimental investigation of algorithm effects on political polarization, *Journal of Broadcasting & Electronic Media* 64, 150–172.

Choi, J. J., D. Laibson, and B. C. Madrian, 2011, $100 bills on the sidewalk: suboptimal saving in 401(k) plans, *Review of Economics and Statistics* 93, 748–763.

Chordia, T., R. Roll, and A. Subrahmanyam, 2000, Commonality in liquidity, *Journal of Financial Economics* 56, 3–28.

Chordia, T., R. Roll, and A. Subrahmanyam, 2001, Market liquidity and trading activity, *The Journal of Finance* 56, 501–530.

Chordia, T., A. Sarkar, and A. Subrahmanyam, 2005, An empirical analysis of stock and bond market liquidity, *Review of Financial Studies* 18, 85–129.

Christiansen, F. B., 1991, On conditions for evolutionary stability for a continuously varying character, *The American Naturalist* 138, 37–50.

Christie, W. G., J. H. Harris, and P. H. Schultz, 1994, Why did Nasdaq market makers stop avoiding odd-eighth quotes? *The Journal of Finance* 49, 1841–1860.

Chung, S. Y., M. Rosenberg, and J. F. Tomeo, 2004, Hedge fund of fund allocations using a convergent and divergent strategy approach, *The Journal of Alternative Investments* 7, 44–53.

Cici, G., A. Kempf, and A. Puetz, 2016, The valuation of hedge funds' equity positions, *Journal of Financial and Quantitative Analysis* 51, 1013–1037.

Clark, A. E., P. Frijters, and M. A. Shields, 2008, Relative income, happiness, and utility: an explanation for the easterlin paradox and other puzzles, *Journal of Economic Literature* 46, 95–144.

Clark, A. E., and A. J. Oswald, 1996, Satisfaction and comparison income, *Journal of Public Economics* 61, 359–381.

Clark, K. A., and K. D. Winkelmann, 2004, Active risk budgeting in action: understanding hedge fund performance, *The Journal of Alternative Investments* 7, 35–46.

Clarke, R. G., S. Krase, and M. Statman, 1994, Tracking errors, regret, and tactical asset allocation, *The Journal of Portfolio Management* 20, 16–24.

Coate, S., and G. C. Loury, 1993, Will affirmative-action policies eliminate negative stereotypes? *American Economic Review* 83, 1220–1240.

Coates, J. M., and J. Herbert, 2008, Endogenous steroids and financial risk taking on a London trading floor, *Proceedings of the National Academy of Sciences* 105, 6167–6172.

Cohen, A., and L. Einav, 2003, The effects of mandatory seat belt laws on driving behavior and traffic fatalities, *Review of Economics and Statistics* 85, 828–843.

Cohen, A., and L. Einav, 2007, Estimating risk preferences from deductible choices, *American Economic Review* 97, 745–788.

Cohen, D., 1966, Optimizing reproduction in a randomly varying environment, *Journal of Theoretical Biology* 12, 119–129.

Cohen, K., S. Maier, R. Schwartz, and D. Whitcomb, 1986, *The Microstructure of Securities Markets* (Prentice Hall, Englewood Cliffs, NJ).

Cohen-Cole, E., and J. Morse, 2010, Your house or your credit card, which would you choose? Personal delinquency tradeoffs and precautionary liquidity motives, Working Paper. Available at SSRN: http://ssrn.com/abstract=1411291.

Cohn, A., E. Fehr, and M. A. Maréchal, 2014, Business culture and dishonesty in the banking industry, *Nature* 516, 86–89.

Collet, C., E. Vernet-Maury, G. Delhomme, and A. Dittmar, 1997, Autonomic nervous system response patterns specificity to basic emotions, *Journal of the Autonomic Nervous System* 62, 45–57.

Comerton-Forde, C., T. Hendershott, C. M. Jones, P. C. Moulton, and M. S. Seasholes, 2010, Time variation in liquidity: the role of market-maker inventories and revenues, *The Journal of Finance* 65, 295–331.

Compte, O., and A. Postlewaite, 2004, Confidence-enhanced performance, *American Economic Review* 94, 1536–1557.

Conley, J. M., C. A. Williams, L. Smeehuijzen, and D. E. Rupp, 2019, Can soft regulation prevent financial crises?: The Dutch central bank's supervision of behavior and culture, *Cornell International Law Journal* 51, 773–821.

Cooper, W. S., and R. H. Kaplan, 1982, Adaptive coin-flipping: a decision theoretic examination of natural selection for random individual variation, *Journal of Theoretical Biology* 94, 135–151.

Corneo, G., and O. Jeanne, 1997, On relative wealth effects and the optimality of growth, *Economics Letters* 54, 87–92.

Cosmides, L., and J. Tooby, 1994, Better than rational: evolutionary psychology and the invisible hand, *American Economic Review* 84, 327–332.

Costa, P. T., and R. R. McCrae, 1992, Normal personality assessment in clinical practice: the NEO personality inventory, *Psychological Assessment* 4, 5.

Counterparty Risk Managment Policy Group II, 2005, *Toward Greater Financial Stability: A Private Sector Perspective* (CRMPG II, New York).

Cover, T., and J. Thomas, 1991, *Elements of Information Theory* (John Wiley & Sons, New York).

Crandall, R. W., and J. D. Graham, 1984, Automobile safety regulation and offsetting behavior: some new empirical estimates, *American Economic Review* 74, 328–331.

Crane, D. B., K. A. Froot, S. P. Mason, A. Perold, R. C. Merton, Z. Bodie, E. R. Sirri, and P. Tufano, 1995, *The Global Financial System: A Functional Perspective* (Harvard Business School Press, Boston, MA).

Crémer, J., 1993, Corporate culture and shared knowledge, *Industrial and Corporate Change* 2, 351–386.

Critchley, H. D., R. Elliot, C. J. Mathias, and R. Dolan, 1999, Central correlates of peripheral arousal during a gambling task, *21st International Summer School of Brain Research*.

Curry, P. A., 2001, Decision making under uncertainty and the evolution of interdependent preferences, *Journal of Economic Theory* 98, 357–369.

Czégel, D., H. Giaffar, I. Zachar, J. B. Tenenbaum, and E. Szathmáry, 2020, Evolutionary implementation of Bayesian computations, *bioRxiv* 685842.

Damasio, A. R., 1994, *Descartes' Error: Emotion, Reason, and the Human Brain* (Putnam Publishing, New York).

Damasio, A., D. Tranel, and H. Damasio, 1991, Somatic markers and the guidance of behavior: theory and preliminary testing, in H. Levin, H. Eisenberg, and A. Benton, *Frontal Lobe Function and Dysfunction*, 217–229 (Oxford University Press, New York).

Damasio, A., D. Tranel, and H. Damasio, 1998, Somatic markers and the guidance of behavior, in J. M. Jenkins, K. Oatley, and N. Stein, *Human Emotions: A Reader*, 122–135 (Blackwell, Oxford).

Daniel, K., and S. Titman, 1999, Market efficiency in an irrational world, *Financial Analysts Journal* 55, 28–40.

Danziger, S., J. Levav, and L. Avnaim-Pesso, 2011, Extraneous factors in judicial decisions, *Proceedings of the National Academy of Sciences* 108, 6889–6892.

Davidson, R. J., and W. Irwin, 1999, The functional neuroanatomy of emotion and affective style, *Trends in Cognitive Sciences* 3, 11–21.

Davison, M., and D. McCarthy, 1988, *The Matching Law: A Research Review* (Lawrence Erlbaum, Hillsdale, NJ).

Dawkins, R., 1976, *The Selfish Gene* (Oxford University Press, Oxford).

de Becker, G., 1997, *The Gift of Fear: Survival Signals that Protect us from Violence* (Little Brown and Co., Boston, MA).

De Blasio, F. V., 1999, Diversity and extinction in a lattice model of a population with fluctuating environment, *Physical Review* 60, 5912–5917.

De Bondt, W. F. M., and R. Thaler, 1985, Does the stock market overreact? *The Journal of Finance* 40, 793–805.

De Bondt, W. P. M., 1993, Betting on trends: intuitive forecasts of financial risk and return, *International Journal of Forecasting* 9, 355–371.

de Castro, L., A. W. Lo, T. Reynolds, F. Susan, V. Vaikuntanathan, D. Weitzner, and N. Zhang, 2020, SCRAM: a platform for securely measuring cyber risk, *Harvard Data Science Review* 2.

de Jong, M., and A. Nguyen, 2016, Weathered for climate risk: a bond investment proposition, *Financial Analysts Journal* 72, 34–39.

De Long, J. B., A. Shleifer, L. H. Summers, and R. J. Waldmann, 1990, Noise trader risk in financial markets, *Journal of Political Economy* 98, 703–738.

De Long, J. B., A. Shleifer, L. H. Summers, and R. J. Waldmann, 1991, The survival of noise traders in financial markets, *Journal of Business* 64, 1–19.

De Martino, B., D. Kumaran, B. Seymour, and R. J. Dolan, 2006, Frames, biases, and rational decision-making in the human brain, *Science* 313, 684–687.

De Nederlandsche Bank, 2009, The seven elements of an ethical culture, Available at http://www.dnb.nl/en/binaries/The%20Seven%20Elements%20of%20an%20Ethical%20Culture_tcm47-233197.pdf.

De Waal, F., S. E. Macedo, and J. E. Ober, 2006, *Primates and Philosophers: How Morality Evolved* (Princeton University Press, Princeton, NJ).

Deason, S., S. Rajgopal, and G. B. Waymire, 2015, Who gets swindled in Ponzi schemes? Working Paper. Available at SSRN: https://ssrn.com/abstract=2586490.

Dekel, E., and S. Scotchmer, 1999, On the evolution of attitudes towards risk in winner-take-all games, *Journal of Economic Theory* 87, 125–143.

Delgado, M. R., L. E. Nystrom, C. Fissell, D. Noll, and J. A. Fiez, 2000, Tracking the hemodynamic responses to reward and punishment in the striatum, *Journal of Neurophysiology* 84, 3072–3077.

Dempster, E. R., 1955, Maintenance of genetic heterogeneity, *Cold Spring Harbor Symposia on Quantitative Biology* 20, 25–32.

Deneubourg, J. L., S. Aron, S. Goss, and J. M. Pasteels, 1987, Error, communication and learning in ant societies, *European Journal of Operational Research* 30, 168–172.

Deng, Y., J. M. Quigley, and R. Van Order, 2000, Mortgage terminations, heterogeneity and the exercise of mortgage options, *Econometrica* 68, 275–307.

Di Pellegrino, G., L. Fadiga, L. Fogassi, V. Gallese, and G. Rizzolatti, 1992, Understanding motor events: a neurophysiological study, *Experimental Brain Research* 91, 176–180.

Diamandis, P. H., and S. Kotler, 2020, *The Future is Faster than You Think: How Converging Technologies are Transforming Business, Industries, and Our Lives* (Simon & Schuster, New York).

Diamond, D. W., and R. E. Verrecchia, 1981, Information aggregation in a noisy rational expectations economy, *Journal of Financial Economics* 9, 221–235.

Diez De Los Rios, A., and R. Garcia, 2011, Assessing and valuing the nonlinear structure of hedge fund returns, *Journal of Applied Econometrics* 26, 193–212.

Dimson, E., P. Marsh, and M. Staunton, 2002, *Triumph of the Optimists: 101 Years of Global Investment Returns* (Princeton University Press, Princeton, NJ).

Dimson, E., P. Marsh, and M. Staunton, 2013, *Credit Suisse Global Investment Returns Yearbook* (Credit Suisse AG, Research Institute, Zurich).

Douglas, M., and A. Wildavsky, 1983, *Risk and Culture: An Essay on the Selection of Technological and Environmental Dangers* (University of California Press, Berkeley, CA).

Dreber, A., C. L. Apicella, D. T. Eisenberg, J. R. Garcia, R. S. Zamore, J. K. Lum, and B. Campbell, 2009, The 7r polymorphism in the dopamine receptor d_4 gene (*drd4*) is associated with financial risk taking in men, *Evolution and Human Behavior* 30, 85–92.

Drehmann, M., J. Oechssler, and A. Roider, 2005, Herding and contrarian behavior in financial markets: an internet experiment, *American Economic Review* 95, 1403–1426.

Duesenberry, J. S., 1949, *Income, Saving, and the Theory of Consumer Behavior* (Harvard University Press, Cambridge, MA).

Duffie, D., and Y. Sun, 2007, Existence of independent random matching, *The Annals of Applied Probability* 17, 386–419.

Dufour, A., and R. F. Engle, 2000, Time and the price impact of a trade, *The Journal of Finance* 55, 2467–2498.

Dunlap, A. S., and D. W. Stephens, 2014, Experimental evolution of prepared learning, *Proceedings of the National Academy of Sciences* 111, 11750–11755.

Dunny, G. M., T. J. Brickman, and M. Dworkin, 2008, Multicellular behavior in bacteria: communication, cooperation, competition and cheating, *Bioessays* 30, 296–298.

Durkheim, E., 1893, *The Division of Labor in Society* (Free Press, New York), Trans. W. D. Halls, intro. L. A. Coser, 1997.

Dyck, I. A., A. Morse, and L. Zingales, 2013, How pervasive is corporate fraud? Working Paper No. 2222608, Rotman School of Management.

Easley, D., and M. O'Hara, 2010, Liquidity and valuation in an uncertain world, *Journal of Financial Economics* 97, 1–11.

Edelman, D., W. Fung, and D. A. Hsieh, 2013, Exploring uncharted territories of the hedge fund industry: empirical characteristics of mega hedge fund firms, *Journal of Financial Economics* 109, 734–758.

Edwards, F. R., and M. O. Caglayan, 2001, Hedge fund performance and manager skill, *Journal of Futures Markets: Futures, Options, and Other Derivative Products* 21, 1003–1028.

Edwards, F. R., K. Hanley, R. Litan, and R. L. Weil, 2019, Crypto assets require better regulation: statement of the financial economists roundtable on crypto assets, *Financial Analysts Journal* 75, 14–19.

Ehrlich, P. R., and S. A. Levin, 2005, The evolution of norms, *PLoS Biology* 3, e194.

Eichengreen, B., D. J. Mathieson, B. Chadha, A. Jansen, L. E. Kodres, and S. Sharma, 1998, *Hedge Funds and Financial Market Dynamics* (International Monetary Fund, Washington, DC).

Eisenbach, T. M., A. Haughwout, B. Hirtle, A. Kovner, D. O. Lucca, and M. C. Plosser, 2017, Supervising large, complex financial institutions: what do supervisors do? *Economic Policy Review* 23, 57–77.

Eisenberger, N. I., M. D. Lieberman, and K. D. Williams, 2003, Does rejection hurt? An fMRI study of social exclusion, *Science* 302, 290–292.

Ekman, P., 1982, Methods for measuring facial action, in K. Scherer and P. Ekman, *Handbook of Methods in Nonverbal Behavior Research*, 45–90 (Cambridge University Press, Cambridge).

Ekman, P. E., and R. J. Davidson, 1994, *The Nature of Emotion: Fundamental Questions.* (Oxford University Press, New York).

Eldredge, N., and S. Gould, 1972, Punctuated equilibria: an alternative to phyletic gradualism, in T. Schopf, *Models in Paleobiology*, 82–115 (Freeman Cooper, San Francisco, CA).

Elster, J., 1998, Emotions and economic theory, *Journal of Economic Literature* 36, 47–74.

Elul, R., N. S. Souleles, S. Chomsisengphet, D. Glennon, and R. Hunt, 2010, What "triggers" mortgage default? *American Economic Review* 100, 490–494.

Eslinger, P. J., and A. R. Damasio, 1985, Severe disturbance of higher cognition after bilateral frontal lobe ablation: patient EVR, *Neurology* 35, 1731–1741.

Espinosa-Vega, M. A., M. R. Matta, M. C. M. Kahn, and M. J. Sole, 2011, Systemic risk and optimal regulatory architecture, Working Paper WP/11/193, International Monetary Fund.

Estes, W., 1950, Towards a statistical theory of learning, *Psychological Review* 57, 94–107.

Estes, W. K., and J. H. Strughan, 1954, Analysis of a verbal conditioning situation in terms of statistical learning theory, *Journal of Experimental Psychology* 47, 225–234.

Evstigneev, I. V., T. Hens, and K. R. Schenk-Hoppé, 2002, Market selection of financial trading strategies: global stability, *Mathematical Finance* 12, 329–339.

Evstigneev, I. V., T. Hens, and K. R. Schenk-Hoppé, 2006, Evolutionary stable stock markets, *Economic Theory* 27, 449–468.

Fabozzi, F. J., 2005, The structured finance market: an investor's perspective, *Financial Analysts Journal* 61, 27–40.

Fama, E. F., 1965, The behavior of stock market prices, *Journal of Business* 38, 34–105.

Fama, E. F., 1970, Efficient capital markets: a review of theory and empirical work, *The Journal of Finance* 25, 383–417.

Fama, E. F., and K. R. French, 1992, The cross-section of expected stock returns, *The Journal of Finance* 47, 427–465.

Fama, E. F., and K. R. French, 1993, Common risk factors in the returns on stocks and bonds, *Journal of Financial Economics* 33, 3–56.

Fama, E. F., and K. R. French, 1995, Size and book-to-market factors in earnings and returns, *The Journal of Finance* 50, 131–155.

Fama, E. F., and K. R. French, 2006, The value premium and the CAPM, *The Journal of Finance* 61, 2163–2185.

Farmer, C. M., A. K. Lund, R. E. Trempel, and E. R. Braver, 1997, Fatal crashes of passenger vehicles before and after adding antilock braking systems, *Accident Analysis & Prevention* 29, 745–757.

Farmer, J. D., 2001, Toward agent-based models for investment, *Developments in Quantitative Investment Models* 78, 61–71.

Farmer, J. D., 2002, Market force, ecology and evolution, *Industrial and Corporate Change* 11, 895–953.

Farmer, J. D., and S. Joshi, 2002, The price dynamics of common trading strategies, *Journal of Economic Behavior & Organization* 49, 149–171.

Farmer, J. D., and A. W. Lo, 1999, Frontiers of finance: evolution and efficient markets, *Proceedings of the National Academy of Sciences* 96, 9991–9992.

Farmer, J. D., P. Patelli, and I. I. Zovko, 2005, The predictive power of zero intelligence in financial markets, *Proceedings of the National Academy of Sciences* 102, 2254–2259.

Farrell, M. J., 1959, The convexity assumption in the theory of competitive markets, *Journal of Political Economy* 67, 377–391.

Fecteau, S., A. Pascual-Leone, D. H. Zald, P. Liguori, H. Théoret, P. S. Boggio, and F. Fregni, 2007, Activation of prefrontal cortex by transcranial direct current stimulation reduces appetite for risk during ambiguous decision making, *Journal of Neuroscience* 27, 6212–6218.

Fehr, E., and C. Camerer, 2007, Social neuroeconomics: the neural circuitry of social preferences, *Trends in Cognitive Sciences* 11, 419–427.

Felsenstein, J., 1976, The theoretical population genetics of variable selection and migration, *Annual Review of Genetics* 10, 253–280.

Feng, S., M. Getmansky, and N. Kapadia, 2013, Flows: the "invisible hands" on hedge fund management, Working Paper, University of Massachusetts, Amherst.

Fenton-O'Creevy, M., N. Nicholson, E. Soane, and P. Willman, 2005, *Traders: Risks, Decisions, and Management in Financial Markets* (Oxford University Press on Demand, Oxford).

Fernholz, R., and C. Maguire Jr, 2007, The statistics of statistical arbitrage, *Financial Analysts Journal* 63, 46–52.

Ferriere, R., and R. E. Michod, 2011, Inclusive fitness in evolution, *Nature* 471, E6–E8.

Fershtman, C., U. Gneezy, and J. A. List, 2012, Equity aversion: social norms and the desire to be ahead, *American Economic Journal: Microeconomics* 4, 131–144.

Fielding, E., A. W. Lo, and J. H. Yang, 2011, The National Transportation Safety Board: a model for systemic risk management, *Journal of Investment Management* 9, 17–49.

Figlewski, S., and S. J. Kon, 1982, Portfolio management with stock index futures, *Financial Analysts Journal* 38, 52–60.

Financial Crisis Inquiry Commission, 2011, *The Financial Crisis Inquiry Report: The Final Report of the National Commission on the Causes of the Financial and Economic Crisis in the United States Including Dissenting Views* (US Government Publishing Office, Washington, DC).

Finger, S., 1994, *Origins of Neuroscience: A History of Explorations into Brain Function* (Oxford University Press, New York).

Finucane, T. J., 2000, A direct test of methods for inferring trade direction from intra-day data, *Journal of Financial and Quantitative Analysis* 35, 553–576.

Fischoff, B., and P. Slovic, 1980, A little learning…: confidence in multicue judgment tasks, in R. Nickerson, *Attention and Performance, VIII* (Erlbaum, Hillsdale, NJ).

Flew, T., and P. Iosifidis, 2020, Populism, globalisation and social media, *International Communication Gazette* 82, 7–25.

Frank, R., 2000, *Luxury Fever: Money and Happiness in an Era of Excess* (Princeton University Press, Princeton, NJ).

Frank, R. H., 1985, *Choosing the Right Pond: Human Behavior and the Quest for Status.* (Oxford University Press, New York).

Frank, R. H., and P. J. Cook, 1995, *The Winner-Take-All Society* (Free Press, New York).

Frank, S. A., 1990, When to copy or avoid an opponent's strategy, *Journal of Theoretical Biology* 145, 41–46.

Frank, S. A., 2011a, Natural selection. I. Variable environments and uncertain returns on investment, *Journal of Evolutionary Biology* 24, 2299–2309.

Frank, S. A., 2011b, Natural selection. II. Developmental variability and evolutionary rate, *Journal of Evolutionary Biology* 24, 2310–2320.

Frank, S. A., 2012a, Natural selection. III. Selection versus transmission and the levels of selection, *Journal of Evolutionary Biology* 25, 227–243.

Frank, S. A., 2013, Natural selection. VII. History and interpretation of kin selection theory, *Journal of Evolutionary Biology* 26, 1151–1184.

Frank, S. A., and M. Slatkin, 1990, Evolution in a variable environment, *The American Naturalist* 136, 244–260.

Fredrikson, M., T. Furmark, M. T. Olsson, H. Fischer, J. Andersson, and B. Långström, 1998, Functional neuroanatomical correlates of electrodermal activity: a positron emission tomographic study, *Psychophysiology* 35, 179–185.

Fretwell, S. D., 1972, *Populations in a Seasonal Environment* (Princeton University Press, Princeton, NJ).

Fuligni, A. J., 2007, *Contesting Stereotypes and Creating Identities: Social Categories, Social Identities, and Educational Participation* (Russell Sage Foundation, New York).

Fung, H.-G., X. E. Xu, and J. Yau, 2002, Global hedge funds: risk, return, and market timing, *Financial Analysts Journal* 58, 19–30.

Fung, W., and D. A. Hsieh, 1997, Empirical characteristics of dynamic trading strategies: the case of hedge funds, *Review of Financial Studies* 10, 275–302.

Fung, W., and D. A. Hsieh, 2000, Performance characteristics of hedge funds and CTA funds: natural versus spurious biases, *Journal of Financial and Quantitative Analysis* 35, 291–307.

Fung, W., and D. A. Hsieh, 2001, The risk in hedge fund strategies: theory and evidence from trend followers, *Review of Financial Studies* 14, 313–341.

Fung, W., and D. A. Hsieh, 2002, Asset-based style factors for hedge funds, *Financial Analysts Journal* 58, 16–27.

Fung, W., and D. A. Hsieh, 2004, Hedge fund benchmarks: a risk-based approach, *Financial Analysts Journal* 60, 65–80.

Fung, W., D. A. Hsieh, N. Y. Naik, and T. Ramadorai, 2008, Hedge funds: performance, risk, and capital formation, *The Journal of Finance* 63, 1777–1803.

Fung, W., D. A. Hsieh, and K. Tsatsaronis, 2000, Do hedge funds disrupt emerging markets? *Brookings-Wharton Papers on Financial Services* 2000, 377–401.

Gaal, B., J. W. Pitchford, and A. J. Wood, 2010, Exact results for the evolution of stochastic switching in variable asymmetric environments, *Genetics* 184, 1113–1119.

Gao, G. P., P. Gao, and Z. Song, 2018, Do hedge funds exploit rare disaster concerns? *Review of Financial Studies* 31, 2650–2692.

Gao, M., and J. Huang, 2016, Capitalizing on Capitol Hill: informed trading by hedge fund managers, *Journal of Financial Economics* 121, 521–545.

Garrett, T. A., 2008, Pandemic economics: the 1918 influenza and its modern-day implications, *Federal Reserve Bank of St. Louis Review* 90, 75–93.

Geczy, C., 2014, The new diversification: open your eyes to alternatives, *The Journal of Portfolio Management* 40, 146–155.

General Accounting Office, 1999, Long-Term Capital Management: regulators need to focus greater attention on systemic risk, *GAO/GGD-00-3*, October.

Geritz, S. A., G. Mesze, J. A. Metz, et al., 1998, Evolutionarily singular strategies and the adaptive growth and branching of the evolutionary tree, *Evolutionary Ecology* 12, 35–57.

Geroski, P. A., 1995, What do we know about entry? *International Journal of Industrial Organization* 13, 421–440.

Gershman, S. J., E. J. Horvitz, and J. B. Tenenbaum, 2015, Computational rationality: a converging paradigm for intelligence in brains, minds, and machines, *Science* 349, 273–278.

Gervais, S., and T. Odean, 2001, Learning to be overconfident, *Review of Financial Studies* 14, 1–27.

Getmansky, M., 2012, The life cycle of hedge funds: fund flows, size, competition, and performance, *The Quarterly Journal of Finance* 2, 1250003.

Getmansky, M., P. A. Lee, and A. W. Lo, 2015, Hedge funds: a dynamic industry in transition, *Annual Review of Financial Economics* 7, 483–577.

Getmansky, M., A. W. Lo, and I. Makarov, 2004, An econometric model of serial correlation and illiquidity in hedge fund returns, *Journal of Financial Economics* 74, 529–609.

Getmansky, M., A. W. Lo, and S. X. Mei, 2004, Sifting through the wreckage: lessons from recent hedge fund failures, *Journal of Investment Management* 2, 6–38.

Ghavamzadeh, M., S. Mannor, J. Pineau, and A. Tamar, 2015, Bayesian reinforcement learning: a survey, *Foundations and Trends in Machine Learning* 8, 359–492.

Gibson, R., C. Tanner, and A. F. Wagner, 2015, Do situational social norms crowd out intrinsic preferences? An experiment regarding the choice of honesty, Swiss Finance Institute Research Paper no. 15–01, April. Available at SSRN: http://ssrn.com/abstract=2557480.

Gigerenzer, G., 2000, *Adaptive Thinking: Rationality in the Real World* (Oxford University Press, New York).

Gigerenzer, G., 2008, *Rationality for Mortals: How People Cope with Uncertainty* (Oxford University Press, Oxford).

Gilbert, M., 2004, Here's how you can get a bigger bonus next year, *Bloomberg News*, December 23.

Gillespie, J. H., 1973, Natural selection with varying selection coefficients—a haploid model, *Genetical Research* 21, 115–120.

Gillespie, J. H., 1977, Natural selection for variances in offspring numbers: a new evolutionary principle, *The American Naturalist* 111, 1010–1014.

Gillespie, J. H., 1991, *The Causes of Molecular Evolution* (Oxford University Press, New York and Oxford).

Gillespie, J. H., and H. A. Guess, 1978, The effects of environmental autocorrelations on the progress of selection in a random environment, *The American Naturalist* 112, 897–909.

Gilovich, T., D. Griffin, and D. Kahneman, 2002, *Heuristics and Biases: The Psychology of Intuitive Judgment* (Cambridge University Press, Cambridge).

Gimein, M., 2005, Is a hedge fund shakeout coming soon? This insider thinks so, *New York Times*, September 4.

Glode, V., and R. C. Green, 2011, Information spillovers and performance persistence for hedge funds, *Journal of Financial Economics* 101, 1–17.

Glosten, L. R., and P. R. Milgrom, 1985, Bid, ask and transaction prices in a specialist market with heterogeneously informed traders, *Journal of Financial Economics* 14, 71–100.

Gneezy, U., and A. Imas, 2014, Materazzi effect and the strategic use of anger in competitive interactions, *Proceedings of the National Academy of Sciences* 111, 1334–1337.

Gneezy, U., and J. A. List, 2006, Putting behavioral economics to work: testing for gift exchange in labor markets using field experiments, *Econometrica* 74, 1365–1384.

Gneezy, U., and J. A. List, 2013, *The Why Axis: Hidden Motives and the Undiscovered Economics of Everyday Life* (PublicAffairs, New York).

Gode, D. K., and S. Sunder, 1993, Allocative efficiency of markets with zero-intelligence traders: market as a partial substitute for individual rationality, *Journal of Political Economy* 101, 119–137.

Goertzel, B., and C. Pennachin, 2007, *Artificial General Intelligence*, volume 2 (Springer, Berlin).

Goetzmann, W. N., J. E. Ingersoll, Jr, and S. A. Ross, 2003, High-water marks and hedge fund management contracts, *The Journal of Finance* 58, 1685–1718.

Gold, J. I., and M. N. Shadlen, 2007, The neural basis of decision making, *Annual Review of Neuroscience* 30, 535–574.

Goldberg, L. R., 1990, An alternative "description of personality": the big-five factor structure, *Journal of Personality and Social Psychology* 59, 1216–1229.

Goldberg, L. R., 1999, A broad-bandwidth, public domain, personality inventory measuring the lower-level facets of several five-factor models, in I. Mervielde, I. Deary, F. D. Fruyt, and F. Ostendorf, *Personality Psychology in Europe*, volume 7, 7–28 (Tilburg University Press, Tilburg).

Goldberg, L. R., J. A. Johnson, H. W. Eber, R. Hogan, M. C. Ashton, C. R. Cloninger, and H. G. Gough, 2006, The international personality item pool and the future of public-domain personality measures, *Journal of Research in Personality* 40, 84–96.

Goldman Sachs & Co. and Financial Risk Management Ltd., 1999, The hedge fund "industry" and absolute return funds, *The Journal of Alternative Investments* 1, 11–27.

Goldman Sachs Asset Management, 2007, The quant liquidity crunch, Goldman Sachs Global Quantitative Equity Group, August.

Goodman, N. D., J. B. Tenenbaum, J. Feldman, and T. L. Griffiths, 2008, A rational analysis of rule-based concept learning, *Cognitive Science* 32, 108–154.

Goodstein, R., P. Hanouna, C. D. Ramirez, and C. W. Stahel, 2017, Contagion effects in strategic mortgage defaults, *Journal of Financial Intermediation* 30, 50–60.

Gordon, G. G., and N. DiTomaso, 1992, Predicting corporate performance from organizational culture, *Journal of Management Studies* 29, 783–798.

Gorski, P., 2008, The myth of the "culture of poverty", *Educational Leadership* 65, 32.

Gorton, G., 2008, The role of incentives and asymmetric information in financial crises, 2008 Jackson Hole Symposium.

Gorton, G., and A. Metrick, 2012, Securitized banking and the run on repo, *Journal of Financial Economics* 104, 425–451.

Gorton, G., and K. G. Rouwenhorst, 2006, Facts and fantasies about commodity futures, *Financial Analysts Journal* 62, 47–68.

Gorton, G., and K. G. Rouwenhorst, 2013, Securities and Exchange Commission: improving personnel management is critical for agency's effectiveness, GAO-13-621, July.

Government Accountability Office, 2005, Securities markets: decimal pricing has contributed to lower trading costs and a more challenging trading environment, Government Accountability Office Report to Congressional Requesters, GAO-05-525.

Graf, V., D. H. Bullock, and M. E. Bitterman, 1964, Further experiments on probability-matching in the pigeon, *Journal of the Experimental Analysis of Behavior* 7, 151–157.

Grafen, A., 1999, Formal Darwinism, the individual-as-maximizing-agent analogy and bet-hedging, *Proceedings of the Royal Society of London. Series B: Biological Sciences* 266, 799–803.

Graham, B., 1952, Toward a science of security analysis, *Financial Analysts Journal* 51, 97–99.

Graham, B., and D. L. Dodd, 1934, *Security Analysis* (McGraw-Hill, New York).

Graham, J., J. Haidt, and B. A. Nosek, 2009, Liberals and conservatives rely on different sets of moral foundations, *Journal of Personality and Social Psychology* 96, 1029–1046.

Grant, D. A., H. W. Hake, and J. P. Hornseth, 1951, Acquisition and extinction of verbal conditioned responses with differing percentages of reinforcement, *Journal of Experimental Psychology* 42, 1–5.

Gray, D., and S. Malone, 2008, *Macrofinancial Risk Analysis* (John Wiley & Sons, New York).

Gray, D., R. C. Merton, and Z. Bodie, 2010, Measuring and managing macrofinancial risk and financial stability: a new framework, in R. A. Alfaro, *Financial Stability, Monetary Policy, and Central Banking* (Central Bank of Chile, Santiago).

Greaves, H., and D. Wallace, 2006, Justifying conditionalization: conditionalization maximizes expected epistemic utility, *Mind* 115, 607–632.

Greene, J. D., 2015, Beyond point-and-shoot morality: why cognitive (neuro) science matters for ethics, *The Law & Ethics of Human Rights* 9, 141–172.

Gregg, D., 2009, Developing a collective intelligence application for special education, *Decision Support Systems* 47, 455–465.

Gregg, D. G., 2010, Designing for collective intelligence, *Communications of the ACM* 53, 134–138.

Griffin, J. M., and J. Xu, 2009, How smart are the smart guys? A unique view from hedge fund stock holdings, *Review of Financial Studies* 22, 2531–2570.

Griffiths, T. L., C. Kemp, and J. B. Tenenbaum, 2008, Bayesian models of cognition, in R. Sun, *The Cambridge Handbook of Computational Psychology*, 59–100 (Cambridge University Press, Cambridge).

Griffiths, T. L., and J. B. Tenenbaum, 2005, Structure and strength in causal induction, *Cognitive Psychology* 51, 334–384.

Griffiths, T. L., and J. B. Tenenbaum, 2006, Optimal predictions in everyday cognition, *Psychological Science* 17, 767–773.

Grossberg, S., and W. E. Gutowski, 1987, Neural dynamics of decision making under risk: affective balance and cognitive-emotional interactions, *Psychological Review* 94, 300–318.

Grossman, S., 1976, On the efficiency of competitive stock markets where trades have diverse information, *The Journal of Finance* 31, 573–585.

Grossman, S. J., and M. H. Miller, 1988, Liquidity and market structure, *The Journal of Finance* 43, 617–633.

Grossman, S. J., and J. E. Stiglitz, 1980, On the impossibility of informationally efficient markets, *American Economic Review* 70, 393–408.

Guidolin, M., and A. Timmermann, 2008, International asset allocation under regime switching, skew, and kurtosis preferences, *Review of Financial Studies* 21, 889–935.

Guiso, L., and M. Paiella, 2008, Risk aversion, wealth, and background risk, *Journal of the European Economic Association* 6, 1109–1150.

Guiso, L., P. Sapienza, and L. Zingales, 2006, Does culture affect economic outcomes? *Journal of Economic Perspectives* 20, 23–48.

Guiso, L., P. Sapienza, and L. Zingales, 2013, The determinants of attitudes toward strategic default on mortgages, *The Journal of Finance* 68, 1473–1515.

Gupta, A., and B. Liang, 2005, Do hedge funds have enough capital? A value-at-risk approach, *Journal of Financial Economics* 77, 219–253.

Gupta, R., and H. B. Kazemi, 2007, Factor exposures and hedge fund operational risk: the case of Amaranth, *Alternative Investment Quarterly* 23, 442–460.

Haghtalab, N., M. O. Jackson, and A. D. Procaccia, 2021, Belief polarization in a complex world: a learning theory perspective, *Proceedings of the National Academy of Sciences* 118, 1051–1057.

Haidt, J., 2007, The new synthesis in moral psychology, *Science* 316, 998–1002.

Hajnal, J., 1976, On products of non-negative matrices, *Mathematical Proceedings of the Cambridge Philosophical Society* 79, 521–530.

Hakansson, N. H., 1970, Optimal investment and consumption strategies under risk for a class of utility functions, *Econometrica* 38, 587–607.

Hake, H. W., and R. Hyman, 1953, Perceptions of the statistical structure of a random series of binary symbols, *Journal of Experimental Psychology* 45, 64–74.

Halpern, J. Y., and R. Pass, 2015, Algorithmic rationality: game theory with costly computation, *Journal of Economic Theory* 156, 246–268.

Hamilton, J. D., 1994, *Time Series Analysis* (Princeton University Press, Princeton, NJ).

Hamilton, W. D., 1963, The evolution of altruistic behavior, *The American Naturalist* 97, 354–356.

Hamilton, W. D., 1964, The genetical evolution of social behavior. I and II, *Journal of Theoretical Biology* 7, 1–52.

Hamilton, W. D., 1971, Geometry for the selfish herd, *Journal of Theoretical Biology* 31, 295–311.

Hammond, K. R., R. M. Hamm, J. Grassia, and T. Pearson, 1987, Direct comparison of the efficacy of intuitive and analytical cognition in expert judgment, *IEEE Transactions on Systems, Man, and Cybernetics* 17, 753–770.

Haney, C., C. Banks, and P. Zimbardo, 1973a, Interpersonal dynamics in a simulated prison, *International Journal of Criminology and Penology* 1, 69–97.

Haney, C., C. Banks, and P. Zimbardo, 1973b, Study of prisoners and guards in a simulated prison, *Naval Research Reviews* 9, 1–17.

Hansson, I., and C. Stuart, 1990, Malthusian selection of preferences, *American Economic Review* 80, 529–544.

Harder, L. D., and L. A. Real, 1987, Why are bumble bees risk averse? *Ecology* 68, 1104–1108.

Hardy, G. H., 1908, Mendelian proportions in a mixed population, *Science* 28, 49–50.

Hare, T., C. Camerer, D. Knoepfle, J. O'Doherty, and A. Rangel, 2010, Value computations in ventral medial prefrontal cortex during charitable decision making incorporate input from regions involved in social cognition, *Journal of Neuroscience* 30, 583–590.

Harlow, J., 1868, Recovery from the passage of an iron bar through the head, *History of Psychiatry* 4, 271–278.

Harlow, J., 1974, Recovery after severe injury to the head, in W. G. Van der Kloot, C. Walcott, and B. Dane, *Readings in Behavior*, 291–309 (Holt, Rinehart and Winston, New York).

Harris, L., 2013, What to do about high-frequency trading, *Financial Analysts Journal* 69, 6–9.

Hasanhodzic, J., and A. W. Lo, 2006, Attack of the clones, *Alpha Magazine*, June/July.

Hasanhodzic, J., and A. W. Lo, 2007, Can hedge-fund returns be replicated?: The linear case, *Journal of Investment Management* 5, 5–45.

Hasanhodzic, J., and A. W. Lo, 2019, On Black's leverage effect in firms with no leverage, *The Journal of Portfolio Management* 46, 106–122.

Hasanhodzic, J., A. W. Lo, and P. Patel, 2009, The CS 130/30 index: a summary and performance comparison, White Paper, Credit Suisse.

Hasanhodzic, J., A. W. Lo, and E. Viola, 2011, A computational view of market efficiency, *Quantitative Finance* 11, 1043–1050.

Hasanhodzic, J., A. W. Lo, and E. Viola, 2019, What do humans perceive in asset returns? *The Journal of Portfolio Management* 45, 49–60.

Hasbrouck, J., 1991, Measuring the information content of stock trades, *The Journal of Finance* 46, 179–207.

Hasbrouck, J., 2007, *Empirical Market Microstructure: The Institutions, Economics, and Econometrics of Securities Trading* (Oxford University Press, Oxford).

Hasbrouck, J., and R. A. Schwartz, 1988, Liquidity and execution costs in equity markets, *The Journal of Portfolio Management* 14, 10–16.

Hasbrouck, J., and D. J. Seppi, 2001, Common factors in prices, order flows, and liquidity, *Journal of Financial Economics* 59, 383–411.

Hauert, C., and M. Doebeli, 2004, Spatial structure often inhibits the evolution of cooperation in the snowdrift game, *Nature* 428, 643–646.

Hawkins, J., and S. Blakeslee, 2004, *On Intelligence* (Macmillan, New York).

Healy, A. D., and A. W. Lo, 2009, Jumping the gates: using beta-overlay strategies to hedge liquidity constraints, *Journal of Investment Management* 3, 11–30.

Hedge Fund Research, 2013, *Global Hedge Fund Industry Report* (Hedge Fund Research, Chicago, IL).

Heer, J., N. Kong, and M. Agrawala, 2009, Sizing the horizon: the effects of chart size and layering on the graphical perception of time series visualizations, in *Proceedings of the SIGCHI Conference on Human Factors in Computing Systems,* 1303–1312 (Association for Computing Machinery, New York).

Heller, Y., and E. Winter, 2020, Biased-belief equilibrium, *American Economic Journal: Microeconomics* 12, 1–40.

Hendricks, D., J. Patel, and R. Zeckhauser, 1997, The j-shape of performance persistence given survivorship bias, *Review of Economics and Statistics* 79, 161–166.

Henriksson, R. D., and R. C. Merton, 1981, On market timing and investment performance. II. Statistical procedures for evaluating forecasting skills, *Journal of Business* 54, 513–533.

Hens, T., and K. R. Schenk-Hoppé, 2005, Evolutionary stability of portfolio rules in incomplete markets, *Journal of Mathematical Economics* 41, 43–66.

Hermalin, B. E., 2001, Economics and corporate culture, in C. L. Cooper, S. Cartwright, and P. C. Earley, *The International Handbook of Organizational Culture and Climate*, 90–109 (John Wiley & Sons, Chichester).

Herre, E. A., and W. T. Wcislo, 2011, In defence of inclusive fitness theory, *Nature* 471, E8–E9.

Herrmann-Pillath, C., 1991, A Darwinian framework for the economic analysis of institutional change in history, *Journal of Social and Biological Structures* 14, 127–148.

Herrnstein, R. J., 1961, Relative and absolute strength of responses as a function of frequency of reinforcement, *Journal of the Experimental Analysis of Behavior* 4, 267–272.

Herrnstein, R. J., 1970, On the law of effect, *Journal of the Experimental Analysis of Behavior* 13, 243–266.

Herrnstein, R. J., 1997, *The Matching Law* (Harvard University Press, Cambridge, MA).

Herrnstein, R. J., and D. Prelec, 1991, Melioration: a theory of distributed choice, *Journal of Economic Perspectives* 5, 137–156.

Heston, S. L., and N. R. Sinha, 2017, News vs. sentiment: predicting stock returns from news stories, *Financial Analysts Journal* 73, 67–83.

Heuson, A. J., M. C. Hutchinson, and A. Kumar, 2019, Predicting hedge fund performance when fund returns are skewed, *Financial Management* 49, 877–896.

Higham, N. J., 2002, Computing the nearest correlation matrix—a problem from finance, *IMA Journal of Numerical Analysis* 22, 329–343.

Hill, C. A., and R. W. Painter, 2015, *Better Bankers, Better Banks: Promoting Good Business Through Contractual Commitment* (University of Chicago Press, Chicago, IL).

Hill, J. M., and F. J. Jones, 1988, Equity trading, program trading, portfolio insurance, computer trading and all that, *Financial Analysts Journal* 44, 29–38.

Hill, J. M., D. Nadig, and M. Hougan, 2015, *A Comprehensive Guide to Exchange-traded Funds (ETFs)* (CFA Institute Research Foundation, Charlottesville, VA).

Hirshleifer, D., and G. Y. Luo, 2001, On the survival of overconfident traders in a competitive securities market, *Journal of Financial Markets* 4, 73–84.

Hirshleifer, D., and T. Shumway, 2003, Good day sunshine: stock returns and the weather, *The Journal of Finance* 58, 1009–1032.

Hirshleifer, D., A. Subrahmanyam, and S. Titman, 2006, Feedback and the success of irrational investors, *Journal of Financial Economics* 81, 311–338.

Hirshleifer, D., and S. H. Teoh, 2009, Thought and behavior contagion in capital markets, in T. Hens and K. R. S. Hoppé, *Handbook of Financial Markets: Dynamics and Evolution,* 1–56 (Elsevier, Amsterdam).

Hirshleifer, J., 1977, Economics from a biological viewpoint, *Journal of Law and Economics* 20, 1–52.

Hirshleifer, J., 1978, Natural economy versus political economy, *Journal of Social and Biological Structures* 1, 319–337.

Ho, K. Z., 2009, *Liquidated: An Ethnography of Wall Street* (Duke University Press, Durham, NC).

Hodder, J. E., and J. C. Jackwerth, 2007, Incentive contracts and hedge fund management, *Journal of Financial and Quantitative Analysis* 42, 811–826.

Hodgson, G. M., 1996, Corporate culture and the nature of the firm, in J. Groenewegen, *Transaction Cost Economics and Beyond*, 249–269 (Kluwer Academic Press, Boston, MA).

Hoffman, D. D., 2016, The interface theory of perception, *Current Directions in Psychological Science* 25, 157–161.

Hogan, W. P., and I. G. Sharpe, 1997, Prudential regulation of the financial system: a functional approach, *Agenda* 4, 15–28.

Hölldobler, B., and E. O. Wilson, 1990, *The Ants* (Belknap Press, Cambridge, MA).

Holt, C. A., and S. K. Laury, 2002, Risk aversion and incentive effects, *American Economic Review* 92, 1644–1655.

Horne, P. J., and C. F. Lowe, 1993, Determinants of human performance on concurrent schedules, *Journal of the Experimental Analysis of Behavior* 59, 29–60.

Horst, J. T., and M. Verbeek, 2007, Fund liquidation, self-selection, and look-ahead bias in the hedge fund industry, *Review of Finance* 11, 605–632.

Houston, A. I., J. M. McNamara, and M. D. Steer, 2007, Do we expect natural selection to produce rational behaviour? *Philosophical Transactions of the Royal Society B: Biological Sciences* 362, 1531–1543.

Howell, M. J., 2001, Fund age and performance, *The Journal of Alternative Investments* 4, 57–60.

Hsu, M., M. Bhatt, R. Adolphs, D. Tranel, and C. F. Camerer, 2005, Neural systems responding to degrees of uncertainty in human decision-making, *Science* 310, 1680–1683.

Hu, H. T., 2012, Efficient markets and the law: a predictable past and an uncertain future, *Annual Review of Financial Economics* 4, 179–214.

Huberman, G., and D. Halka, 2001, Systematic liquidity, *Journal of Financial Research* 24, 161–178.

Huberman, G., and T. Regev, 2001, Contagious speculation and a cure for cancer: a nonevent that made stock prices soar, *The Journal of Finance* 56, 387–396.

Huizinga, H., and L. Laeven, 2010, Bank valuation and regulatory forbearance during a financial crisis, European Banking Center Discussion Paper No. 2009–17. Available at SSRN: http://ssrn.com/abstract=1434359.

Hung, A., A. Heinberg, and J. Yoong, 2010, Do risk disclosures affect investment choice? Technical Report, RAND Labor and Population, September.

Hunter, M., and N. C. Smith, 2011, Société Générale: The Rogue Trader (INSEAD, Fontainebleau, France), Available at: http://cases.insead.edu/publishing/case?code=26046.

Hurtz, G. M., and J. J. Donovan, 2000, Personality and job performance: the big five revisited, *Journal of Applied Psychology* 85, 869–879.

Hutchinson, J. M., A. W. Lo, and T. Poggio, 1994, A nonparametric approach to pricing and hedging derivative securities via learning networks, *The Journal of Finance* 49, 851–889.

Ibbotson, R. G., 2011, *Ibbotson® SBBI® 2011 Classic Yearbook* (Morningstar, Inc, Chicago, IL).

Ibbotson, R. G., 2013, *Market Results for Stocks, Bonds, Bills, and Inflation 1926–2012* (Morningstar, Inc, Chicago, IL).

Ibbotson, R. G., P. Chen, and K. X. Zhu, 2011, The ABCs of hedge funds: alphas, betas, and costs, *Financial Analysts Journal* 67, 15–25.

Ilon, L., 2012, How collective intelligence redefines education, in J. Altmann, *Advances in Collective Intelligence 2011*, 91–102 (Springer, Berlin).

Ineichen, A., 2001, The myth of hedge funds, *Journal of Global Financial Markets* 2, 34–46.

Ingham, C., and E. Ben-Jacob, 2008, Swarming and complex pattern formation in *Paenibacillus vortex* studied by imaging and tracking cells, *BMC Microbiology* 8, 36.

Ipsen, I. C., and T. M. Selee, 2011, Ergodicity coefficients defined by vector norms, *SIAM Journal on Matrix Analysis and Applications* 32, 153–200.

Isen, A. M., and N. Geva, 1987, The influence of positive affect on acceptable level of risk: the person with a large canoe has a large worry, *Organizational Behavior and Human Decision Processes* 39, 145–154.

Isen, A. M., T. E. Nygren, and F. G. Ashby, 1988, Influence of positive affect on the subjective utility of gains and losses: it is just not worth the risk, *Journal of Personality and Social Psychology* 55, 710–717.

Ishii, K., M. H., Y. Iwasa, and A. Sasaki, 1989, Evolutionarily stable mutation rate in a periodically changing environment, *Genetics* 121, 163–174.

Iyer, R., S. Koleva, J. Graham, P. Ditto, and J. Haidt, 2012, Understanding libertarian morality: the psychological dispositions of self-identified libertarians, *PLoS One* 7, e42366.

Jacobs, B., and K. Levy, 2022, The first 75 years of the *Financial Analysts Journal*: prolific contributors and major ideas and innovations, Unpublished manuscript.

Jagannathan, R., A. Malakhov, and D. Novikov, 2010, Do hot hands exist among hedge fund managers? An empirical evaluation, *The Journal of Finance* 65, 217–255.

James, W., 1884, On some omissions of introspective psychology, *Mind* 9, 1–26.

Janis, I. L., 1982, *Groupthink: Psychological Studies of Policy Decisions and Fiascoes* (Houghton Mifflin, Boston, MA).

Jean, E., M. Perroux, J. Pepin, and A. Duhoux, 2020, How to measure the collective intelligence of primary healthcare teams? *Learning Health Systems* 4, e10213.

Jegadeesh, N., and S. Titman, 1993, Returns to buying winners and selling losers: implications for stock market efficiency, *The Journal of Finance* 48, 65–91.

Jen, P., C. Heasman, and K. Boyatt, 2001, Alternative asset strategies: early performance in hedge fund managers, *Lazard Asset Management* 12, 209–218.

Jensen, M. C., 1978, Some anomalous evidence regarding market efficiency, *Journal of Financial Economics* 6, 95–101.

Jensen, M. C., and W. H. Meckling, 1978, Can the corporation survive? *Financial Analysts Journal* 34, 31–37.

Jevons, W. S., 1871, *The Theory of Political Economy* (Macmillan and Company, London).

Jiang, H., and B. Kelly, 2012, Tail risk and hedge fund returns, Working Paper, University of Chicago Booth School of Business.

Joenväärä, J., M. Kaupila, R. Kosowski, and P. Tolonen, 2020, Hedge fund performance: are stylized facts sensitive to which database one uses? *Critical Finance Review* 10, 271–327

Johnson, D. D., and J. H. Fowler, 2011, The evolution of overconfidence, *Nature* 477, 317–320.

Johnson, E. J., and A. Tversky, 1983, Affect, generalization, and the perception of risk, *Journal of Personality and Social Psychology* 45, 20–31.

Jones, J. M., J. F. Dovidio, and D. L. Vietze, 2013, *The Psychology of Diversity: Beyond Prejudice and Racism* (John Wiley & Sons, New York).

Jordan, D. J., and J. D. Diltz, 2003, The profitability of day traders, *Financial Analysts Journal* 59, 85–94.

Jorion, P., 2007, Risk management for hedge funds with position information, *The Journal of Portfolio Management* 34, 127–134.

Jorion, P., 2008, Risk management for event-driven funds, *Financial Analysts Journal* 64, 61–73.

Jorion, P., and C. Schwarz, 2014a, Are hedge fund managers systematically misreporting? or not? *Journal of Financial Economics* 111, 311–327.

Jorion, P., and C. Schwarz, 2014b, The strategic listing decisions of hedge funds, *Journal of Financial and Quantitative Analysis* 49, 773–796.

Jylha, P., 2011, Hedge fund return misreporting: incentives and effects, Working Paper, Aalto University. Available at SSRN: https://ssrn.com/abstract=1661075.

Kahneman, D., 2011, *Thinking, Fast and Slow* (Macmillan, New York).

Kahneman, D., P. Slovic, and A. Tversky, 1982, *Judgment Under Uncertainty: Heuristics and Biases* (Cambridge University Press, Cambridge).

Kahneman, D., and A. Tversky, 1972, Subjective probability: a judgment of representativeness, *Cognitive Psychology* 3, 430–454.

Kahneman, D., and A. Tversky, 1979, Prospect theory: an analysis of decision under risk, *Econometrica* 47, 263–291.

Kahneman, D., and A. Tversky, 2000, *Choices, Values, and Frames* (Cambridge University Press, Cambridge).

Kaminski, K., 2011, *In Search of Crisis Alpha: A Short Guide to Investing in Managed Futures* (Chicago Mercantile Exchange, Chicago, IL).

Kaminsky, G. L., and C. M. Reinhart, 1999, The twin crises: the causes of banking and balance-of-payments problems, *American Economic Review* 89, 473–500.

Kamstra, M. J., L. A. Kramer, and M. D. Levi, 2003, Winter blues: a sad stock market cycle, *American Economic Review* 93, 324–343.

Kane, E. J., 2015, Unpacking and reorienting the executive subcultures of megabanks and their regulators, Working Paper. Available at SSRN: http://ssrn.com/abstract=2594923.

Kao, D.-L., 2002, Battle for alphas: hedge funds versus long-only portfolios, *Financial Analysts Journal* 58, 16–36.

Kao, D.-L., and R. D. Shumaker, 1999, Equity style timing, *Financial Analysts Journal* 55, 37–48.

Kapp, B. S., R. C. Frysinger, M. Gallagher, and J. R. Haselton, 1979, Amygdala central nucleus lesions: effect on heart rate conditioning in the rabbit, *Physiology & Behavior* 23, 1109–1117.

Kat, H. M., and F. Menexe, 2003, Persistence in hedge fund performance: the true value of a track record, *The Journal of Alternative Investments* 5, 66–72.

Kat, H. M., and H. P. Palaro, 2005, Who needs hedge funds? A copula-based approach to hedge fund return replication, Working Paper, Cass Business School, City University, London.

Kat, H. M., and H. P. Palaro, 2006a, Replication and evaluation of funds of hedge funds returns, in H. M. Kat and H. P. Palaro, *Funds of Hedge Funds*, 45–56 (Elsevier, Amsterdam).

Kat, H. M., and H. P. Palaro, 2006b, Superstars or average joes? A replication-based performance evaluation of 1917 individual hedge funds, Working Paper, Cass Business School, City University, London.

Kazemi, H., and Y. Li, 2009, Market timing of CTAs: an examination of systematic CTAs vs. discretionary CTAs, *Journal of Futures Markets* 29, 1067–1099.

Kazemi, H. B., F. Tu, and Y. Li, 2008, Replication and benchmarking of hedge funds, *The Journal of Alternative Investments* 11, 40–59.

Kealhofer, S., 2003a, Quantifying credit risk I: default prediction, *Financial Analysts Journal* 59, 30–44.

Kealhofer, S., 2003b, Quantifying credit risk II: debt valuation, *Financial Analysts Journal* 59, 78–92.

Keasar, T., E. Rashkovich, D. Cohen, and A. Shmida, 2002, Bees in two-armed bandit situations: foraging choices and possible decision mechanisms, *Behavioral Ecology* 13, 757–765.

Kelly, J. L., Jr., 1956, A new interpretation of information rate, *Information Theory, IRE Transactions* 2, 185–189.

Kendall, A., and Y. Gal, 2017, What uncertainties do we need in Bayesian deep learning for computer vision? in M. I. Jordan, Y. LeCun, and S. A. Solla, *Advances in Neural Information Processing Systems*, 1–12 (MIT Press, Cambridge, MA).

Kendall, S., A. Stuart, and J. Ord, 1983, *The Advanced Theory of Statistics*, volume 3, fourth edition (Charles Griffin and Co., Ltd., High Wycombe).

Kenett, D. Y., Y. Shapira, A. Madi, S. Bransburg-Zabary, G. Gur-Gershgoren, and E. Ben-Jacob, 2011, Index cohesive force analysis reveals that the US market became prone to systemic collapses since 2002, *PLoS One* 6, e19378.

Keogh, E., and S. Kasetty, 2003, On the need for time series data mining benchmarks: a survey and empirical demonstration, *Data Mining and Knowledge Discovery* 7, 349–371.

Keynes, J. M., 1936, *The General Theory of Employment, Interest and Money* (Macmillan, London).

Khandani, A. E., and A. W. Lo, 2007, What happened to the quants in August 2007? *Journal of Investment Management* 5, 29–78.

Khandani, A. E., and A. W. Lo, 2011a, Illiquidity premia in asset returns: an empirical analysis of hedge funds, mutual funds, and US equity portfolios, *The Quarterly Journal of Finance* 1, 205–264.

Khandani, A. E., and A. W. Lo, 2011b, What happened to the quants in August 2007? Evidence from factors and transactions data, *Journal of Financial Markets* 14, 1–46.

Khandani, A. E., A. W. Lo, and R. C. Merton, 2013, Systemic risk and the refinancing ratchet effect, *Journal of Financial Economics* 108, 29–45.

Khuntia, S., and J. Pattanayak, 2018, Adaptive market hypothesis and evolving predictability of bitcoin, *Economics Letters* 167, 26–28.

Kim, J. H., A. Shamsuddin, and K.-P. Lim, 2011, Stock return predictability and the adaptive markets hypothesis: evidence from century-long US data, *Journal of Empirical Finance* 18, 868–879.

Kinderman, P., R. Dunbar, and R. P. Bentall, 1998, Theory-of-mind deficits and causal attributions, *British Journal of Psychology* 89, 191–204.

Kindleberger, C. P., 1978, *Manias, Panics, and Crashes: A History of Financial Crises* (Basic Books, New York).

Kirman, A., 1993, Ants, rationality, and recruitment, *Quarterly Journal of Economics* 108, 137–156.

Klepper, S., and E. Graddy, 1990, The evolution of new industries and the determinants of market structure, *The RAND Journal of Economics* 21, 27–44.

Klüver, H., and P. C. Bucy, 1937, "Psychic blindness" and other symptoms following bilateral temporal lobectomy in rhesus monkeys, *American Journal of Physiology* 119, 352–353.

Knight, F. H., 1940, "What is truth" in economics? *Journal of Political Economy* 48, 1–32.

Knoch, D., L. R. Gianotti, A. Pascual-Leone, V. Treyer, M. Regard, M. Hohmann, and P. Brugger, 2006, Disruption of right prefrontal cortex by low-frequency repetitive transcranial magnetic stimulation induces risk-taking behavior, *Journal of Neuroscience* 26, 6469–6472.

Knoll, A. H., and M. A. Nowak, 2017, The timetable of evolution, *Science Advances* 3, e1603076.

Knutson, B., and P. Bossaerts, 2007, Neural antecedents of financial decisions, *Journal of Neuroscience* 27, 8174–8177.

Knutson, B., and R. Peterson, 2005, Neurally reconstructing expected utility, *Games and Economic Behavior* 52, 305–315.

Kocherlakota, N. R., 2010, Modern macroeconomic models as tools for economic policy, *The Region (Federal Reserve Bank of Minneapolis)* 54, 5–21.

Koduri, N., and A. W. Lo, 2021, The origin of cooperation, *Proceedings of the National Academy of Sciences* 118, e2015572118.

Kogan, L., S. A. Ross, J. Wang, and M. M. Westerfield, 2006, The price impact and survival of irrational traders, *The Journal of Finance* 61, 195–229.

Kogler, C., and A. Kühberger, 2007, Dual process theories: a key for understanding the diversification bias? *Journal of Risk and Uncertainty* 34, 145–154.

Koopmans, T. C., 1961, Convexity assumptions, allocative efficiency, and competitive equilibrium, *Journal of Political Economy* 69, 478–479.

Kosowski, R., N. Y. Naik, and M. Teo, 2007, Do hedge funds deliver alpha? A Bayesian and bootstrap analysis, *Journal of Financial Economics* 84, 229–264.

Kouwenberg, R., and W. T. Ziemba, 2007, Incentives and risk taking in hedge funds, *Journal of Banking & Finance* 31, 3291–3310.

Kozup, J., E. Howlett, and M. Pagano, 2008, The effects of summary information on consumer perceptions of mutual fund characteristics, *Journal of Consumer Affairs* 42, 37–59.

Kramer, D., 2001, Hedge fund disasters: avoiding the next catastrophe, *Alternative Investment Quarterly* 1.

Kramer, M. S., K. Demissie, H. Yang, R. W. Platt, R. Sauvé, and R. Liston, 2000, The contribution of mild and moderate preterm birth to infant mortality, *Journal of American Medical Association* 284, 843–849.

Kraus, A., and H. R. Stoll, 1972, Price impacts of block trading on the New York Stock Exchange, *The Journal of Finance* 27, 569–588.

Kreps, D. M., 1990, Corporate culture and economic theory, in J. E. Alt and K. A. Shepsle, *Perspectives on Positive Political Economy*, 90–143 (Cambridge University Press, Cambridge).

Krishnamurthy, A., 2010, Amplification mechanisms in liquidity crises, *American Economic Journal: Macroeconomics* 2, 1–30.

Kritzman, M., 1989, A simple solution for optimal currency hedging, *Financial Analysts Journal* 45, 47–50.

Krivelyova, A., and C. Robotti, 2003, Playing the field: geomagnetic storms and international stock markets, Technical Report, Working Paper 2003-5a, Federal Reserve Bank of Atlanta.

Kroeber, A. L., and C. Kluckhohn, 1952, Culture: a critical review of concepts and definitions, Papers, Peabody Museum of Archaeology & Ethnology, Harvard University.

Kroll, Y., H. Levy, and A. Rapoport, 1988, Experimental tests of the mean-variance model for portfolio selection, *Organizational Behavior and Human Decision Processes* 42, 388–410.

Kronman, A. T., 1983, *Max Weber* (Stanford University Press, Stanford, CA).

Krückeberg, S., and P. Scholz, 2020, Decentralized efficiency? Arbitrage in bitcoin markets, *Financial Analysts Journal* 76, 135–152.

Kruttli, M. S., A. J. Patton, and T. Ramadorai, 2015, The impact of hedge funds on asset markets, *The Review of Asset Pricing Studies* 5, 185–226.

Kubota, J. T., J. Li, E. Bar-David, M. R. Banaji, and E. A. Phelps, 2013, The price of racial bias: intergroup negotiations in the ultimatum game, *Psychological Science* 24, 2498–2504.

Kuhnen, C. M., and B. Knutson, 2005, The neural basis of financial risk taking, *Neuron* 47, 763.

Kundro, C., and S. Feffer, 2004, Valuation issues and operational risk in hedge funds, *Journal of Financial Transformation* 10, 41–47.

Kussell, E., and S. Leibler, 2005, Phenotypic diversity, population growth, and information in fluctuating environments, *Science* 309, 2075–2078.

Kyle, A., and F. A. Wang, 1997, Speculation duopoly with agreement to disagree: can overconfidence survive the market test? *The Journal of Finance* 52, 2073–2090.

Kyle, A. S., 1985, Continuous auctions and insider trading, *Econometrica* 53, 1315–1335.

Lai, C., and M. Banaji, 2020, The psychology of implicit intergroup bias and the prospect of change, in D. Allen and R. Somanathan, *Difference without Domination*, 115–146 (University of Chicago Press, Chicago, IL).

Lake, B. M., R. Salakhutdinov, and J. B. Tenenbaum, 2015, Human-level concept learning through probabilistic program induction, *Science* 350, 1332–1338.

Lakonishok, J., A. Shleifer, and R. W. Vishny, 1994, Contrarian investment, extrapolation, and risk, *The Journal of Finance* 49, 1541–1578.

Lamport, L., R. Shostak, and M. Pease, 1982, The Byzantine generals problem, *ACM Transactions on Programming Languages and Systems* 4, 382–401.

Lawrence, M., P. Goodwin, M. O'Connor, and D. Önkal, 2006, Judgmental forecasting: a review of progress over the last 25 years, *International Journal of forecasting* 22, 493–518.

Lazear, E. P., 1995, Corporate culture and the diffusion of values, in H. Siebert, *Trends in Business Organization*, 89–133 (J.C.B. Mohr (Paul Siebeck), Tübingen).

LeBaron, B., 2001a, A builder's guide to agent-based financial markets, *Quantitative Finance* 1, 254–261.

LeBaron, B., 2001b, Evolution and time horizons in an agent-based stock market, *Macroeconomic Dynamics* 5, 225–254.

LeBaron, B., 2001c, Financial market efficiency in a coevolutionary environment, Proceedings of the Workshop on Simulation of Social Agents: Architectures and Institutions', Argonne National Laboratories, 33–51.

LeBaron, B., 2002, Short-memory traders and their impact on group learning in financial markets, *Proceedings of the National Academy of Sciences* 99, 7201–7206.

LeBaron, B., 2006, Agent-based computational finance, in L. Tesfatsion and K. Judd, *Handbook of Computational Economics*, volume 2, 1187–1233 (Elsevier, Amsterdam).

LeBaron, B., W. B. Arthur, and R. Palmer, 1999, Time series properties of an artificial stock market, *Journal of Economic Dynamics and Control* 23, 1487–1516.

Lebow, C. C., L. P. Sarsfield, W. L. Stanley, E. Ettedgui, and G. Henning, 1999, *Safety in the Skies: Personnel and Parties in NTSB Aviation Accident Investigations* (RAND Corporation, Santa Monica, CA).

LeDoux, J. E., 1996, *The Emotional Brain: The Mysterious Underpinnings of Emotional Life* (Simon & Schuster, New York).

Lee, P., and A. W. Lo, 2014, Hedge fund beta replication: a five-year retrospective, *Journal of Investment Management* 12, 5–18.

Lefcourt, H., 1991, Locus of control, in J. Robinson, P. Shaver, and L. Wrightsman, *Measures of Personality and Social Psychology Attitudes* (Academic Press, San Diego, CA).

Lehmann, B. N., 1990, Fads, martingales, and market efficiency, *The Quarterly Journal of Economics* 105, 1–28.

Lehmann, L., L. Kekker, S. West, and D. Roze, 2007, Group selection and kin selection: two concepts but one process, *Proceedings of the National Academy of Sciences* 104, 6736–6739.

Leibowitz, M. L., 1986a, The dedicated bond portfolio in pension funds—part I: motivations and basics, *Financial Analysts Journal* 42, 68–75.

Leibowitz, M. L., 1986b, The dedicated bond portfolio in pension funds—part II: immunization, horizon matching and contingent procedures, *Financial Analysts Journal* 42, 47–57.

Leibowitz, M. L., 2005, Alpha hunters and beta grazers, *Financial Analysts Journal* 61, 32–39.

Leimeister, J. M., 2010, Collective intelligence, *Business & Information Systems Engineering* 2, 245–248.

Leitgeb, H., and R. Pettigrew, 2010a, An objective justification of Bayesianism I: measuring inaccuracy, *Philosophy of Science* 77, 201–235.

Leitgeb, H., and R. Pettigrew, 2010b, An objective justification of Bayesianism II: the consequences of minimizing inaccuracy, *Philosophy of Science* 77, 236–272.

Lerner, J., 2002, Where does State Street lead? A first look at finance patents, 1971 to 2000, *The Journal of Finance* 57, 901–930.

Lerner, J. S., and D. Keltner, 2001, Fear, anger, and risk, *Journal of Personality and Social Psychology* 81, 146–159.

LeRoy, S. F., 1973, Risk aversion and the martingale property of stock prices, *International Economic Review* 14, 436–446.

LeRoy, S. F., 2004, Rational exuberance, *Journal of Economic Literature* 42, 783–804.

Levenson, H., 1972, Distinctions within the concept of internal-external control: development of a new scale, in *Proceedings of the Annual Convention of the American Psychological Association,* 261–262 (American Psychological Association, Washington, DC).

Levenson, R. W., 1994, The search for autonomic specificity, in P. Ekman and R. J. Davidson, *The Nature of Emotion,* 212–223 (Oxford University Press, New York).

Levin, S. A., D. Cohen, and A. Hastings, 1984, Dispersal strategies in patchy environments, *Theoretical Population Biology* 26, 165–191.

Levin, S. A., and A. W. Lo, 2021, Introduction to PNAS special issue on evolutionary models of financial markets, *Proceedings of the National Academy of Sciences* 118, 1–5.

Levin, S. A., H. C. Muller-Landau, R. Nathan, and J. Chave, 2003, The ecology and evolution of seed dispersal: a theoretical perspective, *Annual Review of Ecology, Evolution, and Systematics* 34, 575–604.

Levins, R., 1968, *Evolution in Changing Environments: Some Theoretical Explorations,* MPB-2 (Princeton University Press, Princeton, NJ).

Lewellen, J., and S. Nagel, 2006, The conditional CAPM does not explain asset-pricing anomalies, *Journal of Financial Economics* 82, 289–314.

Lewontin, R. C., and D. Cohen, 1969, On population growth in a randomly varying environment, *Proceedings of the National Academy of Sciences* 62, 1056–1060.

Lhabitant, F.-S., and M. Learned, 2002, Hedge fund diversification: how much is enough? *The Journal of Alternative Investments* 5, 23–49.

Li, H., X. Zhang, and R. Zhao, 2011, Investing in talents: manager characteristics and hedge fund performances, *Journal of Financial and Quantitative Analysis* 46, 59–82.

Liang, B., 1999, On the performance of hedge funds, *Financial Analysts Journal* 55, 72–85.

Liang, B., 2000, Hedge funds: the living and the dead, *Journal of Financial and Quantitative Analysis* 35, 309–326.

Liang, B., 2001, Hedge fund performance: 1990–1999, *Financial Analysts Journal* 57, 11–18.

Liang, B., 2003, The accuracy of hedge fund returns, *The Journal of Portfolio Management* 29, 111–122.

Liang, B., 2005, Alternative investments: CTAs, hedge funds, and funds-of-funds, in *The World of Hedge Funds: Characteristics and Analysis*, 109–127 (World Scientific, Hackensack, NJ).

Liang, B., M. Getmansky, C. Schwarz, and R. Wermers, 2019, Share restrictions and investor flows in the hedge fund industry, Working Paper, University of Massachusetts, Amherst. Available at SSRN: https://ssrn.com/abstract=2692598.

Liang, B., and H. Park, 2007, Risk measures for hedge funds: a cross-sectional approach, *European Financial Management* 13, 333–370.

Liang, B., and H. Park, 2010, Predicting hedge fund failure: a comparison of risk measures, *Journal of Financial and Quantitative Analysis* 45, 199–222.

Lichtenstein, S., B. Fischhoff, and L. D. Phillips, 1982, Calibration of probabilities: the state of the art to 1980, in D. Kahneman, P. Slovic, and A. Tversky, *Judgment Under Uncertainty: Heuristics and Biases*, 306–334 (Cambridge University Press, Cambridge).

Lieder, F., and T. L. Griffiths, 2020, Resource-rational analysis: understanding human cognition as the optimal use of limited computational resources, *Behavioral and Brain Sciences* 43, E1.

Liew, J., and M. Vassalou, 2000, Can book-to-market, size and momentum be risk factors that predict economic growth? *Journal of Financial Economics* 57, 221–245.

Lillo, F., J. D. Farmer, and R. N. Mantegna, 2003, Master curve for price-impact function, *Nature* 421, 129–130.

Lindholm, E., and C. M. Cheatham, 1983, Autonomic activity and workload during learning of a simulated aircraft carrier landing task, *Aviation, Space, and Environmental Medicine* 54, 435–439.

Lintner, J., 1965a, Security prices, risk, and maximal gains from diversification, *The Journal of Finance* 20, 587–615.

Lintner, J., 1965b, The valuation of risk assets and the selection of risky investments in stock portfolios and capital budgets, *The Review of Economics and Statistics* 47, 13–37.

Lion, S., V. A. A. Jansen, and T. Day, 2011, Evolution in structured populations: beyond the kin versus group debate, *Trends in Ecology and Evolution* 26, 193–201.

Litan, R., and A. Santomero, 1999, *The Effect of Technology on the Financial Sector (Brookings-Wharton Papers on Financial Services)* (Brookings Institution, New York).

Litterman, R., 2011, Pricing climate change risk appropriately, *Financial Analysts Journal* 67, 4–10.

Litterman, R., 2013, The quant liquidity crunch of 2007: an unrecognized crowded trade, S. Donald Sussman Award Lecture, 17 September, accessed 4 January 2014. https://www.youtube.com/watch?v=oIKbWTdKfHs.

Ljung, G. M., and G. E. Box, 1978, On a measure of lack of fit in time series models, *Biometrika* 65, 297–303.

Lo, A. W. (ed.), 1997, *Market Efficiency: Stock Market Behaviour in Theory and Practice, Volumes I and II* (Edward Elgar Publishing, Cheltenham).

Lo, A. W., 1999, The three P's of total risk management, *Financial Analysts Journal* 55, 13–26.

Lo, A. W., 2002a, Bubble, rubble, finance in trouble? *The Journal of Psychology and Financial Markets* 3, 76–86.

Lo, A. W., 2002b, The statistics of Sharpe ratios, *Financial Analysts Journal* 58, 36–52.

Lo, A. W., 2004, The adaptive markets hypothesis, *The Journal of Portfolio Management* 30, 15–29.

Lo, A. W., 2005, Reconciling efficient markets with behavioral finance: the adaptive markets hypothesis, *Journal of Investment Consulting* 7, 21–44.

Lo, A. W., 2008a, Efficient markets hypothesis, in S. N. Durlauf and L. E. Blume, *The New Palgrave Dictionary of Economics*, second edition, 1678–1690 (Palgrave Macmillan, Basingstoke).

Lo, A. W., 2008b, *Hedge Funds: An Analytic Perspective* (Princeton University Press, Princeton, NJ).

Lo, A. W., 2009, Regulatory reform in the wake of the financial crisis of 2007–2008, *Journal of Financial Economic Policy* 1, 4–43.

Lo, A. W., 2012, Adaptive markets and the new world order (corrected May 2012), *Financial Analysts Journal* 68, 18–29.

Lo, A. W., 2013, Fear, greed, and financial crises: a cognitive neurosciences perspective, in J. Fouque and J. Langsam, *Handbook of Systemic Risk*, 622–662 (Cambridge University Press, Cambridge).

Lo, A. W., 2016, The Gordon Gekko effect: the role of culture in the financial industry, *FRBNY Economic Policy Review* 22, 17–42.

Lo, A. W., 2017, *Adaptive Markets: Financial Evolution at the Speed of Thought* (Princeton University Press, Princeton, NJ).

Lo, A. W., 2021, The financial system red in tooth and claw: 75 years of co-evolving markets and technology, *Financial Analysts Journal* 77, 5–33.

Lo, A. W., 2022, Jack Bogle: champion of the people, *Journal of Index Investing* 13, 24–27.

Lo, A. W., and A. C. MacKinlay, 1988, Stock market prices do not follow random walks: evidence from a simple specification test, *Review of Financial Studies* 1, 41–66.

Lo, A. W., and A. C. MacKinlay, 1990, When are contrarian profits due to stock market overreaction? *Review of Financial Studies* 3, 175–205.

Lo, A. W., and A. C. MacKinlay, 1999, *A Non-random Walk Down Wall Street* (Princeton University Press, Princeton, NJ).

Lo, A. W., H. Mamaysky, and J. Wang, 2000, Foundations of technical analysis: computational algorithms, statistical inference, and empirical implementation, *The Journal of Finance* 55, 1705–1765.

Lo, A. W., H. Mamaysky, and J. Wang, 2004, Asset prices and trading volume under fixed transactions costs, *Journal of Political Economy* 112, 1054–1090.

Lo, A. W., K. P. Marlowe, and R. Zhang, 2021, To maximize or randomize? An experimental study of probability matching in financial decision making, *PLoS One* 16, e0252540.

Lo, A. W., and M. T. Mueller, 2010, Warning: physics envy may be hazardous to your wealth! *Journal of Investment Management* 8, 13–63.

Lo, A. W., H. A. Orr, and R. Zhang, 2018, The growth of relative wealth and the Kelly criterion, *Journal of Bioeconomics* 20, 49–67.

Lo, A. W., and P. N. Patel, 2008, 130/30: the new long-only, *The Journal of Portfolio Management* 34, 12–38.

Lo, A. W., and D. V. Repin, 2002, The psychophysiology of real-time financial risk processing, *Journal of Cognitive Neuroscience* 14, 323–339.

Lo, A. W., D. V. Repin, and B. N. Steenbarger, 2005, Fear and greed in financial markets: a clinical study of day-traders, *American Economic Review* 95, 352–359.

Lo, A. W., and J. Wang, 2000, Trading volume: definitions, data analysis, and implications of portfolio theory, *Review of Financial Studies* 13, 257–300.

Lo, A. W., and J. Wang, 2006, Trading volume: implications of an intertemporal capital asset pricing model, *The Journal of Finance* 61, 2805–2840.

Lo, A. W., and R. Zhang, 2021, The evolutionary origin of Bayesian heuristics and finite memory, *iScience* 24, 102853.

Lo, A. W., and R. Zhang, 2022, The wisdom of crowds vs. the madness of mobs: an evolutionary model of bias, polarization, and other challenges to collective intelligence, *Collective Intelligence* 1, 1–50.

Lochoff, R. W., 2002, Hedge funds and hope, *The Journal of Portfolio Management* 28, 92–99.

Loewenstein, G., 2000, Emotions in economic theory and economic behavior, *American Economic Review* 90, 426–432.

Lorig, T. S., and G. Schwartz, 1990, The pulmonary system, in J. Cacioppo and L. Tassinary, *Principles of Psychophysiology: Physical, Social, and Inferential Elements* (Cambridge University Press, Cambridge).

Loveless, J., 2013, Barbarians at the gateways: high-frequency trading and exchange technology, *ACM Queue* 11, 40–52.

Lowenstein, R., 2000, *When Genius Failed: The Rise and Fall of Long-Term Capital Management* (Random House, New York).

Lu, J., and I. Perrigne, 2008, Estimating risk aversion from ascending and sealed-bid auctions: the case of timber auction data, *Journal of Applied Econometrics* 23, 871–896.

Lu, Y., N. Kaushal, X. Huang, and S. M. Gaddis, 2021, Priming COVID-19 salience increases prejudice and discriminatory intent against Asians and Hispanics, *Proceedings of the National Academy of Sciences* 118, e2105125118.

Lucas, D., 2011, Government as a source of systemic risk, Technical Report, MIT Golub Center for Finance and Policy.

Lucas, R. E., Jr., 1972, Expectations and the neutrality of money, *Journal of Economic Theory* 4, 103–124.

Lucas, R. E., Jr., 1978, Asset prices in an exchange economy, *Econometrica* 46, 1429–1445.

Lughofer, E., and M. Sayed-Mouchaweh, 2015, Adaptive and on-line learning in non-stationary environments, *Evolving Systems* 6, 75–77.

Luo, G. Y., 1995, Evolution and market competition, *Journal of Economic Theory* 67, 223–250.

Luo, G. Y., 1998, Market efficiency and natural selection in a commodity futures market, *Review of Financial Studies* 11, 647–674.

Luo, G. Y., 2001, Natural selection and market efficiency in a futures market with random shocks, *Journal of Futures Markets: Futures, Options, and Other Derivative Products* 21, 489–516.

Luo, G. Y., 2003, Evolution, efficiency and noise traders in a one-sided auction market, *Journal of Financial Markets* 6, 163–197.

Lynch, M., and R. Lande, 1993, Evolution and extinction in response to environmental change, in P. M. Karieva, J. G. Kingsolver, and R. B. Huey, *Biotic Interactions and Global Change*, 235–250 (Sinauer Associates, Sunderland, MA).

Lyng, S., 1990, Edgework: a social psychological analysis of voluntary risk taking, *American Journal of Sociology* 95, 851–886.

MacDorman, M. F., and T. J. Mathews, 2008, Recent trends in infant mortality in the United States, *NCHS Data Brief* 9, 1–8.

Macey, J., G. Miller, M. O'Hara, and G. D. Rosenberg, 2008, Helping law catch up to markets: applying broker-dealer law to subprime mortgages, *The Journal of Corporation Law* 34, 789–842.

Madhavan, A., A. Sobczyk, and A. Ang, 2021, Toward ESG alpha: analysing ESG exposures through a factor lens, *Financial Analysts Journal* 77, 69–88.

Madrian, B. C., and D. F. Shea, 2001, The power of suggestion: inertia in 401(k) participation and savings behavior, *The Quarterly Journal of Economics* 116, 1149–1187.

Makridakis, S., 2017, The forthcoming artificial intelligence (AI) revolution: its impact on society and firms, *Futures* 90, 46–60.

Malkiel, B. G., 1973, *A Random Walk Down Wall Street* (W. W. Norton & Company, New York).

Malkiel, B. G., and A. Saha, 2005, Hedge funds: risk and return, *Financial Analysts Journal* 61, 80–88.

Malone, T. W., 2018, *Superminds: The Surprising Power of People and Computers Thinking Together* (Little, Brown Spark, Boston, MA).

Malone, T. W., R. Laubacher, and C. Dellarocas, 2010, The collective intelligence genome, *MIT Sloan Management Review* 51, 21.

Malthus, T. R., 1826, *An Essay on the Principle of Population*, *6th Edition* (John Murray and Library of Economics and Liberty, London).

Mangel, M., and C. W. Clark, 1988, *Dynamic Modeling in Behavioral Ecology* (Princeton University Press, Princeton, NJ).

Mano, H., 1992, Judgments under distress: assessing the role of unpleasantness and arousal in judgment formation, *Organizational Behavior and Human Decision Processes* 52, 216–245.

Mano, H., 1994, Risk-taking, framing effects, and affect, *Organizational Behavior and Human Decision Processes* 57, 38–58.

Manski, C., 1975, Maximum score estimation of the stochastic utility model of choice, *Journal of Econometrics* 3, 205–228.

Manski, C. F., and D. McFadden (eds.), 1981, *Structural Analysis of Discrete Data with Econometric Applications* (MIT Press, Cambridge, MA).

Markowitz, H., 1952, Portfolio selection, *The Journal of Finance* 7, 77–91.

Markowitz, H. M., 1991, Foundations of portfolio theory, *The Journal of Finance* 46, 469–477.

Markowitz, H. M., 2009, Proposals concerning the current financial crisis, *Financial Analysts Journal* 65, 25–27.

Marshall, J. A. R., 2011, Group selection and kin selection: formally equivalent approaches, *Trends in Ecology and Evolution* 26, 325–332.

Mata, J., P. Portugal, and P. Guimaraes, 1995, The survival of new plants: start-up conditions and post-entry evolution, *International Journal of Industrial Organization* 13, 459–481.

Matson, J., 2014, Fact or fiction?: Lead can be turned into gold, *Scientific American*, 14 January. https://www.scientificamerican.com/article/ fact-or-fiction-lead-can-be-turned-into-gold/, accessed 3 November 2022.

Matthews, G., D. M. Jones, and A. G. Chamberlain, 1990, Refining the measurement of mood: the UWIST mood adjective checklist, *British Journal of Psychology* 81, 17–42.

Maynard Smith, J., 1964, Group selection and kin selection, *Nature* 201, 1145–1147.

Maynard Smith, J., 1979, Evolutionary game theory, *Physica D: Nonlinear Phenomena* 22, 43–49.

Maynard Smith, J., 1982, *Evolution and the Theory of Games* (Cambridge University Press, Cambridge).

Maynard Smith, J., 1984, Game theory and the evolution of behaviour, *Behavioral and Brain Sciences* 7, 95–101.

Maynard Smith, J., and G. R. Price, 1973, The logic of animal conflict, *Nature* 246, 15–18.

Mayr, E., 2001, *What Evolution Is* (Basic Books, New York).

McAlmond, R., 2008, Too much emphasis on quantitative methods instead of ethics? *Financial Analysts Journal* 64, 10.

McCrae, R., and P. Costa, 1996, Toward a new generation of personality theories: theoretical contexts for the five-factor model, in J. Wiggins, *The Five-factor Model of Personality: Theoretical Perspectives* (Guilford, New York).

McCulloch, W. S., and W. Pitts, 1943, A logical calculus of the ideas immanent in nervous activity, *The Bulletin of Mathematical Biophysics* 5, 115–133.

McFadden, D., 1973, Conditional logit analysis of qualitative choice behavior, in P. Zarembka, *Frontiers in Econometrics* 105–142 (Academic Press, New York).

McGuffin, P., B. Riley, and R. Plomin, 2001, Toward behavioral genomics, *Science* 291, 1232–1249.

McIntosh, D., R. Zajonc, P. Vig, and S. Emerick, 1997, Facial movement, breathing, temperature, and affect: implications of the vascular theory of emotional efference, *Cognition and Emotion* 11, 171–196.

McKenzie, C. R., 2003, Rational models as theories–not standards–of behavior, *Trends in Cognitive Sciences* 7, 403–406.

McNamara, J. M., 1995, Implicit frequency dependence and kin selection in fluctuating environments, *Evolutionary Ecology* 9, 185–203.

Mehra, R., and E. Prescott, 1985, The equity premium puzzle, *Journal of Monetary Economics* 15, 145–161.

Merton, R. C., 1973, Theory of rational option pricing, *The Bell Journal of Economics and Management Science* 4, 141–183.

Merton, R. C., 1980, On estimating the expected return on the market: an exploratory investigation, *Journal of Financial Economics* 8, 323–361.

Merton, R. C., 1981, On market timing and investment performance. I. An equilibrium theory of value for market forecasts, *Journal of Business* 54, 363–406.

Merton, R. C., 1993, Operation and regulation in financial intermediation: a functional perspective, in P. Englund, *Operation and Regulation of Financial Markets*, 4–67 (Economic Council, Stockholm).

Merton, R. C., 1995a, Financial innovation and the management and regulation of financial institutions, *Journal of Banking & Finance* 19, 461–481.

Merton, R. C., 1995b, A functional perspective of financial intermediation, *Financial Management* 24, 23–41.

Merton, R. C., and Z. Bodie, 1993, Deposit insurance reform: a functional approach, in *Carnegie-Rochester Conference Series on Public Policy*, volume 38, 1–34 (Elsevier, Amsterdam).

Merton, R. C., and Z. Bodie, 1995, Financial infrastructure and public policy: a functional perspective, in D. B. Crane, K. A. Froot, S. P. Mason, A. Perold, R. C. Merton, Z. Bodie, E. R. Sirri, and P. Tufano, *The Global Financial System: A Functional Perspective*, 263–282 (Harvard Business School Press, Boston, MA).

Merton, R. C., and Z. Bodie, 2006, Design of financial systems: towards a synthesis of function and structure, in H. G. Fong, *The World of Risk Management*, 1–27 (World Scientific, Hackensack).

Merton, R. K., 1960, *The Ambivalences of LeBon's The Crowd, Introduction to the Compass Books Edition of Gustave LeBon* (Viking, New York).

Mery, F., and T. J. Kawecki, 2002, Experimental evolution of learning ability in fruit flies, *Proceedings of the National Academy of Sciences* 99, 14274–14279.

Meyn, S. S. P., and R. L. Tweedie, 2009, *Markov Chains and Stochastic Stability* (Cambridge University Press, Cambridge).

Milgram, S., 1963, Behavioral study of obedience, *The Journal of Abnormal and Social Psychology* 67, 371–378.

Minsky, H. P., 2008, *Stabilizing an Unstable Economy* (McGraw-Hill, New York).

Mirollo, R. E., and S. H. Strogatz, 1990, Synchronization of pulse-coupled biological oscillators, *SIAM Journal on Applied Mathematics* 50, 1645–1662.

Mishkin, F. S., 1997, *The Economics of Money, Banking, and Financial Markets*, fifth edition (Addison-Wesley, Reading, MA).

Mitchell, M., and T. Pulvino, 2001, Characteristics of risk and return in risk arbitrage, *The Journal of Finance* 56, 2135–2175.

Mittal, V., and W. T. Ross Jr, 1998, The impact of positive and negative affect and issue framing on issue interpretation and risk taking, *Organizational Behavior and Human Decision Processes* 76, 298–324.

Modigliani, F., and R. A. Cohn, 1979, Inflation, rational valuation and the market, *Financial Analysts Journal* 35, 24–44.

Modigliani, F., and M. H. Miller, 1958, The cost of capital, corporation finance and the theory of investment, *American Economic Review* 48, 261–297.

Montague, P. R., and G. S. Berns, 2002, Neural economics and the biological substrates of valuation, *Neuron* 36, 265–284.

Montier, J., 2007, The myth of exogenous risk and the recent quant problems. Available at: http://behaviouralinvesting.blogspot.com/2007/09/myth-of-exogenous-risk-and-recent-quant.html, accessed 4 January 2014

Moore, G. E., 1965, Cramming more components onto integrated circuits, *Electronics* 38, 114–117.

Mossin, J., 1966, Equilibrium in a capital asset market, *Econometrica* 34, 768–783.

Mozer, M. C., H. Pashler, and H. Homaei, 2008, Optimal predictions in everyday cognition: the wisdom of individuals or crowds? *Cognitive Science* 32, 1133–1147.

Murphy, K. J., 1999, Executive compensation, in O. Ashenfelter and D. Card, *Handbook of Labor Economics*, volume 3, 2485–2563 (North Holland, Amsterdam).

Muth, J. F., 1961, Rational expectations and the theory of price movements, *Econometrica* 29, 315–335.

Neely, C. J., P. A. Weller, and J. M. Ulrich, 2009, The adaptive markets hypothesis: evidence from the foreign exchange market, *Journal of Financial and Quantitative Analysis* 44, 467–488.

Nelson, R., and S. Winter, 1982, *An Evolutionary Theory of Economic Change* (Harvard University Press, Cambridge, MA).

Newcombe, R. G., 1998, Two-sided confidence intervals for the single proportion: comparison of seven methods, *Statistics in Medicine* 17, 857–872.

Newey, W. K., and K. D. West, 1987, A simple, positive semi-definite, heteroskedasticity and autocorrelation consistent covariance matrix, *Econometrica* 55, 703–708.

Nicholson, N., E. Soane, M. Fenton-O'Creevy, and P. Willman, 2005, Personality and domain-specific risk taking, *Journal of Risk Research* 8, 157–176.

Niederhoffer, V., 1997, *The Education of a Speculator* (John Wiley & Sons, New York).

Nolder, C., and T. J. Riley, 2014, Effects of differences in national culture on auditors' judgements and decisions: a literature review of cross-cultural auditing studies from a judgment and decision making perspective, *Auditing: A Journal of Practice & Theory* 33, 141–164.

Nowak, M. A., 2006, Five rules for the evolution of cooperation, *Science* 314, 1560–1563.

Nowak, M., and R. Highfield, 2011, *SuperCooperators: Altruism, Evolution, and Why We Need Each Other to Succeed* (Simon & Schuster, New York).

Nowak, M., and R. M. May, 1992, Evolutionary games and spatial chaos, *Nature* 359, 826–829.

Nowak, M., A. Sasaki, C. Taylor, and D. Fudenberg, 2004, Emergence of cooperation and evolutionary stability in finite populations, *Nature* 428, 646–650.

Nowak, M. A., C. E. Tarnita, and E. O. Wilson, 2010, The evolution of eusociality, *Nature* 466, 1057–1062.

Odean, T., 1998, Are investors reluctant to realize their losses? *The Journal of Finance* 53, 1775–1798.

Odier, P., and B. Solnik, 1993, Lessons for international asset allocation, *Financial Analysts Journal* 49, 63–77.

Office of Personnel Management, 2019, 2019 federal employee viewpoint survey: agency ratings, Available at: https://www.opm.gov/fevs/reports/governmentwide-reports/governmentwide-management-report/governmentwide-report/2019/appendixg-fevs-indices-gsi.xls, accessed 15 March 2022.

Okasha, S., 2013, The evolution of Bayesian updating, *Philosophy of Science* 80, 745–757.

Okasha, S., and K. Binmore, 2012, *Evolution and Rationality: Decisions, Co-operation and Strategic Behaviour* (Cambridge University Press, Cambridge).

Olds, J., and P. Milner, 1954, Positive reinforcement produced by electrical stimulation of septal area and other regions of rat brain, *Journal of Comparative and Physiological Psychology* 47, 419–427.

O'Reilly, C. A., and J. Chatman, 1996, Culture as social control: corporations, culture, and commitment, in B. M. Staw and L. L. Cummings, *Research in Organizational Behavior*, volume 18, 157–200 (JAI Press, Greenwich, CT).

Orr, H. A., 2017, Evolution, finance, and the population genetics of relative wealth, *Journal of Bioeconomics*, 20, 29–48.

Oster, E., 2020, Health recommendations and selection in health behaviors, *American Economic Review: Insights* 2, 143–160.

Oster, G. F., and E. O. Wilson, 1979, *Caste and Ecology in the Social Insects* (Princeton University Press, Princeton, NJ).

Ozik, G., and R. Sadka, 2015, Skin in the game versus skimming the game: governance, share restrictions, and insider flows, *Journal of Financial and Quantitative Analysis* 50, 1293–1319.

Palmer, R. G., W. B. Arthur, J. H. Holland, B. LeBaron, and P. Tayler, 1994, Artificial economic life: a simple model of a stockmarket, *Physica D: Nonlinear Phenomena* 75, 264–274.

Pan, Y., S. Siegel, and T. Y. Wang, 2017, Corporate risk culture, *Journal of Financial and Quantitative Analysis* 52, 2327–2367.

Panageas, S., and M. M. Westerfield, 2009, High-water marks: high risk appetites? Convex compensation, long horizons, and portfolio choice, *The Journal of Finance* 64, 1–36.

Papillo, J., and D. Shapiro, 1990, The cardiovascular system, in J. Cacioppo and L. Tassinary, *Principles of Psychophysiology: Physical, Social, and Inferential Elements* (Cambridge University Press, Cambridge).

Parkinson, B., 1995, *Ideas and Realities of Emotion* (Psychology Press, London).

Pasteels, J. M., J. L. Deneubourg, and S. Goss, 1987, Self-organization mechanisms in ant societies. I: Trail recruitment to newly discovered food sources, *Experientia. Supplementum* 54, 155–175.

Pástor, L., and R. F. Stambaugh, 2000, Comparing asset pricing models: an investment perspective, *Journal of Financial Economics* 56, 335–381.

Pástor, L., and R. F. Stambaugh, 2003, Liquidity risk and expected stock returns, *Journal of Political Economy* 111, 642–685.

Pastor, L., and P. Veronesi, 2020, Inequality aversion, populism, and the backlash against globalization, Technical Report, National Bureau of Economic Research.

Patton, A. J., and T. Ramadorai, 2013, On the high-frequency dynamics of hedge fund risk exposures, *The Journal of Finance* 68, 597–635.

Patton, A. J., T. Ramadorai, and M. Streatfield, 2015, Change you can believe in? Hedge fund data revisions, *The Journal of Finance* 70, 963–999.

Pekalski, A., 1998, A model of population dynamics, *Physica A: Statistical Mechanics and its Applications* 252, 325–335.

Pekalski, A., 1999, Mutations and changes of the environment in a model of biological evolution, *Physica A: Statistical Mechanics and its Applications* 265, 255–263.

Pekalski, A., 2002, Evolution of population in changing conditions, *Physica A: Statistical Mechanics and its Applications* 314, 114–119.

Peltzman, S., 1975, The effects of automobile safety regulation, *Journal of Political Economy* 83, 677–725.

Perner, J., and H. Wimmer, 1985, "John thinks that Mary thinks that…" attribution of second-order beliefs by 5-to 10-year-old children, *Journal of Experimental Child Psychology* 39, 437–471.

Perold, A. F., and W. F. Sharpe, 1995, Dynamic strategies for asset allocation, *Financial Analysts Journal* 51, 149–160.

Perrow, C., 1984, *Normal Accidents: Living with High Risk Technologies* (Basic Books, New York).

Perrow, C., 1999, *Normal Accidents: Living with High Risk Technologies–Updated Edition* (Princeton University Press, Princeton, NJ).

Peters, E., and P. Slovic, 2000, The springs of action: affective and analytical information processing in choice, *Personality and Social Psychology Bulletin* 26, 1465–1475.

Pfennig, D. W., J. P. Collins, and R. E. Ziemba, 1999, A test of alternative hypotheses for kin recognition in cannibalistic tiger salamanders, *Behavioral Ecology* 10, 436–443.

Phelps, E. S., 1972, The statistical theory of racism and sexism, *American Economic Review* 62, 659–661.

Philippon, T., and A. Reshef, 2009, Wages and human capital in the US financial industry: 1909–2006, Working Paper 14644, National Bureau of Economic Research.

Philippon, T., and A. Reshef, 2012, Wages and human capital in the US finance industry: 1909–2006, *The Quarterly Journal of Economics* 127, 1551–1609.

Pinker, S., 1979, Formal models of language learning, *Cognition* 7, 217–283.

Pinker, S., 1991, Rules of language, *Science* 253, 530–535.

Pinker, S., 1994, *The Language Instinct: How the Mind Creates Language* (William Morrow and Company, New York).

Pinker, S., 2012, The false allure of group selection, Technical Report, Edge.com.

Plantin, G., H. Sapra, and H. S. Shin, 2008, Marking-to-market: panacea or pandora's box? *Journal of Accounting Research* 46, 435–460.

Plomin, R., 1990, *Nature and Nurture: An Introduction to Human Behavioral Genetics* (Brooks/Cole Publishing Company, Pacific Grove, CA).

Plomin, R., M. Owen, and P. McGuffin, 1994, The genetic basis of complex human behaviors, *Science* 264, 1733–1739.

Plous, S., 1993, *The Psychology of Judgment and Decision Making.* (Mcgraw-Hill, New York).

Pohley, H.-J., and B. Thomas, 1983, Non-linear ESS-models and frequency dependent selection, *Biosystems* 16, 87–100.

Post, T., M. J. Van den Assem, G. Baltussen, and R. H. Thaler, 2008, Deal or no deal? Decision making under risk in a large-payoff game show, *American Economic Review* 98, 38–71.

Pratt, J. W., 1964, Risk aversion in the small and in the large, *Econometrica* 32, 122–136.

Price, G. R., 1970, Selection and covariance, *Nature* 227, 520–521.

Qi, H., and D. Sun, 2006, A quadratically convergent Newton method for computing the nearest correlation matrix, *SIAM Journal on Matrix Analysis and Applications* 28, 360–385.

Queller, D. C., 1992, Quantitative genetics, inclusive fitness, and group selection, *The American Naturalist* 139, 540–558.

Queller, D. C., and J. E. Strassmann, 1998, Kin selection and social insects, *Bioscience* 48, 165–175.

Quercia, R. G., and L. Ding, 2009, Loan modifications and redefault risk: an examination of short-term impacts, *Cityscape* 11, 171–193.

Rabin, M., and R. H. Thaler, 2001, Anomalies: risk aversion, *Journal of Economic Perspectives* 15, 219–232.

Rajan, R. G., 2006, Has finance made the world riskier? *European Financial Management* 12, 499–533.

Ralston, A., 2004, *Between a Rock and a Hard Place* (Atria Books, New York).

Ramadorai, T., 2012, The secondary market for hedge funds and the closed hedge fund premium, *The Journal of Finance* 67, 479–512.

Ramadorai, T., 2013, Capacity constraints, investor information, and hedge fund returns, *Journal of Financial Economics* 107, 401–416.

Rangel, A., C. Camerer, and R. Montague, 2008, A framework for studying the neurobiology of value-based decision-making, *Nature Reviews Neuroscience* 9, 545–556.

Rasekhschaffe, K. C., and R. C. Jones, 2019, Machine learning for stock selection, *Financial Analysts Journal* 75, 70–88.

Real, L., and T. Caraco, 1986, Risk and foraging in stochastic environments, *Annual Review of Ecology and Systematics* 17, 371–390.

Real, L. A., 1980, Fitness, uncertainty, and the role of diversification in evolution and behavior, *The American Naturalist* 115, 623–638.

Reinganum, M. R., 1981, Abnormal returns in small firm portfolios, *Financial Analysts Journal* 37, 52–56.

Reinganum, M. R., 2009, Setting national priorities: financial challenges facing the Obama administration, *Financial Analysts Journal* 65, 32–35.

Reinhart, C. M., and K. S. Rogoff, 2008, Is the 2007 US sub-prime financial crisis so different? An international historical comparison, *American Economic Review* 98, 339–344.

Reinhart, C. M., and K. S. Rogoff, 2009, *This Time is Different: Eight Centuries of Financial Folly* (Princeton University Press, Princeton, NJ).

Resulaj, A., R. Kiani, D. M. Wolpert, and M. N. Shadlen, 2009, Changes of mind in decision-making, *Nature* 461, 263–266.

Riedl, C., Y. J. Kim, P. Gupta, T. W. Malone, and A. W. Woolley, 2021, Quantifying collective intelligence in human groups, *Proceedings of the National Academy of Sciences* 118, e20057371.

Rimm-Kaufman, S. E., and J. Kagan, 1996, The psychological significance of changes in skin temperature, *Motivation and Emotion* 20, 63–78.

Riniolo, T. C., and S. W. Porges, 2000, Evaluating group distributional characteristics: why psychophysiologists should be interested in qualitative departures from the normal distribution, *Psychophysiology* 37, 21–28.

Rivest, R. L., A. Shamir, and L. Adleman, 1978, A method for obtaining digital signatures and public-key cryptosystems, *Communications of the ACM* 21, 120–126.

Rizzolatti, G., and M. Fabbri-Destro, 2010, Mirror neurons: from discovery to autism, *Experimental Brain Research* 200, 223–237.

Robatto, R., and B. Szentes, 2013, On the biological foundation of risk preferences, Working Paper.

Roberts, H. V., 1959, Stock-market "patterns" and financial analysis: methodological suggestions, *The Journal of Finance* 14, 1–10.

Roberts, S. O., and M. T. Rizzo, 2020, The psychology of American racism, *American Psychologist* 76, 475–487.

Robson, A. J., 1992, Status, the distribution of wealth, private and social attitudes to risk, *Econometrica* 60, 837–857.

Robson, A. J., 1996a, A biological basis for expected and non-expected utility, *Journal of Economic Theory* 68, 397–424.

Robson, A. J., 1996b, The evolution of attitudes to risk: lottery tickets and relative wealth, *Games and Economic Behavior* 14, 190–207.

Robson, A. J., 2001a, The biological basis of economic behavior, *Journal of Economic Literature* 39, 11–33.

Robson, A. J., 2001b, Why would nature give individuals utility functions? *Journal of Political Economy* 109, 900–914.

Robson, A. J., and L. Samuelson, 2007, The evolution of intertemporal incentives, *American Economic Review* 97, 492–495.

Robson, A. J., and L. Samuelson, 2009, The evolution of time preference with aggregate uncertainty, *American Economic Review* 99, 925–1,953.

Robson, A. J., and B. Szentes, 2008, Evolution of time preference by natural selection: comment, *American Economic Review* 98, 1178–1188.

Rodrik, D., 2018, Populism and the economics of globalization, *Journal of International Business Policy* 1, 12–33.

Rodrik, D., 2020, Why does globalization fuel populism? Economics, culture, and the rise of right-wing populism, Technical Report, National Bureau of Economic Research.

Rogers, A. R., 1994, Evolution of time preference by natural selection, *American Economic Review* 84, 460–481.

Roll, R., 1984, A simple implicit measure of the effective bid-ask spread in an efficient market, *The Journal of Finance* 39, 1127–1139.

Roll, R., 2011, The possible misdiagnosis of a crisis, *Financial Analysts Journal* 67, 12–17.

Rolls, E. T., 1990, A theory of emotion, and its application to understanding the neural basis of emotion, *Cognition & Emotion* 4, 161–190.

Rolls, E. T., 1992, Neurophysiology and functions of the primate amygdala, in J. Aggelton, *The Amygdala: Neurobiological Aspects of Emotion, Memory, and Mental Dysfunction*, 143–166 (John Wiley & Sons, New York).

Rolls, E. T., 1994, A theory of emotion and consciousness, and its application to understanding the neural basis of emotion, in M. Gazzaniga, *The Cognitive Neurosciences*, 1091–1106 (MIT Press, Cambridge, MA).

Rolls, E. T., 1999, *The Brain and Emotion* (Oxford University Press, Oxford).

Roncalli, T., and J. Teiletche, 2008, An alternative approach to alternative beta, *Journal of Financial Transformation* 24, 43–52.

Roncalli, T., and G. Weisang, 2010, Tracking problems, hedge fund replication and alternative beta, *Journal of Financial Transformation* 31, 19–29.

Rosano, A., L. D. Botto, B. Botting, and P. Mastroiacovo, 2000, Infant mortality and congenital anomalies from 1950 to 1994: an international perspective, *Journal of Epidemiology and Community Health* 54, 660–666.

Rosenberg, B., and J. Guy, 1976a, Prediction of beta from investment fundamentals: part one, *Financial Analysts Journal* 32, 60–72.

Rosenberg, B., and J. Guy, 1976b, Prediction of beta from investment fundamentals: part two, *Financial Analysts Journal* 32, 62–72.

Ross, C., and A. Wilke, 2011, Past and present environments, *Journal of Evolutionary Psychology* 9, 275–278.

Rothenberg, J., 1960, Non-convexity, aggregation, and Pareto optimality, *Journal of Political Economy* 68, 435–468.

Rothman, M., 2007a, Rebalance of large cap quant portfolio, US Equity Quantitative Strategies, Lehman Brothers Research.

Rothman, M., 2007b, Turbulent times in quant land, US Equity Quantitative Strategies, Lehman Brothers Research.

Rothman, M., 2007c, View from quantland: where do we go now? US Equity Quantitative Strategies, Lehman Brothers Research.

Rubenstein, D. I., 1982, Risk, uncertainty and evolutionary strategies, in S. R. Schulman and D. I. Rubenstein, *Current Problems in Sociobiology*, 91–111 (Cambridge University Press, Cambridge).

Rubinstein, A., 2002, Irrational diversification in multiple decision problems, *European Economic Review* 46, 1369–1378.

Rubinstein, M., 1976, The valuation of uncertain income streams and the pricing of options, *The Bell Journal of Economics* 7, 407–425.

Rubinstein, M., and H. E. Leland, 1981, Replicating options with positions in stock and cash, *Financial Analysts Journal* 37, 63–72.

Russell, J. A., 1980, A circumplex model of affect, *Journal of Personality and Social Psychology* 39, 1161–1178.

Sacks, O. W., 1974, *Awakenings* (Doubleday, Garden City, NY).

Sadka, R., 2010, Liquidity risk and the cross-section of hedge-fund returns, *Journal of Financial Economics* 98, 54–71.

Sadka, R., 2012, Hedge-fund performance and liquidity risk, *Journal of Investment Management* 10, 60–72.

Safarzyńska, K., and J. C. van den Bergh, 2010, Evolving power and environmental policy: explaining institutional change with group selection, *Ecological Economics* 69, 743–752.

Salgado, J. F., 1997, The five factor model of personality and job performance in the European community, *Journal of Applied Psychology* 82, 30–43.

Samuelson, L., 2001, Introduction to the evolution of preferences, *Journal of Economic Theory* 97, 225–230.

Samuelson, P. A., 1947, *Foundations of Economic Analysis* (Harvard University Press, Cambridge, MA).

Samuelson, P. A., 1948, *Economics* (McGraw-Hill, New York).

Samuelson, P. A., 1958, An exact consumption-loan model of interest with or without the social contrivance of money, *Journal of Political Economy* 66, 467–482.

Samuelson, P. A., 1965, Proof that properly anticipated prices fluctuate randomly, *Industrial Management Review* 6, 41–49.

Samuelson, P. A., 1971, The fallacy of maximizing the geometric mean in long sequences of investing or gambling, *Proceedings of the National Academy of Sciences* 68, 2493–2496.

Samuelson, P. A., 1998, How foundations came to be, *Journal of Economic Literature* 36, 1375–1386.

Sanborn, A., and T. L. Griffiths, 2008, Markov chain Monte Carlo with people, in J. Platt, D. Koller, Y. Singer, and S. Roweis, *Advances in Neural Information Processing Systems 20 (NIPS 2007)*, 1265–1272 (Curran Associates Inc., New York).

Sandroni, A., 2000, Do markets favor agents able to make accurate predictions? *Econometrica* 68, 1303–1341.

Sandroni, A., 2005, Market selection when markets are incomplete, *Journal of Mathematical Economics* 41, 91–104.

Santos, M. S., and M. Woodford, 1997, Rational asset pricing bubbles, *Econometrica* 65, 19–57.

Sapra, H., 2008, Do accounting measurement regimes matter? A discussion of mark-to-market accounting and liquidity pricing, *Journal of Accounting and Economics* 45, 379–387.

Saver, J. L., and A. R. Damasio, 1991, Preserved access and processing of social knowledge in a patient with acquired sociopathy due to ventromedial frontal damage, *Neuropsychologia* 29, 1241–1249.

Schein, E. H., 2004, *Organizational Culture and Leadership* (Jossey-Bass, San Francisco, CA).

Schneeweis, T. R., H. Kazemi, and E. Szado, 2011, Hedge fund database "deconstruction": are hedge fund databases half full or half empty? *The Journal of Alternative Investments* 14, 65–88.

Schneeweis, T. R., and R. B. Spurgin, 1998, Multifactor analysis of hedge fund, managed futures, and mutual fund return and risk characteristics, *The Journal of Alternative Investments* 1, 1–24.

Schneeweis, T. R., R. Spurgin, and D. McCarthy, 1996, Survivor bias in commodity trading advisor performance, *The Journal of Futures Markets (1986–1998)* 16, 757–772.

Schneider, D. J., 2005, *The Psychology of Stereotyping* (Guilford Press, New York).

Schoemaker, P. J. H., 1982, The expected utility model: its variants, purposes, evidence and limitations, *Journal of Economic Literature* 20, 529–563.

Schoenemann, P. T., 2006, Evolution of the size and functional areas of the human brain, *Annual Review of Anthropology* 35, 379–406.

Schoenemann, P. T., M. J. Sheehan, and L. D. Glotzer, 2005, Prefrontal white matter volume is disproportionately larger in humans than in other primates, *Nature Neuroscience* 8, 242–252.

Schultz, W., 2002, Getting formal with dopamine and reward, *Neuron* 36, 241–263.

Schumpeter, J. A., 1939, *Business Cycles: A Theoretical, Historical, And Statistical Analysis of the Capitalist Process* (McGraw-Hill, New York).

Schwager, J., 1989, *Market Wizards: Interviews with Top Traders* (New York Institute of Finance, New York).

Schwager, J., 1992, *The New Market Wizards: Conversations with America's Top Traders* (Harper Business, New York).

Securities and Exchange Commission, 2009, *Investigation of Failure of the SEC to Uncover Bernard Madoff's Ponzi Scheme* (Government Printing Office, Washington, DC), Public version. Report OIG-509. August 31.

Securities and Exchange Commission, 2014, *Agency Financial Report: Fiscal Year 2014* (Securities and Exchange Commission, Washington, DC).

Segaran, T., 2007, *Programming Collective Intelligence: Building Smart Web 2.0 Applications* (O'Reilly Media, Inc, Sebastopol).

Seger, J., and H. J. Brockmann, 1987, What is bet-hedging? *Oxford Surveys in Evolutionary Biology* 4, 182–211.

Sender, H., K. Kelly, and G. Zuckerman, 2007, Goldman wagers on cash infusion to show resolve, *Wall Street Journal*, August 14.

Senior, C., 2006, CDOs explode after growing interest, *FT Mandate*.

Serfling, R., 1980, *Approximation Theorems of Mathematical Statistics* (John Wiley & Sons, New York).

Shanks, D. R., R. J. Tunney, and J. D. McCarthy, 2002, A re-examination of probability matching and rational choice, *Journal of Behavioral Decision Making* 15, 233–250.

Shannon, C. E., 1948, A mathematical theory of communication, *The Bell System Technical Journal* 27, 379–423.

Shapira, Z., 1995, *Risk Taking: A Managerial Perspective* (Russell Sage Foundation, New York).

Shapiro, J., and M. Dworkin, 1997, *Bacteria as Multicellular Organisms* (Oxford University Press, New York).

Shapiro-Mendoza, C. K., M. Kimball, K. M. Tomashek, R. N. Anderson, and S. Blanding, 2009, US infant mortality trends attributable to accidental suffocation and strangulation in bed from 1984 through 2004: are rates increasing? *Pediatrics* 123, 533–539.

Sharpe, W., 1964, Capital asset prices: a theory of market equilibrium under conditions of risk, *The Journal of Finance* 19, 425–442.

Sharpe, W. F., 1972, Risk, market sensitivity and diversification, *Financial Analysts Journal* 28, 74–79.

Sharpe, W. F., 2010, Adaptive asset allocation policies, *Financial Analysts Journal* 66, 45–59.

Shaver, P. R., and K. A. Brennan, 1991, Measures of depression, *Measures of Personality and Social Psychological Attitudes* 1, 195–289.

Shawky, H. A., N. Dai, and D. Cumming, 2012, Diversification in the hedge fund industry, *Journal of Corporate Finance* 18, 166–178.

Shefrin, H., and M. Statman, 1985, The disposition to sell winners too early and ride losers too long: theory and evidence, *The Journal of Finance* 40, 777–790.

Shefrin, H. M., and R. H. Thaler, 1988, The behavioral life-cycle hypothesis, *Economic Inquiry* 26, 609–643.

Shelp, R., and A. Ehrbar, 2009, *Fallen Giant: The Amazing Story of Hank Greenberg and the History of AIG* (John Wiley & Sons, Hoboken, NJ).

Shiller, R. J., 2003, From efficient markets theory to behavioral finance, *Journal of Economic Perspectives* 17, 83–104.

Shiller, R. J., 2005a, *Irrational Exuberance*, second edition (Princeton University Press, Princeton, NJ).

Shiller, R. J., 2005b, 'Irrational exuberance'—again, CNN Money, January 25. http://money.cnn.com/2005/01/13/real_estate/realestate_shiller1_0502/.

Sias, R., H. J. Turtle, and B. Zykaj, 2016, Hedge fund crowds and mispricing, *Management Science* 62, 764–784.

Siegel, S., 1960, Decision making and learning under varying conditions of reinforcement, *Annals of the New York Academy of Sciences* 89, 766–783.

Simon, H. A., 1955, A behavioral model of rational choice, *The Quarterly Journal of Economics* 69, 99–118.

Simon, H. A., 1957, *Models of Man; Social and Rational* (Wiley, New York).

Simon, H. A., 1981, *The Sciences of the Artificial*, second edition (MIT Press, Cambridge, MA).

Simon, H. A., 1997, *Administrative Behavior: A Study of Decision-Making Processes in Administrative Organizations*, fourth edition (Free Press, New York).

Singh, M, Q. Xu, S. J. Wang, T. Hong, M. M. Ghassemi, and A. W. Lo, 2022, Real-time extended psychophysiological analysis of financial risk processing, *PLoS One* 17, e0269752.

Sinquefield, R. A., 1996, Where are the gains from international diversification? *Financial Analysts Journal* 52, 8–14.

Sirota-Madi, A., T. Olender, Y. Helman, C. Ingham, I. Brainis, D. Roth, E. Hagi, L. Brodsky, D. Leshkowitz, V. Galatenko, V. Nikolaev, R. Mugasimangalam, S. Bransburg-Zabary, D. Gutnick, D. Lancet, and E. Ben-Jacob, 2010, Genome sequence of the pattern forming *Paenibacillus vortex* bacterium reveals potential for thriving in complex environments, *BMC Genomics* 11, 710.

Sitkin, S. B., and A. L. Pablo, 1992, Reconceptualizing the determinants of risk behavior, *Academy of Management Review* 17, 9–38.

Sitkin, S. B., and L. R. Weingart, 1995, Determinants of risky decision-making behavior: a test of the mediating role of risk perceptions and propensity, *Academy of Management Journal* 38, 1573–1592.

Skyrms, B., 2000, Game theory, rationality and evolution of the social contract, *Journal of Consciousness Studies* 7, 269–84.

Skyrms, B., 2014, *Evolution of the Social Contract* (Cambridge University Press, Cambridge).

Slatkin, M., 1974, Hedging one's evolutionary bets, *Nature* 250, 704–705.

Slovic, P. E., 2000, *The Perception of Risk* (Earthscan Publications, London).

Smaers, J. B., J. Steele, C. R. Case, A. Cowper, K. Amunts, and K. Zilles, 2011, Primate prefrontal cortex evolution: human brains are the extreme of a lateralized ape trend, *Brain, Behavior and Evolution* 77, 67–78.

Smallwood, P., 1996, An introduction to risk sensitivity: the use of Jensen's inequality to clarify evolutionary arguments of adaptation and constraint, *American Zoologist* 36, 392–401.

Smith, C. W., 2005, Financial edgework: trading in market currents, in S. Lyng, *Edgework: The Sociology of Risk Taking*, 203–217 (Routledge, London).

Smith, K., J. Dickhaut, K. McCabe, and J. Pardo, 2002, Neuronal substrates for choice under ambiguity, risk, gains and losses, *Management Science* 48, 711–718.

Smith, W. L., and W. E. Wilkinson, 1969, On branching processes in random environments, *The Annals of Mathematical Statistics* 40, 814–827.

Snow, R., 2013, *I Invented the Modern Age: The Rise of Henry Ford* (Simon and Schuster, New York).

Sobel, R. S., and T. M. Nesbit, 2007, Automobile safety regulation and the incentive to drive recklessly: evidence from NASCAR, *Southern Economic Journal* 74, 71–84.

Sober, E., and D. S. Wilson, 1998, *Unto Others: The Evolution and Psychology of Unselfish Behavior* (Harvard University Press, Cambridge, MA).

Société Générale, 2008, Mission green: summary report, Technical Report, Société Générale. English translation. Accessed 20 September 2014.

Soramäki, K., M. L. Bech, J. Arnold, R. J. Glass, and W. E. Beyeler, 2007, The topology of interbank payment flows, *Physica A: Statistical Mechanics and its Applications* 379, 317–333.

Sørensen, J. B., 2002, The strength of corporate culture and the reliability of firm performance, *Administrative Science Quarterly* 47, 70–91.

Spitzer, M., U. Fischbacher, B. Herrnberger, G. Grön, and E. Fehr, 2007, The neural signature of social norm compliance, *Neuron* 56, 185–196.

Sraffa, P., 1926, The laws of returns under competitive conditions, *Economic Journal* 36, 535–550.

Stanovich, K. E., and R. F. West, 2000, Advancing the rationality debate, *Behavioral and Brain Sciences* 23, 701–717.

Starr, R. M., 1969, Quasi-equilibria in markets with non-convex preferences, *Econometrica* 37, 25–38.

Statman, M., 2009, Regulating financial markets: protecting us from ourselves and others, *Financial Analysts Journal* 65, 22–31.

Steenbarger, B. N., 2002, *The Psychology of Trading: Tools and Techniques for Minding the Markets* (John Wiley & Sons, New York).

Steinberg, L., 2008, A social neuroscience perspective on adolescent risk-taking, *Developmental Review* 28, 78–106.

Stemme, K., and P. Slattery, 2002, Hedge fund investments: do it yourself or hire a contractor? *Journal of Retirement* 2002, 60–68.

Stephens, D. W., and J. R. Krebs, 1986, *Foraging Theory* (Princeton University Press, Princeton, NJ).

Steyvers, M., J. B. Tenenbaum, E.-J. Wagenmakers, and B. Blum, 2003, Inferring causal networks from observations and interventions, *Cognitive Science* 27, 453–489.

Stock, J. H., and M. W. Watson, 2002, Has the business cycle changed and why? *NBER Macroeconomics Annual* 17, 159–218.

Strassmann, J. E., R. E. Page Jr, G. E. Robinson, and T. D. Seeley, 2011, Kin selection and eusociality, *Nature* 471, E5–E6.

Strens, M., 2000, A Bayesian framework for reinforcement learning, *ICML* 2000, 943–950.

Strogatz, S. H., and I. Stewart, 1993, Coupled oscillators and biological synchronization, *Scientific American* 269, 102–109.

Strotz, R. H., 1955, Myopia and inconsistency in dynamic utility maximization, *The Review of Economic Studies* 23, 165–180.

Stroyan, K., 1983, Myopic utility functions on sequential economies, *Journal of Mathematical Economics* 11, 267–276.

Suchow, J. W., D. D. Bourgin, and T. L. Griffiths, 2017, Evolution in mind: evolutionary dynamics, cognitive processes, and Bayesian inference, *Trends in Cognitive Sciences* 21, 522–530.

Sun, Z., A. Wang, and L. Zheng, 2012, The road less traveled: strategy distinctiveness and hedge fund performance, *Review of Financial Studies* 25, 96–143.

Surowiecki, J., 2005, *The Wisdom of Crowds* (Anchor, New York).

Swank, D., and H.-G. Betz, 2003, Globalization, the welfare state and right-wing populism in western europe, *Socio-Economic Review* 1, 215–245.

Swedroe, L. E., 2005, *The Only Guide to a Winning Investment Strategy You'll Ever Need* (St. Martin's Press, New York).

Szpiro, G. G., 1986, Relative risk aversion around the world, *Economics Letters* 20, 19–21.

Tanny, D., 1981, On multitype branching processes in a random environment, *Advances in Applied Probability* 13, 464–491.

Tatham Jr, C., 1945, A brief history of the society, *Financial Analysts Journal* 1, 3–5.

Tattersall, I., 2008, An evolutionary framework for the acquisition of symbolic cognition by *Homo sapiens*, *Comparative Cognition & Behavior Reviews* 3, 157–166.

Tenenbaum, J. B., T. L. Griffiths, and C. Kemp, 2006, Theory-based Bayesian models of inductive learning and reasoning, *Trends in Cognitive Sciences* 10, 309–318.

Tenenbaum, J. B., C. Kemp, T. L. Griffiths, and N. D. Goodman, 2011, How to grow a mind: statistics, structure, and abstraction, *Science* 331, 1279–1285.

Teo, M., 2009, The geography of hedge funds, *Review of Financial Studies* 22, 3531–3561.

Teo, M., 2011, The liquidity risk of liquid hedge funds, *Journal of Financial Economics* 100, 24–44.

Tett, R. P., D. N. Jackson, and M. Rothstein, 1991, Personality measures as predictors of job performance: a meta-analytic review, *Personnel Psychology* 44, 703–742.

Thaler, R. H. (ed.), 1993, *Advances in Behavioral Finance* (Russell Sage Foundation, New York).

Thaler, R. H., and S. Benartzi, 2004, Save more tomorrow^{TM}: using behavioral economics to increase employee saving, *Journal of Political Economy* 112, S164–S187.

Thaler, R. H., and E. J. Johnson, 1990, Gambling with the house money and trying to break even: the effects of prior outcomes on risky choice, *Management Science* 36, 643–660.

Thaler, R. H., A. Tversky, D. Kahneman, and A. Schwartz, 1997, The effect of myopia and loss aversion on risk taking: an experimental test, *The Quarterly Journal of Economics* 112, 647–661.

Thomas, B., 1985, On evolutionarily stable sets, *Journal of Mathematical Biology* 22, 105–115.

Thorp, E. O., 1971, Portfolio choice and the Kelly criterion, *Proceedings of the American Statistical Association (Business and Economics Statistics Section)*, 215–224.

Thorp, E. O., 2006, The Kelly criterion in blackjack, sports betting and the stock market, in S. A. Zenios, and W. T. Ziemba, *Handbook of Asset and Liability Management, Handbooks in Finance*, 385–428 (North Holland, Amsterdam).

Thuijsman, F., B. Peleg, M. Amitai, and A. Shmida, 1995, Automata, matching and foraging behavior of bees, *Journal of Theoretical Biology* 175, 305–316.

Thurstone, L. L., 1927, A law of comparative judgment, *Psychological Review* 34, 273–286.

Tierney, J., 2011, Do you suffer from decision fatigue? *The New York Times*, August 17.

Tinic, S. M., 1972, The economics of liquidity services, *The Quarterly Journal of Economics* 86, 79–93.

Titman, S., and C. Tiu, 2011, Do the best hedge funds hedge? *Review of Financial Studies* 24, 123–168.

Tom, S. M., C. R. Fox, C. Trepel, and R. A. Poldrack, 2007, The neural basis of loss aversion in decision-making under risk, *Science* 315, 515–518.

Tooby, J., and L. Cosmides, 1995, Conceptual foundations of evolutionary psychology, in J. H. Barkow, L. Cosmides, and J. Tooby, *The Handbook of Evolutionary Psychology*, 5–67 (John Wiley & Sons, Hoboken, NJ).

Treynor, J. L., 1961, Market value, time, and risk, Unpublished manuscript.

Treynor, J. L., 1962, Toward a theory of market value of risky assets, Unpublished manuscript.

Treynor, J. L., 1965, How to rate management of investment funds, *Harvard Business Review* 43, 63–75.

Treynor, J., 1995, The only game in town, *Financial Analysts Journal* 51, 81–83.

Treynor, J., and K. Mazuy, 1966, Can mutual funds outguess the market? *Harvard Business Review* 44, 131–136.

Trivers, R. L., 1971, The evolution of reciprocal altruism, *The Quarterly Review of Biology* 46, 35–57.

Trivers, R. L., 1985, *Social Evolution* (Benjamin/Cummings, Menlo Park, CA).

Trivers, R. L., 2002, *Natural Selection and Social Theory: Selected Papers of Robert L. Trivers* (Oxford University Press, Oxford).

Tuljapurkar, S. D., 1990, *Population Dynamics in Variable Environments, Lecture Notes in Biomathematics* (Springer-Verlag, New York).

Turing, A. M., 1950, Computing machinery and intelligence, *Mind* 59, 433–460.

Tversky, A., and D. Kahneman, 1971, Belief in the law of small numbers, *Psychological Bulletin* 76, 105–110.

Tversky, A., and D. Kahneman, 1974, Judgment under uncertainty: heuristics and biases, *Science* 185, 1124–1131.

Tversky, A., and D. Kahneman, 1981, The framing of decisions and the psychology of choice, *Science* 211, 453–458.

Tversky, A., and D. Kahneman, 1983, Extensional versus intuitive reasoning: the conjunction fallacy in probability judgment, *Psychological Review* 90, 293–315.

Tversky, A., and D. Kahneman, 1992, Advances in prospect theory: cumulative representation of uncertainty, *Journal of Risk and Uncertainty* 5, 297–323.

US Treasury, 2013, Legacy securities public-private investment program update—quarter ended September 30, 2013, October 28.

Valukas, A. R., 2010, Report of Anton R. Valukas, examiner: Chapter 11, case no. 08-13555 (JMP), in re Lehman Brothers Holdings Inc., et al., debtors, Technical report, United States Bankruptcy Court, Southern District Of New York, Volume 3. March 11. Available at https://www.jenner.com/en/news-insights/news/lehman-brothers-holdings-inc-chapter-11-proceedings-examiner-s-report, accessed 24 August 2023.

van den Bergh, J. C., and J. M. Gowdy, 2009, A group selection perspective on economic behavior, institutions and organizations, *Journal of Economic Behavior and Organization* 72, 1–20.

Vassalou, M., 2003, News related to future GDP growth as a risk factor in equity returns, *Journal of Financial Economics* 68, 47–73.

Venkatesh, S. A., 2006, *Off the Books: The Underground Economy of the Urban Poor* (Harvard University Press, Cambridge, MA).

Vomfell, L., and N. Stewart, 2021, Officer bias, over-patrolling and ethnic disparities in stop and search, *Nature Human Behaviour* 5, 566–575.

von Neumann, J., and O. Morgenstern, 1944, *Theory of Games and Economic Behavior* (Princeton University Press, Princeton, NJ).

Vul, E., N. Goodman, T. L. Griffiths, and J. B. Tenenbaum, 2014, One and done? Optimal decisions from very few samples, *Cognitive Science* 38, 599–637.

Vul, E., and H. Pashler, 2008, Measuring the crowd within: probabilistic representations within individuals, *Psychological Science* 19, 645–647.

Vulkan, N., 2000, An economist's perspective on probability matching, *Journal of Economic Surveys* 14, 101–118.

Wade, M. J., D. S. Wilson, C. Goodnight, D. Taylor, Y. Bar-Yam, M. A. de Aguiar, B. Stacey, J. Werfel, G. A. Hoelzer, E. D. Brodie III, P. Fields, F. Breden, T. A. Linksvayer, J. A. Fletcher, P. J. Richerson, J. D. Bever, J. D. van Dyken, and P. Zee, 2010, Multilevel and kin selection in a connected world, *Nature* 463, E8–E9.

Waksberg, A. J., A. B. Smith, and M. Burd, 2009, Can irrational behaviour maximise fitness? *Behavioral Ecology and Sociobiology* 63, 461–471.

Waldman, M., 1994, Systematic errors and the theory of natural selection, *American Economic Review* 84, 482–497.

Wallerstein, E., N. S. Tuchschmid, and S. Zaker, 2009, How do hedge fund clones manage the real world? *The Journal of Alternative Investments* 12, 37–50.

Wäneryd, K.-E., 2001, *Stock-market Psychology: How People Value and Trade Stocks* (Edward Elgar Publishing, Cheltenham).

Wang, H., and D.-Y. Yeung, 2020, A survey on Bayesian deep learning, *ACM Computing Surveys (CSUR)* 53, 1–37.

Watts, D. J., 1999, *Small Worlds: The Dynamics of Networks Between Order and Randomness* (Princeton University Press, Princeton, NJ).

Watts, D. J., and S. H. Strogatz, 1998, Collective dynamics of 'small-world' networks, *Nature* 393, 440–442.

Weeks, J., 2004, *Unpopular Culture: The Ritual of Complaint in a British Bank* (University of Chicago Press, Chicago, IL).

Weibull, J. W., 1995, *Evolutionary Game Theory* (MIT Press, Cambridge, MA).

Weinberg, W., 1908, Uber den nachweis der vererbung beim menschen, *Jahreshefte des Vereins Varterländische Naturkdunde in Wurttemberg* 64, 369–382.

White, H., 2001, *Asymptotic Theory for Econometricians*, revised edition (Academic Press, New York).

Wicker, B., C. Keysers, J. Plailly, J.-P. Royet, V. Gallese, and G. Rizzolatti, 2003, Both of us disgusted in my insula: the common neural basis of seeing and feeling disgust, *Neuron* 40, 655–664.

Wickham, H., D. Cook, H. Hofmann, and A. Buja, 2010, Graphical inference for infovis, *IEEE Transactions on Visualization and Computer Graphics* 16, 973–979.

Wild, G., A. Gardner, and S. A. West, 2009, Adaptation and the evolution of parasite virulence in a connected world, *Nature* 459, 983–986.

Williams, G. C., 1996, *Adaptation and Natural Selection: A Critique of Some Current Evolutionary Thought* (Princeton University Press, Princeton, NJ).

Williams, R. W., and K. Herrup, 1988, The control of neuron number, *Annual Review of Neuroscience* 11, 423–453.

Willits, P., 2007, *Guided Flight Discovery: Private Pilot* (Jeppesen Sanderson, Englewood, CO).

Wilson, A. G., and P. Izmailov, 2020, Bayesian deep learning and a probabilistic perspective of generalization, in M. I. Jordan, Y. LeCun, and S. A. Solla, *Advances in Neural Information Processing Systems*, 1–12 (MIT Press, Cambridge).

Wilson, D. S., 1975a, A theory of group selection, *Proceedings of the National Academy of Sciences* 72, 143–146.

Wilson, D. S., and E. Sober, 1994, Reintroducing group selection to the human behavioral sciences, *Behavioral and Brain Sciences* 17, 585–607.

Wilson, D. S., and E. O. Wilson, 2008, Evolution "for the good of the group", *American Scientist* 96, 380–389.

Wilson, E. O., 1975b, *Sociobiology: The New Synthesis* (Harvard University Press, Cambridge, MA).

Wilson, E. O., 1998, *Consilience: The Unity of Knowledge* (Alfred A. Knopf, New York).

Wilson, E. O., 2005, Kin selection as the key to altruism: its rise and fall, *Social Research* 72, 159–166.

Wilson, E. O., 2013, *The Social Conquest of the Earth* (Liveright, New York).

Wilson, E. O., and W. H. Bossert, 1971, *A Primer of Population Biology* (Sinauer Associates, Sunderland, MA).

Wilson, M., and M. Daly, 1985, Competitiveness, risk taking, and violence: the young male syndrome, *Ethology and Sociobiology* 6, 59–73.

Wolford, G., M. Miller, and M. Gazzaniga, 2000, The left hemisphere's role in hypothesis formation, *Journal of Neuroscience* 20, RC64.

Wolford, G., S. Newman, M. Miller, and G. Wig, 2004, Searching for patterns in random sequences, *Canadian Journal of Experimental Psychology* 58, 221–228.

Woolley, A. W., I. Aggarwal, and T. W. Malone, 2015, Collective intelligence and group performance, *Current Directions in Psychological Science* 24, 420–424.

Woolley, A. W., C. F. Chabris, A. Pentland, N. Hashmi, and T. W. Malone, 2010, Evidence for a collective intelligence factor in the performance of human groups, *Science* 330, 686–688.

Woolverton, W. L., and J. K. Rowlett, 1998, Choice maintained by cocaine or food in monkeys: effects of varying probability of reinforcement, *Psychopharmacology* 138, 102–106.

World Bank, 2013, *World Development Report 2014: Risk and Opportunity—Managing Risk for Development* (World Bank, Washington, DC).

Wozny, D., U. Beierholm, and L. Shams, 2010, Probability matching as a computational strategy used in perception, *PLoS Computational Biology* 6, e1000871.

Wright, P., G. He, N. A. Shapira, W. K. Goodman, and Y. Liu, 2004, Disgust and the insula: fMRI responses to pictures of mutilation and contamination, *Neuroreport* 15, 2347–2351.

Wright, S., 1968, *Evolution and the Genetics of Populations, Volume 1* (University of Chicago Press, Chicago, IL).

Wright, S., 1980, Genic and organismic selection, *Evolution* 34, 825–843.

Wright, W. F., and G. H. Bower, 1992, Mood effects on subjective probability assessment, *Organizational Behavior and Human Decision Processes* 52, 276–291.

Wunderlich, K., A. Rangel, and J. O'Doherty, 2009, Neural computations underlying action-based decision making in the human brain, *Proceedings of the National Academy of Sciences* 106, 17199–17204.

Wundt, W., 1897, *Outlines of Psychology* (Wilhelm Engelmann, Leizig), Trans. C. H. Judd.

Wynne-Edwards, V. C., 1962, *Animal Dispersion in Relation to Social Behavior* (Oliver & Boyd, London).

Wynne-Edwards, V. C., 1963, Intergroup selection in the evolution of social systems, *Nature* 200, 623–626.

Xu, F., and J. B. Tenenbaum, 2007, Word learning as Bayesian inference, *Psychological Review* 114, 245.

Yan, H., 2008, Natural selection in financial markets: does it work? *Management Science* 54, 1935–1950.

Yang, C.-H., P. Belawat, E. Hafen, L. Y. Jan, and Y.-N. Jan, 2008, *Drosophila* egg-laying site selection as a system to study simple decision-making processes, *Science* 319, 1679–1683.

Yang, T., and M. N. Shadlen, 2007, Probabilistic reasoning by neurons, *Nature* 447, 1075–1080.

Yoshimura, J., and C. W. Clark, 1991, Individual adaptations in stochastic environments, *Evolutionary Ecology* 5, 173–192.

Yoshimura, J., and V. A. Jansen, 1996, Evolution and population dynamics in stochastic environments, *Researches on Population Ecology* 38, 165–182.

Young, J. S., 1981, Discrete-trial choice in pigeons: effects of reinforcer magnitude, *Journal of the Experimental Analysis of Behavior* 35, 23–29.

Zajonc, R. B., 1980, Feeling and thinking: preferences need no inferences, *American Psychologist* 35, 151–175.

Zajonc, R. B., 1984, On the primacy of affect, *American Psychologist* 39, 117–123.

Zask, E., 2000, Hedge funds: a methodology for hedge fund valuation, *The Journal of Alternative Investments* 3, 43–46.

Zhang, R., T. J. Brennan, and A. W. Lo, 2014a, Group selection as behavioral adaptation to systematic risk, *PLoS One* 9, e110848.

Zhang, R., T. J. Brennan, and A. W. Lo, 2014b, The origin of risk aversion, *Proceedings of the National Academy of Sciences* 111, 17777–17782.

Zimbardo, P. G., 2007, *The Lucifer Effect: Understanding How Good People Turn Evil* (Random House, New York).

Zuckerman, G., 2010, *The Greatest Trade Ever: The Behind-the-Scenes Story of how John Paulson Defied Wall Street and Made Financial History* (Crown Pub, New York).

Zuckerman, G., J. Hagerty, and D. Gauthier-Villars, 2007, Impact of mortgage crisis spreads, dow tumbles 2.8% as fallout intensifies; moves by central banks, *Wall Street Journal*, August 10.

Zuckerman, M., and D. M. Kuhlman, 2000, Personality and risk-taking: common bisocial factors, *Journal of Personality* 68, 999–1029.

Zung, W. W., 1965, A self-rating depression scale, *Archives of General Psychiatry* 12, 63–70.

Zung, W. W., 1971, A rating instrument for anxiety disorders, *Psychosomatics: Journal of Consultation and Liaison Psychiatry* 12, 371–379.

Index

Note: Page numbers followed by n indicate footnotes.